MASTERING

modern British history

WITHDRAWN

Palgrave Master Series

Accounting
Accounting Skills
Advanced English Language
Advanced Pure Mathematics
Arabic
Basic Management
Biology
British Politics
Business Communication
Business Environment
C Programming
C++ Programming
Chemistry
COBOL Programming
Communication
Computing
Counselling Skills
Counselling Theory
Customer Relations
Database Design
Delphi Programming
Desktop Publishing
e-Business
Economic and Social History
Economics
Electrical Engineering
Electronics
Employee Development
English Grammar
English Language
English Literature
Fashion Buying and Merchandising
  Management
Fashion Marketing
Fashion Styling
Financial Management
Geography
Global Information Systems
Globalization of Business

Human Resource Management
International Trade
Internet
Java
Language of Literature
Management Skills
Marketing Management
Mathematics
Microsoft Office
Microsoft Windows, Novell NetWare
  and UNIX
Modern British History
Modern German History
Modern European History
Modern United States History
Modern World History
Novels of Jane Austen
Organisational Behaviour
Pascal and Delphi Programming
Personal Finance
Philosophy
Physics
Poetry
Practical Criticism
Psychology
Public Relations
Shakespeare
Social Welfare
Sociology
Spanish
Statistics
Strategic Management
Systems Analysis and Design
Team Leadership
Theology
Twentieth-Century Russian History
Visual Basic
World Religions

www.palgravemasterseries.com

Palgrave Master Series
Series Standing Order ISBN 0–333–69343–4
(*outside North America only*)

You can receive future titles in this series as they are published by placing a standing order. Please contact your bookseller or, in case of difficulty, write to us at the address below with your name and address, the title of the series and the ISBN quoted above.

Customer Services Department, Macmillan Distribution Ltd.
Houndmills, Basingstoke, Hampshire RG21 6XS, England

MASTERING

modern British history

Fourth Edition

Norman Lowe

palgrave
macmillan

First edition 1984
Second edition 1989
Third edition 1998
Fourth edition 2009

Published by
PALGRAVE MACMILLAN

Palgrave Macmillan in the UK is an imprint of Macmillan Publishers Limited,
registered in England, company number 785998, of Houndmills, Basingstoke,
Hampshire RG21 6XS.

Palgrave Macmillan in the US is a division of St Martin's Press LLC,
175 Fifth Avenue, New York, NY 10010.

Palgrave Macmillan is the global academic imprint of the above companies
and has companies and representatives throughout the world.

Palgrave® and Macmillan® are registered trademarks in the United States,
the United Kingdom, Europe and other countries.

ISBN 978–0–230–20556–7

This book is printed on paper suitable for recycling and made from fully
managed and sustained forest sources. Logging, pulping and manufacturing
processes are expected to conform to the environmental regulations of the
country of origin.

A catalogue record for this book is available from the British Library.

A catalog record for this book is available from the Library of Congress.

10   9   8   7   6   5   4   3   2
18 17 16 15 14 13 12 11

Printed in Great Britain by
CPI Antony Rowe, Chippenham and Eastbourne

Contents

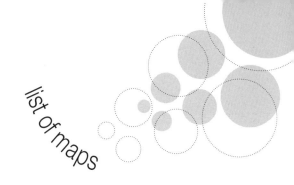

list of maps

list of tables

list of illustrations

list of figures

preface to the fourth edition

The fourth edition of this book takes the story of British history from 1815 right through to Tony Blair's resignation in 2007. It is ideal for students taking AS level and A2 level examinations, and for undergraduates as a general introduction to the period. All the chapters contain new material, taking into account the latest research and the most recent interpretations, and there are new chapters and sections. I hope too that the general reader will find the book informative and interesting, especially as it requires no previous knowledge. For this edition, the questions based on source material can be seen on the accompanying website at www.palgrave.com/masterseries/lowe2.

Once again I am grateful to my friends, Glyn Jones, formerly Vice-Principal of Bede College, Billingham, and Michael Hopkinson, formerly Head of History at Harrogate Grammar School, for their helpful suggestions and advice; to my wife, Jane, who read the entire manuscript and was able to save me from many errors and infelicities of style; and to Suzannah Burywood of Palgrave Macmillan for her patience, encouragement and unfailing good humour. Finally, I would like to thank Keith Povey and Elaine Towns for their help and their careful editing.

NORMAN LOWE

Note about money values and sources

Before the change of currency in 1971, British money consisted of pounds (£), shillings (s) and pence (d); 12 pence (12d) were equal to one shilling (1s, sometimes written 1/-); 20s were equal to £1. In terms of the new decimal coinage, 1s = 5p, 50s = £2.50, and so on.

It is difficult to get an accurate idea of what a monetary value in the past is 'worth' today, and in fact there is no one correct answer. For anyone interested in pursuing this topic in detail, a helpful website is www.measuringworth.com. This explains that in the past, 'an income or price would have been valued in different ways in that time by different people and under different contexts'. It is possible to calculate the present day value using, among other indicators, average earnings, GDP, and the retail price index, all of which give surprisingly wide variations. However, if we simply want to get an idea of the current equivalent of what someone earned in the past and what that person might be able to afford, the best indicator to use is probably the retail price index.

The following list shows how much £1 would be worth in terms of purchasing power in selected years in 2007 values (with thanks to www.measuringworth.com):

1815	£62.24
1830	£73.04
1850	£82.37
1875	£67.55
1900	£77.58
1915	£57.43
1925	£40.88
1930	£45.32
1940	£39.13
1945	£30.93
1955	£18.88
1965	£13.94
1975	£6.04
1985	£2.18
1995	£1.39
2005	£1.08

acknowledgements

The author and publishers wish to thank the following for permission to reproduce copyright material:

Guardian News & Media Ltd. for Figure 33.1, from *The Guardian*, 17 July 1997, Copyright Guardian News & Media Ltd. 1997; Eurostat data is reprinted by permission of the European Communities; Hodder Education for Tables 21.1 and 21.2, from R. W. Wolfson, *Years of Change: European History, 1890–1945* (1979), reproduced by permission of Edward Arnold (Publishers) Ltd; Oxford University Press for Table 15.4, from A. J. P. Taylor, *The Struggle for Mastery in Europe, 1848–1918* (Oxford History of Modern Europe) (1971); Palgrave Macmillan Ltd for Tables 33.1 and 35.1, from D. Childs, *Britain Since 1939: Progress and Decline* (1995); Pearson Education Ltd for Tables 15.2 and 25.1, from C. Cook and J. Stevenson, *Handbook of Modern British History, 1714–1987*, published by Longman (1988); Penguin Books Ltd for Tables 25.2 and 25.3, from J. Stevenson, *British Society, 1914–1945* (1984), pp. 270, 271, Copyright © John Stevenson, 1984, reproduced by permission of Penguin Books Ltd; Taylor & Francis Books UK for Tables 15.1, 15.3, 15.5 and 15.6, from P. Mathias, *The First Industrial Nation*, published by Methuen (1969).

The following new photograph sources are acknowledged:

National Archive, 2.1 (p.20), The People's Charter, 6.1 (p.80), istock, 7.1 (p.87), 9.1 (p.116), 13.1 (p.221), 14.1 (p.239), Wikipedia, 10.1 (p.143), The Art Archive, 12.1 (p.168), 15.1 (p.258), Photos.com, 16.1 (p.289), Getty, 17.1 (p.314), 24.1 (p.478), 22.2 (p.438), 29.1 (p.572), Library of Congress, 22.1 (p.434), 2000 Credit:Topham/PA, 25.1 (p.503), 28.1 (p548), 35.1 (p.730) Rex Features, 27.1 (p.532), 36.1 (p.791), Alamy, 33.1 (p.676).

Every effort has been made to trace all the copyright-holders, but if any have been inadvertently overlooked the publishers will be pleased to make the necessary arrangements at the first opportunity.

For Nathanial, Millie, Anna, Ruby and George

introduction

1.1 prologue: Waterloo

In the late evening of Sunday, 18 June 1815, as the smoke and rain-clouds cleared to reveal the setting sun, the Battle of Waterloo drew to an end. Napoleon's Imperial Guard and the whole French army were in retreat. As they streamed away from the battlefield, leaving behind a mass of artillery and baggage, they were harassed by British and Prussian cavalry. Meanwhile, the two allied generals, Wellington and Blucher, met briefly and congratulated each other on their victory. In the chaos, Napoleon himself was held up for over an hour only four miles from the battlefield, at the village of Genappe. There was utter confusion as several thousand men struggled and fought to cross the only bridge over the River Dyle. With only minutes to spare before the Prussian cavalry caught up, Napoleon at last forced a path through, and galloped away towards Charleroi and Laon.

He reached Paris on 21 June and, realizing the hopelessness of the situation, he abdicated four days later. He was exiled to the tiny island of St Helena in the South Atlantic; the long series of wars that had lasted almost continuously since 1792 (Britain became involved in 1793) was over. Wellington was horrified by the carnage at Waterloo: the British had lost a quarter of their army – over 15,000 dead and wounded – including nearly all Wellington's personal staff. He shrank from ever having to use force again. Wellington was to play a prominent part in public life for over thirty years after Waterloo; and when he was Prime Minister (1828–30), it was this reluctance to resort to force that in 1829 was to lead him to agree to Catholic emancipation rather than risk a civil war in Ireland (see Section 2.7(b)).

1.2 themes of change after 1815

Britain in 1815 was a victorious nation, apparently at the height of its power and prestige. But there was to be no tranquillity after the turmoil of the previous twenty-two years; the period following the Battle of Waterloo turned out to be crammed with important changes and developments. Some of them, such as the Industrial and Agricultural Revolutions, were already under way before the outbreak of war with France in 1793; others, such as falling prices and industrial slumps, came in the aftermath of the wars. These changes brought with them innumerable problems – poverty, discontent and violence. The ruling classes, badly shocked at the fate of the aristocracy during the French Revolution, were nervous in case a similar outbreak occurred in Britain.

(a) industrially and commercially, Britain led the world through much of the nineteenth century

In 1815 Britain was still in the throes of what is known as *the Industrial Revolution,* which lasted from the 1740s until the 1850s. Historians still disagree about exactly when this revolution started and finished; in fact, one can argue that it has never really come to an end and is still happening today. Some historians do not like to use the word 'revolution' because they think it implies too sudden a change and they feel that in reality the process was too gradual to be called a revolution. Nevertheless, 'Industrial Revolution' is still a convenient phrase to describe the introduction of the many new inventions and techniques that transformed the Midlands, the North and parts of Scotland from being mainly rural areas where the majority of people worked in agriculture, and where such industry as existed was carried on in homes or in small factories, into a mainly industrial society of large, power-driven mills and factories concentrated in sprawling industrial towns.

The cotton textile and metal industries were the centrepiece of the revolution. The main inventions included Hargreaves' spinning jenny (1764), Arkwright's water frame for spinning – first used in his big mill at Cromford in Derbyshire (1771), Crompton's spinning mule (1779), Watt's rotary steam-engine (1781) and Cartwright's power loom (1785). In 1785, a steam-engine was used for the first time to power a cotton-spinning mill, and by 1800 at least 500 of them were in operation. The need for armaments during the wars acted as a stimulus to the metal industries and resulted in the widespread adoption of coke-fired blast furnaces for producing iron. At the same time there was an expansion in the coalmining industry.

However, the main expansion of industry took place after 1815. For example, power-loom weaving had not caught on by 1815, even though Cartwright's loom had been available for thirty years. Yet, by 1835, after it had been improved by Horrocks, there were 85,000 of them in use in England and 17,500 in Scotland; whereas imported cotton for weaving amounted to a modest 82 million pounds in weight in 1815, it had soared to 1,000 million pounds in 1860. Coal production rose sharply, from about 15 million tons in 1815 to 44 million tons in 1846. Together with the industrial expansion went a marked population increase, from about 18 million in 1811 to over 27 million in 1851. The increase was most noticeable in the industrial towns and cities, so that by

1851, about 80 per cent of the labouring population worked in some form of manufacturing industry. Another development of crucial importance was the introduction and spread of the railway; the greatest era of railway building was between 1830 and 1860.

During the last quarter of the nineteenth century, Britain began to lose its economic lead, and by the outbreak of the First World War in 1914, Germany and the USA had taken over Britain's position as the world's greatest manufacturing power.

(b) agriculture had also seen the appearance of new techniques and changes, usually referred to as the Agricultural or Agrarian Revolution

Early in the eighteenth century, new crops were introduced – turnips, clover and sainfoin – which provided winter fodder for cattle. Thomas Coke, of Holkham in Norfolk, demonstrated how yield could be increased greatly by using marl to enrich light soils, by using bones as fertilizer, and by improving land drainage. Robert Bakewell, of Dishley in Leicestershire, concentrated on careful and scientific breeding of animals, and showed that by allowing only the best specimens to breed, it was possible to produce far superior cattle and sheep. Another important aspect of the agricultural revolution was *the spread of enclosures.* An enclosure was the fencing- or hedging-in of a large area of medieval strip and furrow land, along with the common pasture land, to form large fields. Enclosures were essential if progress was to be made, because it was impossible to introduce the new scientific farming methods on the open field strips that had survived from medieval times in the counties of eastern and southern England.

Although these improvements had been creeping in throughout the eighteenth century, making possible a marked increase in agricultural production, they were by no means in general use over the whole country. As in industry, the agricultural changes only reached their peak in the years after 1815.

On the debit side, enclosures had the unfortunate effect of depriving many of the smallest farmers of their land. For a variety of reasons, British agriculture went through a serious depression in the twenty years after Waterloo. This was followed by a period of prosperity lasting until about 1875, but then a further period of depression set in. Consequently, another important theme running through the century, even when the industry as a whole seemed prosperous, was *poverty among agricultural labourers,* especially in the South and East of England.

(c) governments began to intervene more in an attempt to solve the new problems caused by industrial and agricultural changes, and by the population growth

There were problems of overcrowded towns, excessively long hours of work, child labour, dangerous conditions in mines and factories, and dire poverty among many working-class people. Another important theme in the nineteenth century was therefore *the emergence of working-class movements such as the Chartists and the trade unions,* which hoped, in their different ways, to improve social and working conditions. The state introduced new regulations dealing with health matters and conditions at work, but ignored some other problem areas. For example, it did very little to help the poor, except provide workhouses for them to live in when they could no longer manage at home.

Towards the end of the nineteenth century there was a great argument going on about whether or not the state – the government – should be expected to do anything to help poor people. *Should the state introduce old-age pensions, health insurance, unemployment insurance and social security?* The traditional Victorian view was known as *laissez-faire:* the belief that the government should interfere as little as possible with people's lives and activities; they should be left alone, with the freedom to organize their own lives. The poor should be encouraged to help themselves and not expect to be helped out by the state. This is known as *individualism* or *self-help.*

The opposing view, which was gradually becoming more widespread after about 1870, is known as *collectivism.* This is the belief that the state has a duty to look after the welfare of its people and to do its best to improve things for the poor. Gradually politicians of all parties (though not all politicians) came to accept that it *was* the state's job to provide social services. One of the great themes of the twentieth century was therefore *the development of the Welfare State.* This means a state in which the government tries to provide the best possible services for everybody, in health care, education, housing, pensions and unemployment benefit. Other ideas that became associated with the Welfare State were the belief that the government should do its best to make sure that everybody had a job, and that arguably the best way of achieving this was for the government to plan and organize the economic life of the country; in other words, there should be *a managed economy.* This, in theory, would help to reduce unemployment and keep costs under control.

The first steps towards a Welfare State were taken by the Liberal governments of 1905–15. Later governments continued to build on these foundations, and the Labour governments of 1945–51 can be said to have more or less completed the Welfare State. They also went some way towards introducing a managed economy by *nationalizing important industries* such as coal, gas, electricity, steel and transport; this means that these industries were taken into state ownership, instead of being privately owned.

During the period of Conservative government from 1979 until 1997, there were worries about the escalating costs of the Welfare State and the burden it placed on the economy. The Conservatives believed that the nationalized industries were not as efficient as they ought to have been, and consequently almost all of them were *privatized*; that is, sold off into private ownership. The individualism versus collectivism debate was re-opened. Many Conservatives believed strongly in self-help, and since the economy was not as successful as it might have been during the 1980s, the future of the Welfare State seemed in some doubt. However, after 1997, the Blair and Brown New Labour governments continued to show commitment to the Welfare State, though the idea of re-nationalizing key industries was quietly dropped.

(d) many changes and developments took place in politics – the way the country was governed

In 1815, Britain was a union of England, Wales, Scotland and Ireland. The country was governed by a monarch (King George III in 1815) and a Parliament of two houses (the House of Commons and the House of Lords) which sat at Westminster. England and Scotland had shared the same monarch since 1603, but it was only in 1707 that the Scots had reluctantly agreed to give up their own parliament in Edinburgh and send MPs to Westminster instead. Wales had been conquered by Edward I of England in 1283 and the country was united with England by an Act of Parliament in 1536. The Welsh had never had a parliament of their own, and their MPs always sat at Westminster.

English kings had claimed control of Ireland since Henry II of England first went over to Ireland in 1172, but it was only in the sixteenth century that it was conquered by the English. After that, the English government encouraged English and Scottish Protestants to settle in Ireland in what were known as 'plantations'. This happened especially in Ulster, and the idea was to 'civilize' the Catholic Irish. The Irish had their own parliament until 1800, but Roman Catholics, who formed almost 90 per cent of the population, had only been allowed to vote since 1793; even then, Catholics were not allowed to become MPs. In 1800, the Irish agreed to give up their parliament in Dublin in return for the promise of *full Catholic emancipation;* this was the granting of full political and civil rights, so that Catholics could become MPs at Westminster. However, for a number of reasons, the British government failed to keep its promise about emancipation. Irish Catholics, poverty-stricken and frustrated, were highly indignant at this betrayal, and throughout the nineteenth century *the country was usually in some sort of turmoil.* This was a constant problem for successive British governments, which tried *different methods of pacifying Ireland.*

The Irish campaigned first for Catholic emancipation (achieved in 1829) and then for the repeal (cancellation) of the 1800 Act of Union so that they could have *Home Rule* – their own parliament in Dublin from which they could control their own internal affairs. This long and bitter struggle dragged on throughout the nineteenth century; it ended temporarily in 1922 with *the setting up of the Irish Free State* (known as the Irish Republic or Eire since 1937). However, this did not include the six counties of Ulster (Northern Ireland), which remained part of the United Kingdom, and many Irish patriots would never rest until Ulster was united with the Republic.

Britain's Parliament, which contained, in the House of Commons, elected representatives of the people, played an important part in governing the country. In comparison with other European rulers, the powers of the British monarch were somewhat restricted; for this reason the British system is sometimes described as *a limited monarchy*. On the other hand, for example, Russia was ruled by the Tsar (Emperor) who was *an autocratic or absolute monarch*. This means that he had complete power; there was no parliament to restrict him, and theoretically he could do exactly as he wished. The British system was therefore the envy of *liberals* all over Europe. Nineteenth-century European liberals (not to be confused with the British Liberal party) were people who wanted to limit the power of autocratic monarchs and replace autocracy with a system in which the middle classes had some say in government.

Although the British Parliament had a great deal of power, *in 1815 the system was not democratic*. Democracy is a system of government through which a country is ruled by elected representatives of the people. However, the House of Lords was not elected – members (peers) inherited their seats. The House of Commons *was* elected, but the franchise (the right to vote) was restricted to men, and only the wealthiest ones at that. Both Parliament and local government were controlled by wealthy aristocratic landowners, who dominated the two main political parties – Whigs and Tories. It was one of the ironies of the early nineteenth century that Britain, the world's greatest industrial power, should be governed by a group of wealthy agriculturalists who, on the whole, knew little about industry.

There was constant pressure for this state of affairs to be remedied. The most striking aspect of the campaign was *the struggle for parliamentary reform:* the extension of the vote to all adult males, and a fairer distribution of seats and constituencies. It was thought in many circles that to get a Parliament that was genuinely representative of all the people was the best way of bringing about an improvement in the miserable conditions of the working classes. Progress towards achieving these aims was made in the Parliamentary Reform Acts of 1832, 1867 and 1884; but in 1900 Britain was still not a democratic country: only 27 per cent of the adult population (aged 21 and over) were allowed to vote. All women and 40 per cent of men were excluded from voting (only householders had the vote), and nothing had been done to make the House of Lords more democratic.

The next stages in the reform of Parliament in the early twentieth century were the campaigns to limit the powers of the House of Lords and to secure votes for women. The reform of the House of Lords was achieved by the Parliament Acts of 1911 and 1949, though members were still not elected. The vote was given to women (aged 30 and over) by the Representation of the People Act (1918), thanks partly to a long and bitter struggle by the suffragettes, and the process was completed by the Equal Franchise Act of 1929, which gave women the vote at 21.

Important changes took place in the party system. In 1815 the Whigs and Tories were the two main political parties. In the mid-nineteenth century *the*

Whigs developed into the Liberal party, which, under the leadership of W. E. Gladstone, appealed to the growing urban middle classes, to skilled workers and to religious Nonconformists. *The Tories developed into the Conservative party;* originally this was a party of rich English landowners and supporters of the Church of England, but under the leadership of Peel and Disraeli it began to attract more widespread support. It was the most successful party at staying in power: since 1874 (when Disraeli won a general election), the Conservatives have been in power themselves, or as leading members of coalitions, for roughly two-thirds of the time.

During the struggle for Irish Home Rule *the Irish Nationalists became an important third party,* but they almost faded out after the Irish Free State was set up in 1922. *The Labour party was formed in 1900,* and by 1924 it had replaced the Liberal party as the main challenger to the Conservatives. The rapid decline of the Liberals and the rise of Labour were two of the most fascinating political developments of the early twentieth century, which historians are still trying to explain. *The Communist Party of Great Britain* was founded in 1920 but it never made much headway. Other important developments were the formation of *the Welsh Nationalist party (Plaid Cymru)* in 1925, and *the Scottish Nationalist party* in 1928. In 1932, Sir Oswald Mosley founded *the British Union of Fascists (BUF).* After the Second World War the fascists resurrected themselves in *the National Front* (1967). In 1982, *the British National Party (BNP)* broke away from the National Front and soon replaced it as the main far-right or neo-fascist party (meaning a new modern version of fascism).

(e) in foreign affairs, Britain's prestige abroad stood high in 1815

This was mainly thanks to the crucial role Britain had played in the defeat of France, and to the country's developing industrial strength. Britain's attitude to Europe and the rest of the world was complex: traditionally, the British were reluctant to get mixed up in European affairs; they had only become involved in the wars against France for reasons of self-defence. After 1815, their instinct was the same, and towards the end of the nineteenth century this policy became known as one of *splendid isolation.* They succeeded in avoiding major foreign entanglements – apart from the Crimean War (1854–6) and the Boer War (1899–1902) – until the outbreak of the First World War in 1914. In practice, however, Britain was never genuinely isolated for long:

▸ Britain found itself drawn into European affairs because of disagreements with autocratic governments, especially those of Austria and Russia, *which were determined to destroy liberalism and nationalism.* Nationalism is the desire of peoples to rid themselves of foreign rulers and have governments of their own nationality. For example, the Greeks wanted to break away from Turkey, the Poles from Russia, and the Italians from Austria. Nationalism could also be the desire to unite all people of the same nationality into one powerful state; this was important in Italy and Germany, which were both divided up into a number of separate states. Britain tended to sympathize with both liberalism and nationalism, especially where it suited the country's interests.

› Britain was also drawn into Europe, whether it chose to or not, by commercial and political interests, since Europe was its most important market for exports until the end of the nineteenth century. British governments *gradually abolished tariffs (import and export duties) and other trade restrictions,* so that British manufacturers could enjoy *free trade.* The British were always on the alert in case another power threatened to dominate Europe. British governments always talked about *preserving the balance of power,* by which they seem to have meant taking measures to make sure that no single country controlled the rest, in the way that Napoleon and the French did in the years before 1815. If that happened, British profits and political influence would suffer. In practice, the five great powers of Europe – Britain, Austria-Hungary, Prussia (Germany from 1870), France and Russia – more or less balanced each other out. On several occasions Britain intervened directly – in 1827, British troops were sent to Portugal, an ally of Britain, to help the Portuguese resist what seemed to be an attempt by the Spanish to take control of the country. Over the so-called *Eastern Question*, the British did their utmost to prevent Russia increasing its power at the expense of the weakening Turkish Empire – the 'Sick Man of Europe'.

› Britain became involved in the pursuit of *imperialism – building up an empire.* The idea was that it would be good for Britain to take over territory abroad that would be valuable for trade. The British already controlled some overseas territories, including India, Canada, the Cape of Good Hope and Hong Kong; in the last quarter of the nineteenth century they joined other European powers in taking over large areas of Africa. This operation took place mainly between 1880 and 1912 and became known as *the 'Scramble for Africa'.* During the 1890s, the phrase *Pax Britannica* became popular, though the ideas behind it had been in circulation long before that; it was the idea that the British Empire was comparable with the Roman Empire, that Britain, all-powerful because of its naval supremacy and economic prosperity, would bring the benefits of peace and civilization to the foreign peoples under British rule. At its largest, Britain's Empire covered something like one fifth of the world's land area, and contained about a quarter of the world's population. After the Second World War ended in 1945, Britain's Empire gradually became independent and the country's world role changed.

› A great variety of continental cultural influences was felt in Britain. British writers were influenced by their European counterparts. Musicians such as Mendelssohn, Verdi, Liszt, Tchaikovsky and Dvorak visited and performed in Britain. In 1858, a German conductor, Charles Hallé, founded the Hallé Orchestra in Manchester.

- After Germany was united in 1870 the situation in Europe began to change with the development of a system of alliances: France and Russia (known as the Dual Alliance) balanced Germany, Austria and Italy (the Triple Alliance). At first, Britain stayed outside the system, sticking resolutely to its *splendid isolation*. But the Boer War (1899–1902) showed how dangerous it was to have no allies; so Britain moved away from isolation, signed agreements with Japan (1902) and France (1904), and became involved in the First World War (1914–18). Some historians have suggested that Britain could have had more influence in Europe and could therefore have done more to prevent the outbreak of war there, if the country had not spent so much time and energy building up its Empire.
- The British continued to show their mixed feelings about Europe and foreign entanglements after the Second World War. They refused to sign the Treaty of Rome (1957) setting up the European Economic Community (EEC), but later changed their minds and eventually joined the community in 1973. When the community began to move towards more political unity, calling itself the European Union (from 1992), the British feared that they would lose their sovereignty (control over their own internal affairs), and resisted moves towards a European super-state.

summary of major themes and developments after 1815

- Britain's industrial supremacy, followed by gradual decline after 1914.
- Agriculture: cycle of depression>prosperity>depression up to 1914; poverty among agricultural labourers.
- Growth of population and towns and associated social problems.
- Working-class movements – Chartists, trade unions, the Labour party.
- Social reform – factories, mines, education, public health.
- The role of the state in society; the individualism versus collectivism debate; development of the Welfare State.
- Problems in Ireland – the struggle for Home Rule.
- The struggle for reform of Parliament – votes for everybody, constituency changes, and changes to the House of Lords.
- Changes in the political parties – decline of the Liberals and rise of Labour.
- Imperialism – the rise and fall of the British Empire.
- Britain and foreign affairs – splendid isolation, the *Pax Britannica*, First and Second World Wars.
- Britain and Europe after 1945 – The European Economic Community and the European Union.

You can follow these themes through the book by using the detailed index; for further study, see the Reading List at the end of the book.

chapter 2

Britain under the Tories, 1815–30

summary of events

In 1815 *King George III* was still on the throne. By then aged 77, he had been King since 1760. Since 1811, he had been suffering from a form of mental derangement, and there seemed no possibility of a cure, though he had recovered from two earlier attacks, in 1788 and 1802. His eldest son, George, acted as Regent, and the period from 1811 to 1820, when the unfortunate George III died, is known as *the Regency*. In 1820, the Prince Regent became *King George IV* and reigned until 1830. He was extremely unpopular and had a bad reputation because of his extravagance, immorality, laziness and selfishness.

Politically, *the Tories were in power.* They had been in government more or less since 1783, though the Prime Minister, the 45-year-old *Lord Liverpool* (Robert Banks Jenkinson) had been premier only since 1812. His predecessor, *Spencer Perceval* (Prime Minister 1809–12), had been shot dead by a bankrupt financier as he entered the lobby of the House of Commons. Liverpool was mild-mannered and modest, and his greatest strength was his ability to manage and reconcile the ministers in his cabinet, who had a disturbing tendency to squabble among themselves. Another strength of the government was *Lord Castlereagh*, a first-rate Foreign Secretary and leader of the Tories in the Commons. Outwardly cold and imperturbable, he was nevertheless deeply sensitive, and was eventually driven to suicide in 1822. The main opposition group to the Tories was known as the Whigs. The modern labels – Conservative and Liberal – were not yet in use.

Liverpool's government was unfortunate in having to deal with probably the most complex set of problems ever faced by a British government up to that date: economic and social distress, the demand for Catholic Emancipation in Ireland, and widespread disturbances suggesting that Britain might be on the verge of a revolution like the one that had broken out in France in 1789. Strong measures were taken to maintain law and order, but very little was done to relieve the distress. However, in 1822, Liverpool brought new blood into the government in the form of some politicians with more progressive ideas – *George Canning, Robert Peel and William Huskisson.* As a result of this, a number of much-needed reforms and improvements were introduced, which caused this phase of the government to be described as *'liberal' Toryism* ('liberal' meaning 'open-minded and favourable to reform').

Early in 1827, Lord Liverpool suffered a stroke, and without his conciliatory skills, the Tories began to fall apart. In April 1827, *George Canning* became Prime Minister, but he died in August of that year. His successor, *Frederick John Robinson, Lord Goderich,* had the greatest difficulty in persuading enough people to serve in his cabinet, and soon resigned in despair. George IV turned next to *the Duke of Wellington,* who, in January 1828, succeeded in forming a government whose most memorable act was the granting of Catholic Emancipation. The Wellington government lasted until November 1830, when *Lord Grey* became Prime Minister of a Whig government.

2.1 what were the British political parties in 1815, and what did they stand for?

The main groups were Whigs, Tories and Radicals, though it is important to realize that they were not as rigidly organized with manifestos and special policies as they are today. Leading figures had their own groups of supporters; sometimes relations between these groups were not good: among the Tories, the rival Castlereagh and Canning groups were notoriously hostile to each other. Parties therefore consisted of loosely linked factions; there was very little idea of party discipline, and MPs often voted as they saw fit. For most of the time there seemed little to distinguish Whigs from Tories, since wealthy landowners formed the backbone of both groups. In fact, historian Boyd Hilton points out that for several years after 1815 the term 'Tory' still had the lingering connotation as a term of abuse, and some Tory ministers tried to avoid the use of the label. It was only in 1827, when Lord Liverpool retired, that the term 'Tory' came into everyday use.

(a) Whigs

The names 'Whig' and 'Tory' originated during the reign of Charles II (1660–85) at the time when there was some controversy about whether or not Charles's brother, James, should be allowed to succeed to the throne on Charles's death. The Whigs were the people who wanted to exclude him on the grounds that he was a Roman Catholic, whereas the Tories were those who were not prepared to exclude him. Both words – Whig and Tory – were terms of abuse flung by each side at the other. 'Whig' was short for 'whiggamor', a nickname for western Scots who came to Leith for corn; while 'tory' was Irish for 'robber' or 'brigand'. By 1815, the origins of the groupings had largely been forgotten. The Whigs had no particular programme or policy and were not even united. Broadly speaking, they stood for:

-   a reduction in crown patronage (the monarch's power to appoint people to certain important positions and offices);
-   sympathy towards Roman Catholics and Nonconformists (Methodists and other Protestant groups who had broken away from the Church of England);
-   care for the interests of merchants and bankers;
-   a vague sympathy towards the idea of some reform of the voting system, although they were unable to agree on a scheme.

Leading Whigs – almost all of them wealthy aristocratic landowners – were Lord Grey, Lord Grenville, Lord Althorp, William Lamb (later Lord Melbourne) and Lord John Russell. Perhaps the most gifted of all was Henry Brougham, a brilliant lawyer, who was rather set apart from the rest by his comparatively modest background.

(b) Tories

On the whole, Tories stood for the preservation of the status quo:

-   They wanted to maintain the powers of the monarch and the Anglican Church (the Church of England); they were much less tolerant of Nonconformists than the Whigs were.
-   They had been badly frightened by the French Revolution and consequently they believed in the strict maintenance of law and order.
-   Unlike some of the Whigs, most Tories opposed any reform of Parliament, though the more progressive among them were in favour of some cautious humanitarian reform.

Leading Tories of the more rigid type, sometimes known as 'high' Tories, were Henry Addington (Lord Sidmouth), Lord Castlereagh, Lord Eldon and the Duke of Wellington. The 'reforming' or 'liberal' Tories included George Canning, Robert Peel, William Huskisson and F. J. Robinson (Lord Goderich). The Tories, like the Whigs, were often deeply divided; in 1809, Castlereagh and Canning had disagreed so violently over the conduct of the war that Castlereagh had challenged his colleague to a duel with pistols. This took place at 6 o'clock one morning on Putney Heath, and ended with Castlereagh slightly wounding Canning in the thigh. The duel caused something of a sensation, and both men had to retire from the Cabinet for a time. After 1812 the Tories were more united, which says much for Liverpool's skill as a manager and conciliator.

(c) Radicals

They had been greatly encouraged by the French Revolution (which began in 1789) and by its slogan, which translated as 'liberty, equality, fraternity'. They only had a handful of MPs in 1815, the most influential being Sir Francis Burdett and Joseph Hume; but outside Parliament, Radical leaders such as Major John Cartwright, Henry 'Orator' Hunt, Francis Place (whose tailor's shop in Charing Cross Road became a famous Radical meeting-place), and William Cobbett (the journalist and publicist of the movement), were busy organizing mass meetings, marches and petitions. The word 'radical' (from the Latin 'radix' – a root) meant someone who wanted fundamental reforms that got to the root of problems. Early-nineteenth-century Radicals were not an organized party, but they had one aim in common: they wanted a thorough reform of the political system and an improvement in the conditions of the working class, though they did not always agree about how these were to be achieved. Most of them did agree, however, that they were not in favour of violent action. They were greatly influenced by the ideas of *Jeremy Bentham* (1748–1832), known as *Utilitarianism.* A lawyer, like his father, Bentham claimed that the function of governments was to promote 'the greatest happiness of the greatest number of people'; this could be achieved in two ways:

1　The government and administration of the country must be made as efficient as possible; anything that was not efficient or useful – whether it was the education system, the penal system, the prison system or the voting system – must be modernized.

2　The government should interfere as little as possible with the lives and activities of individual people, since this was thought to be the best way of achieving the greatest happiness. Such a policy was known as *laissez-faire* (meaning literally 'leave alone') – allowing people to act as they wanted, without government restrictions. Thus one of the Radicals' pet theories was free trade: the belief that import and export duties should be abolished because they interfered with the natural flow of trade.

There was something of a contradiction in these Radical ideas – in fact, more government interference than ever before might be necessary in order to achieve efficiency in, for example, the education system. But this did not prevent Radicalism, with its clubs and debating societies, from swelling to become the great protest movement of the early nineteenth century, supported by the working classes, by middle-class humanitarians (people who wanted society organized in a humane fashion), and by some industrialists.

2.2　why was there so much discontent and distress among ordinary people after 1815?

The trouble was caused by a combination of many different developments. These, for the sake of simplicity, can be divided into three groups.

(a) the industrial and agricultural revolutions caused widespread poverty in both town and country

1 *Enclosures* (see Section 1.2(b)) probably caused hardship in some areas. The movement towards enclosure had been taking place piecemeal since the thirteenth century, but had gathered pace after 1760, and there was a late surge during the war years as farmers took advantage of the high demand for wheat. There has been disagreement among economic historians about how serious and widespread the effects were. It used to be argued that enclosures ruined the yeomen (farmers of medium-sized holdings) and small peasant farmers, who were evicted from their land because they could not afford the expenses involved or because they could not prove their rights to the land at law. However, J. D. Chambers and G. E. Mingay, writing in 1966, argued that this was an over-simplification, that the extent of hardship had been exaggerated and was not supported by the evidence. They suggested that it would be a mistake to blame enclosures for 'developments that were the consequence of a much broader and more complex process of historical change'. And in fact much of the country – including Kent, Essex, Sussex and the West Country – had been enclosed long before 1815, so that poverty in those counties could not have been caused by enclosures. In other areas –including Lancashire, Cheshire, Northumberland and Durham – the open-field system had never existed.

There must therefore have been other reasons for the poverty in these areas in the years immediately following 1815. One obvious explanation is that *the rapid population growth made many farm labourers redundant.* Nevertheless, it is likely that in areas where enclosures did take place during the war years, large numbers of smallholders lost their two or three acres, together with their right to use the common pasture for their animals, and so were reduced to being landless labourers. Marxist historian E. P. Thompson suggested that this was a deliberate policy by wealthy farmers to swell the reserves of cheap labour that could be called on for haymaking, harvesting, road-making, fencing and draining. According to Thompson, 'enclosure (when all the sophistications are allowed for) was a plain enough case of class robbery'.

2 *The Speenhamland System* aggravated rural poverty. The pool of cheap labour kept farm labourers' wages so low that in 1795 the magistrates at Speenhamland in Berkshire decided to supplement wages from the poor rates, either with food or money, depending on the price of bread and the size of a labourer's family. This system spread rapidly, though it was never common in the North of England. Despite the magistrates acting from humanitarian motives (as well as the need to calm unrest and perhaps prevent revolution), the system resulted in two unfortunate effects: farmers reduced wages still further, or refused to employ men for a full week, knowing that,

however inadequate their earnings were, they would be topped-up by the magistrates. In addition, the money had to come out of the poor rate (a special rate charged by the parish for the maintenance of the poor); this meant that the rest of the ratepayers were having to subsidize the wealthy farmers, a highly unpopular state of affairs, particularly as poor rates on average doubled between 1795 and 1812.

3 *The new machines in agriculture, factories and mines* often reduced the demand for labour and caused hardship in certain trades. The best-known example is the hand-loom weavers of Lancashire, Yorkshire and Cheshire, who were gradually being forced out of business by the power-loom. They were already past their heyday in 1800, because their earlier prosperity had attracted too many extra weavers, thus enabling employers to force down wages. But as the power-loom was adopted more widely after 1815, their plight became much worse. One set of statistics puts the average weekly wage for hand-loom weavers at 21s in 1802, 14s in 1809, 8s 9d in 1817, 7s 3d in 1828 and 6s in 1832. And there was worse to come; according to William Cobbett after a visit to Halifax in 1832: 'It is truly lamentable to behold so many thousands of men who formerly earned 20 to 30 shillings per week, now compelled to live on 5s, 4s, or even less' (see the note about money on p. xxii).

4 *In the industrial towns there were unpleasant working and living conditions.* It is difficult to generalize about this, and in fact historians have disagreed about how bad working conditions actually were. However, there is no doubt that in many mills men had to work long hours (a 16-hour day was common); children from the age of five could be expected to work a 14-hour day; and there was resentment at the way wages were paid in some trades – there was the 'truck' system by which workers received part of their wages in goods, or in vouchers that could only be spent at the 'truck' shop or the 'Tommy' shop kept by the mill- or mine-owner. What was also distressing for industrial workers was the loss of freedom, together with the regimentation of factory life, plus the fact that wages probably failed to keep pace with rising prices.

Nor can there be any doubt that the growth of industrial towns was too rapid for proper planning and housing. For example, Liverpool mushroomed from only 82,000 people in 1801 to 202,000 in 1831, Manchester/Salford grew from 95,000 to 238,000 over the same period, and Glasgow from 77,000 to 193,000. Much of the extra population came in from the surrounding countryside, while in Lancashire there was a great influx of Irish immigrants. Cheap, jerry-built housing was thrown up close to the factories, water supplies and sanitation were primitive, and overcrowding was dangerously unhealthy. In Manchester in 1820 at least 20,000 people, including many Irish immigrants, were living in cellars. This excess of cheap labour was one of the reasons why industrial wages stayed so low (see Sections 12.1 and 12.2 for more details).

(b) the after-effects of the wars aggravated these problems

1   *The end of the war brought a sharp fall in corn prices,* causing bankruptcies among poorer farmers. The price reached a peak in 1812 at an average per quarter of 126s 6d; then it fell dramatically to 65s 7d in 1815, and by January 1816 it was down to 55s 6d. The fall was caused by the fact that farmers, having put more land under cultivation to meet demand during the war, were now over-producing. Imported foreign corn was available again, and in addition, the harvests of 1813 and 1814 were outstandingly good. Many small owner-occupiers, already in debt because of the costs of enclosure, high war-time taxes and the increase in the poor-rate, could not stand the reduction in profits, and were forced out of business. Wealthier farmers reduced wages and laid off some of their labourers, thus adding to the unemployment pool.

2   *There was a sudden industrial slump causing widespread unemployment.* The reasons for this were several: now that the war was over, the government stopped buying armaments and uniforms, which meant the loss of orders worth about £50 million. European manufacturers, worried by British competition, brought pressure to bear on their governments to introduce tariffs (import duties), making British goods more expensive in Europe, and thus protecting the developing European industries. After a short boom (a period of increasing exports) in 1815, British exports fell away again, and had dropped 30 per cent by 1818. Roughly half the blast furnaces in the country had to close down, and there was a corresponding reduction in the demand for coal. On top of this, there were over 200,000 demobilized soldiers and sailors flooding the labour market, making a grand total of perhaps half a million unemployed by the end of 1816.

(c) some of the government's actions made the situation even worse

1   *The Combination Laws (1799–1800)* made combinations (trades unions) illegal, and while the laws were not effective, they aroused resentment.

2   *The Corn Laws of 1815* forbade the import of foreign wheat until the price of home-grown wheat had risen to 80s a quarter; this was considered to be a sufficiently profitable level to enable landowners and farmers to keep all their labourers in work. This increased the price of wheat, which rose to 76s 2d a quarter in 1816 and to 96s 11d in 1817, sending the price of a four-pound loaf up from 10d to 1s 2d. Although this pleased farmers, it was disastrous for unemployed workers, and it brought a shower of accusations that the Tory landowners were looking after themselves at the expense of the poor.

3   *Income tax was abolished in 1816.* It had been introduced originally in 1797 to raise extra cash for the war effort. William Pitt, the then Prime Minister, had pledged to remove it as soon as the war was over. Liverpool, under pressure from wealthy industrialists, merchants, bankers and landowners who

wanted to get rid of income tax, kept Pitt's pledge. However, the income tax was bringing in about £15 million a year, which the government could ill afford to lose, especially as the interest they had to pay on the National Debt (money borrowed by the government to finance the war and for other purposes) amounted to over £31 million a year. To make up for the loss, Liverpool's government increased the taxes on a wide range of goods, including tea, sugar, tobacco, beer, paper, soap and candles. While the rich were relieved of income tax, the poor, who had not paid income tax, since it only applied to people earning over £60 a year, now found themselves burdened with at least some of the extra taxes on popular goods. The government's unpopularity reached a new peak.

4 The government showed very little sympathy or understanding when people protested, and replied with a policy of repression which only embittered them further (see Section 2.4).

2.3 how was the discontent expressed?

Some people, like the Radicals, expressed their views peacefully in pamphlets, speeches and petitions; but there were also marches and demonstrations, many of which ended violently. The government was convinced that there was a widespread and centrally organized conspiracy, and that the country might well be on the verge of revolution. In fact this was probably not the case.

(a) the Radicals kept up a constant stream of criticism of the government and the way society was organized

In 1816, William Cobbett began a 2d weekly edition of his pamphlet *Political Register* (known as Twopenny Trash), which was soon selling over 60,000 copies a week. His themes were the crushing burden of taxation on ordinary people, and the need to bring about a reform of Parliament: 'We must have that first, or we shall have nothing good … Any man can draw up a petition and any man can carry it up to London'. He advocated universal male suffrage (the vote for all men) and a general election every year, thereby keeping Parliament firmly in touch with the wishes of the people. This would enable a start to be made on vital social reforms. In 1817, Thomas Wooler began his weekly, the *Black Dwarf*. Scores of local radical papers were founded that both criticized the government and drew attention to local grievances. On the whole, the Radicals favoured peaceful protest, realizing that violence would discredit their cause, though Henry Hunt tended to get involved in agitation.

(b) the Luddite Riots (1811–17)

These had already started before the end of the wars. They involved workers in three trades – the croppers (woollen cloth dressers and finishers) of the West Riding of Yorkshire, the cotton weavers of Lancashire and the framework-knitters of the Midlands, particularly Nottingham. All these workers were suffering economic hardship for a variety of reasons, including the use of new labour-saving machinery. They began to relieve their feelings by smashing machinery and setting fire to factories. Beginning in Nottinghamshire, the movement took its name from Ned Ludd, a youth who was reputed to have smashed up some machinery in a fit of temper. During 1811 almost 1,000 frames valued at over £6,000 were destroyed, and the government retaliated by making frame-breaking punishable by death.

The outbreaks soon spread to Yorkshire and Lancashire; mills were attacked in Leeds, Manchester, Stockport and many other centres. At Rawfolds in the Spen Valley, a mill-owner used troops to fight off the Luddites, killing two of the attackers; at Middleton, near Manchester, a power-loom mill was attacked by a crowd of several thousands, but they were driven back by musket-fire; after ten people had been killed, the crowd retaliated by burning down the mill-owner's house (April 1812). The government took a strong line, using troops to break up demonstrations and hanging seventeen Luddites at York (January 1813). The main phase of Luddism was over by this time, though sporadic outbursts occurred until 1817. The Marxist historian, E. P. Thompson, believed that Luddism was more than just an economic and industrial protest movement, and that it had political aims as well. He saw it as an important step forward in the political consciousness of the working classes, and thought the Luddites were part of a great underground revolutionary movement. Many other historians go along with Thompson on the question of political aims (mainly the reform of Parliament), but are not convinced by his evidence of a widespread revolutionary network. (For a fuller discussion of this debate, see John A. Hargreaves, 'Luddism', in *Modern History Review*, September 1995).

(c) the Spa Fields Meetings in London (1816) led to disturbances

There were three separate meetings (15 November; and 2 and 9 December), the second of which ended in a riot. The main speaker was 'Orator' Hunt, who urged the need for a reform of Parliament, universal suffrage, voting by secret ballot, and annual elections. However, the organizers of the meeting were more extreme than Hunt; they included Arthur Thistlewood and Thomas Preston, who wanted the eventual overthrow of the monarchy. They believed the army was on the verge of mutiny and hoped to excite the crowd into attacking prisons, the Bank of England and the Tower of London. Even before Hunt began to speak, a section of the crowd had rampaged through the streets and ransacked a gunsmith's shop. They were dispersed by troops, but only after several hours' rioting.

(d) the March of the Blanketeers (1817) set out from Manchester to present petitions to the Prince Regent in London

Manchester, full of unemployed weavers, was the centre of an impressive reform movement, and the march was well organized. About 600 men, mainly poor weavers, walked in groups of ten with blankets on their backs, each group carrying a petition (ten was the maximum number allowed by law to present a petition) asking the Prince Regent to help their unfortunate industry. About 200 were arrested at Stockport and most of the remainder were chased away by cavalry at Macclesfield. One man was allowed through to present the petition, but nothing came of this pathetic incident except that thirteen of the leaders were sent to prison.

(e) the Derbyshire Rising (1817) was one of a number of similar incidents that took place in Yorkshire and the Midlands

Encouraged by a government spy known as Oliver (W. J. Richards), about 300 poor stocking-makers and quarrymen from the Derbyshire villages of Pentridge and Ripley, led by Jeremiah Brandreth, set off to seize Nottingham Castle, fourteen miles away. Brandreth had assured his followers that the whole country was about to rise with them, and that a provisional government would be set up that would send relief to the workers. A detachment of cavalry already alerted by Oliver was waiting in Nottingham, and the rising ended ignominiously as the men ran off. Three of the leaders, including Brandreth, were executed.

(f) the Peterloo Massacre in Manchester (1819) was the most famous incident of the period

After a quiet year in 1818 thanks to an improvement in trade and the previous year's good harvest, 1819 brought a slump in exports and a return to unemployment. This led to new Radical demands for reform, and a plan to hold a meeting in London of Radical leaders from all over the country. The Manchester Radicals organized an open-air meeting in St Peter's Fields, to be addressed by Henry Hunt, who was to be Manchester's representative at the London meeting. About 60,000 men, women and children turned up, and while many carried Radical banners, they were not armed and there was no disorder. The magistrates allowed the meeting to begin and had troops standing by in case there was trouble.

While Hunt was speaking, the magistrates apparently lost their nerve, decided the meeting was illegal, and ordered the yeomanry (local volunteer troops) to arrest him. Unfortunately, they had difficulty forcing a way through the solidly packed crowd, and regular troops were sent to help. They charged in with drawn swords, the crowd panicked and stampeded, and eleven people were killed and 400 injured; 161 of the injured had sabre wounds. Hunt was arrested but soon released on bail.

There were protests from all over the country at the magistrates' handling of the situation and the incident soon became known as the 'Peterloo Massacre' – an ironic comparison with the army's activities at Waterloo. However, the government, afraid that the country was on the verge of revolution, congratulated the

Illus. **2.1 The Peterloo Massacre of August 1819**

magistrates on their prompt action and used the incident to justify passing *the Six Acts* – a further tightening up of restrictions on Radical activities (see below, Section 2.4(b), for full details of the Six Acts) – which, among other things, banned any further large meetings.

(g) the Cato Street Conspiracy (1820) was the final and most extreme act in this series of protests

The leaders, who included Arthur Thistlewood (a former army officer and one-time gentleman farmer) and Thomas Ings (a butcher), were apparently moved to desperation by the latest government restrictions. They conceived a half-baked plan to murder the entire Cabinet at a dinner, parade the heads of the ministers on pikes, capture the Tower, Bank and Mansion House (the residence of the Lord Mayor of London) and proclaim a republic. It was hoped that the London 'mob' would rise in support, as had happened in Paris during the

French Revolution. However, government spies knew all about it, and the conspirators were arrested at a house in Cato Street (off the Edgware Road). Five leaders, including Thistlewood, were executed, and five others transported. The incident was not particularly important except that it seemed to justify the Six Acts. Apart from an abortive attempt to start a general strike in Glasgow, the agitation died down towards the end of 1820 as the economic situation improved.

2.4 what steps did Liverpool's government take to combat the unrest in the period before 1820?

(a) the government's attitude to the problem

The government's main concern seems to have been to stem the violence and keep order rather than to remove the causes of grievance. It was because of this that they attracted so much criticism at the time from the Radicals and later from liberal historians. In fact it is easy to understand the reaction of the Tories: they had been elected by the wealthy landlords; they had seen the horrors of the French Revolution, which had started with similar protests in 1789 (Lord Liverpool had witnessed the storming of the Bastille); and their landowning supporters had a great deal to lose if a similar revolution broke out in Britain. It is important to remember that there was no police force at the time, and only a limited number of troops; consequently, the government had to rely for law and order on local magistrates, who had little experience of handling such situations, had no idea of crowd control, and were liable to panic, as they did at Peterloo. The widespread nature of the disturbances after 1815 convinced the Tories that unless firm action was taken, the whole country would erupt into revolution. They were probably mistaken: there is very little evidence of any co-ordinated conspiracy to overthrow the government; the Radicals were not in favour of violence, and extremists such as Thistlewood were only a small minority. Nevertheless, the Tories, ignoring the fact that some of their policies (Corn Laws and the abolition of income tax) were making matters worse, embarked on *a policy of repression* (keeping people under control, restricting liberties, quelling riots and stamping out violence), directed by Lord Sidmouth, the Home Secretary.

(b) repressive policies

1 *The government used spies and informers,* who usually pretended they had been sent by Radical groups in London to help organize agitation in the provinces. Having contacted local reformers, they reported full details back to Lord Sidmouth; sometimes they acted as *agents provocateurs* – they encouraged reformers with violent tendencies to come out into the open and take action. The most notorious of these informers, W. J. Richards (known as

Oliver), while not actually planning such activities as Brandreth's Derbyshire Rising, seemed to have encouraged them enthusiastically. This exaggerated the threat to law and order, but enabled the government to arrest possible revolutionary leaders, and it appeared to justify the rest of their repressive programme. According to E. P. Thompson, 'the government wanted blood – not a holocaust, but enough to make an example'.

2   *The Game Law of 1816* made poaching and even the possession of a net for catching rabbits punishable by transportation to Australia for seven years. This was designed to stamp out the sudden increase in poaching that occurred after the introduction of the Corn Laws, but it was not as effective as the government had hoped, because juries were reluctant to convict when the penalty was so severe for such a minor offence.

3   *The Habeas Corpus Act was suspended in 1817.* This Act (meaning literally – you must have the body) had been passed originally in 1679 and gave the right to demand a written order for a prisoner to appear in court so that he or she could be charged with an offence; this was to protect people from being kept in prison for long periods without being charged. If the Habeas Corpus Act was suspended, a person who had committed no offence could be arrested and held for an indefinite period without charge and without trial to prevent him or her from committing an offence that might have been planned. It was the Spa Fields affair that prompted the government into the 1817 suspension. *Seditious meetings* (meetings that might have discussed or caused disobedience or violence against the government) were banned, and letters were sent to magistrates urging them to be firm with agitators. Together, these government actions were nicknamed the '*Gagging Acts*.' They allowed the arrest of scores of Radical leaders, though not Cobbett, who had left smartly for the USA.

4   *The Six Acts (1819) were the government's reply to Peterloo;* these were the most drastic measures taken so far.

- Magistrates could search houses, without warrants, for unauthorized firearms; there were severe penalties if any were found.
- Drilling and military training by private individuals were forbidden.
- Political meetings to present petitions must involve only people from the parish in which the meeting was taking place; this was to prevent huge gatherings like those at Spa Fields and St Peter's Fields.
- Magistrates could search houses, without warrants, for seditious literature.
- Magistrates could try people charged with political offences immediately, without waiting for the local assizes where they would have been tried by judge and jury. This was because juries were sometimes reluctant to convict when it was obvious that evidence came from informers.
- The stamp duty on pamphlets and periodicals was increased, making them more expensive; most of them now cost at least 6d, and the government

hoped this would reduce the circulation of Cobbett's *Political Register* and other radical publications.

Hundreds of prosecutions followed and during 1820 the agitation and violence gradually died away.

(c) minor reforms

The government introduced a few improvements:

> *The Factory Act of 1819* (the work of Sir Robert Peel senior) forbade the employment of children under 9 in the mills, and limited the working hours of 9–16-year-olds to 12 hours a day. Unfortunately, this was largely ineffective: it applied only to cotton mills, and magistrates were expected to enforce the regulations, a task quite beyond them; what was needed was a large body of professional inspectors.
> Another ineffective reform was *the Truck Act of 1820*, which attempted to control abuses in the system of paying wages in ways other than in money.

In conclusion it has to be said that the gradual disappearance of agitation during 1820 was not caused solely by the government's repression, and certainly not by their reforms. It had much more to do with the recovery in exports, which helped to reduce unemployment; there was also a series of good harvests, which brought down the price of bread. As Cobbett remarked, 'I defy you to agitate a fellow with a full stomach.'

2.5 who were the 'liberal' Tories and why did Lord Liverpool bring them into the government in 1822–3?

(a) the new men

They included George Canning, who became Foreign Minister and Leader of the House of Commons, replacing Castlereagh, who had just committed suicide. Sir Robert Peel (junior), aged only 33, became Home Secretary, replacing Sidmouth who had retired. F. J. Robinson (aged 40) became Chancellor of the Exchequer in 1823, and William Huskisson (aged 50) became President of the Board of Trade in the same year. As well as being open to new ideas, they came from more middle-class backgrounds than the majority of landowning Tories. Canning's father was a barrister and his mother an actress – a profession not then considered respectable; it was a handicap that Canning took a long time to live down. Peel's father was a wealthy Lancashire cotton manufacturer.

(b) they were brought into the government for a number of reasons

> Castlereagh's suicide made a major Cabinet reshuffle necessary. Canning was the obvious candidate to take over as Foreign Secretary; this meant that some

members of Canning's group of supporters, such as Huskisson and Robinson, would be brought in too.

- They were all in their different ways more progressive than the men they replaced, and were prepared to introduce some reforms. By drafting them into the government, Liverpool hoped to improve social and economic conditions sufficiently to win the support of moderate reformers all over the country, as well as the support of the manufacturers. By removing some of the causes of distress, he hoped to reduce the demand for a reform of Parliament, which he and his colleagues certainly did not favour.
- The year 1822 was a suitable time to begin reforms, since law and order had been restored, and it would therefore not look as though the government was being swayed by violence.
- Moderate reform would be a blow to the Whigs, who were split between the aristocratic members, who were not keen on reform, and the left wing of the party, who were sympathetic towards the Radicals.
- The Tories had been seriously embarrassed by what was known as the Queen's Affair (1821). On the death of George III in 1820, the Prince Regent became George IV. Already secretly married to the Roman Catholic Mrs Fitzherbert, he had, in 1795, married Princess Caroline of Brunswick. Since he and Caroline had lived apart for many years, George was determined that she should not be crowned Queen, and he persuaded Liverpool to introduce a Bill of Divorce into parliament on the grounds of Caroline's adultery. The King was himself highly unpopular because of his extravagance and his mistresses; the general public, the Radicals and most of the Whigs rallied to Caroline's support, though she was certainly no saint. Public opinion seemed so solid in its support of Caroline that the government dropped divorce proceedings. In London, huge mobs celebrated, and Cabinet ministers had their windows smashed. George still tried to ignore her, and she threatened to attend George's Coronation if the government failed to increase her financial settlement. This made her appear somewhat mercenary, and gradually her popularity declined. Following the government's refusal to grant any increase in her financial settlement, the London public was treated to the spectacle of the Queen trying to force her way into Westminster Abbey to take part in the Coronation service. She had to abandon the attempt and was hissed by the fickle crowd as she was driven away. Fortunately for George, she died a month later. When he heard the news, the King announced that this was 'one of the happiest moments of my life'. As well as bringing the popularity of the monarchy to its lowest point ever, the Affair had also shown how out of touch the government was with public opinion. This may well have reinforced Liverpool in his decision to bring in some new blood.

2.6 what reforms did the 'liberal' Tories introduce between 1822 and 1830 to deserve this title?

Huskisson and Robinson, both able administrators and financiers, were quick to grasp the importance of overseas trade, and were prepared to remove antiquated restrictions that were hampering Britain as a trading nation. Peel was ready to listen to proposals for reforming prisons and the system of maintaining law and order; he was even persuaded to support Catholic Emancipation, though he had begun by being resolutely against it. Canning favoured Catholic Emancipation and supported his colleagues in their social and economic policies. They were all influenced by the ideas of Jeremy Bentham (see Section 2.1(c)), that governments should aim for greater efficiency. Two important points to remember, however, which have sometimes caused confusion, are:

1 Very few of the Tories were in favour of making Parliament more democratic; only after the death of Canning (1827), who was against political change, did the 'liberal' Tories begin to consider a modest reform of Parliament. Therefore, they were not fully 'liberal' (the word could mean 'in favour of democratic reform' as well as 'wanting a general removal of abuses').

2 The change of policy was not as sudden as some historians have made out. The beginnings of reform had already taken place before 1822. The Factory Act (1819) and the Truck Act (1820) have already been mentioned (see previous section). In addition, there had been the partial abolition of the pillory (1816) and the abolition of the whipping of women (1820); a Commons Committee of Enquiry had been set up in 1819 to study the weaknesses of the legal system; the Board of Trade had already admitted the need for commercial reform before Huskisson arrived. Even Canning's foreign policy, which seemed to favour liberalism overseas (see Section 3.3(a)), had its beginnings under his predecessor, Castlereagh.

However, what had been a mere trickle of reform became a flood after 1822.

(a) Huskisson and the move towards Free Trade

The problem was that British merchants were hampered by numerous *tariffs* (import duties) and other restrictions. Some of these had been imposed originally to protect British industry from foreign competition by making foreign goods more expensive than similar goods produced in Britain. Others had been imposed to raise money during the wars with France. There were, for example, heavy duties on imported raw materials, which were now needed on a much larger scale than ever before, because of the expansion of British industry. In 1820, the merchants of London, Manchester and Glasgow had petitioned the government for *free trade* (the abolition of all duties), since they were convinced that British industry could beat all foreign competitors and no longer needed protection. They also argued that, if Britain continued with tariffs, foreign countries would do the same in order to protect their industries from British goods. Huskisson was a follower of *Adam Smith* (1723–90), a Scottish philosopher and political economist, who, in his book *The Wealth of Nations* (1776), had condemned monopolies and too much state control, and argued in favour of free trade, competition and private enterprise as being the most successful ways of encouraging a nation's economy to develop.

› Huskisson reduced import duties by varying amounts on a wide range of raw materials and other goods: cotton, wool, silk, linen, tea, coffee, cocoa, wine, rum, spirits, books, glassware, china, porcelain, manufactured textiles, iron, copper, zinc, tin and many others. For example, the duty on imported raw silk was slashed from 5s 7½d per pound to 4d per pound. The duty on imported manufactured goods not specifically mentioned in the list was reduced from 50 per cent to 20 per cent.

› He removed restrictions on the trade of Britain's colonies: they could now trade directly with foreign countries for the first time, instead of all such trade having to pass via Britain first. Many goods imported from the colonies now paid lower duties than similar goods from foreign countries (such as wheat and timber from Canada; and wool from Australia paid no duty at all). This was known as *imperial preference* and was designed to encourage trade with the British Empire.

› He modified an obsolete set of restrictions known as the Navigation Laws (introduced in the seventeenth century) which said that goods being imported into Britain and its colonies had to be carried in British ships or in ships of the country where the goods originated. This had been designed to prevent the Dutch from capturing the world's carrying trade, but by the 1820s it was quite unnecessary, and other countries were beginning to retaliate with similar policies; this meant that British ships were being excluded from European ports, or were being forced to pay high duties. Huskisson's *Reciprocity of Duties Act (1823)* enabled the government to sign agreements with foreign governments, allowing completely free entry of each other's ships. During the next six years, fifteen of these agreements were signed, with, among other countries, Prussia, Sweden, Denmark, Brazil and Colombia.

› He modified the 1815 Corn Law by introducing a sliding scale of import duties (1828): if British wheat was selling at over 73s a quarter, there would be no duty on imported foreign wheat; but as the price fell, the amount of duty increased.

In the long term, Huskisson's work bore fruit: cheaper raw materials enabled manufacturers to produce goods at lower prices, so that British exports and shipping increased steadily as the country's industries became more competitive; smuggling began to disappear, since the reduction in duty made it unnecessary.

In the short term, there were a few problems: the government lost the revenue (income) it had collected from the higher import duties, and in December 1825 a sudden slump in exports began, caused mainly by over-production. Unemployment increased again, and in Lancashire there were more outbreaks of machine-breaking. Some people blamed Huskisson, though this was absurd, because many of his reforms only applied from the beginning of 1826. In fact, he had taken Britain through the first crucially important steps towards Free Trade. Sadly, his career was cut short in 1830 when he was knocked down and killed by a locomotive at the opening of the Liverpool and Manchester Railway.

(b) repeal of the Combination Laws (1824)

Since 1800, the Combination Laws had made trade unions illegal. A campaign to have these laws repealed (cancelled) was mounted by Francis Place, the famous Radical tailor of Charing Cross, whose shop was a favourite meeting-place for London Radicals. He was supported in Parliament by the Radical MPs Joseph Hume and Sir Francis Burdett, and by many other Benthamites. *Their arguments were:*

▸ The laws were inefficient – trade unions did, in fact, exist, but called themselves friendly societies; these were organizations into which workers paid in order to receive sickness and unemployment benefit.
▸ Workers were dissatisfied simply because unions were illegal; once they had full rights, workers would co-operate with employers for the greater prosperity of both, and unions would no longer be necessary.

In 1824 Hume succeeded in having a parliamentary committee of inquiry set up to study the situation. Hume and Place trained the workers who gave evidence so well that Huskisson was persuaded to take the extremely liberal step of repealing the Combination Laws. However, the results horrified both Radicals and industrialists. Hundreds of trade unions came out into the open, and hundreds of new ones were formed. In 1825, there was a wave of strikes as workers demanded wage increases – their share of the general prosperity. Under pressure from industrialists, the government was preparing to re-introduce the Combination Laws, but Place and Hume managed to salvage something for the unions: *the Amending Act (1825)* permitted trade unions to exist for the purpose of negotiating about wages and hours of work, but they were not allowed to 'molest' or 'obstruct'. While this made it difficult to conduct strikes, it was an important step forward in trade union organization.

(c) Peel and law and order

Part of Peel's talent was that he was willing to listen to and be persuaded by reasonable arguments. He studied carefully the recommendations of humanitarian reformers such as Sir Samuel Romilly, Sir James Mackintosh, John Howard and Elizabeth Fry. Bentham himself had criticized the inefficiencies of a legal system that had grown up piecemeal over 600 years. *The Penal Code* (the list of punishments for various crimes) was far too severe: over 200 offences, including minor ones such as stealing a loaf of bread, damaging Westminster Bridge and impersonating a Chelsea pensioner, were punishable by death. Another 400 were punishable by hard labour in the convict settlements of Australia. In a notorious case in 1813, a boy had been hanged for stealing a sheep. In practice, the system broke down because juries often refused to convict if it meant execution for a trivial offence, and many criminals went unpunished.

Conditions in prisons were atrocious: they were overcrowded, filthy, insanitary and disease-ridden; child offenders were put together with hardened criminals; jailers were often brutal, and there was a ludicrous system whereby they were unpaid, and had to make a living from fees paid to them by prisoners. Peel introduced a series of reforms which, between 1823 and 1830, radically changed the whole system of law and order:

1 *Penal Code reform:* the death penalty was abolished for over 180 crimes, and in the remainder (apart from murder and treason) it was left for the judge to decide whether the death penalty should be imposed. Punishments for other offences were made less severe. The barbaric practice of burying suicides at crossroads with a stake through the heart was abolished. In addition, the jury system was drastically reorganized, and the government stopped using spies to report on possible trouble-makers. These were splendid liberal and humanitarian reforms, but there was still some way to go: people could still be sent to jail for debt and transported to Australia, while public hangings continued until 1868. Peel was unable to do much about the procedure of the law courts, which remained slow and cumbersome.

2 *The Jails Act (1823)* removed some of the worst abuses from the prison system: magistrates were to inspect prisons at least three times a quarter; jailers were to be paid instead of having to extort cash from prisoners; women prisoners were to be looked after by women jailers; all prisoners were to have some elementary education, and receive visits from doctors and chaplains. However, the Act applied only to the large prisons in London and seventeen other cities – smaller prisons and debtors' prisons remained as before.

3 *The Metropolitan Police Act (1829)* introduced the London police force. The Bow Street Runners and the army of elderly night-watchmen were not very efficient at keeping the peace; Peel was convinced that the law would be more effective if there was some organization to track down and deter criminals. The Act provided for 1,000 paid constables, soon to be increased to 3,000, under the control of a commissioner with headquarters at Scotland Yard. The scheme was to be financed by a special rate. The new police wore top hats and blue coats with belts, but were armed only with truncheons, to

avoid the charge that they were a military force. Soon nicknamed 'bobbies' or 'peelers' after their founder, they reduced the crime rate spectacularly. As criminals moved out of the capital, provincial city authorities, and then country areas, began to copy the London force. *It was a controversial reform:* many people resented the police rate; they felt that the police were just another form of repression, and that the country was moving towards a dictatorship. Even a parliamentary committee set up to consider the problem had announced in 1822: 'It is difficult to reconcile an effective system of police with that perfect freedom of action and exemption from interference which are the great privileges and blessings of society in this country'. However, respect for the police increased as crime and violence were reduced over the whole country.

(d) religious reforms

Peel and Wellington (then Prime Minister) piloted two important and liberal religious reforms through parliament.

1 *The Repeal of the Test and Corporation Acts (1828).* These antiquated laws dating back to the seventeenth century said that only Anglicans (members of the Church of England, the official state Church) could hold important positions in the state and in town corporations. Non-Anglicans included Dissenters or Nonconformists (such as Methodists, Unitarians, Presbyterians and Baptists) and Roman Catholics. For years, the Acts had been ignored as far as Nonconformists were concerned, and their repeal was simply a recognition of what happened in practice. But the repeal was only partial: *the restrictions still applied to Roman Catholics.*
2 *The Catholic Emancipation Act (1829)* was passed amid tremendous controversy, which ruined Peel's popularity with the Tories and finally caused the party to disintegrate (see next section). Roman Catholics could now sit in Parliament and hold all important offices apart from Lord Chancellor of England or Ireland, and Lord Lieutenant of Ireland.

For Canning's 'liberal' foreign policies, see Chapter 3.

2.7 why did the Tory party disintegrate in 1830?

Between 1827 and 1830 a series of events and problems occurred that split the Tory party and allowed the Whigs to form a government.

(a) the resignation of Lord Liverpool

Liverpool resigned at the age of only 57 in March 1827 after suffering a paralytic stroke. This removed the only man among the leading Tories who had the gift of holding together the various factions in the party. The old squabbles re-emerged: George Canning became Prime Minister, but Peel, Wellington and five other ministers resigned because they disapproved of his foreign policy and his sympathy for Catholic Emancipation. Canning even had to bring some Whigs into his Cabinet to make up the numbers, which shows how loose party organization was at that time. After Canning's death in August, Goderich failed to form a Cabinet, and in desperation, George IV asked Wellington to form a government. He succeeded but soon fell out with Huskisson and the other 'liberal' Tories who resigned after a disagreement over parliamentary reform. Though Peel remained in the government, Wellington had lost the support of the 'liberal' Tories (now referred to as Canningites), the left wing of the party.

(b) the crisis in Ireland, culminating in Catholic Emancipation, split the party further

1 *The problem in Ireland* arose from the fact that while almost 90 per cent of the people were Roman Catholics, most landowners and all important government officials were Protestants. Catholics had the vote, but were not allowed to sit in Parliament. This was a source of great bitterness, especially as the Irish had only agreed to the Act of Union (1800), giving up their own parliament, on condition that Catholics were allowed full political and civil rights; that is, Catholic Emancipation. The British government had failed to keep its promise because George III refused to agree to emancipation, on the grounds that he would be violating his Coronation Oath, in which he had sworn to uphold the Protestant religion. Since George IV held the same view, no progress could be made.

2 *The campaign for emancipation was led by Daniel O'Connell,* an Irish Catholic landowner and barrister, and an exciting speaker. After emancipation had been achieved, he hoped to get the Union dissolved and the Irish parliament restored to run internal affairs, though he was quite happy for the link with England to remain as far as foreign policy was concerned. His methods were non-violent: in 1823, he founded *the Catholic Association,* to which Catholics, including poor peasants, paid a penny a month (the Catholic rent). It soon became powerful, with a weekly income of £1,000 and the full support of Roman Catholic priests. At elections, the Association backed Protestant candidates who were pledged to vote for emancipation at Westminster, and anti-Catholic candidates were defeated in two by-elections. The repeal of the Test and Corporation Acts made O'Connell even more determined.

3 *The crisis point was reached with the County Clare election of 1828.* Vesey Fitzgerald, the MP for County Clare, was standing for re-election (he had just been promoted to President of the Board of Trade, and a newly-appointed minister was required to resign his seat and submit himself for re-election). Though Fitzgerald was a Protestant landlord, he was in favour of emancipation and had been a popular MP. O'Connell decided to stand against him to show how strongly Catholics felt about the issue, though as a Catholic he would not be able to take his seat even if he won. The franchise (right to vote)

was restricted: the minimum qualification was the ownership of land worth £2 a year (these voters were known as 40-shilling freeholders). However, there were enough Catholic peasants with the vote to swing the election for O'Connell, who won a triumphant victory. Ireland was seething with excitement at the prospect of scores of Catholics winning seats at the next general election. There seemed every possibility of violence and even civil war if O'Connell and other future Catholic MPs were debarred from Westminster. The Catholic MPs might well set up their own parliament in Dublin, and that could lead to the break-up of the Union.

4 *Faced with this prospect, Wellington and Peel decided to give way.* Both had been bitter opponents of emancipation for years, on the grounds that it would lead to the breaking of the Union between England and Ireland (which it eventually did). Peel had been nicknamed 'Orange Peel' and was regarded as a Protestant hero because of his anti-Catholic stance. But both were convinced that only concessions would prevent civil war. Wellington himself said: 'I have probably passed a longer period of my life engaged in war than most men and I must say this: if I could avoid by any sacrifice whatever even one month of civil war, I would sacrifice my life in order to do it.' Wellington persuaded the rest of the Cabinet to support them, and Peel introduced the Bill for Catholic Emancipation skilfully in the Commons. Wellington bullied the Lords into passing it, and George IV accepted it after a stormy five-hour meeting with Wellington and Peel, during which they both offered their resignation (April 1829). Catholics could now sit in both Houses of Parliament and hold all important offices of state in Britain except monarch, regent, Lord Chancellor of England or Ireland, and Lord Lieutenant of Ireland. As a parting shot, the government forced O'Connell to fight the County Clare election again and raised the property qualification for voting to £10, so that over 100,000 mainly Catholic 40-shilling freeholders no longer had the vote; however, this did not prevent O'Connell from winning again.

The results of emancipation were important: Peel and Wellington could claim to have averted civil war in Ireland, but the treatment of O'Connell and the 40-shilling freeholders lost the government most of the goodwill that emancipation should have won for them from the Irish Catholics. The Protestant Tories, especially the Irish landlords, never forgave Peel and Wellington for their 'betrayal.' Peel resigned, and a bitter joke circulated that he had changed his name from Peel to Repeal. Wellington was so incensed at one of his critics, Lord Winchelsea, that he challenged him to a duel, which took place in Battersea Park. Neither man was wounded. Having earlier lost his left wing over parliamentary reform, Wellington had now lost the support of right-wing Tories (known as the Ultras) and most of the Tory press over Catholic Emancipation.

Nevertheless, as Peel's most recent biographer, Douglas Hurd, points out,

Catholic Emancipation remains one of the great reforms of British history – because of its effect not just in Ireland but on the politics of the nation. For the first time a pressure group from outside Parliament had forced Parliament to alter the Constitution. The Catholic Association had achieved this not by violence but by the peaceful and shrewd use of a legal power, the right of the forty-shilling freeholder in Ireland to vote.

Emancipation was therefore a great encouragement to supporters of parliamentary reform; it showed that the Constitution could be changed peacefully, and by weakening the Tories, it opened the way for the Whigs, who had plans for reform, to come to power the following year.

(c) in 1830 there were new outbreaks of violence all over England

The causes of the outbreaks were complex: bread prices were high following the poor harvest of 1829; there was a sudden slump in exports, which brought unemployment to the Midlands and the North; and revolutions in France and Belgium helped to fuel the unrest. All over the South of England labourers burnt ricks and smashed the threshing-machines that were throwing them out of work. Strong measures were needed, but Wellington's government seemed too weak for decisive action.

(d) the demand for reform of Parliament revived

After a lull during the period of calm and prosperity since 1821, interest in parliamentary reform revived again, for a variety of reasons (see Section 4.3). Many of the Whigs now supported the demand, because they thought it was the best way to prevent revolution. It was Wellington's refusal to consider even the mildest reform measure that brought about his downfall. At the general election in the autumn of 1830 (caused by the death of George IV and the accession of his brother, William IV), candidates who favoured reform did well; when Parliament met in November, there was pressure for reform from Whigs and from 'liberal' Tories. Though he had compromised over emancipation, Wellington remained unmoved by the arguments for reform. In spite of the fact that the election system was hopelessly out of date, he announced that he thought it was the best that could be devised. Soon afterwards he was outvoted by a combination of Whigs and Tories, and immediately resigned. The Whig leader, Lord Grey, became Prime Minister of a joint Whig, Radical and Canningite government.

2.8 verdict on the Tories

No simple, straightforward verdict is possible. Students at AS level and beyond, who look more deeply at these Tory governments, soon realize that historians disagree about several aspects of their policies. Here, there is space only to refer briefly to some of the areas of dispute as an introduction to further study. There is a fuller discussion of some of these points in the articles by Graham Goodlad, 'Liberal and High Tories in the Age of Liverpool' in *Modern History Review*, November 1995, and 'Liberal Toryism' in *Modern History Review*, November 2002. The traditional view, accepted by writers such as Derek Beales, is that the Tories were reactionary (against progress, wanting to put the clock back to an earlier situation) until 1822, when there was suddenly a dramatic change in policy as the 'liberal' Tories gained the ascendancy. More recently, several new points have been suggested:

› There was no sudden change in 1822; the first signs of change were already there, and the process was simply speeded up after 1822 (see Section 2.6). Historians such as J. E. Cookson (1975) and Norman Gash (in his 1984 biography of Lord Liverpool) suggest that the government was not reactionary before 1822: they were just extremely cautious and thorough, and 'were held back by their desire to present reforms which would have the widest possible acceptance'. There was, in fact, a great deal of continuity between the two phases. Canning, Peel and Huskisson had all held important posts before 1822 – Peel had been Chief Secretary for Ireland (1812–18), where he had introduced a new police force (1814), Canning had been Foreign Secretary (1807–9) and Huskisson had been acting as an adviser to Liverpool on economic affairs.

› A clear distinction needs to be made between the Tories' political policies and their economic policies; though they may not have been progressive as far as political matters were concerned (as late as 1827, the majority were against parliamentary reform), they were prepared to make concessions on economic matters.

› The motives of the Tories have provoked argument: the traditional view is that they followed policies (Corn Laws, abolition of income tax) favouring their own class – wealthy landowners – for purely selfish reasons. However, Boyd Hilton (1977 and 2006) believes that they acted through disinterested motives: they wanted to secure food supplies and full employment, and therefore supported agriculture because it seemed the most promising area of expansion. Later, they realized their mistake, and industry was the major growth area, so consequently, in the 1820s, they began to favour industrialists. Philip Harling (1996) argues that 'liberal' Tories set out to reduce indirect taxation and aimed to run the government as cheaply as possible in the hope of winning middle-class support. As Graham Goodlad puts it: 'By demonstrating the responsiveness of the unreformed parliament to middle class interests, Canning staved off demands for thorough constitutional change.' The problem was that economic prosperity dwindled in the years 1929–30, and so the demand for reform was renewed.

› Jonathan Parry (1996) suggests that, whatever reservations there might be about the earlier phase of Tory government before 1822, the 'liberal' Tories were responsible for laying the foundations of the later nineteenth-century Liberal party.

› There is disagreement about the personal achievements of Lord Liverpool. Disraeli described him as 'the arch-mediocrity'. Others see him as the arch-reactionary, responsible for repression and opposition to parliamentary reform. On the other hand, he allowed important reforms to be introduced between 1822 and 1827, and showed enormous skill in holding a difficult Cabinet together for fifteen years. 'If Liverpool was an arch-mediocrity', writes N. H. Brasher (1968) in his defence, 'then it is a pity that Britain has had so few of the breed since'.

QUESTIONS

1 To what extent was the discontent and distress of the period 1815–20 caused by the after-effects of the wars with France?

2 'After 1822 the policies of the Tory governments underwent fundamental changes.' How accurate is this view of the activities of the Tory governments in the period 1815–30?

3 How far would you agree that Lord Liverpool's Tory government simply pursued selfish policies designed to benefit wealthy aristocratic landowners?

A document question about Peterloo can be found on the accompanying website www.palgrave.com/masterseries/lowe1.

foreign affairs, 1815–30

summary of events

The period was dominated by two outstanding Foreign Secretaries: *Robert Stewart, Lord Castlereagh* (from 1812 until his death in 1822); and *George Canning* (1822–7). After Canning's death, the key influence on foreign policy was Wellington, who became Prime Minister in 1828.

The most pressing problems at the end of the Napoleonic Wars were how to deal with the defeated France, and how to redraw the map of a Europe whose frontiers and governments had been drastically reorganized by Napoleon. The Bourbon monarchy was restored in the person of Louis XVIII, and other details were dealt with by *the First and Second Treaties of Paris* (May 1814 and November 1815). In the intervening period, Napoleon escaped from exile on the island of Elba and he had to be crushed once and for all at Waterloo. The wider problems of Europe were settled at *the Congress of Vienna* (1814–15), though the arrangements, like those of most peace treaties, were controversial and were to cause problems later.

The year 1815 saw the formation of *the Holy Alliance*, the brainchild of Tsar Alexander I of Russia; its members pledged themselves to rule their countries according to Christian principles. More important was *the Quadruple Alliance* of Britain, Austria, Prussia and Russia, a continuation of the 1815 alliance that had defeated Napoleon; this became *the Quintuple Alliance* in 1818, when France was allowed to join. Its aims, broadly speaking, were to maintain the Vienna Settlement and preserve peace by holding Congresses to solve any awkward problems that arose. After the initial Congress at *Aix-la-Chapelle* (1818) it gradually became apparent that Britain was not in agreement with the other members of the alliance about how to deal with the revolutions that had broken out in Naples, Spain and Portugal, where liberals (see Section 1.2(d)) were trying to force autocratic monarchs to allow democratic constitutions. Following the Congresses of *Troppau* (1820) and *Laibach* (1821), troops were sent in to suppress the revolutions in Spain and Naples, in spite of strong objections from Castlereagh, who disapproved of interfering in the internal affairs of other states.

There were other revolutions as well, this time caused by nationalism (see Section 1.2(e)): the Spanish colonies in South America were trying to assert their independence, while the Greeks were struggling to break away from Turkish rule. These problems were considered at *the Congress of Verona* (1822). Unlike the outbreaks in Naples and Spain, these revolutions were successful, partly because of British support. In the case of the Greek revolt, Russia and France agreed with Britain, while the Austrians and Prussians were incensed at Canning's attitude. Although further Congresses met in St Petersburg in 1824–5, Britain took no part and the Congress System (sometimes known as the Concert of Europe) came to an end. The general feeling in Britain was that this was no bad thing, since the Austrian and Prussian ideas of preserving peace and the Vienna Settlement seemed to be to keep as many autocratic governments in power as possible.

key events in British foreign affairs, 1815–30

1812	Castlereagh becomes Foreign Secretary
May 1814	First Treaty of Paris
Oct 1814–June 1815	Congress of Vienna
June 1815	Battle of Waterloo – Napoleon finally defeated and exiled to St Helena
Nov 1815	Second Treaty of Paris
Nov 1815	Quadruple Alliance of Britain, Austria, Russia and Prussia signed – Congress System begins
1818	Congress of Aix-la-Chapelle. France joins the Alliance, which becomes the Quintuple Alliance
1820	Revolutions break out in Spain, Portugal, Naples and Piedmont
1820	Congress of Troppau meets – Castlereagh refuses to attend because he knows other members want to crush revolutions
1821	Congress of Laibach – Castlereagh again refuses to attend. Congress decides to send Austrian troops to crush revolutions in Naples and Piedmont
Aug 1822	Castlereagh commits suicide
Sept 1822	Canning becomes Foreign Secretary
1822	Congress of Verona authorizes French army to crush revolution in Spain
July 1823	Canning sends British naval squadron and later 5,000 troops to help Portuguese revolutionaries, who are eventually successful
1825	Britain recognizes Mexico, Colombia and Argentina (former Spanish colonies) as independent republics

July 1827   Canning signs Treaty of London: Britain, France and Russia
                      promise to help Greeks win independence from Turkey
Aug 1827   Canning dies
Oct 1827   Battle of Navarino – British and French fleets destroy
                      Turkish/Egyptian fleet – leads to recognition of Greek
                      independence (1830)

3.1 what were the aims of the statesmen who met at Vienna in 1814–15, and to what extent were their aims fulfilled in the Vienna Settlement?

The leading personalities at Vienna were Prince Metternich (Austrian Chancellor), Tsar Alexander I of Russia, Count Hardenburg (Prussian Minister) and Lord Castlereagh.

(a) their aims were:

> To make sure that the French, who were held responsible for the wars, paid for their misdeeds.
> To further their own interests and make sure that the victorious powers gained some compensation for their pains.
> To prevent any further French aggression which might threaten the peace and security of Europe. This could be done by strengthening the states bordering on France and by making sure that the four leading powers remained on good terms with each other in order *to maintain a balance of power* (no single state would be powerful enough to dominate the rest). Rulers who had been expelled by Napoleon should be restored, as far as possible, as the best guarantee of peace and stability (this was known as the principle of *legitimacy*).

There were disagreements about details: each had different ideas about what constituted a balance of power. Castlereagh was worried in case the settlement was too hard on the French, which might make them bitter and likely to go to war again to recoup their losses; he argued that 'it is not our business to collect trophies, but to try, if we can, to bring the world back to peaceful habits'. There were jealousies lest one country gained more than another: Prussia wanted Alsace-Lorraine (from France) and the Kingdom of Saxony, and Alexander wanted the whole of Poland; in each case, the other states were suspicious and refused to allow it. Austria wanted to make sure that Russia did not take over from France as the most powerful nation on the continent of Europe.

Throughout the entire negotiations Talleyrand, the French representative, was extremely active in protecting French interests and salvaging what he could from the disaster.

(b) how successful were they?

1 The treatment of France was finalized by the Second Treaty of Paris (November 1815); though harsher than the First Treaty, it was still reasonably lenient. France was to be reduced to its 1790 frontiers, which meant losing some territory to Belgium and some to Piedmont (see Map 3.1). The country had to pay an indemnity (a fine) and have an army of occupation until the fine was paid; in addition, it lost many of its overseas colonies. The terms might have been much more stringent if Castlereagh had not been so moderate in his demands, and if Talleyrand had not exploited the mutual suspicions of the other powers so shrewdly; for example, France was allowed to keep Alsace-Lorraine in spite of Prussia's determination to get it, because the other states thought that taking this would make Prussia too powerful. The statesmen were successful in their aim: France was penalized, yet not embittered enough to want a war of revenge (note the contrast with the treatment of the defeated Germany at Versailles in 1919 – see Section 22.6).

2 The victorious powers all gained territory, mainly at the expense of countries that had been unlucky enough to end the war on the losing side. Britain gained Ceylon (Sri Lanka), Mauritius, Trinidad, Tobago, St Lucia, Malta, Heligoland, the Cape of Good Hope, and a protectorate over the Ionian Islands. After some complicated bargaining, Prussia received about two-fifths of Saxony, the Rhineland, Western Pomerania, Danzig and Posen; Russia received Finland (from Sweden) and part of Poland; Austria was given

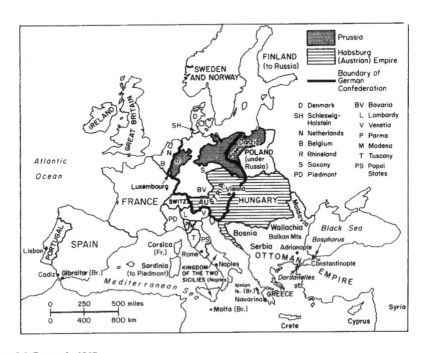

map **3.1 Europe in 1815**

Lombardy and Venetia in North Italy, plus a stretch of Adriatic coast. As compensation for losing Finland, Sweden was given Norway, taken from Denmark; this move was pressed by Britain, so that the entrance to the Baltic would not be controlled by a single power.

3 Two of France's smaller neighbours were strengthened: the Austrian Netherlands (Belgium) were combined with Holland to make a strong barrier state to the north-east. Piedmont (also known as Sardinia) in North Italy on France's eastern frontier, regained most of Savoy and Nice (taken by France in 1796) and was given the port of Genoa. The Bourbon family was restored to the Kingdom of Naples in the person of Ferdinand I, though they had a reputation for misgovernment. The Pope was restored to the Papal States. Also in Italy, the Duchies of Parma, Modena and Tuscany were given to Austrian princes. Austria, in fact, had a firm grip on northern Italy; this was thought necessary to deter a possible French invasion of Italy. In general, therefore, the statesmen's aims seemed to have been fulfilled: a balance of power had been achieved and the Quadruple Alliance of Britain, Austria, Prussia and Russia seemed likely to preserve good relations.

There was, in fact, no major conflict in Europe until the Crimean War (1854–6), though of course there are many other reasons besides the Vienna Settlement for this long period of comparative peace. On the other hand, *there were criticisms of the settlement.* The main one was that it ignored the principle of nationalism: Belgians were placed under Dutch rule, Italians under Austrians; Finns, Norwegians and Poles were placed under foreign governments merely to suit the wishes of the great powers. Even in Britain there were dissenting voices: the Whig MP Sir James Mackintosh said that the way the powers had redrawn the national frontiers of Europe was the most unacceptable arrogance. He was particularly incensed by the way in which Norway had been switched from Denmark to Sweden without the slightest regard for the wishes of the Norwegian people.

German nationalists were disappointed: they wanted Germany united into one powerful state, whereas the settlement reduced the old Germany of over 360 small states to 38 (known as the German Confederation); this was an improvement, but not at all what the nationalists had hoped for. By restoring autocratic rulers such as the Pope and Ferdinand I of Naples, the Congress also ignored the newly developing principle of liberalism. While there was no major war for many years, there were a number of disturbances that resulted directly from the settlement – the Belgian struggle for independence; revolutions in Naples, Piedmont and the Papal States, and the Italian fight to throw off Austrian control. The great powers were concerned in case these disturbances escalated into a major war, as had the French Revolution. In conclusion, it has to be said, in defence of the settlement, that in 1815 nationalism was still a very new principle, produced mainly by the French Revolution. It was hardly to be expected that the statesmen of Europe would allow themselves to be influenced by such a new and, to them, suspect ideal.

3.2 what were the aims and achievements of Lord Castlereagh in foreign affairs after the Congress of Vienna (1815)?

Robert Stewart, Viscount Castlereagh, was an Irish Protestant aristocrat brought up in County Down. At the end of the Congress of Vienna he had enormous prestige among the statesmen of Europe and already had considerable achievements to his credit. He had played an important part in building up and maintaining the alliance that had finally brought down Napoleon. At Vienna, he had successfully played the role of conciliator, persuading Prussia to tone down its demands, so that France gained a lenient peace. He had prevented both Prussia and Russia from gaining too much, and had consequently preserved the balance of power. He must take much of the credit for Britain's territorial gains after the defeat of Napoleon; these confirmed British naval supremacy, providing valuable bases, sources of raw materials and markets – the basis for its future imperial and commercial expansion. Britain's position as a great power had clearly been consolidated.

(a) Castlereagh's aims after the Congress of Vienna.

His main concern was to preserve peace, and he hoped that this could be achieved by continuing the co-operation between the great powers started at Vienna, thereby maintaining the balance of power. He wanted regular meetings of the powers to solve problems and quell disturbances via a *Concert of Europe* (states acting in concerted agreement) instead of by confrontation. However, he did not believe it was right for the great powers to intervene in the internal affairs of other states, and did not want Britain to become involved in any such action. Thus, in 1818, when Alexander I proposed that they should sign a written guarantee to preserve all frontiers and monarchs in Europe, Castlereagh refused. His attitude was summed up perfectly by a statement he issued in December 1815: 'It is the province of Great Britain to encourage peace by exercising a conciliatory influence between the Powers, rather than put herself at the head of any combination of Courts to keep others in check … It is not my wish to encourage on the part of this country, an unnecessary interference in the ordinary affairs of the Continent.' As to specific details, he was keen to get the army of occupation removed from France, and France accepted as an equal again by the other powers; this would boost Louis XVIII's popularity and help to stabilize the country. Castlereagh felt it was wrong to penalize the Bourbon government too heavily for the behaviour of Napoleon.

(b) Castlereagh's achievements.

It seemed as though his policies were beginning well; however, after 1818 his actual achievements were limited.

1 With the help of Metternich, Castlereagh was responsible for *the Quadruple Alliance* (November 1815) of Britain, Austria, Russia and Prussia. They agreed to maintain the peace settlement and to hold regular Congresses to discuss any threats to peace and stability. The frontiers of France were guaranteed, and the powers would intervene in France to prevent any attempt to restore the Bonapartes. This was an important achievement, because regular conferences in peacetime were a new idea in diplomacy.

2 *The Congress System got under way with the Congress of Aix-la-Chapelle (1818).* It met to consider what to do about France, which had paid off the 700 million franc indemnity and was settling down under Louis XVIII. It was decided that the army of occupation should be withdrawn, and that France should take part in future Congresses, transforming the Quadruple into the Quintuple Alliance. Relatively minor problems discussed and agreed upon were the rights of Jews in Europe, Swedish payments to Denmark for the acquisition of Norway, and the treatment of Napoleon on St Helena. A discordant note was sounded when Tsar Alexander I, perhaps carried away by his Holy Alliance (which had been signed by all European rulers apart from George III (who was insane), the Pope and the Sultan of Turkey, but which was dismissed by Castlereagh as 'a piece of sublime mysticism and nonsense'), proposed that the powers should guarantee all frontiers and all monarchs; this would have meant intervening to suppress all revolutions, including those provoked by bad government. Castlereagh was able to carry the Austrians and Prussians with him in rejecting this proposal. Again, Castlereagh seemed to have scored a considerable success: France had been accepted again on equal terms; he had launched his new method of European diplomacy; and had avoided a split in the Alliance. Unfortunately for Castlereagh, the fragile harmony of the Alliance could last only so long as there were no revolutions and no divergent interests among the powers.

3 *The year 1820 was one of revolutions inspired by liberalism,* in protest against autocratic government. In January, Spanish troops gathered at Cadiz, preparing to sail in an attempt to recapture Spain's New World colonies (Mexico, Argentina, Chile, Peru and Colombia), which had declared themselves independent during the wars. Instead, the troops turned on the government and forced King Ferdinand VII to grant a democratic constitution. Similar revolutions in Portugal, Naples and Piedmont also achieved democratic constitutions. Metternich and Alexander, alarmed at the prospect of disturbances spreading from Italy into their own territories, summoned *The Congress of Troppau (1820).*

4 Castlereagh, knowing that they intended to use the Alliance to quell the revolutions and destroy the new constitutions, refused to attend the Congress, merely sending his half-brother, Lord Stewart, as an 'observer'. Castlereagh expressed his attitude in a famous State Paper (May 1820); it was not that he approved of liberal revolutions – in fact, he sympathized with

Metternich's fears; but he was unwilling to involve Britain in general commitments on the continent. It was not morally right for the great powers to force their wishes on smaller countries: 'the Alliance ... was never intended as a Union for the government of the world ... such a scheme is utterly impractical and objectionable'. In addition, he knew that the Opposition in Parliament would be furious if Britain supported intervention, and that even many of his Cabinet colleagues were sick of Britain's involvement in Europe. He was extremely suspicious of Russian motives, since Alexander was itching to send an army through Europe to crush the Spanish revolution. Unimpressed by Castlereagh's objections, the other representatives issued *the Troppau Protocol* (a first draft of terms to be agreed), which asserted their right to intervene in any country where a revolution seemed in danger of infecting other countries. Castlereagh rejected the Protocol, and there was clearly a serious split in the Alliance. The Congress adjourned in disarray.

5 *The Congress of Laibach (1821)* was a continuation of Troppau. To show his disapproval, Castlereagh again sent his half-brother. He did concede, however, that the Austrians should intervene in Naples, provided it was not done in the name of the Alliance. As a result, Austrian troops quelled the revolts in Naples; they went on to deal with the revolt in Piedmont as well, a step Castlereagh did not approve. No action was taken against Spain and Portugal at this stage. Just before the Congress ended, the European situation was further complicated by the outbreak of the Greek revolt against Turkish rule. Relations between Britain and the rest remained tense, and it was obvious that Castlereagh's idea of international co-operation was being misused by Britain's allies, though he could not bring himself to break away from the Alliance completely. A further Congress was planned for Verona in 1822, to consider the Spanish and Greek problems, but before it met, Castlereagh had committed suicide (August 1822).

His mind had given way under the strain of what historian R. J. White calls 'his courageous attempt to be with Europe but not of it, a diplomatic tight-rope act which must have been a nightmare for the chief performer'. He also had the difficult job of leading the unpopular Tory government in the Commons (as an Irish peer, Lord Castlereagh was not entitled to a seat in the House of Lords, and therefore sat in the House of Commons, whereas the Prime Minister, Lord Liverpool, an English peer, was able to sit in the House of Lords). In addition, though he appeared cool and arrogant, Castlereagh was a shy and sensitive man who was deeply hurt and disturbed by his unpopularity, and by the abuse he had to suffer. He was already unpopular with the liberals and radicals in 1815 for allowing the restoration of so many autocratic monarchs. Later, he was blamed for the government's repressive policy (see Section 2.4). Not being a good speaker, he failed to explain his foreign policy clearly; consequently, the opposition in Parliament and the general public thought he was committed to supporting autocracy, which seemed to be borne out by his approval of Austrian intervention in Naples. During the summer of 1821 he was convinced that sinister characters were trying to ruin his reputation by accusing him of being a homosexual. He became so unbalanced that, despite his friends removing his pistols and razors, he succeeded in cutting his throat with a penknife. So great was his unpopularity that crowds hissed and jeered as his coffin was carried into Westminster Abbey.

Though his career was tragically cut short at the age of 53, Castlereagh's achievements after Vienna deserve to be remembered: he must take the credit for the introduction of the Congress System; this was a new departure in international co-operation and personal contact between the statesmen of Europe, a policy that he pursued with commonsense and restraint.

3.3 what were the aims and achievements of Canning in foreign affairs (1822–7), and how did his policies differ from those of Castlereagh?

(a) Canning's aims

Canning was not radically different from Castlereagh in his attitude, though there were differences of method and style.

▸ Canning was not an enthusiastic supporter of liberalism and revolution abroad, but he did believe that whenever there was bad government, change must come.
▸ Like Castlereagh, Canning did not approve of great powers interfering all over the world as they saw fit – if a change was necessary, as for example in Greece, the process should be supervised by whichever of the powers was most closely concerned, and not simply squashed by the whole Alliance.
▸ Whereas Castlereagh had merely protested against the Metternich policy of intervention, Canning intended to be more decisive and actually help the revolutionaries in Greece and Portugal. Even here, though, the difference was not completely clear cut, since just before his death, Castlereagh had been contemplating sending a fleet to help the Portuguese liberals.
▸ Where he differed most from Castlereagh was that his overriding concern was to protect British interests rather than to preserve the Alliance. As Canning's biographer, Wendy Hinde, put it, 'his policy was based on a careful, even opportunist calculation of what would best preserve peace and promote England's prestige and prosperity'. Not being a founder-member of the Alliance, he had no special affection for it, and did not know the European rulers and politicians personally; if it suited Britain's interests, he was quite prepared to withdraw from the Alliance: 'For *Europe*, I shall be desirous now and then to read *England*', he wrote soon after becoming Foreign Secretary.

- Whereas Castlereagh's policies were misunderstood, Canning took the trouble to explain to the public what he was trying to achieve; this gained him public support and popularity, though other politicians often disapproved and thought him rather showy – one critic remarked that Canning's trips round the country 'speechifying and discussing the intentions of the Gov't were ridiculous ... quite a new system among us ... which excites great indignation'.
- Canning's specific aims were to prevent the French from interfering in Spain; to preserve the new Portuguese constitution; maintain the independence of the Spanish colonies with which Britain had developed valuable trade; and to help the Greeks, while at the same time making sure that the Russians did not gain too much advantage from the situation.

(b) Canning's achievements

1 Canning failed in his first specific aim – to keep the French out of Spain. At *the Congress of Verona* (1822) it soon became clear that Britain's representative, Wellington, was isolated, since all the other powers were determined to destroy Spain's new liberal constitution. British protests were ignored and a French army was authorized to invade Spain; by April 1823, the Spanish liberals had been defeated and Ferdinand's full powers restored. It was a diplomatic failure for Britain, and public opinion was outraged at the presence of French troops in Spain again, only ten years after they had been driven out by Wellington. However, Canning's anti-French speeches won him popularity at home, which increased as some important successes followed.

2 He was successful in upholding the liberal constitution in Portugal. Canning's fear was that unless Britain took decisive action, the French and Spanish, carried away by their crusade against liberalism, might invade Portugal and might even be tempted to regain the lost Spanish colonies in the New World. Following an appeal for help by the Portuguese Foreign Minister, a British naval squadron was sent to Lisbon (July 1823), and later, when it looked as though a Spanish army was about to enter Portugal, Canning despatched 5,000 British troops to defend the Portuguese liberals. This was immensely popular with the public at home: it was felt that Canning had restored Britain's prestige after the Spanish failure, and had defied Metternich and the other reactionaries in the Alliance.

3 Together with the USA, Britain was instrumental in preserving the independence of Spain's former colonies. The situation reached crisis point in the autumn of 1823, when Ferdinand VII of Spain proposed another Congress to consider action; it was obvious that Spain and France, and probably the other powers as well, were in favour of a joint expedition to recapture the lost colonies. Canning was determined this should not happen, for several reasons: he felt that the people of South America and Mexico should have the right to remain free from such a reactionary tyrant as Ferdinand VII; he

feared that the French might keep some of the Spanish colonies for themselves; and probably most important of all, Britain stood to lose the valuable export trade that had developed with the new states, as the Spanish refused to guarantee Britain's right to trade with the colonies if they were recovered. By now, Canning was convinced that the Congress System was a waste of time: 'We protested at Laibach and Verona and our protests were treated as waste paper.' Consequently, he rejected the idea of a further Congress, and warned Polignac, the French ambassador, that Britain would use its fleet in the Atlantic to prevent any expedition from reaching South America.

Support for the British stand came from the USA, which had already recognized the colonies' independence. In December 1823, President Monroe told Congress (the US parliament) that if any European power interfered in any part of America, whether it be North, Central or South, the USA would oppose it by force. This American policy became known as *the Monroe Doctrine.* The President's motive was to make Central and South America into a US sphere of influence and to warn off the Russians in case they had designs on the rest of America via Alaska, which belonged to Russia. The Monroe Doctrine was actually anti-British as well as anti-the rest of Europe; moreover, Canning was disappointed that the USA had recognized the colonies as republics – he would have preferred to see monarchies. However, the Americans were well aware that their navy alone would be ineffectual, and that only with the help of British sea-power could they enforce the Monroe Doctrine. In 1825, Canning recognized Mexico, Colombia and Argentina as independent republics, and signed trade agreements with them. Metternich and the others, faced with the double threat from Britain and the USA, abandoned all hope of recovering the colonies.

Canning was triumphant: the Alliance had been thwarted and the British defeat over Spain avenged: 'I called a New World into existence to redress the balance of the Old,' he remarked. Prospects for British trade were good, and Britain had shown that it could take effective action independently of the European powers. The Congress System was almost, but not quite, finished.

4 *Canning became involved in helping the Greeks in their fight against the Turks,* but he died (1827) before he could see it through. Though the Greeks eventually won full independence (1830), the circumstances were not particularly to Britain's advantage.

The origins of the situation lay in what was known as the Eastern Question: the Turkish Empire (also known as the Ottoman Empire) had once stretched far into south-eastern Europe as well as across Northern Africa. In 1683, the Turks had unsuccessfully besieged Vienna, and since that failure, they had gradually been in retreat. The Turkish government usually neglected and misgoverned its outlying provinces; by 1815 it had lost its authority over North Africa and much of the Balkans, though nominally these areas were still part of the Ottoman Empire. It was because of the obvious Turkish weakness that the Greek nationalists were stirred to try to assert their independence.

In essence, the Eastern Question was a Russian attempt to take advantage of the weakening Turkish Empire, and the attempts of other powers, especially Britain, to prevent this happening (see Section 9.2(c), Chapter 10 and Section 14.4 for later recurrences of the Eastern Question).

Canning's motives for intervention in the Greek revolt were:

› The Greeks were not having a great deal of success, since the Sultan of Turkey had received help from Mehmet Ali, the ruler of Egypt. Ali's son Ibrahim had arrived in Greece with a large army, and by 1825 he was well on the way to crushing the rebellion. There was much sympathy in Britain for the Greek cause, and many volunteers, including Lord Byron, had gone out to fight for them. The Greeks themselves sent a deputation to Britain begging for help. All this put Canning under pressure to send active assistance to the Greeks.

› By the early part of 1826, it was clear that the Russians were about to intervene on the Greek side. Alexander I had been keen to help, but Metternich had dissuaded him on the grounds that revolutions, even against the Turks, must not be encouraged. However, Alexander died in December 1825, and the new Tsar Nicholas I was ready for immediate intervention. Russian policy since 1815 had been to suppress revolutions, but this one was different: Nicholas was horrified at the slaughter of Greek Christians by Egyptian and Turkish Muslims; above all, though, Greek success would further weaken Turkey. Canning therefore decided that Britain must act too, in order to make sure, first, that Turkey would not be weakened too much and would still serve as a buffer against Russian expansion in the Balkans, and second, that Russia should not gain too much advantage, such as for example, possession of Constantinople.

› Canning may have intervened in order to break up the Congress System, knowing that Anglo-Russian co-operation would infuriate Metternich.

Consequently, Canning, now Prime Minister, negotiated *the Treaty of London* (July 1827) by which Britain, Russia and France agreed to bring about Greek self-government, by force if necessary; a joint naval expedition set out for Greece. The Austrians and Prussians objected strenuously at this support of revolution, and the Turks refused to negotiate. In August, Canning died (aged 57) from inflammation of the liver and lungs, probably brought on by overwork. Meanwhile, the combined 27-ship fleet was blockading the Turkish–Egyptian fleet of 81 ships in *Navarino Bay*. Though they were under orders to avoid hostilities, the British Admiral Codrington decided to force the issue by sailing into the bay. The Turks opened fire and a full-scale battle developed that lasted four hours. It was a disaster for the Turks and their allies; 61 ships and about 4,000 men were lost (October

1827). This battle was of great importance: Ibrahim was cut off from supplies and reinforcements; French troops landed and organized the evacuation of his troops. There was now no prospect of the Turks recapturing Greece, whose independence was recognized in 1830, although its frontiers were not decided until 1832.

After Canning's death, Wellington reversed his policy and withdrew Britain from the treaty alliance, because he did not approve of aiding and abetting revolutionaries. The government apologized to the Turks and removed Codrington from his command. With no Canning to keep a watchful eye on them, the Russians declared war on the Turks and forced them to sign *the Treaty of Adrianople* (1829) which gave the area round the Danube delta to Russia.

In the end, *Canning's work in the Near East had mixed success.* He had helped to achieve a completely independent Greece, which in 1832 was recognized as a kingdom, with Otto of Bavaria as the first king. However, his wider aim of limiting Russian gains by co-operation with Greece had been ruined by Wellington, who had failed to grasp Canning's intentions. Russia had substantially increased its influence in the Balkans, and Turkey had suffered military defeat.

5 One result of the Greek revolt which, from Canning's point of view, can be seen as an achievement, was that it marked the end of the Quintuple Alliance and the Congress System as an instrument for crushing revolutions: for the first time, Russia was acting *with* Britain and France in opposition to Austria, and there could be no further pretence that Europe was united. Canning had been prepared to break up the Congress System for a variety of reasons: to avoid binding commitments on the continent, to help liberals and nationalists (though this motive must not be exaggerated), but primarily to further Britain's trading and other interests. Metternich had been thwarted; no wonder he was delighted at Canning's death and thanked God for delivering Europe from 'this malevolent meteor'.

QUESTIONS

1 Compare and explain the foreign policies of Castlereagh and Canning.
2 To what extent can British foreign policy be described as 'liberal' in the period 1815–30?

A document question about Lord Castlereagh and his conduct of foreign affairs can be found on the accompanying website www.palgrave.com/masterseries/lowe1.

chapter 4

Parliament and the Great Reform Act of 1832

summary of events

In 1830, the agitation for a reform of Parliament and the system of elections burst out afresh after a lull from 1821, during a period of good trade and comparative prosperity. The demand for reform dated back into the middle of the previous century. William Pitt (premier from 1783 until 1801, and again from 1804 until his death in 1806) tried to introduce some modest changes in 1785; he proposed re-distributing some of the worst 'rotten' boroughs, but the idea was dropped, largely because of opposition from George III. This new agitation seemed more widespread than before; this was shown by the general election held in the autumn of 1830, when candidates who favoured reform did well. Wellington, the Tory Prime Minister, said that he saw no need to change the system, but the Whig government that came to power in November decided to introduce a Reform Bill that would remedy some of the worst faults of the system. The Whigs came up against many problems as they tried to steer their Reform Bill through Parliament. It was defeated once in the Commons and twice in the Lords, but it eventually became law as the 1832 Reform Act, later known as the Great Reform Act. After all the excitement, the reformers found that the terms of the Act were something of an anti-climax; several more Reform Acts were needed before Britain could be regarded as a genuinely democratic country.

4.1 how are laws made?

It will be helpful at this point to outline briefly the stages through which any proposed government measure has to pass before it becomes law.

‣ The proposed changes are known as *a Bill*; this is read out in the House of Commons (*first reading*) and then printed, after which it gets a *second reading*.
‣ Next, the proposals are debated by the MPs and a vote is taken. If a majority of MPs are in favour of the Bill, it passes to the next stage.

- *The committee stage.* Here, each clause is carefully considered by an all-party committee of between sixteen and fifty MPs who have special knowledge about the subject of the Bill. If necessary, they can suggest amendments (changes) to the Bill before sending it back to the Commons, to go through the next stage.
- *The report stage.* MPs consider the suggested amendments and may also propose further changes. When the Bill has been sorted out into its final form ...
- *a third reading* takes place, followed by a short debate and another vote. These votes are known as *divisions*, because MPs register their votes by moving out into the lobbies of the House of Commons and dividing into two groups: those who approve of the Bill file back through one lobby, and those against the Bill, through another.
- A Bill that has passed all three readings in the Commons is sent to the House of Lords, where it goes through all the same stages again. A controversial Bill may well be defeated in the Lords; this happened twice to the Whig Reform Bill. This is one of the main functions of the House of Lords – to act as a check and to make the government think again about Bills or parts of Bills that might be considered to be ill-advised.
- If a Bill is approved by the House of Lords, it is sent to the sovereign (the King or Queen) to be signed. This is known as receiving *the Royal Assent.* Once the monarch has signed it, the Bill becomes *an Act of Parliament* and is ready to be put into operation as a new law. Nowadays the Queen always gives the Royal Assent to Bills that have been passed by both Houses of Parliament. The last sovereign to refuse to do so was Queen Anne in 1707, but since then the monarch has gradually withdrawn from the business of party politics. The Queen is said to be 'above politics', and she has to act 'on the advice' of her Prime Minister; in other words, she has to go along with the wishes of the Prime Minister and Cabinet. However, both George III and George IV could still have some influence on government policy; if the government knew the King disapproved of a certain policy, it could delay introducing a Bill or hold it up in Parliament so that it never reached the King; this happened with Catholic Emancipation, and with Pitt's earlier attempt at parliamentary reform.

4.2 what was wrong with the system before the Great Reform Act?

Very few changes had been made since the mid-eighteenth century, so the system was completely out of date and took no account of population increases or the recent spread of urbanization and shifts in population caused by the Industrial Revolution. Though Britain was rapidly becoming an industrialized nation, Parliament, and therefore the running of the country, was still dominated by landowners.

(a) constituencies were not organized to give fair and equal representation to all parts of the country

There were two types of constituency: *counties* and *boroughs*. There were 122 county MPs, 432 borough MPs, 100 from Ireland and two each from the universities of Oxford and Cambridge.

The absurdities of the system were many:

▸ English and Irish counties were each represented by two MPs, irrespective of size and population. Yorkshire, for example, had 17,000 electors, while Rutland had only 609.
▸ Scottish and Welsh counties had only one MP each, and both Scotland (45 seats) and Wales (24 seats) were under-represented compared with England's 489 seats.
▸ Most English borough constituencies had two MPs, whereas those in Scotland, Wales and Ireland were allowed only one. Again, the electorate (the group of people allowed to vote) varied widely: Westminster, Preston, Bristol, Leicester and Liverpool each had over 5,000 voters, while at the other end of the scale Old Sarum (Wiltshire) had seven, and Gatton (Surrey) had six. These tiny constituencies were known as *rotten boroughs*, because they had fallen into decay. Old Sarum was no more than a field and some earthworks and nobody actually lived there; Gatton had dwindled to six houses, and Dunwich (Suffolk), which had once been a thriving community, had gradually fallen into the sea as the coast had eroded away. In total there were 56 boroughs with fewer than 40 voters each, yet each of them was represented in the House of Commons by two MPs.
▸ Expanding industrial cities such as Birmingham, Manchester, Leeds and Sheffield had no MPs because they had not been boroughs in the late seventeenth century, when the last major redistribution of seats had taken place. Consequently the Midlands and North of England were greatly under-represented compared with the South: in 1831, Lancashire, with a population of 1.3 million, had only 14 MPs, while Cornwall, with 300,000 people, had 42 MPs.

(b) the franchise (right to vote) was restricted and inconsistent

Women were not allowed to vote at all. *In county constituencies* the franchise was fairly straightforward: since 1430 men who owned freehold (land or property) worth 40 shillings had the vote. The fact that the value of money had declined meant that the county electorate was often larger than that in the boroughs. Sometimes the holders of certain church offices were considered to be freeholders – the bellringer at Westminster Abbey was allowed to vote in Middlesex.

Borough constituencies varied widely and there were five different categories:

1 *Freeman boroughs*: these were the most common (Liverpool and Coventry, for example). Here, the vote went to all who had received the freedom of the city, usually by inheritance, by marrying the daughter or widow of a freeman, or by purchase.

2 *Burgage boroughs*: the vote went to owners of certain pieces of land or property; these usually had small electorates; for example, Clitheroe (Lancashire) with fewer than 50 voters.

3 *Scot and lot boroughs*: all male householders who paid local rates had the vote; these varied in size from Westminster (over 5,000 voters) to Gatton (six).

4 *Potwalloper boroughs*: all males who owned a house and fireplace on which to boil a pot had the vote; some of these were large – Preston had over 5,000 voters, Bedford and Northampton both had over 1,000.

5 *Corporation boroughs:* only members of the corporation were allowed to vote; here, the electorates were small: out of 29 such boroughs in England, 26 (including Andover, Bath, Portsmouth, Scarborough and Truro) had fewer than 50 voters.

What they all had in common was that the system of choosing their two MPs was not at all democratic. In the whole of England, only seven boroughs out of a total of 202 had more than 5,000 voters, while 56 had fewer than 50 voters each. In the whole of Britain, which had a population of around 24 million (1831 census), there were fewer than 500,000 voters.

(c) the way in which elections were carried out encouraged bribery and corruption

▸ There was no secret ballot and votes were cast openly, so that the candidates knew how each elector had voted. Electors often had little freedom, particularly if the candidate happened to be their landlord. There were many cases of tenants being evicted because they had dared to vote against the local squire.

▸ In constituencies with large electorates, candidates resorted to outright bribery in the way of cash payments, jobs, government posts, contracts, and sometimes free beer. An election in Liverpool in 1830 cost the two candidates over £100,000 between them. The voting lasted the usual fifteen days, and the state of the contest was known from day to day. They were paying £15 a vote at the beginning, but on the last day, with the candidates neck and neck, each vote was costing £150.

▸ In the very small borough constituencies, dealings were not quite so blatantly sordid. Usually there was no contest: the local landowner would nominate his MP and the handful of voters would approve, probably encouraged by a few gifts. Boroughs of this type were known as *pocket boroughs* (or nomination boroughs) and were a valuable asset to their owners, who could sell the nomination to the highest bidder.

4.3 why did the demand for reform revive in 1829–30?

There had always been a small group of Whig MPs in favour of moderate parliamentary reform. The Whig leader, Lord Grey, had come out in support of reform as far back as 1793; other prominent supporters included his son-in-law, Lord Durham (known as 'Radical Jack'), Lord Brougham and Lord John Russell. By 1829 there were further pressures.

(a) the ever-increasing class of prosperous businessmen and manufacturers

Though many of them were MPs, *they resented the domination of Parliament by landowners.* It seemed as though the latter protected their own interests with measures such as the Corn Laws, whereas the unfortunate manufacturers still had to pay duties on their imported raw materials; they felt they were paying more than their fair share of taxes. Generally referred to as *the middle class,* they wanted the system changed, not to one of complete democracy in which all adults had the vote, but just enough to give themselves a fair representation in the Commons.

(b) the passing of Catholic Emancipation in 1829 (see Section 2.7(b))

This provided an added stimulus, because it split and weakened the Tory party, which was the chief enemy of reform. Some of the right-wing Tories (Ultras) were so furious with Wellington that they came out in favour of reform just to spite him. They hoped to reduce the number of pocket boroughs, many of whose MPs had been used by Wellington to push Emancipation through.

(c) there was a sudden slump in the economy

This hit both agriculture and industry. The effects were seen most dramatically in the Midlands and South of England, where farm labourers' riots broke out in protest against irregular employment and low wages. In some areas, disturbances were sparked off by the introduction of threshing-machines, which reduced the number of labourers needed. In other areas, workers were protesting against having to pay tithes; this was a tax amounting to one-tenth of annual income, payable either in cash or produce, to the local vicar for the upkeep of the church. Beginning at Orpington (Kent) in June 1830, the outbreaks spread rapidly and involved the burning of hayricks and barns, smashing of threshing-machines and attacks on parsons. There was a spate of threatening letters signed 'Swing' or 'Captain Swing' (apparently a reference to the swinging stick of the flail used in hand threshing). The new Whig government acted decisively to curb these *'Swing Riots'*; Lord Melbourne, the Home Secretary, set up special courts, which tried nearly 2,000 offenders. Nineteen were hanged, over 600 sent to gaol, and nearly 500 transported to Australia. By the summer of 1831, order had been restored, but the outbreaks had been alarming enough to convince many Whigs that a moderate reform of Parliament was the best way to avoid revolution.

(d) strikes in the North of England

Here John Doherty had founded a trade union for cotton spinners, and strikes broke out in the Manchester area in protest at wage reductions. In October 1830 there was a coal strike at Oldham, and miners began to join Doherty's union. The signs were ominous: a visitor at the opening of the Liverpool–Manchester Railway (September) noted: 'Tricolour flags (the French revolutionary standard) were displayed at some parts of the line. The spirit of the district was detestable.'

(e) Jeremy Bentham continued to advocate a reform of Parliament

Bentham and his supporters (known as 'Philosophic Radicals') (see Section 2.1(c)) had been pressing their case for many years. In 1817, Bentham had published a pamphlet calling for annual general elections, secret ballots, and the vote for all males at 21. At first these demands were far too extreme for most people, but now some of them began to be taken up in unexpected quarters. *Thomas Attwood*, a Birmingham banker from a Tory background, founded *the Birmingham Political Union* (January 1830); 'The general distress which now affects the country,' he wrote, 'can only be permanently remedied by an effectual Reform in the Commons.' The Union aimed to unite the middle and working classes; similar unions quickly appeared in London and other cities, and later they organized themselves into a nationwide movement known as *the National Political Union.* It won the support of workers because it seemed the only peaceful way to achieve social reform.

(f) revolutions in Europe had an important influence on Britain

Particularly important was the revolution in France that overthrew King Charles X and put Louis Philippe on the throne (July 1830). This probably encouraged the reformers and might have frightened many of the ruling classes (though not Wellington) into giving way.

(g) the death of George IV helped the reformers

The reformers were fortunate that George, who was against any changes in Parliament, died in June 1830. His successor, William IV, was by no means enthusiastic, but was prepared to go along with some changes. It was the practice to hold a general election on the accession of a new monarch. This took place in July–August 1830, and it was no surprise that reform candidates did well. The Tory Prime Minister, Wellington, continued to stick to his view that the existing system was perfect. He told the House of Lords that 'he had never heard of any measure that could in any degree satisfy his mind that the state of the representation could be improved.' Eventually Wellington was outvoted by a combination of Whigs and progressive Tories, and was forced to resign. The King invited the Whig leader, Lord Grey, to form a government (November 1830).

However, the new Whig government was by no means united on how far reform of Parliament should go. They had no plan or programme prepared, and in the following months, until the Bill finally became law in June 1832, it often seemed as though they were responding to events rather than taking the lead. There has been some debate among historians about the Whigs' real motives for pressing ahead with reform. Probably the majority view is that the government was genuinely afraid that failure to introduce some reform measure would lead to revolution, particularly when the violence began to escalate in September 1831. The most disturbing aspect of the violence as far as the Whigs were concerned was that so many business and professional people – the rising middle class – were involved. The eventual aim of the Bill was therefore to do just enough to keep the respectable middle classes on the government's side and separate them from the working-class agitators. Other historians have suggested that the fear of revolution was exaggerated, and that the main aim of the Whigs was to strengthen the existing system and its domination by the aristocracy by giving the wealthier middle classes a stake in the constitution. It has even been suggested that the Bill was a cynical move by the Whigs for party political gain, in the hope that all the new voters would support the Whigs for the foreseeable future. Most of the Tories, led by Wellington, became more determined than ever to oppose reform.

4.4 why was there so much opposition to reform?

It might appear that the case for reform was so strong that no sane-minded person could possibly oppose it. However, the system had plenty of vigorous supporters, whose arguments and motives were:

› It had worked perfectly well in the past, producing stable and successful government, winning a great victory in the wars against France and bringing economic prosperity. Therefore there was no need to change it.
› Rotten boroughs were useful because they allowed both parties to introduce their promising up-and-coming young men into the Commons; they were also essential to provide seats for unpopular ministers.
› All the people who benefited in any way from the system were reluctant to have it changed. For example, corporation members and freemen opposed an extension of the franchise because the more electors there were, the less they could expect to pick up in bribes.
› If the small boroughs were abolished, the resulting loss of the franchise would be an interference with the property rights of those people concerned; it would be like taking away someone's house or land, and once such practices were allowed, no property would be safe.
› The majority of Tories, though certainly not all of them, wanted to uphold the system, because the nomination boroughs (pocket and some rotten

boroughs) provided the basic core of their MPs (well over 200, whereas the Whigs had only about 70).

▸ Even small changes in the system must be restricted because they would encourage demands for more, and appetites would not be satisfied until full democracy had been introduced. This would upset the Constitution and make the House of Commons more powerful than the Lords. This was why Peel was against reform: 'I was unwilling to open a door which I saw no prospect of being able to close.' Some Tories feared that the effects would be even more drastic. Tory MP and friend of Peel, J. W. Croker, wrote that, if the Reform Bill went through, there would be 'no King, no Lords, no inequalities in the social system; all will be levelled to the plane of the petty shopkeepers and small farmers, perhaps not without bloodshed, but certainly by confisca-tions and persecutions'.

▸ Landowners were afraid that their interests would not be well served by a House of Commons dominated by the middle classes, particularly as some of the reformers were also advocating repeal of the Corn Laws.

4.5 the passing of the Bill

Although the Whigs were well aware of the strength of Tory feelings, it is unlikely that they foresaw how bitterly the Tories would fight the Reform Bill. Instead of it taking a few weeks to pass, as they expected, it took fifteen months, and there were riots, marches and a general election before it became law. The stages were:

▸ Lord John Russell introduced the Bill (March 1831), which proposed, among other things, to abolish over a hundred rotten and pocket boroughs, and to give their MPs to the industrial North and Midlands. It would also allow more people to vote. It was quite a mild measure, to change things just enough to bring the new business and manufacturing classes into the system. As Professor Norman McCord puts it, the Bill was designed 'to recruit to the political nation, groups who could be seen as useful ... to admit the respon-sible, respectable, trustworthy few and to exclude the dangerous many ... What the Whigs intended was the enfranchisement of the possessors of property and information ... those who could make an informed use of the vote.'

The Bill was greeted with jeers and howls of derision from the Tories, and while it passed its second reading in the Commons by a majority of one, the Tories were able to defeat it at the committee stage.

▸ The Prime Minister, Lord Grey, persuaded William IV to dissolve Parliament, and a general election followed (April). Naturally, the Tories held on in their rotten and pocket boroughs, but in the counties, where the electorate was larger, the Whigs made sweeping gains and came back with a majority of 136.

- Russell introduced a slightly different version of the Bill, which passed the Commons with a comfortable majority of 109 (September). However, after a debate lasting five nights it was defeated in the Lords by a majority of 41, of whom 21 were bishops. There was an immediate outburst of public anger against the Lords, and the *Morning Chronicle* appeared with black borders as a sign of mourning for the Bill. There were riots in Derby and Nottingham, where the castle was destroyed (it was the property of the unpopular Duke of Newcastle, who had expelled tenants for voting against his candidates). In Bristol, rioters burned down the bishop's palace and other public buildings, and it took three troops of cavalry to restore order; at least twelve people were killed and around 400 seriously injured. Things were more orderly in Birmingham, but about 100,000 people attended Attwood's protest meeting; the Political Unions organized similar meetings all over the country. Several peers and bishops known to have voted against the Bill, and even some who had not, were attacked by mobs, and the Duke of Wellington had his windows smashed (he retaliated by putting up iron shutters).
- A third version of the Bill passed the Commons (March 1832) and two readings in the Lords, but at the committee stage the Tories passed an amendment that would have weakened the Bill (May). Grey asked the King to create fifty new Whig peers, enough to give them a majority; when William refused, Grey resigned.
- With excitement in the country at a new climax, William invited Wellington to form a government. The Duke was prepared to do his duty and help the King: for six days he tried to form a Cabinet, intending to introduce a much watered-down version of the Bill. But most Tories regarded this as another Wellington betrayal, and when Peel refused to support him, the Duke had to admit failure.
- Grey returned to office amid growing agitation. Attwood was urging non-payment of taxes and one MP wrote in his diary, 'the whole country is in a state little short of insurrection'. Now thoroughly alarmed, William agreed to create as many new peers as were necessary.
- Seeing no way out, the Tory peers stayed away in large numbers, and there was no need for the King to create any new peers. Consequently, on 4 June 1832 the Bill passed its third reading in the Lords by 106 to 22, and on 7 June it received the Royal Assent.

There is disagreement among historians about how close Britain was to revolution during the Reform Bill crisis. The traditional view, which is also held by more recent writers such as E. P. Thompson and Boyd Hilton, is that without the Reform Act there would almost certainly have been widespread revolution. According to Thompson, 'Britain was within an ace of revolution', and he went on to argue that only the compromises and concessions provided by the Act averted full-scale revolt.

On the other hand, some writers, including the American historian J. Hamburger, believe that the violent incidents were not as serious as historians have thought. Hamburger thinks that the danger was deliberately exaggerated by James Mill and other Radicals in order to frighten Parliament into passing the Bill. One of the main pieces of evidence to support Hamburger's theory is that during the riots in Bristol, the better-off working class became so disgusted with the behaviour of the rioters (mainly unemployed labourers) that they ignored them and went home; if Britain had been genuinely on the verge of revolution, these riots should have acted as the starting-pistol.

Boyd Hilton argues that 'there is a case for seeing the crisis in genuinely revolutionary terms. For a brief period control passed out of the hands of the parliamentary classes and into those of radicals.' He points out that in the volatile North-West, particularly in Manchester, the situation deteriorated dangerously. This was because of the bitterness among industrial workers left over from earlier incidents such as the Peterloo 'Massacre' and a spinners' strike in 1829. The situation also became threatening in Nottingham, Leeds and some other large urban centres.

There is no escaping the fact that contemporaries had a genuine fear that some great social upheaval was about to take place. Douglas Hurd, Peel's latest biographer, sums the situation up well:

> The pressures from the public were by now [May 1832] overwhelming. Britain was nearer to a violent outburst of popular feeling in these famous Days of May than at any time in the last three centuries. The middle and working classes were in general commotion. Meetings, processions and petitions were organized across the nation; factories and shops closed; there was a run on the banks; citizens declared they would withhold taxes; the King was hissed; men of the Scots Greys in Birmingham said they would not act against a constitutional protest.

4.6 what were the terms of the Act, and how far did they put right the faults of the system?

(a) the terms of the Act changed both the representation and the franchise

1 Boroughs with a population of less than 2,000 (56 in all) lost both MPs.
2 Boroughs with a population of between 2,000 and 4,000 (31 in all) lost one MP.
3 This made 143 seats available for redistribution: 65 were given to the counties (for example, Yorkshire received an extra two, giving it six in all). Sixty-five were given to boroughs that had never had an MP (these included Leeds, Birmingham, Manchester, Sheffield, Bolton, Oldham and Bradford). Eight were given to Scotland and five to Ireland. The total number of MPs in the Commons remained the same (658).

4 In borough constituencies the vote was given to the owners or occupiers of property rated at £10 a year or more.

5 In county constituencies the vote was given to owners of copyhold land valued at £10 a year (copyholders were tenants whose families had held a particular piece of land for generations; the proof of their right to occupy the land was a copy of the original manorial court-roll entry which first allowed their ancestors to hold the land). The vote was also given to holders of land on long leases worth £10 a year, holders of land on short leases worth £50 a year and to tenant farmers who paid £50 a year rent (40-shilling freeholders kept the vote).

6 Eligible voters had to register – that is, have their names put on the electoral roll, for a fee of one shilling (5p).

(b) a few of the worst faults were remedied, but many still remained

▸ Rotten boroughs disappeared but the constituencies still varied enormously in size of electorate: there were 35 boroughs with fewer than 30 voters, while Westminster now had 11,600 and Liverpool 11,300. Although the industrial towns were given MPs, the South was still over-represented: 370 MPs came from south of a line from the Wash to the Severn, whereas the area north of the line (excluding Scotland), which had a larger population, returned only 120. Scotland, Ireland and Wales continued to be under-represented compared with England.

▸ The electorate of Britain increased from about 478,000 to 813,000 (though estimates of the figures vary) out of a total population of 24 million. This was a long way from being democratic: large sections of the population – agricultural labourers and the vast majority of industrial workers – still had no vote. Certain boroughs which already had something approaching a democratic franchise, now had a smaller electorate than before; at Preston, everyone who spent the night before the election in the town had been allowed to vote, but under the new system, all the workers were excluded, and the Radical Henry Hunt lost his seat as a result. The continuing unfairness of the new system was shown in another way: over Britain as a whole, one in seven adult males now enjoyed the vote; however, while this worked out at one in five in England, it was only one in eight in Scotland, and even worse, one in twenty in Ireland.

▸ The Act did not introduce voting by secret ballot: consequently bribery, corruption and 'influencing' of the voters continued unabated. John Hobhouse (a Radical) paid out a total of £6,000 to encourage the electors of Nottingham to support him in the elections of 1834 and 1837. At Ipswich, between £20 and £30 was being paid quite openly for one vote during the election of 1841 (see *Pickwick Papers* for Charles Dickens' hilarious description of a corrupt election, after 1832, in the imaginary borough of Eatanswill).

- The Act did not change the length of Parliaments: this remained at seven years (introduced in 1716), and it stayed at that until 1911, when it was reduced to five years.
- There was no dramatic change in the membership of the House of Commons. Some businessmen and industrialists came in, but the wealthy landowners still predominated. Many of the pocket boroughs had survived, and there were at least fifty boroughs in England and Wales where some member of the local gentry could nominate the MP. In the counties, the position of the landowners was strengthened by the fact that the tenant farmers who now had the vote felt obliged to support their candidates. Since the position of the House of Lords remained unchanged, the Tory fears of being edged out of control were not justified, at least for the time being.

In spite of its limitations, the Great Reform Act was seen by Victorian historians as a great turning point in constitutional history, and this reputation continued well into the twentieth century. J. J. Brierley, writing in 1948, claimed that the Act 'completely shifted the balance of power in the constitution'. Later historians were less enthusiastic about its impact. E. P. Thompson (1963) argued that the working classes were right to be bitterly disappointed by the terms of the Act, since it actually strengthened the state and property rights against the aspirations of the workers. They were thus obliged to look towards Trade Unionism and Chartism. G. M. Brock (1973) remarked dismissively: 'Much the same men continued to run much the same system'. The Whig government elected after the Reform Act was passed was just as full of aristocrats as the previous one had been, and just as repressive, as the unfortunate Tolpuddle Martyrs were soon to discover (see Section 5.6(a)).

Recent historians have tended to emphasize the more positive aspects of the Act. Edward Pearce, writing in 2003, describes its changes as 'drastic and sweeping'. While this is probably overstating the case, there is no doubt that the long-term effects were of great importance:

- The new registration of voters led the political parties to form committees in the constituencies to keep the rolls up to date and to make sure of maximum support. In spite of some initial corruption (such as trying to remove known opponents from the list while keeping dead supporters on it), these committees were eventually to develop into the modern local party organizations, and so the party system was strengthened.
- The disappearance of so many rotten boroughs reduced the Crown's influence in politics. The real importance of the Act turned out to be not the changes it introduced, but the fact that, as Pearce points out, it was the first breach in the system. Many of the speeches during the debates in Parliament gave new publicity to the principle of universal suffrage. Much to the disappointment of Grey and the Whigs, who hoped it would be enough to satisfy appetites, the Act led to demands for further reform of Parliament. These in

turn led to a series of peaceful political changes in which Parliament reformed itself, in 1867, 1884, 1911, 1918 and 1928. The Act also encouraged those who were advocating other types of reform – in factories, mines, Poor Law and local government. It is difficult to imagine the 1834 Poor Law, the Municipal Corporations Act of 1835, or Peel's repeal of the Corn Laws (1846) being passed by the unreformed Parliament.

› The Tory party suffered a heavy defeat in the first election after the Reform Act, being reduced to only 175 seats. However, under the leadership of Sir Robert Peel, the party adapted itself successfully to the new situation, producing a new party structure and new policies designed to appeal to the middle class. In the process, it became the modern Conservative party, which since 1841 has spent longer in power than any other British political party.

› Arguably, it was the way in which the Reform Act had been passed that proved to be of more importance than the terms themselves. In the words of Douglas Hurd: 'Public opinion had mobilised itself to influence the political class, and the political class had decided to listen. The stage was now set for a new kind of politics based on an increasingly coherent party system, on manifestos, party platforms and an ever widening range of appeals to public opinion.'

QUESTIONS

1 To what extent did the 1832 Reform Act fulfil the hopes of the Whig ministers who introduced it?

2 '[After the 1832 Reform Act] much the same men continued to run much the same system' (M. G. Brock).

The changes introduced by the 1832 Reform Act were 'drastic and sweeping' (Edward Pearce).

How do you explain the apparent contradiction between these two views?

A document question about the campaign for parliamentary reform can be found on the accompanying website www.palgrave.com/masterseries/lowe1.

chapter 5

Whig reforms and failures, 1833–41

summary of events

Following the Great Reform Act, a general election was held in December 1832, when the Whigs gained a large majority. They remained in office, except for two short breaks, until the Tory victory in the general election of 1841. Grey remained Prime Minister until 1834, when he resigned at the age of 70. This was partly because he felt that his main ambition – to introduce a moderate reform of Parliament – had been achieved, and partly because there was a split in the Cabinet about how to deal with the continuing unrest in Ireland.

The 55-year-old *William Lamb, Lord Melbourne*, took over the premiership. However, he had difficulty in forming a Cabinet, and in discussions with the King, William IV, he offered to resign. William, who had had enough of the Whig reforms by this time, accepted the offer, and in effect dismissed the government. He invited Peel to form a ministry, even though the Tories lacked a majority in the Commons. A general election had to be held (January 1835), and despite the Tories gaining many seats, Peel was well short of a majority. Nevertheless, he was Prime Minister from December 1834 until April 1835 (known as 'Peel's 100 days'), but he was repeatedly defeated and forced to resign. William had no choice but to recall Melbourne and the government he had sacked; this demonstrated that the traditional practice of the Commons supporting whatever Prime Minister the King wanted no longer applied. It was one of the by-products of the Great Reform Act, and it meant that the monarch would from then on play less and less of a part in politics.

William IV died in 1837 and was succeeded by his niece, *Queen Victoria*, who reigned until her death in 1901. She was the daughter of William's deceased younger brother, Edward, Duke of Kent. The usual general election took place after the death of the monarch, though this was the last time the custom was followed. The Whig majority was greatly reduced, and in May 1839 Melbourne resigned after his government had secured a majority of only five votes in an important division. This dismayed Victoria, who had found Melbourne most helpful and sympathetic when she had taken over the throne at the tender and inexperienced age of 18, and who looked on the Whigs as her friends. It was assumed that Peel would form a government, but an odd incident occurred, which became known as *the Bedchamber Crisis.* Peel, cautious about taking office again without a majority, asked Victoria to remove some of the leading ladies of the Queen's household who were related to the former Whig ministers, and replace them with Tory ladies. Victoria refused, whereupon Peel abandoned the idea of forming a government, and Melbourne returned yet again, for a further two years as Prime Minister. In 1840, Victoria married her cousin, *Prince Albert of Saxe-Coburg,* and became less dependent on Melbourne.

Though Melbourne himself was not interested in change, *the Whigs were responsible for some important reforms,* particularly in the early part of the ministry before they began to run out of steam. There was the abolition of slavery, attempts to improve factory conditions, grants for education, and reform of the Poor Law and of town government. At the same time, the Whig Foreign Secretary, *Lord Palmerston,* conducted a successful and popular overseas policy (see Chapter 9). Much of this programme was welcomed and supported by moderate Tories, and some historians have even suggested that the real ruler of the country, at least for part of the time, was Peel, 'governing in opposition.'

On the other hand *there were problems that the Whigs seemed incapable of understanding:* unrest among the unemployed, the Chartist movement, trade depressions and a failure to balance their budgets, which all help to explain the Whig defeat in 1841.

5.1 the Whig attitude to reform

Most of the members of the Whig government – wealthy aristocrats – seemed to think that the Great Reform Act was the one gesture towards reform that they were required to make; left to themselves, they would have been quite content to meander along without taking any further positive action. Melbourne himself, though amiable and cultured, was against nearly all the reforms being discussed. 'I am for holding the ground already taken,' he remarked, 'but not for occupying new ground rashly.' He claimed that passing new laws was only an incidental duty of governments, and believed that there were no really serious problems to be solved. Two of the most progressive Whigs, Lords Brougham and Durham, were dropped from the Cabinet in 1835. However, Lord John Russell remained in the Cabinet, and he was determined to press ahead with further reforms, even if it meant working with the Radicals and the Irish MPs.

It is easy for historians, and students, with the benefit of hindsight, to be too critical of these nineteenth-century politicians for what might be seen as a lack of vision. It is important to remember that, at the time:

- There was no tradition of wide government intervention in the life of the nation.
- Most people disapproved when governments *did* try to extend their powers, and suspected that their motives were only for party political or personal gain.
- Governments did not have the administrative machinery and resources to operate an interventionist policy.
- Policies of this sort would cost money, and there was a widespread feeling against increasing taxation. Even the Radicals, who wanted efficient government, also demanded 'cheap government'.

In spite of all this, the Whig government came under considerable pressure from several directions to keep up the flow of reforming measures.

(a) the Benthamite Radicals

The ideas of Jeremy Bentham (see Section 2.1(c)) had enormous influence. Ever since the publication of his first pamphlet in 1776, Bentham had persevered with his doctrine of *Utilitarianism:* the acid test of all laws and institutions should be – are they efficient and useful? If not, they must be changed or scrapped. He must take some of the credit for the Great Reform Act; once that had been achieved, why should governments not continue to give way to pressure and concede reform in other areas of inefficiency? Though Bentham himself died in 1832, just before the Reform Bill was passed, his followers kept up the pressure, publishing reports and recommendations, and generally harassing the Whigs. The most important were *Edwin Chadwick*, who produced reports on the Poor Law, public health (see Section 5.3 and Section 12.4(d)) and the police, and *Joseph Parkes*, who investigated the defects of town government. On the other hand, many Radicals were not enthusiastic about factory reform, since they were themselves factory-owners and did not approve of government interference.

(b) the Humanitarian movement

This was composed of people from many different spheres of life, who all had one aim in common – to improve the living and working conditions of the working classes. They were supported by *the Evangelical Movement* of the Church of England, a group which felt that the Church was not showing enough concern for the plight of ordinary people, and was consequently losing support to the Methodists. Evangelicals believed in a life of prayer and service to others, and they saw it as their Christian duty to maintain Christian principles in public life. Many Humanitarians were Tories; for example, Michael Sadler and Lord Ashley (later Lord Shaftesbury), the factory reform campaigners, were Tory MPs as well as Evangelicals. William Wilberforce, leader of the anti-slavery movement and an MP for forty-four years, always maintained that he was independent of party, though he usually voted with the Tories.

(c) progressive factory-owners such as Robert Owen and John Fielden

These two men in particular demonstrated that better conditions and shorter working hours increased rather than reduced output. They tried to influence other industrialists, as well as governments, to follow their example (see Section 12.4(g)).

5.2 the first round of reforms: slavery, factories and education (1833)

(a) the abolition of slavery in the British Empire (1833)

1 The problem was that, while the slave trade had been prohibited in 1807 by the British government, after a long campaign led by the humanitarian MP for Hull, *William Wilberforce*, slavery itself was allowed to continue. This encouraged the smuggling of slaves, who continued to be shipped across the Atlantic in appalling conditions, traders cramming as many slaves as possible into their ships. There were 670,000 slaves in the West Indies alone. In 1821, Wilberforce brought out a pamphlet explaining the arguments in favour of abolition, and although he retired from Parliament in 1824, he continued to be active in the cause. The leadership of the movement in the Commons was taken over by *T. F. Buxton*, a Tory MP, who also founded *the Anti-Slavery Society*. In 1833, the Whig Colonial Secretary, Lord Stanley, introduced an Emancipation Bill. Happily, Wilberforce lived just long enough (he died on 29 July 1833) to be told that all his efforts were about to be rewarded. 'Thank God,' he said, 'that I should have lived to witness a day in which England is willing to give twenty millions sterling for the Abolition of Slavery.'

2 *There was a good deal of opposition to the Bill,* especially from the owners of sugar plantations in the West Indies, and from merchants involved in the sugar trade: abolition would mean loss of property (a good slave might be worth around £50); there would be a labour shortage that would push up production costs, to the advantage of competitors in the USA, who would still have their slaves; and there was the fear of unrest and disturbances if former slaves ran riot after gaining their freedom. Many MPs had money in sugar production and trade: W. E. Gladstone's father was a sugar merchant in Liverpool, and he gave his son, newly elected to Parliament in 1833, strict instructions to vote against the Bill.

3 *The terms of the Act,* which passed with a large majority, were:

  ‣ All slaves were to be set free within a year, and were then to serve apprenticeships of up to seven years to their former owners; this was to ease the transition from a slave economy to a wage-earner system.
  ‣ The government paid £20 million compensation to the slave-owners.

4 *The Act was successful* in the sense that it did away with a system that was morally wrong, though it caused some economic problems. Planters complained that the compensation was insufficient, and many went out of business. In Jamaica and British Guiana (now Guyana), freed slaves preferred to settle in villages of their own instead of working on the plantations. This led to labour shortages and high wages, and helped to cause a general depression in the West Indies. In Cape Colony (South Africa) many Boers, convinced that farming would be unprofitable without slaves, decided to leave, and they embarked on the Great Trek (see Section 14.3(d)). Nowhere was anything done to enable the slaves to make good use of their freedom; instead, black people remained illiterate and exploited.

(b) Althorp's Factory Act (1833)

This was the first effective attempt to improve working conditions in factories. Although the Bill was introduced by the Whig Chancellor of the Exchequer, Lord Althorp, most of the credit for it should go to the Tory Lord Ashley (for full details see Section 12.4(d)).

(c) the first government grant for education

1 Having stipulated in Althorp's Factory Act that children ought to receive at least two hours' schooling a day, the government felt it should try and make this possible. There were no state schools, and the only education for the masses was provided by two rival religious bodies or voluntary societies, one Anglican, one Nonconformist. In 1833, the government gave its first annual grant of £20,000, to be divided between the two societies. This was increased to £30,000 in 1839, and the Privy Council was to keep an eye on how the money was spent (in fact, most of it went on building new schools).

2 The grants established an important principle: that the state should accept some responsibility for educating the poor. On the other hand, the amounts of cash involved were pitifully small, and the system remained totally inadequate. Bentham's proposal that the government should set up its own system separate from the voluntary societies was ignored; consequently religious rivalry continued to be an unfortunate feature of the haphazard system.

5.3 reform of the Poor Law: the Poor Law Amendment Act (1834)

(a) what was wrong with the existing provision for the poor?

▸ The system dated back to the late sixteenth century; each parish was expected to look after its own poor, and it became the traditional practice for paupers (people who were so poor that they were unable to support themselves) to be sent back to the parish of their birth. The cash to provide relief for the poor came from a special rate paid by the inhabitants of the parish. The 1601 Poor Law Act had classified paupers into three groups:

(i)   those who couldn't find work (able-bodied poor);

(ii) those who were too ill, too young or too old to work (impotent poor); and

(iii) those who refused to work (idle poor).

In practice, the system varied widely throughout the 15,000 parishes: in some parishes, relief payments were made to the poor at home; during the eighteenth century it became more common for relief to be given to all types of poor only inside the parish workhouse. From the late eighteenth century onwards, however, the system was unable to cope with the vastly increasing numbers of poor people during periods of unemployment and low wages.

▸ *The Speenhamland System* adopted in the South after 1795 was a well-meaning attempt to deal with the problem, but it made the situation worse (see Section 2.2(a)). Depending on the size of a labourer's family and the price of bread, relief payments were made out of the parish poor rates to supplement low wages. However, this type of *outdoor relief*, as it was known (to distinguish it from the *indoor relief* that was given in the workhouse), encouraged employers to lower wages still further. In addition, it introduced a new principle: poor relief was originally intended for people who, for whatever reason, were out of work; now it was also having to cope with people who were in jobs. This placed a tremendous burden on the parish, much to the disgust of the people who had to pay the ever-increasing rates. In 1795, the total money spent by the 15,000 parishes on poor relief was £2 million; in 1830, it was not far short of £8 million.

▸ *The Swing Riots of 1830–1* (see Section 4.3(c)) highlighted the complete breakdown of the system and frightened the government into taking some action.

(b) a Commission was appointed to investigate the working of poor relief

Appointed in February 1832, its main objective was to find ways of saving money on the poor rates rather than to ease the plight of the poor, which the Humanitarians wanted. The most influential member of the Commission was *Edwin Chadwick*, a Manchester lawyer and a fanatical Benthamite. He was determined that the system should be made uniform and efficient so that it gave value for money. The Commission's Report (February 1834) condemned outdoor relief: 'every penny bestowed ... is a bounty to indolence and vice'. It also disapproved of the slack way in which many workhouses were run: able-bodied poor were being kept at the parish's expense 'in sluggish, sensual indolence'. The Commission's recommendations became the 1834 Act, which, according to Chadwick himself, was like 'a cold bath – unpleasant in contemplation but invigorating in its effects'. On the other hand, some historians have suggested that the old system was not as bad as the reformers claimed, and that the Benthamites exaggerated the evidence to make it look more wasteful and over-generous than it really was.

(c) terms of the Act

› Outdoor relief would no longer be provided for the able-bodied poor, though in some cases help would continue to be given to the sick and aged at home.

› For the able-bodied poor, and for the impotent poor who could not be helped at home, relief would be provided in workhouses.

› In order to make larger and more efficient units, parishes were to be grouped into Unions. It was intended that each Union would contain separate workhouses for the able-bodied, impotent and idle poor.

› Conditions in workhouses were to be made as unattractive as possible, so that the poor would make every effort to find work and only come to the workhouse as a last resort. Existence in the workhouse had to be more miserable than the life of the poorest labourer outside. This would encourage 'self-help' and thriftiness, and prevent the poor from looking on the workhouse as a haven of refuge; it was known as the 'less eligibility' principle.

› Each Union was to have paid officials to operate the system; they were to be appointed by the unpaid Board of Commissioners and their secretary, Edwin Chadwick.

(d) how successful was the new system?

It was a success in the narrow sense that it helped to reduce the poor rates. During 1830–4 the average annual expenditure on poor relief had been around £7 million; but between 1835–9 it averaged only £4.5 million. Thus the Benthamites saw it as an ideal reform, and it was popular with the majority of ratepayers. However, in every other respect, the Act can hardly be seen as a 'reform' at all. It aroused the most bitter criticism, both from the working classes who suffered hardship from it, and from the Humanitarians who thought it cruel and cold-blooded. Most newspapers were severely critical, and there was a flood of pamphlets and petitions, as well as hostile demonstrations and attacks on workhouses and Guardians. *The main criticisms were:*

› The new system ignored the causes of poverty and unemployment, and assumed that to be poor was always the fault of the pauper – lack of initiative, laziness or drunkenness – and that people would be able to find jobs if they tried hard enough. Unfortunately, this theory made no allowances for the regular trade recessions and slumps that caused unemployment.

› The stoppage of outdoor relief for the able-bodied poor caused great hardship in the South. Thousands of labourers in full-time work were not receiving a living wage, and wives and children had to take whatever work they could get in the fields to avoid starvation. The situation would have been much worse had it not been for a series of good harvests, which kept bread prices low, and for railway building, which provided extra jobs.

- In the industrial North, it proved impossible to stop giving outdoor relief. Unfortunately for all concerned, there was a trade recession in 1837–8, just when the Commissioners began to apply the Act in those areas. Outdoor relief was essential as unemployment pay if workers were not to starve in their thousands, and there were far too many to be accommodated in the workhouses. In Huddersfield, a mob organized by Richard Oastler, a local Tory Evangelical, gate-crashed the first meeting of the new Board of Guardians and chased them off; it was a further two years before they were able to begin operating. At Bradford, the Guardians had to be protected by cavalry, while at Todmorden on the Lancashire–Yorkshire boundary, John Fielden, a mill-owner, led a campaign to boycott the election of Guardians. Police constables were attacked and troops had to be quartered in the town to keep order. Not until 1897 was a workhouse built in Todmorden. At Colne in Lancashire, nobody could be found to act as Guardians.
- By 1838 over 13,400 of the 15,000 parishes had been grouped into 573 Unions, but in the majority of them it proved too expensive to provide separate workhouses. Each parish within the Union was still responsible for meeting the cost of its own poor, which meant that the poorest parishes faced the largest expenses. It was not until 1865 that the system was changed, so that parishes within the Union shared the cost more equally. This meant that, in the years immediately after 1834, all types of poor, including children, were herded together with criminals, prostitutes and lunatics. As Charles Dickens showed in *Oliver Twist*, which came out in instalments in 1837, conditions were poor. Some historians have suggested that opponents of the new Poor Law deliberately exaggerated the worst features of workhouse life, and that conditions were in reality fairly tolerable. But it seems certain that during the first fifteen years at least, workhouse life was harsh. Husbands and wives were separated (this was relaxed in 1842), children were separated from parents, meals had to be eaten in silence and diets were sparse; the jobs provided in the workhouses – stonebreaking, bone-grinding and picking old rope to pieces – were either backbreaking or painful on the fingers. There was a famous scandal in the Andover workhouse in 1845, when inmates working on bone-crushing were so hungry that they were found to be eating rotting marrow and fat from the bones. No wonder workhouses became known among the workers as Bastilles (after the notorious fortress-prison in Paris).

Thus the new Poor Law did not end poverty, and consequently thousands of workers were driven to support Chartism (see Chapter 6). While conditions in workhouses improved after 1865, there was still a great stigma attached to people who were forced into them, and the poor always viewed workhouses with fear and suspicion.

5.4 the reform of town government: the Municipal Corporations Act (1835)

(a) why was reform needed?

The governing and running of towns was confused and inefficient. There were about 250 boroughs, each with its own corporation (mayor, councillors and aldermen), which ran the town's affairs. There were wide variations in how the corporations were chosen and how they functioned, but the disturbing feature was that in 186 of them, only the members of the corporation itself were allowed to vote; they normally re-elected themselves or brought relatives or friends on to the council. These small cliques (known as closed corporations) fixed the local bye-laws and taxes, and it was impossible for the mass of ratepayers to get rid of unpopular councils by voting them out. Most of the corporations used their privileges for personal or party advantage, and ignored matters such as water supply, drainage and street cleansing that they were supposed to look after. Even more ludicrous was the fact that the newly expanded industrial towns had not been recognized as boroughs and had no corporation at all. Here, living conditions in overcrowded slums were a threat to public health; in 1831–2 there was a cholera epidemic which began in Sunderland and spread across the country, causing thousands of deaths (see Section 12.5(c)). It was inevitable that once the Whigs had accepted the principle of parliamentary reform, local government reform would soon follow.

Following the same procedure as with the Poor Law, the Whigs appointed a Royal Commission to investigate the problem (July 1833). The Commission secretary, *Joseph Parkes*, a Radical lawyer, was determined to act quickly: 285 towns were investigated, most of which were found to be unsatisfactory. Consequently, with the help of Parkes, a Bill was drawn up and introduced into the Commons by Lord John Russell (June 1835). It became law in September 1835.

(b) terms of the Act

▸ The closed corporations were abolished; borough councils were to be elected by all the male ratepayers who had lived in the town for three years.
▸ Councillors were elected for three years; one-third to be elected annually.
▸ Councillors would choose the mayor (to hold office for one year) and a group of aldermen (for six years).
▸ Each borough was to have a paid town clerk and treasurer, and accounts were to be properly audited.
▸ It was compulsory for councils to form a police force; councils were allowed, if they so desired, to take over social improvements such as proper drainage, and street cleansing and lighting.
▸ Towns and cities which had no councils could apply to become boroughs.

There was plenty of opposition to the Bill. It went through the Commons smoothly enough and its general principles were welcomed by Peel and the moderate Tories. But it received a rough ride in the Lords. Since most of the closed corporations were controlled by Tories, the Tory peers claimed that the Bill was an attack on personal privileges and property, in the same category as the abolition of rotten boroughs, and that it was a further step in the destruction of the constitution. However, although some amendments were made to the Bill, Peel and Wellington restrained the Tory peers from throwing it out altogether.

(c) how successful was the new Act?

There was a marked improvement over the previous haphazard and disorganized system, and the Act established the principle of elected town councils. It led to increasing interest in town party politics, and it gave the middle classes a chance to play an important role in local public life. At the same time, *it had several failings:*

› By making it optional rather than compulsory for the new councils to make social improvements, the Act missed an opportunity to do something positive about the appalling conditions in most towns. By 1848, only 29 boroughs had taken any action. One reason for the poor response was that ratepayers were often only interested in keeping the rates down.
› Many towns failed to apply to become boroughs, because the procedure was complicated and expensive. In 1848, there were still sixty-two large towns without a council.
› While the new system was more democratic than before, it was mainly of benefit to the middle classes; very few working men were wealthy enough to be ratepayers.

However, although progress was slow, the Act did at least set up the machinery that would enable future social and health reforms to be carried out effectively in the towns.

5.5 other Whig reforms

The Whig governments also introduced a number of less spectacular, but none the less important, changes:

(a) the compulsory registration of births, marriages and deaths (1836)

This typically Benthamite measure was extremely important: without it, it would have been impossible to apply the Factory Acts, which sought to protect children and young people; they could now rely on their birth certificates to prove their age.

(b) religious reforms (1836)

The government was responsible for two measures that did something to reduce Nonconformist resentment against the power and privilege of the Church of England:

> ‣ *The Marriage Act* recognized marriages in Nonconformist chapels and Roman Catholic churches as legal, provided that a civil registrar was there.
> ‣ *The Tithe Commutation Act* replaced the tithe (a tax of one-tenth of annual produce to be paid to the church) with a cash rent. Though this was a move in the right direction, non-Anglicans felt it should have been abolished altogether. The Act was popular with Irish Catholic tenant farmers, who tended to come off better with a fixed money rent, and it helped to keep Ireland fairly peaceful until 1841.

(c) limited liability companies were permitted (1836)

These were companies in which the shareholders did not have to pay the full losses if the company became bankrupt. This encouraged investment and proved to be an enormous boost to the spread of the railways. The government sanctioned 1,500 miles of new railway in 1836–7, and the first main line was opened between London and Birmingham.

(d) the Penny Post

The brainchild of *Rowland Hill, the Penny Post* was introduced in 1840. Hill managed to convince the Whigs that the existing letter post, in which charges were made according to the weight of the letter or parcel and the distance it travelled, was actually losing the Post Office money; time was wasted while the postman waited at every house for payment. Hill's suggestion was adopted: the fee was to be paid in advance by means of an adhesive stamp; the charge was one penny for a half ounce letter. The Post Office objected, but Hill was proved right: business soared and so eventually did profits (though the scheme lost heavily for the first few years). The new system was swift and efficient.

5.6 why did the Whigs lose the 1841 election?

The Whigs had a number of failures and showed a fatal lack of understanding in certain areas, all of which contributed to their defeat.

(a) they showed no real understanding of the causes of unemployment

This was the case in both industry and agriculture, and the Whigs tended to fall back on repression. The first instance of this occurred with the Swing Riots (1830–1), and there were several more. When working people began to join Robert Owen's Grand National Consolidated Trades Union (founded in 1833) in their thousands, the government decided to make an example of six farm labourers from the village of Tolpuddle in Dorset who had started their own union. They were sentenced to seven years' transportation to Australia for having sworn an illegal oath (1834). Lord Melbourne personally approved their sentences. The GNCTU soon collapsed in the face of such determined government opposition (for full details see Section 19.2).

(b) important Whig reforms slowed to a mere trickle after 1836

This was partly because of Melbourne's unprogressive attitude, and partly because the Whigs' Commons majority was dwindling all the time. But the unpopular fact remained that the Whigs did nothing to improve either the appalling working conditions in the mines or the unhealthy social conditions in towns. Hardly anything was done to continue Huskisson's commercial reforms, yet there was still a long way to go before Free Trade was achieved. As a result, trade seemed to be stagnating.

(c) further working-class hostility was aroused

The government, already unpopular because of the harshness of the new Poor Law, rejected the first Chartist petition in 1839 (see Chapter 6). By the middle of 1841, Britain was moving into a severe depression; Manchester cotton mills were soon to be at a standstill, and in Birmingham almost 100,000 people were being given poor relief. Just before the election, Feargus O'Connor, one of the Chartist leaders, instructed all Chartists who had a vote to support the Tories as a protest against the Whig Poor Law.

(d) the Tories produced an attractive programme

The Whigs failed to produce a programme that was appealing to the voters. The Tories, on the other hand, were now united under the leadership of Peel, and they had a promising new programme, which had appeared in 1834 as the Tamworth Manifesto (see Section 7.1(b)). Peel's reputation had grown during his ten years in opposition. He had earned admiration in many quarters for the responsible way in which he had led the opposition in the Commons; whereas most of the Ultras had wanted to vote against the Whig government on every available opportunity, Peel preferred to support it when it was doing something useful and necessary, as in the case of the Municipal Corporations Act. It was also known that he had plans for encouraging trade and industry, and therefore employment. The Tories (now known as Conservatives) seemed more likely to be able to deal successfully with the country's emergency than the tired and jaded Whigs.

It was no surprise when the Conservatives won the general election of June 1841, emerging with a comfortable majority of over 70.

1 Why did the Whig reforms arouse so much opposition before they were introduced, and so much criticism afterwards?

2 Explain why the Whigs, after introducing an apparently impressive programme of reforms between 1832 and 1836, lost the general election of 1841 to the Conservatives.

A document question about the reform of the Poor Law can be found on the accompanying website www.palgrave.com/masterseries/lowe1.

chapter 6

Chartism

summary of events

Chartism was a movement that boiled up in the mid-1830s out of working-class discontent and disillusionment with the reforms of the Whig governments. It was the first working-class political organization, and so, in a sense, it was the forerunner of the Labour Party. With branches all over Britain, including Ireland, it aimed to change the parliamentary system so that the working classes would be in control. The Chartists drew up their political demands in a six-point list known as *the People's Charter.* Three times, in 1839, 1842 and 1848, the Charter was presented to Parliament in the form of a gigantic petition containing millions of signatures; and three times it was overwhelmingly rejected by the Commons. After each rejection there were outbreaks of violence organized by the more extreme Chartist leaders, but on each occasion the government took swift action to restore order.

After the failure of the third petition in 1848, the movement gradually died out; it seemed at the time to have been a rather pathetic failure. However, it did have some important effects, and in time, though not until long after the Chartists themselves were all dead, five of its six political aims were actually achieved.

6.1 why did the Chartist movement come into existence?

The movement was caused quite simply by an overwhelming feeling of misery among the working classes, together with the conviction that they were not getting a fair deal at the hands of the wealthy and governing classes. There was a whole range of grievances, some of which, such as the ill-effects of the Industrial Revolution, had been building up and worsening over many years, while others had arisen more recently, in the 1830s.

(a) poor conditions in factories, workshops and mines

The Whig Factory Act of 1833 had brought in a 12-hour limit on the working day for young people of 18 and under, but it only applied to textile factories, and even this was not effective in many cases. Lord Shaftesbury continued the campaign to get a 10-hour day introduced for women and young people. There was no limit on the working hours of men. Serious injury and death were common in many factories, where dangerous machinery was not properly fenced off; the 1840 committee of enquiry mentioned one case of a girl who had been caught by the hair and scalped from the nose to the back of the head. Conditions in mines were even more horrifying (see Section 12.2).

(b) poor living conditions

Industrial towns were generally overcrowded and unhealthy, with no proper sanitation or sewage disposal. Edwin Chadwick's *Report on the Sanitary Condition of the Labouring Population*, which appeared in 1842, revealed some appalling details: one fifth of the inhabitants of Liverpool were living in one-room cellars; in Leeds, the streets were a foot deep in accumulated rubbish; while in London, workers had to drink untreated water from the Thames. No wonder there were constant epidemics of cholera, typhoid, tuberculosis and diphtheria; roughly one-third of all children died before they reached the age of five. In the decade 1831–40, the death rate over the country as a whole was 23 per thousand, which was bad enough; in industrial Lancashire it was 37 per thousand.

(c) disillusionment with the 1832 Reform Act

It soon became clear that the high hopes of the workers that real democracy was about to arrive had not been realized. The working classes were not given the vote, and in some boroughs, such as Preston and Westminster, working men actually lost the vote as a result of the Act. Pocket boroughs, 'influence' and bribery still survived and would continue to do so as long as there was no secret ballot (see Section 4.6(b)). Even the Municipal Reform Act (1835) brought no benefit to working men: again, it was only the middle classes who received the vote.

(d) the collapse of trade unionism

In the late 1820s, a number of trade unions were formed, and Robert Owen attempted to unite them into his Grand National Consolidated Trades Union (formed 1833); but the movement was dogged by all kinds of problems, including government hostility (see Section 19.2(c)). After the affair of the Tolpuddle Martyrs (1834) and the arrest and trial of the Glasgow cotton spinners' leaders (1837), the unions collapsed and many of their members joined the Chartists.

(e) anger at the 1834 Poor Law

This was particularly strong in the North, where the Commissioners first attempted to apply the new system in 1837 (see Section 5.3(d)).

(f) trade depression, unemployment and hunger

The immediate cause of the Chartist outbreaks was always the same. The Reverend J. R. Stephens, a north-country Methodist minister from near Manchester, was a Chartist supporter as well as a Tory. He summed up the situation well when he declared that the movement 'is a knife-and-fork question, a bread-and-cheese question'. It was the Englishman's God-given right 'to have a good coat and hat, a good roof over his head, a good dinner upon his table'. Some categories of workers – the handloom weavers of Lancashire, Wales and Scotland and the Leicester stocking weavers – had all been suffering falling wages and unemployment for years; they were the most consistent supporters of Chartism. But in 1837 a general trade depression set in, which affected workers in most industries, and only began to ease off in 1842. By the summer of 1837 there were 50,000 out of work or on short time in Manchester. In 1839, a Lancashire handloom weaver could expect to earn at best five shillings (25 pence) a week, while a Leicester stocking knitter was managing only four shillings and sixpence. General Napier, who was in charge of the troops sent to keep order in the Midlands and North, noted that 'everywhere people are starving in the manufacturing districts ... and the guardians of the poor are guardians of their own pockets'.

All these grievances could be, and were, blamed on the 'rotten Whigs', as a Leicester Chartist described them in 1840. They were held to be directly responsible for the Reform Act, the New Poor Law and the treatment of the Tolpuddle Martyrs, and indirectly for bad conditions, depression and unemployment, which they had done next to nothing to improve.

6.2 how did the Chartist movement begin, and what sort of people joined it?

(a) the early days – the London Working Men's Association

It is difficult to pinpoint exactly when and where the movement began because there were so many protest groups and societies in different parts of the country, and they didn't necessarily call themselves Chartists to begin with. However, it is usual to take the founding of *the London Working Men's Association* in 1836 as the starting point. It was formed by a number of skilled craftsmen, including *William Lovett*, a cabinet-maker, and *Francis Place*, the veteran Radical tailor. In 1837, at a meeting between the LWMA and some Radical MPs, the Charter from which the movement took its name was drawn up. Almost immediately, other protest groups began to affiliate, until by 1838 there were over 100 branches all over the country. In 1840, the National Charter Association (NCA) was formed, and the movement became well organized, with annual subscriptions and local branch meetings. By 1842, the NCA could boast 400 branches and 50,000 members.

(b) the rank-and-file membership was overwhelmingly from the working class

There was a great deal of middle-class support in the early stages, with the involvement of men such as Thomas Attwood, Robert Owen and Joseph Sturge, a Birmingham corn-miller; but many of them abandoned the movement in the early 1840s as the more violent elements came to prominence. Even so, the remaining leaders tended to come from what Miles Taylor calls 'the persuading professions and vocations – the law, evangelical ministry, quack medicine, the theatre, the bookstall, the newsdesk and the print-shop. In their hands and mouths words became weapons, with the power to capture and convert'.

The most reliable and consistent rank-and-file membership came from the craftsmen who were being forced out of business by new machines (northern handloom weavers and Black Country nail-makers); and from workers in areas of declining industry (Wales, Wiltshire and the South-west, where the old textile industries were in dire straits). Staffordshire potters were consistent supporters, and so were the framework knitters of the East Midlands. In other industrial areas, for example the coalfields of Yorkshire, South Wales and the North-east, workers became involved with Chartism in times of slump and unemployment, but drifted away when trade recovered. In agricultural areas, membership was even less consistent: in Suffolk, for example, though there were Chartist groups in Ipswich and Saxmundham, it was difficult to sustain the involvement of agricultural labourers because of their relatively isolated situation in the countryside.

6.3 what were the Chartists' aims and how did they hope to achieve them?

(a) aims

Basically, the Chartists wanted a drastic change in the parliamentary and political system so that the working classes would be in control. As James Bronterre O'Brien, one of the Chartist leaders, put it in 1833, 'they aspire to be at the top instead of the bottom of society – or rather that there should be no bottom or top at all'. Only when this happened, or so they believed, would anything positive be done to achieve what was arguably their primary aim – to improve the general plight of working people.

The Charter contained their six specific political demands:

1 Universal male suffrage (a vote for all men at the age of 21).
2 Voting by secret ballot.
3 Equal electoral districts (constituencies), so that each MP would represent roughly the same number of voters.
4 No property qualification for parliamentary candidates, to enable working men to stand for Parliament.

5 Payment of MPs, so that working men who had no other income except from their trades would be provided for when they left their jobs to enter Parliament.

6 Annual elections. In the words of a Chartist voter, this would be 'the most effectual check to bribery and intimidation ... though a constituency may be bought once in seven years, no purse can buy a constituency in each ensuing twelvemonth'.

All the branches agreed on the six points, but at different times and in different places, Chartist groups and individuals put forward further aims, some of them economic and social in character. Most of them wanted the abolition of taxes on newspapers. *The London Democratic Association* (a rival group to the LWMA) mentioned 'the repeal of the infamous New Poor Law, an eight hour day for all workers in factories and workshops, and the abolition of child labour'. They were convinced that education for the working classes was vitally important, and supported the promotion of 'public instruction and the diffusion of sound political knowledge'. Their programme was summed up as the destruction of inequality and 'the establishment of general happiness'. The Birmingham group wanted the abolition of the Corn Laws. Another Methodist minister, the Reverend Joseph Barker of Leeds, wanted votes for spinsters and widows as well as for men.

(b) methods

From the outset there were serious differences of opinion about how these aims were to be achieved. Like so much else to do with the Chartists, this is difficult to generalize about, because many of the leaders changed their minds as the campaign developed. For the sake of simplicity, though, they can be divided into the 'moral force' and the 'physical force' Chartists.

▸ *Lovett, Place and the LWMA* (together with Attwood, the Birmingham banker), were probably the most consistent leaders. They were moderate and peaceful, hoping to achieve their aims by discussion and persuasion, by means of orderly meetings and pamphlets. They accepted that this could only happen gradually, but it would be 'without commotion or violence', and without breaking the law. Gradually the methods of the 'peaceful' Chartists became more varied. Not only did they present three petitions to Parliament, but they also, in the words of Miles Taylor, 'debated, lectured, sang and wrote verse, drama and novels in the name of the Six Points ... Long before the mid-Victorian surge in cheap newspapers, the Chartists had the popular market cornered. More than 120 newspapers devoted to the cause were established between the mid-1830s and the mid-1850s'. They also used the hustings during the general elections of 1841 and 1847, and it was here that some of the more fiery leaders came to the forefront.

▸ *Feargus O'Connor* was impatient with the moderates. An Irish Protestant who had become MP for Cork in 1832, he wanted quick results. After founding the

London Democratic Association (1837), he took over the Leeds Radical newspaper, the *Northern Star*, which he soon turned into the main Chartist propaganda weapon, with a weekly sale of 50,000 copies. A brilliant agitator and fiery speaker, he swayed the masses into supporting the idea of a general strike and also seemed to favour an armed revolution. However, he was not himself prepared to risk force, and backed out on more than one occasion. Not surprisingly, he fell out with every other important Chartist leader at one time or another, but somehow retained his popularity with the rank and file.

» *James Bronterre O'Brien*, an Irish lawyer, and *George Julian Harney*, who helped to organize the groups in Sheffield and Newcastle, were two of the real militants, both quite prepared to use force. Harney, who went around in a red cap and fancied himself as the British version of Marat (a French revolutionary leader murdered in 1793), wanted a full-scale revolution on the French model. However, even they cooled down after *John Frost*, another militant, had been sentenced to transportation for life after leading an uprising in Newport (Monmouthshire) in 1839.

6.4 the three phases of the Chartist movement

(a) phase one: 1838–9

» During 1838 there was a series of huge open-air meetings addressed by Chartist leaders: 100,000 people gathered on Glasgow Green to hear O'Connor, at least 30,000 at Manchester, and a similar number at Leeds. When O'Connor tried to address a meeting in Newcastle, the crowd was dispersed by cavalry. O'Connor's activities were remarkable: during 1838–9 he spent sixteen weeks touring the country and addressed no fewer than 147 meetings.

» In February 1839 a National Chartist Convention met in London to organize a petition and its presentation to Parliament. It was here that the first serious differences of opinion occurred as the leaders argued about how best to proceed. Some of the extremists wanted to proclaim a general strike immediately, while Lovett and Attwood hoped to keep within the law. Attwood and the Birmingham contingent walked out in disgust at the extremists, though for the time being the moderates just about kept control. In May, the Convention moved to Birmingham, where there was more support for Chartism, and the petition was completed after some vast meetings in the Bull Ring, at which Lovett, O'Brien and Harney appeared.

» The first Chartist petition containing one and a quarter million signatures was brought to the Commons in a decorated cart. It was introduced by Attwood, who asked that Parliament should grant the six points. The Whig Home Secretary, Lord John Russell, led the attack on the petition and it was overwhelmingly rejected by 235 votes to 46 (July 1839).

‣ This rejection suggested that nothing could be achieved by moderation, and the physical force supporters seized the initiative, attempting to organize a general strike or 'sacred month' as the Chartists called it. There were protest meetings, riots, fights and strikes, with many leaders calling for an armed uprising.

The Whig government, which had reacted cautiously when Lovett and the moral force leaders were in the ascendant, now decided to act. The army was increased by 5000 and new police forces set up in Birmingham, Manchester, Bolton and other industrial centres. General Napier, who was in charge of forces in the North, sympathized with the working classes and blamed the situation on 'Tory injustice and Whig imbecility'. He tried to avoid confrontation and showed local Chartist leaders how suicidal any attempt at revolution would be, given the strength of his artillery and cavalry. This, together with the arrest of many of the leaders, probably prevented any serious outbreak in the Midlands and North.

‣ The most serious violence took place in Wales, where conditions in the mining valleys were probably the worst in Britain. This was *the Newport Rising* (November 1839) organized by John Frost, a local draper and former mayor of Newport. Frost led 5,000 miners in an attack on the town, apparently aiming to release a Chartist leader from gaol. However, the authorities knew about it well in advance, and positioned troops in the Westgate Hotel. As the Chartists approached they were met by volleys of musket fire; at least twenty were killed, and the rising soon ended in confusion. Frost and two other leaders were sentenced to death, though this was later changed to transportation.

Illus. 6.1 The Chartists attempt to seize Newport, 1839

Despite occasional incidents and a number of large open-air meetings, there was a lull in Chartist activity in 1840–1, partly because all the main leaders, even the peaceful ones like Lovett, were in gaol, and partly because there was a temporary revival in trade.

(b) phase two: 1842

▸ As the most influential leaders finished their sentences and emerged from gaol, the Chartists gathered themselves together for another effort. Members were to pay a penny a week each to build up a strike fund.

▸ Another National Convention met and a second petition was drawn up containing three and a quarter million signatures. Reputed to be six miles long, it was carried to Parliament in a huge procession of over 100,000 people, with brass bands playing. It was introduced in the Commons by Thomas Duncombe, supported by John Fielden, and although Peel and the Conservatives were now in power, it suffered a similar fate to that of the first petition – it was rejected by 287 votes to 49 (May 1842).

▸ Again violence followed the rejection, though this was probably caused as much by wage reductions which took place in all industrial areas from Scotland down to the Midlands, as the depression reached its worst. At Wolverhampton, strikers besieged the workhouse and had to be dispersed by dragoon guards. In the Lancashire 'Plug Riots', strikers hammered the plugs out of factory boilers, forcing them to close down. By August, work in the industrial North was at a standstill: there was serious rioting in towns such as Preston, Rochdale, Stockport, Bury and Bolton, while in Manchester several policemen were killed and thousands of strikers looted food shops. The situation seemed close to a general strike and perhaps even a revolution.

▸ O'Connor, who had so often advocated violence, was horrified by this turn of events, and condemned the strike in the *Northern Star*. Peel and his Home Secretary, Sir James Graham, though sympathetic to the plight of the workers, were none the less determined that law and order should be maintained. The government took prompt action and rushed troops to trouble spots, using the new railways. Within a week order had been restored, and hundreds of Chartist leaders were thrown into gaol; strikers had no choice but to return to work. Again there was a lull in Chartism, and membership declined rapidly as trade revived in 1843.

(c) phase three: 1847–8 – the Chartists' last fling

▸ In the mid-1840s, O'Connor, still the most exciting and influential of the Chartist leaders, put all his energies into his *Land Plan*. His idea was to buy country estates where thousands of Chartists from industrial towns could settle, each family with its own smallholding (small area of land). As well as making the settlers independent, this would also ease the unemployment situation in manufacturing areas. O'Connor founded the Chartist Co-operative

Land Society in 1847. Chartists bought shares in the company for £1. 6s each, and eventually four Chartist colonies were started: O'Connorville near Watford, Lowbands and Snig's End near Gloucester, and Charterville near Witney (Oxfordshire). Each family had a two-, three-, or four-acre plot and a cottage, and paid an annual rent of £1. 5s an acre.

▸ Early in 1847 another trade depression set in and unemployment soared. By May there were 24,000 out of work in Manchester and 84,000 on short time. This new wave of distress brought the Chartists back to politics again and in the general election of July 1847 O'Connor was elected MP for Nottingham. Encouraged by the news of a successful revolution in Paris (February 1848), which overthrew King Louis Philippe, the Chartists set about producing their third petition. It was completed early in April 1848 at another National Convention in London; this one contained five points (secret ballot was the one omitted), and it was reported to have been signed by almost six million people.

▸ There was to be an open-air rally on Kennington Common on 10 April (see Source B on the accompanying website) followed by a mass procession to Westminster to present the petition. Some of the speakers at the Convention urged revolution and it was decided that if this third petition was rejected, the Chartists would call a National Assembly to force Parliament to accept the Charter. It was said that O'Connor had even drawn up a new constitution with himself as president of a British republic.

▸ In fact, both O'Connor and O'Brien played down the physical force approach in their speeches, but Russell's Whig government took no chances. The march on Parliament was banned and O'Connor was told that only ten people would be allowed through to present the petition. In a clever propaganda move, the Duke of Wellington, now aged 79, was brought in as commander; he stationed troops at key points in the capital, signed up 150,000 special constables, and made excellent use of the London police force. The Kennington Common rally went ahead, but far fewer people turned up than had been expected and in the afternoon heavy rain dampened the Chartists' enthusiasm. No attempt was made to storm Parliament, since it would have been difficult to force a way across the bridges over the Thames; the event ended lamely with O'Connor and a handful of supporters delivering the petition to the Commons in three cabs.

▸ When it was examined closely the petition was found to contain less than two million signatures, some of which – Queen Victoria, Wellington, Mr Punch, Sir Robert Peel, Flatnose and No Cheese – made it look ridiculous. Again, the Commons rejected it by a huge majority.

▸ At the same time, O'Connor's Land Scheme found itself in serious difficulties: much of the land was poor, the settlers had no experience of farming, the smallholdings were not large enough to support whole families, and O'Connor himself, though certainly not dishonest, made a hopeless muddle of the finances. In August 1851, the National Land Company was wound up in complete failure.

› While there were some violent incidents in the Midlands and North following the rejection of the third petition, Chartism never again achieved the same impact. O'Connor could still draw a crowd of 20,000 in Leicester in 1850, but in general there was a slow fade-out of the movement after 1848. By 1852, the circulation of the *Northern Star* was down to only 1,200 from its 1839 peak of around 50,000. O'Connor became insane and had to be confined in an asylum at Chiswick; he died in 1855.

6.5 why were the Chartists unsuccessful in the 1840s, and what was the significance of the movement?

(a) reasons for their lack of success

From the beginning, the Chartists' demands were too advanced for the time, and they had no chance of having their six political demands accepted at that particular point; there was no way that a Parliament still dominated by aristocratic landowners was going to hand over power to the working and lower middle classes, which is what acceptance of the petition would have amounted to. In addition:

› There were serious divisions and disagreements among the leaders about whether to use moral persuasion or physical force. Lovett was hopeful that the industrial society would eventually lead to prosperity for all, but O'Connor hated the new machinery and wanted a society of small landholders. He and Ernest Jones, the poet and songwriter of the movement, grieved for the loss of the old rural world from which the unfortunate workers had been driven into factories and urban slums. But O'Connor's Land Scheme was condemned as impractical by most of the other leaders. O'Connor outshone all the rest and made much more impact nationally, but unfortunately he was reckless and unstable, seeming to preach violence one minute and drawing back the next.

› There were many local differences which made unity difficult and central organization weak.

› The Chartists never won sufficient middle-class support; many potential backers who sympathized with the six points were frightened off by the Chartists' violence and by their attacks on wealth and property, and they preferred to put their energies and cash into the more respectable Anti-Corn Law League (see Section 7.5). In 1841, when Lovett seemed to be bridging the gap between the classes by attracting the support of Joseph Sturge, a wealthy corn-miller, O'Connor attacked Lovett, accusing him of trying to 'domesticate the charter', and this New Move, as it was called, broke down. Many middle-class people preferred a limited extension of the franchise to include just themselves, and they were not willing to share political power with the workers.

> The Chartists' aims were too complicated: as well as the six points, there were numerous other social and economic aims which meant that they were trying to achieve too much all at once, which tended to confuse people. This was in marked contrast to the Anti-Corn Law League, which knew exactly what it wanted (the total abolition of the Corn Laws) and hammered away at that single aim until it was achieved. A better course of action for the Chartists might have been to concentrate on getting MPs elected, so that they would have had a more effective voice in the Commons (as the League did).

> The authorities kept one step ahead of the Chartists and always knew of their plans; for example, police spies had informed them about the Newport Rising in 1839. Both Whig governments (in 1839 and 1848) and Peel's Conservatives (in 1842) took prompt action, arresting leaders, moving troops swiftly by train to areas of disturbances, and using the new electric telegraph. By the late 1840s, politicians had realized that it was better to pass short sentences of between six months and two years, since this avoided making martyrs of imprisoned Chartist leaders.

> The reforms of Peel's government between 1841 and 1846 (see Sections 7.2 and 7.3) led to some improvement in trade and conditions. Britain was moving into a period of great economic prosperity, which was reflected to some extent in rising wages and increased food consumption: the average price of a four-pound loaf, which had cost 11½d in 1847 was under 7d in 1850. As living standards improved, support for the Chartists and their complicated programme melted away, and workers preferred to join trade unions or the co-operative movement.

(b) the significance of Chartism

It would be wrong to dismiss Chartism as insignificant simply because it failed to achieve its political aims in the 1840s.

It was a remarkable achievement for a largely working-class movement at that time to develop such a high degree of communication, organization and control on such a large scale. Mass meetings like the one on Glasgow Green in 1838 did not happen by accident, and must have taken considerable preparation and planning, especially as most of them passed off peacefully and without violence.

In the words of Boyd Hilton, 'Chartism was a totalizing experience and may even have been for some a substitute for older Christian certainties. There were Chartist sermons, hymns, libraries, reading classes, discussion groups, lectures, clubs, orchestras, choirs and sports teams, all organized by working men themselves.' It encouraged the working class to persevere in developing their own organizations and institutions: the co-operative movement, friendly societies and temperance societies all began to flourish in the second half of the nineteenth century. Arguably, the movement played a part in helping to transform the Whigs into the more radical Liberal party, and in one sense it can be seen as a forerunner of the Labour party.

Chartism's most important immediate achievement was that it focused public attention on the appalling hardships of working people. Politicians in both Whig and Conservative parties were dismayed at living and working conditions in the industrial districts. It was no coincidence that Peel and the Conservatives (1841–6) immediately took steps (Mines Act, Factory Act, Commission on Public Health in Towns – leading to the 1848 Public Health Act, repeal of the Corn Laws) to try to remove the grievances that had given rise to Chartism in the first place. Only when working-class conditions improved could public order be comfortably maintained.

6.6 when was the Chartists' political programme achieved?

Bit by bit over the next eighty years, five of the six points were achieved. First to come was the abolition of the property qualification for MPs, in 1858, followed by the introduction of the secret ballot in elections (1872). Manhood suffrage was achieved in stages by the Reform Acts of 1867 and 1884, and by the Representation of the People Act of 1918, which went further than the Chartists had intended by giving the vote to women aged 30 and over; in 1928, women were given the vote at 21. These acts also redistributed seats so that constituencies became approximately equal (though even today there are some variations: Northern Ireland constituencies contain many more voters than the average constituency in the rest of Britain). Payment of MPs was introduced in 1911. The only one of the points not achieved was annual elections; however, the 1911 Parliament Act did reduce the length of Parliaments, so there has to be a general election every five years instead of every seven.

QUESTIONS

1 How far would you agree with the view that Chartism was 'a glorious failure'?
2 How important do you think disappointment with the 1832 Reform Act was in relation to other factors in explaining the rise of Chartism?
3 'Chartism failed because the leaders could not agree on a strategy.' How accurate is this view of the reasons for the failure of Chartism in the period 1838 to 1848?

A document question about the Chartist campaigns can be found on the accompanying website www.palgrave.com/masterseries/lowe1.

chapter 7

Sir Robert Peel, the Conservatives and the Corn Laws, 1830–46

summary of events

At the end of 1830, the Tory party had disintegrated in the wake of Catholic Emancipation (see Section 2.7(b)) and was also deeply divided about what attitude to adopt towards reform of Parliament. Reaching rock bottom in 1833, the party gradually began to revive under the leadership of Sir Robert Peel. When Melbourne's Whig government began to falter, Peel and his party – now known as Conservatives – held office for a short time (December 1834 to April 1835, known as 'Peel's Hundred Days'), but, lacking a majority, they soon had to resign. However, Peel's reputation grew steadily, and in August 1841 the Conservatives won a large electoral majority. Peel was Prime Minister from 1841 to 1846.

He had to face some alarming problems: an economic slump, appalling working and living conditions in industrial areas, unemployment, agitation and violence from the Chartists, and pressure from the Anti-Corn Law League. Abroad, there were strained relations with the USA and France (see Section 9.3). However, Peel showed the same determination as he had earlier when he was Home Secretary (1822–30). Often facing opposition from many of his own party, he pushed through *important economic reforms* (the re-introduction of income tax, further steps towards free trade, and the Bank Charter Act) and *social reforms* (Mines Act, Factory Act and an enquiry into health conditions in towns).

These were considerable achievements, and all seemed to be going well, when Peel was brought down by *the repeal of the Corn Laws.* Influenced by the Anti-Corn Law League's campaign and by a disastrous famine in Ireland, Peel decided that the Corn Laws must go. Many of the Tory landowners, amounting to about two-thirds of the party, were bitterly opposed to the repeal, convinced that it would damage British agriculture and reduce their profits by letting in too much cheap foreign corn. Whig support enabled Peel to get the repeal act through Parliament, but the rebel section of his party soon forced him to resign, and the Conservatives split into two groups. After doing so much to rebuild his party during the 1830s, it seemed as though Peel had now destroyed it again.

7.1 Peel and the revival of the Tory/Conservative party

(a) Peel's early career

Peel was the son of a wealthy Lancashire cotton manufacturer (also called Robert) who had bought a large estate at Tamworth (Staffordshire), which he represented as a Tory MP from 1790. The elder Peel had great political ambitions for his son; he sent him to Harrow and Oxford and secured him a seat in Parliament in 1809 when he was only 21. The young Peel soon made a good impression with his speeches, and in 1812 Lord Liverpool appointed him Chief Secretary for Ireland, a position he held until 1818. This was a difficult period in Ireland, with the Irish Catholics violently opposing the Act of Union. Peel acquitted himself well, managing to contain the violence by setting up the Irish Constabulary, the first effective police force Ireland had ever had. With his reputation as an able and honest administrator standing high, Peel became Home Secretary in 1822, and was responsible for penal code reform and the

Illus. **7.1** **Sir Robert Peel: founder of the modern Conservative party?**

introduction of the Metropolitan Police (see Section 2.6(c)). Following the downfall of the Tory government in November 1830, the Whigs were in power for most of the next ten years; it was during this time that Peel devoted himself to building up the new Conservative party.

(b) what was Peel's contribution to the development of the Conservative party?

▸ Peel gave the party a new image, both in his speeches in Parliament, and outside Parliament in a document known as *the Tamworth Manifesto*. This was issued in December 1834 as an election address to the people of Tamworth, whom he represented in Parliament after his father's death in 1830. In it he explained that while he had at first opposed parliamentary reform, he now accepted the 1832 Reform Act as 'a final and irrevocable settlement of a great constitutional question'. He and his party were in favour of 'a careful review of institutions ... undertaken in a friendly temper, combining, with the firm maintenance of established rights, the correction of proved abuses, and the redress of real grievances'; in other words, he was prepared to introduce moderate reform wherever there was a genuine need for it, while at the same time preserving all that was good about the British system – the monarchy, the aristocracy and the Protestant Church of England. In a later speech, Peel referred to these aims as 'conservative principles'. The Tamworth Manifesto was important because it formalized the party's new programme; it showed that the Conservatives, as they were now called, stood for a safe programme of cautious reform midway between the old Tories, who were against all change, and the Radicals, whose ideas about reform were alarming to moderates.

▸ He gained wider support for his party from moderate people of all classes, particularly from middle-class manufacturers and businessmen, who felt neglected by the Whigs. The attractiveness of the Tamworth Manifesto and the party's new image were partly responsible for Peel's success, plus the fact that he came from a middle-class background himself.

▸ Under Peel, local Conservative associations and clubs were set up all over the country, so that the party was far more highly developed at local level than the Whigs. However, Peel himself did not take the initiative here, and in fact, he showed very little interest in the day-to-day details of party management. It was left to F. R. Bonham, who was appointed as the first full-time Tory election manager in 1835, to oversee this development. Bonham was also involved in the Carlton Club in London. Opened in 1832, this soon became both a social and an administrative headquarters for Conservative MPs.

As a result, the gap between Conservatives and Whigs gradually closed in the elections of 1835 and 1837, until in June 1841 Peel led his party to a triumphant victory, winning a majority of 76. Reasons for the Conservative success are fully explained in Section 5.6. In less than ten years, Peel had revived and given new direction to a party that had seemed defunct. Some historians, such as Norman Gash, think he deserves to be remembered as the founder of the modern Conservative party; but others feel that Disraeli has a better claim to this distinction. They point out that, at the time of their big election victory in 1841, there was nothing particularly 'new' about Peel's Conservatives, apart from their name – they still drew most of their support from country gentry and defenders of the Church of England. Peel certainly revived the party in the 1830s, but then, having revived it, he almost killed it off again with his repeal of the Corn Laws (see Section 7.6).

7.2 what did Peel do to help the British economy?

The country was facing serious economic problems when Peel became Prime Minister in 1841. Exports had fallen sharply, bringing an industrial slump and inevitable unemployment; industry seemed to be stagnating, and there had been a series of poor harvests since 1837, which kept bread prices high. As well as causing hardship and misery for the workers, the slump was accompanied by a financial crisis in which many small banks collapsed. The Whigs had left a deficit (the amount spent over and above income) of over £2 million. Peel aimed to encourage trade and to do something to ease the problems of the workers. He acted positively.

(a) he took important steps towards free trade

Huskisson had removed many tariffs (import and export duties) in the 1820s (see Section 2.6(a)), but the Whigs had taken no further action; there were still about 1,200 commodities that were subject to tariffs. Peel, influenced by a group of northern industrialists calling themselves *the Manchester School* (they included John Bright and Richard Cobden), came to believe that tariffs were stifling British industry. Their argument was that import duties made raw materials (such as cotton, wool and iron ore) more expensive, thereby keeping production costs too high. Foreign countries resented British tariffs and were less willing to trade than they would otherwise have been. Tariffs, including the duty on imported corn, made imported food more expensive and caused difficulty for the poor. Removal of tariffs would bring down the cost of British goods abroad, increase exports, stimulate industry and provide more jobs. In addition, the cost of living would be cheaper, to the benefit of the working classes. In Peel's own words: 'We must make this country a cheap country for living, and thus induce people to remain and settle here. Enable them to consume more by having more to spend.' In his *budgets of 1842 and 1845* he boldly swept away a large proportion of the remaining duties, so that, after 1845:

‣ duties on over 600 articles had been removed completely; and
‣ duties on about 500 others had been greatly reduced.

To take a few examples, this meant that there were no longer any export duties at all, and there was no import duty on raw cotton, livestock, meat and potatoes. Cheese imported from British colonies paid a duty of only 1s 6d per hundredweight instead of 10s 6d. There was even a slight reduction in the import duty on corn, though not enough to satisfy the Anti-Corn Law League.

These measures worked exactly as Peel had hoped: they helped to bring about a trade revival, exports increased, unemployment fell rapidly, and food was cheaper (though bread was still more expensive than it need have been, thanks to the Corn Laws). Britain began to move out of the 'hungry forties' and into a Golden Age of Victorian prosperity that lasted until around 1873 (see Section 15.1).

(b) income tax was re-introduced

This was at the rate of seven pence in the pound on incomes over £150 a year (1843). This controversial tax had been abolished by the Tories in 1816 (see Section 2.2(c)), but Peel brought it back as a temporary measure for three years to make up for the losses in revenue (annual income) that the government would suffer with the abolition of so many duties. It turned out to be so profitable that Peel persuaded Parliament to renew it for a further three years; since then, no government has been able to afford to abandon it.

Between them, the trade revival and income tax were strikingly successful: Peel had soon turned the Whig deficit of £2 million into a healthy surplus.

(c) the Bank Charter Act (1844)

This was an important financial measure made necessary because many banks were unreliable. The problem was that all banks, no matter how small, could issue banknotes, with no limit on the amount. When demand for currency was high among businessmen (for example, to finance railway building), there was a tendency for banks to issue too much paper money, which they loaned out for investment in new companies. If any companies got into difficulties (as many railway companies did), investors often lost their money and could not repay the bank. Some banks, having over-issued notes, lacked sufficient gold reserves to see them through, and during a slump, some small banks would collapse. This gave the impression that the currency was unsound, and Peel realized that trade could only expand if the currency was stable. The 1844 Act aimed to bring about 'by gradual means the establishment of a safe system of currency'.

- No new banks were allowed to issue notes.
- Existing banks were restricted to their average issue during the three months preceding the passing of the Act; if any existing banks amalgamated, they lost the right to issue notes.
- The Bank of England could issue notes worth up to £14 million, but any paper money issued beyond that had to be covered by gold reserves in the Bank's vaults.

The Act was generally successful: it had the effect of gradually phasing out the note-issuing function of ordinary banks, so that the Bank of England came to control the amount of currency in circulation; there was less danger of over-issuing notes, English currency became extremely stable and London came to be regarded as the world's leading monetary centre.

(d) the Companies Act (1844)

This Act dealt with another finance and business problem: the fact that there were no controls on the formation of companies. Anybody could start a company simply by publishing an advertisement, and could then begin receiving money from foolish investors. During the 1830s, many such dubious companies became bankrupt, or dishonest directors absconded with the capital; either way, the investors suffered. The Act aimed to prevent 'reckless speculation' (investing money when there is a risk that it might be lost): all companies now had to be registered officially and were to issue prospectuses and regular accounts. The Act had some success, but its weakness was that it did not apply to companies that had to get special approval from Parliament; these included railway companies, where some of the worst racketeers operated.

7.3 what did Peel do about Britain's social problems?

Peel was well aware of the disgraceful conditions in some factories, mines and industrial towns. On the other hand he knew that not all manufacturers were blameworthy: his own father had been a humane and enlightened employer. His instinct told him that the best way of dealing with problems was not to pass laws, but to wait until his economic policies bore fruit; then all the workers would have jobs, and would be able 'to consume more by having more to spend'; hardships would gradually disappear. Another reason for not taking direct action was that he might lose the support of middle-class businessmen if he tried to regulate working hours and conditions. However, when unemployment reached a new peak in 1842, and troops had to be despatched to deal with Chartist violence (see Section 6.4(b)), the situation took on a new urgency. Peel was also under constant pressure from Shaftesbury and the Ten-Hour Movement (which wanted a ten-hour working day for women and children). Eventually *the Mines Act (1842)* and *a Factory Act (1844)* did something to improve conditions (for full details, see Section 12.3(e–f)). Most of the credit for these Acts belongs to Shaftesbury rather than to Peel; in fact, Peel himself was responsible for defeating Shaftesbury's proposal of a ten-hour maximum working day, and both Acts had serious weaknesses.

Again under pressure, this time from Edwin Chadwick, the government appointed a Royal Commission to enquire into the 'state of Large Towns and Populous Districts', which produced alarming findings in 1844 and 1845. Peel, now hampered by the Corn Law crisis, took no further action, and it was left to

Russell's government to introduce the first Public Health Act in 1848. Social reform was therefore not Peel's most successful area.

7.4 Peel, O'Connell and Ireland

(a) Ireland after the 1800 Act of Union

Following the passing of this much-hated Act, which took away the Irish parliament (see Section 1.2(d)), nearly every British government in the nineteenth century had to deal with problems of one sort or another in Ireland. We have already seen (Section 2.7(b)) how the Tory party split over Catholic Emancipation in 1829. The Irish were not satisfied with emancipation, partly because success had been soured when, at the same time, the Tories took the vote away from the 40-shilling freeholders.

When the Whigs were in power (1830–41), Daniel O'Connell, the Irish leader who now sat at Westminster as MP for County Clare, did not press his next great ambition – *the repeal of the Act of Union.* For most of the time he co-operated with the Whigs, hoping to win some concessions, such as the abolition of tithes, which were highly unpopular with the Catholic tenant farmers. However, there were some outbreaks of violence, and it was disagreement about how to deal with these that caused Grey to resign as Whig Prime Minister in 1834. O'Connell did secure a few concessions, including the Tithe Act (see Section 5.5(b)) and the inclusion of Irishmen in the Irish police force, but overall he was disappointed.

(b) Ireland during Peel's ministry

Irish affairs had come to the forefront again by 1843, and in 1846 they were instrumental in bringing down Peel and splitting the Conservative party.

1 O'Connell's comparative lack of success after 1829 meant that he was beginning to lose his hold over the Irish; younger and more violent men – Smith O'Brien, Gavan Duffy and John Mitchel, calling themselves 'Young Ireland' – were impatient with O'Connell's moderation. The ageing leader, now 65, decided to stage a last attempt to force the British to repeal the Act of Union, by agitation and the threat of civil war, a policy that had worked with Peel and Wellington in the case of Catholic Emancipation. Supported by the Catholic priests, O'Connell began to address large meetings, stirring up intense excitement; he told a crowd of over 100,000 at Tara (the seat of medieval Irish kings) that within a year the Act of Union would be smashed and the Irish would have a parliament of their own. The climax of the campaign was to be a vast open-air meeting at Clontarf in October 1843.

2 Peel was determined not to be frightened into giving way again; he believed, rightly, that this time Ireland was not on the verge of civil war, as it had been in 1829. He announced that the Union would never be cancelled and that

rebellion would be crushed. Troops were sent to Ireland and the Clontarf meeting banned.

3 This placed O'Connell in a difficult situation: if he allowed the meeting to go ahead, it would be treated as rebellion, while if he cancelled it, 'Young Ireland' could accuse him of surrendering to the British. In the event, he was not prepared to risk violence; he called the meeting off, and it was clear that Peel had outmanoeuvred him in the war of nerves.

4 O'Connell was arrested, tried for conspiracy (remarks in his earlier speeches were said to be seditious), found guilty, sentenced to one year in gaol and fined £2,000. The House of Lords reversed the verdict and O'Connell was released, but there was no disguising his defeat. His influence gradually faded as 'Young Ireland' assumed the leadership. O'Connell died in 1847.

5 Peel combined his firm line with some mild concessions. He was convinced that Ireland would never be calm and stable until the government won the support of the educated Catholic community, and he had been making concessions to them since 1843. He appointed the Devon Commission to investigate problems of land-holding in Ireland; this reported in 1845 but there was no time to act before the government fell. He tried to please the Catholics by increasing the annual government grant to Maynooth College (which trained Catholic priests) from £9,000 to £26,000. However, this aroused hostility among his Protestant supporters, many of whom voted against it; in fact, the grant was only approved by the Commons because the Whigs voted for it.

6 In an attempt to provide wider opportunities for higher education, Peel also set up three non-sectarian university colleges – in Belfast, Cork and Galway. However, this was opposed by Roman Catholics, who wanted a state-funded university college exclusively for them. Consequently, they put pressure on Catholic students not to attend the new colleges. Cork and Galway were not a success; however, Queen's College in Belfast proved to be extremely popular with the Presbyterians, who were in a majority in northern Ireland. These were all courageous moves by Peel, but they left the Conservatives deeply divided, and this prevented him from tackling the country's basic problem – poverty. Once again, religious problems in Ireland had seriously embarrassed the British government (see Section 12.14 for more details). Unfortunately, worse was soon to come, both for Peel and the Irish.

7 By July 1845 it was clear that the Irish potato crop had been ruined by blight; the country was on the verge of famine, bringing new urgency to the Corn Law repeal problem.

7.5 the struggle for the repeal of the Corn Laws, 1838–46

Along with Chartism, the campaign to repeal the Corn Laws was the other great protest movement of the nineteenth century. The two movements provide a striking contrast: Chartism a failure, the Anti-Corn Law League a triumphant success in 1846.

(a) formation of the Anti-Corn Law League

▸ Ever since the introduction of the Corn Laws (1815) banning the import of foreign corn until the price of home-grown corn reached 80 shillings a quarter (see Section 2.2(c)), critics had argued that they should be repealed, because they kept bread prices far too high. Huskisson's sliding scale of import duties (1828) did nothing to alter their general argument that the Corn Laws were in place simply as protection for British agriculture – to guarantee farmers high profits by keeping out as much foreign corn as possible.

▸ Between 1830 and 1835, harvests were good and wheat prices fairly low; in 1835, for example, wheat averaged 39s 4d a quarter, and a four-pound loaf cost 7d, compared with 96s 11d a quarter and 14½d a loaf in 1817. After 1835 there was a run of poor harvests, corn became scarce, and prices rose. In 1839, wheat averaged 70s 8d a quarter and a loaf cost 10d – not as disastrous for the poor as in 1817, but bad enough, bearing in mind the serious industrial depression that began in 1837. The average price of a loaf was 10d, but at times in 1839 it was as high as 13d (1s 1d); this was when unemployment was rising and a Lancashire hand-loom weaver was earning no more than 5s a week; a family of two adults and three children would need at the very minimum five loaves a week.

▸ Agitation for repeal was strong in Manchester, the main distress centre. Here, the Anti-Corn Law Association was started in 1838, followed by similar groups in other cities. In March 1839, they merged into the Anti-Corn Law League with its headquarters in Manchester. It was inspired mainly by manufacturers and businessmen; the leaders were *Richard Cobden*, a southerner who ran a calico factory in Manchester, and the Quaker, *John Bright*, a Rochdale cotton manufacturer.

(b) arguments for and against abolishing the Corn Laws

The case for abolition involved a lot more than just cheaper bread, though that was an important consideration:

1 Removal of the Corn Laws was part of the general move away from protection and towards free trade already started by Huskisson. Like all other duties, protective tariffs were seen by Benthamites as an unnatural restraint on trade; they kept imports of foreign corn to a minimum and forced bread prices up simply to ensure good profits for landowners. According to Cobden and Bright, this was un-Christian. Abolition would bring cheaper bread, to the benefit of the poor. For this reason, the League attracted a good deal of working-class support, so that it became a powerful alliance of the middle classes and workers.

2 Once bread prices fell, real wages would increase (workers would be able to buy more with their wages even though the actual money paid to them was the

same), enabling workers to buy not only more bread, but more of other goods as well. This would provide a much-needed stimulus to British industry.

3 The importing of foreign corn would encourage British farmers to become more competitive so that they would have no need of protective tariffs.

4 Buying corn from abroad would encourage foreign countries to import more British manufactured goods. As trade between nations expanded all round, it would improve international relations and contribute towards world peace. This argument appealed especially to the pacifist Bright and gave the campaign the flavour of a moral crusade.

The case for retaining the Corn Laws was put strongly by the landowners and by their ally, *The Times* newspaper:

1 Removal of the Corn Laws would allow an influx of cheap foreign wheat, which would ruin British farmers and cause mass unemployment among farm labourers, who would migrate to the towns, adding to the existing problems of overcrowding, and leave the countryside depopulated.

2 Britain would become too dependent on foreign corn, which might be cut off in wartime.

3 The whole campaign was a selfish, middle-class capitalist plot: manufacturers only wanted cheaper bread so that they could reduce wages. This argument had some success among industrial workers and helps to explain why the Chartists were hostile to the League.

(c) methods and activities of the League

Their simple and logical case was put, over and over again, by Cobden, Bright and other leaders; there was no violence and they almost always kept within the law:

▸ They used masses of paper propaganda: they published a fortnightly and later a weekly newspaper called *The Anti-Bread Tax Circular* and bombarded the public with millions of leaflets and pamphlets hammering home their arguments and ridiculing their opponents. They made excellent use of the new Penny Post (introduced 1840) and made sure that every elector received at least one batch of League literature.

▸ They held both indoor and open-air mass meetings. In Manchester, the Free Trade Hall was built (1843) to hold 8,000 people; in the same year, a League headquarters was set up in London that organized no fewer than 136 meetings in that year alone. The country was divided into twelve areas, each with a paid agent whose job was to arrange meetings and speakers. Cobden and Bright emerged as expert orators, though in the early days many League speakers had a rough reception from Chartists in industrial towns and from farmers in country areas. At a meeting in Manchester the audience hurled chairs at the speakers on the stage, while at Saxmundham in Suffolk, a speaker was thrown down a flight of stairs and had to be rescued by police.

- Much time and effort was expended on fund-raising – the wealthy middle class often needed persuasion to put their names on the donation lists, and there were bazaars and tea-parties to organize. In 1843, over £50,000 was raised; in 1844, £100,000; a bazaar at the Covent Garden Theatre in May 1845 raised £25,000.
- Cobden won the support of Daniel O'Connell, who provided an enormous boost by ensuring that Irish workers co-operated with the League, rather than with the Chartists. At meetings in the North, Irish labourers often acted as bodyguards against Chartist rowdies.
- Like the Chartists, the Leaguers presented a number of monster petitions to Parliament, but as soon as it became obvious that these were useless, they concentrated on getting as many MPs as possible elected to Parliament. Their first attempt was encouraging: at a bye-election in Walsall (January 1841) they put up J. B. Smith, who stood as an *Abolitionist*. After a violent campaign, Smith was defeated only narrowly by the Tory candidate (363 votes to 336). The League used its funds to enable members who had no vote to buy 40-shilling freehold properties, (these could usually be bought for between £30 and £60), which carried the right to vote; in the general election of 1841, eight Abolitionists were elected, including Cobden himself for Stockport. Bright won a bye-election at Durham in 1843, and by 1845 there were twelve Abolitionist MPs. Now the League could bring constant pressure to bear on the government; as Cobden himself remarked, 'you speak with a loud voice when you are talking on the floor of the House, and if you have anything to say that hits hard ... it reaches all over the kingdom'.

(d) stages in the repeal

1 In the first two years, the League made little progress: there was violent opposition from Chartists and farmers, and Lord John Russell, the Whig Home Secretary, refused to receive deputations and petitions.

2 After the 1841 election, the Abolitionist MPs began to make some impact, so much so that Peel slightly reduced the corn import duties laid down in Huskisson's 1828 sliding scale. He hoped that this would be sufficient to silence the more moderate League supporters, and in fact there was something of a lull in the campaign until 1845.

3 At some time between 1842 and the beginning of 1845 (*before* the Irish famine) Peel himself made up his mind that the Corn Laws were not serving any useful purpose and that British farmers ought to be perfectly capable of maintaining their profits without them, provided they modernized their methods. An up-to-date farming system would make a perfect partnership with expanding industry. No doubt the League's arguments were partly responsible for Peel's change of mind: after Cobden had delivered a particularly effective attack on the Corn Laws in the Commons (March 1845), Peel screwed up his notes and whispered to the MP sitting next to him, 'You must

answer this, for I cannot.' Peel's problem was that, during the 1841 election campaign, the Conservative party had promised to keep the Corn Laws, and if he moved too quickly, he would infuriate the landowners and split the party again. He hoped to prepare the party gradually for repeal, and then allow the country to decide at the next general election, due in 1848.

4 In the summer of 1845 the Irish potato crop was ruined by blight. In a country where the basic diet of the great mass of the population consisted entirely of potatoes, this was disastrous. With the poor facing starvation, Peel arranged for £160,000 worth of maize to be imported from the USA to be sold at 1d a pound to the Irish. But this was soon used up; in hundreds of villages in the west of Ireland there was no food of any sort, and thousands were dying of starvation. At the same time, the English and Scottish potato crop failed and the corn harvest was a poor one; however, corn grown in Ireland was being exported to England. In November 1845, Peel told his cabinet that the Corn Laws must go immediately; this was the only way to get cheap food into Ireland. Whether he really believed this, or whether he was using the Irish famine as an emergency excuse to force repeal through, is not certain. (In fact, the repeal made little difference to the tragic situation in Ireland.) Either way, a majority of the Cabinet opposed the idea, and Peel resigned in December 1845.

5 After Russell failed to form a Whig government, Queen Victoria recalled Peel, who had by then won over most of his Cabinet, but not his party. A Repeal Bill (which would phase out the Corn Laws over the next three years) was introduced into the Commons. There was a fierce debate lasting five months, during which about two-thirds of the Conservative MPs revolted against Peel. The Protectionists were led by Benjamin Disraeli and Lord George Bentinck. They made bitter personal attacks on Peel, claiming that the situation in Ireland was not serious enough to warrant such a Bill, and accusing Peel of breaking his promises and betraying his party again, as he had over Catholic Emancipation. Some said Disraeli's real motive for the attacks was revenge for Peel's refusal to include him in the government in 1841.

6 The Repeal Bill passed the Commons (May 1846), but only with Whig support: the rebel Conservatives (231 of them) all voted against Peel; only 112 Conservatives voted with him. Wellington, though initially unconvinced by Peel's arguments, eventually used his enormous prestige to support Peel once again. He told the House of Lords that 'a good government for the country is more important than Corn Laws or any other consideration.' The Bill passed the Lords without too much trouble and became law in June. But Disraeli and the Protectionists were determined on revenge. To help restore order in Ireland, Peel had introduced a Coercion Bill into the Commons; on the same night as the Corn Law Repeal Bill passed the Lords, Disraeli and some of the rebel Conservatives combined with the Whigs and the Irish MPs to defeat the Coercion Bill. Peel resigned and never held office again.

(e) what were the effects of the Corn Law repeal?

Oddly, after all the controversy and excitement, the results of the repeal were an anti-climax:

▸ There was no dramatic fall in wheat prices, for the simple reason that whenever the British harvest was poor, so was the European one; there was no vast inflow of European wheat, and supplies from North America were not yet available in large enough quantities. However, economists believe that repeal did at least keep British wheat prices steady at a time when world prices generally were rising.
▸ British farmers did not suffer immediate ruin; they soon developed better methods – the use of fertilizers, more mechanization, drainage pipes, stronger strains of wheat – all of which helped to increase yield per acre. As town populations increased steadily, the demand for food grew, and farmers were ensured reasonable profits. It was not until the 1870s that British farming began to suffer competition from massive imports from America (see Section 15.4).
▸ Repeal did not seem to help the Irish significantly; the 1846 potato crop failed as badly as the one in 1845, and 1847 saw only a slight improvement, so that the famine continued until 1848, when there was a good harvest. Since there were no large stocks of life-saving European corn available, and Irish-grown corn continued to be exported to England throughout the famine, the condition of the Irish poor was pitiful. To add to their misery, a cholera epidemic broke out in December 1846. It is estimated that at least a million people died from starvation and disease, and a further million emigrated to Canada and the USA (for the next phase in Irish history, see Section 8.2(a)).
▸ Repeal probably encouraged other countries to reduce duties on goods from Britain, though there were many other reasons for this reduction; there was much more behind the British trade expansion than the abolition of the Corn Laws.
▸ It destroyed Peel and split the party; after this, the Conservatives were out of office (except for two short and ineffective periods in 1852 and 1858) until 1866. However, landowners were still the dominant group in Parliament, whereas the middle classes, the largest section of voters, were still in a minority. Cobden had hoped that the Anti-Corn Law League would develop into a new middle-class political party capable of seriously challenging the landowning class. As time passed, he suffered disappointment: once the single aim uniting all the various sections of the middle class had been achieved, the alliance fell apart; the middle classes were far too diverse and varied in character and interests to be represented by one political party.

Of course, in June 1846 none of these results could be foreseen; as far as the League members were concerned, all else was forgotten as they celebrated their triumph.

(f) why was the Anti-Corn Law League successful?

‣ The League concentrated on the one aim that was simple to understand (unlike the Chartists, who tried to achieve too much all at once), and their arguments were reasonable and logical.

‣ It was a middle-class-inspired movement, which provided it with sufficient funds to form a national organization and mount an effective propaganda campaign (the Chartists – violent and threatening revolution – failed to win significant middle-class support).

‣ They had outstanding and united leaders (especially Cobden and Bright), who were successful in winning twelve seats to put their case effectively in Parliament. It was this continued pressure, plus the strength of their case, that convinced Peel that the Corn Laws must eventually go, though not necessarily immediately (the Chartist leaders were less able, could not agree on what tactics to follow, and failed to make an impact in Parliament).

‣ The Irish famine helped to bring matters to a head, causing Peel, or perhaps giving him the excuse, to abandon the Corn Laws earlier than he would otherwise have done.

7.6 was Peel a great statesman who deserves to be remembered as the founder of the modern Conservative party?

Taking the *Oxford Dictionary* definition of a statesman as 'a person taking a prominent part in the management of state affairs', there can be no disputing that Peel was a statesman. But there have been widely varying views about how 'great' he was. W. Bagehot, writing in 1856, thought that, while Peel was a great administrator, he was not a great statesman, because he was not capable of creative thought; he merely borrowed other people's ideas. Bagehot made the point, well worth thinking about, that Peel had begun by opposing most of the measures that were later considered his greatest achievements (such as Catholic Emancipation and the repeal of the Corn Laws); he was good at repealing things but not so impressive when it came to thinking of something new. G. Kitson Clark, writing his biography of Peel in 1936, believed that, in spite of all his successes, there was 'a lack of vision in Peel'.

On the other hand, Peel's was a career full of striking achievements, first as Irish Secretary (1812–18), then as Home Secretary (1822–30), and finally as Prime Minister. Norman Gash sums up his premiership clearly and simply: 'Financial stability had been achieved, trade revived, Chartism virtually extinguished, O'Connell's repeal movement checked, the great institutions of state safeguarded, and good relations with France and the USA restored ... More than any other one man he was the architect of the early Victorian age.'

Yet how could he be a great statesman if he betrayed his Conservative party and left it in ruins? The answer is simple: Peel believed that the national interest was more important than the party. When the Conservatives refused to go along with him over the Corn Laws, Peel was disgusted with them and disillusioned with party politics. Soon after the split, he wrote: 'Thank God I am relieved for ever from the trammels of such a party.'

Some more recent writers have not been as glowing as Norman Gash in their assessment of Peel; it has been suggested that:

▸ His role as founder of the modern Conservative party has been exaggerated, and that the party and its supporters were basically the same – gentry, landowners and the Church of England – in 1841 as they were in 1830.
▸ Wellington deserves as much credit as Peel for the revival of the party after 1830, and that Disraeli deserves most of the credit for founding the modern Conservative party.
▸ His political judgement was often seriously at fault during his premiership;
▸ He failed to understand the way the party political system was changing after 1832; the new thinking was that party members must stick to party principles – loyalty to the party and party unity should be the prime concerns.

One of Peel's latest biographers, Douglas Hurd, takes a rather more positive view of Peel's achievements and legacy. He argues that what Peel brought to the party in the Tamworth Manifesto was a new and more progressive attitude: 'He believed that the institutions of his country were best protected not by resisting change but by measuring it to the needs of the moment ... He defined the appeal of the new Party based on selective and constructive opposition and the gradual enlisting of sober men of property.' As to Peel's 'betrayal' of his party in 1846, it is important to remember that the role of political parties at that point was still in a transitional stage. Should the Prime Minister carry out the wishes of the monarch, or those of his party rank and file? Peel's conclusion was that he had been recalled by the Queen, and therefore it was his duty to carry on the Queen's government in the interests of the whole nation. If this meant bringing about his own downfall, then so be it. If his party failed to appreciate his reasoning, then so much the worse for them. It is possible to argue that, by acting in this noble and self-sacrificing way instead of leaving it to the Whigs to repeal the Corn Laws, Peel rose above party and showed a certain greatness of spirit. In the words of Douglas Hurd, by making this choice, Peel 'gained something which he had never consciously sought, namely popularity among the great mass of people as the man who brought them cheap bread.' He goes on to suggest that perhaps Peel's greatest legacy was to the world as a whole. 'He proclaimed the message [of free trade] not just to Britain but to all trading nations. Britain should adopt the motto "Advance, not recede" so that others could follow.' Disraeli's contribution was to rebuild the strength of the divided Conservative party on the foundations laid by Peel. 'Those foundations are the basis of the Conservative Party today.'

Peel died unexpectedly in 1850 at the age of 62, from injuries sustained when he was thrown from his horse. While many who knew him in politics thought him dull and cold (O'Connell said that when he smiled it was like the gleam of the silver plate on a coffin lid), the general public certainly felt that the country had lost its most brilliant politician. Shops and factories closed, and in Bury, his birthplace, over £3,000 was raised from ordinary people for his memorial. Lord Aberdeen wrote: 'A great light has disappeared from amongst us. Never did I know such universal grief exhibited by every description of person; high and low, rich and poor, from the Queen to the common labourer; all feel alike and with good reason, for his services were equally rendered to all'. Among the many tributes that poured forth was this excruciating but no doubt sincere verse:

> Talk of Canning and Pitt for their talents and wit,
> And all who upheld that high station,
> Oh! there has ne'er been such a noble Premier
> As Sir Robert before in the nation,
> In every way he carried the sway,
> For the good of his country, God rest him.
>
> (Anon)

QUESTIONS

1 'Peel's place as the founder of modern Conservatism is unchallengeable ... The age of revolt was giving way to the age of stability; and of that age, Peel had been the chief architect' (Norman Gash). How far would you agree with this assessment of Peel's achievement?

2 'Peel was a great Prime Minister but a disastrous leader of the Conservative party.' How valid is this view of Peel's ministry of 1841 to 1846?

A document question about Peel, Disraeli and the repeal of the Corn Laws can be found on the accompanying website www.palgrave.com/masterseries/lowe1.

domestic affairs, 1846–67: Russell, Gladstone, Disraeli and the Reform Act of 1867

summary of events

Despite the mid-1800s being a time of general economic prosperity, *the political scene was confused and unstable* following the Conservative split over the Corn Law repeal. Those Conservatives (112 of them), including W. E. Gladstone and Lord Aberdeen, who had voted with Peel for the abolition of the Corn Laws, were known as *Peelites.* Those who had wanted to keep the Corn Laws (*Protectionists)* were led officially by Edward Stanley, Lord Derby, though it was Disraeli who supplied the leadership of the Conservative party in the Commons. The Peelites and Protectionists would have nothing to do with each other, and the Peelites usually voted with the Whigs. This enabled Lord John Russell, the Whig leader, to form a government with Peelite support, even though the Whigs lacked an overall majority.

The Whigs improved their position in the 1847 general election, winning 325 seats to the Tory Protectionists' 243. However, the Peelites, with 89 seats,[*] held the balance, and the Whigs could not afford to ignore their wishes if they wanted to remain in power. In the 1852 election, the Peelites dwindled to 45 (Peel himself had died in 1850), but they still held the balance, and actually formed a coalition government with the Whigs; the Peelite leader, Lord Aberdeen, was Prime Minister (1852–5). In the election of 1857, the numbers of Peelites slumped to 29, and after that they gradually faded away as most of them joined the Whigs, who were now known as the Liberals. But the Conservatives had still not recovered fully from the split, and were only in government for three short spells during this period. The list of governments shown here (see Box) illustrates the instability.

---

[*] The problem with the Peelites is that they were never an organized party, so it is difficult to be sure who were Peelites and who weren't at any given time. You will probably find different estimates of the numbers of Peelite MPs in different books. The figures used here are from R. Blake, *The Conservative Party from Peel to Thatcher* (Fontana, 1985), p. 46.

Party	Prime Minister	In office
Whig	Lord John Russell	1846–52
Conservative	Lord Derby	Feb–Dec 1852
Whig/Peelite coalition	Lord Aberdeen	1852–5
Liberal	Lord Palmerston	1855–8
Conservative	Lord Derby	1858–9
Liberal	Lord Palmerston	1859–65
Liberal	Lord John Russell	1865–6
Conservative	Lord Derby	1866–8
Conservative	Benjamin Disraeli	Feb–Dec 1868
Liberal	William Ewart Gladstone	1868–74

Domestic politics were for the most part uneventful during these years, with certain exceptions, notably *the final fling of Chartism* in 1848 (see Section 6.4(c)), and *some useful social reforms* introduced by Russell's government of 1846–52. Gladstone, who was Chancellor of the Exchequer for much of the time between 1852 and 1866, continued *the move towards Free Trade,* his policies reaching a climax with a series of remarkable budgets (1860–4). The most striking feature on the domestic scene was not in politics – it was the great surge of industrial and agricultural prosperity sometimes referred to as *the Golden Age of Victorian Britain* (see Section 15.1).

In the middle of the period, much of the public's attention was occupied by events abroad – *the Crimean War of 1854–6* (see Chapter 10) and *the Indian Mutiny of 1857* (see Chapter 11). Public interest in foreign affairs was maintained during Palmerston's second spell as Prime Minister, from 1859 to 1865.

During the 1860s the question that again came to the forefront was the need for a further reform of Parliament. After long wrangling reminiscent of the struggle to get the 1832 Reform Act through, Derby's Conservative government was responsible for *the Reform Act of 1867,* another major step towards a democratic system of parliamentary government. Much to the disgust of the Conservatives, the newly enlarged electorate responded at the general election of 1868 by voting in a Liberal government with a majority of over 100.

8.1 the Whigs become the Liberal party

The *Oxford English Dictionary* gives a variety of definitions of the word 'liberal'. These include 'free', 'in favour of reform', 'not rigorous', 'free from narrow prejudice' and 'open to new ideas'. From the late 1830s, the Whigs began to be called 'Liberals'. The last truly Whig government was Lord John Russell's Cabinet of 1846. As the aristocratic Whig party gained more wealthy middle-class support, it gradually transformed itself into a party that aimed to put into practice middle-class reformist ideas. It drew on the works of economists, philosophers and political theorists such as Adam Smith, David Ricardo, and Jeremy Bentham and his follower, John Stuart Mill. In his famous book *The Wealth of Nations* (1776) Adam Smith argued that economic success depended on a combination of freedom of the individual and division of labour, or specialization. Ricardo put forward powerful arguments in favour of Free Trade.

Classical Liberals therefore viewed society as a collection of unconnected individuals. They believed that individual enterprise was the best way to ensure economic progress. It was important that the government should interfere as little as possible (*laissez-faire*), and only for the purpose of removing obstacles to progress and reforming existing institutions to make them more efficient. It was also important that the government should spend as little as possible. By the 1850s the Liberals' slogan was 'liberty, retrenchment and reform'. Another theme of Liberalism was Jeremy Bentham's Utilitarianism – that governments should be as efficient as possible and should strive to secure 'the greatest happiness of the greatest number of people'.

However, there was some confusion and contradiction in these ideas. Areas such as factory reform, religious affairs, education, poverty and public health needed government action if 'the greatest happiness' was to be secured. But the *laissez-faire* section of the party saw this as unnecessary meddling. Thus, in 1846, it was no surprise when Russell, the Prime Minister, at the time of the famine in Ireland, told Parliament: 'we cannot feed the people', adding later that government interference in the food trade would undermine all private enterprise, and that eventually everything would be 'abandoned to the care of the government'. Fortunately, he was soon moved to change his mind and state funds were used to buy imported corn and other emergency supplies (see next section). Similarly in 1847, the Radicals in the party, including Cobden and Bright, voted against Fielden's Factory Bill, which proposed to introduce a 10-hour limit on the working day of women and children, on the grounds that it was a breach of *laissez-faire* principles. The Bill passed with the support of the Conservative Protectionists. These confusions and contradictions partly explain why the Liberal governments' domestic achievements after 1850 were few and far between.

According to Roy Douglas, it is difficult to pin down exactly when the Liberal party as such came into existence, and 'almost any date between 1830 and 1868 might be chosen'. There was a meeting of 274 Liberal MPs in June 1859 in Willis's Rooms in London, which is taken by some historians to mark the formal beginning of the party. Those present included Whigs, Peelites, Radicals and anyone else who could be relied upon to support them, so that the new Liberal government that had just taken office would have a majority in the House of Commons.

8.2 how successful were the domestic policies of Russell's government of 1846–52?

Broadly speaking, the government had its main successes up to 1850, but after that it ran into trouble and achieved little of any significance.

(a) continuing problems in Ireland

Ireland was again the most pressing problem, with famine, cholera, dysentery and fever continuing until 1852. Clearly, massive amounts of relief were necessary, and while Russell's government did offer some help, it was nowhere near enough. During the first half of 1847, a network of soup kitchens was set up, which provided free soup for about three million people. However, at the same time, stricter rules made it more difficult for the poor to get financial payments, and the government reduced its financial contribution, announcing that, from August 1847, the Poor Law must deal with the problem; in other words, the Irish taxpayers must foot the bill for famine relief themselves. This meant that the Irish Poor Law, which had been intended to cope with perhaps 100,000 paupers, was having to deal with about a million and a half people during the winter of 1847–8. Potato blight was still a problem in some areas as late as 1850; the deaths continued, though the majority were caused not by starvation, but by famine-related diseases. The terrible suffering and loss of life (which was confined to Ireland) demonstrated to the Irish people that Ireland was not being treated on equal terms with the rest of Britain, and it only served to fuel Irish hatred of the English (see Section 13.3(a) for the next phase in Irish history).

(b) the Chartist outburst of 1848

Although this turned out to be the final fling of Chartism, it could well have got out of hand. However, the government acted positively and the situation was dealt with decisively (see Section 6.4(c)).

(c) social reforms

These included *two Factory Acts: Fielden's in 1847 and Grey's in 1850*; both were concerned with limiting the working day for women (see Section 12.4). Another important reform was *the Public Health Act of 1848* (see Section 12.6(a)). This was a pioneering piece of legislation that allowed Local Boards of Health to be set up to improve sanitation and the water supply, but the fact that it was not compulsory robbed it of much of its effectiveness. The government grant for education was increased in 1847 (see Section 12.8(a)).

(d) the government loses its way

After 1850, the government aroused opposition and lost support over several issues:

- The 1851 budget was highly unpopular among manufacturers and businessmen, who had hoped to see income tax (standing at 7d in the £) abolished.
- Russell appeared to be against parliamentary reform when he opposed a private member's bill that would have made the voting qualification the same in both counties and boroughs. The Radicals, already disappointed over the budget, were so annoyed with Russell that they voted for the motion, which was passed against Russell's wishes. At this point, the Prime Minister resigned (February 1851), but the Conservatives, lacking a majority, failed to form a government, so Russell came back for another year. This was long enough to see through the Great Exhibition (see Section 15.1(a)).

But the government grew steadily weaker and was finally brought down by Palmerston in retaliation for his dismissal by Russell a few weeks earlier (see Section 9.4(e)).

8.3 what contribution did Gladstone make to the development of the British economy while he was Chancellor of the Exchequer?

William Ewart Gladstone, the son of a wealthy Liverpool merchant, was educated at Eton and Christ Church, Oxford, and first entered Parliament as a Tory in 1832. For a time he was President of the Board of Trade in Peel's 1841–6 government, helping to formulate Peel's great tariff reforms. When the Conservatives split over the repeal of the Corn Laws, Gladstone remained a Peelite, which kept him out of office until 1852, when he became Chancellor of the Exchequer in the Whig–Peelite coalition (until 1855). The Conservatives tried to entice him back, but he was now moving firmly towards the Liberals, and when Palmerston invited him to take up his old post, Gladstone accepted. He was Liberal Chancellor of the Exchequer from 1859 until 1865, and became Liberal leader in the House of Commons on Palmerston's death.

(a) Gladstone had strong views about economic policy

- While serving with Peel, he had been converted to the idea of Free Trade. The more manufacturers and businessmen could be freed from having to pay tariffs, the more cheaply they could produce their goods. These would be all the more competitive on the world market, and British exports would increase.
- Full employment and low food prices would enable the working class to enjoy a share of the general prosperity.
- Gladstone believed it was important to keep both government expenditure and taxation to a minimum: 'All excess in public expenditure … is not only a pecuniary waste, but above all, a great moral evil.' He hoped to abolish the income tax and generally make government finance more efficient.

- The result of all this would be to create the right environment for people to prosper, to live economically and to build up their savings; in other words, people should help themselves, rather than expect the government to spend vast amounts of cash on welfare schemes.

(b) Gladstone's aims put into practice

1 *The attack on tariffs* began immediately, in the 1853 Budget: he abolished nearly all remaining duties on partially manufactured goods and on food, including fruit and dairy produce, and halved nearly all remaining duties on fully manufactured goods; these changes affected over 250 separate articles. The 1860 Budget continued this trend, import duties being abolished on a further 375 articles; this left only another 48 articles still being taxed. Even this was whittled down further when Gladstone reduced the duty on sugar (1864) and later halved the duty on tea (from 1s to 6d a pound).

2 *Income tax reduction* proved more difficult to achieve; Gladstone hoped to phase it out gradually, ending it altogether in 1859. He was reluctant to abolish it at a stroke in his 1853 budget because he needed the revenue it brought in to make up for that lost from the tariffs he was abolishing. His plans were thwarted by the outbreak of the Crimean War in 1854, which forced him to raise income tax to 10d in the pound on incomes between £100 and £150 a year and 1s 2d on incomes over £150. After the war he realized it was far too valuable a tax to disappear completely, but he reduced it again, to 6d, in 1865, and to 4d in 1866.

3 *The Cobden Treaty (1860) with France* sprang from a mixture of political and economic motives. The details were worked out by Richard Cobden, negotiating with Napoleon III's government in Paris. Cobden was convinced that Free Trade between the great nations would remove many of the causes of international friction. Since the British were eternally suspicious of Napoleon III's intentions, Gladstone was prepared to give Cobden a free hand, in the hope of reducing tension. The agreement was that France reduced import duties on British coal and manufactured goods, and in return Britain reduced duties on French wines and brandy, all of which fitted in well with Gladstone's tariff policy.

4 Gladstone brought in a clever new practice in the way laws dealing with financial matters were passed. Instead of introducing a number of separate bills, he combined them all into one large bill for the 1861 Budget. This brought greater speed and efficiency into the passing of financial legislation. However, his real motive was to manoeuvre the House of Lords into approving the abolition of the duty on paper; in 1860, they had voted out the bill abolishing the duty, in case it encouraged the growth of a cheap left-wing press. The Lords could hardly throw out the entire budget just to save the paper duty; so Gladstone had his way and the combined Budget has remained until the present day.

5 *The Post Office Savings Bank was opened in 1861*, and after only a year it had attracted 180,000 investors, who deposited between them almost two million pounds. This was a most important achievement, not only because it encouraged ordinary people to save, but also because it provided the government with a new supply of cash that it could draw on if necessary.

(c) Gladstone's policies had far-reaching effects

1 Free Trade provided a great stimulus to the British economy. The 1860 Cobden Treaty alone had produced a threefold increase in trade with France by 1880. In general, between 1850 and 1870, British exports increased fourfold, while the outstanding success story was provided by coal exports, which increased in value fivefold during the same twenty-year period. Of course, all this was not due solely to Gladstone's tariff policies: there were other causes, such as the improvement in communications (railways and steamships); but Gladstone certainly created the right atmosphere for the great Victorian boom to develop (see Section 15.1).

2 The working classes were probably better fed, since wages rose rather more than food prices. There was, for example, a marked increase in the consumption of commodities such as tea and sugar. On the other hand, Gladstone's economy drive meant that much-needed social reform in the fields of public health, sanitation, housing and education could not take place.

3 Gladstone's reputation among fellow politicians and with the general public was much enhanced by his achievements. It was no surprise when he became leader of the Liberals in 1868, and his popularity partly explains the Liberal victory in the general election held later that year.

8.4 why did the demand for parliamentary reform revive in the early 1860s?

After the passing of the 1832 Reform Act, most people, including Lord John Russell, who had introduced the bill, believed that this was the end of the matter. But gradually the situation changed, and several influences, both internal and external, combined to bring about a widespread feeling that further reform was necessary.

(a) there had been important population changes since 1832

The total population of Britain increased from 24 million in 1831 to 29 million in 1861; by 1865, the adult male population of England and Wales had risen to over 5 million, and yet of those, only a fraction over a million had the vote. The vast majority of the working class was still voteless. People had continued to move into the ever-expanding industrial areas, but there had been no corresponding changes in constituencies, and no new ones had been created. Clearly, some extension of the vote and some redistribution of seats was necessary.

(b) pressure from Radicals both inside and outside Parliament

The Radicals, with John Bright as their acknowledged leader, kept up constant pressure for reform. Bright was convinced that democracy, as it operated in the USA, Canada and Australia, should be tried in Britain. During the winter of 1858–9, he launched himself into a series of great speeches, which brought reform more publicity than it had enjoyed for a decade; it was time, he argued, that ordinary people were given a share in controlling their own fortunes; 'palaces, baronial castles, great halls, stately mansions, do not make a nation. The nation in every country dwells in the cottage', he told a Birmingham audience in October 1858.

(c) the trade union movement campaigned for reform

During the 1850s, associations of skilled workers, known as Model Unions, began to spread (see Section 19.3). These new craft unions were more moderate than earlier unions, and their leaders, men such as Robert Applegarth of the Sheffield carpenters, and bricklayer George Howell, demonstrated that they were responsible people, concerned to improve standards for the workers and to reform Parliament by legal means, not by revolution. They were in contact with Radical MPs, and succeeded in impressing a large section of the Liberal party, and many of the Conservatives as well, with their sense of responsibility. As early as 1861, working men in Leeds were organizing reform conferences, and in March 1864, *the Reform Union*, an alliance of middle- and working-class reformers, was set up at a meeting in the Manchester Free Trade Hall.

(d) the American Civil War (1861–5) was an important external stimulus

For most Radicals this was a simple case of freedom (the North) struggling to assert itself against tyranny and slavery (the South), and the war provided splendid publicity for the idea of equal rights and opportunities within a nation. The war had another effect: the northern blockade of southern ports cut off cotton supplies to the industrial towns of Lancashire, bringing serious unemployment and hardship during late 1861 and right through 1862. Yet by the end of 1862, as the cotton workers realized that the North stood for the abolition of slavery, they swung their support firmly behind the North, whose warships were the direct cause of their distress. This reaction impressed many politicians as a sign of working-class political maturity.

(e) Gladstone was converted to the idea of reform

Eventually, Gladstone was persuaded by the logic of the arguments put forward by Radicals and trade unionists and he accepted the need for reform. He first revealed his change of mind publicly in the Commons in 1864 when he said: 'Every man who is not incapacitated by some consideration of personal unfitness or political danger, is morally entitled to come within the pale of the constitution.' This angered his Prime Minister, Palmerston, who was still against reform and who retorted, 'I entirely deny that every sane man has a moral right to a vote.' Gladstone's approval of the Lancashire cotton workers' political maturity led him to declare that it was 'a shame and a scandal that bodies of men such as these should be excluded from the parliamentary franchise'. The death of the anti-reform Palmerston in 1865 removed the most serious obstacle to reform within the Liberal party.

(f) the visit of Giuseppe Garibaldi to London (April 1864)

This gave added publicity to the idea of liberal reform. In 1860, he had played a vital and heroic part in the unification of Italy, and was still popular with the British public as a liberal and a democrat. A group of his admirers eventually became *the Reform League* (February 1865), which had extensive Trade Union support.

(g) the Conservatives accepted that pressure would eventually bring about further reform

Disraeli, the Conservative leader in the Commons, was even prepared to introduce limited reform of Parliament himself, provided it did not go too far. His reasoning seems to have been that if further reform really was inevitable, as Bright kept telling everybody, then the Conservatives ought to jump in and take the credit for it. In fact, the Tories did bring in a very mild reform bill (March 1859), but it was thrown out; most of the Liberals voted against it, because it did nothing to extend the vote in the boroughs and would have brought very few workers into the system.

8.5 what were the stages by which reform was achieved?

(a) the Liberal Reform Bill fails

Russell and Gladstone introduced a moderate reform bill in March 1866, which proposed to give the vote in the boroughs to householders paying £7 a year rent (instead of £10) and in the counties to tenants paying £14 a year rent (instead of £50). This was expected to bring an extra 400,000 voters on to the lists. No mention was made of redistributing seats. There was lively opposition in the Commons from:

 ▸ *The Conservatives,* who thought the Bill went too far. *Lord Cranborne (later Lord Salisbury)* compared the state to a joint-stock company, arguing that 'the wildest dreamer never suggested that all the shareholders should hold a single vote without reference to the number of shares they might hold'. Even Disraeli thought the Bill would bring into Parliament 'a horde of selfish and obscure mediocrities, incapable of anything but mischief'.
 ▸ *A section of the Liberals led by Robert Lowe,* who told Parliament: 'You are about to take away the management of affairs from the upper and middle classes, and you are about to place it in the hands of people of whose politics

you know nothing.' He claimed that the working classes were ignorant of politics, would be incapable of deciding who to vote for and would be open to bribery. They were full of 'venality, ignorance, drunkenness and the facility for being intimidated.' Bright nicknamed Lowe and his supporters *the Adullamites* (after the Bible story about the discontented Israelites who left Saul and went to join David in the cave of Adullam – see 1 Samuel 22, verses 1–2).

The opposition introduced an amendment to reduce the number of new voters, and when the Commons passed the amendment, Russell (now aged 74) resigned. It was a sad end to Russell's career in politics, since he had hoped to bow out with parliamentary reform as his crowning achievement.

(b) pressure for reform mounts

The incoming Conservative government hoped to move slowly and introduce some mild reform in 1868. However, public interest was now thoroughly aroused, and *pressure built up for immediate action.* Bright embarked on another speaking tour to campaign for reform; there was a short, sharp economic crisis which developed in 1866, several companies went bankrupt and there was widespread unemployment. Bread was expensive following the poor harvest of 1865, and there was a sudden cholera epidemic that killed 8,000 people in London alone. In July, a demonstration was planned to take place in Hyde Park. When the government closed the park to the meeting, there were some disturbances, during which 1,400 yards of railings were demolished. The combination of all these circumstances convinced the Conservatives that reform could not wait. Derby and Disraeli decided to make a bid for popularity that would prolong their stay in office and, in Derby's words, 'dish the Liberals'.

(c) Disraeli's 'leap in the dark'

Both Disraeli and Derby were prepared to introduce a much more drastic bill than Gladstone's if it would bring the Tories a long period in power. Their problem was that Cranborne and his supporters in the Cabinet threatened to resign if the bill went too far; so in February 1867 a measure was introduced which was so mild that it caused an uproar in the Commons when it was read out. It was obvious that the Liberals would not vote for it, and rather than be forced to resign, Disraeli decided to risk upsetting Cranborne by introducing a more radical measure. Cranborne and two other Cabinet members resigned, but Disraeli pushed ahead with his bill. As it passed its various stages in the Commons, the Liberals proposed several amendments, all of which were accepted; this made the final bill even more extreme. This Conservative bill became law in August 1867, and is usually known as *The Second Reform Act.*

There has been some speculation about the reasons why Disraeli and Derby were prepared to support a more far-reaching bill than they had themselves proposed. Historian Robert Blake explained that there were three main theories:

- The Liberals claimed that it was Gladstone who had forced the bill on the Tories, and that Disraeli had cynically accepted it just so that they could remain in government.
- The 'Tory Democracy' theory, strongly pressed by Disraeli himself, was that the final reform bill was the result of a long-term plan to forge an alliance between the Tories and the urban working class. Far from being browbeaten into accepting it, Disraeli had cleverly manoeuvred the Liberals into going much further than they had intended.
- The left-wing theory suggests that politicians of both parties were greatly influenced by the mass working class demonstrations mounted by the Reform League, which reached a climax in the early months of 1867. However, it seems generally agreed that there was much less violence than might have been expected, less in fact than had occurred in some areas during the 1865 election. Disraeli was apparently not unduly perturbed by the damage to shrubberies, flower-beds and railings in Hyde Park.

Evidence for the 'Tory Democracy' theory is at best unconvincing. Disraeli later claimed that he had been converted to the idea of household suffrage as early as 1859, and that the Second Reform Act was his way of 'educating' his party. Blake himself points out that Disraeli's 1859 conversion was 'simply untrue' and that his 'education' claim was 'a piece of retrospective boasting'. Much more convincing is the argument that Disraeli and Derby were prepared to accept almost anything in the bill provided that the Tories got the credit for it, and in that way would be able to 'dish' Gladstone and stay in power themselves. Also doubtful is the claim that Gladstone was the driving force behind the final form of the bill. It was a group of Radical MPs who hit upon the idea of proposing the more extreme amendments to the bill in its committee stage. Gladstone was horrified when the bill passed and said it was 'a smash perhaps without example'.

8.6 what were the terms and effects of the 1867 Reform Act?

(a) terms

1 *In the boroughs* the vote was given to all householders (both owner-occupiers and tenants) who paid rates, provided they had lived in their house for at least one year. Lodgers paying £10 a year rent also received the vote.
2 *In the counties* the vote was given to all ratepayers paying £12 a year in rates, and to copyholders and leaseholders holding land valued at £5 a year.
3 Boroughs with a population of under 10,000 lost one MP. This released forty-five seats for redistribution; twenty-five of them were given to the counties, fifteen to boroughs which had not had an MP up till then, one was given to the University of London, and a third MP was given to Liverpool, Manchester, Leeds and Birmingham.

4 The franchise in Scotland was brought into line with the English pattern, and seven seats were transferred from England to Scotland.

5 In Irish boroughs, the vote was given to £4 ratepayers.

(b) effects of the 1867 Act

Apart from the obvious one of increasing the size of the electorate, the effects of the Act were something of an unknown quantity at the time. Even Derby admitted that they were 'making a great experiment and taking a leap in the dark', while the historian Thomas Carlyle said it was 'like shooting Niagara'.

1 The size of the electorate was almost doubled, from about 1.36 million to 2.46 million.

2 Most of the new voters were industrial workers living in the towns, so for the first time there was something approaching democracy in the boroughs.

However, there were some other results that showed that the leap in the dark fell a long way short of full democracy:

3 In the counties, the voting qualification was high enough to keep agricultural labourers (the majority of the rural population) and people such as miners who lived in rural pit villages without the vote. This was completely illogical discrimination, but it was designed to preserve the power of wealthy farmers and landowners. If democracy had to be conceded in the boroughs, the wealthy were determined to salvage at least something for themselves in the countryside.

4 Voting was still held in public; the lack of secrecy meant that working-class borough voters were bound to be swayed by their employers and landlords (the 1872 Ballot Act solved this problem – see Section 13.2(f)).

5 The distribution of seats still left a lot to be desired. Many small towns with only just over 10,000 inhabitants – such as Tiverton – still had two MPs, the same as Glasgow, which had over half a million. The South and East were still over-represented compared with the industrial Midlands and North; Wiltshire and Dorset between them were represented by twenty-five MPs for a population of 450,000, yet the West Riding of Yorkshire, with over two million, had only twenty-two MPs.

As time went on, other results became apparent that had not been foreseen in 1867:

6 The increased borough electorates meant that there were too many voters to be able to bribe them all; politicians began to realize that they must explain and justify their policies, and gradually the whole nature of politics changed as the election campaign in the constituencies became the accepted procedure. The Liberals were the first to appreciate this, with Gladstone leading the way in the 1868 general election.

7 The creation of the large, three-member constituencies such as Birmingham and Manchester led to another development: the rule was that each elector could only vote for two candidates; this meant, for example, that one of the three Birmingham Liberal candidates might not poll enough votes to be elected, while the other two received far more votes than was necessary. It was, in fact, the Birmingham Liberals who first realized that this wastage of votes could be avoided by having a local organization to make sure that there was an equal distribution of Liberal votes between the three candidates, so that all three were elected. The Conservatives soon followed suit, and before long, party organizations developed at both national and constituency level to whip up support at election times and to nurse the voters between elections.

In spite of his triumph, Disraeli (who became Prime Minister on Derby's retirement) still lacked a Commons majority, and hoped that the 1868 election would bring its reward. To his intense disappointment, the Liberals won, with a majority of 112.

Reasons for the Liberal victory were:

› Gladstone and Bright conducted a vigorous election campaign, speaking all over the country, whereas Disraeli merely sent a printed election address to his own constituents, and missed a splendid opportunity of winning over the new borough voters with a programme of much-needed social reform.
› Gladstone won middle- and working-class Nonconformist support by announcing that the Liberals would disestablish the Anglican Church in Ireland (the Anglican Church would no longer be the official state Church in Ireland).

QUESTIONS

1 Read the following extract from a speech about electoral reform made by Gladstone in the House of Commons in 1866, and then answer the questions that follow:

> I believe the composition of the House might be greatly improved and that the increased ... representation of the working classes would supply us more largely with the ... members we want, who would look not to the interests of classes, but to the public interest.

(a) Why was parliamentary reform such a controversial issue in 1866–7?

(b) Examine the implications of the Second Reform Act of 1867 for both governments and political parties in the period to 1880.

A document question about the passing of the 1867 Parliamentary Reform Act can be found on the accompanying website www.palgrave.com/masterseries/lowe1.

chapter **9**

Lord Palmerston and foreign affairs, 1830–65

John Henry Temple, Viscount Palmerston, was a leading figure in British politics for much of the nineteenth century. He had a remarkable career lasting from 1807 to 1865, when he died at the age of 80; for the whole of that period he was a member of the House of Commons. This might seem surprising, since English peers normally sit in the House of Lords; but in fact, though Palmerston was born in London, the peerage had been given to the family for their estates in Ireland. Irish peers were not entitled to sit in the House of Lords, and this meant that Palmerston, like Castlereagh, was eligible to become an MP in the Commons.

Palmerston began as a Tory MP for Newport on the Isle of Wight in 1807 and was made Secretary at War in 1809 (aged only 25), a position he held until 1828. He had a reputation as an efficient administrator, but was perhaps better known for his numerous love affairs. He was in sympathy with Huskisson and the 'enlightened' Tories; when Huskisson disagreed with Wellington, Palmerston also resigned and soon joined the Whigs. When the Whigs came to power in 1830, Grey appointed him Foreign Secretary. His career after that is shown in the box below.

Lord Palmerston's career, 1830–65

1830–41	Foreign Secretary in the Whig governments of Grey and Melbourne
1846–51	Foreign Secretary in Lord John Russell's Whig government
1852–5	Home Secretary in Lord Aberdeen's Whig/Peelite coalition
1855–8	Liberal Prime Minister
1859–65	Liberal Prime Minister

During his first two periods at the Foreign Office, Palmerston became immensely popular with the general public because he was prepared to stand

Illus. **9.1 Lord Palmerston**

up to foreign countries, giving the impression that the British were far superior to all other peoples. In his relations with other politicians and ambassadors he could sometimes be arrogant and abrasive; he upset Queen Victoria, who felt he should have consulted her more. In 1851, the Prime Minister, Russell, insisted that Palmerston should resign because he had acted rashly without informing either the Queen or the rest of the Cabinet. In 1852, Lord Aberdeen made Palmerston Home Secretary, a position that would give him less chance of offending foreigners. However, for much of the time he could be approachable, good-humoured and witty, and had a gift for dealing with ordinary people, with whom he remained hugely popular to the end, even though he consistently opposed the extension of the vote to the working classes.

While he was away from the Foreign Office, the Crimean War (1854–6) broke out; without Palmerston to look after foreign affairs, the government ran the war badly (see Section 10.2). Many people felt that only Palmerston had the necessary flair to bring the war to a successful conclusion, and eventually the Queen, against her will, appointed him Prime Minister. This seemed to bring new energy to the conduct of the war, which soon ended with what appeared to be advantageous terms for Britain. From 1859–65, Russell was Foreign Secretary, and though he was not a man to be ignored, Palmerston usually got his own way. With the earlier rift between them now healed, the two men made a good partnership, and successes in foreign affairs continued. After 1862, Palmerston encountered setbacks and suffered a decisive diplomatic defeat at the hands of the Prussian Minister-President, Bismarck. The long run of successes was over, and the two veterans – Russell over 70 and Palmerston nearing 80 – seemed out of step with the times.

9.1 what were the principles behind Palmerston's conduct of foreign affairs?

1 He was determined to defend British interests wherever they seemed threatened, and to uphold Britain's prestige abroad. Whether it was a question of protecting British trade with China, maintaining the British position in India (against Russian ambitions), opposing the spread of French influence in Spain, or looking after the interests of British citizens abroad (such as Don Pacifico), Palmerston was prepared to take whatever action he thought necessary.

2 Like Canning, he wanted the public to be aware of those interests, and he developed a remarkable skill in using the press to publicize the issues and enlist support from all classes in society.

3 He was in favour of the spread of liberalism (the introduction of constitutional governments like the one in Britain). He believed that following the 1832 Reform Act, the British system was ideal, and that similar systems should replace the autocratic monarchies of Europe, even if this had to be achieved by revolution. Thus he welcomed the revolutions in France (1830) and Greece (1843 and 1862). There were limits to his liberalism, however; after 1832 he was strongly against any further extension of the vote in Britain, and he remained so until his death in 1865 (see Section 8.3(e)).

4 He supported nationalism, sometimes actively, especially if British interests were being advanced, as in the Belgian revolt against Holland (1830–9) and Italian unification (1859–60).

5 He hoped to maintain world peace, and wanted Britain to be 'the champion of justice and right'. Ideally, this should be achieved by diplomatic means rather than by interfering militarily in the internal affairs of other states. He hoped to work through the 'Concert of Europe' – the great powers acting together in a concerted effort to preserve peace.

6 He wanted to preserve the balance of power, which, put at its simplest, meant making sure that no single country became strong enough to dominate the rest of Europe.

In practice, none of these principles except the first was binding: this was of paramount importance. Palmerston was a great improviser, using events and circumstances to maintain Britain's status as a great power. Although he approved of nationalism, he sent no help to the Poles or the Danes (1863 and 1864); he wanted liberalism to spread, yet he continually supported Turkey against Russia, and there could hardly have been a less liberal state than Turkey; the important consideration was that this policy protected British interests against Russia: 'We have no eternal allies and we have no perpetual enemies,' he said in Parliament. 'Our interests are eternal, and those interests it is our duty to follow.'

9.2 Palmerston as Foreign Secretary 1830–41: how successful was he?

Palmerston took over at the Foreign Office at a difficult time; he was faced almost immediately with three tricky problems: the Belgian revolt against Holland; revolutions in Spain and Portugal; and the outbreak of war between Egypt and Turkey. All three involved in some way or another, *British relations with France.*

(a) the Belgian revolt

1 While in 1815 it had seemed a good idea to unite Belgium with Holland (see Section 3.1(b)), the arrangement had not been a success. The Belgians felt that their interests were being ignored by the Dutch-dominated government. Revolution broke out in Brussels (August 1830); by October Dutch troops had been chased out and Belgium declared itself an independent state. This could not be ignored by the other powers, since it was a breach of the 1815 Vienna Settlement, which they had all promised to uphold. The situation provided a searching test for Palmerston: if he used it well, he could turn it to advantage for Britain – an independent and friendly Belgium would be good for British trade and naval interests. The new constitutional French king, Louis Philippe, who had himself just been brought to power by the revolution of June 1830, favoured the Belgians and could be expected to support them. But though both Britain and France seemed to be working for the same end – Belgian independence – the danger for Britain was that the new Belgium might turn out to be very much under French influence, and the French were still viewed as the traditional British enemy. A further complication was that the autocratic governments of Austria, Russia and Prussia wanted to suppress the Belgians in order to discourage would-be revolutionaries in their own territories.

2 *Palmerston's aims were:* to co-operate with Louis Philippe so that together they would be strong enough to warn off Austria, Russia and Prussia, thus preventing a European war and ensuring Belgian independence. At the same time he wanted to make sure that, if French troops entered Belgium in response to Belgian requests for help, they would leave smartly as soon as the Dutch were defeated. Palmerston suspected that once French troops were

entrenched in Belgium, Louis Philippe might be tempted to annex the country, and he was determined to resist any such move.

3 *Palmerston took the lead* as chairman of an international conference that met in London in November 1830. Working closely with the French representative, Talleyrand, who wanted to maintain good relations with Britain, Palmerston prevailed upon both sides to accept a ceasefire. Belgian independence was recognized in principle – even, surprisingly, by Austria, Russia and Prussia, probably because their attention was occupied by other revolutions in Poland and Italy. The Dutch king, William, also accepted the decision, though reluctantly (January 1831).

This was by no means the end of the crisis; two questions remained to be settled: to choose a king for the new state, and to fix its frontiers. A new alarm occurred for Britain when the Belgians invited Louis Philippe's second son to become their king. Palmerston, seeing this as tantamount to a union between France and Belgium, threatened war if the French accepted, and began fleet movements; Louis Philippe, who was cautious and sensitive to Britain's feelings, declined the invitation, and the throne was given to the pro-British Leopold of Saxe-Coburg.

The frontier question caused further problems: Leopold demanded that Luxemburg should be included in Belgium, and when the London conference seemed likely to support him, the Dutch king, who was also Grand Duke of Luxemburg, broke the ceasefire and sent troops to occupy Belgium (August 1831). French troops moved in and within ten days had driven the Dutch out.

Thus the situation that Palmerston had dreaded had now come about: French troops, established deep in Belgium, were reluctant to withdraw. Again, Palmerston took a firm line: 'One thing is certain,' he warned, 'the French must go out of Belgium or we have a general war, and war in a given number of days.' Again, Louis Philippe gave way, though French public opinion was outraged at this second climb-down. The dispute dragged on until in 1839 the Dutch at last recognized Belgian independence and neutrality, which all the great powers agreed to guarantee in *the Treaty of London.*

4 *Palmerston had been strikingly successful:* thanks to his efforts, a new constitutional state friendly to Britain had been created in an area vitally close to the British coast. The French had been kept out of Belgium; though relations with France were strained for a time, the two governments worked well together during the later stages of the dispute, especially after Leopold married Louis Philippe's daughter. All this had been achieved without a European war. It gained Palmerston the reputation of being a champion of nationalism, but of course his primary aim had been to do what was best for Britain. Even Talleyrand was impressed: 'Palmerston,' he wrote, 'is certainly one of the most able, if not the most able, man of business whom I have met in my career.'

(b) Portugal and Spain

1 *The problems:* by a strange coincidence, the rightful rulers of both Portugal and Spain were child queens – Maria of Portugal and Isabella of Spain. The supporters of both favoured constitutional (liberal) government, and both were opposed by uncles (Miguel in Portugal and Carlos in Spain), who favoured autocratic government and aimed to destroy the liberal constitutions.

In Portugal Maria had been kept in power by British troops sent by Canning (see Section 3.3(b)), but when Wellington withdrew them, Miguel seized the throne. Early in 1832, Maria's party rose in revolt against Miguel; they captured Oporto, and civil war developed.

Meanwhile, *in Spain,* Isabella's mother, acting as Regent for the three-year-old queen, was in the process of setting up a constitutional government, when Carlos raised an army against her. As a first step, he crossed into Portugal to help Miguel. The situation was similar to the one in Belgium: France strongly supported both constitutional parties, while Russia, Austria and Prussia were itching to interfere in order to maintain autocracy.

2 *Palmerston's aims were clear:* he intended to support the queens, working in close conjunction with the French (who were proposing joint action). As in the case of Belgium, he was determined to prevent the French from gaining more than their fair share of influence; there were important British naval and commercial interests to be safeguarded in the Mediterranean and Gibraltar, at the southern tip of Spain, was a British colony. Finally, he hoped that joint Anglo-French action would deter Russia, Austria and Prussia from intervening.

3 Palmerston was responsible for sending both direct and indirect help; a British fleet cruised menacingly off the Portuguese coast while British finance equipped a naval expedition commanded by British officers. In 1833, this force defeated Miguel and drove him out of Portugal. The following year, Palmerston masterminded a treaty between Britain, France, Spain and Portugal in which they promised joint action against the uncles. This *Quadruple Alliance* began promisingly: Miguel was prevented from returning to Portugal, and Carlos was captured and brought to Britain as a prisoner.

4 *British policy seemed to be successful* in the short term, 'a capital hit and all my own doing,' boasted Palmerston.

In Portugal success was lasting; Miguel never returned, constitutional government of a sort survived, and Portugal became a firm ally of Britain.

In Spain, however, success was only shortlived; Carlos soon escaped, made his way back to Spain and resumed the struggle for the throne. The civil war (known as the Carlist Wars) lasted until the defeat of Carlos in 1839, and by then Britain's relations with Isabella's government were somewhat strained because of a row over Spain's non-payment of debts to Britain. The Quadruple Alliance broke up in 1836 when the French withdrew, apparently annoyed at Britain's good relations with Spain and Portugal. Added to the disagreement over the Near East (see below) it meant that Anglo-French relations were anything but good. But at least French influence in the Iberian peninsula had been kept to a minimum, and the alliance lasted long enough to keep Austria, Russia and Prussia from intervening.

(c) Mehmet Ali, Turkey and the Eastern Question, 1831–41

1 In 1831, a crisis occurred that stemmed from the Greek revolt against Turkey (see Section 3.3(b)) which was to end successfully for the Greeks in 1833. Mehmet Ali, nominally the Turkish governor of Egypt (though he was practically independent), had been promised a reward for helping the Sultan Mahmud against the Greeks, but had received nothing. He demanded Syria, but when Mahmud refused, Mehmet's son, Ibrahim Pasha, moved his troops into Syria. The Turks tried to drive them out but were soundly defeated at Konieh (December 1832). Ibrahim advanced towards Constantinople, the Turkish capital, whereupon Mahmud issued a general appeal for help. Since most of the powers were occupied with Belgium, Tsar Nicholas I of Russia eagerly seized this opportunity for intervention in Turkey. A Russian fleet entered the Bosphorus, while Russian troops moved towards Constantinople, both ostensibly to defend the capital against Ibrahim (see Map 10.1 on page 138).

2 Palmerston was dismayed at the Russian presence in Turkey; he suspected them of wanting to annex the European part of Turkey including Constantinople, so that they could control the Dardanelles, the exit from the Black Sea. Russian warships would be able to sail through the Straits at will, posing a serious threat to Britain's interests in the eastern Mediterranean. The British were also worried that this would be one more step in the general collapse of the Turkish Empire that would ultimately enable the Russians to gain sufficient territory and power to threaten British control of India. It was probably an irrational fear, but to the British, it seemed only too real. Palmerston's aim, therefore, was to end the conflict between Mahmud and Mehmet as quickly as possible, and so remove the Russians' excuse for intervention.

3 *Palmerston sent a British fleet* into the eastern Mediterranean, and Britain, France and Austria, all worried about Russian expansion, threatened and cajoled the Sultan into giving Syria to Mehmet. Ibrahim withdrew his troops from Turkey so that the Russians had no excuse for staying. However, Tsar Nicholas, who was in a strong position, could not resist demanding a high price for his help. He forced Mahmud to sign *the Treaty of Unkiar Skelessi* (July 1833), by which Russia and Turkey agreed to give each other military help whenever necessary; Turkey would allow Russian warships free passage through the Dardanelles, and would close them to ships of every other country in wartime.

4 *This was a setback for Palmerston* and a diplomatic triumph for the Russians who would now be extremely powerful in the eastern Mediterranean; Turkey was reduced almost to being a protectorate of Russia, dependent for survival on Russian military support. Palmerston fumed and fretted and was determined to destroy the Treaty of Unkiar Skelessi. However, Nicholas ignored all protests, and for six years no opportunity offered itself.

5 *Palmerston's chance came in 1839* when the Sultan, who had never intended to let Mehmet keep Syria, suddenly launched an invasion. Once again, Ibrahim was called into action, and yet again the Sultan's armies were decisively defeated. The earlier situation seemed about to repeat itself as Ibrahim moved towards Constantinople. The French complicated the situation by aiding and advising Mehmet on military matters; they were hoping to build up their influence in Egypt to add to their recent capture of Algiers (1830) at the western end of the Mediterranean. The future seemed bleak for Turkey when Mahmud died (July 1839), to be succeeded by a 16-year-old boy.

6 *Palmerston this time was prepared:* he aimed to preserve Turkey as a reasonably strong state capable of standing up to Russian ambitions. Help for Turkey must be provided jointly by several European powers, not just by Russia alone. Another motive for wanting to bolster up Turkey, as Jasper Ridley (one of Palmerston's biographers) points out, was because Palmerston was afraid that 'the collapse of Turkey would lead to a scramble for the pieces, which would trigger off a major European war'. He was also determined to frustrate the French, and he knew he could count on Russian support in that. Above all though, Palmerston hoped to use the situation in order to destroy the Treaty of Unkiar Skelessi. The first step towards all this was to curb Mehmet Ali, who, according to Palmerston, was 'an ignorant barbarian, a former waiter at a coffee shop', but who impressed some Western ambassadors as courteous, witty and charming.

7 *Palmerston made most of the running:* in July 1840 he engineered an agreement in London between Britain, Russia, Austria and Prussia; France was not even consulted. The four powers offered Mehmet Ali terms: he could remain as hereditary ruler of Egypt and keep the southern half of Syria, provided he immediately made peace with Turkey. Though it was not an unreasonable offer, Mehmet rejected it, expecting French military help if the powers moved against him. A major European war seemed likely, and Franco-British relations, which had recently been harmonious over the settlement of Belgium, reached rock bottom. However, Palmerston was convinced that while the French premier, Adolphe Thiers, was in an aggressive mood, the cautious Louis Philippe would never risk taking on four other powers. He instructed the British ambassador in Paris to inform Thiers that 'if France begins a war, she will to a certainty lose her ships, colonies and commerce … and that Mehmet Ali will just be chucked into the Nile'.

8 *Allied action against Mehmet Ali now went ahead:* a British and Austrian force captured his ports of Acre and Beirut, while a British fleet bombarded Alexandria in Egypt. Louis Philippe knew that it would be madness for France to get involved, and Thiers was forced to resign. Mehmet had to accept harsher terms from the powers (this time including France). He was allowed to remain ruler of Egypt but had to return Syria to the Sultan. A further agreement known as *the Straits Convention* was signed in July 1841. By this, all the powers, including Russia, agreed that the entrance to the Black Sea should be closed to the warships of *all* nations while Turkey herself was at peace. This cancelled Russia's special advantage by the Treaty of Unkiar Skelessi; Nicholas made this concession in the hope of gaining British friendship.

9 This complex problem turned out to be probably *Palmerston's greatest triumph:* he had bolstered up Turkey so that there were no disagreements among the powers over who should take what; Russian expansion had been controlled, and, so the British thought, the threat to India reduced. In addition, French ambitions in the eastern Mediterranean had been thwarted – and all without a war. Palmerston's actions showed clearly that his major concern was to protect British interests even if it meant abandoning co-operation with constitutional France and working with the autocratic governments of Russia and Austria which he had opposed over Belgium, Spain and Portugal.

(d) China and the Opium War

1 *Early in 1839 a dispute arose between Britain and China* about the British import of opium from India into the Chinese port of Canton. British merchants had built up the opium trade into a highly profitable operation. The Chinese government claimed that opium smoking was ruining the health of the population, and banned the trade. They seized opium worth over a million pounds belonging to British merchants at Canton, and poured it into the sea. Tension increased when the British refused to hand over to the Chinese some British sailors who had killed a Chinese man in a drunken brawl. The reason given was that the Chinese used torture to extract confessions, and therefore the British refused to accept the jurisdiction of Chinese courts.

2 *Palmerston demanded compensation for the opium,* and guarantees that British merchants would be free from interference. The Chinese rejected both requests, and Palmerston despatched a naval and military expedition to Canton. His aim was partly to defend British honour and win compensation, but more important, to force the Chinese to open up their vast market of 350 million people to more British trade (until now the British had only been allowed to trade at Canton). The fighting that followed is known as *the Opium War.*

3 The British fleet bombarded and captured Canton and had no difficulty in forcing the poorly led and equipped Chinese to sign an agreement based on Palmerston's demands. *The Treaty of Nanking* (signed in August 1842 by Peel's Conservative government after the Whig defeat) allowed the British to trade at five treaty ports (Canton, Shanghai, Amoy, Foochow and Ningpo), exempted British merchants from Chinese law, granted six million pounds compensation and leased the island of Hong Kong to Britain until 1997. Other European powers were granted similar privileges.

4 *The Opium War seemed to be a success,* and a whole new and vast market seemed to be assured for British exports. However, there was to be more trouble later, as the Chinese tried to reduce their concessions. In addition Palmerston was criticized severely in the Commons on the grounds that it was morally wrong to force Britain's will on a weak and defenceless country.

The Whig government fell in August 1841, and Palmerston was away from the Foreign Office for over five years. His policies had been triumphantly successful, especially during his last two years in office. Even the Conservative Disraeli wrote about his 'brilliant performances'; and according to Jasper Ridley, 'by 1841 the Palmerston legend was already firmly established'.

9.3 Conservative interlude, 1841–6

The Conservative Prime Minister, Peel, allowed his Foreign Secretary, Lord Aberdeen, a fairly free hand. Aberdeen was much less aggressive and bombastic than Palmerston, and favoured a policy of calmness and conciliation whenever possible. He did not like the idea of Britain interfering in the internal affairs of other countries, and withdrew the troops Palmerston had sent to Portugal. He settled peacefully a potentially dangerous dispute with the USA over its frontiers with Canada in Maine and Oregon. Much of Aberdeen's time and energy was spent trying to improve relations with France, which Palmerston had left in some disarray. He found he could work amicably with the new French minister, François Guizot, with whom he reached compromise agreements on policing the Atlantic (in a joint attempt to stamp out the slave trade) and on the establishment of a French protectorate over the Pacific island of Tahiti.

More troublesome was the *Affair of the Spanish Marriages.* Louis Philippe was anxious for one of his sons to marry the young Queen Isabella of Spain. The British objected to this, suspicious that some kind of union might take place between France and Spain; this, plus the French occupation of Algiers, made the British nervous about the safety of Gibraltar. They suggested that Isabella (aged 11 in 1841) should marry a Saxe-Coburg prince (who would be friendly to Britain) or one of her own Spanish cousins (which would at least keep the French out). Early in 1846 an understanding was reached that Isabella should marry one of her cousins, and Louis Philippe's son should marry Isabella's younger sister, but only after Isabella had had children, so that there would be little chance of the two crowns becoming united. However, nothing was put in writing, and it was at this stage in the negotiations that Peel's government fell because of the Corn Law crisis, and Palmerston returned to the Foreign Office (June 1846).

9.4 Palmerston at the Foreign Ministry again, 1846–51

Palmerston was less successful at winning specific advantages for Britain during his second turn in office, and he was outmanoeuvred by Louis Philippe over the Spanish Marriages. However, incidents such as the Don Pacifico Affair and the visit of General Haynau, though empty triumphs in themselves, greatly added to Palmerston's popularity with the public.

(a) the Spanish Marriages, 1846

‣ Palmerston had been thoroughly impatient with Aberdeen's delicate handling of this problem and was determined to settle it quickly. The French, deeply distrustful of him and expecting him to press the claim of the Saxe-Coburg prince (a cousin of Prince Albert), saw a chance to get revenge on Palmerston for the Mehmet Ali affair. Following French bribery of the Spanish Queen Mother, two weddings took place: Isabella married her cousin, the elderly Duke of Cadiz, who was rumoured to be sexually impotent, while her sister Luisa married the Duke of Montpensier, Louis Philippe's younger son.

‣ *This was a diplomatic defeat for Palmerston:* if Isabella had no children and Luisa became queen, Spanish and French interests would be closely united. Even Queen Victoria for once found herself in agreement with Palmerston and wrote to Louis Philippe accusing him of breaking the previous agreement. In the end though, the marriages did Louis Philippe no good: the recent co-operation between France and Britain was brought to an abrupt end, which gave great comfort to Russia and Austria. Isabella had children (though probably not her husband's), so that Montpensier was excluded from the Spanish throne, and in 1848 Louis Philippe himself was overthrown by a revolution.

(b) the year of revolutions: 1848

1 During this momentous year (the year of the third Chartist petition), revolutions took place in many European countries, inspired by a mixture of liberalism and nationalism; for example:

‣ Louis Philippe was replaced by a republican government.
‣ The Italians of Lombardy and Venetia tried to throw off Austrian rule.
‣ The people of Hungary and Bohemia fought for more national freedom from Austria.
‣ In Vienna, Chancellor Metternich was forced to flee.

2   *Palmerston's attitude showed his policy in all its contradictions.* He had some sympathy with all the revolutionary movements, particularly the Italians: 'I cannot regret the expulsion of the Austrians from Italy,' he wrote, 'her rule was hateful to the Italians.' With his reputation as a friend of liberals and nationalists, he might have been expected to do all in his power to help the revolutionaries. *But British interests came first:* though he liked the idea of an independent united state of Italy, he wanted the tottering Austrian Habsburg empire to survive as a check to Russian expansion. He was also worried in case the new French republic sent military help to the Italians, which could give the French too much influence in northern Italy.

3   Britain therefore took no direct action, though as usual there was plenty of verbal activity from Palmerston. He tried to persuade the Austrians to grant independence to Lombardy and Venetia before the French intervened; nothing came of it, and the French dithered so long about whether to send help, that the Austrians regained control of Italy. Eventually all the revolutions in Austria, Germany and Italy were brought under control, and all Palmerston could do was protest against the atrocities committed by the Austrians against the Hungarian rebels. He supported the Turks when they refused to hand over to the Austrians the Hungarian nationalist leader, Louis Kossuth, who had escaped to Constantinople; after British warships were despatched to the Bosphorus, the Austrians and Russians took no action.

4   A general war had been avoided and the balance of power preserved; but while Palmerston's support for Kossuth was popular with the British public, there can be no disguising the fact that Britain had made very little impact on the main course of events in 1848.

(c) the Haynau incident, 1850

In September 1850, the Austrian General Haynau came to Britain on an official visit. He was one of the generals responsible for putting down the revolutions in Italy and Hungary, where he had ordered numerous hangings and the flogging of women. While he was visiting Barclay and Perkins' Brewery in Southwark, some of the workmen, realizing who he was, set upon him and chased him through the streets. He took refuge in a public house and had to be rescued by police. Victoria demanded that an apology should be sent to the Austrians; Palmerston sent an official apology, but added that Haynau had been asking for trouble in coming to Britain in view of his unpopularity, and that he regarded Haynau as 'a great moral criminal.' Palmerston showed the Queen a copy of the apology, but only after it had been sent. Victoria was furious with him, particularly as he had recently promised not to send any despatches before she had approved them. It was obvious that if Palmerston continued to act in this way, there would soon be a major showdown.

(d) the Don Pacifico Affair, 1850

1 There was a long-standing dispute between King Otto of Greece, and Britain, France and Russia, arising from the refusal of the Greeks to pay even the interest on the massive loans granted by these governments to help the newly independent Greece to establish itself in 1832. The dispute came to a head when Don Pacifico, a Portuguese-Jewish merchant and money-lender who lived in Athens, had his house burnt down by an anti-Semitic mob. Don Pacifico had been born in Gibraltar and could therefore claim to be a British citizen; when the Greek government rejected his demand for £27,000 compensation, he wrote directly to Palmerston asking for British support.

2 Palmerston threatened force, but for a long time the Greeks ignored him. Early in 1850, a British fleet was in the eastern Mediterranean (protecting Kossuth); Palmerston decided to use it to frighten the Greeks into paying compensation. For a month British warships blockaded Piraeus (the Port of Athens) and other main ports, seizing all Greek merchant ships. After a good deal of haggling, it was agreed that some compensation would be paid, though not the original sum demanded, which was far too high (Don Pacifico was in fact paid £6,550).

3 This was something of a success for Palmerston; British prestige abroad had been maintained, but his high-handedness and belligerence caused a first-rate political row. The French and Russians, who had agreed, along with Britain, to protect the new state of Greece, protested strongly that they ought to have been consulted. Queen Victoria, Prince Albert, the Conservatives and even some of his own Cabinet thought Palmerston had gone too far. When it looked as though his opponents might force him to resign, he rose magnificently to the occasion with a brilliant speech lasting four and a half hours, delivered to a crowded House of Commons. He defended his entire foreign policy since 1830, and ended: 'as the Roman in days of old held himself free from indignity when he could say *Civis Romanus sum* (I am a Roman citizen), so also a British subject, in whatever land he may be, shall feel confident that the watchful eye and the strong arm of England will protect him against injustice and wrong'. When he sat down, the House broke out into enthusiastic cheering and the speech won Palmerston a comfortable vote of confidence (June 1850). However, the blaze of popularity that followed tended to obscure the fact that Britain had gained nothing from the affair except to annoy France, Austria and Russia, who claimed that Palmerston was nothing more than a bully, especially when dealing with weaker states.

The Don Pacifico Affair was one of several incidents that brought relations between Palmerston and Victoria and Albert to breaking point, and culminated in Palmerston's resignation.

(e) the Affair of Louis Napoleon and the downfall of Palmerston, 1851

1 The breaking point between Queen and Foreign Minister came in 1851, and ironically it was concerned with affairs in France. Louis Napoleon Bonaparte, the nephew of Napoleon I, had been elected President of the French Republic in 1848 following the overthrow of Louis Philippe. On 2 December 1851, in a cleverly organized *coup d'état*, he had himself proclaimed president for the next ten years, and became virtually a dictator.

2 Palmerston approved of this, believing that a strong government would prevent France from falling under socialist control and bring economic stability to the country. Queen Victoria would have preferred to see Louis Philippe restored; both she and Russell (the Prime Minister) felt that Britain should remain strictly neutral and make no comment. However, Palmerston acted carelessly: without consulting the Queen or the Cabinet, he told the French ambassador that he congratulated Louis Napoleon on his success.

3 This was the chance the Queen had been waiting for, and she demanded that Palmerston should be sacked immediately. Russell, knowing that this time Palmerston could expect very little support for his action (the British public was still suspicious of all Bonapartes, and feared the worst a year later when Louis Napoleon had himself declared Emperor Napoleon III), asked for and received his resignation.

4 By resigning, Palmerston avoided a confrontation with Victoria and Albert, but left unsettled the question of who really controlled British foreign policy: was it the Foreign Minister, or was it the monarch, who by tradition usually had the last word in foreign affairs? Though he was furious at having to leave the Foreign Office, Palmerston agreed to go in order to avoid a public dispute with the Queen, which might have damaged the monarchy. However, he blamed Russell for not standing by him; early in 1852 he and his supporters took great delight in voting with the Conservatives to bring down Russell's government. This brought in Lord Derby's short-lived Conservative government (February–December 1852), followed by Lord Aberdeen's coalition (a government made up of people from different political parties), which got Britain involved in the Crimean War (1854–6).

9.5 the final phase: Palmerston as Prime Minister, 1855–65

Palmerston became Liberal Prime Minister in February 1855 after Aberdeen's coalition had failed to bring the Crimean war to a speedy conclusion. Except for one short period (Derby's second Conservative government, February 1858–June 1859), Palmerston remained Prime Minister until his death in October 1865. For the first year he was fully occupied with the Crimean War (see Chapter 10). Other problems included the Indian Mutiny of 1857 (see Chapter 11), a second war with China (1857–60), the question of Britain's attitude towards Italian and German unification, and a dispute with the USA that came close to involving Britain in the American Civil War (1861–5).

(a) the second war with China, 1857–60

1 The Chinese had been reluctant to keep to the terms of the 1842 Treaty of Nanking, and tried to keep out as many foreign merchants as possible; the authorities at the treaty ports regularly victimized Chinese merchants who traded with the British. To protect these friendly merchants, the British started granting British registration to Chinese vessels trading at Hong Kong, hoping that the Chinese would not dare to interfere with ships flying the British flag. In 1856, the Chinese authorities in Canton seized a small ship called the *Arrow*, which belonged to a Chinese pirate and had been robbing merchant ships off Canton. The *Arrow* had been registered as a British ship and was flying the British flag; consequently the British consul in Canton demanded the release of the crew and an apology for insulting the British flag. The Chinese released the crew but refused an apology, whereupon British warships from Hong Kong bombarded Canton, causing considerable damage.

2 Palmerston was placed in an difficult situation: since the *Arrow* was a pirate ship (and its British registration had expired) the Chinese had a good case; the British governor of Hong Kong who ordered the bombardment should have consulted Palmerston first. However, Palmerston felt obliged to support the British officials once they had taken their stand. *He had a double motive:* there was the need to uphold British prestige and to avenge the insult to the flag; but more important, he was determined to force the Chinese to accept full-scale trade with Britain, whether they wanted it or not.

3 After winning a general election (in which the Liberal majority was increased) fought on the Chinese issue (March 1857), Palmerston felt justified in sending a strong expedition to press British claims. The French supported the British and together they captured Canton (1858) and Peking (1860), after which the Chinese agreed to all demands. Several more ports, including Tientsin, were opened to trade with Western powers: foreign diplomatic representatives were to be allowed at Peking; the opium trade, instead of being banned, was to be regulated by the Chinese authorities.

4 Palmerston had triumphed again, and his popularity rose to new heights; British merchants were delighted at the prospects of a trade expansion with the Far East; even foreign powers, for once, were happy with Palmerston, since they too hoped to take advantage of the opening-up of China. Again, however, as with the Opium War and the Don Pacifico Affair, Palmerston's actions can be questioned from a moral point of view. The 1856 bombardment of Canton was a breach of international law; the war itself was another example of Palmerston bullying a much weaker country.

(b) Palmerston and Italian unification, 1859–60

1 Early in 1859, Italy was still divided into a number of separate states. Lombardy and Venetia in the north belonged to the Austrians; three small states – Parma, Modena and Tuscany – were ruled by Austrian dukes; the three largest states were independent: Piedmont (including the island of Sardinia) was ruled by King Victor Emmanuel and his Prime Minister, Count Cavour; the Papal States (including Rome) belonged to the Pope; and the Kingdom of Naples (including the island of Sicily) was ruled by Francis II.

2 Italian nationalists wanted to free the northern states from Austrian domination, and Cavour hoped to bring about a united Italy under Piedmontese leadership, with a democratic constitution similar to Britain's. In 1859, the Piedmontese, with considerable military help from Napoleon III, attacked the Austrians, defeated them twice (at Magenta and Solferino) and captured Lombardy. The French pulled out of the operation before Venetia had been captured, but Parma, Modena and Tuscany announced their intention of uniting with Piedmont. The Austrians immediately rushed more troops into Venetia with the clear intention of preventing the union.

3 *At this point, Palmerston acted:* he announced that Britain would not allow armed intervention by the Austrians; 'the people of the Duchies have as good a right to change their rulers as the people of England, France, Belgium and Sweden,' he claimed. The Austrians decided against intervention and the Duchies remained with Piedmont.

4 The next step towards Italian unification began in 1860, when the nationalist leader Giuseppe Garibaldi led an armed force by sea from Genoa (in Piedmont) and captured Sicily from the unpopular king of Naples. Again, the British were able to help: British warships protected Garibaldi's invasion force as it went ashore in Sicily. Later they were in the vicinity as Garibaldi's expedition crossed the Straits of Messina from Sicily to the mainland. Napoleon III had threatened to stop him, but dared not make a move against the British fleet. Consequently, Garibaldi captured mainland Naples, which soon united with Piedmont to form the Kingdom of Italy; all these changes were recognized as legal by the British government.

5 *As usual, Palmerston's motives were mixed:* both he and Russell, as well as British public opinion as a whole (apart from Victoria and Albert) were sympathetic towards Italian nationalism and unification. They disapproved of Austria's repressive rule in northern Italy and of the atrocious government in Naples, which Gladstone had described after a visit there in 1851 as 'the negation of God'. But as usual there was more to it than that: if there was to be a new state of Italy, Palmerston wanted to make sure it would be grateful and friendly to Britain. This would be to Britain's advantage in the Mediterranean, and a valuable counterbalance to French hostility in that

area. Friendship might also lead to a lowering of Italian tariffs against British goods, which would be of great benefit to British merchants.

Palmerston's Italian policy turned out to be his last great success in foreign affairs. He and Russell won the reputation as friends of the new Italy, whose unification had been made possible because Britain had restrained other powers from intervening. British sea-power had enabled it to make this contribution.

(c) Britain and the American Civil War, 1861–5

1 In 1861, war broke out between the North and South of the USA, partly over the question of slavery (which existed mainly in the South) and partly over whether states had the right to leave the Union (which the South was trying to do). Public opinion in Britain was divided in sympathy: middle and working classes, who were very much against slavery, tended to sympathize with the North, especially after President Lincoln promised to abolish slavery throughout the USA (1863). However, in political circles, there was much support for the South (the Confederates), on the grounds that all peoples should have the right to decide who they wished to be ruled by.

2 With sympathies so divided, Palmerston and Russell announced that Britain would remain strictly neutral. However, both North and South hoped to attract British help. Two incidents occurred, both involving ships – the *Trent* and the *Alabama* – that caused tension between Britain and the North.

3 *The Trent Incident* took place in November 1861, when two Confederate agents, Mason and Slidell, were on their way to Europe on board the *Trent*, a British ship, to try to whip up support for the South. A Northern cruiser stopped the *Trent*, and the agents were seized and taken to Boston. This was a breach of international law, and an insult to the British flag, which had to be avenged. Palmerston wrote a very strongly worded protest demanding an apology and the release of Mason and Slidell; extra troops were dispatched to Canada, and feelings ran high on both sides. Fortunately, Prince Albert persuaded Palmerston to tone down some of his more insulting phrases, and Lincoln was sensible enough to give way. The agents eventually arrived in Britain, but had no success with their mission. Prince Albert probably deserves much of the credit for keeping Britain out of the war. It was to be his last contribution to politics; he died from typhoid in December 1861 at the early age of 42.

4 *The Alabama Incident (1862)* could have been avoided if Palmerston or Russell had acted promptly. The South, attempting to build up a navy, had ordered a number of warships from British yards. The first one sailed from Liverpool in March 1862 disguised as a merchant ship, but eventually became the cruiser *Florida*, which proceeded to attack Northern merchant ships. A second ship, destined to become the *Alabama*, was being built at Birkenhead; Lincoln's government protested that this was a breach of the

1819 Foreign Enlistment Act, which forbade the building and equipping in Britain of military vessels meant for either side in a war in which Britain was neutral. While the Northern protest was reasonable, Russell delayed so long before ordering the vessel to be detained, that she slipped out of the Mersey, and for the next two years inflicted severe damage on Northern merchant shipping. The North blamed the British government and claimed compensation; Russell denied all responsibility and refused to pay compensation or to allow the matter to go to arbitration. However, he later had three further ships detained, so avoiding any more friction with the North. (Later still, after the North had won the war, Gladstone accepted arbitration – see Section 13.4(b).)

5 Meanwhile, the Northern blockade of Confederate ports was preventing exports of raw cotton from reaching the Lancashire textile industry. During 1862 *the cotton famine reached its worst,* throwing over half a million people out of work in Britain's most important export industry. The situation eased only in the spring of 1863, as alternative supplies of cotton began to arrive from Egypt.

In the spring of 1863 the 'two dreadful old men', as Queen Victoria called Palmerston and Russell, were still handling foreign affairs with some success. They had made a contribution to Italian unification, and though they had bungled the *Alabama* incident, they had at least kept Britain out of the American Civil War. But in the last two years of his government, Palmerston suffered two failures – over the Polish revolution and the affair of Schleswig-Holstein. Palmerston's inept handling of these two situations was described by Lord Derby, the Conservative leader, as a policy of 'meddle and muddle'.

(d) Palmerston and Poland, 1863

› Poland was in an unfortunate situation; it had once been an independent state, but between 1772 and 1795 it had been divided up between Russia, Austria and Prussia, who all seized large areas for themselves. Like the Italians, the Poles looked forward to the day when they could escape from foreign rule and have a united Poland; but there was little chance of this happening, since the Poles, unlike the Italians, had three lots of foreigners to expel.

› In 1863, the Poles in Russia broke out in revolution, and Russian troops were moved in to crush the rising. Bismarck (the Minister-President of Prussia) gave diplomatic support to the Russians, in case the outbreak should spread to the Polish areas of Prussia.

› Palmerston and Napoleon III protested to the Tsar about his brutal treatment of the rebels, and hinted at some action to support the Poles. However, when Napoleon III proposed a European congress, Palmerston rejected the idea because he suspected Napoleon's motives. No help of any sort arrived, and the Poles were quelled with great cruelty.

- *This was Palmerston's first obvious failure in foreign affairs*, and was a striking contrast to his role in helping the Italian nationalists. In Italy, the presence of the British fleet was enough to warn off the Austrians; the Russians were already in Poland, and only a major military effort by Britain and France could have driven them out. Britain simply did not have the military strength for such an operation. Palmerston and Russell knew from the beginning that such action was out of the question, and should not have made threats that they could not carry out. Their actions only encouraged the Poles to resist longer than was sensible and left them feeling distinctly let down. Britain had been clearly outmanoeuvred by the Tsar, and Napoleon III, who should have been treated as an ally, was mortally offended. All in all, British prestige took a severe knock.

(e) Palmerston, Bismarck and Schleswig-Holstein, 1863–4

1. In 1863, a long-standing dispute came to a head over whether the Duchies of Schleswig-Holstein should belong to Denmark or remain independent (see Map 3.1 on page 38). By *the Treaty of London (1852)* the great powers had decided that the Duchies should remain as independent units, but the new king of Denmark, Christian IX, who also happened to be Duke of Schleswig-Holstein, was under pressure from Danish public opinion to incorporate the Duchies into Denmark. A majority of the people of Holstein were German-speaking, and German nationalists were strongly opposed to any move that would take Germans into Denmark. In November 1863, Christian announced the incorporation of Schleswig, though this was a breach of the 1852 treaty. Bismarck, who had ambitions to extend Prussian control over the whole of North Germany, saw this as an opportunity to take Schleswig-Holstein for Prussia. He threatened military action unless the Danes dropped their claims; he insisted that the 1852 agreement should be kept, but naturally made no mention of his own designs on the Duchies.

2. *Palmerston decided that Britain must support Denmark.* Again, there was the usual mixture of motives: British public opinion was strongly pro-Danish; the Prince of Wales had recently married Princess Alexandra of Denmark, which led the Danes to expect British help. Palmerston was also rightly suspicious of Bismarck: 'what is at the bottom of the German design is the dream of a German Fleet and the wish to get Kiel as a German seaport'. A strong Denmark would increase British influence in Northern Europe.

3. Palmerston therefore told Parliament that, if any state attacked Denmark, 'those who made the attempt would find that it would not be Denmark alone with which they would have to contend'. This was intended to frighten Bismarck off and encourage the Danes.

4. Bismarck, who had Austrian support, guessed that Palmerston was bluffing, and that Britain would need French help, which they were unlikely to get after Palmerston's abrupt rejection of Napoleon III's proposal for a European

congress. In February 1864, a joint Prussian and Austrian force invaded the Duchies; but when the Danes appealed urgently for British help, the Cabinet decided not to risk involvement in a major war against both Prussia and Austria.

5 The Danes had no alternative but to surrender (July 1864). Bismarck dropped the pretence that the Prussian action had been taken to uphold the 1852 treaty, and the two Duchies were handed over to Prussia and Austria.

6 *Palmerston had failed again:* he had seriously underestimated the astuteness of Bismarck and the growing threat of the Prussian army; this led him to make threats that Britain could not carry out with sea-power alone. At the same time, he refused to consider joint military action with the French in case Napoleon seized the Rhineland. From the beginning he had been supporting a state that was in the wrong; if Britain had insisted on a Danish withdrawal from the Duchies, there would have been no treaty violation, and Bismarck would have had no excuse for the invasion. British encouragement of the Danes had played right into Bismarck's hands.

Palmerston – 'Old Pam' as he was affectionately known by his many admirers – died in October 1865 after catching a chill. On the whole, he had been remarkably successful. Theo Hoppen sums his career up neatly:

> Palmerston had made himself the embodiment of a very wide spectrum of opinion. He had done so by being in many respects the most modern politician of his day: by cultivating the press, appealing to public opinion on grounds of national pride, taking his policies to the people. He had done so too by sheer professional skill ... As an orator he could reach considerable, though unpredictable, heights. His progressive rhetoric abroad and support for enough reform to distance himself from complete reaction at home, allowed him to achieve a unique place in political life.

On the other hand, James Chambers, his latest biographer, points out that:

> Palmerston's reputation has not worn well. All too often it has been judged not by what he did but by the way he did it, or by the criticisms in the memoirs of contemporaries, most of whom had been thwarted by him ... Palmerston's achievements are not much more remembered in England today than they are in the islands of the Caribbean.

And yet it was only in the last two years that he seemed to be getting out of touch with important developments. He failed to see that Bismarck, not Napoleon III, was likely to be the main threat to the balance of power, and continued acting as though Britain was still the dominant power in Europe, as it had been immediately after 1815. But circumstances were changing: in less than six years after Palmerston's death, the Prussians had defeated both the

Austrians and the French; Napoleon III was a refugee in England; and Bismarck had united Germany. In all these highly important events, British influence was nil. The balance of power had shifted decisively, and not in Britain's favour.

QUESTIONS

1 Consider the view that 'Palmerston's influence on British foreign policy served British interests less effectively in the period 1846–65 than in the period 1830–41'.

2 Prince Albert wrote to the Prime Minister (Russell) about Palmerston: 'His policy has generally had the effect that England is universally detested, mistrusted and treated with insult even by the smallest powers.' Explain why, if this was the case, Palmerston remained so popular with the British people for so long.

A document question about Palmerston and the reactions to his foreign policies can be found on the accompanying website www.palgrave.com/masterseries/lowe1.

the Crimean War, 1854–6

summary of events

The Crimean War involved Britain, France, Turkey (also known as the Ottoman Empire) and Piedmont, all fighting Russia. It was caused partly by *the Eastern Question* and partly by *the ambitions of Napoleon III of France, which brought him into conflict with Tsar Nicholas I of Russia.*

A joint allied force arrived in the Crimea (September 1854) with the object of capturing Sevastopol, the great Russian naval base. The allies, badly organized and ill-equipped, made heavy weather of the campaign, though they managed to win the three major battles that were fought: *the crossing of the River Alma* (September 1854); *Balaclava* (October), which included the notorious Charge of the Light Brigade; and *Inkerman* (November). Sevastopol eventually fell (September 1855) and the new Russian Tsar, Alexander II, faced with pressing financial and social problems, was prepared to end hostilities. After long negotiations, *the Treaty of Paris* was signed in March 1856. At the time, both Britain and France were highly satisfied with the peace terms, but as it turned out, the war had not solved the Eastern Question permanently; twenty years later it was to flare up again (see Section 14.4).

Apart from its military and political importance, the Crimean War was remarkable for two other reasons. For the first time, a newspaper correspondent, William Howard Russell of *The Times,* sent back detailed reports so that the British public was better informed than ever before about what was happening on the spot. Partly because of Russell's vivid descriptions of the disgraceful conditions, *Florence Nightingale* and her team of nurses went out to try to bring some order to the chaos in the base hospitals where the wounded were looked after.

Historian Andrew Lambert put forward a new interpretation of the Crimean War in a book published in 1990 (*The Crimean War: British Grand Strategy Against Russia, 1853–56*). He points out that the term 'Crimean War' is misleading; it was not used at the time and only came to be applied in the

1890s. He argues that the campaign in the Crimea was only one part of a much wider struggle against Russia, which involved other campaigns in Asia Minor, the White Sea, the Baltic and the Pacific. Events in the Crimea attracted the most attention among contemporaries, and so historians have tended to focus on that campaign and ignore the other areas of fighting.

10.1 what caused the war?

There have been differing opinions over the years about exactly why the war broke out. Some historians believe that Nicholas I of Russia deliberately provoked a war with Turkey so that he could destroy the Ottoman Empire and seize a large slice of the Balkans for Russia. Others believe that none of the countries involved really wanted a war, and that they all drifted into it because of a series of misunderstandings. The second view, held by such historians as A. J. P. Taylor and M. S. Anderson, is the more widely accepted one today. Several issues and rivalries were at stake.

(a) the basic hostility was between Russia and Turkey over the Eastern Question

Section 3.3(b) 4) explained how the Turkish Empire, weak and badly governed, was in decline. Regarded by other states as 'the Sick Man of Europe', it was expected to fall apart in the near future. The Russians wanted to profit from this situation as much as possible; they were handicapped militarily and commercially by the fact that most of their ports were ice-bound for many months of the year, while ships sailing to and from the ice-free Black Sea ports, could, in wartime, be prevented by the Turks from passing through the Bosphorus and the Dardanelles, the two narrow straits that form the outlet from the Black Sea (see Map 10.1). If the Russians could gain influence in the Balkans as far south as Constantinople, it would enable them to control the Straits. In 1833 the Treaty of Unkiar Skelessi had given the Russians much of what they wanted, but their advantage had been cancelled out by the Straits Convention of 1841 (see Section 9.2(c)).

By 1852, the Turks had had no success in reorganizing or strengthening their Empire, and experienced observers were convinced that it would shortly collapse. The British ambassador at Constantinople, Stratford Canning, an admirer of the Turks, resigned in 1852, believing that 'the Turkish Empire is evidently hastening to its dissolution'. There was also the question of religion: the Russians, who were Greek Orthodox Christians, saw themselves as the protectors of the Christian inhabitants of Turkey (in the Balkans and Armenia) against the cruelties of the Muslim Turks.

(b) the Russians seem to have been torn between two possibilities

> ‣ To divide the outlying provinces of Turkey up between themselves (taking parts of the Balkans) and Britain (taking Egypt and Crete). Nicholas had

map **10.1 The Eastern Question and the Crimean War**

suggested this during a visit to Britain in 1844. However, the drawback was that other powers, namely Austria and France, might also want a share.

▸ To try and preserve the Turkish Empire in its weak state in the hope that they, the Russians, would be able to exercise close control over the government at Constantinople; this would reduce the influence of other states to a minimum.

Russian indecision explains why there has been disagreement about their real intentions; A. J. P. Taylor believed that, by 1852, the Russians had decided on the second policy. Either way, there was bound to be friction between Russia and Turkey.

(c) Napoleon III of France begins the crisis that leads on to war

Having recently become Emperor, Napoleon needed a success in foreign affairs and was eager to win the support of French Roman Catholics. In the mid-eighteenth century, the Sultan had granted French Roman Catholic monks the right to look after *the Holy Places* in Palestine. These included the Church of the Nativity and the Grotto of the Holy Manger in Bethlehem, and two churches in Jerusalem, all of which were held sacred by Christians. The republican government that came to power in France in 1793 was hostile to Catholics and withdrew its support from the monks. Gradually, Greek Orthodox monks had taken over control of the Holy Places, and it was this situation that gave Napoleon his chance to interfere. He demanded that the Sultan should grant the privilege of guarding the Holy Places solely to the French monks. After the French ambassador had sailed through the Dardanelles in a 90-gun warship on his way back to Constantinople, the Sultan gave way to the French demands (1852).

(d) Tsar Nicholas fears growing French influence in Turkey

Nicholas was now afraid that the French might soon rival Russian influence in Turkey. He sent Prince Menschikoff to Constantinople to demand that the rights of the Greek Orthodox monks should be maintained, and in addition, that the Tsar should be recognized as the protector of all Christians living in the Turkish Empire. If this were allowed, it would give the Russians a permanent excuse to interfere in Turkish affairs. The Sultan restored the privileges to the Orthodox monks, but rejected Menschikoff's further demands (May 1853), despite the Russians threatening to invade the Turkish provinces of Moldavia and Wallachia.

(e) the British distrust Russia's intentions

The British government suspected, probably wrongly, that the Russians were plotting the destruction of the Turkish Empire, and they hated the idea that Russian warships might be able to come and go through the Dardanelles as they pleased. It was widely believed that Russian influence in Afghanistan was the first step in an attempt to oust the British from control of India. After Russian troops had helped the Austrians to suppress the 1848 Hungarian revolution, British public opinion became violently anti-Russian. However, Lord Aberdeen's coalition government was divided about what line to take:

› Palmerston (who was Home Secretary) and Russell wanted to stand up to the Russians; Russell was convinced that 'the question must be decided by war, and if we do not stop the Russians on the Danube we shall have to stop them on the Indus' (a river in northern India close to the frontier with Afghanistan). Andrew Lambert suggests that Palmerston thought Russia (along with the USA) was likely to become a serious rival to Britain in the league table of the world's most powerful nations, and he saw the situation as a chance to defeat Russia and weaken it so much that its challenge to British interests would be delayed for many years.

› Aberdeen was more cautious: he disliked the idea of supporting the Turks, who often persecuted Christians, against the Christian Russians. He believed the problems could be solved by negotiations; his attitude probably gave Nicholas the impression that Britain would not support Turkey if he were to step up Russian pressure. However, Aberdeen, influenced by Palmerston and Russell, and by British public opinion and the press, agreed to send a naval force to Besika Bay just outside the Dardanelles (June 1853). It was soon joined by a French force.

(f) events escalate towards war

1 Nicholas was not impressed by this British and French action, and thought it was all bluff. Having threatened Turkey, he now felt the threats must be carried out. Confident of support from Austria and Prussia, he sent troops to occupy Moldavia and Wallachia (roughly modern Romania) in July 1853, though they made no further moves towards Constantinople. Palmerston blamed Aberdeen for the Russian occupations, believing that if the British and French fleets had sailed into the Black Sea as he had proposed, instead of remaining outside the Dardanelles, the Russians would not have dared to violate Turkish territory.

2 Palmerston wanted the British fleet to move into the Black Sea and arrest Russian warships, which could be held hostage until Russian forces withdrew from Moldavia and Wallachia. Aberdeen rejected this idea, and the British Cabinet was so divided that no decisive action was taken either to warn the Russians off or to promise support to the Turks.

3 The Austrians, also suspicious of Russian intentions around the Danube, organized a conference in Vienna to find a solution. Attended by Prussians, French and British, the conference produced proposals known as *the Vienna Note*. It was suggested that the Sultan should make a few concessions to the Tsar, and should consult both the Russians and the French about his policy towards the Christians. Nicholas, now realizing that help from Austria and Prussia was unlikely, accepted the proposals, but the Turks rejected them, thinking that Nicholas was weakening.

4 Nicholas met Francis Joseph, the Austrian Emperor, and Frederick William IV of Prussia, in a final attempt to win support, but the most they could agree was to remain neutral if war broke out. However, the British and French, who knew of the meetings but not what had been decided, thought that the three monarchs had hatched a new plot to divide the Turkish Empire up between them. Consequently, on 8 October 1853, the British government ordered the fleet to Constantinople, where it was joined by French warships.

5 The Sultan, feeling certain of British and French support, had already declared war on Russia on 4 October, though Stratford Canning (now Lord Stratford de Redcliffe and back as British ambassador to Turkey) persuaded the Turks to take no immediate action.

6 When the British and French fleets approached Constantinople, the Turks could restrain themselves no longer; on 23 October, their troops crossed the Danube and attacked the Russians in Wallachia. The Russians replied by attacking and sinking part of the Turkish fleet near Sinope on the Black Sea (30 November). Though this was a justifiable action since war had been declared, British public opinion regarded it as a 'massacre', and pressure intensified on the government to declare war on Russia.

7 The British government still dithered about what to do next, and it was Napoleon who took the lead by sending the French fleet into the Black Sea. This forced Aberdeen to order the British fleet to follow (January 1854). But still there was no declaration of war: the allies were there to protect Turkish shipping.

8 Britain and France made one last effort to avoid all-out war: in February, they sent Nicholas an ultimatum demanding the withdrawal of Russian troops from Moldavia and Wallachia. When this was ignored, the two Western allies declared war on Russia (March).

M. S. Anderson sums up the causes clearly: the war 'was thus the outcome of a series of misjudgements, misunderstandings and blunders, of stupidity, pride and obstinacy rather than of ill will'. A. J. P. Taylor makes the point that all the participants got themselves into situations from which they could not retreat without their prestige being seriously damaged, and that the war was caused by fear and suspicion of each other rather than by conscious aggression. The British government must take its share of the responsibility for not taking a tougher attitude towards the Russians much earlier, which might have dissuaded Nicholas from sending his troops into Turkey; once committed to the occupation of Moldavia and Wallachia, the Russians could hardly withdraw without seeming to climb down. But the Cabinet was divided: Aberdeen did his best to maintain peace; Palmerston was more aggressive and wanted to weaken the Russians so that they would be unable to cause any trouble for years to come; while Clarendon, the Foreign Secretary, seemed unable to make up his mind. Governments are usually blamed for involving countries in war, but on this occasion, the pressure of public opinion, expressed through influential newspapers such as *The Times*, played an important role in pushing the British government into action. Theo Hoppen points out that the Sultan's government was just as much influenced by public opinion as was the British government: 'By the autumn of 1853, the Porte (as the Ottoman government was known) was dragging the Western powers in its wake and was doing so with no little skill and diplomatic dexterity.'

10.2 events in the war

(a) the Russians withdraw

The British military expedition commanded by the 66-year-old Lord Raglan, a veteran of the Peninsular War, arrived at Gallipoli and Scutari together with the French, in May 1854. Their objective was to protect Constantinople and to help the Turks drive the Russians from the occupied provinces. As the allied forces moved towards Varna, the Russians unexpectedly withdrew from Moldavia and Wallachia (August). This was not simply through fear of the approaching allied forces, but also because:

▸ They were finding it difficult to maintain their position against Turkish attacks.
▸ The Austrians, afraid that their interests would be threatened by Russian control of the Danube, threatened to declare war on the Russians unless they withdrew.

The Russian withdrawal took the wind out of the allies' sails, since their objective had been achieved without a shot being fired. As Taylor put it: 'they were thus faced with the problem – how to check an aggressive power when it is not being aggressive?' The governments decided that, having progressed so far, a blow of some sort should be struck at the Russians. It was decided that the expedition should sail across the Black Sea from Varna to the Crimean peninsula to capture the naval base of Sevastopol. This, it was hoped, would destroy Russian power in the Black Sea, and make life easier for Turkish shipping.

(b) British and French successes

The 60,000-strong allied force (30,000 French, 26,000 British and 4,000 Turks) landed at Eupatoria to the north of Sevastopol, and in spite of numerous problems, it had some successes:

1 Faced by a Russian army of about 40,000, *the allies managed to force their way across the River Alma* (20 September) and advanced towards Sevastopol. Instead of attacking the city immediately, they marched round it and set up a base at Balaclava, to the south, which was thought to be a good harbour. This would enable supplies to be brought in so that the allies could lay siege to Sevastopol.

2 *The Battle of Balaclava* (25 October) was fought when the Russians launched a surprise attack in an attempt to push the invaders into the sea. The British held off the attack, and the troops distinguished themselves with great bravery, particularly the cavalry. The 'thin red line' of the Heavy Brigade delayed the Russian advance until reinforcements arrived; but more famous was 'the Charge of the Light Brigade', led by Lord Cardigan. This was a courageous but mistaken attack on some Russian heavy artillery which

Illus. **10.1 British troops in the Crimea during the siege of Sevastapol**

achieved nothing and was extremely costly – 113 men were killed and 134 wounded out of 673.

3 A second Russian attack under cover of fog was driven off at *Inkerman* (5 November). Again, the British and French troops acquitted themselves impressively; though 775 of their men were killed, they inflicted four times that number of deaths on the Russians, and took many prisoners.

However, it was almost a year before the allied objective was achieved and Sevastopol fell (September 1855). In the meantime, the troops had to endure the most appalling conditions during the severe winter of 1854–5.

(c) weaknesses in the British military system

By the end of 1854, it was clear that *many mistakes had been made, and that there were serious shortcomings in the British military system*, some of which were revealed by William Howard Russell, *The Times* war correspondent:

‣ There were disagreements between the British and French commanders, the most serious of which was over what to do immediately after the crossing of the Alma. Raglan wanted to advance and make a swift attack on the north side of Sevastopol, but his French counterpart, St Arnaud, refused on the grounds that they lacked sufficient troops for a frontal attack. While the armies were marching round to the south of the city, the Russian engineer Totleben seized his chance to strengthen its fortifications. Whereas an immediate attack would have had an excellent chance of success, the delay probably added months to the campaign. Balaclava was a bad choice for a base – its harbour was too small and it was served by primitive roads. Raglan did nothing to improve them, and so they became almost impassable in the winter.

- The officer class was less efficient than it might have been because of the practice of selling commissions; wealth rather than ability was what counted. A prime example of incompetence was the Charge of the Light Brigade; although the cavalry performed brilliantly, they charged up the wrong valley, thanks to a badly worded order from Raglan and a less than intelligent response from Lords Cardigan and Lucan, who were scarcely on speaking terms. Military organization matched the poor leadership. There had been hardly any modernization or improvement in the army since the Battle of Waterloo, forty years earlier. The troops were poorly equipped, poorly trained and badly paid. In its desire to save money, the government refused Raglan's request for a special corps to handle food and other supplies and transport; thus the army was constantly short of food, clothing and ammunition. In the winter blizzards of 1854–5, the troops were still wearing the summer uniforms they had arrived in; they were completely unprepared for a winter campaign.

- Medical arrangements were grim: the wounded and sick had to endure a nightmare journey across the Black Sea to the base hospitals at Scutari. The hospitals were badly organized and had no properly trained nursing staff. There was a chronic shortage of beds, dressings, bandages, soap, food and medicine. Many patients had to be left lying on the bare floor, and sanitation was non-existent. More people died from dysentery and cholera than from wounds sustained in battle.

(d) Palmerston takes over

Public opinion became increasingly critical of the government for its incompetent handling of the war. In February 1855, Aberdeen resigned and Palmerston became Prime Minister for the first time. The public expected great things from the new leader, and the situation began to improve as soon as he took office. However, this was not all Palmerston's doing. Florence Nightingale (known as 'the Lady with the Lamp') and her team of trained nurses had already begun to reorganize the Scutari hospitals, reducing the death-rate and improving morale. Reinforcements and adequate supplies had started to arrive, and a decent road had been built from the harbour at Balaclava to the trenches around Sevastopol. *Palmerston's contribution was to:*

- send out a 'sanitary commission', which greatly improved conditions both at Scutari and in the Crimea;
- set up a special transport department, which largely solved the problem of supply;
- sack some of the more inefficient administrators in the Crimea – what he called 'that knot of Incapables who have been the direct cause of the disability and deaths of thousands of our brave men'.

(e) the fall of Sevastopol and the end of the war

Gradually, as the allies brought in reinforcements, solved the supply problems, and even constructed a light railway from Balaclava harbour to the trenches, the siege tightened around Sevastopol. Even so, several assaults during the summer of 1855 failed, and it was not until September that Sevastopol was captured. Some sections of the British public, including Queen Victoria, wanted the allies to follow up their victory by forcing the Russians out of the Crimea altogether. However, both sides had had enough: the allies were now occupying Sevastopol, but the Russians had installed heavy artillery on the northern outskirts of the city, and this meant that the allies never felt very secure, and any further advance was out of the question. Nicholas I had died from pleurisy after catching a chill while reviewing his troops (March), and the new Tsar, Alexander II, was anxious for peace so that he could concentrate on Russia's many internal problems. In January 1856, the Austrians threatened to declare war on Russia unless he agreed to peace negotiations. Andrew Lambert believes that what finally convinced Alexander it was time to start talking was a British threat to attack Kronstadt, the Russian Baltic naval base situated on an island just off St Petersburg (the Russian capital). In August 1855, a British fleet had destroyed the Russian dockyard at Sweaborg (near the modern city of Helsinki) on the Baltic Sea. Very little was made of this at the time, because all attention was concentrated on the fate of Sevastopol. The British were planning to follow up this success by a similar but much larger attack using a huge fleet known as the 'Great Armament'. It was to consist of some 350 gunboats, mortar vessels and rocket-firing boats and a force of Royal Marines, which were to bombard and capture Kronstadt. This was timed for April 1856, and if successful, it would leave St Petersburg itself open to a direct British attack. Totleben was already at work fortifying Kronstadt, but it seems likely that Alexander decided to negotiate rather than risk the loss of his vital Baltic naval base.

In the end, Britain and its allies were successful because once the supply problems were solved, their equipment was better than that of the Russians, and their troops were more professional and more adept at coping with the situation. Russian supply lines were poorly organized and most of their generals were as incompetent as the allied commanders.

10.3 the Treaty of Paris (1856) and the results of the war

(a) the Paris Peace Conference

Peace talks opened in Paris in February 1856, much to the delight of Napoleon III, whose prestige reached a high point. *The terms of the treaty (signed in March) were:*

- Moldavia and Wallachia were to have self-government for internal affairs, though they still had to acknowledge Turkish suzerainty (the right of general supervision). The powers agreed to guarantee this new semi-independence, and Russia had to give up its claim to protect the provinces.
- Russia had to hand over the southern part of Bessarabia to Moldavia, which meant that the Russian frontier no longer reached up to the River Danube. In addition, the Danube was to be a free waterway for all nations.
- The Straits Convention of 1841 (see Section 9.2(c)) was repeated: the Black Sea was neutralized – no warships were allowed on it but it was open to merchant shipping of all nations. The treaty added that the Russians must not build any military or naval strongholds along the Black Sea coast.
- Russia had to abandon its claim to protect the Christians in Turkey, and the independence of the Turkish Empire was guaranteed. In return, the Sultan promised to treat his Christians fairly, and to modernize and strengthen his state.

(b) how far were Britain's war aims achieved?

The general idea had been to check Russian expansion in the Balkans, to keep the Russian navy out of the Mediterranean, and to bolster up the Turkish Empire to act as a buffer against Russia. To some extent all three aims were achieved:

1 Russian influence in the Balkans was checked when Moldavia and Wallachia were given semi-independence. When the provinces united to form the new state of Romania (1858), it acted as a real barrier against any further Russian attempt to annex parts of the Balkans.
2 Russia was not allowed to have a fleet on the Black Sea, and so could not threaten British sea-power in the Mediterranean. However, this clause of the treaty was difficult to enforce without keeping a Franco-British fleet permanently cruising around the Black Sea to make sure the Russians behaved themselves. In 1870, during the Franco-Prussian War, the Russians announced that they no longer recognized the ban and that they would build a Black Sea Fleet and fortify the coastline. The neutralization of the Black Sea therefore lasted only just over fourteen years.
3 The Turkish Empire had been protected and saved from collapse, but in fact the Sultan kept neither of his promises, and Turkey remained as weak as before.

Ever since the war there has been debate about whether the results justified the cost in money and lives – Britain alone lost over 22,000 combatants. Cobden and Bright thought it was a waste of time, since the threat from Russia was a 'phantom'. More recently, historians have taken a different view: Asa Briggs, writing in 1959 in *The Age of Improvement*, argued that the war 'dealt a very real blow to Russian influence in Europe as a whole. In the aftermath of the 1848 revolutions, Russian power had reached its peak; it was never to be so strong again until the twentieth century'. Andrew Lambert (1990) pointed out an unexpected *disadvantage* for Britain: *'this check to Russian influence in central Europe left a power vacuum; this enabled Bismarck to create the united Germany which was to prove a much greater threat to Britain than anything ever presented by Russia'*. For the time being, however, British seapower was at its peak: no other state could begin to rival the Royal Navy in sheer size, technical skill and experience. At Sweaborg it had demonstrated that it was powerful enough to destroy any naval arsenal anywhere in the world. As it turned out, the war had not solved the Eastern Question permanently, but when the next Balkans crisis arose in 1875–9 (see Section 14.4), Alexander did not push things as far as another war with Britain.

(c) other results of the war

1 Florence Nightingale was determined to improve the health, living conditions and food of British soldiers. It was through her efforts, and with the support of the Queen and Prince Albert, that a Royal Commission on the Health of the Army was appointed in 1857 under the chairmanship of Sidney Herbert. As a result, sanitation, diet and leisure facilities in barracks and military hospitals were improved, and the Army Medical School was founded.

2 The government made some attempt to improve the military efficiency of the army. A staff college was set up at Camberley to raise training standards for officers. The system of supply was modernized and up-to-date breech-loading rifles were introduced. The price of commissions was reduced by a third. But it was not until Edward Cardwell became Secretary for War in 1868 that a really thorough reform took place, including the abolition of the sale of commissions.

3 Partly because of Florence Nightingale's work, nursing began to be taken more seriously in Britain. Using the £50,000 presented to her by the grateful public, Miss Nightingale set up a training school for nurses at St Thomas's Hospital in London (1861). The idea soon spread over the country, bringing a marked improvement in standards, as well as improvements in medicines and hospitals. On the other hand, some of her critics focus on the limitations of her reforms and try to play down their importance. However, Susan-Mary Grant feels that this is unfair, and that the effects of Florence Nightingale's work were more far-reaching than has been appreciated; she points out, for example, that

> many of the improvements made in medical care during the American Civil War (1861–65) clearly derived from the work done by Florence Nightingale, both in the Crimea and after. Several leading figures of the time including … the Surgeon-General of the US during the Civil War,

acknowledged this, in their own attempts at reform, and in their emphasis on hygiene and hospital administration.

See Section 12.6(b) for more on Florence Nightingale.

4 Britain's poor performance in the early stages of the war probably encouraged Bismarck to risk ignoring Palmerston's warning and go ahead with his invasion of Denmark in 1864 (see Section 9.5(e)). Bismarck's success in this venture, together with the check on Russian power, prepared the way for the unification of Germany.

QUESTIONS

1 How far would you agree that the Crimean War of 1854–6 was caused by miscalculations and misunderstandings rather than by deliberate design and provocation?

2 'Britain's intervention in the Crimean War resulted in a reduction in, rather than an enhancement of, its position as an international power'. How valid is this judgement in respect of the period 1856 to 1870? (Use information from Chapters 9, 10 and 13.4.)

3 How important was the role played by the press and public opinion both before and during the Crimean War?

A document question about the outbreak of the Crimean War can be found on the accompanying website www.palgrave.com/masterseries/lowe1.

chapter **11**

Britain, India and the Mutiny of 1857

summary of events

The British had been in India since the early seventeenth century, when *the East India Company* had established trading settlements (known as factories) at Surat (1612) and Madras (1640), and later at Bombay (1661) and Calcutta (1690). In the early days, the Company was there purely for trade and not to take political control of India. In the early eighteenth century, the central administration of India began to break down; and the Mogul emperor found it difficult to maintain his authority against ambitious local princes. In this situation, the Company trading posts were forced to defend themselves, both against hostile princes and rival French trading companies. Both sides trained and equipped Indian soldiers, known as *sepoys,* to help them defend their settlements.

By 1764, largely thanks to the work of Robert Clive, who successfully supported friendly princes against hostile ones, the French threat had been curbed, and Company control was established in Bengal and Bihar, and in the areas around Madras and Bombay. The job of running these areas was fast becoming too much for the East India Company, so *the 1784 India Act* gave the British government overall authority; this was to be exercised through the Governor-General, based in Calcutta, who would decide the political policy to be followed in the British parts of India, while the Company continued to control trade. During the Franco-British wars (1793–1815) the Company got itself into financial difficulties, and the British government gradually took over most of its functions.

Successive Governors-General after 1800 were anxious to extend the area of British control. By 1857, partly through a series of bloody wars and partly by devious political manoeuvring, the vast majority of India and Burma was either directly controlled by the British government or had accepted British protection.

However, the British became careless and failed to read certain danger signals. British complacency suffered a painful jolt when, in May 1857, the

149

Bengal sepoys suddenly mutinied and murdered all the Europeans they could lay hands on. There were at least five times more Indian troops than Europeans, and for a time it seemed as though the British might lose control of the whole of India. Fortunately for them, however, only the Bengal sepoys mutinied; those in Madras, Bombay and the Punjab remained loyal. Even so, there was a bitter struggle, and terrible atrocities were committed on both sides; it took the British until the end of September to regain control, and it was another full year before all resistance ended. Relations between the British and Indians were never quite the same again.

11.1 how was British power in India extended between 1800 and 1857?

After the 1784 India Act, there was a long line of Governors-General appointed by the British government. The office of Governor-General carried with it enormous personal power and prestige, and every one of them made a contribution to the extension of British power in India. It was not always a case of sheer aggression by the British; sometimes native princes were persuaded to sign alliances with them; sometimes neighbouring tribes raided British territory and had to be subdued, giving the British an excuse to annex new areas. As well as initiating military campaigns, some of the Governors-General introduced reforms to improve administrative efficiency and social conditions.

(a) Lord Wellesley (1798–1805)

He began by attacking the ruler of Mysore, Tipu Sahib, who was supporting the French and had sworn to drive the British from India. Tipu was defeated and killed (1799) and Mysore came under British control, soon to be followed by the Carnatic. Wellesley's attitude towards the remaining independent Indian princes (who were known by various titles such as nawab, rajah, maharajah, nizam (in Hyderabad) and peshwa (in Maratha areas), which meant 'ruler', or 'prince' or 'governor') was to persuade them to sign *subsidiary alliances* with the British: the native ruler could run the internal affairs of his state while British troops would 'protect' him from attack. In return for protection, the ruler had to pay towards the expenses of the troops who would be based in his territory, accept a British resident (an adviser representing the British government) and promise not to sign treaties with other princes. The Nizam of Hyderabad was the first to accept British 'protection', followed by the Nawab of Oudh and by three Maratha chiefs. In seven years, Wellesley had transformed the British position in India. Less impressive, however, were his superior attitude towards the Indians, especially Hindus (Indians were not allowed in top administrative posts and could not attend social events organized by whites), and his excessive vanity, which, so reliable reports had it, caused him to wear his medals and other decorations even in bed.

(b) Lord Minto (1806–13)

Minto did not find life as quiet as might have been expected following Wellesley's exploits: some sepoys had mutinied near Madras, and the Maratha chiefs resented their treatment by the British. The Sikhs of the Punjab, led by Ranjit Singh from his capital at Lahore, had already captured Kashmir from the Afghans and now had designs on neighbouring British territory across the Sutlej river. Minto, however, was soon able to restore internal order, and persuaded Ranjit Singh to sign an agreement at Amritsar promising not to cross the Sutlej river (1809).

(c) Lord Hastings (1813–23)

Like Minto, Hastings had to face possible attacks from tribes outside British territory. Most troublesome were the Gurkhas of Nepal, to the north of Bengal. It took a difficult 18-month campaign (1814–16) in the Nepal mountains to persuade the Gurkhas to abandon their claim to British territory. Most of Nepal

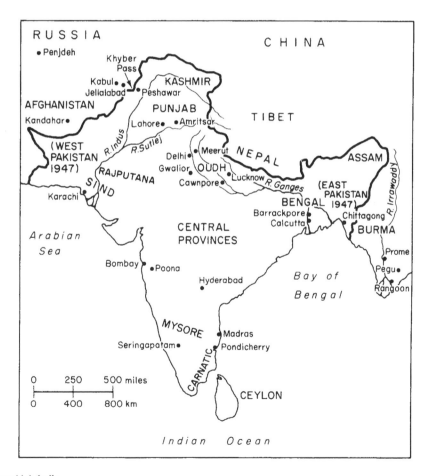

map **11.1 India**

was left as an independent state and the Gurkhas have remained friendly to Britain ever since. Meanwhile the Pindaris, robber bands of Maratha tribesmen, were causing trouble in central India. When Hastings sent troops against them, several of the Maratha chiefs, including the Rajah of Nagpur, rose against the British. In the large-scale campaign that followed, the British deployed over 100,000 troops against more than twice that number, and the Marathas were finally defeated at the Battle of Kirkee (1817). Feeling that subsidiary treaties with such rulers were a waste of time, Hastings decided to annex their territories; the Deccan became part of the province of Bombay, and the Rajah of Nagpur lost some of his territory. Hastings must take the credit for stabilizing the northern frontiers of British India, and after his annexations, the only significant parts of India not under British control (either directly or indirectly) were the Punjab and Sind in the north-west. He even found time for internal improvements, such as the introduction of irrigation schemes and the building of new roads and schools.

(d) Lord Amherst (1823–8)

He was hoping for a peaceful time, but, like his predecessors, he found himself harassed by raids; this time they were on the eastern frontier of Bengal, where the aggressive king of Ava on the Irrawaddy river occupied British territory near Chittagong (1824). Reluctantly, Amherst dispatched an 11,000-strong expedition by sea, which sailed up the Irrawaddy, capturing Rangoon and Prome. As the British approached Ava itself, the king promised to abandon his claims and to hand over to the British the coast of Burma, from Chittagong down to the Irrawaddy delta. However, the cost had been heavy: the British troops had inadequate supplies and were hampered by monsoons and floods. Over half the force perished, most of them from tropical diseases.

(e) Lord William Bentinck (1828–35)

Thanks to the energy of his predecessors, Bentinck was able to enjoy a period of peace in which he put the country's finances on the road to recovery after the enormous expense of the military campaigns, and distinguished himself as a social reformer. It was during his time in India that *two conflicting British attitudes towards the Indians became apparent*:

> ‣ An increasing readiness to accept much of the Indians' own laws and customs and to respect the Indians themselves. *The India Act (1833)* stated that 'the interests of the Native subjects are to be consulted in preference to those of Europeans, whenever the two come into competition; and that therefore laws ought to be adapted rather to the feelings and habits of the natives than to those of Europeans'. It added that 'no native of India ... should be disabled from holding any place, office or employment by reason of his religion, place of birth, descent or colour'. Bentinck's own motto was 'British greatness is founded on Indian happiness'.

▸ The belief that Western culture and methods must be introduced before India could become fully developed.

In fact India was so backward that *the drive towards Westernization became dominant*:

1 Bentinck decided that English should be the language of instruction in all state-aided schools; the government would provide money to set up more schools and colleges of higher education. Thus began the process of imposing on educated Indians a European culture that was probably not appropriate for them, though it can also be argued that the use of English as a common language helped to unite India.

2 He began to stamp out two ancient but barbaric customs:

  ▸ *suttee* – the practice of burning Hindu widows on the funeral pyres along with their dead husbands; and
  ▸ *thuggee* – sacrificial murders by members of a secret society called thugs.

3 He deposed the unpopular Rajah of Coorg for cruelty to his subjects, and the Maharajah of Mysore for incompetent government.

4 Bentinck was influenced by *a new motive – fear of Russian ambitions* in the north-west, through Afghanistan. This led him to renew the alliance with Ranjit Singh of the Punjab, signed originally during Minto's time, while the rulers of Sind were persuaded to sign an agreement allowing merchants to trade along the Indus river, on condition that no weapons or armaments were carried.

(f) Lord Auckland (1835–42)

He was the least successful of the Governors-General before the Mutiny; in fact, his stay in India ended in disaster – British defeat in *the First Afghan War (1839–42)*. Auckland decided that Britain must gain control of Afghanistan in order to keep the Russians out. In 1839 he launched an invasion of Afghanistan with the intention of removing Dost Mahomed, the Amir based at Kabul, and replacing him with Shah Suja, who had previously been driven out by the Afghans themselves.

Auckland's actions are difficult to defend: he had earlier assured Dost Mahomed that he had no intention of interfering in Afghan affairs; Dost was anxious to remain on good terms with him and much preferred the British to the Russians. Shah Suja was extremely unpopular and would never be accepted back by the Afghans. And finally, the British army, lacking sufficient transport and supplies, invaded Afghanistan through Sind, thereby breaking Bentinck's agreement with the rulers of Sind.

The army captured Kabul and set up Shah Suja, but the outraged Afghans rose in revolt and besieged the British forces in Kabul and Kandahar. It was decided to retreat into India, but in January 1842, 4,500 British troops were caught in a narrow pass between Kabul and Jellalabad and were completely annihilated; only one survivor struggled through to Jellalabad.

(g) Lord Ellenborough (1842–4)

He arrived in India soon after the massacre. He sent a large relief expedition which forced its way through the Khyber Pass, recaptured Kabul (September 1842) and rescued the British prisoners still being held. However, the country was too rebellious to hold down for long, so the British withdrew to India. British prestige had been restored to some extent, but they had failed to achieve their original objective: Dost Mahomed was back in power in Kabul, Shah had been murdered, and the Afghans had to be left severely alone.

Carried away by the success of his expedition, Ellenborough sent troops into Sind, defeated the rulers and annexed the territory. This was a totally unjustified and unprovoked attack, of which the British government strongly disapproved. Ignoring their protests, Ellenborough next launched an invasion of the state of Gwalior, which was soon defeated and taken under British 'protection'. Peel's government felt this was going too far, and Ellenborough was dismissed; he was replaced by his brother-in-law.

(h) Lord Hardinge (1844–8)

Hardinge had no sooner arrived in India than he had to deal with a Sikh invasion from the Punjab across the Sutlej into British territory. So long as the capable and popular Ranjit Singh had been alive, the Sikhs had been friendly, but since his death in 1839 the Sikh army had dominated the country. Deeply suspicious of the British because of the activities of Auckland and Ellenborough, the Sikhs were convinced that the Punjab was next on the list for annexation, and decided to strike first. They were savage fighters, but after a series of bloody and costly engagements, the British captured Lahore, the Sikh capital (February 1846). The young Maharajah Duleep Singh was placed on the throne, with Sir Henry Lawrence as resident; though the Punjab was not annexed, it seemed firmly under British control. As Hardinge left India in January 1848, he pronounced that 'it will not be necessary to fire a gun in India for several years to come'. He was wrong.

(i) Lord Dalhousie (1848–56)

Dalhousie, who had been a successful President of the Board of Trade in Peel's government until 1846, was still only 36 when he arrived in India. His period in power was packed with incident: he was responsible for extending British power still further (though not always by design) and for introducing important reforms.

1 Three months after his arrival, the Sikhs of the Punjab rose in revolt again, and another costly campaign was needed to restore order. This time, Dalhousie decide to annex the Punjab, and Duleep Singh was deposed and

sent to Britain. This enabled much needed and, on the whole, popular reforms to be introduced, with such success that the Sikhs remained loyal even during the Mutiny.

2 More of Burma came under British control after the Burmese had broken the agreement signed with Amherst (1826) by harassing British traders on the Irrawaddy river. In 1852, the Burmese attacked some British ships; Dalhousie felt strong action was needed to discourage similar anti-British moves in India. A carefully organized expedition was sent, avoiding Amherst's mistakes; with only 377 casualties, Rangoon and Pegu were captured, bringing the Burmese coast as far south as Tenasserim under British control.

3 Within India, Dalhousie was responsible for bringing under British rule a number of states which until this point had been governed by native rulers. This was achieved by using what was called *'the doctrine of lapse'*: Hindu tradition allowed a childless man to adopt an heir, and this applied to native rulers as well. However, Dalhousie decided that in certain cases of political succession, this should not be allowed to happen – if a native ruler died without an heir, his family's claim to the throne lapsed, and the state reverted to the British. By this method. Dalhousie succeeded in annexing seven states, of which the most important was Nagpur, with a population of four million (1853). He also annexed the large northern state of Oudh after removing the nawab, who had been notoriously incompetent and cruel for many years.

4 There were important advances in administration, communications and education. Dalhousie created a central legislative council and set up a Public Works Department to carry out his ideas. Two thousand miles of road were built, including the Grand Trunk Road from Calcutta to Peshawar; 18,000 miles of irrigation canal were completed, the showpiece being the spectacular Ganges Canal, opened by Dalhousie himself in 1854. He began the construction of railways to link Bombay, Calcutta and Madras, and introduced the Indian telegraph service. A total of 753 post offices were built, and a uniform postal rate adopted. An engineering college which eventually became a university was founded at Roorkee; hundreds of village schools were started, and the education of women was encouraged.

All this was a tremendous achievement, but Dalhousie knew that he had offended many people; at the end of his stay in India he warned the British government to remain alert: 'No prudent man would ever venture to predict a long continuance of peace in India.' Palmerston's government took little notice, and only just over a year had passed when the Mutiny broke out.

11.2 what were the causes of the Mutiny?

In general, the reforms of Bentinck, and especially Dalhousie, though well-intentioned and beneficial in many ways, were too quick and far-reaching for the conservative and traditionally minded Indians. They disliked the drive towards Westernization and the attempt to impose an alien culture on them. Dalhousie left behind a number of individuals and groups nursing grievances, and a sense of injustice, for political, economic and religious reasons.

(a) Indian rulers resented Dalhousie's recent annexations

Dalhousie's annexations using the 'doctrine of lapse', and in particular the annexation of Oudh in 1856, alarmed other Indian rulers, who began to feel that it was the beginning of a British plan to expel them all. They regarded the British behaviour as dishonourable, since in some cases it broke existing treaties. The dispossessed rulers and their supporters were left smarting and eager for revenge. Dalhousie realized how risky the annexation of Oudh would be, but decided it was essential for the welfare of the population. In fact, many ordinary people were as outraged as the nawab himself. One loyal sepoy, writing about his experiences, was certain that 'this seizing of Oudh filled the minds of the sepoys with distrust, and led them to plot against the Government'. Unfortunately for the British, many of the sepoys in the Bengal army came from Oudh.

(b) there were economic grievances in both town and countryside

- The British flooded India with all kinds of cheap, mass-produced goods, which were gradually putting Indian urban craftsmen out of business; one Indian complained that 'the introduction of English articles into India has thrown the weavers, spinners, cotton-dressers, the carpenters, the blacksmiths and the shoemakers, etc., out of employ, so that every description of native artisan has been reduced to beggary'.
- In the countryside, the British tried to make the land more efficient by introducing European practices such as individual ownership of land and fixed money rents. But this caused enormous problems because both peasants and landlords, unaccustomed to making regular cash payments, got into debt and had to sell their land. According to Bernard Porter, 'the pattern of rural life was breaking up in many areas; families were forced to abandon lands they had tilled for generations; the old familiar feudal masters were replaced by new ones, sometimes unsympathetic with rural ways; and the loss of the old *elites* was regretted, apparently, by their faithful peasantry'.
  This was particularly true in Oudh.

(c) there were religious and social grievances among civilians and sepoys

1 The Brahmins (Hindu priests) objected to the abolition of suttee, though to Europeans it seemed a sensible and humane reform. To add insult to injury, in 1856 Dalhousie permitted Hindu widows to re-marry, a further breach of Hindu custom.
2 Much of the resentment arose because of *the caste system:* Hindu society is divided into four castes or classes, which make up the social scale. At the top

are the priests, and below them the rulers and soldiers; third in the social scale are traders and farmers, and fourth artisans (craftsmen). People outside these groups were known as 'untouchables' who were regarded as the dregs of society. Members of different castes did not mix socially. Thus innovations such as the railways, on which all classes were expected to travel together, and the British practice of everybody being equal before the law, seemed to be an insult to the higher castes, and were taken to be an attack on the caste system. Similarly, the spread of education, and in particular the education of women, seemed to threaten the structure of Hindu society. The increasing number of Christian missionaries arriving in India confirmed suspicions that the British were trying to destroy not only Hinduism but Islam and Buddhism as well, and convert all Indians to Christianity.

3 In the Bengal army there were discipline problems caused by the caste system. Since 1830, many high-class Hindus had been allowed to join the army as ordinary private soldiers, but they thought themselves superior to some of their officers and were unwilling to take orders from somebody of a lower caste. When the government tried to improve matters by forbidding the wearing of caste marks, this further offended Hindu principles. A rumour went round that two regiments of sepoys were about to be sent on operations to Burma, and this would involve sailing across the Bay of Bengal to get there. The Hindus were afraid that they would lose caste by crossing water; in fact, there had already been a mutiny for the same reason at Barrackpore (1824), which had quickly been put down by a few well-directed cannon blasts. The British had failed to learn the obvious lesson.

(d) the Indians began to realize that the British were not invincible

British defeats in Afghanistan (1839–42), together with their recent less than impressive performance in the early part of the Crimean War (1854–6) showed the Indians that the British were not invincible. Also encouraging to the Indians was the obvious unpreparedness of the British: the arsenals at Delhi and Allahabad were inadequately guarded; some of the European troops had been withdrawn for service in the Crimea, Persia and Burma; there were scarcely 40,000 European troops in the whole of India, against 230,000 sepoys. In fact, in Bengal itself, the most troubled area, there were only 5,000 Europeans and nearly 55,000 sepoys. The British were far too careless and casual: they seemed unaware of the growing resentment and unconcerned at the prophecy that British rule in India would end on 23 June 1857 (exactly a hundred years after Robert Clive's famous victory over the Nawab of Bengal's army at the Battle of Plassey).

(e) the affair of the greased cartridges was the immediate cause of the Mutiny

Cartridges for the recently introduced Enfield rifle had to be ripped open with the teeth before loading. A rumour spread that the grease for these cartridges was made from cow and pig fat. This caused consternation among both Hindus and Muslims, since the cow is sacred to Hindus and the pig considered unclean by Muslims. It united the two religious groups against the British; they were convinced that it was part of the attempt, deliberately planned by the British Parliament in London, to eliminate the Indian religions. At Meerut, not far from Delhi, the sepoys refused to touch the new cartridges, and eighty-five of them were arrested. With an amazing lack of sensitivity and foresight, the military authorities ordered that they should be stripped of their uniforms, manacled in chains and made to serve long prison sentences. The following day (10 May 1857) the Meerut sepoys mutinied and killed their European officers.

Clearly, all these factors contributed towards the Mutiny. While the affair of the greased cartridges was the immediate cause of the outbreak, it was the culmination of many years of growing resentment and unrest. Joseph Coohill, in an article in *History Today* to mark the 150th anniversary of the Mutiny, points out that 'sepoys had seen their pay (and therefore their status) decline in recent years, and many felt that the new officers serving in the Company army since the 1840s did not have the same respect and sympathy for sepoys that had been a hallmark of the previous generation of officers'. Arguably, the annexation of Oudh under the 'doctrine of lapse' was the final outrage, and was seen as a great cultural insult.

11.3 events in the Mutiny

(a) fighting confined to the north

After the initial shock at Meerut, the Mutiny spread rapidly through Bengal, Oudh and the North-West Provinces. The Punjab, only recently annexed and garrisoned by regiments of Bengal sepoys, might have been a danger area; however, the Sikhs remained loyal and helped the governor, John Lawrence, to disarm the Bengal regiments. After this, the Punjab remained quiet, and there was very little trouble elsewhere, as the Madras and Bombay armies mainly remained loyal. Hyderabad was a critical area with its large Muslim population, but the Nizam turned out to be completely reliable, and so did the King of Nepal, who allowed his Gurkha soldiers to fight for the British. *The main centres of fighting were Delhi, Cawnpore and Lucknow.*

(b) Delhi captured by the rebels

Delhi was crucially important, since it was regarded by the northern Indians as the seat of power. The Meerut rebels quickly marched on Delhi and were joined by the Indian regiments based there. They soon captured the city and slaughtered all the British they could lay their hands on. A small British force of 3,500 set out to relieve Delhi and fought its way to the Long Ridge just outside the city, but it could make no headway against 40,000 sepoys with 114 cannons mounted on the walls. In fact, the British did well to survive until August, when a relief force from the Punjab, under John Nicholson, arrived on the Ridge. In September, the British blasted their way into Delhi with heavy artillery, and after a further week's fierce fighting, the city was recaptured, though Nicholson himself was killed. The British shot three local princes as a reprisal for the slaughter of European women and children.

(c) siege and massacres at Cawnpore

At Cawnpore, early in June 1857, a tiny British force of less than 700 was besieged by 3,000 rebel sepoys commanded by the Nana Sahib, who had had his large pension stopped by Dalhousie (he was the adopted son of the Peshwa of Poona, who had been deposed by the British). After three weeks, the British were almost out of food and water, and since there were about 400 women and children with them, they decided to surrender and accept the Nana Sahib's offer of safe-conduct by boat down the river to Allahabad. As the crowded barges were about to push off, the Nana Sahib turned his cannons on them and sprayed them with grapeshot at point blank range. Only four soldiers and about a hundred women and children survived, and they were held as prisoners. When a British relief force under Sir Henry Havelock was within two days of Cawnpore, the Nana Sahib had the prisoners hacked to death and their bodies thrown down a well. The city was taken on 17 July; the British were horrified at the remains of the massacre and took terrible revenge, although the Nana Sahib insisted that he had never given orders for the killings. Captured sepoys were made to lick up the blood from the floors of the prison huts before being hanged. Some mutineers were tied to cannon barrels and blasted into pulp. The one British regret was that the Nana Sahib escaped and was never captured. In the words of British historian A. N. Wilson: 'The ruthlessness of British reprisals, the preparedness to "punish" Indians of any age or sex, regardless of whether they had any part in the rebellion, is a perpetual moral stain on the Raj.'

(d) Lucknow besieged

At Lucknow, the capital of Oudh, there were only about a thousand European troops holding out against 60,000 rebels, though only 10,000 of these were trained sepoys. Havelock advanced from Cawnpore, but while he managed to force his way into Lucknow (25 September), there were still not enough British troops to drive the rebels off. The siege lasted another two months before Lucknow was relieved by Sir Colin Campbell's force advancing from Calcutta (17 November). However, with over 100,000 rebels still in the area, there remained much for Campbell still to do. Lucknow was not finally secured until March 1858. At this point, the Governor-General, Lord Canning, in an attempt to end resistance in Oudh, announced that all the landowners should forfeit their land. But in an area where hatred of the British was stronger than anywhere else in India, this had the opposite effect to what Canning had intended; it was not until the end of 1858 that the Oudh rebels were finally subdued.

(e) why did the Mutiny fail to achieve its objectives?

There is some disagreement about what the objectives of the rebels were. Some Indian historians see the Mutiny as a national revolution with the ultimate aim of expelling the British from India.; it is sometimes called *the First National War of Independence.* However, this was probably not the case; most recent Indian historians reject the idea, though they believe that memories of the events of 1857 certainly encouraged and inspired supporters of the later Freedom Movement. If the Mutiny had been a war of independence, the whole country would have risen, with the civilian population joining in as well. If this had happened, the Indians would have stood a good chance of success. However, the risings were mainly confined to the North-West of the country. British historians therefore see the Mutiny as a spontaneous response to frustrations and grievances. *The rebels' aims* were to restore their old rulers, customs and institutions; beyond that they were vague – there were certainly no plans for a united India. Therefore *the Mutiny failed because:*

1 It was not a national rising: fewer than half the sepoys actually mutinied, and many important native rulers, for example in Hyderabad, Gwalior and Rajputana, stayed loyal. Some of them even supplied troops to help the British.
2 Except in Oudh, the civilian population was hardly involved, either because they had not been affected by British reforms, or because they had done well out of them. Many upper-class Indians had benefited from an English education and were playing an important part in the commercial life of the big cities. Very few Muslims took any part in the Mutiny.
3 No outstanding Indian leader emerged; there was no co-ordination between the different centres of unrest, and no overall plan of campaign. Fatal mistakes were made: for example, at the beginning of the Mutiny, while the British in Delhi were still stunned with shock, the sepoys waited around for three weeks wondering what to do next.
4 Though individual British commanders made mistakes, the British had much better leadership than the Indians. The Governor-General, Lord Canning, was able to direct operations from Calcutta, while Havelock, Nicholson and Campbell distinguished themselves, though their forces were heavily outnumbered.

11.4 what were the results of the Mutiny?

(a) the Government of India Act (1858)

The British government was forced to admit that something must have gone sadly wrong with the way India had been ruled, to cause such a serious outbreak of violence. In order to secure greater efficiency, Lord Derby's Conservative government (1858–9) introduced *the Government of India Act (1858)*. This abolished the East India Company, which for years had been slack and easy-going, and transferred all its powers, properties and territories to the Crown. A Secretary of State and a Council of fifteen members were created to look after the running of India, and the Governor-General had his title changed to *Viceroy* (meaning 'in place of the king'), to show that he represented the British monarch in India. The Indians were promised that there would be no further interference with their religions (a promise that was largely kept) and that they would have equality of opportunity with the British (which was not kept – see item (d) below).

(b) Lord Canning tries a policy of moderation and reason

Lord Canning was Governor-General from 1856 to 1858, and then Viceroy until 1862. He followed a policy of moderation towards the Indians. He refused to carry out wholesale executions, to the annoyance of much of the British public, which nicknamed him 'Clemency Canning'. Though reforms were continued, the pace was much slower, and care was taken not to offend religious and local customs. The doctrine of lapse was abandoned, and the British went to great pains not to offend native rulers and princes in other ways. This policy was successful, and on the whole, the Indian upper classes, realizing that it was impossible to get the British out by force, remained loyal well into the twentieth century.

(c) no more annexations

The British abandoned their policy of expansion temporarily. In 1863, when civil war broke out in Afghanistan, they wisely refused to become involved, preferring to concentrate on improving the vast territories they already held.

(d) legacy of ill-feeling between the British and Indians

As a result of the atrocities committed by both sides during the Mutiny, there remained considerable ill-feeling between the British and Indians, in spite of Canning's efforts. The British felt they could never trust the Indians again: they sent more troops to India, disarmed the civilian population, and increased the proportion of Europeans in the army. The artillery was kept wholly in British hands. Equality of opportunity was never a reality; for example, while entrance to the Indian Civil Service was thrown open to anyone who could pass an examination, this had to be taken in London, which involved the problem of a candidate losing caste if he crossed the sea. Consequently, only one Indian took the examination before 1871; Indians were relegated to low-level positions. In fact, a much deeper gulf than ever before had come between the British and Indians, and this gulf was never bridged.

1 One of the mottos of Lord Bentinck (Governor-General of India, 1828–35) was 'British greatness is founded on Indian happiness'. To what extent did the British look after the happiness of the Indians during the period 1800 to 1862?

2 To what extent was the Indian Mutiny of 1857 a response to recent events rather than the result of long-term grievances?

A document question about the Indian Mutiny can be found on the accompanying website www.palgrave.com/masterseries/lowe1.

chapter 12

Standards of living and social reform:
factories, mines, public health, education, leisure, religion

summary of events

For the great mass of people in early-nineteenth-century Britain, the quality of life, the conditions in which they lived and worked and spent what little leisure time they had, probably left a lot to be desired. There has been a great debate among historians about how bad conditions really were. Arnold Toynbee, and J. L. Hammond and Barbara Hammond, writing before 1920, gave the left-wing view – that, as a result of the Industrial Revolution, conditions for the workers became worse than ever before – they were shamefully exploited and lived in squalid slums. Sir John Clapham thought this was a gross exaggeration and produced statistics which, he claimed, proved that the living standards of the poor were improving, as real wages (what people could actually buy with their earnings) increased. More recently, it was shown that life for the workers *before* the Industrial Revolution was not the bed of roses that some writers had seemed to suggest: long working hours, slum conditions and families living on the verge of starvation were just as common in rural Britain as they were in the new industrial towns. In 1963, E. P. Thompson, in *The Making of the English Working Class,* questioned some of Clapham's findings and came to the conclusion that in reality the picture was a mixed one: 'If no serious scholar is now willing to argue that everything was getting worse, no serious scholar will argue that everything was getting better.' In fact, there can be no doubt that in the new industrial towns many workers lived and worked in horrifying conditions, which persisted into the second half of the century.

In an age of *laissez-faire,* the instinct of governments was to ignore these problems; the development of the industrial society that had given rise to this situation had taken place without any intervention from the state, and so it was assumed that individuals would find their own solutions, also without interference from the state. *Self-help* was a virtue much prized by the Victorians. And yet there was always a paradox within the concept of *laissez-faire*: even its most fanatical supporters had to acknowledge that, on occasion, governments did have to 'intervene'. For example, they had to raise taxes and ensure that law and order were enforced. As the industrial society became more complex, many people, perhaps even a majority, were not free to do what they wanted – they were exploited by those who *were* free. Therefore government action was needed to protect them, and to ensure that the best conditions existed for the efficient working of the industrial system.

Gradually governments began to pay attention to the mass of evidence being placed before them by political economists about the unacceptable conditions endured by so many workers. After considerable debate, some sections of the ruling classes accepted that only through state intervention could the worst excesses be eliminated. However, even after this principle was accepted, there was determined opposition from some industrialists (though not all) and from other people who resented state interference; effective reform was therefore slow to come, and when it did, it often took the form of a compromise between the opposing factions.

12.1 the great standard of living debate

There can be no doubt that *in the long term* the Industrial Revolution led to a huge improvement in living standards. The question that has occupied economic and social historians is, in the words of E. J. Evans: 'were the benefits of industrial advance enjoyed to any important degree by first-generation industrial workers, or were they sacrificed through long hours, vile conditions and uncertain wages to profit hungry employers while, unintentionally, smoothing the path for future generations?' Marxists and other left-wing historians take a pessimistic view and emphasize the negative results of industrialization, while the optimists, looking at the evidence provided by statistics of wages, prices and consumption of food and other commodities, as well as trends in national physique, argue that life was getting better for the majority of workers.

Reaching a definite conclusion about the national picture is difficult, partly because the statistical evidence available is heavily weighted towards London and the southern counties, whereas in fact most of the industrialization took place in the North of England and the Midlands, and partly because the accuracy of much of the evidence is suspect in any case. In addition, it is important to remember that there are other indicators of living standards that cannot be measured statistically, such as environmental conditions, rent costs, regularity of wage payments, spending power, use of leisure-time, and so on. There are further complications too: other factors besides the Industrial Revolution helped to determine living standards – for example, the effects of the long wars with France, which lasted until 1815, and the fact that the Corn Laws kept the price of bread higher than it need have been, until 1846. Higher wages were no consolation for workers if the cost of food had risen even more. And finally, historians on both sides of the debate have tended to exaggerate or manipulate the evidence in order to support their political standpoint, as did contemporary commentators.

(a) the pessimists

Arnold Toynbee, writing in 1884, claimed that the Industrial Revolution was 'a period as disastrous and as terrible as any through which a nation ever passed ... because side by side with a great increase of wealth was seen an enormous increase of pauperism; and production on a vast scale, the result of free competition, led to a rapid alienation of the classes and to the degradation of a large body of producers'. Much of the evidence certainly supports this view. It seems to be generally accepted now that the first half of the nineteenth century saw a widening gap between rich and poor in terms of income and wealth. Not that all workers suffered hardship: the wages of skilled workers and craftsmen increased substantially; it was the unskilled and general labourers who were the victims – particularly agricultural labourers in southern and eastern England, and the women and children who worked long hours in factories and mines. Local or regional studies show that, at best, their wages remained static. Also badly hit were people such as handloom weavers and woolcombers who had been put out of their jobs by the new machinery. There was also a problem of over-production, and consequent depression and unemployment. This was especially marked in the Lancashire textile industry: in 1842 in Bolton, for example, 60 per cent of all factory workers were unemployed and many more were on short time.

Trends in national physique suggest a marked fall in living standards: statistics show that the average height of 20-year-olds who had been born between 1826 and 1850 fell by about two inches over that period; and mortality rates rose sharply between 1830 and 1850. In the words of Simon Szreter: 'the 1830s and 1840s may well have been the worst-ever decades for life expectancy since the Black Death in the history of those parishes which were now experiencing industrialisation'. Ample evidence of the squalid living environment, and the dangerous and exhausting working conditions, is provided by contemporary accounts and reports, although some were no doubt exaggerated (see the following sections). The large number of disturbances and the repeated Chartist agitation up to 1848 would seem to support the view that all was not well with the workers. Some estimates show that even after 1848 real wages continued to decline until the early 1860s.

(b) the optimists

The optimists set great store by statistics of wages. They emphasize that between 1781 and 1851 the real wages of skilled workers doubled; life expectancy more-or-less doubled (from 25 to 40), and the average height of the population increased steadily. Some surveys show greatly increased consumerism in the industrial areas. In Lancashire and Yorkshire, workers were able to buy more cheap new clothes and a wider range of cheap foods.

The problem is that much of the optimists' evidence is flawed. The wage statistics are averages, which may conceal the fact that labourers' wage levels performed differently from those of skilled workers. Most local studies greatly weaken the optimists' case, at least with regard to the first half of the nineteenth century.

Professor E. J. Evans provides a well-balanced conclusion to the great debate:

> The first generation of workers in industrial Britain, though their real wages probably improved slightly, laboured in worse conditions than their parents had known. The first fruits of industrial progress were harvested by the middle and upper classes, followed at respectful distance by the skilled workers whose jobs were not threatened by machines, particularly those with skills industrialism created. Even in the 1850s and 1860s only slender improvements were made by ordinary workers, who would have to wait until the price depression of the late nineteenth century to enjoy measurable and unequivocal benefits from economic development. By that time, of course, those who lived through the squalor of early-nineteenth-century Manchester were all dead.

12.2 why was factory and mine reform necessary?

(a) there were no restrictions or controls

The factory system, particularly mills and workshops driven by steam, were still comparatively new, and there were no restrictions, controls or checks of any kind. Factory owners were completely free to treat workers as they wished; fierce competition led employers to pay as little as possible for as much work as possible, and to take insufficient safety precautions. With nobody to protect the interests of the workers, it was inevitable that exploitation and abuse of all kinds would creep in.

(b) many factories were dangerous and unhealthy

Since the new machines were expensive, it was tempting for industrialists to keep them running as long as possible. This was highlighted by a parliamentary committee of enquiry in 1832, which produced evidence to show that thousands of small children, especially girls, were working from six in the morning until half-past eight in the evening, with only half an hour allowed for eating. Towards the end of the shift, they began to drop off to sleep, and depending on the foreman, had to be shaken or beaten with a strap to keep them alert. It was common practice to use small children to clean spinning machines and looms while they were still in motion. An adult spinner might use two or three children working as 'piecers'; their job was to crawl under machinery no more than a foot above the floor to tie broken ends. Serious accidents were common; *the 1840 Royal Commission Report* mentioned a case at Stockport where a girl had been caught by her clothing and carried round an upright shaft: 'her thighs were broken, her ankle dislocated, and she will be a cripple for life'. The Report went on to say that, in the Stockport area, 'fatal accidents generally happen from want of boxing-off; there has been a considerable number of accidents and loss of life within the last three months'.

The long-term effect of bending and standing for long periods was that children developed weak, curved legs and arched backs. Sometimes there were respiratory diseases caused by working for so long in the hot and humid atmosphere of a textile mill, where the air was contaminated by clouds of microscopic cotton dust.

There was danger in other industries too: the Staffordshire potteries were notoriously bad for health. Charles Shaw, a Tunstall potter who started work as a mould-runner at the age of 6, recalled that 'my wage was a shilling a week. For this I had to work from between five and six o'clock in the morning and work on till six, seven or eight o'clock at night'. His job was to light the fire in the stove-room and spend the rest of the day rushing backwards and forwards bringing the raw clay to the potter and then running to take the plaster moulds (each bearing a soft plate) into the hot stove-room where the plates were hardened off. Though some employers, like the Wedgwoods, were enlightened and caring, one Stoke-on-Trent doctor wrote: 'the potters as a class are as a rule stunted in growth and frequently deformed in the chest; they become prematurely old and are certainly short lived'. Workers in match factories often developed a disease known as 'phossy-jaw' which caused the teeth to fall out and the jaw bone to rot away.

(c) mines had special problems

As the demand for coal grew, mines became deeper, bringing additional problems of ventilation and the risk of flooding. There were frequent gas explosions since use of the Davey safety lamp was not compulsory. Small children, both boys and girls, sometimes as young as 4 years of age, were employed underground hauling trucks full of coal along passages that were too low for adults; or opening and closing ventilation doors (see Illustration 12.1), or filling coal trucks. *The Royal Commission Report which came out in 1842* revealed some appalling details: a 12-year-old girl had to carry a hundredweight of coal on her back, stooping and creeping through water in a low tunnel; children had to climb dangerous ladders up the pit shaft with huge baskets of coal strapped to their backs. The Report also expressed outrage that naked and semi-naked men, women, girls and boys all worked together, which had a demoralizing effect on the women and girls.

Illus. **12.1 Children working down a mine (sketch from the 1842 Royal Commission Report)**

(d) growing pressure for government intervention

Pressure grew steadily for some government action. The main leader in the early days was a Leeds Tory Evangelical, Richard Oastler, who, after the failure of his career as a merchant, became estate manager at Fixby Hall, near Huddersfield. He was shocked by the horrifying conditions he saw in the Bradford woollen mills. A deeply religious man (he was brought up as a Wesleyan Methodist), he was moved to write a letter to the Leeds *Mercury* (1830) in which he claimed that child workers were being treated worse than slaves: 'Thousands of our fellow creatures, both male and female, the miserable inhabitants of a Yorkshire town, are this very moment existing in a state of slavery, more horrid than are the victims of that hellish system "colonial slavery"'. Soon famous throughout the North, Oastler found himself the leader of a huge movement, publishing pamphlets, and organizing public meetings and demonstrations demanding factory reform. Typical of the campaign were the mass marches that converged on York on Easter Monday, 1832; the result was a petition containing over 130,000 signatures which was handed to Parliament.

Inside Parliament, the movement found an effective voice in another Tory Evangelical, Michael Sadler, who demanded a maximum working day of 10 hours for children. He was supported by other Tories and by humanitarians, who between them made up a formidable alliance. Their case was simple; as Derek Fraser puts it: 'it was a moral or religious crusade against an intolerable evil ... it simply could not be right for these things to persist'. However, there was bitter opposition to *the Ten-Hour Movement* from most factory and mine owners.

12.3 what arguments were used by the opponents of reform?

- Benthamite Radicals (see Section 2.1(c)), many of whom were factory owners, believed that any state intervention was bad because it tampered with the natural working of the economic system. *Laissez-faire* was all important. However, as we saw earlier (Section 2.1(c)), the Radicals were themselves divided: believing as they did in securing 'the greatest happiness of the greatest number of people', some were torn between humanitarian impulses and the pull of market forces. John Hobhouse, for example, was a Radical supporter of factory reform: he acknowledged that workers, especially women and children, needed protection, not simply on humanitarian grounds, but because exhausted and unhealthy workers would be inefficient workers.

- A shorter working day for children would mean restricting adult working hours, since, so it was argued, factories would have to close when the children left. This would cause a reduction in output, which would in turn mean lower profits and thus lower wages. One economist, Nassau Senior, Professor of Political Economy at Oxford, argued that the entire profit of industry was made in the last hour of work each day; therefore, to reduce the working day even by one hour, would destroy profits. This theory had already been shown to be nonsense by Robert Owen, a progressive manufacturer who had reduced working hours in his textile mills in New Lanark, and had continued to make a comfortable profit; but many still clung to the argument.

- Better working conditions would push production costs up, making British goods more expensive on foreign markets. British exports would decline, causing unemployment. On this reckoning, it seemed that the British working classes had only a miserable choice available to them – to endure exhausting working hours and appalling conditions, or to suffer total poverty in unemployment.

- It was pointed out that wage-earners were free agents who could leave and take a job elsewhere if they were not satisfied. However, Richard Oastler retorted that this was simply not true: in fact they were only 'free to starve or to obey the will of their masters'.

- Some argued that children working long hours in industry was acceptable because it had gone on for centuries in agriculture without any protest. It was even suggested that child labour was to be encouraged, since it gave them something to do and kept them out of mischief; too much leisure for the poor could be dangerous.

12.4 what improvements were made, and why did it take so long for the Acts to become effective?

Before 1833, there were no fewer than six attempts via Acts of Parliament to improve conditions in textile mills, but every one was a failure. The business interests, the supporters of the free market and many of the Benthamite Radicals did their best to tone down the terms of the original bills to make them less effective. The most important of the bills are detailed below.

(a) the Health and Morals of Apprentices Act (1802)

This was the work of the elder Sir Robert Peel, who was influenced by the reports of a group of Lancashire doctors concerned at the exploitation of children in industry. The Act was designed to help workhouse children who were being used as apprentices in textile mills:

1 Apprentices were not to work more than 12 hours a day, and must not work after 9 p.m.
2 They should be given two suits of clothes a year and sleep no more than two to a bed, with separate sleeping quarters for boys and girls. This was to regulate those manufacturers who had their workhouse children sleeping at the mill.

The weaknesses of this Act were that it did not apply to 'free' children, and no inspectors were appointed to make sure that it was enforced; instead, it was left to local magistrates, who might be relatives or friends of the mill-owner. Even Peel himself acknowledged that it was hardly ever enforced.

(b) the Factory Act of 1819

Again, this was the work of the elder Peel, who was influenced by his discussions with Robert Owen (see Section 19.2). Owen's cotton mills at New Lanark, with their model villages and model schools for workers, had shown that reasonable profits could go hand-in-hand with humane living and working conditions. Peel's bill began its passage through Parliament in 1815, but by this time the opponents of reform were well organized, and they were able to delay it and water it down in the House of Lords. *The final terms applied only to cotton mills:*

1 No children under the age of 9 could be employed (Peel and Owen had wanted it to be under 10).
2 Young people aged 9 to 16 must not work more than twelve hours a day (the original bill passed by the Commons said 11 hours); the work was to be done between 5 a.m. and 9 p.m., with one and a half hours off for meals.

Again, the weaknesses of the Act were the same: no inspectors were appointed, and magistrates were expected to enforce the new regulations. Peel apparently hoped that the offer of rewards would encourage informers, but very few workers dared to risk the wrath of the mill-owner by reporting him to a magistrate. On the whole, the Act was ignored, and in any case it did not apply to children in other industries. On the other hand, *it was an important step* because it established the principle that Parliament could interfere with parents' decisions about their children: no parent could now choose to send an 8-year-old to work in a cotton factory (at least in theory).

(c) the Factory Act of 1831

This was a good example of the alliance between different political groups. The Act was introduced by Sir John Hobhouse, a Radical, and was carried with Tory support. It extended the 12-hour limit to include 17- and 18-year-olds, but was as disappointing as previous Acts. Lord Althorp, speaking on behalf of the business interests, succeeded in weakening the original bill; consequently, there were still no inspectors; in addition, there was the problem of deciding a child's age, since there was, as yet, no official registration of births. Though these first three Acts were disappointing, nevertheless they *were* important because they showed that governments were prepared to depart from *laissez-faire.*

(d) the Factory Act of 1833

This was the first really effective piece of factory legislation. It was introduced by the Whig Chancellor of the Exchequer, Lord Althorp, though in fact all the credit was due to the Tory Evangelical, Lord Ashley (later the 7th Earl of Shaftesbury). The background was quite complex.

Oastler and other leaders of the Ten-Hour Movement, bitterly disappointed by Hobhouse's Act, redoubled their efforts to achieve a statutory ten-hour day, with Sadler leading the campaign in the Commons. A parliamentary select committee, chaired by Sadler, produced a damning report about the factory system, but the free marketers claimed, with some justification, that he had grossly exaggerated the evidence. However, in the 1832 general election (the first after the Reform Act) Sadler was defeated at Leeds and never managed to get back into Parliament again. This seemed a fatal blow, but the leadership of the movement was taken over by Ashley, who turned out to be just as impressive and as dedicated as Sadler. Ashley introduced Sadler's bill proposing to limit the working day of all textile operatives aged between 9 and 18 to ten hours. The hope was that, by restricting young people's hours in this way, the factories would have to close after ten hours, thus also giving adult workers the benefit of a ten-hour day. The Whig government, under pressure from mill-owners, delayed the bill until a Royal Commission had investigated the situation. Dominated by the Benthamite, Edwin Chadwick, the commission was efficient, detached and unemotional. They accepted that children needed some protection, but felt that Sadler's bill was too drastic. Determined to side-line what they called 'this ruinous measure before the House', they too probably exaggerated their case. Their report (June 1833) recommended that while, ten hours was too long for young children, by the age of 14 they were almost adults and were strong enough to work a longer day. Vitally important was its suggestion that paid inspectors should be appointed to supervise the new regulations.

Impressed by Chadwick's report, the Commons immediately defeated Ashley's Ten Hour Bill (July 1833). Althorp introduced a Whig bill based on Chadwick's recommendations, which quickly became law (August 1833). In some ways the new Act fell short of what Ashley wanted, while in other ways it went far beyond what he and Sadler had in mind. It applied to all textile mills except those making silk and lace:

▸ No child aged under 9 could be employed.
▸ Children aged from 9 to 13 were limited to an eight-hour day, and were to receive at least two hours of education a day.
▸ Young people from 14 to 18 were limited to a 12-hour day, to be worked between 5.30 a.m. and 8.30 p.m.
▸ Four inspectors were appointed at an annual salary of £1,000 each, to supervise the working of the Act; they had the power to enter any mill.

This was obviously a great advance on previous legislation, applying as it did to woollen and worsted as well as to cotton mills, and at long last introducing an inspectorate. *But it was still a disappointment for the Ten Hours supporters*:

▸ Most mill-owners responded by using a relay system of child labour, so that factories could be kept open for the whole time between 5.30 a.m. and 8.30 p.m., and so adults still had to work in excess of 12 hours.
▸ There still remained the problem of establishing a child's age; many parents needed the extra wages and often claimed that their 10-, 11- and 12-year-old children were really 13 years old. However, this difficulty was soon overcome by the compulsory registration of births, marriages and deaths, introduced in 1836.
▸ The education clauses turned out to be ineffective: no money was provided for building schools, and only the most progressive factory owners complied.
▸ Four inspectors were not enough to cover the whole country adequately. After one had died of overwork in 1836, assistants were appointed. Their reports showed that while many manufacturers complied with the regulations, it was still easy for the unscrupulous ones to evade them. However, as historian Edward Royle points out, to dwell on the weaknesses of the Act is to miss the point of its real significance:

> The inspectors were working in a totally new area of legislation; their aim was not to make the factory masters into criminals, but to protect the workers; and they had to be confident of a successful prosecution before bringing a case ... But the Inspectors did their work conscientiously and made some impact. In the first five full years of the Act in the major textile districts of England, an average of nearly 600 charges were laid each year, with success in three out of every four cases. Moreover the Inspectors' experience in working the Act led them to demand further legislation. Their reports to the Home Office became propaganda for

further reform and the Inspectors gave their full backing to Ashley's efforts in the 1840s.

Ashley certainly had no intention of giving up. In 1840, he persuaded Parliament to appoint a committee, with himself as chairman, to investigate the working of Althorp's Act. It was able to use evidence from the Inspectors and soon produced its own report (which included the details about the Stockport mills – Section 12.2(b)), showing that factory work was still extremely dangerous. This led to:

(e) the Factory Act of 1844

In 1841 the Whig government was replaced by the Conservatives under Peel, who was not in favour of a 10-hour day; 12 hours was as low as he was prepared to go. Even so, *the Act was a great advance*:

> Children could start work at the age of 8 (instead of 9), which seemed to be a backward step, but ...
> Children aged 8 to 13 could only work a six-and-a-half-hour day.
> Women over the age of 13 were limited to a 12-hour day.
> Dangerous machinery had to be fenced, and meals were to be eaten in a separate place.

(f) the Mines Act of 1842

Meanwhile, Ashley had been active in other areas; he was equally concerned about conditions in the mines, and pestered Parliament so much that a Royal Commission on the Employment of Women and Children in Mines was appointed. Its report (published in 1842) contained sketches showing some of the dangerous and unpleasant jobs that young children had to do. Until that time, mining conditions had received much less publicity than those in factories, and the public was deeply shocked by what the report revealed. Ashley's Mines Bill passed the Commons comfortably, but ran into trouble in the Lords, which had many aristocratic mine-owners. Led by Lord Londonderry, they were determined to weaken it as much as possible. *In its final form the Act*:

> Forbade the employment of women and girls in the mines, and of boys under the age of 10. (Ashley's original bill said no boys under 13 to be employed.)
> Appointed one inspector to enforce the regulations (though this was obviously inadequate).

(g) Fielden's Factory Act (1847) – the Ten Hours Act

The Ten-Hour Movement lost its leader in Parliament when Ashley resigned (1846) over Peel's decision to abolish the Corn Laws (see Section 7.5). His place was taken by John Fielden, the Radical MP for Oldham and a progressive owner of cotton mills in Todmorden. He introduced a bill to limit the working day of all women and young people up to the age of 18 to ten hours. At the same time, Oastler made sure there were massive demonstrations and marches throughout the North of England, and to the intense jubilation of the movement, the bill passed without amendment, only three years after the Commons had decisively rejected similar proposals.

Reasons for the change in attitude were:

‣ Peel, who had insisted on a 12-hour day, had now fallen from power, and the Conservative party was split. Many Tories who sympathized with Ashley and Fielden but had been unwilling to go against Peel's orders in 1844, were now free to vote for the Ten Hours Bill.
‣ Some Tory landowners, infuriated by the Repeal of the Corn Laws, may have voted for the bill as a way of revenging themselves on the manufacturers, who had supported the Corn Law repeal.
‣ In 1847, there was a trade depression during which demand for British textiles was reduced. For this reason, most factories were only working a ten-hour day, which seemed to upset the mill-owners' argument that they would be forced out of business if a ten-hour day was brought in.

The triumph was short-lived, though: as trade revived, manufacturers began to use the relay system, keeping their mills working from 5.30 a.m. until 8.30 p.m., so that adult males were still required to work for over 12 hours. Ashley, back in Parliament, kept up the agitation for a limit on factory opening hours, and eventually agreed to a compromise with the mill-owning interests. This was passed into law as:

(h) the Factory Act of 1850

‣ Factories should only be open for 12 hours, of which an hour and a half must be for meals.
‣ The working day for women and young people was to be ten-and-a-half hours.
‣ On Saturdays, the factories must close at 2 p.m., and women and young people must only work seven and a half hours.

While some of Ashley's supporters were annoyed with him for agreeing to the extra half-hour, the Act was nevertheless a great achievement. As well as a ten-and-a-half-hour day and the half day off for women and children, it meant that in most cases the men's working day was also limited, even though this was not mentioned specifically in the Act. The shorter working day did not cause the fall in production that many manufacturers had feared. Gradually, the health and efficiency of the textile workers improved, and serious accidents were almost eliminated.

Up to this point, these laws only applied to textile mills; it now remained to extend government control and regulation to those trades and industries where workers were still unprotected. Ashley (who became Earl of Shaftesbury in 1851) could not rest until all workers had been brought under some sort of protection. There were other reformers, of course – he was not personally responsible for all subsequent improvements; but it was usually Shaftesbury who stole the limelight. As late as 1884, at the age of 83, he was still making speeches in the Lords and giving evidence to Royal Commissions (he died in October 1885).

(i) more mining legislation

The 1842 Mines Act had said nothing about safety in the mines, and there continued to be regular explosions and disasters.

- *The Coal Mines Inspection Act (1850)* provided more inspectors to enforce the earlier Act, and to produce detailed reports on conditions and safety standards. However, it was a slow and difficult job to gain even these modest advances, since the coal-owners in the Lords bitterly opposed all attempts at legislation; Lord Londonderry thought the 1850 Act was 'infernal'.
- *The Mines Regulation and Inspection Act (1860)* increased the number of inspectors and said that no boys under 12 must work underground.
- In 1862, it was laid down that every mine must have at least two shafts to improve the chances of escape if there was an explosion. By this time, *the Royal School of Mines* (opened in 1851) was doing invaluable work training inspectors and developing new and safer techniques.
- *The Coal Mines Regulation Act (1872)* insisted on the introduction of some of these safer methods: fan ventilators, stronger timbering, wire ropes, improved winding machinery and better safety lamps.
- Finally, *the 1887 Mines Act* introduced stringent regulations about blasting precautions and the provision of first-aid and ambulance facilities.

(j) more factory and workshop legislation

In 1862, Shaftesbury secured the appointment of a Children's Employment Commission to investigate conditions in the other industries. As a result of the Commission's Reports, *two vitally important Acts were passed in 1867* by the Conservatives: one extended the mill legislation to all other workshops employing more than fifty people (such as iron and steel works, potteries, glass and paper mills and printing works). The other extended the regulations to workshops and ordinary houses where fewer than fifty people were employed.

This was a tremendous victory for Shaftesbury; but he had not quite finished – in 1871, he made a moving speech in the Lords about conditions in the brickfields:

> I saw little children, three-parts naked, tottering under the weight of wet clay, some of it on their hands and some on their shoulders, and little girls with large masses of wet, cold and dripping clay pressed on their abdomens. They had to endure the heat of the kiln, and to enter places where the heat was so intense that I was not myself able to remain more than two or three minutes.

As a result of this speech, brickfields too were brought under the Factory Act regulations.

Disraeli's Conservative government (1874–80) introduced further improvements:

1 *The Factory Act of 1874* reduced the working day to ten hours (from ten and a half). No child could be employed before the age of 10 (previously 8); no young person could work full-time until he or she was 14 (previously 13).
2 *The Factory and Workshops Act of 1878* put right a weakness of the 1867 legislation, which had placed the responsibility for inspecting workshops employing fewer than fifty people on to the shoulders of local authorities, many of which had failed to make regular inspections. The new Act brought these premises under government inspection. This was an important advance, though there were still problems in making sure that the regulations were adhered to within private houses.

Another Conservative measure, *The Factory Act of 1891,* raised the minimum age at which children could be employed in factories to 11 (see Section 16.5(b)).

12.5 what were the main public health problems in industrial towns?

(a) the rapid increase in the population

This was at the root of most of the problems. Between 1801 and 1851, the population of England, Wales and Scotland more or less doubled, from 10.5 million to 20.8 million. This was probably because young people were marrying earlier and therefore producing more children; so that while the death rate remained high, births outstripped deaths. Much of the increase was concentrated in industrial towns and cities, as workers migrated from the countryside to find jobs in the new factories. Most of the industrial towns had grown too quickly for the influx of people to be housed satisfactorily. During that half-century – 1801–51 – the population of Glasgow increased from 77,000 to 357,000, Edinburgh from 83,000 to 202,000, Liverpool from 82,000 to 376,000, Manchester from 75,000 to 303,000, Birmingham from 71,000 to 233,000 and Leeds from 53,000 to 172,000. Even more spectacular was the case of Bradford, whose population increased eightfold during the same period, from only 13,000 to 104,000.* In the late 1840s, the cities of northern England absorbed thousands of starving Irish fleeing from the potato famine. At first empty cellars and attics were pressed into use; later, cheap accommodation was built

---

* Statistics from *Britain 1987*, London, HMSO, pp. 7, 22; B. R. Mitchell and P. Deane, *Abstract of British Historical Statistics,* Cambridge, 1962, pp. 6–7, 24–7.

so that workers could live near the factories. Since there were few building regulations, this tended to consist of rows of cramped back-to-back houses (in northern England) or huge tenement blocks (in Scotland). Everywhere there was the problem of overcrowding – in 1847, a typical street (Church Lane) in the East End of London had 1,095 people living in only 27 houses – an average of 40 people to a house, and probably eight to a room.

(b) lack of proper amenities

Almost without exception in the rapidly growing industrial towns and cities there was a complete lack of what we, in the early twenty-first century, consider to be basic amenities – a pure water supply, drainage and sewage disposal, and street cleansing and lighting.

1 In working-class houses there was no such refinement as the water closet type of lavatory; usually there was an outside privy which might have to serve as many as twenty houses; these privies were not connected to sewers, but drained into cesspits, which had to be emptied manually. A doctor who visited a particularly bad part of Liverpool reported: 'I found the whole court inundated with fluid filth which had oozed through the walls from two adjoining ashpits or cesspools and which had no means of escape in consequence of the court being below the level of the street, and having no drain … The court had remained for two or three years in the state in which I saw it.' A Manchester doctor wrote about 'streets full of pits, brimful of stagnant water, the receptacle of dead cats and dogs'. In Nottingham 'the courts have no back yards, and the privies are common to the whole court; they present scenes of surpassing filth … the refuse is allowed to accumulate until, by its mass and its advanced putrefaction, it shall have acquired value as manure'. Boyd Hilton sums the situation up neatly:

> All large industrial towns had brothels, gin shops, alehouses, thieves' dens, filthy courts, rookeries, communal privies, cesspools, middens, dungheaps, and dangerously ill-paved streets crawling with wild dogs … and rats. Most were noisy, smelly, filthy, smoky, dark at night-time, blisteringly cold in winter, fly-ridden and dusty in summertime, flea- and lice-ridden at all times.

2 Drinking water was usually supplied by private companies, but only the wealthiest people had water piped to their houses. The rest had to use standpipes, taps or pumps outside in the street, which would probably only be turned on for part of the day. Many towns had to use river water, which was always polluted. London's water supply came mainly from the Thames, into which no fewer than 237 sewers were emptied. In 1841, a Leeds newspaper described the River Aire (which supplied much of the city's drinking water) as being 'charged with the contents of about 200 water closets and similar

places, a great number of common drains, the draining from dunghills, the Infirmary (dead leeches, poultices for patients), slaughter houses, pig manure, old urine wash and all sorts of decomposed animal and vegetable substances.'

3 There were unsatisfactory arrangements for funerals and burials, which added to the general health hazards. Corpses were often kept in the house for a week or more (to give the family time to raise cash for the funeral expenses), even when death was due to an infectious disease such as cholera or typhoid. Cemeteries and churchyards were grossly overfilled; according to Edwin Chadwick's report on burial (1834), in London, 'on spaces of ground which do not exceed 203 acres, closely surrounded by the abodes of the living, layer upon layer, each consisting of a population equivalent to a large army of 20,000 adults and nearly 30,000 youths and children is every year imperfectly interred'. Some graveyards contaminated the district's water supply.

(c) high death-rate from infectious diseases

The appalling fact was that, in 1840, one child in three died before reaching the age of five. Cholera was perhaps the most terrible of all these diseases. It first appeared in Britain in Sunderland in 1831 and rapidly reached epidemic proportions, killing 21,000 people in England and Wales, 9,000 in Scotland and 20,000 in Ireland. An even worse epidemic followed in 1848–9, which at its height was killing 2,000 people a week in London alone; in total 90,000 died in that outbreak, and there were further epidemics in 1854 and 1867. It was not known at the time that the cholera bacillus is carried in water that may otherwise be pure, which is why it affected the rich with their piped water supplies as well as the poor. The stages of the disease were horrifying: beginning with vomiting, the skin then turned blue, purple and finally brown or black; eventually the patient was afflicted with severe breathlessness, followed by rigid spasms of the legs and thighs, and almost invariably by death. Much more common were diseases such as typhus (usually referred to simply as 'the fever'), typhoid and tuberculosis (consumption), scarlet fever, diphtheria, measles and even ordinary diarrhoea, all of which were caused by contaminated water and lack of proper sewage disposal. Though they were all killers, the most lethal was tuberculosis, which caused between a quarter and a third of all deaths during the first half of the century.

The national death-rate increased as the industrial towns mushroomed; before 1831, the figure was in the region of 19 per thousand, but during the 1830s it rose steadily to 22.4 (in 1838) and reached a peak of 25.1 in 1849. However, this was the average figure; in crowded urban areas, the death-rate was usually around 30 per thousand, and in Glasgow during the 1830 cholera epidemic it hit 49 per thousand.

All these problems were highlighted by Edwin Chadwick's *Report on the*

Sanitary Condition of the Labouring Population of Great Britain (July 1842). A fanatical Benthamite, always striving for greater efficiency, Chadwick had already been involved in the 1834 Poor Law Commission Report (see Section 5.3) and with the Royal Commission on Factory Conditions (1833) (see Section 12.4(d)). After the Poor Law Amendment Act of 1834, Chadwick was Secretary to the Poor Law Commissioners, and he became interested in the causes of disease. In Chadwick's way of looking at things, sickness cost money and caused people to become paupers, which cost more money. He hoped therefore, by controlling disease, to reduce the expense of supporting the sick. What his report did was to hammer home the point that filthy conditions were the main causes of disease. He produced some startling statistics of life expectancy, which shocked the public; whereas a lawyer in a rural county such as Rutland could expect to live (on average) to be 52, a labourer in a Manchester slum would be lucky to survive until 17, while in Liverpool his average life expectancy would be only 15. Unfortunately, there was no organization or body, either locally or nationally, with the expertise or the funds necessary to tackle such enormous problems, except, of course, the government.

12.6 what advances were made in public health during the nineteenth century?

In his report, Chadwick suggested a number of measures that would improve public health. These included providing all houses with piped water, which could be used for flushing sewage away from the houses into main sewers; instead of being large, square tunnels built of porous brick, sewers ought to be smaller, tube-shaped and made of non-porous (glazed) pottery. The new system should be organized and controlled centrally, like the New Poor Law. But improvements were very slow to come, mainly because of the enormous expense involved. How, for example, did one set about supplying cities the size of Glasgow and Manchester with a system of pure, piped water? In addition, Chadwick's emphasis on compulsion and centralization was completely alien to Victorian *laissez-faire* principles. When progress did take place, it was partly a result of government action, but owed more to advances in medicine, and to some great engineering projects.

(a) government action

Before 1848, any action to improve sanitary conditions was taken on a local basis without any central direction. Liverpool had its own Sanitary Act (1846), which made the town council responsible for drainage, sewerage, cleansing and paving, and it was the first city to have a permanent Medical Officer of Health. But the nature and efficiency of these local *Improvement Committees*, as they were called, varied widely. Chadwick's report had made it obvious that legislation was needed to cover the country as a whole, and after tremendous pressure and agitation, Russell's government introduced the first in a series of new measures:

1 *The Public Health Act of 1848* gave local authorities the power to appoint Boards of Health, whose work was to be supervised by the General Board of Health, headed by Chadwick himself and including Lord Shaftesbury. Unfortunately, the Act had a fatal weakness: there was no compulsion on local authorities to set up Boards; by 1854, only 182 Boards had been appointed in England and Wales, covering only 2 million people out of a population of 18 million. And most of those that were set up were ineffective; only 13 of them had started large-scale water and sewage works. Chadwick had offended many people by his arrogant manner, especially those who opposed the centralization of health control. In 1854, he was sacked from the Board of Health and the government contented itself by passing local acts.

2 In 1858, the Board of Health was terminated, and local initiatives were given more encouragement and freedom. Three million pounds was provided to prevent sewage from being pumped into the Thames above London. Even this did not prevent 10,000 Londoners from dying in the 1866 cholera epidemic, and the national death-rate was still running at over 23 per thousand.

3 *The Sanitation Act of 1866* recognized that the 1848 Act had been a failure, and it therefore compelled local authorities to improve local conditions and remove nuisances such as cesspits and excrement. According to *The Times,* this 1866 Act 'introduces a new sanitary era.'

4 *The Public Health Act of 1872* (introduced by Gladstone's Liberal government) clarified the position by dividing England and Wales into districts under specific health authorities, each of which was to have its own Medical Officer and staff. Unfortunately, this Act was another failure, because it was not clear what the duties of the health boards were, and most of them were reluctant to spend the cash necessary for radical health reform.

5 *The Public Health Act of 1875.* It was left to Disraeli and the Conservatives to rationalize and consolidate the complicated patchwork of health legislation. The Act was the work of Disraeli's Home Secretary, R. A. Cross, and has been rated by some historians as one of the greatest pieces of legislation in the nineteenth century. It laid down in clear detail *what the compulsory duties of local authorities were:* they had to ensure that there was adequate water supply, drainage and sewage disposal; nuisances were to be removed, offensive trades regulated, and contaminated food to be sought out, confiscated and destroyed. Cases of infectious disease were to be notified to the Medical Officer, who had to take appropriate action. Other regulations dealt with markets, street lighting and burials.

6 *The Artisans' Dwellings Act (1875),* also the work of Cross, attempted to deal with the problem of slum housing. Local authorities were given the power, if

they wished to use it, to buy up and demolish insanitary properties and replace them with modern, healthy accommodation. It was the violent opposition of many of his own party, who thought the bill a blatant invasion of landlords' rights, that caused Cross to abandon the idea of making slum clearance compulsory. This weakened the Act seriously, but at least a start had been made. Birmingham, under its mayor, Joseph Chamberlain, was one of the first cities to begin a massive slum clearance programme (see also Sections 14.2(a) and 16.4(d)).

7 *The Housing of the Working Classes Acts (1890 and 1900)* were two more Conservative measures that remedied the deficiencies of the 1875 Act. Now local authorities were *compelled* to demolish unhealthy housing and to provide other accommodation for those made homeless. Owners of slum property could be compelled to sell it to the council for demolition. What was needed next was legislation to carry slum clearance a step further by regulating the planning of towns. Unfortunately, a great opportunity to encourage careful and systematic planning of new building schemes and new towns was missed in the next major piece of legislation.

8 *The Housing and Town Planning Act (1909).* This Liberal measure allowed local authorities to introduce town planning schemes, if they wished, in order to avoid piecemeal building. But there was no compulsion, and the Act was so complicated that only one major scheme was started in the whole country before 1914.

(b) medical improvements

Back in the late 1790s, Edward Jenner had introduced his vaccination technique which controlled smallpox, though the disease was still dangerous. At about the same time, Humphry Davy (who was later to invent the miners' safety lamp) had used nitrous oxide (laughing gas) as a partial anaesthetic for use during operations. But it was another half a century before any further advances were made:

‣ The introduction of chloroform (in the late 1840s) as a general anaesthetic gave surgeons more time to perform operations, though there was still the problem of how to avoid infection in the wound.

‣ A major breakthrough came in the early 1860s, when Louis Pasteur, a French chemist, put forward the germ theory of disease: that decay and putrefaction as well as infectious diseases are caused by micro-organisms or bacteria, not just by filth and bad smells, as Chadwick thought. A Glasgow surgeon, Joseph Lister, building on Pasteur's work, developed an antiseptic technique using carbolic acid, which reduced infection after operations. He first used his new method successfully in 1865; between 1865 and 1869, the death rate after operations in his Male Accident Ward at Glasgow Royal Infirmary fell from 45 per cent to 15 per cent. At first most British surgeons were unconvinced by his claims, but after a triumphant and much publicized demonstration tour of Germany in 1875, his ideas gradually gained acceptance at home. By the early 1880s, the death-rate after operations had fallen substantially; in 1883, Lister was created a baronet in recognition of his work.

› Standards of nursing improved steadily, thanks to the work of Elizabeth Fry, who founded the Institute of Nursing Sisters, and of Florence Nightingale, who developed the Nightingale School of Nursing in St Thomas's Hospital, London. It is only comparatively recently that the wide-ranging nature of Nightingale's work has been fully recognized. According to Lynn McDonald, writing in 2006, 'with the benefit of hindsight we can see her as a major architect of the modern health care system'. One of her great achievements after the Crimean War was to persuade the authorities that trained nurses were needed in workhouse infirmaries as well as in hospitals. In April 1865, Liverpool Workhouse Infirmary became the first poor-law institution to employ fully-trained Nightingale nurses. In the same year she produced a plan to revamp the entire workhouse system by providing three different types of institution: for the sick; for the aged and infirm; and for the insane. The plan also included schools for pauper children; the whole system would be paid for by a general rate. Much of this was incorporated in *the Metropolitan Poor Act of 1867*, but the new legislation was not compulsory, so that improvements had to be fought for, workhouse by workhouse. Nightingale worked tirelessly and won the support of important figures such as Edwin Chadwick and J. S. Mill, by providing them with irrefutable statistical evidence of the problems. Many improvements were made, but unfortunately, at a time when *laissez-faire* was the dominant theory, it proved impossible to implement the broader 'system' that she had in mind. In the words of Lynn McDonald:

> Her vision was of a profoundly reformed system, the private sector largely running the economy, but with measures for income security, savings and pensions, employment stimulation in bad economic times, better housing, provision for the disabled, aged and chronically ill, and a whole system of public health care. This can now be seen as an early conceptualization of the welfare state. It is high time that Nightingale is given due credit as a major social reformer; for her vision of a public health-care system within a broader system of social welfare, and for offering a method by which these reforms could be achieved.

› There were improvements in the education of doctors, and in 1858 the Medical Act set up the General Council for Medical Education and Registration, whose function was to supervise standards of efficiency among doctors.

(c) engineering achievements

This might seem a strange topic to include in a chapter on public health, but in fact the provision of large-scale water, sewage and drainage schemes required some remarkable feats of civil engineering. One of the first cities to attempt such a scheme was Manchester, which in 1847 began work on its huge Longdendale waterworks, which was to cost in the region of three-quarters of a million pounds. When it was completed ten years later, it could supply the city with thirty million gallons a day, whereas the previous private companies had managed no more than two million gallons a day. As soon as a continuous supply of water was available, work could go ahead on laying sewers. Liverpool soon followed with a massive water scheme supplied from reservoirs near Rivington Pike, which by 1857 could hold 3,000 million gallons; by 1875, most of the city's housing had water closets connected to sewers. London's system of waterized sewers was completed by 1866. Most cities and towns of any size had followed suit by 1900.

In spite of these improvements, the death rate was still hovering around 24 per thousand in 1870. Slowly but steadily over the next thirty years, Britain became a healthier place in which to live; the 1901 census showed that over-crowding was beginning to thin out, and the death rate had dropped to below 18 per thousand. Even so, every now and again, some sort of epidemic occurred that upset the growing late-Victorian complacency – a typhoid epidemic in Blackburn in 1881, cholera in London in 1893, and smallpox in several ports in 1902. The investigations of Charles Booth in London (1889–1903) and Seebohm Rowntree in York (1901) showed that there was still some way to go to achieve a final victory over filth and infectious diseases (see Section 20.1(b)).

12.7 what kinds of schools were there before 1870, and why was there no state system of elementary education?

(a) a confusion of different types of school

Before 1870, there was hardly anything that could be described as an educational 'system' in Britain. The government took very little interest in education, and gave no financial support to education before 1833. Existing schools were run by private individuals and religious groups, and sometimes by companies of the City of London. Consequently, there was a confusing hotch-potch of different sorts of school.

1 *Public schools.* There were nine major ones (Eton, Harrow, Westminster, Charterhouse, Rugby, St Paul's, Shrewsbury, Winchester and Merchant Taylors) and many minor ones. Despite being called 'public' schools, they were in fact only open to those members of the public who could afford the fees – namely, wealthy aristocrats, landowners and industrialists. The education these schools provided was based on the classics (Latin and Greek), and in the early part of the century did not even include mathematics. It was only very gradually that the public school curriculum was modernized, thanks to the work of progressive Headmasters such as Thomas Arnold (Headmaster

of Rugby, 1828–42) who insisted on mathematics and French being taught regularly. He also introduced the prefect system and encouraged the ideal of Christian duty.

2 *Grammar schools.* Many of these were ancient foundations going back to the sixteenth century. Unlike public schools, they did not take boarders, but the subjects taught were similar – heavily weighted towards Latin and Greek. Fees were charged, though most grammar schools provided some free places for poor children.

3 *Private schools.* Also fee-paying, these were newer schools started by people who were impatient with the old-fashioned curriculum of the public and grammar schools. One of the earliest was the Liverpool Royal Institution School (1819) which taught mathematics, modern languages and science.

All these schools were completely outside the reach of the great mass of the population, who were lucky to receive a few years of elementary education – basic reading, writing and arithmetic – in what were known as *Voluntary Schools.* These included Sunday Schools (Robert Raikes had founded the Sunday School Union in 1780), dame schools run by elderly ladies and which were often no more than child-minding establishments, and charity schools such as those set up by the Society for Promoting Christian Knowledge (SPCK). After the 1833 Factory Act, a number of factory schools were set up, and during the 1840s large numbers of Ragged Schools were started in deprived areas, with Ashley as president of the Ragged Schools Union. The most widespread and best organized of the Voluntary Schools were those run by the Church of England (Anglican) and the Nonconformist churches.

‣ The Church of England organized its schools through *the National Society,* founded in 1811 by Andrew Bell.

‣ The Nonconformists worked through *the British and Foreign Schools Society (1814),* whose leading light was Joseph Lancaster, who ran his own school for 1,000 pupils in Borough Road, London.

There was bitter rivalry and hostility between these two groups, though their teaching methods – based on *the monitorial system* – were similar. In order to save money, and because of the shortage of teachers, older pupils (known as monitors) taught small groups of children. According to Lancaster: 'the whole system of tuition is almost entirely conducted by boys; the school is divided into classes, and to each of these a lad is appointed a monitor; he is responsible for the morals, improvement, good order and cleanliness of the whole class. To be a monitor is coveted by the whole school.'

There was wide variation in the quality of elementary education provided, and in some industrial areas there were no schools at all for working-class children. In 1818, only 1 in 17 of the population was receiving any elementary education.

(b) why was there no state system of education?

Many people felt that the only way to secure an efficient education system was for the government to organize it. Jeremy Bentham thought it would eliminate the dangerous rivalry between different religious denominations. In 1820, a Whig politician, Henry Brougham, introduced a bill that would have set up schools in parishes where there were none already in existence, but it was easily defeated.

Reasons for lack of progress:

1 The same *laissez-faire* outlook that delayed government intervention in the other problem areas applied equally to education; if the poor wanted education, they must see to it themselves; it was no part of a government's function to provide such an expensive service.

2 There was a strong belief that the education of the working classes was unnecessary; all they needed were the skills of the job for which they were destined, and these could be learnt perfectly well by simply doing the job. And if children spent their time being educated, industrialists would lose their source of cheap labour.

3 An educated working class could be dangerous: one MP, Davies Giddy, told Parliament in 1807 that education would teach workers 'to despise their lot in life instead of making them good servants in agriculture and other laborious employments to which their rank in society had destined them'. He added that it would enable them to read seditious pamphlets and 'render them insolent to their superiors'. In 1825, another MP, afraid of revolution, delivered himself of the view that 'whenever the lower orders of any great nation have obtained a smattering of knowledge, they have generally used it to produce national ruin'. Two years later a Tory MP argued that 'as education has increased amidst the people, vice and crime have increased ... the majority of criminals consist of those who have been educated'.

12.8 how and why the government intervened in education

(a) first government action on education

Gradually, those who were in favour of government intervention gained the ascendancy in Parliament. The Whig government that came to power in 1830 was under pressure from its Radical Benthamite wing, and at last in 1833 the first breakthrough was made. However, *in the period 1833–70* the government itself did not provide any schools; it merely made some funding available and tried to make sure that the voluntary societies used it efficiently:

1 In 1833 the government gave a total of £20,000 to the Anglican and Nonconformist societies, to help them to provide more school buildings, while £10,000 was voted for building schools in Scotland.

2 In 1839, the grant was increased to £30,000, on condition that a committee of the Privy Council was set up to supervise how the money was spent. The secretary of the committee was Sir James Kay-Shuttleworth, who had been a doctor in the slums of Manchester; later, as a Poor Law commissioner, he developed workhouse schools and set up his own training college for teachers. At his suggestion, school inspectors were appointed; and they soon began to produce disturbing reports about the inefficiency of the monitorial system.

3 In the 1840s, teacher training colleges were established by the religious societies, following the example of Kay-Shuttleworth's Battersea College. He also introduced *the pupil–teacher scheme*, by which able students were apprenticed to good voluntary schools at the age of 13 for five years, after which, with the help of government grants, they could go on to teacher training colleges. To finance this new scheme, which gradually replaced the monitorial system, the annual government grant was increased to £100,000 (1847). Within ten years it had reached £500,000, and in 1856 the government set up the Department of Education to look after its administration.

4 *The Newcastle Commission* reported in 1861 that, while one in seven of the population was now receiving some education, the majority were still unable to read a newspaper or write a letter. It recommended that grants to schools, and teachers' salaries, should depend on how well pupils performed in examinations.

5 Robert Lowe, head of the Education Department in Palmerston's Liberal government of 1859–65, accepted this recommendation and introduced a *'payment by results' system* (1862). School inspectors tested the pupils in reading, writing and arithmetic (known as the '3Rs'), and the number who passed determined both grants and salaries. The system aroused tremendous criticism, because, despite making schools more efficient and saving money, it led to a great deal of mechanical cramming and reciting of lists of facts learnt off by heart. It also meant that the curriculum tended to become narrowed to the '3Rs', and it caused considerable nervous strain among teachers. Even so the system lasted until 1897.

The year 1870 saw the beginning of a new era: Gladstone's Liberal government (1868–74) decided that it was up to the state to make sure that every child received some education; if necessary, it would provide the schools itself.

(b) why did the government decide that a state system of elementary education was needed?

1 The 1867 Reform Act, which gave the vote to industrial workers living in the boroughs, meant that they needed some education to enable them to decide how to vote. According to Lowe himself: 'from the moment you entrust the masses with power, their education becomes an imperative necessity; you

have placed the government of this country in the hands of the masses and you must therefore give them an education.'

2 Some historians have suggested that basic education for the masses was seen by its supporters as a way of exercising social control. The working classes would be less dangerous, less prone to revolution, if they received in school from an early age moral teaching from the Bible and instruction in the virtues of hard work, duty and self-restraint. However, the majority view nowadays is that the ruling classes were probably not thinking in terms of such direct control. Gladstone, for example, was anxious for greater efficiency, and genuinely believed in 'equality of opportunity' for everybody.

3 Britain was lagging well behind Prussia and the northern states of the USA in the provision of education, and the two countries seemed to be doing well both militarily and economically. Prussia had defeated Austria-Hungary easily in 1866, and the North had turned out the eventual winner in the American Civil War (1861–5); it was already clear that both would soon be challenging Britain's industrial lead. These developments helped to swing opinion in Britain in favour of education for the masses.

4 The rapid population growth meant that the Voluntary Societies were unable to keep up; in fact they were losing ground – in some large industrial cities fewer than one in ten of the child population was receiving any education.

5 The supporters of education for the masses were waging a more vigorous campaign than ever before; spearheading the movement was Joseph Chamberlain's National Education League, started in Birmingham in 1869.

6 Finally, Britain's economy was booming, so that the government felt able to provide the extra money that would be needed to finance a full state system of education.

(c) Forster's Education Act (1870)

W. E Forster, MP for Bradford, and head of the Education Department under Gladstone, had a difficult problem: he had to find a way of including the existing religious voluntary schools within the new legislation; since there were so many of these schools, they could not simply be ignored, and certainly not abolished. He also had to try not to seem to be favouring either Anglicans or Nonconformists. The result was bound to be a compromise:

1 The existing Anglican and Nonconformist voluntary schools were allowed to continue, with increased grants from the government.

2 In areas where there was no voluntary school, or where the existing schools could not provide enough places, a locally elected School Board was to be set up. Its function was to organize Board Schools for children aged between five and twelve. These schools were to receive government grants as well as extra finance from a special local rate to be collected by the Board.

3 As an attempt to sidestep the religious problem, it was left to each Board to decide whether religious education was to be provided in their schools. If so, it should be restricted to Bible study, and this should be 'undenominational' (it should not be taught with either an Anglican or a Nonconformist bias).

4 Attendance was not made compulsory (because as yet there were not enough school places for every child) and it was not free of charge. However, Boards could pay the fees for poor children, either in the new Board Schools or in the voluntary schools.

Forster's Act caused a great political row: the religious bodies resented the fact that their schools received no money from local rates, and that the new schools might provide no religious teaching at all. Nonconformists were particularly annoyed, because they had hoped that Forster would abolish Anglican schools, whereas he had in fact strengthened the already strong Anglican position in many areas. To add insult to injury, Nonconformists now found themselves having to pay the local education rate, much of which might be used to finance 'godless' Board Schools. Equally galling was the possibility that some Boards would use their rates to pay the fees of poor children being educated in Anglican schools. This unfortunate situation led to bitter struggles in which the different religious groups fought for control of their local School Board. There can be no doubt that this religious feuding made the task of providing an effective education system for working-class children much more difficult and drawn-out than it need have been.

The Act can also be criticized on the grounds that it resulted in a dual system of education – in which church schools were handicapped by a shortage of money. However, it achieved what Forster and Gladstone had in mind – 'to complete the present voluntary system … to fill up the gaps'. B. H. Abbott claims that the Act 'remains a remarkable piece of social legislation, playing a vital part in civilizing the masses in the nation's vast industrial cities'. Certainly, between 1870 and 1880, the number of children receiving elementary education had more than doubled, to almost three million, as the new Board Schools sprang up all over the country – by 1883 there were 3,692 Board Schools. However, there were still over 11,000 Anglican voluntary schools, and even in 1900 the majority of children were being educated in voluntary schools.

(d) further developments in elementary education

▸ *Sandon's Education Act* (1876). Lord Sandon, head of the Education Department in Disraeli's second government (1874–80), decided that local School Attendance Committees should be set up to encourage as many children as possible to take advantage of educational opportunities; parents were to be responsible for making sure that children received basic instruction, and committees *could* help parents who were too poor to pay the school fees, though this was not compulsory.

- *A. J. Mundella's Education Act* (1881) was a Liberal measure that *made attendance at elementary school compulsory* for all children aged between five and ten. There was still the problem of fees, which worked out at around three pence per child per week; this was far too much for poor families to afford, if they had several children.
- *The Fee Grant Act* (1891). This was a Conservative measure which meant that in practice *elementary education was now free.*
- During the 1890s, Lowe's payment by results system was gradually phased out, thanks to recommendations made by *the Cross Commission* (1888). Grants to schools were now based on attendance, and 'bald teaching of facts' was replaced by 'the development of interest and intelligence'.

By the end of the nineteenth century, the vast majority of children were receiving some basic instruction, and the quality of that education was improving.

(e) the Balfour Education Act (1902)

This was the next major landmark, the work of A. J. Balfour, Conservative Prime Minister from 1902 to 1905. He decided that radical changes were needed in the way elementary education was being organized, and that some government policy was needed to deal with secondary education. *His reasons were*:

- Because of a shortage of money, the Voluntary Schools (of which the great majority were run by Anglicans) were much inferior in every way to the Board Schools.
- *The Bryce Commission reported* (1895) that there was a chronic shortage of suitable technical education, while Britain's industrial competitors – the USA, Germany and Belgium – were far ahead in this field.

The details of the new Act were worked out by R. L. Morant, Balfour's educational adviser:

1 The School Boards were abolished; county councils and county borough councils were to run both Voluntary and Board Schools, and were made responsible for organizing secondary and technical education.
2 For the first time, Voluntary Schools were to receive money from the rates to enable them to bring their standards up to those of the Board Schools.
3 Local authorities, working through their own education committees, could help existing secondary schools (mainly old grammar schools) with money from the rates; they were also directed to set up their own fee-paying secondary schools.

The Balfour/Morant Act was vitally important: it meant a general raising of the standards of elementary education and more uniformity, though it perpetuated the dual church/state system. It also meant that the state was going to see to it that secondary education was more widely available; this brought about the appearance of a new phenomenon – the state grammar school. Unfortunately, at first these tended to model themselves on the old private grammar schools with their concentration on Latin and Greek, and with insufficient attention to technical and scientific subjects.

At the time, the Act caused another religious controversy, bitterly disappointing the Nonconformists once again. They had hoped that Balfour would abolish Anglican and Roman Catholic schools, most of which were teetering on the verge of bankruptcy. Instead, they were rescued by money from the local rates (to which the Nonconformists themselves had to contribute). In some country areas, especially in Wales, the only school available was an Anglican one, which Nonconformists had to allow their children to attend.

(f) further steps towards secondary education for all

‣ In 1906, Campbell-Bannerman's Liberal government introduced what in effect became *the 11-plus system.* All secondary schools receiving government grants had to reserve 25 per cent of their places for children coming up from elementary schools; they would be awarded scholarships on the results of a special entrance examination.

‣ *H. A. L. Fisher's Education Act* (1918) was passed by the Lloyd George government shortly before the end of the First World War. It raised the school-leaving age from 12 to 14 and required local authorities to provide what it called 'day continuation classes' or part-time education to the age of 18 for those children who left school at 14. Grants to secondary schools were increased, so that more scholarships could be awarded, and State Scholarships were introduced so that secondary school pupils could go on to university.

Education had clearly come a long way since 1833, but there was still much to be done. In fact, very little was done about Fisher's day continuation classes, because, after the war, governments claimed to be short of the necessary funds. Although much was made of the fact that an 'educational ladder' had been established, it was still very rare for a child from a working-class home to get to university. As J. A. Hobson (a well-known Edwardian expert on politics and economics) put it: 'What is needed is not an educational ladder, narrowing as it rises, to be climbed with difficulty by a chosen energetic few ... it is a broad, easy stair that is wanted ... one which will entice everyone to rise.'

Later developments included the 1926 Hadow Report, (see Section 20.4(f)) and the 1944 Butler Act (see Section 28.7(b)).

12.9 everyday life and leisure in Victorian Britain

(a) the emergence of class

One of the key themes of the nineteenth century was the development of the concept of class. People began to use the labels 'working class' and 'middle class' to describe different groups in society according to their jobs, incomes, living conditions and leisure activities. This was no doubt prompted by the Industrial Revolution and the growth of a large urban labour force – manual workers who made up the new 'working class'. They included workers in factories and mines, engineers, ship-builders, railway workers and general labourers. Agricultural labourers and other rural workers, such as blacksmiths, also belonged to the working class, as did domestic servants. The middle class were deemed to be those who worked with their brains; these included office workers, shopkeepers, teachers, lawyers, doctors, clergymen and, at the top of the scale, factory owners, financiers and businessmen.

However, there were wide variations within both groups, and the classes tended to merge at the margins. For example, in mid-century, a farm labourer in the south of England might earn as little as 6s a week, whereas a skilled worker in a Barrow-in-Furness shipyard could be paid as much as 50s a week, which was probably more than a poorly-paid clerk in the office. Yet the industrialists, financiers and entrepreneurs, like the elder Sir Robert Peel, for example, would have amassed enormous wealth and enjoyed a life-style not dissimilar to some of the upper class aristocracy or gentry, the top group in society.

The aristocracy had dominated British society for centuries; their power, privilege and wealth were based on the ownership of large estates and the income in profits and rents that came from them. With the arrival of industrialization, some of the aristocracy, such as Lord Londonderry, became even wealthier because they were fortunate enough to have coal or iron ore discovered on their land, which brought in huge mining royalties. During the course of the nineteenth century, however, the aristocratic upper class faced a number of challenges to their pre-eminent position. Their political control came under threat as parliamentary reform widened the franchise to include middle-class and even some working-class voters. Yet, even at the end of the century, the aristocrats had not lost political control, though they *were* sharing it with the upper middle class. The other challenge was perhaps more serious: with the agricultural depression of the last quarter of the century came a sharp decline in income from rents; landowners without other sources of revenue found themselves in considerably straitened circumstances, and a large section of the aristocracy began to sink into a gradual decline. At the same time, many of the wealthiest members of the middle class aspired to join the upper class by acquiring large estates and titles. Historians Jeremy Black and Donald MacRaild sum up the class situation well:

> At every level, then, class is a complicated issue. There is no doubt that by the 1880s a classic 'them and us' working-class mentality was in existence. Developed by social stratification, labour conflicts, struggles with employers … and a sense that working men and women were not enjoying their

share of the industrial and imperial honeycomb, a high degree of social polarisation did emerge ... and it had its equivalents within the middle class as well as between the classes; between new wealth and landed privilege. The process of acclimatising the arriving middle class was not entirely simple; behind the statistical picture was layer upon layer of tradition: manners, customs, blood-lines, historical status. Land alone was not enough to guarantee acceptance into what was a social and cultural as well as a political elite.

(b) the Victorians at leisure

In the early part of the nineteenth century, most manual workers had to work a six-day week, and they were long days. There must have been very little leisure time, and very little money left over to spend on leisure in any case. However, the length of the working day was gradually reduced (see Section 12.4), and the 1850 Factory Act specified that factories must close at 2 p.m. on Saturdays; as real wages began to increase (at least according to some historians), there was cash available for leisure to be enjoyed.

One popular leisure activity among all classes was drinking alcohol. The average annual consumption of beer per person in Britain rose from 19.4 gallons in 1845–9 to 33.2 gallons in 1875–9, most of it being consumed in public houses. Pubs were frequented almost exclusively by the working class. One commentator reported in 1852 that 'no person, above the rank of a labouring man or artisan, would venture to go into a public house'. The middle and upper classes drank in their clubs or hotels and at home, mainly spirits and wine, especially claret. As Theodore Hoppen points out, this increased the social gulf between the classes: 'Pubs thus became the great social centres of working-class life, their attractions based upon, but also reaching far beyond, the consumption of alcohol. Some turned themselves into informal working-men's clubs where friendly societies, trade unions, and craft societies met in upstairs rooms.' Some middle-class observers found all this rather alarming and began the temperance movement, which tried to turn people towards tea, coffee and other non-alcoholic drinks, but without much success.

Other popular working-class pastimes in the early part of the nineteenth century were cock-fighting, dog-fighting and bear-baiting; in country areas, these blood-sports were enjoyed by all classes, attracted by the opportunity for gambling. However, the Society for the Prevention of Cruelty to Animals, formed in 1824, campaigned against such sports. Queen Victoria supported the society and gave it the title 'Royal' in 1840. Eventually, these pastimes were all made illegal; it was ironic that laws against cruelty to animals seemed to be more pressing than laws against cruelty to female and child workers! Public executions too were extremely popular entertainments until they were abolished in 1868. When John Wilson was hanged in 1849, an estimated 100,000 people came to watch, many arriving by special train.

Horse-racing became steadily more popular as the century progressed and was patronized by all classes, again attracted by the gambling. As early as the 1840s, bookmakers were operating at the racecourses specifically for the urban working class, who were able to travel cheaply by train to courses such as York, Doncaster, Sandown Park, Ascot and Goodwood. In April 1851, C. C. F. Greville wrote in his diary about the Earl of Derby: 'A few weeks ago he was on the point of being Prime Minister … but now, at Newmarket, he was to be seen in the midst of a crowd of blacklegs, betters, and loose characters of every description, in uproarious spirits, chaffing, rowing and shouting with laughter.'

Hunting and shooting, originally the preserve of the upper classes, began to be shared by the wealthier middle classes in mid-century. Women could take part in foxhunting with the hounds, and there was a sharp increase in the number of packs, from 99 in 1850 to 137 in 1877. During the 1840s, deerstalking was introduced, particularly in the Highlands of Scotland. Shooting birds and small animals was almost an obsession: anything that moved was fair game – pheasants, grouse, partridges, hares and rabbits were the favourite targets.

In the second half of the nineteenth century, with the spread of the free Saturday afternoon, spectator sports such as soccer, rugby and cricket became popular. The Football Association was formed in 1863, and the first FA Cup competition was held in 1871. Some of the early soccer teams were founded by church groups such as Aston Villa Wesleyan Chapel and Christ Church, Bolton, which became Bolton Wanderers. Glasgow Celtic was founded by a Roman Catholic priest in 1887, while Manchester United and Stoke City were railway teams. Soccer developed into a professional game, and despite players being paid tiny amounts by today's standards, it provided a great opportunity for working men to supplement the meagre wages earned from their day jobs. Whereas soccer became mainly a working-class entertainment, rugby was enjoyed by all classes, at least until the 1890s, when it split into an amateur Union game and a professional Rugby League that had strong support in the North of England. Cricket had been the national summer game since the eighteenth century and was played by children and adults of all classes. Almost every village and town had its own cricket team. The game had one unusual characteristic, particularly at county level – the amateurs often paid a few good working-class players to give their team some extra clout. This unfortunately led to the demeaning division between 'gentlemen' and 'players', in which the players were relatively poorly paid and had different, invariably inferior, changing rooms. Foreign observers, as well as having difficulty with the rules of the game, saw it as the very epitomy of the English class system. Nevertheless, during the second half of the century, cricket became an extremely popular spectator sport; the County Championship was introduced in 1873, and the first test matches against a visiting Australian team were played in 1880. Crowds of around 10,000 were the norm. On the other hand, sports such as tennis and golf remained strictly middle- and upper-class preserves.

While Victorian Britain had the reputation, as far as classical music was concerned, of being 'a land without music', as one German observer put it, in fact the Victorians were extremely musical. Music halls became increasingly popular; one of the first was the Star in Bolton, opened in 1832; by 1866, London had no fewer than thirty-six large halls, each seating on average around 1,500 people. Music halls provided a mixture of song, orchestral music, dance, acrobatics and comedy, much of it extremely risqué, and not quite 'respectable'. No doubt because of this, the halls were always packed with both working-class and middle-class audiences; even members of the aristocracy in search of excitement would sometimes venture inside, sitting in the most expensive seats, of course. The comic operas of William Gilbert and Arthur Sullivan enjoyed great popularity in the last quarter of the nineteenth century. With music by Sullivan and librettos full of social and political satire by Gilbert, they appealed to audiences of all classes. Beginning with *Trial by Jury* (1875), which ridiculed the legal system, the series continued with *The Sorcerer* (1877), *H.M.S. Pinafore* (1878), *The Pirates of Penzance* (1879), *Patience* (1881), *Iolanthe* (1882), *Princess Ida* (1884), *Ruddigore* (1887), *The Yeomen of the Guard* (1888), *The Gondoliers* (1889), *Utopia Limited* (1893) and *The Grand Duke* (1896). Each one made fun of some aspect of British society; for example, *The Sorcerer* dealt with the Church, *H.M.S. Pinafore* the armed forces and *Iolanthe* the political system, while *Princess Ida* was a satire on feminism. So successful did they prove that the theatrical impresario Richard D'Oyly Carte built the Savoy Theatre, which opened in 1881, especially for them.

In Wales and the North of England there was a long tradition of amateur choral singing among the working and middle classes; Welsh Male Voice choirs, often consisting mainly of coalminers, were famous throughout the country. In Lancashire and Yorkshire, there were the brass bands with their festivals and contests. Audiences of several thousand would gather in Belle Vue, Manchester, to hear champion bands such as the Black Dyke Mills Band and the Grimethorpe Colliery Band competing.

Religious music was extremely popular, especially oratorios such as Handel's *Messiah* and Mendelssohn's *Elijah*, which were regular favourites, performed both by semi-professionals in London and other major cities, and by countless amateur choirs throughout the country. A new oratorio, *The Crucifixion*, by a British composer, John Stainer, first performed in 1887, soon became just as popular.

Orchestral music had only limited appeal in the early part of the century. There were no British composers of classical music of the calibre of the two great Germans, Beethoven and Brahms, and most of the upper classes were notoriously philistine in their musical tastes. However, the two leading British composers of the mid-Victorian era, Hubert Parry and Charles Villiers Stanford, succeeded to some extent in reviving British music and raising the standards of performance. In London, orchestral concerts could be heard in St

James's Hall and the Albert Hall, with pride of place taken by the Philharmonic Society concerts. Manchester has the distinction of being able to boast the first professional symphony orchestra in Britain, known as Mr Hallé's Band, after its founder, Charles Hallé, who was, ironically, a German. Giving its first concert in 1858, the Hallé Orchestra, as it soon became known, made only a tiny profit at the end of its first season. But Hallé was determined that 'the whole musical education of the public had to be undertaken', and gradually audiences grew until his eighth season brought a handsome profit of £2,000. The lowest-priced seats in the Free Trade Hall were cheap enough to enable working-class music lovers as well as the middle classes to enjoy music by Beethoven, Mozart, Haydn, Mendelssohn, Wagner, Berlioz and eventually the music of the man considered by many to be the greatest British composer of all time – Edward Elgar. So successful was Hallé as a conductor of both orchestral and choral music that in 1888 he was knighted by Queen Victoria. Sadly, the rates of pay for professional musicians remained low, and it was difficult for them to find regular employment. The writer and music critic, George Bernard Shaw complained in 1889 that music was the worst-funded of all the arts. He blamed the aristocracy, because, he claimed, music lacked 'constant and enlightened patronage such as the upper classes accord to racing, millinery, confectionary, and in a minor degree to literature and painting'.

12.10 the position and role of women in Victorian society

In the middle of the nineteenth century, all classes of British women were in many ways treated as second-class citizens. It was thought that women were naturally more caring and less aggressive than men, and that therefore the roles of the two sexes were intended to be different; their responsibilities should lie in 'separate spheres'.

A woman's place was meant to be in the home, acting as 'the angel of the house', being a good wife and mother, doing her best to make life as smooth as possible for her husband, whose function was to bring home the money to support his family. Marriage was considered to be the ideal state for women: statistics show that in 1850, out of every thousand girls aged 15, no fewer than 859 could expect to have been married at least once by the time they reached 50. Women who did not marry, for whatever reason, particularly those of the upper and middle classes, were thought to have failed. Society showed great concern for these 'unfortunate' souls, who might well find themselves in financial difficulties in later life without a husband to provide for them. Nor were they expected to marry outside their own social class. In her 1849 novel, *Shirley*, Charlotte Brontë bemoaned the lot of the single woman: while her brothers were occupied in business or the professions, the unfortunate single woman had 'no earthly employment, but household work and sewing; no earthly pleasure but an unprofitable visiting; and no hope, in all their life to come, of anything better'. It was a prime concern of most parents with young daughters to see to it that they made 'a good marriage'.

Unfortunately, marriage brought with it certain problems:

> When a woman married, all her money and possessions became the property of her husband. A wife had no legal identity as a separate person from her husband.
> If the marriage failed, the husband was legally entitled to keep the children, even if he was responsible for the breakdown and was unsuitable to be caring for children.
> Divorce was only allowed by special Acts of Parliament which were extremely expensive and affordable only by the wealthiest couples. A man could divorce his wife or turn her out, but because she had no legal identity it was almost impossible for a woman to secure a divorce. In 1848, when a Mrs Dawson petitioned the House of Lords for a divorce on the grounds that her husband had beaten her with a riding whip and was an adulterer, it was ridiculed by the all-male peers and thrown out.
> The 1857 Divorce Act introduced a new system (excluding Ireland) by which divorce could be obtained via the courts, but this still cost £100 – much too expensive for the working class. Even then the act was biased in favour of men: they could sue for divorce merely on grounds of adultery, whereas wives could only do so if the husband had been guilty of bestiality, bigamy, incest, rape or cruelty as well.
> Husbands could not always be relied on to hand over their wages to their wives; Friday evenings were a crucial time: immediately after men had received their weekly pay packet, the temptation to spend much of it in the pub on the way home was often irresistible. Drunkenness and wife-beating were common, and there was little protection from the law for wives and children.

Even if a marriage was a happy one, lack of contraception meant that the lives of the majority of married women were dedicated to the bearing and bringing up of children. Pregnancy and birth were especially difficult and dangerous times. Yet even with the high child mortality rate, families tended to be large. G. E. Searle quotes the example of George Lyttelton, a friend of Gladstone, who, between 1840 and 1857, fathered twelve children. His unfortunate wife became so exhausted that she died giving birth to the twelfth child. The Reverend S. Baring-Gould, author of the hymn *Onward Christian Soldiers,* was even more prolific, fathering no fewer than sixteen children (and often having difficulty remembering their names). During the 1840s it was normal for families to have around seven surviving children; anything less than this would have been regarded as a 'small' family. For most working-class women, living in less than ideal conditions and on low incomes, trying to bring up children successfully must have been a constant struggle. Not surprisingly, abortion was fairly common – it was reasonably cheap but dangerous.

Women were not expected to go out to work or to follow professional careers; they were not allowed to take degrees at universities, and they were barred from professions such as medicine, law and accountancy. Nor could they become magistrates, sit on juries, vote in elections or become MPs. Women who did work were paid less than a man doing the same job. One of the justifications put forward by men for this exclusion of women was that women, by their nature, were too emotional to be able to take rational decisions in areas such as medicine, the law and politics. It was all to do with their 'poorly times' which, so it was claimed, rendered them semi-hysterical. As Theo Hoppen explains:

> Most young girls found themselves quite unprepared for menstruation, for which a dictionary of euphemisms was employed: the 'curse', the 'poorly time', the 'relations', the 'dipe', the 'antics', and so forth. Menstruation continued to be used as an argument against female involvement in education, sport and politics, and in favour of female inferiority generally. Not until the 1870s did more positive interpretations begin to be canvassed, though these at first affected only a very small number of women indeed.

A new development in the 1860s that outraged the growing feminist movement was the introduction of *the Contagious Diseases Acts,* the first one in 1864. This was an attempt to apply the continental system of regulated prostitution to British army garrison towns and seaports, in order to control the spread of venereal diseases, especially syphilis, for which there was no cure at the time. The Acts permitted the police to arrest any woman found loitering within a certain radius of a garrison area; she would be treated as a common prostitute and forced to undergo a medical examination.

As A. N. Wilson points out:

> It was taken for granted that British soldiers and sailors needed prostitutes. It now became enshrined in British law that women were a source of contamination. No attempt was made to regulate the spread of the disease by, for example, penalising the men who tried to pay for sex. The women … were 'fallen' women. Their sin was much greater than the man's … In the context of the 1860s the CD Acts were not, by most, seen as an issue of sexual politics so much as of public health … but the abuses caused by the Acts, and the debates which led to their repeal, worked as a powerful stimulus to the Women's Movement.

12.11 Victorian women at work

In spite of the 'separate spheres' concept, the fact remains that many women in Victorian times did go out to work. Working-class women who had not found a husband, for whatever reason, often had no choice but to try to earn their own living. Many married women with large families and a husband who was unemployed, or on short time or earning low wages, felt the need to supplement the household income, since there was no unemployment benefit or social security. The 1851 census revealed that 34.6 per cent of British women (numbering 2.8 million) were in paid work. This proportion remained fairly steady throughout the rest of the century, though the increase in population meant that the actual number of employed women increased considerably, reaching 4.8 million in 1901, whereas 10.2 million did not work outside the home.

In 1851, well over half of employed women – numbering about a million – were described as 'in service'; that is, servants working as maids, chambermaids and cooks in the houses of the upper classes and many of the wealthier middle classes. By 1871 the number had risen to almost 1.5 million. The spread of industrialization brought new job opportunities for women; the second-largest group of employed women were the textile workers of Lancashire and Yorkshire, who numbered some 358,000 in 1841, rising to just over 800,000 in 1911. Women worked as spinners and weavers in the cotton mills, though the better-paid jobs such as tacklers and overlookers were reserved for men. A much smaller number of women worked in the Sheffield and Birmingham cutlery industries, in the finishing and polishing processes. As in the pre-industrial era, large numbers of women worked as dressmakers and tailors. Many women continued to work in agriculture – around a quarter of a million, according to the 1851 census; however, by 1881, this figure had fallen sharply to about 80,000, following the great migration to the towns in the second half of the century.

Married women who went out to work were often criticized on the grounds that they were neglecting their families, and some people blamed the high child mortality on these 'negligent' mothers. However, most recent historians believe there is little evidence that the homes of mothers who went out to earn money were any worse than the rest; in fact, they were likely to be better, since there was more money available. The appallingly high child mortality rate that continued right through the century was more likely to have been caused by the shortage of money and food, and by the generally unhealthy environment. Some women did paid work at home, such as sewing and glove-making; others took in washing, or perhaps a lodger. Very few women could aspire to more elevated jobs, though some educated middle-class women were able to work as governesses and teachers. One occupation that *was* open to any educated woman was to become a writer. Boyd Hilton points out the remarkable fact that, apart from Sir Walter Scott, nearly all the best-selling novelists of the early nineteenth century were women: Maria Edgeworth, Elizabeth Hamilton, Amelia Opie and Mary Shelley (the daughter of Mary Wollstonecraft – see below), who published *Frankenstein* in 1818. The best-known was Jane Austen, followed later by the Brontë sisters and Elizabeth Gaskell. But these were very much the exception: in most occupations and activities where women were in competition with men, it was only very gradually, and after much campaigning, that they began to make progress towards equal rights with men.

12.12 the campaign to improve the status of women

In the early days of the movement for women's rights, a few outstanding individuals led the way. In 1792, *Mary Wollstonecraft (1759–97)*, who had lived in Paris during the French Revolution and who was much in sympathy with the revolutionaries, published *A Vindication of the Rights of Woman.* In it she claimed that the education provided for girls was deliberately designed to be lightweight and frivolous. She argued that if girls and boys were given the same education, young women would be better wives and mothers, and would be able to use their abilities in many professions. This would avoid much wastage of talent and therefore bring benefit to the whole of society. Why should woman be no more than man's 'rattle and toy'? She also advocated free state education for everybody. These ideas were too advanced for the time, but they had considerable influence in the 1840s, when interest in feminism was increasing.

Another remarkable woman who made a vital contribution to feminist ideas was *Elizabeth Fry (1780–1845),* a Quaker and the wife of a wealthy London merchant. She made prison reform her special interest, travelling throughout Britain and parts of Europe inspecting and comparing prison conditions and writing reports and recommendations. She was particularly horrified by the treatment of women in London's Newgate Prison, and recommended that the sexes should be separated, that women should be looked after by female warders, and that they should receive some education while in prison. Her ideas received a sympathetic hearing from the Home Secretary, Sir Robert Peel, and the result was the Jails Act of 1823 (see Section 2.6(c)).

Caroline Norton (1808–77), a grand-daughter of the famous playwright, Richard Brinsley Sheridan, and a friend of Lord Melbourne, began a campaign to secure legal protection for married women. Her marriage to the Honourable George Norton had been a failure – they were ill-matched and he beat her. After three years she left him and he retaliated by forbidding her all access to their three children. As the law stood at the time, she had no way of challenging his decision, unless the law were to be changed. Since she was a published poet and novelist and had sympathetic friends in Parliament, she was able to get *the Infant Custody Bill* introduced, which eventually became law in 1839. It was a very mild measure by modern standards, but it did allow a judge, in cases where a mother had not been guilty of adultery, to grant her custody of any children under seven and rights of access at certain times to older children. Caroline Norton entered the fray again in 1855 when the

Divorce Bill was being debated in Parliament. Her husband was refusing to pay her allowance and was demanding the royalties from her books. She mounted a determined campaign, including sending a moving letter to Queen Victoria explaining the situation; her efforts were instrumental in securing some important extensions of women's rights when the Bill finally became law in 1857: a woman who left her husband, on reasonable grounds, could keep some of her own property and have full possession of any future earnings and income, including inheritances. And now, for the first time, a married woman was given the right to sue and to make contracts in her own right. There was still a long way to go before married women were fully protected, but this was an encouraging beginning.

Probably the best-known of these trail-blazing women was *Florence Nightingale (1820–1910)*. From a wealthy background, she was educated by her father, and went to Germany to be trained as a nurse. In 1853 she became superintendent of the Institution for the Care of Sick Gentlewomen in London, where she soon made a name for herself as a reformer and improver. During the Crimean War (see Section 10.2(d)) she was put in charge of nursing in the military hospitals, where she and her team of trained nurses were able to improve the filthy conditions and inadequate facilities, in spite of opposition from the doctors and administrators, who resented taking orders from a woman. However, her work was fully reported by the war correspondents in the Crimea, and by the time she returned home in 1856 she was a national heroine, with enormous prestige. She devoted herself to improving conditions in the British army as well as the training of nurses. She had several long meetings with Queen Victoria to explain what she saw as her mission. In 1860 she founded a school for nurses, based at St Thomas's Hospital in London. She worked tirelessly to improve conditions for women in workhouses, and was partly responsible for the introduction of trained nurses and midwives into workhouse hospitals.

At about the same time, another pioneering woman, *Elizabeth Garrett (1836–1917)*, was conducting her own campaign to enable women to enter the medical profession. She was refused admission to medical schools in Britain but studied privately with several sympathetic physicians and in the Middlesex Hospital, where she had to cope with the hostility of the male students. She was eventually awarded a degree in Paris and was allowed to work as a doctor in Britain in 1865. She was the first woman to be admitted to the British Medical Association. Her efforts helped towards the foundation of the London School of Medicine for Women in 1874.

By this time, the movement for women's rights was gaining momentum, helped by a number of publications such as the *English Women's Journal* founded by Barbara Leigh Smith in 1858. The campaign also gained support from some men, notably John Stuart Mill (1806–73), whose book *Subjection of Women* (1869) was a plea that men should stop treating women as slaves, and that society should give them equal rights. So far, however, it had been mainly a middle-class and upper-class movement. These pioneering women had all received a 'modern' education rather than the usual 'frivolous' instruction that was thought to be sufficient for young ladies. Clearly, what was needed were schools to educate girls to the same standards as boys. *Frances Mary Buss* founded the North London Collegiate School for Ladies in 1850, and in 1858 *Dorothea Beale* became principal of the new Cheltenham Ladies' College, where she introduced a 'modern' curriculum that included mathematics and science. By the end of the century there were around 12,000 girls' schools in England alone, though they were all private and therefore not available for working-class girls.

Progress soon carried through into higher education: London University led the way by allowing women to take degrees in 1878; this was followed by Owen's College in Manchester, soon to become the Victoria University of Manchester, where Christabel Pankhurst gained a first-class law degree in 1906. In the early 1870s, two women's colleges – Girton and Newnham – were opened in Cambridge, while in 1879 Oxford followed suit, with Somerville College and Lady Margaret Hall. However, women were not actually allowed to take degrees at Oxford until 1920, and almost unbelievably, it was 1948 before they could take degrees at Cambridge!

Further important milestones were:

> The legal status of women was further improved by *the Married Women's Property Act* of 1882, which allowed a woman to continue as the separate owner of her property when she married.
> *The Guardianship of Children Act* (1886) allowed a mother to claim custody of her children if her marriage broke up.
> Largely through the efforts of Josephine Butler, the much-hated Contagious Diseases Acts were repealed in 1886.
> Some progress was made towards securing women's political rights. By 1869, women who owned a house, and were therefore ratepayers, had gained the right to vote in local elections; in 1888, this same small group of women were allowed to vote for the new county and borough councils; and in 1894, both married and unmarried women were given the right to vote for the new urban and rural district councils and could stand for election to these councils.

Yet strangely, after all these successes, the feminist movement seemed to get becalmed, and further progress, particularly in the political sphere, was slow in coming. The most striking injustice was that women were still not allowed to vote in general elections, and it was not until after the First World War in 1918 that the vote was extended, and then only to women aged over 30 (see Section 21.4).

Looking back from our standpoint in the twenty-first century, it is difficult to appreciate just how important religion was in the daily lives of the vast majority of ordinary people in nineteenth-century Britain. It is perhaps even more difficult to understand the intensity of feelings generated by the disputes between adherents of the different religious beliefs, sometimes leading to demonstrations, riots, hatred, violence and death. The remnant of the long-running Protestant–Roman Catholic feud in Ireland still lingers on as a reminder of the troubled past.

In 1800, Britain was an overwhelmingly Christian country, apart from substantial Jewish communities in the large cities. Church attendance was high, but though all the churches were Christian, there were several different groups, known as denominations, each with different beliefs, rituals, styles of worship and ideas about the way a Christian life should be led. There were the Protestant Anglicans, known in England as the Church of England, in Scotland as the Episcopalian Church, and in Ireland as the Church of Ireland. Other Protestant groups were the Methodists, Presbyterians, Baptists, Congregationalist and Unitarians; these were all known as Dissenters and later as Nonconformists, because they refused to conform to the Anglican Church. The third main grouping was the Roman Catholic Church. These religious groups all had one thing in common: in a time of great social and economic change, they fulfilled people's needs by providing them with spiritual support and with membership of a stable and reliable community – at least that was the ideal. As well as Sunday worship, churches provided ceremonies at each stage of life – baptisms, marriages and funerals; they provided moral guidance as well as social events and other activities.

The *Anglican Church* was (and still is in England) recognized as the official state church and is known as the Established Church. The reigning monarch is the head, or Supreme governor of the Church of England, which came into existence in the sixteenth century when Henry VIII broke away from the universal Roman Catholic Church and its head, the Pope. Anglicans and other non-Catholics are known as Protestants because they protested against the practices of the Roman Catholic Church. The Church of England was governed by a hierarchy of archbishops, bishops and archdeacons; it had great influence in politics, since twenty-six of the bishops had seats in the House of Lords. The government controlled the appointment of church leaders and could therefore choose bishops who were sympathetic to their policies. Only members of the Anglican Church could hold important positions in the state and on town corporations; Oxford and Cambridge Universities did not admit non-Anglicans. This privileged position caused great resentment among Nonconformists, who campaigned to get the Anglican Church disestablished, so that it would no longer be the state church. This was achieved in Ireland in 1869, when the Church of Ireland was disestablished, and in Wales in 1920.

Many observers believed that the Anglican Church was in decline in the early nineteenth century, as Nonconformist groups such as Methodists and Baptists grew in strength. However, the fact that it was the state church enabled it to maintain its power and influence. Most Tories were Anglicans because the church opposed radical change – it condemned the French revolutionaries; it opposed parliamentary reform and, later, trade unions; and the prospect of Catholic emancipation roused it to fury. Not for nothing did the Anglican Church earn itself the label 'the Tory party at prayer'. In fact, however, there were different parties within the Church:

- *The Low Church party* took a detached view and tried to avoid confrontation. In the words of B. G. Worrall, 'they had little patience with, or understanding of, religious fervour and ... saw the Church almost as a department of state concerned with morality. Clergy were seen as models and teachers of polite manners, not as mediators between God and man ... fitted more to be observers of theological controversy than participants'.
- *The Evangelicals* were the largest and most influential group. According to the *Oxford Dictionary*, Evangelicals are 'Protestants who hold that the essence of the Gospel consists in the doctrine of salvation by faith in the atoning death of Christ, and deny the saving efficacy of good works.' There had been an evangelical revival in the eighteenth century, in which John Wesley had been a leading participant. They believed in a more emotional response to the teaching of the Gospels, relying on the Holy Spirit for guidance. They took their religion very seriously, living a life of humility, prayer and service to others; they saw it as their duty to maintain Christian principles in public life. Their leaders were mainly rich and influential, and included William Wilberforce (1759–1833) and Zachary Macauley (1768–1838), who were MPs and members of a group called the Clapham Sect. Lord Shaftesbury was an Anglican Evangelical. It was their Evangelical fervour that led Wilberforce to campaign for the abolition of the slave trade and slavery; and Shaftesbury to devote himself to improving working conditions for women and children.
- *The High Church party* was the smallest group. Although they accepted the connection between the Anglican Church and the state, they were not happy when they felt that the government was interfering too much in the Church's affairs (see below 12.15(b)). According to B. G. Worrall, they were 'inclined to stress the Church's spiritual role ... They saw its orders of bishops, priests and deacons as essential to its true life. The sacraments, especially the Eucharist, administered by a priest in apostolic succession, were central to Christian discipleship ... When the time came, they provided the strength for the Oxford Movement'.

The Methodists originated in Oxford in the late 1720s and gradually spread throughout the country, becoming particularly strong in England. The two leading lights of the movement were John Wesley, an Anglican curate, and his younger brother Charles, a student at the University. They formed what they called a Holy Club with the aim of getting back to basics by studying the Greek New Testament. By 1738, John Wesley had become convinced that salvation depended on faith in Jesus Christ alone, and that it was possible for people to achieve something approaching perfection in this life, provided that they did their best to live a moral life. He was also convinced that it was his duty to carry this assurance to others. He advocated that people should read the Bible themselves at home instead of merely having it read to them in church. Methodists preached a strict social and moral code: sexual misbehaviour, the drinking of alcohol and the pursuit of cruel sports such as cock-fighting were all condemned; the goal should be to keep oneself 'unspotted from the world' and to live a life of service to others. This was much too strong a brew for many people, and the early Methodists had to suffer abuse and violence; Wesley's sermons were frequently interrupted and many parish clergy refused to let him preach from their pulpits. Eventually, he took to preaching in the open air, and in spite of Methodism's unpopularity in some quarters, he was able to attract huge audiences. The first Methodist chapel was built in Bristol in 1739. In spite of growing tensions with the Anglican authorities, the Methodists officially stayed as a party within the Anglican Church until John Wesley's death in 1791 at the great age of 88.

After his death, Methodists found themselves increasingly at odds with the Anglican Church. They came to believe that the Anglicans were failing in the Christian mission to minister to the poor and needy, and that, as a state church, they were too subservient to the government. They also criticized the hierarchical structure of the Anglican Church, since they themselves believed in individual freedom in matters of religion. All this forced them into becoming a Nonconformist Church in which the worship and life of its members was centred on the local chapel, where ordinary people took part in the leadership and conducted services. Methodism was the most highly organized of the 'Free Churches', as the Nonconformist groups became known. There was a central Conference which appointed ministers to groups of churches known as circuits. Ministers usually moved on after three years and were assisted by local preachers. Some Methodists considered this control to be too autocratic, and several groups broke away, including the Independent Methodists in 1811. Methodism, and Nonconformism in general, tended to be a mainly middle-class movement that attracted the new business and industrial people. Whereas the Anglican Church was strongly Tory/Conservative, Nonconformists were likely to have Whig or Liberal sympathies. The Independent Methodists, who did not believe in ministers and whose services were taken by ordinary lay people, were strong among urban workers.

The oldest of the dissenting churches were Congregationalists, Baptists and Presbyterians, dating back to the sixteenth century, when they were known collectively as Puritans.

- *Congregationalists* believed in the individual autonomy of each separate congregation. Oliver Cromwell (1599–1658) was a Congregationalist; when he was Lord Protector (1653–8) the Congregationalists enjoyed a certain amount of political power, and Cromwell extended religious toleration. However, after the monarchy was restored in 1660, severe restrictions were imposed on all Dissenters, and these were still in operation at the beginning of the nineteenth century.
- *Baptists* believed that all true professing Christians should be baptized by complete immersion in water as a symbolic cleansing from sin. On the whole they did not approve of infant baptism because they felt that the person being baptized must be able to understand what was happening to them. During the nineteenth century the number of Baptists grew rapidly and they played an enthusiastic part in the campaigns to secure complete equality with the Anglican Church. In 1813, the Baptist General Union was formed; its organ-ization was improved and extended in 1863, when it became known as the Baptist Union of England and Wales. Baptists were strong believers in missionary work abroad: India, the West Indies, the Cameroons, the Congo and even China were all areas in which Baptist missionaries worked to spread the teachings of Christianity.
- *Presbyterians* had a system of local churches governed by presbyters or elders; these churches were grouped into areas each governed by a presbytery – an assembly of ministers and an elder from each individual church; this was a kind of ecclesiastical court above the normal group of elders or kirk-session. They did not have a hierarchy of archbishops and bishops like the Anglican Church, believing that all elders were of equal rank. Presbyterians were numerous in Scotland, but in England many of them had become Unitarians.
- *Unitarians* were different from all the other Protestant denominations in that they did not accept the Trinity – the belief that God consisted of three parts: the Father, the Son (Jesus) and the Holy Spirit. For them, God was a single unitary personality, and therefore Jesus, though he was a great prophet and teacher, was not divine. Nor did they go along with some other parts of accepted doctrine, such as the need for salvation and redemption, and the idea of eternal punishment in hell for unrepentant sinners. They believed in a God of love rather than justice, and they tended to be more relaxed than the other Nonconformists in their attitudes towards austere chapels and 'moral' behaviour. As Boyd Hilton points out: 'Unitarian chapels became increas-ingly ornate, with fine three-decker pulpits and brass candelabra, while danc-ing, cards, theatre, even 'lust of the flesh' were condoned in moderation.' Unitarianism reached a peak of influence in the 1820s; it was popular among

the business classes and had large followings in commercial centres such as Manchester, Hull, Birmingham, Leeds, Liverpool and in the capital itself. They ran their own schools, which were some of the first to teach science and modern languages. Many MPs and doctors were Unitarians.

The Roman Catholic Church in England was at a low ebb at the beginning of the nineteenth century; it was confined to just a few aristocratic families and to Irish labourers; estimates put its numbers at around 100,000. However, there was a rapid increase during the first half of the century, thanks to the immigration of Irish labourers; the total reached perhaps 750,000 by 1851. Roman Catholics recognized the Pope as their head and held the doctrine of *transubstantiation*: this was the belief that during the Communion or Eucharist, though the bread and wine remains the same in appearance, it actually changes into the body and blood of Jesus. Anglicans and Lutherans, on the other hand, do not accept transubstantiation; Lutherans believe in *consubstantiation:* that the body and blood of Jesus co-exist in the bread and wine; while Anglicans consider that the bread and wine symbolize the body and blood of Jesus.

Roman Catholicism was seen as an alien force that posed a threat to the nation's security and freedom. As B. G. Worrall explains: 'This view was fuelled by a collection of myths based on partially understood, or quite misunderstood, theological objections to the authority of the Pope, the doctrine of transubstantiation, the role of priests in Roman Catholic life and the attitude to saints and relics in Roman Catholic devotion ... it was feared as pseudo-magical and despised as superstitious and sinister.'

Roman Catholics were excluded from all public life; when a new monarch took the Coronation Oath, one of the promises made was a pledge to preserve the Protestant religion.

12.14 religion and politics in England and Ireland, 1820–46

In 1800, the Act of Union brought England and Ireland together under the control of the Westminster Parliament, and the Irish lost their own parliament. They had agreed to this on the understanding that Roman Catholics, who made up almost 90 per cent of the Irish population, would be granted full political and civil rights, always referred to as 'Catholic Emancipation'. However, George III refused to sanction it, claiming that it would break the promise to safeguard the Protestant religion that he had made at his Coronation. Understandably, the Irish Catholics felt cheated and embittered, and Daniel O'Connell spearheaded the campaign for emancipation as a first step towards the eventual repeal of the Act of Union. The struggle revealed how bitter Protestant feelings were against Catholics, and it helped to cause a surge of support for the Church of England. Matters reached a climax in 1828–9:

- In 1828, the Tory government *repealed the Test and Corporation Acts,* which had prevented Nonconformists and Catholics from holding important posts in the state and in town corporations. However, for many years, Nonconformists had been enabled to ignore the restrictions by annual government acts of indemnity, but now it was official and legal. But the exclusions had been strictly applied against Catholics, and their hopes of emancipation were dashed when it emerged that the Lords had actually thrown out the clause that would have removed their restrictions.
- As tensions rose, Wellington and Peel agreed to grant full Catholic Emancipation in 1829, in order to avoid civil war in Ireland (see Section 2.7(b)). This outraged the government's Protestant supporters and split the Tory party, which was out of office for most of the next dozen years.

Religious affairs continued to cause problems between England and Ireland even after the achievement of Catholic Emancipation. The fact remained that, while over 90 per cent of the Irish population were Roman Catholics, the state church was still the Anglican Church of Ireland. Catholics had to pay tithes (a tax amounting to one-tenth of annual produce) to the state church to help pay the stipends of state church ministers. Yet in some areas there were literally no state church members. Irish Catholics demanded the abolition of tithes, and some groups resorted to maiming and branding cattle so that they could not be sold. Many people refused to pay tithes; there were numerous violent incidents and several poor Irish farmers were shot and killed by the local yeomanry. In 1833, the Whig government passed a Coercion Act, which enabled order to be restored. Yet the Prime Minister, Grey, acknowledged that some changes were needed:

- Later in 1833, he introduced *the Irish Temporalities Bill,* which proposed to reduce the number of Church of Ireland bishops and dioceses by ten, and to make do with fewer ministers; the money saved (known as 'surplus revenues') would be used to fund various educational and social projects. This apparently modest measure prompted more outraged protests from Anglicans, Tories and even some of the Whigs, partly because O'Connell wanted the 'surplus revenues' to be used to pay the salaries of Catholic priests. Anglicans were determined that church revenues must be used to maintain the Anglican Church, and nothing else; using it to pay Catholic priests was total anathema to them. The unfortunate Whig government found itself hamstrung by Irish church affairs, and in 1834 Grey resigned. Admittedly, he was over 70, but there is no doubt that he was exasperated by the wrangling over his bill in the Cabinet – the 'surplus revenues' clause had been deleted from the bill, and when Russell tried to bring it back, four Cabinet members resigned.
- As part of their general reform programme, the Whigs brought in *the Marriage Act (1836),* which recognized marriages in Nonconformist chapels

and Roman Catholic churches as legal, provided that a civil registrar was present.

▸ Also in 1836, Russell's government passed *the Tithe Commutation Act,* in a further attempt to placate Irish opinion. The tithe now became a money payment instead of a payment in kind, and was to be only three-quarters of its nominal value. All arrears of tithe payments were cancelled. While this was an improvement, O'Connell and his supporters were bitterly disappointed – they were still having to pay for the upkeep of the state church and would be satisfied with nothing less than the total abolition of tithes.

During Sir Robert Peel's Conservative Ministry (1841–6) O'Connell and his Roman Catholic supporters stepped up the campaign for the repeal of the Act of Union. But there was no way that the Conservatives could even contemplate such a move, so strong was the anti-Catholic feeling in England. Peel nevertheless tried to make some concessions, including increased state funding for the Roman Catholic Maynooth College. However, this succeeded only in upsetting Anglicans as well as Nonconformists, and in dividing the Conservative party (see Section 7.4 for full details).

12.15 Anglicanism: crisis and revival

During the early years of the nineteenth century, the Anglican Church in Britain passed through a period of crisis. Attendances at Anglican services seemed to be falling, while Nonconformist chapels and Roman Catholic churches were flourishing and expanding their congregations. Anglicans came under sustained attack from all these rival denominations and from radicals in general. It was clear that Anglicanism did have many faults and weaknesses that needed to be addressed, and during the 1830s and 1840s both Whig and Conservative governments tried to reform the Church. Nor did the Anglicans themselves sit around waiting for the government to improve things; at the same time there was an Anglican revival spearheaded by the Evangelical wing of the Church. One of its most striking forms was the Oxford Movement, which developed in the 1830s. The result of all this activity was a distinct strengthening of the Anglican Church, though at the same time some aspects of the revival, particularly the Oxford Movement, were extremely controversial.

(a) why did the Anglican Church face such strong opposition?

▸ All the other religious denominations and groups opposed it because of its privileged position as the Established Church, and the fact that as Nonconformists, they were excluded from so many posts as well as from the Universities of Oxford and Cambridge. Progress was made towards dealing with some of their grievances in 1828, when the government *repealed the Test and Corporation Acts.* However, this still left the problem of church rates. All property-owners, whether they were Anglicans or not, had to pay annual rates for the upkeep of Anglican churches, and this was bitterly resented by non-Anglicans. *A Church Rate Abolition Society* was formed and several Nonconformist leaders were sent to gaol for encouraging their flocks to refuse to pay the church rates. However, all attempts to find a compromise solution during the 1830s failed, and this intensified demands for the Anglican Church to be disestablished. The struggle dragged on until Gladstone finally abolished church rates in 1868.

› Many people felt that the Anglicans were failing to respond adequately to the new social and economic conditions resulting from the Industrial Revolution. In the new industrial towns with their overcrowded populations it was the Nonconformists and the Roman Catholics who were ministering successfully to the spiritual and sometimes to the social needs of the working classes. In the words of E. J. Evans:

> the Church of England was overstocked with clergymen in the wrong places. Its urban ministry, stronger in 1830 than in 1800, nevertheless remained outmatched by the nonconformists. Too many of its incumbents did not live in their parishes. Too much of its enormous wealth was enjoyed by a tiny handful of opulent clerical princes while curates and vicars had to make do with incomes which were plainly inadequate.

› Another cause for complaint was that many incumbents had charge of more than one parish (this was known as 'plurality'), and it was reported that in 1835 only about half the parishes had a vicar who actually lived in the parish. One reason for this was that many wealthy landowners had the right to appoint vicars to the parishes on their estates. For example, the Marquis of Bath appointed his own son as vicar of three churches that he controlled. This practice (known as 'nepotism') of appointing close family members as incumbents was very common. E. J. Evans quotes the example of Baron Wodehouse of Kimberley: 'Five of the eight Norfolk livings within his gift were bestowed on his sons, and one more on another relative.' These practices obviously raised questions about the suitability of such men for the priesthood, and cast grave doubts about the value of their ministry.

› Many opposed Anglicanism for political reasons, because of the close alliance between Anglicans and the Tory party. They had shown themselves to be the enemies of reform; they had opposed the French Revolution, Catholic Emancipation and parliamentary reform; and they had defended the church rate doggedly. There were many examples of local clergy supporting the aristocratic landowner against the working class. In 1834, when six farm-labourers of Tolpuddle in Dorset were sentenced to seven years' transportation to Australia for allegedly trying to form a trade union, the local Anglican vicar endorsed the court's verdict, as did Lord Melbourne, the Prime Minister (see Section 19.2 for full details).

In spite of all the criticisms and attacks and calls for disestablishment, the Church of England had strong support in many quarters and it maintained much of its power and influence right through the nineteenth century. Its alliance with the Tory party, particularly the High Tories or Ultras, was one of its great strengths; together they stood shoulder to shoulder to preserve the traditional establishment. The landed aristocracy had great vested interests to defend within the Church. As well as the twenty-six Anglican bishops in the House of Lords, many other MPs and peers were Anglicans. Protestants in general saw the Church of England as the best defence against Roman Catholicism, considered to be a 'sinister force', from which the British had been fortunate to escape in the sixteenth century. In the middle years of the nineteenth century, when the Catholic Church in England seemed to be on the offensive, there was a surge of support for Anglicanism. The Universities of Oxford and Cambridge were staffed by Anglicans, and the Church controlled most of the public schools.

(b) government attempts to reform the Anglican Church

Both the leading Whigs, and progressive Tories such as Peel, accepted that unless some attempt was made to eliminate at least some of the worst failings of the Church of England, demands for its disestablishment would become more insistent. We have already seen how the Tories repealed the Test and Corporation Acts (1828) and granted Catholic Emancipation (1829). This was seen by non-Anglicans as just the beginning, but whenever governments tried to go further, they faced determined opposition from Anglicans and reactionary Tory Ultras.

▸ In 1834, the Whig government produced a plan to replace the detested church rate for the upkeep of Anglican churches with a money grant paid out of the land tax. The Tories supported this idea and on this occasion it was the Nonconformists themselves who objected. Their argument was that they would still be contributing to the maintenance of alien churches from the taxes that they had paid. The Whigs, who depended for much of their support on Nonconformist votes, dropped the idea.

▸ It was Peel's short-lived Tory government (it lasted just under four months) that took the bull by the horns and set up *the Ecclesiastical Duties and Revenues Commission* (February 1835). Peel had been careful to get the support of church leaders first, and the Commission included both archbishops, three leading bishops and some leading politicians. Their aims were far-reaching: to get rid of plurality and non-residence, to even-out clergy incomes and make sure that they were all adequately paid, to modernize the church organization and structure, and to build more churches, especially in the industrial towns. Their achievements were considerable; between 1836 and 1840 a series of new laws was passed: they included *the Established*

Church Act, The Pluralities Act, the Ecclesiastical Duties and Revenues Act, and the Tithes Commutation Act (see Section 12.14 for details of this Act). This legislation succeeded in removing the worst of the church's failings and abuses, and put it in reasonably good order. Between 1836 and 1888, eight new dioceses were formed; some, such as Manchester (1847), Liverpool (1880), Newcastle (1882) and Wakefield (1888) were to meet the demands of expanding industrial areas. As the improvements gradually gained recognition, opposition subsided, and after 1868, when Gladstone abolished church rates, there were very few demands for disestablishment.

▸ The other great achievement of the Commission was to set in motion a programme of building new Anglican churches. As E. J. Evans explains, between 1831 and 1851 their efforts 'managed the impressive feat of more than matching the rate of population growth in the major industrial areas of England. In this period the number of Anglican churches in Lancashire increased from 292 to 521 and in the West Riding of Yorkshire from 287 to 556. In the whole country 2,029 new churches were built'. And the church building spree continued for much of the century. Most of them were built with money provided by the church itself or by wealthy supporters, rather than by state funding. One striking example occurred in the new industrial town of Barrow-in-Furness, where, in 1878, four new Anglican churches were opened, costing a total of £24,000, half of which was provided by the Duke of Devonshire.

(c) the Anglican revival and the Oxford Movement

The revival in the Church of England really began in the late eighteenth century, with the so-called *Evangelical Revival*. This was not confined to Anglicans and in fact many Dissenters too were inspired by Evangelical ideas. As noted earlier, they believed in salvation by faith in the atoning death of Jesus Christ – good works alone were not enough! Nevertheless, service to others was an important aspect of a Christian life. They attached great importance to conversion experiences, humility and prayer. They favoured plain worship services, though they were more emotional than Low Church Anglicans, who felt that showing too much emotion or fervour was in some way suspect.

The revival received a great boost in the 1830s and 1840s from *the Oxford Movement,* also known as *Tractarianism* because over the years its members published a series of ninety pamphlets or tracts setting out their ideas. The movement's leaders, all tutors at Oriel College, Oxford, included John Henry Newman, John Keble and Edward Pusey, who was Regius Professor of Hebrew in the University. They had become increasingly concerned at what they saw as the growing liberalism of the Anglican leadership and the way it had weakly allowed the Test and Corporation Act repeal to pass through Parliament in 1829. In 1833, Keble delivered a controversial sermon criticizing the Whig government's *Irish Temporalities Bill*, which was designed, among other things, to abolish ten Irish bishoprics (see Section 12.14). He was supported enthusi-astically by many High Church and Evangelical Anglicans, who saw this as an unacceptable interference by the state in church affairs; in addition, it was yet another weak surrender to religious liberalism, which both groups detested. Liberals in the religious sense were those theologians who were influenced by the growth of biblical criticism on the Continent, which encouraged close study of the scriptures and opened up the possibility of different interpretations. It encouraged the view that any opinion is as good as any other, and that there can be no absolute truth in the scriptures or the teachings of the Church. This, of course, was anathema to High Church and Evangelical Anglicans because it was a threat to their own dogmatic teachings.

The incident that well and truly launched the Oxford Movement came in 1836 when a theological liberal, R. D. Hampden, was nominated as the next Regius Professor of Divinity at Oxford. The alliance of High Churchmen and Evangelicals went on the offensive to get the appointment cancelled; they objected both to his liberality and to the fact that the state had been involved in the appointment. But it was all to no avail – Hampden remained professor and the Tractarians had been made to look mean-spirited. Then, in 1841, Newman caused another controversy when his Tract No. 90 was published. In it he seemed to be saying that the Thirty-Nine Articles (the Church of England's official list of doctrinal beliefs) were not anti-Catholic, and could even be interpreted as supporting the doctrine of transubstantiation. This upset many of Newman's fellow Anglicans who took it as an attack on the Protestant nature of the Church of England; it also contributed towards a split between the Tractarians and the Evangelicals.

Church of England leaders and the University authorities now began to move against the Tractarians. Pusey was banned from preaching in the University after delivering a sermon in which he too appeared to favour transubstantiation (1843). Some bishops claimed that the Oxford Movement was a deliberate attempt to subvert the Church of England from the inside. According to Boyd Hilton, 'it is true that many Tractarians *were* destructive, demanding tolerance and understanding for themselves, but rarely willing to extend those qualities to others'. To be fair to Newman, he had tried his best to remain an Anglican and genuinely wanted to purify and stimulate the Church of England from within. This is why the Movement opposed state interference and the Ecclesiastical Commission – the clergy should be left in freedom, independent of the state, to put things in order in their own way. Eventually, in October 1845, Newman came to the conclusion that he had no alternative but to become a Roman Catholic; over the next fifty years, some 500 Anglican clergy followed his exam-ple. However, Keble and Pusey remained High Church Anglicans. Strictly speak-ing, this was the end of the original Oxford Movement.

One of the innovations that had appeared during Newman's final years in the Church of England was greater emphasis on ceremonial in the services.

Hymn-singing, choirs, organs, more regular communions and congregational responses became the norm in many parish churches. A minority of churches experienced the phenomenon of 'ritualism', a distinctly Anglo-Catholic development and a by-product of the Oxford Movement. This involved the use of altar candles, incense and bells during the Eucharist; the clergy wore coloured stoles or vestments over their white surplices; many people seemed to like ornate services and ornate church buildings with stained glass windows. However, others felt that it smacked too much of 'Popery', and this fuelled the traditional anti-Catholic prejudice. Ritualism became highly controversial: its critics staged protests that sometimes led to violence and even riots. There were two violent confrontations in Exeter, in 1845 and 1848; in 1850–1 mobs burst into St Barnabas, Pimlico, protesting against what they called 'Romish goings-on'. Queen Victoria felt that the ritualists were far too Catholic, and reportedly remarked that the Catholics 'are dreadfully aggressive people who must be put down – just like our Ritualists'.

When Disraeli became Prime Minister in 1874, perhaps wanting to please his beloved Queen, he was responsible for the *Public Worship Regulation Act*, which banned some of the most objectionable rituals such as the wearing of vestments and the use of water to dilute the communion wine in the chalice. Unbelievably, five priests were actually given jail sentences for failing to comply with the new law; one of them, S. F. Green of Miles Platting, Manchester, was kept in prison for over eighteen months. Many felt that this was an over-reaction, and some bishops began to step in to prevent prosecutions going ahead. The fact was that ritualism was becoming popular, particularly in urban parishes, and though it probably spread to no more than 15 per cent of Anglican churches by the end of the nineteenth century, it was certainly not eliminated and survives to this day.

(d) effects of the Oxford Movement

Assessments of the impact of the Oxford Movement on the religious life of the nation are inevitably coloured by historians' own religious views, or lack of them. Critics see them as exemplifying everything that was wrong with Anglicanism: they were reactionary, doctrinally illiberal, and appealed only to the highly educated. Its most lasting effect was to split the Church irrevocably between High and Low Anglicans, and to encourage too many different viewpoints, which only confused people. It failed to rise to the challenges posed by a rapidly changing Victorian society, and had nothing to offer the industrial working class.

On the other hand, it is possible to present a much more sympathetic assessment:

› They genuinely wanted to revitalize the Church of England, which certainly needed it. Their first great contribution was to bring about a revival of religious and theological discussion and debate, and a re-examination of what did comprise Anglican doctrine. They made the Church of England wake up and start putting its house in order instead of waiting for the state to do it for them.

▸ Some commentators have claimed that the new ritualism in services attracted working people in urban centres. A. N. Wilson claims that 'the churches where these rituals were practised tended to be the poorer parishes. Clergy who laid on incense-drowned and candle-lit ceremonials brought colour and mystery into the lives of people who had nothing'.

▸ The Movement had a profound effect on the clergy. In the words of B. G. Worrall, it 'clearly set before the clergy a pattern of spiritual and moral commitment more searching than they had known for several generations. Many learned to take their priestly role as mediators between God and man far more seriously than had become the custom'.

▸ On the whole, the pastoral care provided by priests was carried out more conscientiously and successfully than for many years. There is plenty of anecdotal evidence to show that clergy influenced by Tractarianism dedicated themselves to working in poverty-stricken areas. Men like Charles Lowder, vicar of the slum parish of St Peter's, Wapping, and Lincoln Wainwright (educated at Marlborough and Wadham College, Oxford) who became his curate in 1873, remaining there for fifty-six years, lived among their poor parishioners and devoted their lives to helping them. Wainwright used to say: 'One cannot understand poverty unless one knows what it is to be poor'. High churchmen of this calibre, whether ritualist or not, were not primarily concerned with theological debate: their mission was to bring Christianity to the poor. Scott Holland, himself an Anglican priest, quoted in *The Church Times* in 1987, said that the Ritualist movement was 'the recovery in the slums by the Oxford movement of what it had lost in the university … It wore poverty as a cloak and lived the life of the suffering and the destitute … Nothing could hold it. It won in spite of all that could be done by authorities in high places, or by rabid Protestant mobs, to drive it under'.

▸ Another by-product of the Oxford Movement was the founding of several religious orders living in communities. Some of these, such as Park Village West in London, were for women. Members of these communities did charity work and also worked as nurses and teachers among the poorest people.

(e) F. D. Maurice and Christian Socialism

Although the Tractarians and ritualists did impressive work in the slums, they rarely criticized the society that permitted the existence of such problems, or suggested any alternative way of organizing society. All the Churches were steeped in what became known as 'Victorian values' – the belief in self-help, hard work, cleanliness and temperance; drink was seen as the great evil, hence the constant campaign for moderation and abstinence. F. D. Maurice (1805–72) was the first Christian leader in the nineteenth century to put forward an alternative – *Christian Socialism.* The son of a Unitarian minister, he became an Anglican and was appointed Professor of History and Theology at King's College, London. He was converted to socialism following the 1848 revolutions in Europe, particularly by the attempt to form communes. His supporters included Charles Kingsley and Thomas Hughes (author of *Tom Brown's Schooldays*). Their aim was to publicize the appalling conditions of the working-class and to show the workers, particularly the Chartists, that at least some Anglicans sympathized with their difficulties and their programme. They produced a series of *Tracts on Christian Socialism* in which they suggested that low wages and unemployment were caused by the *laissez-faire* capitalist system, which focused too much on profit and competition. Their solution was to set up workers' co-operatives: by 1850, they had already set up associations of tailors, shoemakers, bakers and needlewomen. Maurice and his supporters organized themselves into the *Society for Promoting Working Men's Associations.* Using biblical texts that criticized the rich and advocated justice for the poor, they preached sermons explaining that society is a body made up of many members, all of which should work together and not compete; justice, not self-interest, should be the guiding principle.

This aroused considerable opposition among the more traditional Anglicans, and it didn't help matters when, after a few years, all the co-operatives failed, probably because they were operating on too small a scale. Maurice was sacked from his professorship at King's College, though he was soon appointed Principal of a new Working Men's College that opened in 1854. It seemed as though Christian Socialism had been a failure, but in fact it turned out to be only the first phase of the movement. In the words of B. G. Worrall, there were some successes that should not be overlooked:

> They had drawn attention to the needs of working men and had aroused a sense of responsibility and compassion in many churchmen. They had given working men some vision of what they could achieve and they had given an impetus to the co-operative movement … They had assisted, and continued to assist the developing Trade Union movement. Perhaps their greatest achievement, though least measurable, was the vision they gave to others. It is remarkable how many Christians who later became leaders of various movements of social concern looked back, directly or indirectly, to the influence of Maurice.

(f) the 'Papal Aggression' and Nonconformist developments

While the Anglicans were experiencing all the excitement of the Oxford Movement and ritualism, the other denominations were not exactly standing still. In 1850, sensational events took place in the Roman Catholic Church when Pope Pius IX re-introduced in England and Wales a similar hierarchical structure to that of the Anglicans. The problem for the Roman Catholic Church was how to cope with the large numbers of Irish Catholic immigrants without a proper system of parishes, dioceses and bishops to organize an effective pastoral ministry for its mainly working-class flock. While this was a reasonable enough step, it provoked a hostile reaction from Anglicans and Nonconformists, which showed how unpopular Roman Catholicism still was with the majority of British people outside Ireland. *The Times* labelled it *'The Papal Aggression'.* Lord John Russell, the Prime Minister, called the Pope's action 'insolent and insidious'. Anti-Catholic riots broke out in Liverpool and Birkenhead in November 1851; over the next twenty years, anti-Catholic speakers toured the country trying to stir up violent attacks on Catholics.

On the whole, Wales remained calm, since there were relatively few Catholics living there. But in mainly Presbyterian Scotland the great fear was that their turn to have a Catholic hierarchy would be next, particularly as many Irish Catholics had moved into the industrial area stretching eastwards from the Clyde through Glasgow and across to Edinburgh. One of the leading anti-Catholic lecturers, John Sayers Orr, who called himself 'Archangel Gabriel', toured these areas delivering inflammatory harangues. After one of his performances at Greenock, the local Catholic chapel was ransacked by a mob. After speaking in Edinburgh and Dundee with similar results, he reappeared in Liverpool. What exacerbated the situation in Scotland was that many of the Irish immigrants were Presbyterians, who brought the Orange Order with them. Gradually a climate of Orange versus Green developed in Scotland, and there were frequent riots. One of the worst occurred in 1875, when a pitched battle took place between the two, and it was several days before the police could restore order. In 1878, the Pope restored the Catholic hierarchy in Scotland, more or less guaranteeing that the feud between Orange and Green would continue into the twentieth century.

In spite of all its problems, the Catholic Church was extremely successful at ministering to its flock, the vast majority of whom were working-class Irish immigrants. Living in an often hostile environment, they found church membership and attendance a great comfort and support. Robert Blatchford, a leading socialist, believed that Catholic priests were 'the most devoted and unselfish of all clergymen'. According to Theo Hoppen, 'working-class Catholics certainly felt more at home in their religion than did many of their Protestant counterparts – less alienated, more integrated. Their priests responded with affections at once autocratic and relaxed'.

Alongside the controversial 'Catholic Aggression' came some important developments among Nonconformists. *Revivalism* was a popular mid-century phenomenon that originated among the Methodists and involved powerful preaching and songs, often accompanied by apparently uncontrolled excitement, weeping, trances and dramatic conversion experiences. One strand of revivalism originated in the USA, and many Americans carried out preaching tours in Britain. Perhaps the most famous and most powerful British revivalist was the Baptist, Charles Spurgeon, who attracted huge crowds in London during the 1850s to hear him preach. He could fill theatres and music halls, and eventually in 1861 a group of wealthy supporters built a new chapel especially for him near the Elephant and Castle in London – the Metropolitan Tabernacle, which could hold 5,000 people. All denominations had their revivalist wing, and their style of worship attracted people from across the social spectrum; for a time there was a remarkable increase in church and Sunday School attendance.

One of the most striking offshoots of revivalism was *the Salvation Army*, founded by William and Catherine Booth during the early 1870s. Booth believed in 'active Christianity' – if people refused to come to church, he would go out and speak to them where they were, in the pubs, music-halls, theatres and on the streets. Using brass bands, military terms and uniforms, parades and rousing sermons, the Army tried to take the message of Christianity to the poorest members of society. He used reformed drunks and criminals and redeemed prostitutes to talk about their sins and explain how they had benefited from their repentance and conversion. This drew huge crowds, and within twenty years the General, as he styled himself, could boast that his 'army' had 3,000 'corps' and 10,000 full-time 'officers'. The Salvation Army was one of the few organizations in which women played an equal role with men. Catherine Booth was already an outstanding Methodist preacher when the Army was formed.

The Army provoked ridicule in many quarters, and Booth himself was dismissed as an absurd fanatic. Sometimes their open-air meetings and parades were attacked by drunken mobs paid by the brewers. According to Theo Hoppen, 'the Army's impact upon slums can easily be exaggerated'. However, others would not entirely agree: Roy Hattersley sees Booth as one of England's great social reformers as well as one of the world's greatest revivalist preachers, and feels that he is continually underrated. By 1890, when his book *In Darkest England and the Way Out* appeared,

> part of his plan for redemption by hard work had already been put into practice. The Salvation Army had run workshops, cheap food stores, women's refuges and workmen's shelters for years … He found thousands of jobs for the unemployed and, over the years, millions of beds for homeless and unemployed workers. Salvation Army vans still distribute tea and sandwiches under the London bridges where the sight of sleeping beggars so offended William Booth a hundred years ago … William and Catherine Booth represented much of what was best in nineteenth-century Britain. They deserve a place in the pantheon of Great Victorians.

QUESTIONS

1 Robert Lowe, Liberal Head of the Education Department from 1859 until 1865, said in 1867: 'You have placed the government of this country in the hands of the masses and you must therefore give them an education.' In the light of this statement:

(a) Why did it take so long for the state in Britain to introduce a satisfactory system of elementary education?

(b) To what extent can Forster's Education Act of 1870 be seen as a turning point in the provision of elementary education?

2 Why were Whig politicians determined to change the system of poor relief in the 1830s, and how successful were their attempts?

3 Why did the Anglican Church attract so much opposition during the 1820s and 1830s, and how successfully did it deal with this opposition?

4 Why and in what ways have historians disagreed about the effects of industrialization on the living standards of the working classes between 1780 and 1830?

A document question dealing with the case for factory reform can be found on the accompanying website www.palgrave.com/masterseries/lowe1.

chapter 13

Gladstone's first ministry, 1868–74

summary of events

Following the Second Reform Act (1867), the Liberals won the 1868 general election (see Section 8.6(b)), taking 387 seats to the Conservatives' 271. The Conservatives had failed to receive the hoped-for reward for introducing the Reform Act. William Ewart Gladstone became Prime Minister for the first time (December 1868), taking over from his great Conservative rival, Benjamin Disraeli, whose first government had lasted only since February 1868. During the late 1860s and the 1870s, the confusion in British politics, which had lasted since the Conservative party split in 1846, resolved itself. Politics became a well-defined struggle between two more-or-less united parties – Liberals and Conservatives – who alternated in government until the Liberals split in 1886 over the question of Irish Home Rule.

Parliament was dominated by the two party leaders, Gladstone and Disraeli. They came from vastly different backgrounds – Gladstone was the son of a wealthy Liverpool merchant of Scottish ancestry, and Disraeli the son of a comfortably-off Jewish writer and novelist whose family had come to England from Italy. Both were brilliant speakers and debaters, and they heartily detested each other, losing no opportunity to attack each other's policies, sometimes with thrilling oratory. Disraeli once described Gladstone as 'a sophisticated rhetorician, inebriated with the exuberance of his own verbosity', and later, more directly, as 'that unprincipled maniac'. Gladstone had something to say about Disraeli's principles too: 'his doctrine is false, but the man is more false than the doctrine'. It was a real 'duel of the giants', which lasted for almost twenty years. As historian M. R. D. Foot put it: 'To the popular imagination, in the days before the entertainment industries had distracted so much attention from politics, Disraeli and Gladstone appeared a pair of Titans, locked in colossal combat.'

Gladstone's career in politics

1832	Enters Parliament as Tory MP for Newark, aged 22
1843–5	President of the Board of Trade under Peel
1846	Supports Peel over repeal of Corn Laws; remains a Peelite
1852–5	Chancellor of the Exchequer in Aberdeen's coalition
1859–66	Chancellor of the Exchequer in Palmerston's and Russell's Liberal governments
1868–74	**His first ministry** – Gladstone Liberal Prime Minister
1875	Resigns party leadership after Liberal election defeat
1879	His Midlothian Campaign
1880–5	**His second ministry**– Gladstone Liberal leader and Prime Minister, after great election victory
1886 (Jan)	**Forms third ministry**
1886 (June)	Irish Home Rule Bill defeated; Liberal party splits and Gladstone resigns
1892–4	**Gladstone's fourth ministry**
1893	Lords reject second Home Rule Bill
1894	Gladstone resigns as Prime Minister
1898	Death of Gladstone

Whatever Disraeli thought about Gladstone's principles, or lack of them, Gladstone now had his chance in this first ministry, to put into practice what he saw as the principles of Liberalism. There was a rush of long-overdue reforms, which so dismayed Queen Victoria that she referred to Gladstone as 'that half-mad firebrand'. Much of his time was taken up with his largely unsuccessful attempts to solve the problems of Ireland. As so often happens when a government introduces radical changes, so many different people had been offended by the reforms and were looking for revenge that the Liberals were soundly beaten in the 1874 election, and the Conservatives were back in power with a majority for the first time in almost thirty years.

13.1 what were Gladstone's principles and aims?

(a) a committed Christian

Gladstone was deeply religious, and for a time when he was a young man, he thought of becoming an Anglican priest. Throughout his career, politics and religion were closely related, and his policies were often dictated by what he thought was morally right. He saw politics as a means of carrying out God's will. One critic remarked that he did not object to Gladstone always having the ace of trumps up his sleeve, but only to his claim that God had put it there.

During his years as a Tory, he believed that the Anglican Church, as the official (established) state church, had an important part to play in directing the moral life of the nation, and that its special position and privileges must be defended at all costs. However, while he himself remained a committed Anglican, his attitude gradually softened, and he was prepared to be tolerant towards Nonconformists and Roman Catholics. He even came to accept that in Ireland, where the vast majority of people were Roman Catholics, it was unreasonable to have a state church that was Anglican. Not all historians accept that religion *was* Gladstone's great driving motive: A. B. Cooke and John Vincent argue that political expediency usually came first, especially with regard to his Irish policy, which he saw as a way of pleasing all shades of Liberal opinion.

Illus. **13.1 William Ewart Gladstone**

(b) equality of opportunity

He believed that the government should try to make sure that everybody had 'equality of opportunity'. He was determined, as he put it, to 'liberate' people from outdated restrictions, and he aimed to abolish special privileges which he considered unjust, wherever they existed, whether in the army, the Civil Service, the universities or in religious matters. He once declared 'all the world over, I will back the masses against the classes'. As Graham Goodlad explains, 'his dominance was built on a special relationship with the lower-middle and working-class people who made up the rank and file of Liberalism. To them the 'Grand Old Man' was a heroic figure'. On the other hand, he did not exactly enthuse about upward social mobility. In 1875, he told a large gathering of artisans in Greenwich: 'Be not eager to raise your children out of the working class but be desirous that they should remain in that class and elevate the work of it.'

(c) free trade and laissez-faire

Gladstone was committed to the principles of free trade and *laissez-faire*, and the idea that free enterprise was the best way to encourage economic growth and prosperity. However, this did not mean that the state had no role to play – he believed that the state had a duty to foster the Benthamite virtues of efficiency and economy, even though the two might be contradictory. According to his biographer, Philip Magnus, Gladstone 'loathed waste because he regarded all money as a trust committed by God to man'. One of his favourite words was 'retrenchment', which meant cutting back on government expenditure, and keeping taxation low – hence his determination to abolish income tax.

(d) lukewarm on social reform

Oddly enough his religious beliefs did not convince him of the necessity of practical social reform to improve working and living conditions and public health. Apart from the expense involved, too much government help might destroy the moral fibre of the nation. It was for individuals to make the best of their circumstances. 'The best thing the government can do for the people,' he once remarked, 'is to help them to help themselves.' The 1872 Public Health Act was Gladstone's only reform to improve actual material conditions, and that was not a success.

(e) peace and tranquillity in foreign policy

In foreign affairs, Gladstone's religious views led him to favour a policy of peace and tranquillity, and to respect the rights of other countries. This was in great contrast to Lord Palmerston's methods of conducting overseas affairs, which Gladstone saw as being far too aggressive (as well as too expensive). However, there was a risk that foreign governments might interpret Gladstone's methods as a sign of weakness, though he did protect Britain's interests in Egypt and the Sudan during his second ministry.

(f) a desire to pacify Ireland

Gladstone had a burning desire, which became almost an obsession during his later ministries, to find solutions to the problems of Ireland. It was here that Gladstone was at his most radical, and where some of his solutions did attempt to help the poor and the exploited.

(g) build up support for the Liberals

Gladstone aimed to win support for the Liberals among the prosperous working classes (who had been given the vote in the 1867 Reform Act) and the religious Nonconformists. He deliberately aimed to make himself into a 'populist' leader, making full use of all the available publicity. He toured the country, addressed mass meetings, especially in industrial areas, and won over many of the leading newspaper editors, so he always got plenty of favourable press coverage. This was seen at its most successful in his Midlothian Campaign in 1879: incredible as it seems today, there were occasions when up to 5,000 working men stood for two or three hours in the open air listening to Gladstone speak. And it was this apparent commitment to ordinary people that won him support and goes a long way towards explaining the big Liberal election victories of 1868 and 1880.

(h) hold the Liberal party together

Gladstone's relationship with the Liberal party was never straightforward. It is important to remember that he began his political career in 1832 as a Tory, and opposed nearly all the Whig reforms of the 1830s.When the Conservatives split over Peel's repeal of the Corn Laws in 1846, Gladstone supported Peel and remained a Peelite for many years. He only really committed himself to the Liberal party in 1859, when Palmerston persuaded him to become Chancellor of the Exchequer. Despite having been a Liberal for over thirty years when he retired in 1894, Gladstone never quite succeeded in breaking away from some of his early Tory principles, and many of the Liberals never fully understood Gladstone or his motives. The party was a difficult coalition of several different groups that didn't see eye to eye: aristocratic Whig landowners, Benthamite radicals, Nonconformists and Anglicans; they had also split over the need for further parliamentary reform in 1866 (see Section 8.5). Gladstone was constantly on the lookout for some cause that would unite the different factions; this was probably one of the reasons why he disestablished the Anglican Church in Ireland (see Section 13.3 below).

13.2 Gladstone's domestic reforms: necessary but unpopular

Every one of the Liberal reforms succeeded in upsetting at least one influential group of people, and sometimes more, but Gladstone pressed on in spite of all protests, fortified by the belief that he was carrying out God's will.

(a) Forster's Education Act (1870)

By the late 1860s it was clear that the patchwork of elementary schools provided by the religious voluntary societies was totally unable to cope with the rapidly increasing population. The Forster Act was a creditable attempt to 'fill the gaps' and 'cover the country with good schools'; there could never be 'equality of opportunity' unless the whole population had the benefit of elementary education. Equally important in Gladstone's eyes was that education would enable the working classes to read the scriptures for themselves. However, the Act aroused tremendous opposition from the Nonconformists (for full details see Section 12.8(c)).

(b) the University Tests Act (1871)

This was a clear case of Gladstone removing a glaring injustice and promoting equality of opportunity in the universities. Action was needed because there was an ancient statute still in operation which allowed only Anglicans to become teachers or members of the administration, or to hold fellowships at Oxford and Cambridge Universities.

The new Act abolished this special privilege of the Church of England and threw these posts open to all suitable candidates, whatever their religion. Nonconformists were pleased, but not enough to make them drop their opposition to the Education Act. Many of Gladstone's fellow Anglicans acknowledged that it was a just reform, but others resented their loss of privilege; Lord Salisbury, the future Conservative Prime Minister, led a bitter but unsuccessful attack on the bill in the House of Lords. In practice, however, there was no really dramatic change in the teaching or the social exclusiveness of the Oxbridge colleges before the First World War.

(c) Civil Service reform (1871)

The problem with the Civil Service was that appointments were still made according to recommendations from an MP or a peer. It depended on who the aspiring candidate knew and what strings he could pull, and even sometimes how much he could afford to pay for the post. Inevitably, many of the men appointed in this way were lazy or incompetent. As the administration of the country became more complex, a more efficient Civil Service was needed.

Gladstone, with the strong support of his Chancellor of the Exchequer, Robert Lowe, another efficiency fanatic, introduced the principle that recruitment must be by examination. This was a first-rate reform, which opened up the Civil Service to the best brains in the country, and its efficiency and professionalism increased accordingly. But it took time. Many of the aristocracy, who had previously dominated the Civil Service, were bitterly opposed; in fact, the Foreign Office had to be excluded from the reform because Gladstone's own Foreign Secretary, Lord Granville, flatly refused to agree to it for his department. The Home Office managed to delay its implementation for three years, and even then it was 1880 before the first open entrants were admitted.

(d) trade union reform (1871)

The legal position, privileges and powers of trade unions had never been precisely defined; the Liberals came up with two measures, both in 1871, to clarify this state of affairs:

- *The Trade Union Act* recognized unions as legal bodies with rights to own property and funds, to protect their property and funds at law, and to strike. Trade unionists greeted the Act with delight, but almost immediately this turned to disgust at the second measure.
- *The Criminal Law Amendment Act.* This stated that although unions could organize strikes, picketing of all types, even peaceful, was forbidden. In practice, it would be impossible to make a strike effective.

Some historians believe that this Act was Gladstone's most serious miscalculation in home affairs, since it lost it him much working-class support. His religious views probably explain his attitude: he was utterly against the use of any kind of force to sway opinion, and picketing could easily lead to violence.

(e) the Public Health Act of 1872

This was a half-hearted attempt to deal with Britain's chaotic health problems. It was a great disappointment to those who were looking to the government for positive leadership and a large-scale injection of cash. Gladstone was not sufficiently interested, and the people who ran the local boards of health seemed to think that their most important function was to keep expenditure to a minimum. It was a classic example of the Benthamite contradiction – efficiency being sacrificed to economy (see Section 12.6(a)).

(f) the Ballot Act (1872)

Voting in elections was still carried out in public by a show of hands, a system that lent itself to bribery, corruption and intimidation of all kinds. *Gladstone's Act made voting secret,* but while it made elections more orderly affairs, it did not completely remove bribery and corruption: there were still ways of buying votes – free beer in pubs and free transport for voters being the most obvious. It was not until the Corrupt Practices Act (1883), passed during Gladstone's second ministry, that corruption was brought under control.

Although it was a necessary measure leading to more efficient electoral processes, the Ballot Act was highly unpopular with landlords and employers, who could no longer control the way their tenants and workers voted. Lord Hartington, leader of the right-wing Liberals, was one of the most severe critics of the bill.

(g) the Licensing Act (1872)

Widespread drunkenness was one of the most striking features of mid-nineteenth century Britain. Gladstone and his Home Secretary, Henry Bruce, looked on this as a moral issue; they felt that there were too many public houses and that the massive profit made by brewers ought to be controlled. Bruce was forced to tone down the original version of his bill, so fierce was the outcry from the brewers and from supporters of *laissez-faire*, who believed that the bill was a prime example of state interference going too far. The final version was a very mild measure:

▸ It gave magistrates the power to issue licenses for the opening of public houses, so that in areas where it was felt there were already too many, magistrates would be able to close some pubs down.
▸ Pubs must close at midnight in towns and at 11 p.m. in country areas.
▸ The adulteration of beer was forbidden; one of the most common practices was to add salt to the beer, which increased the thirst and therefore sales as well.

Though mild, the Act was highly unpopular with the working classes, and there were a number of near riots when police tried to enforce closing hours. Brewers resented what they saw as an attack on their independence and profits; others disliked the Act because it interfered with personal liberty. The Bishop of Peterborough, attacking the bill in the Lords, voiced his opinion that he would prefer to see 'England free better than England sober.' Some historians believe that the liquor trade became solidly Conservative because of the Licensing Act, which was consequently a major cause of the Liberal defeat in 1874. It certainly gave the Conservatives the chance to present themselves as the defenders of the beer-drinking working man's chief haven of retreat and relaxation – the pub.

(h) the Judicature Act (1873)

The British legal system was in an unbelievable muddle. It had developed piecemeal from medieval times, with new courts being created to meet specific demands. By the nineteenth century, there were seven major courts, including Queen's Bench, Common Pleas and Exchequer, and the legal processes were slow and inefficient. The whole shameful system was immortalized by Charles Dickens in *Bleak House.* Lord Selborne (Gladstone's Lord Chancellor) prepared the successful Act that simplified the situation greatly, uniting the seven courts into one Supreme Court of Judicature.

This was the least controversial of the Liberal reforms, though there were some objections to the clause depriving the House of Lords of its right to act as the final court to which people could appeal if they were dissatisfied with any verdict in a lower court. In 1876, Disraeli's government restored this right.

(i) Edward Cardwell's army reforms

The glaring faults and inefficiencies of the army had been exposed by the Crimean War (1854–6) and the Indian Mutiny (1857). The root cause of the trouble was that the army, like the Civil Service, acquired its officers not on merit, but by the purchase of commissions. Any wealthy young man could buy himself into the officer class, whether he knew anything about military matters or not. For example, a rank of lieutenant-colonel could be bought for between £4,500 and £7,000; the price variations were because commissions were often auctioned to the highest bidder. An officer was free to sell his commission whenever he chose; money, not brains was what counted in the promotion stakes. The Commander-in-Chief was the Duke of Cambridge, a cousin of Queen Victoria, who often referred to him as 'poor George'; this was apparently because he had the reputation of being an expert at making bad situations even worse. He was slow-witted and against all change. For the Liberals, army reform was essential as an attack both on inefficiency and on privilege (the army was considered the natural preserve of the aristocracy). It was made more urgent by Prussian victories over Austria (1866) and France (1870–1), which revealed a new, highly professional and potentially dangerous military power.

Edward Cardwell, the Secretary for War, was responsible for planning the reforms, which were introduced at intervals throughout the ministry:

▶ Troops were withdrawn from Britain's self-governing colonies, which were encouraged to raise their own forces.
▶ Flogging was abolished in peacetime.
▶ The Commander-in-Chief was made subordinate to the Secretary for War.
▶ The purchase of commissions was abolished – selection and promotion of officers was to be on merit.
▶ The different sections of the war department were all combined under one roof in the War Office.
▶ The regiments, which had previously been known only by numbers, were reorganized. Cardwell divided Britain into sixty-nine districts, each with its own county regiment of two linked battalions, one on active service overseas, the other at home in Britain. The new regiments were given the name of their home county (for example, Durhams, Gloucesters).
▶ The length of service was reduced from twelve years overseas followed by a period in the reserves, to six years overseas and six in the reserves. This was a more sensible arrangement, since many men ended up broken in health after twelve years in India.

- The Martini–Henry breech-loading rifle was introduced as the main infantry weapon.

The reforms inevitably aroused a lot of opposition from the aristocracy, whose privileges were being threatened, and who believed that the main qualification for an officer was to be a gentleman and a sportsman rather than a professional. The Duke of Cambridge was suspicious of officers who had been to Staff College; 'Brains!' he said, 'I don't believe in brains!' Faced with this sort of mentality, it was not surprising that Cardwell's bill to abolish the purchase of commissions was defeated in the Lords. It was only when Gladstone showed that he was prepared to bypass the Lords by persuading Queen Victoria to issue a royal warrant to the same effect, that the Lords decided they had better pass the bill. This was quite an achievement by Gladstone, since Victoria herself considered the army reforms 'unwise'.

Cardwell's work was an outstanding success. The more humane and civilized conditions of service encouraged a better type of recruit and made possible a large and efficient reserve (increased from only 3,500 to almost 36,000). The artillery received an extra 5,000 men and 156 large horse-drawn guns (bringing the total to 336). In fact, thanks to Cardwell, Britain had the beginnings of an efficient modern army that made possible successful overseas campaigns such as the one in Egypt in 1882 (see Section 16.2(c)).

On the other hand, *Cardwell would have gone much further if the opposition had been less violent:*

- He failed to create a permanent General Staff of the type already in existence in Prussia and France; this was one of the causes of the disasters in the early part of the Boer War.
- Incredibly, artillery officers preferred to continue using old-fashioned muzzle-loading cannon, even though recent Prussian victories had been achieved with breech-loading artillery.
- He had failed to get rid of the Duke of Cambridge, who continued with his stubborn blocking of all further change until his retirement in 1895.

Though he was one of the most brilliant men in the Liberal party, Cardwell was so exhausted and disillusioned by his long struggle that he retired from active politics in 1874.

13.3 Gladstone and Ireland

(a) Ireland since 1846

The plight of Ireland can probably best be illustrated simply by looking at the population figures: from a peak of 8.2 million in 1841, the population fell dramatically over the next decade to 6.5 in 1851, and continued to fall until, by 1911, the figure was only 4.4 million.

The Irish suffered the utmost miseries during the famines of 1846–8; at least a million people died of starvation and cholera, and in desperation another million emigrated to the USA and Canada. During the 1850s and early 1860s, Ireland slipped from the forefront of the British newspapers, but that did not mean that the basic problems of Irish society had disappeared. The majority of the poverty-stricken Irish were still engaged in a grim struggle for survival. Occasionally, their frustrations broke out in acts of violence against the property of wealthy landlords. British governments responded by ignoring the root causes of the problem and merely sent more troops to hold the Irish down.

A new phase in Irish affairs opened in 1867, when a society known as *the Fenians* (formed in the USA in the 1850s) began operations in Britain. They were pledged to revolution and wanted an Irish republic completely separate from Britain. There were several risings in Ireland in 1867. Manchester was the scene of a violent incident in which a group of Irishmen rescued two Fenians from a prison van; a policeman was killed and three of the rescuers were later hanged. An attempt to free two Fenians from Clerkenwell Gaol in London by blowing a hole in the prison wall with gunpowder went sadly wrong: twelve people were killed and over 100 seriously injured. The Fenians had limited support in Ireland itself, but their activities were important because they helped to convince Gladstone that something must be done to help the Irish. Apart from anything else, he was acutely conscious of the cost of keeping Ireland under control – there were more troops stationed in Ireland than in India.

(b) What were the grievances of the Irish in 1868?

They fell into three main areas – *religious, economic and political*:

1 *The Protestant Church of England (Anglican) was the official state or 'established' Church in Ireland.* However, about 88 per cent of the Irish were Roman Catholics (just over 5.3 million out of a population of 5.8 million, according to the 1861 census). They had to pay tithes (a tax amounting to 10 per cent of their annual income) to the Protestant Church, even though they never attended its services, and since they also had to support their own churches and priests, the burden was heavy.

2 *There was intense poverty,* especially in the west of Ireland, because of the lack of industry and the land situation. Until the Act of Union (1800) there had been a prosperous Irish linen industry, but the Act introduced free trade between Ireland and England, and competition with the more advanced British ruined the Irish linen industry, causing widespread unemployment. Another problem was the partial collapse of the herring fishing industry along the west coast of Ireland, caused by the mysterious disappearance of the herring. These problems forced more and more people to rely on farming, and the Irish economy came to depend very much on agriculture being

organized efficiently. However, most of the land was owned by wealthy Anglo-Irish landlords, many of whom lived in England, leaving agents to manage their property in Ireland. Irish people could only obtain land by renting it from absentee landlords.

As the population grew rapidly during the nineteenth century, demand for land increased and original tenants sub-let part of their holding; sometimes holdings were subdivided several times, so that by 1841, at least half the agricultural land of Ireland consisted of plots of less than five acres. The potato was the staple crop because it was possible to produce enough from one acre to keep a family of eight alive, whereas two acres would be needed to provide wheat for making bread. If tenants improved their holdings (by ditching, fencing or hedging) so that the value was enhanced, landlords would increase rents.

The whole system was uneconomic; many landlords were only interested in profits, and being dissatisfied with their paltry income from rents, took to evicting tenants so that small plots could be consolidated into large farms, on which modern methods of agriculture could be introduced. Between 1860 and 1870 the number of people seeking poor relief almost doubled, and desperate people could only retaliate against evictions by joining secret societies and indulging in acts of violence.

3 *There was a feeling of separateness among the Irish*, who looked on the English as aliens. Many Irish people blamed the English for the decay of their country, which was obviously not regarded as an equal partner in the Union. Such was the English lack of sympathy for the hardships of the Irish, and the lack of understanding of Ireland's problems, that the feeling grew among the Irish that only when they were allowed to manage their own affairs would the country recover and prosper. *The Home Rule League*, formed in 1870 by Isaac Butt, a Protestant barrister, campaigned for a separate Irish parliament in Dublin to look after Irish internal affairs. At this stage the majority of the Irish were not thinking in terms of a complete break with Britain, and would have been happy for the Dublin parliament to be subordinate to Westminster for foreign affairs.

(c) what measures did Gladstone take, and how successful were they?

Gladstone was anxious to solve the religious and land problems, though at this stage he was not interested in Home Rule. He was the first British politician to show a real understanding of Ireland's problems and a genuine desire to do something constructive about them instead of simply holding the Irish down by force. His concern sprang from his religious conviction that all people have certain basic rights of freedom and fair treatment; it seemed to him that, in both religious and economic matters, the Irish were being denied these rights. When the news was brought to Gladstone in 1868 that he was about to be called on to form the next government, he was busy felling a tree on his

Hawarden estate. The story goes that he laid down his axe and announced: 'My mission is to pacify Ireland.' That is not to say that political tactics did not come into it as well; one of his biographers, Edgar Feuchtwanger, points out that when Gladstone introduced his first great Irish reform, the Irish Church bill, 'he was acting largely for tactical political reasons. It was the issue which enabled him to pull the warring factions of the Liberal party together after the split over parliamentary reform'.

Gladstone did not have a great deal of success with his Irish policies, either during his first ministry or later. One of his difficulties was that Irish demands kept changing, becoming step-by-step more extreme; so Gladstone found that each of his concessions came too late and had already been overtaken by events. This was not necessarily the fault of the Irish: in fact, the situation demanded the sort of drastic remedies that Gladstone was not prepared to take. This was not always because he was unwilling; more often than not he had to face deeply entrenched opposition from groups in the British Parliament – such as Anglican bishops and Anglo-Irish landlords – whose interests were threatened.

1 *The Irish Church Act (1869)* disestablished the Anglican Church in Ireland. This meant that, while the church still existed in Ireland, Anglicanism was no longer the official state religion, and Roman Catholics no longer had to pay tithes to it. Much of its property and wealth were taken away and used to improve hospitals, workhouses and schools. There was strenuous opposition to it in the Lords, and the bill only passed after Queen Victoria had intervened.

   The Act was the first major breach in the Union between Ireland and Britain, and was naturally well received by the Catholics. However, its effect on the general situation was slight, since the other grievances still remained. It won Gladstone some popularity with the Roman Catholic Church leaders, but this was later lost by the failure of his attempt to convert Trinity College, Dublin, into a University that could be attended by both Catholics and Protestants (Catholics were refusing to attend the College in its existing form because it was a Protestant institution). However, Catholic leaders wanted their own university, while Protestants objected to Catholics being admitted. In the end, the bill pleased nobody and it was defeated in the Commons (1873).

2 *The First Irish Land Act (1870)* was an attempt to give some sort of protection to tenants:

▸ The courts were to make sure that landlords did not charge exorbitant rents;
▸ Evicted tenants who had improved their holdings were to receive some compensation even if they had been evicted for non-payment of rent.
▸ A scale was introduced showing how much damages people could claim for having been evicted. The amount to be paid varied according to the size of

the holding, but no damages would be paid if tenants had been evicted for failure to pay their rent.

Unfortunately, the Act was an almost total failure. It did not define how high an exorbitant rent was, and so landlords raised rents to ridiculously high levels, which tenants could not possibly afford, and then evicted them for non-payment of rent. The courts, which were intended to protect tenants, almost always supported landlord against tenant. In such cases, though evicted tenants might receive a little compensation if they had improved their plots, they would get nothing on the scale of damages. What the Irish tenants most wanted – security of tenure (that is, to be safe from eviction) – was therefore not provided by the Act.

Why did Gladstone allow such an obviously ineffective measure to be introduced? The main reason was probably opposition in his own Cabinet from Whig landowners such as Clarendon and Argyll, who held strongly to the view that the state should not be able to interfere with the rights of property-owners, who should be free to do exactly as they wanted on their own estates; a more radical bill – for example, one specifying a fair rent and forbidding evictions – would not have passed the House of Lords. The Act, far from solving the land problem, only served to dash expectations and arouse more ill-feeling. Frustration led to further violence and outrage in the countryside.

The situation became so serious that Gladstone introduced a *Coercion Act (1871)* giving the police extra powers of arrest and imprisonment. In spite of his good intentions, Gladstone had been forced back on the old policy of repression. This was a tragedy: if only he could have produced an effective Land Act, all the bitterness might have been taken out of the situation. In that case, as Karl Marx suggested, Ireland might have been more docile than Wales, and the demand for Home Rule would have been limited. On the other hand, the Act did have important long-term effects. As Theo Hoppen points out, 'it can be seen to have heralded the beginnings of the collapse of the landlord class in Ireland'. The 3rd Marquess of Salisbury realized this almost immediately, remarking in the House of Lords in June 1870 that the Irish landlords were now a wounded and enfeebled class.

3 *The demand for Home Rule left Gladstone unmoved during his first ministry,* though he was to change his mind later (see Sections 16.1(e) and 16.8(b)). There was hardly any support for it among English MPs, though nobody could have been more reasonable in his demands and his approach than Isaac Butt. When it became clear that the Irish were making no progress using reasoned arguments and gentle persuasion, Butt was cast aside in favour of more extreme leaders, such as Charles Stewart Parnell, who were prepared to use less gentlemanly tactics.

13.4 how did Gladstone's foreign policies cause him to become unpopular?

Gladstone was hampered in his foreign policies by his desire to protect Britain's interests while at the same time respecting the rights of other nations and avoiding foreign entanglements that might involve Britain in war. He felt that war must be avoided at all costs: Britain's army, even with Cardwell's improvements, was not in the same class as the German professional army. There were also financial considerations: Gladstone had been very critical of Palmerston, whose aggressive overseas policies had been expensive. Unfortunately for the Liberals, these considerations caused Gladstone to follow reasonable and realistic policies, which often appeared weak and spineless, in marked contrast to Palmerston's general approach.

(a) Britain and the Franco-Prussian War (1870–1)

The British government decided to remain neutral in this struggle, which began in July 1870. There was no clear-cut reason why Britain should support one side or the other, and indeed there was no other realistic possibility: the Germans already had nearly half a million troops in the field, whereas Britain, at a pinch, could have managed to get 10,000 across the Channel. However, British interests were involved in the war in two ways:

▸ *There was a danger that Belgium might be invaded,* and it was well known that Napoleon III of France hoped to annex it sooner or later. Britain had traditionally been concerned to make sure that no major power controlled this stretch of European coastline, strategically placed as it was, so close to the British coast and the Thames estuary. In August, Gladstone persuaded both Prussia and France to sign an agreement with Britain, guaranteeing Belgian neutrality. This was seen as a triumph for Gladstone: both countries kept to the agreement, Belgian neutrality was preserved and British interests safeguarded.

▸ After France had suffered crushing defeats at Sedan (September) and Metz (October), *the Russian government, with the support of Bismarck, announced that it no longer considered itself bound by the Black Sea clauses of the 1856 Treaty of Paris* (see Section 10.3): Russia would patrol the Black Sea with its fleet, build bases and fortify the coastline. This destroyed one of the main British advantages gained from the Crimean War and provoked a storm of anti-Russian feeling in Britain. But the Russians had timed their announcement to perfection: with France, Britain's ally in the Crimea, on the verge of collapse, there was very little Britain could do about it. After some diplomatic manoeuvring, a conference of the powers was held in London in January 1871 to review the situation.

Britain suffered a clear diplomatic defeat: it was agreed that the Black Sea clauses be cancelled, though Lord Granville, the British Foreign Minister, saved face to some extent by securing a general agreement that from then on, no government must break parts of a treaty unless all the other signatories agreed. The British government probably did as well as could be expected in the circumstances; A. J. P. Taylor (in *The Struggle for Mastery in Europe*) believed that the Russians signed the general agreement in all good faith and that, because of it, they were prepared to agree to a re-negotiation of the Treaty of San Stefano in 1878 (see Section 14.4(e)). But the British public felt that Gladstone had acted weakly in allowing the Russians to steal a march over Britain – he had let Britain down in a way that Palmerston would never have allowed.

▶ When it emerged at the end of the war that *Bismarck was to take Alsace and Lorraine from France*, Gladstone was prepared to make a strong formal protest to Prussia. However, this time it was the rest of the Cabinet who refused to go along with Gladstone, claiming there was no point in protesting when they were in no position to do anything about it if the protest was ignored. But once again the impression given was one of weakness.

(b) Gladstone and the Alabama case

Since the American Civil War (1861–5), the American government had claimed compensation from Britain for the damage caused by the *Alabama* and other ships built in Britain (see Section 9.5(c)). In 1868, Disraeli's government had expressed Britain's readiness to submit to arbitration, but it was Lord Granville, the Liberal Foreign Minister, who represented Britain at the arbitration conference in Geneva. It was decided that Britain should pay the USA £3.25 million in compensation, a decision which Gladstone accepted in 1872. This was probably the sensible and moral thing to do, but coming after the Black Sea affair, it seemed to confirm the impression that Gladstone lacked backbone. There was a widespread feeling that the amount was unjustifiably high, and that Gladstone should have said so. There is no doubt that the incident contributed to the Liberals' growing unpopularity. One Conservative MP remarked that they showed 'a strange mania for eating dirt'. Shortly afterwards, Gladstone was booed as he entered St Paul's for a thanksgiving service for the recovery of the Prince of Wales from typhoid; when Disraeli arrived, there was tumultuous applause.

13.5 why did the Liberals lose the 1874 general election?

In January 1874, Gladstone decided that the time was ripe for a general election (though the Liberals had lost seven by-elections during 1873 and a total of thirty-two during the life of the government) and Parliament was dissolved. The background to his decision was his long-standing desire to get rid of income tax once and for all. The Chancellor of the Exchequer, Robert Lowe, had reduced the tax from 6d to 4d, but had been made to look inept when extra expenses on military improvements and colonial campaigns forced him to put it back up to 6d again in 1871. Despite succeeding in bringing it down to 3d in the pound by 1873, this was not good enough for Gladstone: he sacked Lowe and took over the Exchequer himself. He decided to go to the country and make the final abolition of income tax the main pledge of his election campaign, confidently assuming that this would be enough to swing the electorate. He was astonished and dismayed at the result: a decisive Conservative victory. The figures were: Conservatives 342, Liberals 251, Irish Home Rulers 59. The latter appeared in Parliament for the first time, because the 1872 Ballot Act made it possible for Irish tenants to vote as they wished without fear of reprisals from landlords. The Liberals were defeated partly because Gladstone's policies had offended so many influential people, and because the Conservatives, for the first time for many years, appeared to offer a realistic alternative to the Liberals.

(a) unpopularity of the Liberal reforms

Many of the Liberal reforms outraged *the upper and wealthy classes,* whose special privileges had been attacked – for example, the Civil Service and army reforms (especially the abolition of the purchase of commissions). Many Anglicans resented the disestablishment of the Irish Church and the University Test Act; some industrialists were annoyed at the legal recognition of trade unions. The Ballot Act was unpopular because it reduced landlords' influence at elections.

The working classes were offended by Gladstone's apparently contradictory behaviour of offering help to the unions with one hand and taking it back with the other, when he made picketing illegal. There was disappointment that the Liberals had introduced so little effective social reform and no further extension of the franchise. Gladstone himself thought that the Licensing Act was the decisive cause of his defeat: 'We have been borne down in a torrent of gin and beer,' he told his brother, though Robert Blake believes that while it may have cost him some votes, it was not the main reason for the defeat.

Nonconformists were still smarting over the Forster Education Act; they vented their disapproval by abstaining rather than by voting Conservative, but it was still damaging, since, traditionally, Nonconformists were the mainstay of Liberal support. And there was widespread dissatisfaction in all classes with Gladstone's handling of foreign affairs. For a combination of reasons, therefore, Gladstone had lost the support of the two big groups – the working classes and the Nonconformists – which had been most responsible for the Liberal victory in 1868.

(b) the Conservatives present a new image

The Conservatives, ably led by Disraeli, had been mounting an effective attack on the government since April 1872, when Disraeli addressed a huge meeting in Manchester's Free Trade Hall. In a blistering speech lasting over three hours, during which he fortified himself with two bottles of white brandy, Disraeli ridiculed the Liberals as 'a range of exhausted volcanoes – not a flame flickers on a single pallid crest'. He went on to give the Conservative party a new image – a party that stood for building up the British Empire and aimed to improve 'the condition of the people'. Disraeli was seeking to cash in on Gladstone's areas of weakness, and his popularity grew appreciably.

During the election itself, the party had the benefit of a highly efficient organization built up by John Gorst and his new Conservative Central Office. Finally, Robert Blake makes the point that many householders who had been enfranchised by the 1867 Reform Act voted for the first time in 1874, and voted Conservative – a belated 'thank you' to Disraeli.

QUESTIONS

1 'I will back the masses against the classes'. How far did Gladstone live up to his promise during his First Ministry of 1868–74?
2 Consider the view that 'Gladstone was more of a liability than an asset to the Liberal party in the period 1865–1894' (see also Chapter 16).

A document question about the Liberal government's foreign policies can be found on the accompanying website www.palgrave.com/masterseries/lowe1.

chapter 14

Disraeli and the Conservatives in power, 1874–80

summary of events

This was the first Conservative government to have real power since the collapse of Peel's ministry in 1846. The Conservatives were now more or less united under Disraeli's leadership and enjoyed a comfortable majority over the Liberals and Irish Home Rulers, who usually voted with the Liberals. The results of the election were: Conservatives 342, Liberals 251, Home Rulers 59.

It was an eventful ministry: Lytton Strachey, in his biography of Queen Victoria, called it 'six years of excitement, of enchantment, of felicity, of glory, of romance'. Disraeli was much more to the Queen's liking than Gladstone; the Liberal leader exhausted her with complicated documents and explanations – she complained that 'he speaks to me as if I were a public meeting'. Disraeli on the other hand was careful to charm and flatter her; 'Everyone likes flattery,' he said, 'and when you come to royalty you should lay it on with a trowel.' In 1876, Disraeli accepted a peerage, taking the title *Earl of Beaconsfield*.

In keeping with his ideas of *'Tory Democracy'* or *'New Conservatism',* the early part of the ministry saw *important social reforms* dealing with housing, public health, factories, education and trade unions. *In overseas affairs* he was determined to restore Britain's prestige, which was felt to have waned under Gladstone. When *the Eastern Question* flared up again, Disraeli took a firm stand against the Russians, culminating in *the Congress of Berlin in 1878;* this was hailed as a great triumph for Britain and a resounding diplomatic defeat for the Russians. He took measures *to defend and strengthen the British Empire*, in Egypt, India, South Africa (Zulu War) and Afghanistan, though in South Africa and Afghanistan it was the British officials on the spot who took the initiative, against Disraeli's wishes.

In the meantime, *all was not well with the British economy:* in the late 1870s, industry ran into a serious depression, while agriculture suffered a near-disaster because of rapidly-growing foreign competition. Even so, most people were surprised when the general election of March 1880 reversed the situation in Parliament, bringing Gladstone and the Liberals back with an overall majority of around fifty. Disraeli took his defeat well, but his health was deteriorating, and he died just over a year later (April 1881).

14.1 Disraeli's earlier career and his political outlook – Tory Democracy

(a) background and earlier career

Benjamin Disraeli was the son of a Jewish writer and scholar whose family had come to England from Venice in the middle of the eighteenth century. The young Disraeli was educated at an obscure private school; he did not go to university, and when he left school, he worked as a solicitor's clerk. He wrote several novels and tried unsuccessfully to get into Parliament – as a Whig. At the fourth attempt he was elected MP for Maidstone (1837), having changed his allegiance to the Tories. He already had a reputation as something of a gambler and a flashy dresser. He had appeared at one society dinner dressed in green velvet trousers, a canary coloured waistcoat, low shoes with silver buckles, lace at his wrists, and his hair in tightly curled ringlets. His maiden speech in Parliament was a disaster: he used such flowery language that he was shouted down with catcalls and shrieks of laughter. He soon improved his technique and was furious when Peel refused to offer him a place in his government in 1841. Perhaps because of this *he led the attack on Peel over the Corn Law repeal in 1846* (see Section 7.5(d)). After that his career ran as follows:

‣ He was Chancellor of the Exchequer in the Conservative governments of 1852, 1858–9 and 1866–8.
‣ He was largely responsible for the 1867 Reform Act (see Section 8.4), though apart from that he achieved nothing of great significance.
‣ He was Prime Minister for a few months in 1868 after Lord Derby's retirement. This in itself was a remarkable achievement, given his unconventional background and the fact that he was viewed as an outsider. Although he had been baptized a Christian (Anglican) at the age of 13, he had to put up with a great deal of anti-Semitic feeling.

It speaks volumes for his brilliance as a politician that, in spite of all his disadvantages, he was able, as he put it, to 'climb to the top of the greasy pole', leader of a party still dominated by wealthy landowners. John Charmley claims that Lord Derby's support for Disraeli was vitally important to his rise: 'Without Derby, Disraeli would have been nothing; on their own, the country gentlemen of England would never have consented to be led by a Jewish literary adventurer; but if he was good enough for Derby, that was sufficient for most Conservatives.'

Illus. **14.1** Benjamin Disraeli

(b) Tory Democracy/New Conservatism

By the time he became Prime Minister for the second time in 1874, Disraeli seemed to have clear ideas about the direction he wanted the Conservative party to take. He spoke about this new approach in two famous speeches he made while in opposition in 1872, one in Manchester and the other at the Crystal Palace; the ideas are sometimes referred to as *Tory Democracy* or *New Conservatism*:

1 He believed that there was value in privilege and tradition, and wanted to preserve the power of the long-established institutions – the Anglican

Church, the aristocracy and, above all, the monarchy. But it was essential that these institutions used their power wisely and unselfishly, for the good of the whole community.

2 It was vitally important for the government and the privileged classes to help working people. In his novel *Sybil* (1845), Disraeli had written that there were really two separate nations living in Britain – the Rich and the Poor; though he had no intention of upsetting the class structure, he believed that something must be done to improve the conditions of the poor. He said so in his Manchester speech in 1872: 'Pure air, pure water, the inspection of unhealthy habitations, the adulteration of food … it is impossible to overrate the importance of the subjects; after all, the first consideration of a Minister should be the health of the people.' This was a paternalistic approach; that is, treating the poor kindly, like a benevolent father looking after his children. It became known as 'one nation Toryism' and was followed by some later Conservative leaders, notably Baldwin, Macmillan and Heath.

3 Disraeli hoped that social reform would lead to an alliance between the privileged classes and the mass of the population, which would strengthen the monarchy and aristocracy; as he remarked revealingly: 'the Palace is unsafe if the cottage is unhappy'.

4 The Conservative party must, in other words, adapt itself and come to terms with the new democratic and industrial age. If it failed to win working-class support, it would be condemned to remain a permanent party of opposition. Disraeli was highly critical of the Liberals because of their attack on privilege and their weak foreign policy. He called them an 'anti-national' party and despised them because they seemed to look after the interests of the middle class at the expense of the workers. This, he said, made them 'odious to the English people'.

5 In the early 1870s, before he became Prime Minister, he made it clear that he intended the Conservative party to commit itself to upholding Britain's power and prestige in the world, including defending and perhaps extending her Empire, so that the British could continue to compete successfully with the great continental empires of the USA, Germany and Russia.

(c) Disraeli's motives have aroused some controversy

The Tory Democracy theory was accepted without question until the 1960s, when some historians began to question Disraeli's motives. Paul Smith was one of the first to point out that, apart from his rather generalized speeches, Disraeli had no specific programme of social reform prepared when he took office; the reforms that were introduced were piecemeal responses to particular problems that happened to come to prominence in the first half of his ministry. The 1876 Merchant Shipping Act, for example, reached the statute book thanks to a campaign organized by a Liberal MP, Samuel Plimsoll. Robert Blake argued that Disraeli was not really interested in the details of social reform, and this is why so much of the work was carried out by Richard Cross, his Home Secretary. According to Blake, 'it is an exaggeration to see in them some concept of paternalistic Tory democracy'. He took up social reform primarily to score points over Gladstone, who neglected it. Political hard-headedness probably did come into it: it was an obvious way to attract and hold on to working-class support.

T. A. Jenkins took the argument a stage further, suggesting that too much has been made of Disraeli's supposed attitude towards imperialism, as well as his Tory Democracy. He suggests that this was 'part of the mythology that developed around Disraeli's memory after his death ... in reality Disraeli's comments about social reform were vague and non-committal, and his criticisms of what he alleged was the Liberals' hostile attitude towards the British empire were entirely negative and did not anticipate a new era of imperial expansion'.

However, it is important not to lose sight of the fact that, whatever Disraeli's motives were, the social reforms themselves were extremely significant. At that time, it was simply not the practice for governments to intervene by introducing extensive social reforms, partly because it would be expensive, and partly because the *laissez-faire* climate reacted strongly against any increase in government control. Given the standards and expectations of the time, Disraeli's social reforms, though limited in scope, were a remarkable achievement. He had talked and written sympathetically about the conditions of the poor as far back as the 1840s; it was not something he had suddenly taken up in 1872 because of Gladstone's failings. As Ian St. John points out, 'Disraeli could have resisted moves to reform and ignored the reports of Royal Commissions. Instead he made time available for reform and championed the process with supportive rhetoric ... he enriched late nineteenth century Conservatism, allowing it to develop policies appealing to the working-class electorate.' The working class had certainly come to expect great things from the Conservatives – in Lancashire, the heart of the new industrial England, the Conservatives won 18 out of the 25 seats in the 1874 general election.

14.2 what did Disraeli's government do for working people?

(a) improvements in public health and living conditions

> *The Public Health Act* and *the Artisans' Dwellings Act*, whose details were worked out by Richard Cross, Disraeli's Home Secretary, were passed in 1875 (see Section 12.6(a)).

> *The Sale of Food and Drugs Act* (also 1875) laid down stringent regulations about the preparation and adulteration of food.

> *The Enclosures Act* (1876) was designed to protect the public's right to use the common pasture land; landowners were restricted from absorbing such land

into their estates, so that it would be kept free from building. Thus the idea of the green belt was born.

› It was made illegal to tip solid industrial waste into rivers (1876) and liquid waste could only be discharged if it was non-poisonous.

All these Acts met with success, though the Artisans' Dwellings Act would have made more impact if it had been compulsory. Even so, as B. H. Abbott points out, 'the legislation of those years laid the foundations of modern public health so thoroughly and lastingly that no major changes were required for over 60 years'.

(b) the Factory Acts of 1874 and 1878

These introduced important new limitations on working hours (see Section 12.4(j)).

(c) labour relations and trade union legislation

1 *The Conspiracy and Protection of Property Act* (1875). Trade unionists had been bitterly disappointed by their treatment at the hands of the Liberals in 1871: despite unions being given legal recognition, picketing, even if peaceful, was not allowed, which meant that it was more-or-less impossible to make a strike effective. This new measure, again introduced by Cross, made peaceful picketing legal and allowed unions to carry out as a group whatever actions an individual was permitted to take, in support of their case; unions could not be charged with conspiracy for taking such action.

2 *The Employers and Workmen Act* (1876), another Cross measure, put both employer and worker on an equal footing in cases of breach of contract. Previously, if a workman broke his contract, it was treated as a criminal offence, whereas if an employer did it, it was regarded only as a civil offence, for which the penalties were much lighter. Now both were treated as civil offences.

These two Acts mark a vitally important breakthrough in the development and recognition of trade unions as acceptable and respectable bodies (see Section 19.3). Union leaders were delighted, and so was Disraeli, who remarked that these laws 'will gain and retain for the Conservatives the lasting affection of the working classes'. In reality, there was still some way to go: most of the existing unions represented skilled workers; it was when semi-skilled and unskilled workers began to organize themselves – the so-called 'New Unionism' of the late 1890s – that further problems developed (see Sections 19.4 and 19.5).

(d) Sandon's Education Act (1876)

This was less effective than it might have been, because it lacked the element of compulsion (see Section 12.8(d)).

(e) the Merchant Shipping Act (1876)

This was passed after a vigorous campaign by its author, Samuel Plimsoll. The problem was that there were no regulations governing the loading and repair of merchant ships. It was not unknown for unscrupulous ship-owners to overload decrepit and over-insured vessels so that they could make a handsome profit if the ships sank. Plimsoll's bill was designed to prevent this scandalous sacrifice of seamen's lives, but the ship-owning interests in Parliament delayed it as long as they could. Plimsoll became so exasperated that he caused a scene in the Commons, literally jumping up and down with rage and shaking his fist at Disraeli. This produced results, and the bill was passed. A line (known as the Plimsoll Line) was to be painted on the side of every ship to show the maximum loading point. However, the ship-owners had the last laugh, for the time being, because the Act allowed *them* to paint the line where they thought fit. Only in 1890 did Board of Trade officials begin to apply the regulations as Plimsoll had intended.

14.3 What is meant by the term 'imperialism', and how successful was Disraeli in pursuing it?

(a) imperialism and the British Empire

Imperialism has existed throughout history, and on many different continents. British imperialism in the nineteenth century was just one in a long succession of systems of imperialism which came and went. Imperialism involves the domination and exploitation of a weaker people by a stronger power. The dominant people, or colonizers, run the territory of the weaker people to suit their own interests, as sources of raw materials or markets; the wishes of the exploited peoples always take second place.

Britain had already had one empire, founded in the early seventeenth century, on the east coast of North America. By the time the Americans broke away from British rule in their war of independence (1775–83), Britain already had a second empire in the making; by the end of the wars with France in 1815, the British controlled a large collection of territories in India, Africa, Australasia and the Caribbean.

Disraeli added a new dimension to the idea of Empire: it should not simply be a case of Britain making use of its overseas possessions; it had a duty to bring the benefits of British civilization – 'courage, discipline, patience, reverence for the public law, and respect for national rights' – to primitive peoples. Kipling later described this duty as 'the white man's burden'. Other European countries acted in the same way. Late-nineteenth-century imperialism therefore carried with it the false assumption that Europeans were racially superior to all other peoples, and the idea that European culture, religion and systems of government should be forced on other peoples, for their own good. Disraeli also had in mind that the Empire could be called on for military help if Britain became involved in a major war.

Later, 'imperialism' became a term of abuse; Gladstone was one of the first critics who claimed that imperialism was not to be encouraged, because it interfered with the rights and freedom of overseas peoples. In addition, it was expensive – a waste of British wealth and manpower; defence of the empire would be a constant strain on Britain's resources. The other major criticism made by historians is that imperialism was motivated by sheer greed – weaker peoples and their resources were exploited simply so that the British (and other Europeans) could make big profits.

However, in a controversial article ('The British Empire', in *History Today*, February 1996), historian Max Beloff put forward a spirited defence of British imperialism, arguing that historians should 'search out the positive factors both in what was attempted and in what was done'. He believed that the profit motive was very much a secondary one: 'there were many easier ways of making money than acting as the overseas representative of the Crown at any level from royal governor to local magistrate'. The real motive, according to Beloff, was the British desire to bring other parts of the world under their rule so that they could be given the benefits of law and order; 'the core of Empire was not profit but governance'. Niall Ferguson also defended British imperialism (in *Empire: How Britain made the Modern World*, published in 2003), claiming that while Britain's record as a colonial power was certainly not unblemished, British rule brought genuine benefits for their peoples.

In fact, Disraeli had no specific plans for pursuing imperialism, but in the early years of his ministry he made excellent use of circumstances. This, together with his successful stand against the Russians at the Congress of Berlin in 1878 (see Section 14.4), coming after six years of Gladstonian 'weakness' in foreign affairs, dazzled the public. Towards the end of his term, however, the imperialist adventures in South Africa and Afghanistan, though they both ended successfully, were badly mishandled along the way.

(b) Disraeli and Egypt: the Suez Canal shares (1875)

▸ The Suez Canal (opened in 1869) was controlled jointly by the French and the Khedive Ismail, the ruler of Egypt. In 1875 the Khedive, who was in serious financial difficulty, decided to sell his shares, which amounted to seven-sixteenths of the total. There was a strong possibility that a French company would buy them, posing the threat of complete French control of the canal, which had already proved itself to be a vital link between Britain and India.

▸ The Khedive was asking for £4 million, which the French company had difficulty in raising. Disraeli seized the opportunity: after securing the approval of the Cabinet, not without difficulty, he stepped in and bought the shares for the British government, using £4 million loaned by the banking house of Rothschilds.

▸ It is difficult to imagine any other politician of the time acting with such flair and panache, and there is no doubt that it was a splendid piece of opportunism –the kind of 'grand gesture' that Disraeli liked so much because it would dazzle the public. While Britain had fewer than half of the shares in the canal, the important point was that France had been prevented from gaining exclusive control, which would have given them great bargaining power over the Khedive; in addition, the shorter trade route to India had been safeguarded. The British were soon able to get the tolls reduced, and the ownership of the shares turned out to be profitable; by 1898 they were valued at over £24 million. The cost of transporting cargo to and from Australia and New Zealand was reduced by 75 per cent. Gladstone was highly critical of the purchase, calling it 'a ruinous and mischievous misdeed'. He believed that it would lead to an eventual British occupation of Egypt, and although Disraeli denied any such intention, Gladstone was later proved to be right (see Section 16.2(c)).

(c) Victoria becomes Empress of India (1876)

This was not Disraeli's idea; it had been discussed on and off since the Mutiny in 1857, and the Queen herself was eager for it. Disraeli was anxious to oblige, and *the Royal Titles Act* duly passed through Parliament, though only after surprisingly strong resistance from both houses. Gladstone called it 'theatrical bombast'. However, there seemed good reasons for Victoria to take the title:

1 It demonstrated that the British had every intention of staying in India, and it was hoped that the new personal link with the Queen would mean more to the Indians than their relationship with an impersonal Parliament.
2 It was a symbolic gesture to warn off the Russians, who were extending their influence into Persia and Afghanistan, and who, it was feared, had designs on India.

(d) South Africa: the Zulu War (1879)

Again, this had not been planned by Disraeli; it was forced upon him by the actions of the men on the spot, and Disraeli was furious when the situation developed into war.

▸ *The background was complicated:* the Cape of Good Hope was originally colonized by Dutch settlers, but as a result of the Congress of Vienna (1815), ownership passed to Britain. Many of the Dutch farmers, known as Boers (or Afrikaners), disliked British rule, and in 1836 many thousands of them left the Cape in what was called *The Great Trek.* They founded two new states of their own: Transvaal and the Orange Free State. The British still claimed sovereignty over them, and for many years, relations between the new Boer republics and the two British colonies – the Cape and Natal – remained strained. Tension eased after the British recognized the independence of the Transvaal (by the Sand River Convention, 1852) and the Free State (by the Convention of Bloemfontein, 1854) (see Map 17.1 on page 311).

• A constant threat to both the British and the Boers was the presence on the Transvaal/Natal border of the large and aggressive Zulu tribe under their king, Cetawayo. The Boers had already had one major clash with the Zulus at Blood River (1838), in which 3,000 Zulus were slaughtered. Cetawayo was eager to avenge this defeat, though he was not unfriendly to the British.

• Disraeli's Colonial Secretary, Lord Carnarvon, who in 1867 had been responsible for uniting the four provinces of Canada into a single federation (see Section 18.1(e)), had similar plans for South Africa. He hoped to bring the Transvaal and the Orange Free State under British control in a union with the Cape and Natal. The snag was that the circumstances in South Africa were completely different from those in Canada: the Boers were hostile to the idea, and the Cape and Natal, where many Boers had remained, were unenthusiastic.

• Carnarvon decided that the Boers, who were also being harassed by another tribe, the Bapedi, as well as by the Zulus, would be glad of British protection. He sent Sir Theophilus Shepstone, an ex-governor of Natal, to the Transvaal to sound the Boers out. He found them extremely nervous about Cetawayo's intentions, and also nearly bankrupt, with only 12s 6d in the treasury. Reluctantly, President Burgers of the Transvaal agreed to a British annexation of the republic (though he was allowed to protest in public); Shepstone promised the Boers self-government later.

• Carnarvon also appointed Sir Bartle Frere as High Commissioner for South Africa, with instructions to set up a federation. Frere was a well-known supporter of expansionist policies and was indignant when he discovered that Shepstone had promised the Boers self-government. He decided that the Zulu threat would have to be removed before a peaceful federation of South Africa could be achieved. Disraeli and the Cabinet did not want a war in South Africa at this time, as they were preoccupied with the situation in the Balkans, and the British were already involved in hostilities in Afghanistan. Frere was given strict instructions not to start a native war, but he deliberately disobeyed orders and took it upon himself to launch an invasion of Zululand (January 1879).

• The beginning of the war was disastrous for the British: the commander, Lord Chelmsford, and his section of the invading army, were surprised by a 20,000-strong Zulu army at Isandlwana. Chelmsford had ignored advice from the Boers to *laager* his wagons (arrange them in a circle), and suffered a crushing defeat, losing over 1,000 men. The same night, a much smaller force, which had *laagered* correctly, held out against the Zulus at Rorke's Drift, though casualties were heavy. In June, there was a further blow when the Prince Imperial (son of the former French emperor, Napoleon III), who had gone along as an observer, was killed by a Zulu raiding party. These events caused a public outcry in Britain.

▶ Disraeli was intensely angry with Frere, but dithered over whether to sack him or back him up. Frere received a severe reprimand but at the same time Disraeli felt he had to send reinforcements to South Africa. In the end, Chelmsford redeemed himself by decisively defeating the Zulus at Ulundi, Cetawayo's capital, in July 1879. Cetawayo was captured and deported, and the Zulu threat was finally removed.

▶ However, much criticism had been aroused; the Liberals enjoyed themselves complaining about the unprovoked attack on the Zulus, the loss of life and the expense involved; although Carnarvon and Frere were to blame, Disraeli had to take the responsibility. Even the victory left a new problem: now that the Zulu threat had been removed, the Transvaal demanded its independence again. It was clear that a more subtle approach would have been to delay or even abandon entirely the complete destruction of Zulu power, so that the continuing menace would frighten the Transvaal into remaining under British protection. It was a problem Gladstone inherited in his next ministry (see Section 16.2(b)).

(e) the Second and Third Afghan Wars (1878–80)

The British were interested in what happened in Afghanistan because they looked on it as a buffer state to protect India from Russian attentions. An earlier British attempt to control the country (the First Afghan War, 1838–42) had been thwarted by the Afghans. Now Disraeli wanted to build up good relations with the Amir of Afghanistan, Sher Ali Khan, in the hope that he would have nothing to do with the Russians, who also had thoughts of bringing Afghanistan within their 'sphere of influence'.

▶ Disraeli appointed Lord Lytton as Viceroy of India, with instructions to persuade Sher Ali to accept a British mission at his capital, Kabul. Lytton, like Sir Bartle Frere, was a well-known advocate of expansionist or 'forward' imperialist policies, and as it turned out, he too could not be relied on to obey orders. According to Robert Blake, 'he was curiously unbalanced in judgement' and became dangerously impatient when he failed to make progress with Sher Ali. It was not a wise appointment.

▶ In July 1878, a Russian military mission arrived in Kabul. Disraeli ordered Lytton to take no action until the situation had been discussed with the Russians through proper diplomatic channels. However, the Viceroy, itching to get the Russians out, ignored this and sent 35,000 troops under Sir Frederick Roberts into Afghanistan. The Russians withdrew, Sher Ali was driven out and his son Yakub Khan was placed on the throne. In May 1879 he signed a treaty of friendship with Britain; a British minister and staff took up residence in Kabul. Though Disraeli was secretly displeased with Lytton, this Second Afghan War seemed to have been completely successful.

- The achievement did not last long: in September 1879, the British minister and the entire mission were murdered by rebel tribesmen, and a Third Afghan War was needed to re-establish British control. Roberts again took Kabul, but it was now clear that a large section of the Afghans resented British interference, and serious fighting broke out in the south of the country. Before order was restored, Disraeli's government had been defeated (April 1880), and it was left to Gladstone to preside over the final stages of the problem. Roberts carried out a brilliantly executed 300-mile march from Kabul to Kandahar, the main centre of resistance, and in August he completely annihilated the rebel army. Again, British control was complete.
- The Liberals criticized the 'wanton invasion' of an independent nation, and even Lord Salisbury, the Conservative Foreign Minister, thought that Disraeli should have kept tighter control over Lytton. The Gladstone government removed Lytton and withdrew British troops and the British mission from Afghanistan. It looked as though all Roberts' efforts had been a waste of time. However, the new Amir, who owed his position to Roberts, remained friendly to Britain for the next twenty years, and the Russians refrained from interfering in Afghanistan again, apart from the Penjdeh incident in 1885 (see Section 16.2(e)). It is possible to argue, therefore, that Disraeli's policy had been a success after all – British military efficiency made a deep impression both in Afghanistan and in Russia.

(f) Disraeli and Ireland

In general, Disraeli had no understanding of small nations, such as those in the Balkans, which were struggling for independence. He saw Ireland in the same light – a troublesome possession trying to break away from Britain in the same way that the Balkan peoples were trying to win freedom from Turkey. Given his desire to consolidate the empire, he naturally did not see Home Rule as the solution to Ireland's problems. Towards the end of his government, the situation in Ireland deteriorated further, because of a severe agricultural depression; an increasing number of tenants failed to pay their rents, and landlords evicted them on a larger scale than ever before. But Disraeli was unmoved; according to Blake, 'he was at heart wholly out of sympathy with the Irish ... and he never did or said anything helpful to them'. One of his last pronouncements before the general election of 1880 was to warn the British government of the dangers of Home Rule.

14.4 the Eastern Question and the Congress of Berlin, 1875–8

(a) background to the Balkans crisis

The crisis that erupted in the Balkans in 1875 was a recurrence of the Eastern Question that had plagued international relations since early in the nineteenth century. For a full explanation of its origins, see Section 3.3(b). It was hoped that the Eastern Question had been solved by the Treaty of Paris (1856), which ended the Crimean War: the Russians were not allowed to have warships on the Black Sea – a severe check to their ambitions in the Balkans and Near East. The Sultan of Turkey had promised to treat his Christian subjects fairly, so that the usual Russian excuse for intervention in the Balkans – that they wanted to protect the Christians living under Turkish rule – would no longer be valid. But British calculations were upset in two ways:

1 In 1870 (during the Franco-Prussian War), the Russians announced that they no longer felt bound by the Black Sea clauses (see Section 13.4(a)).
2 The Turks ignored their promises and continued to over-tax and generally to persecute their Balkan Christians. This led to a rebellion in Bosnia and Herzegovina, which soon spread to Serbia, Montenegro and Bulgaria.

The main European powers – Germany, Austria-Hungary, Russia, France and Italy (but excluding Britain) sent the Berlin Memorandum to the Turks, protesting about their harshness and calling on them to make peace and behave themselves.

(b) what was Disraeli's attitude?

1 He was deeply suspicious about Russian intentions – if Britain intervened to help the Balkan Christians, there seemed every chance that the whole of the Balkans, perhaps even Constantinople and the Dardanelles, would fall under Russian control.
2 He also mistrusted the motives of the Austrians and Germans and suspected them of scheming with the Russians to partition the Ottoman Empire.
3 He therefore wanted to preserve Turkish power as the best way of maintaining British interests in the Near East. He had no sympathy with the peoples of the Balkans in their struggle for independence.
4 For these reasons, he refused to support the Berlin Memorandum, but this refusal encouraged the new Sultan, Abdul Hamid, to think that he could rely on British support no matter what happened. The Turks redoubled their efforts to crush the rebels, and in Bulgaria some terrible atrocities were committed. Turkish irregular troops, known as Bashi-Bazouks, carried out vicious reprisals on Bulgarian peasants, slaughtering at least 12,000 men, women and children. This was embarrassing for Disraeli: he felt bound to condemn the Turks, though he did not change his determination to support them against Russia if necessary.

(c) Gladstone's attack on the Turks

Gladstone's attitude was the direct opposite of Disraeli's. He saw it as a purely moral issue – the threat from Russia paled into insignificance beside the appalling Turkish massacres of innocent Christians. He was so incensed that he published a pamphlet, *The Bulgarian Horrors and the Question of the East* (September 1876), which rapidly became a best-seller. It contained a blistering attack on the evils of Turkish rule, their 'abominable and bestial lusts', and the foul deeds by which women had been violated, roasted and impaled. He hoped that the Turks 'one and all, bag and baggage, shall clear out from the province they have desolated and profaned', and went so far as to urge the Russians to expel the Turks from Bulgaria as soon as possible.

As a result, much of British public opinion turned against the Turks, making it more difficult for Disraeli to maintain an anti-Russian front. He retorted that Gladstone was worse than any Bulgarian Horror, and relations between the two men became irretrievably embittered. In fact, many Liberals thought Gladstone had over-reacted and was tempting fate by encouraging the Russians.

(d) war between Russia and Turkey

- The Russian Tsar, Alexander II, possibly influenced by Gladstone's attitude, announced that he could no longer stand by and allow Turkish atrocities to continue (November 1876). Frantic negotiations followed during which the Russians gave assurances that they would not capture Constantinople and the Dardanelles, and that they had no intention of interfering with the Suez Canal and India; consequently, Britain agreed to remain neutral.

- The Russians declared war on Turkey (April 1877); their forces marched southwards into the Balkans and besieged the fortress of Plevna which held out from June to December. The Russians did not perform particularly well and progress was painfully slow against unexpectedly strong Turkish resistance. However, by January 1878, they had reached Adrianople, not much more than 100 miles from Constantinople.

- Doubts began to creep in; would the Russians keep their promises? Now that Constantinople was threatened, British public opinion veered round to become pro-Turkish; mobs hooted Gladstone in the streets and smashed his windows.

- Disraeli acted promptly: he demanded an armistice and ordered British warships to Constantinople, where they arrived in February 1878. By now, Russian troops were in San Stefano, on the outskirts of Constantinople. Disraeli warned that, if they captured it, Britain would declare war. Tension was high and a European war seemed imminent as the British prepared an expeditionary force. The chorus of a popular music-hall song of the time ran:

  > We don't want to fight, but by jingo if we do,
  > We've got the ships, we've got the men, we've got the money too.

- The attack on Constantinople never came. The Russian commanders realized that the Turks would throw everything into the defence of their capital; the

Russian troops were nearing exhaustion and there were not enough of them to defeat 100,000 Turks. Disraeli claimed, perhaps with some justification, that the British threats had also influenced the Russians. Peace negotiations opened and eventually agreement was reached ... .

(e) the Treaty of San Stefano (March 1878)

This was signed between Russia and Turkey, and naturally the terms were very favourable to Russia. As soon as the details became known, *there was an immediate outcry from Britain and Austria-Hungary.* The terms were:

1 Serbia, Montenegro and Romania were recognized as being independent of Turkey.
2 Russia took Bessarabia from Romania, giving it control of the mouth of the Danube. This alarmed the Austrians, who depended on the Danube as a vital trade outlet into the Black Sea; there was no mention of Bosnia and Herzegovina being given to Austria-Hungary, which the Russians had referred to as a reward for Austria remaining neutral.
3 A large independent state of Bulgaria was set up; referred to as 'Big Bulgaria', it stretched right across the Balkan Peninsula and had a coastline on both the Black Sea and the Aegean Sea. For 'an initial period', Bulgaria would be administered by Russian army officers. This was the most sensational clause of all; the British and Austrians were convinced that 'Big Bulgaria' would be a satellite of Russia, giving it the use of a port on the Aegean, so that it would be able to by-pass the Dardanelles. It seemed that the Balkan peoples had exchanged rule by Turkey for rule by Russia.

Britain and Austria protested in the strongest possible terms: Disraeli called up the reserves and sent 7,000 Indian troops to Malta. Moderate opinion prevailed in Russia and it was decided not to risk a conflict with both Britain and Austria-Hungary. Bismarck, the German Chancellor, offered to act as 'honest broker', and the Russians agreed to attend an international Congress in Berlin to renegotiate the peace terms.

(f) the Congress of Berlin (June–July 1878)

Many of the issues had been settled at preliminary discussions, but there were still some important points to be decided when the representatives met. Disraeli himself led the British delegation, ably assisted by his new Foreign Secretary, Lord Salisbury. Disraeli dominated the Congress with his vitality and the force of his personality, though most of the detailed negotiation was carried out by Salisbury. Between them, they achieved nearly everything they wanted, and still had time to enjoy the incessant round of receptions, parties and banquets. *The terms of the new agreement were:*

1 The idea of a 'Big Bulgaria' was dropped; it was divided into three:

› a small independent state of Bulgaria in the north ('Little Bulgaria');
› in the centre, an area known as Eastern Roumelia, belonging to Turkey but having self-government under a Christian governor; and
› the rest – Macedonia – was to remain part of the Turkish Empire, with no Christian governor.

2 The Austrians were allowed to occupy and administer Bosnia and Herzegovina, though nominally it still belonged to Turkey.
3 The Turks allowed Britain to occupy Cyprus in return for military help if Russia should attack again; there were more Turkish promises of fair treatment for the Christians.

(g) how successful was the Congress?

At the time, it was regarded as a great British victory, and a personal triumph for Disraeli, who drove from the station to Downing Street through cheering

map **14.1 Balkan frontiers after the Congress of Berlin, 1878**

crowds. 'We have brought back peace with honour,' he declared. It was the crowning achievement of his career: not only was he a successful Prime Minister, he was also now a highly respected statesman who had achieved most of what he hoped for at Berlin:

- Russia had been checked in its advance through the Balkans towards the Dardanelles, and British interests in the Near East had been safeguarded – and all without war.
- The association of Austria, Germany and Russia (the *Dreikaiserbund* – League of Three Emperors) which Disraeli had so mistrusted, had been destroyed. Russia was now on poor terms with Austria, and its relations with Germany (which had failed to support Russia at Berlin) were never the same again.
- Turkey had been bolstered up against further Russian expansion attempts, and Britain had a strong position in the eastern Mediterranean with the acquisition of Cyprus.

Robert Blake believes that Disraeli deserves immense credit, because the Congress gave Europe over thirty years of peace. However, some other historians have emphasized the drawbacks of the settlement:

- Bulgaria, far from becoming a Russian puppet state as expected, was determined to maintain her independence and turned out to be strongly anti-Russian. Salisbury later admitted that he and Disraeli had 'backed the wrong horse', meaning that from the British point of view it would have been better to have kept 'Big Bulgaria'.
- The Austrian occupation of Bosnia aroused resentment in Serbia, which had hopes of expanding in that area. In the words of A. J. P. Taylor, this 'contained the seeds of future disaster'; it was the beginning of the friction between Austria and Serbia, which was to culminate in the outbreak of the First World War in 1914.
- The Turks again failed to keep their promises and made no attempt to reform or strengthen their state. Many of the Balkan peoples remained under Turkish rule which was therefore unacceptable to them. Thus the Eastern Question had still not been solved permanently and there would be further disturbances and crises.

In the autumn of 1878, however, none of this was apparent, and if a general election had been held then, there is little doubt that Disraeli and the Conservatives would have won easily.

14.5 why did the Conservatives lose the 1880 general election?

After a surprise by-election victory in which the Conservatives won the Liberal stronghold of Southwark, Disraeli judged that the tide was running in his favour. However, the general election of April 1880 showed that he had miscalculated badly; the results were: Liberals 353, Conservatives 238, Irish Home Rulers, 61. Yet it was less than two years since Disraeli's triumph at Berlin. *What had gone wrong?*

‣ There was disappointment and criticism about some events overseas, *after* the Congress of Berlin, which spoiled Disraeli's image as the international diplomatic master – the mishandling of the Zulu War and the fiasco in Afghanistan, which had not been resolved when the election took place.

‣ The lack of social reform aroused growing disapproval. While the government had begun well, after 1876 no major reforming measure was introduced. This was partly because Disraeli was occupied with foreign affairs, and partly because the fifty-nine Irish MPs, having failed to secure Home Rule by reasoned argument, resorted to tactics of obstruction; more than once they kept the Commons up all night talking about Irish affairs, and the government could find no way of dealing with them.

‣ There was an industrial slump, which caused unemployment to shoot up rapidly. In 1872, only about 1 per cent of trade union members were out of work, but by 1879 the figure was as high as 11 per cent. In some trades, the situation was even worse – 22 per cent of registered engineers were without work. It was the first taste of the foreign competition that was to oust Britain from her economic leadership of the world, and the beginning of what became known as *The Great Depression* (see Sections 15.2 and 15.4).

‣ There was an even more severe agricultural depression caused by a massive influx of cheap corn from North America, and by a series of wet summers. Hundreds of farmers went bankrupt and thousands of farm labourers were put out of work. Most other European countries introduced tariffs, but Disraeli refused to do so, and was naturally criticized for this by the farming interests; ironically, his argument (which he had opposed in 1846) was that free trade in corn would keep down the cost of living for the workers.

‣ Gladstone, who had retired from the Liberal leadership after their defeat in 1874, re-emerged as the real Liberal leader and conducted a stunning campaign, starting in his constituency of Midlothian and travelling the length of the country. He attacked Disraeli's policies as 'immoral and iniquitous': the Afghan War was 'a crime against God', and Cyprus was 'a valueless encumbrance'. Perhaps his most successful speech was the one in St Andrew's Hall, Glasgow, to a crowded audience of over 6,000 people. For a man of over 70, *The Midlothian Campaign* (November–December 1879) followed by a repeat performance just before the election, was a remarkable achievement. Disraeli, approaching 80 and in failing health, was unable to provide an effective answer.

- Finally, the Liberal party organization had reached peak efficiency under the guidance of Joseph Chamberlain (see Section 17.1(b)), whereas the Conservative organization had stagnated since 1874 and was caught unprepared for an election.

14.6 assessment of Disraeli

Soon after Disraeli's defeat, Gladstone crowed: 'the downfall of Beaconsfieldism is like the vanishing of some vast magnificent castle in an Italian romance'. Did Disraeli's career have any lasting effect on British politics, or was Gladstone right? Opinions are divided:

- Robert Blake, probably Disraeli's best-known biographer, and historian of the Conservative party, believes that Disraeli's great and lasting achievement was to hold the Conservative party together through a difficult period, and then to demonstrate that it was still capable of forming an effective government. After all, when a political party has failed to win a general election for over thirty years, even its staunchest supporters could be forgiven for writing it off. He also made it the party of the Empire and the party with a strong foreign policy; that is, the party of British nationalism. By showing concern for the social conditions of the poor, Disraeli enabled the Conservatives to attract a large enough slice of the working-class vote to keep them in existence as a major party.
- In his 1996 biography, T. A. Jenkins suggests that Disraeli's greatest contribution was to make the Conservatives into a genuinely national party, able to attract support from all classes in society. While this might not have seemed clear in 1880, at the time of the big Conservative election defeat, 'in fact the image of a national party promoted by Disraeli was soon to stand the Conservatives in good stead, especially after Gladstone's Liberal party split over the question of Irish Home Rule in 1886. Already, by that time, the belief was gaining ground that Disraeli had laid the foundations for a "Tory Democracy", an idea that was to inspire the Conservatives for generations to come'.
- Some other historians feel that Disraeli's impact has been overestimated. Paul Smith claims that Peel had already made the Conservatives into a modern party when they won the 1841 general election, and that Disraeli actually retarded its development by leading the attack on Peel over the Corn Laws. The next leader of the party, Lord Salisbury, abandoned the social reform policy, so that aspect of Beaconsfieldism certainly did not survive long.

Whichever view one accepts, there is no escaping the fact that Disraeli was a first-rate parliamentarian; Blake calls him 'an impresario, an actor manager … there is a champagne-like sparkle about him which has scarcely ever been equalled and never surpassed among statesmen'.

1 'The domestic reforms of Disraeli and the Conservative government of 1874 to 1880 brought major advances in modernizing Britain.' How far do you agree with this judgement?

2 Judging by the social reforms of his 1874–1880 government, to what extent can it be argued that Disraeli was 'a champion of the working classes'?

3 To what extent did Disraeli's government of 1874 to 1880 follow a carefully planned programme in foreign and imperial affairs?

A document question about Disraeli and Conservative policies can be found on the accompanying website www.palgrave.com/masterseries/lowe1.

chapter 15

Victorian prosperity and depression

summary of events

During the first few years of Queen Victoria's reign – from 1837 until about 1844 – industrial prosperity seemed variable, and there were several short trade depressions. The situation began to stabilize with a great surge of railway building from 1844 to 1847, and after that, industry moved into *a period of remarkable prosperity that lasted until 1873*. Agriculture enjoyed a similar 'Golden Age', usually known as the period of *High Farming;* this demonstrated that all the prophets of doom, who had forecast that the repeal of the Corn Laws in 1846 would ruin British farming, were wrong, at least for the time being.

The period from 1873 to 1896 is usually referred to as the Great Depression, though there is some controversy among historians about exactly how serious this so-called depression was. Some parts of British industry went through a difficult period: while exports of most commodities continued to increase, prices and profits were falling, mainly because of overseas competition. There was something of a recovery between 1896 and 1914, but by the outbreak of the First World War in 1914, it was clear that the USA and Germany had toppled Britain from its position as the world's leading manufacturing nation. In agriculture, the depression was much more severe, and despite a slight recovery around the turn of the twentieth century, it was only during the war years (1914–18), when foreign wheat was difficult to obtain, that British farming began to revive.

15.1 illustrate and account for Britain's industrial prosperity in the mid-nineteenth century

(a) The Great Exhibition of 1851

This is probably the best illustration of Britain's prosperity during the mid-nineteenth century. The suggestion for it came from the Royal Society of Arts,

Illus. **15.1 The Great Exhibition, in the Crystal Palace, 1851**

whose president, Prince Albert, was full of enthusiasm for the idea. The exhibition was housed in *the Crystal Palace,* a vast construction of glass and cast iron, designed by Joseph Paxton and erected in Hyde Park. One-third of a mile long and over 100 feet high, it contained a display of every conceivable type of British machinery (much of it working) and manufactures: railway engines, steam ploughs, steamship engines, cranes, steam hammers for heavy industry, printing machines, screw-making machines, Lancashire cottons and Nottingham lace; there was even a silent piano (made out of papier-mâché) and an unsinkable deckchair. To demonstrate that Britain was a free-trade country, exhibits were included from foreign countries – Dresden china, and silks and tapestries from France. There were over six million visitors during the five months the exhibition was open, many of them from abroad, and many new export orders followed. Britain was rightly regarded as 'the workshop of the world'.

(b) the great export boom

Over the next twenty years, British industry enjoyed a remarkable export boom, the like of which had never been experienced before. This can best be illustrated by looking at the export figures shown in Table 15.1. Table 15.2 shows how the total value of exports from Britain increased.

Another way in which prosperity showed itself was that the wages of the industrial working class increased, on average, by about 50 per cent in the

table **15.1** **export figures for the main manufacturing industries**

(a) Annual average for each five-year period

Year	Iron and steel (in thousand tons)	Coal (in million tons)
1845–9	458	2.5
1850–4	1 225	3.2
1855–9	1 411	5.99
1860–4	1 536	7.83
1865–9	2 027	9.86
1870–4	2 965	12.31

(b) Annual average per decade

Year	Cotton textiles (in million yards)	Woollen goods (including carpets) (in thousand yards)
1840–9	978	93 316
1850–9	1 855	161 563
1860–9	2 375	236 267
1870–9	3 573	311 601

Source: P. Mathias, *The First Industrial Nation* (Methuen, 1969), pp. 481–7.

table **15.2** **total value of exports from Britain**

Year	£ millions
1840–9	124.5
1860–9	159.7
1870–9	218.1

Source: C. Cook and J. Stevenson, *Handbook of Modern British History, 1714–1987* (Longman, 1988), p. 194.

period 1850–75. Prices also rose, but only by about 20 per cent on average; this meant that workers enjoyed a rise of about 30 per cent in *real wages* (what they could actually buy with their money).

(c) reasons for the prosperity

1 The basis was that Britain was still enjoying the advantage of having been the first nation to industrialize. As yet there was no real competition from abroad, and the countries that were to become serious competitors later were still lagging far behind, for one reason or another. The USA was having difficulty in supplying its own rapidly increasing population and was held back by the Civil War (1861–5); and Germany did not become a unified state until 1871. Both these countries were important buyers of British manufactures.

2 Further inventions were made, and these helped to keep Britain in the forefront; most important were the new processes in the metal industry which resulted in mild steel taking over from malleable iron as the most popular metal.

Henry Bessemer patented a converter system that could produce steel in large quantities at much lower prices (1856); this caused railways and shipping-lines to change to steel for rails and metal plating. William Siemens, a German engineer working in Britain, patented his open-hearth process (1867), which could produce a stronger type of steel.

3 The population growth increased the demand for manufactured goods at home. Between 1851 and 1871 the population of Britain rose from 27.4 million to 31.5 million, and this acted as a stimulus to industry.

4 Gladstone as Chancellor of the Exchequer (1853–5 and 1860–5) made an important contribution to the prosperity by removing almost all the remaining tariffs (see Section 8.2). This meant that there were no artificial restrictions on trade: Britain could obtain cheap raw materials from its overseas territories – its Empire – and flood the world with cheap manufactured goods.

5 As trade increased, so the merchant shipping and ship-building industries expanded: the Clyde, Tyneside, Merseyside, Belfast and Barrow-in-Furness all flourished; new docks were built, particularly in London: the first two were Poplar Dock and the Royal Victoria Dock, opened in 1852 and 1855, respectively. By 1886, the Millwall, Royal Albert and Tilbury Docks were in operation.

6 The spread of railways contributed to the boom in many ways. In 1843 there were less than 2,000 miles of track, but the rest of the decade saw an enormous investment of cash in railway building. This 'Railway Mania' as it became known, resulted in the construction of a further 5,000 miles of track by 1850, and in 1875 a total of 14,510 miles of track was open. Thousands of extra jobs were provided, as well as a large market for the iron industry, for rails, locomotives, coaches and wagons. Railways became an important consumer of coal, and railway towns such as Crewe and Swindon mushroomed as workshop and repair centres. The cheap, fast transport provided by the railways enabled new inland coalfields to be developed, notably in South Wales, together with the iron ore mines in North Yorkshire. Most important of all, they made it possible to transport manufactured goods of all kinds to the ports much more quickly. This, together with the rapid spread of steam-power in merchant shipping after 1850, played a vital part in increasing British exports.

7 There was plenty of capital available for investment in industry. There were more reliable banking and credit facilities since the 1844 Bank Charter Act (see Section 7.2(c)). Once industrial progress had got under way, the vast profits which were earned from, for example, exports of cotton textiles, provided a continuous flow of capital that was used to finance further expansion. There was even some left over to be invested abroad – in 1875, at least £12,000 million of British capital was invested in railway and factory projects overseas. Much of this cash was used by foreigners to buy British goods. The discovery of gold in California (1849), Australia (1851) and New Zealand (1861) added to the capital available and further increased the demand for British manufactures.

On the other hand some economic historians have suggested that it would not be entirely accurate to think of the Victorian boom as a single unbroken phase of growth and expansion. F. Crouzet pointed out (in 1981) that between 1850 and 1873 there were several short periods of sudden depression, the most serious one in 1858, followed by two less serious crises in 1861–2 and 1866. At times like this, workers found themselves laid off or put on short time.

15.2 in what ways and why can Britain be said to have suffered an industrial depression after 1873?

(a) no serious industrial slump

The last quarter of the nineteenth century used to be thought of as the time of the Great Depression; and certainly contemporaries took a very gloomy view of the situation, bemoaning the success of the USA and Germany in overtaking Britain economically. However, since the Second World War, historians have begun to question just how serious the 'Great Depression' really was. It has been pointed out that there was no serious industrial slump with sharply falling exports, as there was in the depression of the early 1930s (see Section 25.2). In most industries, the general trend of production and exports was still rising. The steel industry enjoyed a massive expansion during the so-called depression; in coal and cotton textiles, output and exports continued to increase, though *the rate of growth was slowing down;* and while production of iron decreased, this was only to be expected as steel became more widely adopted. One economic historian, S. B. Saul, even went so far as to call his book about the period, *The Myth of the Great Depression* (1985). However, economists described it as a depression because:

▸ Prices were falling, and therefore although exports continued to increase, they were worth less in cash; this is shown by the statistics in Table 15.3.
▸ Consequently, profits were declining; as the economists put it, profit margins were being squeezed.
▸ Employers often tried to cut down costs and maintain profit levels by laying off workers, causing periodic bursts of unemployment. In the twenty years before 1874, the average rate of unemployment among trades union members was 4.6 per cent, but from 1875–95 the average was 5.4 per cent. Some individual years were serious: the 1879 figure was 11 per cent and 1886, 10 per cent. However, it was not a period of sustained unemployment: 1882–3 and 1888–90 were good years when no more than 2 per cent were out of work.

Pressure from businessmen, never slow to voice their concern when profits take a turn for the worse, caused the government to appoint a Royal Commission in 1886 to investigate the problem. Its conclusion merely stated

table **15.3** **exports of cotton textiles after 1870**

Year	Cotton cloth exported (millions yards)	Value (£ millions)
1870–9	3573	71.5
1880–9	4675	73.0
1890–9	5057	67.2

Source: P. Mathias, *The First Industrial Nation* (Methuen, 1969), pp. 468, 486.

the obvious: there was 'a diminution, and in some cases, an absence of profit, with a corresponding diminution of employment for the labouring classes'.

(b) what caused the 'depression'?

Some historians have tried to explain it in terms of a single cause: falling prices were the result of the world economy running short of gold. Another favourite single explanation was that the depression, if indeed it was a 'depression', was the inevitable downturn in the economy following a boom. In fact, the situation was much more complex than that; historians have suggested a wide variety of factors that could have played a part:

1 There was a reduction in railway building: between 1845 and 1870 an average of 2,000 miles of new track was opened in each five-year period. After 1870 the figure fell by half, and between 1885 and 1900 an average of only 750 miles of track were built in each five-year period. Thus there was a gradual falling-off in demand for metals, and a loss of jobs.

2 Britain was beginning to suffer serious competition from abroad, especially from the USA and Germany. This was probably inevitable: once other countries learned the techniques for themselves and began to industrialize, they were bound to challenge Britain's lead. The USA had enormous natural resources and a growing labour force (thanks to immigration). The statistics in Table 15.4 show how the USA and Germany were overtaking Britain, and how Britain's growth rate was much smaller than theirs. One set of statistics puts Britain's economic growth rate in the period 1873 to 1913 at 1.3 per cent, whereas Germany's was 3.9 per cent, and the USA's 4.8 per cent.

3 The British were now experiencing the disadvantages of having been the first nation to industrialize: their machinery and equipment were old and in some cases obsolete, whereas the Americans and Germans could start with the latest technology available. The Germans, for example, were able to install the Siemens furnaces for making steel; they also took full advantage of a later invention by the cousins Percy Gilchrist (a Welsh steelworks chemist) and Sydney Gilchrist-Thomas (a clerk in a London law-court), who in 1878 discovered how to manufacture steel from iron-ore that had a high phosphorous content. The British were saddled with the earlier Bessemer converters, which the Germans had abandoned and which were more expensive to run than the Siemens and Gilchrist-Thomas methods.

Similar advances had been made in other industries: in the American cotton industry there was the introduction of ring-spinning instead of the slower and more expensive mule-spinning still used in Lancashire. America pioneered new machines such as the typewriter and the sewing-machine. The Belgians made advances in the glass industry, enabling them to produce better-quality glass more cheaply than the British. Over the whole range of industry the British were therefore suffering in two ways: they were being gradually pushed out of their markets in Europe and America (most states introduced tariffs to protect their developing industries); and foreign imports were making an increasing impact on the British market. The British government, still committed to *laissez-faire*, would not introduce tariffs.

4 There was a failure of management and businessmen generally to respond positively to the new challenges. Eric Hobsbawm, a Marxist historian writing in 1968, claimed that the British class system was at least partly responsible for this failure: the upper classes despised industrialization and the industrial middle classes tried to imitate the aristocracy, preferring to put their profits into land, hunting and shooting instead of ploughing them back into industry. Martin Wiener (1981) produced a similar argument: he believes that while by the early 1870s Britain was the most advanced industrial nation, the new economic forces did not change the structure of society; 'pre-modern elements remained entrenched within the new society'; in other words, successful businessmen tried to behave like aristocrats, buying land and 'adopting a new culture of enjoyment'. Most other historians reject this 'class and culture' theory, though they do accept that there were serious management failures:

  ‣ The most common unit was the family firm; top management tended to be chosen not because of ability but because of family connections; unfortunately, inspiration and interest often deteriorated by the time a firm had reached its third or fourth generation of owners. In the USA and Germany, recruitment depended much more on ability.
  ‣ There was not enough effort to develop new industries, with the result that the British export trade relied too heavily on a few staple products. The Germans meanwhile surged ahead in the 'new' industries such as electrical engineering, chemicals and dyestuffs.
  ‣ There was not enough effort to improve designs and reduce costs by introducing the latest machinery; this might have enabled the British to hold on to their European and American markets. However, they preferred to switch exports to India, to other parts of the Empire and to China; this was especially true of the cotton industry. Management was too complacent, preferring to repair the old machinery rather than invest profits in new premises and equipment; in fairness, though, the fall in profits during the 'depression' probably goes some way towards explaining the lack of investment.

- Even when they were prepared to invest, industrialists sometimes made the wrong decisions: between 1896 and 1914 there was a boom in cotton exports, and hundreds of new mills were built in Lancashire; but instead of taking the opportunity to install the latest automatic looms already widely used in the USA and Germany, manufacturers on the whole decided to invest in the traditional types of looms.
- Too little attention was paid to the importance of science, especially in chemicals and electrical engineering.

5 Martin Wiener blames Britain's education system for not being geared to producing academically trained scientists and engineers. The public schools concentrated on the classics and worked on the assumption that gentlemen did not involve themselves in practical training. A nationally organized system of elementary and secondary education was very slow in arriving (see Section 12.6), and even when it did, the science taught was not designed to prepare students for top-level technological training. In the 1870s, science was scarcely taught in British universities except to medical students; yet in 1872 there were already eleven purely technical universities and twenty other universities in Germany, all organized and financed by the government.

6 Trade unions may have held up the introduction of some new machines and processes in an attempt to make sure that skilled workers were not pushed out of their jobs.

7 The middle-class obsession with *laissez-faire* meant that Britain remained a free trade country at a time when many European states and the USA were introducing tariffs. By 1886, Germany, France, Russia, Austria and the USA were all protecting their main industries with import duties. Particularly serious was the USA's McKinley tariff introduced in 1891, which had an immediate adverse effect on exports of British woollen goods. The British had profited from free trade while theirs was the world's leading economy, but once other countries caught up, they were exposed to the full blast of competition.

If we accept these arguments, it seems clear that British industry was already suffering, long before 1914, from many of the major weaknesses that were to afflict it after the First World War and which were to cause Britain's long economic decline. However, not all historians go along with this interpretation. S. B. Saul argued that the depression was largely a myth (see Source D on the website). W. D. Rubinstein (1993) rejected Hobsbawm's and Wiener's theory that Britain's economy was mainly an *industrial* economy whose industrial and manufacturing lead had vanished through decline after 1870. Rubinstein argues that Britain's economy was *never* fundamentally an industrial and manufacturing economy; it was a commercial, financial and service-based economy whose comparative advantage always lay with commerce and finance: 'What is so often seen as Britain's industrial decline or collapse can be seen, with greater

table **15.4 Coal, pig-iron and steel production of the three leading powers**

Coal production (in millions tons)

	1850	1860	1870	1880	1890	1900	1910	1914
Germany	6	12	34	59	89	149	222	277
USA	–	3.4	10	64.9	143	244	350	455
Britain	57	81	112	149	184	228	268	292

Pig-iron production (in millions tons)

	1850	1860	1870	1880	1890	1900	1910	1914
Germany	–	–	1.3	2.5	4.1	7.5	9.5	14.7
USA	–	0.8	1.7	3.9	9.4	14	27	30
Britain	2.2	3.9	6	7.8	8	9	10	11

Steel production (in millions tons)

	1850	1860	1870	1880	1890	1900	1910	1914
Germany	–	–	0.3	0.7	2.3	6.7	13.8	14
USA	–	–	–	1.3	4.3	10	26	32
Britain	–	–	0.7	1.3	3.6	5	5.9	6.5

Source: A .J. P. Taylor, *The Struggle for Mastery in Europe, 1848–1918* (Oxford University Press, 1971), pp. xxix–xxx, tables vii, VII, IX. By permission of Oxford University Press.

accuracy, as a transfer of resources and entrepreneurial energies into other forms of business life ... In moving from industry to commerce, Britain's entrepreneurs were responding intelligently to perceived opportunities.' The service sector was vitally important, as it meant that Britain's invisible earnings more than offset the fall in income from exports.

Martin Pugh (1994) argues that Britain's so-called manufacturing decline was only relative, and points out that 'there was an impressive range of new enterprises in late Victorian Britain which is difficult to square with the pessimistic view of some businessmen'. He mentions the major expansion of the motor car, bicycle, telephone, soap and chemical industries, the spread of grocery store chains such as Sainsbury's and Lipton's, and even the rapid spread of fish-and-chip shops! Even the so-called decline in the traditional industries did not mean that exports were reduced. The statistics of coal, pig-iron and steel production given in Table 15.4 reveal that British exports continued to increase between 1850 and 1914; true, *the rate of increase slowed down*, but there was no absolute fall in exports of these three products. It was Britain's world share that fell, mainly because of competition from the USA and Germany. Other areas of industry where a similar trend took place were shipbuilding, textiles and coal, all of which reached new peaks in the 1890s. For example, in 1890, Britain built 90 per cent of the world total of ships and had the world's largest merchant fleet. Britain was also the centre of the world's financial system. In fact, Britain still had one of the world's leading economies.

Theo Barker, in an article in *History Today* ('Workshop of the World 1870–1914', June 1994), challenged many of the traditional arguments. He pointed out that Britain, though apparently lagging behind the USA in the 'new' industries such as electric lighting, electric traction and car manufacture, was later able to take advantage of the delay by introducing, before 1914, improved and more efficient techniques, which had been developed abroad by trial and error. Barker also claims that the old industries such as cotton and shipbuilding *were* showing a willingness to introduce changes. Nor does he accept the claim that the education system neglected science: he points out that there was ample opportunity to study science at grammar schools, technical schools and colleges, and at the expanding redbrick universities. In fact, according to Barker, on the eve of the First World War, all was set fair for the continuing growth of British industry. What threw everything off course was the First World War: 'the war accelerated trends with which, given the slower pace of peace, British manufacturers could have coped as they had been doing before 1914. Does anyone believe that Lancashire cotton in the 1920s would have been suffering as it did if there had been no war? Or British shipbuilding? Yet it has been after looking back from this side of the 1914–1918 war that historians have reached their gloomy conclusions about Britain's industrial performance on the other side of that disastrous conflict.' (see Section 22.5(g) for the effects of the war on the British economy). On the other hand, not all historians put the blame for the continued economic decline on the First World War (1914–18). Black and MacRaild argue that the war did not cause the weaknesses mentioned in Section 15.2(b) above, which were all there in varying degrees; it merely exacerbated them. But that came later; they concede that, in 1914, 'the British economy was still far stronger in absolute terms than it had been 50 years earlier and Britain was one of the three leading economies in the world and, in some spheres, the foremost. Modern British leaders would be happy to be in this situation.'

15.3 what is meant by the term 'High Farming', and why was the period 1846–74 one of prosperity for British agriculture?

(a) High Farming

High Farming was the title of a pamphlet written by a Wigtownshire farmer, James Caird, and published in 1849. In it he explained his ideas about how farmers should respond to the threat of foreign competition following the abolition of the Corn Laws in 1846. They should farm their land more intensively, using all the latest techniques and inventions, in order to increase yield and lower costs; it would thus be possible to cope with the lowering of prices which cheap foreign imports would bring, while still maintaining profits. According to F. M. L. Thompson, the early part of this period (1846–53) was one of faltering prosperity, and it was only in 1853 that prices of farm produce stabilized at an encouraging level. The period of 'High Farming', the real Golden Age of British agriculture, lasted for only about twenty years after 1853;

it was when farmers with money to spare 'opened their purses and embarked on the new course in a big way'. It was a period of prosperity for farmers, whose incomes probably doubled; even farm labourers were becoming slightly better off as far as wages, housing and food were concerned.

(b) what were the reasons for the prosperity?

1 The new 'High Farming' techniques resulted in much greater productivity. Widespread use of clay piping improved land drainage; there was an increase in 'mixed farming'; that is, growing wheat and root crops, *and* raising cattle, sheep and pigs as well. Artificial fertilizers – nitrate of soda, superphosphates, sulphate of ammonia, Peruvian guano and German potash – came into use. Pedigree breeds of cattle – Hereford, Aberdeen Angus, Ayrshire and Channel Island – were improved; by the early 1870s the major profit for most farmers came from their livestock. There were also improvements to ploughs and hoes, and the spread of the horse-drawn reaper. More spectacular were the steam threshing-machines and steam ploughs, though these were not so important; Thompson calls them 'the white elephant of high farming, a plaything of rich landowners with money to spare for anything new in farm gadgetry'.

2 Scientific farming was encouraged by the Royal Agricultural Society of England (founded 1838), which published a journal and organized agricultural shows. An experimental station was set up in 1842 at Rothamsted in Hertfordshire to carry out research into soils and fertilizers.

3 Britain's growing population meant an ever-increasing demand for the farmers' products, and therefore meant higher prices and profits. While wheat prices remained steady, the prices of all types of meat, butter, cheese and wool (for clothing) rose by close on 50 per cent.

4 Vitally important was the fact that, because of the lack of fast shipping and of refrigeration facilities, there was very little competition from foreign produce, except Russian and American wheat. Imports of wheat gradually increased during the 1860s, which explains why wheat prices were steady while prices of meat and dairy produce rose.

5 Railways enabled livestock and perishable goods such as meat, milk and market garden produce to be transported quickly and cheaply over long distances for sale in the cities. Farmers who had previously been too far away from towns and cities now had a whole new market at their disposal. Counties such as Norfolk and Herefordshire could produce milk for London, and Aberdeenshire was supplying meat to industrial Lancashire and London.

6 Finally, even the weather was kind to the farmers with a run of mainly good summers and good harvests between 1850 and 1873.

15.4 why and with what results was there a depression in agriculture after 1873?

The Golden Age changed quite suddenly into a depression, which was especially severe in areas that relied heavily on wheat and cereal production. Prices and profits fell, harvests were smaller, and many fields went out of cultivation. However, livestock and dairy farming were not so badly affected; the boom in this area of farming lasted well into the 1880s, when foreign imports began to bring down prices.

(a) reasons for the depression

1 Bad weather played an important role; the summer of 1873 was wet and the harvest poor; the autumn of 1875 was exceptionally wet, and after that came twelve years of above average rainfall and below average temperatures. Crops were ruined and harvests disappointing. Worse still, the wet weather helped to spread pneumonia and foot and mouth disease among livestock; there were also epidemics of liver rot among sheep, and swine fever, causing farmers to suffer heavy losses.

2 The most important cause of the depression was the import of cheap foreign food which was now available to make up the shortages. The building of the trans-continental railways opened up the fertile prairies of North America as vast wheat-growing areas, and the development of large merchant steamships enabled American, and later Canadian, Indian, Australian and Argentinian wheat to be transported swiftly and cheaply to Britain. For example, in 1868, the cost of transporting a ton of wheat from Chicago to Liverpool was 65s; in 1882 it had fallen to only 24s. Consequently, the price of wheat fell, on average, by half; at one point it hit a record low level of 17s 6d a quarter. These trends are illustrated in Tables 15.5 and 15.6.

3 The ill-effects of the 1846 repeal of the Corn Laws, which farmers had feared but which had been obscured during the period of 'High Farming' were now making themselves felt. Increasing wheat imports forced prices down at a time when a series of poor harvests in the twelve years after 1875 resulted in a

table **15.5 Imports of wheat and flour into the UK (average per decade)**

Year	(thousands of cwt)
1840–9	10 667
1850–9	19 326
1860–9	33 697
1870–9	50 406
1880–9	70 282
1890–9	85 890
1900–9	102 85

Source: P. Mathias, *The First Industrial Nation* (Methuen, 1969), pp. 472–5.

table **15.6 Wheat prices (annual average for 5 year periods)**

Year	(shillings per quarter)
1840–4	57.85
1845–9	54.00
1855–9	57.62
1865–9	53.62
1870–4	55.00
1875–9	47.67
1885–9	31.58
1895–9	27.82
1900–4	27.37
1910–14	32.93

Source: P. Mathias, *The First Industrial Nation* (Methuen, 1969), pp. 472–5.

dramatically reduced domestic output. In spite of intense pressure from farming interests, which expected help from the government of Disraeli (1874–80) – the man who had opposed repeal in 1846 – the government took the decision not to protect British agriculture by the reintroduction of tariffs.

4 In the 1880s, the introduction of refrigerated ships brought frozen mutton from Australia and New Zealand and chilled beef from Argentina. At the same time, according to Thompson, 'the traditional English breakfast of Danish bacon and eggs was being established'.

(b) results of the depression

▸ Farmers who relied heavily on wheat and cereal growing, particularly in southern and eastern counties, had a hard time; many became bankrupt, some tenant farmers fell into arrears with rents, and landowners suffered reduced profits from rents. The area of land producing cereal crops fell substantially, from 9.6 million acres at the height of the Golden Age in 1872, to 6.5 million acres in 1913. On the other hand, in the Midlands, in Lancashire and Cheshire, and in Scotland, where mixed farming was common, the depression was comparatively mild.

▸ There were important political effects: the domination of Parliament by wealthy landowners began to break down. Though most of the top landowning aristocrats, such as the Salisburys and the Roseberys, were able to continue their political activities, many of the middling and smaller landowners were no longer able to afford the money or the time to make any significant contribution to politics. The House of Commons gradually filled up with middle-class members – businessmen, industrialists, bankers and lawyers, and even a few working men. In the words of E. J. Evans, 'the old political order was finally being dismantled, without revolution but in response to substantial economic changes'.

▸ Many farmers survived by turning arable land over to pasture, and switching to livestock, dairy and poultry farming. Others turned to orchards and market gardening, producing fruit, vegetables, flowers and bulbs. The area under pasture increased from 17.1 million acres in 1872, to 21.5 million in 1913. Although it is true that meat, butter and cheese prices fell during the late 1880s and the 1890s in the face of foreign imports, this was not as disastrous as the fall in cereal prices. There were three reasons for this:

(i)   The price of animal feed fell substantially;
(ii) British meat was of a higher quality than imported frozen and chilled meat; and
(iii) The growing demand for milk in the industrial towns and cities could only be met by British cattle.

‣ There were important social effects. In areas where arable farming was abandoned, many agricultural labourers were thrown out of work, and there must have been considerable hardship for a time. In 1851, the agricultural labour force reached a peak of 2.1 million – almost twice as many as worked in mills and factories. By 1891, the number had fallen to 1.6 million; but worse was to come: by 1901, there were only just over 600,000. Some had moved to London and other industrial centres, while others had emigrated to the USA, Canada, Australia and New Zealand.

‣ Thanks to the continued absence of tariffs in the form of import duties, the depression brought the benefit of cheaper food, so that working-class people who were lucky enough to have jobs could enjoy a higher standard of living. For the remaining agricultural labourers, falling prices meant that, despite their money wages falling, their real wages probably remained steady. However, agricultural labourers were poorly paid compared with industrial workers – their average real wages never reached much above half of those in industry, and they were still working longer hours than industrial workers. Sharply falling food prices meant that workers had more money left over so they could now buy goods which were previously too expensive for them; some chose to spend their extra cash on leisure activities, which explains why professional football became such a popular entertainment during the later part of the century.

(c) agriculture recovers slightly after 1900

By 1914, total output of agriculture had increased by 5 per cent since 1900, and prices, even of wheat, were rising again. This apparent recovery took place because the blast of foreign competition had forced farmers to adapt and become more efficient, or go under. *The Eversley Commission* (1893–7) urged more people to take up dairy and poultry farming, or turn to market gardening. Many took this advice, further slimming down the less profitable cereal-producing sector. The government helped by forbidding the import of live cattle (1892); while the prime purpose of this move was to control cattle diseases, it removed an important element of competition. In the end, therefore, it was not so much a recovery as that the survivors had learned to live with world-wide foreign competition.

QUESTIONS

1 Read the following extract about the agricultural depression in the late nineteenth century, from *British Economic and Social History* by C. P. Hill, and then answer the questions that follow.

> Wheat prices ... reached rock bottom in 1894. In 1874 there had been 3,630,000 acres under wheat in Great Britain; by 1900 the total was only just over half that figure ... In thirty years some 300,000 agricultural labourers had left the countryside.

(a) Why was British agriculture in depression between the late 1870s and the early 20th century?

(b) 'Far more people benefited from than were harmed by the agricultural depression'. Examine the validity of this claim.

2 How accurate is it to describe the period c.1875–c.1914 in Great Britain as one of economic decline?

A document question about the 'depression' in British industry in the late nineteenth and early twentieth centuries can be found on the accompanying website www.palgrave.com/masterseries/lowe1.

chapter 16

Gladstone and Salisbury, 1880–95

summary of events

This period was very much dominated by events in Ireland; governments of both parties tried to solve the problems by a combination of coercion and pacification, but without any lasting success. Of the six governments which held office, four were directly brought down by Irish affairs.

governments, 1880–95

Party	Prime Minister	In Office
Liberal	W. E. Gladstone (2nd ministry)	1880–Jun 1885
Conservative	Lord Salisbury (1st ministry)	Jun 1885–February 1886
Liberal	W. E. Gladstone (3rd ministry)	Feb–Aug 1886
Conservative	Lord Salisbury (2nd ministry)	1886–92
Liberal	W. E. Gladstone (4th ministry)	1892–Mar 1894
Liberal	Lord Rosebery	Mar 1894–Jun 1895

Gladstone began his second ministry with a large majority, but very little went right for him. His *Second Irish Land Act (1881)* failed to satisfy the Irish Nationalists and their leader, Charles Stewart Parnell, who would settle for nothing less than Home Rule. Disraeli had left Gladstone several problems abroad – in Afghanistan, the Transvaal, Egypt and the Sudan. Gladstone's handling of these situations aroused criticism, and though his policies resulted in Egypt in effect becoming part of the British Empire, he was also held responsible for the death of the popular General Gordon in the Sudan. There was time for a few domestic reforms, notably *the Parliamentary Reform Act of 1884,* but the Radicals felt that there ought to have been many more.

Believing that there was more to be gained for Ireland from the Conservatives, Parnell had no hesitation in using Irish Nationalist votes to turn out Gladstone and put in Salisbury and the Conservatives (June 1885). When it was revealed that Gladstone had been converted to Home Rule, despite the opposition of many of his own party, Parnell switched his support back to the Liberals. However, Gladstone's *1886 Home Rule Bill* was defeated in the Commons, when 93 Liberals voted against it. The Liberal party, deeply split over Ireland and other matters, was defeated in the following general election.

During the six years of Conservative rule, there were several important developments: Ireland was given firm treatment along with some modest concessions; in foreign affairs, Salisbury was concerned to keep Britain aloof from binding agreements with other powers – a policy that became known, misleadingly, as *'splendid isolation';* and there were the early stages of the *Scramble for Africa*, during which the powers of Western Europe managed to divide Africa between them without a war. This was not exciting stuff for ordinary working people, who were more concerned with the unemployment situation and the cost of living; the attentions of many of them were turning towards trade unions and events such as the successful dockers' strike of 1889.

In the 1892 election, the Liberals won just enough seats to form a government, with Irish Nationalist support. The main aim of the 83-year-old Gladstone was to secure Home Rule for Ireland; but his *Second Home Rule Bill,* though it passed the Commons, was defeated by the Conservative-dominated House of Lords, and Gladstone resigned. Lord Rosebery's short government was notable for the way in which the Lords continually prevented Liberal bills from becoming law. This was the beginning of the growing confrontation between the two houses, which was to reach its climax with *the Parliament Act of 1911.* With Gladstone's retirement, the Liberals had lost their main attraction for the electorate, and they were heavily defeated in the election of 1895. Ten years of unbroken Conservative rule followed.

16.1 how did Gladstone try to pacify Ireland between 1880 and 1886, and why did he fail?

(a) the deteriorating situation in Ireland

The situation in Ireland had deteriorated during Disraeli's government (1874–80). The agricultural depression, caused by cheap American corn, made farming in Ireland even less profitable than before. Many landlords reacted by evicting more tenant-farmers in order to consolidate holdings; violent incidents were common as desperate tenants retaliated. To make matters worse, the potato crop failed again for several years in succession, especially in Connaught in the west. All over Ireland, a series of wet summers helped to cause epidemics among farm animals and ruined hay crops. Nor was there much industry for the farmers to fall back on; the once-flourishing domestic textile industry had been killed off even before the famine, by competition from cheap factory-produced cloth made in England and Scotland. For some reason, probably lack of suitable coal resources, the Irish had failed to develop their own textile mills.

Smallholders and tenant-farmers combined to form *the Irish Land League (1879)* under the leadership of Michael Davitt. He was an Irish Catholic whose family had been evicted from their land when he was a child; he had spent seven years in Dartmoor after being convicted of involvement in Fenian outrages. The League soon gained massive support throughout Ireland, and it demanded three concessions which, it was thought, would ease the situation. *Known as the 'three Fs', these were*:

› a fair rent;
› fixity of tenure (a guarantee that tenants would not be evicted provided they paid the rent); and
› free sale (the right to sell their land, or their interest in a holding, without interference from the landlord, so they could get the best possible price).

According to historian Michael Winstanley, the traditional view of these demands, that they were 'the reaction of a poverty-stricken peasantry to mounting landlord exploitation, excessive rents and widespread evictions', has now been discredited. He argues that, during the prosperity of the previous thirty years, rents had in fact lagged behind profits; the Land League's motive therefore was to force landlords to reduce rents still further so that smallholders and farmers could hold on to their gains. The League's official tactic was for farmers to refuse to pay rents, though in some areas they resorted to violence – the maiming of cattle and burning of landlords' haystacks.

Whatever its exact motives, the League was soon working closely with the Home Rule Movement and its formidable leader, Charles Stewart Parnell. He seemed an unlikely choice for an Irish nationalist leader, since he was a Protestant landlord, descended from an English family and seemed the typical English land-owning country gentlemen – the very type detested by Irish Catholics. However, he was much influenced by his mother, who was American and strongly anti-English. Aloof, icily disdainful and withdrawn, he detested the English, once remarking: 'We will never gain anything from England unless we tread on her toes.' He had been MP for County Meath since 1875 and had organized the successful Irish Nationalist obstruction campaign in the Commons.

(b) Gladstone tries to give the Irish concessions

Gladstone was determined to be reasonable and go as far as he could towards giving the Irish what they wanted. At this stage, however, he was not prepared to consider Home Rule. He was hampered all the way by opposition from the House of Lords, from the Land League, and from a section of his own party which felt he was being too lenient with the Irish.

1 A Bill was introduced (1880) to give compensation to Irish tenants who had been evicted, but the Lords, many of whom owned land in Ireland, rejected it by a huge majority (282 to 51). More than 10,000 people had been evicted in that year alone, and there was widespread misery and desperation. The Land League retaliated by boycotting anyone who took over a farm from which the previous tenant had been evicted; he should be 'isolated as if he were a leper'. The first person to be dealt with in this way was Captain Boycott, the agent of a wealthy landowner in County Mayo; after evicting a tenant for non-payment of rent, Boycott found that servants, shopkeepers, labourers, in fact everybody, would have nothing to do with him, and troops had to be sent in to protect his property. A new word was thus added to the language, and the boycott idea spread rapidly.

2 The government replied with a *Coercion Act (1881)*, which suspended habeas corpus (see Section 2.4(b)).

3 Gladstone would not be content with repression alone, and he was soon responsible for *the Second Irish Land Act (1881)*, which gave the Irish what the League wanted – the three Fs, plus Land Courts to decide fair rents. The Act was a remarkable achievement and shows how genuinely committed Gladstone was to easing the misery of the Irish. It took fifty-eight sittings in the Commons and all Gladstone's tremendous skill and experience to pilot it through. The Lords only passed it thanks to Queen Victoria's influence. Unfortunately, it did not solve the Irish problem, though there was very little wrong with the Act itself, except that it was ten years too late. Parnell decided that since his campaign had squeezed such a great concession out of Gladstone, then continued pressure might bring the ultimate prize – Home Rule. The Land League therefore boycotted the new Land Courts, ordered a non-payment of rent campaign, and did all it could to sabotage the working of the Act. Evictions and violence continued.

(c) Gladstone, Parnell and Irish Nationalism

While Isaac Butt was leader of the Home Rule League (formed in 1870) its campaign for a separate Irish parliament in Dublin to look after internal affairs, was moderate and respectable. Poverty and the land problem were probably behind the growth of nationalism during the last thirty years of the century, but there was much more to it than that. There was a deep feeling of separateness from the English, and the Home Rulers talked about 'the inalienable right of the Irish people to self-government'. Charles Stewart Parnell (who became leader in 1877) was much more aggressive than Butt. He pointed out that 'Ireland is not a geographical fragment of England; she is a nation'. The fact that New Zealand had been given self-government in 1856 and Canada dominion status in 1867 encouraged the Irish to hope for something similar. In the 1880 general election, the Irish Nationalists won 61 seats, and their success in pressurizing Gladstone in the Second Land Act was a great boost to their confidence.

However, Gladstone was shocked and disgusted by their refusal to co-operate with the Act, and he had Parnell and other leaders arrested and imprisoned in Kilmainham Gaol, Dublin. This solved nothing, violence increased and a rash of secret extremist societies broke out.

1 After six months, both Gladstone and Parnell were anxious to break the stalemate; Parnell was afraid that he might lose control of the movement while he was absent in gaol. An understanding (sometimes known as *the Kilmainham Treaty*) was reached, through intermediaries (April 1882). Parnell agreed to call off the rent strike and control the violence, and in return Gladstone promised an Arrears Bill to let tenants off their rent arrears which had accumulated during the recent campaign. Parnell was released. This agreement was an admission by Gladstone that only Parnell, who was now regarded as 'the uncrowned king of Ireland', could control the Irish. It was probably around this time that Gladstone realized that Home Rule would have to come sooner or later.

2 *The Phoenix Park murders* ruined chances of immediate progress. Only four days after Parnell's release, Lord Frederick Cavendish, the new Chief Secretary for Ireland (and brother of Lord Hartington, leader of the Whigs), who had only been in the country a few hours, and T. E. Burke, the permanent under-secretary, were attacked and stabbed to death with surgical knives while they were walking in Phoenix Park, Dublin. The murderers were members of an extremist group known as the 'Invincibles'. Parnell was shocked and denounced the group, but more murders followed, and it seemed as though Parnell's influence was declining. The English public was now convinced that the Irish were impossible to deal with, and opinion hardened against Home Rule.

3 Gladstone bowed to pressure and an even more severe Coercion Act was passed, which enabled the government to track down and arrest the 'Invincibles', five of whom were hanged.

4 Gladstone and Parnell tried hard to make the Kilmainham agreement work. The Arrears Act was passed and the Second Land Act began to operate, resulting in a general reduction of rents by an average of 20 per cent. During 1883, affairs in Ireland gradually settled into a period of comparative calm, which lasted until June 1885. This must be seen as a partial success for Gladstone, but it was not a permanent solution.

(d) Parnell puts the Conservatives in power

Parnell still wanted Home Rule and still controlled a powerful group of sixty Nationalist MPs. He decided that instead of obstructing the government, there might be more to be gained by co-operation with one of the major parties. There seemed little prospect of the Liberals giving him what he wanted, since there was strong right-wing opposition to any further concessions. However,

Lord Randolph Churchill, a brilliant up-and-coming young Conservative, eager to gain Irish votes, seemed to be offering major concessions. It made no difference to Parnell which party helped him, so he decided to take a chance with the Conservatives. In June 1885, the Nationalists voted with the Conservatives to defeat the Liberal government on an increase in the beer and spirit duties. Gladstone resigned and a Conservative government took office, with Robert Cecil, Marquis of Salisbury, as Prime Minister. He was totally dependent on Irish votes to stay in office, and consequently gave them two major concessions:

▸ The Coercion Acts were dropped.
▸ *Lord Ashbourne's Act (1885)* introduced a scheme that provided £5 million for loans to enable tenants to buy holdings from their landlords. During the following six years, around 25,000 Irish farmers took advantage of this offer, and more and more landlords were prepared to sell holdings, since their income from rents was declining. The terms for borrowers were quite generous – an interest rate of 4 per cent, and 49 years to pay back the loan.

A general election was held in November 1885, and Parnell, delighted with his gains so far, instructed all Irishmen living on the mainland to vote Conservative. The election result was a strange one: the Liberals lost 18 seats but still had a majority of 86 over the Conservatives (335 Liberals to 249 Conservatives). By a strange coincidence, the Irish Nationalists won 86 seats, which meant that, if the Parnell–Salisbury alliance continued, the result was a dead heat. The Conservative government carried on, with Parnell holding the balance: he could keep the Conservatives in office, or he could withdraw his support and allow the Liberals back in. By now Gladstone realized that only Home Rule would pacify the Irish, though he kept his feelings to himself. He hoped that the Conservatives would be the ones to introduce it, since they would have a better chance of getting the approval of the Lords. By early December, it was clear that Salisbury was not prepared to go so far as Home Rule; and it was only a matter of time before Parnell removed him.

(e) Gladstone and the First Home Rule Bill (1886)

Gladstone decided in favour of Home Rule during the summer of 1885. *There were several reasons for his change of mind*:

▸ Violence was on the increase again following the Conservatives' removal of the Coercion Acts, and Gladstone was afraid the campaign would spread to England.
▸ Some leading British officials in Dublin, including Sir Robert Hamilton (successor to the murdered Burke), who knew the situation at first hand, believed that Home Rule was the only way to get consistent government in Ireland.

- Above all Gladstone realized that Irish nationalism, like Italian and Belgian nationalism (both of which the British government had supported) was such a deeply felt desire that the only just and reasonable course was to satisfy it.

Gladstone did not reveal his conversion to Home Rule, because he hoped that the Conservatives would introduce it, and because he was afraid of splitting the Liberals, many of whom were opposed to the idea and would require gradual persuasion. Lord Hartington, brother of Lord Frederick Cavendish and leader of the Liberal right-wing (Whigs), was a bitter opponent of any further concessions to the Irish. However, a series of sensational developments took place:

1 On 15 December 1885, Gladstone's son, Herbert, leaked the news to the press of his father's conversion. Having the news sprung on them so suddenly outraged Hartington and his supporters, and made Gladstone's job of winning them over almost impossible. Hartington announced that he would never support Home Rule, but Gladstone was determined to go forward. The Conservative government was defeated by the combined Liberal and Irish votes, and Gladstone became Prime Minister for the third time (January 1886).

2 *The First Home Rule Bill* was introduced in April. It proposed that Ireland should have its own parliament in Dublin, and that no Irish MPs would sit at Westminster. The Dublin parliament would control all internal affairs; foreign affairs, defence and trade would remain under the direction of Westminster. The bill met bitter opposition in the Commons from the Conservatives. Lord Randolph Churchill stirred up religious prejudices with the argument that the Protestant minority in Ulster would not be well treated by a Dublin government dominated by Catholics; it would, he said, amount to 'Rome Rule', not Home Rule, and so Ulster should therefore oppose Home Rule by every means possible. His slogan was 'Ulster will fight and Ulster will be right.' There was also opposition to the bill from Lord Hartington and his Whig supporters; Hartington, the future Duke of Devonshire, owned large estates in southern Ireland and was afraid that an Irish parliament would take action to end Whig land ownership in Ireland. More opposition came from Joseph Chamberlain, leader of the Radical wing of the Liberal party; he was convinced that Home Rule for Ireland would threaten the unity of the British Empire. In June, the bill was defeated by 343 votes to 313; 93 Liberals voted against it.

3 Gladstone decided to appeal to the country, but in the following general election the Liberals lost heavily and were reduced to only 191 seats, against 317 Conservatives. The mainland electorate had given its verdict decisively against Home Rule, and once again Irish affairs had brought down a British government. More than that, the Liberal party was now deeply divided and would take years to recover from the split. The anti-Home Rule Liberals remained as a separate group of 77 MPs (in addition to the 191 Gladstone

supporters) and, under the leadership of Chamberlain, were known as *the Liberal Unionists* (because they wanted to preserve the union between England and Ireland). Many later joined the Conservatives and it was twenty years before the Liberal party recovered (see Section 16.6 for Ireland under the Conservatives, 1886–92).

(f) why did Chamberlain oppose Home Rule?

There has been disagreement about his motives:

‣ Irish historians put it down to sheer ambition; it was widely expected that Gladstone would resign the leadership if Home Rule was defeated; this would leave the way clear for Chamberlain to become Liberal leader. His English biographers feel this is unfair on Chamberlain, who was not the only Liberal to consider that Gladstone had become so obsessed with Ireland that he was out of touch with politics in the rest of Britain. Gladstone had ignored all Chamberlain's suggestions for reform, and Home Rule was threatening to split the party. Arguably, Chamberlain genuinely believed that he was the man to reunite the party after Gladstone's retirement.

‣ Chamberlain believed that improved administration and social conditions would pacify the Irish, and felt that these could be achieved by a system of county boards, which would be a less drastic solution than complete Home Rule. Gladstone rejected this idea.

‣ Chamberlain, who was a great supporter of imperialism and the British Empire, disliked Home Rule because it meant the separation of Ireland from the rest of Britain; this might cause other British territories to demand independence, leading to the disintegration of the Empire.

‣ He was annoyed, with some justification, that Gladstone had not consulted him at any stage during the drawing up of the bill, and felt that the government's time would have been better spent on introducing social reform.

16.2 the Liberals and the Empire

Gladstone's views on imperialism were well known – he disapproved of it because it interfered with the rights and freedom of overseas peoples to govern themselves; also, it would be expensive – the Empire would have to be defended, causing a constant drain on British resources. He had criticized Disraeli unmercifully (see Section 14.3), but once back in office, he found to his annoyance that he was saddled with several imperial problems left by Disraeli. Gladstone wanted to disentangle Britain, but it was not as easy as he had expected.

(a) withdrawal from Afghanistan

Gladstone reversed Disraeli's policy (see Section 14.3(e)) by withdrawing British troops from Afghanistan. This was regarded by the Conservatives as a typical example of Liberal weakness abroad, but in fact relations with Afghanistan remained good for the next twenty years.

(b) the Transvaal wins independence

Shortly before the outbreak of the Zulu War in 1879, the Transvaal, recently annexed by Britain, had been promised self-government once the Zulu threat had been removed. Since this had been achieved by the Zulu War, the Transvaal Boers expected immediate independence, given Gladstone's powerful condemnation of the annexation. However, nothing happened, partly because Gladstone was busy with financial affairs, and because he was beginning to think about setting up a South African federation, to include the Transvaal and the Orange Free State. In January 1881, he told the Transvaal that immediate self-government was out of the question. The Boers rose in revolt, and in February defeated a tiny British force of 359 men at *Majuba Hill;* a hundred of the British were killed, including the commander, Sir George Colley. Gladstone was in a dilemma, faced with two possible courses of action:

1 He could send out more troops to avenge the defeat and crush the Boers, which public opinion, the Queen and the Conservatives demanded.
2 He could make peace and concede independence to the Transvaal.

Showing great courage, Gladstone took the unpopular second course: *the Pretoria Convention* (August 1881) recognized the Transvaal's independence, 'subject to the suzerainty [overlordship] of her Majesty'. When the Boers protested at the suzerainty clause, Gladstone agreed that it should be dropped. There was an angry public outcry at this 'surrender', and Queen Victoria sent Gladstone a strongly worded letter of protest. But Gladstone was unrepentant – he had no intention of involving Britain in an expensive colonial war. It was probably the right decision in the circumstances, but he had handled the situation badly, with unfortunate consequences:

▸ He had given way to force, whereas if he had allowed independence earlier, British prestige would have been preserved.
▸ The Boers took it as a sign of British weakness, and became more arrogant in their relations with Britain. Their attitude was a contributory cause of the Boer War, which broke out in 1899 (see Section 17.3).

(c) the British occupy Egypt

Gladstone had to accept that Britain was deeply involved in Egypt as a result of its ownership of almost half the Suez Canal shares (see Section 14.3(b)), and events compelled him, against his will, to intervene in Egypt to safeguard British interests. The Egyptian government was in worse financial difficulties than before as it tried to pay the interest on massive French and British loans that had been made to finance railways, roads, docks and agricultural projects.

When an epidemic of cattle plague broke out in 1878, the country was brought to the verge of bankruptcy.

1 Britain and France, concerned about their financial interests, tried to force the ruler, the Khedive Ismail, to allow European advisers to control his country's finances. When he refused, they prevailed upon his overlord, the Sultan of Turkey, to replace Ismail with his son Tewfik (1879).

2 There was widespread resentment in Egypt at this foreign interference, and a strong, anti-foreign Egyptian Nationalist party emerged, led by an army officer, Arabi Pasha, who, by May 1882, seemed on the point of deposing Tewfik. There was every chance that Arabi would seize the Canal and repudiate Egypt's debts.

3 Gladstone, acting jointly with the French, sent a fleet to Alexandria as a warning gesture, but this provoked serious anti-European rioting in Alexandria, in which about eighty Europeans were killed. Arabi, far from being overawed by the presence of the foreign fleets, began to fortify Alexandria. At this point, the French decided to take no further action, but Gladstone authorized the bombardment of Alexandria's defences. A 12-hour artillery battle followed, which ended with British troops occupying the city (July 1882).

4 Gladstone asked Parliament for £2.3 million for an expedition 'to substitute the rule of law for that of military violence in Egypt'. The money was granted, and 16,400 British troops under Sir Garnet Wolseley were soon en route for Egypt. Having landed at Alexandria, they destroyed Arabi's army at *the Battle of Tel-el-Kebir* (September) and captured Cairo. Arabi was exiled to Ceylon, and Tewfik restored to the throne.

5 Sir Evelyn Baring (later made Lord Cromer) was appointed Consul-General of Egypt, and virtually ruled the country for the next twenty-three years. He was a highly efficient administrator: as early as 1888 he had balanced the Egyptian budget, and he went on to introduce irrigation schemes and other reforms. Egypt had all the appearance of being a British colony, though Gladstone did not annex it, and claimed that the British occupation was only temporary. The British stayed in Egypt until 1954.

Gladstone's decisive action astonished the public and boosted his popularity. He might have been expected to sympathize with the Egyptian nationalists, and yet it was a more 'forward' policy than anything Disraeli had initiated. It shocked the veteran pacifist John Bright, who resigned from the Cabinet, remarking that Gladstone's intervention was 'simply damnable – worse than anything ever perpetrated by Dizzy'.

(d) why did Gladstone agree to the occupation of Egypt?

The reason was simply that financial and strategic considerations outweighed sympathy for the nationalist movement. The possibility of Arabi repudiating

Egypt's debts horrified Gladstone; if Arabi seized the Suez Canal, British shipping would be at a disadvantage and the route to India threatened. It was Britain's duty 'to convert the present interior state of Egypt from anarchy and conflict to peace and order'. *The policy was viewed as an outstanding success:* British interests had been safeguarded, and British prestige abroad enhanced. However, some imperialists felt that Gladstone ought to have annexed Egypt outright, or at least declared it to be a British protectorate.

(e) General Gordon and the Sudan

There was soon another opportunity for Britain to seize territory, in the Sudan, but this time Gladstone acted predictably and did not take it. The affair was so badly mishandled that it turned out to be the most spectacular failure of the entire ministry. The Sudan had been ruled by Egypt since 1823, and the Sudanese, especially in the north, resented Egyptian rule because it was corrupt; it had abolished the profitable slave-trade; and it had close connections with Europeans, who were non-Islamic. Muhammed Ahmed, a local religious leader, proclaimed that he was the *Mahdi* – the saviour of Islam from foreign influence, and roused most of the country against the occupying Egyptian troops.

1 Tewfik, the newly restored ruler of Egypt, sent an Egyptian army commanded by a British officer, Hicks Pasha, to subdue the rebels, but the force, Hicks Pasha included, was slaughtered by the Mahdi and his Dervishes (November 1883).

2 Gladstone was faced with a difficult decision: should he send a British army to conquer the Sudan, or should he leave it to the Mahdi? He decided against sending a British expedition, partly because Sir Evelyn Baring advised that the only reasonable course was to withdraw, so great was the Mahdi's popular support. Gladstone also sympathized with the Sudanese in their nationalist struggle against the Egyptians.

3 However, there were still a number of Egyptian garrisons in the Sudan, commanded by British officers, who could not be left at the mercy of the Mahdi. The government therefore sent out General Charles Gordon, with orders to organize the evacuation of the garrisons as quickly as possible. This was where the first mistake lay: Gordon was not the sort of man to be relied on to organize a retreat. He had made himself famous through military exploits in China, Africa, India and the Crimea. In the words of Philip Magnus (one of Gladstone's biographers), 'fearless, erratic, brilliant, perverse, always notoriously undisciplined, he exercised an extraordinary fascination over his fellow-countrymen'. Gordon had already been governor of the Sudan (1877–9), and early in 1884 he told the press that he considered it quite feasible to resist the Mahdi.

4 Gordon arrived in Khartoum, the Sudanese capital, in February 1884, but instead of hurrying on with the evacuation while there was still time, he

decided to stay put; a fanatical Christian, he believed it was his duty to save the country from the Mahdi, and he asked for British troops to be sent to keep open the Nile route from the Sudan into Egypt. This request was refused. By the end of March, the Mahdi's forces had closed in and Gordon was besieged in Khartoum.

5 Public opinion and the Queen demanded that help be sent immediately, but Gladstone, furious with Gordon for disobeying orders, hesitated. All through the summer the Cabinet argued about what action to take, and it was not until October that a relief force under Wolseley left Cairo on its 1,600 mile journey up the Nile. It arrived at Khartoum on 28 January 1885, only to find that the city had fallen to the Mahdi two days earlier, and Gordon was dead.

The nation was stunned and Gladstone was blamed. Angry crowds hooted and jeered in Downing Street, and instead of being the GOM (Grand Old Man) he became the MOG – murderer of Gordon. In April, Gladstone outraged public opinion further by withdrawing Wolseley's forces and leaving the Sudan to the Mahdi. While Gordon had brought disaster on himself by disobeying orders, there is no doubt that the Cabinet could and should have sent help much sooner, and the Liberals were deeply unpopular.

(f) the Penjdeh incident (1885)

This crisis in Anglo-Russian relations was well handled by Gladstone. On 30 March 1885, encouraged by British embarrassment over the Sudan, the Russians seized the Afghan village of Penjdeh, a few miles from the Russian frontier. Gladstone responded vigorously, warned the Russians that Britain would not tolerate such aggression, and called up the reserves. The Russians withdrew and agreed to submit their claim for Penjdeh to arbitration. Gladstone had shown that he could be firm when international morality had been violated; unfortunately, the effect was spoilt when the arbitrators awarded Penjdeh to the Russians; but this was after Gladstone's government had fallen.

Gladstone's record in imperial and foreign affairs during this ministry was not particularly impressive. Contemporaries found it difficult to understand his motives, and his actions seemed contradictory: he had abandoned the Transvaal and tried to give Ireland Home Rule with the one hand while occupying Egypt with the other. All these situations were to cause further trouble later. Worst of all, he had allowed the national hero, Gordon, to get himself killed in Khartoum.

16.3 what were the domestic achievements of the Liberal government?

There were several important domestic reforms.

(a) the repeal of the Malt Tax (1880)

This removed a long-standing grievance of farmers, who had campaigned against it more vigorously than ever as they began to feel the pinch of the agricultural depression. Disraeli had disappointed the farmers, but Gladstone obliged, even though he had to increase income tax by a penny in the pound to make up the lost revenue.

(b) the Married Women's Property Act (1882)

This was designed to protect the property of married women. When a woman married, her husband became the owner of all her worldly goods; he could spend her savings and sell her house, and the system was an open invitation for unscrupulous fortune-hunters to take advantage of innocent and unsuspecting but wealthy young ladies. The new Act gave a married woman the right to continue as the separate owner of property of all kinds.

(c) the Corrupt Practices Act (1883)

This went a long way towards removing abuses and corruption during general elections, including bribery and intimidation of voters. It specified the amount of money a party could spend on the campaign in each constituency, the sum being based on the number of voters. It also introduced rules about the type and number of carriages that could be used to take voters to the polls.

(d) the Parliamentary Reform Act (1884) and the Redistribution of Seats Act (1885)

These two Acts were the major domestic achievement of Gladstone's second ministry.

The demand for further parliamentary reform came from Joseph Chamberlain and the Radical wing of the Liberal party, who were disappointed with Gladstone's reforms to date in this ministry. Their case was unanswerable: the 1867 Reform Act had given the vote to householders in towns, but in the counties, the voting qualification was still high enough to prevent agricultural labourers and other workers from voting; thus the power of wealthy farmers and landowners was preserved. This was undemocratic, and Chamberlain was bitterly critical of the landowners; he described them as a class 'who toil not, neither do they spin ... whose fortunes have originated by grants made in times gone by ... and have since grown and increased while they have slept'. Another anomaly of the system was that the distribution of seats was still unfair, with many small towns having the same representation – two MPs – as large industrial cities (see Section 8.5(a)). Chamberlain carried a majority of the Cabinet with him, and a Reform (or Franchise) Bill passed the Commons comfortably (June 1884).

There was strong opposition from the Conservatives in the Lords, who demanded that a Redistribution Bill should be passed first. They hoped that this would cause so many local difficulties that both bills would be delayed indefinitely. Chamberlain retaliated with a series of violent speeches, warning the Lords of dire consequences if they continued to block Liberal legislation; his rallying cry was 'the Peers versus the People'. The Queen, worried about a constitutional crisis, suggested that Gladstone and Salisbury should meet for tea and have talks. After secret negotiations between Liberal and Conservative leaders, an acceptable compromise was worked out:

- *The Reform (Franchise) Act* gave the vote to all householders in the counties, adding over two million voters to the list. In total, 5.7 million people had the vote by this time. The same system was extended to Ireland.
- *The Redistribution Act* took away both MPs from boroughs with fewer than 15,000 inhabitants, while those with fewer than 50,000 lost one MP. This released 142 seats, which were redistributed among more densely populated areas. The system was reorganized so that 647 out of 670 constituencies were represented by one MP each (these were known as single-member constituencies). The exceptions were large cities with well in excess of 50,000 inhabitants, the Scottish universities, and Oxford and Cambridge Universities. Redistribution went some way towards achieving one of the Chartists' demands – equal electoral districts. Cornwall, for example, lost 37 seats, while Lancashire gained 44 and London 37.

Joseph Chamberlain claimed that these acts were 'the greatest revolution that this country has ever undergone'. But in fact *they did not complete the transition to full democracy:* it still remained to give the vote to women and to about a third of all men; and to abolish plural voting (the right of a man to vote in every constituency where he owned property). It was to be almost half a century (1928) before full modern democracy was achieved – when women were allowed to vote at the age of 21.

There were two other important results: the disappearance of most of the two-member constituencies put a stop to the Liberal practice of running one Whig and one Radical candidate in each constituency. This meant that fewer Whigs could gain acceptance as candidates: the aristocratic Whig section of the party began to shrink and the Radicals became the dominant wing of the party. In Ireland, the changes meant that Parnell's nationalists swept the board and could always guarantee winning at least 80 seats.

These domestic reforms, though excellent in themselves, were disappointingly few for a government with a large majority, which lasted for over five years. Part of the trouble was that Irish affairs and Irish obstruction consumed far too much of the government's time. Parnell became a master at obstructing parliamentary business, forcing late-night and sometimes all-night sittings, and calling for endless divisions. According to K. H. Flynn, he 'became the most hated man in the Commons. Whenever he stood up the House broke into howls and jeers, sometimes keeping him standing for several minutes before he could speak'. Another reason for the relatively few social reforms was that the Liberal party was deeply divided over a number of issues. These are examined in the next section.

16.4 why was there so much tension within the Liberal party, 1880–6?

(a) divisions between the left (Radical) and right (Whig) wings of the party

The Whigs, mainly aristocratic landowners such as Lord Hartington (later Duke of Devonshire), Lord Granville, Lord Spencer and the Duke of Argyll, were much less progressive than the Radicals, whose main figures were Joseph Chamberlain, Sir Charles Dilke and John Bright. Gladstone, careful to please the Whigs, gave them all but two of the Cabinet posts, but of the Radicals, only Chamberlain and Bright were included. The Radicals felt slighted and the two wings did not work smoothly together.

(b) Gladstone was difficult to work with

Gladstone caused problems by his methods of running the government. As well as being Prime Minister, he took on the office of Chancellor of the Exchequer (1880); this meant that he was overwhelmed with a mass of financial details, which prevented him from giving sufficient attention to other matters (such as independence for the Transvaal). Though he resigned the Chancellorship in 1882, much damage had been done. He often acted on impulse without consulting the Cabinet, and was generally a difficult man to work with.

(c) the Bradlaugh case was an embarrassment for the government

Charles Bradlaugh was elected Liberal MP for Northampton in 1880. A Radical of somewhat unorthodox views (for the time), he was an outspoken atheist and an advocate of contraceptives. The trouble started when he refused to take the normal oath of allegiance because it included the words 'So help me God'. After a Commons select committee decided that he must take the oath, Bradlaugh agreed, but a group of young Conservative MPs led by Lord Randolph Churchill (father of Winston) stirred the Commons up to vote for Bradlaugh's expulsion. He was obliged to stand for re-election, but after he had again won Northampton, the same procedure was repeated when he tried to take his seat. Churchill and his friends (nicknamed 'the Fourth Party') exploited the situation to divide the Liberals. Gladstone and many Radicals supported Bradlaugh, but the Nonconformist Liberals were outraged at the presence of such an avowed atheist, and Bradlaugh was again expelled. He was re-elected and expelled a further three times, and was prevented from taking his seat until the next Parliament, in 1885.

(d) disagreement over social reform

Joseph Chamberlain was keen on social and local government reform. A successful industrialist in the West Midlands and a convinced Nonconformist Christian (he was a Unitarian) (see Section 12.13), he had started his political career as Mayor of Birmingham. He believed that it was the role of both national and local government to take action to improve the social conditions of ordinary people. He had been responsible for building a fine new city centre in Birmingham, and for providing a clean water supply. However, these matters bored Gladstone, who believed that government intervention in such things should be kept to a minimum. But while Gladstone was merely bored, Hartington, the Whig leader, was positively hostile. Before the 1885 election, Chamberlain launched a campaign for reform – *the Unauthorized Programme,* so called because Gladstone had not approved it. Amid mass meetings and processions, Chamberlain outlined his programme:

‣ Free primary education.
‣ Payment of MPs.
‣ County councils to look after rural areas.
‣ Graduated income tax, to make the wealthy foot the bill.
‣ With one eye on the new county voters, he also proposed that agricultural labourers should be given smallholdings; this became known as 'the three acres and a cow' policy.

In one of his speeches, Chamberlain declared:

> I am told if I pursue this course that I shall break up the Party ... but I care little for the party ... except to promote the objects which I publicly avowed when I first entered Parliament. In this rich country, an honest, a decent, an industrious man should be able to earn a livelihood for himself and his family, and should be able to lay aside something for sickness and old age. Is that unreasonable? Is that impossible?

Chamberlain and his programme were largely responsible for the Liberal success in the 1885 election, yet Gladstone made no concessions to him and ignored the case for social reform. 'Chamberlain's socialism repels me,' Gladstone noted in his diary.

(e) mixed reactions to foreign and imperial policies

Gladstone's foreign and imperial policies – especially independence for the Transvaal and the disaster in the Sudan – made the government unpopular with the public. Yet when he scored a success with the occupation of Egypt, some of the Radicals objected and Bright resigned from the Cabinet.

(f) Irish affairs were a major cause of tension

Whatever Gladstone did, he offended one section or another of the party. When he tried to make concessions to the Irish, the Whigs objected; Chamberlain's plan for Irish local self-government on a county basis was defeated in the Cabinet because all the Whigs (except Granville) opposed it (May 1885). Shortly afterwards, when Gladstone tried to take a hard line by stepping up coercion, the Radicals objected, and Chamberlain and Dilke resigned from the Cabinet. Gladstone's determination to secure Home Rule at all costs during his 1886 government was disastrous for the Liberals: most of the Whigs and the main Radical leaders opposed it, and the party split; Chamberlain led the breakaway group of Liberal Unionists. Without Chamberlain, the Liberals had little to offer, and the voters turned to the Conservatives. Some historians believe that the Liberal party never fully recovered from the split over the First Home Rule Bill (see Section 23.4).

16.5 what contribution did the Conservatives make to domestic reform, 1886–92?

(a) Lord Randolph Churchill and Tory Democracy

When Salisbury's Conservative government (317 seats) took office they could usually rely on the support of the 77 Liberal Unionists, which gave them a large majority over the 191 Liberals and 85 Irish Nationalists. At first it seemed as though it might turn out to be a great reforming ministry. The Chancellor of the Exchequer was the 37-year-old Lord Randolph Churchill, who had made a name for himself with his brilliant attacks on Gladstone; he seemed to have a gift for making the Liberal leader look ridiculous. He was easily the most exciting and dynamic personality in the government, and he aimed to follow the Disraeli brand of Conservatism – reform and modernization – in order to retain working-class support. In his famous *Dartford Speech* (October 1886) he announced his programme of Tory Democracy:

› improvement of public health and housing;
› compulsory national insurance;
› smallholdings for agricultural labourers;
› reform of parliamentary procedure; and
› provision of parks, art galleries, museums, and public baths and wash-houses.

However, Churchill soon left the government after a disagreement over his controversial Budget proposals. These included increases in death duties and house duties, and reductions in income tax and in tea and tobacco duties, to be paid for by cuts in defence expenditure. W. H. Smith, the War Minister, naturally

Illus. **16.1 Robert Cecil, third Marquis of Salisbury**

objected strongly, and when Salisbury supported Smith, Churchill suddenly resigned from the Exchequer (December 1886). He apparently thought that he was indispensable, and that his action would force Salisbury to bring him back and overrule Smith. But Churchill had completely miscalculated: he had shown himself to be far too radical for the right wing of the party, and Salisbury was probably relieved to be rid of such an embarrassment. Salisbury did not ask Churchill to withdraw his resignation and instead appointed Sir Edward Goschen, a Liberal Unionist, as Chancellor. With Churchill's departure, any chance of far-reaching reform disappeared. He never again held Cabinet office, and died in 1895 at the early age of 45. His biographer, R. F. Foster, and Robert Blake, the historian of the Conservative party, both feel that the whole concept of Tory Democracy has been exaggerated, and that as far as Churchill was concerned, it amounted to little more than opportunism – he wanted to be Conservative leader and Prime Minister.

(b) Salisbury's reforms

The Conservative reforms were few in number for a government that lasted six years. Salisbury believed that the function of government was to preserve and

Illus. **16.2 Lord Randolph Churchill**

extend individual freedom, with a minimum of interference by the state in
social and economic matters. He was a strong advocate of self-help: 'No men
ever rise to any permanent improvement in their condition of body or of mind
except by relying upon their own personal efforts.' He was not a complete reactionary, though, and in a speech at Exeter early in 1892 he claimed that the

greatest service a government could render for a poor man was 'so to shape matters that the greatest possible liberty for the exercise of his own moral and intellectual qualities should be offered to him by law'. Measures which attempted to 'shape matters' in this way were:

- *The Labourers' Allotment Act (1887)*. This gave local authorities the power to acquire land for allotments, so that the working classes could 'elevate themselves into a position of manly independence by their industry'. The results were disappointing: since the Act was not compulsory, many local authorities ignored it.
- *The Mines Regulation Act (1887)* was more successful, extending legal protection for miners while they were at work.
- *The Tithe Act (1890)* made tithes (the annual tax, amounting to one-tenth of income or produce, paid to support the Anglican church) payable by the owner of land and not by the occupier. This removed a long-standing cause of friction by ending the practice of seizing tenants' cattle and other possessions in lieu of cash payment.
- *In education*, the government was responsible for the appointment of *the Cross Commission* (see Section 12.8(d)) and for *the Fee Grant Act (1891)*, which abolished fees for elementary education.
- *The Factory Act (1891)* raised the minimum age at which children could be employed in factories to 11, and specified that the maximum working day for women was to be twelve hours, with one and a half hours for meals.

(c) the Local Government Act (1888) – the Conservatives' major reform

This was the work of C. T. Ritchie (President of the Local Government Board) and Sir Edward Goschen. A change was necessary because the 1835 Municipal Corporations Act had only reformed the boroughs; in the counties, local government was carried out by about 27,000 different boards, which dealt separately with matters such as sanitation, drainage and street-lighting. Goschen called it 'a chaos of authorities, a chaos of jurisdictions, a chaos of rates, a chaos of franchises, a chaos, worst of all, of areas'. Unlike the town corporations, these bodies were not directly elected; local Justices of the Peace (JPs), usually landowners, appointed their members. In 1884, agricultural labourers had been given the right to vote for their MPs, so it was only logical that they should be able to choose the people who governed them at the local level. *The terms of the Act were*:

- The old boards were abolished and replaced by sixty-two elected county councils. They had wide compulsory powers over matters such as the maintenance of roads and bridges and the provision of police, and they took over the administrative functions of the JPs.
- Over sixty towns of more than 50,000 inhabitants were made into county boroughs: they were to have elected councils with the same powers as county councils.

- London was regarded as a county in its own right; subdivided into twenty-eight Metropolitan boroughs, its overall government was to be in the hands of the London County Council.
- An important feature of the voting rules for these new councils and for the borough councils was that *unmarried women were given the vote*, though they were not allowed to be members of councils.

The following year (1889) this new system was extended to cover Scotland.

After a slow start the new councils gradually took over more and more functions. There was a marked improvement in the quality of local government, and the powers and influence of the land-owning gentry were reduced. Further refinements were added by the Local Government Act of 1894 (see Section 16.8(a)).

While these reforms were worthy enough, in one sense they were irrelevant to the main social and economic problem of late Victorian Britain – that a large proportion of the working class were living in conditions of extreme poverty. In February 1886, mobs smashed shop windows in the West End of London and set fire to cabs and carriages, as some of them put it, 'to frighten the idle rich'. Many workers were turning towards the Labour movement and the formation of unions for unskilled workers (see Section 19.4). In 1889, the London dockers came out on strike, and public support for their demand for a standard wage of 6d an hour was so great that after four weeks the dock companies gave way. Salisbury was worried by these developments, but despite acknowledging that they arose from genuine hardship, he could see no cure for the problems, beyond self-help. Under his leadership, the Conservatives took up an anti-trade union stance (see Section 19.5).

16.6 how did the Conservatives deal with the problems of Ireland, 1886–92?

This period saw a mixture of firm government and mild concessions; there was also high drama, with the downfall and ruin of Parnell in a divorce case. Evictions of tenants were still continuing, and the Irish retaliated with *the Plan of Campaign,* organized by William O'Brien and John Dillon. All the tenants on an estate would offer what they considered to be a fair rent; if the landlord disagreed, they would refuse to pay any rent and put the money into a 'fighting fund'. The plan spread rapidly, but inevitably provoked more mass evictions and violence. It was the job of Arthur Balfour (Salisbury's nephew), the new Chief Secretary for Ireland, to deal with this situation.

(a) 'Bloody' Balfour

The government's first response was a new *Crimes Act (1887),* which gave police and magistrates extra powers to deal with offenders, including the right to suspend trial by jury. Balfour applied the Act rigorously, jailing anyone who broke the law. An ugly incident occurred at Mitchelstown, in which police shot and killed three members of a crowd demonstrating against some evictions. Balfour ignored all protests and went calmly on, earning himself the nickname 'Bloody' Balfour. This caused opinion among left-wing and moderate Liberals to swing back towards Parnell.

(b) Parnell: triumph and downfall

The next developments in Irish affairs concerned Parnell. *The Times* newspaper, always strongly anti-Irish, ran a series of articles to try to discredit Parnell by showing that he was deliberately encouraging violence in Ireland. In April 1887, it published a letter reputed to have been written by Parnell to a friend, expressing his approval of the Phoenix Park murders. Parnell protested that the letter was a 'barefaced forgery', but very few people in England believed him. In 1888, during a libel action against *The Times*, more alleged Parnell letters were produced. The government appointed a special commission of three judges to investigate the charges. The enquiry dragged on for months, but eventually it emerged that all the letters had been forged by an Irish journalist called Pigott, whose motive had been to make money by selling them. Before he could be arrested for perjury, he fled to Spain and shot himself in a Madrid hotel (March 1889). Parnell was shown to be completely innocent; he was given a standing ovation when he appeared in the Commons, and there was a rush of public sympathy both for him and for Home Rule. It was the climax of his career; he was indeed 'the uncrowned king of Ireland'.

However, disaster and tragedy soon followed in 1890, when Parnell was named as co-respondent in a divorce case. For nine years he had been living with Katherine O'Shea, who had separated from her husband, Captain W. H. O'Shea, before she met Parnell. The affair was conducted so discreetly that the general public knew nothing about it. O'Shea kept quiet, hoping for political advancement from Parnell, and also for a share of the large fortune which his wife was expecting to inherit from a wealthy aunt. Although the aunt died in 1889, there was a legal wrangle over the will, and the fortune was not forthcoming. O'Shea grew tired of waiting, started proceedings against his wife, naming Parnell as co-respondent, and in November 1890 was granted a divorce.

The news that Parnell was an adulterer came as a bombshell. The Victorian moral code was such that affairs were acceptable provided they were conducted discreetly. But once they became public in the divorce courts, the guilty parties were disgraced. Overnight, Parnell was shunned by many of his supporters. Nonconformist Liberals refused to co-operate with the Nationalists unless they changed their leader; the Irish Roman Catholic Church turned against him, and 44 of the Nationalist MPs deserted him. Yet he refused to resign the leadership, and damaged his health trying to re-establish his authority. Exhausted and suffering from kidney disease, he died in October 1891, leaving the Nationalist party hopelessly split. It was a tragic end to one of the great Irish patriots, and it was ironic that he was brought down, not by the hated English, but by his own people, the Irish, who turned against him.

(c) more concessions for the Irish

Parnell's disgrace and the chaos in the Nationalist party turned English opinion against Home Rule, and the government seized the opportunity to introduce some improvements. A *Land Purchase Act (1891)* extended the earlier Ashbourne Act and enabled thousands more Irish farmers to buy land, with government help. *The Congested Districts Board* was set up (1891) to help over-populated areas. Using government money, it introduced a variety of improvements such as draining and fencing of land, better farming methods, training schemes, railways and harbours. Living conditions gradually improved, and since Irish leaders were preoccupied in attacking each other instead of organizing protest campaigns against the English, Ireland became comparatively calm.

16.7 foreign and imperial affairs under the Conservatives

Salisbury's main interest was in foreign affairs; as a young man he had worked as a journalist and had written many book reviews, mainly of the works of contemporary European historians and political philosophers, including French and German. He was therefore well versed in European history and political theory, and had studied, among other things, the works of Karl Marx. From 1887 to 1892 he acted as Foreign Secretary as well as Prime Minister, and often remarked that he would willingly step down from the premiership so that he could concentrate on diplomatic affairs.

(a) Salisbury's aims in foreign policy

- He would do his utmost to maintain peace and regarded war as 'the final and supreme evil'.
- He wanted to protect British interests and 'to uphold England's honour steadily and fearlessly and always be prone to let actions go along with words rather than to let it lag behind them'.
- He expected the main threats to British interests to come from France and Russia, and hoped to use diplomatic means to counter these threats. However, he also realized that, since German unification in 1870–1, Germany was potentially the most powerful state in Europe. But he shrank from the idea of binding alliances, because these might involve Britain in war. This attitude became known as a policy of '*splendid isolation*', a phrase first coined in the Canadian parliament in 1896. It was then used by *The Times* to describe a speech by Joseph Chamberlain, in which he argued that Britain's strength lay in the support of its Empire; later, it was applied to Salisbury's

foreign policy. However, it is a misleading phrase: Britain was never completely isolated from Europe – Salisbury was quite happy to sign agreements with other countries, as he did with Germany, Italy and Portugal, provided they did not commit Britain to military action in certain circumstances. In other words, Salisbury wanted to retain a free hand; Robert Taylor calls it a policy of 'limited liability' – seeking to influence events, without commitment, rather than initiating new policy.

▸ He recognized the value of Britain's colonies but, unlike Joseph Chamberlain, he was not anxious to expand the Empire further, and was unhappy about the British occupation of Egypt which he regarded as 'a disastrous inheritance'. 'However strong you may be, there is a point beyond which your strength will not go … it is madness and ruin if you allow yourself to pass it.'

▸ It followed that if Britain was to influence events, continue to be the world's greatest trading nation and remain secure, it was vital to maintain naval supremacy. Hence the passing of the *Naval Defence Act (1889)*, which laid down what was known as a 'Two Power Standard'. This meant that the strength of the Royal Navy must be kept equal to that of the combined navies of the two states regarded as the most serious threat to Britain – still at that point considered to be France and Russia. Sufficient money was provided to build ten new battleships.

The main events during this Conservative government (1886–92) were as follows.

(b) the Balkans crisis and the Mediterranean Agreements

1 Almost immediately, Salisbury was faced with a serious international crisis. In 1885, Eastern Roumelia had declared itself united with Bulgaria, a clear breach of the 1878 Berlin Settlement (see Section 14.4(f)). Now that Bulgaria had turned out to be hostile to Russia, the Russians wanted Eastern Roumelia returned to Turkey; they even went to the length of organizing the kidnapping of King Alexander of Bulgaria, in an attempt to control the country. However, this misfired when the Bulgarians, with Austrian and Italian support, chose as their new king the anti-Russian Ferdinand of Saxe-Coburg.

2 At the same time, relations between France and Germany were strained. General Boulanger, the French War Minister, was calling for revenge and the recovery of Alsace-Lorraine, taken by the Germans at the end of the Franco-Prussian War (1871). Bismarck, the German Chancellor, had formed the Triple Alliance of Germany, Austria-Hungary and Italy, and was hoping for a breach between Britain and France, so that France would be completely isolated. The prospects for peace did not seem good. Salisbury had to try to influence the Triple Alliance powers to take some action to curb Russian designs in the Balkans, while at the same time avoid involving Britain so closely that it would be drawn into a war against France. Events worked out

quite successfully for Britain, although at no stage did Salisbury take the initiative.

3 He supported Germany and Austria in their decision to oppose Russian demands for the return of Eastern Roumelia to Turkey, and for the removal of King Ferdinand from the Bulgarian throne. The Russians had to accept this check to their Balkan ambitions.

4 Responding to a suggestion from the Italian government, Salisbury signed *the Mediterranean Agreement* with Italy (1887). Britain would help Italy maintain the status quo in the Aegean, Adriatic and Black Sea areas. Italy would support British interests in Egypt, and the British navy would protect the Italian coast, though only in the event of an *unprovoked* French attack on Italy. Six weeks later, Austria-Hungary also signed the Mediterranean Agreement. Bismarck was pleased that the British were moving towards the Triple Alliance, and promised Salisbury unofficially that Germany would support British interests in Egypt.

5 Bismarck proposed a formal alliance with Britain (1889), intending it to have a strong anti-French flavour. Salisbury wanted it to include a promise of German assistance in case of Russian aggression, but Bismarck, hoping to remain on good terms with Russia, would not commit himself. Salisbury therefore declined the offer. Nevertheless, relations between Britain and the Triple Alliance remained excellent right up to the resignation of Bismarck (March 1890) and while his successor, Caprivi, was in power (1890–4).

(c) Salisbury and the 'Scramble for Africa'

The 'Scramble for Africa', lasting roughly from 1881–1900, was the operation in which the European powers established control over most of the parts of Africa that had not already been claimed. *Their motives were mixed*:

‣ sometimes governments were forced to act to protect trading companies against local rulers or against rival companies;

‣ it was hoped that there would be economic advantages – cheap raw materials and large markets;

‣ sometimes, as in the case of Egypt, European investments needed protection;

‣ some people genuinely believed it was their duty (the 'white man's burden') to Christianize and civilize the African natives; and

‣ there was the question of national prestige and the need to protect areas already taken by extending control into a neighbouring area (the British decided to subdue the Sudan in order to consolidate their hold on Egypt) (see Section 14.3(a) for more about the motives behind imperialism).

The operation was well under way when Salisbury came to power; the French (who already owned Gabon and Algeria) started the Scramble in 1881 by declaring a protectorate over Tunisia. The British (who already controlled Cape Colony, Natal, the Gambia, Sierra Leone and the Gold Coast) occupied Egypt

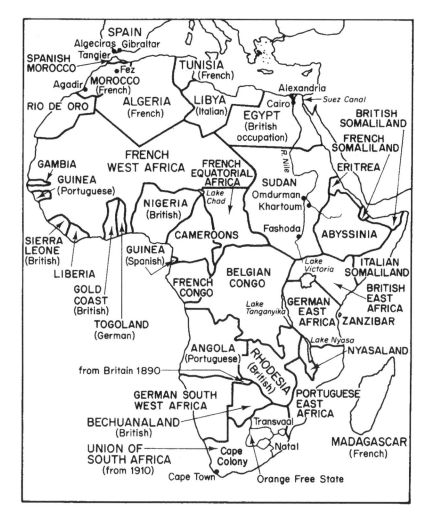

map **16.1** 'The Scramble for Africa'

(1882) and added Somaliland (1884) and Bechuanaland (1885) as protectorates. The Germans took South West Africa and the Cameroons (1884), followed by Tanganyika (1885), while the Italians acquired Eritrea (1885). In an attempt to avoid friction, *the Berlin Conference (1884–5)* had laid down rules of procedure which powers were to follow. Each government was to inform the others which areas it was planning to settle and develop as colonies.

Nevertheless, disputes did occur and Salisbury was worried in case these led to war:

› *The French* were highly indignant at the British occupation of Egypt, where French interests were involved with the Suez Canal.
› *The Italians* were aggrieved at the French occupation of Tunisia, which they had been hoping to control.

Salisbury was unwilling to get involved: as Robert Taylor puts it, 'his aim was not to splash Africa with the red of the British Empire'. But he was driven to intervene by the need to protect British interests in Egypt and along the Nile, and to protect the trading companies in other parts of Africa – the Royal Niger Company clashed with the French, who were trying to control the same area. The British East Africa Company was having problems with both German and French rivals, while Cecil Rhodes's South Africa Company was extending its operations northwards into what became known as Rhodesia, causing friction with the Transvaal Boers and the Portuguese.

In 1890, Salisbury signed a series of remarkable agreements that did much to reduce friction

- The frontier between Portuguese East Africa (Mozambique) and the British areas was fixed, leaving Britain in control of Nyasaland and Rhodesia. The French accepted British control of Zanzibar in return for French control of Madagascar, and the northern frontier between Nigeria and French West Africa was agreed.
- The Germans recognized British control of Zanzibar, Uganda and Kenya (British East Africa); in return, Britain accepted German control of German East Africa (Tanganyika), the Cameroons and South West Africa; Britain also gave Germany the North Sea island of Heligoland, which it had taken from Denmark in 1807.
- The Italians and British agreed on the frontier between Eritrea and the Sudan.

(d) the Franco-Russian alliance

A new and potentially dangerous problem appeared during the last year of Salisbury's government: Russia and France, the two powers most hostile to Britain, began to draw together in the friendship which was to lead to a full treaty of alliance in 1894. Salisbury was anxious to improve Britain's relations with France, but before he could do much about it, the Conservatives were thrown out of office.

16.8 the last of Gladstone, 1892–4

In the election of July 1892, the Conservatives lost 48 seats, but this was not enough to give the Liberals a decisive majority. There were 272 Liberals to 268 Conservatives; in addition, there were 46 Liberal Unionists, who would vote with the Conservatives, and 80 Irish Nationalists. This meant that Gladstone was able to form a government, but only with the support of the Irish Nationalists. The Liberals were disappointed by the smallness of their majority, since they had been hoping to attract massive support with their *Newcastle Programme*; this included Home Rule for Ireland; Welsh and Scottish disestablishment; a general election every three years; allotments for workers; employers to be held liable for accidents to workers; and payment for MPs. However, Philip Magnus calls the programme 'a hotch-potch which had been hastily compiled with the object of attracting as many votes from as many different sources as possible'. Graham Goodlad believes that Gladstone's acceptance of the programme was 'a belated and half-hearted conversion'. The Conservative defeat was probably caused as much by the electorate's boredom with their record over the previous six years as it was by the Newcastle Programme.

(a) the Local Government Act (Parish Councils Act) of 1894

This was the major achievement of Gladstone's Fourth Ministry. The problem needing attention was that most of the county councils set up by the 1888 Act were finding it difficult to cope with the mass of detail involved, since the counties were so large. This new Act:

- subdivided the counties into urban districts and rural districts, each with its own elected council;
- further divided rural districts so that each village had its own parish council; and
- allowed married as well as single women to vote in elections for these councils, and *to stand as candidates,* an important new step.

The district councils gradually developed into efficient units looking after public health, roads and education. But the parish councils were never very important because the Lords insisted that their powers should be kept to a minimum. This framework of county and district councils remained the basis of local government until a new system was introduced in 1974 (see Section 30.6(f)).

(b) Gladstone and the Second Irish Home Rule Bill

This was Gladstone's final attempt to solve the Irish problem. Introduced in February 1893, it was similar to the 1886 Bill, except that Irish MPs were to be allowed to sit at Westminster. There was a tremendous struggle to get the Bill through the Commons. Chamberlain led the attack on it, and Gladstone himself, 'alert and tireless, hardly ever left the House; he gloried in every episode of the battle, and his performance, at the age of 83, must be ranked among the supreme achievements of his life' (Magnus). Once, fighting broke out on the floor of the House, and it was not until September that the Bill finally passed (by 309 votes to 267). However, it was rejected overwhelmingly by the Lords (419 votes to 41). Gladstone wanted the government to resign and force a general election, so that he could appeal to the country on the grounds that the unelected Lords were thwarting the wishes of the democratically elected Commons. The rest of the Cabinet refused, and after further disagreements about naval spending, Gladstone resigned (March 1894) and retired from politics. He died in May 1898.

(c) assessment of Gladstone

Although his first ministry (1868–74) was impressive, looking at his achievements after that, it is sometimes difficult to see why his reputation remained so high. Was he a great statesman or just a self-righteous bigot, as some of his fiercest critics claimed? He certainly had his faults – he was self-opinionated and his reluctance to discuss policies fully with his colleagues made him difficult to work with. His religious convictions led him into the irritating habit of claiming that he was at all times trying to carry out the will of God. More serious, in the words of R. T. Shannon, was that 'he had no real awareness of what the masses thought and did not care very much what they wanted ... he was moving not from right to left in the conventional manner, but rather into a lofty station of his own, remote from the main political course'.

But he also had qualities that made him the outstanding figure of Victorian politics: he was prepared to fight on behalf of fair play and freedom of the individual against traditional attitudes and restrictions; this led to the great reforms of the first ministry. Above all there was his determination to stick to a course of action if he thought it was morally right and necessary, hence his obsession with Ireland and Home Rule, where his attitude was far ahead of his time. This was unfortunately his greatest failure, and the tragedy was that if the Lords had passed the Second Home Rule Bill in 1893, all the problems and calamities of Ireland since that date might have been avoided. And yet for all Gladstone's declared belief in 'backing the masses against the classes', he did not support the idea of government intervention to bring about 'social equalization'; self-help and self-improvement were the ways forward.

Another area of controversy in Gladstone's career is his role in the rise and fall of the Liberal party. Many historians, like Paul Adelman, believe that Gladstone did the Liberal party a great service by winning the support of the skilled working classes, thus helping to make it a national and classless party (see Section 13.1(g)). Adelman goes on to argue, however, that by continuing as leader of the party until 1894, when he was well into his eighties, his resistance to radical social reform prevented the Liberal party from devoting itself to improving social and economic conditions, and so it was never able to fulfil the expectations of the working classes. 'It is no coincidence therefore', argues Adelman, 'that two years after the death of Gladstone in 1898, a new political party was formed which, unlike the Liberals, did claim to be a class party. That party was the Labour party; and its formation is an instructive comment on the weaknesses and failures of the last phase of Gladstonian Liberalism.' The Liberals missed a golden opportunity to rethink their mission by turning themselves into the party of the trade unions and the workers; but the *laissez-faire* ethic remained too strong among Liberals for this to happen. The result was that working-class radicals and moderate socialists, who would have voted Liberal, began to look towards the Labour Party.

Jonathan Parry also suggests that Gladstone's leadership had unfortunate long-term effects on his party, but for different reasons. He claims that it is misleading to talk about 'Gladstonian Liberalism', as if it was something invented by Gladstone. He points out that Gladstone did *not* invent Liberalism, and he argues that the aristocratic Whig section of the party carried the real Liberal tradition; Gladstone was the outsider, the former Tory, who soon upset the traditional Liberals by his so-called 'moral' approach to foreign policy. His support for Irish Home Rule in 1886 completely undermined the Whig-Liberal tradition, and brought about the disastrous split in the party, so that it was never again the 'natural' party of government.

16.9 the Liberals in decline: Lord Rosebery's ministry, 1894–5

(a) Rosebery's government an anti-climax

It was probably inevitable that, immediately after all the brilliance of the larger-than-life Gladstone, a Liberal government led by anybody else would seem to be an anti-climax. When Gladstone handed in his resignation to the Queen, he did not recommend a successor. The two obvious candidates for the leadership of the party were Lord Rosebery and Sir William Harcourt; most of the Liberal MPs favoured Harcourt, but Rosebery was supported by most of the Cabinet and by the Queen. Rosebery was chosen, leaving Harcourt feeling cheated and resentful, though Rosebery did appoint him Chancellor of the Exchequer. The government achieved very little because:

1 Rosebery, though able and popular with the public, had never sat in the Commons and lacked experience of leadership and party management. The fact that he was a wealthy aristocrat who owned racehorses made him unpopular with the Radicals, and especially with Nonconformists (he owned the winner of the Derby in 1894 and 1895, while he was Prime Minister).
2 After the bitter leadership campaign, the relationship between Rosebery and Harcourt deteriorated to the point where they were scarcely on speaking terms. This was disastrous: since Rosebery was in the House of Lords and therefore isolated from everyday Commons business, it was vital that he should have a close relationship with Harcourt, who was acting as party leader in the Commons. This made it difficult for the Liberals to formulate new policies of social reform in order to retain their working-class support.
3 The Lords rejected almost all of the government's measures, with the excuse that the Liberal majority in the Commons was too small for them to claim that they had a mandate from the electorate.

Their only achievements came in Harcourt's budget of 1894: its most important point was *the introduction of death duties on all forms of estate*, on a graduated scale. This was designed to raise an extra £1 million in the first year, rising to around £4 million in subsequent years, mainly to pay for increased naval building. The Conservatives were highly critical of the new duties, which penalized the rich, but the Lords did not reject them because they were included in the budget, and it was the tradition that the Lords never interfered with finance bills.

In June 1895, Rosebery resigned, hoping that public disapproval of the Lords' actions would produce a big Liberal victory in the following general election. Instead, they suffered a crushing defeat: they slumped to 177 seats against 340 Conservatives and 71 Liberal Unionists. There was the usual contingent of Irish Nationalists (82 this time) who would vote with the Liberals, but even so, Salisbury, with Liberal Unionist votes, could count on a majority of around 150.

(b) why did the Liberals lose so decisively?

▸ The Liberal party was still suffering from the split over Home Rule; there was a widespread feeling that the government should have resigned after the failure of the Second Home Rule Bill, so that instead of sympathy for their treatment at the hands of the Lords, there was only impatience.
▸ Working-class disappointment at the lack of social reform led many to vote for the Unionists, who consequently won almost all the seats in the big cities.
▸ The election coincided with a surge of public enthusiasm for imperialism, which the Conservatives and Unionists seemed to stand for.

QUESTIONS

1 'A combination of exaggerated hope and over-heated anxiety'. How adequate is this interpretation of the reasons for British Imperial expansion in the period 1880–1902? (See also information in Chapter 17.)
2 'Gladstone decided to support Home Rule for Ireland in 1885 because he genuinely believed in it, not because he saw it as a way of uniting the Liberal party behind him.' How far would you agree with this view?
3 'The parliamentary reforms of 1883 to 1885 caused both Conservative dominance and Liberal decline during the years 1885 to 1905.' How adequate is this assessment of the development of party politics during this period?
4 'Gladstone did more harm than good to the Liberal party in the years 1880 to 1894.' To what extent do you think this verdict is a fair one?

A document question about Gladstone and Irish Home Rule can be found on the accompanying website www.palgrave.com/masterseries/lowe1.

chapter 17

ten years of Conservative rule, 1895–1905

summary of events

Lord Salisbury was Prime Minister from 1895 until 1902. He also acted as Foreign Secretary until 1900, when Lord Lansdowne took over the Foreign Office. When Salisbury retired in July 1902, his nephew, Arthur James Balfour, became Prime Minister. The Liberal Unionists were now almost indistinguishable from the Conservatives, and two of their leaders, the Duke of Devonshire (formerly Lord Hartington) and Joseph Chamberlain, were members of Salisbury's Cabinet. In fact, the Conservatives and their Liberal allies were often referred to simply as *Unionists* to denote their commitment to maintain the full union between Ireland and the rest of the United Kingdom, as well as the union between Britain and the Empire.

Joseph Chamberlain, the Colonial Secretary, was an outstanding figure in the government, often seeming to eclipse the Prime Minister himself. He chose to be Colonial Secretary because of his belief that it was important to build up the British Empire as a great political and economic unit; this period is therefore regarded as the heyday of *imperialism.* British influence was extended in China, and the Sudan was successfully reconquered (1898). In southern Africa, Britain became involved in *the Boer War (1899–1902)* against the Transvaal and the Orange Free State; though the war eventually ended successfully, the British victory did not come easily, and they were made painfully aware that they lacked friends. The policy misleadingly known as *splendid isolation* seemed thereafter to be transformed into a search for allies.

Two important agreements were signed, one with Japan (1902) and the other – the famous *Entente Cordiale* – with France (1904). The following Liberal government completed the transformation by signing an agreement with Russia in 1907 (see Section 21.8(c)). As Britain's relations with France and Russia improved, those with Germany deteriorated, because of economic and naval rivalry.

Queen Victoria, who had always exercised a restraining influence on her grandson, the German Kaiser Wilhelm II, died in January 1901. She had reigned since 1837 and had lived long enough to celebrate both her Golden and Diamond Jubilees (1887 and 1897). She was succeeded by her son, the 59-year-old Edward VII.

Ireland remained comparatively quiet and during Balfour's government, some important concessions were made, including *Wyndham's Land Act (1903)*. In home affairs, social reforms were very few, though *Balfour's Education Act (1902)* was an important measure. In spite of the investigations of Charles Booth and Seebohm Rowntree, which revealed serious poverty among the working classes, nothing much was done to help them, and many people began to be attracted to the newly formed Labour Party (see Section 19.7–8).

Yet at the half-way stage of the period, the Conservatives still retained their popularity; in the general election of October 1900, they won an overall majority of around 130, probably thanks to a great surge of *jingoism* (aggressive or excessive patriotism) during the Boer War. It was during Balfour's premiership that public opinion began to grow tired of the Conservatives. In the election of January 1906, the Liberals won an astonishing victory, with 400 seats against the Conservatives' 157. One reason for the Conservative defeat was Chamberlain's controversial campaign in favour of *tariff reform*, which fatally divided the party. It was to be 1922 before the Conservatives were able to form another government.

17.1 Lord Salisbury and Conservative dominance

(a) Salisbury: the last of the great aristocrats?

Robert Cecil, the third Marquis of Salisbury, like Gladstone, was Prime Minister of four governments: 1885–6, 1886–92, 1895–1900 and then after the 'Khaki' election of 1900, held during the Boer War, from 1900 until his retirement in 1902. In fact, he was Prime Minister for slightly longer than Gladstone during a twenty-year period when the Conservatives, with Liberal Unionist support, dominated the British political scene. Yet, compared with Disraeli, Gladstone and Joseph Chamberlain, Salisbury remains a rather shadowy figure to later generations, and historians have paid less attention to him than to these other, more charismatic figures.

The general feeling seems to have been that the Conservative domination during these twenty years had very little to do with any initiatives taken by Salisbury, but was the result of circumstances, mainly the fact that the Liberals were split over Home Rule for Ireland, and the anti-Home Rule Liberals supported the Conservatives. Unflattering things have been written about Salisbury: according to Paul Smith, for example, he was 'the last great aristocratic figure of a political system that died with Victoria, or even before, a great whale irretrievably beached on the receding shore of the nineteenth century'.

He never accepted that democracy was a fair and proper way to govern a country, and always did his best to minimize the effects of change and to maintain the status quo. Despite being a committed Christian (Anglican), this did not encourage him to try to improve working-class conditions, and he remained a staunch supporter of self-help. When Lord Randolph Churchill developed a programme of social reform, Salisbury was quite happy to let him resign (see Section 16.5(a)). When Joseph Chamberlain brought his radical proposals into the Conservative government in 1895, Salisbury succeeded in limiting them to the Workmen's Compensation Act (1897).

(b) a positive contribution to the Conservatives' dominance?

In 'Lord Salisbury and Late Victorian Conservatism' (an article in the *Modern History Review*, February 1996), Dr Graham Goodlad suggests that Salisbury deserves more credit for the long period of Conservative dominance than historians have given him. He argues that Salisbury did much more than just passively enjoy the advantages of favourable circumstances, and that his role was a positive one in several ways:

‣ Although he disapproved of democracy, he took the trouble to appeal to the new urban voters and developed an effective speaking style addressing large audiences in the Midlands and North.
‣ It was Salisbury who did a deal with Gladstone over parliamentary reform in 1884 (see Section 16.3(d)): in return for the Conservative majority in the Lords passing the Franchise Act (giving the vote to rural workers), Gladstone agreed to a Redistribution Act, which left the vast majority of seats represented by one MP. This worked to the advantage of the Conservatives in suburban areas, because it meant that Conservative supporters in 'respectable' middle-class London suburbs, and later in the suburbs of other cities, could elect their own Conservative MPs instead of being swamped in large multi-member constituencies. Salisbury described this new development as 'Villa Toryism'.
‣ Salisbury encouraged the development of efficient, professionally organized Conservative associations in the constituencies, run by full-time agents. These were complemented by the Primrose League (founded by Lord Randolph Churchill in 1881) which also had branches in every constituency, and which attracted members in large numbers with it social programmes of fetes and concerts, used to spread the Conservative message to all social classes.
‣ Salisbury did all he could to widen the split in the Liberal party; for example, in the 1886 election, the Conservatives did not run candidates against sitting Liberal Unionist MPs.
‣ Above all, as Dr Goodlad points out, Salisbury showed great skill in managing and holding together a Conservative party which itself had the potential

for serious divisions. Within little over a year of Salisbury's retirement in 1902, Joseph Chamberlain had split the party disastrously over the question of tariff reform.

Clearly, then, Lord Salisbury led the party with great authority and did make a positive contribution to the long period of Conservative dominance. On the other hand, it seems inescapable that the direction in which he pointed the party during those twenty years was firmly backwards. As Dr Goodlad himself concludes: 'politics for Salisbury had been a slow, stubborn rearguard action against change'.

17.2 Joseph Chamberlain and imperialism

Born in 1836, the son of a prosperous London boot and shoe manufacturer, Chamberlain went to Birmingham at the age of 18 to become a partner in a screw-making factory owned by his uncle, J. S. Nettlefold. With his acute business sense, he quickly became the driving force behind the enterprise and developed it into a highly profitable firm. In 1876 he was able to retire and live on his personal fortune, devoting most of his time to politics. The appalling conditions in Birmingham led him to stand for the town council in 1869; he spent the rest of his life deeply involved in local and national politics, though after a severe stroke in 1906 he remained an invalid. He died in July 1914.

Chamberlain's career

1869–76	Member of Birmingham council; Mayor 1873–6
1876–86	Liberal MP for Birmingham; President of Board of Trade 1880–6
1885	Publishes his *Unauthorized Programme*
1886	Opposes Home Rule for Ireland and votes against Liberal government; at least partly responsible for Liberal split
	Leads breakaway group of Liberal Unionist MPs
1886–95	Liberal Unionist MP for Birmingham
1895	Joins Salisbury's Conservative government
1895–1910	Conservative/Unionist MP for Birmingham
1895–1903	Colonial Secretary
1903	Resigns from Cabinet to lead the campaign for tariff reform
	Conservative party splits between supporters and opponents of tariff reform and is heavily defeated in election of Jan. 1906

(a) Chamberlain's work in Birmingham

In the mid-1860s, the people of Birmingham were suffering all the evils of a new industrial city: child labour, long working hours in dangerous conditions, overcrowded slums, and no proper disposal of sewage and refuse. The town council, reluctant to spend money, had ignored opportunities for improvement. Chamberlain was determined on action: 'The town,' he declared, 'shall not, with God's help, know itself.'

- Using his business skills and methods, he organized the Birmingham Liberal Association, which enabled him and some of his friends to win seats on the council. By 1873, the Liberals were in a majority.
- He gave £1,000 to the Birmingham (later the National) Education League, and soon became its chairman. The League campaigned for free, compulsory and undenominational education for all. Chamberlain felt that, after the 1867 Reform Act, it was essential to educate the new working-class borough voters. The League played a part in the passing of Forster's Education Act in 1870 (see Section 12.8(c)), though it far from satisfied them.
- The council bought up the town's two gas companies and its waterworks, which were then modernized and expanded. A Medical Officer of Health was appointed and a new hospital built. A Drainage Board was set up to deal with the proper disposal of drainage and refuse. Street paving and lighting were extended, and six public parks opened. Chamberlain even organized a national conference in Birmingham to encourage other authorities to follow Birmingham's example.
- His most remarkable achievement was *the Improvement Scheme* made possible by the 1875 Artisans' Dwellings Act (see Section 12.6(a)). About 90 acres of slums in the town centre were demolished and replaced by a fine new shopping area – Corporation Street – and by high-quality housing for workers.
- New libraries, museums and art galleries were opened, and in 1900 Chamberlain founded the University of Birmingham. Thanks to Chamberlain, Birmingham was recognized as a city in 1889 and was widely regarded as a model of progressive local government.

(b) Chamberlain as a Liberal MP

Right from his first appearance in the Commons, Chamberlain was full of self-confidence; he was an excellent speaker and soon established a reputation as 'Radical Joe', the champion of the working classes. He was not afraid to criticize anyone or anything that stood in the way of social reform, whether it was the monarchy, the House of Lords, or other members of the Liberal party. He believed that the party could only survive if it dropped its Whig elements, and he was impatient with Gladstone for his lack of interest in social questions and his obsession with Ireland. He wanted the government to 'intervene on behalf of the weak against the strong, in the interests of labour against capital, of want and suffering against luxury and ease'. Gladstone never understood or liked Chamberlain, who was not exactly a modest man and was as difficult to work with as Gladstone himself. It was with the greatest reluctance that Gladstone made Chamberlain President of the Board of Trade in 1880. Working closely with his friend Sir Charles Dilke, another Radical, Chamberlain was able to make a valuable contribution:

- In 1877, he had formed *the National Liberal Federation*, with the aim of helping Liberal candidates fight elections. Using the same techniques as his local party 'caucus' in Birmingham, the Federation provided efficient organization in many constituencies – producing pamphlets and posters, collecting subscriptions, attracting new members and holding public meetings and social events. This contributed to the Liberal victory in the 1880 general election.
- Pressure from Chamberlain and the Radicals resulted in the introduction of the *Third Parliamentary Reform Bill in 1884* (see Section 16.3(d)).
- Before the 1885 election, Chamberlain produced his *Unauthorized Programme* of social reform (see Section 16.4(d)). Lloyd George later paid him a handsome compliment: 'I am convinced that our victory [in the 1885 election] is all due to Chamberlain's speeches. Gladstone had no programme at all that would draw.'
- He was concerned at the growing unemployment, and urged the Poor Law Guardians to use their powers to provide work for the unemployed (1886).

Chamberlain was the most dynamic of the leading Liberals; he was ambitious, and was viewed in many quarters as the most likely leader when Gladstone eventually retired. However, this was not to be: serious trouble began when Chamberlain, a passionate imperialist, opposed Gladstone's decision to give Home Rule to Ireland (see Section 16.1(e)), thereby splitting the Liberal party.

(c) Chamberlain as Colonial Secretary

When Chamberlain joined Salisbury's government in 1895 there was a hysterical chorus of criticism from Liberals; they said he was inconsistent, a turncoat, a traitor, a Judas. 'It seems to me,' remarked Gladstone, 'that Chamberlain is the greatest blackguard I have ever come across.' However, Chamberlain believed that he was being perfectly consistent; he was convinced that the best way of curing the trade depression was by developing and expanding the British Empire – the larger the Empire, the more profitable British commerce would become; this would reduce unemployment and help the workers. He also believed in Britain's 'national mission' to take the benefits of peace and civilization to backward peoples. This was the heyday of the *Pax Britannica*, a phrase at its most popular during the 1890s (see Section 1.2(e)). Since the Conservatives were more committed to imperialism than were the Liberals, it was only logical that Chamberlain should eventually join them. So strongly did he feel about imperialism that he chose to be Colonial Secretary instead of Chancellor of the Exchequer.

Nor had he abandoned his radicalism: he hoped to push the Conservatives towards social reform, and was responsible for the *Workmen's Compensation Act (1897)*, which enabled workers to claim compensation for injuries suffered at work. The Act had its weaknesses – seamen, domestic servants and agricultural labourers were not included; but at least the government had accepted the principle that employers must bear the responsibility for accidents; eventually, by 1908, all categories of workers were included. Chamberlain also urged Salisbury to introduce *Old Age Pensions*, but nothing came of this, partly because the expenses of the Boer War used up all the available funds. Chamberlain's main energies were lavished on his imperial policies:

1 In 1896, Chamberlain negotiated a successful conclusion to a dispute with Venezuela about its frontier with British Guiana. The American President Cleveland resurrected the Monroe Doctrine (see Section 3.3(b)), threatening war if Britain tried to seize any Venezuelan territory. Tension was high, but Salisbury allowed Chamberlain to visit the USA, where he persuaded the Americans to submit the case to international arbitration. The verdict awarded Britain almost the entire territory it had claimed.

2 An expedition under Wolseley was sent to the Gold Coast to deal with the Ashanti tribesmen, who were constantly raiding areas claimed as British. Early in 1896 the Ashantis were defeated and British control assured.

3 In 1897 a dispute arose with France about the frontier between the French colony of Dahomey and the British territory of Nigeria. French troops occupied two small towns, Busa and Nikki, claimed by the British. Chamberlain retaliated by organizing the West African Frontier Force, commanded by Sir Henry Lugard. This firm action resulted in a compromise (June 1898) by which France kept Nikki but gave Busa to Britain.

4 The Sudan was reconquered (1898), and the Fashoda incident, another dispute with the French, was concluded successfully (see Section 17.4(a)).

5 Britain leased the Chinese port of Wei-hai-wei (1898) in response to the German seizure of Kaiochow and the Russian occupation of Port Arthur.

6 As a result of the Boer War (see next section), the Transvaal and the Orange Free State were brought under British control, and in 1910 they became part of the new Union of South Africa.

It was not simply a case of acquiring as much territory as possible; Chamberlain tried to improve the British possessions. 'We are landlords of a great estate.' he remarked; 'it is the duty of a landlord to develop his estate.'

7 He encouraged the formation of Joint Stock Companies, which, in return for a monopoly of trade in an area, undertook to develop it by providing amenities such as harbours and railways.

8 Government money was sometimes given directly to finance projects such as, for example, a railway in Uganda. *The Colonial Loans Act (1899)* provided £3 million, which was spent on a variety of projects – railways in

Sierra Leone, Lagos (Nigeria) and the Gold Coast; irrigation and railway systems in Cyprus; and harbours and railways in Jamaica.

9 Chamberlain's initiative led to the founding of Two Schools of Tropical Medicine, one in London, the other in Liverpool, to investigate the causes of the diseases that were holding up progress.

10 He was responsible for organizing *the Colonial Conference of 1897*, where he explained his ideas for an Empire customs union. He wanted the colonies to remove the duties by which they protected their industries against imported British goods, but they would only agree if Britain promised to give preference to their goods on the British market. This would require Britain to place tariffs on goods imported from countries outside the Empire, but since Britain was a free-trade country, this was not possible. At the 1902 Colonial Conference, attended by members from Australia, New Zealand, Newfoundland, Cape Colony and Natal, the result was the same, and Chamberlain also failed to persuade them to join in an imperial federation.

Although his imperial policies had a great deal of success, Chamberlain was deeply disappointed at his failure to organize the Empire into a great customs union. Consequently, he took the disastrous decision to campaign for a return to tariffs, which would enable a system of imperial preference to be introduced. He resigned from the Cabinet so that he could devote himself fully to the campaign. This was to be his greatest failure, splitting the Conservatives and contributing to their crushing defeat in 1906. Peel had also split the Conservatives, and Lloyd George was to do the same to the Liberals during the First World War; but Chamberlain is the only politician to have split two major parties.

17.3 the Boer War, 1899–1902

(a) what caused the war?

Since the First Boer War of 1881, after which the Transvaal was granted independence (see Section 16.2(b)), its relationship with Britain had not been a comfortable one, though the Orange Free State remained friendly towards Britain. Relations gradually deteriorated; by 1897, the Orange Free State had joined the Transvaal and events escalated into war. The reasons were:

1 *President Paul Kruger of the Transvaal wanted to extend his country's boundaries,* but was continually frustrated by the British, who occupied Bechuanaland on the Transvaal's western frontier in 1885. Cecil Rhodes, head of the British South Africa Company, was granted a charter which enabled him to develop Rhodesia (1888–91), hemming in the Transvaal to the north.

2 *Cecil Rhodes was the central figure in British South Africa.* Sent out to his brother in Natal on a health cure (for tuberculosis) in 1870, when he was only 17, Rhodes became involved in the diamond mining recently opened up at Kimberley. By 1881, he had secured control of virtually all the Kimberley mines for his company, the de Beers Corporation, and he was immensely rich. His burning ambition was to use his wealth to extend the Empire until Britain controlled the whole of southern Africa. He had grandiose plans to build a railway linking the Cape with British-controlled Cairo in the north. A confrontation between Rhodes and Kruger was inevitable: if Rhodes had his way, the Transvaal must become part of the British Empire.

3 *The discovery of gold in the Transvaal in 1886 complicated the situation.* From being a poor agricultural country, the Transvaal was suddenly transformed into one of the wealthiest areas in Africa. By 1894, it seemed to Rhodes that it was becoming richer than Cape Colony; it was also becoming less dependent on the Cape, since the Boers could now import and export goods along a new railway to Delagoa Bay in Portuguese East Africa, and there was no need to pass through British territory at all. Kruger began to buy armaments from Germany and there were rumours that he was planning to take over the whole of South Africa. This was not as unlikely as it might sound; there were thousands of Boers living in the Cape, and if they co-operated with Kruger, such a plan would have been perfectly feasible. More

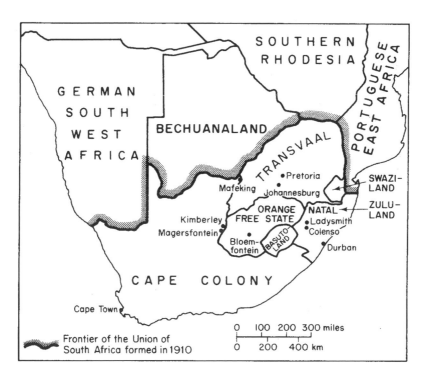

map **17.1 Southern Africa during the Boer War**

than ever it seemed essential to Rhodes that some action must be taken against 'Krugerism'.

4 *Rhodes, who became Prime Minister of Cape Colony in 1890, decided on direct intervention.* Thousands of settlers, many of them Cape British, had moved into the Transvaal to work in the goldmines. By 1895, these *uitlanders* (outsiders), as the Boers called them, outnumbered the Boers themselves. Kruger, afraid of being swamped, and anxious to preserve the character of his country, refused them all political rights and taxed them heavily. Rhodes decided to stir up *uitlander* unrest into revolution which, with some outside help, might be strong enough to overthrow Kruger. The result of his efforts was ...

5 *The Jameson Raid (December 1895).* Dr Leander Starr Jameson, an associate of Rhodes, was to lead an invasion of the Transvaal from Bechuanaland to coincide with an uprising of *uitlanders* in Johannesburg. However, *uitlander* unrest, genuine though it was, was too disorganized to produce revolution, and when Jameson rode into the Transvaal at the head of only 500 troops, he was easily defeated by the Boers. Chamberlain, the Colonial Secretary, claimed that he knew nothing about the raid, but historian Elizabeth Longford has shown that he was deeply implicated, and suggests that the probable understanding was that if the exploit failed, Rhodes should take the responsibility, which he did by resigning as Cape Prime Minister. *The results of the affair were disastrous:* to the rest of the world it seemed that Britain had authorized the unprovoked invasion of a foreign state, and the German Kaiser sent a telegram to Kruger congratulating him on successfully defending his country. The raid offended the Orange Free State and the Cape Boers; it confirmed all Kruger's fears about British intentions and he continued to arm heavily. War was not inevitable at this stage, though, provided the British abandoned their designs on the Transvaal.

6 *Sir Alfred Milner, chosen by Chamberlain to be High Commissioner for South Africa in 1897, must bear much of the responsibility for the outbreak of war, along with Chamberlain.* A passionate imperialist, as Chamberlain well knew, Milner suspected that Kruger might try to expand the Transvaal southwards, with backing from the Germans and the Cape Boers. In order to destroy Kruger, he deliberately set about provoking a crisis that could be turned into war. Given Kruger's belligerent attitude, this was not too difficult, though in fact the old man was prepared to make some concessions. The *uitlanders* sent a telegram to Queen Victoria protesting about their 'frightful' treatment at the hands of the Boers. This prompted the British government to demand that some improvement be made in the *uitlanders'* position. Kruger agreed to meet Milner at Bloemfontein, the capital of the Orange Free State, in June 1899. He offered to give the *uitlanders* the vote after a residential qualification of seven years, and there seemed a good chance of a peaceful compromise. However, Milner rejected this and

demanded a five-year qualification, which Kruger would not hear of; the meeting broke up without progress. Chamberlain, genuinely hoping to avoid war, attempted to reopen negotiations, but without a satisfactory response. British troops now began to move up to the Transvaal frontiers.

7 *The Boers, also moving troops, responded by sending an ultimatum to the British government.* This suggested independent arbitration, but demanded the withdrawal of British troops from Boer frontiers and the return home of all British forces that had recently arrived in South Africa. When this was rejected, the Transvaal and Orange Free State Boers immediately attacked Natal and the Cape. Kruger had therefore played into Milner's hands and, as Salisbury put it, he had 'liberated us from the necessity of explaining to the people of England why we are at war'.

(b) events in the war

1 The Boer armies moved swiftly and besieged Ladysmith in Natal, and Mafeking and Kimberley (where Rhodes himself was trapped) in the west. Sir Redvers Buller, British Commander-in-Chief, split his troops into three divisions in an attempt to relieve all three towns. But in the same week in December 1899 – Black Week as it became known to the British public – all three armies were defeated:

› Buller himself, advancing to relieve Ladysmith, was checked by Louis Botha's troops at Colenso;
› the division moving along the road to Kimberley was heavily defeated by Cronje's forces at Magersfontein; and
› the third division, attempting to relieve Mafeking, was driven back at Stormberg.

In January 1900, Buller tried again to relieve Ladysmith but failed more disastrously than before, losing 1,700 men at Spion Kop.

2 The British failures were not difficult to explain. The Boer forces outnumbered the British by two to one, they were all mounted and they were excellent marksmen who knew the country well; they had superior German Krupps artillery and rifles. The War Office had not studied the situation properly and sent too many unmounted troops, who had to operate at great disadvantage in unfamiliar territory where the local population was hostile. Most historians have blamed the incompetence of the generals, particularly Buller, but Thomas Pakenham, in his book about the Boer War, defends Buller, claiming that he was learning fast under the most difficult circumstances, and would eventually have been just as effective as Roberts and Kitchener, the men sent out to supercede him. What was needed was large numbers of extra troops.

3 As vast reinforcements poured in, Lord Roberts, with Kitchener as his Chief-of-Staff, outmanoeuvred Cronje and relieved Kimberley (February). Soon afterwards, Cronje was forced to surrender at Paardeberg. After that, things

Illus. **17.1 The first Welsh regiment make camp during the Boer War**

happened quickly: Buller relieved Ladysmith (February), Roberts captured Bloemfontein (March), Mafeking was relieved (May) after a siege lasting 217 days, and finally Johannesburg and Pretoria (capital of the Transvaal) were captured (June). Kruger escaped to Europe and the Boer republics were taken over by Britain. It seemed as if the war was over, and Roberts returned home. British successes at this stage were a result partly of the fact that they now had many more troops at their disposal, including some from Canada, Australia and New Zealand, and partly because the Boers made the mistake of keeping too many of their troops tied up in the sieges of Ladysmith, Kimberley and Mafeking.

4 The Boers, however, refused to surrender or negotiate, and continued to fight in small guerrilla groups, constantly harassing the British forces. Helped and sheltered by the friendly local populations, they raided Natal and Cape Colony, destroying crops and attacking railways. Kitchener found these tactics difficult to deal with, and eventually resorted to a drastic policy of 'scorched earth': farms and crops were destroyed to deny the guerrillas food; forts or blockhouses were built to protect railways; the civilian population, including women and children, were rounded up into concentration camps to prevent them helping the guerrillas. Kitchener's methods were effective: the Boer leaders agreed to negotiate and a peace treaty was signed at Vereeniging in 1902.

5 British tactics aroused world-wide criticism, since the concentration camps were overcrowded and badly mismanaged; epidemics broke out that killed

over 20,000 people during 1901. Sir Henry Campbell-Bannerman, the Liberal leader, denounced government policy as 'methods of barbarism'.

(c) results of the war

> *The Treaty of Vereeniging was reasonable and generous in its terms:* despite the two Boer republics being annexed, they were promised eventual self-government; English was to be the official language, but Afrikaans (the language of the Boers) was to be allowed in schools and law-courts. The British government gave £3 million to help the Boers repair damage and re-stock farms. On the whole, this settlement was satisfactory to both sides, though some Boer leaders demanded more money and doubted whether the promise of self-government would ever be kept. In fact, Campbell-Bannerman's Liberal government did carry it out in 1906, and as relations between British and Boers steadily improved, the Transvaal and the Orange Free State agreed to join the Union of South Africa, along with Cape Colony and Natal, in 1910 (see Section 21.2).

> The war revealed Britain's isolated position in the world: the other major European powers – Germany and Austria-Hungary, France and Russia – all sympathized with the Boers. Consequently, the British made determined efforts to find new allies or, as some historians see it, sought new ways of safe-guarding their Empire, the real source of their strength (see next section).

> As the war dragged on through 1901 and into 1902, the public tended to grow disenchanted with it. It had cost at least £200 million and over 20,000 British lives, and people began to question whether it had all been worth it. The effect was to turn a large section of public opinion against the Conservatives and against imperialism, which became discredited.

17.4 foreign affairs, 1895–1905

For the sake of simplicity, it is usual to divide this period into two phases:

> 1895–1900, when Britain continued the policy known as *splendid isolation*; and

> 1900–1905, when Britain looked for, and found, allies – Japan (1902) and France (1904).

However, some historians have challenged this interpretation of the second phase, arguing that the situation was in reality much more complex than a simple quest for allies. K. M. Wilson, in his 1985 book *The Policy of Entente: The Determinants of British Foreign Policy 1904–1914*, argued that three 'myths' continue to exist about the period 1900 to 1914. These are that:

1 The British policy of isolation came to an end.
2 Britain joined the alliance system of the other European powers.

3 Britain's commitment to the Empire ceased to be the main concern of British governments; this was replaced by a concern to preserve the balance of power in Europe.

Wilson claims there is a plausible alternative interpretation to each of the three so-called myths:

1 Britain had never been completely isolated, and in fact the previous British policy of avoiding binding alliances continued as before, since the strength of the empire was thought to be sufficient for Britain to maintain its paramount position.
2 Britain's agreements with France and later Russia were different from those of Germany, Austria-Hungary and Italy (the Triple Alliance), which all had military commitments. Britain's agreements with France and Russia were not military alliances – they were made to solve imperial differences that had been dragging on for years.
3 It follows, therefore, that defending and preserving the British empire was still very much the prime concern of British governments; there was already a military balance of power in Europe. Russia was seen as the greatest threat to the Empire, in India and the Far East; therefore the prime objective of British foreign policy was achieved with the signing of the agreement with Russia in 1907. Consequently, there was no need for Britain to get involved in affairs on the continent of Europe.

A concise version of Wilson's arguments appeared in his article, 'British Foreign Policy, 1900–14' in *Modern History Review*, November 2001. The disturbing conclusion that could perhaps be drawn if these theories are accepted is that Britain need not, and should not, have entered the First World War in 1914, since the hostilities posed no threat either to Britain or to the Empire. Not everybody is convinced, but this conclusion was indeed reached by John Charmley and Niall Ferguson (see Section 21.8(f)).

(a) splendid isolation

Salisbury had started the 'splendid isolation' policy during his previous government of 1886–92. His aims in foreign policy are set out in Section 16.7(a). But in fact it is a misleading term: it was not that Britain deliberately refused to have anything to do with the rest of the world – Salisbury signed the Mediterranean Agreements and negotiated boundary settlements in Africa. However, Britain *was* isolated in the sense that Salisbury kept the country aloof from binding alliances in case they committed it to military action.

By the time Salisbury came to power again in 1895, an important change had taken place: the two countries he most feared, *France and Russia, had signed an alliance with each other in 1894.* Germany, Austria-Hungary and Italy were already bound together in *the Triple Alliance*, so that left Britain as the only major European country not associated with an alliance bloc. Nor was Salisbury anxious to commit Britain to either of the blocs. He preferred to try to revive the old Concert of Europe, in which *all* the powers would co-operate in times of crisis. In other words, according to John Charmley, his policy was now 'more flexible and sensitive to the international situation ... he retained a free hand for British diplomacy'. Sadly, he had little lasting success; he was getting old – he was 66 in 1895 – and his health was deteriorating; and he came under increasing pressure from some of his Cabinet, particularly Chamberlain, Goschen and Lansdowne, for a more positive policy. Chamberlain was full of enthusiasm for an alliance with Germany, but Salisbury did all he could to avoid it. The main events illustrate the different strands:

1 *The Venezuela dispute (1895–6)* was settled in Britain's favour (see Section 17.2(c)), but not before it had demonstrated a lack of support for Britain.
2 *New problems arose in Turkey in 1896,* when the Turks, breaking their promise made at Berlin (1878), began wholesale massacres of Christian Armenians. Salisbury tried to persuade the European powers to take joint action to restrain the Turks, but the Germans, who were cultivating the Sultan as an ally, would not co-operate, and the attempt failed.
3 *British intervention in the war between Greece and Turkey (1897–8)* was one of Salisbury's successes. The Greeks tried to capture the Turkish island of Crete in the Mediterranean, but the Turks were too strong for them and retaliated by occupying a large part of Thessaly in mainland Greece. Salisbury managed to get the Concert of Europe to bring about a Turkish withdrawal from Thessaly, but Germany and Austria-Hungary would take no action in Crete itself. This time, however, the British fleet could be brought into play; Salisbury used it to expel Turkish troops from the island, after which Prince George of Greece was appointed governor.
4 *Britain's position in China and the Far East was being threatened by both Russia and Germany.* In 1894, the Japanese had surprised Europe by sending troops into the Chinese territory of Korea, ostensibly to help put down revolution, and then by defeating Chinese forces that tried to prevent them. China was forced to agree to *the Treaty of Shimonoseki (1895),* which gave Japan the Liaotung Peninsula, including the first-class harbour of Port Arthur. This was too much for the Russians, who themselves had designs on Port Arthur, which was ice-free. With the support of France and Germany, they forced Japan to hand back Liaotung. The following year, the Russians signed a treaty with the Chinese promising to defend China, and receiving in return the right to build a railway across the Chinese province of Manchuria, bordering on Russia. Then suddenly, in 1897, the Germans seized the Chinese port of Kiaochow; ignoring Salisbury's attempts to dissuade them, the Russians followed this up by forcing the Chinese to grant them a 25-year lease on Port Arthur. It seemed as though China was about to be carved up,

much against the wishes of Salisbury, who preferred an 'open-door' policy – to keep China open for trade but politically independent. The best Britain could do was to fall in with the trend and lease Wei-hai-wei.

5 *The reconquest of the Sudan* was achieved by an army under the command of Sir Herbert Kitchener. Salisbury agreed to the campaign for several reasons. Since Gordon's death (1885) the Sudan had been controlled by the Dervishes. Though the Mahdi had died soon after Gordon, his successor, known as the Khalifa, was a constant threat to Egypt itself. In 1889, his forces had invaded Egypt, and Kitchener had played an important part in repelling the attack. The Dervishes were also threatening the Italian colony of Eritrea, and the Italian government, with German support, urged Britain to destroy the Khalifa. Salisbury was suspicious of French ambitions in southern Sudan: in June 1896, the French Captain Marchand had set out from French West Africa with a small force, heading for Fashoda on the Nile above Khartoum; thus it was important to assert British control of the Sudan before the French became established (see Map 16.1 on page 297).

Setting out in 1896, Kitchener's expedition advanced slowly up the Nile, building a railway as they went and fighting off repeated Dervish attacks. Other hazards included cholera outbreaks, and torrential rain which washed away a section of the newly constructed railway. The climax came in September 1898, when the Khalifa's army was heavily defeated at *Omdurman*, just outside Khartoum. Dervish power was destroyed and British control of the Sudan was assured, though the French still had hopes in the area.

6 *The Fashoda incident (1898) seemed likely to bring war between Britain and France.* Only a few days after the Battle of Omdurman, news was brought to Kitchener that Marchand, having struggled through marshes and jungles for weeks on end, had finally arrived at Fashoda, and had claimed the Upper Nile for France. Kitchener moved southwards to Fashoda with two battalions of Sudanese troops and four field guns. Marchand came aboard Kitchener's gunboat and Kitchener, who spoke fluent French, invited Marchand to withdraw, pointing out with perfect courtesy that if it came to a showdown, his force was much larger (by at least ten to one) than Marchand's. After an initial coolness, Kitchener offered Marchand a whisky and soda, whereupon Marchand brought out a bottle of champagne. It was agreed that the matter should be decided by their respective governments. The two governments negotiated, and while the press in both countries adopted warlike attitudes, good sense prevailed. The French government ordered Marchand to withdraw from Fashoda. They had decided not to risk war because:

▸ they could not compete with the British fleet, which was cruising in the Eastern Mediterranean;
▸ their Russian ally was unable to help; and

> they were afraid that the Germans might profit in some way if France became embroiled in a war with Britain.

This was viewed as a personal triumph for Salisbury, though he hated confrontations of this nature and immediately began to look for ways of improving relations with the humiliated French.

7 *The Boer War (1899–1902)* was the climax of the Salisbury period in foreign affairs (see previous section).

8 *Britain's relations with Germany* were generally good while Bismarck and his successor, Caprivi, were in power. But after Caprivi's resignation in 1894, Kaiser Wilhelm II began to play a leading role in the conduct of German foreign affairs. He wanted to build Germany into a great colonial and world power. His attitude towards Britain was difficult to understand. Envious of its naval power and at the same time full of grudging admiration, he was sometimes belligerent and arrogant, sometimes co-operative. Some historians think that he really wanted an alliance with Britain and was hoping to frighten it into joining the Triple Alliance by a show of strength:

> In January 1896, Wilhelm sent his famous telegram to Kruger congratulating him on defeating the Jameson Raid (see Section 17.3(a)). Whether the Germans intended to take any action is doubtful, though three German cruisers were in Delagoa Bay off Portuguese East Africa. In case they were intending to act, Salisbury despatched a small fleet described as a 'flying squadron', and Wilhelm realized he had gone too far. The incident had important effects: coming so soon after the Franco-Russian alliance (1894), it shocked the British to find the Germans so hostile. On the German side, it justified an expansion of the German navy, so that any future British flying squadrons could be dealt with. Britain had thirty-three battleships and 130 cruisers, whereas Germany had only six and four, respectively. Tirpitz, the Minister of Marine, was responsible for the 1897 Navy Laws, which provided for the building of seven battleships and nine cruisers. In 1900, it was proposed to build three new battleships a year for the next twenty years.

> Twice, in 1898 and 1899, Chamberlain proposed an alliance with Germany, but the Germans refused on the grounds that Britain wanted to use the Germans to check Russian expansion in the Far East.

> During the Boer War, Wilhelm behaved correctly and refrained from interfering; when Kruger arrived in Germany, the Kaiser refused to meet him.

> *The Boxer Rising in China (1900)* brought Britain and Germany together in close co-operation. The Boxers, a Chinese nationalist group, besieged the foreign legations in Peking in protest against the increasing outside intervention in their country. Britain played an important role in organizing an international expedition to relieve the legations. At the suggestion

of the British, a German officer was placed in overall command; the besieged foreigners were rescued and order restored.

‣ At the Kaiser's suggestion, an Anglo-German convention was signed (October 1900), sometimes known as *the Yangtze Agreement*. Both promised to maintain the 'open-door' in China to the trade of all nations and to check foreign aggression.

(b) why and with what results did Britain look for allies after 1900?

The reasons why Britain began to search for allies with more urgency after 1900 (most of them already mentioned) can be summarized briefly:

1 All the other major European powers had allies, whereas British isolation had been clearly demonstrated by the Jameson Raid, the Venezuela incident and the Boer War. It had been difficult to defeat the Boers; what would happen if Britain were to be attacked by one or more of the great powers?

2 France was still hostile, smarting over diplomatic defeats in Nigeria and at Fashoda, and resenting the British presence in Egypt and the Sudan.

3 Russia was viewed as a likely enemy, with designs on India and northern China.

4 Though Germany was seen as the most probable ally, the Kaiser himself was unpredictable and the Navy Law of June 1900 suggested that the Germans were setting out to match Britain's naval power. Naval rivalry was later to become the main cause of Anglo-German friction.

5 In October 1900, Salisbury at last gave up the Foreign Office, and Lord Lansdowne took his place. Lansdowne, like Chamberlain, had long been in favour of a more positive approach to finding Britain an ally.

6 The matter became urgent with the growth of Russian power in northern China. Towards the end of 1900, Russian troops occupied the northern part of Manchuria, and in January 1901, the details of a Russo-Chinese agreement became known; this meant that, in practice, Manchuria was now part of Russia. Lansdowne was determined to form some sort of alliance to check Russian ambitions.

The search for allies:

1 Lansdowne first tried to arrange a joint Anglo-German action under the Yangtze Agreement, but the Germans refused to co-operate, arguing that this only applied to the Yangtze Valley and not to Manchuria. The real reason was that they were happy that the Russians were occupied in Manchuria, since that kept them out of the Balkans, where they might clash with Germany's ally, Austria-Hungary. Yet another attempt at a formal agreement with Germany had failed; the Germans were convinced that Britain would be unable to find allies elsewhere.

2 *The Anglo-Japanese Alliance was signed in January 1902.* Lansdowne realized that the power which had the closest interest in checking the growth of Russian power in the Far East was Japan. The Russians were already turning their attention towards Korea, and the Japanese were determined not to allow Russia to control Korea as well as Manchuria. The terms of the agreement were:

▶ Japan recognized Britain's interests in China and the Pacific, and Britain recognized Japan's rights in Korea.
▶ If Japan was involved in a war with Russia, Britain would remain neutral, but if another power (presumably France) joined in to help Russia, Britain would help Japan.

The alliance had important results: the position of both powers in the Far East was greatly strengthened; if Russia continued to press its ambitions, there was now a much greater chance that Japan would resist by force. This is in fact what happened – war between Russia and Japan followed in 1904–5, and it was Japan that emerged victorious.

How does this square with the Wilson theory? In fact, it fits in rather well: if Russia was the greatest threat to the British Empire, it made good sense to draw close to Japan, the only power strong enough to resist Russia in the Far East. It worked brilliantly, in that Russia was weakened by its defeat. In fact, claims Wilson, 'if anything, the Anglo-Japanese Alliance was geared towards maintaining British isolation, certainly from the Great Powers of Europe, rather than towards ending it'. The alliance also played a part in gaining Britain a second ally, France.

3 *The Anglo-French Entente Cordiale* (friendly understanding) was signed in April 1904. On the face of it, it was a highly unlikely development: for years relations had been strained over colonial matters; and during the Boer War the French press had been violently anti-British and extremely rude about Queen Victoria and Edward VII. But pressures for an understanding had built up on both sides: though the French resented British colonial power, they did not want a war with Britain, and still viewed Germany as their main enemy. They were alarmed at the Anglo-Japanese alliance and the growing danger of war between Japan and their ally, Russia. The Russians would expect help from France, but this might also provoke British help for Japan, and the French would find themselves involved in war with Britain.

Delcassé, the French Foreign Minister, worked hard to improve relations. On the British side, it was Chamberlain who made the first move; his motive was a desire to sort out the colonial squabbles. Lansdowne was probably thinking in terms of a counter-move against the build-up of German naval strength, though the government denied that it was an anti-German agreement. In fact, Lansdowne also explained in a memorandum that 'a good understanding with France' would probably lead to 'a better understanding with Russia'. Edward VII helped the process of reconciliation by paying an official visit to Paris (May 1903), during which he went to great lengths to show Britain's readiness to co-operate. The outbreak of the Russo-Japanese War (February 1904) made an agreement urgent and speeded up the final negotiations. *The terms were*:

› France would give Britain a free hand in Egypt and the Sudan, while Britain recognized French interests in Morocco.
› France gave up its claim to the Newfoundland coast in exchange for land in the Gambia (West Africa). Agreement was reached in disputes over Siam, Madagascar and the New Hebrides.

Results of the Entente: It had the desired effect of limiting the Russo-Japanese War. There was one tense incident in October 1904, when the Russian Baltic fleet fired on some British trawlers near the Dogger Bank, apparently mistaking them for Japanese torpedo boats. The French mediated and the Russians apologized and agreed to pay compensation. The Entente was just a settling of differences, not a military alliance. However, the Kaiser soon began to view it as an anti-German move, and announced that Germany too had interests in Morocco. This was clearly a challenge to the new Entente; over the next few years the German attitude pushed Britain into a closer commitment to France and away from the German camp. The next move was to be a similar agreement with France's ally, Russia, in 1907 (see Section 21.8(b)).

17.5 Ireland under the Conservatives

Although the situation in Ireland was comparatively calm, the basic problem was still there – the majority of the Irish were still without land of their own and were living in extreme poverty. George Wyndham, who became Chief Secretary for Ireland in 1900, believed that the best solution was to enable as many tenants as possible to buy land; the more content they were, the more likely they would be to forget their desire for Home Rule. *Wyndham's Land Purchase Act (1903)* allowed the loaning of money to tenants who wanted to buy farms of their own in cases where a reasonable price could be agreed with the landlord. The loans were at a low rate of interest – only $3\frac{1}{4}$ per cent – and the repayments were spread over 68 years. All parties involved approved, and by 1910 some 250,000 tenants had taken advantage of the measure. Earlier, the administration of the country had been improved by the introduction of elected county councils on similar lines to those in Britain.

17.6 what were the achievements of Balfour's government (1902–5), and why had it become so unpopular by 1905?

Arthur James Balfour had had a distinguished career – a successful Chief Secretary for Ireland (1887–91) (see Section 16.6) and First Lord of the

Treasury (1895–1902). As Salisbury's health deteriorated, Balfour took on more and more of the burden of government. He was able, cultured and witty, though he often seemed to lack a strong commitment to any particular direction. Lloyd George dismissed him contemptuously as 'just like the scent on a pocket handkerchief'. He remained leader of the Conservative party until 1911, but his reputation is tarnished by the fact that he led the Conservatives into the crushing electoral defeat of 1906, and then lost two further general elections in 1910. No party leader could survive that record. Yet during his short period as Prime Minister, there were some important achievements.

(a) Balfour's achievements

1 *The Education Act of 1902* was probably his greatest achievement (see Section 12.8(e)), though it was a disappointment to Nonconformists.
2 *Wyndham's Land Purchase Act of 1903* (see previous section).
3 *The Licensing Act of 1904* dealt with the problem of whether brewers should be compensated when a public house was closed down by having its licence withdrawn. The brewers naturally felt that they were entitled to compensation in cases where licences were withdrawn because there was an excess of public houses; but in 1891 the House of Lords had decided that liquor licences were to last only for one year, and that there should be no compensation for licences not renewed. The situation became urgent in 1902, when magistrates in certain areas launched what seemed to be a determined effort to reduce the number of public houses – in Birmingham alone, over fifty – had their licences withdrawn. Balfour felt that his Act achieved a masterly compromise:

>) If a public house was closed because there were too many in the area and not because of any misconduct, the brewer should receive compensation.
>) However, the compensation would come, not from public money, but from a fund paid into by the brewers themselves.

Opposition was therefore aroused on both sides: the anti-drink movement objected to the payment of any compensation, no matter where it came from, while the brewers were not happy at having, in effect, to compensate themselves.

4 *Measures to improve defence.* Balfour, like other politicians, had been profoundly disturbed by Britain's poor military showing in the early stages of the Boer War. There was also the realization that the navy, although more efficient than the army, might well have to face a challenge from Germany within a few years.

>) The Prime Minister became Chairman of the Committee of Imperial Defence, and a thorough investigation was started into the Empire's military requirements. This had made little progress when the government

fell, but at least a beginning had been made for Lord Haldane, the subsequent Liberal War Minister, to build on (see Section 21.7(a)).

▸ Sir John Fisher was appointed First Sea Lord, and Lord Cawdor became First Lord of the Admiralty. They took two crucial decisions: they created a third fleet – the Atlantic Fleet based at Gibraltar – in addition to the existing Channel and Mediterranean Fleets; and they authorized the building of a revolutionary new battleship, the *Dreadnought,* launched in February 1906. Weighing 17,900 tons, equipped with eight 12-inch guns, driven by steam turbines and capable of reaching a speed of 21 knots, the *Dreadnoughts* made all other battleships obsolete. The plan was to build four *Dreadnought*-type battleships every year.

5 *The Anglo-French Entente of 1904* (see Section 17.4(b)).

6 *The Aliens Act of 1905.* Previously, there had been no restrictions on who could enter the country, except in wartime. Consequently, Britain was seen as a haven of freedom and economic potential, and from around mid-century people arrived from all over the world. However, this new act was prompted by the unprecedented influx, during the 1880s and 1890s, of some 50,000 poor Jews from Eastern Europe, who had been forced from their homelands by increasing restrictions and pogroms. They tended to concentrate in and around London in poorer areas such as Spitalfields, which were already overcrowded before they arrived. Inevitably this produced complaints that these 'alien paupers' were driving English workers out of the labour market by working for very low wages.

The 1905 Aliens Act required immigrants arriving in ships carrying more than twenty steerage passengers to be examined by an immigration officer and a medical officer. The only ones to be allowed in were:

▸ those who could prove that they were genuine political or religious refugees;

▸ those possessing at least £5 to meet expenses until they were able to find a job; and

▸ those who could show that they were likely to be able to earn their own living.

Anybody suffering from a contagious disease, from mental problems or having a criminal record would not be allowed entry.

In the years up to 1914 there was a clear decline in the number of immigrants, though many people thought that the act was too lenient.

(b) why did Balfour's government become unpopular?

Balfour was unfortunate: though some of his own policies aroused criticism, he and the Conservative party paid the price for the shortcomings and mistakes of Salisbury's governments:

1 *There had been an almost complete absence of major social reform from the Conservatives for the previous twenty years.* This was because both Salisbury and Balfour, unlike Disraeli, had very little conception of the problems and needs of the working classes; strong believers in self-help, they were not prepared for the state to take on responsibility for the problems of old age, sickness and unemployment. And yet there was an example to follow – in Germany, the conservative Bismarck had introduced successful schemes for sickness insurance (1883) and old age pensions (1889).

2 *The trade union movement was hostile to the Conservatives* because of the Taff Vale case, in which the House of Lords, acting as the final court of appeal, had ordered the Amalgamated Society of Railway Servants to pay heavy damages following a strike in 1900. This made it impossible for any union to hold a strike without at the same time risking bankruptcy (see Section 19.6(b)). This decision, and the failure of Balfour's government to take any action to reverse it, caused a surge of support for the Labour party.

3 *There was a reaction after the Boer War* against the shortcomings of the government and the military, against the 'methods of barbarism' in Kitchener's concentration camps, and against imperialism itself.

4 *Balfour's Education Act (1902) and the Licensing Act (1904)* were vote losers.

5 *The 'Chinese slavery' affair caused a political storm.* Balfour made a serious mistake by allowing thousands of Chinese labourers to be taken into the Transvaal to work in the gold mines. They were not treated as free people, and were confined in barrack-like compounds even in non-working hours. There were around 50,000 of them by the end of 1905, working for very low wages. There were protests from Canada, Australia and New Zealand, and the trade union movement was outraged at this inhuman treatment of fellow labourers. Possibly the real reason for working-class outrage was that the Chinese were filling jobs in South Africa that might have been taken by emigrant workers from Britain. The Liberal opposition made the most of it, but again Balfour showed his lack of awareness and sensitivity, merely claiming that the situation had been exaggerated.

6 *The tariff reform controversy split the Conservative party.* It was clear that Britain's period of industrial and commercial predominance was rapidly coming to an end. Most other countries had introduced tariffs, but since Britain persisted in remaining a free-trade country, British manufacturers and farmers were suffering intense competition from abroad. German and American manufactured goods were doing most of the damage to British industry. Joseph Chamberlain was convinced that the time had come to abandon free trade and return to a policy of tariffs. This would have two advantages:

- It would protect British industry against cheaper foreign imports and would therefore help maintain full employment.
- It would make possible the introduction of a system of imperial preferences; this would encourage a closer union among the Empire by having low tariffs or perhaps no tariffs at all on imports from the Empire, and comparatively high tariffs on imports from foreign countries outside the Empire.

Chamberlain announced his policy in May 1903, and while there was a lot of support for him in the party, most of the Cabinet was against his ideas. He therefore resigned from the Cabinet and launched a propaganda campaign backed by *the Tariff Reform League.* Balfour proposed a compromise, in which Britain would only place import duties on goods from countries which had imposed tariffs on British goods, but this only annoyed both sides – it did not go far enough for Chamberlain, while for the free-traders, any tariff at all was anathema. The row in the Conservative party enabled the Liberals to forget their differences and spring to the defence of free trade. Their argument was that free trade guaranteed 'cheap food', whereas tariffs would put up the cost of living for the workers.

(c) the Conservative defeat

Early in December 1905, Balfour suddenly resigned, but did not ask for Parliament to be dissolved. This was a gamble on Balfour's part. If he asked for a dissolution, there would have to be an immediate general election in which Conservative prospects could not be too bright. However, if the Liberals formed a minority government, there was a chance that disagreements in the Liberal party between imperialists and anti-imperialists might suggest that they were still unfit for government.

Sir Henry Campbell-Bannerman formed a Liberal government, not without some difficulty; but is soon became clear that Balfour had miscalculated. The leading Liberals were far too shrewd to waste such a golden opportunity. They patched up their differences and began to campaign for a general election in mid-January 1906. The election result was a massive Liberal victory; the figures were: Liberals 400, Conservatives and Unionists 157, Irish Nationalists 83, and Labour 30. No doubt all the issues mentioned above played a part in the Conservative defeat, but possibly the question of tariff reform was the crucial one. Liberal election posters showed a large loaf representing the cheap food provided by free trade, and a small loaf representing the more expensive food that would result from tariffs. Even Balfour lost his seat at Manchester, which he had held for twenty years, though Chamberlain's popularity in Birmingham was so great that he held his seat with an increased majority.

1 To what extent did the British government abandon 'splendid isolation' in the period 1895 to 1905 through fear of Germany?

2 'The Liberals did not win the General Election of 1906; the Conservatives lost it because they were divided.' How far would you agree with this interpretation of the reasons for the Conservative defeat at the 1906 General Election?

A document question about the outbreak of the Boer War can be found on the accompanying website www.palgrave.com/masterseries/lowe1.

the Dominions: Canada, Australia and New Zealand before 1914

summary of events

At the 1907 Colonial Conference it was decided to use the word *'dominion'* instead of 'colony' to describe all the parts of the British Empire which were self-governing – Canada, Australia, New Zealand, Newfoundland and South Africa (from 1909). In the early days of overseas settlement, the theory was that colonies existed simply for the benefit of the mother country. After Britain lost its American colonies in the American War of Independence (1775–83), the idea gradually became accepted that colonies with predominantly European and British populations would eventually be allowed to rule themselves. *Lord Durham's Report on the Affairs of British North America (1839)* played a vitally important part in persuading the British government that this was the only way to hold the Empire together.

Canada, Australia and New Zealand passed through similar stages of development:

1 Direct rule by a Governor with a council chosen by himself.
2 Representative government – an elected council that could advise the Governor, but had no real power itself.
3 Responsible government – an elected assembly that had the power to appoint and dismiss ministers, and control internal affairs.
4 Federal government – the separate colonies or provinces united in a federation, keeping their own separate parliaments, but also joining in a central, federal parliament.

Canada achieved independent federal dominion status in 1867, and Australia in 1901. New Zealand became a federal self-governing state in 1856, and then in 1876 decided to abandon the federal system in favour of a single parliament at Wellington. South Africa had a rather different and more troubled history, which eventually resulted in the Union of South Africa in 1910 (see Sections 17.3 and 22.1(b)).

Dominion status was rather a vague term, since it had never been stated precisely how much control the British government had in the last resort over the dominion governments. In 1926, a definition was produced which seemed to satisfy all concerned: in effect, the dominions were completely free from British control, but they retained a link with Britain through the monarchy.

18.1 Canada

(a) The early settlement of Canada

Representatives of rival French and British trading companies were the first European settlers in Canada. The French were defeated in the Seven Years' War (1756–63), and by *the Treaty of Paris (1763)*, Canada, with its considerable French population, became British.

▸ *The Quebec Act (1774)* was designed in part to placate the French settlers. Canada (still called Quebec at this point) was to be ruled by a British governor who would choose a council of up to twenty-three members to advise him. There was no elected parliament.

French civil law was recognized, but English criminal law was introduced. The French Roman Catholics were given freedom of worship. At this time, the Maritime Provinces of modern Canada – Nova Scotia, Prince Edward Island, Newfoundland and New Brunswick (founded 1784) – were treated as separate colonies.

▸ *Pitt's Canada Act (1791)* arose from the changing situation brought about by the American War of Independence (1775–83). Many Americans, wanting to remain loyal to Britain, left the USA and moved into Canada. Known as *United Empire Loyalists*, some stayed on the coast in New Brunswick, while others travelled inland and settled along the northern shores of Lake Ontario. At the same time, immigrants were flocking in from Britain, especially from Scotland and Ireland. With the influx of English-speaking settlers, Quebec began to split into a French-speaking east and an English-speaking west. Pitt's Act therefore recognized this by dividing Quebec into two provinces: *Upper Canada* (Ontario) for the British; and *Lower Canada* (Quebec), which was overwhelmingly French.

Each had its own Lieutenant-Governor with an elected assembly that could advise the Lieutenant-Governor and his nominated council, but had no legislative powers and could not dismiss the Lieutenant-Governor. There was also a joint governor for both provinces together. Canada had secured representative government, but there was over half a century to wait before responsible government was achieved.

(b) unrest and the rebellions of 1837

During the Napoleonic Wars, the USA fought against Britain (1812–14). American forces attacked Canada and burnt down the Upper Canada

Assembly building in York (later called Toronto). The Canadians and British retaliated by setting fire to the American presidential residence in Washington. Gradually, however, both Upper and Lower Canada became impatient with British rule, for a variety of reasons:

- In British Upper Canada there was still a feeling that the Lieutenant-Governor and his advisory council gave preferential treatment in matters such as allocation of land, and in civil service and political appointments, to United Empire Loyalists and their families. Another grievance was that large areas of land – known as clergy reserves – were controlled by the Church of England.
- In French Lower Canada, the elected assembly was naturally predominantly French, but the Lieutenant-Governor and his advisory council, who had the final say in politics, were British. The French became more suspicious of British motives in 1833, when a new company, calling itself the British American Land Company, began to sell land to British non-Catholic immigrants.
- There was a demand in some quarters, particularly among commercial interests, for a union of the two provinces, since it was felt that the existence of two separate customs systems was hampering the smooth flow of trade along the St Lawrence River.
- During the 1830s, the major issue in both provinces was the demand for responsible government, so that the elected assemblies could enforce their will over the Lieutenant-Governors. In 1834, Lord Grey's Whig government sent out a commission of enquiry, but when it became clear that it was not prepared to recommend any major concessions, extremists in both provinces could restrain themselves no longer.

In 1837, there were two separate rebellions. The one in Lower Canada was led by Louis Papineau, a French-Canadian member of the assembly, while the one in Upper Canada was organized by a Scottish-Canadian journalist, William Lyon Mackenzie. Both were easily suppressed, but they acted as a warning to the British government that they must treat Canadian grievances seriously.

(c) Lord Durham and the Canada Act (1840)

Melbourne decided to send out Lord Durham, the leading Radical Whig, to investigate and report on the situation. Durham, who took with him as adviser his imperialist friend, Edward Gibbon Wakefield, had vague ideas about a federation of *all* the Canadian colonies, but was disappointed to find that the maritime colonies were very cool towards the idea. He was only in Canada from May until November 1838, when he was recalled because his dictatorial attitude made him unpopular; but it was long enough for him to size up the situation.

Lord Durham's Report, published in 1839, was an important document, often

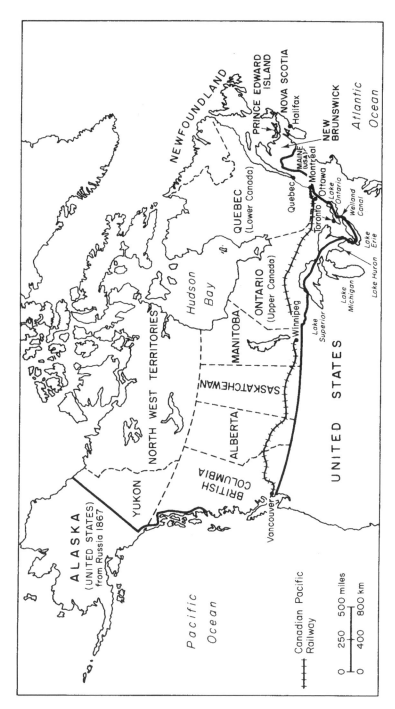

map **18.1 Canada before 1914**

regarded as setting the guidelines not just for Canada, but for the whole of the Commonwealth. He believed that representative government was not enough to keep the colonists happy and loyal; they would have to be given responsible government, otherwise there was likely to be a Canadian War of Independence. He suggested that the two Canadas should be reunited, in the mistaken hope that the French Canadians would eventually be absorbed into the language and culture of the British population, so making a completely united people. There should be one Governor with his advisory councils, and an elected assembly which would control internal affairs, defence and foreign policy. This last proposal was too radical for Lord Melbourne, but most of Durham's other suggestions were carried out in *the Canada Act of 1840*:

▸ Upper and Lower Canada were united under a Governor-General.
▸ He was to have an advisory council whose members were nominated for life.
▸ There was to be an elected House of Assembly containing equal numbers of members from each province.

This was a disappointment for supporters of responsible government, since the Assembly still had very little power. However, Lord Elgin, who became Governor-General in 1847, was a liberal Scotsman (and Durham's son-in-law). He came to an agreement with the parties in the Assembly that, provided they maintained the connection with Britain, he would accept laws proposed by them. In effect, therefore, Canada had responsible government. At about the same time, Nova Scotia, New Brunswick and Newfoundland were also given responsible government.

(d) Canada's relations with the USA

Since the birth of the hostile USA, Canadians had been worried about the threat to their largely undefended frontiers. The events of 1812–14 had shown that their fears were justified, and it seemed that the Americans were trying to outdo the Canadians at every opportunity. The Canadians retaliated effectively:

▸ In 1825, the Americans opened the Erie Canal, which joined Lake Erie to the Hudson River, and threatened to take trade away from the St Lawrence. The Canadians retaliated by building the Welland Canal, joining Lakes Erie and Ontario. This proved to be a great success, but commercial rivalry continued.
▸ A dispute about the frontier between Canada and Maine was settled by *the Ashburton Treaty (1842)*. Called after the British negotiator who worked it out with the Americans, the treaty was unpopular with Canadians, who felt it had given too much away.
▸ More popular was *the Oregon Treaty (1846)*, which solved a dispute about possession of the Pacific coast. The Americans claimed the whole of the coastline right up to Alaska (owned by Russia until 1867, when it was bought by the USA for $7 million), which would shut Canada out completely from

the Pacific. There was considerable tension between Britain and the USA, whose extremists wanted war. President Polk gave way and the treaty fixed the boundary to Canada's advantage along the 49th parallel, with a detour so that the whole of Vancouver Island could be included in Canada.

(e) the move towards federation and the Dominion of Canada (1867)

In the early 1850s, the idea of a federation of all the Canadian colonies began to be widely discussed. There were different motives:

‣ Time showed that Lord Durham had been wrong in thinking that the French Canadians would be assimilated into their British surroundings. In fact, they became more determined to preserve their French customs and language, and more worried as English-speaking immigrants continued to flood in. When gold was discovered in the Fraser River canyon in the far west in 1858, there was the prospect of thousands more flocking into the west, tipping the balance even more heavily against the French. In 1830, the English-speaking population of Upper Canada totalled only half the population of French Lower Canada; by 1861, because of massive immigration, there had been a dramatic turnaround – there were now 1.4 million people in Upper Canada and 1.1 million in Lower Canada. The Upper Canadians were protesting that they ought to have more MPs than the Lower Canadians. The French Canadians decided that a federal system might be the best way of saving themselves from being submerged: Upper and Lower Canada could be separated again and they would at least have their own assembly for internal affairs.
‣ All the colonies realized the need for a railway to link Halifax (Nova Scotia) with Quebec. This intercolonial scheme received very little support from London, and the separate colonies seemed unable to agree on a joint policy. The idea spread that only if British North America became united would the railway be built.
‣ The colonies had economic problems. As Britain moved towards complete free trade, Canada lost its preferential rates for timber exported to Britain. The American Civil War (1861–5) adversely affected Canada's trade. The Canadians realized that the only way to survive was by closer co-operation between the provinces.
‣ The American Civil War gave a decisive impetus to federation in another way. The Northern States and Britain were close to war, and British troops shipped out to Halifax had to travel by sleigh through New Brunswick to Quebec. This convinced the British government that a united defence and an inter-colonial railway were needed.

The Canadians began discussions at the Quebec Conference (1864). This broke up without agreement, but the matter became urgent in 1866, when the Fenians (see Section 13.3(a)) attacked from the USA and captured Fort Erie in

Upper Canada. British troops were able to drive them back, but the constant threat from the USA convinced all the colonies that unity was essential. Talks were resumed, and the Canadians produced their own plan, which the British government accepted in *the British North America Act of 1867.*

Upper and Lower Canada were separated again and became the provinces of Ontario and Quebec; they joined New Brunswick and Nova Scotia to form the Dominion of Canada. It was understood that other provinces would join later as they became more populated and developed. Manitoba joined in 1870, British Columbia in 1871, Prince Edward Island in 1873, and Alberta and Saskatchewan in 1905. The last to join was Newfoundland (1949), which had been a dominion in its own right. Each province had its own parliament (which pleased the French in Quebec) which had certain specific powers over local affairs. There was a federal parliament containing representatives from all the provinces, which was to sit at Ottawa, the new Canadian capital; this controlled matters such as defence, taxation and overseas trade. The Act also contained provision for the long-needed railway to link all the provinces. The word *dominion* was chosen to solve the problem of what title to give the new confederation. 'Kingdom' of Canada offended many people, so Samuel Tilley of New Brunswick suggested a text from Psalm 72: 'He shall have dominion also from sea to sea.' Thus the Dominion of Canada came into existence.

(f) important developments since 1867

- The first Prime Minister of Canada was Sir John A. Macdonald, who had played a leading part in drawing up the details of the 1867 Act. He went on to point the new state towards successful development, the first step in which was the completion of the Intercolonial Railway from the St Lawrence to Halifax in 1876.
- After initial problems, Macdonald was able to promote the building of the Canadian Pacific Railway linking Montreal with Vancouver on the Pacific coast. When this was completed in 1885, it enabled more and more pioneer farmers to move out west and made possible the vast expansion of wheat farming.
- There was one unpleasant episode in 1885. The Federal government had in 1869 bought up the territory of the Hudson's Bay Company, which had been trading in furs for the previous 200 years. These huge Northern Territories came under Federal control, but the government had been surprised when Louis Riel, a French Indian, led a rebellion of buffalo hunters who farmed along the banks of the Red River. Macdonald agreed that their settlements should become the province of Manitoba, and calm was restored. However, in 1885 Riel appeared again, leading a rebellion along the Saskatchewan River. This was quickly suppressed by troops rushed from the east along the new railway. Macdonald made himself unpopular by having Riel hanged, which reawakened much of the resentment between French and British, and

helped to keep alive Quebec nationalism, which has survived until the present day.

▸ Macdonald encouraged the development of Canadian industries by introducing high protective tariffs against American goods, though British goods were given preference.

▸ The link with Britain remained strong. During the Boer War, Canada unhesitatingly sent troops to help the British, while during the First World War no fewer than 650,000 Canadian troops played an important role in the eventual defeat of the Central Powers.

18.2 Australia

(a) New South Wales: the first Australian colony

The first European settlers – 750 convicts – arrived at Botany Bay in 1788, under the command of Captain Arthur Phillip. Australia was already peopled by the native Aborigines, whose ancestors are thought to have reached the country from Java or South East Asia some 40,000 years ago. It was estimated that in 1788 there were between 300,000 and a million Aborigines living in Australia, but the discovery of a huge burial site in New South Wales in 1994 has led archaeologists to revise that figure upwards to something like three million.

The first European settlement was at Port Jackson, and soon afterwards Sydney was founded. The first free settlers arrived in 1793, but the early years were violent ones: the convicts had to be kept in order by troops, and floggings and executions were common. Under pressure from the free settlers, the British government stopped the transportation of convicts to New South Wales in 1840, though the penal settlements remained open until 1866, when the last convicts in New South Wales finished their sentences. Convicts continued to be sent to Western Australia until 1868.

Sheep farming was the vital factor in the early prosperity of New South Wales, and of the other colonies as well. The Spanish merino sheep had been introduced from South Africa in 1796 by Captain John Macarthur. At first, sheep farmers stayed in the coastal area, but in 1813 an expedition led by William Lawson, Gregory Blaxland and W. C. Wentworth crossed the Blue Mountains and discovered the rich pastureland of the Bathurst plains. A rapid expansion of sheep farming followed, and by 1850, Australia, producing high-quality wool, was the world's largest wool exporter, and the British woollen industry came to rely heavily on Australian supplies.

Gold became the other mainstay of Australian prosperity. It was first discovered at Bathurst in New South Wales in 1851, and soon afterwards at Ballarat and Bendigo in Victoria, which had separated from New South Wales the previous year. It was in Victoria that the largest deposits were found.

(b) the other Australian colonies

Explorers began to move into the interior and around the coasts. Midshipman Samuel Flinders and Surgeon George Bass sailed round Van Diemen's Land (later called Tasmania) in 1798, and by 1803 Flinders had sailed all the way round Australia, mapping the entire coastline.

- *Tasmania* was the second colony to be founded, taken by the British in 1803 to prevent the French claiming it. Hobart was the capital, but in the early days it was used as a penal settlement for the worst type of convicts. The free settlers distinguished themselves by their brutal treatment of the Aborigines, who were eventually placed on Flinders Island in the Bass Straits. By 1869, all the Aborigines of Tasmania had died.
- *Victoria* began as a sheep-rearing settlement around the village founded in 1835 and became known as Melbourne, named after the British Prime Minister. Development was rapid: by 1850, there were 77,000 settlers and five million sheep in Victoria, and in that year it was recognized as a separate colony. When gold was discovered the following year, there was a frantic rush of immigrants, both from the other colonies and from Britain.

   The total for the year 1852 was around 84,000, with 19,000 people arriving in Melbourne in the month of September alone. There were enormous problems of administration and law and order, and there were some unpleasant confrontations between miners and the government of Victoria. In December 1854, what amounted almost to an armed insurrection took place at the Eureka mine in Ballarat. The miners complained that over the previous three years they had been subjected to unfair treatment, insensitive policing and exorbitant mining licence fees, and that all attempts to reason with the mine-owners had come to nothing. In protest, several hundred miners burnt their permits and barricaded themselves in. The authorities brought in government troops who stormed the stockade, killing around thirty-five miners. Public opinion was with the workers, and at their trials in Melbourne, their leaders were acquitted of charges of high treason. Eventually, the industry settled down and the mining was taken in hand by large companies.
- *South Australia* was the other important colony (see below). *Queensland* was first used in 1824 as another dumping-ground for convicts; it became a separate colony in 1859, though its population was only 25,000. The first settlers arrived at Perth in *Western Australia* in 1829, but development was slow and difficult because of the way the land was distributed. The government sold land at less than a shilling (5p) an acre, so colonists bought far more than they needed but lacked sufficient labour to work the land. They even petitioned the government to send them convicts who could work as labourers. The government gratefully obliged, sending 10,000 between 1850 and 1868. Another boost to the colony's development was the discovery of gold at Coolgardie (1892) and Kalgoorlie (1894).

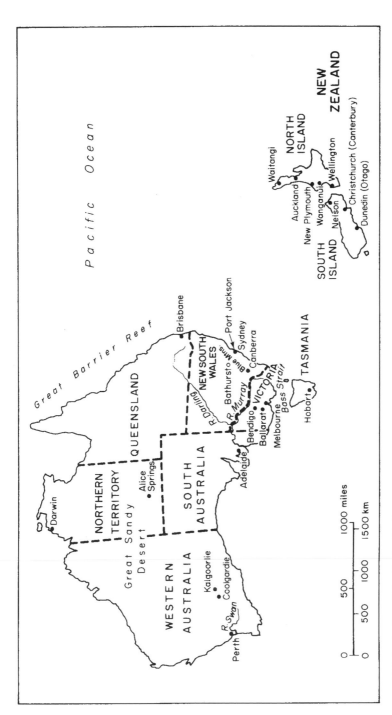

map **18.2 Australia and New Zealand before 1914**

(c) Edward Gibbon Wakefield and South Australia

Edward Gibbon Wakefield came from a Quaker and Radical background, his father having been a close friend of Bentham and Place. The young Wakefield was wild and undisciplined. He eloped with one rich heiress and later kidnapped another who happened to be under age; this earned him three years in Newgate Prison, London. Here he had plenty of time to ponder the plight of criminals and convicts, particularly those in Australian penal settlements. He developed a theory about how overseas colonization should be organized; this was explained in his *Letter from Sydney* written in 1829 while he was still in prison.

The idea was that, if emigration was properly organized by the government, *it could be the perfect solution for unemployment and poverty in Britain.* As things were at that time in Australia, he believed it was too easy to get land and too difficult to find labourers to cultivate it. The government should therefore sell land at a 'sufficient price', which would be high enough to ensure that only responsible people acquired it, and acquired only a workable area. The money raised would be used to pay the passages of more immigrants, who would have to work as labourers until they had saved enough money to buy farms for themselves. The purchase money could then be used to bring out more immigrants, so that the balance between the demand for and supply of labour would always be kept. Thus convicts would no longer be needed.

‣ In 1830, as soon as he emerged from prison, Wakefield started a *Colonial Society,* and almost immediately many of his ideas were adopted in the existing colonies. Between 1832 and 1842, 7,000 free settlers arrived in New South Wales; since land was priced at five shillings (25p) an acre (by 1842 it was £1 an acre), most of the new arrivals initially had to do their stint as labourers. Transportation of convicts was duly stopped in 1840. This was in marked contrast to what happened in Western Australia, where land was sold too cheaply (see above).

‣ Wakefield, wanting to found a colony of his own, started *the South Australia Association (1834)* and persuaded the government to agree to the setting up of South Australia. The first settlers arrived in 1836 and work began on the capital, Adelaide (named after William IV's queen). Land was offered at 12 shillings (60p) an acre. Soon, however, the problems of starting a new colony from scratch under Wakefield's system became apparent. The government provided no financial help; this was expected to materialize from land sales and loans, but the price per acre proved to be too expensive to attract enough buyers, so not enough cash was raised. And a great deal of cash was needed, since there was a complete lack of facilities and not even a reasonable harbour. Wakefield quarrelled violently with the other members of the governing body – he wanted to raise the price of land to 72 shillings an acre, but they rightly felt this was unrealistic. He withdrew from the whole project and started a New Zealand Association instead.

South Australia was saved from disaster when G. F. Angas floated a company that raised £320,000, enough to provide most of the vital facilities. Progress was slow even then, but by 1850 the colony was well and truly launched. It had a population of 63,000, with around a million sheep and 60,000 cattle. The land proved to be fertile enough for wheat growing, so that the new colony developed into the granary of Australia. The discovery of copper in 1846 brought an added boost to the economy, and in 1850 total exports were valued at £570,000. The success of South Australia had little to do with Wakefield, but at least it was his inspiration that founded it.

(d) political developments: the move towards a united Australia (1901)

The colonies moved towards responsible government without the agitations and disturbances that characterized Canada. New South Wales became a Crown colony in 1826 under a Governor-General who nominated his own advisory council. From 1842, two-thirds of the members of the council were allowed to be elected. The other colonies followed a similar pattern until, in 1855, responsible elected assemblies – with the power to decide policies – were granted in New South Wales, Victoria, Tasmania and South Australia. Responsible government came to Queensland in 1859 and to Western Australia in 1890.

For many years there was little interest in federation. The six colonies had developed separately and communication between them were so poor that any sort of union seemed impractical, at least until after 1870, and it was only after 1890 that federation began to be discussed seriously. The reasons for discussing federation were:

› *External threats began to worry many Australians.* Both Germany and Japan had ambitions in the Pacific. After 1890, the Germans began to follow an aggressive policy of expansion wherever possible, and the Japanese showed their potential by defeating the Chinese decisively in 1894. A strong and united defence was essential to dissuade any foreign ambitions of expansion into Australia.
› *The early 1890s were a time of economic difficulty,* culminating in the crisis of 1893. In fact, South Australia had been in difficulties since around 1880 because of drought and plagues of rabbits that ruined the wheat harvests. In 1886, a sudden fall in world wool prices threw many farmers into debt in all the colonies. Though Australia had experienced an industrial revolution after 1850, much of the new industry was inefficient, and in 1890 a depression set in, bringing widespread unemployment. In 1893, the crisis worked its way through to the banks as people rushed to withdraw deposits. Panic followed, and of the thirty-two major banks in Australia, twenty-two had to suspend payments. While prosperity gradually returned, the crisis had been a profound shock for the Australians, and was probably the main stimulus to

the federation movement. Union would remove the troublesome customs barriers between the states; the increased confidence would enable Australians to borrow from abroad. Improved communications made the idea feasible: Melbourne and Sydney were linked by rail in 1883, Melbourne and Adelaide in 1887, and Sydney and Brisbane (Queensland) in 1889.

The Commonwealth of Australia Act was passed by the British Parliament in 1900 and came into operation on 1 January 1901. The Federal parliament was to control defence, foreign policy and treaties, trade and customs duties, postal services, marriage and divorce, banking and currency, and immigration. Everything not specifically mentioned in the list was left to the state parliaments. These had more power than their counterparts in Canada, controlling social services, health, education, labour and industry, agriculture, mines, police, rivers and railways. To avoid inter-state jealousies, a new federal capital was to be built at Canberra, between Sydney and Melbourne.

(e) the Dominion or Commonwealth of Australia

The new state did not become prosperous overnight, but by 1914 the policies of the Federal government had stabilized the economy and the depression had disappeared. Important measures of the Federal parliament were:

- *The Immigration Restriction Act (1901)* in effect allowed only white people to enter the country. This was because Australians were afraid that Asian and Pacific labourers would work for very low wages, thus forcing down wages paid to white Australians. There was also the fear that the white population would be swamped if unrestricted immigration was allowed from such countries as Japan and India.
- *An Arbitration Court was introduced (1904)* to fix 'fair and reasonable' wages and to mediate in industrial disputes. The novelty of this was that the court's decisions were binding on all parties.
- Old age pensions (1908), invalid pensions (1911) and maternity allowances (1912) were introduced.
- In defence matters, conscription was introduced (1911) and the first ships of the Australian navy were launched in 1913. Australia played an important part in the First World War, sending more than 300,000 troops to Europe.

18.3 New Zealand

(a) early colonization

When the first Europeans arrived, New Zealand was already inhabited by the Maoris, a Polynesian race with light-brown skins. Captain James Cook had mapped both the North and South Islands in 1769, and had claimed them for Britain. The British government had ignored their existence, and there was no large-scale attempt to colonize New Zealand until well into the nineteenth century. The only European settlers were missionaries – the first of whom arrived in 1814 – attempting to convert the Maoris, and there were some whalers and escaped convicts.

Edward Gibbon Wakefield was responsible for the first organized settlement. After he had washed his hands of the South Australia project, he formed *the New Zealand Association* (1837) which, the following year, was allowed by the British government to become a chartered company. The first expedition of 1,200 people arrived and four settlements were started – Wellington, Wanganui and New Plymouth on North Island, and Nelson on South Island. The British government announced that it had annexed the colony, just in time to forestall a French colonizing party which was off the coast.

The first Governor, William Hobson, signed *the Treaty of Waitangi (1840) with the Maoris of North Island.* It was agreed that:

▸ The Maoris would regard Victoria as their queen.
▸ In return, the British guaranteed the Maoris the possession of their lands.
▸ The British government would buy any Maori land offered for sale, provided the whole tribe agreed. This was designed to prevent settlers acquiring land cheaply from individual Maoris.

Unfortunately, many settlers and officials of the company broke the treaty and simply evicted Maoris from their lands. The Maori tribes retaliated and there was some spasmodic fighting, sometimes referred to as the *First Maori War (1842–6).* By 1845 the new colony was not a success: the Maoris were hostile, the settlements were not expanding and exports were non-existent.

(b) The New Zealand Federation (1852)

Sir George Grey became Governor of New Zealand in 1845, and immediately matters took a turn for the better. Aged only 33, he had already made a reputation as a successful governor of South Australia. He quickly subdued the Maoris, mainly by a show of military strength, but then showed great sympathy and understanding, and made a study of Maori language and literature. He stopped the private sale of land and negotiated the purchase of almost the whole of South Island, where there were only about 2,000 Maoris. He developed a close friendship with many of the chiefs and spent money on schools, hospitals, law-courts and agricultural advice. The farmers began to prosper as exports of foodstuffs and livestock to Australia increased in the early 1850s because of the rush to the Australian goldfields.

As the numbers of settlers increased, they began to campaign for self-government, though Grey wanted to postpone it until the land and Maori problems had been settled completely. The first major step was taken in 1852, while Grey was still Governor: *the New Zealand Federation was established by an Act of the British Parliament.* The six main settlements – Auckland, New Plymouth (later called Taranaki) and Wellington in North Island; and Nelson, Canterbury and Otago in South Island – were given their own elected councils, and there was a central federal assembly. While this was representative government, it was not yet responsible government, since in the last resort the Governor was still in charge. Grey ended his first period as Governor in 1853, and the British Parliament agreed that the New Zealanders could have full responsible self-government in 1856.

(c) relations with the Maoris deteriorate again

▸ There was a great influx of new settlers after self-government was achieved. In 1856 there were still no more than 60,000 Europeans in New Zealand, but the number soared to 350,000 by 1878. There was tremendous pressure for land, causing settlements to spread from the coastal towns into the interior of North Island, where the Maoris had previously been left undisturbed. Now they gathered themselves for the final desperate defence of their lands, and the *Second Maori War (1860–71)* broke out.

▸ The Maoris fought bravely, but against the superior military strength of the Europeans there was no chance of a Maori victory. Grey was recalled for a second term as Governor (1861–8), and though he did his best to bring peace, he had very little power since the introduction of self-government. However, he managed some concessions: the Maoris were allowed to have at least four representatives in the federal assembly (1867) and an agreement was reached that allowed them to live undisturbed in an area amounting to about one-third the size of North Island. Fighting gradually fizzled out, but the fact remained that the Maoris had been deprived of much of their most fertile land, sometimes by purchase, but more often by straightforward confiscation.

(d) the united New Zealand (1876)

In the early 1870s, a group of leading politicians, including Julius Vogel of Otago, became convinced that the provincial assemblies were largely inefficient and lacking in vision, and that government could be carried on more effectively without them. An Act to abolish them passed the federal legislature and came into operation in 1876. There was to be a single parliament in Wellington.

Economically, New Zealand went through a difficult period until the mid-1890s. Then prices of foodstuffs and wool began to recover, and farmers enjoyed a period of great prosperity, lasting right through the First World War. The development of refrigerator ships enabled them to export lamb to Britain.

The Liberal governments of Richard John Seddon (1893–1906) introduced some remarkable reforms: votes for women (1893), old age pensions, cheap loans to farmers, improved working conditions and a system of compulsory arbitration of industrial disputes (the first country in the world to have such a system).

During the First World War a remarkably high proportion of New Zealand's population served in the armed forces. About 100,000 men served overseas, and many distinguished themselves, and lost their lives, in the Gallipoli Campaign of 1915 (see Section 22.1(d)).

QUESTIONS

1 New South Wales was the first Australian colony to be founded, in 1788; it was followed by Tasmania (1803), Western Australia (1829), South Australia (1836), Victoria (1850) and Queensland (1859).

   (a) Show how sheep-farming and gold-mining were important in the early development of the Australian colonies.
   (b) How important was the work and influence of Edward Gibbon Wakefield in the development of Australia?
   (c) What problems delayed the development of Western Australia, and how were similar difficulties avoided in New South Wales?
   (d) Why, during the 1890s, did the six colonies begin to think about joining together, and what arrangements were made by the Commonwealth of Australia Act of 1900?

A document question about Lord Durham and the development of Canada can be found on the accompanying website www.palgrave.com/masterseries/lowe1.

chapter **19**

$\overset{the}{\overset{growth}{}}$ of the trade unions and the Labour party to 1914

summary of events

Between 1799 and 1824, the *Anti-Combination Laws* made trade unions (and employers' associations) illegal. Though they were given legal recognition in 1824 (see Section 2.6(b)), their powers were more-or-less non-existent. Between 1829 and 1834, various attempts were made to form national unions, culminating in *Robert Owen's Grand National Consolidated Trades Union of 1834*. All the attempts failed, and it was to be the last quarter of the century before there were any serious efforts to form unions for the lowest-paid workers.

In the 1850s, associations known as *'New Model' trade unions* were successfully founded for skilled workers. The first was *the Amalgamated Society of Engineers (1851)*. After a long campaign, the Trade Union Act of 1871 granted legal protection for union funds, and in 1875 peaceful picketing was allowed.

As some areas of Britain experienced varying degrees of depression during the late 1870s, the low-paid workers were driven to form trade unions. These so-called *'New Unions'*, unlike the Model Unions, contained some socialists, though just how great the differences were between the two types of union has been the subject of some debate among historians. The first major triumph of the New Unionism was the successful *dockers' strike of 1889*. From 1900 to 1913 the unions were involved in legal wrangles – *the Taff Vale case (1900) and the Osborne Judgment (1909)* – with the courts and the House of Lords. Both were eventually resolved in a way that was satisfactory to the unions, but for a number of reasons there was considerable bitterness in labour relations, resulting in a wave of strikes in the years 1910 to 1913.

During the 1890s, the Labour party began to develop; in 1900, representatives of several socialist groups, and of some trade unions, came together to form *the Labour Representation Committee (LRC)*, which is usually taken as the beginning of the Labour party. Working closely with the trade unions, Labour won 29 seats in the general election of 1906, and 42 seats in 1910.

19.1 early trade union developments and failures

(a) repeal of the Combination Laws

There had been unions of labourers and workmen for centuries in the form of local trade associations. Towards the end of the eighteenth century, the Industrial Revolution caused skilled tradesmen to combine together to protect their interests. It was unfortunate that these early combinations happened to coincide with the French Revolution, so in the eyes of the ruling classes, unions were dangerous and revolutionary.

▸ *The Combination Acts* introduced by Pitt's government in 1799 and 1800 made it illegal for workers to form Combinations 'for obtaining an Advance of Wages ... or for lessening ... their Hours of working'. These Acts remained in operation throughout the wars with France and the period of unrest which followed after 1815.

▸ A campaign for the repeal of the Acts, led by Francis Place and Joseph Hume, was eventually successful in 1824 (see Section 2.6(b)), but so great was the resulting crop of new unions and strikes that the government immediately introduced an *Amending Act (1825)*: trade unions could exist to negotiate about wages and hours of work, but were forbidden to obstruct or intimidate. While some progress had been made, it was still almost impossible to hold a strike without breaking the law.

(b) the attempt to form nationwide unions (1829–33)

The year 1825 saw the beginning of a trade depression, which made it difficult for trade unions to have any impact. There were many attempts at local strikes, usually in protest at wage reductions, but employers broke them by bringing workers (nicknamed 'blacklegs') in from nearby areas. The idea therefore grew that, instead of having separate local unions, it was essential to form nation-wide unions of all the workers in a particular trade. Only in this way could the interests of the workers in that trade be protected. Beyond that, some leaders were already thinking in terms of uniting these national unions into a single national union for all trades.

▸ *The National Union of Cotton Spinners* (1829) was the first effective national union in a single trade. Founded by John Doherty in Manchester, it soon gained massive support, encouraging Doherty to go one step further and set up a *National Association for the Protection of Labour* (1830). This attracted the support of 150 trade unions throughout the North and Midlands, but both unions had died out by 1832 because of cash shortages, a failure to co-ordinate their activities, and an improvement in trade.

▸ An *Operative Builders' Union* was founded in Manchester (1832), bringing together all the various crafts in the building trade. Headed by a Grand Lodge and publishing its own journal, the new union seemed stronger than Doherty's creations, but it too had faded out by the end of 1834.

> The climax of this phase of trades unionism was the formation of Robert Owen's *Grand National Consolidated Trades Union* in 1834.

19.2 Robert Owen and the Grand National Consolidated Trades Union (GNCTU)

Born in Newtown, Montgomery, in 1771, Robert Owen became one of the most remarkable industrialists and reformers of the nineteenth century. From a modest background – his father was a postmaster – he was apprenticed to a draper in Stamford and, after a spell in London, he became a draper's assistant in Manchester. At the age of 18 he went into partnership with a mechanic to produce the recently introduced spinning machines, and soon became manager of a large spinning mill employing 500 workers. In 1794 he set up his own factory in Manchester, where he introduced the spinning of American Sea Island cotton, the first British manufacturer to do so.

(a) Owen as an enlightened manufacturer

In 1800, Owen moved to Scotland and became a partner in the New Lanark cotton mills. Before long, he had factories of his own, where he put into practice his advanced theories, so that the New Lanark mills and community facilities became a showpiece. His ideas were later published in a pamphlet, *A New View of Society*, in 1813.

> He believed that people's characters were a product of their environment; if miserable living and working conditions and grinding poverty drove people to crime, it was wrong to blame them. It was the duty of men with power and influence to improve the environment.

> He turned New Lanark into a vast experiment to prove his theories. He enlarged the factories, making them lighter and more airy, and reduced working hours. All this was in marked contrast to the usual practices. He built new cottages for the workers and a school for the local children, where there was an emphasis on outdoor activities – rambling and botany. He had parks and gardens laid out for the workers and introduced a scheme enabling them to buy goods at cost price.

> He believed that capitalists should take only limited profits and that surplus profits should be used on services and facilities for workers – a theory he certainly put into practice. He astonished his fellow manufacturers by continuing to pay wages when trade was slack and when cotton supplies were cut off during the war with the USA (1812–14). He was a strong supporter of the movement to limit children's working hours, and played an important part, along with Sir Robert Peel senior, in securing the 1819 Factory Act, though

he was bitterly disappointed with its terms (see Section 12.4(b)). While this Act was not a success, the effects of Owen's methods at New Lanark were vitally important: he had demonstrated that a manufacturer could still make a reasonable profit while at the same time reducing working hours and caring for his employees instead of exploiting them.

(b) Owen and the Co-operative movement

Although his ideas were arousing a great deal of interest and attracting supporters and followers, Owen was disappointed at the lack of response from government and from other industrialists. Consequently, he carried his logic further, influenced by a theory of David Ricardo, a leading economist of the time. Ricardo argued that the value of a manufactured article depended entirely on the amount of labour put into it, and that workers were therefore not receiving a just reward for their labours. If Ricardo was right, then capitalists were not necessary; society should be reorganized to rid it of landowners and capitalists. *Co-operative communities of workmen,* jointly owning the means of production, would produce the goods and fix prices according to the relative quantity of labour in each product. Sometimes they might exchange their products for the goods they wanted. He thought up a scheme for co-operative villages laid out in quadrangles, some producing food, others manufacturing goods. Oddly enough, Owen did not see this scheme as an attack on the rich, and he disapproved of strikes and violence to achieve it. Like the later Fabians (see Section 19.8(a)), he tried to appeal to the employers' better nature; he hoped that as they realized the attractions of this new 'socialism', they would voluntarily give up their property and join in the experiment.

▸ As a preliminary experiment, a 'Labour Exchange' was set up in Gray's Inn Road, London, for the exchange of goods. Workers brought their products and received certificates stating how much each article was worth in hours' work. The certificates entitled them to other goods of equivalent value. This was not a success, mainly because there proved to be too much of some goods and not enough of others – particularly food; the experiment was abandoned in 1834.
▸ He started the London Co-operative Society (1824), which opened several co-operative shops. These had only limited success, but the idea was taken up with spectacular results by the Rochdale pioneers in 1844 (see Section 19.2(d)).
▸ Owen himself went to the USA in 1824 to set up an experimental co-operative village at New Harmony in Indiana, but this collapsed in 1828 and he returned to Britain.

(c) Owen and the trade unions

When he arrived back in Britain, Owen found that his co-operative ideas had great appeal among workers, and some union leaders were attempting to put them into practice. In 1833, the Derby silk-throwers declared that the factories in which they worked were now co-operatives; the employers, not sharing Owen's enthusiasm, announced that they would not employ any labourer who was a member of a trade union, and proceeded to lock out their workers. Union leaders looked to Owen for guidance; his response was to set up *the Grand National Consolidated Trades Union* (GNCTU) towards the end of 1833. All existing trade unions were invited to join, and within a few weeks it had attracted over half a million members. On paper it had an impressive organization; in every district there was to be a branch of each separate trade, together with a joint branch linking the different trades. In central control was a Grand Council, which would meet twice a year. Members were to pay a shilling a year, and co-operative workshops were to be set up. Schools, recreational facilities and other services would be provided on the New Lanark model.

When these were established, the next step, as Owen himself explained, would be 'the union of master traders and manufacturers with the operatives and manual producers'. Finally 'the Government will not only feel the necessity of uniting with them, but it will also discover the advantages to the whole empire of this national bond of union'. What Owen was aiming for was a complete reorganization of society, in which workers' control replaced private ownership, and in which, ultimately, the GNCTU would control the government. He hoped it could be achieved voluntarily and without violence. If not, there would have to be a general strike, or 'sacred month' as it was called. However, the problems were enormous, and by August 1834 the GNCTU had more-or-less collapsed. *Reasons for its failure were*:

- Four of the most important unions – builders, potters, spinners and clothiers – decided not to join; they were apparently afraid of losing their separate identities. In fact, skilled workers tended to remain aloof.
- There were problems of communication between one district and another; it was impossible to make sure that all branches knew what action they were supposed to be taking, and to discipline branches that failed to co-operate.
- There were disagreements between different trades and branches, some wanting immediate strikes, others wanting to wait until a nationwide general strike could be organized. Some leaders merely wanted to improve conditions, while others wanted a revolution.
- Employers everywhere reacted with hostility. The Derby silk-throwers were soon defeated, and so were the London tailors and the Leeds clothiers. Some employers insisted on their workers signing a statement known as 'The Document', swearing that they were not members of the GNCTU. Anybody refusing to sign it was sacked.
- Probably most important was that the Whig government, alarmed at the wave of rick-burning and machine-breaking in the southern counties, decided to support local magistrates who dealt harshly with trade unionists. The most famous example occurred at the village of Tolpuddle in Dorset,

where there was a branch of the Friendly Union of Agricultural Workers. Although there had been no violence or even strike action, the union leader, George Loveless, who was also a Methodist preacher, was arrested and convicted, along with five other men, on a charge of 'administering illegal oaths'. For this, the five *Tolpuddle Martyrs* were sentenced to seven years transportation to Tasmania (1834). Lord Melbourne, the Home Secretary, upheld the sentence. In the face of such harsh measures by government and employers, trade unionists became discouraged, and while many individual unions survived, the GNCTU collapsed.

Owen himself and his group of supporters continued to publicize his ideas. Calling themselves socialists (what *they* meant by the word were people who believed that capital and land should not be held in private hands) they founded the co-operative settlement of Queenwood (East Tytherly) in Hampshire (1839), which survived until the mid-1840s. While none of Owen's ideas had much success outside New Lanark, he was important because he was the first person to publicize socialism.

The immediate results of the failure of the GNCTU were to turn workers towards Chartism and the Anti-Corn Law League. One of Owen's ideas that *was* taken up seriously later was the co-operative shops experiment.

(d) the Rochdale Pioneers and the Co-operative movement

In 1844, two Rochdale weavers, G. J. Holyoake and Charles Howarth, persuaded five fellow weavers to join them in setting up a co-operative store. It was partly an act of self-help and a defence against the ineffectiveness of the 1820 Truck Act (see Section 2.4(c)). They pooled their savings, bought their goods in the usual markets like any other shopkeeper, and sold them at normal retail prices. The difference was that most of the profits, instead of remaining in the hands of a single shopkeeper, were shared out among the people who had bought at their shop, in proportion to their purchases. By the end of 1844, the Pioneers, as they became known, had attracted twenty-eight members who shopped regularly at their store. The following year the store became well established, and other co-operative societies began to spring up, so that by 1850 there were over a hundred. In 1863, all the stores joined together to form the *Co-operative Wholesale Society (CWS)*, which bought goods in bulk for sale in the local shops. In 1873, the society began to open its own factories, and by 1900, when there were over two million members, it had even bought its own tea plantation in Ceylon.

19.3 show how the 'New Model' unions were established in the 1850s, and how they gained legal recognition

After the collapse of the GNCTU in 1834, the unions went through a difficult period, which lasted into the early 1840s; there was a serious trade depression, unemployment and wage reductions. Yet many unions of skilled workers survived, and as the country moved into the prosperity of the 1850s there were new and more successful attempts, mainly by skilled workers, to form large national unions.

(a) the 'New Model' Unions

1 In 1851, William Allan and William Newton formed *the Amalgamated Society of Engineers.* Its aim was not to change society, but simply to improve the position of its members within the capitalist system, by securing better wages and conditions. They were prepared to negotiate and to co-operate with employers; they were desperately keen to be respectable and looked on strike action very much as a last resort. With 11,000 members each paying the high membership fee of a shilling (5p) a week, it had an income of over £500 a week, and was rich enough to provide unemployment and sickness benefits for its members. It had its own headquarters and (paid) officials.

2 Other national unions soon followed, deliberately modelling themselves on the ASE, hence the phrase 'New Model' unionism. In 1860, *the Amalgamated Society of Carpenters* appeared, which became a national organization in 1862 when Robert Applegarth was appointed general secretary at a salary of £1.10s (£1.50) a week. Much smaller than the ASE to begin with, Applegarth built it up into an effective craft union; in 1870 it had over 10,000 members and 230 branches, and it was financially sound. Other amalgamated societies were the Shoemakers and Tailors, while in the North, the National Union of Miners was revived, and the Union of Lancashire Cotton Operatives was formed to deal with the problem of fixing piece rates.

3 The secretaries of these unions became powerful men; some of them – Allan, Applegarth, George Odger (Shoemakers) and Daniel Guile (Iron Founders) – used to meet regularly for consultations, and were nicknamed *the Junta* (a word usually used for a group of army officers running a country) by critics who resented their influence. The Junta, who seemed to see their members as a kind of 'labour aristocracy', superior to ordinary unskilled workers, went to great lengths to convince society that their New Model unions were moderate and respectable, and in no way revolutionary. The 1867 Royal Commission Report (see below) was a great help in this respect. Applegarth was particularly successful, winning respect from politicians and the press. The Junta was also responsible for the first *Trades Union Congress (TUC),* which met in 1868; this turned into an annual meeting and soon became a permanent organization, guiding and advising individual member unions and even being in contact with government ministers.

(b) the unions run into difficulties, 1866–7

While it was now accepted that unions had the right to negotiate with employers, there were two areas of trade union activity which had never been settled specifically: one was whether striking and picketing were to be legalized or not; and the other was the question of the legality of a trade union's funds. Though the Junta disapproved of strikes on the whole, every union had its firebrands who were eager for action. Many employers were waiting for an excuse to mount an attack on the unions, whether the leaders were moderate or not:

▸ The so-called *Sheffield outrages* gave the unions' opponents their opportunity. Union extremists sometimes used crude intimidation to force workers to join or make members pay their dues, and a number of unsavoury incidents occurred in Sheffield. Workers' tools and equipment were smashed, a small workshop was blown up, and in 1866 a can of gunpowder exploded in the house of a workman who had just withdrawn from the local Saw Grinders' Union. The culprit, the union treasurer, was arrested, and it emerged that he had been responsible for a whole string of similar outrages in several other towns. The employers demanded a Royal Commission to enquire into the conduct of trade unions, and the government obliged.
▸ A further crisis arose for the unions in 1867 when the Boilermakers' Society sued the treasurer of its Bradford branch, who had pocketed £24 of union funds. It was thought that union funds were protected by the 1855 Friendly Society Act, but when the case (known as *Hornby* v. *Close*) came before the Court of Queen's Bench, it was ruled that a trade union was not a Friendly Society, it was an organization 'in restraint of trade', and therefore its funds were not protected.
▸ The Royal Commission, to the disgust of the employers, came out in grudging support of the unions (1868–9). Applegarth had presented a skilful defence of their activities, emphasizing their disapproval of strikes, and pointing out the financial and social benefits gained by members. The Commission decided that outrages were in decline, and that union funds should be protected by law. This was a major triumph, preparing the way for the complete legalization of trade union activities that came during the 1870s.

(c) legal recognition for the unions (1871–6)

Two considerations probably influenced the government's thinking:

▸ Following the Royal Commission Report, unions were widely considered to be 'respectable'.
▸ Many union members had been given the vote by the 1867 Reform Act, and both parties were anxious to win this new working-class vote.

The vital measures were:

1 *Gladstone's Trade Union Act (1871)* recognized unions as legal bodies with the right to strike and to protect their funds at law. However, Gladstone followed this up with *The Criminal Law Amendment Act (1871)*, which made

picketing illegal (see Section 13.2(d)), so that strikes were impossible to enforce.

2 *Disraeli's Conspiracy and Protection of Property Act (1875)* made peaceful picketing legal, while the *Employers and Workmen Act (1876)* put both employer and worker on an equal footing in cases of breach of contract (see Section 14.2(c) for full details).

19.4 the 'New Unionism' for unskilled workers

(a) why did the 'New Unionism' emerge?

Though trade unions had achieved full legal recognition by 1876, most of them represented skilled workers, and the vast majority of unskilled workers were still unorganized and unprotected. During the 1880s, an increasing number of semi-skilled and unskilled labourers began to show an interest in forming their own unions. The main reason was the depression of the last quarter of the century: during the serious slumps of 1879 and 1886, it was always the unskilled labourers who were laid off first and who seemed to be exploited the most. The spread of education meant that intelligent labourers were literate, and they were perfectly well aware of the advantages that members of the 'Model' unions enjoyed. It was quite logical that they should try to follow this example. The spread of the factory system meant that there were greater concentrations of unskilled labour than ever before, which tended to encourage working-class solidarity. Joseph Arch had already formed the *National Agricultural Labourers' Union (1872)* which soon attracted 100,000 members. But when it asked for a wage increase from 13s to 14s for a 54-hour week, the farmers in Suffolk reacted decisively, locking out 10,000 labourers. The union almost went bankrupt, paying out over £20,000 in strike pay, and the agricultural depression killed it off completely. Eventually, however, the 'New Unionism' had some successes:

> • *In 1888, there was a strike of 700 girls working at the Bryant and May match factory in London.* Encouraged by the Fabian socialist, Annie Besant, they were protesting about having to work in an atmosphere full of choking, poisonous phosphorous fumes, which had caused many of the girls to develop 'phossy jaw', a type of bone cancer. Amid great public sympathy, the match girls won their case.
> • In 1889, Will Thorne, a stoker at Beckton gasworks, East Ham, formed a *Gasworkers' Union.* When the union demanded an eight-hour day, the owners granted it without argument.

(b) the London dockers' strike of 1889

This was the most spectacular success of the 'New Unionism'. Encouraged by the success of the Gasworkers and the match girls, Ben Tillett, Tom Mann and

John Burns formed a *General Labourers' Union,* and asked for a minimum wage for dockers of 6d an hour ('the dockers' tanner'). In fact, there was more behind the strike than simply wanting more money: the dockers wanted the right to work more hours a day, and they objected to having to hang around the docks at all hours of the day and night on the off-chance that they might be taken on. A further objection was that more often than not they had to bribe the hirer to get any work at all. The dock owners refused to negotiate, so the entire dock labour force came out on strike (14 August 1889). The dispute lasted almost five weeks, and the employers tried to break the strike by bringing in blackleg labour. In the end, however, they gave way and agreed to allow the men their tanner. *A number of reasons contributed to the dockers' victory*:

- They received solid support from skilled stevedores and watermen who had their own unions, and there were soon about 100,000 men on strike; the entire port of London was paralysed and cargoes were rotting in the hot weather.
- The strike was conducted in a peaceful way, with huge processions and mass meetings to publicize the justice of their claim. These won over public opinion and brought a rush of donations from sympathizers. This was vitally important, since the union had no funds of its own for strike pay.
- Just when it seemed that the cash would run out, the dockers received an unexpected gift of £30,000 from the Australian trade unions, which enabled them to continue.
- Finally, Cardinal Manning, head of the Roman Catholic Church in Britain (he was an old Harrovian Tory and a former Anglican Archdeacon who had joined the Catholic Church), supported the dockers, and together with the Lord Mayor of London, he persuaded the employers that the men's demands were reasonable.

The dockers' strike was a vital turning point in trade union development. It showed that even the lowest paid and most exploited and despised labourers could take on their employers and beat them, provided their demands were reasonable and provided they conducted their strikes in an orderly fashion. 'New Unionism' received an enormous boost, as all types of unskilled workers formed new unions or rushed to join existing unions that had been struggling to find their feet. There was also an increase in the membership of the older 'Model' unions.

19.5 the unions run into problems during the 1890s

The year 1889 – the year of the dockers' strike – was a year of triumph for the unions. Yet within a very short time 'New' unionism ran into all sorts of difficulties, which slowed up development. Many strikes took place, often involving dockers and seamen, during the years 1890–3, usually to try to enforce the 'closed shop' (this would take the form of an agreement with the owners that they would only employ union members). All the strikes were unsuccessful.

(a) what were the problems?

> The country moved into another period of depression, when, again, unskilled workers were the first to be laid off. It was impossible to run a successful strike when there was unemployment, since the owners could simply sack the strikers, knowing that they would be able to fill the vacancies with unemployed men desperate for a job.
> Employers also began to fight back by taking on non-union labour, with police protection where necessary. This applied mainly to dockers and seamen, and was the main reason for the failure of their strike at Hull in 1893; as *The Times* put it: 'At Hull, as elsewhere, the New Unionism has been defeated, but nowhere has the defeat been so decisive, or the surrender so abject.'
> There were quarrels within the trade union movement between the older 'Model' unions and the 'New' unionism.

(b) what were the differences and similarities between the 'Model' and 'New' unionism?

There is some debate among historians about how great the differences were. Superficially there seemed to be some fairly obvious differences, at least in the 1880s and 1890s:

1 The 'New' unions were much poorer, since their membership fees – usually about 1d a week – had to be lower than those for the skilled unions. Nor did they undertake Friendly Society benefits and pensions, believing instead that the state ought to provide them.

2 They tended to be more militant than the 'Model' unions, which seemed reluctant to face up to the problems of unemployment. According to Mann and Tillett, writing in 1890: 'A kind of deadly stupor covered them and they really appeared to be dying of inanation [lack of nourishment].'

3 Many of the leaders of the 'New' unions were socialists, who wanted political as well as industrial action. They believed that it was the duty of the state to provide a decent standard of living for everybody via the introduction of social benefits. In the early years of the twentieth century, some of these unionists threw their weight behind the Labour party. Tillett and Mann complained that the leaders of the old 'Model' unions 'do not recognise, as we do, that it is the work of the trade unionist to stamp out poverty from the land ... A new enthusiasm is required, a fervent zeal ... The cause we have at heart is too sacred to admit of time being spent quarrelling amongst ourselves' (see Source A on the website).

These quarrels used to be seen as the struggle between the reactionary 'old-guard' leaders who were trying to cling on to power, and the brash new unionists, many of them socialists, who were trying to hijack the trade union movement. However, many historians now recognize that this interpretation is too simplistic: the 'old guard' were not as conservative as used to be thought. Paul Adelman points out that between 1885 and 1887 the three presidential speeches at the TUC all spoke in support of two of the favourite aims of 'New' unionism:

» the eight-hour maximum working day; and
» the nationalization of land.

They also criticized the existing capitalist system. Henry Pelling is of the same opinion, believing that the differences have been exaggerated: 'It is clear that Marxist historians have completely got the wrong end of the stick: militancy was much more likely to be found among the better-off than among the poorer workers' (see Source B on the website).

Whatever the differences, there is no doubt that the 'New' unionism found it hard going during the 1890s. As J. Savile points out, 'outside the highly skilled trades, to win even an approximation to the closed shop or to ensure that blackleg labour did not swamp a strike, militant tactics were demanded which the older unionists … believed they no longer needed; the employers' first reaction was to smash these new upstart organizations' (see Source C on the website). By 1900, the total membership of the 'New' unions was at most only 200,000, whereas membership of all unions was about two million. Even the 200,000 was only a tiny fraction of the total unskilled labour force of perhaps 15 million. However, 'New' unionism survived and struggled on into the twentieth century.

(c) how did 'New' unionism manage to survive the problems of the 1890s?

» Workers in some industries which were expanding – such as gas, water and electricity – coped better than the dockers and seamen. These expanding industries were often owned by the local councils, which might be held accountable by voters if there were constant gas and electricity cuts. Thus the workers had more power, and employers needed to have a good relationship with them, since industrial action would affect the customer more immediately than would a dock strike.
» Unions of gas, water and electricity workers tended to be better-led than the dockers' and seamen's unions, and they gradually became more like the old craft unions in organization and general outlook. For example, the Gasworkers' Union aimed to build up its strength in certain large works rather than over the industry as a whole.
» They also concentrated on building up the idea that they were 'specialized' workers and therefore indispensable, and this helped them to pressurize employers to recognize their union. Many employers did so; once this had been achieved, 'collective bargaining' would follow; and this was when the union would negotiate for better conditions of work for the entire industry.

As 'New' unionism gradually won the battle for survival, according to Paul Adelman, 'the frontiers between "old" and "new" unionism began to become blurred'. For example, in 1892, the Amalgamated Society of Engineers (an 'old' union) relaxed its rigid qualifications for membership, so that unskilled workers in the engineering industry could join. Between 1891 and 1893, the TUC adopted the eight-hour day as one of its policies.

(d) what was the real significance of the 'New' unionism in the 1890s?

If this question had been put in 1889, immediately after the dockers' strike, the answer would have seemed obvious – it was going to have great industrial importance. But in fact this industrial significance did not develop in any big way before 1914. However, it did have great political significance. According to Ben Tillett, 'it marked the beginning of that close alliance in thought and purpose between the Trade Union Movement and the Socialist Movement which produced, in due time, the Labour Party'. Both agreed on the need for working-class solidarity and state action against poverty. The alliance became closer because of legal problems facing the unions.

19.6 what legal problems faced the trade unions in the early twentieth century, and how were they overcome?

Most manufacturers and men of property were genuinely afraid of trade unionism, and some were determined to smash the movement. The Federation of Engineering Employers, for example, refused to discuss a workers' demand for an eight-hour day. The men were locked out from July 1897 until January 1898, while the management moved in blackleg labour. The employers won, and while the unions survived, there was great bitterness. Even more serious for the unions was the fact that the law courts seemed biased against them; several adverse judgments had serious implications for both skilled and unskilled unions.

(a) the Lyons v. Wilkins case (1899)

In a dispute between the Society of Fancy Leather Workers and a workshop owner named Lyons, the Appeal Court issued an injunction that prevented union members from picketing Lyons' premises; if the same thing were to happen every time there was a strike, it could eventually reverse the 1876 Trade Union Act. It prompted the TUC to vote (with a small majority) for a meeting with the various socialist societies; it was this meeting which set up *the Labour Representation Committee* (February 1900). Its purpose was to put up independent Labour candidates for election to Parliament. Many trade unionists had come to the conclusion that, if strikes were failing and the law was against them, the only option left was to work through Parliament. However, at this stage there was only lukewarm support – only ten unions affiliated to the Labour party out of a total of over 1,300 unions.

(b) the Taff Vale case (1900–1)

This arose from a strike by the workers of the Taff Vale Railway Company in South Wales. They wanted better working conditions and the right to join the Amalgamated Society of Railway Servants, which recognized the strike as official. The company refused to negotiate, and broke the strike by bringing in blackleg labour. After two months the men had to return to work on the old terms (August 1900). The company decided to press home its advantage by suing the ASRS for damages suffered through loss of profits during the strike. After months of argument, the House of Lords judged in favour of the company, and ordered the ASRS to pay £23,000 damages, plus costs, making a grand total of £42,000. This was a disastrous decision for the trade unions, since it meant that no union could call a strike without risking bankruptcy; strike action was now virtually impossible.

The only way to defeat the Taff Vale decision was for the government to pass an Act changing the law in the unions' favour. The unions had therefore to concentrate on political means to restore their powers. The Conservatives declined to co-operate, so many union leaders advised their members to support the Labour party instead. By the end of 1903, a further 168 unions had affiliated to Labour, which won 29 seats in the 1906 general election. Twenty-four trade unionists were elected as Liberal MPs, and one of the first measures of the new Liberal government was *the Trade Disputes Act (1906)*. This stated that unions could not be sued for damages, and accepted that peaceful picketing was legal. This Act, possibly the most important in trade union history, left the unions more powerful than ever before, and made possible the strike wave of 1910–14.

(c) the Osborne Judgment (1909)

This was another legal decision which displeased the unions, though it was the Labour party that suffered directly from it.

1 The situation was that the unions charged their members what was called *the political levy* – a small weekly payment on top of their normal union subscription, which was used mainly to provide financial help for Labour Members of Parliament, since at that time MPs were not paid a salary. Not all union members were supporters of the Labour party, and W. V. Osborne, a Liberal, and secretary of the Walthamstow branch of the Amalgamated Society of Railway Servants, challenged the right of his union to demand the political levy. The House of Lords ruled that it was illegal for unions to demand such a payment for the purpose of helping a political party. This was a serious blow for the Labour party, which was chronically short of funds and

could not afford to pay the salaries of around sixteen of its MPs. The Osborne Judgment drove many trade unionists towards syndicalism (see Section 19.7).

2 Again, it was only by parliamentary means that the Osborne Judgment could be defeated, and the unions and Labour launched a campaign to pressurize the Liberal government into action. This was slow to materialize, since the government was beset by many other serious problems (see Sections 21.3–21.5), but eventually the Liberals gave satisfaction:

  ▸ In 1911 an annual salary of £400 was introduced for MPs. This fulfilled one of the Chartists' demands and eased the difficulties caused by the Osborne Judgment. But union pressure continued, and the result was:
  ▸ *The Trade Union Act of 1913*, which, in effect, reversed the Osborne Judgment. The political levy was legal, but any individual who objected to contributing to the Labour party could 'contract out'. Since this required some personal effort and the filling-in of forms, the vast majority of trade union members did not bother to 'contract out', and Labour party funds accordingly received a life-saving boost.

On the eve of the First World War, therefore, trade unions had overcome all legal obstacles; they had the power to strike, to picket, and to play an important role in politics.

19.7 syndicalism and trade union militancy

In the years 1910–14, many of the 'New' trade unions became much more militant and violent, influenced by French and American syndicalism or revolutionary trade unionism (*syndicat* is the French word for a trade union).

(a) syndicalist ideas

  ▸ The trade union movement, not the state, was destined to become the main democratic organization of the future, owning industries and land, and controlling the country's economic and social policies.
  ▸ Party politics were too full of compromises to be worth wasting time on; Ben Tillett called them 'a farce and a sham'.
  ▸ Syndicalist aims must therefore be achieved, not by political action through Parliament, but by direct action outside Parliament. They introduced the idea of the 'sympathetic' strike – if a union was conducting a strike, other unions in different industries would strike in sympathy, so that maximum pressure could be brought to bear on employers and government. Ultimately, they hoped to disrupt the country by a general strike so that the capitalist system would be overthrown and the trade union movement would take charge. There was some similarity here to Robert Owen's ideas, though he never liked the idea of violence.

(b) why did syndicalism develop in Britain?

There was serious labour unrest because of unemployment and because, while prices were rising, wages were in fact falling in real terms. As usual, it was the unskilled, low-paid workers who suffered most. The results achieved by the skilled unions and by the Labour party in Parliament were disappointing. The Osborne Judgment seemed designed deliberately to cripple the Labour party. Some historians see the rejection of Lloyd George's budget by the House of Lords in November 1909 (see Section 21.3) as an important stimulus: 'If the peers can sabotage the constitution for their own ends, why can't we?' was the question on the lips of many trade unionists. If parliamentary action was impossible, there remained only direct action outside Parliament.

(c) the strike wave, 1910-14

The wave of strikes began in July 1910 with action by railway workers, soon followed by Lancashire cotton workers, boilermakers and Welsh miners. In 1911 there was a successful dock strike which affected all ports, and in Liverpool there was a transport strike during which troops were moved in and two men were killed. There seemed to be a lull in the strikes on the mainland in 1913, though there was a major syndicalist strike in Dublin lasting over six months.

In fact, the unskilled workers were gathering themselves for another onslaught. Several small railway unions united to form the National Union of Railwaymen (NUR), and in 1914 the powerful *Triple Alliance* was formed, consisting of the new NUR, the Transport Workers' Federation and the Miners' Federation. The outbreak of the First World War may have prevented a massive Triple Alliance strike in 1914, but the Alliance survived and moved into action later during the general strike of 1926.

19.8 the causes of the rise of the Labour party, and the main stages in its development to 1914

It is an oversimplification to talk about the rise of the Labour party as if it were a single homogeneous body. In fact, it was an amalgamation of three different socialist groups – the Social Democrat Federation, the Fabians and the Independent Labour party – with some trade unions. Despite all these groups being described as socialist, their aims and methods were not always the same. The word 'socialist' meant different things to different people. One thing that all the members did agree on, however, was that their aim was to represent working-class interests in Parliament, and to do their best to improve life for the workers. The origins of the party lay in the conditions and circumstances of late-Victorian Britain.

(a) poverty and poor social conditions

During the last quarter of the nineteenth century, at least 30 per cent of the working class were living close to starvation level. Agricultural and industrial depressions had worsened the situation, bringing unemployment. Often wages were so low that families were living in dire poverty even when the breadwinner was in full-time employment. Many people were becoming disturbed at the striking contrast between this poverty and the comfortable existence enjoyed by the upper and middle classes (see Section 20.1 for more details).

▸ *Progress and Poverty*, a book by an American economist, Henry George, published in Britain in 1881, focused attention on the tremendous contrasts of wealth and poverty. George blamed the problems on the greed of the landowners and advocated a massive land tax as the cure for all ills. In a time of severe agricultural depression, the book was bound to have an impact both on middle-class intellectuals and on the working classes. Thanks to the spread of education following Forster's Education Act (1870), working people could read George's book and other socialist propaganda, such as Robert Blatchford's influential newspaper, *The Clarion*.

▸ There was growing impatience among Radicals with Gladstone's second government (1880–5), which virtually ignored their suggestions for social reform. This was ill-advised, since many workers had been given the vote by the 1867 Reform Act, and Gladstone himself had extended the franchise to many more in 1884.

(b) two important socialist groups were formed in 1884

1 *The Social Democratic Federation (SDF)* was set up by an old-Etonian, H. M. Hyndman, and included John Burns and Tom Mann. Advocating violent revolution to overthrow the capitalist system, they achieved publicity by organizing marches and demonstrations. The most famous demonstration, held in Trafalgar Square in 1887, was broken up by police and is remembered as *Bloody Sunday* because of the violence on both sides.

2 *The Fabian Society* was a group of middle-class intellectuals that included Sidney and Beatrice Webb and George Bernard Shaw. They believed that land and industrial capital should be owned by the community, but unlike the SDF, they did not believe in violence. They took their name from Fabius, the Roman general who defeated Hannibal by waiting patiently and avoiding battle, knowing that time was on his side. The Fabians believed that society would gradually change from capitalism to socialism, and that their function was to persuade the political parties to accept socialism. At first they preferred this policy of 'gradual permeation', instead of creating a separate Labour party, but they changed their minds when it became clear that the Liberals and Conservatives were not impressed by their ideas.

(c) a slump in the Yorkshire woollen industry led to the formation of the ILP

The Independent Labour Party (ILP) was formed by James Keir Hardie, secretary of the Scottish Miners' Federation, in 1893. He had already formed *the Scottish Labour Party* in 1888 because he was disgusted with the complacency and ineffectiveness of the Liberal party. He became the first Labour MP in 1892 (for West Ham South), deliberately choosing to wear a cloth cap – the badge of working-class solidarity – for his first appearance in the Commons. He was soon to play a crucial role in the formation of the Labour party. He was convinced that the needs of working people could only be properly satisfied by a Labour group completely independent of other parties.

A slump in the Yorkshire woollen industry in the early 1890s, caused by foreign competition and American tariffs, gave Hardie and his associate, John Burgess, who ran a newspaper called *The Workman's Times*, the chance to form a new party. In the winter of 1890–1, the whole woollen area was badly hit by unemployment and wage reductions, and the unions were weak. Wool workers at Manningham Mills in Bradford went on strike in protest against wage cuts, but they found themselves up against the combined forces of mill-owners, local politicians and police, who prevented them from holding public meetings. The strike failed, but the treatment of the workers and the hostile attitude of local Liberals (many of whom were mill-owners) gave great impetus to the idea of a separate Labour party. The area was bristling with Labour clubs – twenty-three of them in Bradford alone, where the old Chartist tradition lingered on. Hardie organized a conference in Bradford in 1893 which led to the formation of *the Independent Labour Party.*

Its ultimate aim was *the collective ownership of the means of production*; in other words, the state should own land, gas and electricity, water and railways, and important industries such as coal, iron and steel. Hardie knew this was a highly controversial programme, so initially the new party aimed to concentrate on improving social conditions. The ILP was a northern working-class organization, but Hardie wanted a Labour party that was a national body with middle-class support.

(d) the growth of trade unions contributed to the formation of the Labour party

The trade unions gradually moved towards the idea of a Labour party, following incidents such as the great engineering lock-out of 1897–8 and the *Lyons* v. *Wilkins* case of 1899 (see Section 19.6(a)). The TUC proposed a meeting with the socialist groups. Representatives of some unions, the SDF, the Fabians and the ILP attended the meeting at the Memorial Hall, Farringdon Street, London (February 1900) and decided to form a distinct Labour group in Parliament. *The Labour Representation Committee* was appointed to organize their election campaign, and James Ramsay MacDonald, later to become the first Labour Prime Minister (1924), was its unpaid secretary. This is usually taken as the beginning of the Labour party. Its aim was simply to represent working-class interests in Parliament. About socialism, it was very vague.

There has been some debate about what part Marxism played in the formation of the Labour party. Karl Marx (1818–83) was a German Jew who spent most of his life after 1848 in Britain. His economic and political ideas were explained in *The Communist Manifesto (1848)* and *Das Kapital [Capital] (1867)*. He believed that economic factors are the real cause of historical change, and that workers (the proletariat) are everywhere exploited by capitalists. This must inevitably lead to a struggle between the classes, to revolution and to the setting up of a classless society. His ideas certainly appealed to syndicalists and became the basic doctrine of communism. However, it is easy to exaggerate his influence on politics in Britain. *Das Kapital* did not appear in English translation until 1887; Hyndman had read it in a French translation in 1880–1, and the SDF was the most Marxist of the socialist groups. Tom Mann was a convinced Marxist and remained so until his death in 1941; he eventually left the Labour party and in 1920 became a founder member of the Communist Party of Great Britain. The ILP, which was more important than the SDF in the emergence of the Labour party, arose out of the practical problems of the working class in Scotland, in the Yorkshire wool towns and in Lancashire, though Marx's theories may have had an indirect influence.

(e) stages in Labour party development, 1900–14

The major priority after the formation of the LRC was to get Labour MPs elected. Keir Hardie and two other Labour MPs had been successful in 1892, but all three lost their seats in 1895. The immediate impact of the new party was disappointing. In spite of the interest shown by the TUC, there was only lukewarm support; only ten unions decided to affiliate (associate themselves with, and give financial support) to the Labour party, and their members numbered only about 200,000, about a tenth of total union membership.

› In the election of October 1900, the LRC put up fifteen candidates, but only two were successful – Hardie himself at Merthyr Tydfil, and Richard Bell at Derby. Both of them were two-member constituencies, and the Liberals won the other seat in both. It was unfortunate for the new party that the election came so soon after its formation, when it was suffering from a severe cash shortage and had very little union support.

› *The Taff Vale case (1900–1)* changed the situation dramatically (see Section 19.6(b)). Ramsay MacDonald wrote to all trade unions stressing the need for a large Labour representation in Parliament, and this produced a surge of trade-union support. By the end of 1903, a further 168 unions had affiliated to Labour; this brought an immediate improvement in the financial situation, thanks to the political levy.

- *The electoral pact between the LRC and the Liberals, agreed in 1903,* brought an important boost in terms of seats in Parliament. MacDonald came to an arrangement with Herbert Gladstone, the Liberal Chief Whip, who agreed that, at the next election, the Liberals would not run candidates in certain constituencies, thus giving Labour a straight fight against the Conservatives. The Liberal motive was not to help Labour, but to avoid three-cornered contests in constituencies where the Conservatives were not thought to have much of a chance of winning. If both Labour and Liberal candidates ran, this would split the anti-Conservative vote, and allow the Conservatives to win. There was a financial consideration too for the Liberals: they would save election expenses in those constituencies that did not field a Liberal candidate. It was this electoral pact which allowed Labour to make the first breakthrough: in the 1906 election, Labour put up fifty candidates, thirty of whom were not opposed by the Liberals. Twenty-nine were successful, and when they took their seats in Parliament they decided to call themselves simply 'the Labour party'.
- At first, Labour had some success in Parliament. *The Trade Disputes Act (1906),* which reversed the Taff Vale decision, was based on the Labour party's own bill, and they were able to add small improvements to the Workmen's Compensation Act, and to the School Meals and Medical Inspections Act (see Section (20.3(a) and (b)). However, after 1907, they had very little influence on the government; they seemed to have run out of ideas and simply accepted the Liberal reforms.
- Important developments were taking place outside Parliament: the unions were grateful to Labour for the Trade Disputes Act, and more of them decided to affiliate to the Labour party instead of to the Liberals. Another reason for the move to Labour was that the steady fall in real wages and the increasing number of disputes with employers (who often happened to be Liberals) made socialist ideas seem more attractive. The most important catch for Labour was *the National Union of Mineworkers* in 1909, one of the largest unions in the country. If all the miners voted Labour instead of Liberal, this could swing as many as 60 seats to Labour. This is what happened in fact after 1918, when the electoral pact was no longer in operation.
- *The Osborne Judgment of 1909* (see Section 19.6(c)) damaged the party financially and its funds were further strained by the fact that there were two general elections in 1910. In January, Labour won 40 seats, and this increased to 42 in December. However, only two of these had defeated Liberal candidates; the other 40 were successful because of the continuing electoral pact.
- By 1914, the Labour party, though making some progress in local council elections, had failed to break away from its dependence on the Liberals. Convinced socialists were disappointed with Labour's showing, particularly when MacDonald claimed in 1911 that the party was 'not socialist', but was a federation organized for 'immediate political work'.

(f) was the rise of the Labour party inevitable?

This question, along with the parallel one – was the decline of the Liberal party inevitable? – has long been the subject of debate among historians. Henry Pelling and Ross McKibbin believe that by 1906 the rise of Labour was more-or-less inevitable.

Pelling stresses that long-term social changes: the growth of large industrial cities and the greater concentration of industry, together with the steadily rising cost of living, were gradually turning large sections of the working class towards the Labour party. McKibbin attaches special importance to the growth of trade unionism, which he thinks had already undermined Liberal strength before 1914. Another handicap for the Liberals was that they were against votes for women, and this led many supporters of female suffrage to back Labour. He argues that the reasons why the Labour party did not do better before 1914 were that:

‣ the party was financially handicapped by the Osborne Judgment, and this prevented it from improving its organization and campaigning; and
‣ in spite of the Reform Acts of 1867 and 1884, voting was still restricted, and many working men did not qualify to vote; this meant that Labour was deprived of many of its 'natural' supporters. *If all workers had been able to vote before the First World War,* the rise of Labour and the decline of the Liberals would have been obvious in 1914. *The Representation of the People Act (June 1918)* was therefore the crucial factor in the Labour breakthrough. By trebling the electorate, it brought the industrial working classes into a majority for the first time.

However, other historians, such as P. F. Clarke and Trevor Wilson, do not go along with this 'inevitable rise of Labour' theory. Clarke argues that, with the coming of 'New Liberalism', there was still plenty of life left in the Liberal party before 1914. Legislation such as the National Insurance Act of 1911 and the other Liberal reforms showed that they were doing their best to win working-class support. Wilson believes that the First World War was the crucial factor, because it split and discredited the Liberal party and opened the way for Labour to step in. Without the war, there was no way that Labour could have become the main opposition party to the Conservatives.

Two more recent writers, Duncan Tanner and Martin Pugh, also reject the idea that the Labour party would inevitably take over from the Liberals. Martin Pugh thinks this view is the product of hindsight; he argues that, before the First World War, it was difficult for Labour to project itself as a party radically different from the Liberals, except by advocating socialism, which was not popular with the vast majority of the working class nor with the Labour MPs at that point. He also highlights the weakness of Labour's constituency organizations and the fact that in the elections of 1910, although the Liberals lost many of the seats gained in 1906, these went back to the Conservatives, and not to Labour. The Liberals held on to most of their seats in the industrial North, Midlands, Scotland and Wales. It seemed that Labour could only win in constituencies where there was no Liberal candidate. Nor were there any Labour by-election successes between 1910 and 1914. In fact, it may be that Labour was in reality losing support because of the wave of strikes that caused great disruption between 1910 and 1912. Middle-class voters who had voted Labour in 1910 could well have been put off Labour by the prospect of militant trade unions trying to browbeat the legally elected government (for a further discussion of Labour's rise and the Liberals' decline, see Section 23.4).

QUESTIONS

1 Examine the influences that (a) encouraged, and (b) limited, the growth of the Labour party before 1914.
2 How far can the London Dock Strike (1889) be considered a turning-point in the history of trade unions in the period 1871–1914?
3 How far would you agree with the view that, by 1914, it was inevitable that the Labour party would take over from the Liberals as the main party of opposition to the Conservatives?

A document question about the 'Old' and the 'New' unionism can be found on the accompanying website www.palgrave.com/masterseries/lowe1.

the state and the people from the 1890s to 1939

summary of events

For most of the nineteenth century, the state did very little to organize society in Britain. The government did provide some cash for education, and several Acts of Parliament were passed to organize and improve education. The state had also introduced regulations dealing with health matters and working conditions (see Chapter 12). But there were many problem areas that the state made no attempt to deal with: it did nothing, for example, to try to plan the nation's economy; it did very little to help the poor, except to provide workhouses for them to live in when they could no longer cope at home. However, this gradually changed, and one of the major themes of British history in the twentieth century is *the development of the Welfare State.* This means a state in which the government tries to provide the best possible services for everybody, in health care, education, housing, pensions and unemployment benefit. It is also accepted that in a Welfare State the government does its best to make sure that everybody has a job.

The Welfare State was not achieved without a great deal of debate and struggle. There was never any overall plan or blueprint for setting up such a system, and it happened in a piecemeal fashion, in fits and starts. The first big steps were taken under the Liberal governments of 1905–15, and another important 'surge' took place between 1940 and 1948, mainly as a result of the Second World War (see Section 28.7 and Chapter 29).

In 1900, there was a great debate going on about whether or not the state – the government – should be expected to do anything to help the poor. Was it the function of the state to introduce old age pensions, health insurance and unemployment benefit? There were two opposing views.

‣ *Individualism or self-help* – this was the traditional Victorian view, which went hand-in-hand with the theory of *laissez-faire*: the belief that the government should interfere as little as possible with people's lives and activities; they should be left alone with the freedom to organize their own lives. The poor should be encouraged to help themselves and not expect to be helped out by the state.

• *Collectivism* – this was gradually becoming more widespread after about 1870, and was the belief that the state had a duty to look after the welfare of its people and to do its best to improve things for the poor.

The Liberal governments of 1905–15 were partially converted to the idea of collectivism, and though they could never fully tear themselves away from their *laissez-faire* background, they did introduce some important social reforms. During the period between the wars (1919–39) politicians of all three parties (though not *all* politicians) came to accept that it *was* the state's job to provide social services. The social reforms of the Liberals were gradually extended, but not without difficulty, mainly because of the enormous cost of financing unemployment benefit, which was far greater than anybody had expected. These problems led some politicians, especially those in the Labour party, to suggest that the government should play a part in planning and organizing the economic life of the country; in other words, there should be *a managed economy.* This, in theory, would help to reduce unemployment and keep costs under control.

20.1 individualism versus collectivism: the main arguments in the debate

(a) the case for individualism or self-help

1 Throughout the nineteenth century, as part of the general *laissez-faire* attitude, there was a strong feeling that the state should interfere as little as possible with the lives and activities of individual people, who should be left in freedom to act as they wanted, without any government directions or restrictions. As early as 1776, Adam Smith, in his book *Wealth of Nations,* put forward the theory that the economy would function most efficiently if people were free to pursue their own self-interest. He thought this applied to individuals as well as to nations, and so it followed that individual people were more likely to be successful at making money if the government did not interfere.

2 One of the supreme Victorian virtues was thought to be self-help. This was the belief that, given complete freedom, everybody had an equal chance to do well; initiative and hard work would always be rewarded. Samuel Smiles was one of the best-known supporters of self-help, and he published a book about it in 1859: 'Heaven helps them who help themselves', he wrote. 'Even the best institutions can give a man no active help. Perhaps the most they can do is to leave him free to develop himself and improve his individual condition.' And in fact Victorian Britain was full of examples of men who, by their own determination and dedication, had pulled themselves to the top from modest or poor backgrounds. Nor did Smiles believe in unemployment

benefit: 'every working man should strive, in times of prosperity and good wages, to save something and accumulate a fund in case of bad times'. Friendly Societies were a good example of workers helping themselves; they were insurance schemes run by workers to provide burial expenses, sickness and unemployment benefits, and even old age pensions.

3 There was also the question of cost – who would foot the bill for old age pensions and other benefits? If the government was expected to provide funding, that would mean increased taxation, which would be unpopular with electors. If the cash was to come from local authorities, that would mean higher rates – another certain vote-loser. One of the main motives behind the new Poor Law of 1834 had been to reduce rates. There was another possible source of cash – tariffs (import and export duties); but these were also out of the question – the Liberals were committed to free trade, and the Conservatives were split on the issue (see Section 17.6(b)).

4 If success was a result of self-help, it must follow (so the theory went) that poverty occurred when people failed to help themselves because of some character defect such as laziness, drunkenness, a weakness for gambling, or just a general inability to cope with life's stresses. This was the belief underlying the new Poor Law system, under which conditions in workhouses were made as unattractive as possible, so that the poor would make every effort to find work, and only come to the workhouse as a last resort. Life in the workhouse was deliberately made more miserable than the existence of the poorest labourer outside. The idea was known as the *'less eligibility' principle*, and was expected to encourage self-help and prevent the poor from looking on workhouses as comfortable refuges (see Section 5.3).

5 Finally, it was thought that state help for the poor was not a good idea, because it would destroy the initiative of the working class; they would stop trying to help themselves and expect the state to do everything for them. Samuel Smiles was convinced of this: 'whatever is done for men ... takes away the stimulus and necessity of doing for themselves ... and the inevitable tendency is to render them comparatively helpless'. Individualism was therefore the best way of dealing with the working class because it encouraged people to work hard, live a moral life and save money.

(b) the case for collectivism – state intervention to help the poor

1 During the final quarter of the nineteenth century there was a great deal of unemployment – this was the time of the so-called 'Great Depression', caused mainly by increasing competition from Germany and the USA (see Section 15.2). Things improved around the turn of the century, but 1904 and 1905 were years of high unemployment. With no unemployment insurance to support them, many workers and their families had to endure severe hardship. This was where the self-help theory seemed to be breaking down – often, no matter how hard a man tried to find work, there were simply no

jobs available. Freedom was useless if circumstances beyond his management had caused him to lose control of his life. The 'freedom' that he really wanted was freedom from unemployment and freedom from poverty.

2 There was a growing realization that the Poor Law was completely inadequate in a situation like this. Able-bodied poor who could not support themselves were expected to move into workhouses run by local authorities, which received no financial help from the government. As the population of mainland Britain increased from 29.7 million in 1881 to 37 million in 1901, so the number of paupers (poor people) grew, and the burden on the local rates became heavier. In 1900, working people still viewed workhouses with fear and suspicion. Inmates were treated almost like criminals, losing their personal freedom and their right to vote. Many families, especially in London and the industrial cities, were living close to starvation level, trying to survive as long as possible before entering the dreaded workhouse. It was clear that in times of high unemployment this system was inappropriate; something more was needed to support the overburdened Poor Law.

3 There were plenty of charity organizations and the churches did a lot to help, but they could not cope in a systematic enough way with the unemployment of the 'Great Depression' period. Charity had another drawback – it tended to be degrading to those receiving it, producing the feeling that they were inferior beings humbly accepting crumbs of comfort passed down by their wealthy superiors.

4 Poverty received more publicity in the last quarter of the nineteenth century than ever before:

   ▸ Recruitment for the Boer War (1899–1902) drew attention to the problem of poverty when it was found that almost half the men who volunteered for the army were physically unfit for military service. This convinced many people that the time had arrived for government action to help the poor, otherwise Britain might be unable to defend its Empire adequately in the event of a major war. The popular turn-of-the century theories of Social Darwinism played their part in encouraging this attitude: it was a question of 'the survival of the fittest' – the nations that were the strongest, both physically and mentally, would inevitably dominate the rest.

   ▸ Between 1886 and 1903, Charles Booth, a Liverpool ship-owner and manufacturer who was a Christian and had a social conscience, carried out a series of investigations which showed that over 30 per cent of the population of London were living in serious poverty. Among old people, the situation was worse: possibly 45 per cent of the old people of London were living in dire poverty. Booth also showed that, in a time of depression, a worker might be unable, through no fault of his own, to find a job. Another point revealed by the survey was that some men were living in poverty because they were too ill to work. These discoveries were important because they probably did more than anything to explode the Victorian myth that poverty was always the result of laziness or some other character defect.

> Seebohm Rowntree, a Quaker and a member of the famous York chocolate and cocoa manufacturing family, found it difficult to believe that London's poverty level would be repeated over the rest of the country. So he carried out his own survey in York. His findings, published in 1901, showed that 28 per cent of the population of York were living in serious poverty. 'We are faced with the startling possibility,' he wrote, 'that from 25 to 30 per cent of the town population of the United Kingdom are living in poverty.' And he discovered something worse – that in York wages were so low that even men in full employment, working long hours every day, were forced to live close to starvation level. The work of Booth and Rowntree was vitally important, because it provided the hard statistical evidence needed to boost the case for state intervention to help the 'deserving poor.'

5 It followed that, if nearly a third of the population needed help, only the state could afford the necessary cash, and only the state had the necessary powers to provide what was needed. The next question for those who accepted that some state intervention was required was: *what was the best way to help the poor?*

Charles Booth suggested a pension of five shillings (25 pence) a week at the age of 65. Another of his ideas was for the state to take care of the poorest 10 per cent of the population, which he described as 'the incapable.' He believed that this would remove them as competitors to the other 20 per cent of poor people, so enabling them to get work and earn a reasonable living. He described this as 'limited socialism' and he said that if the state intervened in the lives of this small percentage of the population, it would be possible 'to dispense with any Socialistic interference in the lives of all the rest.'

Seebohm Rowntree suggested that the state should introduce a minimum wage, and he recommended that 21s 8d (£1.08p) a week was needed to keep a couple with three children in what he called 'Spartan physical efficiency.'

The most drastic suggestions came from the various socialist groups (see Section 19.8) that wanted *a redistribution of wealth*. They all agreed on *the collective ownership of the means of production*. This means that important sources of wealth such as land, coal-mines, heavy industries – for example, iron and steel, industries producing power (gas and electricity) and transport should all be jointly owned by the people. The state should organize and run these industries and take all the profits, which would be shared out among all the people, possibly in the form of lower prices, instead of going into the pockets of a few wealthy industrialists. In this way, wealth would be spread more fairly and poverty should disappear. However, suggestions like this were enough to strike terror into the hearts of the wealthy, and so ...

6 *Fear of socialism* became an important argument in favour of some less drastic state action. Many ordinary working people had been given the vote in 1867 and 1884, and might well be attracted to socialist ideas if the Liberals and Conservatives failed to do something about poverty. Moderate social reform would improve conditions for the workers, and be sufficient to turn them away from socialism. This would kill off the infant Labour party, which had been formed in 1900, and would preserve the capitalist system. This had been the motive of Bismarck, the German Chancellor: when he introduced state old age pensions, and sickness and unemployment benefit schemes in the 1880s, he too was hoping to put a stop to the growth of German socialism.

(c) what was the government's response to the growing pressure for state intervention?

Arthur Balfour's Conservative government (1902–5) (see Section 17.6) responded to the arguments and suggestions with two pieces of action. First came *the Unemployed Workmen Act (1905)* which allowed local committees to be set up to provide work for the unemployed, using voluntary subscriptions. This was a failure, because the government had missed the point that some state help with financing was necessary. More important was *the Royal Commission on the Poor Laws, set up in 1905*. This was a committee of experts, including Charles Booth and Beatrice Webb (a leading Fabian), who were to investigate the shortcomings of the Poor Law system and suggest ways of improving it. Unfortunately, the committee took a long time to reach any conclusions, mainly because of disagreements among the members, which reflected the individualism versus collectivism debate. Beatrice Webb, George Lansbury (a future Labour MP) and two other members wanted to abolish the Poor Law system altogether and set up a national system for helping the poor, to be run by a new Ministry of Labour. There would be labour exchanges, retraining schemes and public works programmes to provide jobs in times of depression. Another department would look after people who were unable to work because of ill-health. However, the chairman, Lord George Hamilton, and fourteen other members of the committee merely wanted to extend the Poor Law system and make more use of charities. They found it difficult to tear themselves away from their belief in individualism, and there was no way in which the two groups would ever agree. In the end, they brought out two separate reports:

1 *The Minority Report* was written by Beatrice Webb and her three supporters. They argued that, basically, problems brought about by the state of the national economy (such as depression and unemployment) were the main causes of poverty, and that consequently poverty should be dealt with at a national level by state intervention.

2 *The Majority Report* was produced by Hamilton and his fourteen supporters. They pointed out that, in their view, 'the causes of distress are not only economic and industrial; in origin and character they are largely moral'; in other words, it was very much a man's own fault if he found himself in poverty.

The arguments dragged on so long that it was 1909 before the Reports were published. The Conservative government, which had appointed the Commission, had been replaced in December 1905 by a Liberal government. By 1909, this Liberal government had already done something to deal with the problem of poverty.

20.2 why did the Liberals introduce social reforms, 1906–14?

The Liberal governments in office from December 1905 to May 1915 were the first governments in Britain to do anything in a systematic way for the poor, apart from providing them with workhouses. Starting in 1906, they introduced a series of social reforms: measures to help children, old age pensions, new laws to help people at work, and labour exchanges to help people find jobs. Lloyd George's National Insurance Act of 1911 provided health and unemployment insurance for many workers.

Given the strength of support for individualism and self-help, it is astonishing that the Liberals did so much, and it should be no surprise that the reforms can hardly be described as fully collectivist. In fact, the Liberals had no master plan for reform prepared when they came to power. Each reform was a response to a particular problem or situation, and politicians had mixed motives for acting as they did.

(a) the New Liberalism

In the last twenty years of the nineteenth century, many Liberals on the left wing of the party realized the need for more social reform, in particular to help the unemployed, the old and the sick. Influenced by the economist J. A. Hobson and the sociologist L. T. Hobhouse, they accepted that the time had come for the Liberal party to turn away from *laissez-faire*; only when the state intervened could these nationwide social problems be tackled effectively. These New Liberals were a minority at first, but they gradually influenced and won over the moderate centre of the party (see Section 21.1 for more details about New Liberalism).

(b) compassion and a desire for justice and fairness

Many Liberals felt that it was simply not right for a third of the population to be living in such misery at a time when the country as a whole was enjoying a fair degree of prosperity. It did not seem fair that, when the profits of most industrialists were showing a healthy increase, the wages of those who were helping to earn those profits were hardly keeping up with the rise in prices. Statistics showed that half the total national income was going into the pockets of one-ninth of the population, and it seemed that prosperity and good times were passing the working class by. However, if this had been the only consideration, it is doubtful whether much would have been done.

(c) the need for a healthy working class for military and economic purposes

This was probably a more important motive. The poor physical condition of many working-class volunteers for the Boer War (1899–1902) had shocked the nation. If Britain were to be involved in a major war, an efficient army would be necessary to defend the Empire, and so it was vital that Britain's children should be properly fed and cared for. This was why in 1904 the Committee on Physical Deterioration suggested school meals and regular medical inspections. The Birmingham Chamber of Commerce called for health insurance on the grounds that a healthy workforce would be more efficient and more profitable. It was a question of national survival – the 'struggle for existence'.

(d) pressure from the Labour party and the trade unions

Thirty Labour MPs had been elected in January 1906, and twenty-four Liberal MPs were trade unionists; they were now able to make their demands for free school meals and old age pensions heard in the House of Commons. When the Liberals began to lose by-elections to Labour, they decided that a limited amount of social reform would attract voters away from socialism and so defeat the challenge from the infant Labour party. This was certainly one motive for the introduction of old age pensions in 1908 – Lloyd George remarked: 'it is time we did something that appealed straight to the people – it will, I think, help to stop this electoral rot and that is most necessary'. This became even more urgent after the two general elections of 1910, which left the Liberals with only 272 seats compared to the 400 won in 1906. Labour had gone up to 42, the Irish Nationalists to 84, and with the Conservatives also on 272, the Liberals were dependent on Irish and Labour support to stay in office. The need to 'steal Labour's thunder' was one motive for Lloyd George's National Insurance Act of 1911.

(e) the need for policies to distinguish the Liberals from the Conservatives

Some Conservatives, for example, had wanted to introduce free school meals, but Balfour refused because of the cost, which would have to be met by increasing taxes or local rates. Here was an excellent chance to show that the Liberals had something different to offer.

(f) liberal politicians wanting to make a name for themselves

Both Lloyd George and Churchill, who were responsible for most of the reforms, were ambitious politicians keen to make a name for themselves. They genuinely wanted to help the poor, but they wanted to further their own careers as well. As historian Derek Fraser put it, writing about the campaign to get National Insurance introduced: 'it had always been Lloyd George's intention to make a great stir, to do something really big that would attract public attention.' An observer wrote of Churchill in 1908: 'He is out for adventure; he follows politics as he would follow the hounds. I wonder whether he has any driving motive save ambition.'

20.3 what were the Liberal reforms, and how far did they go towards creating a Welfare State?

(a) trade union legislation

▸ *The Trade Disputes Act (1906).* Since 1901, the trade unions had been agitating for some action to reverse the Taff Vale decision (see Section 19.6(b)), which made it almost impossible for a union to conduct a strike without risking bankruptcy. The Cabinet agreed that something ought to be done to protect trade union funds, and thus keep the support of organized labour, but it got into a tangle trying to draw up a bill that gave the unions only limited powers. The Labour party had its own bill prepared, so Campbell-Bannerman decided to accept it as it stood, to save time. The resulting Act was therefore more drastic than many Liberals intended: unions could not be sued for damages, and peaceful picketing was allowed. Critics felt this gave far too much power to the unions, which were now more or less immune from the law.

▸ *The Trade Union Act (1913)* remedied the situation caused by the Osborne Judgment of 1909 (see Section 19.6(c) for full details). It was prompted by the desire to soothe union militancy and, given the Liberals' much weaker position following the 1910 general elections (see Section 21.3(c)), by the need to keep the support of the Labour MPs, now 42 in number.

(b) measures to help children

1 Local education authorities were given the power, if they wished to use it, to provide free school meals for needy children (1906). This developed from a Labour bill, but its immediate effects were not as great as had been hoped, since *it was not compulsory.* By 1914, less than half the education authorities in England and Wales were providing meals, so in that year the government made it compulsory and provided some funds to help towards the cost.

2 There were to be compulsory medical inspections in schools, and education authorities could provide free medical treatment (1907). Again, this was a hesitant measure, since many authorities ignored the second part of the Act. However, in 1912, government grants were made available to provide treatment, and school clinics began to be set up.

3 Child offenders were to be tried, not in ordinary law courts, but in special juvenile courts, and were to be sent to corrective schools (borstals) instead of to ordinary prisons. Probation officers were to be appointed for after-care. There were to be stiff penalties for people ill-treating children or selling them cigarettes and tobacco, or alcohol in unsealed bottles or jugs (1908).

4 The Liberals took action on the academic side of education. Already by 1900 the state had taken over the responsibility for financing and organizing elementary education, which was free and compulsory for all children. However, secondary education was a different matter. Balfour's Education Act of 1902 gave local authorities the power to help existing voluntary secondary schools with money from the rates; they were also directed to set up their own secondary schools. However, these were fee-paying, and very few working-class parents could afford the fees. The Liberals therefore introduced the 'free place' system – all secondary schools had to reserve 25 per cent of their places free of charge for children from elementary schools; they would be awarded scholarships on the results of a special entrance examination.

In spite of its weaknesses, this *Children's Charter*, as it became known, was important because it was the first time any government had intervened so directly in the lives of ordinary people. It was providing help not as a charity, as the Poor Law did, but as a right, and it was a service to which all were entitled. The state was at last beginning to admit that it had a responsibility to look after the poor.

(c) old age pensions

These were introduced at the rate of five shillings (25p) a week at the age of 70, not at 65, as Charles Booth had suggested. It was a non-contributory pension (people did not have to pay anything towards it). It was to be financed by the government out of taxation, and it would be paid through post offices. No one could receive the pension if his or her income from other sources exceeded £21 a year, or if he/she had a conviction for drunkenness or some other offence. The Labour party complained that five shillings was too little, and that many people would not survive until 70 to enjoy it. Nevertheless, the pension was enormously popular and Lloyd George gained credit for it. However, it left a strange situation in that Britain had two parallel systems for dealing with the poor; the new system was operating alongside the Poor Law.

(d) measures to help working people

1 A *Workmen's Compensation Act (1906)* extended the earlier Conservative Act of 1897 to include all categories of worker, and allowed compensation for injury to health caused by industrial conditions as well as for injuries caused by accidents.

2 *The Merchant Shipping Act (1906)* introduced stringent regulations covering standards of food and accommodation for crews on British registered ships. This was the work of Lloyd George, who was already showing considerable drive at the Board of Trade, where he was also responsible for a *Patents Act* that gave inventors more protection.

3 *The Mines Act (1908)* introduced a maximum eight-hour working day for miners. This was a remarkable milestone, since it was the first time the British government had intervened to regulate the working hours of adult males. In 1912 came *the Minimum Wage Act*, which set up local boards to fix minimum wages in each district in order to help miners working in difficult seams. This sounds impressive, but the Act was an emergency measure forced through Parliament to end the damaging coal strike which had lasted from February to April. Nor did it fully satisfy the miners, who had been campaigning for *a national minimum wage* of five shillings (25p) a day for a man and two shillings for a boy.

4 *Labour Exchanges* were set up (1909) by Churchill and William Beveridge at the Board of Trade. This was an idea pressed on the government by Beatrice Webb and recommended in her Minority Poor Law Report. With unemployment rising steeply in 1908 and 1909 – in some trades it was double the 1907 figure – Churchill decided to act. Employers with vacancies were to inform the Labour Exchanges, so that unemployed workers could easily find out what jobs were available. By 1913, there were 430 exchanges in Britain and the system was working well; but again it could have gone further – it was only voluntary at this stage.

5 *The Trade Boards Act (1909)* was another of Churchill's achievements; it dealt with the problem of low-paid and depressed workers in what were called the 'sweated' industries. These usually employed female and child labourers working excessively long hours in their own homes or in 'sweatshops' for outrageously low wages. Described by Charles Booth as 'a body of reckless, starving competitors for work', their plight had been publicized by the National Anti-Sweating League, since the nature of their work made trade union organization impossible. Churchill's Act set up boards to fix minimum wages in four occupations: tailoring, lace-making, box-making and chain-making. In 1913 this was extended to cover six more 'sweated' trades, so that now almost 400,000 workers were protected and were ensured a reasonable wage. This certainly broke new ground, showing that the state was prepared to make a move towards establishing a minimum wage, as Seebohm Rowntree had suggested; but it was a pity that only a small fraction of the total workforce was covered.

6 *The Shops Act (1911)* gave shop assistants a statutory half-day holiday each week, but unfortunately it did not limit hours of work. This meant that assistants were often required to make up for the half-day off by working later at other times during the week.

(e) the National Insurance Act (1911)

This was the most important of the Liberal measures to help working people, and it was Lloyd George's greatest achievement before 1914. It was a compulsory scheme in two parts: one provided some health insurance, the other unemployment insurance. The Act introduced a new principle – unlike old age pensions, which were non-contributory, this was to be *a contributory insurance scheme* into which workers themselves had to pay. The Labour party wanted the scheme to be non-contributory, but Lloyd George believed it would be far too expensive to finance the whole thing from the Treasury, especially as the cost of old age pensions had turned out to be much higher than anybody had expected. It had been partly to offset the high cost of pensions and other future reforms that Lloyd George had introduced his controversial budget of 1909, which taxed the rich in order to help the poor; in that sense this was a collectivist action by Lloyd George (see Section 21.1(a)). The reason for the introduction of health insurance was very much the drive for greater national efficiency, though Lloyd George was genuinely concerned at the large number of deaths from tuberculosis – estimated at 75,000 a year. Unemployment insurance was a response to Labour party and trade union pressure. Both were an attempt by the Liberals to head off socialism.

▸ *Health insurance* was provided by a fund into which the worker paid 4d, the employer 3d and the state 2d a week. When the worker was off work ill, he/she would receive ten shillings (50p) a week sick pay for 13 weeks, and was entitled to free medical attention and medicines, a maternity grant of 30 shillings and a sanatorium allowance if he or she fell ill with tuberculosis. The obvious drawback was that benefits (apart from the maternity grant) did not apply to the worker's wife and children, nor to those earning more than £160 a year.

The whole scheme caused bitter controversy: although Labour moderates accepted the contributory principle, strong socialists such as Keir Hardie were against it, and they demanded even higher taxes on the wealthy so that the scheme would be a genuinely collectivist solution to the problem of poverty. Another complaint, bearing in mind the small state contribution, was that, instead of providing sickness benefit, the state was merely forcing workers to provide their own.

The Conservatives succeeded in turning many workers against it by arguing that the government had no right to force people to pay into the scheme directly from their wages. There was also opposition from doctors, who feared they would lose their independence, and from Friendly Societies and insurance companies, who were afraid of losing business. It was here that Lloyd George showed his skill in reconciling all the conflicting interests; it was decided, for example, that the scheme would be operated by 'approved societies', usually insurance companies, as it turned out, which workers would join. However, these would be under state supervision.

‣ *Unemployment insurance* applied only to workers in certain trades where the demand for labour fluctuated most; these were building, shipbuilding, mechanical engineering, iron-founding, vehicle construction and sawmilling. Worker and employer both paid 2½d into the fund and the state 2d. The unemployment benefit was seven shillings a week up to a maximum of 15 weeks in any 12-month period. Very soon 2.25 million men were protected by this scheme, though its obvious drawback was that it covered only the handful of trades listed above. There was also the question of what would happen after 15 weeks if the worker was still unemployed; and there was the criticism that, again, as with health insurance, the state's contribution was too small. It is important to remember, however, that Lloyd George intended both parts of the Act to be an experimental beginning, to be extended as soon as possible; but unfortunately the First World War intervened. Nevertheless, it was an important extension of state aid and established the principle that health and unemployment schemes should be contributory.

(f) the Housing and Town Planning Act (1910)

This introduced compulsory slum clearance schemes and gave local councils the power to build council houses. New regulations specified that houses should not be built more than twelve to an acre and banned the building of back-to-back houses. Again, this Act had its faults – while it resulted in the demolition of some of the country's worst slums, very few councils took up the option to build new houses to replace them, because there was no government money forthcoming to help with the cost.

(g) how successful were the reforms?

Although individual reforms had varying degrees of success, taken together they must have done something to relieve the worst effects of poverty. However, in 1914, there were still some areas that had not been touched by any of this legislation. For example, hardly any of the recommendations of the Poor Law Commission Reports (apart from Labour Exchanges) had been carried out, leaving the country with an unsatisfactory dual system in which the new state aid was being provided alongside the old Poor Law, with its stigma of charity, which continued until 1929. Nothing had been done for agricultural labourers, who remained the worst-paid of all workers. The trade unions were not impressed by the reforms, and they showed this by their increasing militancy between 1910 and 1914. Another disturbing fact was that, in 1914, the percentage of army volunteers rejected as physically unfit was almost as high as it had been in 1900. However, this was only to be expected; there was bound to be a time-lag before the benefits of the new state aid made themselves felt.

It is easy, with the benefit of hindsight, to be critical of the Liberals for being too cautious. But it is important to remember that they had to face determined opposition from the Conservatives, and sometimes from the right wing of the

Liberal party itself – in the election of January 1910, about twenty-five Liberal MPs stood down rather than support a programme which they saw as being too left-wing. Given the strong support still around for individualism and self-help, the Liberals deserve credit for going as far as they did. The vitally important point was that the government had laid the foundations on which Lloyd George and Churchill intended to build later. They weren't to know that, following the First World War and the rapid rise of the Labour party, there would not be another Liberal government after May 1915.

(h) how far had Britain moved towards a Welfare State by 1914?

There are differing opinions about this.

▸ Jo Grimond (Liberal leader from 1956 to 1967) claimed that the Liberal reforms were so novel for the times that they established all the necessary basic principles and therefore as good as created the Welfare State.
▸ Historian Arthur Marwick believes that the full Welfare State was not created until after the Second World War, by the Labour governments of 1945–51.
▸ Another historian, Donald Read, came up with a good compromise conclusion: he suggests that what the Liberals had achieved – and it *was* a new departure – was the beginnings of a *social service state* rather than a *welfare state.* The difference is this: a *social service state* is one in which certain minimum standards are ensured by the government; a *welfare state* is one where the government provides the best possible services for everybody.

20.4 state social policy between the wars: problems and successes

(a) effects of the First World War

Historians disagree about how profound the effects of the First World War were on British society. Arthur Marwick and Derek Fraser, both writing in 1973, agreed that the effects were quite dramatic There can be no doubt that the war did have important effects on the role of the state in British society. Whether it wanted to or not, the government was forced to abandon *laissez-faire* so that the war could be fought more efficiently. The government controlled and directed the life of the nation in a way that would have been unthinkable before the war.

Coalmines and merchant shipping were taken over directly by the state, factories were told what to produce, strikes and lockouts were prohibited, farmers were obliged to cultivate more land, wages and prices were controlled, and food was rationed. While most of this was abandoned at the end of the war, people had become used by then to the idea of state intervention. Martin Pugh, writing in 1994, claimed that in reality the war merely speeded up developments that had already started (see Section 22.5 for more about the effects of the war on British society).

As the war dragged on, people began to talk about post-war 'reconstruction'. In July 1917, the government set up a Ministry of Reconstruction and a Ministry of Pensions; it seemed to be taken for granted that the state would plan and carry out this reconstruction. Clearly, state collectivism was much more widely accepted then than it had been before the war.

The idea began to spread that working-class people deserved some rewards for their sacrifices during the war; Lloyd George talked about building 'homes fit for heroes'; H. A. L. Fisher, the Minister for Education, wanted better education for everybody. Other areas mentioned for improvement were unemployment insurance and health. In a speech in 1917, Lloyd George said: 'the country will be prepared for bigger things immediately after the war ... it will be in a more enthusiastic mood'. Improvements were certainly made in all four areas mentioned: education, housing, health and unemployment insurance, and in health insurance and pensions as well, as the following sections 20.4(d–i) show. However, the amount of legislation introduced up to 1939 may seem disappointing, given all the brave talk in 1917–18. The truth is that a variety of problems arose that limited the extent of state intervention in the inter-war years.

(b) problems limiting state intervention – slump, economic decline and unemployment

▸ Soon after the end of the war, starting at the beginning of 1921, there was a severe slump that threw about two million people out of work by the end of the year. There was a reduction in government revenue (money flowing into the Treasury from taxation) caused partly by the general falling-off of trade, and partly by the enormous expense of unemployment benefit. It meant also that there was less government money to be spent on other social welfare policies such as education and health.

▸ Some parts of British industry went into a slow but permanent decline, which became apparent during the 1920s, causing a steady rise in unemployment. This is known as *structural unemployment* – people were unemployed because there was something wrong with the structure of the economy. Unemployment caused by a slump is known as *cyclical unemployment*, since it is caused by the operation of the trade cycle – trade flows in a fairly regular cycle of boom followed by a slump, which gradually develops into another boom. People in cyclical unemployment tend to be out of work for short periods until the next boom arrives, but people in structural unemployment are likely to be out of work for much longer periods; they have difficulty finding other jobs because there is something seriously wrong with the structure of the economy. This was the case in Britain in the 1920s and 1930s when unemployment in certain areas refused to go away. These areas were

Scotland, Tyne-Tees, Cumberland, Lancashire, Northern Ireland and South Wales, where the older staple export industries – coal, textiles, shipbuilding, iron and steel – were situated (for detailed statistics of unemployment see Section 25.4(a)).

(c) reasons for Britain's economic decline

▶ Even before the First World War these *older industries had begun to suffer competition from abroad.* During the war these industries concentrated largely on supplying the needs of the war effort, which meant that Britain's customers who had bought British products either had to buy them from somewhere else or to start up their own industries. Immediately after the war, there was a short period during 1919 and early 1920 when British industry, including the old staple industries, enjoyed a great surge in exports, and it looked as though trade would recover to its pre-war level. This encouraged investment in the staple industries. However, this short boom soon fizzled out as the other states that had been involved in the war also gradually got their economies moving again. It soon became clear that many countries were not going to resume buying British goods, because they had found alternative sources. There was fierce competition from more highly mechanized and more efficient foreign industries and cheaper foreign goods, such as Japanese and East European textiles. India, the main market for British textiles before the war, was rapidly developing its own industry. Coal exports were badly hit by cheap coal from Germany, Poland and Holland, and the world demand for coal was decreasing in any case, as oil, gas and electricity came into wider use. By 1939, over half the world's merchant ships were using oil instead of coal. More efficient rival shipyards had opened in the USA, Japan, Holland and Scandinavia. By the end of 1920, exports were falling again, and by Christmas 1921 there were around 2 million people unemployed. While this figure varied during the inter-war period, it never fell below 1 million unemployed – 10 per cent of the working population – until 1940, when the war effort resulted in full employment. The bulk of the unemployment was in Wales, Northern Ireland, the North of England and Scotland.

▶ *Many foreign countries introduced tariff barriers* to protect their home industries; and some governments began to subsidize their industries to enable them to compete more successfully. However, in Britain, *very little was done to modernize these struggling industries,* and there were no state subsidies. There were far too many small coal mines, which were expensive to operate and therefore uncompetitive; the cotton industry was slow to adopt automatic looms and electric power; and the more profits fell, the less cash was available for reinvestment in new techniques and equipment. Worse still was that foreign rivals were gaining a foothold in the British market: as noted above, there were textiles from India, as well as foreign ships, iron and steel.

- *The World Economic Crisis*, which began in the USA with the Wall Street Crash in October 1929, made unemployment in Britain much worse. As the world moved into a slump, demand for British goods declined. Employers could see no alternative to laying men off; this threw more people out of work in the already depressed areas, and caused cyclical unemployment in other areas. By the winter of 1932–3, there were almost 3 million people out of work – around 23 per cent of the insured workforce. In the old staple industries in the depressed areas the figures were appalling – 59.5 per cent in shipbuilding, 48.5 per cent in iron and steel, and 41.2 per cent in coal. Unemployment benefit was costing the Treasury well over three times the amount it was getting from contributions.
- The governments were constantly having to wrestle with the problem of *how to finance unemployment benefit and other social policies*. From 1930 onwards, no matter how well-intentioned a government was, its first priority was always to restrict expenditure so that it could balance the budget without having to raise taxes. Often, it tried to deal with this problem by pressurizing local authorities to pay more towards the cost of social services. Another device was to keep benefits lower than wages, and to make them *means tested;* this is when the total income and assets of the household were taken into account in deciding the level of benefit to be paid. This aroused considerable resentment among respectable working people, who felt they were being cheated out of what was rightfully theirs.

(d) unemployment and poverty

Governments spent more time and energy on this area of social welfare than on any other, which was not surprising, since unemployment was the most pressing problem of the inter-war years.

1 At the end of the war in 1918 there was an immediate crisis as demobilized soldiers returning home, and munitions workers who were surplus to requirements, were all looking for jobs at the same time. The government introduced what was called *the Out-of-work Donation (OWD)*, a non-contributory payment calculated according to the size of the unemployed person's family, to continue until the worker found a job. This was an important innovation because it set a precedent: it was the first time a worker's family had been provided for. OWD was discontinued in 1920 when it was superseded by two new Acts.

2 *The Unemployment Insurance Act, 1920* brought in a great expansion of Lloyd George's 1911 scheme to include most workers with incomes of less than £250 a year (except agricultural labourers, domestic servants and self-employed people). Contributions were increased, but so were benefits – from seven shillings to fifteen shillings a week for up to fifteen weeks per year. In 1921, extra allowances were made for an unemployed man's wife and

family. These were admirable steps forward: not far short of two-thirds of the entire labour force were now insured against unemployment. But unfortunately, there were problems almost immediately: the scheme was expected to be self-supporting, but unemployment rose so sharply during 1921 that it was soon running deeply into debt.

3 Lloyd George's coalition government (1918–22) accepted that the state would have to contribute more, since many workers had still failed to find jobs at the end of the fifteen weeks. In theory, any worker still unemployed after the fifteen weeks benefit had been exhausted would have to apply to the local Poor Law for further relief. This was an intolerable prospect for most workers, and in any case the Poor Law would hardly be able to bear the additional cost. There was unrest in industrial areas, and the danger of riots and perhaps even revolution if nothing was done to help. It was under these pressures that in 1921 Lloyd George extended the benefit to two sixteen-week periods per year, with a gap in between. The extra payments were called 'uncovenanted' benefits (meaning that the worker had not contributed anything towards them), and they later became known as the 'dole'. Because the dole was in a sense a 'gift' from the treasury, it was means-tested; careful checks were made into family circumstances to make sure that the unemployed person did genuinely need the extra payments. Lloyd George had accepted a new principle: *unemployment benefit was no longer just an insurance scheme; it was in many cases long-term maintenance by the state.* The first Labour government (1924) removed the gap between the two periods of benefit.

4 *The Unemployment Insurance Act 1927* (the work of Neville Chamberlain, Minister of Health in Stanley Baldwin's Conservative government) abolished the distinction between 'covenanted' and 'uncovenanted' benefit. Benefit would be paid for an unlimited period, provided an unemployed person could show that he or she had genuinely been seeking work. The extra benefit over and above what had been received as 'covenanted' benefit (which had been paid for by his or her contributions), was now known as 'transitional' benefit. Here, the Conservatives were accepting *the principle of long-term maintenance by the state,* though workers' contributions were increased and benefits decreased.

5 The Conservatives were also responsible for another major step forward – *the end of the Poor Law (1929–30).* While Beatrice Webb had been advocating this since 1904, all governments had shied away from such a daunting problem. It was still the last resort for people not covered by state welfare provision. According to John Stevenson, 'between one third and one fifth of those dying in the larger cities and towns could expect to end their days in the workhouse or Poor Law infirmaries'. At times of high unemployment, as many as 1.5 million people were claiming financial help from the Poor Law, and the burden on the local rates was becoming unbearable.

Neville Chamberlain (as part of his 1929 Local Government Act) abolished the entire Poor Law system and handed all the workhouses and other buildings over to the county and county borough councils, which were expected to appoint Public Assistance Committees (PACs) to be responsible for the care of the poor. Local authorities were to receive a grant from the government towards the cost of these services. The new system was much more efficient, but it was still not perfect; one drawback was that the local authorities still had to use the same buildings, and though the names and the administration had changed, the poor still thought of them with loathing as 'the workhouse'. It was only very gradually that this attitude changed.

6 *Unemployment benefit was cut by 10 per cent in 1931,* bringing it down to 15s 3d a week. This was the result of the financial and political crisis that, in August 1931, brought down the second Labour government (1929–31) (see Section 25.2). The world economic crisis sent unemployment shooting up to over 2.5 million, causing a massive increase in 'transitional' benefits from the Treasury. In 1931, the state paid out £120 million in benefits, but only took in £44 million from contributions. Foreign bankers would only make new loans to the government on condition that expenditure was reduced, and this included unemployment benefit. The Labour government resigned rather than comply, but the National government that took over from Labour had no hesitation in introducing the 10 per cent cut.

7 *The Unemployment Act of 1934* (the National government's next attempt to deal with the problem) introduced yet another new scheme distinguishing between 'covenanted' benefit paid from insurance contributions, and 'unemployment assistance', paid by a new *Unemployment Assistance Board (UAB)* financed by the treasury. Branches of the new UAB all over the country would pay out means-tested 'assistance', taking over this function from the PACs. This aroused massive protests in some areas when it was discovered that the new 'assistance' rates were less than the old relief rates paid locally by the PACs. There were demonstrations in South Wales, and eventually the government gave way and allowed payment of whichever rate was higher. The 10 per cent cut was restored, and benefit was payable from the age of 14. In certain areas the assistance rates were in fact higher than some wages – so the 'less eligibility' principle had gone at last. However, the means test was bitterly resented, especially when a person was refused benefit because other members of his/her family were working, or because he or she had some savings. It could be demoralizing when a man seemed to be penalized because he had been careful and thrifty, or when he had to be supported financially by his own children.

8 *Agricultural workers were insured for the first time in 1936.* By this time, pressure on the Treasury was beginning to subside, and by 1937 unemployment was down to 1.4 million, the lowest level since the end of 1929.

Provision for the unemployed was probably the most successful of the state's welfare policies during the inter-war period, though the amounts paid were perhaps inadequate and the means test unsatisfactory. Some historians believe that Lloyd George's extension of the scheme in 1920–1 saved the country from revolution. Later developments, though haphazard and unplanned, did at least get rid of the old Poor Law and the 'less eligibility' principle. Most important of all, the state had accepted responsibility for financing 'transitional benefits'. (For the effects of long-term unemployment, see Section 25.4(c)).

(e) housing

This was an area in which great things were expected of the government, bearing in mind Lloyd George's promises to build 'homes fit for heroes'. Very few new houses had been built during the war and it was estimated that 600,000 were needed. All the large cities had slums that were insanitary, unhealthy and generally unfit for human habitation. A report published in 1919 gave this description of Leeds:

> The City of Leeds is perhaps confronted with the most difficult problem to be found in any of the provincial towns owing to the enormous number of back to-back houses, the building of which continued up to a comparatively recent date … There are altogether 72,000 of these houses in the city. About 27,000 are built in blocks of eight which open directly onto the street and have their sanitary conveniences provided in the open spaces between each pair of blocks. These conveniences can only be reached by passing along the streets.

At the same time, as Roy Hattersley shows, half the houses in Salford and Glasgow did not have a fixed bath, while in Bootle and Hull 'two out of every three families had to manage with a zinc bath which they kept under the kitchen sink and brought out into the living room when needed'. In Scotland, the problem of overcrowded slums was worse than in England. In Glasgow and Edinburgh most low-income families lived in apartment blocks or tenements. In Clydebank half the housing was described as 'over-crowded'.

In many areas it was the Church of England that led the campaign for improved housing. Cyril Garbett, Bishop of Southwark and later Archbishop of York, said that it was a Christian's moral duty to press for a change in national policy towards housing and slum clearance; the church should set up housing improvement schemes to show how the job could be done. In 1924, William Temple, Archbishop of York and later Canterbury, and a socialist, organized a series of conferences to discuss how Christians could best respond in a practical way to the social challenges facing society. In 1925, Basil Jellicoe, an Anglican priest, and his St Pancras House Improvement Society began to buy up and recondition slum houses in Somers Town in the borough of St Pancras. In 1930, they graduated to building new houses on land where slums had been demolished. While this was a small-scale operation, Jellicoe travelled around the country to publicize what was happening in Somers Town, and the idea was taken up by other clergymen, notably Charles Jenkinson, vicar of Holbeck, Leeds. But these housing improvement schemes only scratched the surface of the slum problem. What was needed was determined government action backed by government cash; but slum clearance and house building were expensive exercises, and although successive governments began initiatives, they were always among the first policies to be abandoned whenever the economy ran into difficulties.

1 *The Addison Housing Act, 1919* (the work of Christopher Addison, Minister of Health in Lloyd George's coalition government) provided government cash for local authorities to build houses for the working classes. This was an important milestone: the principle was now established that provision of reasonable housing was the responsibility of the state. By the end of 1922 more than 213,000 new houses had been built, but the scheme was abandoned in 1922 as part of the government's economy drive during the slump. By this time, Addison had already been sacked by Lloyd George because he was spending too much money.

2 *The Wheatley Housing Act of 1924* was an attempt by the first Labour government to get house-building moving again. It provided grants of £9 million a year to local authorities to build council houses, which would be for rent only. Rents were to be at pre-war levels, so that working people would be able to afford them. This scheme ran successfully until 1933, when over half a million new houses had been built under the Act.

3 So far, the housing legislation had benefited mainly the middle class and better-off working classes. Hardly any slum clearance had taken place. *The Greenwood Housing Act, 1930,* another Labour measure, required every local authority to draw up a plan for slum clearance and new houses, and provided government subsidies to local authorities to carry out the plans. The National government suspended the scheme from 1931 to 1934, when the slump was at its worst, though in fact thousands of jobs could have been created if the scheme had continued, using money that was otherwise paid out on unemployment benefit. It also decided to end the subsidy provided by the Wheatley Act, in the belief that private enterprise ought to build working-class houses that were not direct replacements for demolished slums. When the worst of the slump was over, the scheme was started up again, and by 1939 more than 700,000 council houses had been built to re-house slum dwellers.

Clearly, housing conditions improved considerably between the wars, with the building of well over a million new council houses (plus about 3 million built by private enterprise). The new council houses tended to be far superior to the houses they replaced: they were brighter, more spacious and easier to clean, and had more bedrooms and better sanitary facilities. Between 1918 and

1939, the government spent more than £208 million on housing and slum clearance – a staggering amount for those days, bearing in mind the economic difficulties. The average number of people per house was reduced from 5.4 to 3.5. But there was still a long way to go – many of the new houses only replaced those that had been demolished. Roy Hattersley points out that, out of a grand total of over 4 million new houses built, only 26,000 had been built to relieve overcrowding and allow the demolition of unfit property. There was still serious overcrowding in some areas: a 1936 survey showed that in Birmingham there were 39,000 back-to-back houses and 51,000 houses without lavatories. In Scotland in 1939, there were still 66,000 slums, and at least 200,000 new houses were needed to put an end to overcrowding.

(f) education

▸ *H. A. L. Fisher's Education Act, 1918* was a product of the war. Fisher believed that the working class deserved a better education in order to avoid 'intellectual wastage'. There was to be full-time compulsory education for all up to the age of 14, and more free places at secondary schools for bright children from poor backgrounds. Teachers' salaries were made uniform throughout the country. Local authorities could provide 'continuation schools' for young people up to the age of 16, as well as nursery schools for under-fives. Unfortunately, only the first part of the Act was carried out. From 1921, government attempts to economize fell heavily on education; hardly any continuation or nursery schools were built.

▸ The Labour party deplored the fact that the vast majority of working-class children did not receive any education beyond the age of 14. C. P. Trevelyan, Labour's Minister of Education, was a strong believer in *'Secondary Education for All'*, and he appointed a committee chaired by Sir Henry Hadow to look into how this might be achieved (1924). *The Hadow Report (1926)* was an important milestone in education: it recommended the break between primary and secondary education at the age of 11, and a school-leaving age of 15. There should be two types of secondary school:

1 The existing ones, now to be called 'grammar schools', were to provide an advanced academic education; and
2 'Modern schools' which most children would attend until the age of 15.

Although these recommendations were generally accepted, very little was done immediately, because of economic difficulties. No government legislation followed, and by 1939 only a tiny fraction of working-class children were getting any 'advanced' secondary education; this was not seen as a priority area.

(g) pensions

1 The non-contributory old age pension of five shillings a week at 70, first introduced in 1908, was increased to ten shillings a week in 1919 by the

Lloyd George coalition government. Many socialists pressed for it to be paid at 60, but all governments thought that a non-contributory pension for so many extra people would be an impossible burden on the treasury.

2 *The Widows, Orphans' and Old Age Contributory Pensions Act (1925)* was the main development – another Conservative measure steered through by Neville Chamberlain. It was a compulsory insurance scheme into which both workers and employers paid, and to which the state would also contribute. It provided a worker with a pension of ten shillings a week from the age of 65 to 70 (without means test), £1 for a married couple, ten shillings a week for a widow, extra payments for children (five shillings for the first child and three shillings each for any other children), and seven shillings and sixpence a week for orphans. The scheme was extended to self-employed workers in 1937.

This was in many ways a welcome extension of pensions, *but there was much controversy over the principle behind it.* The Labour party complained that workers were really paying for their own pensions, and that if the Conservatives had not kept on reducing income tax, the whole scheme could have been financed from the Treasury; in fact, under Chamberlain's scheme the Treasury contributions were quite small. According to R. C. Birch, Chamberlain 'had neither the resources nor the imagination to practise generosity'. Another criticism was that the system of pensions was now unnecessarily complicated: the old non-contributory pension at 70 still continued, and the insured worker had to transfer to this scheme on reaching the age of 70.

(h) health insurance

This was the most disappointing area of state welfare activity between the wars, with *no major change to the 1911 health insurance provision.* The weekly payment was raised from ten to fifteen shillings in 1919, but in 1926 the state reduced its contribution. A Royal Commission on National Health Insurance (1926) recommended that it should be extended to cover a worker's wife and children. Another point made was that some of the 'approved societies' that administered the scheme were offering better services than others; it was suggested that the insurance companies should pool their resources in order to provide wider and better services for all. However, the larger and wealthier insurance companies (such as the Prudential and the Pearl) objected to being expected to subsidize the smaller ones. They were in business primarily for profit, not to improve the nation's health. So powerful was their influence that the system survived without any improvements or extensions until after the Second World War. *The most glaring criticisms were:*

‣ no provision for workers' families to have medical treatment;
‣ no payments towards the cost of hospital treatment; and

> not enough hospitals provided by local authorities. This was because the new Ministry of Health set up in 1919 had taken no action to *compel* local authorities to provide hospitals.

(i) how effective were government social policies by 1939?

There can be no doubt that the average citizen was much better provided for in 1939 than in 1914 in the areas of housing, unemployment insurance and pensions. State spending on social services increased dramatically, from £22 million in 1913–14 to £204 million in 1935–6, though one striking point about these statistics is that the proportion of government expenditure devoted to the social services remained almost exactly the same – about a third.

The most obvious areas of failure were in health insurance and education. Left-wingers deplored the acceptance of the insurance principle, believing that this was not a genuine state collectivist solution to the problem of poverty, but merely a device to shift the responsibility for decent social services on to the workers themselves and their employers.

While most people were in work and enjoying an increase in real wages after 1935, there was still some appalling poverty in the depressed areas, which could have been given more help. Seebohm Rowntree carried out another survey in York, which was reasonably prosperous in the late 1930s. His conclusion, published in 1941, was that the standard of living of the workers in York was about 30 per cent higher than in 1899, thanks to smaller families, the increase in real wages, and 'the remarkable growth of social services'. But he went on to point out that 'there is no cause for satisfaction in the fact that in a country so rich as England, over 30 per cent of the workers in a typical provincial city have incomes so small that it is beyond their means to live even at the basic subsistence level … nor in the fact that almost half the children of working class parents spend the first five years of their lives in poverty'. In 1939, there was still no generally planned social policy and certainly no planned economy. (For social conditions during the unemployment of the 1930s, see Section 25.4).

20.5 why was the idea of a planned economy discussed between the wars, and what plans were suggested?

(a) why was the idea discussed?

During the 1920s many people began to feel that *something was seriously wrong with the British economy.* The main symptom was the persistently high level of unemployment, which never fell below a million between the wars. There had been spells of unemployment during the nineteenth century, but these had usually been fairly short-lived – most workers found jobs again when the next boom came along. However, after the First World War, the next boom was very slow to arrive in the old-established industries (coal, iron, steel and shipbuilding), which were now clearly seen to be in decline. Reasons for the decline are explained in Section 20.4(b and c).

Structural unemployment therefore seemed to be here to stay. To make matters worse, the depression in world trade from 1929 to 1933 affected most British industries, adding *cyclical unemployment* to the existing structural unemployment. British exports in 1932 were only half what they had been in 1913, and unemployment reached a new peak at 2.8 million. The economy recovered gradually, and unemployment began to fall; by 1937 the Midlands and the South were prosperous again, with only 7 per cent of the workforce unemployed; but in the North of England, Wales, Scotland and Northern Ireland, structural unemployment lingered stubbornly on, with, on average, 20 per cent of the insured workers out of a job.

Some people believed that unemployment had become a permanent feature and was an unavoidable evil of modern economies. They concentrated on trying to work out the best way of caring for the unemployed. A more imaginative approach was to argue that it ought to be possible to defeat unemployment by careful planning or managing of the economy; a wide variety of suggestions appeared both from the right and the left of politics.

(b) what policies were suggested?

1 *The Liberals put forward some good ideas in their 1929 election manifesto,* written with the guidance of John Maynard Keynes, a leading economist and Liberal supporter. Keynes believed that the vast amounts of government money being paid out in unemployment benefit would be far better spent financing works schemes and new industries, which would create lots of new jobs. The workers in these new jobs would receive wages instead of unemployment benefit and would be able to afford to buy more than if they had been unemployed; this in turn would help to revive trade. What Keynes was suggesting was that *a government should spend its way out of a depression* instead of following the usual practice of cutting government expenditure and wages, which, Keynes thought, would only reduce people's purchasing power and so make the depression worse. The Liberals therefore proposed spending £250 million on public works – building new roads and houses, and extending electricity to all homes.

2 *Many Conservatives had similar ideas;* one of their leading thinkers was Harold Macmillan, MP for Stockton-on-Tees. They produced a document called *Peace and Reconstruction* (1935) setting out detailed public works schemes which could be organized by government and local authorities, using cash that would have been spent on unemployment benefit.

3 *A group known as Political and Economic Planning (PEP)* involved a wide cross-section of people – Liberal and Conservative politicians, businessmen, bankers, economists, architects and town-planners. They believed that the needs of industry and the social services should be investigated carefully, so

that things could be planned well in advance instead of in the haphazard fashion of the 1920s. Starting in 1931, they produced a flood of reports on every conceivable subject, from housing and the health service to the reorganization and relocation of industry.

4 *The Mosley Memorandum (1930)* was an interesting plan worked out by Sir Oswald Mosley (Chancellor of the Duchy of Lancaster in the second Labour government), after consultations with Keynes, to deal with the economic crisis of 1930–1. He suggested import restrictions, subsidies for farmers (to reduce food imports), government control of banks to ensure that industry was allowed more credit (to enable new industries to expand), old age pensions at 60 and the school-leaving age at 15 (instead of 14). These last two measures would have made an immediate impact on unemployment. Although there was much support in the Labour party for Mosley's plan, the leaders rejected it.

5 *Later there were other plans within the Labour party*, which was gradually taking on Keynes's ideas of a planned economy, together with a greatly expanded network of social services. The most radical cure suggested for the ailing economy was the socialist idea of *nationalization*. In a pamphlet entitled *The Theory and Practice of Socialism (1935)*, John Strachey argued that boom, overproduction and slump were inevitable in an uncontrolled capitalist economy. Nationalization (taking into state ownership and control) of the main industries would enable careful forecasting and planning to take place so that production could be limited to need, and slumps and unemployment therefore eliminated.

(c) lack of government action

Successive governments largely ignored all this good advice. Some action was taken by the National governments after 1931, but it was the usual piecemeal approach and it failed to get to the root of the problem.

› *Free trade was abandoned in 1932*, when a 10 per cent duty was placed on imports (see Section 25.3(c) for full details).

› *The Special Areas Act (1934)* appointed two unpaid commissioners and gave them £2 million to try to revive Scotland, Cumberland, Tyneside and South Wales. This had little effect, because employers could not be compelled to move into depressed areas. Businessmen were much more attracted to the Midlands and South-East and the ready markets of the London area. Later, the government offered rates, rent and income tax remission to encourage firms to move in. This resulted in the setting up of trading estates such as the ones at Treforest (South Wales) and Larkhall (near Glasgow); but these provided only a few thousand jobs, many of them for women.

› *An attempt was made to revive the steel industry* by imposing a tariff on foreign steel and setting up the British Iron and Steel Federation.

Government pressure brought about the building of two new steelworks, at Ebbw Vale and Corby, but the federation was criticized bitterly for refusing to allow one to be built at Jarrow, where the unemployment rate was the highest in the country.

> From 1936 onwards, *the rearmament programme helped to create extra jobs,* and loans were made available to encourage shipbuilding, including the completion of the *Queen Mary.*

But by 1939 there was still no sign of any long-term strategy emerging to plan the economy and eliminate unemployment.

(d) why was more not done?

1 Despite many of the ideas suggested being supported by people in all three political parties, there were never enough of them to form a majority. The Mosley Memorandum, for example, had a lot of support in the Labour party, and many Liberals would have voted for some of its proposals. But it was never even considered in the Commons because a majority of Labour MPs, including Ramsay MacDonald (the Prime Minister) and Philip Snowden (Chancellor of the Exchequer), were against it.

2 A majority of MPs in all three parties were still convinced that unemployment was incurable, and that the only way to deal with it was to try to make unemployment insurance as effective as possible.

3 All the proposals would be expensive, and the leading politicians were very cautious. They all felt, as did the Bank of England and the Treasury, that the most important requirement was to keep government expenditure as low as possible in a time of depression in order to balance the budget. Borrowing should also be kept to a minimum. They believed that Keynes' proposals to 'spend your way out of a depression' were far too risky – not sound economics. This was why MacDonald and Snowden refused to contemplate Mosley's plans in 1930, and why, from 1931 until 1940 Neville Chamberlain took very little notice of the suggestions put forward by PEP. For the next major steps, the country had to wait until after the Second World War (see Chapters 29 and 30).

20.6 the state of the people

(a) problems of rural society

In general, living standards gradually improved as real wages continued to rise, up to around 1908. Though there was no dramatic rise, it was sufficient to make it possible for the working classes to buy more food. However, there were still important groups of workers facing difficulties, and foremost among them were agricultural labourers employed in arable farming. By 1894, foreign imports had forced the price of wheat down to 22s 10d. a quarter – less than half the price in 1874. Between 1886 and 1903, over 5 million acres of arable farmland ceased to be cultivated; and thousands of labourers were forced to leave their home villages to find work in the cities. In the words of G. R. Searle, 'a severe psychological blow was delivered to British farming, from which it took decades to recover'. Labourers employed in livestock farming fared better, and this was most noticeable in areas adjacent to large towns, where average wages actually rose slightly. On the whole, though, the morale of agricultural labourers was low, and the failure of Joseph Arch's Agricultural Labourers' Union did not help matters.

As for the farmers themselves and the landowners, they too had problems. Arable farmers suffered the worst; even when sympathetic landowners reduced their rents, many did not survive. On average, rents on arable land were reduced by around 40 per cent during the 1890s, and yet in those years almost 500 farmers a year went bankrupt. Many avoided bankruptcy but abandoned the struggle and tried another line of business. From the mid-1880s onwards the owners of arable land found that their incomes from rents were much reduced, and consequently that the values of land also fell, by around 60 per cent on average, between 1875 and 1910. There was a brief recovery between 1910 and 1921 in response to the rise in prices, but then between 1925 and 1931 there was another collapse in land values. According to David Cannadine, 'by the mid-1930s land was selling for barely one-third of the sum it had fetched during the mid-Victorian period'. This caused a further problem: it deprived aristocrats, who depended entirely on income from land of the ability to raise loans, using their estates as collateral. Nor were they helped by Harcourt's 1894 death duties and new taxes in Lloyd George's 1909 budget. As David Cannadine put it:

> At a time when confidence in the land was already undermined, they served only to erode it still further. To many estates already burdened with heavy debts, fixed outgoings and reduced income, the effect of these duties at the margin might be quite crippling. There would be no surplus income to put away in anticipation; there might be no scope for further mortgaging; and loans might be impossible to obtain ... this meant that from the 1890s, the traditional territorial classes found themselves caught between a world economy that operated to their disadvantage, and British governments that seemed equally ill-disposed.

(b) social improvement for industrial workers?

In spite of fluctuations in trade and employment towards the end of the nineteenth century, there is much evidence to suggest that the standard of living was showing clear signs of improvement. It was calculated that, for those in work, average real income increased by over a third between 1882 and 1899. This suggests that there was probably an improvement in diet, certainly for the better-off working-class families, who could now afford to buy a healthier range of food, including more meat and vegetables and less bread. It was also noted that the working class were drinking less alcohol – between 1876 and 1910, expenditure on alcohol fell from over 15 per cent of the average working class family budget to under 9 per cent.

Another striking sign of greater prosperity was the growth of Friendly Society membership. These were mainly working-class organizations that encouraged people to save their spare cash to be invested and the interest used for mutual assistance in times of hardship. It was estimated that, between 1877 and 1904, membership had risen from around 2.7 million to 5.6 million, and savings deposits from £12.7 million to £41 million. By 1911, at least half the male labour force probably belonged to a friendly society – more than belonged to a trade union. These societies were seen as being highly respectable and much praised by the middle classes as fine examples of self-help. Other self-help initiatives were Post Office savings accounts, burial societies, doctors' clubs and the Co-operative Movement. According to F. M. L. Thompson, by 1900 probably around 90 per cent of the population could rely on some sort of insurance protection, thanks to their own self-help initiatives.

On the other hand, there were still reasons for concern. While death-rates fell and average life expectancy rose (from 42 in 1880 to 53.5 in 1911), the infant death-rate also rose during the 1890s, reaching 163 per thousand in 1899. This was partly the result of streptococcal infections which caused a variety of illnesses, including pneumonia, and which were responsible for the majority of deaths of babies under the age of one. Whooping cough was a deadly childhood disease, killing around 40 per cent of children who died before the age of five. In addition, there were all the usual killers that were so difficult to control before the days of antibiotics – dysentery, bronchitis, typhoid and diphtheria. One reason suggested for the rise in child mortality was that, as more and more children were attending school, diseases were spread more widely.

One encouraging sign was that some diseases, such as typhus and cholera, that were spread by impure water had almost been eliminated, apart from the occasional outbreak. This was partly thanks to the 1875 Public Health Act, which had led to clean water supplies being provided for most urban areas by 1900. Water closets were being fitted in even the cheapest new houses, even though most of them in working-class houses were outside in the back yard. Another sign of progress was that, by 1900, smallpox had been almost conquered thanks to the recently introduced programme of vaccination.

Much depended on social class and area of residence. According to G. R. Searle, 'the infant death-rate was generally about twice as high among the working class as among the comfortably off. Moreover the damp and unhealthy accommodation in which hundreds of thousands of poor families were doomed to live directly contributed to many premature deaths, notably from tuberculosis (consumption). By 1900 mortality from this dreaded disease had halved since mid-century, but there were still 250 000 sufferers, making TB the main killer of the adult population.'

On balance, many historians see the 1890s as a time of optimism. During the mid-1880s the propertied classes had been alarmed at the prospect of some sort of uprising by discontented workers. By 1900, this fear had passed and society seemed to have settled down into an uneasy calm. Searle concludes that 'it had become a society within which each class accepted the institutionalized role assigned to it and sought to settle its differences with others through negotiation and compromise, not violence'.

Nevertheless, within a few years more problems arose. By 1908, real wages were stagnating and between 1910 and 1913 the cost of living rose sharply, causing a wave of strikes. In early 1914, many observers felt that Britain was a nation in crisis (see Section 21.6).

QUESTIONS

1 Why were the revelations of Charles Booth and Seebohm Rowntree about poverty at the turn of the century both surprising and significant for British government and society?

2 'Unemployment in Britain between the two world wars was caused more by structural weaknesses in the economy than by short-term factors during the period'. How valid is this judgement?

3 How far would it be accurate to claim that Britain had a Welfare State by 1939?

A document question about poverty and self-help can be found on the accompanying website www.palgrave.com/masterseries/lowe1.

the Liberals in power, 1905–14

The Liberal government that took office in December 1905 and then won a landslide victory in the general election of January 1906 (see Section 17.6(b–c) for statistics and reasons) in many ways marked the beginning of a new era. For the first time Britain had a government which was not dominated by wealthy landowners and aristocrats. The radical wing of the Liberal party had come to the forefront, and though there were some aristocrats in the Cabinet (such as Sir Edward Grey, the Foreign Secretary), most of the senior posts were filled by lawyers (Asquith, Lloyd George and Haldane), with a sprinkling of writers and journalists. As president of the Local Government Board there was John Burns, who had worked as an engineer, had helped to organize the 1889 dock strike and had for a time been a member of the SDF before joining the Liberals. Also in Parliament were the thirty new Labour MPs and twenty-four Liberal MPs sponsored by the miners' unions, who usually sat with the Labour men.

This radical predominance has led historians to describe these years as the era of *New Liberalism*. The Prime Minister, the 69-year-old Sir Henry Campbell-Bannerman, was a successful Scottish businessman who had been Liberal leader in the Commons since 1898. Generally regarded as a radical and known affectionately in the party as CB, he was level-headed, kindly and sympathetic, but he was also tough and determined. Though he was not a brilliant speaker and not in robust health, he turned out to be an expert at managing his Cabinet, which was full of brilliant men. Herbert Henry Asquith was Chancellor of the Exchequer, and David Lloyd George, a fiery young Welshman from a modest background, was President of the Board of Trade.

Campbell-Bannerman died in April 1908, his greatest achievement having been *the settlement of the South African problem*. Asquith became Prime Minister, and a Cabinet reshuffle made Lloyd George Chancellor of the Exchequer and brought Winston Churchill in as President of the Board of Trade.

The government had an enormous majority, and carrying its policies into effect should have been plain sailing. However, it was a period full of tensions and crises:

- The built-in Conservative majority in the House of Lords decided to block much of the Liberals' programme, which inevitably led to *a bitter confrontation between the two houses, settled eventually by the Parliament Act of 1911.*
- *The suffragettes* mounted a determined and violent campaign to secure the vote for women.
- From 1910 there was *serious labour unrest and a wave of strikes.*
- There was *new trouble in Ireland*, where civil war was averted only by the outbreak of the First World War at the end of July 1914.
- Foreign affairs were characterized by Britain's growing friendship with France, and, in spite of Grey's efforts, the deterioration of relations with Germany, which brought Britain into the war in 1914.
- In spite of all these distractions, the Liberals found time to introduce *important reforms to help trade unions and working people* (see Section 20.2–20.3). Though in some ways their social reforms were disappointing, it is usual to regard them as the beginning of the welfare state.

The period from 1901 to 1914 is known as the Edwardian era, after Edward VII, who reigned from the death of his mother, Queen Victoria, in 1901, until 1910. He was succeeded by his son, George V, who reigned until 1936.

21.1 the New Liberalism

During the last twenty years of the nineteenth century, many left-wing Liberals moved away from the old-fashioned Gladstonian Liberalism, which had developed from the theories of David Ricardo, Jeremy Bentham and John Stuart Mill. These traditional Liberals believed that society was simply a collection of unconnected individuals, and economic growth could only be brought about by individual enterprise. The government's job should therefore be as insignificant as possible – confined to removing any obstacles in the way of individual enterprise and providing, at most, limited social services. This *laissez-faire* approach would make for individual liberty and ensure cheap and efficient administration.

The leading New Liberals included Asquith, Churchill and Lloyd George, who all acknowledged that if the party was to survive and attract working-class votes, it was essential for the state to play a new and decisive role in bringing about social reform. The leading thinkers of New Liberalism were the economist J. A. Hobson and the sociologist L. T. Hobhouse, both of whom had been influenced by the Fabians. They argued that 'old' Liberalism had been too concerned with individual liberty, and that it was ridiculous to talk about liberty and freedom in connection with the poorest ranks of the working class, because their freedom of action had been taken away from them by their poverty. And yet the people making vast profits from their business activities could not have done so without the efforts of their workers. In fact, as the influential Oxford don, T. H. Green, pointed out, society was much more than just a collection of individuals – it was 'organic', like a living creature in which all the parts worked together and depended on each other for progress and success. It followed therefore that there should be a fairer distribution of wealth, which could only be achieved by state action.

New Liberals proposed that the state should take the lead in introducing far-reaching social reforms, such as old age pensions and a minimum wage, to be financed by increased taxes on the land and incomes of the wealthy. By redistributing wealth in this way, the purchasing power of the working class would be increased, and this would stimulate the economy and the general prosperity. There was certainly much that was new in all this, but it must be emphasized that New Liberal ideas were by no means a complete break with classical Liberalism. The leaders were constantly at pains to point out that they still valued individual initiatives, that their social reforms were merely extensions of Gladstone's policies, and that, like classical Liberals, they did not plan to restructure society in the way that the socialists did, and most certainly did not intend to provide welfare for *all* workers, only for the 'deserving' poor; as for the 'undeserving' poor, they would have to take responsibility for their own welfare.

Both Hobson and Hobhouse were prolific writers and their ideas had enormous influence – men such as Seebohm Rowntree and C. P. Scott (the editor of *The Manchester Guardian*) were committed New Liberals. The New Liberals gradually influenced the moderate centre of the party, though it would not be true to say that the *entire* party had been converted by 1906. Nevertheless, the Liberal reforms of the next few years showed how deeply New Liberal thinking had penetrated, and so did Lloyd George's famous budget of 1909, which contained many elements of New Liberalism. When the Liberal government scored its big triumph over the House of Lords in 1912 (see Section 21.3(c)), it seemed that there was plenty of life left in the party, and it was the New Liberals who were at the forefront.

21.2 the Liberals and South Africa

Many of the New Liberals, in particular Hobson, were against imperialism. In his book *Imperialism* (1902), Hobson argued that imperialism held back the progress of social reform because it diverted both attention and financial resources away from the domestic scene, and only benefited the upper classes and capitalists, such as arms manufacturers and merchants. Campbell-Bannerman agreed and the New Liberals saw him as an ally. He had no hesitation in dealing decisively with two of the most pressing imperial problems, both in South Africa.

(a) Chinese slavery

This problem, which had embarrassed Balfour so much (see Section 17.6(b)), was settled immediately. The government simply made it illegal to bring any more Chinese labourers into the Transvaal. The existing workers had to serve out their contracts, but when this was completed in 1910, the problem disappeared.

(b) the Transvaal and the Orange Free State

After their defeat in the Boer War, these two Boer republics had been annexed by the British government; however, in the Treaty of Vereeniging (1902) they were promised eventual self-government (see Section 17.3(c)). Campbell-Bannerman saw no sense in delaying it any longer: complete self-government was granted to the Transvaal (1906), and the following year to the Orange Free State. The Boer leaders were much impressed by the government's speed and had retained great respect for Campbell-Bannerman ever since he had described Kitchener's concentration camps as 'methods of barbarism'. For these reasons, they decided to join Cape Colony and Natal to form *the Union of South Africa*, which came into existence officially in 1910. Though this took place after CB's death, the creation of the new dominion and the reconciliation of the Afrikaners and the British were very much his achievement. South Africa supported Britain in two world wars and stayed in the Commonwealth until 1961.

There was one major criticism: no provision was made to safeguard the rights of non-whites, and no guarantee was given that they would eventually be allowed to vote. However, if the government had insisted on such guarantees being written into the new constitution, the Boers would not have agreed to join the Union. The Liberals hoped that in time the more progressive attitude of English-speaking South Africans would prevail and ensure that non-whites received equal treatment. Unfortunately, this did not happen and the policy of *apartheid* was later introduced by the Boer-dominated South African government (see Section 34.5(e)); but it is hardly fair to blame Campbell-Bannerman and Asquith for this.

21.3 the Liberals and the dispute with the House of Lords

(a) the House of Lords in 1906

The House of Lords contained 591 members, known as 'peers of the realm', of whom 561 had inherited their seats from their fathers or from another male relative. The other thirty, whose seats were not hereditary, consisted of four law lords, the two Archbishops (Canterbury and York) and twenty-four bishops. Roughly two-thirds of the peers were Conservatives, and the rest were Liberals, which gave the Conservatives a built-in, permanent majority in the Lords. New peers could be created by the sovereign on the advice of the Prime Minister.

In theory, the powers of the Lords and Commons were equal: bills could be introduced in the Lords as well as in the Commons. In 1900, the Conservative Prime Minister, Lord Salisbury, sat in the Lords, though he was the last Prime Minister to do so. However, two traditions had gradually developed during the nineteenth century:

▸ all bills dealing with finance and taxation started life in the Commons; and
▸ the House of Lords did not reject finance bills.

(b) what were the causes of the dispute?

While the Commons was in the process of becoming the more important of the two houses, the Lords could still change bills radically, and even prevent a government passing laws if there seemed to be a good reason for doing so (see Section 4.1 for the stages in passing a bill through Parliament). The basic cause of the dispute was that the House of Lords, with its permanent Conservative majority, continually rejected Liberal bills, although during the previous ten years of Conservative rule, it had not once interfered with a Conservative bill. The Liberal government, in spite of having been elected with a huge majority, was being prevented from carrying out its policies by a House of Lords that had not been elected; democracy was being denied. *The confrontation built up gradually*:

1 Gladstone's Second Irish Home Rule Bill had been rejected by the Lords in 1893 (see Section 16.8(b)) and this was followed by the defeat of most of Lord Rosebery's attempted measures (1894–5) (see Section 16.9). The Lords' justification was that the Liberals had only a tiny majority.

2 After lying dormant for ten years, the House of Lords woke up and in 1906 defeated two of Campbell-Bannerman's most important bills – an Education Bill and a Plural Voting Bill (which would have removed the right of people owning premises in several constituencies to vote more than once). The following year, two more important bills were rejected, and two more were changed so drastically by the Lords that they turned out to be almost worthless.

3 In 1908, the Lords rejected the Licensing Bill, designed to reduce the number of public houses, though Edward VII advised them to pass it. There could be no excuse that the Liberals had a flimsy majority, and Campbell-Bannerman warned the Conservatives that if this continued, an attempt would be made to restrict their powers. It seemed to the Liberals that the Conservative leaders, Balfour and Lord Lansdowne, were making blatant use of the Lords' powers to protect the interests of their own party and class. According to historian Robert Blake (who himself became a Conservative peer), 'this was a denial of parliamentary democracy ... many Conservatives behaved as if the verdict of 1906 was some freak aberration on the part of the electorate and that it was their duty, through the House of Lords, to preserve the public from the consequences of its own folly till it came to its senses'.

4 The Lords were also preparing to oppose old age pensions, but Asquith thwarted them by using an important loophole – *the tradition that the Lords never interfered with a finance bill, usually the annual budget.* Asquith shrewdly designated the pensions bill as a finance bill and it passed without controversy.

5 The dispute came to a climax in 1909, when the Lords *broke the constitutional tradition by rejecting Lloyd George's entire budget for that year.* It was Lloyd George's first budget and was designed to raise an extra £15 million to pay for pensions, labour exchanges and *Dreadnought* battleships. The wealthy were to foot the bill:

> income tax up from a shilling to 1s 2d in the pound on incomes over £3,000;

> supertax of 6d in the pound on incomes over £5,000;

> higher taxes on tobacco and spirits (a bottle of whisky went up from 3s 6d to 4s), and higher charges for liquor licences;

> taxes on petrol and cars;

> taxes on mining royalties; and,

> most controversial of all – a 20 per cent tax on the increased value of land when it was resold.

6 The budget was debated in the Commons from April until November – much longer than usual. The Conservatives assaulted it viciously, both in the Commons and outside, forming a Budget Protest League. They claimed that it was a deliberate attack on the wealthy, especially on landowners, and that it was the beginning of socialism: the new land tax would require all land to be valued, and this, they feared, could be the preliminary to the nationalization of land. The Duke of Beaufort said he would like to see Lloyd George and Churchill 'in the middle of twenty couple of foxhounds'; Lloyd George hit back in his famous Limehouse speech, accusing landlords of being selfish creatures whose sole function was 'the stately consumption of wealth produced by others'. In November 1909, the budget passed the Commons with a huge majority (379 to 149), but later the same month the Lords rejected it, even though Edward VII was anxious for it to pass. Lord Lansdowne, the Conservative leader in the Lords, justified this on the grounds that such a revolutionary measure ought to be put before the public in a general election. Balfour said that the Lords were merely carrying out their proper function as the 'watchdog of the constitution' (meaning that its function was to make sure that no irresponsible laws were passed, and that all proper rules and procedures were adhered to), but Lloyd George retorted that the Lords were acting as if they were 'Mr Balfour's poodle'.

It has been suggested that Lloyd George deliberately produced a controversial budget to trap the Lords into rejecting it, so that the Liberals would have a cast-iron case for restricting their powers. But there is little evidence of this; the government needed the money and were determined to make the wealthy pay a fair share. On the other hand, the budget was cleverly framed to embarrass the Conservatives: if they did not oppose the tax increases, their landowning supporters would be furious; and if they *did* oppose them, they would lay themselves open to charges of selfishness for refusing to contribute towards defence and help for the poor. Very few Liberals could have expected the Lords to break the tradition by rejecting the entire budget.

(c) the constitutional crisis and the two elections of 1910

The 'insane decision' (as Robert Blake calls it) of the Conservative Lords to reject the budget immediately caused a constitutional crisis. No government can continue unless its budget is approved by Parliament, so it can go ahead and collect taxes. If the Lords were allowed to get away with it, the basic principle of democracy that had developed in Britain would be overturned: the hereditary House of Lords and not the elected House of Commons would control government policy. Asquith declared that the Lords had breached the Constitution, and he prepared to do battle to reduce their powers. It was a long and bitter struggle, which was only resolved in August 1911, over eighteen months after the rejection of Lloyd George's 'People's Budget'.

1 Parliament was dissolved and a general election held (January 1910) on the issue of 'Peers versus People'. The results were disappointing for the Liberals, who lost over 100 seats; the figures were: Liberals 275, Conservative and Unionists 273, Labour 40, Irish Nationalists 82. Liberal losses can probably be explained by the fact that some traditional Conservative seats that had fallen to the Liberals in the landslide of 1906, now returned to the Tories. Many people who had voted Liberal in 1906 might have been frightened off by the government's radical policies.

2 In spite of their heavy losses, the Liberals continued in government because they could usually count on Irish and Labour support. However, Asquith's dependence on the Irish meant that the constitutional crisis became mixed up with the Irish Home Rule question. The Irish Nationalist leader, John Redmond, agreed to vote for Lloyd George's budget (which now had to pass the Commons again), but at a heavy price – he demanded two rewards:

  › another Irish Home Rule Bill; and
  › a bill to restrict the powers of the House of Lords so that it would not be able to throw out the Home Rule Bill, as it had in 1893.

3 April 1910 was therefore a busy month: a Parliament Bill designed to reduce the Lords' power passed the Commons easily, closely followed by the budget. The following day, the Lords approved the budget, perhaps hoping to escape the Parliament Bill.

4 The next problem for Asquith was how to manoeuvre the Lords into passing the Parliament Bill, which would significantly reduce their own powers.

Asquith tried to persuade Edward VII to create about 250 new Liberal peers, enough to defeat the Conservatives in the Lords. The king would only agree if the Liberals could win another election on the issue, but Asquith dared not risk another one so soon. Edward died suddenly in May 1910, and the new king, George V, suggested a conference. This met and discussed the situation for the next six months. A compromise solution was almost reached, but the conference broke down over the problem of Ireland. The Conservatives wanted special loopholes in any new bill, which would enable them to block Home Rule, but Asquith would not agree.

5 In November 1910, Asquith resumed battle by sending the Parliament Bill up to the Lords. When they refused to pass it, he met the king and secretly secured a promise that if the Liberals won another general election, George V would create the required peers. Armed with this promise, Asquith went into the general election of December 1910, which had a remarkably similar result to the previous one: Liberals 272, Conservative and Unionists 272, Labour 42, Irish Nationalists 84. The Liberals and their allies had maintained their support, and the Parliament Bill again passed the Commons with a comfortable majority (May 1911).

6 In July 1911, Asquith announced in the Commons that the king had promised to create as many as 500 new Liberal peers if necessary, to get the bill through the Lords. The furious Conservatives, led by Lord Hugh Cecil (Salisbury's son) howled Asquith down with shouts of 'Traitor!' and he was unable to complete his speech. It caused a split in the Conservative ranks between the outright opponents of the bill (nicknamed the 'Ditchers') and the moderates (the 'Hedgers'). The moderates decided that it would be better to accept a reduction of their powers rather than be permanently swamped by the Liberals,, and many of them abstained when it came to the vote. But it was a close-run thing – the bill was passed by 131 votes to 114 (August 1911). The Parliament Act became law and the constitutional crisis was over.

(d) terms of the Parliament Act and its results

1 The Lords were not allowed to amend or reject a finance bill, and the Speaker of the House of Commons was to decide which were finance bills.

2 The Lords could still amend and reject other bills, but if a bill passed the Commons in three successive sessions of Parliament and was rejected three times by the Lords, it would automatically become law on its third rejection by the Lords. In simple terms, this meant that the Lords could delay a bill for two years.

3 There was to be a general election at least every five years instead of every seven.

The Act was of major importance in the development of the Constitution. Democracy had been safeguarded – the Lords had no control over the country's finances; they could delay other legislation for two years, but could not prevent it becoming law eventually, provided the government remained in power long enough. There can be no doubt that it was a vitally important step in the reduction of the powers of the aristocracy, many of whom now began to withdraw from politics. The Duke of Northumberland remarked in 1917: 'I have almost abandoned politics as hopeless – at any rate for a peer.'

On the other hand, the Lords still had the power, if they felt like using it, to paralyse a government for the last two years of its five-year term. As for immediate results, the Lords were so incensed at the Liberals that they used their remaining powers to the full: they rejected the Irish Home Rule Bill, a Welsh Disestablishment Bill (which would have meant that the Anglican Church was no longer the official state church in Wales) and another Plural Voting Bill; not one of these perfectly reasonable bills had passed into law when war broke out in 1914. Nor had the Parliament Act done anything to make the membership of the House of Lords more democratic – most peers still inherited their seats instead of having to win them in an election. For the next reduction of the Lords' powers in 1949, see Section 29.3(b).

21.4 votes for women: suffragists and suffragettes

The campaign to secure votes for women in parliamentary elections was basically a middle-class movement at the beginning, but it soon attracted strong working-class support, especially in the North. These demands were nothing new – there had been women's suffrage societies since the late 1860s, when the question of votes for women was raised during the debates on the 1867 Reform Act. They did not attract a lot of attention until the Edwardian period, when interest began to revive for several reasons: women had just been given the vote in New Zealand; the new Independent Labour Party, particularly Keir Hardie, were encouraging; and given that women could now vote for rural and district councils, and could stand for election to these councils, it was logical to expect that they would soon have the right to choose their MPs.

(a) suffragists and suffragettes

The National Union of Women's Suffrage Societies (NUWSS), formed in 1897, campaigned non-violently for votes for women on the same terms as men; they did not want the vote for *all* women. Historian Martin Pugh believes that, by 1906, a majority of MPs had been won over to the general principle of votes for women by Mrs Millicent Fawcett, the suffragist leader, and her peaceful campaign. The problems were: finding time for legislation in a crowded parliamentary timetable, and deciding exactly which women should be given the vote – should it be given to all women, or just to unmarried women and widows, since married women were not considered to be householders.

A much more vocal pressure group than the suffragists was *the Women's*

Social and Political Union (WSPU) founded in 1903 by Mrs Emmeline Pankhurst, helped by her daughters Christabel, Sylvia and Adela. Both Emmeline and her husband Richard, a left-wing Manchester barrister, were members of the Independent Labour Party (ILP). After Richard's death in 1898, Emmeline worked as a registrar in a working-class area of Manchester. She was shocked by the poor conditions and hardship suffered by many of the women she dealt with, and became convinced that only when women had the vote could sufficient pressure be brought on governments to improve social conditions. The suffragettes, as the *Daily Mail* mockingly called them, had high hopes for the new Liberal government, since it was well known that Campbell-Bannerman and Lloyd George were sympathetic. Their hopes were further raised by *the Qualification of Women Act (1907)*, which allowed women to become members of county and borough councils and to act as mayors.

However, later the same year, a private member's bill to give women the vote was heavily defeated in the Commons. In fact, both Liberals and Conservatives were divided on the issue; the Liberal government would not introduce a bill for women's suffrage, their excuse being the difficulty about which classes of women to include; but the real reason was probably that Asquith, who became Prime Minister in 1908, was against the whole idea. Further private members' bills suffered the same fate in 1908, 1909 and 1911.

(b) the case against votes for women

Outright opponents put forward the old argument that women, by their nature, were too emotional to have sound political judgement. It was not that they were thought to be inferior to men; it was simply that the women's role was seen as rearing children and looking after the home; politics and earning the family income was the role of the male.

Even pro-suffragist supporters had to admit that there was a genuine problem about which women should be included. The pro-suffragist Liberals were undecided whether to give the vote to *all women* or to restrict it to women who owned property. They were not happy at the prospect of women voters outnumbering men if *all* women were allowed to vote. On the other hand, if only propertied women were included, that might benefit the Conservatives, since rich women might be more inclined to support the Conservatives. The increasing militancy of the suffragettes only served to strengthen the opposition by discrediting the whole women's rights movement for a time.

(c) the suffragette campaign turns to militancy

Faced with what they saw as the government's stubbornness, the WSPU became more militant.

› Since 1905, they had been disrupting meetings addressed by Liberal politicians; Christabel Pankhurst and Annie Kenney, a Lancashire cotton worker, spent a week in gaol after being ejected from the Manchester Free Trade Hall for heckling Sir Edward Grey. Next, they turned to smashing windows, chaining themselves to the railings of Buckingham Palace and Downing Street, kicking and scratching policemen who tried to move them on, and holding massive demonstrations and processions.

- By 1912, Asquith and the Cabinet had accepted the principle of women's suffrage, and, to save time, made a late addition to the Plural Voting Bill, which was already under discussion. The amendments gave the vote to certain categories of women. However, in January 1913, the Speaker ruled that the additions could not be allowed, since they changed the nature of the bill.

- This decision drove the suffragettes to desperate measures – they resorted to setting fire to post boxes, churches and railway stations, and there were physical attacks on Cabinet ministers, particularly Asquith. Some extremists tried to tear his clothes off on the golf-course at Lossiemouth, and others beat him over the head with dog-whips. Lloyd George's new house, which he had fortunately not moved into, was badly damaged by a bomb explosion, for which Mrs Pankhurst was given a three-year gaol sentence (she only served six weeks). The most horrifying incident occurred at the 1913 Derby, when Emily Davidson was killed as she threw herself in front of the king's horse.

These outrages, as the press called them, were really unnecessary: the Liberals had accepted the principle of votes for women and had only failed to get it through the Commons on a technicality. It is more than likely that they would have tried again later in 1913, and that the Commons would have approved it by 1914. But the government hesitated to try again because it did not want to seem to be giving way to violence. Mrs Fawcett and the moderates of the NUWSS, which had played no part in the violence, were disgusted with the WSPU, because it was clear that their behaviour was delaying the granting of votes for women. Even within the WSPU itself, the Pankhursts were losing support because of their dictatorial attitude. In 1912, for example, Emmeline expelled half the WSPU membership, including her daughter Sylvia, some because they wanted to call off the militancy, others because she thought they were challenging her leadership in other ways. Emmeline and Christabel disagreed with Sylvia over a number of policy issues, particularly the fact that Sylvia and her East London branch of the movement had allied with various socialist and trade union organizations, and this was against WSPU policy.

- As the suffragettes became more militant, the government response became more unpleasant and insensitive. When suffragettes went on hunger-strike in prison, the government authorized them to be forcibly fed. When this provoked criticism, the government responded with the farcical 'Cat and Mouse' Act of 1913; this permitted the release from prison of women who were in a weak physical state because of hunger-strike, and allowed them to be re-arrested when they had recovered.

- The campaign of violence continued into 1914: in the first seven months, around a hundred buildings were set on fire, including the historic White Kirk in East Lothian and the refreshment pavilion in Regent's Park, London.
- As soon as Britain entered the war in August 1914, the suffragettes called off their campaign, although they had failed to achieve their objective. Emmeline was extremely patriotic and pointed out that it was ludicrous to continue campaigning for the vote if you had no country to vote in.

(d) assessment of the suffragettes and the Pankhursts

Understandably, the Pankhursts have attracted a great deal of attention from historians, and many of them have been uncomplimentary. Martin Pugh, writing in 2001, argues that they were more of a hindrance than a help in furthering the cause of votes for women, and that Emmeline was a failure both as a leader and as a mother. He sees Sylvia as the real heroine of the family, sticking loyally by her socialism and her support for trade unionism, and consequently suffering humiliation and expulsion from the movement by her own mother and elder sister, Christabel. Jill Liddington (2006) is more sympathetic to Emmeline, paying tribute to her skill as an inspiring speaker and to her ability to fire up her supporters, though she still feels that the suffragettes did more harm than good.

June Purvis (2002) takes issue with Martin Pugh for ignoring the most recent interpretations of Emmeline's career. She claims that he largely bases his conclusions on Sylvia Pankhurst's book *The Suffragette Movement*, published in 1931. In it, Sylvia presents her mother as a traitor to the socialist cause: she had resigned from the ILP in 1907 and after the First World War she joined the Conservative party and stood, unsuccessfully, as a Conservative candidate. In addition, embittered at her expulsion from the movement and her rejection by Emmeline and the detested Christabel, Sylvia accused Emmeline of being a failed mother and a weak leader who allowed herself to be too easily swayed by Christabel. However, as June Purvis points out, 'the souring of Emmeline's relationship with Sylvia during the last years of Emmeline's life undoubtedly helped to shape the way the daughter represented the WSPU leader in *The Suffragette Movement*'. Moreover, Pugh and others fail to mention that much of what Sylvia wrote about her mother contradicts what she wrote in an earlier book published in 1911, and in a biography of her mother that came out in 1935.

Whichever interpretation one favours, there can be no escaping the fact that the Pankhursts were a remarkable family who, though they may have failed in their main aim in the short term, nevertheless made a considerable impact on society and political life. Ethel Smyth, a well-known composer and feminist champion, and a close friend of Emmeline, claimed that 'the supreme achievement of Mrs Pankhurst was creating in women a new sense of power and responsibility, together with a determination to work out their destiny on other lines than those laid down for them since times immemorial by men'.

(e) votes for women at last

Over the four years of the First World War, women made such a vital contribution to the war effort, taking over important jobs so that the men would be free to join the army, that it appeared even more ludicrous that they were denied full political rights. In 1918, the Lloyd George government's *Representation of the People Act* gave the vote to all men at the age of 21, and to women at the age of 30. Women were also allowed to become MPs. Later that same year, women were granted the right to sit on juries, to become magistrates and to enter the legal profession. The franchise situation was not equalized until 1928, when Baldwin's Conservative government gave the vote to women at 21. Martin Pugh is not convinced that the role of women in the war *was* the vital factor in securing them the vote. He points out that this theory ignores the changes of attitude which had already taken place before the war: 'During the war', he writes, 'not surprisingly votes for women simply vanished from the agenda for some time. The issue returned only because the politicians grew anxious to enfranchise more men, many of whom had lost their qualification as a result of moving home for war service. It was this that led to the scheme of parliamentary reform in 1917 in which women were included.'

The first woman elected to Parliament was the Countess Markievicz, a Sinn Fein (see Section 21.5 below) MP, who, ironically, along with the other 72 Sinn Feiners elected in 1918, refused to take her seat at Westminster (see Section 26.2(c)). The first woman to actually take her seat in the House of Commons, in 1919, was the American Lady Nancy Astor, elected as Conservative MP for Plymouth Devonport, which she continued to represent until 1945.

21.5 why did the Liberals' attempts to settle the Irish question fail before 1914?

Since the rejection of Gladstone's Second Irish Home Rule Bill by the Lords in 1893, the issue had been pushed into the background, and there was no prospect of Home Rule during the ten years of Conservative rule from 1895–1905. However, it was a period full of important developments for the Irish people. *There was a growing emphasis on all things Irish, to keep alive the idea that Ireland was a separate nation with its own culture and heritage.* There was a revival of interest in Irish sports, such as Gaelic football and hurling. *The Gaelic League,* founded in 1893, aimed to spread the Gaelic language and culture – folk music, dancing and literature. It culminated in a great Anglo-Irish literary movement involving outstanding writers such as the poet W. B. Yeats and the playwright J. M. Synge. The new Abbey Theatre was opened in Dublin in 1904 and quickly became a centre of the Irish revival. The cultural revival affected politics as well: *in 1905 Arthur Griffith founded a new political group called Sinn Fein (Ourselves Alone).* Griffith believed in self-reliance – there was no reason why the Irish could not be economically prosperous provided they were given political freedom, which he hoped could be achieved by passive resistance to Britain.

The Irish Nationalists, led by John Redmond, were hopeful of quick satisfaction from Campbell-Bannerman and the Liberals, especially when he was so ready to give the Boers self-government. However, the most they were prepared to allow in the immediate future was *an Irish Executive Council* to look after certain affairs, such as the Congested Districts Board and education. This was not a genuine Irish parliament, and the proposal was rejected by Redmond.

The situation changed dramatically with the general election of January 1910, which left Asquith heavily dependent on the Irish Nationalists to stay in office. As the price for their support for Lloyd George's budget, Asquith had to promise to reduce the powers of the House of Lords so that another Irish Home Rule Bill could be passed. The Parliament Act of August 1911 (see Section 21.3(c)) opened the way for the Third Irish Home Rule Bill, which passed the Commons in 1912. It was immediately rejected by the Lords and the same thing happened again in 1913. However, under the terms of the Parliament Act, the bill only had to pass the Commons a third time to become law at some point during 1914; but things turned out not to be so simple. In August 1914, a solution to the Irish problem was as far away as ever, and the country was on the verge of civil war. *The reasons were complex.*

(a) the Irish Nationalist Party was being eclipsed by Sinn Fein

Irish opinion was bitterly disappointed by Redmond's failure to get anything like Home Rule from the Liberal government before 1910, and this caused more people to look towards Sinn Fein. Griffith wanted a similar solution to the one that had settled the problems of the Habsburg Empire, where the Hungarians had been campaigning for independence from Austria. In 1867, Austria and Hungary became separate countries, each with its own parliament, but they kept the same ruler, Franz Josef, who was to be Emperor of Austria and King of Hungary. It was known as the Dual Monarchy. Griffith could see no reason why Ireland could not be treated like Hungary – having its own parliament with full powers, but keeping the monarchy as a link between the two. Eventually, as their ideas were ignored, Sinn Fein moved to the position of demanding an independent republic. Another group which was gaining support was the Irish Republican Brotherhood (IRB) or Fenians, which also wanted a complete break with Britain. This was not necessarily fatal for chances of a solution, but it meant that at the very time when Home Rule was imminent (thanks to the Parliament Act), a large section of the Irish wanted something that went much further.

(b) the problem of Ulster was more serious than before

At the time of the First Home Rule Bill (1886), Lord Randolph Churchill had tried to stir up the Ulster Protestants against the Bill with warnings that they would be swamped by the Catholics of Southern Ireland. At the time this was probably not a major issue: Parnell, the Nationalist leader, was himself a Protestant; but by 1912, the situation had changed. Ulster had developed industrially, especially shipbuilding at Belfast, and there was also linen manufacture and whisky distilling. Ninety per cent of all Ireland's manufactured exports were made in the area around Belfast, while the rest of Ireland remained largely agricultural and backward. Griffith's talk of introducing tariffs to protect Irish industries worried Ulster businessmen, who were afraid that Home Rule would mean the loss of their valuable markets in the rest of Britain. The Protestant Ulstermen felt themselves to be a separate community, both economically and in religious matters. Four counties – Antrim, Armagh, Down and Derry – had large Protestant majorities and they were strongly against becoming part of an independent Ireland in which, they feared, they would be dominated and discriminated against by a Catholic government in Dublin. They were determined to keep as much of Ulster as possible united with Britain.

Even before the Home Rule Bill was introduced into the Commons, *the Ulster Unionists* began to organize themselves to resist Home Rule. Appointing Sir Edward Carson, a prominent barrister and Unionist MP, as their leader, they held massive demonstrations and threatened to set up a provisional government if the bill passed. Hundreds of thousands of Ulstermen signed a Covenant swearing to fight any government that tried to force Home Rule on them.

(c) the Conservatives (Unionists) intensified the crisis by encouraging the Ulster Unionists

There is no doubt that the unfortunate Nationalists were the victims of the bitterness between Liberals and Conservatives in the aftermath of the 1911 Parliament Act. The Conservatives, still smarting from the Parliament Act and their failure to win three consecutive general elections were, in the words of Roy Jenkins, 'sick with office hunger'. The Ulster situation was the perfect weapon with which to embarrass Asquith and might even be used to bring the government down. When Carson openly organized a military force, the Ulster Volunteers, and held drills and parades, Andrew Bonar Law, the new Conservative leader, went over to Ireland to take the salute at a review. He told a Conservative Party rally at Blenheim Palace in July 1912: 'I can imagine no length of resistance to which Ulster will go, which I shall not be ready to support.' In other words, the leader of the British Conservative Party was encouraging armed rebellion against a law about to be passed by the legally elected British government. The Conservatives even called themselves Unionists at this time, to show how strongly they felt about maintaining the union between England and Ireland.

(d) Asquith and the Liberal government were partly to blame for the stalemate

Asquith realized that the Conservatives were only using the Irish situation as a lever to get the government out, and he decided to let events take their course, or as he put it, 'wait and see'. He could have eased the situation from the beginning by discussing the possibility of a partition, allowing the four counties with a Protestant majority to remain under British rule. There would have been opposition from the Nationalists, but it was not out of the question for them to have accepted a compromise of this sort, and it would have avoided the formation of the Ulster Volunteers. Not until early in 1914 did Asquith show that he was prepared to exclude Ulster. By this time the Nationalists had also organized their private army, *the Nationalist Volunteers.* This was another fatal omission by Asquith: he should have taken immediate action to ban all private armies and arms imports. He took no action, and both sets of volunteers openly imported arms, built up their manpower and drilled their troops. Only in March 1914 did Asquith decide to send British troops into Ulster to guard arms depots and other strategic points.

(e) the 'Curragh Mutiny' seemed to undermine the government's position

This was not a true mutiny, just the threat of one. When the government's intention to send troops to Ulster became known, about sixty army officers stationed at the Curragh in Dublin threatened to resign if they were ordered to force Ulster into accepting Home Rule. The Secretary for War, J. E. B. Seely, assured them, in an astonishing statement, that they would not be used to force Home Rule on Ulster. At this, Asquith insisted on Seely's resignation and took over the War Office himself. However, the damage had been done – the impression had been given that, in the event of fighting breaking out, the government might not be able to rely on the loyalty of its own army; this could only encourage the Ulster Volunteers into bolder action.

(f) the Larne gun-running incident inflamed the situation further

The Ulster Volunteers were allowed to smuggle 30,000 rifles and 3 million rounds of ammunition into Ireland via Larne (April 1914) without any interference from the police, though by this time there was an official ban on arms imports.

(g) the Home Rule Bill passed through the Commons for the third time in May 1914

However, it still contained no provision for a separate Ulster. Frantic negotiations followed, culminating in an all-party conference (July). At one point, a solution seemed near, as Redmond, faced with civil war, was apparently prepared to agree to the exclusion of the four mainly Protestant counties from Home Rule, at least temporarily. But the Unionists stepped up their demands and insisted that Ulster should include Fermanagh and Tyrone, whose population was at least 50 per cent Catholic. Redmond could not agree to this and the conference broke up.

On 26 July there was *the Howth incident*, which showed how precarious peace was in Ireland. The Nationalist Volunteers smuggled in a large shipment

map **21.1** Ireland showing the provinces and counties

of rifles, despite the efforts of troops sent to prevent them. A hostile crowd gathered, angry that the Nationalists should be treated differently from the Ulster Volunteers. Stones were thrown at the troops, who opened fire, killing three people and wounding thirty-eight. Tensions ran high, and Ireland seemed on the verge of civil war. A few days later, Britain entered the First World War, and though the Home Rule Bill had been placed on the statute book, the government decided to suspend its operation until one year after the war was over. No solution had been found to the stalemate, but it was generally hoped that the Irish would remain quiet and support the war effort. Many did, but the convinced republicans had other ideas, as they showed at Easter 1916 (see Section 26.2).

21.6 why was there so much political and industrial unrest between 1909 and 1914, and how did Asquith's government deal with it?

Most of the information to answer the question has appeared earlier in the chapter, but it will be helpful to summarize the points briefly.

(a) the Commons versus Lords conflict

This was brought to a climax by Lloyd George's so-called 'People's Budget' of 1909; skilfully handled by Asquith, probably his greatest achievement.

(b) the suffragette agitation

This was not particularly well handled by the government, which ought to have introduced a women's suffrage bill before the situation got out of hand; Asquith, however, opposed votes for women.

(c) the Irish situation

This was made worse by the attitude of the Conservatives, but again, ineptly handled by Asquith and his 'wait and see' approach.

(d) the Osborne Judgment

This contributed towards trade union unrest. The situation was put right by the Trade Union Act of 1913, though only after a delay of four years.

(e) industrial unrest

This was sometimes caused by unemployment, especially in 1908–9, but more often by the fact that wage increases were not keeping pace with rising prices. Some statistics show that in 1908, 1909 and 1910, average real wages were lower than in 1900 (see Cook and Stevenson, p. 207), and the cost of living rose sharply in 1910–13. Syndicalism also played a part in causing the strike wave (see Section 19.7). The government tried to handle the strikes with a mixture of conciliation and firmness. Churchill sent troops to deal with a mining dispute at Tonypandy in South Wales (though they were not used). Asquith's attitude was that essential services must be maintained at all costs, and he authorized the use of troops during the 1911 railway strike, resulting in the deaths of two men at Llanelly. This sort of approach was an over-reaction and did nothing to calm the situation. Eventually, Asquith handed the railway strike over to Lloyd George, who had developed considerable skill as a conciliator. In one way or another he soothed tempers, and within four days had found a compromise. The 1912 coal strike was settled when the government manoeuvred both sides into accepting the Minimum Wage Act (see Section 20.3(d)).

Historians have disagreed about how serious the threats to law and order were; the country seemed to be in total disarray, given the amount of violence and unrest. George Dangerfield, in his vividly written book, *The Strange Death of Liberal England 1910–1914*, first published in 1936 and reissued in 1997, argued that, at the beginning of 1914, Liberal Britain had been 'reduced to ashes' and was standing on the verge of anarchy and revolution. He claimed that the year 1910 was a fatal landmark during which Asquith's Liberal party was first undermined and then destroyed by four vicious attacks:

- the attack from the die-hard Tories in the House of Lords culminating in the struggle over Lloyd George's budget;
- the attack from the Conservatives against the Irish Home Rule bill;
- the attack from revolutionary syndicalism in the strike wave of 1910–13; and
- the attack on the government by militant suffragettes.

Dangerfield believed there would have been a massive general strike led by the Triple Alliance, probably in October, 'an appalling national struggle over the question of the living wage'. Coinciding with civil war in Ireland, this would have placed an enormous strain on the government's resources, and he clearly felt that the Liberals would not have been equal to the task. Only the outbreak of the First World War saved Britain from internal social catastrophe. He also suggested that one reason why the Cabinet was so ready to enter the war was to save the country from descending into total anarchy.

However, all the most recent research suggests that Dangerfield's theories are rather exaggerated, even though his book still provides a good read. True, there were many problems for the Liberals to deal with, but they were steadily being overcome, one by one. The 1911 Parliament Act brought the House of Lords under control; the worst of the strike wave was over by 1914, and even the big syndicalist strike in Dublin, which had lasted over six months, ended in January 1914. Syndicalism was never more than a minority interest in British trade unionism. T. O. Lloyd points out that there were the beginnings of a trade depression early in 1914, which would have made a strike less likely. Although people were uneasy about what might happen, 'England in 1914 was not on the verge of plunging into disorder and chaos'. As for the suffragettes, their numbers and influence had dwindled by 1914, and as soon as war broke out, they called off the campaign and supported the war effort.

The situation in Ireland, where the Ulster Unionists, apparently supported by some Conservative leaders, were preparing to fight against Home Rule, did present a real threat. However, Trevor Fisher believes that, even if the situation had developed into civil war, 'it is unlikely that the violence would have spread to the mainland. What was happening here was the strange death of Liberal

Ireland ... It is by no means clear that the Irish problem ... marked a systemic collapse of Liberalism in the rest of the UK'.

The conclusion has to be, therefore, that the Liberal party was not in terminal decline on the eve of the First World War. In fact, if the war had not happened, it is arguably possible that the Liberals could have rallied their supporters and beaten off the challenge from the Labour party. It was the difficulties posed by having to run the war, and the divisions this caused between the Lloyd George and Asquith supporters that brought about the Liberal decline. As Trevor Wilson put it, the Liberal party was run over by the rampant omnibus of the First World War (see Section 22.5(a)).

21.8 liberal defence and foreign policies, 1905–14

(a) problems facing Sir Edward Grey

Britain's foreign policy was conducted largely by Sir Edward Grey, who was Foreign Secretary from December 1905 until December 1916. The period from 1905 until the outbreak of war was full of international tensions, and there were a number of incidents which seemed likely to cause a major European conflict; these were the Moroccan Crisis (1905–6), the Bosnia Crisis (1908), the Agadir Crisis (1911) and two Balkan Wars (1912 and 1913). When Grey took over at the Foreign Office, Britain had already moved a long way from the comparative isolation of Salisbury's time, having recently signed an agreement with Japan (1902) and the Entente Cordiale with France (1904) (see Section 17.4(b)). *Grey's aims were to build on these agreements while at the same time working to maintain good relations with the Germans*, who, as we saw earlier, viewed Britain's understanding with France as a hostile gesture against them.

Grey's task was difficult:

▸ The British were bound to see the build-up of the German fleet (which started with the 1897 Navy Laws) as a challenge to their naval supremacy.
▸ Although Britain was well ahead in numbers of ships, the problem was that, whereas the British fleet was strung out across the world defending the Empire, the German fleet would be concentrated in the North Sea, where it might on occasion outnumber the available British ships.
▸ There was a need therefore for Britain to press ahead with its *Dreadnought* programme, as well as to make some improvements in its army, which was pitifully small by European standards.
▸ Yet the more Britain increased its military strength and the closer it drew in friendship towards France, the more difficult it would be to improve relations with Germany.

On the whole, Grey performed with great skill and steered Britain successfully through the crises. But the general trend of events was for Britain to find itself supporting France against Germany, and consequently Grey failed to reconcile Britain and Germany.

(b) Britain's defences improved

1 *In the army*, very little had changed since the days of Cardwell's reforms during Gladstone's First Ministry (1868–74). Some reorganization was needed, as the army's performance in the Boer War had shown. The Liberal Secretary for War, R. B. Haldane, had been educated partly in Germany, at Göttingen and Dresden, and was an expert on German affairs. He used his experiences to good effect in bringing the British army up to date. Beginning in 1907, he introduced a General Staff to give an efficient and co-ordinated direction to army leadership. An Expeditionary Force was organized, consisting of six infantry divisions and a cavalry division – 160,000 troops in all, together with the necessary accessories of artillery, transport, medical units and reserves. The various volunteer and part-time soldiers were organized into the Territorials – around 300,000 men who were to be fully equipped and trained so that they could compare in efficiency with the regulars. To improve the supply of officers, Haldane brought the Officers' Training Corps at the public schools under the control of the War Office. This was a fine achievement by Haldane; when he left the War Office in 1912 to become Lord Chancellor, the only drawback, though it was a big one, was that the army was not large enough (see Table 21.1).

2 *The navy was Britain's great strength*, but it was also expensive to maintain. Campbell-Bannerman decided to reduce the Cawdor–Fisher Plan (see Section 17.6(a)); instead of building four *Dreadnoughts* a year, only three were built in 1906, and two in 1907. CB hoped this would induce the Germans to slow down their naval programme and prepare the way for disarmament, but it had the opposite effect – Tirpitz, the German Navy Minister, saw it as a chance to catch up, and the Germans built three ships in 1906, and four each year from 1907 to 1909. This caused a public outcry in Britain, and when the government announced a plan to build six *Dreadnoughts* in 1909, the First Sea Lord, still the forceful and determined Fisher, urged the press into mounting a campaign for eight; 'We want eight

table **21.1 numbers of men in the armed forces, 1880–1914**

	Germany		Great Britain	
	Army	**Navy**	**Army**	**Navy**
1880	401 650	7 350	198 200	59 000
1891	511 650	17 000	209 000	97 600
1901	604 100	31 200	773 500	114 900
1911	622 500	33 500	247 000	128 000
1914	791 000	73 000	247 000	146 000

Source: R. Wolfson, *Years of Change: European History, 1890–1945* (Edward Arnold, 1979), p.137.

table **21.2 fleet sizes, 4 August 1914 (figures in brackets indicate ships under construction)**

	Germany	Great Britain
Battleships	33 (+7)	55 (+11)
Battlecruisers	3 (+3)	7 (+3)
Cruisers	9	51
Light cruisers	45 (+4)	77 (+9)
Destroyers	123 (+9)	191 (+38)
Torpedo ships	80	137 (+1)
Submarines	23 (+15)	64 (+22)
Dreadnoughts	13	20

Source: R. Wolfson, *Years of Change: European History, 1890–1945* (Edward Arnold, 1979), p.137.

and we won't wait', ran the slogan. The public got their eight *Dreadnoughts*, though the expense was alarming and led to Lloyd George's controversial budget. A further five were built in 1910, and five more in 1911. Fisher and the government had already, in 1906, created the Home Fleet based on the Nore (London). When he retired in 1912, Fisher left Britain with a marked superiority in numbers of ships and in gunpower, though it was discovered during the war that individual German ships were better-equipped than their British counterparts (see Table 21.2).

(c) events leading up to the outbreak of war

1 *The Moroccan Crisis (1905–6) was already under way when Grey arrived at the Foreign Office.* It began as a German attempt to test the new Anglo-French Entente, with the implication that France would soon add Morocco to her overseas empire. The Germans announced that they regarded Morocco as independent and would assist its ruler to maintain that independence. They demanded an international conference to discuss Morocco's future. A conference was duly held at Algeciras in Spain (January 1906). Grey believed that, if the Germans had their way, it would be tantamount to acknowledging German diplomatic control of Europe and North Africa. At the conference, he came out strongly in support of the French demand to control the Moroccan bank and police. Russia, Spain and Italy also supported France, and the Germans suffered a serious diplomatic defeat. This was an impressive start for Grey; he had shown that the Anglo-French Entente meant something, and he had helped to preserve the balance of power. The French were grateful and Anglo-French 'military conversations' were started.

2 *The British agreement with Russia (1907) was another blow to Germany.* Britain's motive was not to build up an anti-German bloc; it was more a desire to settle differences with the Russians. For years, the British had viewed Russia as a major threat to her interests in the Far East and India, but recent events had changed all that. Russia's defeat in the war with Japan had weakened the country, and it no longer seemed so much of a danger. The remaining area of dispute was Persia (Iran), and it seemed desirable to both

sides, particularly the Russians, who were anxious to attract British investment, to eliminate rivalry. Such an agreement was only logical, since Russia had signed an alliance with France, Britain's Entente partner, as far back as 1894. Persia was divided into 'spheres of influence'. The north was to be Russian, the south (bordering on Afghanistan and India) British, and the central area to remain neutral. The British could now relax, knowing that the north-west frontier of India was secure, but unfortunately, the Germans took the agreement to be confirmation of their fears that Britain, France and Russia were planning to 'encircle' them.

3 *The Bosnia Crisis (1908) caused great tension.* The Austrians, taking advantage of a revolution in Turkey, annexed Bosnia (still technically Turkish territory) as a deliberate blow against Serbia, which also hoped to acquire Bosnia. The Serbs appealed for help to their fellow Slavs, the Russians, who called for a European conference, expecting French and British support. When it became clear that Germany would support Austria in the event of war, the French drew back, not wanting to become involved in a war in the Balkans, and Grey, anxious to avoid a breach with Germany, contented himself with a formal protest to Austria. Austria kept Bosnia; it was a triumph for the Austro-German alliance, *but it had unfortunate consequences:* Serbia remained bitterly hostile towards Austria and it was this quarrel that developed into the First World War. The humiliation stimulated Russia into a massive military build-up; and Grey and Asquith were now convinced that Germany was out to dominate Europe, an impression confirmed when Tirpitz seemed to be speeding up the naval building programme. The outcome was the hysterical 'We want eight' campaign and an intensification of the naval arms race.

4 *The Agadir Crisis (1911)* arose when French troops occupied Fez, the Moroccan capital, to put down a rebellion against the Sultan. A French annexation of Morocco seemed imminent; the Germans sent a gunboat, the *Panther,* to the Moroccan port of Agadir, hoping to browbeat the French into giving them some compensation – perhaps the French Congo. Grey was concerned in case the 'compensation' turned out to be the German acquisition of Agadir, a vital naval base which could be used to threaten Britain's trade routes. With the intention of strengthening French resolve, Lloyd George (with Grey's permission) made a famous speech at the Lord Mayor of London's banquet at the Mansion House, warning the Germans that Britain would not stand by and be taken advantage of 'where her interests were vitally affected'. Eventually, the gunboat was removed, and the Germans agreed to recognize the French protectorate over Morocco in return for two strips of territory in the French Congo.

This was seen as a further triumph for the Anglo-French Entente, but in Germany public opinion became intensely anti-British. Inevitably, the French and British were driven into closer co-operation; a joint naval strategy was discussed, and to ease the burden on both, it was agreed (1912) that the British fleet would patrol the Atlantic and the Channel while the French would concentrate on the Mediterranean. The French pressed for a definite written alliance with Britain, but Grey felt unable to agree for fear of committing Britain irrevocably against Germany.

5 *The Balkan Wars. The First Balkan War (1912)* began when Serbia, Greece, Montenegro and Bulgaria (calling themselves the Balkan League) attacked Turkey and captured most of her remaining territory in Europe. All the great powers felt their interests were threatened: the Russians were afraid of the Bulgarians taking Constantinople, the Austrians feared that Serbia would become too powerful, and the Germans thought that their hopes of controlling Turkey via the railway to Baghdad would be disappointed if the Balkan states became too powerful and the Turkish Empire collapsed. Grey seized the opportunity to show that Britain and Germany could still work together; *a peace conference met in London,* where it was decided which territories the Balkan states should take from Turkey. The Serbs were not pleased with the outcome, since they wanted Albania, which would give them an outlet to the sea; but the Austrians, with German and British support, insisted that Albania should become an independent state. This was yet another attempt by Austria to prevent Serbia from becoming too strong.

The Bulgarians were also dissatisfied: they were hoping for Macedonia, but most of it was given to Serbia. *Bulgaria therefore attacked Serbia, starting the Second Balkan War (1913),* but her plan misfired when Greece, Romania and Turkey rallied to support Serbia. The Bulgarians were defeated, and by *the Treaty of Bucharest,* lost most of their gains from the first war. Grey was pleased with the outcome, feeling that joint British and German influence had prevented an escalation of the wars by restraining the Austrians, who were itching to attack Serbia.

Unfortunately Grey did not realize at the time the seriousness of the consequences:

▸ Serbia had been strengthened and was now determined to stir up the Serbs and Croats inside the Austrian Empire; war between Austria and Serbia was only a matter of time.
▸ Turkey was now so weak that it fell more and more under German influence.
▸ The Germans took Grey's willingness to co-operate as a sign that he was ready to be detached from France and Russia.

6 *The naval race was still continuing.* From time to time, the British proposed a joint slow-down in the naval building programme. In 1911, shortly after Agadir, Haldane went to Berlin, but while the Kaiser expressed an interest in a slow-down, he wanted Britain to promise not to intervene again in disputes between Germany and another state. This, of course, Haldane could not

map **21.2 The Balkans in 1913, showing changes of territory after the Balkan Wars (1912–13)**

accept. The British tried again in 1912 and in 1913, hoping that their joint action during the Balkan Wars would encourage the Germans to co-operate. Churchill proposed that there should be a 'naval holiday', during which all building of warships should stop; the Germans declined. However, right through 1913, Anglo-German relations were good. According to A. J. P. Taylor, the naval rivalry had lost its bitterness: 'the British had come to tolerate the German navy and were outstripping it without undue financial strain.'

In June, an Anglo-German agreement was reached over a possible partition of the Portuguese colonies of Mozambique and Angola, which were being badly ruled by the mother country. In the words of G. R. Searle, 'the Anglo-German relationship appeared almost sunny'.

7 *The assassination of the Austrian Archduke Franz Ferdinand in Sarajevo (28 June 1914) was the event that sparked off the war.* The Archduke was the nephew and heir to the Habsburg Emperor Franz Josef. Against all advice, he paid a visit to Sarajevo, the Bosnian capital. He and his wife were shot dead by a Serb terrorist, Gavrilo Princip. The Austrians blamed the Serbian government and sent them a stiff ultimatum. The Serbs accepted most of the points in it, and the Austrian government, its armies unprepared for war, was divided about whether to take military action or not. However, with German encouragement and promises of support, the Austrians declared war on Serbia (28 July). The Russians, determined not to let the Serbs down this time, ordered a general mobilization (29 July). The German government demanded that this should be cancelled (31 July), and when the Russians failed to comply, Germany declared war on Russia (1 August) and on France (3 August). When German troops entered Belgium on their way to invade France, Britain, who had promised (in 1839) to defend Belgian neutrality, demanded their withdrawal. When the Germans ignored this, Britain entered the war (4 August). Austria-Hungary declared war on Russia on 6 August, and other countries joined later.

(d) what caused the war?

It is clear that the Austrian quarrel with Serbia precipitated the outbreak of war. Austria was genuinely afraid that if Serbia acquired Bosnia (which contained about three million Serbs), all the other Serbs and Croats living inside the Habsburg Empire would want to join Serbia; other national groups such as Czechs, Poles and Italians would be encouraged to demand independence, and the result would be the collapse of the multinational Habsburg Empire. For the Austrians, it was an essential 'preventive' war.

It is more difficult to explain why this should have escalated into a major war, and historians have still not managed to agree. Some blame Russia, the first country to order a general mobilization; some blame Germany for making Austria more aggressive with her promises of support; and some blame the British for not making it clear that they would support France; this, it is argued, might have dissuaded the Germans from declaring war on France. Many other reasons have been suggested, and some have been rejected by other historians.

1 *The existence of the two opposing alliance systems or armed camps is thought by some to have made war inevitable.* The blocs were:

  › *The Triple Alliance* – Germany, Austria-Hungary and Italy; and
  › *The Triple Entente* – Britain, France and Russia.

But these had not proved binding earlier – Britain and France had not supported Russia during the Bosnia Crisis and Austria-Hungary kept aloof from Germany during the Agadir Crisis. Italy, though a member of the Triple Alliance, entered the war *against* Germany in 1915. It is just as arguable that the existence of two fairly evenly balanced power blocs acted as a deterrent to war during the 20 years before 1914.

2 *Colonial rivalry.* This had caused friction in the past, but in 1914 there were no specific quarrels; as late as June 1914, Britain and Germany had reached agreement about the future of the Portuguese colonies in Africa.

3 *Anglo-German naval rivalry.* This was probably no longer a major cause of friction, since, as Winston Churchill pointed out, 'it was certain that we (Britain) could not be overtaken as far as capital ships were concerned'.

4 *Economic rivalry.* It has been argued that the desire for economic mastery of the world caused German businessmen to want war with Britain. However, Germany was already well on the way to economic victory; one leading German industrialist remarked in 1913: 'Give us three or four more years of peace and Germany will be the unchallenged economic master of Europe'. The last thing they needed was a war.

More plausible suggestions are:

1 *The Russians should bear some responsibility for the escalation of the war.* They were deeply worried about the Balkans, where both Bulgaria and Turkey were under close German influence. Russian existence depended on the free passage of merchant ships through the Dardanelles, and this now seemed threatened. Once Austria declared war on Serbia, the Russians felt they must mobilize. There was also the need to maintain Russian prestige as leader of the Slavs. The Russian Tsar, Nicholas II, though not exactly relishing the prospect of war, nevertheless was well aware that it could be useful to divert the public's attention away from domestic problems. On the other hand, they must also have been aware that involvement in a major war would be a gamble that would put a severe strain on the country and the tsarist regime.

2 *German backing for Austria was vitally important.* In 1913, Germany had restrained the Austrians from attacking Serbia, yet in 1914 the Kaiser egged them on and promised unconditional German help – the so-called 'blank cheque'. This could mean that the Germans now felt ready for war and wanted to get on with it, for one of two reasons:

> ‣ either because they were set on world domination, as the German historian Fritz Fischer suggested. (He based his theory partly on evidence from the diary of Admiral von Müller, who wrote about a 'war council' held on 8 December 1912; at this meeting, General von Moltke remarked: 'I believe war is unavoidable; war the sooner the better'.); or

▶ because they felt encircled and threatened by British naval power and by the Russian military build-up. In this case, a preventive war, a war for survival, was necessary before the end of 1914. After that, they thought, the Russians would be too strong.

3   *The mobilization plans of the great powers were blamed by A. J. P. Taylor.* He believed that there was very little evidence to show that Germany deliberately timed the war for August 1914, and suggested that all the countries involved became the victims of their own mobilization plans and timetables, and of the belief that the opening battles would be the decisive ones – as had been the case in the Balkan Wars. The German *Schlieffen Plan* assumed that, in the event of war, France would automatically join Russia; therefore the bulk of the German forces were to be sent through Belgium to knock France out in six weeks, after which they would be rushed across Europe by train to face Russia. Once Moltke, the German Commander-in-Chief, knew that Russia had ordered a general mobilization, he demanded immediate German mobilization, which, under the Schlieffen Plan, required German troops to enter Belgium. The Kaiser suggested a partial mobilization, just against Russia, hoping that Britain would stay neutral if Germany refrained from attacking France. But Moltke insisted on the full plan; he said there was no time to change all the railway timetables to send the troop trains to Russia instead of to Belgium. This suggests that, even if Britain had announced on 31 July that it would definitely support France, it would have made no difference: it was the full Schlieffen Plan or nothing, even though Germany at that point had no specific quarrel with France.

However, in 2002, doubt was cast on the Schlieffen Plan theory by American historian Terence Zuber, who argued that the Schlieffen Plan was only one of about five alternatives being considered by the German High Command. He concludes that Schlieffen had never committed himself to one particular plan: he thought that if there was a war in the west it would be started by a French attack on Germany, and never intended that the Germans should take the offensive against France first. According to Zuber, it was only after the war that the Germans tried to blame their defeat on the rigidity of the so-called Schlieffen Plan, which had, in fact, never existed in the form they tried to suggest.

Whatever the truth, it is clear that, as Fritz Fischer claimed in 1961, Germany must take much of the responsibility for the war. For years, the Kaiser's aggressive attitude had alarmed Britain, France and Russia, and given the impression that Germany wanted to dominate Europe. Her encouragement of Austria and the invasion of Belgium were vital factors. The decision for war had probably been taken as early as 1912 at the infamous 'war council'. Some West German historians were not happy with Fischer's interpretation. H. W. Koch pointed out that the meeting was not a proper war council, since

Chancellor Bethmann-Hollweg and other ministers were not present. In fact, as soon as Bethmann-Hollweg discovered what had happened he cancelled all the 'decisions' that had been taken. According to John Charmley, writing in 1999, this suggests three things about the German leadership: 'that the military were quite prepared to go to war – but that the politicians remained firmly against it, and that they were in control'.

At the time of writing, the majority of historians, including many Germans, accept Fritz Fischer's theory as the most convincing one: that the outbreak of the war was deliberately provoked by Germany's leaders. In a collection of essays edited by Richard Hamilton and Holger Herwig (2002), Herwig argues that the Kaiser, his advisers and his generals believed that time was running out for them as Russia's armament plans neared completion, or so they thought. The German leaders gambled on a victorious war, in the words of von Moltke, 'in order to fulfil Germany's preordained role in civilization', which could 'only be done by way of war'.

(e) why did Britain enter the war?

The immediate British instinct on the outbreak of war was to remain neutral. The public knew little about Serbia, and Britain did not seem to be threatened directly. The prospect of a war with Germany dismayed many people in Britain. Businessmen knew that Germany was Britain's second largest customer, after India, and that Britain obtained a wide range of raw materials and manufactured goods from Germany which would be difficult to obtain elsewhere; these included pig-iron, steel, glass and sugar-beet. In addition, there were close commercial and financial relationships with British finance houses providing capital for German industry. Nothing could be worse for the economies of both nations than a major war. There was considerable admiration in Britain for German achievements – her scientists, philosophers, writers and musicians. Anglo-German ties were also strengthened, as G. R. Searle points out, by the fact that 'so many Britons and Germans were studying at each other's universities – among them the young Germans at Oxford who were being funded by Rhodes scholarships'. Indeed, Britain possibly enjoyed a greater variety of contacts with Germany than with any other country, particularly in all matters affecting social policy.

Sir Edward Grey was in a difficult situation because the majority of the Liberal Cabinet wanted to avoid war. Grey hoped to limit the conflict as he had during the Balkan Wars; he tried to organize a conference to discuss Serbia, but the Germans refused. Grey then warned the Germans not to count on British neutrality and warned the French and Russians not to count on British help. This did not prevent Germany declaring war on Russia (1 August) and then on France (3 August). Events moved so quickly that there was no time for negotiation.

- *Defence of Belgium?* It was the German invasion of Belgium, on the way to attack France, that convinced a majority of the Cabinet that war was unavoidable. Grey sent an ultimatum to the Germans, warning them to withdraw. Britain had promised in the 1839 Treaty of London, along with France and Prussia, to guarantee the neutrality of Belgium. When the ultimatum was ignored, Britain declared war on Germany (4 August). Only two ministers resigned.

- *Though the defence of Belgium was given as the official reason for Britain's entry, there was more to it than that.* There was the moral obligation to the French; having given them solid diplomatic support since 1904, to desert them in their hour of greatest need would have damaged Britain's international prestige.

- Probably more important, a German victory would endanger Britain's trading interests and ruin the balance of power in Europe. As Asquith wrote: 'It is against Britain's interests that France should be wiped out as a great power … We cannot allow Germany to use the Channel as a hostile base.' *The real reason for Britain's entry was therefore the need to resist German domination of Europe.* The attack on Belgium was convenient, because it enabled Grey to unite the Liberals and so bring Britain into the war as early as possible.

- A rather different reason for Britain's entry to the war was put forward by K. M. Wilson. He argued that both Grey and Lansdowne, his Conservative predecessor, considered the security of the British Empire, and particularly India, as their main concern. Since Russia was the main threat to India, it was vitally important to maintain the cordial relations that had begun with the 1907 agreement. When Austria declared war on Serbia (28 July), it was clear to the Russians that they must help Serbia, and that this would involve them in war with Germany. Consequently, the Russians were anxious for British support and they informed the British ambassador that, unless help was forthcoming, 'your friendship is valueless, and we shall act on that assumption in the future'. This was taken as a veiled threat to India and was treated seriously by the Foreign Office; officials admitted that India was the part of the Empire most vulnerable to attack from Russia, and therefore India is 'our main concern'. In the words of K. M. Wilson, '*it was this Russian blackmail, on imperial issues,* rather than considerations to do with the balance of power in Europe or with obligations to Belgium, which swung Asquith and Grey in their turn into blackmailing their non-interventionist colleagues with their resignations if Britain did not participate in the war' [emphasis in original].

(f) should Britain have stayed neutral?

In spite of all the compelling arguments in support of Britain's entry into the war, it is possible to make a strong case for neutrality, as indeed Niall Ferguson has done. He suggests that there was a fundamental flaw in Fritz Fischer's theory – the assumption that Germany was aiming for world domination. In fact, the Germans were so anxious to secure Britain's neutrality that, on 29 July, Bethmann told the ambassador that he was prepared to guarantee the territorial integrity of both France and Belgium in return for British neutrality; there were no plans for German control of the Belgian and French Channel coast. Would Germany's limited war aims have posed a direct threat to British interests? 'Hardly,' concludes Ferguson. 'Germany's European project was not one with which Britain, with her maritime empire intact, could not have lived.' Of course, the problem with Bethmann's offer was that it made Germany's plan to attack France obvious, and came at the time that both France and Russia were pressing Grey to make Britain's position clear. Grey, still trying to keep both sides guessing, rejected the German offer. But there was no real risk of a German invasion of Britain –British naval superiority was far too great for that, and there is no evidence that the Germans had serious thoughts about trying.

And so the debate continues. A recent writer, Andrew Roberts (2006), disagrees totally with Ferguson, partly because he pays too little attention to the attitudes of the Kaiser himself. Roberts believes that, while Bethmann might have been a moderate, Kaiser Wilhelm II wanted nothing less than a German-dominated Continent, what Wilhelm himself later called 'a United States of Europe under German leadership'. According to Roberts, if the British had remained neutral, 'they would have faced the bleak prospect of being isolated, dishonoured and with an implacable foe's huge battle fleet in the Channel ports'. In these circumstances, a victorious Germany 'would ultimately have posed a mortal danger to Britain's continued existence as an independent power'.

Wilson's theory that Britain entered the war in order to protect India is difficult to sustain. If that *was* the real reason for Britain's entry, it can be seen as somewhat exaggerated. Russia was going to be far too preoccupied fighting Germany to be able to think seriously about attacking India. And even if the Russians did threaten India, the British, neutral in the European struggle, would have had no difficulty in concentrating all their forces in the defence of India.

Grey has often been accused of being too indecisive, and of not making it clear that Britain would support France. But this is probably unfair. It was hardly possible for him to have acted differently, because the Cabinet was not united in favour of intervention until the last minute, and even then two leading members resigned. One thing is certain – the Cabinet was extremely reluctant to commit Britain to war. They tried to console themselves with the thought that Britain's contribution would be mainly naval. Grey told the Commons on 3 August: 'if we engage in war, we shall suffer but little more than we shall suffer if we stand aside'. As he looked gloomily out of the Foreign Office window late on the evening of 4 August, he made his most memorable remark: 'The lamps are going out all over Europe; we shall not see them lit again in our lifetime.'

1 'Ulster will fight and Ulster will be right'. Why was Unionist opposition to Irish Home Rule so strong during the period 1906–14, and to what extent was this responsible for the Liberals' failure to find a solution to the Irish problem before 1914?

2 How far can it be argued that Sir Edward Grey was a successful Foreign Secretary in the period 1906 to 1914?

A document question about the suffragettes can be found on the accompanying website www.palgrave.com/masterseries/lowe1.

chapter 22

Britain, the First World War and its aftermath

summary of events

the two opposing sides in the war were:

The Allies or Entente Powers	*The Central Powers*
Britain and the Empire	Germany
France	Austria-Hungary
Russia (left December 1917)	Turkey (entered November 1914)
Japan	Bulgaria (entered October 1915)
Italy (entered May 1915)	
Serbia	
Belgium	
Romania (entered August 1916)	
USA (entered April 1917)	

Most people in Britain, and certainly the Germans, thought the war would only last a matter of weeks. In Britain, there was a general feeling that 'it would all be over by Christmas'. But Lord Kitchener, the newly appointed Secretary for War, was not so sure; he dismayed the Cabinet by telling them that it would last nearer three years than three months. Once the German Schlieffen Plan had failed to achieve the rapid defeat of France, Kitchener was proved right. Though the Germans penetrated deeply, Paris did not fall, and *stalemate quickly developed on the Western Front,* with all hope of a short war gone. Both sides dug themselves in and spent the next four years attacking and defending lines of trenches which were difficult to capture because the increased fire-power provided by magazine rifles and machine-guns made frontal attacks suicidal and rendered cavalry useless. The British, desperately looking for a way to break the stalemate, *opened up a new front by attacking Turkey at the Dardanelles (1915);* but everything went wrong and the troops had to be withdrawn.

In eastern Europe there was more movement, with Russian successes against the Austrians, who constantly had to be helped out by the Germans, causing friction between the two allies. But by December 1917, the Germans had captured Poland (which was Russian territory) and forced the defeated Russians out of the war. Britain, suffering heavy losses of merchant ships through submarine attacks, and France, whose armies were paralysed by mutiny, seemed on the verge of defeat.

Gradually, the tide turned; the Allies, helped by the entry of the USA in April 1917, wore the Germans down. The last despairing German attempt at a decisive breakthrough in France failed in the spring of 1918. The success of the British navy in blockading German ports and defeating the submarine threat by defending merchant convoys, was also telling on the Germans. By the late summer of 1918, they were nearing exhaustion. An armistice was signed on 11 November 1918, although Germany itself had scarcely been invaded. A controversial peace settlement was signed at Versailles the following year.

The war had important effects on the political and social scene in Britain, causing the resignation of Asquith; the end of the Liberal government and the fatal split in the Liberal Party; the move to coalition governments; and the remarkable premiership of Lloyd George, remembered by many as 'the man who won the war'.

main political changes during the war

May 1915	End of the Liberal government. Asquith forms coalition, bringing Conservative leaders and Henderson (Labour leader) into government. Lloyd George becomes Minister of Munitions.
July 1916	Lloyd George becomes Secretary for War after death of Kitchener.
December 1916	Asquith resigns and Lloyd George becomes Prime Minister of second coalition government.
August 1917	Labour leader Henderson resigns from government after disagreements with Lloyd George.
May 1918	Maurice debate shows seriousness of Liberal split as 98 Liberals vote against government.
December 1918	Lloyd George's coalition wins landslide victory in 'coupon' election. He remains in power until October 1922, when Conservatives withdraw support.

(a) the British Expeditionary Force (BEF)

This was quickly mobilized under the command of Sir John French and sent to join the French army at Maubeuge. It was extremely small – only four divisions, compared with seventy French and seventy-two German divisions, but it made an important contribution towards slowing down the German push towards Paris. The Schlieffen Plan had already been held up by unexpectedly strong Belgian resistance, and it took the Germans over two weeks to capture Brussels. This was a vital delay, giving the French time to make full preparations, and leaving the Channel ports free for the BEF to land. Instead of sweeping around in a wide arc, capturing the Channel ports and approaching Paris from the west, the Germans found themselves making straight for Paris just east of the city. They penetrated to within twenty miles of the capital, and the French government withdrew to Bordeaux. But the nearer they got to Paris, the more the German impetus slowed up; there were problems in keeping the armies supplied with food and ammunition, and the troops became exhausted by long marches in the August heat.

› *The first British engagement took place at Mons (23 August),* where the BEF suddenly found itself in the path of the advancing German 1st Army under von Kluck. The British distinguished themselves by fighting back the Germans, who had been surprised to encounter any British troops. However, when the French army retreated to the River Marne, the British had no alternative but to move with them.
› *At the Battle of the Marne (September 1914),* the French under Joffre attacked the wilting Germans and drove them back to the River Aisne, where the Germans were able to dig trenches. The British played a valuable supporting role and suffered only a few casualties. The battle was vitally important; some historians have called it one of the most decisive in modern history. It ruined the Schlieffen Plan once and for all; France would not be knocked out in six weeks; hopes of a short war were dashed, and the Germans would have to face full-scale war on two fronts. The war of movement was over; the trench lines eventually stretched from the Channel coast to the Alps and there was time for the British navy to bring its crippling blockade to bear on German ports.
› *The BEF was suddenly moved northwards into Flanders* to protect Ypres from the German advance following their capture of Antwerp. In the bloody *First Battle of Ypres (October–November 1914),* the British managed to hang on to the city, though it proved to be a vulnerable point right through the war. This British success probably saved the Channel ports of Dunkirk, Calais and Boulogne, making it possible to land and supply more British troops. This is

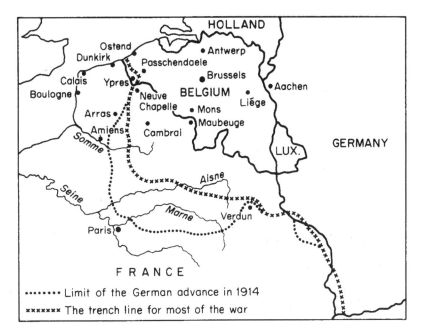

Holland

Ostend
Dunkirk
Calais
Boulogne
Arras
Amiens
Somme
Seine
Paris

• Antwerp
Passchendaele
• Brussels
Ypres
Neuve
Chapelle
• Mons
Cambrai
Maubeuge

BELGIUM
• Liège
• Aachen

LUX.

GERMANY

Aisne
Marne
Verdun

F R A N C E

•••••• Limit of the German advance in 1914
×××××× The trench line for most of the war

map **22.1 The Western Front**

usually taken to mark the end of the BEF. Casualties were extremely high at Ypres; over half the force was wounded and about one-tenth killed. For its size, it made a remarkable contribution to the early stages of the war. Von Kluck paid it the highest compliment, claiming that it was British resistance that had prevented him from taking Paris.

Niall Ferguson draws the conclusion from all this that if the BEF had never been sent, 'there is no question that the Germans would have won the war. Even if they had been checked at the Marne, they would almost certainly have succeeded in overcoming the French army in the absence of substantial British reinforcements'. The war would indeed have been over by Christmas, since there would have been little point in Britain continuing the fight once France had been eliminated. This opens up a whole series of fascinating consequences. 'Had Britain stood aside,' argues Ferguson, 'continental Europe could have been transformed into something not wholly unlike the European Union we know today – but without the massive contraction in British overseas power entailed by the fighting in two world wars'. Perhaps the revolutions in Russia would not have occurred, so there would have been no Communism, and with Germany victorious, no Third Reich either, and no Second World War. British participation in the war, which could have been over in a matter of weeks, therefore prolonged the conflict over four years, with all the extra death and destruction that entailed, and ultimately brought about the defeat of the Germans and their humiliation at Versailles. 'The historian is bound to ask,' concludes Ferguson, 'if acceptance of a German victory on the continent would have been as damaging to British interests as Grey claimed at the time, and as the majority of historians have subsequently accepted. The answer suggested here is that it would not have been ... The First World War was something worse than a tragedy ... It was nothing less than the greatest *error* of modern history.'

(b) Kitchener raises a new army but runs out of ideas

Kitchener decided that Britain needed an army of seventy divisions, and since Asquith refused to introduce conscription (compulsory military service), Kitchener mounted a propaganda campaign to encourage volunteers. Soon Britain was bristling with huge posters of Kitchener pointing his finger, and the words: 'Your country needs You'. The response was amazing: 10,000 men volunteered within a few days, and by mid-September the total was 500,000. By the end of February 1915, a further 500,000 had been recruited. The dominions sprang to the call – Canada and Australia sent 30,000 men each and New Zealand 8,500.

Having arrived at the front, the new troops found that they could make no headway against the German trench lines. The stalemate on the Western Front continued throughout 1915, though several attempts were made to break through. The British tried at *Neuve Chapelle in March 1915 and at Loos (September)*, where they suffered heavy casualties. The Germans attacked again in Flanders *at the Second Battle of Ypres (April–May)*, but all attempts failed. *The reasons for these continued failures right through until 1918 were always the same*:

‣ There was no chance of a surprise attack because a massive artillery bombardment always preceded the infantry attack to clear the barbed wire away from no-man's-land between the two lines of trenches, and generally to soften up the enemy.
‣ Reconnaisance aircraft and observation balloons could spot troop concentrations on the roads leading up to the trenches.
‣ Even when a trench line was breached, advance was difficult because the ground had been churned up by the artillery barrage and there was deadly machine-gun fire to contend with.

   Any ground won was difficult to defend, since it usually formed a *salient* or bulge in the trench line; the flanks of a salient were always vulnerable.
‣ Another method of attack that turned out to be unpredictable was the use of poison gas. The Germans used it at Ypres, but when the wind changed direction it was blown back towards their own lines and they suffered more casualties than the Allies, especially when the Allies released some gas of their own.

Nevertheless, when all possible allowances have been made, it seems clear that Sir John French was not an outstanding commander. He was therefore replaced by Sir Douglas Haig. But French was not the only one to find himself at a loss in these new conditions: Kitchener commented to Grey: 'I don't know what is to be done. This isn't war.'

(c) the Eastern Front

The Russians, having mobilized more quickly than the Germans expected, made the mistake of invading both Austria and East Prussia at the same time, though they were successful against Austria, occupying the province of Galicia. The Germans called Hindenburg out of retirement and twice defeated the Russians *at Tannenberg (August 1914) and the Masurian Lakes (September)*, driving them out of Germany. Worse was to come: in 1915, the Germans occupied Poland, and the Turks began to blockade the Dardanelles, severing the most convenient supply lines to the Russians and hampering their import and export trade.

(d) the Gallipoli (Dardanelles) Campaign (1915)

This was launched by the British partly to open up the vital supply lines to Russia. It was an idea strongly pressed by Winston Churchill (First Lord of the Admiralty) to escape the deadlock in the west by eliminating the Turks, who were thought to be the weakest of the Central Powers because of their unstable government. Success against Turkey would enable help to be sent to Russia and might also bring Bulgaria, Romania and Greece into the war on the allied side; it would then be possible to attack Austria from the south.

The campaign was a total failure. The first attempt, in March, was an Anglo-French naval attack through the Straits to capture Constantinople; this failed because the Turks had laid lines of mines across the channel. This ruined the surprise element, so that when the British attempted landings at the tip of the Gallipoli peninsula, the Turks had strengthened their defences and no advance could be made (April). Further landings by Australian and New Zealand troops (Anzacs) in April, and by the British in August were equally useless and positions could be held only with great difficulty. In December the entire force was withdrawn.

The consequences were serious: besides being a blow to Allied morale, it turned out to be the last chance of relieving Russia via the Black Sea and probably caused Bulgaria to join the Central Powers. A Franco-British force landed at Salonika in neutral Greece to try to relieve Serbia, but it was too late. When Bulgaria entered the war in October, Serbia was quickly overrun by Bulgarians and Germans. The year 1915 therefore was not a good one for the Allies: casualties at Gallipoli had been heavy: 250,000 wounded and 43,000 British, Australians and New Zealanders dead.

On the other hand, Turkish losses were even heavier, and the Turkish army probably never fully recovered. So, arguably, Gallipoli weakened the Turks and made possible the later British victories against them in Palestine in 1917. But this was very much in the future, and there were more British disasters to come before then. A British army sent to protect Anglo-Persian oil interests found itself surrounded by Turks at *Kut-el-Amara in Mesopotamia.* After a siege lasting from December 1915 until April 1916, General Townshend surrendered with 12,000 men, of whom some 8,000 later died in the dismal conditions of the Turkish prison camps.

(e) the Battle of the Somme (1916)

This was the major operation involving the British on the Western Front in 1916. In February, the Germans, under Falkenhayn, launched *a massive attack on the French fortress town of Verdun,* but the French defended stubbornly. It was partly to relieve pressure on the French that Haig decided to attack the German lines near the River Somme; he also hoped that by keeping the Germans fully committed, they would be unable to risk sending any more troops to the Eastern Front against Russia. The campaign began on 1 July, with disastrous results: the preliminary artillery bombardment failed both to destroy the barbed wire in no-man's-land and to soften up the Germans, who merely waited in heavily fortified dugouts. When the British troops left their trenches, under orders to advance at a slow walking pace, many were caught up in the wire and all came under murderous German machine-gun fire. *21,000 were killed and over 35,000 wounded on the first day, with no gains to show for it.* Yet incredibly, Haig continued with these attacks until November.

Illus. 22.1 **A British trench during the Battle of the Somme, 1916**

At the end of it all, the Allies had made only limited advances, varying between a few hundred yards and seven miles along a thirty-mile front. *The real importance of the battle was the blow to German morale* as they realized that Britain (where conscription was introduced for the first time in May 1916) was a military power to be reckoned with. Losses on both sides, killed or wounded, were appalling (Germans, 650,000; British, 418,000, French, 194,000), and Haig came under severe criticism for persisting with suicidal frontal attacks. However, they probably helped to wear down the German armies: Hindenburg himself admitted in his *Memoirs* that the Germans could not have survived many more campaigns like Verdun and the Somme. The Somme also contributed to the fall of the Prime Minister, Asquith; as criticisms of British tactics mounted, Asquith resigned and was replaced by Lloyd George.

(f) Asquith's failings as a war leader

Asquith had been a competent peace-time Prime Minister, handling many problems well, particularly the clash with the House of Lords. However, his 'wait and see' attitude to the Irish and suffragette problems was not a good omen for his performance during the war. Unfortunately, he continued his detached approach after hostilities had started. He believed it was the generals' job to run the war and was most reluctant to interfere, even when French turned out to be incompetent, and when there was a serious shortage of shells in 1915. There was a complete lack of urgency in all departments just at the time when decisive leadership was needed. As A .J. P. Taylor put it: 'Asquith was as solid as a rock, but like a rock, incapable of movement.' In May 1915, Asquith tried to counter the growing criticism by bringing some leading Conservatives – Bonar Law, Lansdowne, Balfour, Carson and Lord Curzon – together with the Labour Party leader, Arthur Henderson, into the Cabinet. This was the end of a purely Liberal government (the last Liberal government, as it turned out), and the beginning of government by coalition.

Asquith's most important move was *the appointment of Lloyd George as Minister of Munitions.* He soon emerged as the outstanding member of the Cabinet, his vigour and panache contrasting sharply with Asquith's detachment and lack of energy. After Kitchener's death (he was drowned on his way to Russia when his ship, the *Hampshire,* struck a mine), Lloyd George took his place as Secretary for War (July 1916). Relations between Asquith and Lloyd George deteriorated steadily, the introduction of conscription being the main area of dispute. Lloyd George felt it was the only way to win the war, but Asquith was totally opposed, believing it to be against all Liberal principles. As news of the terrible casualties on the Somme became known, moves began to oust Asquith and replace him with Lloyd George. Asquith was manoeuvred into resigning, much against his will, and Lloyd George became Prime Minister of another coalition government (December 1916). However, he had the support of only about half of the Liberal MPs, the other half remaining loyal to Asquith. It was the Conservatives who had put Lloyd George into power, because he seemed to be the only man with sufficient drive to win the war for Britain.

22.2 Lloyd George at the helm

(a) Lloyd George as Minister of Munitions

Lloyd George immediately began to show, in his new job, as he had as Chancellor of the Exchequer, that he was a man who got things done instead of just talking about them. He sliced through all the official red tape in the most unconventional ways. He began by requisitioning a hotel to house his new ministry and appointed businessmen to important positions in the government, because he thought they were more decisive than politicians. He made sure that the supply of shells increased, and was responsible for the widespread adoption of the machine-gun. At the outbreak of war, the army had been totally unprepared; each battalion had only two machine-guns, which, in Haig's view, was 'more than sufficient'. Kitchener thought four would be a good idea, but the British Army School of Musketry had recommended six. Lloyd George is reputed to have said: 'Take Kitchener's figure. Square it. Multiply it by two. Then double it again for good luck.' This figure was achieved. There were two further occasions on which Lloyd George superseded Kitchener (who was still Secretary for War):

› In January 1915, Wilfred Stokes demonstrated his new light mortar, but the War Office thought it was too dangerous. Lloyd George persuaded a wealthy Indian prince to finance the first thousand Stokes mortars and it soon proved to be one of the most effective weapons of the war.
› Kitchener was apparently not impressed with the tank, which had been developed from an idea of Major E. D. Swinton, and first demonstrated in February 1916. Lloyd George was most enthusiastic, and the first order for forty tanks was placed.

Lloyd George was also behind the Munitions of War Act, giving the government power to take control of factories responsible for armaments and other war work. Strikes and lockouts were prohibited, and measures taken to combat drunkenness, so that the war effort would not be impaired. Most controversial of all, Lloyd George at last got his way over conscription, which was introduced in May 1916 and applied to all males aged 18 to 45.

This compulsion caused great protest on religious and moral grounds; the anti-conscription campaign was led by the No Conscription Fellowship (NCF) and its chairman, Clifford Allen. The Quakers issued a statement in which they declared: 'We believe that the man who regards military service as contrary to his deepest religious or moral conviction – a service which denies his sense of personal responsibility – is right in refusing obedience to the state.' Around 4,000 men declared themselves to be 'conscientious objectors' and refused to fight. Some were sent to do non-combatant work as drivers or stretcher-bearers; others, known as 'absolutists', refused to do even that. One absolutist, Howard Marten, was court-martialled and sentenced to death in June 1916, but his sentence was commuted to ten years' penal servitude. He later explained: 'It was more than just an objection to fighting. It was an objection to having one's life directed in that way by an outside authority.' There was support across a wide spectrum of society for such courageous stands; it was particularly strong among what Howard Marten called 'the aesthetic group: artists, musicians and all that'. Jonathan Atkin, for example, has shown how some, though by no means all, members of the so-called Bloomsbury Group of artists, writers and academics – G. L. Dickinson, Philip and Ottoline Morrell, Bertrand Russell, Clive Bell, Duncan Grant and Virginia Woolf, among others – were strongly pacifist. Bell described the war as 'purposeless horror'.

(b) Lloyd George as Prime Minister

Even after he became Secretary for War in July 1916, Lloyd George was prevented from doing all he wanted by the dithering Asquith. But as soon as he became Prime Minister, he began to run the country almost like a dictator. According to one of his biographers, K. O. Morgan, 'Lloyd George's war premiership was without parallel in British history. No previous Prime Minister had ever exercised power in so sweeping and dominating a manner.' Almost everything he did provoked controversy and offended somebody, but so great was the crisis facing the country that he was able to get away with it:

‣ He set up a small war Cabinet of five men – himself, Bonar Law (the Conservative leader), Curzon, Henderson (the Labour leader) and Milner (the former governor of Cape Colony) – which took all the main decisions. He appointed men from outside Parliament to head important ministries: Sir Joseph Maclay, a Glasgow ship-owner, made an excellent ship-building organizer; and Lord Beaverbrook, owner of *The Daily Express*, a brilliant Minister of Propaganda.

‣ He introduced the Cabinet Secretariat under Sir Maurice Hankey to organize Cabinet business. This was so successful in co-ordinating the different departments and their advisers that it was continued after the war. Lloyd George also had his own private secretariat and advisers, including Waldorf Astor, owner of *The Observer*. This was known as the 'Garden Suburb' because it met at first in huts in the garden behind No.10 Downing Street.

‣ More government controls than ever before were introduced. All merchant shipping was brought under government direction, to defeat the submarine threat. Farmers were ordered to cultivate extra land to meet the food shortages, factories were told what to produce (for example, army blankets and khaki cloth for uniforms), and the coal industry was taken directly under government control. The new Ministry of National Service decided which men would be called up, depending on whether their jobs were vital or could be done by women. Food was rationed and prices and wages controlled.

› Lloyd George was able to do less on the military side of the war. However, he was mainly responsible for the adoption of the convoy system (see Section 22.3(e)), which saved Britain from starvation in 1917. He disapproved of Haig's costly and unimaginative tactics, but could find nobody better to replace him. However, he did manage to have the French Marshal Foch appointed as Supreme Allied Commander on the Western Front, which reduced Haig's influence to some extent.

Unfortunately for Lloyd George and his future in politics, his policies, and the style in which he carried them out, made him many enemies. Asquith and his supporters never really forgave him for the way in which Asquith was removed from the premiership, thus causing a fatal split in the Liberal Party. Lloyd George has therefore been blamed for the decline of the Liberal Party; but it has to be said in his defence that, like Peel before him, he was never primarily a party man. For Lloyd George, the paramount aim was to win the war, not to preserve the Liberal Party. Most historians would agree that, if Asquith had remained Prime Minister for another year, Britain would have lost the war.

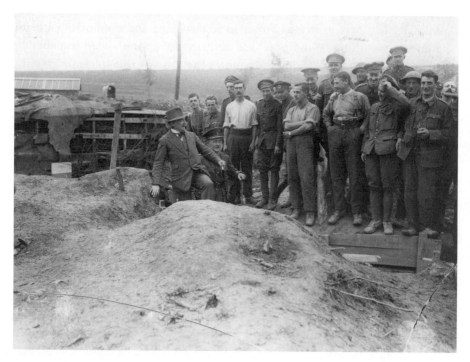

Illus. 22.2 Lloyd George on a visit to the front – talking to British soldiers

22.3 the war at sea

The general public in Germany and Britain expected a series of naval battles rather like the Battle of Trafalgar, in which the rival Dreadnought fleets would confront each other. But both sides were cautious and dare not risk any action which might result in the loss of their main fleets. The British Admiral Jellicoe was particularly careful; as Churchill pointed out, 'he was the only man on either side who could have lost the war in an afternoon'. Nor were the Germans anxious for a confrontation, because they only had thirteen of the latest Dreadnoughts against Britain's twenty.

(a) the Allied blockade and the Battle of the Falkland Islands

The Allies aimed to prevent goods entering or leaving the Central Powers, thus cutting off their trade and slowly starving them out. At the same time, trade routes had to be kept open between Britain, its Empire and the rest of the world, so that the Allies themselves would not starve. A third function of the navy was to transport British troops to the Continent and keep them supplied via the Channel ports. The British were successful in carrying out these aims, and they went into action against German units stationed abroad.

The most important battle in the early stages of the war took place off *the Falkland Islands (December 1914).* Admiral von Spee with a squadron of two cruisers and three light cruisers was about to bombard the Falklands when he was attacked by a much stronger British squadron (which included two battle-cruisers) commanded by Admiral Sturdee. The Germans were no match for the superior fire-power of the British battle-cruisers, and von Spee's entire squadron was destroyed. By the end of 1914, most of the German armed surface vessels had been sunk or badly damaged and the Falklands engagement made the Kaiser unwilling to lose any more ships. One fleet continued to block-ade the Baltic in order to cut off supplies to Russia, but the main German fleet did not venture out of port until the Battle of Jutland in 1916. The Kaiser had some idea of keeping his fleet intact as a bargaining counter in peace negotia-tions, and the British were happy with this situation which left them in control of the surface, though not of the submarines. The navy made an important contribution during 1915 to the Gallipoli campaign, though this was not one of its successes (see Section 22.1(d)).

(b) the Allied blockade causes problems

Britain was trying to prevent the Germans using the neutral Scandinavian and Dutch ports to break the blockade. This involved stopping and searching all neutral ships and confiscating any goods suspected of being intended for enemy hands. The USA objected strongly to this, being anxious to continue trading with both sides.

(c) the Germans retaliate with mines and submarine attacks

This was their only alternative, since their surface vessels had either been destroyed or were being blockaded in port. At first they respected neutral shipping and passenger liners, but it was soon clear that the German U-boat blockade was not effective, partly because they had insufficient U-boats, and partly because of problems of identification – the British tried to fool the Germans by flying neutral flags and by using passenger liners to transport arms and ammunition. In April 1915, the British liner *Lusitania* was sunk by a torpedo attack. In fact, the *Lusitania* was armed and carrying vast quantities of arms and ammunition, which the Germans knew all about; hence their claim that the sinking was not just an act of barbarism against defenceless civilians. *The sinking had important consequences:* out of the thousand dead, 118 were Americans. Woodrow Wilson, the US President, found that the USA would have to take sides to protect its trade. Whereas the British blockade did not interfere with the safety of passengers and crews, German tactics certainly did. For the time being, however, American protests made the Germans tone down their submarine campaign, making it even less effective.

(d) the Battle of Jutland (31 May 1916)

This was the only time in the war that the main battle-fleets emerged and engaged each other; the result was indecisive. The German Admiral von Scheer tried to lure part of the British fleet out from its base, so that section could be destroyed by the numerically superior Germans. However, more British ships came out than he had anticipated. After the two fleets had shelled each other on and off for several hours, the Germans decided to retire to base, firing torpedoes as they went. On balance, the Germans could claim that they had won the battle, since they lost only eleven ships to Britain's fourteen. But the real importance of the battle lay in the fact that the Germans had failed to destroy British sea power. The German High Seas Fleet stayed in Kiel for the rest of the war, leaving Britain's control of the surface complete. In desperation at the food shortages caused by the British blockade, the Germans embarked on a campaign of 'unrestricted' submarine warfare.

(e) 'unrestricted' submarine warfare (January 1917)

The Germans had been concentrating on the production of U-boats since the Battle of Jutland, and so this campaign was extremely effective. They attempted to sink all enemy and neutral merchant ships in the Atlantic, and although they knew that this was bound to bring the USA into the war, they hoped that Britain and France could be starved into surrender before the Americans was able to make any vital contribution. They almost did it: the peak of German success came in April 1917, when 430 ships were lost. Britain was down to about six weeks' supply of corn, and while the USA came into the war in April, it would be several months before their help became effective. However, the situation was saved by Lloyd George, who insisted that the Admiralty adopt the convoy system – a large number of merchant ships sailed together so that they could be protected by escorting warships. This reduced the losses dramatically, and the German gamble failed.

In an attempt to finish off the U-boat threat completely, the navy carried out daring raids on the captured Belgian ports of Ostend and Zeebrugge, which the Germans were using as submarine bases. On the night of 22 April 1918, under cover of smoke-screens, ships loaded with cement were brought in and sunk to block the exits from the ports. The operation at Zeebrugge was the more successful one, and although not as much damage was inflicted as had been hoped, Zeebrugge was rendered almost useless as a German base. This, together with extra defences at the Straits of Dover, made it almost impossible for the Germans to attack the Straits, and increasingly difficult for submarines to slip through.

The German 'unrestricted' submarine campaign was important because it brought the USA into the war. By mid-1918, the British navy, helped by the Americans and the Japanese, had achieved their three aims mentioned under section 22.3(a), above, and played a vitally important role in the defeat of the Central Powers.

22.4 Vimy Ridge to the armistice, 1917–18

(a) the failure to gain a negotiated peace

One reason why the war continued to drag on for so long, apart from the difficulties of breaking the stalemate of trench warfare and the fact that both sides were so evenly balanced, was the failure of all attempts at negotiation. By the summer of 1915, when it was clear that it would not be a short war, there were people on both sides who felt that the cost in men and money had already been too high, and that it should be possible for intelligent, civilized people to get together and negotiate peace terms that would be acceptable to both sides. After the terrible slaughter at Verdun and the Somme in 1916, several serious attempts were made to start negotiations, but all failed. The reasons were:

› There were people on both sides who thought outright victory was still possible. In Germany, the generals were more powerful than the politicians. Chancellor Bethmann-Hollweg was ready to negotiate, but General Ludendorff wanted to fight on.
› In Britain, Lord Lansdowne and the Labour Party were keen to negotiate, but Lloyd George was a hard-liner who still believed in the 'knock-out' blow.
› Negotiations would mean compromise, and neither side was prepared to make sufficient concessions. The Germans, for example, insisted on keeping some sort of control over Belgium and parts of Poland.

Woodrow Wilson tried all through 1916 to get talks started before the USA was drawn into the conflict. When Bethmann-Hollweg eventually agreed to talk in December 1916, Britain and France rejected the offer. They took it as a sign that Germany was weakening; it later emerged that German demands would have been too high in any case.

After the overthrow of Tsar Nicholas II in March 1917, the Russian socialists proposed 'peace without annexations or indemnities' and suggested a conference in Stockholm, to be attended by socialists from all the countries involved in the war. However, the British and French governments would not allow their socialists to attend. Henderson was told that he would be a traitor if he went, because he would have to talk to Germans. This was the major reason for Henderson's resignation from the government.

The Pope also proposed a peace conference (August 1917), but this came to nothing when the Germans refused to attend. The German generals had persuaded the Kaiser to dismiss Bethmann-Hollweg on the grounds that he was too weak. With that, all chances of a negotiated peace disappeared. The German armies were doing well at that point, and Russia was on the verge of collapse; Ludendorff was determined on a fight to the finish.

(b) limited Allied successes on the Western Front during 1917

In April, the Canadians captured Vimy Ridge, north of Arras. This was an impressive achievement, though at the time it was not followed up. In March 1918, allied possession of the ridge turned out to be a serious obstacle in the way of the German spring offensive. The allied campaign at Vimy was accompanied by a massive French offensive under their new commander, Nivelle, on the Aisne. It achieved absolutely nothing and provoked the French army to mutiny. Nivelle was replaced by Pétain, who calmed the situation successfully.

From June to November, the British fought *the Third Battle of Ypres*, usually remembered as *Passchendaele*, in appallingly muddy conditions. British casualties were enormous – 324,000 compared with 200,000 Germans for a four-mile advance. More significant was *the Battle of Cambrai*, which demonstrated that tanks, properly used, might break the deadlock of trench warfare; 381 massed British tanks made a wide breach in the German line, but lack of reserves prevented the success from being followed up.

However, the lesson had been observed: Haig belatedly realized that the best tactic was to stop the advance once a breach had been made in the German line, and to start another attack at a different point. The technique was therefore a series of short, sharp jabs instead of a prolonged push at one point. This avoided creating a vulnerable salient and would force the enemy to fall back at several points, eventually withdrawing the whole line.

Meanwhile, the Italians were heavily defeated by Germans and Austrians at *Caporetto (October 1917)* and retreated in disorder. Unexpectedly, this proved to be an important turning point. Italian morale revived, perhaps because they were faced with having to defend their homeland against the hated Austrians. The defeat also led to the setting up of an Allied Supreme War Council. The new French premier, Clemenceau, a great war leader in the Lloyd George mould, rallied the wilting French.

(c) the Eastern Front

Disaster struck the Allies when the Russians withdrew from the war (December 1917). Continuous defeat by the Germans, lack of arms and supplies in the right places and incompetent leadership caused two revolutions (March and November 1917), and Lenin and the Bolsheviks, who seized power in November, were willing to make peace. This meant that, in 1918, the entire weight of German forces could be thrown against the west; without the Americans, the Allies would have been hard pressed.

On the other hand, encouragement was provided by British victories against the Turks. More troops and supplies were sent out, and Kut was taken at the end of February 1917. The capture of Baghdad (March) encouraged the Arabs of Syria and Palestine to revolt against Turkish rule, which was an important reason for the Turkish defeat. The British supplied the Arabs with arms, and T. E. Lawrence (Lawrence of Arabia), an archaeologist working with the Arab bureau, helped to organize an Arab campaign which captured the port of Aqaba and ruined Turkish communications by constantly blowing up railway lines. Allenby captured Jerusalem (December 1917) and after a delay during the first half of 1918, when some of his forces were rushed to the Western Front to help stem the German spring offensive, he entered Damascus (October 1918). The way was clear to Constantinople, and the Turks signed an armistice with Britain on 30 October.

(d) the USA enters the war (April 1917)

This was provoked partly by the German U-boat campaign, and partly by the Zimmermann Telegram. This was sent in January 1917 by Arthur Zimmerman, the German Foreign Secretary, to the German Minister in Mexico; it contained proposals for an alliance between Germany and Mexico. With help from Germany, Mexico was to attack the USA, and would receive Texas, New Mexico and Arizona in return. This finally convinced the Americans that they had no choice but to enter the war against Germany. The Americans had also hesitated about siding with the autocratic Russian government, but the overthrow of the Tsar in the March revolution removed this obstacle. The USA made an important contribution to the Allied victory: they supplied Britain and France with food, merchant ships and credit. Actual military help came more slowly. By the end of 1917, only one American division had been in action, but by mid-1918 over half a million men were fighting. Most important was the psychological boost that the American potential in resources of men and materials gave the Allies, and the corresponding blow it struck to German morale.

(e) the German spring offensive (1918)

This was launched by Ludendorff in a last desperate attempt to win the war before too many US troops arrived, and before discontent in Germany led to revolution. It almost came off: throwing in all the extra troops released from the east, the Germans broke through on the Somme (March). By the end of May they were only forty miles from Paris, and the Allies seemed to be disintegrating. However, under the overall command of the French Marshal Foch, they managed to hold on as the German advance lost momentum and created an awkward bulge. Lloyd George, helped by Sir Joseph Maclay, organized the recall and transportation to the front of 88,000 British troops who were at home on leave, and others were brought from Palestine.

(f) the Allied counter-offensive

This began on 8 August 1918, near Amiens. With Haig using his new tactics, hundreds of tanks attacked in short, sharp jabs at many different points and forced the Germans to withdraw their entire line. Slowly but surely, the Germans were forced back until, by the end of September, the Allies were through the Hindenburg Line. Though Germany itself had not yet been invaded, Ludendorff was convinced that they would be defeated in the spring of 1919. He insisted that the German government ask President Wilson for an armistice (3 October), hoping to get less severe terms based on Wilson's fourteen points (see Section 22.6(a)). By asking for peace in 1918, he hoped to save Germany from invasion and preserve the army's reputation. Fighting continued for another five weeks, but eventually an armistice was signed on 11 November.

(g) why did Britain and its allies win the war?

The reasons can be summarized briefly:

1 Once the Schlieffen Plan had failed, removing all hope of a quick German victory, it was bound to be a strain on their resources. They had not intended to fight a long war, nor a war on two fronts.
2 Allied sea power was decisive, enforcing the crippling blockade that caused desperate food shortages, while at the same time keeping Allied armies fully supplied.
3 The German submarine campaign was defeated by the use of convoys protected by British, American and Japanese destroyers. The campaign itself was a mistake because it brought the USA into the war.
4 The entry of the USA brought the Allies vast new resources of men and materials.
5 Allied political leaders at the critical time – Lloyd George and Clemenceau – were arguably more competent than those of the Central Powers. The unity of command under Foch in 1918 probably helped, while Haig learned lessons from his 1917 experiences about the effective use of tanks and the

avoidance of salients. However, the performance of the British High Command has been the subject of some debate over the years. The traditional view was that, while British soldiers fought like lions, their generals were as stupid as donkeys – 'lions led by donkeys'. As recently as 1988, John Laffin wrote that the generals were 'butchers and bunglers'.

John Terraine was one of the first to present a defence of Haig (1963), and this was followed by Gary Sheffield (2001) who argues that, given the fact that the British had no experience of trench warfare, and that they were the junior partners to the French, Haig learned remarkably quickly and proved to be an imaginative and even visionary commander. Peter Hart (2008) believes that Haig has been denied the credit he deserves for the victorious operations of 1918; these, he argues, were 'a series of daring triumphs that smashed the seemingly eternal deadlock of the trenches'. However, there seems no escaping the fact, as Niall Ferguson points out (1998), that Haig *was* responsible for a number of serious mistakes. To mention just two: originally a cavalry officer, he took a great deal of convincing that mechanical warfare was the way forward, and later he ignored expert advice on how best tanks could be used. Second, before the Somme Offensive in 1916 he rejected Sir Henry Rawlinson's draft plan, which was to seize points of strategic importance and then wait for the Germans to counter-attack; he insisted that a breakthrough could be achieved by a massive assault; the result – 56,000 British casualties on the first day (1 July) compared with 8,000 suffered by the German defenders. Yet the offensive continued off and on until November!

6 The continuous strain of heavy losses told on the Germans – they lost their best troops in the 1918 offensive and the new troops were young and inexperienced. An epidemic of deadly Spanish 'flu did not help the situation, and morale was low as they retreated.

7 Germany was badly let down by its allies, and was constantly having to help out the Austrians and Bulgarians. The defeat of Bulgaria by the British (from Salonika) and Serbs (29 September 1918) was the final straw for many German soldiers, who could see no chance of victory after that. When Austria was defeated by Italy at Vittorio-Veneto, and Turkey surrendered (both in October), the end was near.

The combination of military defeat and dire food shortages produced a great war weariness, leading to mutiny in the navy, destruction of morale in the army and a revolution in Germany, which forced the Kaiser to abdicate (9 November).

22.5 effects of the war on British society

The whole question of the ways in which major wars have affected societies is a fascinating and a controversial one. Some historians believe that 'total' wars, like the First and Second World Wars, were bound to have profound effects on the countries involved. Arthur Marwick has made a special study of the ways in which these two major conflicts have affected British society. Although he concludes that the effects of the Second World War were more drastic, he nevertheless argues in his book *The Deluge: British Society and the First World War* (1973; second edition 1991) that the Great War had vitally important political, social and economic consequences for Britain. Derek Fraser goes along with this: 'The war quite simply swept away a whole world and created a new one,' he writes, 'and the Edwardian epoch became a vision of the distant past.' However, Martin Pugh, in *State and Society* (1994) is more cautious: 'On investigation,' he writes, 'many of the trends and innovations attributed to the great war turn out to be not so much the direct product of war as the outcome of long-term developments whose origins lie in the pre-1914 period.'

It is possible to find evidence to support both points of view. Some changes have to be seen in the context of long-term trends already well under way, which were perhaps accelerated by the war: the move towards more complete democracy in the 1918 Representation of the People Act falls into this category. Other changes do seem to have been largely the result of the war – the sudden decline of the Liberal Party may be the best example of this (though some historians believe that the party was already in terminal decline *before* the First World War).

(a) important effects on the political parties

The war sent the Liberal Party into a disastrous decline. The party had not enhanced its reputation with its fumbling conduct of the first nine months of war, and then came the split between the Lloyd George and Asquith supporters. The seriousness of the Liberal divisions was demonstrated in May 1918 in the House of Commons, during what was called the Maurice debate. General Maurice had accused the government of holding back army reserves at the critical moment when they were needed to stem the German spring offensive. Lloyd George defended himself and his government in a brilliant speech, but the opposition insisted on a vote being taken (the only time this happened during the entire war). Lloyd George won easily, having shown that Maurice's statistics were wrong, but 98 Liberals voted against the government. The split continued after the war was over, keeping the party fatally divided and demoralized.

This allowed the Labour Party to become the viable alternative opposition to the Conservatives. The war helped the Labour Party in other ways – it gave at least two of its members Cabinet experience and caused it finally to assert its independence from the Liberals. While he was a member of the War Cabinet, Henderson had more than once been offended by Lloyd George's high-handed attitude. He decided it was time for Labour to establish its identity as a separate party. He resigned from the government (August 1917) and gave Sidney

Webb the job of producing a new and attractive manifesto, *Labour and the New Social Order*, which included the following points:

- Common ownership of the means of production – nationalization of mines, iron, steel, railways, canals, armaments, shipping, gas, electricity and land; (this was the famous Clause 4).
- A statutory basic wage for men and women.
- Full employment, unemployment insurance and abolition of the Poor Law.
- The development of health services.
- A special tax on capital.
- Abolition of conscription.
- Freedom for Ireland and India.

Henderson himself was responsible for encouraging the formation of party organizations at constituency level (see Section 23.4 for a full discussion of the Liberal decline and the rapid rise of Labour).

The war also benefited the Conservative Party, which had been in such disarray before the war, after losing two elections in 1910 and having to concede the 1911 Parliament Act. As early as May 1915, some Conservatives were back in government after Liberal failures forced Asquith to form a coalition. The Liberal split meant that there was no strong party of the left or centre to oppose them. So dominant did they become that for the thirty years after 1915 there were only three years (1924 and 1929–31, when Labour was in power) when there were no Conservatives in the government.

(b) greater government intervention and control than ever before

Section 22.2(b) showed how there was much greater government control of industry and labour than had ever been known in Britain, and ordinary people found that the government interfered with their lives as never before:

- From May 1916, conscription meant that most men aged 18 to 45 were compelled to join the armed forces, and the age limit was later extended to 51. Consequently, the majority of wives were left struggling on inadequate army pay, while children often missed their father's discipline and there was an increase in child crime.
- Early in the war, trade unions were not happy about the regulations which prevented workers leaving jobs in munitions factories and other vital industries. However, Lloyd George won them over by guaranteeing reasonable minimum wages and by favouring firms that used union labour. This encouraged more workers to join trade unions, which generally enhanced their reputation, with their responsible attitude throughout the war. The unions did not have things all their own way, however; while strikes were illegal under the Munitions of War Act, there were several strikes, mainly about wage rates. In July 1918, during a strike of munitions workers in Coventry, Churchill, who

was now Minister of Munitions, gave them a choice – either return to work or be called up for military service; they returned to work. An important feature of the wartime industrial unrest, particularly in engineering and shipbuilding, was the emergence of a new type of union leadership – the shop-steward, who organized workers in individual factories and workshops.

▸ The food situation caused problems. At first there were no real shortages, but prices increased substantially: in June 1916, food prices on average were 59 per cent above the level of July 1914. Towards the end of 1916, supplies of imported goods began to dwindle and long queues formed outside shops. In some areas, local rationing schemes were started and worked extremely well. The government adopted the idea nationally in 1918, rationing meat (to one pound per head per week), sugar (half a pound), bacon, ham and jam. This eased the situation and the queues disappeared. One highly unpopular government policy was its interference with drinking habits. It was felt that much absenteeism from work was caused by drunkenness; in 1915, therefore, opening hours of public houses were restricted (normally from midday to 2.30 pm, and from 6.30 pm to 9.30 pm), and beer was made weaker and more expensive. Most of these changes came to an end when the war was over, but the 'afternoon gap' in public house opening hours survived into the 1990s.

(c) important steps forward in the emancipation of women

As more and more men joined the army, women began to fill the vacancies in a wide variety of jobs that had previously always been done by men. Girls worked in munitions factories, on farms and on the buses, railways and docks. Even more remarkably, women were to be found in the police, and as window cleaners, blacksmiths and quarry workers; some did very heavy work in gasworks and foundries, carrying sacks of coal and coke, and stoking furnaces. 'Many is the time,' recalled one lady, 'that the girls would be affected by the gas, the remedy being to walk them up and down in the fresh air and then [get them to] drink a bottle of Guinness.' Middle-class women went into banking and took clerical jobs in administration, commerce and education.

Many became nurses and worked both at home and in Europe, like Vera Brittain, who wrote a moving account of her experiences in *Testament of Youth*. Women had made such a vital contribution to the war effort that their whole position in society was changed. Many men were amazed at what women had proved themselves capable of, and women's confidence in themselves increased accordingly. However, Gerard DeGroot feels that the positive effects on the status of women have been grossly exaggerated; women never attained the status of skilled workers and were usually paid much less than men for doing the same work; this only 'increased antagonism between the sexes, and, needless to say, did nothing for gender equality.' Martin Pugh points out that most women were forced to leave their wartime jobs once the men came home from the war; there was still a long way to go before women would be accepted as the complete equals of men.

(d) huge step forward in the move towards full democracy

In 1914, in spite of three parliamentary reform Acts and the 1911 Parliament Act, Britain was still not a genuinely democratic country, since no women were allowed to vote for MPs, and about 40 per cent of all adult males were still without the vote. The war gave an enormous boost to the development of full democracy. By 1918, a general election was long overdue (under the terms of the 1911 Parliament Act there should have been an election no later then December 1915) and the government felt it was important to hold one as soon as the war was over. Voting rights were widely discussed during the war, and the government was influenced by two points:

» Many men serving in the armed forces had lost their right to vote because they were out of the country; this was because there was a rule that you had to live in a constituency for one year before an election to be entitled to vote.
» Many working-class men who had never had the vote had made an indispensable contribution to the war effort, fighting in the armed forces or working in vital industries.

It was widely felt that both groups must be given the right to vote in recognition of their contribution. It was also felt, in view of *their* vital role in the war effort, that women could not be left out if there was to be another extension of voting rights. All these points were taken into consideration in the *Representation of the People Act (July 1918)*. The vote was given to all males at the age of 21, and to women at the age of 30 (it was 1928 before women were given the vote at 21). As we saw earlier, however (Section 21.4(e)), Martin Pugh believes that women would have received the vote by 1918 even if there had been no war. The new Act also introduced the practice that all voting in general elections was to take place on the same day instead of being spread over several weeks. The idea of the 'deposit' was introduced: in order to exclude the lunatic fringe from standing in elections, every candidate had to pay a deposit of £150; if the candidate failed to win one-eighth of the total votes, the deposit was forfeited.

(e) important effects on education

The Education Act of 1918 was a product of the war. Lloyd George's Minister of Education, historian H. A. L. Fisher, believed that the war had created an 'increased feeling of social solidarity' and that the contribution of the working class to the war effort entitled them to a better education (see Section 20.4(f) for full details).

(f) important effects on housing

The war caused an almost complete stoppage of house building, which affected the working class most of all. In 1913, it had been calculated that 120,000 new houses were needed, and by the end of the war the figure was in the region of 600,000. Lloyd George talked of providing 'homes fit for heroes', and during the twenty years following the end of the war, great progress was made with council house building (see Section 20.4(e)).

(g) stimulus to aviation and broadcasting

Apart from the obvious effects of stimulating scientific and technological research in order to produce better weapons, the war did not have a great impact on pure science. However, it led to two striking developments which otherwise might not have taken place so quickly: aviation and broadcasting. Commercial companies soon realized the potential of these, and began to exploit them for profit. The first regular commercial passenger flight was introduced between London and Paris in July 1919. Also important was the growth of the mass media – there were soon six private companies broadcasting for profit; in 1922, these amalgamated to form the British Broadcasting Company. The government decided that radio had far too great a potential to be left in private hands, and in 1926 the Conservatives made it into a public corporation – the British Broadcasting Corporation (BBC) (see Section 24.2(a)).

(h) repercussions in Ireland

At Easter 1916, the Irish Republican Brotherhood decided to turn Britain's preoccupation with the war to their own advantage (see Section 26.2(a)).

(i) appalling loss of life and limb – the 'lost generation'

Something like 745,000 British men were killed and 1.6 million wounded, many so severely that they could never work again. Between the wars, people talked about the 'lost generation' and the shortage of young men. Marwick suggests that one of the reasons for the political weakness of Britain during the inter-war years was the loss of so much young talent during the war. Recent demographic research has shown that in fact there was no great shortage of men in the 1920s and 1930s, because the war caused an almost total stoppage of emigration from Britain; after 1918, emigration never returned to its pre-war levels of several hundred thousand men every year. But as Peter Clarke points out, in *Hope and Glory: Britain 1900–1990* (1996),

> It was not the demographic but the human impact of the losses which burned so deep ... it is the sheer cumulative impact of the losses, week by week and month by month which is staggering ... Women at home bore this special burden, dreading the arrival of a telegraph boy on his bicycle – in working class streets telegrams were only received from the War Office, with their invariable bad news ... The 'lost generation' was an emotional and psychological reality which made a life-long impact on its surviving members.

The sheer horror of life in the trenches and the atmosphere of wartime life in general are admirably caught in Robert Graves' *Goodbye to All That,* and in the trilogy of novels by Pat Barker, *Regeneration, The Eye in the Door* and *The Ghost Road.*

(j) serious economic effects on Britain's world position

Britain had lost some 40 per cent of its merchant shipping and run up enormous debts, mainly to the USA, which had to be repaid with interest. While Britain was pre-occupied with the war, many other countries either developed their own industries or bought goods from elsewhere; consequently, Britain never regained many of the export markets that had been lost during the war. Compared with the USA, and even Germany, Britain's economic position had deteriorated sharply; this was one reason for the high unemployment between the wars.

(k) economic effects on the different social classes

Increased taxation to help finance the war fell most heavily on the aristocracy and the middle classes. The landowning aristocracy were especially badly hit; many were forced to sell their estates, so that, although they were still wealthy, they had lost their position as the dominant political and land-owning class. The middle classes found that their living standards fell; for example, they were unable to maintain such large households. Fewer servants were needed, and the number of domestic servants fell by about 50 per cent over the whole country.

The working class, on the other hand, benefited from government intervention. Wage rates doubled on average, the average working week was reduced from 55 hours to 48 hours, and food rationing meant that some working-class families could afford meat for the first time. Admittedly, some of these changes were not permanent, but as Marwick puts it, 'the working class in 1914 was large and it was poor. In the early 1920s it was not quite so large and it was not quite so poor.'

(l) less respect for authority

Before the war, only a small minority of people criticized society and the establishment. But partly as a result of the war, people had less respect for, and became more ready to challenge, authority, and were less willing to accept propaganda from the government. This was especially true among working-class men who had fought in the trenches and had experienced at first-hand the incompetence and lack of imagination of many of the generals and officers. After the war there was a marked decline in church attendance; there seemed to be a reaction especially against the Anglican Church, because it had supported the government line and the war so solidly.

22.6 Britain and the peace settlement

A peace conference met at Versailles in January 1919 to decide what should be done with the defeated powers. The three most important people at the conference turned out to be Lloyd George, Clemenceau (representing France) and the American President, Woodrow Wilson. It quickly emerged that, depending on their war aims, they had rather different ideas about how to treat the Central Powers, and Germany in particular.

(a) war aims of the Allied leaders

Britain's war aims had been vague at the outset. The public was told that the intention was to defend Belgium. In January 1918, probably to encourage the troops by presenting them with some clear objectives to fight for, Lloyd George spelled out Britain's war aims in more detail. They included the defence of democracy and the righting of the injustice done to France in 1871 (in other words, the return of Alsace and Lorraine, which the Germans had taken from France at the end of the Franco-Prussian War), the restoration of Belgium and Serbia, an independent Poland, democratic self-government for the nationalities of Austria-Hungary, self-determination for the German colonies, and an international organization to prevent war.

In an off-the-cuff speech made in December, which he later regretted, Lloyd George said that Germany should be made to pay the whole cost of the war. Sir Eric Geddes, one of the businessmen brought into the government by Lloyd George, suggested that Germany should be 'squeezed until you can hear the pips squeak'. These were popular slogans in preparation for the election, which the Lloyd George coalition won with an overwhelming majority in December 1918 (see Section 23.1(a)). Once the election was safely over, Lloyd George toned down his language, and at the conference argued that a lenient approach to Germany was essential so that it would not become embittered, and so that international trade could settle down to normal again. On the other hand, he now felt that Britain ought to be given Germany's African colonies, and should be allowed to keep the Turkish territories in the Near East, with their valuable oil supplies.

Clemenceau and the French wanted the harshest possible treatment of Germany in revenge for France's defeat in the Franco-Prussian War of 1870–1, and in payment for all the damage inflicted by the Germans over the previous four years. Germany must be completely crippled so that it could never again invade the sacred soil of France.

Woodrow Wilson's peace aims were set out in his Fourteen Points, also issued in January 1918. They were similar to Lloyd George's aims, but emphasized the idea of national self-determination – peoples should have democratic governments of their own nationality. It was difficult to reconcile these conflicting aims, but eventually a settlement was hammered out.

(b) the Treaty of Versailles dealt with Germany

The Germans had to lose territory in Europe: Alsace and Lorraine to France; Eupen, Moresnet and Malmédy to Belgium; North Schleswig to Denmark (after a plebiscite); West Prussia and Posen to Poland, though Danzig, the main port of West Prussia, was to be a free city under League of Nations administration, because its population was wholly German. Memel was given to Lithuania; the Saar was to be administered by the League of Nations for fifteen years, when a plebiscite would decide whether it should belong to France or Germany. In the meantime, France was to have the use of its coalmines. Germany's African colonies were taken away and became 'mandates' under League supervision. This meant that various member states of the League 'looked after' them. In particular, it meant that Britain acquired Tanganyika, and Britain and France divided Togoland and the Cameroons between them. German armaments were strictly limited: a maximum of 100,000 troops and no conscription; no tanks, armoured cars, military aircraft or submarines, and only six battleships. The Rhineland was to be permanently demilitarized (this meant that German troops were not allowed in the area). The War Guilt clause (Article 231) fixed the blame for the outbreak of the war solely on Germany and its allies. Germany was to pay reparations for damage done to the Allies; the actual amount was not decided at Versailles, but announced later (1921), after much argument and haggling, as £6,600 million. A League of Nations was set up, its aims and objectives being set out in the League Covenant; its main aim was to settle international disputes by discussion, and so prevent war.

(c) treaties dealing with Germany's defeated allies

Germany's defeated allies were each dealt with by a separate treaty. When Austria was on the verge of defeat, the Habsburg Empire disintegrated as the various nationalities declared themselves independent. Austria and Hungary separated and declared themselves republics, but both lost huge areas, some of which went to make up the new states of Czechoslovakia and Yugoslavia; some parts were given to a much-enlarged Romania, and the rest went to make up the newly reconstituted state of Poland. By the Treaty of Sèvres (1920), Turkey lost its Arab territories: Iraq, Transjordan and Palestine became mandated territories supervised by Britain, and Syria became a French mandate.

(d) was the peace settlement too hard on Germany?

Both Lloyd George and the general public seemed happy with the terms, and Lloyd George was given a hero's welcome on his return from Paris. However, it gradually emerged that there were many faults with the settlement. The Germans themselves indignantly rejected the terms presented to them. They claimed that they were not solely to blame for the war – they had been provoked into it by the encirclement policies of Russia and France. But, as well as that, as Ruth Henig points out, 'they did not believe that their country had been honourably defeated on the battlefield ... and Germany had not been invaded by Allied troops ... They believed that, at the worst, they had fought to an honourable draw on the Western Front, while being totally victorious in the East'.

The most common criticisms of the terms from the Allied side are that they were far too hard on the Germans, and that some of them – especially reparations

map **22.2 European frontiers after the First World War and the peace treaties**

payments and German disarmament – were impossible to carry out. There was much controversy about the size of the reparations bill: J. M. Keynes, a British economic adviser at the conference, argued that £2,000 million was a more realistic figure, which the Germans could afford to pay without bankrupting themselves. On the other hand, some of the British and French extremists were demanding £24,000 million, so the final figure of £6,600 million was kinder to the Germans than it might have been. Even the territorial losses, as David Stevenson points out, could be justified on the grounds that most of the territories were peopled by non-Germans, and Germany was still the largest country in Europe east of Russia.

Any settlement was bound to be a compromise, and this one had the unfortunate effect of dividing Europe into the states that wanted to revise it (Germany being the main one) and those that wanted to preserve it, and on the whole, even they turned out to be lukewarm in their support of the settlement. Within a year, the victorious coalition had disintegrated. The US Senate failed to ratify the settlement, much to the disgust of Woodrow Wilson, and the USA never joined the League of Nations. This in turn left France completely disenchanted with the whole business, because the Anglo-American guarantee of its frontiers could not now apply. The Italians felt cheated because they had not received the full territory promised them in 1915, and the Russians were ignored because they were now under communist rule. All this tended to sabotage the settlement from the beginning, and it became increasingly difficult to apply the terms fully. Worst of all, it *did* embitter the Germans, yet did not weaken them enough to prevent further aggression. But while the settlement did produce some of the preconditions for another war, that is not the same as saying that it was the cause of Hitler's war. As Ruth Henig concludes, 'it was the total failure of the three powers (USA, Britain and France) to work closely together after 1919 that was one of the contributing factors to the outbreak of a second world war 20 years later'.

QUESTIONS

1 Given that most people expected the war to be over by Christmas 1914, why did it take Britain and its allies until 1918 to defeat Germany and its allies?
2 How decisive were the land campaigns of 1918 in bringing about the defeat of the Central Powers in the First World War?
3 How far would you agree with the theory that Britain would have done better to remain neutral in the First World War?
4 Assess the importance of the various effects of the First World War on Britain.

A document question about munitions and change during the First World War can be found on the accompanying website www.palgrave.com/masterseries/lowe1.

politics in confusion, 1918–24

summary of events

At the end of the war, politics did not return immediately to the normal two-party system. Lloyd George was still Prime Minister of the wartime coalition, consisting of his own section of the Liberal party supported by most of the Conservatives under the leadership of Andrew Bonar Law. The coalition won an overwhelming victory in the election of December 1918, and stayed in government for the next four years.

The problems of peacetime Britain proved to be as difficult to deal with as the problems of war, and Lloyd George was unable to find permanent solutions to the post-war depression and to the chronic difficulties encountered by the coal industry. His popularity gradually ebbed away, and when his Conservative supporters decided to withdraw from the coalition to fight the next election on normal party lines, Lloyd George was left with less than half a party to lead, as the Liberal split continued. This enabled the Labour party to make a major breakthrough, coming in second place to the Conservatives in the election of November 1922.

Although the Conservatives seemed set to rule for the next five years, the revival of the old tariff reform issue caused another general election only a year later. The Labour party won enough seats to form a government, with James Ramsay MacDonald as the first Labour Prime Minister (January 1924). Lacking a majority, this government proved to be only a short-lived experiment, and yet another election followed (October 1924). This was won decisively by Stanley Baldwin and the Conservatives, who remained in office for the next five years. The Liberals slumped badly at that election, confirming that Labour was now the alternative party of government to the Conservatives.

Date	Government	Prime Minister
Dec 1918–Oct 1922	Coalition	David Lloyd George
Oct 1922–Jan 1924	Conservative	Andrew Bonar Law (Oct 1922–May 1923)
		Stanley Baldwin (May 1923–Jan 1924)
Jan–Oct 1924	Labour	James Ramsay MacDonald
Nov 1924–Jun 1929	Conservative	Stanley Baldwin

23.1 the Lloyd George coalition, 1918–22

(a) the election of December 1918

This was the first general election since December 1910, and it must have been confusing for the voters, especially those who were voting for the first time – some six million women and two million extra men who had been enfranchised by the recent *Representation of the People Act* (see Section 22.5(d). The confusion arose because the election was not fought on normal party lines; Lloyd George, as the successful leader of the wartime coalition of Liberals and Conservatives (Labour had withdrawn in 1917), decided to continue the coalition, but since the Liberal party was still split, it meant that in most constituencies there were two Liberal candidates – a Lloyd George coalition Liberal and an Independent or Asquith Liberal. It became known as the 'coupon election', because Lloyd George and Bonar Law issued coupons (signed letters) to their candidates, so that the electors would know which were genuine coalition candidates.

The coalition won easily, mainly because of Lloyd George's popularity as the man who had led Britain to victory, and his promises to create 'a fit country for heroes to live in' and to make Germany pay 'the whole cost of the war'. The coalition won 478 seats, made up of 335 Conservatives, 133 Lloyd George Liberals and 10 Labour and other supporters. The main opposition consisted of 63 Labour members, 28 Asquith Liberals and 48 Conservatives who refused to support the coalition. There were also 73 Sinn Feiners, but they refused to take their seats at Westminster and set up their own parliament in Dublin. The election result was a disaster for the Liberals, whose representation in Parliament was almost halved; even Asquith lost his seat. Though in one sense it was a triumph for Lloyd George, he was left very much dependent on the Conservatives, who had enough seats to form a government of their own. However, this was out of the question for the time being, since their leader, Bonar Law, was a great admirer of Lloyd George and he acknowledged that the Conservatives owed their success to Lloyd George's popularity.

(b) what problems faced Lloyd George, and how successfully did he deal with them?

The situation in the aftermath of the war was chaotic, and all Lloyd George's brilliance was needed to bring the country through such a difficult period.

1 Difficulties arose with demobilization of the troops from the army. The government began by releasing holders of key civilian jobs first, leaving the ordinary rank-and-file troops until last. Some alarming protest demonstrations broke out, and the government changed its tactics smartly, adopting a 'first in, first out' policy. This worked well, and by the autumn of 1919 over four million troops had been successfully 'demobbed'. Most of them found jobs, thanks to the post-war boom – an encouraging beginning.

2 There was a sudden period of inflation at the end of the war, caused partly by the removal of government wartime controls on prices, profits and guaranteed wage levels. Prices and profits rose but wages lagged behind. Trade unions were determined to protect their members, and during 1919 and 1920 there were over 2,000 strikes. However, it was not simply a desire for higher wages; there were other reasons for labour unrest: there was serious disillusionment and bitterness among the working class, caused by their experiences in the trenches; this seemed to emphasize the gulf between the workers on the one hand, and on the other, capitalists and profiteers who had done well out of the war. The Russian Revolutions (1917) gave tremendous publicity to nationalization and worker control, and some of the strikes in Britain in 1919 threw the government into a panic in case they developed into something more serious.

 In February and March 1919, a strike of Clydeside engineers and shipbuilders demanding a 40-hour week seemed ominously like the start of a revolution: huge demonstrations, rioting, and a red flag hoisted in George Square, Glasgow, caused the government to move in troops and tanks. Order was quickly restored and two of the leaders, Willy Gallacher and Emmanuel Shinwell, were sent to jail. The Miners' Federation threatened a national strike if their demands for a six-hour day, a 30 per cent wage increase and continued government control of mines through nationalization were not accepted. This time, Lloyd George avoided a confrontation and played for time: he offered a seven-hour day, continued government control for the present, and a Royal Commission (the Sankey Commission) to investigate the problem. The miners accepted his offer.

3 There was a slump beginning early in 1921, which threw about two million people out of work by the end of the year, and the unemployment figure never fell below a million again until the Second World War. The slump had a variety of causes; in a sense it was the continuation of the slow decline of the British economy that had begun in the 1870s. The requirements of the war economy had stimulated the steel, coal and textile industries, but as soon as

peace returned, this extra demand disappeared. Many foreign buyers, who had been unable to obtain British goods during the war, had found alternative sources of supply, or had developed their own manufacturing industries. Thus demand for traditional British exports – ships, textiles, coal, iron and steel – never revived to its pre-war level. By 1920 the government had extended the 1911 National Insurance Act so that unemployment payments were made, for not more than 15 weeks in any one year, to *all workers* earning less than £250 year (except agricultural labourers, domestic servants and civil servants). At that point, boom conditions still applied, and mass unemployment was not expected. When it came in 1921, the new scheme could not cope: payments to the unemployed far outweighed contributions. However, having once conceded the principle of state benefit for the unemployed, the government could hardly do a U-turn simply because unemployment had increased. During 1921, therefore, benefit was extended to two 16-week periods in the year with a gap between (see Section 20.4(d) for more details). The government aid probably eased the situation, and may even have prevented revolution. Nevertheless, it was criticized by Labour because it only treated the symptoms and did nothing to remove unemployment. Labour MPs claimed that the benefits were too low and were 'mocking the poor', while Conservatives condemned them on the grounds that they would demoralize the workers.

4 The trouble in the coal industry over whether it should remain under government control or be returned to private ownership, had been simmering since the appointment of the Sankey Commission. Matters came to a head on 1 April 1921, when the entire industry came out on strike. This was because the Sankey Commission had been unable to agree on a solution to the problem. Some members recommended nationalization and others recommended the return of the mines to private ownership. This bitterly disappointed the miners, who wanted nationalization, but it gave Lloyd George the opportunity to avoid permanent nationalization: the government announced that mines and railways would be handed back to private control on 1 April.

Mine-owners informed the men that wages would have to be reduced because of the slump in exports. For a time, the miners' strike threatened to develop into a general strike, but on 15 April the miners' allies in the Triple Alliance – the railwaymen and transport workers – decided to abandon the idea. This the miners regarded as a betrayal, and the day was remembered as the 'Black Friday' of the trade union movement. The miners continued alone, and their strike lasted three months; but without support, their position was hopeless and they had to give way on all points. Soon afterwards, workers in other trades (engineering, shipbuilding, docks, building, textiles, printing and railways) had to accept wage reductions. Lloyd George had solved the problem in the sense that the strike had failed and a general strike had been averted, but he was fast losing his popularity with the workers.

5 There was a reduction in government revenue (money flowing into the Treasury from taxation). This was caused partly by the general falling-off of business during the slump and partly by the enormous expense of unemployment benefits. A committee under Sir Eric Geddes recommended 'retrenchment' (drastic cuts in expenditure); the government took this advice, saving itself £64 million. The policy became known as *the Geddes Axe* and it involved greatly reduced expenditure on the army, navy, education, health services and council house building. The economy measures were successful, but highly unpopular with the Labour party, who criticized the government for 'making the children pay while the ladies of Mayfair spend extravagantly on dresses and the rich betake themselves to St Moritz.' Left-wing or progressive Liberals were not happy either: it seemed to these critics that Lloyd George was no more than a prisoner of the Conservatives, who were using him to do their dirty work for them.

6 Trouble flared up in Ireland immediately after the election, when the 73 Sinn Fein MPs (who wanted Ireland to be independent from Britain) set up their own parliament (Dail) in Dublin and proclaimed the Republic of Ireland. The IRA began a campaign of terrorism against the police, and the government retaliated by using the Black and Tans. Although Lloyd George found a temporary settlement by partitioning Ireland (see Section 26.2(a) for full details), he had made enemies in doing so: many Liberals resented his use of the Black and Tans, whereas the Conservatives were furious at the way the union between Britain and Ireland had been destroyed. This was serious for Lloyd George, because the survival of his coalition depended on continued Conservative support. On the other hand, Kenneth Morgan believes that 'he surely found the only workable compromise at the time and brought fifty years of peace to that tormented island, until the late 1960s. Where Pitt, Peel and Gladstone had failed, he could claim to have triumphed.'

7 There were numerous problems in foreign affairs, which took up a large proportion of the Prime Minister's time throughout the four years. Sometimes – at the Paris Peace Conference, for example – he was successful; but there were also failures, and the overall impact of his foreign policies was to damage his reputation.

> Under strong pressure from his Conservative supporters, Lloyd George sent British troops to help the anti-Bolshevik forces in the Russian civil war. By the end of 1919 the Bolsheviks (later known as communists) were victorious and the British troops were withdrawn, having achieved nothing. The Russian communists, and many among the British working class who admired them, resented Lloyd George's intervention. In fact, he was anxious for a reconciliation and consequently an Anglo-Russian trade treaty was signed (March 1921).

- *The Genoa Conference (1922)* took place, on Lloyd George's initiative. There was growing tension between Germany and France over reparations, since the Germans were already complaining that they would not be able to afford the next instalment. Lloyd George hoped to calm the situation by persuading the French to reduce their demands. Other problems to be discussed were the need to resume diplomatic relations with Russia, and Europe's war debts to the USA. The conference was a dismal failure: the French refused all compromise and insisted on full reparations payments; the Americans refused to attend; and the Russians claimed to be insulted at the suggestion that they should honour all debts owed by the Tsarist government. The Germans and Russians withdrew and signed a separate agreement at nearby Rapallo: Germany officially recognized the Soviet government, and both countries wiped off their mutual debts. The other nations were alarmed at this reconciliation between two 'suspect' states, and blamed Lloyd George. To be fair, though, the fault was more that of the French premier, the bitterly anti-German Poincaré, for his refusal to compromise.

- *The Chanak incident (1922), though concluded successfully by Lloyd George, was the event that triggered his downfall.* The Turks threatened to break the Versailles settlement by moving troops into a neutral zone, thereby clashing with the British occupying force based at Chanak on the Dardanelles (see Map 22.2 on page 454). Lloyd George took a strong line, warning the Turks that if the neutral zone was violated, they would face war not only with Britain but with the British Empire as well. Eventually a compromise was reached by *the Treaty of Lausanne (1923)*, allowing Turkey to keep Eastern Thrace and Smyrna. The crisis passed, war was averted, and it seemed that Lloyd George had triumphed. Unfortunately, he had made the mistake of not consulting the Commonwealth Prime Ministers before committing them to a possible war against Turkey. Many of the Conservatives were outraged at what they saw as his unforgivable rashness, and his days in power were numbered.

(c) the coalition found time for some important political and social reforms

1 *The Sex Disqualification Removal Act (1919)* allowed women to stand for Parliament; the first woman to take her seat was Nancy Astor, the American-born wife of Viscount Waldorf Astor, owner of the *Observer* newspaper.
2 *The Addison Housing Act (1919)* (see Section 20.4(e)).
3 The extension of unemployment insurance mentioned above (see Section 20.4(d)).
4 Increases in old age pensions (see Section 20.4(g)).
5 *The Rent Act (1920)* protected working-class tenants against exorbitant rent increases.

(d) the fall of the Lloyd George coalition (October 1922)

Unfortunately for Lloyd George, his achievements were not enough to save the coalition. He had been losing working-class support steadily, and it was significant that Labour won thirteen by-elections between 1918 and 1922. Much depended on whether the Conservative MPs would continue to support him at the next general election, which he intended to hold fairly soon. A meeting of Conservative MPs held at the Carlton Club (29 October) was expected to endorse the decision to continue supporting the coalition. However, when a vote was taken, it was 185 to 85 *in favour of ending their support of Lloyd George.* The main anti-Lloyd George speech that swayed the meeting was made by Stanley Baldwin. Lloyd George immediately resigned and Andrew Bonar Law became Prime Minister of a Conservative government.

The Conservatives decided to abandon him because he had outlived his usefulness. They resented his solution of the Irish problem and his handling of the Chanak incident, and they criticized him because he allowed the sale of knighthoods and other honours to unsuitable candidates. More than that, they were afraid that if the coalition continued much longer, Lloyd George would split the Conservative party permanently (between those who supported the coalition and those who opposed it) in the same way that he had split the Liberal party. This was the point made forcibly by Baldwin when he said that while Lloyd George was a dynamic force, such a force was 'a very terrible thing'.

He was still only 59, but he was never again to hold an important political office, though he remained an MP until the end of 1944 when he became Earl Lloyd George of Dwyfor. He died in March 1945. A. J. P. Taylor calls him 'the most inspired and creative British statesman of the twentieth century', and 'the greatest ruler this country has known since Oliver Cromwell'. If this is so, then it must be seen as a national tragedy that Lloyd George had to sit on the side-lines during the problems of the 1920s and 1930s, while, in the words of C. L. Mowat, 'the pygmies, the second-class brains, frittered away Britain's power in the world'. Kenneth Morgan perhaps presents the most balanced view of Lloyd George:

> He was a rogue elephant among political animals ... he was a thoroughly modern politician in his handling of the media, very image-conscious with his mane of white hair and his long cloak ... But he never sought power for its own sake. Always he was a man interested in policies, in ideas, in results. The welfare reforms he generated were the starting point for all future debates on social provision. He pioneered a new role for the interventionist state and for the mixed economy during the First World War ... But he aroused distrust and hostility to an astonishing degree.

And so, in the end 'ideas were not enough. He needed also supporters, organisation, a party base – above all, public trust. These were assets which Lloyd George, however fertile in ideas and initiatives, conspicuously lacked'.

23.2 the Conservatives and tariff reform again

(a) the Conservative election victory, November 1922

The Conservatives won a decisive victory: they had 345 seats and a majority of 75 over all other parties combined. It was a disaster for the Liberals, who fought the election in two separate groups: the Asquith Liberals won 62 seats, and the Lloyd George Liberals 54. The combined Liberal total of 116 seats was well behind Labour's 142, and it was clear that *Labour had emerged as the main opposition party to the Conservatives.*

However, the new Conservative government did not last long. After Bonar Law's resignation through ill-health in May 1923, Stanley Baldwin became Prime Minister. After only a few months in office he decided that another general election was necessary, though the Conservatives still had their comfortable overall majority.

(b) tariff reform again

Joseph Chamberlain's cure for all ills, tariff reform (see Section 17.6(b)), was the question at issue. Baldwin had decided that Joseph Chamberlain was right after all – tariffs must be reintroduced. But since Bonar Law had earlier promised that this was exactly what the Conservatives would *not* do, Baldwin felt it was only fair to give the voters a chance to express their views. Many Conservatives thought it was a totally unnecessary exercise, and Lord Curzon called it an 'idiotic' decision.

Baldwin's argument was that tariffs would make foreign goods more expensive in Britain and thus give a much-needed boost to British industry; the growing unemployment problems would be solved at a stroke. The two sections of the Liberal party reunited under Asquith's leadership and campaigned for free trade, the traditional Liberal policy. Together with Labour, they argued that continued free trade and foreign imports would keep down the cost of living for the workers. The results were: Conservatives 258, Labour 191 and Liberals 159, a clear defeat for protection, and a further confirmation that Labour had replaced the Liberals as the alternative party to the Conservatives.

23.3 the first Labour government (January–October 1924)

(a) formation of the Labour government

When the election results were announced, it was not immediately clear what would happen next. Baldwin remained as Prime Minister for six weeks while discussions took place. The Conservatives could not remain in office for long, because, despite being the largest single party, they had lost their overall majority; both Labour and Liberals would vote against a Conservative Bill to introduce tariffs. Some Conservatives felt they should patch up their differences with the Liberals over tariffs, and form a government of national unity to keep Labour out. But Baldwin was quite happy for a Labour government to go ahead: he knew that if MacDonald tried to do anything unacceptable, the Tories and Liberals between them could vote Labour out. When Asquith decided to promise Liberal support in the Commons for a Labour government, Baldwin encouraged him, because he knew it would outrage right-wing Liberals such as Winston Churchill, who were likely to join the Conservatives. Baldwin was right again, and this proved to be yet another nail in the Liberals' coffin. Therefore, Labour, as the second-largest party, formed a government on the understanding that Liberal support would be forthcoming, and James Ramsay MacDonald became the first ever Labour Prime Minister.

(b) James Ramsay MacDonald

It was an exceptional achievement for MacDonald to become Prime Minister. Born at Lossiemouth, the illegitimate son of poor parents, his only formal education was at the local board school and then as a pupil teacher. He went to London where he worked as a clerk and a political journalist, and after joining the ILP (1893) he became secretary of the Labour Representation Committee (1900) and Labour MP for Leicester in 1906. After opposing Britain's entry into the war, he was forced to resign the leadership, and lost his seat in 1918. Re-elected to Parliament in 1922, his prestige had recovered sufficiently for him to become leader of the party again.

There was near panic in some quarters when it was realized that there was going to be a Labour government. Some people thought that everybody's savings would be confiscated, and that there would be a period of profound social revolution; but nothing spectacular happened: MacDonald's Cabinet, with only two exceptions, consisted of moderates – Philip Snowden as Chancellor of the Exchequer, Arthur Henderson, J. H. Thomas and Sidney Webb. He even brought in three former Liberals, including Haldane as Lord Chancellor. In fact, this Labour government, and the one that followed in 1929–31, were a great disappointment to its socialist supporters. Snowden was a cautious Chancellor: instead of introducing a wealth tax, which socialists had hoped for and which the wealthy had feared, he did his best to reduce taxes.

(c) why didn't the two Labour governments have more success?

1 Both were minority governments lacking an overall majority, and dependent on Liberal votes to stay in office. They had therefore to pursue moderate policies, and it was out of the question to introduce nationalization and disarmament even if MacDonald had wanted to. This meant that their policies were very little different from those of Liberal governments.

2 Labour had difficulty in projecting itself as a genuinely national party, since from the beginning it had claimed to be the party of the industrial workers,

and was closely tied to the trade unions. It was distrusted by people of property, who feared nationalization and the link with militant trade unionism.

3 Labour could not break its ties with the trade unions because they provided most of the party's funds. In return, the unions expected to be able to control the party, which caused serious friction because union leaders were preoccupied with furthering the interests of their members. They gave very little support to the 1924 Labour government, and made no allowance for its dependence on Liberal support, criticizing its 'half-measures'. Almost immediately there was a dockers' strike in support of a demand for an extra two shillings a day. This was organized by Ernest Bevin, general secretary of the Transport and General Workers' Union. Following the success of this strike, London Transport workers also came out, and the situation became serious enough for MacDonald to proclaim a state of emergency, enabling the government to use armed lorries for moving essential supplies. In the end this was not necessary, because the employers gave way and made an acceptable wage offer; but it was embarrassing for the government and left its relationship with the unions strained.

4 It proved impossible to work out a joint plan of action between the parliamentary Labour party and the trade unions. When some Labour intellectuals suggested that the two should co-operate to avoid a repetition of the 1924 fiasco, Bevin dismissed the idea, claiming that left-wing intellectuals and Fabians did not understand the working class.

5 Both governments were unfortunate enough to have to deal with serious economic problems: a million unemployed in 1924 and the world economic crisis in 1930–1. Labour had no answer beyond nationalization, and since that was out of the question, they were helpless.

6 The divisions between left and right in the party were shown up by MacDonald's attitude. He immediately offended the left by not giving them a fair representation in the Cabinet, and affronted them by calmly accepting the limitations of a minority government. The Scottish Clydeside MPs and the ILP wanted him to bring in genuinely socialist measures; though these would be defeated in the Commons, it would give Labour a chance to appeal to the electorate. MacDonald had no intention of attempting such heroics; he wanted moderate policies to gain the confidence of the country, and he condemned strikes for wage increases as 'not socialism'. It wasn't long before the left decided that MacDonald himself was really no socialist.

(d) social reforms of the first Labour government

The 1924 government could claim a few achievements in spite of the disappointments:

› *Wheatley's Housing Act* provided grants of £9 million a year for the building of council houses (see Section 20.4(e)).

- Old age pensions and unemployment benefit were increased, and the gap between the two 16-week benefit periods was removed.
- The number of free places in grammar schools was increased, and state scholarships to universities brought back. Sir Henry Hadow was appointed to work out the needs of education (see Section 20.4(f)).

(e) achievements in foreign affairs

MacDonald acted as Foreign Secretary as well as Prime Minister, and had clear ideas about what he hoped to achieve. Like Lloyd George, he felt it was essential to improve relations between Germany and France, which had deteriorated sharply during 1923. Following the German refusal to pay their reparations instalment, the French sent troops to occupy the Ruhr (the important German industrial region that includes the cities of Essen and Dusseldorf), in an attempt to force the Germans to pay. MacDonald was also anxious to resume normal diplomatic relations with Russia, to promote disarmament, and to support the new League of Nations as the best hope for the maintenance of peace. His policy produced quick and impressive results.

- *He was largely responsible for the Dawes Plan (1924),* which solved the problem of Franco-German relations for the present time. By the end of 1923 the French occupation of the Ruhr had succeeded in producing only galloping inflation and the collapse of the German mark. MacDonald invited Herriot, the new French premier, and Stresemann, the new German Foreign Minister, to a conference in London, and persuaded the Americans to participate as well. The conference was chaired for part of the time by the American representative, General Dawes. No reduction was made in the total amount that Germany was expected to pay, but it was agreed that it should pay annually only what it could reasonably afford, until the country became more prosperous. A foreign loan of 800 million gold Marks (about £40 million), mainly from the USA, was to be made to Germany. France, now assured of at least some reparations from Germany, agreed to withdraw its troops from the Ruhr. The plan was successful: the German economy began to recover on the basis of the American loans, and international tensions gradually relaxed. MacDonald was fortunate that the formidable Poincaré had fallen from office, and his successor, Herriot, was anxious for reconciliation. Nevertheless, he made excellent use of the situation and showed that a Labour government could conduct a successful foreign policy, which many people had doubted.
- MacDonald gave full diplomatic recognition to the Soviet regime in Russia, signed a trade treaty and opened discussions about a British loan to Russia. This was a realistic policy, but the Conservatives and Liberals strongly disapproved.
- MacDonald made a serious effort to make the League of Nations work; he attended its meetings in Geneva, and tried to strengthen it by introducing *the*

Geneva Protocol, a proposal which would have made arbitration of international disputes compulsory. Unfortunately, the Labour government fell before the Protocol was accepted, and the Conservative government that followed felt unable to ratify it.

(f) the fall of the first Labour government (October 1924)

The end of the government came rather suddenly over *the Campbell Case*. J. R. Campbell, editor of the communist *Workers' Weekly*, was arrested and charged with incitement to mutiny, for writing an article urging soldiers not to fire on their fellow workers in the event of a strike. However, the Labour Attorney-General withdrew the prosecution, and both Conservatives and Liberals, already alarmed by MacDonald's opening of relations with Russia, accused the government of being sympathetic towards communists. The Liberal demand for an enquiry into the matter was carried in the Commons by 364 votes to 198. MacDonald took this as a vote of no confidence and resigned.

The following election was complicated by the affair of *the Zinoviev Letter*. This appeared in the *Daily Mail* four days before polling; the paper claimed it was from one of the Russian Communist leaders, Grigori Zinoviev; it was addressed to the British Communist party, marked 'very secret', and contained instructions on how to organize a revolution. The fact that the Foreign Office protested to the Russians about this interference in British affairs made the letter appear genuine, though it was in fact a hoax; it had actually been written by a group of White Russian émigrés, in collaboration with some members of Conservative Central Office and the Intelligence Service. But it caused a sensation at the time and was taken to show that Labour sympathy towards Russia was encouraging the British communists. Labour dropped to 151 seats, the Liberals lost disastrously, winning only 40 seats, while the Conservatives emerged triumphant with 419 seats.

Labour blamed their defeat on the Zinoviev Letter, but historians seem to agree that the Conservatives would have won in any case. Although short, the first Labour government was not without significance: it proved that a Labour government could work, which had been MacDonald's main aim in what was clearly going to be a short stay in power; and Labour had won respect both at home and abroad. This was probably also the point of no return for the Liberal party.

23.4 why did the Liberal party decline so rapidly?

The decline of the Liberal party was one of the most dramatic developments in recent British history because of the speed with which it happened. At the time of the great Liberal landslide victory of 1906, very few people could have foreseen that in less than twenty years Labour would have formed a government and the Liberals would have slipped into a poor third place. Worse was to come: in the election of 1935 they could muster only 21 seats and 6.4 per cent of total votes cast. Historians have had a long debate about whether the Liberal party decline was inevitable as the Labour party began to grow, or whether different courses of action by the Liberal leaders could have kept them in contention and squeezed Labour out. Another point at issue is whether the Liberal decline began before the First World War or whether it was the war which caused the decline.

(a) some historians believe that the Liberal party was in serious difficulties long before 1914

They had split over the question of Ireland in 1886 when 93 Liberal MPs led by Joseph Chamberlain voted against Gladstone's First Irish Home Rule Bill (see Section 16.1(e–f)). The Bill was defeated and the Liberal government fell, leaving the party weak, divided and out of office for the next ten years. A different split developed between the left or progressive wing of the party, which favoured the so-called New Liberalism (state action to bring about social reform – see Section 21.1), and the right wing, which favoured old-fashioned Gladstonian *laissez-faire* (wanting government intervention kept to a minimum). George Dangerfield argued in his book *The Strange Death of Liberal England* (1935) that the many problems facing Asquith's government were too complex for the divided Liberals to cope with. The combination of the clash with the House of Lords, potential civil war in Ireland, the suffragette campaign and industrial unrest stretched the Liberals beyond the limits of their capabilities and, according to Dangerfield, left Britain in 1914 on the verge of anarchy and perhaps revolution. The Liberal decline was shown in the general elections of 1910 when they lost heavily and were only able to stay in office because the Irish Nationalists and Labour MPs supported them.

(b) other long-term causes are stressed by Henry Pelling and Ross McKibbin

Pelling, writing in 1965, claimed that long-term social changes – such as the growth of large industrial cities, the greater concentration of industry, and the steadily rising cost of living were gradually causing large sections of the working class to look towards the Labour party. McKibbin (1974) believed that the growth of trade unionism was especially important and had already undermined Liberal strength before 1914 (see Section 19.8(e)). Between 1909 and 1913, trade union membership rose from something like 2.47 million to 4.13 million; unions were switching support steadily from the Liberals to Labour, and in 1913 the political levy became legal again, so that unions could use funds for political purposes. *The 1918 Representation of the People Act* can therefore be seen as a crucial factor in the Labour breakthrough. By trebling the electorate it brought the industrial working classes into a majority for the first time. It was this new mass electorate that the Liberals had to attract if they were to survive as a major party. Unfortunately for them, the Liberals did not produce sufficiently attractive policies and did not choose enough working-class candidates. Labour, on the other hand, with its new party organization and its new programme, projected itself successfully as the party of working people. In the elections of 1918 and 1922, Labour was much better organized than the Liberals, and in 1922, for the first time, won more seats than the Liberals (142 to 116).

(c) some historians reject the 'inevitable rise of Labour' theory

Paul Adelman believes that Dangerfield's whole argument 'seems hopelessly exaggerated'. Peter Clarke argued, in his famous book *Lancashire and the New Liberalism* (1971), that there was plenty of life left in the Liberal party in 1914; they had adapted to the social changes taking place and their social reform policies *were* attracting support among the workers. He based his conclusions on by-election results and local election results in Lancashire, which showed that Labour was losing ground to the Liberals after 1910. Even where the Liberals did lose seats, it was often to the Conservatives, not to Labour. More recently, Martin Pugh (1982) and Duncan Tanner (1990) also rejected the idea that Labour would inevitably take over from the Liberals (see Section 19.8(e)). If these historians are correct, and the Liberals were not already in a terminal decline before 1914, the question remains: why had they slumped into third place only eight years later?

(d) the First World War was the key factor, according to another group of historians

Trevor Wilson, in his book *The Downfall of the Liberal party 1914–35* (1966), compares the war to a 'rampant omnibus', which first knocked down and then ran over the unfortunate Liberal party. First of all its prestige was ruined by the hesitant and inappropriate way in which it tried to run the war on traditional *laissez-faire* principles. Then Lloyd George split the party by the way in which he manoeuvred Asquith into resigning so that he could form a coalition government with the Conservatives and Labour (December 1916). Asquith's supporters never forgave Lloyd George for this 'betrayal', and the party remained divided. The split between the two was highlighted during the Maurice debate in the Commons (May 1918), when only 72 Liberals voted for Lloyd George and 98 voted against him (see Section 22.5(a)). The party entered the first two elections after the war – in 1918 and 1922 – still fatally divided just as the Labour party was presenting a strong challenge.

While the war divided the Liberal party, it worked to the advantage of Labour. Arthur Henderson, the Labour leader during the war, gained Cabinet experience as a member of the wartime coalitions. When he left the government after disagreements with Lloyd George, he concentrated on providing the party with a new constitution, a new manifesto and new constituency organizations. The war caused Labour to adopt a new foreign policy: they wanted a pacific approach to foreign affairs as well as what they called 'open diplomacy'

– no more secret diplomacy, since this only led to misunderstandings and suspicions – plus an internationalist attitude to foreign policy. This attracted many converts from the left wing of the Liberal party, who also felt that there would be more chance of social reform from Labour than from the other two parties (see Section 22.5(a) for more details of Labour's new programme). Labour therefore entered the 1918 election united and better prepared than the Liberals, and was able to put forward 350 candidates, as opposed to only 72 in December 1910. Another boost for Labour was the increase in trade union membership during the war, from 4.14 million in 1914 to 7.9 million in 1919; this again damaged the Liberals, because by this time most of the big unions had affiliated to the Labour party.

The real disaster for the Liberals came in 1922, when they were still divided into the Lloyd George and Asquith factions. For the first time, Labour won more seats than the Liberals, and there seemed to be every chance that Labour would become the main opposition party to the Conservatives unless the Liberals were able to unite and produce the necessary policies.

(e) the Liberal party leaders were a liability after 1918

While the Liberals did succeed in reuniting under Asquith's leadership for the general election of December 1923 (in defence of free trade), Asquith was now aged over 70 and out of touch with most of the electorate, while Lloyd George had lost his popularity with the workers. This was because of his close co-oper-ation with the Conservatives, especially during the coalition of 1918–22, when on many occasions his policies had seemed unsympathetic towards the work-ers. Asquith did not retire from the leadership until 1926, when it was too late for the party to recover. If the party's leaders were not impressive, neither were its policies: all the important things the Liberals had stood for were ceasing to be major issues: Irish Home Rule, for example, was no longer an issue after the 1921 partition. Nor could the Liberals compete with Labour's new social poli-cies and their attractive leader, Ramsay MacDonald.

Even so, with all these disadvantages, the Liberals were not all that far behind Labour in the 1923 election, polling 4.31 million votes (29.6 per cent of votes cast) to Labour's 4.43 million (30.5 per cent). This gave Labour 191 seats to the Liberals' 159 (there were 258 Conservatives). Arguably, all was not lost at this point: dynamic leadership, some new creative policies and the right decisions might well have tipped the balance back in favour of the Liberals. However ...

(f) the Liberals made fatal mistakes after the 1923 election

Chris Cook argues that Asquith and the Liberals made the fatal mistake of allowing MacDonald and the Labour party to form a government 'without any understandings or conditions, and without having considered how they would fare if Labour refused to cooperate'. This played into the hands of both MacDonald and Baldwin, who each had strategies of their own:

- MacDonald was not interested in co-operation with the Liberals; his aim was to destroy them as the rival left-wing party. This could be done, he believed, by pushing them permanently into third place, so that the British electoral system, which always works against smaller parties, would work to the advantage of Labour.
- Baldwin encouraged the Liberals and their promises of support for Labour because he knew that many right-wing or middle-class Liberals would disapprove of the way Asquith was allowing Labour into office, and would switch to voting Conservative as the best way of keeping Labour out.

Both strategies worked perfectly: during the 1924 Labour government, MacDonald ruthlessly rejected all suggestions of an alliance with the Liberals, even though Labour was totally dependent on Liberal votes to stay in office. At the next election (October 1924) the Liberals were crushed, winning only 40 seats and 17.6 per cent of the vote; their total vote fell by 1.4 million. The Conservatives won the election with 419 seats and Labour lost 40 seats, but the Labour vote increased by well over a million, from 30.5 per cent to 33 per cent.

This was the end of the road for the Liberals: a precedent had been set – they had allowed Labour to show that it was capable of forming a government without the expected social upheaval. From now on, anti-Conservatives began to vote Labour as the best way of keeping the Tories out. The loss of their right-wing, middle-class and business support was serious for the Liberals because it deprived them of much of their financial backing. Four expensive election campaigns between December 1918 and October 1924 left them short of funds, while Labour could rely on financial support from the trade unions. With the benefit of hindsight it is clear that Asquith had missed an opportunity which was never to come the Liberals' way again: he could have insisted on a coalition government with Labour, which might have been able to introduce a proportional representation system of voting.

(g) the Liberals were at a disadvantage because of the electoral system

With three parties contesting many seats, a high proportion of MPs won their seats on a minority vote; many Liberals came second and their votes were not reflected in the Commons. The 1924 election revealed how unfair the system was. The percentages of votes polled were: Conservatives 48.3, Labour 33 and Liberals 17.6; under the 'first past the post system' this gave the Conservatives 419 of the 615 seats, Labour 151 and Liberals 40. Under some kind of proportional representation system that would have given a fairer distribution of seats, the result might have been something like: Conservatives 312, Labour 205 and Liberals 98.

The 1929 election is usually regarded as the Liberals' last chance: Lloyd George led a united party with an attractive programme, but they could scrape together only 59 seats (23.4 per cent) to Labour's 288 (37.1 per cent); the

Conservatives actually polled more votes than Labour (38.2 per cent), but this gave them fewer seats (260). There was a lack of confidence in Lloyd George and a feeling that Baldwin and MacDonald, though less exciting, were more solid and reliable. Again, the electoral system worked against the Liberals; under a different voting system they could have had as many as 140 seats, while the Conservatives would have been the largest party in the Commons. Many people now stopped voting Liberal, believing it to be a 'wasted vote'. The election of 1935 saw the Liberal share of the vote slump to only 6.4 per cent, giving them just 21 seats.

Perhaps the simplest conclusion is that, given the circumstances after the First World War, with the Conservatives firmly established as the party of the property-owners and the ratepayers, and Labour in alliance with the trade unions as the party of the workers, there was no remaining interest group large enough to keep the Liberal party going as a serious contender for power. On the other hand, it has to be remembered that if the Liberals could have come up with the right policies and the right leader to attract working-class votes, there may well have been nothing inevitable about their decline.

QUESTIONS

1 'An interlude of sheer futility'. Do you think this is a fair verdict on the Labour government of 1924?
2 Explain why Lloyd George's coalition government collapsed in 1922, and why he never held office again.
3 'The First World War was like a rampant omnibus which first knocked down and then ran over the Liberal Party' (Trevor Wilson). How far is this an adequate explanation of the decline of the Liberal party?

A document question about the decline of the Liberal party can be found on the accompanying website www.palgrave.com/masterseries/lowe1.

chapter 24

Baldwin, the Conservatives and the General Strike

summary of events

With a massive overall majority in excess of 200, the reunited and revitalized Conservative Party was in a powerful position. The rebel wing of the party, which included Austen Chamberlain (Joseph's son) and Lord Birkenhead, which had wanted to continue supporting the Lloyd George coalition, was now safely back in the fold; Chamberlain was Foreign Secretary. Winston Churchill, who had drifted back to the Conservatives after twenty years as a Liberal, became Chancellor of the Exchequer. He had left the Liberals because he disapproved of their co-operation with the Labour government. Neville Chamberlain, another of Joseph's sons, was one of the most successful members of the government; as Minister of Health, he was responsible for steering no fewer than twenty-one bills through Parliament. The government lasted for almost its full term of five years, introducing a mass of solid, if unspectacular, legislation. The only dramatic incident was the General Strike of 1926, which aroused considerable emotion, fear and excitement, though it lasted less than two weeks. Throughout the period, with his image of a plain and honest man puffing contentedly at his pipe, Stanley Baldwin presided over the country's fortunes.

24.1 the Conservative revival

The party had gone through a difficult period after its disastrous defeat in 1906, failing to win the general elections of 1910 and suffering a further split over the Parliament Bill of 1911. However, signs of recovery were there before the First World War.

(a) organizational improvements

Balfour set up a committee to improve party organization (1910), which resulted in two major changes:

> A new post was invented to help the Conservative Chief Whip – *Chairman of the Party Organization*. Previously the Chief Whip had been responsible

for all organization both inside and outside Parliament, and the job had become too much for one person. The Chairman was now responsible for all matters outside Parliament.

› Conservative Central Office was found to be inefficient, with no proper accounts or records being kept. This was put right and there was to be much closer contact between Central Office and the National Union of Conservative Associations.

› Another important change was that, by 1914, local constituency branches had gained the right to control propaganda and speakers and to choose their own candidates instead of being told what to do by Central Office.

› Conservative working men's associations were set up in many constituencies, and after women were given the vote in 1918, women's branches were introduced.

(b) a new party leader – Bonar Law

Balfour, having lost three consecutive elections, resigned as leader in 1911. There were two candidates for the leadership – Austen Chamberlain, from the 'progressive wing' of the party, and Walter Long, from the 'die-hards'. Since support seemed to be evenly divided, the choice of either of them would have been unacceptable to the other camp, and a party split would have been perpetuated. In the end, both agreed to stand down in the interests of party unity, and Andrew Bonar Law, who was acceptable to both camps, was chosen. Bonar Law had been born in Canada; his father was a Scottish Presbyterian minister and there were family connections with Ulster. Robert Blake calls him 'a melancholy teetotal widower', but he had great fighting qualities – he was 'a hard-hitting debater' and was full of 'bluntness, vigour and invective'. In addition, he was passionately against Irish Home Rule, and was prepared to go to almost any lengths to keep Ulster British. It was fortunate for the party that the Ulster issue came to the forefront at this point, because it gave them a cause they could all agree on. For the first time since 1900, the party was able to unite, under the leadership of Bonar Law, and the tariff issue slipped into the background (see Section 21.5(c)).

(c) First World War benefits the Conservatives

Liberal failures and splits during the war led to some Conservatives being included in the Asquith and Lloyd George coalitions (1915–18) (see Section 22.1(f)). According to Robert Blake, 'on almost every issue that came up, Conservative tradition and ideology was better suited than Liberal to meet the needs of the hour'. They were the party who stood for patriotism, strong defence and conscription; despite Lloyd George being recognized as 'the man who won the war', the Conservatives could claim some of the credit too, and this was reflected in the fact that 335 coalition Conservatives were elected in the 1918 'coupon' election. The continuing Liberal split after the war meant that there was no strong party of the left or centre to challenge the Conservatives.

(d) the changed Irish situation helps the Conservatives

When the Anglo-Irish Treaty partitioning Ireland came into operation in 1922 (see Section 26.2), it meant that there were no longer any Irish Nationalist MPs in the Commons. Up to 1918, there had always been at least 80 Irish Nationalists, who had almost always supported the Liberals, and had kept the Liberals in office after the 1910 elections. Now the only Irish MPs in the Commons were largely Ulster Unionists, who always voted Conservative.

(e) another new leader – Stanley Baldwin

Baldwin was the son of a wealthy Worcestershire iron and steel manufacturer. After leaving Cambridge, he worked in the family business and was aged over 40 when he first became an MP (1908). He was President of the Board of Trade in Lloyd George's coalition (1921–2), but grew to dislike Lloyd George's methods; it was his speech at the Carlton Club (October 1922) attacking Lloyd George that established him as one of the leading Conservatives, and Bonar Law made him Chancellor of the Exchequer when the party took office at the end of 1922. When Law resigned in 1923, Baldwin was the surprise choice as the next leader and Prime Minister. The obvious candidate, Lord Curzon, was unpopular with the party because he was pompous and arrogant. When told of the choice, Curzon is reported to have described Baldwin as 'a person of the utmost insignificance'. In fact, he was an extremely able politician and a much better manager of people than Lloyd George, who offended many of his colleagues. He gave the impression of being honest and lacking in deviousness, unlike Lloyd George, whom Baldwin regarded as 'a corrupter of public life'. Baldwin wanted a return to 'clean government', and donated to the Exchequer a large slice of the profits he had made from the manufacture of armaments during the war.

He put forward his ideas in a pamphlet – *Looking Ahead* – in 1924: he believed essentially in a moderate consensus, a partnership between employers and workers, and he utterly rejected the idea of a class war. He treated his own workforce with sympathy and understanding, and applied the same methods to national labour relations (though at the time of the General Strike the more extreme members of the Cabinet gained the upper hand). He was highly respected by Labour MPs, to whom he could often be seen chatting in the smoking-room of the House of Commons. In the atmosphere of industrial unrest between the end of the war and the General Strike, it could have been disastrous if the Conservatives had adopted anti-working-class policies. In a splendid Commons speech in 1925, he killed off a 'die-hard' Conservative private member's bill to reduce trade union powers, and ended with the plea: 'Give peace in our time, O Lord.' He was certainly a popular figure in the country and a great electoral asset; even in the 1929 election, which was won by Labour, the Conservatives polled more votes than Labour. Probably his greatest achievement was in helping to reunite the Conservative Party and holding it together until his retirement in 1937.

On the other hand, he was later blamed for neglecting Britain's defences in the face of the threat from Nazi Germany, especially when he was Prime Minister of the National Government (1935–7). His main failing, apart from his lack of originality, was his reluctance to take the initiative. According to John Charmley, the most recent historian of the Conservative Party, Baldwin was 'an idle man who disliked work, and he had what amounted to a chronic inability to take decisions until they were forced upon him. As chairman of the Cabinet he would listen to his colleagues but give little, if any, indication of his thoughts; he may not have had any, but his colleagues had to assume that he did, and were thus left in a state of uncertainty whilst trying to divine them'. Neville Chamberlain was the real driving force behind most of the domestic achievements of the government.

(f) why has the Conservative Party remained such a dominant force in British politics?

For over 120 years – since the first Liberal split over Irish Home Rule in 1886 – the Conservatives have been the most consistently successful party on the British political scene, and many people see them as the natural party of government. By the time of the Conservative defeat in 1997, they had been the largest party in the House of Commons for 76 out of the 111 years that had passed since 1886: over two-thirds of the time – a remarkable record. So far, this section has analysed how the party recovered successfully from its disaster of 1906, but there were other general factors that played a part in making the Conservatives such a dominant force:

> They could always rely on the support of the majority of the upper classes and the upper middle classes – broadly speaking, people of wealth and property – as well as much of the lower middle class; all these sections of society felt that the Conservative Party could best be relied on to safeguard their interests. These were people who had the education, the financial resources, the influence and the press support needed to keep a political party at the forefront.

> The Conservatives also proved to be adept at winning sufficient working-class support – probably in the region of a third of working-class votes – to tip the overall balance in their favour. It was not until 1945 that Labour actually polled more votes than the Conservatives in a general election.

> One reason for the party's continuing popularity was its readiness to adapt to changing circumstances. Its basic principles were quite vague: provided the existing capitalist power structure was preserved, so that political power was

kept in the hands of the wealthy, property-owning class, the Conservatives were prepared to introduce important reforms. Disraeli took the initiative by introducing the 1867 Reform Act, which was followed by various social reforms. Under Baldwin and Neville Chamberlain, the party again showed its readiness to pursue social reform, and even moved towards collectivism (the idea that the state should intervene directly to guide social policy and plan the economy). This trend continued during and after the Second World War in the period of consensus politics, when the Conservatives largely accepted the social and nationalization policies of the Attlee Labour governments (1945–51).

24.2 Conservative achievements, 1924–9

(a) important domestic achievements

1 *The Widows, Orphans and Old Age Contributory Pensions Act (1925).* See Section 20.4(g) for full details and criticisms of the Act.

2 The vote was extended to women at the age of 21. Labour objected strongly because the plural vote was not abolished.

3 *The Unemployment Insurance Act (1927)* increased contributions and reduced benefits, but had the great advantage that benefit would be paid for an indefinite period, provided an unemployed person had been genuinely seeking work. The Conservatives had accepted the principle of long-term maintenance by the state (see Section 20.4(d) for more details).

4 *The Local Government Act (1929)* was Neville Chamberlain's greatest achievement. It provided a complete overhaul of local government organization, rates and provision for the poor: Poor Law Unions and their boards of guardians, who had provided relief for the poor since 1834, were abolished, and their functions taken over by county and county borough councils (see Section 20.4(d) for full details). Agricultural land and farm buildings were to be exempt from payment of rates, and industrial property and railways were to pay only a quarter of the previous rate. This was designed to encourage farmers and industrialists to expand operations and provide more jobs. Local councils would receive a block grant from the government to cover the cost of services to the poor, and of other functions such as public health, slum clearance, roads, and town and country planning. This was a much fairer system, because expenses were being shared by the whole body of taxpayers in the country, instead of poor areas with high unemployment having to foot the bill from rates collected locally. However, the Labour Party protested bitterly that it was an attack on the independence of local councils, since the government could now cut off grants to local councils that did not follow their wishes. Many Labour-controlled councils had been running up huge debts paying wages and benefits well above the approved levels; this was

Illus. **24.1** Neville Chamberlain (left) and Stanley Baldwin arriving at the House of Commons

known as 'Poplarism' after the London borough where the practice originated. Now these councils would have to obey the rules.

5 *The Central Electricity Board* appointed by the Minister of Transport was
made responsible for the distribution of electricity. The National Grid was
started, with its thousands of pylons connecting the generating stations; it
was completed in 1933.

6 *The British Broadcasting Company* became a public corporation, to be
controlled by governors appointed by the Postmaster-General. John Reith,
the first Director-General of the BBC, was determined that it should provide
more than just light entertainment. He built the BBC up into an important
educational and cultural influence, with its own symphony orchestra. There
were regular news bulletins and educational programmes, and leading politicians were invited to broadcast. Baldwin and Philip Snowden soon developed an excellent radio technique, but Lloyd George and MacDonald, used
to addressing huge live audiences, never mastered the new medium.

7 Depending on one's viewpoint, it is possible to argue that the government's
handling of the General Strike was an achievement. The strike lasted less

than two weeks, and has never been repeated. The 1927 Trade Disputes Act reduced the powers of the trade unions (see next section).

(b) overseas affairs

These were in the hands of Austen Chamberlain, the Foreign Secretary.

1 He made an important contribution to the signing of *the Locarno Treaties (1925),* a number of different agreements involving Germany, France, Britain, Italy, Belgium, Poland and Czechoslovakia. The most important one was that *Germany, France and Belgium promised to respect their joint frontiers;* if one of the three broke this agreement, Britain and Italy would assist the state that was being attacked. Germany signed agreements with Poland and Czechoslovakia providing for arbitration over possible disputes. The agreements were greeted with wild enthusiasm all over Europe, and the reconciliation between Germany and France was referred to as the 'Locarno honeymoon'. Later, historians were not so enthusiastic about Locarno: there was one notable omission from the agreements – *no guarantees were given about Germany's eastern frontiers with Poland and Czechoslovakia.* By ignoring this problem, the signatories at Locarno were also ignoring the fact that by signing the League of Nations Covenant they had already undertaken to guarantee all members against aggression. Locarno gave the impression that no action need necessarily be taken if Germany attacked Poland and Czechoslovakia, and that Britain had turned its back on eastern Europe. Indeed Chamberlain talked of Poland's frontier with Germany as something 'for which no British government ever will or ever can risk the bones of a British grenadier'.

However, more recent research suggests that Austen Chamberlain's long-term aims, far from being isolationist, were for Britain to become increasingly involved in European diplomacy; he saw Locarno as just the beginning of a long process, of which the next phase would be for Britain to support Stresemann, Chamberlain's German opposite number, in his attempts to get a revision of some of the more objectionable terms of Versailles. After Germany was allowed to join the League of Nations in 1926, the three foreign ministers, Chamberlain, Stresemann and Briand (France) held regular informal meetings (which became known as the 'Geneva tea parties'). In fact, it was Chamberlain who persuaded the French to begin a phased withdrawal of their troops from the Rhineland. Richard Grayson concludes that 'Chamberlain was as much interested in allying with Germany, as he was in being a friend to France. And his policy very much depended on British involvement in Europe after Locarno, rather than any kind of withdrawal from diplomacy.' Given time, it should have been possible to calm both Germany and France and to sort out the most important European problems. Tragically, the premature death of Stresemann and the beginnings of the world economic crisis in 1929 completely changed the situation by allowing extremist politicians to come into power.

The situation was not helped by the fact that the Conservatives continued to be cool towards the League of Nations; Chamberlain had already rejected MacDonald's Geneva Protocol. Whatever Chamberlain's private intentions were, many historians continue to see in Locarno the beginnings of appeasement (see Section 27.1). For the time being, though, as the world enjoyed a period of great economic prosperity, any uneasy thoughts were pushed into the background. The 'Locarno spirit' culminated in:

2 *The Kellogg–Briand Pact (1928).* This originated in an idea of Briand, who proposed that France and the USA should sign a pact renouncing war. Frank B. Kellogg, the American Secretary of State, suggested that the whole world should be involved; eventually sixty-five states, including Britain, signed the pact, agreeing to renounce war as an instrument of national policy. This sounded impressive, but was completely useless because no mention was made of sanctions against any state which broke its pledge. Japan, for example, signed the pact, but was not prevented from waging war against China only three years later.

3 No attempt was made to develop the new relationship with Soviet Russia, started by the 1924 Labour government. The Conservatives had no love for the Communists. Chamberlain immediately told the Russians that Britain would not keep to the treaties that the Labour government had signed with them. The British attitude became even more hostile when evidence appeared that Russian propaganda was partly responsible for the unrest in India (see Section 26.4). Police raided the British Communist Party headquarters in London (1925) and the premises of Arcos, a Soviet trading organization based in London (1927), and claimed to have found evidence that Russians were plotting with British communists to overthrow the capitalist system. The government expelled the trading mission and broke off diplomatic relations with the Russians, who responded by arresting some British residents in Moscow. It has been argued that conciliation would have been a more rational approach, which might have persuaded the Russians to emerge from their isolation.

4 The way was prepared for *the Statute of Westminster* (eventually signed in 1931), which defined the relationship between Britain and the rest of the Commonwealth (see Section 26.1(b)). Baldwin also set up *the Simon Commission (1927)* to report on the situation in India (see Section 26.4(b)).

24.3 what caused the General Strike of 1926?

As usual, there was a combination of long-term causes that had been building up for several years, and short-term causes that triggered off the whole thing.

1 In the background was the post-war economic depression, which brought falling exports and mass unemployment. During the war the government had nationalized the coal mines in order to control the industry directly. This brought a great advantage for the miners: they were paid a national wage instead of miners in different pits receiving wage levels which varied according to the profitability of the mine. The miners naturally wanted nationalization to continue, but once the immediate post-war crisis was over in 1921, Lloyd George returned the mines to private control.

2 On the whole, industrialists failed to promote greater efficiency and more mechanization, which would have enabled them to compete better with other countries. They tended to blame declining profits on higher wages, and their attempts to reduce wages caused strained relations with their workforces.

3 The problems of the coal industry were important, because it was here that the stoppage began. Coal sales were probably worse hit than those of any other industry, partly because more gas, electricity and oil were being used, and because there was stiff competition from Germany and Poland, which had more modern mechanized pits. In 1925, only 20 per cent of British output was produced by coal-cutting machines; the rest was produced by hand-picks. In addition, France and Italy were receiving free coal from Germany as part of reparations.

4 The government refused to nationalize the mines, though it was widely believed that only government control could bring about the essential modernization that would enable the industry to survive. Mine-owners were unwilling to take any initiatives.

5 The return to the gold standard in April 1925 worsened the export position of all British industries, not just coal. According to the economist, J. M. Keynes, Churchill, the Chancellor of the Exchequer, though acting on the best available advice, had over-valued the pound by 10 per cent, making British exports that much more expensive.

6 The situation worsened in June 1925, when there was a sudden drop in coal exports, following a brief revival while the German mines in the Ruhr were closed during the French occupation. The owners announced that they would have to lower wages, abandon the national wage rate and increase hours. The miners protested and threatened action; Baldwin saved the situation temporarily by providing a government subsidy for nine months to keep wages at the existing levels until a Royal Commission under Sir Herbert Samuel could come up with a solution. This was viewed by the miners as a victory, and the day the subsidy was announced became known as 'Red Friday'. Many Conservatives claimed that by granting the subsidy, Baldwin had surrendered to the miners' threats; and in fact some of the more militant trade unionists did take Baldwin's sympathetic action to mean that the mere threat of a strike would be enough to get what they

wanted. However, the government began to make preparations so that it would not have to give way if the miners tried the same tactic again.

7 Meanwhile the Trades Union Congress (TUC) made it clear that they would support the miners, because if miners' wages were reduced, it was more than likely that wages of other workers would soon follow. Their concern was to protect the wages and living standards of all workers. This promise of support stiffened the attitude of the miners, but the TUC, hoping that the mere threat of a general strike would cause the government to back down, and relying on the Samuel Commission to find a way out, made no special preparations for a general strike. After all, a general strike was the syndicalists' method of attempting to overthrow a government, and the TUC leaders were far too moderate to be considered as syndicalists.

8 Everything hinged on whether the Samuel Commission could find a solution. Its report appeared in March 1926 and was an eminently sensible document. It recommended that mine-owners should press ahead with reorganization and modernization, should not insist on longer hours (which would only lead to over-production) and should not reduce wages (which would simply enable them to avoid reorganization). The government should not continue the subsidy. For the present, until the crisis had passed, miners must accept some wage reductions. Neither the owners nor the miners would accept the report, though the TUC welcomed it and tried to keep negotiations going because they were still not prepared for a general strike. The government made no attempt to force acceptance of the report, though one moderate mine-owner, Sir Alfred Mond, urged Baldwin to do so.

9 The mine-owners brought a showdown one step nearer by announcing that wages would be reduced on 30 April, to which the miners replied that they would strike on 1 May. The owners got in first and staged a lock-out on 30 April. The coal strike had begun. Ernest Bevin announced that a general strike would begin on 3 May if a settlement was not reached.

10 The TUC General Council, still hoping that the threat of a general strike would bring results, continued to negotiate with the government on behalf of the miners. However, negotiations between Cabinet and TUC were hampered all through 2 May because the miners' leaders had gone home, leaving the TUC to handle the talks. Baldwin heard that the *Daily Mail* compositors had refused to print an article claiming that a general strike would be a revolutionary action. He described this as an 'overt act', a sign that the general strike had begun; in fact, it was an unofficial action by the printing workers. Baldwin called off the negotiations, and while TUC representatives went to Downing Street in the early hours of 3 May to protest about the abrupt ending to the talks, they found that the Cabinet had dispersed and Baldwin had gone to bed. No solution had been found, so the General Strike began.

(a) why did it prove impossible to prevent the General Strike?

Left-wing historians have had no hesitation in laying the blame for this on Baldwin. They argue that he should have followed Mond's advice and insisted on all parties accepting the Samuel Report; nor should he have broken off negotiations so abruptly when the TUC was prepared to go on talking. There is a lot of evidence to suggest that many members of the government wanted a showdown so they could deal with the trade union threat once and for all. Churchill was one of the hard-liners, and so was the Home Secretary, Sir William Joynson-Hicks, who claimed that a communist revolution was about to be launched. In fact the communists had very little influence in any of the unions involved and certainly not in the TUC. So the government was well prepared, and they knew that the TUC had made very few plans. On the other hand, the miners were completely inflexible, their favourite slogan being 'Not a minute on the day, not a penny off the pay.' The mine-owners (with a few exceptions) were equally inflexible, insisting on district wage agreements (instead of a national wage rate), longer hours and lower wages. Even Lord Birkenhead, no friend of the miners, remarked that he thought the miners' leaders were the most stupid men in the country until he had the misfortune to meet the mine-owners.

24.4 the General Strike and its aftermath

The strike was an impressive show of working-class solidarity. In the industries called out (road, rail, docks, printing, gas, electricity, building, iron, steel, chemicals and, finally, textile workers), the response was almost 100 per cent, which seemed to show how alienated workers had become from employers and government. Over three million workers were on strike, and it soon affected other industries too, as factories ran out of raw materials and workers had to be laid off. Since the aim was to paralyse industry, workers in essential service industries such as sewage, rubbish collection and domestic electricity were not called out, so that the general public would not be inconvenienced more than was necessary. It was hoped that once industry was at a standstill, the government would soon be forced to intervene and make the mine-owners see reason. The TUC made it clear that it was not a political strike: they did *not* want to bring the government down; they did *not* want to run the country; what they *did* want was to force the government to defend miners' wages and jobs.

Despite the strike lasting for only nine days, there were many violent incidents, especially in Scotland, the North of England and in London itself. In Glasgow, a crowd attacked the tram depots where volunteers were about to drive off, throwing stones and smashing shop windows. Strikers detested the volunteers in particular, seeing them as middle-class strike-breakers. In Leeds, a crowd of some 5,000 threw coal and stones at trams driven by volunteers, injuring a number of passengers. In Middlesbrough, a crowd tried to wreck a train by blocking the track with stolen cars. In Aberdeen, strikers attacked buses being driven by student volunteers. Striking miners from Cramlington derailed 'The Flying Scotsman' by removing a rail from the track, while in Preston a crowd of some 5,000 attacked a police station, trying to free a man who had been arrested for throwing stones at a bus driven by a volunteer. After nine days the violence seemed to be getting worse, though, so far, both sides in the dispute had shown restraint. The TUC insisted that the strikers must not take up arms, and Baldwin managed to control the more extreme Cabinet members. When Churchill demanded that the Bank of England should freeze all trade union accounts, King George V helped by advising against it and expressing his concern about 'the dangers of the PM being rushed by some of his hot-headed colleagues which might have disastrous effects'. The Bank rejected Churchill's request. When the strike was over, the King wrote in his diary: 'Our old country can well be proud of itself, as during the last nine days there has been a strike in which four million people have been affected, not a shot has been fired and no-one killed. It shows what a wonderful people we are.' By 11 May there was no sign that the government would give way. When Sir Herbert Samuel offered to act as mediator, the TUC accepted. He produced *the Samuel Memorandum*, suggesting a short-term renewal of the subsidy to maintain wage levels, no wage reductions until reorganization was assured, and a National Wages Board. On 12 May the TUC suddenly called off the General Strike, hoping that the Memorandum would be accepted, though it was strictly unofficial and Baldwin had given no guarantees. The strike lasted unofficially until 14 May, but the miners refused to go back. Since the mine-owners refused to compromise, the coal strike dragged on until December. In the end the miners had to give way and go back to longer hours and lower wages. There was much bitterness about the TUC's 'betrayal'.

(a) why did the TUC call the General Strike off so soon?

They were dismayed when at the end of the first week there was no sign of a softening in the government' attitude; in fact, the extremists in the Cabinet were talking about 'unconditional surrender'. The TUC, completely unprepared for a general strike, was anxious to end it before provocative government actions caused events to take a more violent turn (see below). There were doubts about the legal position – Sir John Simon, a Liberal MP who was also a lawyer, said in the House of Commons that the strike was 'an illegal proceeding', not an industrial dispute, and that the leaders were liable to be sued for damages – 'to the utmost farthing' of their possessions – and then sent to jail. The Labour Party's attitude was unhelpful – MacDonald was against sympathetic strikes and was afraid that they would simply lose the party votes. The strike was proving too expensive – the TUC had already used £4 million out of their total strike fund of £12.5 million.

(b) how well did Baldwin handle the strike?

This question has evoked sharply contradictory views:

▸ The critical view is that Baldwin acted in his usual indolent way, scarcely 'handling' the strike at all. Worse still, he allowed the right-wing 'fire-eaters' in his Cabinet (Churchill and Joynson-Hicks) to take aggressive action, which might have provoked the strikers into violence. There is plenty of evidence to support this view. As A. N. Wilson points out, 'Churchill was in his element. He forgot that the job of the Chancellor was merely to look after the economy and moved immediately into dictatorial mode.' J. C. C. Davidson (former private secretary to Bonar Law) complained to Baldwin that Churchill 'thinks he is Napoleon', so Baldwin put Churchill in charge of the *British Gazette*, the government emergency newspaper. This printed uncompromising articles and fighting exhortations to the police and special constables, though the TUC had given strict orders that all violence was to be avoided. The tone of the *British Gazette* became so strident that King George V, who showed himself in a very favourable light throughout the strike, protested to Baldwin, and the *Gazette* became more restrained. It was Churchill's idea to use armoured cars to protect food convoys; 'We are at war', he declared; 'we must go through with it; either we crush the strike or the strike will crush us.' In fact, the special constables had been protecting the food convoys perfectly adequately.

▸ The sympathetic view is that Baldwin played a skilful waiting game, knowing that the TUC had no stomach for a prolonged strike. He took the view that the strike was an attack on the constitution and not an ordinary industrial dispute; therefore he refused to negotiate until the strike was called off. He concentrated on operating emergency plans prepared months earlier, and these worked efficiently. Volunteers kept food supplies moving, unloaded ships, and drove trains and buses. Food convoys were organized and protected by special constables (and later by Churchill's armoured cars) while the navy manned power stations. At the same time, Baldwin was usually conciliatory in tone – in a broadcast on 8 May he told the country that he was a man of peace and appealed to the strikers to trust him to secure a fair deal for everybody.

Whichever view one accepts, the fact remains that the General Strike failed, and the government claimed the credit.

(c) what were the results of the strike?

Historians and trade unionists are still divided in their views about the significance of the General Strike in trade union and labour history. Some see it as a watershed, a turning-point, the climax of the last period of labour militancy, when the failure of the strike caused the working classes to concentrate on political action through Parliament. Others feel this is exaggerated; Margaret Morris, for example, believes that it is difficult to isolate the effects of the General Strike from those of the coal strike. As she points out, although important developments did take place in working-class attitudes, these might well be the product of other factors such as mass unemployment and structural changes in industry, as old industries declined and contracted and new industries expanded. However, here are some of the developments which can be at least partly attributed to the General Strike and the coal strike:

› There was a good deal of working-class disillusionment with the TUC for its 'betrayal' of the miners. Membership of unions dropped from over 5.5 million before the strike to 4.9 million in 1927, reaching a lowest point of 4.4 million in 1933. After that it began to recover and had reached 6 million in 1938. In fact, there had been a much bigger fall in union membership following 'Black Friday', when the railwaymen and transport workers failed to support the miners' strike (April 1921) – from a peak of 8.3 million in 1920, membership fell to 5.6 million in 1922.

› The TUC abandoned the idea of a General Strike, convinced that one could never succeed.

› There was no solution to the problems in the coal industry and no modernization. The industry continued in slow decline with exports falling steadily. In 1913, 73 million tons had been exported; by 1929 the figure had fallen to 60 million tons, and even more disastrously, to 39 million tons in 1932.

› The government introduced the *Trade Disputes Act of 1927*, which was designed to make another general strike impossible. Baldwin had earlier rejected proposals for such legislation but now he could not resist right-wing pressure within the Conservative party. In future, sympathetic strikes and intimidation were illegal, and union funds could be seized during a dispute. Trade union members were not required to contribute to the union's political fund (the political levy paid to the Labour Party) unless they chose to do so and gave written notice of their intention. This was known as 'contracting-in', which now replaced the 'contracting-out' system introduced by the 1913 Trade Union Act. The new Act placed the responsibility on the member; many did not bother to contract in, and this caused a fall of over 25 per cent in the Labour Party's income.

The Act seems to have been largely unnecessary, since the TUC had had enough of general strikes. It was bitterly resented by the unions, but was not repealed until 1946.

› The working classes realized that parliamentary action offered the best chance of achieving their aims. Bitterness at the Trade Disputes Act and unemployment standing at over a million helped to bring trade unionists and the Labour Party together again. There is evidence that many working-class voters who had formerly supported the Conservatives and Liberals now began to look towards Labour as the party most likely to safeguard their interests. From 1927 onwards, Labour made extensive gains in local elections, and in the general election of 1929 increased its seats from 151 to 288. This was not an overall majority but it meant that, for the first time, Labour was the largest party in the Commons, and was able to form its second government.

The strike was not without some beneficial effects for the workers. It acted as a warning to other employers who, on the whole, were more reasonable than the mine owners and avoided drastic wage reductions. Some employers made genuine efforts to improve labour relations; for example, Sir Alfred Mond, founder of Imperial Chemical Industries (ICI), began a series of talks with Ernest Bevin of the Transport and General Workers' Union, and with other leading trade unionists.

(d) the general election of 1929

The election was a strangely quiet affair, with no dramatic issues under debate. The main Conservative slogan was 'Safety First', while the Labour programme played down full socialism and concentrated on immediate reforms. Much the most interesting was the new Liberal manifesto, *We Can Conquer Unemployment*. Liberal politicians had been having long consultations with leading economists, such as J. M. Keynes and William Beveridge, and had taken on many of their ideas. Under the leadership of Lloyd George, the party proposed a series of far-reaching reforms for agriculture, town-planning, housing, road-building and railway modernization; these were to be financed by state spending and could be expected to create at least half a million new jobs. The Conservatives lost over 140 seats and slumped to 260. Labour, though winning fewer votes than the Tories, emerged with 288 seats, while the Liberals, in spite of having the best ideas, were bitterly disappointed to take only 59 seats.

Why did the Conservatives lose? The government had done nothing to solve unemployment, which, though lower than when they took office, still stood at over a million. The coal-mining industry continued to decline and the balance of payments was unhealthy (this means that the value of goods imported was greater than the value of goods exported, causing a drain on gold and foreign currency reserves to make up the difference). The government – with the exception of Neville Chamberlain –seemed dull and lacking in inspiration and energy.

Probably the main reason for the swing to Labour was the aftermath of the General Strike: the 1927 Trade Disputes Act backfired on the government: it was seen by many in the centre and on the left as being vindictive as well as unnecessary, and it gave the trade unions and the Labour Party a common cause to unite against. The government's attitude towards the miners probably alienated much of their normal support among the working classes. As Martin

Pugh points out, 'in most working class communities the General Strike had been solidly supported, and the subsequent six-months miners' strike generated immense sympathy for the men and their families who were driven to the poor law authorities for assistance'. A. N. Wilson reached this damning conclusion: 'The General Strike ... was a yelp of pain and anger, not an organized political programme ... It had been an ugly episode. It did not show what a wonderful people the British were. It showed how selfish their middle classes were, and how strong was their monied power'.

In a sense, though, the election result was indecisive: Labour lacked an overall majority, and more people had voted Conservative (8.6 million) than Labour (8.4 million). The Liberal vote of 5.3 million was not fairly reflected in their 59 seats. Over 60 per cent of the electorate did not want a Labour government, but there was no possibility of a coalition between Conservatives and Liberals because Baldwin detested Lloyd George so much.

QUESTIONS

1 Read the following extract about the General Strike of 1926 from *Empire to Welfare State: English History 1906–1976* by T. O. Lloyd, and then answer the questions that follow.

> The miners' stand was not flexible: 'not a minute on the day, not a penny off the pay'. Nor were the owners more helpful: district agreements, longer hours, and lower wages was their answer.

   (a) How far was the General Strike caused by lack of flexibility on the part of both mine workers and mine owners?
   (b) Why did the General Strike fail?
   (c) How important was the General Strike in the development of trade union and working-class history between the wars?

2 Why did the Conservative Party have such a dominant position in British politics in the inter-war period? (See also Chapter 25.)
3 Lord Grey, writing in the *British Gazette* in May 1926, said that the General Strike was 'an attempted revolution'. How far do you think the events of 1926 and the actions of the government and the unions support this view?

A document question about Baldwin, the General Strike and its aftermath can be found on the accompanying website www.palgrave.com/masterseries/lowe1.

political and economic crises, 1929–39: the second Labour government (1929–31), the world economic crisis and the National Governments

summary of events

Labour was again in a minority, though this time the government was slightly stronger, since Labour was the largest single party. With 288 seats to the Conservatives' 260, they needed the support of the 59 Liberals to get any contentious legislation through the Commons. This time, MacDonald did not attempt to combine the premiership with the Foreign Office, which went to Arthur Henderson. The Cabinet was again solidly moderate, with a sprinkling of former Liberals; it contained one left-winger, George Lansbury, in a minor post, and for the first time ever in Britain, a woman, Margaret Bondfield, who became Minister of Labour.

The government's main achievements were in foreign affairs, but its promise was blighted by *the world economic crisis (sometimes known as the Great Depression)*, which began with *the Wall Street Crash,* a dramatic fall in share prices on the New York Stock Exchange (October 1929). By May 1931, the unemployment figure in Britain had risen to 2.5 million and there was a financial crisis. The Labour Cabinet could not agree on what measures to adopt, and consequently MacDonald handed in the government's resignation (August). However, he himself stayed on as Prime Minister of a coalition government of Labour, Conservative and Liberal MPs, to the intense fury of the majority of the Labour movement, which accused him of betraying the party. The new *National Government* as it was called, introduced emergency measures and then won an overwhelming victory in a general election held in October 1931. The country began to recover gradually from the worst effects of the depression, though unemployment remained a serious problem in certain areas.

MacDonald was Prime Minister until his retirement in June 1935, when Baldwin took over. The following November, the National Government won another election, which proved to be the last one until July 1945. Baldwin was Prime Minister until May 1937, when he too retired, to be succeeded by Neville Chamberlain who was premier until May 1940, when he was replaced by Winston Churchill. The main issues of these last years were the question of rearmament in the face of the worsening international situation (see Sections 27.2–27.3), and the abdication crisis of 1936.

25.1 Labour policies at home and abroad

(a) domestic problems and policies

These included *the Housing Act of 1930*, which was the work of Arthur Greenwood, the Minister of Health. It renewed the government subsidy for council-house-building and organized the speeding-up of slum clearance. The Act was suspended during the financial crises of 1931–4, but then the National Government began to apply it later in 1934, and by 1939 vast slum areas had been cleared. Another advantage of the Act was that it created extra jobs (see Section 20.4(e)). *The Coal Mines Act (1930)* reduced the miners' working day from eight hours to seven and a half. But there was little else to show; an attempt to repeal parts of the 1927 Trade Disputes Act was defeated by the Liberals, and an Education Bill to raise the school-leaving age to 15 was rejected by the House of Lords, showing its remaining teeth again after slumbering for five years.

(b) overseas affairs

1 Henderson was anxious to continue Britain's conciliatory attitude towards Germany and was involved in *the Young Plan (1929)*. This aimed to settle the remaining problem of reparations – the Dawes Plan (1924) had left the total amount payable uncertain. The French were willing to compromise, and a committee chaired by an American banker, Owen Young, decided to reduce reparations from £6,600 million to £2,000 million, to be paid on a graded scale over the next fifty-nine years. This was the figure that Keynes had urged at Versailles, and its acceptance ten years later was an admission of error by the Allies. The Plan was welcomed in Germany, as was the withdrawal of Allied troops from the Rhineland five years ahead of schedule, at Henderson's suggestion.

   Unfortunately there was hardly time to put the Young Plan into operation before a series of events following in rapid succession destroyed the fragile harmony of Locarno:

   ‣ The death of Stresemann, the German Foreign Minister (October 1929), removed one of the outstanding 'men of Locarno'.
   ‣ The Wall Street Crash in the same month soon developed into the world economic crisis, bringing mass unemployment in Germany. Hopes of

peace and tranquillity were kept alive by the Lausanne Conference (1932), at which Britain and France released Germany from most of its remaining reparations payments.

- In January 1933, Hitler became German Chancellor, and after that, international tension mounted.

2 Relations with Russia improved again when the Labour government, encouraged by the new pro-western Foreign Minister, Maxim Litvinov, resumed diplomatic relations in 1929 and signed another trade agreement the following year; but the improvement was only short-lived: the Conservative-dominated National government cancelled the trade agreement in 1932.

3 Henderson was an enthusiastic supporter of the League of Nations and was highly respected by foreign governments. He worked unceasingly for disarmament and was rewarded by being chosen as president of the World Disarmament Conference, planned to open in Geneva in 1932. Bitter disappointment was to follow, though: by the time the conference met, Henderson was out of office, and the proceedings ended in failure when the Germans walked out in October 1933.

4 MacDonald scored a personal triumph with his visit to the USA (1929) when he became the first British Prime Minister to address the US Congress; his visit did much to heal the rift caused by disagreements over Britain's war debts to the USA. MacDonald followed this up by organizing a conference in London (1930) attended by the Americans and Japanese, at which the three states re-affirmed the 5:5:3 ratio of cruisers, destroyers and submarines that had been agreed at an earlier conference in Washington (1921–2). This was successful in re-establishing friendship between the USA and Britain, but the Japanese soon exceeded their limits.

Less successful were Labour's attempts to deal with the problems in India (see Section 26.4), Palestine (see Section 26.5) and Egypt. Most serious of all were the economic problems that led to the downfall of the government.

25.2 how did the economic crisis bring down the Labour government in 1931?

It was the financial crisis resulting from the world economic disaster that caused the government's resignation.

(a) why was there an economic crisis?

1 The root of the problem lay in the USA, where American industrialists, encouraged by high profits and helped by increasing mechanization, were producing too many goods for the home market to absorb, at a time when foreign countries were becoming increasingly reluctant to buy American goods. This was partly because the Americans had introduced tariffs to keep

foreign goods out; this prevented European states from making the profits they needed, both to buy American goods and to pay their war debts to the USA. The result was a general stagnation of trade which began to show itself during 1929, and which caused some of the better-informed American investors to sell their shares. Confidence in the future was shaken, and in a panic, thousands more investors rushed to sell their shares. However, with the future now so uncertain, very few people were prepared to buy shares, and share prices tumbled on the New York Stock Exchange in Wall Street. One especially bad day was 24 October 1929 – Black Thursday – when nearly 13 million shares were 'dumped' on the stock market at depressingly low prices. This was the so-called Wall Street Crash, which ruined millions of investors and almost half the country's banks. As the demand for goods of all types fell away, workers were laid off and factories closed. By 1933, almost 14 million Americans were out of work.

2 The crisis in the USA affected most European countries. Europe's prosperity since 1924 (particularly in Germany) had much to do with American loans under the Dawes Plan, which enabled Germany to revive its industries and pay reparations to Britain, France, Belgium and Italy. This in turn enabled these countries to pay their war debts to the USA, and thus Europe and America were closely linked in a circle of loans and repayments. Disaster in one part of the circle inevitably had repercussions elsewhere. The USA ceased to import goods from Europe, stopped all further loans to Germany and called in the short-term loans already made. The effects were most serious in Germany, where in 1931 unemployment was approaching four million. Austria and Hungary were badly affected and a number of banks collapsed; the Austrian government had to ask for loans from the League of Nations to get through the crisis.

(b) unemployment in Britain

The effects of the world economic crisis in Britain were not as sudden or as dramatic as in the USA and Central Europe. This was partly because in Britain there had been nothing like the same boom in the late 1920s as had been experienced in the USA, and certainly nothing like the same speculation in shares. Britain was spared the disastrous bank collapses that ruined so many people in the USA and Europe. But the effects were serious enough: unemployment was already standing at over a million when the Labour government took office; by December 1930 it had shot up to 2.5 million, and in the depths of the depression in 1932, exports had fallen by a third from the 1928 figure, and unemployment had passed the three million mark; this was about 23 per cent of insured workers (see Section 20.4(d)) for full details).

The government seemed stunned by the enormity of it all, and took no action to try to reduce unemployment. There was no shortage of advice: economic radicals among both Labour and Liberal supporters proposed that the government should create jobs by spending money. Sir Oswald Mosley (Labour's Chancellor of the Duchy of Lancaster) produced a plan, after consultations with J. M. Keynes, suggesting import restrictions, subsidies for farmers (to reduce food imports), bulk purchase from the Dominions, government control of banks to ensure that industry was allowed more credit (to enable new industries to expand), old age pensions at 60 and the school leaving age being raised to 16 (from 14). The last two measures would have been expensive, but would have made an immediate impact on unemployment (see Section 20.5(b) for other ideas put forward at the time).

MacDonald and Snowden were far too cautious; they ignored all advice, and cut expenditure as much as possible, hoping that the free market would generate its own recovery. The government's minority position was no excuse for its inaction, since the Liberals would have voted for a big programme of government investment to create jobs. There was much support for Mosley within the Labour Party, but when the leaders rejected his proposals, he left Labour and launched the New Party. This was not successful, and so in 1932 he founded the British Union of Fascists (see item (f) below).

(c) the financial crisis and the fall of the Labour government

Payment of unemployment benefit was placing a severe strain on the government's finances, with nothing to show for it. A committee was appointed under Sir George May to investigate national expenditure; its report, published in July 1931, was an extremely gloomy document. It forecast that, by April 1932, there would be a budget deficit of £120 million. To stave off the crisis, it proposed a general reduction of salaries in public-sector jobs (such as the armed forces, civil servants, judges and police). Teachers were singled out for the largest cut of all – 20 per cent, and the report recommended that unemployment benefit should be cut by the same amount.

Unfortunately, foreign bankers were extremely nervous at this time, following the recent collapse of the largest bank in Austria, the Credit Anstalt. The May Report led them to the conclusion that Britain must be on the verge of bankruptcy, and they rushed to withdraw gold, plunging the country into a deeper financial crisis. The Bank of England informed the government that immediate economies were needed to restore confidence in sterling; American and French bankers said that further loans could be made if unemployment benefit was cut by 10 per cent. MacDonald and Snowden were prepared to implement most of the May Report's recommendations, together with the 10 per cent reduction in unemployment benefit. However, this was too much for some of their colleagues: after a fierce argument in Cabinet, the cut in benefit was approved, but only by 11 votes to 9.

MacDonald claimed that the minority was too large for the government to continue; there was nothing else for it but to resign. He went to Buckingham Palace to hand in the government's resignation to George V, but to the amazement of almost the whole of the Labour Party, he stayed on as Prime Minister of what was called a National Government, with a Cabinet consisting of Conservatives, Liberals and just three other Labour MPs (24 August 1931).

(d) did MacDonald betray his party?

The majority of the Labour Party was furious with MacDonald; they condemned him as a traitor to the Labour movement and expelled him from the party. They accused him of being vain, ambitious and out of touch with the grass-roots of the party, and claimed that he had been planning to ditch them for some time, so that he could remain in power. There is no solid evidence to support this view; his biographer, David Marquand, believes that George V and Baldwin persuaded MacDonald to put national concerns above the interests of his party and to stay on as Prime Minister of an all-party government. This, they convinced him, was the best way of restoring confidence and avoiding a general election.

Robert Skidelsky suggests that MacDonald's real betrayal of the party occurred not in August 1931, but in the earlier part of his government, when he ignored advice and failed to take action, which might have avoided the crisis of 1931. Arguably, MacDonald did betray his party in the sense that he abandoned Labour policies when he agreed to the cuts in unemployment benefit. MacDonald also laid himself open to criticism by not discussing in Cabinet the possibility of a coalition government before he met the king and other party leaders at Buckingham Palace on 24 August. This certainly gives the impression that he was deliberately misleading his colleagues.

More recently, Philip Williamson has put forward a different interpretation: he suggests that Neville Chamberlain proposed a National Government in preference to a Conservative government, because 'this would shield their party from the electorally damaging accusations that it was a rich man's party cutting the incomes of the poor'. MacDonald would get the blame for an unpopular but necessary policy, and the Conservatives would win a decisive victory at the next election. This was expected to take place within a matter of weeks rather than years: the National Government was seen as a temporary expedient to deal with the national emergency; once that had been achieved, there would be a return to normal party politics. It would seem therefore that MacDonald did not betray his party by forcing it out of office. After all, the Labour Cabinet had already agreed that he should hand in its resignation, and the evidence suggests that MacDonald hoped to be able to return to the party once the crisis was over. Very few people could have foreseen at the time that the National Government would last for the next fourteen years.

25.3 the National Government and its attempts to promote recovery

The new government had a small Cabinet of only ten – four Labour (MacDonald, Snowden, Thomas and Lord Sankey), four Conservatives (Baldwin, Neville Chamberlain, Sir Samuel Hoare and Sir Philip Cunliffe-Lister) and two Liberals (Sir Herbert Samuel and Lord Reading).

(a) emergency measures

These were introduced by Philip Snowden, the Chancellor of the Exchequer; his emergency budget implemented much of the May Report to try to restore confidence and save the pound. Income tax was raised from 4s 6d to 5s in the pound, and salaries of public employees and unemployment benefits were reduced by 10 per cent. However, these changes did not produce the desired effect, and foreign bankers continued to withdraw funds from Britain. Nor was the situation helped by *the Invergordon Mutiny* in September 1931, when naval crews protested against the proposed salary cuts, though this soon petered out when the government assured them that cuts would not exceed 10 per cent. In the end, the government went off the gold standard (21 September), so that the value of the pound fell by about 25 per cent on the foreign exchanges. The National Government had failed in its original aim of staying on the gold standard, but at least the financial crisis was more or less over. Though the devaluation of the pound might have been expected to help British trade by making exports cheaper, there was no immediate revival: unemployment continued to rise and topped the 3 million mark during the winter of 1932–3.

(b) the general election of October 1931

By October 1931, the leaders of the National Government had decided that a general election was necessary. The government was originally intended as a temporary crisis measure, so now that the financial crisis was over, most people expected an election on normal party lines. However, MacDonald and Baldwin had worked well together; Baldwin seemed to like the arrangement which gave him (as Deputy Prime Minister) plenty of power, but left MacDonald to bear the final responsibility. The Labour members were prepared to go along with the Conservatives' main idea for dealing with unemployment – the introduction of tariffs in the form of import duties; even some leading Liberals such as Sir John Simon had been converted to protection. There seemed to be very good reasons for staying together and continuing the National Government, and MacDonald appealed to the country for 'a doctor's mandate' to do whatever was necessary for recovery, including the introduction of tariffs.

In the general election of October 1931, the National Government won a landslide victory with 554 MPs, which included 473 Conservatives, 13 Labour, 35 Simon Liberals (who supported tariffs) and 33 Samuel Liberals (who supported free trade). The opposition consisted of 52 Labour MPs led by Arthur Henderson, and 4 Lloyd George Liberals. Despite MacDonald being Prime Minister, it was in effect a thinly disguised Conservative government; Neville Chamberlain became Chancellor of the Exchequer, replacing Snowden, who retired to the House of Lords.

The Labour party probably did so badly in the election because the electors blamed the Labour government for the depression; unemployment had more than doubled since Labour came into office, and there was a feeling, rightly or wrongly, that the government had 'run away' from the crisis by resigning. Under Henderson's leadership, the party had moved further to the left, and was suggesting that real socialism was the only way to cure Britain's economic problems. This enabled their opponents to wage an alarmist campaign just before the election: Snowden called Labour's programme 'Bolshevism run mad', and there were rumours that a Labour government would seize everybody's money in the Post Office savings bank. Against this, the National Government offered what seemed to be an attractive immediate solution to the country's economic problems – tariffs.

(c) further government measures to help the economy

Free trade was abandoned when Neville Chamberlain fittingly introduced his father's policy, in the *Import Duties Act* of 1932. This placed a 10 per cent tariff on most imports, except those from the Empire. As well as increasing sales of British goods at home, this brought in extra revenue, so that Chamberlain was able to avoid raising income tax again. However, an attempt at the Ottawa Conference to develop Empire trade met with little success (see Section 26.1(c)). Defence expenditure and interest on war loans were reduced. Some attempt was made to reorganize iron and steel, shipbuilding, textiles and coal, and to persuade new industry to move into areas of high unemployment, though without much success (see section 25.4(e) below). Remaining off the gold standard made British goods cheaper abroad and led to an increase in exports. The bank rate was reduced from 6 per cent to 2 per cent, mainly to reduce debt charges; however, many local authorities took advantage of low interest rates to borrow money for house-building. This provided extra jobs not only for builders but for all the allied trades, including gas and electricity.

These measures helped to boost the economy and to increase sales at home and abroad, though it can be argued that foreign manufacturers, deprived of markets in Britain by the new import duties, became competitors in export markets. Derek Aldcroft points out that while by 1937 'Britain had achieved a strong cyclical recovery with income and production levels well above the former peaks of 1929 ... exports failed to regain previous levels. The recovery was very much a domestically-based one, being powered by housing and the newer industries.' Since this was a cyclical recovery, it seems likely that it was more a result of increasingly favourable circumstances than of the efforts of the National

Government, though to be fair their policies did have some unintentional, indirect benefits, such as the boost to house-building provided by low interest rates.

(d) favourable circumstances

These would probably have occurred in any case as part of the normal economic and trade cycle, whatever action the government had chosen to take:

> Prices of all products (both British and imported) fell during the depression, including the prices of raw materials, which reduced production costs for British industry and brought down the cost of house-building. The cost of living also came down, and even with wage reductions, there was an increase in real wages (what people could actually buy with the cash available).
> This enabled people in jobs to spend their extra cash on British consumer goods and even on luxuries such as radios and holidays, which stimulated the creation of jobs.

(e) signs of prosperity

Unemployment gradually fell from a peak of over 3 million in late 1932 to around 2 million in 1935. This encouraged Baldwin to hold an election in November of that year. This brought another convincing victory for the National Government with 432 seats; Labour recovered to 154 but the independent Liberals slumped to only 21. As the recovery continued after 1935, the economy in the Midlands and the South was booming, the most striking success being the expansion of new industries such as motor car manufacturing, with factories in Coventry and Oxford. The majority of the population began to enjoy a higher standard of living than ever before. New council houses were available and the sales of consumer goods increased rapidly – radios, electric cookers, refrigerators, modern furniture and telephones. Some workers were able to afford an Austin or Morris car – the number of private cars registered doubled between 1930 and 1939. Cinemas and dancehalls were packed and the annual holiday at the seaside became a national institution; the first Butlin's holiday camp was opened at Skegness in 1937. Higher real wages also meant an improvement in diet – more fresh fruit, vegetables and dairy produce were eaten, helping to improve the health of the nation.

However, there was one disturbing fact – while much of the country seemed to have recovered from the depression by 1937–8, unemployment would not go away completely. This was *structural unemployment*, something quite separate from the world economic crisis, which had caused *cyclical unemployment*, and it needs to be examined separately.

(f) communists and fascists

During the 1920s and 1930s Britain experienced its own versions of communist and fascist parties. However, whereas communists in the USSR and fascists in

Italy and Germany came to power, with catastrophic results for millions of people, in Britain they remained merely fringe groups. It seemed that the vast majority of British people considered them to be undemocratic and foreign, and therefore to be avoided.

The Communist Party of Great Britain was formed in 1920 by the British Socialist party together with the Socialist Labour Party of Glasgow. Its early members were inspired by the success of the 1917 Bolshevik Revolution in Russia and the ideas of Karl Marx, the nineteenth-century German political theorist. They believed in a classless society in which all people were considered equal, all property would be held in common, the workers would control the means of production and the economy would be centrally planned; in other words, the dictatorship of the proletariat. They also accepted that this could probably only be achieved when some great crisis in the capitalist system enabled them to seize power, as Lenin and the Bolsheviks had done in Russia. Naturally this horrified the property-owning classes, especially when it became known that the party was being financed and to some extent directed from Moscow. Even the Labour party distanced itself from the communists and rejected their request for affiliation.

Nevertheless communism attracted some support in the depressed areas, in parts of London's East End, and within some trade unions. Two communist MPs were elected in 1922, one at Battersea North, and the other at Motherwell, though neither made much of a mark. Membership of the party reached a peak of perhaps 17,000 in 1926 immediately after the General Strike, but membership soon fell again, and was usually around 5,000. Between 1929 and 1935 there were no communist MPs, but party members played an important role in organizing hunger marches and providing soup kitchens. They were able to claim that the depression and mass unemployment proved that the capitalist system had failed the workers. But the party was too weak numerically to have any chance of launching a revolution. The most they could do during the 1930s was to harass the increasingly aggressive fascist movement. In spite of their weaknesses, the Conservatives still saw communists as being more dangerous than fascists.

The British Fascisti were founded in 1923 by a remarkable woman called Rotha Lintorn Orman, mainly as a reaction against socialism and the new British Communist party. They were afraid of a Bolshevik revolution and were convinced that the 1926 miners' strike and the General Strike were the beginnings of the British Bolshevik revolution. Membership increased to perhaps 3,000 at this time. Once it became clear that the British communists were too weak to attempt an uprising, even during the General Strike and the depression of the early 1930s, membership declined to no more than about 300 by 1933. Many had defected to the new *British Union of Fascists (BUF)*, founded in 1932 by *Sir Oswald Mosley*.

After the Labour party's rejection of his plans for economic recovery, his resignation and then the failure of his New Party, Mosley was disillusioned with party politics. Full of admiration for what Mussolini had apparently achieved in Italy, he believed that a similar system was the answer to Britain's problems. The national decline could be reversed and poverty eliminated by placing the needs of the nation above those of the individual. At best, this would involve 'the fusion of the individual in something far greater than himself'. This approach needed strong and 'robust' leadership, though this often led to violence; it also included many of the trappings of the continental fascists and Nazis: the cult of the heroic leader (Mosley himself), the black shirts, military uniforms, jackboots, parades and fascist salutes. The movement was also anti-communist and anti-Jewish. The BUF soon gained considerable support from some Conservatives, who liked Mosley's plans for tariffs and public works; other influential supporters included Lord Rothermere, the owner of the *Daily Mail.* They were all afraid of a Bolshevik revolution and they liked Mosley's anti-communist stance. In January 1934, under the headline 'Hurrah for the Blackshirts', the *Daily Mail* proclaimed that 'the spirit of the age is one of national discipline and organisation'. Britain's survival depended on 'the existence of a Great Party of the Right with the same directness of purpose and energy of method as Hitler and Mussolini have displayed'. Many of Mosley's supporters genuinely believed that if there was a Labour victory at the next election, even the Conservative party would welcome 'a Fascist counter-revolution'.

There has been some debate among historians about whether Mosley had any real chance of gaining power. The majority view is that the possibility was remote. However, Robert Skidelsky and Martin Pugh suggest that if the depression had lasted longer, voters might well have turned in desperation to Mosley. On the other hand, the fascists made very little headway in the areas worst hit by unemployment, and in the 1935 election there were signs that people were turning to the Labour party rather than towards the right. Pugh also claims that the abdication crisis was Mosley's best chance: 'December 1936 was the closest that Fascism came to obtaining a share of power in interwar Britain'. His theory is that the King, who admired Mosley, could have dismissed Baldwin and appointed Mosley as Prime Minister instead. Only the King's sudden decision to abdicate deprived Mosley of his opportunity. But again, the argument is not convincing: as Ferdinand Mount points out, 'if the king had attempted to dismiss Baldwin and appoint as prime minister Mosley or some other member of the "King's Party", the House of Commons would have erupted in fury and the king would have been dethroned in days'.

The truth is that, by the end of 1936, Mosley's popularity had slumped disastrously; membership of his party plummeted from a peak of 50,000 in the summer of 1934 to less than 5,000. There were several reasons for this dramatic decline:

- Many people were appalled by the violence that seemed to be an integral part of fascism. Mosley had formed what he called his Defence Force, ostensibly to protect his supporters. But they soon became notorious for their violence. In the words of Stephen Dorril: 'Even within the BUF its members had a reputation for brutality ... they used rubber hoses loaded with lead shot and some used knuckledusters to attack a jeering crowd in Rochdale's town hall square ... The BUF strategy was to carry out campaigns in working-class districts where the Defence Force actively sought a fight.' They called it 'doing over the Reds'. In June 1934, Blackshirt stewards at the BUF mass meeting in London's Olympia attacked hecklers. In October 1936, in the so-called 'Battle of Cable Street', a BUF march through Stepney ended in a pitched battle with police and anti-fascist demonstrators.
- The movement's anti-Semitism aroused opposition. In his 1975 biography of Mosley, Robert Skidelsky claimed that the violence was 'at least as much the result of anti-fascist demonstrators interrupting meetings or attacking Fascists', and that the anti-Semitism had been exaggerated. Mosley 'regarded the Jewish issue as more of a liability than an asset, a diversion from his main task'. However, Stephen Dorril disputes this: on the contrary, he argues, the BUF's anti-Jewish policy was 'not cynical political opportunism, but a genuine, integral part of the movement'.
- By 1935, the economy was well on the way to recovery and the Communist party was losing support and presenting much less of a threat. The National Government therefore decided to risk an election. It could now be seen that the BUF was at a disadvantage – Mosley had concentrated on building it into a paramilitary movement rather than a parliamentary party, and so it was not sufficiently organized to be able to fight an election. Perhaps he was afraid that his candidates would do badly. Whatever his reasons, Mosley decided not to contest the election, and the BUF remained without any MPs. Nor did they ever manage to get a single local councillor elected. They did eventually contest a few by-elections, but only scored a few hundred votes.
- Baldwin's National Government took decisive action to curb the violence. *The Public Order Act* of 1936 banned the wearing of military-style uniforms by political parties, the use of stewards at outdoor political meetings and the use of inflammatory language; police were given the power to ban marches. This reduced the impact of the BUF's campaign.
- In the end, therefore, circumstances and conditions in Britain were never as serious as they were in Germany or Italy. The economy improved, so that, except in the depressed areas, people were better off at the end of the 1930s; and the threat of a communist revolution was never as serious as in Germany and Italy. On top of all that, Mosley seemed to have developed delusions of grandeur with his Blackshirts and strutting parades, and people came to feel that he could not be trusted. When the Second World War began, the BUF

was seen as having been corrupted by Nazi influence; in 1940, the party was banned and Mosley and other leading fascists were imprisoned.

25.4 unemployment in the 1930s

(a) the two-economy problem

There were really two economies in Britain: the Midlands and the South were, on the whole, prosperous and booming, once the effects of the world economic crisis had passed; but the North and West – Wales, the North of England, Scotland and Northern Ireland – remained depressed. Tables 25.1, 25.2 and 25.3 show the magnitude of the unemployment problem and how badly the North suffered in comparison with the Midlands and South.

In some towns in the depressed areas the individual figures were startling: Jarrow had 68 per cent of its total workforce unemployed in 1934; and in Merthyr Tydfil the figure was 62 per cent, while in St Albans at the same time it was only 3.9 per cent. The Midlands and the South were much better off

table **25.1 total numbers registered unemployed, average over 12 months (in millions)**

1927 = 1.08	1932 = 2.75	1937 = 1.48
1928 = 1.22	1933 = 2.52	1938 = 1.79
1929 = 1.22	1934 = 2.16	1939 = 1.51
1930 = 1.91	1935 = 2.04	1940 = 0.96
1931 = 2.63	1936 = 1.76	1941 = 0.35

Source: C. Cook and J. Stevenson, *Handbook of Modern British History, 1714–1987* (Longman, 1988), p. 217.

table **25.2 percentage unemployed in staple trades compared to national average**

	1929	1932	1936	1938
Coal	18.2	41.2	25.0	22.0
Cotton	14.5	31.1	15.1	27.7
Shipbuilding	23.2	59.5	30.6	21.4
Iron and steel	19.9	48.5	29.5	24.8
Average for all industries	9.9	22.9	12.5	13.3

Source: J. Stevenson, *British Society 1914–45* (Penguin, 1984), p. 270.

table **25.3 Unemployed as a percentage of insured workers in different regions**

	1929	1932	1937
London and S.E. England	5.6	13.7	6.4
S.W. England	8.1	17.1	7.8
Midlands	9.3	20.1	7.2
Northern England	13.5	27.1	13.8
Wales	19.3	36.5	22.3
Scotland	12.1	27.7	15.9
Northern Ireland	15.1	27.2	23.6

Source: J. Stevenson, *British Society 1914–45* (Penguin, 1984), p. 271.

because they had the new industries – motor cars, electrical goods, aircraft and chemicals.

(b) why was unemployment so persistent in the depressed areas?

These areas had specialized in the older, export-based staple industries – coal, textiles, ship-building, and iron and steel – which had flourished until the 1880s, and then, for a variety of reasons, the export trade declined (see Section 20.4(b) for a full analysis of reasons for the decline). Sadly, very little was done to modernize these declining industries; machinery and techniques were out-of-date, and they were inefficient and over-staffed compared with their main foreign competitors; but as profits fell, there was less chance of re-investment to make them more competitive. Employers laid men off, and this is why unemployment was so high in the North of the country even before the world economic crisis. This is termed *structural unemployment* because it was caused by faults in the structure of the economy.

The depressed areas had concentrated exclusively on the staple industries, so there was very little alternative employment to be had. Some historians have suggested that unemployment benefit took away the worst effects of unemployment and therefore prevented people moving to more prosperous areas. But the evidence does not support this claim: in the first place, many workers moved from South Wales into the London area, and second, many of the new industries in the South wanted young men or women to work on production lines for comparatively low wages; married men with families simply could not afford to move long distances to low-paid jobs in areas where housing was expensive. So they were forced to remain, and become part of the reservoir of long-term unemployed.

(c) the effects of long-term unemployment

The effects could be devastating. In areas of high unemployment, shops and other businesses, and even sometimes pubs, were forced to close, and places such as Jarrow and Merthyr became like ghost towns to which it was difficult to attract investment and new industries. Seebohm Rowntree carried out another survey in York, discovering that 31 per cent of working-class families were living in serious poverty. In Stockton-on-Tees the average income of families where the wage-earner was unemployed was less than £1.50 a week, and clearly, unemployment benefit was insufficient. Men had to resort to casual labour, which brought very poor rewards. Families fell into debt and many were evicted for non-payment of rent. Diet suffered and health deteriorated. This was reflected in the infant mortality rate, which in 1935 in the South was 42 per thousand live births, while in South Wales it was 63 and in Durham and Northumberland, 76. In Jarrow it was as high as 114. There was an increase in diseases such as rickets and anaemia. The longer a worker was unemployed, the more difficult it became for him/her to find another job, even

Illus. **25.1 A hunger march to London, 1932**

when the economy began to recover, because prospective employers suspected that the long-term unemployed would have forgotten whatever skills they once had, or that they must have some character defect that made them incapable of holding down a job. This sort of experience often caused a loss of confidence and self-esteem, and in some cases nervous depression and mental disorders.

As early as 1921 the National Unemployed Workers' Movement (NUWM) was formed, and by 1932 it had perhaps 100,000 members. The Communist Party of Great Britain co-operated with them and together they planned and carried out a programme of demonstrations and hunger marches. The most famous hunger march took place in 1936 when some 200 men, mainly unemployed shipbuilders, walked the 300 miles from Jarrow in the north-east of England to London, where they presented a petition to Parliament. Known as the Jarrow Crusade, the march caught the public imagination and aroused a lot of sympathy, though sadly, it made little difference to the plight of the unemployed.

(d) government action to deal with unemployment

There was no shortage of suggestions for dealing with unemployment. These ranged from Keynesian ideas of state investment to stimulate new industries, through radical Conservative schemes for job creation, to the socialist solution of a planned economy (see Section 20.5(b) for full details). But like the Labour government before it, the National Government ignored most of the advice offered, partly because it shrank from spending any large amounts of cash, and partly because it refused to accept that the problem could be solved (see Section 20.5(c–d)). Its response was unimaginative and its measures failed to get to the root of the problem. They included *The Unemployment Act (1934)*, which was based on the highly unpopular *'means test'* introduced in 1931 (see Section 20.4(d)). *The Special Areas Act (1934)* appointed two unpaid commissioners and provided them with £2 million to try to revive Scotland, Cumberland, Tyneside and South Wales; they did not have a great deal of success (see Section 20.5(c)). The Bank Rate reduction from 6 per cent to 2 per cent helped the housing boom and encouraged local authorities to embark on road-building. This was in fact a Keynesian measure, but it was unintentional: the government's prime motive was to reduce its own debt charges. It showed that it did not really appreciate the potential of what it was doing, because it was constantly urging local authorities to economize. An attempt was made to revitalize the steel industry by imposing a tariff on foreign steel and setting up the British Iron and Steel Federation (see Section 20.5(c), and by 1937, it was showing signs of revival.

By the end of 1937 total unemployment had fallen to 1.4 million, but there had been little improvement in the depressed areas where most of the unemployed were concentrated. The government had failed to produce any positive strategy for planning the economy or reducing long-term unemployment. There was another recession in 1938, which sent unemployment over 1.8 million; only in 1940, as the war effort intensified, did the figure fall below 1 million.

25.5 Baldwin and the Abdication Crisis, 1936

(a) the popularity of Edward VIII

George V died in January 1936 and was succeeded by his 41-year-old unmarried son, Edward VIII. The new king was popular and unconventional and seemed genuinely to care about the problems and hardships of his people. In November he paid a visit to some of the South Wales mining valleys where unemployment was still high. Appalled by the poverty, he is reported to have said, 'terrible, terrible, something will have to be done about this'.

Edward had fallen in love with Wallis Simpson, an American woman who had been divorced from her first husband and was now married to a London stockbroker. In October 1936, Mrs Simpson was granted a divorce from her second husband, and Edward intended to marry her; however, the story was not mentioned in the British press, and the general public knew nothing about it.

(b) objections to the marriage

Baldwin decided, for once, that decisive action was needed. He pointed out to Edward that his marriage to a twice-divorced American lady would not be popular with the government or the British people, and tried to dissuade him from going ahead. There was the prospect of a serious constitutional crisis if Edward acted against his Cabinet's wishes, since presumably Baldwin would resign and no other party leader would serve as Prime Minister under Edward. It was an agonizing dilemma for the king, especially when the whole affair was reported in the newspapers on 3 December. There was some support for the king in the country; many people, including Churchill and Mosley, and the powerful newspaper-owners, Beaverbrook and Rothermere, believed that he ought to be allowed to marry any woman he wished. But the majority opinion supported Baldwin and the government; the Archbishop of Canterbury, Dr Lang, was against the marriage on the grounds that the king, as Head of the Church of England, ought not to marry a divorcee. *The Times* announced self-righteously that the monarchy would be fatally weakened if 'private inclination were to come into open conflict with public duty and be allowed to prevail'.

(c) Edward decides to abdicate

Edward hoped that an arrangement could be made, to allow Mrs Simpson to marry him and remain a private citizen, without becoming queen (this is known as a morganatic marriage). When the Cabinet refused to agree to this, Edward decided that he must abdicate the throne. This he did on 11 December, and was succeeded by his brother, George VI. Edward took the title Duke of Windsor and married Mrs Simpson the following year. The Windsors spent most of their married lives in exile from Britain.

It was generally agreed that Baldwin had handled the situation well, and his popularity, which had waned considerably earlier in 1936 at the time of his limp conduct of foreign affairs (see Section 27.2(d–e)), was suddenly restored. He had avoided an awkward constitutional crisis, saved the monarchy from a damaging controversy and secured the smooth succession of George VI and his wife, Queen Elizabeth, both of whom became popular with the public. Baldwin retired to the House of Lords soon after the Coronation in May 1938. Before long, however, his reputation lay in ruins: when the Second World War started (September 1939), Baldwin was blamed for having left Britain with inadequate defences.

QUESTIONS

1 'The Second Labour government fell in 1931 because Ramsay MacDonald was prepared to betray his party in order to remain in power.' How far would you agree with this verdict?

2 Explain why the National Government was formed in 1931 and why there was no return to party politics before the outbreak of the Second World War.
3 What measures did the National Governments of 1931 to 1939 take to help Britain recover from the depression, and how successful were these measures?
4 'Increased consumption by individuals pulled Britain out of the slump.' In the light of this statement, examine the reasons for the recovery of the British economy in the 1930s.
5 How would you explain the failure of both fascism and communism as political forces in Britain in the 1920s and 1930s?

A document question about the formation of the National Government in August 1931 can be found on the accompanying website www.palgrave.com/masterseries/lowe1.

chapter 26

Britain and the problems of Empire between the wars

summary of events

The British Empire was the largest in the world; it included vast areas in Africa, Malaya, India, Burma, the West Indies, and the Arab territories of Iraq, Transjordan and Palestine; these last three areas had been acquired from Turkey as mandates at the end of the First World War. And there was a special feature which no other empire could boast – the white dominions – Australia, Canada and New Zealand, as well as South Africa. During and after the First World War, nationalist movements developed in some parts of the Empire, aiming at independence from Britain; these were mainly in India, Egypt and the Arab mandates. The Irish did not wait until the end of the war – republicans staged the Easter Rising in 1916. Even the white dominions were unhappy about what the term 'dominion status' meant, and pressed for a clear definition.

The attitude of British governments was that territories would be allowed to proceed to independence in gradual stages, though it often seemed to the nationalists that these stages were so gradual that they could scarcely be detected. Southern Ireland was granted dominion status in 1922; Egypt took steps towards independence in 1922 and 1936; and Iraq gained full independence in 1932. *The Statute of Westminster (1931)* satisfied the dominions about their relationship with Britain and saw the formation of the British Commonwealth; however, progress in India was far too gradual for the nationalists' liking, and their relationship with Britain was uneasy. It was only in 1947 that India was granted independence.

26.1 Britain and its relations with the Commonwealth

(a) Britain's white dominions

Australia, Canada and New Zealand, as well as South Africa and the Irish Free State (since 1922) were already self-governing as far as internal affairs were concerned, but traditionally acted along with Britain for foreign policy, which was one of the reasons they all fought on Britain's side in the First World War. By the end of the war, a desire to run their own foreign affairs had developed; this was partly because the war had made them more aware of their importance as separate nations (together they had put over a million men in the field); in addition, they were encouraged by Woodrow Wilson's support for the principle of national independence, and they were worried in case Britain tried to drag them into another war. Consequently, Canada and South Africa refused to help Britain during the Chanak incident in 1922 (see Section 23.1(b)), and they all refused to sign the Treaties of Lausanne (1923) and Locarno (1925) (see Section 24.2(b)). South Africa became increasingly hostile to Britain and seemed determined to leave the Empire. Clearly, some initiative was needed, and happily for the future of the Commonwealth, as it was beginning to be called, this was taken at the Imperial Conference of 1926.

(b) the Imperial Conference of 1926

Under the chairmanship of Arthur Balfour, the former Conservative Prime Minister, the conference showed that Britain was prepared to conciliate the dominions. Balfour produced a formula which defined the dominions as 'free countries, equal to each other and to Britain, and in complete control of their own internal and foreign affairs'; they were to be 'freely associated as members of the British Commonwealth of Nations'. This satisfied the dominions (even South Africa for the time being) and was passed through the British Parliament as *the Statute of Westminster (1931)*. The Commonwealth was a unique experiment in international organization, but because of the degree of independence enjoyed by the dominions, the achievements of the new 'white man's club', as it was described, were often something of a disappointment. There was no Commonwealth parliament or other set machinery for co-operation to take place, though from time to time conferences were held.

(c) the Imperial Conference in Ottawa (July–August 1932)

This met during the depression, soon after Britain had introduced tariffs. Baldwin and Chamberlain hoped that they could increase trade within the Empire by offering preferential rates for Commonwealth goods in return for concessions by the dominions for British manufactured goods. The discussions were often heated, and more than once the conference almost broke up. Eventually, twelve agreements were signed: among them, Britain agreed to give preference to foodstuffs and certain other commodities from the Empire; the dominions on the whole would not agree to lower tariffs on British goods, but they did raise tariffs on foreign goods. It was a kind of preference, but not quite what the British had hoped for, since the tariffs against British goods were already too high.

(d) the Imperial Conference, May 1937

This took place while the dominions' Prime Ministers were in London for the Coronation of George VI. It was unremarkable except that they all expressed support for Britain's policy of appeasing Hitler (see Section 27.1–27.2). This was predictable, since they had no wish to find themselves involved in another war.

26.2 events leading up to the partition of Ireland, 1922

In the summer of 1914, the operation of the Third Irish Home Rule Bill, which had passed through all its stages in Parliament, and which would have given self-government to Ireland, was postponed until the end of the war. Thus the future of Ireland and the dilemma of whether to include Ulster in Home Rule (see Section 21.5) was put on ice for the time being. The British government hoped that Ireland would remain quiet for the duration of the war, but their hopes were dashed when violence broke out again at Easter 1916.

(a) the Easter Rising 1916

When Britain entered the war in August 1914, the majority of the Irish people *were* prepared to wait until the war was over for Home Rule to come into operation. Thousands volunteered to fight for Britain against the Germans, and the nationalist leader, Redmond, pledged the full support of the Nationalist Volunteers. However, not all of them were happy about this, and a minority group led by Patrick Pearse split off to form the Irish Volunteers. Working with the revolutionary Irish Republican Brotherhood (IRB), they saw Britain's preoccupation with the war as a chance to seize Irish independence, perhaps with help from Germany. Plans were made for a rebellion to take place on Easter Sunday 1916, and Sir Roger Casement tried to persuade the Germans to send support. When it became clear that no German help would be given, some of the leaders tried to call the rebellion off, but others went ahead. On Easter Monday they proclaimed a republic and seized several key points in Dublin, including the General Post Office, hoping that the rest of the country would rise in sympathy and force the British to withdraw. However, no sympathetic rising took place, and the police, together with British troops, soon put an end to the rebellion, which was militarily a complete failure. Most Irish people condemned it; one nationalist called it 'this piece of criminal folly'.

Much has been written about the motives of the 1916 rebels. One theory is that their actions had no serious military objectives; their aim was to force the British into a severe reaction in order to stiffen the backbone of those nationalists who were prepared to await the British government's convenience. It was said that Pearse himself was motivated by the idea of a 'blood sacrifice, whereby Ireland might be spiritually resurrected'. According to Charles Townshend, while many of the rebels certainly expected to die, they did not share Pearse's doctrine of self-sacrifice. If they *did* hope to provoke the British government, their ploy worked brilliantly. On the other hand, the events of Easter Monday were not what was intended: the original idea was for a much wider uprising in several parts of Ireland on Easter Sunday. Townshend believes that if the full operation had gone ahead, it would have stretched the British forces severely.

(b) British treatment of the rebels changes the situation

Although the rebellion was over in a few days, British treatment of the rebels caused a wave of disgust throughout Ireland and the USA, which had a large Irish population. Sixteen of the leaders were executed; one of them, James Connolly, already dying of gunshot wounds and unable to stand, was shot sitting in a chair. The government defended its actions on the grounds that the rebels were guilty of treason in a time of war, and therefore deserved the most severe punishment. But it was a monumental miscalculation: it made the leaders into martyrs and heroes and caused a great outburst of anti-British feeling; more and more people were now wanting not just Home Rule, but complete independence from Britain. Nationalist influence was waning rapidly, and Sinn Fein won four by-elections in 1917. Another insensitive move by the government came early in 1918 when it was proposed to extend conscription to Ireland. All the Irish Home Rule MPs walked out of the House of Commons in protest, and support for complete independence increased still further.

However, there was still the problem of Ulster, with its Protestant majority, who wanted to remain under British rule. By now the British government had accepted that Ireland would have to be partitioned; Lloyd George was thinking in terms of excluding the six most Protestant counties of Ulster (Antrim, Armagh, Down, Derry, Fermanagh and Tyrone) from any further Home Rule legislation. The Ulster Unionists were prepared to sacrifice the other three counties of the historic Ulster (Donegal, Cavan and Monaghan) because Roman Catholics were in a majority in those counties. In a six-county Northern Ireland, the Protestants would have a 3 to 1 majority; if all nine counties were included, the Protestant majority would be much less secure.

(c) the Irish Republic declared, January 1919

In the British general election of December 1918, Sinn Fein won 73 out of the 105 Irish seats; the Nationalists were reduced to 6. Only in Ulster were things different: here, the Unionists, committed to staying with Britain, won 26 seats. Nothing less than full independence would now satisfy the majority of the Irish people. Instead of going to the British Parliament at Westminster, the Sinn Fein MPs proclaimed an independent Irish republic with their own parliament, *Dail Eireann* (Assembly of Ireland) in Dublin. They elected as President Éamon de Valera, one of the few surviving leaders of the Easter Rising, who had escaped execution because his mother claimed American citizenship; de Valera now became the symbol of Irish republicanism. Together with Michael Collins and Arthur Griffith, he organized an effective government which ignored the British and ran the country in its own way, collecting taxes and setting up law courts.

Lloyd George wanted a quick settlement of the Irish problem so that he could concentrate on Britain's many other difficulties. The government's Irish Committee came up with an ingenious compromise plan: it involved setting up two governments – one in Belfast for the nine counties of Ulster, one in Dublin for the rest of Ireland, and a Council of Ireland to act as a link between the two. Sinn Fein rejected this. Next Lloyd George introduced *the Government of Ireland Act* (February 1920) which he hoped would win moderate support back for the British. This was really a revised version of the Third Home Rule Bill: it involved partitioning the country, with a parliament in Belfast for the six most Protestant counties of Ulster, and one for the rest of Ireland in Dublin. Ulster reluctantly accepted its parliament, but Sinn Fein rejected the entire Act because it only gave them control of certain domestic matters, whereas they were determined on a complete break with Britain; they also wanted control of Ulster.

(d) escalating violence

The Irish Republican Army (IRA), formed in January 1919, carried out a campaign of terrorism against the police. Lloyd George retaliated by letting loose the notorious Black and Tans (recently demobilized British soldiers) against the IRA, and both sides committed terrible atrocities. One Sunday in November 1920, for example, fourteen British officers living in Dublin were shot dead in their beds. Later the same day, British troops retaliated by opening fire at a football match at Croke Park, Dublin (Dublin were playing Tipperary); twelve people were killed, including one of the Tipperary players, and about seventy injured. The Black and Tans especially went too far in their brutal reprisals; even the *Times* said that their cruelty was 'enough to make Englishmen hang their heads in shame', and Lloyd George had to admit that there had been 'deplorable excesses'.

(e) the Irish Free State established, 1922

By the spring of 1921, both sides were beginning to feel that the violence had gone on long enough; after Lloyd George had put out peace feelers, a truce was agreed in July 1921 and talks began in London. *Why were they both prepared to negotiate?*

- King George V was very distressed by the situation in Ireland, and made a speech appealing for 'all Irishmen to forgive and forget and join in making for the land which they love, a new era of peace, contentment and goodwill'.
- The Liberal and Labour parties, many of the Conservatives and a majority of the general public in mainland Britain realized the strength of the Irish desire

for independence. Although it might have been possible by sending some-where in the region of 100,000 troops, to subdue Ireland, it would be impos-sible ever again to have the consent or the co-operation of the Irish people.

▶ On the Irish side, the IRA, who never had more than about 3,000 men, were close to exhaustion.

An Irish delegation led by Michael Collins and Arthur Griffith came to London, though de Valera refused to join the negotiating team. According to Roy Hattersley: 'For reasons which might have been noble or squalid, political or personal, de Valera had decided that when Sinn Fein failed to achieve its objec-tive – as fail it must – Michael Collins, [who was] thought to have developed ideas above his subordinate station, must be associated with the failure.' Lloyd George used all his skills as a negotiator, and after both sides had made some concessions, agreement was reached on *the Anglo-Irish Treaty* which involved a partition of Ireland (December 1921):

▶ Southern Ireland was to become independent as *the Irish Free State,* with the same status as dominions like Australia and Canada. This gave the Irish much more than had been offered in the 1920 Government of Ireland Act, but on the other hand they had to drop the idea of a republic, and they still had to recognize the British monarchy. In addition, they had to allow the British navy to use three ports – Queenstown, Berehaven and Lough Swilly.

▶ To satisfy the Ulster Unionists, *Northern Ireland,* consisting of the six counties of Antrim, Armagh, Londonderry, Down, Fermanagh and Tyrone, remained part of Britain, with its own parliament at Belfast. Here, again, the Irish had to make concessions: some were against the idea of partition and wanted Northern Ireland included in the Free State. Even many of those who accepted partition felt that some areas where Catholics were in a majority should have been in the Free State; these areas included south Fermanagh, south Armagh, south Down and much of Tyrone. However, *a Boundary Commission* was included in the treaty and it was hoped in the south that the necessary adjust-ments to the frontier would be made in due course (see Map 21.1 on page 412). It has to be seen as a considerable achievement by Lloyd George, in the circum-stances, that an agreement of any sort was reached, though in the last resort he had to threaten the Irish delegation with a renewal of the war to get them to sign. Arthur Griffith became the first president of the new Irish Free State and Michael Collins the Commander-in-Chief of the army.

Unfortunately, the troubles in Ireland were still not over. A section of Sinn Fein led by de Valera, refused to accept the treaty because of the partition and the remaining connection with Britain. Nothing less than a completely inde-pendent republic would do for de Valera, and his critics suggested that his atti-tude was because he wanted to be president himself. Whatever the truth, de Valera certainly chose to fight the treaty with violence and a vicious civil war broke out between the two Sinn Fein factions. Michael Collins was killed in a cowardly ambush and Arthur Griffith died of a brain haemorrhage. Nevertheless, the war ended in April 1923 with a victory for supporters of the treaty. The Irish Free State came into existence officially in December 1922.

26.3 relations between Britain and the independent Ireland

Relations between the two states were never easy. As A. J. P. Taylor put it: 'the Irish had won, but they were not reconciled or friendly. Their victory had come after terror and troubles, not as a work of conciliatory statesmanship, and they had nothing to be thankful for'. The vast majority of the people of the Free State resented the existence of a separate Northern Ireland just for the benefit of the Ulster Protestants. They felt that most of these Protestants were not genuinely Irish, since their ancestors had been moved in (or 'planted') from Scotland and England during the sixteenth and seventeenth centuries to 'civilize' the Catholics. Both main political parties in the Free State had as part of their programmes the ultimate unification of Ireland. On the other hand, British governments felt obliged by the strength of Protestant Unionist feeling in Northern Ireland to maintain its union with Britain. No compromise seemed possible on either side, and so relations could never be close. And yet some important ties remained. The Dublin parliament, the Dail, voted to recognize 'the common citizenship of Ireland with Great Britain'. This meant that Irish people were still British citizens and could still vote in British elections. There were close trade ties, with almost all Ireland's food exports going to Britain. The major landmarks after 1922 were the following.

(a) the failure of the Boundary Commission

The treaty had promised a Boundary Commission to consider possible changes to the frontier between the Free State and Northern Ireland. Hints had been dropped to the Irish during the negotiations (though nothing had been put in writing), that Britain might be prepared to give parts of Fermanagh and Tyrone to the Free State. However, when the Commission met in 1924, Lloyd George was out of office, and Baldwin's Conservative government made it clear that it had no intention of making any major changes. The Commission folded in 1925 after confirming the original frontier, leaving the Irish feeling cheated and doing no good at all for Anglo-Irish relations.

(b) de Valera cuts the links with Britain

Éamon de Valera remained implacably hostile to Britain. He formed a new party, *Fianna Fail* (Soldiers of Destiny), which won the 1932 election largely because the slump and unemployment had made the government of William Cosgrave highly unpopular. For the next sixteen years, de Valera served as Prime Minister, gradually breaking all the remaining ties with Britain:

- Using the 1926 Statute of Westminster by which the British Parliament ceased to have any control over the dominions parliaments, de Valera abolished the oath of loyalty to the Crown, introduced separate Irish citizenship and took away all power from the governor-general (the representative of the Crown). This was perfectly legal, but the British government, instead of accepting the inevitable with dignity, placed trade sanctions on the Free State. In response, de Valera refused to hand over money owing to the British government in the form of annual loan repayments from farmers who had bought land under the Land Purchase Acts after 1870. Trade between the two countries all but ceased, which did neither of them any good. Trade gradually resumed during 1935, but de Valera had made his point, and the Irish treasury benefited from the cash still owing to Britain.
- In 1937, de Valera took the chance offered by the abdication of Edward VIII to introduce a new constitution, making Eire, as it was now called, completely independent in practice.
- Neville Chamberlain (British Prime Minister, 1937–40) made concessions in an attempt to win Eire's friendship. He accepted the new constitution, wrote off most of the cash still owing (about £100 million by 1938) and gave up the right to use the three naval bases. However, Eire remained uncooperative. Chamberlain failed to realize how deeply de Valera felt about the situation: he would never be reconciled with Britain until Northern Ireland became part of Eire.
- Eire remained neutral during the Second World War and refused to allow the British navy to use ports on its west and south coasts. This left British shipping more vulnerable to German submarine attacks and contributed to their heavy losses in the Atlantic. This caused great bitterness in Britain, especially since the food convoys were bringing supplies to Eire as well as to Britain.
- In 1948, Eire refused to take part in the discussions that led to the formation of NATO. She would only consider joining if Ireland became united.
- In 1949, Eire declared itself an independent republic. (For events in Northern Ireland after 1922, see Section 32.1.)

26.4 the Indian struggle for independence

(a) the growth of Indian nationalism

Nationalist feelings began in the late nineteenth century, when many middle- and upper-class Indians, having received a British-style education, often at Oxford or Cambridge, felt frustrated that their country continued to be run by the British, while they were allowed no say in the government and had only a very minor role in local affairs. They founded a party called *the Indian National Congress* (1885) to press for greater participation by Indians in government.

They were encouraged by the Japanese victory over the Russians in 1905, which raised hopes that this new Asian power might help the Indians in their struggle against British colonialism. A decision by the British in 1905 to divide the huge province of Bengal into two upset the Hindus greatly, because it divided the Bengali-speaking Hindus and reduced their potential power.

In response to this pressure, the British introduced the 1909 *Morley–Minto reforms* (Morley was the Secretary of State for India, and Lord Minto the Viceroy, who ruled India on behalf of the king). Indians were allowed to sit on the executive councils which advised the provincial governors; later, the partition of Bengal was abandoned. This was not enough to prevent unrest increasing, however, and there was an attempt on the Viceroy's life in 1912. After 1914, nationalist feeling intensified, probably encouraged by the important contribution made by the Indians to the war effort, and perhaps by the successful revolutions in Russia and by Woodrow Wilson's talk of self-determination for subject peoples.

(b) how did British governments deal with demands for Indian independence?

For years the British tried to ignore Indian nationalism, having apparently convinced themselves that there were too many differences in Indian society for the Indians ever to form a united movement; there were social, regional and, above all, religious differences, especially between Hindus and Muslims. However, during the war, Hindus and Muslims began to work together to pressurize the British, who were slowly coming round to the idea that India would have to be given a measure of self-government. In 1917, the Indians were promised 'the gradual development of self-governing institutions with a view to the progressive realization of responsible government in India as an integral part of the British Empire'. However, many Conservatives, including Winston Churchill and Lord Birkenhead (Secretary of State for India from 1924 to 1928), were utterly opposed to the idea. Seeing India as 'the brightest jewel in the imperial crown', they could not come to terms with the idea of 'giving it away'; Indian independence would be the beginning of the end of the British Empire. Lord Curzon, Viceroy from 1898 until 1905, the year in which he partitioned Bengal, claimed: 'With India we are everything. Without it we are nothing.' Not surprisingly, the pace was far too slow for the impatient nationalists, whose leaders, Mahatma Gandhi and Jawaharlal Nehru, both lawyers educated in London, organized an anti-British campaign. The stages in the gradual move towards independence were:

1 In 1918, Edwin Montagu (Secretary of State for India, 1917–22) and Lord Chelmsford (the Viceroy) put forward plans that eventually became *the Government of India Act (1919)*. There was to be a national parliament with two houses, and parliaments or assemblies for the provinces. About five million of the wealthiest Indians were given the vote; in the provincial

governments, the ministers of health, education and public works could now be Indians; a commission would be held ten years later to decide whether India was ready for further concessions. Congress was bitterly disappointed because, despite the new parliament having some powers, the really important decisions were still taken by the governor-general; the British also kept control of the key provincial ministries such as law and order and taxes.

In addition, the Indians were enraged at the slowness with which the British put even these limited advances into operation. Rioting broke out, and at Amritsar in the Punjab, after five Europeans had been murdered, General Dyer dispersed an excited crowd of over 5,000 Indians with machine-gun fire, killing 379. Order was soon restored, but the Amritsar Massacre was an important turning-point: it provoked so much fury that Congress was transformed from a middle-class party into a mass movement. Even Churchill said privately that Dyer's action was murder, or at least manslaughter. Historian Nigel Collett called his recent biography of Dyer (2005) *The Butcher of Amritsar.*

However, Andrew Roberts (2006) mounts a strong defence of Dyer's actions. He points out that Dyer had issued a proclamation against public meetings 'at no fewer than nineteen prominent places in the city, with beating drums and much ceremony ... No inhabitant of Amritsar could have possibly been under any doubt about the possibly fatal consequences of attending a political rally that day.' It was all a matter of maintaining British prestige; 'without it the British Empire in India would have simply evaporated overnight'. Thanks to Dyer's action, 'it was not necessary for another shot to be fired throughout the entire region. A deputation of Indian merchants and shopkeepers soon afterwards thanked the General for preventing looting and destruction.'

British control of India may not have evaporated overnight, but it does seem as though the events at Amritsar finally lost the British the support of the moderate Indians who until then had trusted them to do the right thing eventually. 'After Amritsar', wrote Martin Gilbert, 'no matter what compromises and concessions the British might suggest, British rule would ultimately be swept away.'

By this time, Gandhi was the leading figure of Congress. He believed in non-violent protest and the equality of all classes. Always dressed as a simple peasant, he somehow managed, by sheer force of personality, to persuade Indians to refuse to work, stage sit-down strikes, fast, stop paying taxes, and boycott elections. Unfortunately, he was unable to control some of his more extreme supporters, and violence often developed. In 1922 he called off his first non-cooperation campaign.

2 The next British move, apart from putting Gandhi and Nehru in gaol, was that Baldwin, acting a year early, appointed *the Simon Commission* (1928), as the 1919 Act had recommended. In 1930, this proposed self-government for

the provinces, but was treated with contempt by the Indians who, amazingly, were not even represented on the commission – Gandhi and Nehru, who ought to have been consulted, were not allowed out of gaol to attend the talks, and no other Indians were invited. That in itself outraged Indian opinion, and they proceeded to demand immediate dominion status. As soon as he was out of gaol, Gandhi began his second civil disobedience campaign by breaking the law that only government-approved factories could manufacture salt. After a symbolic 250-mile march to the sea, he produced salt from sea-water; but again violent incidents developed, and again Gandhi was arrested.

3 Lord Irwin (later Lord Halifax) (Viceroy, 1926–31), a committed Christian and a humane and enlightened politician, was sympathetic to the Indians. Before the Simon Report appeared in 1930 he had expressed the view that dominion status must come; this is why the Indians had felt so let down when the report made no mention of it. Irwin was convinced that negotiations must take place, and he was fully supported in this view by Ramsay MacDonald, who had just become Prime Minister. Consequently, *two Round Table Conferences were held in London (1930 and 1931)*. The first was unsatisfactory because, despite the Indian princes being represented and accepting the idea of an Indian federation, no Congress representatives were there, because most of them were in prison. Irwin had them released and prevailed upon Gandhi to travel to London to attend the second conference, much to the horror of Churchill, who refused to meet him and described him as 'this malignant and subversive fanatic'. Again, little progress was made, this time because of disagreements about Muslim representation in an independent Indian parliament.

4 *The Government of India Act of 1935* was a major step towards independence. It was introduced as a result of co-operation between MacDonald and Baldwin, and in spite of bitter opposition from Churchill, who called it 'this bogus act'. The elected Indian assembly was to have a say in everything except defence and foreign affairs; the eleven provincial assemblies were to have more-or-less full control over local affairs. The nationalists were still not satisfied, however: the Act fell short of dominion status (the white dominions controlled their own defence and foreign policies), and the princes who still ruled certain areas of India refused to co-operate; thus their areas remained outside the system.

Another failure of the Act was that it ignored the religious rivalry between Hindus and Muslims. Roughly two-thirds of the Indians were Hindus, and the next largest group, the Muslims (who followed the Islamic religion), were afraid that in a democratic India they would be dominated and unfairly treated by the Hindus. When Nehru's Congress Party, which was overwhelmingly Hindu, won control of eight out of the eleven provinces in the 1937 elections, the Muslim League, under its leader M. A. Jinnah, demanded a separate state of their own called Pakistan, while Congress and Gandhi were determined to preserve a united India. No further developments took place before the Second World War, but mounting Hindu/Muslim hostility boded ill for the future, and provided some justification for the British reluctance to grant full self-government. (For events leading to independence in 1947 see Section 34.2.)

26.5 Britain and the Middle East mandates

In 1916, the Arabs in the Turkish empire rose in revolt, and helped by the British colonel, T. E. Lawrence (Lawrence of Arabia), and later by British troops under Allenby, they played an important part in liberating the Arab territories from Turkish control. As a bribe to win Arab support against Turkey, the British had made vague promises that, when the war was over, the Arabs would be allowed to set up independent states; but about the same time (1916), the British had also made the contradictory *Sykes–Picot agreement* with France, whereby Turkey's Arab lands would be divided between the two of them. In 1919, therefore, to their intense disappointment, the Arabs found their territories handed over as mandates (to be 'looked after' and prepared for self-government) to Britain (which was given Iraq, Transjordan and Palestine) and France (which was put in charge of Syria and Lebanon).

Britain was reluctant to sever all connections with its mandates because of the Middle East oil resources, especially in Iraq, and wanted to be allowed to station troops there to guarantee a sure supply of oil. On the other hand, the British dared not offend the Arabs too deeply or its oil supplies might equally be threatened. Consequently, steady progress towards independence was made in Iraq and Transjordan, though with strings attached; however, the situation in Palestine was complicated by the Jewish/Arab problem.

(a) Iraq

After some initial nationalist rioting in Iraq, the British set up an Iraqi national government in which each minister had a British adviser. The Amir Faisal (who had just been driven out of Syria by the French) was accepted as king. Though extreme nationalists did not approve, this arrangement was agreed by *the Anglo-Iraqi Treaty of 1922* and seemed to work well. An elected parliament was introduced in 1924 and Faisal, a man of great personal charm and political ability, proved to be an excellent ruler. With British help, industry and agriculture were organized, and an efficient administrative system was introduced. The British won Iraqi support by successfully opposing Turkish claims to the province of Mosul with its vast oil resources. In 1932, Iraq became fully independent, though Britain was allowed to keep two air-bases. According to one Arab nationalist, George Antonius, 'the modern state of Iraq owes its existence largely to the efforts and devotion of its British officials'.

(b) Transjordan

Here the British set up Faisal's brother, Abdullah, as king, and allowed him to run the country's internal affairs, which he did competently. However, Transjordan was a poor state, lacking in resources, especially oil, and was therefore dependent on Britain for subsidies and for defence. In 1946, it was given complete independence, though Abdullah kept on the British officers who led his army.

(c) Palestine

Palestine proved to be the most troublesome mandate, because of the growing hostility between Jews and Arabs. The problem had originated about 2,000 years earlier, in AD 71, when most of the Jews were driven out of Palestine, their homeland, by the Romans. In fact, small communities of Jews remained behind in Palestine, and during the following centuries there was a gradual trickle of Jews returning from exile, though until the end of the nineteenth century there were never enough to cause the Palestinian Arabs to feel threatened. However, in 1897, some European Jews founded *the World Zionist Organization* in Basel (Switzerland), an event which was to be of profound importance for the Middle East. Greatly disturbed by the recent persecution of Jews in Russia, Germany and France, the Zionists demanded a Jewish national home in Palestine. Even before they were given the mandate over Palestine, the British had become involved in the controversy, and must take much of the blame for the chaos that followed, especially after 1945:

‣ During the First World War, the British had made three contradictory promises, which were bound to lead to frustration and hostility. There were the two already mentioned: independent states for the Arabs, and the partition of Arab territories between Britain and France. The third was *the Balfour Declaration* (November 1917), in which the British Foreign Secretary pledged British support for a Jewish 'national home' in Palestine. The British motive, apart from genuine sympathy with the Zionists, was a belief that the Jews would help to safeguard the Suez Canal and provide a buffer between the Canal Zone and the French in Syria.

‣ Faced with bitter Arab protests both against the British failure to grant independence and against the arrival of increasing numbers of Jews, the British government stated (1922) that there was no intention that the Jews should occupy the whole of Palestine, and that there would be no interference with the rights of the Arabs in the country. The British hoped to persuade Jews and Arabs to live together peacefully in the same state; however, they failed to understand the deep religious gulf between the two.

‣ Jews continued to arrive, equipped with Zionist money, bought land from Arabs who were at first willing to sell, started industries and reclaimed land. It was soon clear that they intended to develop not just a national home, but a Jewish national state; by 1928 there were 150,000 of them. The Arabs rioted and began murdering Jews; in 1929, the British Labour government decided that Jewish immigration must cease for the time being. Now it was the turn of the Zionists to rage against the British, to such an extent that MacDonald felt obliged to allow immigration to continue.

▸ The situation took a turn for the worse after Hitler came to power in Germany (1933); Nazi persecution of the Jews caused a flood of refugees, until by 1935 about a quarter of the total population of Palestine was Jewish. Arabs again began to attack Jews, while British troops struggled to keep order.

▸ In 1935, the British *Peel Commission* suggested dividing Palestine into two separate states, one Jewish, and one Arab, but the Arabs rejected the idea.

▸ As war loomed in 1939, the British felt the need to win Arab support, and in a White Paper they agreed to limit Jewish immigration to 10,000 a year, and promised to set up an independent Arab state within ten years, thus guaranteeing an Arab majority in the new state. At this point, with nothing resolved, the British hoped to shelve the problem until after the war (see Section 34.3 for later developments).

QUESTIONS

1 Outline the developments that led to the Anglo-Irish Treaty of 1921, and explain why the British government agreed to the partition of Ireland.

2 Explain the demands for Indian independence during and after the First World War. How far had the Indians achieved their aims by 1939, and why was progress so slow?

3 How successfully did the British deal with the mandated territories (Iraq, Transjordan, Palestine) that they acquired at the end of the First World War?

A document question about the Amritsar Massacre (1919) and Indian independence can be found on the accompanying website www.palgrave.com/masterseries/lowe1.

appeasement and the outbreak of the Second World War: foreign affairs, 1931–9

summary of events

British foreign policy during this period was dominated by one principle – *appeasement*. This was the practice of making what were thought to be reasonable concessions to aggressive foreign powers – Japan, Italy and Germany – in the hope that it would avoid war. The National Governments of MacDonald (1931–5) and Baldwin (1935–7) followed this policy, and Neville Chamberlain, Prime Minister from 1937 until 1940, was its main exponent, though he did abandon it belatedly in March 1939. In one sense the policy failed completely, since it culminated in the outbreak of the Second World War (1939–45); for this reason 'appeasement' came to be looked on as a dirty word, a term of abuse. But on the other hand, Chamberlain himself claimed that his policy bought time for Britain to rearm and prepare for war.

Between 1924 and 1929, following the Dawes Plan (1924) and the Locarno Treaties (1925), international relations were harmonious. But the Great Depression plunged the world's industrial powers into severe economic crisis, with dwindling markets and mass unemployment. The Locarno spirit of sweetness and goodwill suddenly disappeared and it was a case of every country for itself. Three states – Japan, Italy and Germany – all of which had right-wing nationalist governments, tried to solve their economic problems by territorial expansion, which meant aggression against other states. The League of Nations, vainly trying to operate a policy of *collective security* (joint action to keep the peace), but lacking strong support, failed to curb the aggressors. Britain and France, instead of backing the League and collective security, preferred appeasement. Consequently, all three aggressors successfully defied the League and the majority of world opinion until 1939.

▸ The Japanese were the first aggressors, with their successful invasion of the Chinese province of Manchuria (1931).

- Adolf Hitler, who became German Chancellor in January 1933, began cautiously by announcing the reintroduction of conscription (March 1935), a breach of the Versailles Treaty.
- Mussolini, the Italian fascist dictator, sent troops to conquer Abyssinia (October 1935).
- In 1936, German troops reoccupied the Rhineland, another breach of the Versailles Treaty.
- During the summer of 1936, the Spanish Civil War broke out, and Hitler and Mussolini sent help to General Franco, leader of the Spanish right-wing in their revolt against the left-wing republican government. By 1939, Franco was victorious and a third fascist dictator had been installed in Europe.
- Since the League of Nations was completely ineffective against these acts of aggression, Hitler was encouraged to carry out his most ambitious project to date – the annexation of Austria (known as the *Anschluss* or union – March 1938).
- Next, he turned his attention to Czechoslovakia and demanded the Sudetenland, an area containing some 3.6 million Germans adjoining the frontier with Germany. When the Czechs refused Hitler's demands, Chamberlain, anxious to avoid war at all costs, attended a conference at Munich (September 1938) at which it was agreed that Germany could have the Sudetenland, but no more of Czechoslovakia. War seemed to have been averted.
- However, the following March, Hitler broke this agreement and sent troops to occupy Prague, the Czech capital. At this Chamberlain decided that Hitler had gone too far and must be stopped.
- Hitler next demanded Danzig from Poland. The Poles rejected his demand, and Britain and France promised to help Poland if the Germans attacked. Hitler was not sufficiently impressed by these British and French threats and grew tired of waiting for Poland to negotiate.
- Having first secured a non-aggression pact with Russia (August 1939), the Germans invaded Poland on 1 September. Britain and France accordingly declared war on Germany on 3 September.

27.1 what was appeasement, and why did Britain follow such a policy?

(a) the two phases of appeasement

Appeasement was the policy followed first by the British and later by the French, of avoiding war with aggressive powers such as Japan, Italy and Germany by making concessions to them, provided their demands were not too unreasonable. It was based on a realization of the devastating financial and human costs of another war. There were two distinct phases of appeasement:

1 From the mid-1920s until 1937 there was a vague feeling that it was vital to avoid war, and Britain and sometimes France, drifted along accepting the various breaches of the Versailles Treaty and the acts of aggression as *faits accomplis.*

2 When Neville Chamberlain became British Prime Minister in May 1937 he gave appeasement new drive. He believed in taking the initiative: he would find out exactly what it was that Hitler wanted, and show him that reasonable claims could be met by negotiation rather than by force.

The origins of appeasement can be seen in British policy during the 1920s with the Dawes and Young Plans, which tried to conciliate the Germans, and with the Locarno Treaties and their significant omission: *Britain did not agree to guarantee Germany's eastern frontiers,* which even Stresemann, the 'good German', said must be revised. When Austen Chamberlain, the British Foreign Secretary (and Neville's half-brother), remarked at the time of Locarno that no British government would ever risk the bones of a single British grenadier in defence of the Polish Corridor, it seemed to the Germans that Britain had turned its back on Eastern Europe. Appeasement reached its climax at Munich, where Britain and France were so determined to avoid war with Germany that they made Hitler a present of the Sudetenland and so set in motion the destruction of Czechoslovakia. Even with concessions as big as this, appeasement failed.

(b) justifications for appeasement

At the time appeasement was being pursued, however, there seemed much to commend it, and the appeasers, who included MacDonald, Baldwin, Sir John Simon (Foreign Secretary, 1931–5), Sir Samuel Hoare (Foreign Secretary, June–December 1935) and Lord Halifax (Foreign Secretary, 1938–40), as well as Neville Chamberlain, were convinced of the rightness of their policies.

1 It was essential to avoid war, which was likely to be more devastating than ever before, as the horrors of the Spanish Civil War showed. One of the most appalling incidents was the German bombing of the defenceless Basque town of Guernica in which at least 1,600 people were killed. The fear was that, in any future war, British cities and the civilian population would be at risk, since 'the bomber will always get through'. Moreover, Britain, still in the throes of the economic crisis, could not afford vast rearmament and the crippling expense of a major war. British governments seemed to be supported by a strongly pacifist public opinion. In February 1933, the Oxford Union voted that it would not fight for King and Country. In July 1935, the Peace Pledge Union organized a nationwide public opinion poll in which 92.5 per cent (10.05 million) of people questioned said they were in favour of all-round reduction of armaments by international agreement. In November 1935, Baldwin and the National Government won a huge general election

victory shortly after he had declared: 'I give you my word of honour that there will be no great armaments.'

2 Many people felt that Italy and Germany had genuine grievances: Italy had been cheated at Versailles, Germany treated too harshly. Millions of Germans had been denied self-determination and found themselves living outside Germany's frontiers in Poland and Czechoslovakia. Even Churchill said that the economic terms were 'malignant and silly to an extent that made them obviously futile.' Therefore Britain should react with sympathy, and in the case of Germany, try to revise the most hated clauses of the Versailles Treaty. This would remove the need for German aggression and lead to Anglo-German friendship. *The Times*, one of the world's most respected and influential newspapers, and its editor, Geoffrey Dawson, followed this line of argument, and supported appeasement, even up to the point when Chamberlain attempted to wriggle out of the guarantee to Poland in 1939.

3 Since the League of Nations seemed to be helpless, Chamberlain believed that the only way to settle disputes was by personal contact between leaders; in this way, he mistakenly thought, he would be able to control and civilize Hitler, and Mussolini into the bargain, and bring them to respect international law.

4 Economic co-operation between Britain and Germany would be good for both; if Britain helped the German economy to recover, the internal violence would die down.

5 Fear of Communist Russia was great, especially among British Conservatives, many of whom believed the Communist threat to be greater than the danger from Hitler. Many British politicians were willing to overlook the unpleasant features of Nazism in the hope that Hitler's Germany would be a guarantee against Communist expansion westwards; better still would be a war between Nazi Germany and Communist Russia ending in the destruction of communism; in fact, some British politicians admired Hitler's drive and achievements. According to Ian Kershaw, Lord Londonderry (a Conservative who was Secretary of State for Air from 1931 to 1935), found Hitler 'a kindly man, very agreeable', and he was full of praise for the way Hitler got things done: 'What takes us weeks or months to do in Parliament, Germany can do by a stroke of the pen.'

6 Underlying all these feelings was the belief that Britain ought not to take any military action in case it led to a full-scale war, for which the country was totally unprepared. British military chiefs told the government that Britain was not strong enough to fight a war against more than one country at the same time. Even the navy, which was still the strongest in the world apart from the American navy, would have been hard pressed to defend the far-flung Empire and protect merchant shipping in the event of war against Germany, Italy and Japan simultaneously. The army chiefs were working on

what they called the principle of 'limited liability'. This meant in simple terms that there was no question of immediately sending a large army to France as they had done in 1914; at most there were only four divisions available. At the same time, the USA stood firmly for isolation, while France was weak and divided. The air force was woefully short of long-range bombers and fighters.

Some British politicians thought there was an alternative to appeasement. Winston Churchill, for example, thought the government should make no concessions to the dictators and should concentrate on building up a Grand Alliance, including Russia if necessary. He was convinced that people like Hitler and Mussolini would only take notice of military force. On the other hand, given Britain's military difficulties, it is clear that Chamberlain's options were fairly limited. Historian John Charmley mounts a spirited defence of Chamberlain in his book *Chamberlain and the Lost Peace* (1989), arguing that Chamberlain's policies were far more realistic that those suggested by Churchill and Eden. Philip M. Taylor also takes a sympathetic view in his article on appeasement in the *Modern History Review* (November 1989). He suggests that Chamberlain's real achievement was to prove to the world that Hitler would never be satisfied with concessions, and was determined to achieve his aims by force.

27.2 appeasement in action

(a) the Japanese invasion of Manchuria (September 1931)

This act of aggression brought a Chinese appeal for help to the League of Nations, which condemned Japan and ordered the country's troops to be withdrawn. However, there was a certain amount of sympathy in Britain for the Japanese, and Sir John Simon attempted to put both sides of the case at the League Assembly in Geneva. Unfortunately, according to A. J. P. Taylor, Simon had one serious defect, which made him unfit to be British Foreign Secretary – he was 'too cool and rational'. He pointed out that Japan had been involved in the province since the 1890s and had been given a privileged position in south Manchuria as a result of the Russo-Japanese War. Since then, the Japanese had invested millions of pounds in Manchuria in the development of industries and railways. China seemed to be growing stronger under the rule of Chiang Kai-shek, and the Japanese were afraid that he would try to exclude them from Manchuria. They could not stand by and see themselves gradually squeezed out of such a valuable province with a population of some 30 million, especially when they were already suffering economic hardship because of the great depression.

At Simon's suggestion, the League appointed an investigating commission under Lord Lytton which decided (1932) that there were faults on both sides and proposed that Manchuria be governed by the League. However, Japan rejected this and withdrew from the League (March 1933). The question of economic sanctions, let alone military ones, was not raised, because Britain and France had serious economic problems and were reluctant to apply a trade boycott to Japan in case it led to war, which they were ill-equipped to win, especially without American help. It is possible to argue that Simon's policy was the only realistic one, but it meant that Japan had successfully defied the League, a fact that was carefully noted by Hitler and Mussolini.

(b) the failure of the World Disarmament Conference (1932–4)

The final collapse of the conference came when the French refused to agree that the Germans should be allowed equality of armaments with France. This gave Hitler an excuse to walk out of the conference and to take Germany out of the League, marking the end of MacDonald's great hope – to maintain peace by disarmament and collective security, working through the League. This led to the publication in March 1935 of a government White Paper called *Statement Relating to Defence,* which announced that since Britain could no longer rely on collective security, its own military strength must be built up. It was in fact the decision to rearm; this new policy was put into operation, though very gradually at first.

The White Paper gave Hitler the excuse to announce that he intended to introduce conscription and build the German army up to 600,000 men; both actions were breaches of the Versailles Treaty. In response, MacDonald, now physically almost on his last legs, met Mussolini and Laval (French Foreign Minister) at Stresa in Northern Italy; they condemned Hitler's actions and promised to resist any further unilateral breaches of treaties which might endanger the peace of Europe. This agreement was known as *the Stresa Front* (April 1935); it was significant that both the British and French carefully avoided discussion of the Abyssinian crisis, which was already brewing; Mussolini took this to mean that they would turn a blind eye to an Italian attack on Abyssinia, regarding it as a bit of old-fashioned colonial expansion.

(c) the Anglo-German Naval Agreement (June 1935)

The Stresa Front lasted only a matter of weeks before it was broken by the naval agreement. This astonishing move occurred when Hitler, shrewdly realising how frail the front was, offered to limit the German navy to 35 per cent of the strength of the British navy. Britain eagerly accepted this offer and even went further, allowing Germany to build up to 45 per cent of Britain's total of submarines. This agreement was reached without any consultation at all with the French and Italians; it meant that Britain was condoning German rearmament, which proceeded with gathering momentum. This was Sir Samuel Hoare's first action as Foreign Secretary; his justification was that, since the Germans were already breaking Versailles by building a fleet, it would be as well to have that fleet limited. However, it convinced Mussolini of Britain's cynicism and self-interest, and disgusted Laval, who decided there was more to be gained from co-operation with Mussolini.

(d) the Italian invasion of Abyssinia (October 1935)

1 It had been obvious for months that Mussolini was preparing for an invasion of Abyssinia (Ethiopia), the last major African territory not subject to European control. Abyssinia was a member of the League, and Baldwin was in the difficult position of wanting to support the League in preserving Abyssinian independence while at the same time avoiding a confrontation with Italy. The British hoped that the Stresa Front still had some meaning and wanted to use Italy as an ally against Germany, which was now perceived as the real threat to the peace of Europe. This dilemma helps to explain Britain's apparently weak and sometimes contradictory policy throughout the crisis.

2 Sir Anthony Eden, Minister for League of Nations Affairs, was sent to Rome to make an offer to Mussolini – he could take part of Abyssinia, and Britain would give Italy part of neighbouring British Somaliland as compensation. Mussolini rejected this, arguing that Italy ought to have a similar position in Abyssinia to that of Britain in Egypt – a difficult point for the British to answer.

3 Sir Samuel Hoare made what sounded like a fighting speech at the League Assembly in Geneva (September 1935). Hoping to warn Mussolini off, he affirmed that Britain would support the League against acts of unprovoked aggression. Mussolini ignored the warning and went ahead with the invasion of Abyssinia (3 October). The League, responding to a moving appeal from the Abyssinian emperor, Haile Selassie, immediately imposed economic sanctions on Italy; these included a refusal to buy Italian goods and a ban on exports of iron ore, rubber, tin, scrap iron and other metals to Italy. Britain seemed to be taking the lead in support of the League and of collective security, and public opinion generally approved.

4 With collective security apparently working, Baldwin decided that this was a good time to hold a general election (November 1935). During the campaign he told the voters 'I give you my word of honour that there will be no great armaments'; he wanted a mandate simply to 'remedy the deficiencies which have occurred in our defences'. This was what the people wanted to hear at the time, and the National Government won a convincing victory (see Section 25.3(e)); later, Baldwin was accused of having deliberately misled the country by keeping quiet about the need for rearmament.

5 By the time the election was over, it was clear that the sanctions were not working; Italy had not been brought to its knees. Chamberlain suggested further sanctions to stop the export of oil and coal to Italy, which Mussolini later admitted would have forced him to make peace within a week. The

Cabinet rejected this idea, fearing it would provoke Mussolini to declare war, for which Britain was unprepared. The League's prestige suffered a further blow when it emerged that Hoare had been to Paris and made a secret deal with Laval (December) to hand over a large section of Abyssinia to Italy, provided military action ceased. This was more than the Italians had succeeded in capturing at the time, and when news of *the Hoare–Laval Pact* leaked out, public opinion in Britain and France was so outraged that the plan had to be dropped. Hoare, who had made the agreement without Cabinet approval, resigned in disgrace. No further action was taken, and by April 1936 the Italian conquest of Abyssinia was complete. In June it was decided to discontinue the ineffective economic sanctions.

6 *The results were disastrous:* the League and the idea of collective security were finally discredited; Mussolini was annoyed by the sanctions and began to be drawn towards friendship with Hitler, who had not criticized the invasion and refused to apply the sanctions; in return, Mussolini dropped his objections to a German takeover of Austria; Hitler took advantage of the preoccupation with Abyssinia to send troops into the Rhineland. Baldwin's popularity slumped dramatically.

(e) German troops reoccupy the Rhineland (March 1936)

Since this was another breach of Versailles, Hitler gave his troops orders to withdraw at the first sign of any French opposition; however, no resistance was offered beyond the usual protests. Hitler, well aware of the mood of pacifism among his opponents, soothed them by offering a peace treaty for twenty-five years. Baldwin and Eden (the new Foreign Secretary) judged that British public opinion would not have supported military action, since the Rhineland *was* part of Germany. Indeed, Lord Londonderry was reported to have sent Hitler a telegram congratulating him on his success, while Lord Lothian remarked that the German troops had merely entered their own 'back garden'.

(f) the Spanish Civil War (1936–9)

In June 1936, an army revolt broke out against the Spanish left-wing republican government. General Franco soon assumed the leadership of the revolt, and a quick victory was expected. However, the republicans controlled most of the south, including Madrid, and a bitter struggle developed in which both sides committed terrible atrocities. Most of the states of Europe, including Britain, France, Germany and Italy, signed an agreement promising not to interfere in Spanish affairs. Mussolini and Hitler broke the agreement and sent extensive help to Franco – some 50,000 Italian troops and many planes, together with hundreds of German planes and tanks. In Britain opinion was divided; some left-wing groups – the ILP and the Communist party – wanted the government to support the republic against Spanish fascism; however, the Labour party, under its new leader Clement Attlee, did not want to become involved and shrank from any action which meant co-operation with communists. Baldwin and Chamberlain were determined on non-intervention, since most of the Conservatives disapproved of the Spanish republican government with its anarchist and communist connections. Volunteers were allowed to go – about 2,000 Britons, many of them unemployed miners, fought for the Spanish republic in the International Brigade; but no official help was sent.

British policy reached rock bottom in April 1938 when the Foreign Secretary, now Lord Halifax, tried to resurrect the Stresa Front by agreeing to recognize Italian possession of Abyssinia in return for the withdrawal of Italian troops from Spain. However, Mussolini ignored his side of the bargain, and the British government had been made to look weak and treacherous, condoning Mussolini's aggression and betraying the efforts of the League of Nations. Eventually, Italian and German help proved decisive in securing victory for Franco.

(g) the German occupation of Austria (March 1938)

This was Hitler's greatest success to date. Having first reached an understanding with Mussolini (the Rome–Berlin Axis of 1936) and signed the Anti-Comintern Pact with Japan, Hitler carried out the *Anschluss* (union) with Austria, a further breach of Versailles. Matters came to a head when the Austrian Nazis staged huge demonstrations in Vienna, Graz and Linz, which Chancellor Schuschnigg's government could not control. Realizing that this could be the prelude to a German invasion, Schuschnigg announced a plebiscite (referendum) about whether or not Austria should remain independent. Hitler decided to act before this took place, in case the vote went against union; German troops moved in and Austria became part of the Third Reich. It was a triumph for Germany: it revealed the weaknesses of Britain and France, who again did no more than protest; it demonstrated the value of the new understanding with Italy, and it dealt a severe strategic blow to Czechoslovakia, which could now be attacked from the south as well as from the west and north. All was ready for the beginning of Hitler's campaign to acquire the German-speaking Sudetenland, a campaign which ended in further triumph at the Munich conference in September 1938.

27.3 Munich to the outbreak of war: September 1938 to September 1939

(a) Hitler's aims

Hitler's most pressing aims in foreign affairs when he came to power were to destroy the hated Versailles settlement, to recover lost territory such as the Saar (this was returned to Germany by a plebiscite in 1935) and the Polish Corridor, and to bring all areas containing German people within the Reich.

map **27.1** Hitler's gains before the Second World War

Much of this, culminating in the annexation of Austria, had already been achieved; the rest would require the acquisition of territory from Czechoslovakia and Poland, both of which had large German minorities.

There is some disagreement about what, if anything, Hitler intended beyond these aims. Most historians believe that the annexation of Austria and parts of Czechoslovakia and Poland was only a beginning, to be followed by the seizure of the rest of Czechoslovakia and Poland and by the conquest and permanent occupation of Russia as far east as the Ural Mountains (see Map 27.1). This would give him what some Germans called *Lebensraum* (living space), which would provide food for the German people and an area in which the excess German population could settle and colonize. An additional advantage was that communism would be destroyed. However, not all historians agree about these further aims; A. J. P. Taylor, for example, claimed that Hitler never intended a major war and at most was prepared only for a limited war against Poland.

(b) Hitler, Chamberlain and Czechoslovakia

It seems likely that Hitler had decided to destroy Czechoslovakia as part of his *Lebensraum* policy; he hated the Czechs for their democracy and for the fact that their state had been created by the Versailles Settlement. His excuse for the opening propaganda campaign was that the 3.6 million Sudeten Germans under their leader Konrad Henlein were being discriminated against by the Czech government. It is true that unemployment *was* higher among Germans, but apart from that, they were probably not being seriously inconvenienced.

The Nazis organized huge protest demonstrations in the Sudetenland, and clashes occurred between Czechs and Germans. The Czech president, Benes, feared that Hitler was deliberately stirring up trouble so that German troops could march in 'to restore order'. Chamberlain and Daladier, the French Prime Minister, both feared that war between Germany and Czechoslovakia was imminent.

At this point, Chamberlain took the initiative. He was full of self-confidence (some people called it arrogance) and was determined to play a leading role in international affairs. He once remarked, 'I have only to raise a finger and the whole face of Europe is changed!' And now he felt it was his duty to go to almost any lengths to prevent war. His aim was to prevail upon the Czech government to offer Hitler concessions that would make a German invasion unnecessary. Under pressure, Benes agreed that the Sudeten Germans might be detached from Czechoslovakia. Chamberlain flew to Germany (his first-ever flight) and had talks with Hitler at Berchtesgaden (15 September) explaining the offer. Hitler seemed to accept, but at a second meeting at Godesberg (22 September) he stepped up his demands: he wanted more of Czechoslovakia and the immediate entry of German troops to the Sudetenland. This Benes would not agree to, and immediately ordered the mobilization of the Czech army.

When it seemed that war was inevitable, Hitler invited Chamberlain and Daladier to a four-power conference which met at Munich (29 September). Here, a plan produced by Mussolini (but drafted by the German Foreign Office) was accepted. The Sudetenland was to be handed over to Germany immediately, but Germany, along with the other three powers guaranteed the remainder of Czechoslovakia. Neither the Czechs nor the Russians were invited to the conference; the Czechs were told that if they resisted the Munich decision, they would receive no help from Britain or France, even though at Locarno the French had guaranteed the Czech frontiers.

The following morning, Chamberlain had a private meeting with Hitler at which they both signed a statement, 'the scrap of paper', prepared by Chamberlain, promising that Britain and Germany would renounce warlike intentions against each other and would use consultation 'to deal with any other question that may concern our two countries'. When Chamberlain arrived back in Britain, waving the 'scrap of paper' for the benefit of the newsreel cameras at Heston airfield (see Illus. 27.1), he received a rapturous welcome from the public, who thought war had been averted. Chamberlain himself declared: 'I believe it is peace for our time'. However, not everybody was so enthusiastic: Churchill called Munich 'a total and unmitigated defeat', and Alfred Duff Cooper, the First Lord of the Admiralty, resigned from the Cabinet, saying that Hitler could not be trusted to keep to the agreement. It is open to debate as to whether Chamberlain really understood the sort of man Hitler was; he persisted in treating him as a responsible statesman and ignored his ill-treatment of the

Illus. 27.1 On his return from Munich, Neville Chamberlain waves the scrap of paper containing Hitler's promise of peace

Jews and the mass of evidence (for example, the way he increased his demands at Godesberg when he realized how committed Chamberlain was to maintaining peace at all costs) suggesting that Hitler was not reliable. On his return from Godesberg, Chamberlain told the Cabinet that he had established some influence over Hitler, a man who would be 'rather better than his word'.

Duff Cooper and Churchill were right; Czechoslovakia was crippled by the loss of 70 per cent of its heavy industry and almost all its fortifications to Germany. Slovakia began to demand semi-independence, and when it looked as though the country was about to fall apart, Hitler pressurized president Hacha into requesting German help 'to restore order'. Consequently, in March 1939, German troops occupied the rest of Czechoslovakia. Britain and France protested but took no action: according to Chamberlain, the guarantee of Czech frontiers did not apply because technically Czechoslovakia had not been invaded: German troops had entered by invitation. However, the German action caused a great outburst of criticism: for the first time the appeasers were unable to justify what Hitler had done – he had broken his promise and seized non-German territory. Even Chamberlain and Halifax felt this was going too far, and their attitude hardened. After the outbreak of war, critics of Munich pointed out that if Chamberlain *had* genuinely believed, as he later claimed, that Hitler would have to be stopped eventually, it would have been better for Britain and France to have fought alongside Czechoslovakia, which was militarily and industrially strong and had excellent fortifications.

(c) Hitler, Chamberlain and Poland

After taking over the Lithuanian port of Memel (which was admittedly peopled largely by Germans), Hitler turned his attentions to Poland. The Germans resented the loss of Danzig and the Polish Corridor as part of the Versailles Treaty, and now that Czechoslovakia was safely out of the way, Polish neutrality was no longer necessary. At the end of March 1939, Chamberlain, still outraged at the German occupation of Prague, wrote to the Polish government promising that if their independence was threatened, Britain and France 'would at once lend them all the support in their power'. In April, Hitler demanded the return of Danzig, and a road and railway across the Corridor to link East Prussia with the rest of Germany. This demand was, in fact, not unreasonable, since Danzig was largely German-speaking; but coming so soon after the seizure of Czechoslovakia, the Poles were convinced, probably rightly, that the German demands were only a prelude to invasion. Already fortified by the British promise of help, the Polish Foreign Minister, Colonel Beck, rejected the German demands and refused to attend a conference, no doubt afraid of another Munich. Chamberlain now began to have second thoughts as the threat of war increased again. Britain urged the Poles to surrender Danzig, but Beck stood firm.

Meanwhile, there was pressure from certain quarters in Britain for some sort of alliance with the USSR. The Labour Party, Lloyd George and Churchill all pointed out that the promise of British help to Poland was meaningless without military help from the Russians, who could threaten Germany's eastern frontier. Stalin was anxious for an understanding with Britain, and negotiations opened in April 1939. However, both Chamberlain and Halifax detested communism and were sceptical of Russia's military strength. An added difficulty was that the Poles were as nervous of the Russians as they were of the Germans, and would not agree to Russian troops crossing Poland to take up positions on the frontier with Germany. The negotiations dragged on without any result, and in the end the Russians grew tired of British stalling and signed a non-aggression pact with Hitler (24 August). Also agreed at the same time was a partition of Poland between Germany and the USSR, though this was kept secret.

Hitler was now convinced that with Russia neutral, Britain and France would not risk intervention; when the British ratified their guarantee to

Poland, Hitler took it as a bluff. When the Poles still refused to negotiate, a full-scale German invasion began early on 1 September 1939. Chamberlain had not completely given up on appeasement and still shrank from committing Britain to war. He suggested that, if German troops were withdrawn, a conference could be held – but there was no response from the Germans. Only when pressure began to mount in Parliament and in the country did Chamberlain send an ultimatum to Germany. When this expired at 11 am on 3 September, Britain was at war with Germany. Soon afterwards France also declared war.

(d) Britain's defences

Britain had never begun actively to disarm, though in the years before Hitler came to power, the government had been spending progressively less each year on armaments. For example, the Conservatives had spent £116 million in 1926–7, Labour £110 million in 1930–1, and the National Government £103 million in 1932–3. As soon as Hitler became the German Chancellor (January 1933) Churchill pressed the government to build up Britain's armaments, and in particular its air defences. He warned that if war broke out, Britain would be subjected to heavy bombing: 'the crash of bombs exploding in London, and cataracts of masonry and fire and smoke will warn us of any inadequacy in our aerial defences'. The government responded, though slowly. In July 1930, it was announced that over the next five years an extra 820 planes would be built, bringing the strength of the RAF up to 1,304 front-line planes. Churchill thought this inadequate; in May 1935, Hitler told Simon that his air force was already larger than Britain's. This was an exaggeration, but it helped to speed up British rearmament, especially after German troops entered the Rhineland (March 1936).

Before Munich, German rearmament was much more rapid than Britain's; in 1937–8, Britain spent £350 million on armaments, whereas Germany spent £1,600 million. At the end of that year, Germany had 2,800 front-line planes, while Britain still had fewer than 1,000. After Munich, Chamberlain was responsible for a dramatic surge in arms production, though it was only in the spring of 1940 that British aircraft production overtook that of Germany, and Germany was still in the lead at that point. There was also a fourfold increase in the numbers of anti-aircraft guns; perhaps the most vital of all in the air-defence system was the building-up of a chain of twenty radar stations to track enemy planes.

However, there are still doubts about how committed Chamberlain really was. Cabinet papers and Chamberlain's letters show that he hoped Munich would turn out to be a permanent understanding with Germany, so that rearmament would be unnecessary. With unemployment approaching two million on the eve of war, Britain was certainly not rearming to full capacity.

27.4 who or what was to blame for the war?

The debate is still going on about who or what was responsible for the Second World War.

▸ The Versailles Treaty has been blamed for filling the Germans with bitterness and the desire for revenge, while at the same time leaving the states of central Europe (Czechoslovakia, Poland, Austria, Hungary) too weak and divided to be able to defend themselves against Hitler.
▸ The League of Nations and the idea of collective security have been criticized because they failed to secure general disarmament and to control potential aggressors.
▸ The world economic crisis has been mentioned, since without it, Hitler would probably never have come to power.
▸ It has even been suggested that the USA should take some of the blame for the war. They refused to ratify the Treaty of Versailles; they refused to join the League of Nations, which without them was an almost complete failure; they allowed the economic crisis to develop, which spread to Europe and enabled Hitler to come to power in Germany; and they insisted on remaining isolated as events in Europe moved towards war.

While these factors no doubt helped to create the sorts of tensions that might well lead to war, something more was needed. It is worth remembering that, by the end of 1938, many of Germany's grievances had been removed: reparations were largely cancelled, the disarmament clauses had been ignored, the Rhineland was remilitarized, Austria and Germany were united, and 3.6 million Germans had been brought into the Reich from Czechoslovakia. Britain had even offered some compensation for lost German colonies. Germany was, in fact, a great power again. So what went wrong?

(a) was Hitler to blame?

During and immediately after the war there was general agreement outside Germany that Hitler was to blame. By attacking Poland on all fronts instead of merely occupying Danzig and the Polish Corridor, Hitler showed that he intended not just to get back the German areas lost at Versailles, but also to destroy Poland. Martin Gilbert argues that his motive was to remove the stigma of defeat in the First World War; 'for the only antidote to defeat in one war is victory in the next'. Hugh Trevor-Roper and many other historians believed that Hitler intended a major war right from the beginning. They argue that he hated communism and wanted to destroy the USSR and control it permanently; this could only be achieved by a major war. The destruction of Poland was an essential preliminary to the invasion of Russia. The German non-aggression pact with the Russians was simply a way of lulling Russian suspicions and keeping them neutral until Poland had been dealt with.

Evidence for this theory is taken from statements in Hitler's book *Mein Kampf* (My Struggle) and from the Hossbach Memorandum, a summary made by Hitler's adjutant, Colonel Hossbach, of a meeting held in November 1937, at which Hitler explained his plans to his generals. Another important source of evidence is Hitler's *Secret Book* which he finished around 1928 but never published.

If this theory is correct, appeasement cannot be blamed as a cause of war, except that it made things easier for Hitler. Hitler had his plans, his 'blueprint' for action, and this meant that war was inevitable sooner or later. Germans, on the whole, were happy with this interpretation too. If Hitler was to blame, and Hitler and the Nazis could be viewed as a kind of grotesque accident, a temporary 'blip' in German history, that meant that the German people were largely free from blame. However, it seems certain that Hitler had no intention of starting a *world war.* He believed that Poland and Russia were weak and would be knocked out swiftly by lightning strikes (*Blitzkrieg*).

(b) were the appeasers to blame?

Some historians claim that appeasement was equally to blame; as early as 1940 the appeasers were being castigated as 'the guilty men'. The argument is that Hitler was prepared to get what he wanted, either by war or by diplomatic means. Britain and France therefore ought to have taken a firm line with him before Germany became too strong: an Anglo-French attack on western Germany in 1936 at the time of the Rhineland occupation would have taught Hitler a lesson and might have toppled him from power. By giving way to him, the appeasers increased his prestige at home; with each success, Hitler's position became progressively stronger and he became increasingly contemptuous of the Western powers. As Alan Bullock wrote: 'success and the absence of resistance tempted Hitler to reach out further, to take bigger risks'. He may not have had definite plans for war, but after the surrender at Munich, he was so convinced that Britain and France would remain passive once again, that he decided to gamble on war with Poland.

Chamberlain has also been criticized for choosing the wrong issue over which to make a stand against Hitler. It is argued that German claims over Danzig and routes across the Corridor were more reasonable than the country's demands for the Sudetenland (which contained almost a million non-Germans and had never been part of Germany). Poland was difficult for Britain and France to defend, and was militarily much weaker than Czechoslovakia. Chamberlain therefore should have made his stand at Munich and backed the Czechs. R. A. C. Parker argues that, if Churchill had been Prime Minister rather than Chamberlain, he might well have prevented war by building up a 'Grand Alliance' of Britain, France, Russia, Poland, Romania and Czechoslovakia. This would have presented Germany with the prospect of war on two fronts, and after the experiences of the First World War, this would have deterred even the Nazis from starting another one. In fact, the Russians were not invited to the Munich conference and neither were the Czechs, even though it was their country that was being dismembered.

However, Chamberlain has had many defenders; his most recent biographer, Robert Self (2007), presents a balanced view, arguing that while he made some mistakes – such as persisting for too long with his delusion that Hitler was a moderate Nazi, whereas he was actually 'a half-mad lunatic' – Chamberlain had very few viable alternatives and deserves great credit for trying to prevent war. Andrew Roberts believes that the 'Grand Alliance' idea was never truly a possibility 'through its internal contradictions'. For example, Stalin was far too suspicious of British motives, especially if Churchill was involved; the Poles hated the Red Army and would never allow Russian troops on to their territory, since they had 'a habit of overstaying their welcome'.

Chamberlain's defenders also claim that his main motive at Munich was to give Britain time to rearm for an eventual fight against Hitler. Philip M. Taylor makes the point that it was only during the year after Munich that Hitler gave proof that he intended to achieve his aims by force: 'the forceful incorporation into Germany of Czechs and Slovaks in March 1939 demonstrated what kind of man Hitler was ... this proof was essential if a vulnerable British public was to enter the war united behind the government'. In the words of Andrew Roberts, this policy of

> buying time to develop armaments was one of the primary reasons that Britain had enough Hurricanes and Spitfires to win the Battle of Britain in 1940. That victory should be ascribed to Chamberlain quite as much as to Air Marshal Sir Hugh Dowding, and far more than to Churchill who only became prime minister long after the vast majority of planes had already been produced.

(c) A. J. P. Taylor and his 'Origins'

A. J. P. Taylor, in his book *Origins of the Second World War* (1961), came up with the most controversial theory about the outbreak of the war. He believed that Hitler did not intend to cause a major war, and expected, at the most, a short war with Poland. According to Taylor, Hitler's aims were similar to those of previous German rulers – Kaiser Wilhelm II and Stresemann; only his methods were more ruthless. Hitler was a brilliant opportunist, taking advantage of the mistakes of the appeasers and of events such as the crisis in Czechoslovakia in February 1939. Taylor thought the occupation of the rest of Czechoslovakia in March 1939 was not the result of a sinister long-term plan: 'it was the unforeseen by-product of events in Slovakia' (the Slovak demand for more independence from the Prague government). Whereas Chamberlain miscalculated when he thought he could civilize Hitler, Hitler misread the minds of Chamberlain and the British. How could Hitler foresee that the British and French would be so inconsistent as to support Poland (where his claim was much more reasonable) after giving way to him over Czechoslovakia (where his case was much less valid)?

Thus, for Taylor, Hitler was lured into the war almost by accident after the Poles had called his bluff. Many people in Britain were outraged at Taylor, because they thought he was trying to 'whitewash' Hitler. But he was not defending Hitler; just the opposite, in fact – Hitler was still to blame, and so were the German people, for being aggressive: 'Hitler was the creation of German history and of the German present. He would have counted for nothing without the support and cooperation of the German people ... Many hundred thousand Germans carried out his evil orders without qualm or question.'

(d) did the USSR make war inevitable?

The USSR has been accused of making war inevitable by signing the non-aggression pact with Germany. It is argued that Stalin ought to have allied with the West and with Poland, thus frightening Hitler into keeping the peace. On the other hand, it has to be remembered that *Stalin wanted an agreement with Britain*; it was the British who delayed and stalled and were most reluctant to ally with the Russians, especially once they discovered that the Nazis were also trying to work out some sort of agreement with Stalin. Like the Poles, Chamberlain distrusted the Russians (because they were communists), and he thought they were militarily weak, following Stalin's purge of the Red Army officer class which was said to have removed or liquidated around three-quarters of the high command. Also, Chamberlain continued to cling to the belief that an agreement with Hitler was still possible, and that any agreement between Britain and the USSR would alienate Hitler. Russian historians justify the pact on the grounds that it gave the USSR time to prepare its defences against a possible German attack.

So, what conclusion are we to reach? Today, almost half a century after Taylor published his famous book, very few historians accept his theory that Hitler had no long-term plans for war. Some recent writers believe that Taylor ignored a lot of evidence that did not fit in with his own theory. Hitler *was* largely responsible for the war. As D. C. Watt puts it: Hitler's 'will for war was able to overcome the reluctance with which virtually everybody else approached it'. What Hitler had in mind, as Neil Gregor points out, was 'a racial war of destruction quite unlike that experienced in 1914–18. It began with the dismemberment of Poland, continued with the attack on the USSR, and culminated in an horrific genocidal war – the destruction of the Jews and other groups which the Nazis considered inferior to the German master race'. While he probably did not have a step-by-step plan worked out, he clearly had a basic vision, which he was working towards at every opportunity. That vision was a Europe dominated by Germany, and it could only be achieved by war.

Alan Bullock believed that Hitler genuinely did not want a war with Britain, and certainly not a *world* war. All he asked was that Britain should not interfere with his expansion in Europe and should allow him to defeat Poland and the USSR in separate campaigns. But this does not exonerate Hitler from blame for the war. His most recent biographer, Ian Kershaw, sees no reason to change the general conclusion that Hitler must take the blame:

> Hitler had never doubted, and had said so on innumerable occasions, that Germany's future could only be determined through war ... War – the essence of the Nazi system which had developed under his leadership – was for Hitler inevitable. Only the timing and direction were at issue. And there was no time to wait.

QUESTIONS

1 (a) To what extent was the British policy of appeasement in the 1930s evident before Chamberlain became Prime Minister (May 1937)?

 (b) How far was Chamberlain's policy of appeasement in 1937–8 defensible?

2 Explain why Neville Chamberlain (a) followed a policy of appeasement from 1937 until 1939; (b) apparently abandoned appeasement in 1939; (c) gave guarantees of help to Poland but failed to enlist the help of the USSR in order to make the guarantee effective.

3 How far do you think Britain's leaders were responsible for the outbreak of war in 1939?

A document question about the Munich Conference (1938) and the policy of appeasement can be found on the accompanying website www.palgrave.com/masterseries/lowe1.

chapter 28

Britain and the Second World War, 1939–45

summary of events

Though Britain had declared war on Germany ostensibly to help Poland, there was very little that the British themselves could do; their army was minute in comparison with those of Germany and France. It would be possible to send only a token force to the Western Front, until a larger army had been assembled. Until then it would be a question of defending Britain against the expected bombings. However, there was a long delay, and it was July 1940 before the expected onslaught on Britain arrived. There were other surprises too: unlike the 1914–18 war, the Second World War was one of rapid movement and was altogether a more complex affair. Major campaigns took place in western and central Europe, in the heart of Russia, in Burma and the Far East, and in the Pacific and Atlantic Oceans. *The war falls into four fairly clearly defined phases.*

(a) opening moves: September 1939 to December 1940

By the end of September, the Germans and Russians had defeated and occupied Poland. After a five-month pause (known as the 'phoney war'), the Germans took over Denmark and Norway (April 1940). A British attempt to dislodge them failed and caused Chamberlain to be replaced as Prime Minister by Winston Churchill, who proved to be an outstanding war leader, like Lloyd George in the First World War. In May, the Germans attacked Holland, Belgium and France, which were soon defeated. Mussolini had reached an agreement with Hitler in 1936 that he called the '*Rome–Berlin Axis*'; he said that the Axis was a line drawn between Rome and Berlin 'around which all European states that desire peace can revolve'. Ironically, he declared war in June 1940 just before the fall of France. Hence Germany and Italy were often described as 'the Axis powers' during the war. Next, Hitler attempted to bomb Britain into submission, but he was thwarted in *the Battle of Britain* (July to September 1940). However, this did not prevent Mussolini's armies from invading Egypt and Greece.

(b) the Axis offensive widens: 1941 to summer 1942

The war now began to develop into a worldwide conflict. First, Hitler, confident of victory over Britain, launched an invasion of Russia (June 1941), breaking the non-aggression pact signed less than two years previously. Then the Japanese joined the Axis powers, forcing the USA into the war by attacking the American naval base at Pearl Harbor (December 1941). The Japanese followed this by capturing the British territories of Hong Kong, Singapore, Malaya and Burma, as well as the Philippine Islands. Hitler declared war on the USA, and there seemed to be no way of stopping the Germans and Japanese, though the Italians were less successful.

(c) the offensives held in check: summer 1942 to summer 1943

This phase of the war saw three important battles in which Axis forces were defeated:

» In June 1942, the Americans drove off a Japanese attack on *Midway Island*, at the north-west end of the Hawaiian chain, inflicting heavy losses.
» In October, the Germans, advancing into Egypt, were halted by the British at *El Alamein* and later driven out of North Africa.
» The third battle was in Russia, where, by September 1942, the Germans had penetrated as far as *Stalingrad*. Here, the Russians put up such fierce resistance that, the following February, the German army was surrounded and compelled to surrender.

Meanwhile, the war in the air continued, with both sides bombing enemy cities, and at sea, where, as in the First World War, the British and Americans gradually got the better of the German submarine menace.

(d) the Axis powers defeated: July 1943 to August 1945

The enormous power and resources of the USA and the USSR, combined with an all-out effort from Britain and its Empire, slowly but surely wore the Axis powers down. Italy was eliminated first, and this was followed by an Anglo-American invasion of Normandy (June 1944) which liberated France, Belgium and the Netherlands. Later, Allied troops crossed the Rhine and captured Cologne. In the east, the Russians drove the Germans out and advanced on Berlin via Poland. Germany surrendered in May 1945, and Japan in August, after the Americans had dropped two atomic bombs there, one on Hiroshima and the other on Nagasaki.

28.1 early setbacks: Norway and Dunkirk

(a) why did the British declare war, and how well prepared were they?

The answer to the first question may seem obvious: Britain declared war on Germany because Hitler had ignored the British ultimatum to reverse the invasion of Poland launched on 1 September 1939, after being clearly warned that any violation of Poland's frontiers would result in Britain giving the Poles 'all the support in their power'. But the British government knew perfectly well that there was no way of sending direct help to the Poles in time to save them from defeat. Britain's basic war aim was to stop Hitler going any further, and then, if possible, to destroy Nazi power. Lord Halifax had put it simply in a Cabinet meeting in March 1939 when he advised that, if Hitler's aggression continued, 'we should attack Germany, not in order to save a particular victim, but in order to put down a bully'. In other words, it was the traditional British policy of resisting the domination of Europe by a hostile power that might be a threat to British interests. British resolve may have wavered at the time of the fall of France, but with Churchill as leader, determination stiffened again, and the war aim eventually became 'unconditional surrender of the Axis powers'.

Immediately after the First World War, government defence spending was reduced drastically, and all branches of the armed forces were allowed to stagnate to such a point that they could just about defend the Empire. It was only in 1934, with the collapse of the Disarmament Conference, that spending was slightly increased and Britain slowly began to rearm. By the time of the Munich Conference in September 1938, the picture was mixed. The navy was the weakest of the three military arms, since it was more-or-less completely occupied around the world guarding the Empire. More progress had been made in expanding and modernizing the army, particularly in the sphere of mechanization. It was in the RAF that the picture was brightest (see Section 27.3(d) for more details).

(b) the defeat of Poland and the 'phoney war'

The Poles were swiftly defeated by the German *Blitzkrieg* (lightning war); this consisted of rapid thrusts by motorized divisions and tanks (*Panzers*) with air support; the *Luftwaffe* (the German Air Force) put the Polish railway system out of action and destroyed the Polish Air Force. This was the first demonstration of the vital role that air support was destined to play in the war. Polish resistance was heroic but hopeless; Britain and France did little to help directly, because the French mobilization procedure was slow, and it was difficult to transport sufficient troops to Poland to be effective.

The main British actions were to begin a blockade of German ports, as in the First World War, in the hope that Hitler would soon lose heart; and to send troops across to France. Chamberlain brought Churchill into his War Cabinet as First Lord of the Admiralty, and there were several successful naval actions, including the defeat of the German pocket battleship *Graf Spee* by three British cruisers. It was soon clear, however, that submarines would be just as dangerous as in the previous war: in October a U-boat slipped through the defences at the Scapa Flow naval base in the Orkneys and sank the battleship *Royal Oak*. Despite this, though, throughout the winter of 1939–40 there was no large-scale military action; this led American journalists to call this the 'phoney war'.

(c) German victory in Norway

On 4 April 1940, Chamberlain unwisely said that Hitler had 'missed the bus', but his complacency was rudely shattered a few days later when Hitler's troops occupied Denmark and landed at the main Norwegian ports. Admiral Raeder, the German navy chief, realized that the fjords would be excellent naval bases from which to attack Britain's transatlantic supply lines, and when a British destroyer chased the German vessel *Altmark* into a Norwegian fjord and rescued 300 British prisoners who were on board, Hitler decided it was time to act. On 9 April, the Germans landed at Oslo, Kristiansand, Stavanger, Bergen and Trondheim; and despite British and French troops arriving a few days later, they were unable to dislodge the Germans, who were already well-established. After a temporary success at Narvik, all Allied troops were withdrawn by early June, because of the growing threat to France itself. One reason for the British failure was that they had no air support, whereas the German Air Force constantly harassed the Allies.

The Norwegian campaign had important results: the Germans had lost three cruisers and ten destroyers, which rendered the navy less effective at Dunkirk than it might have been. It showed up the incompetence of Chamberlain's government, which, in the words of Churchill, had been 'forestalled, surprised and outwitted'. In the Commons debate on the campaign, it became clear that a large number of Conservatives were turning against Chamberlain and wanted a more decisive leader. Leo Amery, quoting Oliver Cromwell's remarks to the Long Parliament, told Chamberlain: 'You have sat too long here for any good you have been doing. Depart, I say, and let us have done with you. In the name of God, go.' In the vote, Chamberlain's majority dropped to 81 from the usual 240, and he resigned soon afterwards, expecting Lord Halifax, the Foreign Secretary, to succeed him. Halifax did not seem anxious for the job, and it was Churchill who formed a new government, on the same day (10 May) that Hitler's forces attacked the Netherlands, France and Belgium.

(d) Churchill as war leader

Aged 65 when he became Prime Minister, Churchill was generally regarded as something of a failure in his parliamentary career up to that point. In 1970, when historian and Conservative MP Robert Rhodes James wrote his biography of Churchill covering the years 1900 to 1939, he subtitled it *A Study in Failure*. Churchill was blamed for using troops to disperse rioting Welsh miners at Tonypandy (1910), though in fact the troops were not used, and the job was done by unarmed police. He was blamed for the failure of the Gallipoli campaign (1915), for his mistaken revaluation of the pound (1925), for his aggressiveness during the General Strike (1926), for his opposition to the India Act (1935), and for his support of Edward VIII (1936). For all these reasons, it was thought that his judgement was questionable. He had changed parties –

from Conservative to Liberal and back to Conservative again – so that many regarded him as unreliable and inconsistent. However, two things he had always been consistent about were the need to rearm and the need to stand up to Hitler. His aggressiveness, which had so often seemed inappropriate in peacetime, was exactly the quality needed for an effective war leader. As A. J. P. Taylor put it, 'it was as if all his life had been an unconscious preparation for this hour'.

Churchill set up a War Cabinet of five men: himself as Prime Minister and Minister of Defence, Neville Chamberlain (who died in November 1940), Halifax, and from the Labour Party, Clement Attlee and Arthur Greenwood. Churchill became leader of the Conservative Party on Chamberlain's death; and he later brought into the Cabinet Beaverbrook as Minister of Aircraft Production, and Ernest Bevin as Minister of Labour. Other Labour men included were Herbert Morrison and Hugh Dalton, while the Liberal leader, Sir Archibald Sinclair, became Air Minister. It was a genuinely national government, and it turned out to be extremely effective, steering Britain through a very difficult year when she stood alone against Germany and Italy (June 1940 to June 1941), and organizing the entire nation, including the civilian population, to meet the demands of 'total war'. *The Emergency Powers Act (May 1940)*, which was rushed through Parliament in one day, gave the government almost unrestricted power to take whatever action was thought necessary.

Some historians took the chance provided by the 50th anniversaries of key events in the war to offer reassessments of Churchill's war leadership, some of them not very complimentary. Andrew Roberts, in his book *Eminent Churchillians* (1993), makes much of Churchill's mistakes during the war, while John Charmley is even more controversially harsh in two books – *Churchill: The End of Glory* (1993) and *Churchill's Grand Alliance* (1995). In the first of these he outraged many people by suggesting that Churchill would have done better for Britain if he had secured a negotiated peace in 1940 (see Source G on the website); by defeating Hitler he allowed Stalin and communism, an even greater threat, into central Europe. A more balanced view is presented in a collection of twenty-nine essays edited by Robert Blake and William Roger Louis, entitled *Churchill: A Major New Assessment of his Life in Peace and War* (1993). Eleven of the essays are devoted to aspects of Churchill's role during the Second World War. In their introduction, the editors argue that the choice of Churchill as Prime Minister in May 1940 was one of the most crucial decisions in modern British history (see Source F on the website). The general conclusion seems to be that, while Churchill certainly made mistakes, in the end that does not detract from his 'greatness' as a war leader. David Reynolds (in Chapter 14 of the collection entitled *Churchill in 1940*) claims that

> recognition of Churchill's remarkable role in 1940 must be balanced by acknowledgement that he was not always right in his decisions ...

[however] a sober examination of Churchill's performance as war leader in 1940 does not belittle his greatness. On the contrary, it makes him a more human and thereby a more impressive figure than the two-dimensional bulldog of national mythology. Churchill's greatness is that of a man, not an icon.

Equally fair and well-balanced are assessments by Roy Jenkins (2001), A. N. Wilson (2005) and Richard Toye (2007). Wilson suggests that, despite all his blunders as a strategist, the British people should be grateful to Churchill for three achievements: 'By his rhetoric in 1940 he had stiffened their resolve, and the gamble had paid off. He had stood up to Hitler, and from that autumn and winter of resistance had made possible the ultimate victory'. Second was his refusal to bow to pressure from Stalin and Roosevelt to open up a Second Front by invading France before 1944; Churchill had learned a lesson from the disastrous raid on Dieppe in August 1942, which demonstrated the foolishness of attempted invasions of France too early – before a weakening of the German position in France. And, third, he succeeded in drawing together in his government representatives of all classes in society, a truly national government; in the words of A. N. Wilson, 'Churchill had formed what was in effect the first working socialist government in English history'. Churchill dealt with general strategy and diplomacy; his mind was brimming with original ideas, some of which were impractical and even dangerous. The Chief of the Imperial General Staff, Sir Alan Brooke (from the end of 1941), spent much of his energy persuading Churchill to drop some of his wilder suggestions (see Source C on the website). Even so, mistakes were made: possibly his most serious error was to completely underestimate the aggressiveness and strength of the Japanese, and he would not be swayed from his conviction that 'Fortress Singapore' was impregnable. He must therefore take much of the responsibility for the loss of Singapore, and he was at least partly responsible for the defeats in Libya. He was very slow to appreciate the importance of air support in naval operations and underestimated the deadliness of aircraft to large surface vessels – hence the disaster off Crete (see Section 28.3(a)).

On the other hand, the great advantage of Churchill's methods was that they kept all the military leaders constantly on the alert, so that failures became fewer as the war went on. According to Michael Carver (in Chapter 20 of the collection entitled *Churchill and the Defence Chiefs*),

up to the end Churchill maintained his 'ceaseless prodding', inveighing against the caution of generals ... in the last years of the war, the military leaders, not least Brooke, Alexander, Montgomery and Mountbatten, had learned how to deal with Churchill: never to complain about the 'ceaseless prodding'; to stand firm but to keep him sweet by a constant stream of information and by an adroit balance of flattery, cajolery and frankness. They knew that they could not do without him, and did not want to, and he knew that they were indispensable to him.

Churchill's greatest contribution to the war effort was the sheer impact of his larger-than-life personality and his will to win. He provided an all-important psychological boost to a country which, within a few days of his taking office, seemed on the verge of defeat. For a 65-year-old, he had remarkable physical vitality and mental energy; he was full of bulldog pugnacity, and everybody soon realized that, with Churchill in command, decisive action would be taken. He actually seemed to be enjoying himself and this came over in his broadcasts. He had a brilliant command of words, and his speeches in the Commons, and particularly over the radio, were highly effective. He spoke in language ordinary people could understand, rallying the nation in one supreme co-operative effort – the Dunkirk spirit. He left people in no doubt about what to expect; three days after becoming premier he told them: 'I have nothing to offer you but blood, toil, tears and sweat.' Britain's war aim was simple: 'Victory – victory at all costs, victory in spite of all terror, victory, however long and hard the road may be; come then, let us go forward together with our united strength.' With a man like this in charge, the majority of people did not think about defeat.

(e) Dunkirk and the fall of France (May–June 1940)

German troops attacked the Netherlands, Belgium and France simultaneously on 10 May, and again *Blitzkrieg* methods brought swift victories. The Dutch, shaken by the bombing of Rotterdam, which killed almost a thousand people, surrendered after only four days. Belgium held out longer, but its surrender at the end of May left the British and French troops in Belgium trapped in a pincer movement as German motorized divisions swept across northern France; only Dunkirk remained in Allied hands. The British navy played a vital role in evacuating over 338,000 troops, two-thirds of them British, from Dunkirk between 27 May and 4 June. This was a remarkable achievement in the face of constant *Luftwaffe* attacks on the beaches; it would perhaps have been impossible if Hitler had not ordered the German advance towards Dunkirk to halt (24 May), probably because the marshy terrain and numerous canals were unsuitable for tanks.

The events at Dunkirk were important: a third of a million troops were rescued to fight again, and Churchill used the rescue brilliantly for propaganda purposes to boost British morale with the 'Dunkirk spirit'. In reality, it was a serious blow for the Allies: the armies at Dunkirk had lost all their arms and equipment, so it became impossible for Britain to help France. The British government unfairly tried to blame the disaster on King Leopold of the Belgians for his 'treachery' in surrendering when he did, and, equally unfairly, criticized the French for their 'panic and cowardice'.

Churchill flew to France several times to try to rally the government, and even offered them an Act of Union to turn Britain and France into one nation. But the position was hopeless. The Germans now swept southwards; Paris was captured on 14 June, and France surrendered eight days later. At Hitler's insistence the

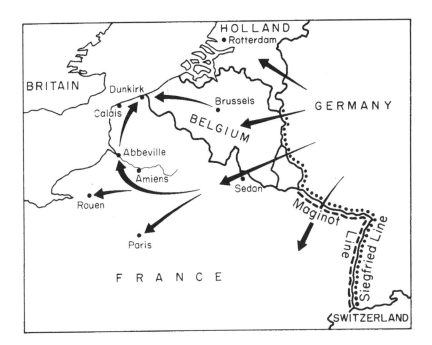

map **28.1 German attacks in May 1940**

armistice was signed at Compiègne, in the same railway coach that had been used for the 1918 armistice. The Germans occupied northern France and the Atlantic coast, giving them valuable submarine bases, and the French army was demobilized. Unoccupied France was allowed its own government under Marshal Pétain at Vichy, but it had no real independence and collaborated with the Germans. The fall of France was the high-water-mark of Hitler's achievements. Britain and its Empire stood completely alone against the dictators, and Hitler immediately began to prepare for Operation Sealion – the invasion of Britain.

What the general public did not know at the time, but which is now clear from sources that have become available more recently, is that during the last week of May, the British Cabinet seriously discussed the possibility of opening peace negotiations with Nazi Germany. Churchill was determined to fight on, at least for a few months, but Halifax, who thought the war was already lost, wanted to appeal to Mussolini (who was still neutral) to act as a mediator. Chamberlain agreed with him about the need to put out peace feelers, but crucially, did not believe that an approach via Mussolini would bring 'decent terms'; so the war must continue for the time being. Attlee and Greenwood were in full agreement with Churchill, and Halifax was outmanoeuvred. However, during the summer of 1940, Halifax continued to make unofficial soundings via the British embassy in Stockholm about what German peace terms might be. Eventually, Halifax was dropped from the War Cabinet and sent as ambassador to the USA.

28.2 the Battle of Britain (August–September 1940)

(a) Hitler prepares to invade Britain

In July 1940, Hitler began to assemble an invasion fleet of barges to carry the first wave of 260,000 troops, which would land between Brighton and Folkstone. But he had his problems: he had neglected the German navy, not expecting a full-scale war with Britain; it was therefore up to the *Luftwaffe* to clear the British navy out of the Channel and destroy the RAF so that the invasion could go ahead unhindered. In one of his most stirring broadcasts, Churchill warned of the vital importance of what was about to happen:

> Hitler knows that he will have to break us in this island or lose the war. If we can stand up to him, all Europe may be free and the life of the world may move forward into broad, sunlit uplands. But if we fail, then the whole world, all that we have known and cared for, will sink into the abyss of a new Dark Age ... Let us therefore brace ourselves to our duties, and so bear ourselves that, if the British Empire and its Commonwealth last for a thousand years, men will say, 'This was their finest hour.'

Already by July the *Luftwaffe* was attacking convoys in the Channel, though without much success; the Germans lost twice as many aircraft as the RAF lost fighters. In August the *Luftwaffe* switched to bombing RAF aerodromes and communication systems; 8 August saw the fiercest battles so far: the RAF shot down thirty-one German planes, and lost twenty themselves. On 12 August,

Illus. 28.1 Winston Churchill inspecting air-raid damage, September 1940

the radar station at Ventnor (Isle of Wight) was put out of action, but shortly afterwards Goering, head of the *Luftwaffe*, called off these attacks, underestimating the importance of radar. The Germans made their greatest effort on 15 August, believing that the British must soon run out of fighters; but again their losses were heavy – seventy-five German to thirty-four British.

(b) the failure of the Luftwaffe

The crucial period of the battle was the fortnight from 24 August to 6 September. The RAF began to lose heavily – on 6 September alone they lost 161 planes against 190 German planes shot down. Many of the British fighters were bombed on the ground, and the aircraft factories could not keep up with losses of this magnitude. Also serious was the loss of pilots – during that fortnight, 103 were killed and 129 wounded; again, it was impossible to make up these losses with experienced pilots. Six out of seven major airfields in the south-east were badly damaged. Then, not realizing how close they were to victory, Goering switched to bombing London and other large cities – in retaliation, it was claimed, for a British raid on Berlin. He was hoping to destroy civilian morale and reduce industrial production; but while enormous damage was caused and thousands of civilians were killed, the German bombers suffered heavy casualties in daytime raids and were forced to change to night bombing.

After the shock of the first raids in the 'Blitz' (over a thousand people were killed in the first three days in London), morale rallied well as the civilian population soon learnt how to cope with the resulting chaos and disruption. On 15 September, the Germans lost sixty aircraft to Britain's twenty-six. The Germans had failed to gain air superiority, and two days later Hitler called off the invasion of Britain. However, bombing raids continued until May 1941, when Hitler was almost ready to launch his attack on Russia. The Battle of Britain is usually taken as finishing at the end of September 1940, when it was clear that Britain had been saved from a German invasion.

(c) reasons for the British victory

Vitally important was the chain of fifty-one radar stations, which gave plenty of warning of German attacks; this worked right through the battle, and the Germans failed to realize the importance of disrupting this system. German bombers were poorly armed, and German Messerschmitt fighters, though not significantly inferior to the British Spitfires and Hurricanes, were hampered by limited range; they carried enough fuel for 90 minutes' flight, which gave them only a few minutes over London before they had to head for home. The switch to bombing London was a major error – it caused great damage and loss of life, but it relieved pressure on British airfields and fighters at a critical moment. British aircraft production was highly effective; the monthly output of fighters had been running at 250 early in the war, but this increased to 325 in May 1940, and reached a peak of 496 in July; even in September, at the height of the blitz, 467 were produced. The Germans could not match this, and Britain always had more reserves than the *Luftwaffe*. Finally, there was the skill and spirit of the fighter pilots and the careful strategy of Air Marshals Dowding and Park. As Churchill remarked when he paid tribute to them: 'Never in the field of human conflict was so much owed by so many to so few.'

(d) importance of the Battle of Britain

For the first time in the war, the Germans had been checked; this showed that they were not completely invincible, and was therefore probably the first major turning-point of the war. To the general surprise of the rest of the world, Britain was able to remain in the struggle and the country's prestige was high. It meant that Hitler, who was poised to begin his invasion of Russia, would be faced with war on two fronts, a situation which had proved fatal to Germany in the First World War.

28.3 the Axis offensive widens

As the war developed into a worldwide conflict during 1941, Britain, having survived the immediate danger of invasion, now had to counter the threat to the Empire – in Egypt and the Far East.

(a) Greece and Crete

Mussolini, who had already captured Albania, wanted a large Balkan empire. His forces invaded Greece in September 1940 but were soon driven back into Albania. Mussolini was clearly going to be an embarrassment to Hitler, who began 1941 by helping out his faltering ally. Churchill decided to support Greece as a matter of prestige, to encourage other countries such as the USA and Turkey to enter the struggle; 60,000 British, Australian and New Zealand troops arrived in Greece, only to be driven out immediately by a massive German invasion which soon overran the Greek mainland (April 1941). The Allies withdrew to the Greek island of Crete, which had been under British occupation for six months. However, they had failed to fortify the island adequately, and it was captured by the Germans in a spectacular parachute attack, which forced the Allies to withdraw again in June, with heavy losses. They had no air protection, and lost some 36,000 men, and their equipment. The government was criticized for intervening in Greece, but the Germans also suffered, losing a third of their troops and 220 aircraft; they did not attempt another operation of this sort again. It has also been argued that Hitler's involvement in Greece and Crete delayed his attack on Russia by about five weeks. It this was so, it may well have saved Moscow.

(b) Mussolini invades Egypt

Mussolini had opened hostilities in North Africa by invading Egypt from the

Allied advances and offensives 1942–4

map **28.2 North Africa and the Mediterranean**

Italian colony of Libya in September 1940. A mixed army of British, Indian, Australian, New Zealand, French and Polish troops, commanded by Wavell, pushed the Italians out of Egypt and back into Libya, defeating them at Bedafomm and capturing 130,000 prisoners and 400 tanks. This was a great boost to British morale, and helped to keep hopes of ultimate victory alive. Tobruk and Benghazi were captured, but in February 1941 the British advance was stopped on Churchill's orders, so that many of Wavell's troops and planes could be used in the Greek campaign. This was unfortunate, since only a few days later Hitler had sent Rommel, one of his best generals, to Tripoli with a large German army, to stiffen Italian resistance. By April 1941, Rommel had driven the British out of Libya, though they managed to hold on to Tobruk behind the German lines. The unfortunate Wavell was replaced by Auchinleck, who succeeded in relieving Tobruk in December but made no further headway.

(c) British difficulties in North Africa

The main problem was that the further west the British advanced, the more their lines of communication and supply with Egypt became strained. The other source of supply was from the sea across the Mediterranean, but there was a constant battle for control of the Mediterranean, where Britain's vital naval base was Malta; this was subjected to the most intense German and

Italian bombing, and was in danger of being starved into surrender. Between January and July 1941, very few ships managed to get through to Malta, though the situation eased after Hitler withdrew most of the *Luftwaffe* for the attack on Russia. The loss of the aircraft carrier *Ark Royal* was a serious blow, and for much of 1941–2, British troops in Egypt had to be supplied by ships sailing round the Cape of Good Hope and up through the Suez Canal. Crisis-point was reached in June 1942, when Rommel's forces suddenly struck, capturing Tobruk and penetrating deep into Egypt until they were only seventy miles from Alexandria.

(d) the Battle of El Alamein (October 1942)

This was the real turning-point in North Africa, when Rommel's *Afrika Korps* was driven back by Montgomery's Eighth Army, chased out of Egypt and almost out of Libya too by the British and New Zealanders. Tripoli was captured in January 1943. *The Allies were successful partly because* massive reinforcements had arrived, so that the Germans and Italians were heavily outnumbered – they had only 80,000 men and 540 tanks against 230,000 troops and 1,440 tanks. Allied air power was vital: Axis forces were constantly attacked and their supply ships sunk as they crossed the Mediterranean. By October there were serious shortages of food, fuel oil and ammunition; at the same time the RAF was strong enough to protect the Eighth Army's own supply routes. Montgomery's skilful preparations probably clinched the issue, though he has been criticized for being over-cautious and for allowing Rommel and half his forces to escape into Libya.

However, there is no doubt that the *El Alamein victory was one of the three major turning-points in the war* (the other two were Midway Island and Stalingrad). It prevented Egypt and the Suez Canal from falling into German hands, and ended the possibility of a link-up between the Axis forces in the Middle East and those in the Ukraine. More than that, it led on to the complete expulsion of Axis forces from North Africa; it encouraged landings of American and British troops in the French territories of Morocco and Algeria, to threaten the Germans and Italians from the west, while the Eighth Army closed in on them from Libya. Trapped in Tunisia, 275,000 Germans and Italians were forced to surrender in May 1943, and the Allies were well-placed for an invasion of Italy. The desert war had been a serious drain on German resources that could have been used in Russia where they were badly needed.

(e) the Far East: Malaya, Singapore and Burma

Here there was nothing but disaster for Britain. The Japanese, after their successful attack on Pearl Harbor (7 December 1941), in which nineteen American ships were sunk or disabled and over 2,000 lives lost, went on to invade British territories in the Far East, all of which were inadequately defended. Hong Kong was taken, and Japanese troops landed on the coast of northern Malaya, capturing all the airfields. This deprived the British of air

map **28.3 The war in the Pacific**

protection, and Japanese planes sank the *Repulse* and the *Prince of Wales* (10 December) with the loss of 600 lives. These were the two main capital ships, which were intended to maintain control of the area. Meanwhile, Japanese troops advanced down the Malay peninsula until by the end of January 1942 only Singapore remained in British hands. The Australians now seemed on the verge of panic, fearing that they were next in line for a Japanese attack; it was mainly to satisfy them that Churchill sent more troops to Singapore. But it was too late: the fortress was primarily a naval base, not equipped to withstand a land assault. On 15 February, with the supply of fresh water cut off, the British commander surrendered, with 60,000 troops.

Though it was not the knock-out blow that Hitler had hoped, it was a serious setback to Britain's prestige as an imperial power. For the first time, Britain had suffered a major defeat at the hands of an Asian power. This encouraged opposition to British rule in India, and meant that after the war the Indians would be content with nothing less than full independence. Australia began to look towards the USA as its main defence against Japan. The loss of Singapore led to the Japanese occupation of Burma (March 1942), and the fall of India seemed imminent. However, although the British did not realize it at the time, they need not have worried: the Japanese were mainly concerned with the Pacific and had no immediate plans to conquer India.

28.4 the war at sea

As in the First World War, the British navy had a vital role to play. This included protecting the merchant ships bringing food supplies; sinking German submarines and surface raiders; blockading Germany; and transporting and supplying the Allied troops in North Africa, and later in Italy. At first success was mixed, mainly because the British failed to understand the importance of air support in naval operations and had few aircraft carriers. Thus they suffered defeats in Norway and Crete, where the Germans had strong air superiority. In addition, the Germans had numerous naval bases in Norway, Denmark, France and Italy. British weakness in the Far East led to the fall of Hong Kong, Malaya, Singapore and Burma. However, there were some successes:

1 Aircraft from the carrier *Illustrious* sank half the Italian fleet at Taranto (November 1940); and the following March, five more warships were destroyed off Cape Matapan.
2 The threat from surface raiders was removed by the sinking of the *Bismarck*, Germany's only battleship at the time (May 1941).
3 The navy destroyed German invasion transport on its way to Crete (May 1941), though they could not prevent the landing of parachute troops.
4 The navy provided escorts for convoys carrying supplies to help the Russians; these sailed via the Arctic to Murmansk in the far north of Russia. Beginning in September 1941, the first twelve convoys arrived without incident, but then the Germans began to attack them, until convoy 17 lost twenty-three ships out of thirty-six (June 1942). After this disaster, convoys did not fully resume until November 1943, when stronger escorts could be spared. In total, forty convoys sailed: 720 out of 811 merchant ships arrived safely, with valuable cargo for the Russians, including 5,000 tanks and 7,000 aircraft, as well as thousands of tons of canned meat.
5 The navy's most important contribution was its victory in *the Battle of the Atlantic*. This was the struggle against German submarines attempting to deprive Britain of food and raw materials. At the beginning of 1942, the Germans had ninety U-boats in operation, and 250 being built. In the first six months of that year the Allies lost over 4 million tons of merchant shipping and destroyed only twenty-one U-boats; losses reached a peak of 108 ships in March 1943, almost two-thirds of which were in convoy. However, after that, the number of sinkings began to fall, while U-boat losses increased. By July 1943, the Allies could produce ships at a faster rate than the U-boats could sink them, and the situation was under control. *Reasons for the Allied success were*

that more air protection for convoys was provided by long-range Liberators, both escorts and aircraft protection improved with experience, and the British introduced the new centimetric radar sets, which were small enough to be fitted into aircraft, so that submarines could be detected in poor visibility and at night. This victory was as important as Midway, El Alamein and Stalingrad: Britain could not have remained in the war for much longer if she had continued to sustain losses as heavy as in March 1943.

6 Sea and air power together made possible the great invasion of France in June 1944 (see Section 28.6(b)).

28.5 the war in the air

1 The first significant achievement from the British point of view was the Battle of Britain (1940), when the RAF beat off the *Luftwaffe* attacks, causing Hitler to abandon his invasion plans.

2 In conjunction with the British navy, aircraft played a varied role: the successful attacks on the Italian fleet at Taranto and Cape Matapan, the sinking of the German battleship *Tirpitz* by heavy bombers in Norway (November 1943), the protection of convoys in the Atlantic, and anti-submarine operations. In fact, in May 1943, Admiral Doenitz, the German navy chief, complained to Hitler that since the introduction of the new radar devices, more U-boats were being destroyed by aircraft than by naval vessels.

3 The American air force, together with the navy, played a crucial part in the Pacific War victories against the Japanese, winning the Battle of Midway Island in June 1942. Later, in the 'island-hopping' campaign, marines landed on the Mariana Islands (1944) and the Philippines (1945). American and RAF transport planes kept up a flow of essential supplies to the Allies during the campaign to recapture Burma.

4 The RAF took part in specific campaigns which would have been hopeless without them; for example, during the desert war, operating from bases in Egypt and Palestine, they constantly bombed Rommel's supply ships in the Mediterranean and his armies on land.

5 British and American planes flew in parachute troops to aid the landings in Sicily (July 1943) and Normandy (June 1944), and provided air protection for the invading armies. However, a similar operation at Arnhem in Holland in September 1944 was a failure.

(a) allied bombing of German and Japanese cities

This was the most controversial action by the Allied air forces. The Germans had bombed London and other important British cities and ports during 1940 and 1941, but these raids dwindled during the German attack on Russia, which required all the *Luftwaffe's* strength. The British and Americans retaliated with what they called a 'strategic air offensive' – this involved massive attacks on military and industrial targets, to hamper the German war effort. The Ruhr, Cologne, Hamburg and Berlin all suffered badly. Some raids seem to have been carried out to undermine civilian morale – about 50,000 people were killed during a single night raid on Dresden (February 1945). Early in 1945, the Americans launched a series of devastating raids on Japan from bases in the Mariana Islands. In a single raid on Tokyo in March, 80,000 people were killed and a quarter of the city destroyed.

There has been some debate about how effective the bombing was in hastening the Axis defeat, beyond merely causing inconvenience. Critics also point to the heavy losses suffered by air-crews – over 158,000 Allied airmen were killed in Europe alone. Others argue that this type of bombing, which caused the deaths of so many innocent civilians (as opposed to bombings that targeted industrial areas, railways and bridges) was morally wrong. Estimates of German civilian deaths from Allied bombing vary between 600,000 and a million. German raids on Britain killed over 60,000 civilians. In 2001, a Swedish writer, Sven Lindquist, in his book entitled *A History of Bombing*, suggested that the Allied bombings of German cities should be regarded as 'crimes under national humanitarian law'. In 2002, a German historian, Jorg Friedrich, published a controversial account (*Der Brand* or The Fire) of the horrific suffering inflicted by Allied bombers on German civilians; an English translation came out in 2007. He blames specifically Churchill and Arthur 'Bomber' Harris, the head of Bomber Command, and clearly believes that the bombing raids were war crimes.

Friedrich's book caused great controversy: many British historians condemned it immediately; Corelli Barnett, for example, called it 'a historical travesty' intended to justify Hitler's actions, or at least to move the spotlight away from Nazi atrocities. To mark the appearance of the English edition, York Membery, writing in *History Today* (January 2007), sought the views of some leading British historians. Richard Overy feels that while it is time for a proper assessment of the bombing strategy, Friedrich plays down the contribution and responsibility of the Americans, and the general tone of his book is not helpful, since it is bound to antagonize British and American readers. Overy insists that the bombing 'was neither immoral nor strategically useless … [it] played an important, if not vital, part in distorting Germany's strategy and undermining its war effort'. Also in *History Today*, Adam Tooze, an expert on the Nazi economy, has some controversial views of his own:

> If the war was right – and it surely was – then the only criterion is whether the bombing helped to win it effectively. And in my view it did. But I would go further: I feel that we would have been more justified in using the atomic bomb against Germany, the target for which it was intended, than against Japan.

Bruce Kent, a peace campaigner and former secretary of CND, feels that the bombing raids *were* war crimes, but that Friedrich fails to set the bombings in the political and military context in which they took place. He takes no account of the fact that the Nazis were the first to begin bombing innocent civilians – in Guernica, Warsaw and Rotterdam; and the Nazis themselves were simultaneously committing their own war crimes in Poland and Russia, and exterminating six million Jews. As Robin Niellands points out in his own book about Harris and the bombings (2001), this is what happens during a total war – in the context of what the Germans had done in eastern Europe and the Japanese in their occupied territories, this was the necessary 'price of peace'. The German civilian population were just as much victims of the war as the rest; unfortunately, in the words of Adam Tooze, 'if you start a war with Britain as Germany deliberately did, then this is the kind of war you have to be prepared to fight'.

As to the question of whether the bombing helped to shorten the war, the most recent research suggests that the campaign was effective much earlier than used to be thought; that is, from the autumn of 1944. Evidence from German archives shows that the RAF attack on the Ruhr in the spring of 1943 had an immediate impact on production. From July 1944, thanks to the increasing accuracy of the raids and the use of the new Mustang fighter escorts that could outmanoeuvre all the German fighters, the effects of the bombings reached disaster proportions. Synthetic oil production fell rapidly, causing acute fuel shortages, and then in October the vital Krupps armaments factories in Essen were put out of action permanently. The war effort ground to a halt in 1945. By June 1945, the Japanese had been reduced to the same state.

In the end, therefore, after some wasted early effort, the Allied strategic air offensive was one of the decisive reasons for the Axis defeat: besides strangling fuel and synthetic oil production and destroying rail communications, it caused the diversion of many aircraft from the Eastern Front, thus helping the Russian advance into Germany.

28.6 the defeat of the Axis powers

(a) the fall of Italy

This was the first stage in the Axis collapse. British and American troops landed in Sicily from both sea and air on 10 July 1943 and quickly captured the whole island. This caused the downfall of Mussolini, who was dismissed by the king. Allied troops crossed to Salerno, Reggio and Taranto on the mainland and captured Naples in October 1943, by which time Marshal Badoglio, Mussolini's successor, had signed an armistice and brought Italy into the war on the Allied side. However, the Germans, determined to hold on to Italy, rushed troops through the Brenner Pass to occupy Rome and the north. The Allies landed a force at Anzio, thirty miles south of Rome in January 1944, but bitter fighting followed before Monte Cassino (May) and Rome (June) were captured; Milan in the north was not taken until May 1945. The campaign could have been finished much sooner if the Allies had been less cautious in the early stages and if the Americans had not insisted on keeping many divisions back for the invasion of France. Nevertheless, the elimination of Italy did contribute towards the final victory: it provided air bases for the bombing of the Germans in central Europe and the Balkans, and kept German troops occupied when they were needed to resist the Russians.

(b) the invasion of France – Operation Overlord (6 June 1944)

Operation Overlord (also known as the 'Second Front') began on 'D-Day', 6 June 1944. It was felt that the time was ripe now that Italy had been eliminated, the U-boats controlled and Allied air superiority achieved; the Russians had been urging the Allies to start this Second Front ever since 1941, to relieve pressure on them. The landings took place from both sea and air on a sixty-mile stretch of Normandy beaches (codenamed Utah, Omaha, Gold, Juno and Sword) between Cherbourg and Le Havre. There was strong German resistance, but at the end of the first week, 326,000 men had landed safely, with tanks and heavy lorries.

It was a remarkable operation: it made use of prefabricated 'Mulberry' harbours, which were towed across from Britain and positioned close to the Normandy coast, mainly at Arromanches (Gold beach), and of PLUTO – pipelines under the ocean – carrying motor fuel. Eventually over 3 million Allied troops were landed; within a few weeks, most of northern France was liberated (and Paris on 25 August), putting out of action the sites from which the German V1 and V2 rocket missiles had been launched with devastating effects on south-eastern Britain. In Belgium, Brussels and Antwerp were liberated in September.

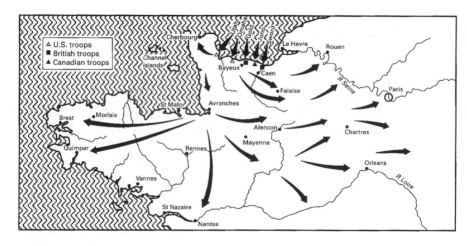

map 28.4 The D-Day landings – 6 June 1944

(c) the assault on Germany

The assault on Germany followed, but the end was delayed by desperate German resistance and by disagreements between the British and Americans. Montgomery wanted a rapid thrust to reach Berlin before the Russians, but the American General Eisenhower favoured a cautious advance along a broad front. The British failure at Arnhem in Holland in September 1944 seemed to support Eisenhower's view, though in fact the Arnhem operation (an attempt by parachute troops to cross the Rhine and outflank the German Siegfried Line) might have worked if the troops had landed nearer to the two Rhine bridges.

Consequently, Eisenhower had his way and Allied troops were dispersed over a 600-mile front, with unfortunate results: Hitler was able to launch a final offensive through the weakly defended Ardennes towards Antwerp; the Germans broke through the American lines and advanced sixty miles, causing a huge bulge in the front line (December 1944). Determined British and American action stemmed the advance and pushed the Germans back to their

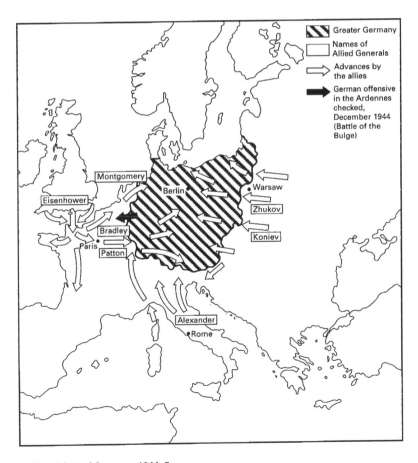

map **28.5** The defeat of Germany, 1944–5

original position, but *the Battle of the Bulge* as it became known, was important because Hitler had risked everything and had lost 250,000 men and 400 tanks, which at this stage could not be replaced. Early in 1945, Germany was being invaded on both fronts, from east and west. The British still wanted to push ahead and take Berlin before the Russians reached it, but supreme commander Eisenhower refused to be hurried, and Berlin fell to Stalin's forces in April. Hitler committed suicide and Germany surrendered on 7 May 1945.

(d) the defeat of Japan

This took longer, and was not achieved until August 1945. Since the Battle of Midway in June 1942, the Japanese had not recovered from their losses of aircraft carriers and strike planes; the Americans always maintained their lead. Under the command of General MacArthur, they began to recover the Pacific islands, beginning in August 1942 with the landings on the Solomon Islands. It was a long and bitter struggle which continued through 1943 and 1944 by a process known as 'island hopping'. The British contributed to the Japanese defeat by prising them out of Burma after capturing Rangoon, the capital, in April 1945. This was a humiliating defeat for the Japanese, who lost 53,000 of their 85,000 troops in Burma.

The end came for Japan in August 1945. On 6 August, the Americans dropped an atomic bomb on Hiroshima, killing perhaps as many as 84,000 people and leaving thousands more slowly dying of radiation poisoning. Three days later. they dropped an atomic bomb on Nagasaki, which killed perhaps another 40,000. After that, the Japanese government surrendered (14 August). *The dropping of these bombs was one of the most controversial actions of the entire war.* President Truman's justification was that he was saving American lives, since the war might otherwise have dragged on for another year. Many historians believe that the bombings were not necessary, since the Truman government knew that the Japanese had already put out peace feelers in June by sending an envoy to Russia. One suggestion is that the real reason for the bombings was to end the fighting swiftly before the Russians (who had promised to enter the war against Japan) gained too much Japanese territory, which would entitle them to share the occupation of Japan. A demonstration of the awesome power of the bomb would help the USA to gain a diplomatic advantage over the USSR, which at that time did not possess any nuclear weapons. According to the American Admiral Leahy, 'the scientists and others wanted to make this test because of the vast sums that had been spent on the project – two billion dollars'.

(e) why did the Axis powers lose the war?

The basic reason was that they simply took on too much; by attacking Russia before Britain had been eliminated, Hitler was facing two powerful enemies; declaring war on the USA as well was a fatal mistake. The Allies learned how to check *Blitzkrieg* attacks and began to appreciate the importance of air support and aircraft carriers. Italian incompetence was a constant drain on German resources, and the longer the war went on, the more the strain began to tell. Italy and Germany suffered from a shortage of raw materials, and even Germany was short of rubber, cotton, nickel and, after mid-1944, oil. On the other hand, the combined resources of the USA, the USSR and the British Empire were potentially overwhelming. The Russians moved their industry east of the Ural Mountains and so were able to continue production even though the Germans had occupied vast areas in the west. By 1940, they had four times as many tanks as the Germans, and could put twice as many men in the field. When the American war machine reached peak production it could turn out over 70,000 tanks and 120,000 aircraft a year, which the Germans and Japanese could not match.

(f) East–West relations at the end of the war

Towards the end of the war, the harmony that had existed between Britain, the USA and the USSR began to show signs of strain, as the old mutual suspicions revived. The deterioration could be seen in two conferences – at Yalta and Potsdam (February and July 1945).

1 *The Yalta Conference (February 1945)* was held in Russia – in the Crimea, and was attended by Churchill, Roosevelt and Stalin. At the time it was generally thought to be a success, agreement being reached on several points: the United Nations Organization was to be set up; Germany was to be divided into zones – Russian, American and British (a French zone was included later); Berlin, which would be in the Russian zone, would be split into corresponding zones; similar arrangements were to be made for Austria. Free elections would be allowed in the states of eastern Europe. Stalin promised to join the war against Japan on condition that Russia received the whole of Sakhalin Island and some territory in Manchuria. However, there were ominous signs over Poland: when the Russians swept through Poland as they pushed the Germans back, they had set up a communist government in Lublin, even though there was already a Polish government-in-exile in London. It was agreed at Yalta that some members (non-communist) of the London-based government should be allowed to join the Lublin government, while in return Russia could keep the strip of eastern Poland she had occupied in 1939; but Roosevelt and Churchill refused to agree to Stalin's demands that Russia should be given all German territory east of the Rivers Oder and Neisse.

2 *The Potsdam Conference (July 1945)* was held in Berlin and revealed a distinct cooling-off in relations. The main representatives were Stalin, Truman (replacing Roosevelt, who had died in April) and Churchill (subsequently replaced by Clement Attlee after Labour's election victory). The war

Land taken by Poland from Germany: territory east of the *Oder-Neisse* Line and part of East Prussia

Land acquired by the USSR during the war

Occupation zones in Germany and Austria:
1 Russian   3 French
2 British   4 American

map **28.6 Europe after 1945**

with Germany was over, but no agreement was reached about the country's long-term future beyond what had been decided at Yalta; it was understood that Germany would be disarmed, the Nazi party disbanded and its leaders tried as 'war criminals'. Moreover, Churchill and Truman were annoyed because Germany east of the Oder–Neisse line had been occupied by Russian troops and was being run by the pro-communist Polish government, which expelled some four million Germans living there; this had certainly not been agreed to at Yalta. Churchill was given the latest information about the successful atomic bomb tests; but while Truman told Stalin that the USA had a powerful new weapon, he did not go into precise detail, and did not tell Stalin that it was about to be used against Japan. A few days after the conference closed, the two atomic bombs were dropped on Japan, and the war ended quickly on 14 August without the need for Russian aid (though the Russians declared war on Japan on 8 August and invaded Manchuria). Though they annexed south Sakhalin, as agreed at Yalta, they were allowed no part in the occupation of Japan.

28.7 what were the effects of the war on Britain?

(a) the civilian population experience 'total war'

Civilians were involved in this conflict more directly than in the First World War. It was a 'total war', summed up perfectly by Churchill in one of his speeches:

> The whole of the warring nations are not only soldiers, but the entire population, men, women and children. The fronts are everywhere. The trenches are dug in the towns and the streets. Every village is fortified, every road is barred. The workmen are soldiers with different weapons but the same courage.

Immediate measures included the mass evacuation of children from cities and large towns to escape the expected bombings, the frantic digging of air-raid shelters and piling up of sand-bags, and the issue of gas-masks to civilians, in case of poison gas attacks. A complete blackout was imposed, so that no chinks of light would remain to guide the German bombers; this had the unfortunate effect of doubling the number of road accidents, and before the end of 1939, partial or 'glimmer' lighting of streets was allowed. Theatres and cinemas were closed and football matches banned, in case of bombing, but regulations were relaxed before Christmas 1939 and never reimposed.

In 1940, with the German invasion imminent, the government began to take more drastic action. *The Emergency Powers Act (May 1940)* gave the authorities full power to do whatever was thought necessary. Signposts, place-names and station name-boards were removed to confuse the Germans (if they arrived). Rationing of bacon, butter, cheese and meat was introduced, and during 1941, as the German submarine campaign reached its peak, regulations were further tightened. The weekly rations per person were austere, to say the least: eight ounces of meat, one ounce of cheese, four ounces of bacon or ham, eight ounces of sugar, two ounces of tea, two ounces of butter and two ounces of jam or marmalade. A 'points' system was introduced for other foods: each person was allowed sixteen points for four weeks, so the wealthy were prevented from buying up all the supplies. Goods available on the points system included tinned foods, rice, sago and tapioca, peas and tomatoes, breakfast cereals and condensed milk, and syrup, treacle and biscuits. People were exhorted to grow their own food – 'dig for victory' was the slogan. Bread, beer and tobacco were never rationed, but beer was watered until it had no more than two-thirds its original alcohol content. Later, clothing and fuel were rationed. There were chronic shortages of all household goods as the war effort drew in most of the available raw materials. On the whole, people accepted the rationing without too much complaint because it seemed to be fair.

Conscription was introduced immediately and applied to unmarried women as well as men, if they were required. The Women's Land Army was formed in 1940 and women took over jobs in the civil service, until almost half the civil service staff were women. The government also called for local volunteers, aged 40 to 65, to act as a Home Guard in the event of an invasion; by mid-1940 over a million men had joined. Though their potential value as a fighting force has been questioned, they fulfilled a useful function in guarding the British coast, so that the professional army was free to undergo intensive training.

German bombing was the worst trial. Starting in early September 1940, London was bombed for seventy-six consecutive nights and the attacks continued through into May 1941. Other cities also suffered – Coventry, Liverpool, Manchester, Plymouth, Hull, Glasgow, Belfast and many more took a battering. About 60,000 people were killed, around half of them in London, and perhaps 100,000 seriously injured. Hundreds of thousands of people were made homeless and had to be housed in emergency centres – cinemas, theatres, schools, or whatever was convenient. In London, thousands took refuge in the tube stations, since government preparations for civil defence were largely inadequate. This caused a great deal of resentment, particularly in London's East End, but on the whole morale stayed remarkably high, and American journalists were amazed at the calmness with which ordinary people tried to continue business as usual among the damage and disruption.

The war economy produced full employment for the first time since 1918, and the poorer working-class groups probably benefited from this. The government tried to keep prices under control to avoid inflation, and while it did not succeed completely, wages rose faster than prices. The increase in wages was partly a result of the rising number of strikes, particularly from 1942 onwards. With full employment, workers were in a strong position, and most employers settled by agreeing to higher wages. At the beginning of the war, average weekly earnings were around 53s, while at the end they were 96s. Bevin had the power to direct workers to where they were needed, and he did his job with such tact and sensitivity that, with very few exceptions, the workers were reasonably happy. It was an impressive achievement by the government to mobilize almost the entire population so effectively that all the demands of the war effort were met.

(b) long-term social effects of the war

These are more difficult to be sure about. Some historians believe that the war caused a social revolution, while others, such as Angus Calder, think this is an exaggeration and that, at most, it hastened British society 'in its progress along the old grooves'. Henry Pelling believes that society emerged from the war basically unchanged. The problem is that there were many different forces – political, economic and social – at work causing changes, and it is difficult to isolate which developments were caused solely by the war and which would probably have happened in any case. Arthur Marwick feels that, while caution is desirable, 'in the end it does not do full justice to the complex range of human reactions touched off by war'. He argues that the war caused, if not exactly a social revolution, certainly some vital changes in attitudes:

1 The enormous cost of the war caused the government to follow Keynes's policies of high spending and high taxation to meet the war effort: income tax went up from 25 pence in the pound in 1939 to 50 pence in 1945. This eliminated unemployment and demonstrated that such policies, admittedly in special circumstances, did in fact work. The question was bound to be faced: why could these policies not be continued after the war?

2 The war increased the sense of social solidarity and created, as John Stevenson puts it, 'a climate of common endeavour, which blunted some of the pre-war objections to increased social spending'. As early as 1940, the state took the unprecedented step of introducing free school milk, and later free school meals, orange juice, cod-liver oil, and nurseries.

3 Middle- and upper-class families were appalled by the deprivation of many of the evacuee children from the big cities who came to stay with them. Often poorly-clothed and under-nourished, these deprived children did a lot to arouse the nation to a realization that they deserved something better.

4 Even Calder admits that, in a total war, 'the nation's rulers, whether they liked it or not, depended on the willing co-operation of the ruled, including even scorned and under-privileged sections of society, manual workers and women'. It was widely felt that the poor, by their co-operation and all-out efforts, had earned concessions – better education, a higher standard of living and better welfare services. There was the added incentive that, if the workers were not given what they wanted, they might try to take it by revolution.

The new thinking showed itself in a number of ways:

- The Christian churches began to speak out on matters of social concern. In 1942 William Temple, a socialist, became Archbishop of Canterbury, and his widely read book *Christianity and the Social Order* set out the minimum social standards that people ought to be able to expect in a Christian society, and left no doubt that it should be the state's responsibility to enforce these standards.
- *Political and Economic Planning (PEP)* produced a plan in July 1942, proposing a new Ministry of Social Security and a National Health Service, as well as a national minimum wage and family allowances for everybody.
- *The Beveridge Report (1942).* The government appointed a committee under Sir William Beveridge, a Liberal, to investigate the problems of social insurance. His report claimed that *the five giant evils to be overcome were want, disease, ignorance, squalor and idleness,* and suggested that the government should fight them with insurance schemes, child allowances, more houses, a national health service, a policy of full employment, and secondary education for everybody. The Report received widespread publicity and was debated in Parliament in February 1943. The Labour Party wanted to carry out its proposals immediately, but Churchill was more interested in finishing the war successfully. This explains why so little was done immediately to implement Beveridge's proposals. Only one of its recommendations was introduced before the end of the war – payment of child allowances at the rate of 5s a week for each child after the first. It was left to the Labour governments of 1945–51 to introduce a welfare state (see Section 29.2). Arthur Marwick is convinced that the war *was* very much responsible for these further developments in state social policy. As he points out in an article in the *Modern History Review* (September 1990), the difference between the welfare state after the war and social policies before the war is the principle of 'universality': 'the new provisions after 1945 were designed to cover the whole nation, rich and poor, the idea being that if you have services which are only for the poor, which was basically the situation before 1939, they will be second rate services, a debate which faces us again at the present time'.
- *The Butler Education Act (1944).* The work of R. A. Butler, the Conservative President of the Board of Education in the coalition government, this Act made secondary education available to all, free of charge and without restriction, and raised the school-leaving age to 15 (to take effect in 1947). A new Ministry of Education was set up to 'direct and control' local authorities, which were now expected to provide secondary schools 'sufficient in number, character and equipment to afford all pupils such variety of instruction and training as may be desirable in view of their different ages, abilities and aptitudes'. Most local authorities took this to mean the system suggested in the 1926 Hadow Report –three different types of secondary school: grammar,

technical and modern. This was a disappointment for many educational experts, who believed this system did not offer equality of opportunity and argued in favour of comprehensive schools. However, the new system was a great improvement, and it enabled many working-class children to go on to university. Calder calls the Act 'the most important gesture towards democracy made in the twentieth century, a fitting product of the People's War'.

▸ Although no more government legislation came before the end of the war, Clement Attlee, who was Labour leader and Churchill's deputy Prime Minister, kept up pressure in the Cabinet so that the Beveridge Report would not be shelved permanently. A Minister for Reconstruction, Lord Woolton, was appointed, and 1944 saw the appearance of three government White Papers (statements of policy which a government hopes to carry out) on a National Health Service, Employment Policy, and Social Insurance.

(c) political effects

The main political effect was to cause the election of a Labour government with a huge majority in July 1945. In normal circumstances, a general election would have been due in 1940, and looking at the trends during the 1930s, it seems most unlikely that Labour would have won. Even if they had, they would have lacked the programme and the experience to act in the way they did after 1945. The war provided them with both (see Section 29.1 for the reasons for Labour's victory). The trade union movement seemed to be strengthened during the war, with membership rising from 6.05 million in 1938 to almost 7.9 million in 1945.

(d) a growing sense of complacency

Many historians have commented on the growing feeling of complacency apparent in Britain in the years after the war. Understandably, people felt that Britain had done well to survive the supreme test of war and come out on the winning side. They drew the conclusion that the system – both political and economic – must have worked so well that nothing needed changing – except social conditions for a people whose efforts during the war had earned them the right to a better life. Corelli Barnett argues that under the Labour governments of 1945–51, too much was spent on social reform and not enough on economic improvement, and that no serious attempt was made in Britain to modernize industry, roads and railways, which put Britain at a disadvantage in relation to its European competitors (see Section 29.4(c) for a further discussion of this point).

(e) the war was economically ruinous for Britain

In 1939, Britain's gold reserves stood at £864 million, but by March 1941 they had plunged to only £3 million. This came about because the war had interrupted Britain's overseas trade: there was so much concentration on producing armaments and other goods for the war effort that hardly anything was made for export. This meant that the income that would have been earned from those exports was lost, and Britain had to use its gold reserves to pay for imports of food and raw materials. At that point, the US Congress passed *the Lend–Lease Act*, which enabled the British to obtain crucial supplies from the USA on credit, to be paid for later. American help kept Britain going during the war, but the Americans had driven a hard bargain – by the autumn of 1945 Britain's overseas debts (not all to the USA) stood at well over £3,000 million.

On the defeat of Japan, Truman, the new American president, abruptly and without warning, ended Lend–Lease, leaving Britain with much of its foreign investments sold off and its capacity to export sadly reduced. It would take time to reconvert factories to peacetime production, so there would be no quick recovery of lost markets, and no guarantee that those markets would ever in fact be recovered. In August 1945, J. M. Keynes told Attlee that 'the country is virtually bankrupt and the economic basis for the hopes of the people non-existent'. The only solution seemed to be to request more help from the USA, and Keynes himself was sent to Washington with the aim of negotiating an interest-free loan of US$6,000 million. This the Americans refused: although a loan of US$3,750 million was agreed, at 2 per cent interest, and this was not finally paid off until 2006. In the words of Andrew Marr, the new financial arrangements 'placed the country firmly under the economic control of the United States, which through the later forties and early fifties would also be steadily advancing into former British markets round the world'.

(f) Britain's world position changed

Although Britain's Empire had survived intact, the defeats at the hands of the Japanese had destroyed Britain's image of superiority and invincibility. The victorious Japanese stirred up nationalist feelings, especially in India and the Far East. Within twenty years, most of Britain's Empire had become independent, though within the Commonwealth. The war revealed that the USA and the USSR were the world's most powerful states, while Britain, though on the winning side, according to most historians, was now a former great power in decline. As Corelli Barnett puts it, at the end of the war, the British people had 'the psychology of the victor although their material circumstances approximated more to those of a loser', and he goes on to chronicle the failures of a Britain in almost terminal decline until Margaret Thatcher rides on to the scene to rescue the nation in 1979.

On the other hand, there are some who take a different view. American historian George L. Bernstein points out that 'a discussion of Britain's decline as a world power must distinguish between absolute and relative decline ... It is interesting that the period of greatest prosperity in British history coincided with the end of empire. The loss of empire thus represented a decline only in how much the world map was coloured red'. It was in fact only the loss of territory that undermined the image of Britain as a world power. Even before 1939 the Empire had reached the stage where the cost of defending it outweighed any economic advantage it might bring. 'In shedding its empire therefore, Britain may well have lost an encumbrance rather than power' (for more on this, see Section 33.4(i)). Bernstein went so far as to call his book *The Myth of Decline – The Rise of Britain Since 1945* (2004). Nor did the British lose an Empire and fail to find a new role, as some have suggested. According to Andrew Marr, 'Britain refocused on its new role as a junior partner in the Cold War, close to Europe but never quite European, speaking the same language as Americans, but never meaning exactly the same.'

(g) there was no all-inclusive peace settlement

There was no big peace conference like the one held at Versailles at the end of the First World War. This was mainly because of the suspicion and distrust that had re-emerged between Russia and the west in the final months of the war, which made a comprehensive settlement impossible. The results of a number of separate treaties are summarized briefly below.

The Italians lost their African colonies. The Russians held on to Estonia, Latvia, Lithuania and eastern Poland, all of which they had occupied in 1939. They refused to agree to any settlement over Germany and Austria, except that they should be occupied by Allied troops, and that East Prussia should be divided between Russia and Poland. Later, in San Francisco (1951), Japan agreed to surrender all territory acquired during the previous ninety years, which included a complete withdrawal from China.

QUESTIONS

1 How successfully did the British government mobilize the population to meet the demands of total war?
2 How far would you agree that the effects of the Second World War on Britain amounted to a 'social revolution'?
3 What impact did the Second World War have on the British economy and on Britain's place in the world?
4 Assess the importance of Allied air power in the eventual defeat of the Axis powers.

A document question about Churchill as a war leader can be found on the accompanying website www.palgrave.com/masterseries/lowe1.

chapter **29**

Labour in power: the Attlee governments, 1945–51

summary of events

As soon as Germany was defeated (7 May 1945), the Labour Party was anxious to withdraw from the wartime coalition and fight a general election, since the existing Parliament was ten years old. Churchill would have liked to fight the election as leader of a national government, as Lloyd George had done in 1918, but Labour's attitude made this impossible. Voting day was 5 July, though the results were not declared until three weeks later, to allow the armed forces to vote.

Labour won a massive victory, with 393 seats to the Conservatives' 213; the Liberals could only muster 12, and there were 22 others. This was the first time Labour had enjoyed an overall majority, and it would now be able to achieve its most cherished objectives – a welfare state, nationalization, work for everybody, and an open foreign policy based on genuine co-operation – without too much opposition (except from the House of Lords). Unfortunately, the government was hampered by the most appalling economic problems in the aftermath of the war; the USA had immediately stopped Lend–Lease, two-thirds of Britain's export trade had disappeared, much of the merchant fleet had been lost in the war, and without American aid, the British lacked the capital to bring the economy back to normal peacetime production, so that they could begin to recover overseas markets. There were problems of international relations and the Cold War (see Section 33.1), and there was the dilemma of what to do about India (see Section 34.2) and Palestine (see Section 34.3).

The government was responsible for a remarkable, though controversial, set of achievements – social reforms, nationalization of key industries, financial measures, economic recovery, and independence for India. Inevitably, aspects of their policies aroused opposition, and in the general election of February 1950, Labour's position weakened as their overall majority fell to only five. The government struggled on until October 1951, when another election gave the Conservatives a slim overall majority of 17.

29.1 the Labour victory in 1945

(a) why did Labour win so decisively?

There was a high turnout in this first election for ten years, with over 72 per cent of the electorate voting. There was general amazement at the election result, which gave Labour an overall majority of 146. Most people expected that after Churchill's splendid leadership during the war, the Conservatives would win comfortably. However, Churchill himself had doubts: 'I am worried about this damned election,' he remarked in June; 'I have no message for them now.' The basic reason for their defeat was that, while Churchill was still popular, the Conservatives were not. Now that the war was almost over (Japan surrendered on 10 August), many people remembered the depression and miseries of the 1930s, and they held the Conservatives responsible, just as they blamed them for getting Britain into the war. As Harold Macmillan put it, 'it was not Churchill who lost the 1945 election; it was the ghost of Neville Chamberlain.' The Conservatives seemed to have shown little enthusiasm for the Beveridge Report, and despite the government preparing three White Papers (see Section 28.7(b)) about its proposed social policy, these received relatively little publicity. Labour, on the other hand, promised to implement the Beveridge Report, offering what people wanted to hear – jobs for everybody, plenty of new houses and a national health service.

Some Conservatives blamed their defeat on the classes arranged by the Army Education Corps and the Army Bureau of Current Affairs (ABCA), which were said to have a pronounced left-wing bias, influencing many of the troops to support Labour; however, Henry Pelling thought this had been greatly exaggerated. More damaging for the Conservatives was a radio broadcast in which Churchill asserted that a Labour government would bring with it 'the kind of features that were associated with the Gestapo'; many people thought this excessive, since he had been working closely and successfully for the previous five years with Attlee, Morrison and Bevin, who could hardly be described as revolutionaries. The Labour leaders had gained ministerial experience during the wartime coalition, and there could be no doubt about their moderation and competence.

(b) the new men in power

The new Prime Minister, Clement Attlee, came from a middle-class background; educated at public school and Oxford, he had intended to become a barrister, but, having a strong social conscience, he became interested in social work in the poverty-stricken East End of London. He was elected MP for Limehouse in 1922, and leader of the Labour party in 1935. In appearance he was mild and inoffensive; he was quietly-spoken and did not waste words, and this led many people to underestimate him. Churchill described him as 'a sheep

Illus. 29.1 The Labour big three: Bevin, Attlee and Morrison, after their victory in 1945

in sheep's clothing', and later as 'a modest little man with plenty to be modest about'. But this was far from the truth; Attlee was shrewd and determined, and, like Lord Liverpool, was an excellent manager of the Cabinet, which contained several strong-minded and potentially difficult people. According to historian Peter Hennessy, he was good at 'using silence as a weapon, cutting off wafflers, absolutely brutal with the inadequate and the incompetent, far more effective than any Prime Minister since'.

The Foreign Secretary was Ernest Bevin; the son of a Somerset farm labourer, he had started work at the age of 11 as a farm boy. Later he became a drayman and then leader of the Transport and General Workers' Union. After the 1926 General Strike he had turned against industrial action, and was an outstanding success as Churchill's wartime Minister of Labour. Other leading members of the government were Hugh Dalton as Chancellor of the Exchequer (replaced by Sir Stafford Cripps in 1947); Herbert Morrison, leader of the House of Commons; and Aneurin Bevan, Minister of Health. All of them, apart from Bevan, had served in Churchill's coalition, and formed a capable and experienced team.

29.2 Labour and the Welfare State

(a) significance of the Beveridge Report

The phrase 'welfare state' means one in which the government tries to provide the best possible social services for everybody. The Labour governments of

1945–51 are usually given most of the credit for setting up such a system in Britain. *The Beveridge Report of November 1942* (see Section 28.7(b)) had provided plenty of ideas about what a welfare state should aim for – the elimination of want, disease, ignorance, squalor and idleness – though it is now recognized as being far from the revolutionary document that many took it to be at the time. Many of its proposals were just a rationalization and an extension of existing schemes, they were not exactly generous, and they discriminated against working women (see Robert Pearce's article 'Beveridge 1942: Reconstruction or Reform?', *Modern History Review,* September 1993).

In fact the Labour party had its own plans for social reform before the Beveridge Report appeared. The 1942 party conference committed a future Labour government to a comprehensive social security scheme, family allowances and a National Health Service (NHS). In spite of the country's economic difficulties, Attlee was determined to press ahead with this programme; a mass of new legislation reached the statute book, and by July 1948, Britain had a welfare state. It was not perfect, but an attack had been made on all five of Beveridge's 'giants': three of them – want, disease and idleness – had been well and truly tamed, though with the other two – squalor and ignorance – there was still some way to go. Some historians have called this a 'peaceful revolution', though others argue that the changes were merely evolutionary – they occurred naturally as the result of a long process of development. As Derek Fraser puts it: 'the British Welfare State was not born – it had evolved.'

(b) the National Health Service

This was the most spectacular of Labour's social reforms. It was the work of the Minister of Health, Aneurin Bevan, a former Welsh miner. Many people thought the task would be beyond him, but Bevan was an outstanding personality: he had educated himself and had read widely, he was a fluent speaker and a formidable debater – one of the few who could stand up to Churchill successfully. Within a very short time he had mastered the intricacies of the health and hospital situation, and he had the vision to see exactly what he wanted, and the courage to make sure that he got it, in the face of some strong opposition from the medical profession. Starting on 5 July 1948, the system entitled everybody to free medical care in a range of services from general practitioners, specialists and dentists, to hospital and ophthalmic treatment – from spectacles, false teeth, medicines and drugs, to midwifery, maternity and child welfare services. The scheme was financed mainly from taxation, but some of the revenue came from National Insurance contributions. To make sure that the same standard of health care was provided in all parts of the country, Bevan decided that the hospitals should be nationalized. For health purposes, England and Wales were divided into fourteen areas, each under a regional hospital board; Scotland had five regional boards. Appointed by the Minister himself, these boards controlled general policy, while the day-to-day running of the hospitals was looked after by local management committees, of which there were 388 in England and Wales and 84 in Scotland.

There was considerable opposition to the scheme from family doctors, who disliked the proposal that they should be paid a salary by the government. This, they argued, would deprive them of their professional independence and reduce them to the status of civil servants, which, they seemed to think, was beneath their dignity. It would also in some mysterious way, interfere with the doctor–patient relationship. In February 1948, 90 per cent of the members of the British Medical Association threatened to boycott the whole scheme. Bevan finally overcame their hostility by a clever device: instead of being paid a salary, doctors would receive fees based on the number of patients they had on their lists. This made all the difference, and when the scheme was introduced on 5 July 1948, 90 per cent of GPs took part.

The service turned out to be more expensive that had been expected, costing more than £400 million in the first year. Prescriptions, which had been running at just under seven million a month under the old system, more or less doubled in September 1948 and had reached 19 million a month by 1951. No fewer than five million pairs of spectacles were given out by opticians in the first year, and the demand for false teeth was double what was expected. This led the government to begin charging adults half the cost of false teeth and spectacles (1951). Bevan resigned from the government, furious that his principle of a free health service had been violated. It was a sad end to his ministerial career, but he will always be remembered as the architect of the NHS.

The system worked remarkably smoothly and soon brought a striking improvement in the health of the working class, while deaths from tuberculosis, pneumonia and diphtheria were greatly reduced. Andrew Marr writes about the queues of poor people arriving at hospitals and doctors' waiting rooms for the first time 'not as beggars but as citizens with a sense of right. If there was one single domestic good that the British took from the sacrifices of the war, it was a health service free at the point of use.' In the words of Alan Sked and Chris Cook, it 'constituted an almost revolutionary social innovation since it improved the quality of life of most of the British people ... it was soon to become the social institution of which the British would feel most proud.'

(c) the National Insurance Act (1946)

This extended the original 1911 Act to cover all adults. The scheme was compulsory; in return for a weekly contribution from worker, employer and government, the individual was entitled to sickness and unemployment benefit, old age pensions for women at 60 and men at 65 (26s a week for an individual, and 42s for a married couple), widows' and orphans' pensions, maternity allowances, and death grants to help with funeral expenses. These were all more generous than Beveridge had anticipated, though some Labour left-wingers thought they should have been even higher.

(d) the National Assistance Act (1948)

This was designed to fill in any loopholes not covered by the National Insurance Act, which was intended to apply to the entire population. However, people joining the insurance scheme for the first time were not entitled to full pension benefits for ten years, and there were tens of thousands of old people whose only income was the non-contributory pension (now 10s a week, but still inadequate) introduced in 1908. Other people not covered were women whose husbands were in jail, unmarried mothers, and the blind, the deaf and the crippled. The Act set up *National Assistance Boards* to which they could apply for further assistance. This was a real innovation, a decisive break with the past, since despite applicants having to undergo a 'means test', the money for the extra relief was provided by the government from taxation, and it was a move away from the idea that poverty was a matter for local administration. As well as cash benefits, the Act also provided services for people in need; and here the government did make use of local authorities, placing on them the duty of providing homes and other welfare services for the elderly and handicapped. Together with the National Insurance Act, this measure provided a whole new social security structure. It was generally welcomed, and unusually the Conservatives in opposition chose not to vote against either bill. They had moved a long way since 1900.

(e) the National Insurance Industrial Injuries Act (1946)

This was a vast improvement on the old Workmen's Compensation Acts, under which it had been difficult and expensive for a worker to prove that an injury or disability had been caused by his/her job, and since the employer had to foot the bill, it had been even more difficult to win adequate compensation. The new Act made it compulsory for both workers and employers to join the state in making weekly contributions to a fund which would provide compensation to injured workers and pensions for those who were disabled.

(f) education

The government concentrated on implementing *the Butler Education Act of 1944* (see Section 28.7(b)), making secondary education until the age of 15 free, and providing meals, milk and medical services in schools. An examination (the 11-plus) was introduced to select which children were thought to be suitable for a grammar school education (or for a secondary technical school in the few areas where these existed), and which would go to secondary modern schools. In one sense, the new system was an outstanding success: it allowed a whole new generation of talented working-class children to move up the educational ladder, many of them as far as university, which would have been unthinkable before 1939. A successful Youth Employment Service was set up, and the government embarked on an expansion of university and technical education. Many Labour supporters and educational experts felt that by merely accepting the Butler Act, the government showed a disappointing lack of imagination.

Two main criticisms soon emerged:

1 The education provided varied in type and quality from area to area. Some counties, such as Lancashire, which could afford to provide technical schools as well as grammar schools, could boast that up to 40 per cent of their secondary places were in grammar and technical schools; but in other counties, such as Surrey, the figure was as low as 15 per cent. The 11-plus examination therefore did not indicate which children were suitable for which type of school: it simply selected the required number of children to fill the places available. In Surrey, children who would have been 'suitable' for a grammar school education had they lived in Lancashire, had to go to a secondary modern school because there were not enough grammar school places.

2 The system was divisive: the view rapidly developed that secondary modern schools were second-class institutions to which the 11-plus failures went; a new type of class distinction was therefore created. Many experts argued that if primary education could work successfully without different types of school, then it ought to be possible for secondary education to be conducted successfully in 'comprehensive' schools, to which all children went at the age of 11, without selection. It was felt that Labour had missed a splendid opportunity to introduce a comprehensive system, free from class distinction, before the Butler system became established.

Another disappointment was that the Labour government, faced with heavy defence spending at the time of the Korean War (which began in June 1950), reduced the spending programme on education, so that fewer new schools, nurseries and colleges were built than had been intended.

(g) housing was a major problem

On top of the housing shortage already existing in 1939, a further 700,000 houses had been destroyed in the war. In March 1945, Churchill's government announced that 750,000 new houses would be needed as soon as the war was over. Housing came under the control of Bevan's Ministry of Health, and despite being preoccupied with the NHS, he still found time and energy to launch a housing drive. Economic conditions were not helpful – raw materials were in short supply and expensive. Nevertheless, Bevan had considerable success. Only 55,400 new houses were completed in 1946, but this rose to almost 140,000 in 1947, and to over 284,000 in 1948 (this figure included prefabricated houses ('prefabs'), which Bevan himself privately described as 'rabbit-hutches'). There was a slight decline after that, but in 1949–51 Labour still averaged well over 200,000 houses a year, most of which were council houses.

Bevan had provided far more houses than Churchill had asked for; and what is more, he had insisted that the new council houses were built to higher standards than ever before, including three bedrooms and an indoor bathroom and lavatory. Unfortunately, Churchill's figure of 750,000 turned out to be an underestimate; what nobody had foreseen was the increase in marriages and the rapid increase in the birth rate after the war, so, in spite of Bevan's undoubted achievement, given the difficult economic situation, there was still a serious housing shortage when Labour left office in 1951. One estimate put it as high as 750,000 houses fewer than households. Finally, Bevan protected tenants who lived in houses owned by private landlords, by introducing rent controls.

(h) legislation to improve the environment

1 *The New Towns Act (1946)* – this gave the government power to decide where new towns should be built, and to set up development corporations to carry out the projects. The aim was to create towns which were healthy and pleasant to live in, as well as being geared to the needs of the townspeople, unlike the ugly monstrosities that had grown up without any planning during the nineteenth century. The first to be completed was Stevenage, followed by Crawley, Hemel Hempstead and Harlow. In total, fourteen New Towns were operational before the end of the Labour governments, and these were not just in the south; successful examples elsewhere were East Kilbride, Peterlee and Glenrothes.

2 *The Town and Country Planning Act (1947)* was another Bevan measure designed to make life more pleasant. It gave the job of planning to the county authorities, which were all required to produce land development plans for the next twenty years. The planning authorities were given much wider powers of compulsory purchase, and the right to control advertisements and historic buildings. Government grants were available when necessary. If there was any increase in land values as a result of profitable development, the government had the power to levy a development charge on the increase.

(i) the Trade Disputes Act (1946)

This repealed Baldwin's 1927 Act with the same title (see Section 24.4(c)). The political levy was now legal again, and it was up to individuals to 'contract out' if they did not wish to make a financial contribution to the Labour party.

29.3 why and how did Labour attempt to introduce a planned economy?

(a) the ideas and motives behind a planned economy

The idea of a planned economy had been discussed between the wars (see Section 20.5). The Labour government was the first to make a serious attempt to carry out some of the suggestions put forward. Their motives were mixed: the immediate need was to restore trade and prosperity, which had been affected badly by the war – it was calculated that about two-thirds of Britain's export trade had disappeared. Declining industries had to be revived so that exports could increase and the massive balance of payments deficit could be eliminated. Over £3,000 million was owed, much of it to the USA for goods supplied on credit during the war.

Labour felt that the best way of restructuring and modernizing industry was to nationalize it; that is, to take the most important industries away from their private owners so that they became the property of the state. In this way, the government would be able to control 'the means of production, distribution and exchange'. It would permit more efficient planning and more co-operation between industries, and would ensure fair treatment and better conditions for the workers. The coal-mining industry was a prime example of inefficiency and poor labour relations, which, Labour felt, could be improved only by government control. Above all, it was hoped that better planning would eliminate unemployment, the problem that had plagued all the governments between the wars.

(b) nationalization

This was the most striking of Labour's attempts at planning. Nationalization was a matter of principle for socialists; they believed that it was only right for the country's most important industries to be owned by the state, so that profits would go into the Treasury rather than into the pockets of private owners; and this would provide much of the extra cash needed to pay for the new welfare state. The programme was carried through under the general direction of Herbert Morrison.

First came the nationalization of the Bank of England (1946), which meant that money would now be available whenever the government needed it for investment. Later the same year, air transport was nationalized and reorganized into three companies: the British Overseas Airways Corporation (BOAC), British European Airways (BEA) and British South American Airways (BSAA). In 1947, it was the turn of coal-mining, and cable and wireless. In spite of Conservative opposition, some 1,500 collieries and about 400 smaller mines were handed over to state ownership, to be controlled by *the National Coal Board*. There was great rejoicing among the miners, who felt that at last they were about to get a fair deal. The main Conservative criticism was that the industry, with close on three-quarters of a million workers, was too large to be controlled centrally. The nationalization of cable and wireless meant that the government now controlled all international radio and telegraph services.

Public transport (1948) was to be controlled by *the British Transport Commission*, which was divided into five executive boards: Docks and Inland Waterways; Railways; London Transport; Road Haulage; and Road Passenger

Transport. The government hoped to create an efficient transport network in which all the different branches were co-ordinated to provide a well-planned system which would serve the whole population, including those living in remote areas. The generation and supply of electricity were also nationalized in 1948. The Central Electricity Board, with its national grid of pylons and power lines, had been owned by the government since 1926. Now the state took over the separate generating companies – about 500 of them – and set up fourteen area electricity boards that were able to standardize voltages and prices, and provide a more efficient service over the whole country. Similar reasoning lay behind the nationalization of the gas industry in 1949. The government was able to organize the hundreds of small companies into an efficient national system.

Iron and steel was the most controversial of Labour's targets for nationalization, and showed that the consensus of opinion between Labour and Conservatives on the issue of nationalization had its limits. The iron and steel industry was reasonably prosperous and efficient; Labour was determined that it should be nationalized (though Morrison himself had doubts), since it was clearly one of the 'commanding heights' of the economy. However, the Conservatives believed that nationalization was only justified if an industry was in need of help because it was inefficient or old-fashioned. Profitable industries should be left in the hands of private people who knew how best to run them. They opposed Labour's plans bitterly in Parliament, and the House of Lords refused to pass the Bill. To overcome this opposition, the government passed *the Parliament Act (1949)*, which reduced the powers of the House of Lords: instead of being able to delay bills for three sessions of Parliament (two years), the delay could now only be for two sessions (one year in actual time). At the same time, plural voting was abolished and the universities lost their representation in Parliament. With all the delays, it was only after the 1950 election that the nationalization of iron and steel came into effect; if Labour had lost the election, the bill would have been scrapped. The Conservatives swore that they would de-nationalize iron and steel as soon as possible, and they did so in 1953.

(c) American aid and the Marshall Plan

In August 1945, an immediate injection of cash was needed to get the economy moving again after the war. Since the Americans had stopped Lend–Lease, J. M. Keynes, the famous economist, was sent to Washington to negotiate an interest-free loan of US$6,000 million. The Americans were unsympathetic and drove a hard bargain – as noted earlier, they were prepared to lend only US$3,750 million at 2 per cent interest, with repayments to start in 1951; in 1947, Britain would be required to make the pound sterling freely convertible (exchangeable) for dollars. The loan was made available in July 1946, but within a year it had almost been used up. Industry was recovering and exports had reached 17 per cent above the 1939 level, but this was not enough – the balance of payments deficit stood at £438 million.

However, help was on the way: the American Secretary of State, George Marshall, worried about the poor prospects for American exports and about the possible spread of communism in a poverty-stricken Europe, launched his *European Recovery Programme*, offering grants to any country in Europe that cared to accept them. In 1948, Britain gratefully took the lead (see Section 33.1(d)), accepting what amounted to a gift of £1,263 million (known as Marshall Aid). This enabled the recovery to be completed, and by 1950, British exports stood at 75 per cent above the 1938 level.

(d) close control of all aspects of the economy

This was another feature of Labour's attempts at planning; a new *Economic Planning Council* was set up (July 1947) under Sir Edwin Plowden, together with a whole host of planning committees, such as the Import Programme Committee and the Production Committee. Control was especially marked in 1947–50 after Sir Stafford Cripps had replaced Dalton as Chancellor of the Exchequer. Descended from an aristocratic family, educated at public school, and with a successful career as a barrister behind him, Cripps was 40 when he was converted to socialism. He was a devout Anglican, moral and upright (many thought him sanctimonious), a teetotaller and a vegetarian. However, his recent biographer, Peter Clarke, reveals that he was no puritan – he smoked and gambled, he had a great sense of humour and his officials found him fun to work with. He also had a highly developed sense of duty and service to his fellow humans and believed that *austerity* was the way to conquer Britain's economic problems. Only increased production and exports would provide the necessary resources to make Britain a fairer country. He left people in no doubt about his priorities: 'First are exports, second is capital investment in industry, and last are the needs, comforts and amenities of the family.' The public must 'submerge all thought of personal gain and personal ambition'. No wonder an observer listening to a Cripps speech once remarked: 'you can just see the home-made lemonade boiling in his veins'. *Control measures included*:

▸ Since there was still a world shortage of food, 'fair shares' wartime rationing was continued. Bread rationing was in operation from 1946 to 1948, and potato rationing was introduced in December 1947; in almost all cases, the allowances were lower than the wartime average. As the situation improved, certain commodities were de-rationed, but even in 1951, meat, bacon, butter, tea and sugar were still rationed. However, the government provided subsidies to keep food prices down, and gave help to farmers (price guarantees, subsidies for modernization, and the National Agricultural Advisory Service to provide the expertise). This helped to bring about a 20 per cent increase in agricultural output between 1947 and 1952, and made Britain's farming industry one of the most mechanized and efficient in the world.

- During the disastrously cold winter of 1946–7, demand for coal and electricity was so enormous that all fuels were severely rationed. For several weeks it was illegal to use electricity in the home between 9am and midday, and between 2pm and 4pm. Many factories had to close through lack of coal, throwing two million people temporarily out of work (March 1947).
- Building materials were rationed and licences had to be obtained for all new buildings; this was to make sure that resources went into building factories, schools and council houses instead of into less essential projects such as dance-halls and cinemas.
- Rents, profits and interest rates were controlled and a tight rein kept on foreign currency, so that holidays abroad were out of the question for most people.
- Imports were controlled in the struggle to achieve a favourable balance of payments. The government bought supplies of raw materials for industry and allocated them to those industries which would contribute towards the export drive: cars, motor-cycles, tractors, ships, engineering products, aircraft and chemicals. Cripps' exhortations to businessmen to export at all costs certainly worked, but it left a chronic shortage of consumer goods for the home market.
- Cripps persuaded the trade unions to accept a policy of wage restraint between 1948 and 1950; at a time of rising prices, this was a considerable achievement.
- In August 1949, in response to a recession in the USA and a drain of Britain's gold reserves, Cripps devalued the pound so that it was worth $2.80 instead of $4.03. Many thought that he had over-reacted, but other experts think the pound had been over-valued after the war and that devaluation was a sensible policy, facing up to reality. Although at the time it was seen as a setback for the government, the immediate effects were good: the devaluation made imports more expensive and British exports cheaper, so that for a time exports were boosted.

29.4 how successful were the policies of the Labour governments?

Labour was responsible for a huge body of reform, but inevitably with such controversial policies, historians are divided about their success and their long-term effects. Broadly speaking, there are three different interpretations:

- The sympathetic view – Labour was largely successful in carrying out its policies and achieving its main aims, and deserves to be remembered above all as the creator of the welfare state and the party that led Britain to recovery after the Second World War.
- The unsympathetic left-wing view – Labour missed an opportunity to introduce real change and real socialism; their policies were half-hearted and nowhere near radical enough.

- The unsympathetic right-wing view – Labour was so obsessed with its welfare state that it neglected industry and the economy, with disastrous long-term results.

(a) the sympathetic view

Historians Kenneth Morgan and Paul Addison are leading exponents of this view. They believe that Labour, boosted by a great vote of confidence in the 1945 election, carried out its mandate for radical change; its social policies were innovative and highly successful, setting the pattern for the next quarter of a century until the appearance of Thatcherism. Labour's attempts at planning the economy surpassed anything previously seen in Britain, and brought considerable success. By 1950, Britain was well on the way to recovery: inflation seemed to be under control, there was full employment, exports were increasing, and there was a healthy balance of payments. Especially impressive was the export of British cars to North America. The 1951 Festival of Britain could be seen as a triumphant symbol of Britain's recovery and revitalization. According to Kenneth Morgan, 1948–50 'was amongst the most thriving periods economically that the country as a whole had experienced since the late Victorian era'. Most Labour supporters were full of praise for the 'mixed economy', that is, partly nationalized and partly privately owned; they hoped that this new 'middle way' (between full capitalism, in which everything was privately owned, and communism, in which everything was owned by the state) would be an example for the rest of the world to follow. Economist Alec Cairncross believes that, given the awesome problems facing the government in 1945, it achievements could hardly have been greater. There were notable achievements in foreign policy too, with Bevin playing an important role in the Marshall Plan and the formation of NATO (see Section 33.1(d) and (f)), and Attlee handling Indian independence well in difficult circumstances (see Section 34.2).

However, in the final year of its life, the Labour government suffered an economic setback when Britain became involved in the war in Korea (see Section 33.1(g)). The USA, leading the attack on the communists, chose massive rearmament, forcing up prices of raw materials on the world market, and causing a sharp increase in the price of goods imported into Britain. When Britain also decided to increase its rearmament programme, it led to a period of inflation, shortages and further economies; to save money, Hugh Gaitskell (who had replaced the exhausted and ailing Cripps as Chancellor) introduced charges for spectacles and dental treatment, causing a split in the party. Peter Hennessy sums up the sympathetic view well: in spite of the economic setback of 1951, 'the achievements of the Attlee administration between 1945 and 1951 probably make it the most hyper-achieving peacetime government this century in economic and, especially, social terms. Virtually all the promises in its manifesto were implemented by 1951'.

(b) the unsympathetic left-wing view

Historians such as John Saville believe that Labour was a great disappointment to real socialists; while the social reforms were quite impressive, the government failed to introduce a genuine socialist system and ended up merely strengthening capitalism:

‣ The people running Labour's economic policy – Morrison, Dalton, Cripps and Shinwell – were not expert planners and were reluctant to listen to advice. Even a sympathetic historian such as Morgan admits that 'Britain's economic planning under Labour was distinctly weak at the centre ... advisers found themselves often frustrated by a government of the left that steadfastly refused to plan.' Their whole approach was piecemeal and indirect, and they tended to deal with specific problems and situations as they arose rather than working out an overall plan to be followed. In spite of all the various planning committees, the government did not succeed in drawing up real targets for investment, production and consumption.

‣ Nationalization was not carried out in the way many socialists had hoped. Morrison set the newly nationalized industries up as public corporations, like the Central Electricity Board and the BBC, which had been introduced by the Conservatives in the 1920s. Each industry was controlled by a small board of experts responsible to a government minister, but there were no workers on the boards, they had no share in decision-making and no share of the profits. This tended to make the structure too bureaucratic and inflexible, and the workers felt excluded, which meant that the mass support for nationalization, which in theory there should have been among the working classes, did not exist. It was felt that the previous owners had been compensated excessively: the mine-owners received £164 million and the iron and steel owners £240 million; it was clear that many years' profits would be needed to pay off such large sums. What the government had in fact done was to buy out the former owners while keeping the same, often inefficient, management.

‣ Only about 20 per cent of the nation's industries were nationalized, and apart from iron and steel, they were either unprofitable, or in need of investment for development and modernization, or both. Profitable industries remained firmly in the hands of private enterprise. Yet the government felt unable to provide sufficient investment to do the job properly, and consequently the nationalized industries, particularly coal and transport, continued to provide an inefficient service and ran up large deficits. The hope that profits would help to meet the cost of the welfare state proved false. This whole approach convinced the public that nationalization automatically implied inefficiency and waste, and Labour failed to point out that the problems were of long standing, and that the payment of compensation to the previous owners was using up most of the profits. There was a strong case for nationalizing other profitable industries – for example, those producing consumer goods – to show that state ownership need not be limited to 'commanding heights' industries and failing industries.

However, the Labour leaders were cautious men who had gone as far as they dared. They had no plans to take over any more industries after iron and steel. Instead of being the beginning of a new era of collectivist planning of which socialists had been dreaming, the Attlee government turned out to be the climax of fifty years of economic and social reform. What remained now was not further development, but, as Morrison himself put it, 'consolidation'.

▸ Labour made the mistake of assuming that Britain must continue to act as if it were a great power, when in fact the country's economy was incapable of sustaining such action. Holders of this view believe that the government should not have taken the decision to become an atomic power in 1947, and should have kept out of the Korean War.

(c) the unsympathetic right-wing view

This view was first put clearly by Corelli Barnett in his book *The Audit of War* (1986) and later in *The Lost Victory* (1995). Barnett would certainly agree with Peter Hennessy that, by 1951, Labour had fulfilled virtually all the promises in its manifesto, but he believes that this had disastrous effects. The government was led astray into the 'utopian' schemes of Beveridge, which the economy was incapable of supporting. Labour's obsession with the welfare state used up resources that should have been put into modernizing industry, and then left the country saddled with a long-term burden which hampered the economy and reduced Britain's competitiveness for the next half-century. True, the country needed social reform, but this should have waited until industry had been brought into the highest possible state of efficiency, thus maximizing profits, which would have helped towards the cost of the welfare state. Holders of this view believe that the Beveridge Report and Attlee's government between them must bear a heavy responsibility for Britain's post-war decline.

(d) conclusion?

Some more recent writers, including Martin Pugh, Robert Pearce, Nick Tiratsoo and Jim Tomlinson, have swung the argument firmly back in favour of the sympathetic view. They feel that Corelli Barnett overstated his case; there were clearly far more forces at work causing Britain's economic decline for it to be pinned on the Labour government and excessive public spending. Robert Pearce points out that while welfare spending did increase rapidly after 1945, 'this was also the case among Britain's economic rivals and so cannot constitute a distinguishing feature explaining poor economic performance'. Martin Pugh mounts a strong defence of Labour's record, arguing that while huge sums of money *were* spent, especially on the NHS, expenditure did not get out of control. The three Labour Chancellors – Dalton, Cripps and Gaitskell – were all extremely careful to keep expenditure within bounds. Pugh makes the important point that the amount of ill-health that had gone untreated before 1945 was also very damaging to the economy; 'any genuine audit of welfare policy would have to include some assessment of the economic gain from a fit and healthy labour force'. David Kynaston believes that if they had achieved nothing else, Labour deserves praise for their immense success in creating the first full employment economy in modern British history.

Nick Tiratsoo and Jim Tomlinson, in their joint study of Labour's economic policy, argue that Labour did not ignore industrial development; on the contrary, important steps were taken:

‣ the government made sure that the building of new factories was given priority over hospitals, schools and houses;
‣ working parties of experts, employers, workers and trade unionists were set up to investigate certain key industries and recommend improvements;
‣ the *British Institute of Management* was set up in 1948 to improve standards in management;
‣ industrialists and workers went to the USA with government backing, to find out what the latest techniques were; and
‣ there was an official government campaign to encourage joint production committees in factories, where employers and workers could come together to sort out differences and improve performance.

If the achievement was less than might have been hoped, this was partly because of a lack of co-operation from employers. In the words of George L. Bernstein, British industry was 'resistant to any change that would make the manufacturing sector more efficient ... it was suspicious of Labour's intentions and was determined to return to an economy free of wartime government interference. Hence, even the most modest admonitions were resented'. Moreover, the idea of consulting trade unions was thought to be a sign of weakness, which would also lead to a loss of control by management.

29.5 why did Labour lose the 1951 election?

The question has to be faced: if Labour was as successful as these historians suggest, why did the party lose the general election in 1951? Several factors seem to have been at work.

1 The country was tired of rationing and the housing shortage, and there was a feeling that austerity had gone on too long. There was a new round of restrictions and shortages as a result of the government's decision to increase its armaments programme when Britain became involved in the Korean War (1950–3); and above all, the cost of living was rising. The period of compulsory

military service (introduced in 1947) was increased from 18 months to two years in 1950, and this was an unpopular move.

2 The government had just had to deal with a crisis in Iran (Persia) when the Iranian government suddenly nationalized the oil refinery at Abadan owned by the Anglo-Iranian Oil Company, in which the British government held most of the shares. The Conservatives urged the government to send troops to recapture the refinery, which was the largest single supplier of oil to Britain. The Labour Cabinet took no action, and thus laid itself open to the charge of weakness. The opposition was able to cash in with the cry that in situations such as the Korean War and the crisis in Iran, Churchill was the man to lead the country. (A compromise was reached in 1954, allowing British Petroleum 40 per cent of the shares.)

3 The Conservatives produced an attractive programme promising to build 300,000 houses a year, to give people 'more red meat', a tempting proposal at a time when meat was still strictly rationed, and to 'set people free' from socialist rules and restrictions. Results suggest that on the whole, working-class voters, especially in the north and west, continued to support Labour; but middle-class voters, especially in the south-east (where Labour lost twenty seats), continued the drift away from Labour that had begun in the 1950 election. Many middle-class voters resented the continuing high taxes to pay for a welfare state from which they benefited disproportionately. They also resented the fact that their incomes were falling while working-class incomes were rising.

4 Labour campaigned on its achievements in office, which were certainly impressive. However, with the resignation of Bevan and Harold Wilson (President of the Board of Trade) over the introduction of National Health charges, the party seemed to be split, and the government had a general air of exhaustion after its six frantically busy years in office.

5 It is thought that Liberal supporters in constituencies where there was no Liberal candidate (only 109 Liberals stood for election) tended to vote Conservative. Even so, the Labour defeat was very narrow: Labour actually polled more votes than they had ever done before (13.95 million, compared with 13.26 million in 1950), and *more votes than the Conservatives* (13.7 million, up from 12.5 million in 1950), yet they won only 295 seats to the Conservatives' 311. The main reason for this strange state of affairs was that many Labour MPs in safe seats were elected with huge majorities, whereas, on the whole, Conservative majorities tended to be smaller. The Liberals, who won only 6 seats, saw their vote slip from 2.6 million in 1950 to only 0.7 million.

QUESTIONS

1 How successful were the Labour governments of 1945–51 in establishing a welfare state?

2 How effectively did Attlee's governments deal with the economic problems facing them between 1945 and 1951?

3 'Nationalization of key industries was a more important achievement of the Labour governments of 1945–51 than the establishment of a welfare state.' Assess the validity of this statement. [AQA]

4 'The achievements of the Attlee governments of 1945–51 make it probably the most hyper-achieving government this century.' In the light of this statement, explain why Labour lost the general election of 1951.

A document question on Labour and nationalization can be found on the accompanying website www.palgrave.com/masterseries/lowe1.

the rise and fall of consensus, 1951–79

The Conservatives were in power for thirteen years following their narrow election victory in October 1951; however, they won the next two elections – in 1955 and 1959 – much more convincingly, with majorities of 58 and 100. This period saw four Tory Prime Ministers: Churchill (1951–5), Sir Anthony Eden (1955–7), Harold Macmillan (1957–63) and Sir Alec Douglas-Home, the 14th Earl of Home (1963–4). On the whole it seemed to be a period of prosperity when, as Macmillan put it, people had 'never had it so good'. Eventually, after losing three consecutive elections, Labour succeeded in winning a tiny overall majority of 4 in October 1964. This was soon increased to 96 in the election of 1966, and Labour remained in power, with Harold Wilson as Prime Minister, until 1970.

By this time the economy was far from healthy, and in the election of June 1970 there was a swing from Labour big enough to give the Conservatives an overall majority of 30. Edward Heath was Prime Minister until February 1974, when a confrontation between the government and the miners led to a narrow Conservative defeat and the return of Wilson as Prime Minister, though without an overall majority. In October 1974, Wilson went to the country again, and despite Labour strengthening its position, the results fell well below Wilson's hopes. With 319 seats, Labour had a comfortable lead over the Conservatives (277) and Liberals (13), but there were 26 assorted Nationalist and Northern Ireland MPs, leaving a Labour overall majority of only 3. In spite of this, Labour remained in office until May 1979, though Wilson himself resigned in April 1976; James Callaghan was Prime Minister for the remainder of the Labour government. The election of May 1979 brought a decisive result: the Conservatives won a comfortable overall majority of 43, and Margaret Thatcher became Britain's first woman Prime Minister.

summary of the different governments, October 1951–May 1979

Date	Government	Prime Minister
Oct 1951–May 1955	Conservative	Sir Winston Churchill (Oct 1951–Apr 1955) Sir Anthony Eden (from Apr 1955)
May 1955–Oct 1959	Conservative	Sir Anthony Eden (until Jan 1957) Harold Macmillan (from Jan 1957)
Oct 1959–Oct 1964	Conservative	Harold Macmillan (until Oct 1963) Sir Alec Douglas-Home (Oct 1963–Oct 1964)
Oct 1964–Mar 1966	Labour	Harold Wilson
Mar 1966–Jun 1970	Labour	Harold Wilson
Jun 1970–Mar 1974	Conservative	Edward Heath
Mar–Oct 1974	Labour	Harold Wilson
Oct 1974–May 1979	Labour	Harold Wilson (until Apr 1976) James Callaghan (Apr 1976–May 1979)

30.1 what is meant by consensus politics?

The period from 1951 until the early 1970s is usually described as *the era of consensus politics.* This means that there seemed to be very little fundamental difference between the policies of the two main parties, though of course there were differences of detail and emphasis. Strictly speaking, consensus began during the Second World War, when the Conservatives and Labour worked so well together during the wartime coalition. This continued during Attlee's governments, when the only really bitter clash was over iron and steel nationalization, leading to a further reduction in the power of the House of Lords.

When the Conservatives came to power in 1951, there was no dramatic change in policy. In spite of all the party propaganda, the generally Keynesian approach continued: the welfare state was safeguarded and even extended, and the government accepted Labour's policy of full employment, and the mixed economy; only steel and road haulage (which Labour had been less than enthusiastic about in any case) were denationalized. The term *'Butskellism'* was coined by *The Economist* from the surnames of R. A. Butler (Churchill's Chancellor of the Exchequer) and Hugh Gaitskell (Labour leader from 1955 until his death in 1963), to show how close Conservative and Labour policies were. This consensus lasted through the thirteen years of Conservative government (1951–64), and during Harold Wilson's Labour governments (1964–70).

This does not mean that there was *total* agreement about every policy; there were people in both parties who felt impatient with the consensus approach. Some Conservative right-wingers, for example, were appalled at Macmillan's decolonization policies (see Sections 34.5 and 34.6) and felt that too much was being spent on welfare provision. Some Labour left-wingers were bitter critics of the official Labour line on defence, which was to go along with the Conservative policy of rearmament and build up nuclear weapons. However, the Conservative leadership kept the right-wingers out of key positions in the government and the consensus was able to continue, but with the failure of Edward Heath's government (1970–4) and the election of the right-winger Margaret Thatcher as Conservative leader (1975), the period of consensus came to an end.

30.2 the Conservative governments, 1951–64

(a) Churchill and Eden

At the age of 77, when he became Prime Minister for the second time, Churchill was no longer the dynamic leader of the early 1940s; and he left much of the heavy work to his acknowledged successor, Anthony Eden. When Churchill retired in April 1955, Eden became Prime Minister and immediately held a general election, in which the Conservatives increased their slim lead to an overall majority of 58. Reasons for their victory were the country's growing prosperity and rising living standards, together with the fact that the Labour Party was seriously split over defence policy. While the official Labour line was to go along with the government's rearmament programme in an attempt to keep up with the USA and the USSR, Aneurin Bevan and his supporters – Harold Wilson, Richard Crossman, Barbara Castle and others – criticized it bitterly; Bevan was on the verge of being expelled from the party after his attacks on Attlee.

When Eden eventually became prime minister after waiting in the wings for so long, his premiership was a disappointment. Much was expected of him: his reputation as an international statesman stood high, he had a social conscience, and since he was charming and handsome, he even looked the part of the successful statesman. Within a few months, however, he was giving the impression of not being in full control of his Cabinet, and even the Conservative press mounted an attack against him, claiming that what was needed was a 'smack of firm government'. His disastrous handling of the Suez Crisis in 1956 (see Section 33.2) and his deteriorating health caused him to resign (January 1957).

(b) the Macmillan era

Harold Macmillan was chosen as Conservative leader in preference to R. A. Butler, and was prime minister for over six years (1957–63). Macmillan was a member of the famous publishing family, and had aristocratic connections, having married the daughter of the Duke of Devonshire. According to Sked and Cook, he was 'a fascinating personality, a strange mixture of the hard-headed professional politician and the amateurish country gentleman, indulging a somewhat theatrical, Edwardian style of political presentation'. Andrew Marr comments on 'the tight little world' of the leading Conservatives during the Churchill and Macmillan eras: 'If they were not dining in the Commons ... they were shooting grouse together or meeting in villas in the south of France'. Out of Macmillan's Cabinet of sixteen, only two had not been to one of the great public schools; at one point, Macmillan 'was leading a government in which thirty-five ministers out of eighty-five were related to him by marriage'.

However, during the 1930s, when he was MP for Stockton-on-Tees, he had been horrified by the poverty and demoralization that he witnessed in his constituency. He had acquired a well-deserved reputation as a progressive, forward-looking and radical Conservative with his plans for dealing with unemployment and his book *The Middle Way* published in 1938, in which he set out his radical, but non-socialist solution to the depression. Macmillan was a 'one nation Tory', believing that the Conservatives should follow Disraeli's example, as Quintin Hogg (another Tory reformer) put it, 'to lead and dominate revolution by superior statesmanship instead of to oppose it, to by-pass the progressives by stepping in front of current controversy instead of engaging in it'. In the words of Peter Hennessy, in his book *Having It So Good*, 'in the end Macmillan was a "never-againer" – a man of the centre left, the essentially social democrat middle ground staked out by the combined experiences of Thirties slump and Forties war ... which is why he would never sympathize with the outlook of the young woman who four months later would be adopted as prospective Conservative candidate for Finchley, the 32-year-old Margaret Thatcher'. As Housing Minister, Macmillan had recently demonstrated his social awareness by building more houses per year than the previous Labour government. He soon restored party morale, which was in tatters after the Suez debacle, and revealed himself as a natural leader, commanding the respect of his Cabinet and establishing a rapport with the public through his television appearances. By the time the next election took place (October 1959) the country seemed to have forgotten Suez, the economy was booming, and the Conservatives coasted to an easy victory under 'Super-Mac's' leadership. It was the third successive election victory for the Tories and a personal triumph for Macmillan.

The Macmillan years were a crucial period in British history; despite the prime minister's many gifts, even he was unable to disguise permanently the fact that Britain was no longer a great power. Most of the Empire gained independence and the British gained no compensatory influence in Europe. When they missed an opportunity to join the Common Market (1957) and were refused entry in 1963, Macmillan's foreign policy had largely failed (see Section

33.3(d–f)). In home affairs, Britain enjoyed a period of prosperity and rising living standards. But in the early 1960s the economy seemed to be stagnating and by January 1963 almost 900,000 people were out of work. Later that year, Macmillan, approaching 70 and in poor health, decided to resign. Sir Alec Douglas-Home was prime minister for a year until the Conservatives lost the 1964 election.

30.3 what did the Conservative governments achieve?

(a) an improvement in living standards

This was the most striking feature of the thirteen years of Conservative rule.

1 The first sign of improvement was the government's decision to move away from 'austerity' by reducing as many of Labour's controls as possible. During Churchill's government, restrictions of all sorts were swept away: all types of rationing and restrictions on building were ended, income tax was reduced and limits on hire-purchase sales and even on the right to strike were removed.

2 Between 1951 and 1963 wages rose on average by 72 per cent while prices rose by only 45 per cent; this meant that people could afford more consumer goods than ever before. For example, the number of cars rose from under 3 million to well over 7 million, while licensed TV sets rose from 340,000 to almost 13 million. In 1961, the working week was reduced from 48 hours to 42 hours. However, one reason for the wage increases was that Walter Monckton, the Minister of Labour from 1951 until 1955, tried to avoid strikes by giving way to trade union demands for higher wages. This meant that trade unions became increasingly powerful, especially in times of full employment, and that prices rose at a faster rate than prices in other European countries.

3 There was an increase in house building, thanks to the efforts of Macmillan at the new Ministry of Housing. He was determined to outdo the previous Labour government's record – their best year had been 1947 when 284,230 new houses had appeared. Macmillan threw all his energies into the 'national housing crusade', as he later described it. Unlike Labour, he encouraged local authorities to allow private contractors to build more houses, and abolished Labour's tax on land development. Churchill told him he must produce 300,000 new houses a year, but Macmillan did even better – 327,000 in 1953, and 354,000 in 1954. The worst of the housing shortage was clearly over.

(b) important extensions of the Welfare State

Benefits were raised, and *the Mental Health Act (1959)* laid down that mental illness was to be regarded no differently from physical illness. However, the introduction of a 2s prescription charge aroused the Labour opposition to fury. There was also criticism that very few new hospitals were built during the 1950s. In 1962, the government announced that ninety new hospitals would be built over the next ten years, but the Conservatives were out of office before the programme got under way.

(c) help for agriculture

Help was provided for agriculture in the form of grants and subsidies, to encourage farmers to use new fertilizers, new machinery, new techniques and new animal feeds. It was calculated that in the year 1960/1 alone, over £100 million was given to farmers by the state. Farming became increasingly mechanized and highly efficient, and production continued to rise.

(d) an expansion of education

About 6,000 new schools were built and eleven new universities, while the existing universities were encouraged to expand. Realizing the importance of technological education, the government introduced Colleges of Advanced Technology. In 1963, the government accepted the Robbins Report on higher education, which recommended a doubling of university places over the next ten years. The great debate in education during the 1950s was about the relative merits of comprehensive and grammar schools. By the time of the 1959 election, Labour was committed to supporting comprehensive education, on the grounds that it would reduce class distinction, and because the 11-plus examination was not thought to be a reliable method of predicting future academic development and achievement. For most of their thirteen years in office, the Conservatives supported the grammar schools and prevented county councils from introducing comprehensive systems. However, by 1963 they were beginning to recognize the possible advantages of comprehensive education, and their support for grammar schools was weakening.

Achievements in other areas included the opening of the first motorway in 1959, and the setting up of the Ministry of Science in 1962. However, critics of the government pointed out that the list of achievements did not seem particularly impressive compared with what Labour had achieved in a much shorter period. As time went on, more attention began to focus on criticism of the government.

30.4 on what grounds can Conservative policies be criticized?

(a) inconsistent economic policies

The Conservatives did not find a permanent solution to the interconnected problems of how to stimulate economic growth, while at the same time keeping inflation under control and maintaining a favourable balance of trade.

Successive Chancellors of the Exchequer tried different methods, sometimes attempting to limit spending, sometimes allowing more freedom; this approach came to be known as 'stop–go.'

1 R. A. Butler, Churchill's Chancellor, inherited an unhealthy economic situation from Labour. The Korean War (1950–3) caused a rise in world raw material prices, so that the cost of Britain's imports increased appreciably; Butler found that the balance of payments deficit was approaching £700 million. He decided that he must bring about a reduction in demand; a package of restrictions was introduced, including controls on credit (bank rate was raised from 2 per cent to 4 per cent, to discourage people from borrowing money) and strict limits on imports. This was the first of the Conservative 'stop' phases; it seemed to work: by the end of 1952, the deficit had been converted into a surplus of £300 million. It was generally thought that Butler's 'stop' had been responsible for the improvement, but it is now clear to economists that the main reason was that the increase in import prices caused by the Korean War lasted only a short time. During 1952, import prices fell to the old levels, whereas Britain's exports continued to sell at roughly the same prices. The deficit would probably have righted itself without any interference from Butler, whose measures had the unfortunate effect of reducing investment in industry at a time when industrialists ought to have been aiming for rapid growth. The disturbing fact was that, while there was a trade surplus at the end of 1952, British exports were in fact falling. The significance of this did not seem to be appreciated at the time: the Tories seem to have drawn the conclusion that whenever an unfavourable balance of payments seemed likely, a quick 'stop' was all that was needed to work the economic miracle. The fact that these stops hindered economic growth was ignored.

2 During 1953 and 1954, Butler operated a 'go' phase, cutting the bank rate, encouraging investment and producing some industrial expansion. There was full employment, exports increased and the economy moved into a period of boom. The situation seemed so promising that, shortly before the 1955 election, Butler took sixpence off income tax. Now a different problem developed: full employment brought rising wages, and the demand for goods at home increased, causing rising prices – inflation. The increasing demand was met partly by increasing imports. At the same time, exports were affected adversely by large numbers of strikes, and 1955 saw another unfavourable balance of payments. Butler tried to reduce home demand by raising purchase tax and hire purchase deposits. This change of tack so soon after the income tax reduction gave the impression that Butler's judgement was at fault, and he was soon replaced as Chancellor by Macmillan.

3 Macmillan continued Butler's 'stop' policy, raising the bank rate to 5.5 per cent, so that it was more expensive to borrow cash. This was known as a *credit squeeze:* an attempt to reduce spending in order to check inflation and

reduce imports, thereby improving the balance of payments. This was successful in that it produced a favourable trade balance for 1956.

4 With the economy apparently going well, the next Chancellor, Peter Thorneycroft (1957–8), who had taken over from Macmillan when the latter became Prime Minister, decided to relax the squeeze and risk a 'go'. Taxes and credit restrictions were reduced and an export boom followed; but at the same time, more cash was available to spend at home, causing an increase in demand and a consequent rise in prices and imports. Price rises led to wage demands and strikes, so that exports were soon affected and the balance of payments was threatened again. Thorneycroft believed the time had come to get inflation under control by holding down expenditure for 1958/9. There was some opposition to this in the Cabinet, since it might mean less cash for social policies; Macmillan, with one eye on the possibility of a 1959 election, also opposed Thorneycroft, who therefore resigned (January 1958).

5 Macmillan pressurized his next Chancellor, Derick Heathcoat Amory, to produce a budget that would be popular with voters. The Chancellor obliged with his 1959 tax-cutting budget, as well as relaxing credit controls and allowing wage increases. This certainly helped to woo the voters, but once again, it contributed to a consumer boom, which brought a new flood of imports and an unhealthy trade balance. This laid the government open to the charge that they were more interested in winning votes than in securing a stable, well-managed economy. The Chancellor tried to hold down wage increases and began a further credit squeeze in 1960. This was not enough, and his successor, Selwyn Lloyd, took tougher measures: he raised interest rates, put 10 per cent on purchase tax and raised import duties. He also tried a new idea – a pay pause, which succeeded in holding wages of government employees down for almost a year, but was repeatedly breached after that. This was the first attempt at a definite pay policy, but it failed. By the early 1960s the repeated 'stops' were holding back industrial expansion and Britain was lagging behind its European competitors.

6 The Conservatives realized that a new approach was needed: first in 1961, they applied for membership of the European Economic Community (EEC), but the application was turned down by France. Later the same year they set up *the National Economic Development Council (NEDC) – commonly known as 'Neddy'*, followed by a *National Incomes Commission* in 1962. The idea was to bring together representatives of government, business and trade unions to discuss production targets and wages, and generally to encourage more central planning.

(b) failure to join the EEC

The Conservatives can be criticized for failing to join the European Economic Community at the outset in 1957, which had unfortunate consequences for British production and exports (see Section 33.3(d–f)).

(c) not enough investment in industry

Not enough cash was directed into important industries; this was partly because the 'stops' discouraged industrialists from risking long-term investment, and because too much of the available money was invested abroad. Many argued that the government was spending far too much on defence, manufacturing the hydrogen bomb in a vain attempt to keep up with the USA and the USSR. Thus certain industries declined, particularly textiles (hampered by competition from Portugal, Japan and India), and shipbuilding (competition from Japan). Other industries were expanding (aircraft, cars and chemicals), but production costs were high, which often made British goods expensive. In the face of some strong foreign competition, exports did not boom as much as they might have done; consequently, there was a constant struggle to keep costs down. Unemployment became more of a problem in the early 1960s, especially in the North of England and in Scotland; early in 1963 there were almost 900,000 out of work. A combination of the failure to enter the EEC, economic stagnation and a final 'go' period, which caused a sudden surge in imports, resulted in a record balance of payments deficit of £748 million for 1964.

(d) not enough expenditure on social services

Rising unemployment enabled the Conservatives' critics to claim that their social policies favoured the better-off, leaving the North of England and the industrial areas of Scotland permanently disadvantaged. Statistically it was true that expenditure on the welfare state increased under the Conservatives, as Kevin Jefferys pointed out, 'this was a natural consequence of population growth and did not reflect a positive vision for the welfare state'. For example, while the government was successful in building houses for the better-off, the building of council houses had been neglected, and it was left to impoverished local authorities to build the notoriously unsatisfactory tower block flats for the rest.

(e) scandals and cover-ups

In addition to its economic problems, the government's reputation was tarnished by scandal. First, in October 1962, John Vassall, a clerk at the Admiralty, was found guilty of spying for the Russians; he had been blackmailed because he was a homosexual, and it was suspected that two government ministers had attempted a cover-up. Though the two ministers, Thomas (Tam) Galbraith and Lord Carrington, were cleared by an enquiry, the affair left an uncomfortable atmosphere. The next scandal was much more damaging to the government, since it involved the Minister for War, John Profumo, directly. In June 1963, it emerged that he had been having an affair with a call-girl, Christine Keeler, who at the same time happened to be associating with a Russian naval attaché. There was the obvious security risk, plus the fact that

Profumo had lied to the House of Commons, denying that there was anything improper in his relationship with Miss Keeler. Macmillan had accepted his statement and was therefore made to look foolish when the truth came out. Profumo was forced to resign, and the new Labour leader, Harold Wilson, seized the opportunity to make a scathing attack on Macmillan for not treating the matter seriously enough at the outset.

Finally, after Macmillan's retirement, there was a rather unseemly squabble to choose his successor. There were three main candidates: Lord Hailsham (Quintin Hogg), who resigned his peerage so that he could become a member of the Commons, R. A. Butler (who seemed the most likely choice), and Reginald Maudling. However, after 'consultations' and 'soundings', Lord Home (Foreign Secretary since 1960) emerged as the new leader. He also had to resign his peerage and became Prime Minister as Sir Alec Douglas-Home. Although he was amiable, honest and popular within the party, and was much more shrewd than the opposition gave him credit for, there was some resentment among Conservatives about the way he had been chosen, which compared unfavourably with Wilson's straightforward election as Labour leader in 1963, following the death of Hugh Gaitskell. There was no established method of choosing a Conservative leader; much depended on the preference of the retiring leader, and Macmillan, unimpressed by the three candidates, pushed his own favourite for the post – his Foreign Secretary. Two of the younger rising stars of the party, Enoch Powell and Iain Macleod, refused to serve in Home's government, thereby destroying the claim that he was the man to unify the party. Labour was able to claim that Home's aristocratic background, his lack of experience in the Commons and his remoteness from ordinary people made him totally unsuitable for the leadership of the country.

All these Conservative failures and tribulations contributed to the Labour victory in October 1964. Another important factor was that Wilson had succeeded in reuniting the Labour party after Gaitskell's divisive leadership (he was in favour of Britain retaining its nuclear weapons, while the Labour left wanted Britain unilaterally to disarm). Wilson had gone on to revitalize the party, presenting an attractive programme of improved welfare services, modernization and planning of the economy. He also stressed the need for the government to sponsor scientific and technological development as well as a managerial revolution, so that Britain could catch up with the USA and Japan in these areas. The Conservatives looked tired and devoid of new ideas after their thirteen years in power, whereas Labour, having largely dropped its obsession with nationalization and nuclear disarmament, looked like the modern party of the future. Even so, it was clear that the Conservatives' record was far from being a disaster, and they retained their popularity with large sections of the population. The Labour victory was a narrow one – 317 seats against 304 Conservatives and 9 Liberals – but it was enough to bring to an end the years of Conservative rule.

Assessments of the thirteen Conservative-led years vary widely. Some historians, pointing to the increasing prosperity and *the affluent society,* as economists called it, claimed they were largely successful years. The Conservatives themselves emphasized this as their main achievement. However, critics of the government suggested that the 'affluent society' had developed from the improvement in world trade, which had very little to do with the government's policies. Some economists go further and argue that the government's 'stop–go' policies hindered the country's economic development: Britain's prosperity under the Conservatives should have been even more marked than it was. They see the period as 'the thirteen wasted years', a time full of missed opportunities – and the greatest was the failure to enter the EEC at the outset in 1957. Some historians believe that Macmillan himself ruined Britain's chances of getting into the EEC in 1962–3 by concentrating too much on Britain's 'special relationship' with the USA (see Section 33.1(h)).

30.5 the Wilson governments, 1964–70

With a tiny overall majority of four when it took office in October 1964, Wilson's new government was precarious. After an encouraging by-election victory at Hull North in January 1966, Wilson decided to risk a general election the following March, in the hope of increasing Labour's majority. He had already been Prime Minister long enough to make a good impression on the electorate; his superb television technique, together with his familiar pipe and Gannex raincoat, combined to project the image of the capable and reliable father-figure who had the country's fortunes well under control. At the same time, the Conservatives had a new and untried leader in Edward Heath (elected by ballot in July 1965); their election campaign seemed flat and uninspiring, and their manifesto had no great vision for the future. A majority of the voters apparently still blamed the Conservatives for the country's economic problems and saw no reason to desert Labour so soon. Wilson won the mandate he had asked for, securing 363 seats against 253 Conservatives, 12 Liberals and 2 others. In spite of their large majority, Labour's path was far from smooth: Wilson and his Cabinet seemed to spend most of their time wrestling with insoluble economic problems and strikes; matters were further complicated by the situation in Rhodesia and by violence in Ireland.

(a) the economy and the balance of payments deficit

The most pressing problem was the £800 million balance of payments deficit inherited from the Conservatives:

▸ The Chancellor of the Exchequer, James Callaghan, borrowed heavily from the International Monetary Fund to replenish Britain's rapidly dwindling gold reserves, which were being used up to cover the deficit. Many economists have pointed out that there was an excellent case for a devaluation of the pound at this point, since all the evidence suggested that it was overvalued against the dollar, and especially against the German Mark. A quick devaluation would make British exports cheaper and lead to an export boom. However, Wilson decided against it, feeling that, having already devalued once in 1949, Labour's prestige would be ruined if they decided on a second devaluation. Callaghan was therefore forced to fall back on yet another squeeze, holding wages down and raising import duties. The government's efforts were ruined by a dockers' strike in May 1966, which brought trade almost to a standstill and caused a drastic fall in exports. Some foreign bankers feared that the unions were getting out of control, and the pound was adversely affected on the foreign exchanges. Even after the strike was settled the value of the pound continued to fall, and some members of the Cabinet suggested devaluation. Callaghan, who still saw devaluation as a political humiliation, would not hear of it: 'devaluation is not the way out of Britain's difficulties', he declared in July 1967. Soon another dock strike, affecting London and Liverpool, reduced exports again, and it was clear that there would be a massive trade deficit by the end of the year. With the drain on gold reserves increasing, the government decided that the only alternative was to devalue the pound from US$2.80 to US$2.40 (November 1967). It was hoped that, apart from stabilizing the financial situation, devaluation would cause a surge in exports. However, the immediate effect was to bring about Callaghan's resignation; after his declaration against devaluation only a few months earlier, it was felt that he could hardly remain at the Treasury. He was replaced by Roy Jenkins.

Unfortunately the main results of the first three years of Labour economic policy turned out to be little different from the previous Conservative 'stop–go' years – economic stagnation. The devaluation did not help Wilson's reputation either; he appeared on television and told the nation: 'devaluation does not mean that the pound in the pocket is worth 14 per cent less to us now than it was'. The problem, as Ben Pimlott, Wilson's biographer, pointed out, was that 'the Prime Minister had persistently argued that devaluation did matter to ordinary people. Now that it had happened, he appeared to be standing on his head, cleverly arguing that it did not ... this did the premier's already slippery image limitless harm in the subsequent, inflationary years'.

▸ During 1968, the new Chancellor cut government spending by £750 million and raised taxes on cigarettes, alcohol and petrol, arousing bitter criticism from the left wing of the party. But Jenkins was determined to stick by his policies, and eventually they began to show results – a balance of payments surplus of £387 million for 1969. Unfortunately, the ending of the pay restraint policy in 1970 led to steep wage increases, which in turn brought rising prices; the government had failed to escape from the 'stop–go' economy.

(b) the failure to reform the trade unions

The economy was damaged by large numbers of strikes, particularly among dockers and in the motor vehicle industry. The number of working days lost through strikes increased from 1.75 million in 1963 to 2.9 million in 1965, and to 4.69 million in 1968. One disturbing point was the rapidly-growing number of unofficial or 'wildcat' strikes, when shop stewards led walk-outs instead of going through official union procedures. While a survey in 1969 showed that 57 per cent of people still thought trade unions were a 'good thing' (the figure had been 70 per cent in 1964), there was a growing feeling among the general public that unions must be more disciplined, and unofficial strikes curbed. In 1968, *the Donovan Commission on Industrial Relations* recommended improved voluntary agreements rather than new laws to deal with trade unions.

Wilson, however, decided that public opinion would support some moderate reform, and Barbara Castle, the Employment and Productivity Secretary, published a White Paper in January 1969 called *In Place of Strife*, outlining the government's plans. There was to be a ballot of all members before a union could call a strike, followed by a 28-day period for further discussions before the strike went ahead; there would be fines for those who broke the rules. There were howls of protest from the TUC and from all sections of the Labour party, and there were real doubts as to whether a bill based on these proposals would have enough support to get it through the Commons. Even the Home Secretary, Callaghan, opposed it, reportedly telling Wilson: 'You won't get it through. You'd better head it off ... If it's [trade union reform] so inevitable, let the Tories pass it.' There were plots to replace Wilson with Callaghan if he tried to push the bill through, and eventually he was forced to accept defeat and drop the proposals. It was a humiliating climb-down: the government had admitted that reform was needed, and had then shown itself incapable of carrying through any reform.

(c) the problem of Rhodesia

The situation in Rhodesia was handled sensitively and skilfully by Wilson (see Section 34.5(d). Economic sanctions were placed on the Smith regime, though they were ineffective. Wilson twice met Smith, aboard HMS *Tiger* (1966) and HMS *Fearless* (1968), but no solution was reached.

(d) violence in Northern Ireland

Northern Ireland had been comparatively calm since Lloyd George's 1922 settlement (see Section 26.2). However, the IRA would never rest until the north was reunited with Eire, while the Protestant-dominated Northern Ireland parliament would never agree to this. Violence between Catholics and Protestants escalated, and in August 1969 Wilson sent troops to Belfast and

Londonderry to restrain the two factions, and in particular to protect Catholic areas from attacks by Protestants (see Section 31.1(d)–(e) for full details).

(e) Labour's achievements

There were constant crises and many of Labour's plans had to be abandoned because of the economic situation. For example, prescription charges were abolished from February 1965, but were reintroduced early in 1968 as part of the emergency measures. But there were some constructive achievements:

- The introduction of rent rebates and votes at 18.
- The abolition of the death penalty and the creation of the Ombudsman, to investigate complaints against inefficient administrators.
- *The Abortion Act (1967)* legalized abortion provided it was approved by two doctors who were satisfied that it was medically or psychologically necessary.
- *The Sexual Offences Act (1967)* legalized sexual acts between consenting male adults over the age of 21 in England and Wales (Scotland had to wait until 1980 for this Act to come into force, and Northern Ireland until 1982).
- *The Race Relations Act (1968)* made it illegal to discriminate against people on racial grounds in employment, housing, insurance, education and other areas. This had some success, and meant that West Indians, Pakistanis and Indians, for example, were able to work as lawyers, teachers and doctors, and to join the police (see Section 31.7(d)).
- *The Divorce Reform Act (1969)* ended the need for proof of some blame or guilt before a divorce could be granted. The sole grounds for divorce were now that 'the marriage has broken down irretrievably' (for full details of these Acts see Section 31.3).
- Many would see Labour's most lasting achievement to be in the field of education. There was a determined move towards comprehensive secondary education, and the Open University was created, using radio and television to enable people to receive a university education at home.
- In general, living standards continued to improve, with a larger proportion of households than ever before having refrigerators, washing-machines and TV sets.

(f) assessment of the Wilson governments

Labour's achievements were not enough to dispel the impression, apart perhaps from their last year in office, that they had made many of the same mistakes as the Conservatives and had not 'got the economy right'. Several key industries – coal-mining, shipbuilding, textiles and railways – continued to contract, and this caused unemployment to rise from around 400,000 to just over 600,000 in 1970. Wilson could have waited until the following year, but some favourable by-election results and opinion polls convinced him that an election victory was possible in June 1970. Unfortunately for Labour, though, many of their traditional supporters felt that the government had failed to live up to its promises; Jenkins stuck to his severe policies and failed to provide a give-away budget before the election, and this may well have lost the party crucial support. David Marquand claims that 'few modern British governments have disappointed their supporters more thoroughly', and describes the Wilson years as 'an era of lost innocence, of hopes betrayed'. Many historians pinpoint the devaluation of November 1967 as the moment when Labour support began seriously to drift away. The Labour vote fell by almost a million, while the Conservative vote went up by 1.7 million, enough to give them an overall majority of 30.

On the other hand, it is possible to present a defence of Labour's record. Dominic Sandbrook argues that Wilson and his government have been unfairly maligned. As he explains,

> for all the fuss at the time about their economic record, in historical terms it was not all that bad. Unemployment never rose above 2.7 per cent; inflation for much of the sixties remained below 4 per cent; and annual economic growth never dipped below 1.8 per cent. By the standards of, say, the 1970s and the 1980s these are pretty impressive figures.

Nicholas Timmins claims that, bearing in mind that government spending on health, education, research, transport, social security and housing increased on average by more than 6 per cent a year between 1964 and 1970, the Wilson governments' record on social services and public welfare was unmatched by any later government. In fact, the mid-1960s can be seen as the golden age of the welfare state. Wilson also deserves some credit for his handling of foreign policy, particularly the British withdrawal from the Far East, which was achieved without too much trauma, and his refusal to become embroiled in the Vietnam War, in spite of considerable pressure from the USA.

30.6 the Heath government, 1970–4

Edward Heath was a 'one nation' Tory, in the tradition of Disraeli and Macmillan, and keen to maintain the Welfare State. He also believed in planning, and in January 1970 held the Selsdon Park conference to work out policies to be followed when the party was next in office. Much time was spent discussing trade union reform and the reduction of state intervention in the economy. This has been seen by some historians as the beginning of the end of consensus politics; Wilson strengthened this impression when he talked about the emergence of a new right-wing type of Tory called 'Selsdon Man'. In reality, when the Heath government was in office, many elements of consensus continued.

Heath believed it was possible to escape from the 'stop–go' trap by reducing controls to a minimum and taking Britain into the EEC, which, it was hoped, would stimulate British industry. Unfortunately, the government almost imme-diately suffered a tragic blow with the death of Iain Macleod, the Chancellor of the Exchequer, after only a month in office. He was the most charismatic member of the government – a politician of enormous ability and expertise who had been working on plans for tax reform. His successor, Anthony Barber, lacked Macleod's experience and authority. After this, very little went right for the government.

(a) continuing economic problems

Barber introduced decisive measures, cutting taxes and reducing restrictions on hire purchase and credit; Britain's entry into the EEC was secured at last in 1972 (to take effect in January 1973), considered to be Heath's greatest achieve-ment (see Section 33.3(g)). However, the hoped-for investment in industry failed to materialize and inflation became serious again. This caused Heath to do a sharp U-turn to a policy of holding wages down and re-imposing controls; but there was no rapid improvement: 1973 showed a balance of payments deficit of close on £1 billion (a new record), unemployment hovered at around the million mark, and inflation was still rising.

(b) help for poor families

Heath strengthened his 'one nation' credentials by introducing the Family Income Supplement, together with rates and fuel rebates to help poor families; but these were criticized by many right-wing Conservatives as being too much like socialism.

(c) help for ailing industries

When Rolls-Royce, Britain's biggest manufacturer of aircraft engines (as well as luxury cars), seemed to be on the verge of bankruptcy, the government rescued it by stepping in and nationalizing it (1971). Later, Upper Clyde Shipbuilders was saved from collapse by a government subsidy of £35 million, preserving thousands of jobs in the Glasgow area.

(d) the Industrial Relations Act (1971)

This was an attempt to introduce the sort of moderate trade union reform that had eluded Wilson. Designed to cut down strikes and curb escalating pay demands, the Act set up a National Industrial Relations Court with the power to enforce ballots for strikes, and a sixty-day 'cooling-off' period before a strike began. While in many quarters this was seen as a mild and sensible measure, similar to the one Labour had intended to introduce, the unions opposed it bitterly. There was a loophole in the Act, which enabled the TUC to defy it successfully: unions were required to register under the Act, and the court would be unable to deal with any union which refused to do so. The TUC instructed all unions not to register, and threatened to expel any union that did.

In 1972 there was a wave of strikes in protest at the new legislation, and a record 23.9 million working days were lost.

The most serious was the miners' strike (January–February 1972). The background to the dispute was the steady decline in the coal industry, which had reduced numbers of miners from over 700,000 in 1957 to less than 300,000, plus the fact that miners' wages had lagged behind those of other industrial workers. The National Union of Miners (NUM) put in a large pay demand and, when this was refused by the National Coal Board, a national miners' strike began. Arthur Scargill, leader of the Yorkshire miners, masterminded a campaign of mass picketing, using 'flying pickets', who would converge on coal depots and prevent the movement of coal stocks. Soon power stations had to close down, the government declared a state of emergency and a million and a half people were thrown out of work. Heath eventually gave way and conceded to all the miners' demands. Meanwhile the Industrial Relations Court largely stood idle.

(e) continuing disturbances in Ireland

The British army found itself in the impossible situation of trying to prevent Catholics and Protestants from slaughtering each other, while at the same time having to endure attacks from the IRA and another group calling itself the Provisional IRA (for the Heath government's reaction, see 32.1(f)–(g)).

(f) the Local Government Act of 1972

This was the most important local government reform since 1888, when county councils were introduced. It was intended to improve administrative efficiency and remove anomalies; it combined some small counties, creating new units such as Humberside and Cleveland, while tiny counties such as Rutland and the Isle of Ely ceased to exist. However, this was not popular in places where centuries-old county loyalties were outraged by the new boundaries.

(g) the Arab–Israeli War and the oil crisis

This problem began in the autumn of 1973, following the short Arab–Israeli War of October 1973, which was won decisively by the Israelis. The Arab oil-producing states decided to show their displeasure towards certain countries that, they felt, had been too friendly towards Israel. Britain found that its oil imports were cut by 15 per cent, while the Arabs imposed a series of price increases which more than trebled the cost of Britain's oil imports. Not only did this cause a petrol shortage, it also ruined any faint chance that there would be a favourable balance of payments for 1973. However, worse was to follow.

(h) renewed confrontation with the miners

Heath's U-turn in favour of wage restraint soon produced another confrontation with the miners. They had just put in a demand for a large wage increase

(September 1973) when the oil crisis seemed to strengthen their position. After the failure of talks, the NUM introduced an overtime ban (November), to which Heath responded by declaring a state of emergency and appointing the moderate, William Whitelaw, as Employment Secretary. A similar ban by electricity workers and railway drivers soon followed, adding to the general fuel shortage. Although the miners' leader, Joe Gormley, was also a moderate, they were unable to find a compromise. Heath was determined not to allow his wages strategy to be breached and would make no increased offer to the miners. Instead, a series of drastic emergency measures was introduced to save power: from January 1974, industry was allowed to work only a three-day week, there was to be a 50mph speed limit and, the most unpopular move of all in the eyes of many – TV was to close down at 10.30 pm. As a strike began to look more likely, the TUC offered Heath guarantees that if he would treat the miners as a special case, other unions would not seek to breach his pay policy. When Heath rejected this offer, the miners held a ballot in which 81 per cent voted in favour of a strike (4 February 1974). Heath decided on a general election, hoping to win public support for his stand against the miners.

(i) the general election of February 1974

The election was a bitter and dramatic affair. Heath campaigned on the need for strong government. 'Who governs Britain,' asked the Conservatives, 'Parliament or the unions?' Labour seemed to have very little to offer that was new. However, the miners presented their case well, while a few days before the election two sets of statistics were published that might well have swayed voters: the first showed that food prices had risen by 20 per cent during 1973; and the second showed that the trade deficit had just reached another all-time high. Enoch Powell, a leading (if rather eccentric) Conservative, urged people who, like him, were against Britain's membership of the EEC, to vote Labour.

The election result was a strange one: there was no great surge of support for Heath's anti-union stand, and the Conservative vote fell by over a million. It was clearly a vote of no confidence in the Conservatives, but it was hardly a positive vote for Labour either, since they polled around half a million fewer votes than in 1970. The Liberals, who had won several sensational by-election results over the Tories, saw their total shoot up to over 6 million (from only 2.1 million in 1970), as they took votes from both major parties. However, the strange British electoral system meant that they still won only 14 seats – the vast majority of Liberal votes were wasted in constituencies where Liberal candidates came second. The final figures were: Labour 301 seats, Conservatives 297, Liberals 14, Nationalists and others 23.

Heath did not resign immediately, but had talks with Jeremy Thorpe, the Liberal leader, about a possible coalition. He justified this on the grounds that the Conservatives had polled more votes (11.87 million) than Labour (11.64 million) and that there was agreement between the two parties on Europe and on an incomes policy. However, the Liberals wanted the Conservatives to support proportional representation, and when the Conservatives refused, Thorpe withdrew from the talks. Heath had little choice but to resign, and Wilson formed a minority Labour government.

Historians, even Conservative ones, have not dealt kindly with the unfortunate Heath. Andrew Roberts is highly critical of his government's U-turns, pointing out that it

> performed a spectacular and comprehensive U-turn on all its major industrial policies, ditching every commitment it had made only two years earlier in its election manifesto ... All its promises, of tax cuts, free-market reforms, immigration controls, law and order measures and legislation to control the trade unions, were abandoned overnight in an act of mass collective funk.

Robert Blake criticized Heath's timing, particularly in calling the election. He could have called it earlier, before the situation became too bad; or he could have delayed it until as late as June 1975. February 1974 was arguably the worst possible time to hold an election, in the middle of winter and at a time when the public was 'shivering and darkened'. On the other hand, Heath deserves great credit for taking Britain into the EEC in 1973, though even this was bitterly condemned by many Conservatives. Andrew Marr takes a more sympathetic view: he believes that Heath was 'a genuinely compassionate and unusually brave politician whose analysis of what was wrong with Britain in the seventies was far more acute than Wilson's'. But he was unfortunate in being prime minister at the wrong time. He realized that trade unions needed to be controlled, 'but he was up against forces too big to conquer quickly'. It was a time when public sympathy was more with the unions than with the government, and when huge rises in oil prices were throwing European economies disastrously off course. 'His strategic mistake was to attack union power head-on and in a single act, rather than piecemeal,' as Margaret Thatcher did later.

30.7 Labour in power again, 1974–9

(a) Wilson's brisk beginning

Wilson faced an unenviable task in trying to 'get the economy right', as he put it. In spite of the government's small majority, he began briskly. He made a left-winger, Michael Foot, Secretary of State for Employment, which pleased the unions. He settled the miners' strike, though only by allowing their full wage claim, and ended the three-day week. The government's *Trade Union and Labour Relations Act* repealed most of Heath's Industrial Relations Act, and later the National Industrial Relations Court was abolished (July 1974). This was followed by a rash of other wage increases, which helped to push up prices and fuel inflation; industrial wages went up by 19 per cent in 1974 and by 23 per cent in 1975. Wilson now introduced a new strategy known as the 'Social Contract'; this was an attempt to improve industrial relations by government and TUC working out agreements on wage levels.

Wilson decided that the situation had stabilized sufficiently for him to hold an election in October 1974, hoping for a repeat of the big Labour victory of October 1966. However, there was only a slight improvement in Labour's position, as they emerged with an overall majority of three. By the end of 1974 there was still no sign that the government would be able to remedy the basic weakness of the economy, though in 1975 the Social Contract began to show some results. The TUC agreed to a £6 a week limit on wage rises; and the Chancellor of the Exchequer, Denis Healey, introduced a tough budget, reducing defence spending, raising income tax to 35p in the pound and raising VAT (which he had introduced in 1974 at 8 per cent) to 25 per cent on certain luxury items.

(b) the EEC referendum (June 1975)

As well as all the economic problems, Wilson was also faced by difficulties within the Labour Party. The left wing of the party, whose leading personalities were Michael Foot, Barbara Castle and Tony Benn, was becoming stronger. Many constituency party organizations began to be taken over by left-wing activists, who bitterly opposed any sort of wage restraint and felt that Wilson was not delivering real socialism; some of them were members of the Trotskyite Militant Tendency. This alarmed right-wingers such as Callaghan and Jenkins, but Wilson succeeded in holding the party together by including both Foot and Benn in the Cabinet and by appeasing the trade unions. Another potential split in the party was over membership of the EEC: right-wingers such as Roy Jenkins and Shirley Williams supported Britain's continued membership, but Benn and the left wanted to withdraw. When Benn suggested a referendum on the issue, expecting a vote in favour of withdrawing, Wilson agreed. The result appeared to be decisive: 67.2 per cent of those who voted favoured continued membership (but see Section 33.3(g)). The left was defeated temporarily, Benn was demoted to the Department of Energy (from Trade and Industry), and Wilson had maintained party unity once again.

(c) Wilson resigns (April 1976)

Although there had been rumours about it, Wilson's sudden resignation came as a complete surprise to the country; however, it was something he had been planning for some time, and had told several people, including the Queen, of his decision as early as the previous December. He said that he had had enough of the strains of top-level politics, and, though he was only 60, did not want to lead the party into another general election, having already gone through four. He therefore felt it was only right that his successor should be given a chance to establish himself before the next election. Wilson's unkindest critics claimed that his real motive was the desire to escape the humiliation of failure, since he knew that he was incapable of solving the country's economic problems. However, Ben Pimlott, writing in 1992, dismissed this idea, explaining that Wilson 'was not ill, but he was ageing. The years of buffeting had left their mark ... He had lost none of his acuteness, but he no longer had the same energy, the same aggression or the same ambition ... He felt he owed it to Mary [his wife] not to go on too long.' In fact we know now that Wilson *was* ill, with the beginnings of Alzheimer's disease, and was anxious to retire before his symptoms became too obvious.

(d) Callaghan in charge

Aged 64, James Callaghan was older than Wilson. He was on the right of the party and had vast experience, having been Home Secretary, Foreign Secretary and Chancellor of the Exchequer. He was a fatherly figure who seemed to inspire confidence, and his style was relaxed and reassuring; he was particularly successful at dealing with the new Conservative leader, Margaret Thatcher, in the House of Commons.

He certainly needed all his coolness, since the government was soon hit by a financial crisis caused by a combination of the huge balance of payments deficit following the oil crisis, inflation running at 16 per cent, and rising unemployment, which had risen well above the million mark for the first time since 1939. Confidence in sterling was badly shaken and the pound fell to US$1.57. Healey was forced to ask the International Monetary Fund (IMF) for a loan; this was granted, but only on condition that the government made massive spending cuts. Callaghan told the party conference in September: 'You cannot now, if you ever could, spend your way out of a recession.' In December 1976, Healey announced cuts of over £2.5 billion over the next two years, and price increases on alcohol and tobacco. Some experts see this crisis period in 1976 as the point when Keynesian policies were abandoned. These were unpopular moves, and Labour soon lost four by-elections, depriving them of their Commons majority.

The government's stringent policies, together with the fact that Britain was beginning to enjoy the advantage of its own North Sea oil soon brought an improvement in the situation. In 1974, Britain imported over 100 million tons of oil and exported less than one million; by 1980, imports and exports of oil almost balanced. By the end of 1977, Britain was able to repay much of the loan to the IMF, and the balance of payments had moved into surplus. The annual inflation rate, which had touched 24 per cent in 1975, had fallen below 10 per cent. Two other important developments were:

› *The Devolution Act (December 1978)* provided for the establishment of regional assemblies in Scotland and Wales, on condition that 40 per cent of the electorate showed themselves to be in favour. However, in a referendum held the following March, only 12 per cent of the Welsh electorate approved, while in Scotland the figure was 33 per cent. Consequently, devolution was quietly shelved for the time being (see Section 32.2(d) and 32.3(c)).

▸ *The Lib–Lab Pact.* By January 1977, Labour's overall majority was down to one. To ensure that his government survived, Callaghan made a pact with the new Liberal leader, David Steel. The Liberals would vote with Labour in Parliament and in return they would be allowed to see Labour's proposed bills before they were introduced into the Commons. The Liberals would then indicate whether they were prepared to support Labour's proposals, so that in effect they could veto future legislation. Steel was angling for a possible deal on a reform of the electoral system – the introduction of some form of proportional representation, which would give the Liberals a fairer representation in the Commons. Nothing came of Steel's hopes, but from Labour's point of view the pact was a success, lasting until the autumn of 1978 and helping to prolong Callaghan's government.

(e) the winter of discontent (1978–9) and the election of May 1979

Most informed observers expected that Callaghan would hold an election in the autumn of 1978, to take full advantage of the improving economic situation. However, he decided to wait until 1979, and this turned out to be a fatal delay. Callaghan proposed to extend the Social Contract for a further period by limiting wage increases to 5 per cent. Given the fact that inflation was still running at 10 per cent and living standards were falling steadily, this was always going to be difficult to enforce. The TUC rejected it, and even more seriously, so did the Labour Party Conference (October 1978). Neither side would compromise, and after the Ford car workers had won a big wage increase by going on strike, there was a surge of strikes, especially among public sector workers, whose wages had been tightly controlled for the previous three years. This was extremely embarrassing for the government, especially when NHS workers, refuse collectors and even Liverpool grave-diggers went on strike. Strike action dragged on through the winter, 'the winter of discontent' as it became known, and ruined Labour's claim that they could control the unions. In addition, there were almost 1.4 million people out of work, and the government seemed to have run out of ideas and reforming zeal. The election was forced on Callaghan by the government's defeat in a vote of confidence. Disappointed by the failure of the devolution referendum, the Scottish Nationalists voted against the government, which lost by one vote. Callaghan was forced to face an election on 3 May 1979, with the opinion polls running strongly against Labour.

By contrast, the Conservatives were full of new purpose, the unfortunate Heath having been dropped after suffering two election defeats in 1974. It was Heath himself who called the leadership election in November 1974 in an attempt to silence his critics, and was surprised when Margaret Thatcher put herself forward as a candidate, supported by two right-wingers – Enoch Powell and Sir Keith Joseph. She had been much influenced by their arguments that

Heath was too weak to be a successful leader, and that the Conservatives (and the country) needed a strong leader who would stand up to the unions and follow monetarist economic policies. Heath expected to win comfortably, but Thatcher's campaign was cleverly directed by another sympathetic Conservative MP, Airey Neave. Heath was devastated when Thatcher defeated him on the first ballot and he resigned immediately. She went on to win the second ballot, her nearest rival being William Whitelaw. And so it was that, on 11 February 1975, in the words of Robert Blake, 'for the first time in British history a woman became leader of one of the great political parties'.

By the time the 1979 election arrived, Margaret Thatcher had proved herself an effective leader. She was aggressive and self-confident, making the most of Labour's failures, particularly the chaos of 'the winter of discontent', and deploring what she saw as Labour's drift towards the far left. In their manifesto, the Conservatives made promises designed to please the middle classes, who were tired of Labour's policies. Foremost was the pledge to reduce the power of the unions, which were 'holding the nation to ransom'; there would be improvements in health care and education, and increased spending on defence and police. On the economy, the proposals were deliberately vague; inflation would be reduced and restrictive practices removed, but beyond that, there was little detail about monetarism. It was hoped that the proposal to sell council houses to tenants at a reduced price would attract working-class voters. The Conservatives left nothing to chance; they hired Saatchi and Saatchi, a leading advertising agency, to mastermind their campaign. Mrs Thatcher herself, who had been accused of seeming overbearing, arrogant and 'headmistressy', took lessons in how to appear relaxed and genuine when delivering speeches and being interviewed. The results of the election were: Conservatives 339, Labour 269, Liberals 11, others 16, giving a Conservative overall majority of 43. Much was made by some analysts of the argument that Labour had suffered because one of their main groups of supporters – manual workers – was declining in numbers, and this was a trend destined to continue. Labour, or 'Old Labour' as it eventually became known, was to be in opposition for the next eighteen years.

(f) what was wrong with the British economy?

As we have seen throughout this chapter, successive governments were dogged by the problem of how to stimulate economic growth, while at the same time keeping inflation under control and maintaining a favourable balance of trade. The economy did grow every year up to 1973, even during the recession of 1957–8. The trouble was that the economies of Britain's rivals grew faster. The simple fact was that British industry was not producing enough goods for export at the right prices; foreign competitors could produce more cheaply and secured a larger share of the market.

In 1950, the British were still responsible for around 25 per cent of the world export of manufactured goods, but by 1979 their share had fallen dramatically

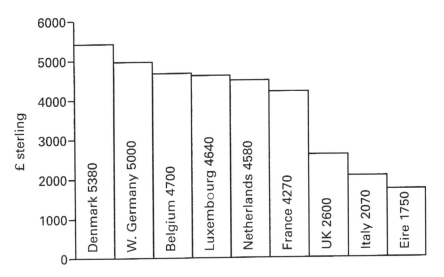

figure **30.1 GDP per head of population, selected European countries, 1977 (in £ sterling)**

Source: Based on statistics in Jack B. Watson, *Success in World History Since 1945* (John Murray, 1989), p. 150.

to under 10 per cent. They were also losing out on the home market: in 1948, Britain imported goods valued at £2.4 billion, but by 1979 these had soared to £54 billion. The statistics of gross domestic product (GDP) for 1977 are very revealing; GDP is the cash value of a country's total output from all types of production. To find out how efficient a country is, economists divide the GDP by the population of the country, which shows how much is being produced per head of the population.

Figure 30.1 shows that, economically, Britain was one of the least efficient nations in the European Community, while Denmark and West Germany were top of the league. The traditional industries of coal, textiles, steel and shipbuilding were all in rapid decline, soon to be followed by motor vehicle and computer manufacture.

Nor did the situation improve during the Thatcher era: in 1993, Britain's performance was still below the EEC average (see Table 35.2 on page 753). *The reasons for this inefficiency are a matter of controversy*:

‣ Management blamed unions for excessive wage demands and opposition to new techniques and processes; certainly, the power of the unions had increased over the previous decade, and both Wilson and Heath had failed to control them. The number of strikes increased from 1,339 in 1950 to 3,906 in 1970, reaching a peak of 4,583 in 1979. Problems of inefficiency and over-manning were not tackled, and many inefficient firms – which should have become more streamlined – stayed in business. The *Financial Times* went so far as to call the unions 'the robber barons of the system', while Mrs Thatcher labelled them 'the enemy within'.

- On the other hand, the unions denied that they were to blame for the country's economic problems; they claimed they were simply trying to defend their jobs, and blamed unimaginative management for the decline of their industries. Some economists also criticized management on the grounds that they were inefficient and lacking in vision. They were accused of being so greedy for profit that too little was ploughed back for research and development, and there was not enough investment in new machinery and techniques. It was suggested that manufacturers concentrated too much on the home market instead of trying to produce goods for export at competitive prices. The drawback was that the domestic market was more volatile and profits were smaller – another reason for the lack of research and modernization.

- It was also suggested that governments should have spent more on grants to develop industry and less on social services and defence. Some government actions were hard to understand; for example, apparently accepting that the textile industry was in terminal decline, the government gave grants to manufacturers to take old looms out of production, whereas a better investment might have been to provide larger grants to enable them to buy modern looms.

- Manufacturers themselves claimed that the 'stop–go' policies, which neither political party had been able to avoid, slowed down industrial expansion. However, some economists believe that they were using this as an excuse for their own incompetence. There is no doubt, however, that the over-valuing of sterling made British exports more expensive and therefore even more uncompetitive.

- The oil crisis that began in 1973 following the Arab/Israeli war disrupted the economies of most of the industrialized world, including Britain. The price of oil, which had been US$2 a barrel in 1972, rose to US$35 a barrel in 1980, causing a surge in inflation and a huge balance of payments deficit. However, the worst effects of this were mitigated when Britain's own North Sea oil supplies began to flow.

- Some historians have suggested that one explanation for poor management is that, unlike in the USA, business was not considered to be a profession until comparatively recently. According to George L. Bernstein, 'there was a real hostility in the business community to the formal training of managers which was shown in the 1950s and 1960s as they resisted American pressures to introduce business training into the universities ... Even when the first business schools were formed in Manchester and London in the mid-1960s, business showed relatively little interest.'

(g) Britain in decline?

Much has been written about Britain's post-Second World War decline: the staple manufacturing industries became uncompetitive and suffered a disastrous contraction; the British suffered humiliation at Suez and lost their Empire; as former American Secretary of State, Dean Acheson, put it in 1962, 'Britain had lost an Empire but had not yet found a role'. Corelli Barnett claimed that the entire period up to 1979 was one of failure and missed opportunities, with Britain teetering on the edge of bankruptcy for most of the time. Newspapers lamented that Britain's diplomatic power and prestige had disappeared for ever.

However, not all historians take this view. Andrew Marr feels that, in spite of the crisis in the 1970s, which he calls 'a national nervous breakdown', the British have had 'rather a good sixty years … The years before Thatcher were not a steady slide into disaster'. And Harold Macmillan did tell people that they had never had it so good, though that was in 1957. Dominic Sandbrook writes about the 'Swinging Sixties' as a time of 'full employment, rising incomes and rampant consumerism. People took home more money than ever before and spent it on a bewildering array of new appliances … The affluent society was in full swing'. *So what is the true picture?*

American historian, George L. Bernstein, makes an excellent attempt to put everything into perspective, though the title of his book, *The Myth of Decline – The Rise of Britain Since 1945*, does tend to reveal his general thesis. According to Bernstein, 'the very evidence of decline is partial and ambiguous. It is shaped by the judgements of economists first and foremost, and by politicians following in their wake'. He points out that in fact the British economy had never performed as well as it did in the twenty-five years after the war. The fact that much of the rest of the industrialized world apart from the USA was performing even better than Britain does not alter the fact that this was an era of unique prosperity for the British people, a period of exceptional performance that was not matched in the 1980s and 1990s. Bernstein argues that Britain's so-called decline in the period from 1945 until 1973 has been exaggerated,

> because when evaluating economic performances, economists discount measures of social wellbeing … Britain's performance in providing for the wellbeing of its people – as measured by employment, a safety net that kept them out of poverty, and improved standards of living – was outstanding.

So too was the quality of Britain's financial services and the efficiency of its retail distribution, which went a long way towards counterbalancing its contracting manufacturing industries (for full details of social developments and the affluent society, see Chapter 31).

QUESTIONS

1 'Thirteen wasted years.' How accurate is this assessment of the record of the Conservative governments of 1951 to 1964?
2 Explain why the Labour party was able to win the elections of 1964 and 1966, but lost the election of 1970.

3 Explain how the growing power of the trade unions influenced the success or failure of both Conservative and Labour governments between 1970 and 1979.

4 'In spite of the occasional short-term boom, the real story of Britain between 1945 and 1979 was one of continuous decline'. In your opinion, how accurate is this assessment?

A document question about Harold Macmillan's premiership can be found on the accompanying website www.palgrave.com/masterseries/lowe1.

the state of the people: social and cultural change since 1945

The period after 1945 saw tremendous social and cultural change, though it was not necessarily confined to any specific years. Some changes – for example, advances in the status of women – had begun long before 1945; while others, such as immigration, have continued until the present day.

> There was a significant rise in living standards, which led some observers to talk about 'the affluent society', and in many ways British society became more equal.

> There were ground-breaking legal changes related to marriage, divorce, abortion and sexual behaviour, some of which greatly increased women's control over their own lives.

> It was in the 1950s that business and the media discovered the 'teenager'; this was followed by the development of a specific teenage culture, centring in the beginning on rock 'n' roll music.

> All this led to a more relaxed attitude towards moral and sexual issues, and people felt free to organize protest movements and challenge authority in ways never before seen in Britain. The 1960s were later described as the 'Swinging Sixties', a phenomenon that many of the older generation condemned as the 'permissive society'.

> Throughout the period, immigration continued, and by 1950 was causing serious racial tension.

31.1 social revolution

(a) rising living standards

From 1945 until the mid-1970s there was a continuous and sustained rise in the standard of living of all social classes in Britain. When Seebohm Rowntree carried out his survey of York in 1899 he found that almost 28 per cent of the population were living in poverty. By 1936, when he conducted his second survey of York, this figure had fallen to just under 18 per cent. In 1953, in his third and final survey, Rowntree discovered that only 2.8 per cent of York's working class (not of the population as a whole) were living in poverty. Of course, York was more prosperous than many of the old industrial towns in the North of England and South Wales. In 1932, for example, the poverty rate for the Liverpool area was 30 per cent of the total population. Sydney Pollard calculated that, as late as 1953, around 20 per cent of Britain's population were living in 'abject' poverty, but by 1973 the figure was only 2.5 per cent for the whole country. Clearly something remarkable had taken place and a number of factors had made it possible.

In the first place, most families had more money to spend than ever before. According to George L. Bernstein, 'between 1951 and 1974, real wages roughly doubled, despite the accelerating inflation of the last decade of the period'. Hours of work for trade union members had shrunk to a 40-hour week, and there was plenty of opportunity to work overtime, which swelled the weekly wage packet even more. By 1950, most workers were entitled to at least two weeks' holiday a year with pay. The Welfare State helped to improve life for the poorest people: there was a wide range of benefits available, including family allowances for all children after the first (later known as child benefit); widows' benefits; more generous unemployment insurance, sickness and disability benefits; and old age pensions. There was even a system of income support supplements for those who were still struggling to make ends meet.

The great symbol of affluence was the motor car, which was now affordable for the working class, thanks to the increasing availability of credit. Sales rose from 1.5 million in 1945 to 5.5 million in 1960. In 1951, only 14 per cent of households owned a car, but by 1970 the number had risen to 52 per cent. The single most popular item in this orgy of consumerism was the television set – hardly anybody owned one in 1945, but by 1973 ownership was virtually 100 per cent. Another important development was that more people were able to buy their own homes, rather than renting: 'No greater social revolution occurred in the twentieth century,' claims Bernstein, 'than the rise of home ownership as the norm.' On the eve of the Second World War, barely a third of all houses were owner-occupied, but this had risen to two-thirds by 1981. At the end of the war, about 40 per cent of all houses in England and Wales had no indoor lavatory, and no bath or shower; 65 per cent did not have hot water; however, by 1990, virtually all houses had these amenities, and around half of working-class people were home-owners.

As well as spending their extra money on consumer goods, people were able to spend on leisure. Eating out became something of a national pastime, especially in the growing number of Chinese, Indian, Italian and Greek restaurants. The annual holiday became a national institution, even for the working class. In the late 1940s and the 1950s the domestic holiday resorts such as Blackpool, Southend, Brighton and Bournemouth, enjoyed their heyday. In the 1960s, holidays abroad, particularly in Spain, became popular. Arthur Marwick shows how the number of holidays taken by British people either at home or abroad rose steadily: 27 million in 1951, 34 million in 1961, 41 million in 1971, to a peak of 49 million in 1973. There was a slight fall in 1976 and 1977, and then the figure recovered again to 48 million in 1978. In 1951, only 2 million holidays were taken abroad, rising to 9 million in 1978, about a third of them to Spain. Continental travel was having its effects on British society in all sorts of ways: as Marwick puts it, 'often now the traditional fish-and-chip shop might be run by Indians, Pakistanis or Greeks, offering curry or kebabs in addition to the old standard fare.'

The country's health improved spectacularly after 1948, thanks partly to the new National Health Service (see Section 29.2(b)) which, in spite of the enormous cost, succeeded in providing treatment free for everybody at the point of delivery. Two good indicators of success were the infant mortality rate and the life expectancy rate. In 1938, the number of children in Britain dying before their fifth birthday was 55 per thousand; in slums and areas of overcrowding the death rate was much higher – in Newcastle it was 91 per thousand in 1937. However, by 1981, the national average had fallen to 15 per thousand, thanks largely to vaccination programmes and the increase in the proportion of births taking place in hospital. The introduction of free school milk in 1945 and regular medical inspections at school were part of the government's drive to secure children's welfare. Average life expectancy for men rose from 66 in 1950 to 70 by 1979, and for women it rose from 71 in 1950 to 75 in 1979.

Advances in medicine contributed to these improvements. The development of penicillin, the first antibiotic, which became available on prescription in 1946, soon proved its effectiveness against diseases such as pneumonia, meningitis and various bacterial infections. Soon the entire child population was being immunized against dangerous diseases such as diphtheria and measles. Tuberculosis, which had been a great killer well into the twentieth century, was brought under control by the use of a new antibiotic – streptomycin – introduced during the 1950s.

Education was another area that experienced improvement and expansion as the effects of the 1944 Butler Education Act began to spread (see Section 30.3(d)). Thousands more schools were built and new universities opened; by the early 1950s, it was possible for large numbers of children from working-class backgrounds to go on to university and, it was hoped, rise in the social scale. Of course, not everybody shared in the affluent society; some benefited more than others, and some hardly at all, as the next section will show. And by the early 1980s, with unemployment rising alarmingly, the gap between the 'haves' and 'have-nots' began to widen again.

31.2 a more equal society?

There seems to be little doubt that during the quarter of a century following the end of the Second World War, the gap between the rich and the poor in terms of income and property was narrowing. In fact, the trend was first noticed after the First World War. In the 1920s, the wealthiest 5 per cent of the population owned over 80 per cent of the nation's wealth; but at the end of the 1950s that figure had fallen to between 70 per cent and 60 per cent, and by the mid-1970s it had fallen to about 40 per cent. This distribution of wealth remained fairly static after the mid-1970s, but then income equality worsened again: a report by the Office of National Statistics in 2000 showed that the incomes of the top 10 per cent of the population rose by 38 per cent during the 1980s, but those of the bottom 10 per cent rose by only 5 per cent. This was partly because, as Bernstein points out, 'the Thatcher and Major governments cut the taxes of the richest [and] increased taxes for the poor'. He also shows that the inequality was not spread evenly over the country: 'prosperity was disproportionately concentrated in the South, while poverty was disproportionately concentrated in the regions of the Industrial Revolution'. In reality, in 2000, this meant in Wales, Scotland, Northern Ireland and the North of England. However, in the last two years of John Major's government (1995–7), the income gap between the top and bottom 10 per cent of the population began to narrow again.

Another striking development was the change in the definition of what was meant by 'class', together with an increase in social mobility. Sociologists introduced new classifications based on information about occupations and incomes given in the census returns, to enable them to analyse changes in social mobility. Anthony Heath and Clive Payne (in Halsey and Webb, 2000) defined six groups:

1 Higher salaried professionals and administrators.
2 Lower salaried semi-professionals and administrators.
3 Routine white-collar workers.
4 A petite-bourgeoisie of farmers, small employers and the self-employed.
5 Skilled manual workers and supervisors.
6 Semi-skilled and unskilled manual workers.

These sociological classes were not quite the same as the traditional upper, middle and lower classes. There is no landowning aristocracy as a separate group, which is indicative of one of the most radical changes in society since the nineteenth century. In 1873, a small group of about 7,000 people owned 80 per cent of the entire land in Britain. In 1967, there were only 200 peerage families still owning large estates, and the majority of agricultural land was in the hands of owner-farmers. Possession of wealth was now probably the main indicator defining membership of the upper class; the aristocracy had shrunk to just a small section of the upper class; and they had been joined by large numbers of industrialists, entrepreneurs, financiers, bankers, media personalities, lawyers, footballers and pop stars. Another indicator of being of the upper class remained an elite education at one of the best public schools – Eton, Harrow, Winchester or Rugby – followed by a university degree course at

Oxford or Cambridge – 'Oxbridge'. This was the kind of education which opened doors to the most prestigious jobs in the land. In Heath and Payne's classification, groups 1 and 2 correspond roughly to the upper and upper-middle class, the difference being mainly the size of business in which they are involved; 5 and 6 correspond to the upper and lower working class; leaving 3 and 4 as middle and lower-middle class. These divisions are not entirely satisfactory, because if the classification is made purely on grounds of income, it could be, for example, that a skilled worker earns more than a white-collar worker. But at least they provide a way of attempting to measure whether social mobility has increased or not.

Heath and Payne discovered that between 1964 and 1997 there was a marked increase in upward mobility, most strikingly into groups 1 and 2; 65 per cent of those in group 1 and 70 per cent of those in group 2 had moved up from a lower group; and what is more, 40 per cent of those joining group 1 and 50 per cent of those joining group 2 had moved up from the working class. The amount of downward mobility was much less – only about 20 per cent of those in the working-class groups had moved down from another group. As A. H. Halsey put it in 1995, 'Two out of every three middle class men today were not born into a middle class family.' A good education was the vital factor leading to upward mobility; a university degree was important for anybody from a working-class background hoping to move higher. Grants for tuition and lodging fees made it possible for rapidly increasing numbers of working-class young people to take university degrees from the late 1940s onwards.

However, some observers are convinced that this is not as impressive as it sounds. Gallie (in Halsey and Webb, 2000), for example, argues that while many people have moved up from the working class, this has not succeeded in breaking the privileged position of the upper and middle classes with their public school and Oxbridge backgrounds. He makes the point that the Heath and Payne survey and others like it only tell part of the story. Much of the upward movement from the working class took place because the number of manufacturing jobs was shrinking; in the 1980s alone, manufacturing employment fell by around 25 per cent, while jobs in service industries increased. In 1951, the working classes made up about two-thirds of the population; in 1991, the figure was not much above a third, while 56 per cent of the labour force were white-collar workers. It was almost as though the working class was disappearing into the middle class. Many skilled workers now thought of themselves as lower-middle-class, equivalent to clerical workers, whereas the clerical workers rejected this notion entirely. Bernstein concludes that there is much more than incomes to be considered when attempting to classify people: 'we need to look at what happened to British culture after 1945, since some of the most important constituents of class identity were cultural'.

The disturbing aspect of all this is that many of those people in groups 5 and 6 who failed to move up, for whatever reason, were likely to be worse off than before, as unemployment rose. In 1955, only some 298,000 people were out of work, but the figure fluctuated considerably after that: 621,000 in 1959; 376,000 in 1965; and 868,000 in 1971. Then the situation became more serious: 1.15 million in 1975, and 1.6 million in 1978. Clearly, poverty had not been eliminated in the 1960s and 1970s, though there were fewer poor people than before the war. The poor included the unemployed, especially those with families and young children; the elderly, the sick and the disabled; and women who were separated, divorced or widowed. Unemployment soared during the 1980s as a result of the Thatcher governments' economic policies, and consequently so did numbers of people falling below the poverty line. A survey carried out in 1999 concluded that 16 per cent of the population had an income that was below what was needed to achieve a minimum standard of living.

31.3 legal changes

During Wilson's governments of 1964–70, the Home Secretary for much of the time, Roy Jenkins, was able to put into practice what he saw as some of the essential requirements of a civilized society. One observer, Peter Hitchens, claimed that Jenkins revolutionized British social behaviour, 'from how long we stayed married, who we went to bed with and what sort of punishments we faced if we broke the law ... [his] programme had more effect on the way that life is lived in this country than the thoughts of any other post-war politician, including Margaret Thatcher'. On the other hand, conservatives in all parties later accused Labour of being responsible for the 'permissive society'. The main reforms were:

) *Abolition of the death penalty, 1965.* There had been growing disquiet for some time about the continuing practice of hanging convicted murderers. Labour MP, Sidney Silverman, had led a long campaign for capital punishment to be abolished. Jenkins described hanging as 'barbaric and useless', and many Conservatives, including R. A. Butler, a previous Home Secretary, supported this view. There had been several recent high-profile executions of people who had been convicted on very thin evidence. As opponents of hanging pointed out, if such convictions were later shown to be unsafe, there was no way of putting right a tragic miscarriage of justice. Accordingly, in 1965 the death penalty was abolished for a trial period of five years. Ironically, the general public was not strongly in favour of abolition: in June 1966, a survey suggested that barely 20 per cent of the population supported the government. In the 1966 election, Sidney Silverman found himself opposed in his Lancashire constituency of Nelson and Colne by an independent pro-hanging candidate who won more than 5,000 votes. Nevertheless, at the end of 1969 the death penalty was abolished for all crimes except treason.

) *Legalization of abortion, 1967.* Previously, abortion had been illegal but it was well-known that thousands of so-called 'back-street' abortions and self-induced miscarriages took place every year. Films such as *Alfie* and *A Taste of Honey* had shown both how common and how dangerous these unsupervised abortions were, and various women's groups campaigned for abortion to be made legal and obtainable on the NHS. Anglican churchmen were involved in the movement, suggesting that abortion could be justified 'if there was a threat to the mother's life or well-being', and including 'the life and well-being of the family'. A young Liberal MP, David Steel, with government support, introduced the bill which became the *Abortion Act*. Abortion was now legal, provided that two doctors thought it was medically or psychologically necessary. Private clinics soon appeared, charging affordable fees, and abortions were available on the NHS, though there was usually a wait for these. Unlike the abolition of hanging, surveys showed that around 70 per cent of the population supported the Abortion Act. Opponents of the Act included the Roman Catholic Church, which argued that abortion was 'legal murder' of unborn children; and those who believed it would lead to increased promiscuity. However, according to Dominic Sandbrook, while the number of abortions increased, 'there is no evidence that the legislation encouraged promiscuity, despite the conservative folk myth to the contrary. In fact a survey in 1972 of unmarried women who had had an abortion suggested that most were naïve and sexually inexperienced' rather than motivated by 'wilful self-indulgence'. The important thing was that the Act 'gave women the feeling that they controlled their own lives and bodies, so that pregnancy need not be a life-changing disaster'.

The Sexual Offences Act, 1967. Previously, all sexual acts between men were illegal, and homosexuality was regarded as an illness, a failure to grow up, or evidence of moral degeneracy and a sin. The majority of the general public were hostile to homosexuals, who had little alternative either to suppress their instincts and try to appear 'normal', or to risk arrest and a gaol sentence. The odd thing was that sexual acts between women were never illegal. Attitudes towards male homosexuality gradually became more liberal, so that it was viewed not as a sin or a crime to be punished, but a sickness that needed medical treatment. In the early 1960s the Homosexual Law Reform Society campaigned for a change in the law, and was supported by a number of Anglican bishops. In the Commons, the campaign was led by Welsh Labour MP, Leo Abse, and in the Lords by the Earl of Arran, a Liberal peer. The Act, which became law at the end of July 1967, legalized sexual acts in private between consenting male adults over the age of 21. The age of consent for heterosexual acts was lowered to 16, but was fixed at 21 for homosexual acts to avoid teenagers being corrupted by older men. The new law did not apply to Scotland or Northern Ireland, where feelings against homosexuality were much stronger; it was extended to Scotland in 1980, and to Northern Ireland in 1982.

Ironically, by then one of the unforeseen results of greater sexual freedom for homosexuals was becoming apparent – it was in 1981 that AIDS (acquired immune-deficiency syndrome) was first identified as a separate disease. One of the first victims in Britain was a gay man called Terrence Higgins. A group of his friends started a charity, the Terrence Higgins Trust, to warn gay men about AIDS and to encourage the use of condoms. The Trust soon became a national organization, and as knowledge about the disease spread – that it could be caught from infected needles used by drug-addicts and from blood transfusions – it led to a new openness in the way that sexual behaviour was discussed.

▸ *The Divorce Reform Act, 1969.* This removed the requirement that one of the partners in the divorce must admit some fault or guilt. Now the sole grounds for divorce were that 'the marriage has broken down irretrievably'. This Act was followed by *the Matrimonial Property Act (1970)*, which acknowledged for the first time that a wife's contribution to the marriage must be take into account when dividing up the property, which meant that a divorced woman would no longer be left penniless. Together, these Acts were a great step forward in improving the status of women and transforming marriage from a rather one-sided contract into an equal partnership. But it was a controversial development: critics saw it as a further step towards a permissive society. Britain already had the highest divorce rate in Europe, and during the first year following the passing of the Act, the total had almost doubled to 100,000. By 1981, it had reached around 150,000, and by 1985 it was calculated that almost half of all marriages ended in divorce.

31.4 changes in the status of women

(a) women at work

The campaign for women's political rights had been successful earlier in the century, when the vote was given to women aged over 30 (in 1918) and to women at the age of 21 (in 1929); women were first allowed to stand for Parliament in 1919. But there were still many other ways in which women were treated as second-class citizens. For example, they did not receive equal pay for doing similar jobs to men; in certain occupations, such as teaching and the civil service, women were often dismissed when they got married, on the grounds that they would be less reliable and would be prone to absenteeism when they had children. Many employers claimed that men deserved higher wages because they were more efficient, they were physically stronger, they were more committed to a career, and they needed higher pay to support a family. A further grievance for women was that too much emphasis was placed on their role as wives and mothers, and there was no assumption that 'women had the right to work'.

During the 1940s and 1950s, women's movements concentrated on achieving equal pay and fair treatment for women at work. Some occupations –

university lecturers, doctors, architects, MPs and people working for the BBC – already had equal pay for equal work, but the numbers of women working in these jobs were relatively small. However, the civil service, local government and teaching, which employed a much larger proportion of women, did not provide equal pay for equal work. Influential women's groups included the London and National Society for Women's Service, and the National Council of Women, which pressed for new laws to enforce equal pay. The Trades Union Congress (TUC) supported their aims, but favoured different methods. They encouraged women to join unions and hoped to win equal pay through union pressure and collective bargaining with employers. They were also supported by medical experts, who rejected the old argument that women's problems – menstruation and the menopause – made them less efficient than men, pointing out that women needed and deserved higher pay to bring their standards of health up to a level equal to those of their male counterparts.

Progress was slow; in 1944, a clause in the Butler Education Act that would have given women teachers equal pay with men was thrown out on the grounds that it would damage the morale of the men in the profession. The first success came in 1955, when women in the civil service were granted equal pay by the Conservatives. No further progress was made through legislation, however, until the mid-1970s, when the prospect of Britain joining the EEC brought the matter into prominence. During the thirty years from 1951 to 1981 the numbers of women in full-time work remained fairly steady at between five and six million. But the numbers in part-time work increased significantly, from less than a million to just over 4 million, or about 44 per cent of the total. Previously, most married women had given up work when they had children, but during the 1960s many began to return to work after having a family. This change was at least partly responsible for the rapid increase of women in part-time work. As George L. Bernstein puts it: 'At least initially, many of these women went into part-time work as a way of increasing the family income, especially as hard times hit in the 1970s and 1980s. They then came to see work as a good thing in itself … not only did it give them a sense of independence; it provided a social life outside the home.'

Some working-class women in trade unions made more progress by going on strike. The one that attracted the most publicity was in 1968, when women sewing-machinists at the Ford plant in Dagenham went on strike for equal pay. They were upholstering car seats, but were paid only 85 per cent of men's wages for doing the same job. Barbara Castle, the Minister of Labour, intervened in the dispute and Ford agreed to close most of the gap.

(b) feminism and the Women's Liberation Movement

During the 1960s, women's protest groups, influenced by feminist writers such as Germaine Greer and Kate Millett, became more radical. They soon became known collectively as the Women's Liberation Movement (WLM) or 'women's lib' for short. As well as equal pay, they demanded higher wages for poorly-paid women, and wages for housewives. But their aims were much wider than the earlier women's groups. They focused on issues such as the recognition of women's right to have the same sexual freedom as men, to be able to enjoy sex before marriage, and to use contraceptives whenever they chose to do so. Other demands included the availability of divorce and abortion, and a recognition of gay and lesbian rights. They were highly critical of violence and the authoritarian role of men within the family; and of any form of sexism at work, in the media, in organizations and institutions, and in general behaviour in everyday life. Some feminists totally rejected the traditional expectation that women must become wives and mothers; they wanted equal opportunities with men, and the right to work whenever, at whatever and for how long they chose. Some extremists saw lesbianism as the ultimate expression of women's freedom from male domination.

Gradually, the feminist movement convinced the Labour party that at least some of their demands were reasonable; the Wilson governments of 1964–70 went some way towards satisfying them. As we saw in the previous section, the *legalization of abortion in 1967* and *the Divorce Reform Act of 1969* were important steps forward. They allowed women more choice over their lives and so increased their personal freedom. However, feminist critics of the new laws complained that:

▸ Decisions about whether or not abortion was appropriate were still in the hands of doctors, most of whom at that time were male. This eventually became less of a problem, as more women doctors qualified.
▸ Divorced women, even those who received a reasonable financial settlement, were often doomed to a lower standard of living, at least until equal pay for women became a reality.

In 1970, the Women's Liberation Movement held its first national conference at Ruskin College, Oxford, attended by over 500 women. They drew up a list of four main demands: equal education and opportunity; equal pay; free and automatically available contraception and abortion; and nursery provision for young children over the whole country. Later that same year, Germaine Greer's influential bestselling feminist classic, *The Female Eunuch* appeared. According to Dominic Sandbrook, this was 'a sparkling argument for female liberation from stereotyping, passivity and male condescension'. Over the next decade, thanks to a combination of the feminist campaigns and the efforts of working-class women such as the Ford sewing-machinists, many of the women's demands were met.

1 In 1970, *the Equal Pay Act* was hurried through Parliament but proved to be something of a disappointment; it was watered down so as not to upset the Conservatives too much, and while it helped some women, it did not apply to part-time workers and was only voluntary for employers. But at least the principle of equal pay for equal work had been acknowledged.

2 *The Sex Discrimination Act of 1975*, and another *Equal Pay Act*, both Labour measures, made inequalities of pay illegal and banned discrimination on gender grounds in appointments, promotions, dismissals, redundancies, and access to training, education and credit. However, discrimination in matters such as social security, taxation and pension rights were not included. Even so, the new legislation made quite an impact on the treatment and employment of women. There was a whole series of cases in which female employees were successful in eliminating discriminatory practices; the two which probably gained the most publicity were those against the Civil Service in 1977, and one against the shipbuilders, Cammell Laird, in 1983.

3 A striking development in education was *the increasing numbers of women in higher education*. Between 1970 and 1989, the numbers of full-time male undergraduates at universities increased by 20 per cent, while the numbers of women increased by 30 per cent, helping to rectify an earlier imbalance against women. Most of the women came from the middle class, though, with very few from the unskilled working class.

The range of female participation expanded into other areas. In sport, for example, women regularly played soccer, rugby and cricket, and there were women's teams right up to national level. Women were first ordained as priests in the Church of Scotland in 1968, and in the Church of England in 1994. Margaret Thatcher became leader of the Conservative party (1975), the first female leader of a British political party, and then the first British woman Prime Minister in 1970. Numbers of women MPs gradually increased; in the 1997 election, 100 women Labour MPs were elected and the new government had five women in the Cabinet.

On the other hand, it has to be acknowledged that there were still limits to what women could hope to achieve. For example, the vast majority of discrimination cases brought by women to industrial tribunals are unsuccessful: in 1984, no fewer than 380 cases were brought, but only 63 were upheld. Women in the workplace still tended to encounter informal or unofficial types of discrimination, which made it more difficult for them to gain promotion and were difficult to bring complaints against. Nevertheless, this should not detract from the fact that, between them, these middle- and working-class women, by expanding into the workforce and asserting their equal status with men, were responsible for huge advances. In the words of Dominic Sandbrook, 'they had a profound effect on the way men saw women and women saw themselves. If we are looking for a genuine revolution, then perhaps this was it.'

31.5 the Swinging Sixties – a permissive society?

In March 1982, the Prime Minister, Margaret Thatcher, blamed the recent riots in Brixton and Toxteth on what had happened during the 1960s: 'We are reaping what was sown in the 1960s,' she declared. 'Fashionable theories and permissive claptrap set the scene for a society in which the old virtues of discipline and self-restraint were denigrated.' Historians have written at great length about the 'permissive society' of the late 1950s through to the early 1970s, and about the more tolerant and relaxed attitude towards many social issues and practices. These included the relaxation of censorship rules in literature, films and the theatre, greater sexual freedom, feminism and the Women's Liberation Movement, a series of protest movements, a decline in religious practices, and the emergence of a distinct youth culture. Clearly, some significant changes did take place, though a few historians, most recently Dominic Sandbrook, believe that Britain changed much less in the 1960s than is generally argued.

(a) censorship changes

Before the 1960s, strict controls were applied to films, the theatre and literature regarding how far they could go in showing and writing about explicit sex and violence. The British Board of Film Classification was the first to adopt a more lenient attitude when, in 1959, it allowed *Room at the Top* to be shown. Adapted from the novel by John Braine, the film won approving reviews; the *Daily Express* enthused: 'at long last a British film has got its teeth into those subjects which have always been part and parcel of our lives, but have hitherto been taboo subjects on the prissy British screen – male ambition in all its ruthlessness, and sex in all its earthy compulsion.' It had an 'X' certificate, which meant that it could only be seen by people over the age of 18. *Room at the Top* was soon followed by other 'New Wave' films – *Saturday Night and Sunday Morning* (1960), *A Taste of Honey* (1961) and *This Sporting Life* (1963).

The new leniency was seen at the same time in literature. Some famous novels had been banned for years for what was considered to be their obscene content, including James Joyce's *Ulysses* and D. H. Lawrence's *Lady Chatterley's Lover*. In 1955, a London bookshop owner was sent to gaol for stocking copies of *Lady Chatterley's Lover*. However, in 1959, the government passed the *Obscene Publications Act*, which allowed 'literary merit' to be presented as a defence against criminal charges. Lawrence's publisher, Penguin Books, decided to test the new legislation by printing 200,000 copies of *Lady Chatterley's Lover* . The Director of Public Prosecutions brought a case against Penguin Books for obscenity, and in 1960 the nation was treated to a famous trial at the Old Bailey that lasted six days and made headlines around the world. The counsel for the prosecution, Mervyn Griffith Jones, began by listing the obscenities used by Lawrence in his novel; but he did not help his case when he asked the largely working-class jury: 'Is this a book that you would have lying around in your own house ... a book you would wish your wife or your servants to read?' Eventually, Penguin Books were acquitted on all charges and the novel became a bestseller. Lawrence's stepdaughter remarked, 'I feel that a window has been opened and fresh air has blown right through

England.' Soon afterwards, *Ulysses* was published without being prosecuted, and this was followed by even more sexually explicit novels such as *Last Exit to Brooklyn* and *The Tropic of Cancer*. The theatre had to wait longer, and it was 1968 before theatre censorship was abolished.

(b) sexual freedom

There were certainly some remarkable changes in sexual behaviour during the 1960s and 1970s. As we saw earlier (see Section 31.3), abortion and divorce became much easier to obtain, and homosexual acts in private were decriminalized in the late 1960s. Oral contraceptives became available in Britain during the early 1960s, and from 1967 local authorities set up family planning clinics which could provide 'the pill'. In the 1970s contraceptive pills became available on the NHS. This meant that the risk of unwanted pregnancy declined, and people could indulge in more casual sex if they wanted to. Whether this did in fact lead to a significant increase in casual sex is unclear. What certainly did happen was that more people began to live together before marriage; the age at which they married increased; and more children were born outside marriage. At the same time, as George L. Bernstein points out, 'feminists saw the loosening of constraints on sexual behaviour (when there was no implication of marriage to follow) as central to ending the double standard which had accepted such sexual activity for men but not for women'. All this, and in particular the contraceptive pill, gave women a sense of being in control that they had never had before. As Bernstein puts it: 'All this change reflected the new attitude that women did not have to feel guilty about sex any more – either about wanting it, having it or liking it.'

(c) a rash of protest movements

The late 1950s and the 1960s was a time of protest movements, most of them peaceful, and most of them directed towards the aim of securing and maintaining world peace.

▸ *The Campaign for Nuclear Disarmament (CND)* was started in 1958 by a group of writers, Quakers, politicians (including the socialist, Michael Foot) and churchmen (including Canon John Collins of St Paul's Cathedral). Many people had been particularly incensed to learn that American bombers carrying hydrogen bombs were patrolling the skies above the UK (see also Section 33.1(h)). The CND immediately attracted great publicity: over 5,000 people attended the inaugural meeting at Westminster, and some were arrested when they went on to protest in Downing Street. Ultimately, the campaign failed, both to persuade the political parties to renounce nuclear weapons and to stop the build-up of American nuclear weapons on British soil. On the other hand, in the words of Andrew Marr: it was successful in 'seizing the imagination of millions of people. For a ramshackle left-wing organization, it behaved in a thoroughly modern and media-savvy way ... its symbol, based on semaphore, became an international brand'.

- *The New Left* movement developed around the same time from an alliance of former communists who had left the party because they disapproved of the Soviet invasion of Hungary in 1956, and radical members of the Labour party who were fed up with the official Labour consensus politics and its support for retaining nuclear weapons. In 1957, four Oxford radicals – Stuart Hall, Gabriel Pearson, Raphael Samuel and Charles Taylor – founded a new left-wing magazine which eventually merged with another publication run by a Marxist historian, E. P. Thompson. They called the new magazine the *New Left Review*, which is still published at the time of writing. They lent their support to most of the protest organizations of the time, particularly the CND and the anti-Vietnam War movement. One of the most influential members of the New Left was Raymond Williams, who was responsible for putting forward an alternative view of what was meant by culture. He argued that, when people talked about 'culture', what they really meant was the culture of the elite, because it was the elite themselves who had defined it. He suggested that the culture of ordinary people – such as cinema, sport and popular music – should not be dismissed as being of no importance; it should be just as worthy of investigation as the culture of the elite.

This new approach to culture became the basis of the new discipline of cultural studies, which developed at the University of Birmingham under the leadership of Stuart Hall in the late 1960s and the early 1970s. A similar approach was taken up by social historians in the USA, and by the Marxist historians E. P. Thompson and Eric Hobsbawm in the UK. As George L. Bernstein puts it, this new history was 'from the bottom up' instead of 'from the top down'. They aimed to rescue ordinary people 'from simply being the masses or the mob, ignorant and purposeless in their actions, reacting to what others imposed ... Rather they showed how these people constructed their lives for themselves'. In this way the British New Left made an important contribution to the renewal of the international left. For the British right, however, this was absolute anathema, the sort of thing Norman Tebbit later called 'the insufferable, smug, wet, pink orthodoxy of the third-rate minds of that third-rate decade, the 1960s'.

- *The anti-Vietnam War movement* included members of the New Left as well as assorted believers in an 'alternative society' or a 'counter-culture'. It began in 1965 as the British Council for Peace in Vietnam, which organized peaceful demonstrations outside the American Embassy in Grosvenor Square in London. By 1968, the movement was attracting a great deal of publicity, and in March, Britain saw its biggest anti-war march to date. One of the organizers was Tariq Ali, a charismatic young Pakistani who had been president of the Oxford Union. Around 25,000 people gathered in Trafalgar Square and marched to the American Embassy. Violent clashes soon broke out between police and demonstrators, and eventually ranks of mounted police charged into the crowd, sparking off what became known as the 'Battle of Grosvenor Square'.

Some accounts blame the police, who seem to have been rather 'truncheon-happy', and others blame the demonstrators, many of whom were said to be 'spoiling for a fight and were delighted to be given the opportunity'. Another large demonstration in October 1968 passed off without serious incident. This proved to be the peak of the movement, however, and it seemed to have lost momentum by the end of the 1960s. Dominic Sandbrook dismisses its effectiveness, arguing that it never appealed to the general public, and that it was mainly a movement of young, middle-class students who were copying 'the style of American protest movements because they thought they were fashionable'. Most historians would probably not agree entirely with this analysis; there can be little doubt that these protests helped to persuade Wilson's government to resist American pressure and stay out of Vietnam.

▸ *A wave of student protest movements* took place in the late 1960s, also following the example of American campus protests. The trouble began at the London School of Economics (LSE) in January 1967 with the appointment of a new director who had previously been principal of University College, Rhodesia. The student union accused him of being 'an accessory to racism' and organized demonstrations to have the appointment cancelled. By January 1969, the LSE seemed to have become ungovernable, but eventually the students realized they could not win, and the protests fizzled out. During 1968 there were protest demonstrations and sit-ins at many other universities and colleges demanding more student control, more up-to-date teaching methods, and an end to military research in universities. A few concessions were made – most universities relaxed some of their more old-fashioned rules and allowed student representatives to sit on committees; and in the end the authorities were able to restore order. There was no comparison between the UK student protests and those taking place at the same time in the USA, France and Germany, possibly because British students had less to complain about. There is disagreement among historians about how significant these 'counter-cultural' movements were. Arthur Marwick, writing in 1998, claims that they 'permeated and transformed' mainstream culture. Dominic Sandbrook (2006) disagrees: in his view they 'made little difference to the lives of most ordinary people ... it is very hard to point to any substantive changes that came about as a result'.

(d) the decline of religious practices

Some historians see the decline of religious practices, at least those connected with traditional organized religion, as a sign of the permissive society; yet this was a trend that had started, significantly, soon after the First World War. It has been estimated that church attendance roughly halved between 1900 and 1995. However, some observers believe that a large proportion of those who went to church in the earlier part of the century did so mainly for the social life and because it was thought to be a sign of middle-class respectability, not because they were especially 'religious'. So in fact the decline of religion may be something of myth; while only about 10 per cent of the population were regular churchgoers in 1950, they were arguably the more committed members – the true believers. In fact attendances at Roman Catholic churches increased between 1950 and 1970; reasons for this included the continued arrival of migrant workers from Ireland, and the modernizing reform of church practices introduced as a result of the Second Vatican Council.

Nevertheless, the traditional churches were concerned about the decline in numbers; consequently, the Anglican Church brought out a new translation of the Bible and a modern Alternative Prayer Book to the 1666 Book of Common Prayer. Robert Runcie (Archbishop of Canterbury from 1980 until 1991) tried to re-create the Church's traditional role as moral and social conscience of the nation, presenting the Church as the protector of the urban poor and the underclass. He also criticized the self-centredness and the materialism of the early 1980s, and this caused tensions with the Thatcher government. In 1994, the modernizers were successful in at last winning the struggle for the ordination of women as priests, though this caused a split in the Anglican Church, and many left to join the Roman Catholic Church, which still refused to ordain women or to allow priests to marry. However, in spite of the changes, the slow fall in church attendance continued; even the Catholic Church began to show signs of decline. Worst affected were the Nonconformists, whose numbers declined so disastrously that many of their chapels were demolished or converted to other uses.

But while most of the traditional churches seemed to be in decline, the newer 'alternative' Christian churches were growing, particularly the Pentecostal churches with their emphasis on the Holy Spirit and the development of charismatic spiritual gifts. Some members of the Church of England have also moved in this direction, and Anglican churches that have elements of Pentecostalism in their services tend to find their congregations increasing. In a survey carried out in the mid-1980s, well over half of those questioned said they believed in God and prayed to God, though the vast majority of them were not happy with organized religion. Summing up the evidence, Bernstein concludes that, apart from the acceptance of sex outside marriage and the new freedom for women, 'religiously based values held up very well among the British people ... There was only a hint in 1984 of more permissive attitudes among the young (those aged eighteen to thirty-four)'. And in the late 1970s a reaction set in against the permissive society, as Margaret Thatcher proclaimed a return to Victorian values.

31.6 youth culture, consumerism and the media

(a) the emergence of youth culture

Many observers date the beginning of a distinct youth culture to 1956, with the arrival of rock 'n' roll in Britain from the USA. Bill Haley and the Comets in the film soundtrack to *Rock Around the Clock* gave the British public its first chance to sample the new music being provided by the likes of Elvis Presley, Little Richard and Jerry Lee Lewis, who were taking the USA by storm. Home-grown British rock acts such as Cliff Richard and Tommy Steele soon came to the forefront, and before long they had influenced groups such as the Beatles, the Animals and the Rolling Stones. This was just one aspect of the American influences on Britain at the time; everything 'American', including jeans and T-shirts, fast food, coffee bars and rock music, was thought to be glamorous, and the new American music was especially appealing to young people. In fact, many people felt that 'Americanization' was going too far and was threatening to overwhelm British culture. The BBC was one of the leading organizations that tried to resist this trend, favouring British artists in preference to Americans. However, young people soon grew impatient with only British groups – they wanted American artists, whom they saw as the real thing. Potential rivals to the BBC were quick to seize the opportunity to satisfy this demand: Radio Luxembourg and ITV began operations, and later 'pirate' radio stations such as Radio Caroline began to broadcast from ships moored off the English coast.

The idea soon caught on that young people were a potentially important market to be targeted, using rock 'n' roll as a key product; and so the idea of the 'teenager' as a separate group with a distinct identity was born. It was also a much larger group than ever before, because of the so-called 'baby boom': these were the children born during or just after the war, who were reaching their teens in the later 1950s and early 1960s, just as the economy was emerging from austerity. Working-class school-leavers were likely to be able to find jobs and to have money to spend. Many members of the older generations were horrified at rock 'n' roll, and Parliament even tried to ban certain records. Politicians were disturbed by this new preoccupation of young people; some on the left felt that teenagers were focusing too much on leisure and not enough on serious pursuits such as politics; some on the right felt that it was all undermining moral standards. The British record industry did well out of the new music, and people began to claim that rock 'n' roll was the spearhead of much of the social and cultural change that took place during the 1960s. Later, the 1960s were labelled as the 'Swinging Sixties' and 'the permissive society', a time of liberation and relaxed morals. The media exaggerated all this and people accepted it as gospel. But in fact, whatever effect rock 'n' roll had was only incidental – basically it was an economic phenomenon in which the record companies and agents went to extraordinary lengths to market their new products.

Nevertheless, it was a very effective campaign; during the 1960s there was a great flowering of the British version of the new music: the Beatles, the Shadows, the Rolling Stones and many others were taken up by major record labels. Liverpool and other cities in the North, together with London, were the main centres of the new culture, drawing on black rhythm and blues music. Liverpool seemed to produce most of the musicians, and London handled the marketing. Soon the unbelievable reverse had happened – British groups became popular in the USA and began to influence American music; and they were a huge financial success. In 1965 the Beatles were awarded MBEs, partly because of the popularity of their music but partly thanks to their financial success. In fact, with their collarless jackets and distinctive hairstyles, they were a product of clever management and marketing by their record producers and image creators. Clearly, by this time, the new music had been accepted as harmless and even respectable. By 1970, rock music was viewed as mainstream and various new genres were being pushed on to the market – reggae, folk-rock and progressive rock, and teeny-bop.

The new culture also involved clothes, general lifestyle and behaviour. It was a time of self-expression and a refusal to conform. Instead of imitating their parents, young people wanted to copy their heroes' clothes and hairstyles. Again, commercial companies were quick to realize that teenagers had plenty of money to spend, thanks to the growing economic prosperity of the country and to the fact that most of them were free agents, with no children or mortgages to finance. The clothes and record industries, hairdressers, makers of transistor radios, and owners of coffee bars all did well out of the new culture, and did their best to encourage teenagers to become aware of their special identity – and to spend more money. The coffee bar became the vital meeting place for young people, where they could listen to music played on juke boxes; sometimes there was even live music.

(b) a social, economic, political and cultural revolution?

Street gangs of working-class youths were nothing new in Britain, and there were plenty of them in the 1940s and 1950s. There were often fights between rival groups, and they were generally viewed as hooligans or juvenile delinquents. However, until 1960, young men were required to do National Service, which tended to socialize them and make them conform. After National Service was abolished in 1960, they no longer had this sobering experience, and as older teenagers, were free to continue with their earlier lifestyle and take full advantage of the new relaxed social and economic climate. Some historians have described the new teenage culture as a 'social revolution'. Others believe it was exaggerated out of all proportion, and was perhaps no more than a creation of the media and the way in which the media chose to portray it. Film-makers and television producers targeted young people by providing them with films and programmes that were relevant to their own experience. Even the BBC, which had stoutly resisted playing rock music for years, eventually gave way to market demands and created 'Radio 1'. Films such as *Alfie*, and TV programmes such as *Ready, Steady, Go!*, *The Old Grey Whistle Test* and *Top of the Pops* appeared. By the end of the 1960s there can be little doubt that popular tastes had been influenced by the products aimed at young people in record and clothes shops, in the cinema, and on radio and television.

On the other hand, most British young people were not rebels, and certainly not revolutionaries. As George L. Bernstein explains, the perception that they *were* rebels 'resulted from the fact that adults often mistook youth *subcultures* as representative of youth in general ... These subcultures often *were* rebellious. They were also more visible than mainstream youth, got much more media attention and so generated anxiety and even panic among adults'. The first of the subcultures – the Teddy Boys – appeared in the 1950s, and were mainly from the unskilled working class. Their distinctive style of dress was part Edwardian dandy and part American river-boat gambler. The American influence was strong – they stood for rebellion against authority, they got into fights in dance-halls and cinemas, they were generally seen as thugs and hooligans – and, like all the subcultures, they liked rock music.

By the end of the 1950s, the Teddy boys had almost faded out and the new subcultures were the Mods and Rockers, who emerged in the mid-1960s. They first came into prominence at Easter 1964, when clashes occurred between the two groups at Clacton, a seaside resort in Essex. Other incidents occurred at Margate and Brighton during the summer; they were eagerly seized on by the press, which reported them in lurid detail. The Mayor of Margate complained that they were encouraging more violence by such over-sensational reporting, but the *Daily Mirror* indignantly rejected any such suggestion. The Rockers were mainly from the unskilled working class and cultivated a macho image like the 1950s motorcycle gangs. They wore black leather jackets and had their hair long and greasy. The Mods came largely from the lower ranks of middle-class white-collar workers. They had more money to spend than the Rockers; they dressed stylishly – Italian high fashion was popular – and they rode scooters. They helped to bring middle-class youth into a culture that had been mainly working class. Carnaby Street in London became the centre of men's fashions; and girls had their own styles too – Mary Quant mini-skirts and the cheaper designs of Biba (designed by Barbara Hulanicki). According to Andrew Marr: 'This was the beginning of the buy-and-throw-away consumer culture applied to clothing, and though it would brim with moral dilemmas later, in the sixties it seemed simple freedom for millions of women. This was underscored by the Biba look, that Audrey Hepburn gawkiness.'

Another aspect of youth culture that developed in the late 1960s was the 'hippy' sub-culture or counter-culture, fuelled by now easily obtainable drugs (particularly LSD and cannabis). Hippies dressed in a deliberately shabby way and wore their hair long; they claimed to worship nature and talked about 'flower power'; their slogans were 'Love' and 'Peace'. The movement had its own magazines such as *Oz*, *Rolling Stone* and *International Times*, and took up radical political causes. They were involved in the student movement campaigning for more control over their academic studies, in the anti-Vietnam War protests, in the CND, and in the movement for women's liberation. The numbers involved in these political protests were in fact quite small and mainly middle class, though the original youth culture sprang from working-class origins. Both middle- and working-class young people shared the same rock music, which gave them a sense of a separate cultural identity. The counter-culture did have its own special influences, which were perhaps most obvious, apart from their so-called 'underground' magazines, in films such as *If ...* and *Oh, Lucky Man*, in which film producer Lindsay Anderson mocked the British public school and class system; and in *How I Won the War*, in which Richard Lester, famous for his Beatles film *A Hard Day's Night*, switched styles and treated the cinema-going public to a parody of British war films. By the early 1970s, the hippy movement had passed its peak.

From around 1969, as the economy ran into trouble and unemployment increased, the subcultures became more aggressive. The skinheads presented a tough, working-class image and they attacked other minority groups that they perceived as being middle-class, including hippies, immigrants and homosexuals. The year 1976 saw the launch of punk, which brought with it a whole new range of fashion and lifestyle products and its own magazine. Punk bands seemed to be, or so the media claimed, an expression of working-class anger at unemployment, consumerism and authority in general. Groups such as the Sex Pistols shocked the nation with their overtly political and vulgar lyrics, and by swearing on TV. Ironically, this musical culture was developed as an art form by middle-class musicians and then taken up by working-class youth. The establishment saw the punks as a sign of Britain's continuing decline, which was exactly the kind of reaction the punks had hoped to generate. Some punk bands played an important part in the anti-racist movement of the 1970s. Rock against Racism was formed in 1976, with the Clash and their lead singer Joe Strummer at the forefront. The following year, they helped to organize the much wider Anti-Nazi League.

In the light of all this evidence, it seems certain that some sort of revolution was taking place among young people, and it was arguably an economic one. Andrew Marr believes that the youth culture of the 1960s influenced many things in Britain, 'but not in order to usher in some kind of anarcho-socialist paradise full of hairy people in boiler-suits, dropping acid, indulging in free love and cultivating allotments. No, the older Britain was being pushed aside so that our current democracy of shopping and celebrity could nose its way smoothly in'. It was the economic power of young people as a group that was entirely new, and it was this that made possible the associated cultural, rather than a social or political, revolution.

31.7 immigration and race relations

(a) immigration before 1945

Immigration to Britain did not begin in 1945. Robert Winder, in his book *Bloody Foreigners* (2004), shows that there have been continuous waves of immigration since 7000 BC. Immigrants included French Huguenots (Protestants) escaping from Catholic persecution in the sixteenth century; Irish labourers looking for a better life, (though legally they were classed as internal migrants, not foreigners) – over half a million by 1900; and European Jews fleeing from persecution in Russia and Poland (around 150,000 by 1900). Hostility and even violence towards immigrants was a marked feature of life in large urban areas; in east London, for example, local groups blamed immigrants for overcrowding and rent increases, and complained about their cultural differences. It was in response to such protests that Balfour's Conservative government introduced the *Aliens Act of 1905*. This was designed to limit entry into Britain to those who were financially self-supporting, and to keep out criminals and other undesirables. One of the government's motives was the hope that the Act would win them working-class votes in the imminent election.

In 1919, after the end of the First World War, another Aliens Act further tightened up the rules. Immigrants now had to have a work permit before they were allowed into the country, they had to register with the police, and faced deportation if they caused trouble. During the 1930s there was a steady influx of German Jews fleeing from Nazi persecution, so that by 1939 there were well over 300,000 Jews in Britain. However, they had been carefully chosen according to their wealth, skills and political outlook. Even so, there was a great deal of anti-Jewish feeling, despite many of the Jews making a valuable contribution to the war effort between 1939 and 1945. The hostility towards immigrants always sprang from the belief that they were causing overcrowding, poor housing conditions and an increase in unemployment, and that they were taking jobs away from local people. On the other hand, there are two important points to bear in mind:

- while between 1900 and 1939 around 10 million people came to live in Britain, during the same period over 14 million Britons emigrated, mainly to the USA, Canada and Australia; and
- blaming unemployment during the inter-war period solely on immigrants fails to take into account the dire economic situation and the depression of the 1930s.

(b) after the Second World War

Immediately after the Second World War there was full employment and a labour shortage, which caused the new Labour government to recruit what were called 'displaced persons' – Poles, Latvians, Lithuanians, Estonians, Belgians, Ukrainians and Italians who had been forced out of their homeland as a result of the war. Some were living in displacement camps in Europe, others had already escaped to Britain and simply stayed on. They were able to play an invaluable part in post-war reconstruction. In 1948, the Attlee government introduced the *British Nationality Act*, which allowed all citizens of Commonwealth countries entry into Britain. Many West Indians took advantage of this, and later that year the first group of Jamaicans arrived in a converted troopship, the MV *Empire Windrush*, soon to be followed by thousands more. Many of them worked as doctors and nurses in the new National Health Service; others got jobs as public transport workers. As the labour shortage continued into the early 1950s, recruitment spread to India and Pakistan; many businesses and firms encouraged people to come to Britain by advertising in Commonwealth countries for workers; thousands of Pakistanis came to work in the north-west's textile industry and in the West Midlands. As members of the British Empire and Commonwealth, they had been brought up to admire the British way of life, and they hoped to improve their standard of living by coming to work in a country presented to them as both affluent and welcoming.

During the 1950s, on average, about 30,000 immigrants a year entered Britain. During the early 1960s the numbers increased, averaging about 60,000 a year. The peak years were 1961, with 115,000 and 1962, with 108,000. This sharp increase in immigration in the 1960s was caused by rumours that the British government was planning to restrict further immigration, which it did in 1962, so during the 1970s immigration was much lower. In 1971, there were about 2 million non-whites living in Britain; roughly two-thirds of them had come from Commonwealth countries, mainly from the West Indies, India, Pakistan and Hong Kong. The other third had been born in Britain. Non-whites were only a tiny proportion of the population, at most only 4 per cent.

(c) the British government restricts immigration

Unfortunately, these new British citizens were often received with some hostility by local people. Just as in the 1930s, the immigrants were blamed for problems such as shortages of affordable housing, and there were fears for jobs. Now there was the added racial dimension: there were anti-black riots in Liverpool and Birmingham (1948–9) and in various parts of London. Tensions between black and white communities increased, and trouble exploded in the Notting Hill riots of 1958. The surge of immigration in 1961 and 1962 was the final straw – the fear was that if this continued it would cause serious economic and social problems. There might not be enough jobs to go round, and if there was unemployment among immigrants, that would place an extra burden on the social services. There were calls for the government to put a stop to the influx of Commonwealth citizens, and successive governments duly obliged. Restrictions gradually reduced immigration to a trickle.

1 Harold Macmillan's *Commonwealth Immigrants Act (1962)* limited immigration from the Commonwealth or the colonies to people who could show that they had a job to come to, or who had special skills needed in Britain, and to people who already had close relatives in Britain. This was criticized by both the Labour and Liberal parties because it did not apply to people from non-Commonwealth countries who could still come in without restriction. This seemed deliberately racist, designed specifically to keep out unskilled black workers.

2 Harold Wilson's Labour government (1964–70) tightened restrictions further, in spite of Labour having criticized the Conservatives for starting the policy. But public opinion seemed to be firmly against unlimited immigration. In the 1964 election the sitting Labour MP for Smethwick (Birmingham), which had a large immigrant population, Patrick Gordon Walker, had been defeated by an anti-immigration candidate. Faced with such a vote-loser, Labour felt that it had no choice but to act. From 1965, only 8,500 Commonwealth immigrants were allowed into Britain each year, and the quota was later reduced to 1,500 a year. This was to keep out thousands of Asians who were leaving Kenya to escape hostile treatment by the Kenyan government. When, in 1968, all Asians were expelled from Kenya, most of them were obliged to go elsewhere – mainly to Canada, Australia, New Zealand and India, even when they held British passports. In the middle of the crisis over the Kenyan Asians, leading Conservative MP Enoch Powell made his inflammatory 'rivers of blood' speech in Birmingham. Although Heath immediately sacked Powell from the shadow Cabinet, the speech suggested that a Conservative government would be even tougher on immigration than Labour. London dockers, Smithfield meat market workers and Heathrow airport staff all demonstrated in support of Powell. During the 1970 election some Conservatives campaigned on the slogan 'Keep Britain White', which may well have helped to swing the election in the Conservatives' direction.

3 Edward Heath duly obliged with his *1971 Immigration Act*. This limited entry to people from the Commonwealth who could prove that they had some connection or family ties with the UK; nor could they bring in members of their families. On the positive side, the government could, on occasion, be persuaded to make exceptions on humanitarian grounds. For example, in 1972, when Idi Amin expelled Uganda's Asian citizens, the Conservative government allowed around 29,000 to come to Britain, in spite of strong objections from Powell, who consequently resigned from the party.

4 The Thatcher governments of the 1980s tended to be more in sympathy with the viewpoint of Enoch Powell, who once famously remarked 'to be born in Britain does not make West Indians or other immigrants British'. The *1981 Nationality Act* redefined the requirements for British citizenship. Being born in Britain was not sufficient – you had to be able to show familial links

to British citizens. As Lawrence Black (writing in 2004) explains, 'government suspicion of immigrants ran deep in the 1980s, visa controls became widespread and only limited numbers of affluent, skilled residents were allowed into Britain when Hong Kong passed into Chinese sovereignty in 1997 ... Today, Britain's are the tightest entry controls within the European Union.'

(d) race relations

On the whole in Britain there was nothing like the bitterness and violence seen in the USA and South Africa, and all immigrants had full civil rights. But racism was still evident; many white people refused to accept non-whites as equals and showed their prejudice in a variety of ways – such as refusing to serve non-whites in pubs and restaurants, and refusing to give them jobs or allow them to rent houses, flats and rooms. The sign 'NO DOGS, NO COLOUREDS' was common. When jobs and houses became fewer, whites felt more threatened, and their hostility to West Indians and Asians increased. Non-whites felt that the police were prejudiced against them, and relations with the police were often tense.

The irony was that government attempts to limit immigration helped to convince people that immigrants really were dangerous and threatening to British culture and the British way of life. While most politicians were careful not to make racist comments in public, the trade unions complained bitterly about 'all the blacks coming in to take their jobs' and at lower rates of pay. It was at street level that hostility showed itself at its worst, especially among young working-class white men who lived in the areas into which immigrants were moving. But it was only the black and Asian immigrants who aroused so much resentment. Migrants were also arriving in Britain from Europe: about 20,000 came from Hungary in 1956 following the Soviet invasion; by the mid-1950s about 10 per cent of the population of Bedford was Italian; workers from the Irish Republic also continued to arrive – about a million of them between 1945 and 1960. But they were not conspicuous and seemed to integrate without too many problems. So it was the non-whites who became the targets; gangs of young poor whites went 'nigger hunting' or 'black-burying'.

Tensions came to a head in 1958; starting in St Ann's, a poor district of Nottingham, anti-immigrant violence spread to the Notting Hill area of London, where there was a mixed population of resentful whites, West Indians, Irish and gypsies. In the words of Andrew Marr,

> into this honeycomb poured ... hundreds of white men, armed first with sticks, knives, iron railings and bicycle chains, and soon with petrol bombs too ... They began by picking on small groups of blacks caught out on the streets, beating them and chasing them. They then moved to black-occupied houses and began smashing windows. The crowds

swelled until they were estimated at more than 700 strong ... though some local whites protected and even fought for their black neighbours, this was mob violence of a kind Britain thought it had long left behind.

There were some 140 arrests, mainly of young white men. And black people began to fight back, using the same weapons as the whites.

British politicians and governments were, on the whole, more sympathetic to non-white people than were the general public, and did their best to encourage racial harmony. There were two important exceptions:

1 Conservative MP Enoch Powell believed that continued immigration of non-white people would lead to great social tensions and violence between the different races. In 1968, in what became known as 'the rivers of blood' speech, he said: 'We must be mad, literally mad as a nation, to be permitting the annual inflow of 50,000 dependents. It's like watching a nation busily heaping up its own funeral pyre. As I look ahead I am filled with foreboding; like the Roman, I seem to see the River Tiber foaming with much blood.' He suggested that all non-whites should be sent back to the countries of their birth. However, most of the leading Conservatives were more liberal on the issue, and Heath sacked Powell from the Shadow Cabinet.

2 The National Front (NF) and its offshoot, the British National Party (BNP) were political parties that campaigned for a 'white' Britain. They failed to win any seats in Parliament, though in 1993 a BNP councillor was elected to Tower Hamlets in London. Most politicians were dismayed by the election of a BNP member, because both the NF and the BNP were extremist parties that stirred up racial hatred and violence.

(d) government attempts to encourage racial harmony

The Labour Party hoped to improve race relations, especially after the increase in immigration in the early 1960s threatened to exacerbate tensions even further. Another disturbing aspect of the situation was that most of the media seemed to be hostile to non-white immigrants. Wilson realized that Acts of Parliament could not force people of different races to love and respect each other, but he believed it was the duty of the government to show people what sort of behaviour was and was not acceptable in a civilized society. *Labour governments introduced three Race Relations Acts.*

1 1965: set up *the Race Relations Board* to work towards fair treatment for non-whites. People could be taken to court for inciting racial disorder and for discriminating in public places, such as refusing to serve black and Asian people in pubs and restaurants. However, the act did not apply to employment and housing, arguably the two most important areas of discrimination.

2 1968: introduced *the Community Relations Commission;* its job was to keep an eye on what was happening in areas of mixed race. It was now illegal to

discriminate in housing, jobs, and in the provision of commercial or other services, and anyone who did so could expect to be prosecuted. The Act also encouraged the formation of *Community Relations Councils* in local areas. No further progress was made during Heath's Conservative government (1970–4), but the succeeding Labour government tried again.

3 1976: this set up *the Commission for Racial Equality* in place of the largely ineffective Race Relations Board. It was designed to actively encourage better relations and understanding between peoples of different races. People could be prosecuted for trying to incite racial hatred by using language that was 'threatening, abusive or insulting'. However, the army and the police were exempt from the act, on the grounds that it might undermine their morale.

(e) how successful were these Acts?

The new Commissions did excellent work, but progress was slow. During the 1980s there were some disturbing developments.

▸ As unemployment increased to three million, it became more difficult for non-whites to find jobs; unemployment was twice as high among Asians and West Indians as among whites. Many young black and coloured people, resentful of their unfair treatment, joined protest demonstrations that often ended in violence. There were riots in Brixton and Liverpool in 1981, and in London and Birmingham in 1985.

▸ Non-whites, especially Asians, began to suffer harassment: houses were covered with insulting graffiti, windows smashed, property vandalized, and people beaten up and stabbed. Black people felt that the police harassed them unfairly, and some police officers seemed to treat crimes against non-whites less seriously than crimes against whites.

▸ In 1993, Bernie Grant, a black Labour MP, said that many black people were disgusted and disillusioned by the way they were treated in Britain, and felt that there was no future for them there. He suggested that they might be better off going to live in their country of origin.

Clearly it was going to take generations for attitudes to change sufficiently for there to be perfect racial harmony.

On the other hand, there were some positive developments. As Lawrence Black points out,

> to stereotype immigrants solely as an oppressed group ignores their impact on whole areas of Britain: writing, sport, music and business success, to name but a few. Popular and everyday culture is today blatantly multicultural. The Notting Hill Carnival, an assertion of that community's identity, is now Europe's largest carnival ... Italian, Indian and Chinese restaurants are a feature of every high street, and a recent survey argued that Britons were addicted to curry.

1 'The British people enjoyed a time of unprecedented social advance and rising living standards between 1945 and 1973.' How accurate is this assessment of the period?

2 To what extent did the social and economic changes of the 1960s and 1970s improve the position of women in British society?

3 In what ways did the development of a 'teenage culture' manifest itself from the late 1950s to 1979? How far would you agree that 'the new teenage culture brought with it a great social revolution'?

4 Why and in what ways did British governments try to limit immigration to Britain between 1945 and 1979?

A document question on the problems of immigration can be found on the accompanying website www.palgrave.com/masterseries/lowe1.

Britain and its parts: England, Ireland, Scotland and Wales

summary of events

In 1900, Great Britain, or the United Kingdom (UK), consisted of four parts – England, Ireland, Scotland and Wales, with one Parliament, which met in London. Scotland was a separate country until 1707, when *the Act of Union* united Scotland and England. The Scots ceased to have their own parliament, which had met in Edinburgh, and instead sent their MPs to the London Parliament. Ireland had its own parliament until 1800, when it was abolished by the British government; like the Scots, the Irish MPs then had to travel to London to sit in the British Parliament. The Welsh had never had a parliament of their own and Welsh MPs always sat at Westminster.

The UK was dominated by England, which had by far the largest population. The 1901 census showed that, out of a total UK population of 41.5 million, 30.5 million (around 73.5 per cent) lived in England; 4.5 million (about 10.8 per cent) lived in Scotland; 4.5 million in Ireland; and 2 million (about 4.8 per cent) in Wales. London, the capital of England, was also capital of the UK, and the fact that the Parliament of the UK happened to meet in England only underlined this domination. Many English people saw nothing wrong in this; they thought that to be English was the same thing as being British and vice-versa, and they seemed to assume that, as time went on, the Irish, Scots and Welsh would become more like the English. However, *in Ireland, Scotland and Wales there were people who were far from happy with this relationship:*

‣ They believed that they did not receive a fair deal from the English-dominated Parliament in London, and blamed all their problems on the English. This feeling was especially strong in Ireland.
‣ They had no wish to become 'English' and were determined to preserve their separate identity and culture. In Wales, for example, they were keen to preserve the Welsh language.
‣ There were demands for self-government, or *devolution*, as it was later called. These feelings were strongest in Ireland, where the Irish Nationalist party,

and later Sinn Fein, had massive support (see Sections 7.4; 16.1 and 16.8(b); 21.5). Southern Ireland was allowed to become independent as *the Irish Free State* in 1922, but most of Ulster, in the north-east, remained part of the UK (see Section 26.2).

Nationalist feelings were never so strong in Scotland and Wales, though both had nationalist political parties: the Welsh Nationalist Party was founded in 1925, and the Scottish Nationalists in 1928. Their campaigns for separate parliaments came nearest to success in 1979, when the British government allowed a referendum in Wales and Scotland to find out whether the majority of people really were in favour of devolution. *The Welsh voted four to one against devolution.* Although a majority of Scots who voted were in favour of it (51.6 per cent to 48.4 per cent), this was only 33 per cent of the total electorate rather than the required 40 per cent; so *devolution for Scotland could not go ahead.* Meanwhile, Northern Ireland had its own parliament at Stormont, but when serious violence broke out between Roman Catholics and Protestants, the British government felt obliged to suspend the Stormont parliament and bring Northern Ireland under the direct rule of London (1972). All attempts to restore power to Stormont came to nothing. When the Labour Party, which had committed itself to allowing parliaments in both Scotland and Wales, won the 1997 general election, prospects for some kind of devolution seemed brighter.

32.1 Northern Ireland since 1922

From 1921 until 1972, Northern Ireland was governed by its own parliament created by the 1920 Government of Ireland Act , which had begun to operate even before the 1921 Anglo-Irish Treaty set up the Irish Free State. The Northern Ireland parliament was usually known as Stormont, after the place where the new parliament building was situated. It consisted of two houses: a lower house called the House of Commons, and a second chamber known as the Senate. The Commons had 52 members, each representing one constituency, while the Senate had 24 members elected by the House of Commons. There was a Prime Minister and Cabinet, and the parliament had very wide powers; only a few matters such as foreign affairs, defence and income tax were still controlled by the British Parliament.

Once the excitement at the partition of Ireland had passed and the civil war in the Free State had ended in 1923, most people in the rest of Britain forgot about Ireland and assumed that life in Northern Ireland was going on in much the same way as it was in the rest of Britain. But this was not the case – from the beginning, Northern Ireland suffered from a number of problems that British governments tended to ignore.

(a) problems in Northern Ireland

> The new province had a long frontier with the Free State, and this frontier had a distinctly artificial look about it. It included many areas, such as parts of Tyrone and Fermanagh, south Armagh and south Down, which contained a large number of Catholics who were strongly nationalist and wanted their areas to be in the Free State. They were bitterly disappointed by the failure of the Boundary Commission to change the frontier (see Section 26.3(a)). This meant that just over a third of Northern Ireland's population were Roman Catholics, many of whom felt that the whole of the province, not just the Catholic areas, should be part of the Free State. Only the most sympathetic treatment by the Protestant majority could have reconciled these Catholics to remaining citizens of Northern Ireland.

> During the depression of the late 1920s and 1930s, Northern Ireland suffered massive unemployment. In 1929, over 15 per cent of insured workers were without jobs, and this soon shot up to more than 30 per cent by 1931. Even in 1937, when the rest of Britain had recovered to some extent, nearly a quarter of insured workers were still jobless, the highest unemployment rate in Britain. There was a shortage of cash for housing, roads, schools and health care, and so all these facilities in Northern Ireland were of a lower standard than anywhere else in Britain.

> Political life in Northern Ireland did not run along normal party lines as it did in the rest of the UK. There were no Conservative, Liberal or Labour parties – political groupings reflected the sectarian divisions in society: Protestants were represented by the Unionist Party, and Catholics by various nationalist groups. The Protestant/Unionist-dominated Stormont government deliberately did its best for the Protestants, while Catholics were discriminated against in housing, jobs, education, apprenticeships and public appointments. Constituency boundaries were fixed to give maximum advantage to Unionist candidates in elections (known as 'gerrymandering'). The Royal Ulster Constabulary (RUC) was armed and was supported by a second armed force known as the 'B Specials', whose main function seemed to be to keep the Catholics under control.

> The Catholic population felt frustrated and helpless, since the Stormont government was always Unionist. There was no way they could ever win a majority at Stormont, and no chance of changing the government, as there was in a normal liberal democracy. Nor did the British government intervene on behalf of the Catholics. Sometimes sectarian violence broke out between Catholics and Protestants (a dictionary definition of a 'sectarian' is 'a bigoted supporter of a particular sect or religion'). The worst case occurred in 1935, when several people were killed in sectarian riots in Belfast.

(b) Northern Ireland during the Second World War (1939–45)

The province took on a new importance and enjoyed unexpected prosperity during the war years. Londonderry played a vital role as a naval base, and industry flourished, as it did in the rest of Britain, producing material for the war effort. The famous Harland and Wolff's shipyard in Belfast was kept busy replacing ships sunk by German submarines, and it also manufactured aircraft.

(c) the situation after 1945

Despite its comparative prosperity and deceptive calm, the problems of Northern Ireland were still there at the end of the war. In the twenty years after 1945, one of the most striking things about the province was *the continued unfair treatment of the Catholic population.* The unemployment rate among Catholics was three times higher than among Protestants. Well over 90 per cent of the workers at Harland and Wolff's were Protestant, and so were 94 per cent of senior civil servants and 90 per cent of the RUC. Eamonn McCann, a Catholic leader of the civil rights movement, recalled: 'The Education Act of 1944 gave Catholic working class children the chance to go to grammar school and university, but we couldn't even get a job as a lavatory cleaner at Derry Guildhall. That made us angry.'

Protestants were more likely than Catholics to get council houses, and there were property qualifications for voting in local elections, which excluded many more Catholics than Protestants. According to historian C. J. Bartlett, 'nowhere else in the western world were Catholics so much excluded from positions of influence. The great majority of Catholics were convinced that they were victims of deliberate discrimination'. Protestants defended their behaviour on the grounds that Catholics were enemies of Northern Ireland and were working for unification with the Republic. In 1956, the IRA began a terrorist campaign against what they described as 'British rule in occupied Ireland', but this only made the Protestants more determined to defend their position.

(d) O'Neill, reform and the civil rights campaign, 1963–8

In 1963, a new Unionist Prime Minister, Terence O'Neill, came to power. He had more progressive ideas than the old Unionists and felt it was time to treat Catholics more fairly, so that they would become reconciled to living in Northern Ireland. He believed that greater economic prosperity and closer relations with the Republic would help. A programme of gradual reform was started, to increase Catholic rights, and a plan was drawn up for industrial expansion, including new towns at Antrim, Ballymena and Craigavon. In 1965, O'Neill met the Prime Minister of the Republic and a friendly relationship seemed to have been established. Encouraged by this, the Roman Catholic community, after years of helpless inaction, began to organize themselves, and in 1967 they founded *the Northern Ireland Civil Rights Association.* This was a non-violent group which had some support from moderate Protestants. Until then things had been peaceful, but tensions began to creep in, which soon turned to violence.

> Harold Wilson's Labour government urged O'Neill to speed up his reform campaign, but this alarmed the extreme Protestants, who were already suspicious of his meeting with the Irish Prime Minister. They were afraid that further reforms would threaten their supremacy, and leaders such as the Reverend Ian Paisley, who had founded an extreme Protestant sect of his own, inflamed the situation by making violently anti-Catholic speeches. In 1971, Paisley formed a breakaway group from the official Unionist Party, known as *the Democratic Unionist Party (DUP).*
> The Civil Rights Association planned a large protest march to take place in Londonderry, a mainly Catholic city, but it was banned by Home Affairs Minister, William Craig.
> In spite of this, the march went ahead, on 5 October 1968, but violence erupted when it was broken up by the RUC using water cannon and baton charges.

(e) British troops sent to Northern Ireland (August 1969)

During 1969, violence escalated as more and more protest marches were held. In January, the Civil Rights Association attempted to march from Belfast to Londonderry, but the march was again broken up by the RUC. After more marches, the Protestant Loyalist Associations such as *the Orange Order* and *the Apprentice Boys* began to hold counter-demonstrations. The Unionist Party was now split, and the extremists, blaming O'Neill for the deteriorating situation, forced him to resign (April 1969). Violence reached a new peak in August 1969, when the Protestant Apprentice Boys held a march. When Catholic crowds tried to hold a counter-march, they were attacked by the RUC and the Protestants and driven back into the Bogside, the Catholic area of the city. Feeling themselves under siege, the Catholics barricaded themselves into the Bogside and declared 'Free Derry'. Riots followed in other cities; in the Falls Road area of Belfast, Protestant gangs throwing petrol bombs destroyed over a hundred Catholic homes. The Northern Ireland government had lost control and was forced to ask the British government for help. James Callaghan, the Home Secretary, decided to send British troops to restore order, though he made it clear that they were there not to maintain Protestant supremacy, but to safeguard the rights of all Northern Ireland citizens. Troops moved into the Bogside and the Falls Road, and the RUC and the 'B Specials' withdrew. Catholics welcomed the troops, feeling that they would now be protected from further Protestant attacks.

(f) direct rule imposed (March 1972)

For a time it seemed as though the presence of British troops and the actions of the British government might stabilize the situation. The Westminster government tried to show its impartiality by holding an enquiry (under the chairmanship of Sir John Hunt) into the activities of the RUC and the 'B Specials'. When this condemned their policing methods, Callaghan did not hesitate to act: he reorganized and disarmed the RUC and abolished the 'B Specials', who were hated by the Catholics. Callaghan also began an impressive programme of local government reform – a fairer system of electoral districts, a fairer system of allocating council houses, and a new body to which people could appeal if they felt they were being unfairly treated. All these measures, it was hoped, would show the Catholics that the British government cared about them and would therefore calm the situation. By the time Labour was defeated in the election of June 1970, *the position of Catholics in Northern Ireland had been transformed for the better.* Unfortunately, though, instead of stabilizing, the situation continued to deteriorate until Edward Heath's government felt it had no alternative but to bring the province under direct rule from Westminster.

‣ The concessions to Catholics provoked riots from Protestants, especially in October 1969, when the 'B Specials', whom many Protestants saw as their guardians, were disbanded. A number of Protestant paramilitary groups was formed, it was claimed, in self-defence. In January 1970, the Reverend Ian Paisley was elected to the British Parliament in London.

‣ The IRA began to play an important role. In December 1969 they split into the Officials, who were more moderate, and the Provisionals, who were committed to military action. Their ultimate aim was to drive the British out of Northern Ireland. There were some non-violent Catholic organizations such as *the Social Democratic and Labour Party (SDLP)* led by Gerry Fitt and John Hume, who were both elected to Stormont. But they were always in danger of being overshadowed by the Provisional IRA, whose tactics were to turn the Catholic population against the British troops. In this they succeeded: they launched a campaign of terrorism, and the troops found themselves having to search Catholic households for weapons and IRA suspects. Some unpleasant incidents occurred; the first major clash between Catholics and troops took place in April 1970, and the first British soldier was killed in February 1971; in July, troops killed two young Derry men.

‣ Brian Faulkner, the new Northern Ireland Prime Minister, with the full support of the British government, responded by introducing *internment* (August 1971) – arresting and imprisoning people indefinitely without trial. Over 300 people were held in an attempt to stamp out the IRA. However, this only served to infuriate the Catholics, and the riots continued. So did Protestant attacks on Catholics, and many Catholics began to seek refuge over the border in the Republic.

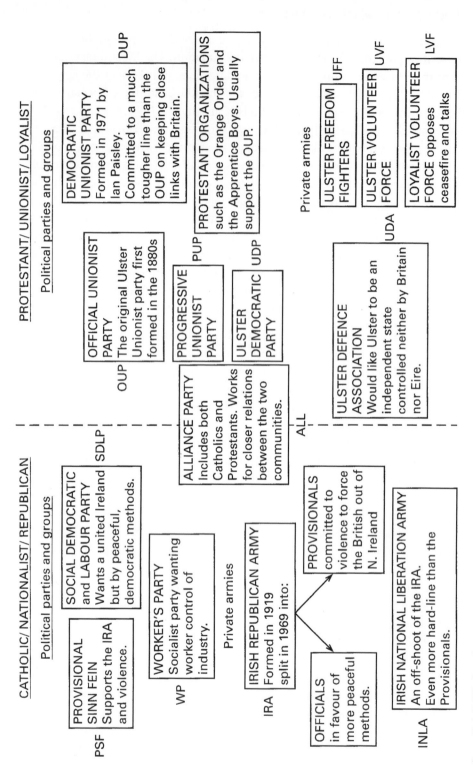

PROTESTANT/ UNIONIST/ LOYALIST

Political parties and groups

DEMOCRATIC UNIONIST PARTY Formed in 1971 by Ian Paisley. Committed to a much tougher line than the OUP on keeping close links with Britain. **DUP**

OFFICIAL UNIONIST PARTY The original Ulster Unionist party first formed in the 1880s **OUP**

PROTESTANT ORGANIZATIONS such as the Orange Order and the Apprentice Boys. Usually support the OUP.

PROGRESSIVE UNIONIST PARTY **PUP**

ULSTER DEMOCRATIC PARTY **UDP**

Private armies

ULSTER FREEDOM FIGHTERS **UFF**

ULSTER VOLUNTEER FORCE **UVF**

LOYALIST VOLUNTEER FORCE opposes ceasefire and talks **LVF**

ULSTER DEFENCE ASSOCIATION Would like Ulster to be an independent state controlled neither by Britain nor Eire. **UDA**

CATHOLIC/ NATIONALIST/ REPUBLICAN

Political parties and groups

SOCIAL DEMOCRATIC and LABOUR PARTY Wants a united Ireland but by peaceful, democratic methods. **SDLP**

PROVISIONAL SINN FEIN Supports the IRA and violence. **PSF**

WORKER'S PARTY Socialist party wanting worker control of industry. **WP**

ALLIANCE PARTY Includes both Catholics and Protestants. Works for closer relations between the two communities. **ALL**

Private armies

IRISH REPUBLICAN ARMY Formed in 1919 split in 1969 into: **IRA**

PROVISIONALS committed to violence to force the British out of N. Ireland

OFFICIALS in favour of more peaceful methods.

IRISH NATIONAL LIBERATION ARMY An off-shoot of the IRA. Even more hard-line than the Provisionals. **INLA**

figure **32.1 Political parties and organizations in Northern Ireland since the 1970s**

- A new peak of violence was reached on *'Bloody Sunday,'* 30 January 1972, in the Bogside, Londonderry. A Catholic civil rights march clashed with troops who over-reacted, shooting dead thirteen unarmed civilians and wounding many more. There was worldwide condemnation of British policy in Northern Ireland. The situation was chaotic: even with 20,000 troops there, it seemed impossible to govern the province. The Catholic side was split between the IRA/Sinn Fein and moderates such as the SDLP; and the Unionists were split into at least three groups: the official Unionists (led by Faulkner) who, on the whole, were prepared to go along with what the British government wanted, the Democratic Unionists (led by Paisley) who wanted complete integration with Britain, and a group who seemed prepared to consider an independent Ulster (see Figure 32.1).

It was in this impossible situation that Edward Heath decided to suspend Stormont and bring Northern Ireland under direct rule from London. William Whitelaw as Secretary of State for Northern Ireland had the unenviable job of trying to prevent civil war.

(g) the failure of the new Executive (May 1974)

Whitelaw tried to please the Catholics by beginning a phase-out of internment. But this further angered the Protestants, who were already annoyed by the suspension of Stormont. There was bitter and violent opposition from Protestant groups such as *the Ulster Defence Association (UDA)*, and the IRA continued its bombing campaign, extending it to England, where six people were killed at the Aldershot army base. In spite of this, the British government made a brave attempt to set up a new and fairer government in Northern Ireland.

- Plans were announced (March 1973) for a new Assembly of 80 members elected on the single transferable vote system, and a new Executive (the group whose job it is to make sure that laws are carried out), in which power would be shared between Protestants and Catholics.
- Elections for the new Assembly were held in June 1973, but were disappointing for the British government. Faulkner's Official Unionists (who supported the plans) won only 23 seats, while the 'Loyalist' Unionists, who opposed the plans because they were against sharing power in the Executive with Catholics, won 27 seats.
- The new Executive was set up in November 1973, consisting of six Faulkner Unionists, four members of the Catholic SDLP, and one member of the Alliance Party (which included both Catholics and Protestants who wanted to be non-sectarian). There was bitter opposition to this from Loyalist Unionists.
- *The Sunningdale Agreement* seemed to be an encouraging development. This was negotiated in December 1973 by Whitelaw, with representatives of the

Eire government and of the new Northern Ireland Assembly. It supported the idea of the power-sharing Executive to be led by Brian Faulkner, with Gerry Fitt of the SDLP as his deputy. To calm Protestant fears, it was agreed that no change would take place in the status of Northern Ireland without the approval of a majority of Northern Ireland voters. Also suggested was a Council of Ireland to include MPs from both parts of Ireland, which would gradually move towards joint control of certain matters.

▸ The new Assembly and Executive formally came into operation on 1 January 1974, but they had to face the most extreme opposition from so-called 'Loyalist' Unionists. In the British general election of February 1974, Protestant opponents of the new system, calling themselves *the United Ulster Unionist Council*, won 11 out of the 12 Northern Ireland seats at Westminster. In May, *the Protestant Ulster Workers' Council* organized a massive general strike in protest against power-sharing. Soon the province was at a standstill, with no power and no food supplies. Faulkner had little choice but to resign (28 May 1974); the Executive collapsed, and the attempt at power-sharing had failed because of opposition from extreme Protestants.

(h) IRA violence continues

From 1974 to 1997 all attempts to provide Northern Ireland with a viable government allowing Catholics some say in the running of the province failed, mainly because of the unwillingness of so many Unionist politicians, especially Paisley, to consider any compromise. On the other hand, it has to be said that the continued IRA campaign of violence, both in Northern Ireland and in England, did not help progress towards a solution. For a time they targeted and killed well-known individuals – three examples were Ross McWhirter, a right-wing critic of the IRA (1975); Conservative Northern Ireland spokesman Airey Neave (1979); and Lord Mountbatten (1979). Most outrageous of all was an attempt to blow up Mrs Thatcher and her Cabinet at the Grand Hotel, Brighton, where they were staying for the 1984 Conservative Party Conference. Though five people were killed and others permanently disabled by their injuries, the top politicians escaped.

(i) the Anglo-Irish Agreement (November 1985)

Margaret Thatcher was determined to do all she could to bring peace to Northern Ireland. She had already had a summit meeting with Irish Prime Minister, Dr Garrett Fitzgerald, in November 1981; they met again in November 1985 and signed *the Hillsborough Agreement* (also known as *the Anglo-Irish Agreement*). This acknowledged that any change in the status of Northern Ireland could only come about with the consent of a majority of the people of the province. Britain and Eire would confer regularly about the situation in the North, and about security along the border. This was seen by many people as a statesmanlike initiative by the two leaders, especially in the wake of the Brighton bombing. The difficulties facing both governments, no matter how willing they were to talk, were illustrated by the reactions to the agreement. Amid massive demonstrations, the two main Protestant Unionist groups, who appeared to have learnt nothing since 1922, denounced it as a sell-out, while on the other side Charles Haughey, leader of the Eire Fianna Fail party, called it 'a very severe blow to the concept of Irish unity'.

However, in spite of all the setbacks, it was clear that some progress had been made:

- blatant discrimination against Catholics in Northern Ireland was a thing of the past; and
- successive British governments since 1963 had poured many millions of pounds into Northern Ireland to improve facilities for *all* its citizens.

On the other hand, the province suffered badly from the recessions of the 1980s and early 1990s; it had the highest unemployment rate in Britain, especially in Catholic working-class areas such as Newry and Londonderry, where it was sometimes as high as 40 per cent. The gulf between Catholics and Protestants seemed as wide as ever, and British troops were still there vainly trying to prevent them from killing each other. People in the rest of Britain, where Catholics and Protestants for the most part lived amicably side by side, grew impatient with the problems of Northern Ireland and could not understand why the people continually failed to move away from sectarian bitterness and forgive and forget the past.

(j) the IRA ceasefire (August 1994–February 1996) and the failure to find peace

The IRA, financed by Irish Americans, still persisted with its pointless campaign of bombings and assassinations: there was the Remembrance Day bombing that killed eleven people at Enniskillen (November 1987) and the murder of Conservative MP Ian Gow in 1990. Later they changed tactics and began placing bombs in business premises and even in shopping areas. When two small boys were killed by a bomb in Warrington (April 1993) there was widespread condemnation of IRA tactics throughout Britain and the Republic. Meanwhile, the Protestant paramilitary groups continued to retaliate in Northern Ireland by shooting and blowing up Catholics. Pressure was beginning to mount on the IRA to call off the campaign of violence, which was getting nowhere. Secret talks had been going on between representatives of the British government and the IRA; and John Hume, the SDLP leader, worked tirelessly to persuade Sinn Fein to use its influence to bring an end to the violence. President Clinton of the USA threw his weight behind the search for peace; apparently, the British government promised that if a ceasefire held for three months, Sinn Fein would be allowed to join peace talks.

John Major took the initiative and had several meetings with the Irish Prime Minister, Albert Reynolds. The two leaders produced a joint statement (known as *the Downing Street Declaration*) setting out the requirements for peace talks to begin. It was emphasized again for the benefit of the Unionists that no changes would take place in the status of Northern Ireland without the approval of a majority in the province. Any party could join in negotiations if it renounced violence (August 1994). After some hesitation, the IRA declared 'a complete cessation of violence' and this was followed by a similar declaration from Loyalist paramilitary groups. There was immense relief and rejoicing in Northern Ireland, where over 31,000 people had been killed since the violence began in 1969.

Progress was very slow. In February 1995, the government published a framework plan that peace negotiations might follow, and there was a proposal for a joint Ulster–Ireland legislative body which could have limited powers. Although this was only a proposal, Unionists were outraged: Paisley called it 'totally and absolutely repugnant' and 'a declaration of war on the union and the unionist people'. In March 1995, the British government demanded that the IRA should begin handing over its weapons before all-party talks could begin, but this was rejected, and stalemate seemed to have been reached. Only at the end of November did things move forward, when the British and Irish governments set up a three-member international panel headed by Senator George J. Mitchell of the USA, to try to find a compromise on the decommissioning of weapons. Immediately afterwards, President Clinton visited Northern Ireland, where he received an enthusiastic welcome from both Catholics and Protestants (30 November 1995).

Senator Mitchell announced his recommendations on 24 January 1996: he dismissed the demand for weapons to be handed over *before* talks began as unrealistic, since paramilitary groups on both sides had rejected it. He proposed that the parties should commit themselves to a phased disarmament, in parallel with talks, and should undertake to abide by six principles:

1 No guns to be relinquished ahead of talks.
2 Decommissioning would be considered once negotiations started.
3 All paramilitary groups would eventually disarm totally.
4 Destruction of all weapons would be monitored by an independent international commission.
5 All punishment attacks should end.
6 All groups should renounce violence and commit themselves to peaceful and democratic means.

This was widely seen as a sensible and realistic document, which provided a basis for all-party talks to get under way. The Irish government, the SDLP, the IRA and the other paramilitary groups accepted it. However, John Major, under pressure from the Unionists and needing their votes to maintain his dwindling Commons majority, tried to sidestep the main thrust of the report and proposed instead elections to a constitutional convention, an idea already put forward by the Unionists. An exasperated John Hume accused him of buying

Unionist votes in the Commons. Whether the IRA was genuine in its acceptance of the Mitchell proposals was never put to the test, and the opportunity was lost. In February 1996, the IRA broke the ceasefire on the mainland by exploding a huge bomb in London's docklands, killing two people. Later, another massive bomb destroyed part of the city centre of Manchester, and it was only by a miracle that nobody was killed.

John Major pressed ahead with his elections in Northern Ireland for delegates to a negotiating forum, drawn from all parties committed to renouncing violence (June 1996). Sinn Fein took part and won 17 out of the 110 seats; however, because of the continuing IRA violence, they were not admitted to the forum. In October 1996, the IRA broke the ceasefire in Northern Ireland and the whole dreary tale seemed set to repeat itself. In the British general election of May 1997, Sinn Fein won two seats and took 16 per cent of the Northern Ireland vote, its best performance for forty years, in spite of the continued violence.

(k) Blair and the Good Friday Agreement, 1998

Tony Blair, the new Labour Prime Minister, was determined to make peace in Northern Ireland a top priority. His first visit was to Belfast, and he appointed Mo Mowlam, one of the government's most feisty personalities, as the new Northern Ireland Secretary. No doubt sensing the new atmosphere, both sides made concessions: in July 1997, after the Orange Order had called off some of their provocative marches, the IRA responded by announcing another ceasefire. A complex series of talks began in September 1997. All the Northern Ireland political parties joined negotiations chaired by George Mitchell – their job was to produce a power-sharing assembly in which they could all sit. A second set of talks involved the parties talking to the British and Irish governments about issues likely to become important in the future – these included the frontier and the constitution of the North. And finally there were talks between the Westminster and Dublin governments about matters such as security and the general situation.

The talks dragged on well into 1998, and when no agreement seemed to be in sight, Blair imposed a deadline: if no settlement had been reached by 1 May, the government would impose its own solution and put it to a referendum. Against all expectations, a deal was finally reached – and with time to spare – on 10 April, Good Friday 1998. The terms were similar to those offered earlier at Sunningdale: Northern Ireland would remain part of the UK for as long as a majority of the population wanted it; the Republic of Ireland would give up its claim to the North; all parties would join in a new power-sharing assembly; and there would be a North–South council which would help the two to co-operate smoothly. Prisoners would be released and the paramilitary organizations would give up or destroy their weapons; this process would be monitored by an independent body.

The agreement was approved by a huge majority in the Republic, and by a roughly three-quarters majority in the North. David Trimble, leader of the

Ulster Unionists, and John Hume, leader of the SDLP, were later awarded the Nobel Peace Prize. Even so, about half the Protestants voted against the agreement. The republican side had its problems as well: a few months after the agreement a group of extremists calling themselves the 'Real IRA' exploded a bomb in Omagh, killing 29 people and injuring 200. It was a terrible setback, but it did not prevent the peace process from advancing. However, putting it all into operation proved to be far from easy, and it was the weapons issue that was the main stumbling block. The IRA seemed reluctant to begin disarmament, and so in February 2000 the Ulster Unionist leader, David Trimble, withdrew his party from the power-sharing government. However, later in the year, the IRA agreed to allow inspection and sealing of some of their weapons, and the Unionists returned. This tedious process repeated itself, neither side trusted the other, and eventually in October 2002 the Westminster government suspended the Stormont assembly. Just before Christmas there was yet another crisis when a £26 million bank robbery was blamed on the IRA. The peace process seemed to have stalled completely and the voters were losing patience. At the next election for the assembly in 2003 the moderates lost ground and the DUP (Ian Paisley) and Sinn Fein (Gerry Adams) emerged as the strongest groups. At the election in May 2005 the moderate Ulster Unionists were almost wiped out and David Trimble resigned the leadership. Soon after the election, Paisley and Adams had separate talks with Tony Blair, since the DUP leader refused to meet the republicans face to face. Paisley told reporters that it was time to give the Good Friday Agreement a decent burial: 'Peace,' he said, 'depends on complete and verifiable decommissioning to the IRA's weapons and an end to criminality.' Real peace seemed as far away as ever.

(l) peace at last

Against all expectations, during the summer of 2005, attitudes began to change. The IRA ordered all its units to 'dump arms'; by the autumn, the Canadian General John de Chastelain, the official monitor, was satisfied that the IRA had finally put much of its weaponry 'beyond use'. More talks began, and at the end of 2006 the St Andrews agreement was drawn up, setting out a timetable for restoring devolved government through the power-sharing assembly. After some delay, both the DUP and Sinn Fein accepted it. In March 2007, the new power-sharing government came into operation with the Revd Ian Paisley as first minister and Martin McGuinness as his deputy. There were extraordinary scenes at the opening ceremony as the former bitter enemies, Paisley on one side, and Adams and McGuinness on the other, stood side by side, laughed and joked and paid tribute to each other.

(m) why was peace finally achieved after so many years of conflict?

▸ By 2005, there was little doubt that the vast majority of the Catholic population wanted peace of some sort, even if it meant staying in the UK. One of the main reasons for their desire to join the Republic – that they were treated as second-class citizens – had more or less been put right, as the Westminster government imposed what the civil rights movement was demanding.

- Northern Ireland had benefited economically from Britain's economic recovery and from the foreign investment in high-tech industries that had taken place during the peaceful periods since the first IRA ceasefire in 1994. Unemployment was at its lowest level for years, and it was obvious that it was in people's interests for a permanent peace to be secured.

- The terrorist bombings in the USA in 2001 led to the American 'war on terror'. This meant that the USA stopped financing the IRA and threw its full weight into the quest for a lasting peace.

All of this provided the right circumstances for the peace process to progress, but it needed the efforts of a number of key individuals to overcome the main obstacles to progress: the IRA's continued reluctance to disarm and the DUP's reluctance to accept that the IRA was genuine in its desire for peace.

- John Hume, the SDLP leader, was the first to realize that the IRA were at last ready for serious negotiations about laying down their arms. He had talks with Gerry Adams during 2004 and convinced him that Ian Paisley might be ready to do a deal.

- Successive Northern Ireland Secretaries – Mo Mowlam, Peter Mandelson and Peter Hain played important roles. Mo Mowlam won the trust of the nationalists and convinced them that there was a bright future for Catholics in Ulster. Peter Mandelson was tougher with the nationalists and therefore was able to keep the Unionists reasonably happy. Peter Hain introduced several unpopular policies – water rates were introduced, homosexuals were given full rights, and a plan announced to abolish grammar schools. According to Andrew Rawnsley (writing in the *Observer* in April 2007), this was a deliberate ploy to make the Northern Ireland parties hate him more than they did the idea of sharing power: 'If they didn't want to carry on being governed by the cunning Mr Hain, the local politicians had to compromise with each other.'

- Tony Blair himself made a major contribution, and most of the key figures in Northern Ireland acknowledged that the final breakthrough would not have happened without him. Andrew Rawnsley is fulsome in his praise: Mr Blair showed 'courage, ingenuity and persistence. He breathed new life into the peace process and then sustained it through all those exhausting years ... He had showcased his best qualities: his negotiating skills, his flair for creative ambiguity, a certain degree of deviousness, his capacity to take risks, and sheer effort of will.'

- Finally, the hard-liners on both sides were prepared to make compromises. Gerry Adams and Martin McGuinness accepted that violence was not going to achieve their aims, and that power-sharing was better than having no power at all. Ian Paisley responded positively, once he was convinced that the IRA were genuinely intending to lay down their arms. He too admitted that the bigotry, hatred and violence could not go on for ever. It has also been suggested that the prospect of his becoming first minister was an added incentive for him to co-operate.

As the 81-year-old Paisley prepared to retire as first minister and DUP leader in May 2008, Martin McGuinness said that they had had a positive and constructive working relationship. But there was still some opposition to the power-sharing by extremists of both parties. Paisley's fiercest critic, Jim Allister, formed a breakaway party called 'Traditional Unionist Voice'; in the local elections in County Down in February 2008, the new party split the DUP vote and the seat was lost. On the other side, the Real IRA, which had carried out the Omagh bombing in 1998, still refused to renounce violence.

32.2 relations between Britain and Scotland

(a) Scotland in 1900

Most Scots were well aware that their country had been a separate kingdom with its own parliament until 1707. Like Ireland, Scotland had had its traumatic times: the most notorious were *the Highland Clearances* of 1782–1820 and 1840–54, when the clan chieftains of the Highlands and Islands had evicted thousands of their tenants to make way for sheep farms. Though there were problems in Scotland – for example, there was considerable economic hardship with the decline of sheep-farming in the 1880s – there was no great desire at this time for Home Rule as there was in Ireland. Most Scots agreed that their country had done reasonably well out of the union with England and felt that it should continue.

While there was no Scottish parliament, the Scots did have some control over their own affairs. They continued their own system of law and law-courts, their own churches and their own education system, which had existed before 1707 and were quite different from those in the rest of Britain. The Scots believed, with some justification, that their education system was superior to England's. The literacy rate was higher than in England or Wales, and Scottish children from poor backgrounds had a better chance of making it to the top. Scotland had four universities, and this meant that a higher proportion of young people could go on to university than anywhere else in the UK. Since 1872, Scotland had had its own Education Department. In 1884, Gladstone's government set up *the Scottish Office* and created a new official known as *the Secretary of State for Scotland,* whose department looked after matters such as the Poor Law, health, roads, bridges and fisheries. Politically, Scotland was strongly Liberal: if there had been a Scottish parliament it would have had a permanent Liberal majority.

(b) the Home Rule for Scotland movement up to 1914

When the campaign for Irish Home Rule gained momentum, it encouraged some Scots to think along the same lines. At the time of the First Irish Home Rule Bill in 1886, a Scottish Home Rule Association was formed in Edinburgh, and the Scottish Liberal Party had some sympathy with the idea of separate parliaments for Scotland, Wales, Ireland and England, within some sort of federal system. In 1908, a bill to give Home Rule to Scotland was introduced into the Commons and passed with a majority of over 100. Of the Scottish MPs, 41 voted in favour and 12 against. The Conservatives opposed it strongly, as they did Home Rule for Ireland. Not surprisingly, the Bill was defeated in the Lords. This happened four times before 1914; when the First World War broke out in 1914, the matter was quietly dropped.

(c) the campaign for Scottish devolution

During the 1920s, Scottish nationalism revived, in a rather different form. The Liberal party was in rapid decline by this time, and so the National Party of Scotland was formed in 1928; another group calling itself the Scottish Party was formed in 1930. They amalgamated in 1934 to form *the Scottish National Party (SNP)*, and talked about 'the urgent need and necessity of self-government for Scotland'. Their motives were both economic and cultural:

- *Economic motives:* like the rest of Britain, Scotland suffered from the inflation at the end of the First World War (see Section 23.1(b)). There was rioting in Glasgow, and the government, convinced that it was the beginning of revolution, brought in troops and tanks to restore order. Scotland also suffered badly from the depression of the early 1930s. In 1932, almost 30 per cent of insured workers in Scotland were out of work, higher than any other region in Britain except Wales. In Motherwell in 1934, over 37 per cent of insured workers were without jobs; in Glasgow alone, 90,000 people were out of work in 1936, when the worst of the depression was over in England. Many Scots felt that Scotland was paying more into the Treasury and receiving less than was fair, but the English argued that Scotland was not paying its fair share and was receiving more than it deserved.
- *Cultural motives:* people such as Hugh MacDiarmid wanted to preserve what they saw as a genuine Scottish culture against English and American influences, and some Scottish nationalists believed in reviving the old Celtic alliance of Scots, Welsh, Irish and Cornish against the English. They also hoped to revive the Gaelic language, which was hardly spoken outside the Highlands and Islands.

The movement generated a lot of interest, but it made no impact on Parliament, and no more Scottish Home Rule Bills were introduced. Instead, the English-dominated Westminster Parliament gave the Scots slightly more control of their own affairs within the existing system. The SNP succeeded in winning one by-election in Motherwell in April 1945, but lost the seat to Labour in the general election of July 1945. Interest was maintained, however, and in January 1949 John MacCormick founded *the Scottish Covenant,* which collected two million signatures of people who wanted a separate Scottish parliament.

(d) the SNP begins to take off

During the late 1960s the SNP began to take off. Again it was economic forces that seemed to be important. The economic performance of Britain as a whole was not impressive towards the end of the 1960s, and many Scots were convinced that Scotland could do better on its own, especially after the discovery of North Sea oil, which was piped ashore to Scotland. The SNP regarded this as Scotland's oil, and they could imagine an independent Scotland enjoying new wealth from oil revenues. At the same time, many Scots resented the rising unemployment, which was again worse than it was in England. Also unpopular was the arrival of American Polaris nuclear submarines based at Holy Loch.

‣ In 1967, the SNP candidate, Winifred Ewing, won Hamilton in a sensational by-election; it had previously been held by Labour with a 16,000 majority. The SNP also won sweeping victories in local government elections, taking control of local councils in Glasgow, Dundee, Cumbernauld and East Kilbride.
‣ Membership of the SNP grew rapidly; by the end of 1968 it had more members than any other party in Scotland and was drawing support from a wide range of people – workers, owners of small businesses, housewives and members of the professional middle classes. Other parties, especially Labour, were losing support to the SNP, which was shown most dramatically by Winifred Ewing's by-election victory.
‣ The other parties therefore found themselves pushed towards the idea of devolution to win back support from the SNP. In 1968, Edward Heath, the Conservative leader, revealed to the Scottish Conservatives that he was in favour of a Scottish Assembly, and a committee was set up to investigate how this could best be introduced.
‣ The 1964–70 Labour government appointed *the Kilbrandon Commission (1968)* to draw up plans for both Scottish and Welsh devolution. These were eventually published in 1973 and involved setting up elected parliaments for Scotland and Wales. However, there had been some problems during the discussions, partly because some of the members felt it was unfair not to give England devolution as well.
‣ The general election of October 1974 was a great success for the SNP: they won 11 seats and took 30 per cent of the votes in Scotland.

- The Labour government, which won the election, decided to go ahead with devolution; one reason for this was no doubt because it had an overall majority of only six, and needed the support of the 11 SNP and 3 Plaid Cymru (Welsh Nationalist) MPs.

However, as the prospect of devolution became brighter, problems and disagreements arose that held things up, and eventually caused the idea to be dropped altogether.

- There was disagreement about how much power the Scottish parliament should have. The SNP wanted it to have full power over taxation, and over industrial and economic policy. The London government was not prepared to allow this, and insisted on the Secretary of State for Scotland having the power to veto laws passed by the Scottish parliament. Another problem was whether there should be a reduction in the number of Scottish and Welsh MPs sitting at Westminster.
- The discussions again raised the question of a separate Parliament for England. Many people in the north of England felt their area had problems that were just as serious as those of Scotland and Wales, and they resented the fact that these areas seemed about to be given special treatment.
- The government eventually produced a Bill for Scottish devolution: there would be a Scottish parliament in Edinburgh, but it would have no powers of taxation and no real control over industry and agriculture; the Secretary of State for Scotland would have the final say over most matters. This was a very weak affair and satisfied nobody.
- The government decided to hold a referendum to find out whether a majority of the Scottish and Welsh people themselves were in favour of devolution. A condition attached was that 40 per cent of the total electorate must vote in favour, not just 40 per cent of those who voted, in order for the Devolution Bill to be passed. When the referendum was held (March 1979), a majority of those who voted (51.6 per cent to 48.4 per cent) were in favour of devolution. But over 36 per cent of the electorate did not bother to vote at all, and this meant that only about 33 per cent of the total electorate had shown that they wanted a separate Scottish parliament. Plans for devolution were dropped and Nationalist support declined sharply; the SNP won only two seats in the general election of 1979, two in 1983, and three in 1987, when their total vote was less than half what it had been at its peak in October 1974.

(e) Labour in the ascendant

The most striking thing about Scotland, judging by the general election of 1987, was the strength of the people's support for Labour: out of the 72 seats in Scotland, the Conservatives could muster only 10 against Labour's 50. The main reason for this was that Thatcherite economic policies had devastated Scottish manufacturing industry, including some new industries that had been introduced since the 1960s. Scotland's manufacturing capacity fell by over 30 per cent between 1976 and 1987, and unemployment reached a peak of 15.6 per cent. Some large firms that had survived began to be taken over by larger companies based in England or abroad. Christopher Harvie points out that during 1985/6 alone, takeovers by British firms halved Scottish manufacturing capital from £4.7 billion to £2.3 billion. On the other hand, Conservative policies did mean that the Scots were forced to diversify their economy, bringing in more high-tech and financial firms. Ultimately therefore the economy was strengthened: by 2000, unemployment had fallen and Edinburgh was one of the most prosperous cities in Britain. However, in 1987 none of this was apparent and prospects seemed bleak.

Both Margaret Thatcher and John Major were adamant against devolution which, they claimed, would lead to the break-up of the UK. Nor did the introduction of the unpopular poll tax improve the Scots' opinion of the Conservatives. Meanwhile, the Labour Party became more enthusiastic about devolution, and under Tony Blair's leadership, pledged itself to a Scottish parliament with the power to raise taxes and able to control all matters except foreign affairs, defence, immigration, social security and macroeconomics. The massive Labour victory in the 1997 election made Scottish devolution much more likely. For Scottish Conservatives the election was a catastrophe: the swing away from them was completed and they lost all 10 of their MPs; 6 of them went to Labour, which emerged with a record 56 seats in Scotland; the Scottish Nationalists doubled their seats to 6, and the Liberal Democrats won 10.

During the summer of 1997, the new Labour government, together with the Scottish Nationalists and the Liberal Democrats, campaigned vigorously in favour of devolution. In the referendum held in September 1997, 60 per cent of the Scottish electorate voted; 74.3 per cent of those who voted wanted a Scottish parliament, and 63.5 per cent wanted it to have tax-raising powers. Devolution for Scotland could now go ahead. The first elections for the new 129-seat parliament in Edinburgh took place in May 1999.

(f) Scotland and the Scottish Parliament

The elections were held using a system of proportional representation, which meant that the new government was almost certain to be a coalition. As expected, Labour emerged as the largest single party, with the SNP second, followed by the Liberal-Democrats. The first Scottish devolved assembly was a Labour/Lib-Dem coalition with Donald Dewar, the Labour leader, as 'first minister'. The SNP was the main opposition party. The parliament quickly got down to business, introducing new laws that made Scotland quite different from England in many ways. As noted above, the Scots already had their own separate legal and education systems, which many experts regarded as being superior to those in England. Now there was more generous provision for the elderly, and no fees for higher education for Scottish students (though students in England, and English students at Scottish universities still had to pay); there were new property laws to enable people in the Highlands to compulsorily purchase the land they occupied. And Scotland banned smoking in public places long before England did.

It was not all plain-sailing however; Donald Dewar, the popular and capable first minister, died suddenly in 2000, and there was nobody with his ability and authority to fill the gap adequately. There were a number of scandals, not least the soaring cost of the new parliament building. This was expected to be £55 million but ended up costing £470 million; not surprisingly, this aroused considerable criticism and the cynics had a field-day, so for a time the parliament became an object of ridicule rather than pride. Once the building was completed and the assembly took up residence in 2004, most people began to forget the problems and took the parliament seriously again. The SNP still wanted greater powers for the Scottish parliament and by the end of 2006 public opinion seemed to be moving in their direction. In fact, polls showed that over half the Scots were in favour of complete independence from Britain. In the elections of May 2007, the SNP became the largest single party in the Scottish parliament, with a one-vote majority over Labour. Alex Salmond, the SNP leader, became first minister. Could this be a further step towards complete independence for Scotland? As Andrew Marr graphically puts it: Scotland and England were 'like two pieces of pizza being gently pulled apart, still together but now connected only by strings of molten cheese'.

32.3 Relations between Britain and Wales

(a) Wales up to 1914

Although Wales had been officially united with England since 1536, the Welsh people had kept a strong feeling of national identity, preserving their own culture, religions and language. Unlike the Irish and Scots, the Welsh tended not to emigrate to the USA and Canada, though one famous group settled in Patagonia (South America) in 1865. Instead, as industry developed, they moved to the coal-mining valleys of South Wales, which were one of the most prosperous parts of Britain in 1900. Well over half the population of two million spoke Welsh, and probably 30 per cent of these did not speak English at all. The British government was quite sympathetic towards Welsh cultural interests, and in 1880 it was agreed that the education system in Wales should help to preserve the Welsh language and cultural heritage. There was a university college at Aberystwyth, and two more were founded, at Bangor and Cardiff; in 1893 the colleges were organized into the University of Wales. Issues at stake before 1914 included:

1 *The row over the 1902 Education Act.* Balfour's Education Act (see Section 12.7(e)) caused a major controversy in Wales. Though this was in many ways an excellent reform, it was bitterly disappointing to religious Nonconformists, who were strong in Wales, because it gave money out of the rates to support Anglican schools. The Nonconformists had been hoping that Balfour would abolish Anglican and Catholic schools, which were mainly on the verge of bankruptcy, but now they were to be rescued by money from local rates, to which Nonconformists had to contribute. In Wales, most of the schools were Anglican, whereas about three-quarters of churchgoers were Nonconformists. There was much ill-feeling that so many children of Nonconformist parents would have to continue attending Anglican schools. There was a great outburst of opposition in both Wales and England, but it was in Wales that the desire to safeguard Nonconformist education was strongest.

A campaign of passive resistance was mounted, which usually involved a refusal to pay rates. David Lloyd George, the Welsh-speaking Liberal MP for Caernarvon Boroughs, himself from a Baptist family background, led the attack on the Act in Parliament. In the general election of January 1906, the Conservatives failed to win a single seat in Wales, so strong was Welsh feeling against the Balfour Act. However, when the victorious Liberals tried to introduce an Education Bill more acceptable to the Nonconformists, it was thrown out by the Conservative majority in the Lords. The row over Nonconformist education was mixed up with another issue:

2 *The Campaign against the Anglican Church.* The Anglican Church (the Church of England) was the established church (that is, the official state church) in both England and Wales (as it had been in Ireland until it was 'disestablished' in 1869 – see Section 13.3(c)). Welsh Nonconformists objected to having the 'English' church forced on them, and they expected the Liberal government to do something about it. *The Welsh Disestablishment Bill,* by which the Anglican Church would cease to be the state church in Wales, was introduced in 1912. Despite passing the Commons three times by 1914, it was held up by the Conservatives in the Lords. Many Conservatives were staunch Anglicans; in fact, the Anglican Church used to be referred to as 'the Conservative Party at prayer'; they opposed the Bill with what now seems rather un-Christian bitterness. F. E. Smith, a leading Conservative MP, even went so far as to say that the bill 'shocked the conscience of every Christian community in Europe'. In spite of the Lords' disapproval, the bill eventually became law in 1914, though its operation was postponed until the end of the First World War.

3 *Home Rule for Wales.* The campaign got under way in 1887 with the founding of an organization called *Cymru Fydd (Coming Wales),* whose aim was a separate Welsh parliament. Its president was Tom Ellis, who called himself a Welsh Nationalist, although he was Liberal MP for Merionethshire. After

Ellis's death in 1899, Lloyd George took over the leadership, and in 1911 the Welsh Liberal Party announced its support. However, there was no great interest in Home Rule; a Welsh Home Rule Bill was introduced into the Commons in 1914, but it was dropped when the war broke out.

(b) Wales between the wars

The most striking thing about Wales between the wars was its economic decline. Heavily dependent on coal-mining, Wales was badly hit by both structural and cyclical unemployment in the 1920s and 1930s (see Sections 20.5 and 25.4), and for much of the time it had the highest unemployment in Britain, even worse than in Northern Ireland. In 1932, 36.5 per cent of all insured workers were without jobs, and the figure was still over 22 per cent in 1937, when the worst of the depression was officially over. In some towns the situation was disastrous: in 1934, for example, 74 per cent of all male workers were without jobs in Brynmawr, 73 per cent in Dowlais, and 66 per cent in Merthyr. Unemployment was worst among coal-miners, especially in the Merthyr and Rhondda valleys: in 1935, about half the miners in these areas were out of work.

In 1934, Wales was named as a 'Special Area', along with Scotland, Cumberland and Tyneside. This seemed to do very little good, though a trading estate was set up at Treforest and a new steelworks was built at Ebbw Vale. These economic difficulties did not cause any marked outburst of Welsh nationalist feeling. The *Plaid Cymru (Welsh Nationalist Party)* was founded in 1925 with a programme of self-government for Wales, but it won no seats in Parliament and only had about 2,000 members by 1939. In South Wales people seemed to be more interested in supporting the Labour Party, which wanted to maintain the union of England and Wales, and which hoped to introduce socialist reforms that would benefit both the English and the Welsh.

(c) Plaid Cymru and Welsh Nationalism since 1945

For the first fifteen years after the Second World War, Plaid Cymru continued its campaign but won very little support. The 1945–51 Labour governments were unsympathetic, but the new Conservative government appointed *a Minister for Welsh Affairs,* acknowledging that Welsh interests deserved to be given special attention. It was also hoped that the announcement in 1956 that Wales was for the first time to have its own capital city – Cardiff – would please nationalist opinion. There was much investment in Welsh industry during these years, and this brought a marked improvement in the economy. Most people seemed happy for Wales to continue as part of the UK, and Plaid Cymru could make no headway in elections. In the 1959 general election the party ran only nine candidates, and all lost their deposits. Only about 5 per cent of the Welsh electorate voted Plaid Cymru. However, during the 1960s there was a surge of support, which led to some successes.

- In 1962, the veteran nationalist leader, Saunders Lewis, dismayed at the decline in the speaking of Welsh, made an impassioned radio broadcast calling for a campaign to protect the Welsh language and culture which, he said, were being ignored by the English-dominated London government. This led to the formation of *the Welsh Language Society,* and to an enthusiastic campaign of civil disobedience, in which Welsh language supporters defaced road signs written in English and damaged TV masts that transmitted English-language rather than Welsh-language programmes. Later, some of the extremists became more violent, attacking Post Offices, and holiday homes in Wales owned by English people.

- Plaid Cymru began to attract more votes, and in 1966 Gwynfor Evans, the party's president, won a by-election at Carmarthen, their first ever seat in Parliament. It was said that many people had voted Plaid Cymru as a protest at the recent closing of the Carmarthen to Aberystwyth railway line. In 1967 and 1968 they came close to winning the safe Labour seats of Rhondda West and Caerphilly; these were coal-mining areas where pit closures and rising unemployment were causing criticism of the Labour government (1964–70).

- Labour made some concessions to Welsh opinion. *The Welsh Language Act (1967)* gave the Welsh language equal legal status with English; Welsh began to be used more in government business, and there were more TV programmes in Welsh and more Welsh-speaking primary schools. Even the Royal Family became involved in the campaign to please the Welsh: Prince Charles was invested by the Queen as Prince of Wales at Caernarvon Castle (1969) and he also spent a term at Aberystwyth University College to learn Welsh. In 1968, a Royal Commission was appointed (later known as *the Kilbrandon Commission)* to look into devolution for both Wales and Scotland.

- Plaid Cymru election successes continued when, in the general election of October 1974, the party won three seats.

- A separate Welsh parliament now seemed to be a distinct possibility. The Labour government had only a tiny overall majority, and in order to make sure of support from the Welsh and Scottish Nationalist MPs, seemed prepared to go ahead with devolution. In 1978, a Bill agreeing in principle to a Welsh assembly passed the Commons, though the actual proposal was for an even weaker body than that proposed for Scotland – little more than a glorified county council.

Plaid Cymru was in line for an even bigger disappointment. In March 1979, when a referendum was held in Wales to find out exactly how strong support for devolution was, the vote went overwhelmingly against it: 243,048 in favour and 956,330 against. There was even a majority against in the Welsh-speaking area of Gwynedd, which had two Plaid Cymru MPs. It seemed that this decisive vote against a separate Welsh assembly was because the Labour Party, which had massive support in industrial areas, campaigned against devolution, believing that Wales would be worse off separated from the English economic and social structures. This was a debatable question though; ten years later the Welsh economy was far from healthy. The coal-mining industry, which had once been such a vital element in Britain's prosperity, had declined beyond recognition. In 1912, over 250,000 men worked in the Welsh coal mines; in 1990, the figure was less than 5,000 and still falling; by 1992, only four collieries were left, employing 1,300 men. The steel industry was suffering too: in 1979, British Steel employed 79,000 men in Wales; in only four years this number plummeted to 19,000.

As the 1997 general election approached, while a section of New Labour still opposed devolution for Wales, official party policy under Tony Blair had swung round to favour some sort of Welsh assembly. In the election, the Conservatives lost all six of their seats in Wales, five to Labour and one to the Liberal Democrats. Plaid Cymru held on to the four seats won in 1992. With Labour now holding 34 out of the 40 seats in Wales, the chances of a 'yes' vote in the referendum due to be held in September 1997 seemed strong. However, the result was extremely close: 559,419 (50.3 per cent of those who voted) wanted a Welsh parliament, while 552,698 (49.7 per cent) voted against it. The turnout was only just over 50 per cent, which meant that the plan had been backed by only 25 per cent of the population. Nevertheless, the government was determined to press ahead with the legislation to set up a 60-member assembly to begin business in Cardiff in the summer of 1999. In the 1999 elections, Labour won 37.6 per cent of the vote, Plaid Cymru 28.4 per cent. The Welsh assembly had fewer powers than the Scottish parliament, and could not levy taxes. It seems to have kept a much lower profile than its counterpart in Scotland; even its move into the fine new building designed by Richard Rogers in 2006 went ahead without much publicity outside Wales.

QUESTIONS

1 In what ways did the nationalist movements in Northern Ireland, Scotland and Wales differ from each other? Why were there still no separate parliaments for these areas in 1997?

2 Explain why and how Northern Ireland gained its own devolved assembly in 2007.

A document question on the events of 'Bloody Sunday' in Londonderry in 1972 can be found on the accompanying website www.palgrave.com/masterseries/lowe1.

chapter 33

Britain and its place in the world after 1945

summary of events

The twenty years after the end of the war saw Britain declining from its pre-war position as one of the world's leading powers, to become a second- or perhaps third-rate power, in comparison with the two super-powers – the USA and the USSR. However, British governments, both Labour and Conservative, seemed unwilling to accept what was happening, and, displaying what some historians have called 'delusions of grandeur', tried to act as though Britain was still on an equal footing with the USA and the USSR. In 1946, the British Empire was still intact, and Britain had troops in Germany, Greece, Iran, India, Egypt, Palestine, Malaya and Singapore. This was extremely expensive to maintain for a country whose resources had been strained to the limit by the war effort, and there were some disagreements in the Labour Cabinet about how long Britain could go on maintaining this worldwide military presence; Hugh Dalton, the Chancellor of the Exchequer, was anxious to economize, and felt that at least British troops could be withdrawn from Germany. However, Ernest Bevin, the Foreign Secretary, was a dominating figure who enjoyed the full support of Attlee, the Prime Minister. They were both determined that Britain should play a world role for as long as possible, even to the extent of producing nuclear weapons.

The problems that were soon to unfold before Bevin were complex: the need for a settlement of Germany; the Indian demands for independence; and the Jewish/Arab violence in Palestine. There was also the question of what role Britain should play in the Cold War, and the war in Korea. Bevin negotiated these problems with great skill, though he failed to resolve the Arab/Israeli situation, which in desperation he handed over to the UN.

After the Conservatives came to power in 1951, foreign affairs were dominated by Anthony Eden, first as Foreign Secretary (1951–5) and then as Prime Minister (1955–7). He seemed to be handling affairs well until the 1956 Suez War ended in humiliation for Britain and caused his downfall. To many people, this seemed conclusive proof that Britain, incapable of conducting an independent foreign policy without American approval, was no longer a world power. However, while Harold Macmillan was Conservative Prime Minister (1957–63), he succeeded in keeping up the illusion for a little longer by seeking to renew and develop Britain's 'special relationship' with the USA, though it was during his premiership that Britain gave up most of its Empire (see Chapter 34)

At the same time as the British were withdrawing from their Empire, they missed an opportunity to join the other states of Western Europe, when they decided against membership of the European Economic Community (EEC) on its formation in 1957. When Macmillan eventually decided that it would be advantageous for Britain to join after all, their entry was blocked by the French (January 1963). Britain was thus left largely isolated from the rest of Europe and at the same time had offended the Commonwealth by applying to join the EEC. Britain seemed to be floundering, and it was to be another ten years before Europe opened its ranks to British membership. Dean Acheson, a former American Secretary of State (who was reasonably pro-British) made the much-quoted remark (in December 1962) that Britain 'has lost an Empire but has not yet found a role'. To what extent Britain was 'in decline' has been the subject of some debate among historians; the most recent trend is to suggest that Britain's so-called decline was something of a myth; arguably, Britain was still a great power, but it was a different kind of greatness.

33.1 Britain and the Cold War

(a) what was the Cold War?

Towards the end of the Second World War, the harmony that had existed between the USA, the USSR and the British Empire began to evaporate, and all the old suspicions came to the fore again. Relations between Soviet Russia and the West became so difficult that, while no actual armed conflict took place directly between the two opposing camps, the decade after 1945 saw the first phase of what became known as *the Cold War*. This continued, in spite of several 'thaws', until the collapse of communism in Eastern Europe in 1989–91. What happened was that, perhaps deterred by the fear of a nuclear war, instead of allowing their mutual hostility to express itself in open fighting, the rival powers confined themselves to attacking each other with propaganda and economic measures, and with a general policy of non-cooperation.

Both super-powers gathered allies around them: between 1945 and 1948 the USSR drew into its orbit most of the states of Eastern Europe. A communist government was established in North Korea in 1948, and the communist bloc seemed to be further strengthened in 1949 when Mao Zedong was at last victorious in the long civil war in China. On the other hand, the USA hastened the recovery of Japan and fostered the country as an ally; and worked closely with Britain and fourteen other European countries, as well as with Turkey, providing them with vast amounts of economic aid in order to build up an anti-communist bloc. Whatever one bloc suggested or did was viewed by the other as having ulterior and aggressive motives. There was a long wrangle, for example, over where the frontier between Poland and Germany should be, and no permanent settlement for Germany and Austria could be agreed on.

In the mid-1950s, after the death of Stalin (1953), the new Russian leaders began to talk about 'peaceful co-existence', and the icy atmosphere between the two blocs began to thaw. It was agreed to remove all occupying troops from Austria (1955); however, relations did not warm sufficiently to allow agreement on Germany, which remained divided until 1990.

(b) what were the causes of the Cold War?

The basic cause lay in the differences of principle between the communist states and the capitalist or liberal-democratic states. Ever since the world's first communist state was set up in Russia in 1917, the governments of most capitalist states viewed it with distrust and were afraid of communism spreading to their countries. Only the need for self-preservation had caused both sides to ignore their differences; as soon as it became clear that the defeat of Germany was only a matter of time, both sides, and Stalin in particular, began to plan for the post-war period. He aimed to take advantage of the military situation to strengthen Russian influence in Europe; this involved occupying as much of Germany as possible as the Nazi armies collapsed, and acquiring as much territory as he could get away with from other states such as Finland, Poland and Romania. When Stalin extended Russian control over most of Eastern Europe, the West became more and more alarmed at what seemed to be Russian aggression; they believed that he was committed to spreading communism over as much of the globe as possible.

In the final phase of the Second World War, President Roosevelt had been inclined to trust Stalin, but Churchill thought differently. He wanted British and American troops to make a dash for Berlin before the Russians took it, but he was overruled by the Americans. However, after Roosevelt died in April 1945, his successor, Harry S. Truman, was much more suspicious of the Russians, and his misgivings were confirmed at the Potsdam Conference in July 1945, when Stalin refused to come to any agreement about Germany's future. Some historians believe that Truman's main motive for dropping the atomic bombs on Japan was to show Stalin what might happen to Russia if he dared to go too far. Even so, it was not until early in 1947 that Truman completely abandoned his belief in Stalin's good faith.

Ernest Bevin's attitude in this situation was similar to Churchill's. He had no love for communists and thought that Britain must stand up to the Russians in order to maintain a balance of power in Europe. The best way to achieve this was by co-operation with the Americans, and he hoped for a concerted Anglo-American effort to prevent the expansion of Russian power and communism in

Eastern Europe. But the Americans, even Truman, were reluctant to interfere in the affairs of Eastern Europe, believing that, even if Poland and Hungary fell under Russian influence, Stalin would allow them to have democratic governments if they wished. The Americans soon received an unpleasant shock, however: by the end of 1947, communist governments had been established, under Russian influence, in Poland, Hungary, Romania, Bulgaria and Albania. In addition, Stalin treated the Russian zone of Germany as if it belonged to Russia, banning all political parties except the communists, and draining it of vital resources.

(c) which side was responsible for the Cold War?

During the 1950s, most Western historians blamed Stalin, arguing that his motives were sinister and that he intended to spread communism as widely as possible through Europe and Asia. The formation of NATO and the American entry into the Korean War in 1950 were the West's self-defence against communist aggression.

On the other hand, Soviet historians, and during the 1960s and early 1970s some American historians, argued that the Cold War ought not to be blamed on the Russians. Their theory was that the USSR had been so weakened by the war that Stalin's motives were purely defensive, and that there was never any real threat to the West from Russia. Some Americans claim that the USA should have been more understanding and should not have challenged the idea of a soviet 'sphere of influence' in Eastern Europe. The actions of American politicians, especially Truman, provoked Russian hostility unnecessarily. This is known among historians as the 'revisionist' view.

Later, a third view – known as the 'post-revisionist' interpretation – became popular among American historians during the 1980s. They had the benefit of being able to look at many new documents and visit archives that had not been open to earlier historians. The new evidence led them to take a middle view, arguing that both sides should share responsibility for the Cold War. They believe that American economic policies such as Marshall Aid (see below) were deliberately designed to increase US political influence in Europe. However, they also believe that while Stalin had no long-term plans to spread communism, he was an opportunist who would take advantage of any weakness in the West to expand Soviet influence. With their entrenched positions and deep suspicions of each other, the USA and the USSR created an atmosphere in which every international act could be interpreted in two ways. What was claimed as necessary for self-defence by one side was taken by the other side as evidence of aggressive intent. Sections 33.1(d)–(h) show how this happened.

(d) the Truman Doctrine and the Marshall Plan

The situation in Greece led to a closer American involvement in European affairs.

- British troops had helped liberate Greece from the Germans in 1944 and had restored the monarchy. However, they were now feeling the strain of supporting the king against communist guerrillas, who were receiving help from Albania, Bulgaria and Yugoslavia. If Greece fell to the communists, there was every chance that Turkey and Iran would follow. In Bevin's view, only Britain stood between Russian control of the eastern Mediterranean, the Dardanelles and the Middle East.

- Churchill responded to what was happening with a speech at Fulton, Missouri (USA), in which he tried to stir the Americans into action (March 1946). He repeated a phrase he had used earlier: 'From Stettin in the Baltic to Trieste in the Adriatic, *an iron curtain has descended across the Continent* [emphasis added].' Claiming that the Russians were intent on 'indefinite expansion of their power and doctrines', he called for *a Western alliance* which would stand firm against the communist threat, 'since our difficulties and dangers will not be removed by merely waiting to see what happens'. The speech helped to widen the rift between East and West; Stalin was able to denounce Churchill as a 'warmonger', while over a hundred British Labour MPs signed a motion criticizing Churchill.

- An added difficulty was that Anglo-American relations were strained by the abrupt ending of Lend–Lease, and by the unfavourable terms insisted on for the American loan in 1945 (see Section 29.3(c)). Many Americans were hostile to Britain's Empire and continued to view Britain as a serious trade rival. This was one reason for the lack of enthusiasm for Britain's anti-communist stand in Greece.

- In February 1947, Bevin told the Americans clearly that Britain's economic position made it impossible to continue the struggle in Greece. If they wanted Greece and Turkey saving from communism, they would have to do it themselves. Truman responded with what became known as *the Truman Doctrine:* the USA would 'support free peoples who are resisting subjugation by armed minorities or by outside pressures'. Greece immediately received massive amounts of arms and other supplies, and by 1949 the communists were defeated. Turkey, which also seemed under threat, received aid worth about US$60 million.

- *The Marshall Plan* (announced June 1947) was an economic extension of the Truman Doctrine. American Secretary of State, George Marshall, produced his European Recovery Programme (ERP), which offered economic and financial help wherever it was needed. 'Our policy', he declared, 'is directed not against any country or doctrine but against hunger, poverty, desperation and chaos.' Its aim was to promote the economic recovery of Europe, thus ensuring markets for American exports. In addition, communism was less likely to gain control of a prosperous Western Europe. The only proviso was that the European nations themselves must co-operate with each other to produce a plan for the best use of American aid.

Bevin eagerly took the lead and, together with the French Foreign Minister, called an international conference in Paris. By September, sixteen nations (Britain, France, Italy, Belgium, Luxembourg, the Netherlands, Portugal, Austria, Switzerland, Greece, Turkey, Iceland, Norway, Sweden, Denmark and the three Western zones of Germany) had drawn up a joint plan for using American aid. During the next four years, over US$13 thousand million of Marshall Aid flowed into Western Europe, fostering the recovery of agriculture and industry, which in many countries were in chaos as a result of war devastation. The Russians were invited to the conference but declined to attend. They were well aware that there was more to Marshall Aid than pure benevolence.

Although in theory aid was available to Eastern Europe, Molotov, the Russian Foreign Minister, denounced the whole idea as 'dollar imperialism'. The Russians saw it as blatant American device for gaining control of Western Europe, and worse still, for interfering in Eastern Europe, which Stalin considered to be in the Soviet 'sphere of influence'. Russia rejected the offer, and neither its satellite states nor Czechoslovakia, which was showing interest, were allowed to take advantage of it. By now the 'iron curtain' seemed a reality and the Cold War was well under way.

(e) the Berlin blockade and airlift (June 1948–May 1949)

This brought the Cold War to its first big crisis, which arose out of disagreements over the treatment of Germany:

1 At the end of the war, as agreed at Yalta and Potsdam, Germany and Berlin were each divided into four zones. While the three Western powers did their best to organize the economic and political recovery of their zones, Stalin, determined to make Germany pay for the damage inflicted on Russia, continued to treat his zone as a satellite, draining away its resources.
2 Early in 1948, the three Western zones were merged to form a single economic unit whose prosperity, thanks to Marshall Aid, was in marked contrast to the poverty of the Russian zone. At the same time, outraged at the Russian-backed coup in Czechoslovakia (February 1948), the Western powers began to prepare a constitution for a self-governing West Germany, since the Russians had no intention of allowing complete German reunification. However, the Russians were alarmed at the prospect of a strong, independent West Germany, which would be part of the American bloc.
3 When in June 1948 the West introduced a new currency and ended price controls and rationing in their zone of Germany and in West Berlin, the Russians decided that the situation in Berlin had become impossible. Already irritated by this island of capitalism deep in the communist zone, they felt it was out of the question to have two different currencies in the same city, and were embarrassed by the contrast between the prosperity of West Berlin and the poverty of the surrounding areas.

The Russian response was immediate: all road, rail and canal links between West Berlin and West Germany were closed. Their aim was to force the West to withdraw from West Berlin by reducing it to starvation point. The Western powers, convinced that a retreat would be the prelude to a Russian attack on West Germany, were determined to hold on; they decided to fly in supplies, rightly judging that the Russians would not risk shooting down the transport planes. Truman had thoughtfully sent a fleet of B29 bombers to be positioned on British airfields. Over the next ten months, the Americans and British airlifted 2 million tons of supplies to the blockaded city in a remarkable operation which kept the 2.5 million West Berliners fed and warm right through the winter. In May 1949, the Russians admitted defeat and lifted the blockade.

The affair had important results: the outcome gave a great psychological boost to the Western powers, though it brought relations with Russia to their worst ever point. It caused the Western powers to co-ordinate their defences through the formation of NATO. It meant also that since no compromise seemed possible, Germany was doomed to remain divided for the foreseeable future. The German Federal Republic (West Germany) came into existence in August 1949; the Russians set up their zone as the German Democratic Republic (East Germany) in October 1949.

(f) the formation of NATO (North Atlantic Treaty Organization) – April 1949

The Berlin blockade demonstrated the West's military unreadiness, and frightened them into making definite preparations. Bevin had already made the first moves to bring about closer co-operation in Western Europe: in March 1948, Britain, France, Belgium, the Netherlands and Luxembourg had signed *the Brussels Defence Treaty*, promising military collaboration in case of war. Now they were joined by the USA, Canada, Denmark, Portugal and Norway. All signed *the North Atlantic Treaty*, agreeing to regard an attack on any one of them as an attack on them all, and placing their defence forces under a joint NATO Command Organization which would co-ordinate the defence of the West. This was a highly significant development: the Americans had abandoned their traditional policy of 'no entangling alliances' and for the first time had pledged themselves in advance to military action. Stalin took this as a challenge and tension remained high.

Bevin was justifiably exultant, seeing NATO as the crowning achievement of his career: he had contributed to the formation of the Truman Doctrine, taken the lead in planning for Marshall Aid, played an important part in preparations for the Brussels Treaty, and supported Truman in the Berlin airlift; the climax of the process was NATO. On the debit side, however, Britain was widely criticized for its handling of the situation in Palestine (see Section 34.3).

(g) the war in Korea (1950–3)

The origins of the war lay in the fact that the country had been divided into two zones in 1945 at the end of the Second World War. It was divided at the 38th parallel by agreement between the USA and the USSR for purely military reasons – so that they could organize the surrender of the occupying Japanese forces; it was not intended to be a permanent political division. However, the unification of communist North Korea with the non-communist South soon became part of the Cold War rivalry, and no agreement could be reached. In 1949, Russian and American troops were withdrawn, leaving a potentially dangerous situation: most Koreans bitterly resented the artificial division forced on their country by outsiders. Without warning, North Korean troops invaded South Korea in June 1950.

The communists had just gained control of China under the leadership of Mao Zedong. Truman was convinced that the attack on South Korea, coming so soon after Cold War events in Europe, was part of a vast Russian plan to advance communism wherever possible in the world; he believed it was essential for the West to take a stand by supporting South Korea. American troops in Japan were ordered to South Korea *before* the United Nations Organization had decided what action to take. The UN Security Council called on North Korea to withdraw its troops, and when this was ignored, asked member states to send assistance to South Korea. This decision was reached in the absence of the Russian delegation, who were boycotting meetings in protest against the UN's refusal to allow Mao's new Chinese regime to be represented, and who would certainly have vetoed such a decision. In the event, the USA and fourteen other countries (including Britain, Australia, Canada and New Zealand) sent troops, though the vast majority were Americans. All forces were under the command of the US General MacArthur.

Their arrival was just in time to prevent the whole of South Korea from being overrun by the communists. By September 1950, communist forces had captured the whole country apart from the south-east, around the port of Pusan. UN reinforcements poured into Pusan, and there was soon a complete turnaround – communist forces were chased out of the South, and by the end of October UN troops had occupied two-thirds of North Korea, and reached the Yalu River, the frontier between North Korea and China. The Chinese government was seriously alarmed: in November they launched a massive counter-offensive, with over 300,000 troops described as 'volunteers'. By mid-January 1951 they had driven the UN troops out of North Korea and crossed the 38th parallel; Seoul, the capital of South Korea was captured again. MacArthur was shocked at the strength of the Chinese forces; he argued that the best way to beat them and stop the spread of communism was to attack Manchuria, with atomic bombs if necessary.

At this point, Clement Attlee, still British Prime Minister, paid a surprise visit to Washington to urge Truman not to use atomic bombs on China. Possibly influenced by Attlee, Truman decided that this would be too risky and might cause a large-scale war, which the USA did not want. He decided to settle for merely 'containing' communism; MacArthur was removed from his command. In June, UN troops drove the communists out of South Korea again and fortified the frontier. Peace talks at Panmunjom lasted for two years, ending in July 1953 with an agreement that the frontier should be roughly along the 38th parallel.

While Britain sent the second largest contingent of troops, and suffered over 4,000 casualties (with almost 700 killed), these were small numbers compared with the American commitment (over 33,000 of their combatants were killed). Yet, as Jeremy Black points out, 'it was difficult to defend the commitment in terms of traditional British interests, and the Americans tended to take decisions without much or any consultation.' The main importance of the war for the British was the way in which it set back their economic recovery (see Section 29.4(a)). The increase in armaments spending forced the government to economize in other areas, including the introduction of NHS prescription charges. This caused a split in the Labour Party, which contributed to its defeat in the election of 1951 (see Section 29.4). A revealing incident occurred during the war after Britain officially recognized the new Communist government of China in 1950. The USA had refused to do so, and continued to treat the exiled Chinese government in Taiwan as the rightful regime. The Americans resented British attempts to follow an independent line, and in 1951, when the USA signed the ANZUS Pact with Australia and New Zealand, the Americans refused Britain's request to join. It was at Suez in 1956 that the Americans committed what some historians see as their greatest 'betrayal' of Britain (see next section).

(h) Britain and its defences

Attlee and Bevin had authorized the manufacture of an atomic bomb, though this was not given much publicity. The nuclear policy was thought to be absolutely vital for Britain's security and influence. The formation of NATO in 1949 meant that the USA had committed itself to defending Western Europe, but the Americans expected Britain to play an important part as well. It was under strong American pressure that Britain began a rearmament programme, including nuclear weapons. An atomic bomb was tested successfully in 1952, and it was thought that this put Britain back on a level with the USA and the USSR. However, the development of atomic weapons moved fast; before long, Britain had to decide whether to produce a hydrogen bomb. In 1954, Churchill announced that Britain would go ahead with its manufacture, and by 1957 the first British H-bomb had been exploded successfully.

However, the nuclear arms race soon became far too fast and too expensive for a small country to compete. The production of the H-bomb meant that Britain was spending as much on defence as during the Second World War, thus ruining much of the economic progress made since 1948. But that was not the end – the next development (by the Russians) was the inter-continental ballistic missile (ICBM), a nuclear warhead carried by a rocket so powerful that it could reach the USA even when fired from inside the USSR. When Britain tried to develop its own rocket system – *Blue Streak* – it proved impossibly expensive and was abandoned in 1960.

At about the same time, *the Campaign for Nuclear Disarmament (CND)* was started. Its supporters argued, on moral grounds, that Britain should withdraw from the nuclear arms race and disarm unilaterally; it was hoped that the USA and the USSR would follow Britain's lead and scrap their nuclear weapons too. Their case was strengthened when evidence began to build up showing that nuclear tests carried out in the atmosphere caused highly dangerous radioactive fallout. CND held mass demonstrations and rallies, and every year at Easter staged a protest march from London to Aldermaston (where there was an atomic research base) and back. No British government dared to risk unilateral disarmament, which, they believed, would leave Britain vulnerable to a nuclear attack from the USSR; they would only consider abandoning their nuclear weapons as part of a general agreement by all the major powers (multilateral nuclear disarmament).

Harold Macmillan quickly built up an impressive reputation as an international statesman. He was convinced that Britain's future was inextricably bound up with the USA and was anxious to renew the 'special relationship' between the two states that had been seriously damaged by the Suez war (see next section). He saw this as the best way of maintaining Britain's 'great power' status. He formed good relationships with Presidents Eisenhower and Kennedy; he was a great believer in the value of summit conferences between world leaders and worked hard to organize one. He visited Moscow (February 1959) and established good relations with Nikita Khrushchev, the Russian leader. Macmillan could claim to be at least partly responsible for Khrushchev's decision not to press for a Western withdrawal from Berlin. Soon afterwards, Macmillan went to Paris, Bonn and Washington, and as the Cold War tensions eased, he was able to persuade the Western leaders that a summit with the Russians might be fruitful. Unfortunately, when the conference eventually met in May 1960, it was unsuccessful. An American U-2 spy plane had just been shot down over a thousand miles inside Russia. The Russians demanded an apology, and when Eisenhower refused, Khrushchev walked out.

By 1963, it was clear that Britain had ceased to be a world power. The British had been humiliated at Suez in 1956; they simply lacked the economic strength and the resources to remain on a level with the two super-powers, and had been forced to abandon the idea of manufacturing their own nuclear weapons. The best Macmillan could manage was to persuade President Kennedy (at a meeting in Nassau in December 1962) to supply Britain with American nuclear Polaris missiles, which could be fired from British nuclear submarines. During

Illus. 33.1 Harold Macmillan and President Kennedy of the USA working at 'the special relationship'

the Cuban missile crisis in October 1962, Britain was unable to play any useful role. The crisis occurred when Kennedy demanded the removal of Russian missiles from Cuba, less than 100 miles from the American coast. The two powers seemed to be on the verge of nuclear war, but common sense prevailed and Khrushchev eventually agreed to remove the missiles. Soon afterwards Britain was refused entry to the EEC (see Section 33.7(f)), and at the same time had lost most of its Empire.

Macmillan had one final achievement before his retirement: he played an important role in the signing of *the Nuclear Test Ban Treaty (August 1963)* by the USA, the USSR and Britain. It was agreed that, in order to avoid polluting the atmosphere, nuclear tests would only be carried out underground. The Americans had not been enthusiastic about the treaty, and it was Macmillan's persistence that eventually brought success. Kennedy paid Macmillan a handsome tribute, acknowledging that the British premier's role in limiting nuclear testing had been indispensable.

33.2 Britain and the Suez Crisis, 1956

(a) the causes of the crisis were complex

It was partly a continuation of the Arab–Israeli conflict; partly a struggle between Arab nationalism (in the person of the Egyptian leader, Colonel Nasser) and the

British (and French), who wanted to prolong British influence in the Middle East; and it was an episode in the Cold War between the USA and the USSR.

1 Colonel Gamal Abdel Nasser, the new ruler of Egypt (who came to power in 1954 soon after the overthrow of the unpopular King Farouk), was aggressively in favour of Arab unity and independence, including the liberation of Palestine from the Jews. Almost everything he did irritated the British, the French or the Americans. He organized guerrilla bands (*fedayeen* – self-sacrificers) to sabotage and murder inside Israel, and blockaded the Gulf of Aqaba, leading to the Israeli port of Eilat.

2 He insisted that Britain evacuate its military base at Suez (the agreement signed in 1936 allowing Britain to keep the base expired in 1956), sent aid to the Algerian Arabs in their struggle against France, prodded the other Arab states into opposing the British-sponsored Baghdad Pact, and forced King Hussein of Jordan to dismiss his British army chief of staff.

3 In September 1955, Nasser signed an arms deal with Czechoslovakia for Russian fighters, bombers and tanks, and Soviet experts went to train the Egyptian army. The Americans saw this as a Russian attempt to 'move into' the Middle East, and tried to placate Nasser by offering to finance the building of a dam at Aswan. However, Nasser upset the West further by officially recognizing communist China, and in July 1956 the Americans cancelled the promised grant of US$46 million.

4 Nasser immediately retaliated by nationalizing the Suez Canal, intending to use its revenues to finance the dam. Shareholders, the majority of whom were British and French, were promised compensation.

5 Anthony Eden, Britain's new Conservative Prime Minister, convinced that Nasser must be removed, took the lead at this point. He believed that Nasser was on the way to forming a united Arabia under Egyptian control and communist influence. Two-thirds of all Britain's oil supplies came via the Suez Canal, and these could now be cut off at Nasser's whim. Eden viewed Nasser as another Hitler or Mussolini, and according to historian Hugh Thomas, 'saw Egypt through a forest of Flanders poppies and gleaming jackboots'. He was also influenced by the fact that the Conservatives had criticized the Labour government when it failed to take action in a similar situation in 1951 (when Iran had nationalized the Anglo-Iranian Oil Company), and he was infuriated by the taunts of the Tory press that he was indecisive. Eden had plenty of support for some sort of action against Nasser; Churchill remarked: 'we can't have this malicious swine sitting across our communications', and the new Labour leader, Hugh Gaitskell, agreed that Nasser must not be appeased in the way that Hitler and Mussolini had been in the 1930s. Most people in Britain seemed to ignore the fact that Nasser had offered compensation to the shareholders and had promised that the ships of all nations (apart from Israel's) would be able to use the canal.

(b) Anglo-French-Israeli plans

Secret talks took place between the British, French and Israelis, and a plan was hatched: Israeli troops would invade Egypt across the Sinai peninsula, whereupon Britain and France would issue an ultimatum to both sides to withdraw from the canal. The Egyptians would not be able to agree to this, since they were in their own territory, so British and French troops would attack Egypt and occupy the Canal Zone, on the pretext that they were protecting it from damage in the fighting. In the words of Anthony Nutting, a Foreign Office minister who resigned in protest at this policy: 'This meant that Britain and France, who were pretending to put a stop to the fighting, were ordering the victim of aggression to withdraw 134 miles, while the aggressor was being allowed to advance up to 115 miles!' Anglo-French control of the canal would be restored, and the defeat, it was hoped, would topple Nasser from power.

Recent research, most notably by Eden's biographer, D. R. Thorpe (2003) has shown that the war could easily have been avoided, and that Eden was more in favour of removing Nasser by peaceful means. The Americans had made it clear that they had no desire to get involved in military action in the Middle East; and President Eisenhower was facing an election in November, and did not want to appear too aggressive. In fact, there was a secret Anglo-American plan (*Omega*) to overthrow Nasser using political and economic pressures. In mid-October 1956, Eden was still willing to continue talks with Egypt; he had called off the military operation, and there seemed a good chance of compromise being reached over control of the canal. However, Eden was under pressure from several directions to use force. MI6 (the British intelligence service) and some members of the Cabinet, including Macmillan (the Chancellor of the Exchequer) and Selwyn Lloyd (the Foreign Secretary) were in favour of military action. Macmillan assured Eden that the USA would not oppose a British use of force: 'I know Ike [Eisenhower's nickname]', he told Eden. 'He'll lie doggo!' In the end, it was probably pressure from the French government that caused Eden to opt for the joint military operation with France and Israel.

(c) the war against Egypt

The plans were duly put into operation and militarily were a brilliant success. The war began with the planned Israeli invasion of Egypt (29 October 1956), which within a week had captured the entire Sinai peninsula. Britain and France delivered their ultimatum and proceeded to bomb Egyptian airfields and land troops at Port Said, at the northern end of the Suez Canal. The attacks caused an outcry from the rest of the world: the Americans were furious: they were afraid of upsetting all the Arabs and forcing them into closer ties with the USSR; the last thing Eisenhower wanted just before the election was Britain rocking the boat. Consequently, the USA refused to support Britain; at the UN both the Americans and Russians, for once in agreement, categorically condemned the British and French action and the UN accused them of aggression. The UN went on to demand an immediate ceasefire, threatened oil sanctions and prepared to send a peacekeeping force of its own. With the pressure of world opinion against them, Britain, France and Israel agreed to a ceasefire (6 November) and began to withdraw, while UN troops moved in to police the frontier between Egypt and Israel.

(d) the outcome of the war

The war was a diplomatic disaster for both Britain and France; as Peter Clarke puts it: 'once the cover story was blown, the British appeared doubly guilty – not only of aggression against Egypt but guilty too of calculated deceit of their great ally'. None of their aims was achieved. They had failed to overthrow Nasser, and his prestige as leader of Arab nationalism against European interference was greatly enhanced. He simply replaced the American and Western aid he had lost with aid from the USSR. The Egyptians blocked the canal and the Arabs reduced oil supplies to Western Europe, where petrol rationing was introduced for a time. To back up its condemnation in the UN, the USA withdrew its support for the pound, and blocked Britain's access to the International Monetary Fund until their troops were withdrawn from Suez. This caused a disastrous fall in Britain's gold reserves – a quarter of its entire gold and dollar reserves were lost in November 1956 alone. The British action soon lost them a valuable Middle East ally in Iraq, where the pro-British King Feisal and his premier, Nuri-es-Said, came under increasing attack from other Arab governments; both were murdered in 1958. Even more serious, the Anglo-American alliance was weakened at a time when it needed to present a strong front against the Russians, who were in the process of crushing the Hungarian uprising. Jonathan Haslam recently showed in *Chill Shadow: A History of the Cold War* (2007) that the Soviet leaders had decided to withdraw their troops from Hungary on 30 October; however, the Anglo-French invasion of Egypt encouraged them to reverse this decision and overthrow the anti-communist regime in Hungary. The British climbdown showed the British government as being weak and incapable of conducting a foreign policy independent of the USA. It has been suggested that Britain's humiliation helped to speed up decolonization by encouraging independence movements in Africa. In the words of Dominic Sandbrook, 'in the aftermath of the crisis, no one could doubt that Britain's days as a great international power had passed, and Suez became the symbol of British retrenchment and reassessment'. For the pessimists, this was indisputable proof that Britain was a nation in terminal decline; they found it hard to accept, and blamed the Americans for letting Britain down. Worse still, the French were furious with Britain for 'running out' on them before the whole of the Canal Zone had been captured, and arguably, this was the main reason why Charles de Gaulle rejected Britain's application to join the Common Market in 1963.

On the other hand, some historians have sought to play down the ill-effects of Suez. David Carlton (1988) points out that, while Nasser was still in power, Egypt had in fact suffered a devastating defeat at the hands of Israel, losing at least a third of its army and its equipment. British influence in the Middle East was not completely finished, since pro-British regimes survived in both Jordan and Kuwait. The breach with the USA was soon healed when Macmillan became Prime Minister, the British government did not fall, and only one politician – Eden – was forced to resign. Dominic Sandbrook also sees another side to Suez: instead of taking it as a sign of decline, it is possible to see it as a watershed leading into a new era and a new role for Britain:

> The heavy grey clouds that had hung over British life for almost twenty years were beginning to lift. Only two years previously meat rationing had still been in force, but now high-street sales of cars, televisions, washing-machines and records were reaching record levels ... To many people Britain felt like a country on the verge of an exciting new era of opportunity and possibility.

(e) The war a personal disaster for Eden

In some quarters, Eden was criticized for having sent troops into Egypt in the first place, without any real moral case (the fact that Nasser had offered compensation was consistently ignored). Others thought that, having gone in, Britain should have ignored the UN and captured the whole Canal Zone, which would have been possible within a few days. What would have happened then is not certain; it seems that Eden had not thought through the consequences clearly enough, and Britain's actual war aims were vague. Finally, to make matters worse, he had lied to the House of Commons, denying that the British had planned to attack Egypt or had known in advance of the Israeli invasion. Always highly strung, he was exhausted by the crisis and, on his doctor's orders, resigned in January 1957. His political career was finished.

The irony was that while Eden is remembered as the scapegoat for Suez, he was succeeded as Prime Minister by Macmillan, who was arguably just as responsible for the disaster as Eden had been. Macmillan had urged Eden to opt for military action, and after talking to Eisenhower, he misled Eden into thinking that the Americans would not oppose it. Despite being Chancellor of the Exchequer, he failed to tell the Cabinet how serious Britain's balance of payments was, or that the Treasury had warned him that it was vital that 'we do not go it alone and that we have the maximum US support'. Then, having to preside over Britain's rapidly dwindling reserves, Macmillan was the one who changed his tune and urged a ceasefire, realizing that this was the only way to get back American support for sterling. A possibly even greater irony is suggested by Andrew Roberts (2006): 'there is even a tantalising possibility that the Eisenhower Administration privately wanted Nasser overthrown and was only criticizing France and Britain in public because of electoral considerations ... The subsequent history of Iraq, and especially her recent history, would have been very different if Nasser had been toppled.'

33.3 Britain, Europe and the European Community

(a) reasons for wanting more unity

In every country in Western Europe there were people from all parts of the political spectrum who wanted more unity. They had different ideas about exactly what sort of unity would be best, however: some simply wanted the nations to co-operate more closely; while others (known as *federalists*) thought in terms of a politically united Europe with a federal system of government similar to the one in the USA. Their reasoning was simple: only by a co-operative effort and a pooling of resources could Europe recover from the ravages of the war; and the countries were too small to be economically and militarily viable separately in a world dominated by the super-powers – the USA and the USSR. The more the countries of Western Europe worked together, the less chance there would be of war breaking out between them again, and it seemed the best way for a speedy reconciliation between France and Germany. Finally, it was thought that the threat to Western Europe from Russia and communism could best be met by joint action. West Germany was especially keen on the idea, because it would gain the country early acceptance as a responsible nation again.

Winston Churchill was one of the strongest advocates of European unity; in March 1943 he spoke of the need for a Council of Europe, and in a speech in Zurich in 1946 he suggested that France and Germany should take the lead in setting up 'a kind of United States of Europe'.

(b) first steps in co-operation

The first steps in economic, military and political co-operation were soon taken, but the federalists were bitterly disappointed that a United States of Europe had not materialized by 1950.

▸ *The Organisation for European Economic Co-operation (OEEC)* was the first move towards unity; it was created in 1948 as a response to the American offer of Marshall Aid, when Ernest Bevin took the lead in organizing sixteen European nations to draw up a plan for the best use of American aid (see Section 33.1(d)). The 16-nation committee became the permanent OEEC, and it was extremely successful in apportioning American aid and encouraging trade among its members by reducing restrictions.
▸ *NATO was another example of European co-operation,* set up in 1949 as a mutual defence organization in case of an attack on one of the member states (see Section 33.1(f)). However, France withdrew in 1966.

- *The Council of Europe (1949)* was the first attempt at some sort of political unity. Its founder-members were Britain, Belgium, the Netherlands, Luxembourg, Denmark, France, the Republic of Ireland, Italy, Norway and Sweden. By 1971, all the states of Western Europe (except Spain and Portugal) had joined, and so had Turkey, Malta and Cyprus, making eighteen members in total. Based at Strasbourg, the Council consisted of the Foreign Ministers of the member states, and an assembly of representatives chosen by the parliaments of the states. It had no powers, however, since several states, including Britain, refused to join any organization that threatened their own sovereignty. It could debate pressing issues and make recommendations, and it did useful work in sponsoring human rights agreements; but it was a grave disappointment to the federalists.

(c) the European Economic Community (EEC) set up (1957)

Known in Britain in its early years as *the Common Market*, the EEC was set up by *the Treaty of Rome (1957)* and came into operation on 1 January 1958. There were six founder-members – France, West Germany, Italy, Belgium, the Netherlands and Luxembourg. Britain refused to join. *The stages in the evolution of the Community were*:

1 *Benelux* – in 1944 the exiled governments of Belgium, the Netherlands and Luxembourg formed *the Benelux Customs Union,* a customs and trading association that came into operation in 1947.

2 *The Treaty of Brussels (1948)* – by this treaty, Britain and France joined the three Benelux countries in pledging 'military, economic, social and cultural collaboration'. The military collaboration eventually resulted in NATO; the next step in economic co-operation was the ECSC.

3 *The European Coal and Steel Community (ECSC) set up in 1951.* This was the brainchild of Robert Schuman, the French Foreign Minister, who hoped that involving West Germany would improve relations between France and Germany and at the same time make European industry more efficient. Six countries joined – France, West Germany, Italy, Belgium, the Netherlands and Luxembourg. All duties and restrictions on trade in coal, iron and steel between the Six were removed, and a High Authority was created to administer the community and organize a joint programme of expansion. However, the British refused to join, because it would mean handing over control of their industries to an outside, supranational authority. The ECSC was an outstanding success; steel production rose by almost 50 per cent during the first five years, and the Six decided to extend it to include all production.

The British decision not to join is usually seen as a serious mistake; but it is easy to be wise with the benefit of hindsight. In defence of the government, it has to be pointed out that they were in the throes of nationalizing iron and steel, and coal had just been nationalized; these would be pointless exercises if the industries were to be handed over immediately to the High Authority. Nor were there any guarantees that the ECSC would be a success; at that point, the six states which joined were much weaker economically than Britain. As historian Stephen George points out, 'by joining in, Britain might have been tying itself to a sinking ship which could pull down the British economy with it'. Attlee therefore announced that, while the British sympathized with any activities that improved Franco-German relations, they could not undertake to join the scheme immediately.

4 *The Treaty of Rome (1957)*, setting up the EEC, specified that the Six would gradually remove all customs duties and quotas so there would be free competition and a common market. Tariffs would be kept against non-members, though even these were reduced. The treaty also mentioned improving living and working conditions, expanding industry, encouraging the development of the world's backward areas, safeguarding peace and liberty, and working for an ever-closer union of European peoples; obviously something much wider than just a common market was in the minds of the statesmen of the Six. Jean Monnet, for example, the French chairman of the ECSC High Authority, set up an action committee to work for a United States of Europe. The EEC was soon off to a flying start; within five years it was the world's biggest exporter and biggest buyer of raw materials, and was second only to the USA in steel production. Once again, however, Britain had refused the invitation to join.

By 1967 the machinery to run the EEC had been refined to include the following:

‣ *The European Commission* based in Brussels was the body which managed the day-to-day work of the Community. It was staffed by civil servants and expert economists who took important policy decisions. It had strong powers so that it would be able to stand up to criticism and opposition from the governments of the Six, though in theory its decisions had to be approved by the Council of Ministers.

‣ *The Council of Ministers* consisted of government representatives from each of the member states. Their job was to exchange information about their governments' economic policies and to try to co-ordinate them and keep them running along similar lines. There was some friction between the Council and the Commission: the Commission often seemed reluctant to listen to the advice of the Council, and kept on producing masses of new regulations.

‣ *The European Parliament* met at Strasbourg and consisted of 198 representatives chosen by the parliaments of the member states. They could discuss issues and make recommendations, but had no control over the Commission or the Council. From 1979, the representatives (Euro MPs) were elected directly by the people of the Community.

- *The European Court of Justice* was set up to deal with any problems that might arise out of the interpretation and operation of the Treaty of Rome. It soon came to be regarded as the body to which people could appeal if their government was thought to be infringing the rules of the Community.
- Also associated with the EEC was *EURATOM,* an organization in which the Six pooled their efforts towards the development of atomic energy.

In 1967, the EEC, the ECSC and EURATOM formally merged and became known simply as *the European Community (EC).*

(d) why did Britain refuse membership of the EEC?

It was ironic that while Churchill had been one of the strongest supporters of the idea of a unified Europe, when he became Prime Minister again in 1951 he seemed to have lost any enthusiasm he might have felt for Britain's membership. Attlee had drawn back from entering the ECSC, and both Churchill and Eden were doubtful about any deeper co-operation. Both Eden and Macmillan were very cool towards the negotiations that preceded the signing of the Treaty of Rome.

Their main objection was that Britain would no longer be in control of its own economy, which would be at the mercy of the European Commission in Brussels. Although the governments of the other six states did not seem unduly worried by this prospect and were prepared to make the sacrifice in the interests of greater overall efficiency, the British government was not.

There was also the fear that Britain's relationship with the Commonwealth might be ruined if it were no longer possible to give preference to Commonwealth goods such as New Zealand lamb and butter. Around 40 per cent of all Britain's exports went to the Empire (or what would soon become the Commonwealth). The Commonwealth, with a population of around 800 million, seemed a more promising market than the EEC, which had less than 200 million.

Britain's 'special relationship' with the USA had to be taken into consideration too; this was not shared by the other states of Europe, and if the British became too deeply involved in economic integration with Europe, it could damage their special relationship with the Americans. Underlying all this was the fact that most British politicians were deeply suspicious that economic unity would lead to the political unity of Europe, and that was even less appealing to the British, who were determined that British sovereignty (that is, supreme control of their own internal affairs) must be preserved.

On the other hand, Britain and some of the other European states outside the EEC were worried about being excluded from selling their goods to EEC members because of the high duties on imports from outside the Community. Consequently, in 1959 Britain took the lead in organizing a rival group, *the European Free Trade Association (EFTA).* Britain, Denmark, Norway, Sweden, Switzerland, Austria and Portugal agreed that they would gradually abolish tariffs among themselves. Britain was prepared to join an organization such as

EFTA because there was no question of common economic policies and no Commission to interfere with the internal affairs of states. By 1961, however, the British had had a complete change of mind, and Macmillan announced that they wished to join the EEC.

(e) why did the British change their minds and apply to join the EEC?

In the first place, it was clear by 1961 that the EEC was an outstanding success – without Britain. Since 1953, French production had risen by 75 per cent, while German production had increased by almost 90 per cent. Britain's economy was much less successful – over the same period, British production had risen by only about 30 per cent. Britain's economy seemed to be stagnating in comparison with the economies of the Six, and in 1960 there was a balance of payments deficit of some £270 million. While EFTA had succeeded in increasing trade among its members, it was nothing like as successful as the EEC; and the Commonwealth, in spite of its huge population, had nothing like the same purchasing power as the EEC; with so many colonies now gaining independence, there was no guarantee that trade with them would continue at the same level, whether they were in the Commonwealth or not. Macmillan now thought that there need not be a clash of interest between Britain's membership of the EEC and trade with the Commonwealth, especially as dominions such as New Zealand and Australia were showing more interest in trading in their own regions. There were signs that the EEC was prepared to make special arrangements to allow Commonwealth countries and some former European colonies to become associate members.

Another argument put forward was that, once Britain joined, competition from other EEC members would stimulate British industry to greater effort and efficiency. Macmillan also made the point that Britain could not afford to be left out if the EEC developed into a political union. He seems to have had some idea that Britain could take over the leadership and build up the Community into a strong defensive unit against the USSR, and in partnership with the USA. This may well have been Macmillan's primary motive, though he could hardly give it much publicity. Meanwhile, the Labour Party opposed British entry; Wilson said it would mean 'selling our friends and kinsmen down the river … for a marginal advantage in selling washing-machines in Dusseldorf'.

Macmillan gave the job of negotiating Britain's entry to Edward Heath, who had been an enthusiastic supporter of European unity since he first entered Parliament in 1950. Talks opened in October 1961, and despite some difficulties, it came as a shock when, in 1963, the French president, de Gaulle, broke off negotiations and vetoed Britain's entry.

(f) why did the French oppose British entry to the EEC?

The Dutch and Belgians welcomed Britain's application to join, seeing British membership as a counter-balance to the danger of Franco-German domination;

the West Germans too saw Britain as a promising market. However, de Gaulle claimed that Britain had too many economic problems and would only weaken the EEC. He objected to any concessions being made for the Commonwealth, arguing that this would be a drain on Europe's resources. Yet the EEC had just agreed to provide economic and technical aid to France's former colonies in Africa. The British believed that de Gaulle's real motive was his desire to continue dominating the Community. Britain would be a serious rival. Nor was de Gaulle happy about Britain's 'American connection'; he thought that Britain's close ties with the USA would allow the Americans to have a major and unwelcome influence in European affairs. 'England is insular and maritime,' he complained. 'The entry of Britain would completely change the Common Market which would become a colossal Atlantic grouping under American dependence and control.' Some suggested that he was still disgusted with Britain for pulling out of Suez in 1956 before the job was finished. He was probably also annoyed that Britain, without consulting France, had just agreed to receive Polaris missiles from the USA. He was certainly furious with President Kennedy for not having made the same offer to France. He was determined to prove that France was a great power and had no need of American help. It was this friction between France and the USA that eventually led de Gaulle to withdraw France from NATO in 1966.

In fact, some of de Gaulle's suspicions may well have been close to the mark. According to Alan Sked and Chris Cook,

> Macmillan had no intention of making Britain a European power. The real reason behind the British application was the need for Britain to find somewhere to act a leading role and improve her international reputation. Once inside the Common Market, Macmillan planned to organize it in co-operation with America, as part of an extended Atlantic partnership.

Finally, there was the problem of French agriculture: the EEC protected its farmers with high tariffs (import duties) so that prices were kept much higher than in Britain. Britain's agriculture was highly efficient and subsidized to keep prices relatively low. If this continued after Britain's entry, French farmers, with their smaller and less efficient farms, would be exposed to competition from Britain and perhaps also from the Commonwealth.

Meanwhile, the EEC success story continued. The Community's exports grew steadily, and the value of its exports was consistently higher than that of its imports. Britain, on the other hand, usually had a balance of trade deficit, and Harold Wilson's Labour government (1964–70) was forced to begin its term in office by borrowing heavily from the IMF to replenish its dwindling gold reserves (see Section 30.5(a)). This convinced Wilson that the only solution was for Britain to join the EEC, though until then Labour had opposed it. However, in 1967 de Gaulle once again vetoed the British application.

(g) Britain enters the Community at last (1973)

The British application for membership remained on the table and eventually, on 1 January 1973, along with the Republic of Ireland and Denmark, Britain was admitted to the Community. The Six became the Nine. Britain's entry was made possible mainly by the resignation of de Gaulle in 1969, and the fact that his successor, Georges Pompidou, was more friendly towards Britain. The French were beginning to feel somewhat perturbed by the increasing economic power of West Germany, and hoped this might be offset by Britain's membership. Conservative Prime Minister Edward Heath (1970–4) was in a good position to press Britain's claims strongly. He negotiated with great skill and tenacity, and it was fitting that, having been a committed European for so long, he was the Prime Minister who finally took Britain into Europe.

Public opinion in Britain was divided over whether it was a wise move to join the Community, and many people were worried about how far British sovereignty would be affected. The Labour Party was split on the issue, and after coming to power in 1974, Wilson held a referendum (see Section 30.7(b)). The people were asked to vote in 1975 about whether or not they wanted Britain to stay in the EC, and 67 per cent of those who voted expressed approval of Britain's membership. But this was not as decisive as it might seem, since only two-thirds of the electorate voted. This meant that less than half the voters were convinced that membership was a good thing; the rest either did not want to stay in the Community or did not care enough either way to bother to vote.

33.4 Britain and the Community since 1973

The main developments and problems since Britain became a member of the Community in 1973 were as listed below.

(a) the Lomé Convention (1975)

Responding to criticism that it was too inward-looking and self-centred, EC representatives, meeting in Lomé, the capital of Togo in West Africa, agreed that goods produced in over forty countries in Africa and the Caribbean, mainly former European colonies, could be brought into the Community free of duties. The agreement also promised economic aid, and other poor Third-World countries were later added to the list.

(b) direct elections to the European Parliament (1979)

Despite being in existence for over twenty years by this time, the EC was still remote from ordinary people. One reason for introducing elections was to try to arouse more interest and to bring 'the people in the street' into closer contact with the affairs of the Community.

The first elections took place in June 1979, when 410 Euro MPs were chosen.

table **33.1 British seats in the European Parliament**

	1979	1984	1989	1994	1999	2004
Labour	17	32	45	62	29	19
Conservatives	60	45	32	18	36	27
Lib Dems				2	10	12
UKIP					3	12
Greens					2	2
SNP	1	1	1	2	2	2
Plaid Cymru					2	1
Official Unionist	1	1	1	1	1	1
Democratic Unionist	1	1	1	1	1	1
SDLP	1	1	1	1	1	
Sinn Fein						1

Sources: Website of the UK Office of the European Parliament (www.europarl.org.uk);
D. Childs, *Britain Since 1987: Progress and Decline* (Macmillan, 1995), p. 241.

Britain, France, Italy and West Germany were allowed 81 each; the Netherlands 25; Belgium 24; Denmark 16; the Irish Republic 15; and Luxembourg 6. For Britain, the elections came immediately after Margaret Thatcher's victory in the UK general election of May 1979 (see Section 30.7(e)), so it was no surprise when the Conservatives swept the board in the Euro elections as well: they won 60 out of the 81 seats, while Labour could muster only 16. The turnout was disappointing – less than a third of the British electorate was interested enough to bother voting. Overall, in the new European Parliament, the right-wing and centre parties had a comfortable majority over the left.

Elections were to be held every five years; and by the time the next elections came round in 1984, Greece had joined the Community, and was allowed 24 seats, bringing the total to 434. This time in Britain the Conservatives lost ground to Labour, winning 45 seats to Labour's 32; overall, the centre and right kept a small majority. For the results of later elections, see Table 33.1. In July 1997, the new Labour government announced that a proportional representation system of voting would be introduced for the 1999 elections, replacing the 'first past the post' system. This would bring Britain into line with the rest of the Community. The new system would be based on large multi-member constituencies, in which electors would vote for lists of candidates drawn up by the parties. It meant that smaller parties, such as the Greens and the UK Independence party would be able to win seats for the first time, while the Liberal Democrats were able to increase the number of their seats from two to ten in 1999.

(c) the introduction of the Exchange Rate Mechanism (ERM) (1979)

This was introduced to link the currencies of the member states in order to limit the extent to which individual currencies (Italian lira; French, Luxembourg and Belgian francs; and German Mark) could change in value against the currencies of other members. A country's currency could change in value depending on how well its domestic economy was performing: a strong economy usually meant a strong currency. It was hoped that linking the currencies would help to control inflation and lead eventually to a single currency for the whole of the Community. Britain decided not to take the pound sterling into the ERM; though Chancellor Nigel Lawson wanted Britain to join in 1985–6, when the economy was booming, Mrs Thatcher refused (see Section 34.4(b)). By the time Britain did eventually join the ERM in October 1990, the economy was weaker and the exchange rate relatively high. This meant that the pound was over-valued and difficult to defend; within less than two years (September 1992), Britain was forced to withdraw sterling from the ERM, and John Major's government suffered a humiliating blow (see Section 35.6(c)).

(d) Community membership grows

Greece joined the Community in 1981, followed by Spain and Portugal in 1986, bringing the total membership to twelve and the Community population to over 320 million. Spain and Portugal had not been allowed to join earlier because their political systems were undemocratic. However, their arrival caused new problems: they were among the poorest countries of Europe, and their presence increased the influence within the Community of the less industrialized nations. From then on there would be increasing pressure from these countries to help the less developed states, and so improve the economic balance between rich and poor nations. Membership increased again in 1995, when Austria, Finland and Sweden, three relatively wealthy states, joined.

(e) Britain and the EC budget

During the early years of their membership, many British people were disappointed that Britain did not seem to be gaining any obvious benefit from the EC. The Irish Republic, which joined at the same time, immediately enjoyed a surge of prosperity as its exports, mainly agricultural produce, found ready new markets in the Community. Britain, on the other hand, seemed to be stagnating in the 1970s, and while its exports to the Community did increase, its imports from the Community increased far more. Britain was not producing enough goods for export at the right prices; the statistics of GDP for 1977 show that Britain was one of the least efficient nations in the EC, while Denmark and West Germany were at the top of the league (see Section 30.7(f) for more details and explanations; and 35.6(c)).

A major crisis erupted in 1980, when Britain discovered that its budget contribution for that year was to be £1,209 million, whereas West Germany's was £699 million and France only had to pay £13 million. Britain protested that its contribution was ridiculously high, given the general state of the country's economy. The difference was so great because of the way the budget contribution was worked out: this took into consideration the amount of import duties received by each government from goods coming into that country from outside the EC; a proportion of those duties received had to be handed over as part of the annual budget contribution. Unfortunately for the British, they imported far more goods from the outside world than any of the other members, and this was why their payment was so high. Margaret Thatcher was determined to have it reduced, and after some ruthless bargaining, a compromise was reached: Britain's contribution was reduced to a total of £1,346 million over the next three years. Similar wrangling took place during the summer of 1983 and again in 1984 before a compromise agreeable to Britain could be arrived at. By that time, Mrs Thatcher had offended most of the other European leaders and was being referred to as 'Lady de Gaulle'. However, her efforts saved the British taxpayer billions of pounds over the next thirteen years.

(f) the 1986 changes

Encouraging developments occurred in 1986 when all twelve members, working closely together, negotiated some important changes which, it was hoped, would improve the EC. They included a move, by 1992, to a completely free and common market with no restrictions of any kind on internal trade and movement of goods. There was to be more Community control over health, safety, protection of the environment, and protection for consumers; there would be more encouragement for scientific research and technology, and more help for backward regions. The most controversial changes were those affecting the Council of Ministers and the European Parliament: there was to be majority voting on many issues in the Council of Ministers; this would prevent a measure from being vetoed by just one state which felt that its national interests might be threatened by that measure. The European Parliament was to have more power, so that measures could be passed with less delay. This meant that the domestic parliaments of the member states were gradually losing some control over their own internal affairs.

Those people who favoured a federal United States of Europe were pleased by these developments, but in some countries, especially Britain and Denmark, they stirred up the old controversy about national sovereignty. Mrs Thatcher upset some of the other European leaders again when she spoke out against any movement towards a politically united Europe: 'a centralized federal government in Europe would be a nightmare; co-operation with the other European countries must not be at the expense of individuality, the national customs and traditions which made Europe great in the past' (for Mrs Thatcher's later policies towards Europe, see Section 35.4(c)).

(g) the Common Agricultural Policy (CAP)

One of the most controversial aspects of the EC was its Common Agricultural Policy. In order to help farmers and encourage them to stay in business, so that the Community could continue to produce much of its own food, it was decided to pay them subsidies (extra cash to top up their profits). This would ensure them worthwhile profits and at the same time would keep prices at reasonable levels for the consumers. This was such a good deal for farmers that they were encouraged to produce far more than could be sold. Yet the policy was continued, until by 1980 about three-quarters of the entire EC budget was being paid out each year in subsidies to farmers. Britain, West Germany and the Netherlands pressed for a limit to be placed on subsidies, but the French government was reluctant to agree to this because it did not want to lose the votes of French farmers, who were doing very well out of the system.

In 1984, maximum production quotas were introduced for the first time, but this did not solve the problem. By 1987, the stockpiling of produce had reached ridiculous proportions. There was a vast wine 'lake', and a butter 'mountain' of 1.5 million tonnes – enough to supply the entire EC for a year. There was enough milk powder to last five years, and storage fees alone were costing £1 million a day. Efforts to get rid of the surplus included selling it off cheaply to the USSR, India, Pakistan and Bangladesh, distributing butter free of charge to the poor within the Community, and using it to make animal feed.

All this helped to cause a massive budget crisis in 1987: the Community was £3 billion in the red and had debts of £10 billion. In a determined effort to solve the problem, the EC introduced a harsh programme of production curbs and a price freeze to put a general squeeze on Europe's farmers. This gradually brought down the surpluses and improved the situation, but ten years later, in 1997, CAP was still absorbing almost half of the Community's budget – about £27 billion a year. Among other reforms introduced in 1992 were changes designed to protect the environment and promote more ecologically friendly farming methods. It was calculated that by 1997 these had reduced the use of fertilizers and pesticides by up to 30 per cent.

Further reforms proposed for 1998 included reducing subsidies paid to farmers and introducing a more open market for agricultural products. Experts predicted that while this would mean British farmers losing some £450 million in annual subsidies, this would be more than offset by the freedom to sell on the world market.

(h) greater integration – the Maastricht Treaty (1991)

A summit meeting of all the heads of the member states was held in Maastricht (Netherlands) starting in December 1991, and an agreement was drawn up (February 1992) for 'a new stage in the process of creating an even closer union among the peoples of Europe'. Some of the points agreed were:

› more powers for the European Parliament;
› greater economic and monetary union – this was intended to culminate in the adoption of a common currency (the euro) shared by all the member states, around the end of the century;
› a common foreign and security policy; and
› a detailed timetable of the stages by which all this was to be achieved.

The Community was to be known as *the European Union (EU).*

Britain objected very strongly to the ideas of a federal Europe and monetary union; the treaty therefore did not mention the phrase 'federal state', and it was agreed that Britain and Denmark could opt out of a single currency of they decided to do so. In fact, most British businessmen seemed to favour a common currency, believing that it would eliminate the uncertainties of fluctuating exchange rates between currencies.

Britain also objected to a whole section of the treaty known as *the Social Chapter*, which was a list of regulations designed to protect people from exploitation at work. There were rules about safe and healthy working conditions, equality at work between men and women, consultation with workers so that they were kept informed about what was going on, and protection of workers made redundant. Britain argued that these would increase production costs and therefore cause unemployment. The other members seemed to think that proper treatment of workers was more important. In the end, because of British objections, the Social Chapter was removed from the treaty and it was left to individual governments to decide whether to carry it out.

This caused protests among European businessmen, who claimed it would give British business an unfair advantage, since British firms did not have to keep to the same rules on working terms and conditions as the rest of the European Union. These opt-outs and omissions were seen as a personal achievement by John Major (see Section 35.6(a)). The rest of the Maastricht Treaty had be to ratified by the national parliaments of the twelve members, and this was achieved by October 1993.

The French, Dutch and Belgian governments supported the treaty strongly because they thought it was the best way to make sure that the power of the reunified Germany was contained and controlled within the Community. However, the ordinary people of the Community were not as enthusiastic about the treaty as their leaders. The people of Denmark at first voted against it, and it took determined campaigning by the government before it was approved by a narrow majority in a second referendum (May 1993). The Swiss people voted not to join the EU (December 1992), and so did the Norwegians; even in the French referendum, the majority in favour of Maastricht was tiny. In Britain, where the government would not allow a referendum, the Conservatives were split over Europe, and the treaty was approved only by the narrowest of majorities in Parliament. Major was harassed by the Conservative anti-Europeans (Eurosceptics) for the rest of his premiership (see Section 35.6(c)).

(i) Britain and the EU since 1997

The Labour victory in the 1997 election heralded a different British approach to Europe. Though the Labour Party was doubtful about a federal Europe, their general approach under Tony Blair's leadership, in striking contrast to that of the Conservatives, was 'Euro-friendly', and the new Prime Minister said that he wanted Britain's attitude to the EU to be positive and constructive. By the

Treaty of Amsterdam (June 1997) it was agreed that the Social Chapter would be put back into the Maastricht Treaty, after Britain had now indicated a willingness to accept it. The Council of Ministers was given the power to penalize member states that violated human rights; and the European Parliament was given more powers. These changes came into effect on 1 May 1999.

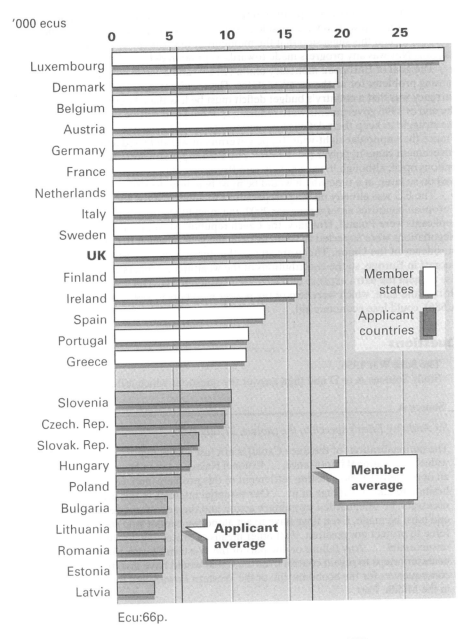

figure **33.1 GDP per head of the population of EU members and applicants, 1995**

Source: The Guardian, 17 July 1997, p. 12. Copyright © Guardian News & Media Ltd 1997.

The goal of European monetary union (EMU) and a single currency by 1999 caused problems for all the member states. The requirement for joining the single currency was that a country's budget deficit must be less than 3 per cent of its GDP. By the end of 1996, governments were reducing spending and cutting welfare benefits in the struggle to keep their deficits low, and this provoked criticism and ill-feeling. The British government said it was keeping its options open, and in the event, decided not to switch to the euro, though France, Germany, Italy, Spain and Portugal joined. The EU was making preparations to admit some eastern European countries, including Poland, Hungary and the Czech Republic, among others. These countries were among the poorest and least efficient in Europe, so the contributions of the existing members could be expected to rise in order to fund economic aid to the new members. The worry for the UK and Eire, which were two of the poorest members in 1995, was that they might lose economic aid (see Figure 33.1 on p. 693).

In February 2001, the *Treaty of Nice* was formally signed, introducing new voting rules in the Council of Ministers and changing the composition of the European Parliament to reflect more closely the size of each member's population. Partly in order to accommodate the new members that were due to join in 2004, all existing members apart from Germany (which had the largest population) and Luxembourg were to have fewer MEPs, and Britain and France were each to have 72 seats instead of 87. Before the treaty could be put into operation in January 2005, it had to be approved by all fifteen member states. However, in June 2001, Ireland voted in a referendum to reject it. A further setback occurred in December 2003 when a summit meeting in Brussels collapsed without reaching agreement on a new EU constitution.

(j) has Britain found a role?

Dean Acheson's famous 1962 statement that 'Great Britain has lost an Empire and has not yet found a role' aroused great resentment in Britain, and the White House immediately tried to distance itself from his remarks. George L. Bernstein suggests that Acheson's remark implied that Britain had been one of the world's great powers until decolonization in the late 1940s and 1950s, and that it had been a great power primarily because of the Empire. However, he argues that Britain's leaders completely misread the situation in 1945. They too believed that the Empire was the source of their strength; between 1945 and 1964 they were trying to do more than ever before – keeping an army in Europe, building a nuclear deterrent, and, for the first few years, pursuing a new imperialist phase: 'This was not trying to prevent Britain's decline. It was aspiring to achieve something very new. For Britain had not been the world's, or even Europe's, greatest power in 1900. It was simply one of many ... Now British governments dreamed of a power status far above any that Britain had attained earlier.' In other words, the British were not a nation 'in decline'; they were a nation aiming higher than ever before, and in fact were pursuing an impossible goal.

The things that some people saw as disasters during those years of 1945 to 1962 were not necessarily signs of new weaknesses; they were simply a demonstration of reality. These developments included the end of Empire, the humiliation at Suez, the loss of independence over a nuclear deterrent, and the realization that the Commonwealth was not going to provide the basis for a strengthening of British power and influence. The first reaction of British leaders was to attempt to develop the 'special relationship' with the USA. Sometimes this worked, but more often than not it was an unequal relationship. The USA often pursued its own interests with complete indifference to the impact this might have on Britain. Therefore the British eventually, but very slowly, came round to the view that membership of the EU was the best way forward. Even then it was primarily for economic reasons that they found the EU attractive; the idea of a United States of Europe did not appeal to the majority of Britain's people. Though joining the EU would mean losing some sovereignty, British governments resisted every step that involved a further reduction of Britain's sovereignty. Mrs Thatcher tried to call a halt, but then from 1997 Tony Blair seemed to have a stronger commitment to Europe. However, even he drew the line at joining the European currency. Britain therefore seems to have gone some of the way towards developing its new role, but has not committed itself fully. This makes it more difficult for the British to fulfil the other role that appeals to many of them – to nurture the special relationship with the USA. Bernstein concludes that Britain's relationship with the USA could perhaps enable it to act as a vehicle of communication between the USA and Europe, 'but it could only be so if it was fully part of Europe and trusted as such by its European friends'.

Andrew Roberts offers a rather different interpretation of Britain's role. He argues that Britain has succeeded in balancing its commitments in all three directions: to the special relationship, the European Union *and* the Commonwealth; and not only these three – also add NATO, G7, The General Agreement on Tariffs and Trade (GATT) and the United Nations Organization:

> Far from being 'played out', over four decades after Acheson's speech, she was in as strong an international position as she had enjoyed in any period since the Suez crisis, without having had to ditch her commitments. In the European Union, but not in the euro currency or federal constitution; 'shoulder-to-shoulder' with the United States in the War against Terror; a nuclear power with an assured seat on the Security Council; a leading member of the (expanding and largely democratic) Commonwealth; and the world's fifth largest economy despite having only 1.3 per cent of global population, Britain protected her status well between 1945 and 2005.

Significantly, Bernstein calls his book *The Myth of Decline: The Rise of Britain Since 1945*. His main theme is that while there may have been some economic decline and a reduction of Britain's influence in the world, there are other criteria which must be taken into account. He argues that Labour and Conservatives between them 'made a real social and cultural revolution ... it is difficult not to see progress in all this – and progress of a very far-reaching and radical kind, which far outweighs in importance whatever economic and political decline may have occurred over these years'. Andrew Marr sums up Britain's 'rise' since 1945 very well. While not denying that the British have had their problems since 1945, he argues that

> we came out on the other side to find ourselves on the cutting edge of the modern condition, a post-industrial and multi-ethnic island, crowded, inventive and rich ... a well-educated and busy people, [with] a relatively uncorrupt and law-abiding national tradition, and an optimistic relish for the new technologies ... Modern Britain had made great advances in science, culture and finance which have benefited, and will benefit, the world.

Add to that one of the most enduring and successful democratic political systems in the world; and a remarkably generous welfare system with unemployment benefit and a National Health Service which is still the envy of most of the world, and understanding begins to dawn as to why so many people want to come and settle in Britain today.

QUESTIONS

1 How far would you agree that Bevin's foreign policy was a reasonable and successful response to Britain's circumstances after the Second World War?
2 How useful to Britain in the period 1945 to 1973 was the 'special relationship' with the USA?
3 Explain why Britain joined NATO in 1949, but refused to join the EEC in 1957.
4 Explain why the British changed their minds and applied for membership of the EEC in 1961. Why did they fail to achieve membership until 1973?

A document question on the Suez War (1956) can be found on the accompanying website www.palgrave.com/masterseries/lowe1.

chapter 34

Britain and the end of Empire

summary of events

In 1946, the British Empire was still intact, and Britain had troops in Germany, Greece, Iran, India, Egypt, Palestine, Malaya and Singapore. This was extremely expensive to maintain for a country whose resources had been strained to the limit by the war effort, and there were some disagreements in the Labour Cabinet about how long Britain could go on maintaining this worldwide military presence; Hugh Dalton, the Chancellor of the Exchequer, was anxious to economize. It was under Macmillan's premiership that Britain gave up most of its Empire, though the vast majority of the newly independent states chose to remain within the Commonwealth. India (1947) and Ceylon (which became Sri Lanka in 1972) and Burma (1948) had already been granted their independence under Labour. They were soon followed by Malaysia and Gold Coast (renamed Ghana, 1957); Nigeria and Cyprus (1960); Tanganyika and Zanzibar (together forming Tanzania), and Sierra Leone (1961); Uganda, Jamaica, and Trinidad and Tobago (1962); and Kenya (1963).

Soon after Macmillan's retirement in 1963, other territories became independent: Nyasaland (renamed Malawi), Northern Rhodesia (renamed Zambia), Guiana (renamed Guyana) and Malta (1964); The Gambia (1965); Bechuanaland (renamed Botswana), Basutoland (renamed Lesotho) and Barbados (1966); Aden (renamed South Yemen, 1967); Mauritius and Swaziland (1968); Fiji (1970); the Bahamas (1973); Grenada (1974); the Seychelles (1976); Dominica (renamed the Dominican Republic) and the Solomon Islands (1978); St Lucia and St Vincent (1979); Southern Rhodesia (renamed Zimbabwe, 1980); and finally British Honduras (renamed Belize) and Antigua (1981).

34.1 the Empire in its heyday and at the beginning of the end

(a) the Empire in its heyday

Arguably, the British Empire reached its peak just before the First World War, when it covered about a fifth of the world's land surface and contained over 400 million people – an Empire 'on which the sun never set'. Much of it had been acquired during the forty or fifty years leading up to the outbreak of war in 1914. Gladstone and Disraeli between them, for example, had taken control of Egypt and the Suez Canal (see Sections 14.3(b) and 16.2(c)); and there was the 'Scramble for Africa' from around 1881 until 1900 (see Section 16.7(c)). But what was it all for? The supporters of Empire themselves had different ideas, motives and priorities, including:

› The economic motive – the desire to increase Britain's wealth (as well as their own) by obtaining raw materials from the colonies and using the colonies as new markets for British manufactured goods. Originally, there was no desire to control the territory politically; it was only when trading interests were threatened by the 'natives' that the British began to take political control, as in the case of India, by making agreements with local rulers. It was only in the last quarter of the nineteenth century that Britain evolved a specific policy of acquiring territory. This is why Bernard Porter described the British as 'the absent-minded imperialists'.

› The motive behind the 'Scramble for Africa' was arguably the drive to make up lost ground. This was the time when Britain was clearly being overtaken as the world's greatest industrial and trading power by the USA and Germany. Britain's share of world trade was dwindling, and people such as Joseph Chamberlain embraced imperialism as a way of winning back British pre-eminence.

› A motive which was probably incidental, though imperialists themselves would perhaps have been unwilling to admit it, was to bring the benefits of civilization – by which they meant British attitudes, values and general way of doing things – to the 'natives'. It was felt that this was a duty of the colonizers, who had no doubt that the British were best. Joseph Chamberlain, the Colonial Secretary, firmly believed that 'the British race is the greatest of governing races the world has ever seen'. Lord Curzon (Viceroy of India from 1898 until 1905) declared that the British Empire was 'the greatest empire for good that the world has seen'.

› Christian missionaries played an important role, especially in the African colonies, carrying out their mission of 'taking the Gospel to all nations'.

› Finally, the Empire was seen as an excellent training ground for administrators, governors and army officers. The vast majority of people who benefited from such training were members of the upper classes who had been to public school, where they had been imbued with a sense of duty, respect for discipline, and the team spirit.

(b) the beginning of the end

At the end of the First World War, Britain acquired the Arab territories of Iraq, Transjordan and Palestine from Turkey as mandates; the intention was that these areas should be supervised and prepared for independence. This is what happened in the case of Iraq, which was given independence in 1932, and Transjordan, which became fully independent in 1946, though Palestine proved to be an insoluble problem (see Section 34.3). However, these were not seen as significant for the future of the Empire. It was with India that the great withdrawal from Empire began in 1947.

However, this did not mean that the British government had a plan for handing out independence to its entire Empire. In fact, the Labour government of 1945–51 fully intended to maintain and develop it economically as a vital part of Britain's economy. One of its motives was to strengthen the sterling area; this consisted of the countries of the Empire and Commonwealth, which had the pound sterling as their reserve currency, enabling Britain to act as banker to all these countries. Britain aimed to continue selling raw materials from the colonies, such as rubber from Malaya and cocoa from the Gold Coast in order to bring dollars into the sterling area. Britain could then buy the dollars in exchange for sterling that the colonies could only spend on British goods; the other advantage was that it would build up Britain's dollar reserves which, it was hoped, would prevent a repeat performance of the financial crises of the mid-1940s. In 1948, the government set up *the Colonial Development Corporation* to encourage and increase production in the colonies. Hundreds of new staff were taken on at the Colonial Office in what some historians have described as 'a second colonial occupation'. Consequently, Britain took a tough line in colonies such as Cyprus and Kenya, where violent independence movements developed. Another motive for keeping control of the Empire was to prevent the spread of communism. In Malaya, communist guerrillas were challenging British rule, but were eventually defeated.

In the early 1950s, it became clear that the colonial development plan was not going well. There were some successes, such as the opening up of oilfields in Kuwait, but most of the schemes, including the major East African Groundnut Scheme, ended in failure, and in the late 1950s and early 1960s there was a rapid withdrawal from most of Britain's overseas possessions.

(c) what were the reasons for the rapid decolonization?

The British Empire was so huge and diverse, and there were such different pressures at work in its various parts, that it is difficult to pin decolonization down to one cause. It was usually a combination of some or all of the following:

‣ Nationalist movements in the colonies, encouraged, among other things, by Britain's loss of areas such as Singapore and Burma to the Japanese during the Second World War. Some historians have suggested that the economic policies of the 'second colonial occupation', especially in Africa, antagonized the native population because they were so obviously designed to exploit the colonies. If this is true, as Graham Goodlad points out, 'ironically, policies designed to exact greater benefit from the empire played a part in bringing about its demise.'

▸ Britain emerged from the Second World War severely weakened economically, and it was becoming increasingly difficult to defend such a far-flung Empire with such limited resources. The failure of the development schemes meant that whatever profit Britain was now making from the Empire was far less than it was costing to maintain it. The prospect of having to fight a continuous series of campaigns against nationalist movements was extremely depressing for the British government, especially at the time when the Cold War was in full swing and Britain was trying to play its part by developing its own nuclear weapons. The British were keen to avoid the problems experienced by the French, who had fought a long, expensive and unsuccessful war to hold on to Algeria.

▸ The new situation in which the world was dominated by the USA and the USSR made it more difficult for Britain to maintain the Empire. Both super powers were hostile to the British Empire in different ways. The Americans wanted to force their way into Britain's imperially protected markets, which they saw as giving Britain an unfair trading advantage. The USA refused to support Britain at the time of Suez in 1956 (see Section 33.2), forcing the British to withdraw from Egypt. This humiliation demonstrated Britain's weakness and vulnerability, and may well have strengthened and encouraged the independence movements, though not all historians agree on this. The USSR was hostile to imperialism in general, because they saw it as one of the evils of capitalism. There was the danger that a prolonged colonial war would lead to Russian intervention to support the nationalists.

▸ By 1960, world opinion was turning against imperialism. Newly independent territories such as India and Pakistan had joined the United Nations and were beginning to stir up anti-colonial attitudes. It was becoming almost a question of international respectability in the climate of the Cold War. How could holding on to colonial peoples who wanted independence be justified when the West was criticizing the USSR for doing the same in Eastern Europe?

There was considerable criticism of Macmillan's decolonization policies from right-wing Conservatives, especially the League of Empire Loyalists. The fifth Earl of Salisbury resigned from the Cabinet in 1957 over the question of Cyprus. Enoch Powell said that in 1947, when India became independent, he 'walked the streets that night trying to come to terms with it.' But most people accepted it all as inevitable, especially as Macmillan and Iain Macleod (Colonial Secretary from 1959 until 1961) hoped that the former colonies would join the Commonwealth. As Graham Goodlad explains,

> the intention behind this process of decolonization was to reach agreement with moderate nationalist leaders ... [and] transfer power to new, independent states, without terminating Britain's connections with

those countries. Rather, the former imperial power sought to maintain links with its ex-colonies in the diplomatic, military or economic spheres ... Decolonization was a realistic response to a situation in which the imperial power's scope for manoeuvre was becoming increasingly restricted.

34.2 why and how did the British leave India in 1947?

(a) why did the British leave India in 1947?

By 1945 and the end of the Second World War it seemed clear that Indian independence could not be delayed much longer. The nationalist campaign had been gathering strength for many years (see Section 26.4), and in 1942 Sir Stafford Cripps, acting on behalf of the war Cabinet, had offered India dominion status once the war was over; the Labour government, wanting to show that it disapproved of 'exploiting' the Indians, was anxious to go ahead. Bevin had earlier toyed with the idea that independence might be delayed for a few years, to enable the British government to finance a development programme for India, but this idea was abandoned, partly because the Indians would be intensely suspicious of any delay, and partly because Britain could not afford the expense, given its own economic difficulties. India became independent and was divided into two states – India and Pakistan – in August 1947.

The reasons why the British eventually decided to leave India have been the subject of some lively debate in recent years. In the period immediately after independence, the withdrawal seemed a perfectly straightforward affair: it was presented by official sources as the culmination of a process going back to the 1919 Government of India Act, by which British politicians carefully moved India towards independence. It had been intended all along and was a triumph of British planning and statesmanship. It was not just British historians who held this view: V. P. Menon, Indian constitutional adviser to the Governor-General for the last five years before independence, believed that Britain's decision to quit India was 'her finest hour ... it not only touched the hearts and stirred the emotions of India ... it earned for Britain universal respect and goodwill'.

This view was later challenged by a number of Indian historians, including Sumit Sarkar and Anita Inder Singh. They argued that Indian independence never was a long-term British goal, and that the 1919 and 1935 Government of India Acts were designed not to prepare for independence but to postpone it. The credit for Indian independence belongs entirely to Congress. As Anita Inder Singh puts it:

> drawing on popular anti-imperialist sentiment, the Congress became one of the biggest mass movements in history; it engaged the Raj in a

protracted trial of strength, and through an adroit mixture of negotiation and civil disobedience, it led India to independence. Generally, Indians do not perceive independence as a gift from the British or as an easy success. To them independence was the hard won fruit of struggle and sacrifice made by millions of Indians against an oppressive Raj, symbolised by the imprisonment of Gandhi and Nehru for eleven and nine years respectively.

True, the Labour government offered independence in March 1946, but that was only because the pressures from below – agrarian troubles, demands for the overthrow of the Raj, mutinies in the Royal Indian Air Force and Navy – had become intolerable, and the government knew that Britain was too weak and the financial burden too great for them to hang on if widespread revolution broke out. In any case, India was no longer of any value to Britain: instead of being a source of profit, it was now a drain on British resources. The value of Britain's trade with India had begun to decline soon after the First World War. By 1945, Britain was running a trade deficit with India, and amazingly, India was the largest holder of sterling balances at the time. As George L. Bernstein puts it: the problem for Britain was 'how to get out in a way that would keep India within the British financial network as a member of the Commonwealth.'

Some other historians take a middle view: while accepting that inter-war Conservative-dominated governments did everything in their power to thwart progress towards Indian independence, they believe that great credit is due to the Labour government for its positive role in 1945–7. Howard Brasted, for example, presents a fair and balanced view: he disputes the claim that the government made its India policy up as it went along and ended up running away from the problem. He points out that the Labour Party had already, *before* the Second World War, produced a clear policy on British withdrawal from India; this was embodied in *the Attlee Report on India (1934)*, which was subsequently discussed by Attlee, Cripps and Nehru in 1938, when they worked out a framework of British withdrawal by a future Labour government, to be preceded by democratic elections. Nehru and Gandhi knew that, with the massive Labour victory of July 1945, Indian independence could not be far away. On 20 February 1947, Attlee announced the timetable for unconditional independence, during which the Indians would work out their own constitution through a representative Constituent Assembly. If the plan was not carried through in the way Attlee envisaged, this was partly because, as Brasted points out, the Viceroy, Lord Wavell, was not in sympathy with Labour's plans: 'proclaiming, despite constant briefings, that he did not know what Labour's itinerary was, the Viceroy persistently departed from the route Labour had long proposed to take; hence his dismissal.' The other problem was the difficulty of preserving the unity of India, and it was this problem that proved impossible to solve.

(b) why was the partition of India necessary?

1 The problem sprang from the religious hostilities between Hindus, who made up about two-thirds of the population, and the rest, who were mainly Muslims. After their victories in the elections of 1937, the Hindu Congress Party unwisely called on the Muslim League to merge with Congress. This alarmed the League, who were by then convinced that an independent India would be dominated by Hindus. M. A. Jinnah, the Muslim leader, demanded a separate Muslim state of Pakistan.

2 Attempts to draw up a compromise constitution acceptable to Hindu leaders (Nehru and Gandhi) and to Jinnah, failed. The British proposed a federal scheme in which the central government would have only limited powers, while those of the provincial governments would be extensive. Provinces with a Muslim majority would be able to control their own affairs, and there would be no need of a separate state. Both sides accepted the principle but could not agree on details.

3 Violence broke out in August 1946, when the Governor-General, Lord Wavell, invited Nehru to form an interim government, still hoping that details could be worked out later. Nehru formed a cabinet which included two Muslims, but Jinnah, convinced that the Hindus could not be trusted, called for 'direct action' to achieve Pakistan. Fierce rioting followed in Calcutta, where 5,000 people were killed; and it spread to Bengal, where Muslims set about slaughtering Hindus. As Hindus retaliated, the country seemed on the verge of civil war.

4 To try to force the Indians into a more responsible attitude, Attlee announced in February 1947 that the British would leave no later than June 1948. The new Viceroy, Lord Mountbatten, turned out to be an inspired choice by Attlee. He quickly decided that partition was the only way to avoid civil war. He realized that there would probably be bloodshed in any case, but felt that partition would produce less than if Britain tried to insist on the Muslims remaining inside India. Within six weeks of arriving, and in spite of all the complexities, Mountbatten had produced a plan by which the country could be divided and power transferred from the British. This was accepted by Nehru and Jinnah (though not by Gandhi). Afraid that delay might cause more violence, Mountbatten advanced the date for British withdrawal to August 1947.

(c) how was the partition carried out?

The Indian Independence Act was rushed through the British Parliament (August 1947) separating the Muslim majority areas (the north-west and north-east of India) from the rest of India as the independent state of Pakistan, which was in two sections, over a thousand miles apart. But it was not easy to carry out the terms of Act:

- It had been necessary to split the provinces of the Punjab and Bengal, which had mixed Hindu and Muslim populations, and inevitably millions of people found themselves on the wrong side of the new frontiers.
- Fearing persecution, millions headed for the border, Muslims trying to get into Pakistan, and Hindus into India. Clashes occurred which developed into near-hysterical mob violence, especially in the Punjab, where about 250,000 people were murdered. Violence was not quite so widespread in Bengal, where Gandhi, still preaching non-violence and toleration, managed to calm the situation.
- Violence began to die down before the end of 1947, but in January 1948 Gandhi was shot dead by a Hindu fanatic who detested his tolerance towards Muslims. It was a tragic end to a disastrous set of circumstances, but the shock seemed to bring people to their senses, so that India and Pakistan could begin to think about their other problems.

Attlee insisted, probably rightly, that Britain could not be blamed for the violence that followed independence; this was because of, he said, with his inimitable knack of understatement, 'the failure of the Indians to agree among themselves'. Howard Brasted believes that a less sensitive handling of the situation by the British government could have produced an even more catastrophic bloodbath. 'The fact that a constitutional settlement was achieved which transferred power to chosen successors, legally, legislatively and amicably rather than through bitter armed struggle, should not be taken for granted.' On the other hand, A.N. Wilson feels that there could have been less violence if Mountbatten had acted differently. There was insufficient policing, he was unwilling to provide peace-keeping forces, which could have protected the migrant populations, and the borders were decided with insufficient care: 'By his superficial haste, his sheer arrogance and his inattention to vital detail ... Mountbatten was responsible for as many deaths as some of those who were hanged after the Nuremberg trials.'

34.3 Britain withdraws from Palestine

In 1945, Britain was still heavily committed in the Middle East; Palestine had been a British mandate since 1919, British troops were still stationed in the Suez Canal zone of Egypt, and Britain owned a controlling interest in the Anglo-Iranian Oil Company. Serious problems arose in all three areas, but it was in Palestine that the first crisis occurred.

(a) what caused the crisis in Palestine?

1 The problem originated soon after the First World War when large numbers of Jews began to settle in Palestine, hoping to set up a Jewish 'national home' (see Section 26.5(c)). The Arabs in Palestine were implacably hostile to the

idea of a separate Jewish state in what they considered to be their homeland. In order to retain Arab friendship and their own oil supplies, the British limited Jewish immigration to 10,000 a year (1939).

2 The Second World War intensified the problem, with hundreds of thousands of refugees from Hitler's Europe looking for somewhere to go. In 1945, the USA pressed Britain to admit 100,000 of them into Palestine; this demand was echoed by David Ben Gurion, one of the Jewish leaders, but the British refused, not wanting to offend the Arabs. The British were particularly exasperated by Truman's attitude: he criticized the British government for not admitting the refugees, yet would give no help and refused to allow any more Jews into the USA.

3 The Jews, after all that their race had suffered at the hands of the Nazis, were determined to fight for their 'national home'. They began a terrorist campaign against both Arabs and British; the most spectacular incident was the blowing up of the King David Hotel, the British headquarters in Jerusalem, with the loss of 91 lives (1946). The British responded by arresting Jewish leaders and by turning back ships such as the *Exodus*, which was crammed with some 4,500 intending immigrants.

4 Bevin hoped to be able to find some sort of compromise to satisfy both Jews and Arabs, and one that would preserve British influence. He met the leaders of both sides, but no compromise was possible: the Jews wanted their own state, the Arabs refused all concessions, and neither side would budge. By February 1947, therefore, Bevin invited the United Nations to deal with

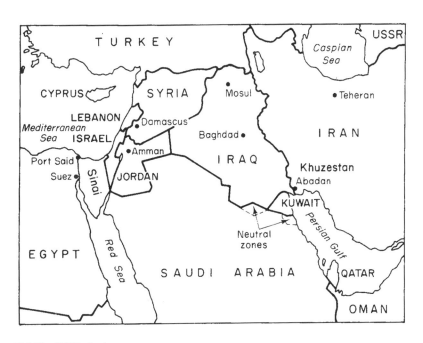

map **34.1 The Middle East**

the problem, and in November the UN voted to partition Palestine, setting aside roughly half of it to form an independent state of Israel for the Jews. The UN also suggested that Britain should put the plan into operation. Bevin was against partition, even though the UN announced that the existing Arab population would be able to continue living in Israel. His argument was: why should the Palestinian Arabs be forced to become a minority in a Jewish state when the Jews were refusing to become a minority in an Arab state? Consequently the British refused to carry out the partition, and in May 1948 they withdrew altogether from Palestine, thus ending the mandate.

(b) why did the British decide to withdraw?

There were several motives. British public opinion had gradually turned against the Jews because of their terrorist outrages; the peace-keeping operation had already proved expensive, and the prospect of enforcing the partition (of which they did not approve, and which would be even more costly, at a time when Britain was in economic difficulties) to the advantage of the Jews, appalled Bevin. Nor did Bevin see why the British should have the sole obligation of acting as international policemen in the Middle East; there was a strong feeling that since the Americans had taken up a pro-Jewish stance, then they ought to be allowed to get on with carrying out the partition. Finally, there was the possibility that British troops might be needed in Europe, given the growing tension over Berlin.

When the British withdrew, fighting had already broken out between Jews and Palestinians, who bitterly resented the loss of half of their homeland. Ben Gurion declared the new state of Israel independent and it was immediately attacked by Egypt, Syria, Jordan, Iraq and Lebanon. Amid general surprise, the Israelis defeated their enemies and their new state soon became established. They have defended it successfully ever since.

The most tragic result of the war was the plight of the Palestinian Arabs who found themselves inside the new state of Israel. After Jewish terrorists had slaughtered the entire population of an Arab village, nearly a million Palestinians fled into Egypt, Lebanon, Jordan and Syria, where they lived in miserable refugee camps.

(c) who was responsible for the tragedy?

▸ Most of the rest of the world, and the Conservatives, blamed Britain's Labour government for its handling of the situation. It was said that British troops should have stayed on to ensure that the partition of Palestine was carried out smoothly. The Arabs accused the British of being pro-Jewish for letting far too many Jews into Palestine in the first place, and for causing them to lose half their homeland, while the Jews accused the British of being pro-Arab for trying to limit Jewish immigration.

▸ Bevin defended his actions and blamed the USA for the chaos; there is some evidence to support his case. It was US President Truman who pressured

Britain to allow 100,000 extra Jews into Palestine in April 1946. Despite this being bound to upset the Arabs even more, Truman refused to provide any American troops to help keep order in Palestine, as well as refusing to allow any more Jews to enter the USA. It was Truman who rejected the British *Morrison Plan of July 1946*, which would have set up separate Arab and Jewish provinces under British supervision. It was the Americans who pushed the plan for partition through the UN, even though all the Arab nations voted against it; this was bound to cause more violence in Palestine.

▸ Some historians have defended the British, pointing out that they were trying to be fair to both sides, and that in the end, it was impossible to persuade both Arabs and Jews to accept a peaceful solution. The British withdrawal was understandable: it would force the Americans and the UN to take more responsibility for the situation they had helped to create. It would save Britain a great deal of expense: since 1945 they had spent over £100 million and used 80,000 troops trying to keep the peace; they simply could not afford to continue.

34.4 Britain, Malaya and Cyprus

(a) problems involved in the British withdrawal from Malaya

Malaya was liberated from Japanese occupation in 1945, but there were two main problems to be faced before the British could think of withdrawing:

▸ How could such a complex area be organized? It consisted of nine states, each ruled by a sultan; two British settlements, Malacca and Penang; and Singapore, a small island less than a mile from the mainland. The population was multiracial: mainly Malays and Chinese, but with some Indians and Europeans. It was decided to group the states and the settlements into *the Federation of Malaya* (1948) while Singapore remained a separate colony. Each state had its own legislature for local affairs; the sultans retained some power, but the central government had firm overall control. Since everybody had the vote, the Malays, the largest group, usually dominated affairs.

▸ Chinese communist guerrillas, who had led the resistance to the Japanese, now began to stir up strikes and violence against the British, and the situation was serious enough for a state of emergency to be declared in 1948. The British dealt with the problem successfully, though it took time: all the Chinese suspected of helping the guerrillas were re-settled into specially guarded villages; it was made clear that independence would follow as soon as the country was ready for it; this ensured that the Malays remained firmly pro-British and gave little help to the communists, who were mainly Chinese. Even so the emergency remained in force until 1960.

The move towards independence was accelerated when the Malay party, under their capable leader, Tunku Abdul Rahman, joined forces with the main Chinese and Indian groups to form *the Alliance Party*, which won 51 of the 52 seats in the 1955 elections. This seemed to suggest stability, and the British were persuaded to grant full independence in 1957, when Malaya was admitted to the Commonwealth.

(b) the Federation of Malaysia founded (1963)

Malaya soon settled down under the leadership of Tunku Abdul Rahman, and its economy, based on exports of rubber and tin, was the most prosperous in South East Asia. Thus in 1961, when Abdul Rahman proposed that Singapore and the three British colonies of North Borneo (Sabah), Brunei and Sarawak should join Malaya to form the Federation of Malaysia, Britain agreed. The Tunku had an ulterior motive: the island of Singapore, with its prosperous port, would be a valuable acquisition, but since three-quarters of its population were Chinese, the Malays would be outnumbered if union took place just between Malaya and Singapore; if the other three colonies, with their predominantly Malay populations, also joined the federation, the Malay majority would be preserved. Singapore, Sarawak and Sabah were in favour of joining, but *objections came from two quarters*:

‣ In Brunei, groups of people opposed to joining the federation started a revolt (December 1962). Although this was quickly suppressed by British troops flown in from Singapore, the Sultan of Brunei decided not to join. This was a disappointment for Abdul Rahman, since Brunei had rich oil resources.
‣ President Sukarno of Indonesia protested because he hoped that Sabah and Sarawak would become part of Indonesia once the British had left.

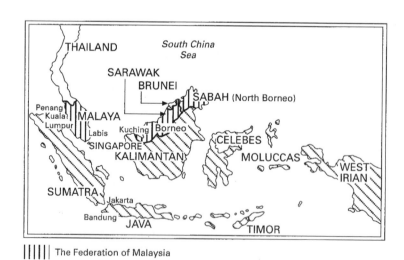

||||| The Federation of Malaysia

\\\\ Indonesia (formerly Dutch East Indies)

map **34.2 Malaysia and Indonesia**

After a United Nations investigation team reported that a large majority of the populations concerned were in favour of the union, the Federation of Malaysia was officially proclaimed (September 1963). Malaysia survived an attempt by neighbouring Indonesia to bring about its disintegration (1963–6). Britain, Australia and New Zealand provided vital military assistance to enable the Malaysians to control the situation. However, in 1965, Singapore, under the leadership of Lee Kuan Yew, chose to leave the Federation, becoming an independent republic. Brunei ceased to be a British colony and became an independent state within the Commonwealth in 1984.

(c) complications in Cyprus

The Labour government (1945–51) considered giving Cyprus independence, but progress was delayed by complications, the most serious of which was the mixed population – about 80 per cent were Greek-speaking Christians of the Orthodox Church, while the rest were Muslims of Turkish origin. The Greek Cypriots wanted the island to unite with Greece (*Enosis*), but the Turks were strongly opposed to this. Churchill's government (1951–5) inflamed the situation in 1954 when their plans for self-government allowed the Cypriots far less power than Labour had envisaged. There were hostile demonstrations, which were dispersed by British troops.

Eden, Churchill's successor, decided to drop the idea of independence for Cyprus, believing that Britain needed the island as a military base to protect its interests in the Middle East. He announced that Cyprus must remain permanently British, though the Greek government promised that Britain could retain its military bases even if *Enosis* took place.

The Greek Cypriots, led by Archbishop Makarios, pressed their demands, while a guerrilla organization called *EOKA*, led by General Grivas, waged a terrorist campaign against the British, who declared a state of emergency in 1955 and deployed about 35,000 troops in an attempt to keep order. British policy also involved deporting Makarios and executing terrorists. The activities of Colonel Nasser in Egypt only served to strengthen Eden's resolve that Britain must keep its foothold in the Middle East.

(d) Macmillan favours compromise

The situation became even more difficult in 1958 when the Turks set up a rival organization, which favoured dividing the island. Eventually, to avoid civil war between the two groups, Macmillan (who became Prime Minister in 1957 when Eden resigned following Britain's humiliation over Suez) decided to compromise. He appointed the sympathetic and tactful Hugh Foot as governor, and he soon negotiated a deal with Makarios: the Archbishop dropped *Enosis* and in return Cyprus was granted full independence; Turkish interests were safeguarded, Britain retained two military bases, and, along with Greece and Turkey, guaranteed the independence of Cyprus. In 1960, Makarios became the first president, with a Turkish Cypriot, Fazal Kutchuk, as vice-president. It seemed a masterly solution, but unfortunately it only lasted until 1963, when civil war broke out between the Greeks and Turks. In 1974, Turkey sent troops to help establish a separate Turkish state in the north, and the island has remained divided ever since. The Turks occupy the north (roughly one-third of the island's area), and the Greeks the south, with UN troops keeping the peace between the two.

34.5 the end of the British Empire in Africa

(a) why did the British decide to leave Africa?

During the 1990s, as more and more government documents dealing with decolonization became available, historians have had a great time investigating the motives behind the withdrawal of all the European powers, not just Britain, from their empires, and the different ways in which these withdrawals were conducted. The main debate that has developed (as we saw in the case of India in Section 33.2) is about the extent to which decolonization was caused by the local nationalist movements, and how far it was brought about by outside political and economic considerations. Robert Holland, a leading exponent of what has become known as the *'metropolitan thesis',* believes that outside forces – metropolitan factors – were more important: 'The great colonial powers,' he writes, 'divested themselves of their subordinate possessions, not because internal pressures within their colonies left them with no other choice, but in the wake of a revisionist process whereby imperial roles came to be seen as incongruent with more "modern" goals in the fields of foreign and economic policy.'

Other historians feel that more credit must be given to the strength of local nationalist movements, and they acknowledge that in some cases the imperial power was quite simply expelled by sheer force. The sorts of questions that historians have to try to answer are, for example: would the British have left East Africa and Central Africa for purely 'metropolitan' reasons *if there had been no nationalist movements in those areas?* However, each case was different, and more research will be needed before clearer conclusions can be reached.

What can be said with certainty is that African nationalism spread rapidly after 1945; this was because more and more Africans were being educated in Britain and the USA, where they were made aware of racial discrimination. Colonialism was seen as the humiliation and exploitation of blacks by whites, and working-class Africans in the new towns were particularly receptive to nationalist ideas. The British, especially the Labour governments of 1945–51, were prepared to allow independence, and were confident that they would still be able exercise influence through trade links, which they hoped to preserve by including the new states as members of the Commonwealth. This practice of exercising influence over former colonies after independence by economic means is known as *neo-colonialism,* and it became widespread in most of the new states of the Third World. Even so, the British intended to move their colonies towards independence very gradually, and the African nationalists had to campaign vigorously and often violently to make them act more quickly.

There were plenty of 'metropolitan factors' at work too. The USA, the USSR and the UN were all against imperialism. Britain had been seriously weakened economically by the Second World War, and the sheer cost of maintaining its Empire, while at the same time developing its own nuclear weapons, was spiralling out of control. It was Macmillan who accelerated Britain's decolonization, apparently because he thought it foolish for a country that was so economically weak to attempt to maintain an imperial role. According to Martin Pugh, it was more than just a loss of nerve after Suez; already as Chancellor of the Exchequer, Macmillan 'had drawn up a profit and loss account for every colony in order to determine where the balance of advantage lay'. His conclusion was: withdraw with as much dignity as possible, while presenting it as a generous and noble response to rising African nationalism. As Macleod, Macmillan's Colonial Secretary, later put it: 'we could not possibly have held by force our territories in Africa; the march of men towards freedom cannot be halted; it can only be guided'.

The British colonies in Africa fell into three distinct groups. They had important differences in character, and these affected progress towards independence.

(b) West Africa: Gold Coast, Nigeria, Sierra Leone and the Gambia

Here, there were relatively few Europeans, and they tended to be administrators rather than permanent settlers with profitable estates to defend. This made the move to independence comparatively straightforward.

Gold Coast

Gold Coast was the first black African state south of the Sahara to win independence after the Second World War, taking the name *Ghana* (1957). It was achieved fairly smoothly, though not without some incident. The nationalist leader, Kwame Nkrumah, educated in London and the USA, and since 1949 leader of *the Convention People's Party (CPP),* organized the campaign for independence. There were boycotts of European goods, violent demonstrations and a general strike (1950), and Nkrumah was twice imprisoned. However, the British, realizing that he had mass support, agreed to allow a new constitution, which included the vote for all adults, an elected assembly and an eleven-person Executive Council, of which eight members were chosen by the assembly. In the 1951 elections, the first under the new constitution, the CPP won 34 seats out of 38. Nkrumah was invited to form a government and became Prime Minister in 1952. This was self-government but not yet full independence.

Gold Coast had a small but well-educated group of politicians and other professionals who, for the next five years, gained experience of government under British supervision. In 1957 Ghana received full independence.

Nigeria

Nigeria was easily the largest of Britain's African colonies, with a population of over 60 million. It was a more difficult proposition than Ghana because of its great size and because of its regional differences between the vast Muslim north, dominated by the Hausa and Fulani tribes, the western region (Yorubas), and the eastern region (Ibos). The leading nationalist was Nnamdi Azikiwe, popularly known to his supporters as 'Zik'. He had been educated in the USA, and after his return to Nigeria in 1937 he soon gained enormous prestige. In 1945, he showed that he meant business by organizing an impressive general strike, which was enough to prompt the British to begin preparing Nigeria for

The Central African Federation 1953–63
Northern Rhodesia (Zambia), Southern Rhodesia (Zimbabwe) and Nyasaland (Malawi)

R Ruanda 1962
B Burundi 1962

map **34.3 Africa becomes independent**

independence. It was decided that a federal system would be most suitable; in 1954 a new constitution introduced local assemblies for the three regions with a central (federal) government in Lagos, the capital. The regions assumed self-government first and the country as a whole became independent in 1960. Sadly, in spite of the careful preparations for independence, tribal differences caused civil war to break out in 1967, when the Ibos declared the eastern region independent, calling it Biafra. Only after long and bloody fighting was Biafra defeated (1970) and Nigerian unity preserved.

Sierra Leone and the Gambia
These two remaining British colonies in West Africa achieved independence without serious incident – Sierra Leone in 1961, and the Gambia in 1965.

(c) East Africa: Tanganyika, Uganda and Kenya

Here, especially in Kenya, things were complicated by the 'settler-factor' – the presence of European and Asian settlers who feared for their future under black governments.

Originally, the British thought that independence for the colonies of East Africa was not as necessary as for West Africa, and that when independence did come, it would be in the form of multiracial governments, in which the European and Asian settlers would play a significant part. But Macmillan (Prime Minister 1957–63) was responsible for the important change in British policy towards the remaining African colonies. He had come to realize the strength of black African feeling and the strain it would place on the British if they attempted to crush it. In a famous speech in Cape Town in 1960 he talked of 'the wind of change blowing through the continent. Whether we like it or not, this growth of national consciousness is a political fact, and our national policies must take account of it'.

Tanganyika
In Tanganyika, the nationalist campaign was conducted by *the Tanganyika African National Union (TANU)* led by Dr Julius Nyerere, who had been educated at Edinburgh University. He insisted that the government must be African, but he also made it clear that whites had nothing to fear from black rule. Macmillan's government, impressed by Nyerere's ability and sincerity, conceded independence with black majority rule (1961). The island of Zanzibar was later united with Tanganyika and the country took the name *Tanzania* (1964). Nyerere was president until his retirement in 1985.

Uganda
In Uganda, independence was delayed for a time by tribal squabbles; the ruler (known as the Kabaka) of the Buganda area objected to the introduction of democracy. Eventually a solution was found in a federal constitution, which

allowed the Kabaka to retain some powers in Buganda. Uganda itself became independent in 1962 with Dr Milton Obote as Prime Minister.

Kenya

Kenya was the most difficult area to deal with, because there were some 66,000 white settlers who were violently opposed to black majority rule. They refused to negotiate with the African nationalist leader, Jomo Kenyatta, and his *Kenya African Unity Party (KAU)*, and were determined to prolong white settler rule. They provoked a confrontation, hoping that violence would destroy the African party. The British government was under pressure from both sides, and the white settlers were supported by certain big business interests in Britain; even so, it did not handle the situation with much imagination. KAU was able to make little progress, the only British concession being to allow six Africans to join the Legislative Council of 54 members.

African impatience burst out in a campaign of terrorist attacks on European-owned farms and on black workers. It was organized by the *Mau Mau* secret society, whose members were mainly from the Kikuyu tribe, who had been deprived of much of their best land by the white settlers, and had either been forced to move into reservations or work as tenant farmers. A state of emergency was declared (1952) and Kenyatta and other nationalist leaders were arrested. Kenyatta was kept in jail for six years (1953–9) although he had publicly condemned terrorism. The British committed 100,000 troops to flush out the terrorists, and over the next eight years, thousands of people, most of them Africans, were killed, and well over 100,000 Kikuyu were imprisoned in what can only be described as concentration camp conditions. There was a scandal in 1959 with revelations of brutal treatment of prisoners at the Hola detention camp, where savage beatings left eleven dead and sixty seriously injured. However, the British government managed to hide from people at home the scale of what was going on in Kenya. It was only in 2005 that the full horrifying details were revealed in two separate books, by historians David Anderson and Caroline Elkins. During the period of the emergency, the British hanged more than a thousand Kikuyu, and killed some 20,000 in combat. In addition, up to 100,000 died in detention camps, where there was a culture of brutality, routine beatings, killings and torture of the most grotesque kinds. One police chief later admitted that conditions in the camps were far worse than those he had suffered as a prisoner of war in Japan. By contrast, less than a hundred whites were killed.

The terrorists had been defeated by 1960, but by then, ironically, the British, encouraged by the 'wind of change', had performed their policy U-turn. They realized that Kenyatta was, after all, a moderate, and allowed him to become Prime Minister when Kenya became independent in 1963. In spite of his treatment by the British, Kenyatta favoured reconciliation; whites who decided to stay on after independence were fairly treated provided they took Kenyan citizenship.

(d) Central Africa: Nyasaland, Northern Rhodesia and Southern Rhodesia

This was the most difficult area for Britain to deal with because this was where the white settlers were most numerous and most deeply entrenched, particularly in Southern Rhodesia. Another problem was that numbers of well-educated Africans were much smaller than in West Africa, because the settlers had made sure that very little money was spent on further and higher education for black Africans. Alarmed at the spread of nationalism, the whites decided that their best policy was to combine resources. They persuaded Churchill's government to allow them to set up a union of the three colonies – Nyasaland and the two Rhodesias – to be known as *the Central African Federation* (1953). Their aim was to preserve the supremacy of the white minority –about 300,000 Europeans out of a total population of around 8.5 million. The federal parliament in Salisbury (the capital of Southern Rhodesia) was heavily weighted to favour the whites, who hoped that the federation would soon gain full independence from Britain, with dominion status.

The Africans watched with growing distrust, and their leaders, Dr Hastings Banda (Nyasaland), Kenneth Kaunda (Northern Rhodesia) and Joshua Nkomo (Southern Rhodesia) began to campaign for black majority rule. As violence spread, a state of emergency was declared in Nyasaland and Southern Rhodesia, with mass arrests of Africans (1959). However, in Britain there was much support for the Africans, especially in the Labour Party and among moderate Conservatives. The Conservative Colonial Secretary, Macleod, was sympathetic and the government appointed *the Monckton Commission* to investigate the situation. In 1960, this recommended votes for Africans, an end to racial discrimination and the right of territories to leave the federation.

Nyasaland and Northern Rhodesia

The British government introduced new constitutions in Nyasaland and Northern Rhodesia, which in effect allowed the Africans their own parliaments (1961–2). Both wanted to leave the federation, which was therefore terminated in December 1963, signalling defeat for the settlers. The following year both Nyasaland and Northern Rhodesia became fully independent, taking the names *Malawi* and *Zambia.* There was bitter opposition from some Conservative right-wingers, led by Lord Salisbury, who were strongly pro-settler; but most Conservatives were reconciled to decolonization by this time, and the government was able to ignore their protests.

Southern Rhodesia

Rhodesia, as it was now known, took much longer to deal with, and it was 1980 before the colony achieved independence with black majority rule. It was here that the white settlers fought most fiercely to preserve their privileged position. There were just over 200,000 whites, about 20,000 Asians, and four million black Africans; *the Rhodesia Front,* a right-wing racist party, was determined never to surrender control of the country to black African rule. The black African parties were banned.

When Zambia and Malawi were given independence, the whites assumed that Rhodesia would get the same treatment and requested independence. The Conservative government refused, making it clear that independence would be granted *only if the constitution was changed to allow black Africans at least a third of the seats in parliament.* Ian Smith (who became Prime Minister of Rhodesia in 1964) rejected this idea, arguing that continued white rule was essential in view of the problems being faced by the new black governments in other African states, and because the Zimbabwe nationalists seemed bitterly divided. When the Labour government (1964–70) refused to compromise, Smith declared Rhodesia independent, against the wishes of Britain, in November 1965 (this was known as UDI – unilateral declaration of independence).

There were mixed reactions to UDI. Harold Wilson soon decided it was out of the question to use force against the illegal Smith regime, and hoped to bring the country to its knees by economic sanctions. The UN condemned UDI and called on member states to place a complete trade embargo on Rhodesia. The Commonwealth was divided – Ghana and Nigeria urged Britain to use force, while Zambia and Tanzania hoped economic sanctions would suffice. However, South Africa, also ruled by a white minority government, and Portugal, which owned neighbouring Mozambique, were sympathetic to Smith, and Rhodesia was able to continue trading through these countries. Many Commonwealth countries felt that Britain was soft-pedalling sanctions, especially as Zambia was suffering more from them than Rhodesia. When Wilson twice met Smith (aboard HMS *Tiger* in 1966 and HMS *Fearless* in 1968) to put forward new ideas, there were howls of protest in case he betrayed the black Rhodesians. Perhaps fortunately for the future of the Commonwealth, Smith rejected both sets of proposals.

In 1970, Rhodesia declared itself a republic, and the rights of black citizens were gradually whittled away until they were suffering similar treatment to that being experienced by blacks living under *apartheid* in South Africa (see Section 34.5(e) below). In 1976, the first signs began to appear that the whites would have to compromise, and they were eventually forced to give way:

> Mozambique's independence from Portugal (June 1975) was a serious blow to the Smith regime. The new president, Samora Machel, applied economic sanctions and allowed Zimbabwean guerrillas to operate from Mozambique. Thousands of black guerrillas were soon active in Rhodesia, straining white security forces to their limits.

- The South Africans became less inclined to support Smith, fearing that the USSR and Cuba (who were involved in Angola) might start interfering in Rhodesia unless some compromise could be found. Both Americans and South Africans urged Smith to make concessions to the blacks before it was too late.

By 1978, nationalist guerrillas controlled large areas of Rhodesia, and the whites were on the verge of defeat.

Smith still tried everything he knew to delay black majority rule as long as possible. He was able to present the divisions between the nationalist leaders as his excuse for the lack of progress, and this was a genuine problem:

- ZAPU (Zimbabwe African People's Union) was the party of the veteran nationalist *Joshua Nkomo*.
- ZANU (Zimbabwe African National Union) was the party of *the Reverend Ndabaningi Sithole*. These two parties, representing different tribes, seemed to be bitter enemies.
- UANC (United African National Council) was the party of *Bishop Abel Muzorewa*.
- *Robert Mugabe*, leader of the guerrilla wing of ZANU, was another powerful figure.

Smith tried to compromise by introducing his own scheme, a joint government of whites and UANC, the most moderate of the nationalist parties, with Bishop Muzorewa as Prime Minister (April 1979). However, it was ZANU and ZAPU that had mass support, and they continued the guerrilla war. Smith had to admit defeat and the new Thatcher government called *the Lancaster House Conference* in London (September–December 1979). All parties were represented, and after some skilful manoeuvring by Lord Carrington, the Foreign Secretary, the conference reached agreement:

- There was to be a new constitution, which would allow the black majority to rule.
- In the new republic of Zimbabwe, there would be a 100-seat parliament in which 80 seats were reserved for black Africans.
- Muzorewa would step down as Prime Minister and the guerrilla war would end.

In the elections that followed, Mugabe's ZANU won a sweeping victory, taking 57 of the 80 black African seats. This gave him a comfortable overall majority, enabling him to become Prime Minister when Zimbabwe officially became independent in April 1980. The transference to black majority rule was welcomed by all African and Commonwealth leaders as a triumph for common sense and moderation. However, some Conservatives accused the government of betraying Muzorewa and allowing Zimbabwe to fall to

Marxism. Civil war between ZANU and ZAPU, which many had feared, did not materialize; the two parties merged in 1987, when Mugabe became the country's first president. He was re-elected for further terms and was still hanging on as president at the time of writing, in 2008, after three obviously rigged elections.

(e) South Africa

The situation in the Union of South Africa was different from that in the other British parts of Africa. South Africa had enjoyed dominion status since 1909 (see Section 21.2) and therefore had more say over its own affairs than the other areas, which were colonies. The majority of the white population was of Dutch Boer origin and therefore did not have the same close affiliations with Britain as the whites in the British colonies. While the colonies gained independence under black majority rule and stayed within the Commonwealth, South Africa preserved white minority rule and left the Commonwealth in 1961.

The whites formed less than 20 per cent of the population. In 1974, there were almost 18 million black Africans, known as Bantus; 2.3 million coloureds; 700,000 Asians; and 4.2 million whites. Roughly two-thirds of the whites were of Dutch origin (known as Afrikaners) and the rest were of British origin. With the granting of independence to India and Pakistan in 1947, white South Africans became alarmed at the growing racial equality within the Commonwealth and were determined to preserve their supremacy. Most of the whites were against racial equality, but the most extreme were the Afrikaner Nationalists, led by Dr Malan, who claimed that the whites were a master race and that non-whites were inferior beings. The Dutch Reformed Church (the official state church) supported this view, though the Christian Church in general believes in racial equality. The Nationalists won the 1948 elections with promises to rescue the whites from the 'black menace'. Malan's policy was *apartheid.*

What was apartheid? This was a policy that involved separating or segregating the different races, in order to preserve the racial purity of the whites, and thus their supremacy. There had been some segregation before 1948; for example, Africans were forbidden to buy land outside special reserve areas. But Malan's apartheid was much more systematic: Africans had to live in special reserves and townships, with separate and inferior facilities. If an existing black township was thought to be too close to a 'white' area, the whole community was uprooted and 'regrouped' somewhere else to make separation as complete as possible. There were separate buses, trains, coaches, cafés, toilets, park benches, hospitals, beaches, picnic areas, sports facilities and even churches. Black children went to separate schools and were given a much inferior education. Every person was given a racial classification and an identity card, and marriage and sexual relations between whites and non-whites were forbidden. Black Africans had no political rights and were not represented in parliament.

There was mounting criticism of apartheid from all over the world. Most of the Commonwealth members were strongly opposed to it, and early in 1960 Macmillan had the courage to speak out against it in the South African parliament in Cape Town, during his famous 'wind of change' speech. His warnings were ignored, and shortly afterwards the world was horrified by the Sharpeville massacre, when 67 Africans were killed in clashes with the police.

At the 1961 Commonwealth Conference, criticism of South Africa was intense, and many thought it should be expelled from the Commonwealth. In the end, the Prime Minister, Hendrick Verwoerd, withdrew South Africa's application for continued membership (in 1960, it been declared a republic rather than a dominion, thereby severing the connection with the British crown; because of this, they had to apply for readmission to the Commonwealth), and the country ceased to be a member of the Commonwealth.

The end of apartheid and white supremacy. Apartheid continued without any concessions to black people until 1980. But pressure for drastic change was building up. It was a serious blow to the white South African regime when, in 1975, the white-ruled Portuguese colonies of Mozambique and Angola achieved independence. The African takeover of Zimbabwe in 1980 removed the last of the white-ruled states that had been sympathetic to South Africa and apartheid. Now South Africa was surrounded by hostile black-ruled states, and many Africans in these new states had sworn never to rest until their fellow Africans in South Africa had been liberated. Moderate Afrikaner leaders realized that they had to make concessions or risk losing everything. In the early 1980s, much of the apartheid system was dropped: in 1990, the African National Congress (ANC) was legalized and Nelson Mandela was released after twenty-seven years in jail.

President F. W. de Klerk (elected 1989) had privately decided that black majority rule would have to come eventually; and he wanted to move the country towards it in a controlled way rather than have it imposed by violence. He deserves great credit for the courage and determination he showed in the face of bitter opposition from right-wing Afrikaner groups. Nelson Mandela, now leader of the ANC, responded well, condemning violence and calling for reconciliation between blacks and whites. After long and difficult negotiations, a new constitution was worked out (1993), and a general election was held in which the ANC won almost two-thirds of the votes (May 1994). Mandela became the first black president of South Africa. It was a remarkable achievement, shared by both Mandela and de Klerk, that South Africa was able to move from apartheid to black majority rule without civil war.

34.6 a balance sheet of Empire

One of the questions that has exercised commentators and historians for many years is: was the British Empire a good thing or a bad thing? In 2002, the director of a centre-left 'think tank' called Demos suggested that the Queen should go on 'a world tour to apologize for the past sins of Empire as a first step to making the Commonwealth more effective and relevant'. As yet, the Queen has not obliged, though her Prime Minister, Tony Blair, did get so far as to express 'deep sorrow' for Britain's role in the evil of slavery and the slave trade. On the other hand, Gordon Brown, Blair's successor, after a recent visit to East Africa, said that 'the days of Britain having to apologize for its colonial history are over'; on the contrary, we should be proud of the Empire. So where does the truth lie?

(a) the debit side

Criticism of Britain's imperial policies goes back a long way. In 1902, J. A. Hobson published an influential book entitled *Imperialism: A Study*, in which he argued that empire-building was a capitalist conspiracy to seize the assets and markets of other, weaker countries for their own profit and against the public good. He accepted that some people supported imperialism for genuine liberal motives – the desire to protect, help and 'civilize' weaker peoples who needed to be ruled by others until they were able to rule themselves, but he was convinced that the interests of the colonialists always came first in any clash of interests. As Lord Salisbury remarked, 'India must be bled, [but] the bleeding should be done judiciously.' As Piers Brendon puts it, the Empire's real purpose 'was not to spread sweetness and light but to increase Britain's wealth and power. Naturally its coercive and exploitative nature must be disguised'. George Orwell said that the Empire 'was a despotism with theft as its final object'. Bertrand Russell called the Empire 'a cesspool for British moral refuse', by which he apparently meant that many of the British administrators and officials were racist bullies.

Sadly, there is a great deal of evidence to support this negative view. Although by no means all officials were racist bullies, there is no doubt that most of them treated the native peoples with arrogance and considered them to be inferior beings or lesser breeds. After the Indian Mutiny of 1857, the army vowed to spill 'barrels and barrels of the filth which flows in these niggers' veins for every drop of blood' they had shed. As Piers Brendon shows, 'the history of India is punctuated by famines which caused tens of millions of deaths'. Yet Lord Lytton insisted on holding his durbar (ceremonial gathering) in 1876 in the middle of a famine, remarking that to stop it 'would be more disastrous to the permanent interests of the Empire than twenty famines'. During the severe famine in Bengal in 1943–4, Churchill refused to divert shipping to take supplies to Calcutta, remarking that the starvation of already underfed Bengalis was less serious than that of sturdy Greeks, particularly as Indians would go on breeding like rabbits.

Also on the debit list must go the slaughter of thousands of Aborigines in Australia and Maoris in New Zealand. Wherever there was any resistance, retribution was always disproportionate. Afghanistan, Ceylon, Jamaica, Burma, Kenya and Iraq were all subjugated violently. During the Boer War in South Africa, the British set up concentration camps in which about a sixth of the entire Boer population died. If one adds the slave trade and atrocities such as the Amritsar massacre (1919) and the notorious detention camps in Kenya, it amounts to a damning indictment of British imperialism.

As to the benefits that imperialism was meant to bring, there is evidence suggesting that, at best, these were thinly spread. Many of the territories were left economically underdeveloped, they had little industry, and were often dependent for revenue on just one product – for example, cocoa in Ghana and oil in Nigeria. In Malawi, for example, when the British left in 1964, there were only two secondary schools for its two million Africans, no roads to speak of, only one railway line and not a single industrial factory. The governor of Bengal wrote a shocking report on his province shortly before India became independent: 'Bengal has, practically speaking, no irrigation or drainage, a medieval system of agriculture, no roads, no education, no cottage industries, completely inadequate hospitals … and no adequate machinery to cope with distress. There are not even plans to make good these deficiencies.'

And finally, most of the newly independent countries had been inadequately prepared for independence. They lacked experience of how to work democratic forms of government and they were left to cope with frontiers, drawn by their European masters, that ignored existing tribal differences. All the African states contained a number of different tribal groups, which had only been held together by the British presence, and had united in the nationalist struggle against the British. Once the British withdrew, tribal rivalries re-emerged and caused trouble, most seriously in Nigeria, which soon descended into a terrible civil war. In fact, as Piers Brendon concludes, 'the British Empire was in grave moral deficit', and he quotes the eighteenth-century historian, Edward Gibbon, who wrote: 'The history of empires is the history of human misery.'

(b) the credit side

Back in the early days of the empire in the eighteenth century, Edmund Burke claimed that the business of empire was a trust, and that colonies should be governed for the benefit of the subject peoples, who would eventually achieve their natural right to rule themselves. In 1921, Lloyd George told the Imperial Conference that the British Empire was unique because 'Liberty is its binding principle'. Some historians believe that the majority of empire-builders were quite sincere in their claims of wanting to improve the welfare of their subjects, though others point out that the native peoples only enjoyed liberty so long as they did as the British told them. Nevertheless, most of the administrators genuinely tried to do 'the right thing'. For example, they tried to eradicate slavery in Africa, practices like thuggee and suttee in India (see Section 11.1(e)), and cannibalism in New Zealand. Lord Curzon (Viceroy of India, 1898–1905) made it his mission to provide India with the best administration it had ever had. He encouraged trade and education, improved communications and the justice system, developed irrigation schemes, and provided famine relief. There is much of evidence to suggest that, while senior administrators tended to be arrogant and aloof, most of the lower civil servants were sympathetic and concerned about the well-being of their charges. Niall Ferguson, who makes a very strong case in defence of the Empire, points out that:

> whenever the British were behaving despotically, there was almost always a liberal critique of their behaviour from within British society. Indeed, so powerful and consistent was this tendency to judge Britain's imperial conduct by the yardstick of liberty that it gave the British Empire something of a self-liquidating character. Once a colonized society had adopted the other institutions the British brought with them, it became very hard for the British to prohibit that political liberty to which they attached so much significance for themselves.

Ferguson admits that there were some dreadful blemishes on Britain's colonial record (though he fails to mention the atrocities in Kenya), but argues that these must be set against the positive benefits of British rule, which were considerable. He goes on to list what he sees as the main benefits:

‣ the triumph of capitalism as the optimal system of economic organization;
‣ the Anglicization of North America and Australasia;
‣ the internationalization of the English language;
‣ the enduring influence of the Protestant version of Christianity; and
‣ the survival of parliamentary institutions, which far worse empires were poised to extinguish in the 1940s.

In addition to all that, the British developed a global network of modern communications made possible by the spread of English as a worldwide language, they spread a system of law and order, and 'maintained a global peace unmatched before or since'. 'What the British Empire proved', he concludes rather controversially, 'is that empire is a form of international government which can work – and not just for the benefit of the ruling power. It sought to globalize not just an economic but a legal and ultimately a political system too.'

(c) how did the loss of Empire affect Britain?

Many observers took the end of the empire as a major sign of Britain's decline from being a great power. Yet there are several different ways of looking at it.

Jeremy Black argues that 'decolonization was not a central issue in British politics. Colonies appeared less necessary in defence terms, not least because in 1957 Britain added the hydrogen bomb to the atom bomb'. Moreover, the near disappearance of the Empire was 'relatively painless because interest in much of it was limited'. And in fact, Bernard Porter, in his book *The Absent-Minded Imperialists*, argues that the Empire had a far lower profile in Britain than it did abroad, and that, certainly during the nineteenth century, many Britons were probably hardly aware that it existed. Those who were aware were mostly among the upper-middle and the upper classes who took part in empire-building and administration, or who had connections with the Empire and followed its development with interest from home. Emigrants from the working and middle classes went to settle in Canada, Australia, New Zealand and South Africa, but since most of them did not return, they can have had little influence on the wider population of Britain.

By the twentieth century, more people knew about the Empire, but certainly in the last forty years of the century 'imperialism' had come to be regarded by a majority of those who knew about it as a 'bad thing' – something morally indefensible. In 2002, a BBC website cited by Niall Ferguson had this to say: 'The Empire came to greatness by killing lots of people less sharply armed than themselves and stealing their countries, although their methods later changed: killing lots of people with machine-guns came to prominence'. According to George L. Bernstein, once India had gone, 'the rest of the empire was irrelevant to British power, while all the empire had become impossible to defend ... Its demise freed Britain from the untenable financial burden, and so made possible a foreign policy that genuinely pursued the national interest'.

In addition, decolonization proceeded relatively smoothly because it could be presented by the British as the long-time ultimate aim of their imperial policies – to bring the benefits of civilization to backward parts of the world in order to prepare them for self-government. A further point that was stressed: Britain was not losing the Empire, it was simply changing it into the Commonwealth. Among the vast majority of the British people, therefore, apart from a few Conservatives, there was no great outburst of despair; as Bernard Porter puts it: 'it was just another of those marginal issues of politics, which might interest their politicians, but not themselves'.

However, Bernstein makes a further significant point: though most Britons were not greatly interested in their Empire, other countries saw the possession of this enormous Empire as a symbol of what made Britain a great power. Even though the Empire no longer contributed to the actual strength of Britain, it was the *perception* that mattered: 'Thus, the loss of the empire not only meant that others might not take the British as seriously in world affairs. More importantly it meant that the British did not take themselves as seriously'.

1 What were the motives behind Britain's move to decolonization after 1945, and how smoothly was the process carried out in the period 1945 to 1964?

2 Analyse the reasons that led to the end of British rule in India. Why did it prove necessary to partition India, and how successfully was the partition carried out?

3 How far would you agree that decolonization was a serious blow to Britain's power and prestige?

4 'The British Empire was in grave moral deficit' (Piers Brendon); 'The British Empire has been a force for good unrivalled in the modern world' (Alan Massie). How would you explain these contradictory judgements?

A document question about decolonization in Africa can be found on the accompanying website www.palgrave.com/masterseries/lowe1.

chapter 35

Thatcherism and the New Right, 1979–97

summary of events

With a comfortable overall majority of 43 after the election of May 1979, Mrs Thatcher, Britain's first woman Prime Minister, prepared to grapple with the country's problems, following Callaghan's 'winter of discontent'. She called the strikes 'a reversion to barbarism', and made it clear that she would stand no more nonsense from the unions. She offered a new policy – monetarism – to cure the country's economic ills and revitalize capitalism. She was firmly on the right of the party, having none of the traditional Conservative paternalism of Disraeli, Macmillan or William Whitelaw, who had been her chief rival for the leadership. By the early 1980s, her beliefs and policies were being referred to as 'Thatcherism' and her supporters were described as the New Right.

During *her first government (1979–83)* Mrs Thatcher and her team applied monetarism with mixed success. The most disturbing result was the rise in unemployment, to over 3 million. The Conservatives' popularity waned rapidly and they began to lose by-elections to the Liberals and to the newly-formed Social Democratic Party (which split from the Labour Party in March 1981). However, Conservative fortunes revived after Mrs Thatcher's decisive handling of the Falklands crisis and Britain's victory in the war with Argentina (April–June 1982). In the election of June 1983, with the Labour Party in complete disarray, the Conservatives won a landslide victory, giving them an overall majority of 144.

The second Thatcher government (1983–7) is regarded as the heyday or 'high noon' of Thatcherism, during which New Right policies such as privatization, 'rolling back the state' and controlling government spending were pursued vigorously. Mrs Thatcher again decided to go to the country early, after local election results seemed favourable. In June 1987, the Conservatives were once again victorious; though losing some seats to Labour, they still emerged with an overall majority of just over 100.

But storm clouds were soon gathering over *the third Thatcher government (1987–90)*. Mrs Thatcher insisted on pushing ahead with a new and extremely unpopular policy, the poll tax, though most members of her Cabinet were against it. There were disagreements within the party over Europe, and criticism of Mrs Thatcher increased. By the autumn of 1990, many Conservatives saw her as a liability, and to the amazement of most of the nation, who knew little about the back-stage manoeuvrings, she was forced to resign (November 1990). John Major was elected leader of the party and became Prime Minister.

John Major began well, dropping the disastrous poll tax, but unemployment was soon rising again, and the Conservatives had to fight the next election (April 1992) in the middle of a recession. Against all expectations, Major won a small overall majority of 21. But things soon began to go wrong for the new government; later the same year, Britain was forced to leave the ERM (see Section 33.4(c) for an explanation of the ERM), and the Conservatives' traditional reputation for being good managers of the economy was left in tatters. Differences in the party over Europe became ever more serious.

Meanwhile, the Labour Party, under its new leader, Tony Blair, had been busy modernizing itself and projecting its non-socialist image of New Labour, so it was no surprise when the Conservatives lost the election of May 1997. What *was* surprising was the magnitude of the Conservative defeat: Labour emerged with 418 seats and an overall majority of 179, and the Conservatives were reduced to only 165 – their lowest total since 1906.

35.1 what is meant by 'Thatcherism'?

Margaret Thatcher was the daughter of a Grantham grocer, Alfred Roberts, who was also a local Conservative councillor and alderman. After reading Chemistry at Oxford, she married Denis Thatcher, a rich industrialist. She stood for Parliament, unsuccessfully, in 1950, at the age of 23, and was eventually elected MP for Finchley in 1959. Before her election as leader in 1975, her experience of high office had been unusually limited – her only major post was Secretary of State for Education under Heath. She was influenced by the ideas of Enoch Powell and Sir Keith Joseph, two right-wing Conservative MPs, who believed that during the years of consensus politics under Macmillan and Heath, the Conservatives had strayed too close to socialism and the mixed economy; it was time to return to 'economic liberalism'. This involved reducing state intervention to the absolute minimum and allowing what they called 'market forces' to rule the economy. Powell and Joseph had themselves been influenced by an Austrian, F. A. Hayek, who had set out New Right ideas in his book *The Road to Serfdom*, first published in 1944. *Thatcherism, as it developed from these ideas, was basically an attack on socialism and collectivism.*

(a) the role of the state in society must be reduced

There was too much planning and too many restrictions; people should be given more freedom to show their initiative in business: it was not the responsibility of the government to provide full employment. This sounded very much like the old nineteenth-century *laissez-faire* ideas, and in fact Mrs Thatcher talked about a return to Victorian values. The economy must be left free to develop according to the demands of the markets (market forces). Hard work and enterprise would be rewarded, and the power of the trade unions, which Mrs Thatcher saw as 'wreckers', must be curbed. Direct taxes must be reduced, so that people could spend their money largely as they wished. It was acknowledged that there would be inequalities of wealth in such a system, but this was to be welcomed in an 'enterprise culture', where the prospect of wealth must be the great driving motive behind people's desire to advance themselves. Eventually (though not much was said about this in the 1979 manifesto), the state would be 'rolled back' even further by privatizing all the nationalized industries. The belief was that privately-owned concerns were always more likely to produce positive results – greater efficiency and greater profits – than those owned by the state.

(b) monetarism was the best way to make Britain prosperous again

Another influence on the New Right was the American economist, Milton Friedman, who believed that governments and businesses ought to spend less; this was the opposite of Keynes' theory, that governments should spend their way out of depressions. Previous governments, during their 'stop' phases, had controlled the money supply temporarily by raising the bank rate. Mrs Thatcher aimed to pursue this policy wholeheartedly and without any relaxation. The theory was that a tight hold must be kept on the money supply via the Bank of England by maintaining high rates of interest, so that firms and individuals were forced to reduce borrowing. Management must therefore keep costs down by laying off workers and streamlining operations for greater efficiency. There would be no government grants to prop up inefficient firms, so that only those that made themselves competitive would survive. Such a policy meant a high unemployment level, but its supporters claimed that it was like a major surgical operation – drastic, but effective in the long term: British industry, though much contracted, would be more efficient and competitive overseas.

With purchasing power reduced as unemployment rose, inflation would be controlled and wage demands moderated accordingly. One advantage of monetarism was that the control it exercised was more impersonal than Heath's wage restraint, and therefore there was less chance of a direct confrontation between government and unions. A further advantage, particularly attractive to the Conservatives, was that trade unions would be less powerful: workers, thankful to be in a job during a time of high unemployment, would be less willing to strike. It was expected that, in due course, job losses would be offset by the creation of large numbers of new jobs in the service industries (such industries as leisure, tourism, advertising, banking, insurance and information technology); many of these would be less well-paid, less secure, and less trade-union-dominated than before. Monetarism would keep inflation low – always one of the government's main aims – and this would encourage people to save more.

(c) self-help and individualism

Mrs Thatcher rejected the idea that it was the job of the state to care for people from 'cradle to grave'. Individuals must make their own provision for sickness and old age and not expect the welfare state to do it for them. Only those who were incapable of looking after themselves would be helped by the state. This would enable the government to save vast amounts of money, but seemed to herald less commitment to the welfare state – the health service, education and social services – than under any government since 1945. One popular item in the 1979 Conservative manifesto was the sale of council houses to sitting tenants at well below market prices.

(d) a strong element of British nationalism

Many right-wing Conservatives had not come to terms with the loss of Britain's Empire in the 1950s and 1960s (see Chapter 34) and her general decline as a great power. Nor had they approved of Heath's enthusiasm for joining the EEC. Mrs Thatcher was prepared to do all she could to safeguard Britain's sovereignty and to stand up for Britain's rights in Europe, and she would not be pushed around by foreigners. Later, she enjoyed being portrayed in *Sun* cartoons 'handbagging the Frogs', and she revelled in it when the Russians dubbed her the 'Iron Lady'. She preferred to foster Britain's special relationship with the USA, especially with President Ronald Reagan, another committed monetarist and market forces enthusiast. Other objects of Mrs Thatcher's disapproval were Scottish and Welsh Nationalists who, she believed, wanted to break up the UK.

(e) Thatcherism was radical and anti-Establishment

Mrs Thatcher felt herself to be an outsider in terms of the traditional Tory leadership: she was from a lower-middle-class background and she was a woman; her beliefs marked her out as being different from most of the Tory 'grandees' like Lord Carrington, William Whitelaw and Sir Ian Gilmour who, she felt, had taken the party perilously close to socialism. She was impatient with civil servants who had spent their careers making consensus politics work. In particular, she resented the Foreign Office diplomats, whom she saw as over-cautious, patronizing and far too liberal. She disapproved of the Rhodesia settlement reached in December 1979 (see Section 34.5(d)), blaming Carrington and the Foreign Office because it gave power to a socialist government. This experience made her determined to follow her instincts against their advice if necessary (as in her refusal to support sanctions against South Africa and her insistence on launching the campaign to recapture the Falklands). Eventually she fell out with most sections of the British Establishment, including the universities, the BBC and the Church of England. When a group of Anglican bishops expressed disquiet at the plight of the poor in Liverpool, Mrs Thatcher was displeased, feeling that the Church of England had become tainted with socialism; she had apparently missed the point that it was Christianity that was motivating the bishops. Her suspicion of the 'Establishment' mentality was the reason why Mrs Thatcher always took care to ask the question, when making appointments both in government and administration, 'Is he one of us?', and why she surrounded herself with reliable New Right advisers.

In practice, many of these Thatcherite principles had to be modified. As Peter Clarke points out, Mrs Thatcher 'was a political opportunist in the best sense, always quick to seize the opportunities which came her way and exploit them ... She made up policies as she went along and used off-the-cuff public utterances to bounce her colleagues into accepting initiatives that had not been previously agreed'. Monetarism eventually had to be abandoned as unworkable, though the government never admitted it. Although Mrs Thatcher opposed too much state interference and wanted people to have more freedom in economic affairs, more restrictions than ever were introduced on civil liberties, and the government took on more powers in areas such as education and local government. However, all this was in the future; in April 1979, Mrs Thatcher seemed exactly the sort of decisive, forceful, strong-willed and self-assured leader that Britain needed. 'The mission of this government,' she announced soon after her election victory, 'is much more than economic progress. It is to renew the spirit and the solidarity of the nation. At the heart of a new mood in the nation must be a recovery of our self-confidence and our self-respect.'

35.2 the first Thatcher government, 1979–83

(a) Rhodesia becomes Zimbabwe

The crisis in Rhodesia had dragged on since 1964, when Ian Smith declared Rhodesian independence. Wilson, Heath and Callaghan all failed to find a solution to the deadlock, but against a background of changing circumstances, Mrs Thatcher was seen at her most flexible and pragmatic. She called the Lancaster House Conference in London in September 1979, and eventually, largely thanks to the skill of Lord Carrington, the Foreign Secretary, a settlement was reached transforming Rhodesia into the new republic of Zimbabwe, under black majority rule (1980). This was seen by most people as a triumph of common sense and moderation, and a good beginning for Mrs Thatcher (see Section 34.5(d)).

(b) monetarism in practice

Mrs Thatcher had to proceed cautiously at first, since only three other members of her Cabinet (Sir Geoffrey Howe, Sir Keith Joseph and John Biffen) shared her ideas; all the rest she regarded, in varying degrees, as 'Wets'. Nevertheless, with Howe as Chancellor of the Exchequer, she was able to make the first moves towards monetarism. Howe's budget of June 1979 was designed to control inflation, which was running at 10 per cent when the government took office. The basic rate of income tax was reduced from 33 per cent to 30 per cent, VAT was raised from 8 per cent to 15 per cent (to offset the losses from income tax), cash limits were introduced on public spending, which affected housing, education and transport, and there was a cripplingly high minimum lending rate, which had gone up to 17 per cent early in 1980. At first the problems seemed to get worse: the annual rate of inflation soared to 22 per cent by May 1980, but this was partly because the government had honoured pay rises agreed under Labour. Thatcher and Howe confidently predicted that the inflation rate would be down to 10 per cent by the end of 1981. Their predictions were not far wrong; in fact, by 1983 the rate had fallen to 4.5 per cent, and the government had therefore achieved its primary aim.

Unfortunately there were some drastic side-effects:

‣ The British economy suffered the worst depression for fifty years, partly because the pound was strong, and this made exports more expensive and encouraged imports. There was also a deepening world recession which would in any case have affected Britain.

Illus. **35.1 Margaret Thatcher and Sir Geoffrey Howe**

- Hundreds of firms went bankrupt, as the high interest rates and tightly controlled money supply prevented people from borrowing, and there was no help forthcoming from the government. In 1981 alone the economy shrank by 2 per cent, and by the end of 1982 something like 25 per cent of British manufacturing capacity had been destroyed. The de-industrialization of Britain was well under way.
- Unemployment shot up to 2.8 million in the autumn of 1981, almost double the figure when the Conservatives came to power. A year later it had reached 3.3 million. Most of the jobs lost were in the manufacturing industry, and the worst hit areas were the north of England, Wales and Scotland. In the summer of 1981 there were riots in Brixton and Southall (London), in Toxteth (Liverpool) and in the Moss Side area of Manchester.

Opinion polls showed that the government was extremely unpopular, but Mrs Thatcher stuck doggedly to her policies. She had already told the party conference in October 1980, 'You turn if you want to. The lady's not for turning'. Whatever her private thoughts, Mrs Thatcher seemed obsessed with self-help and apparently showed little sympathy for the plight of the 3 million unemployed. Michael Heseltine was more concerned; he went to Liverpool many times to see for himself how bad conditions really were. Dismayed by what he saw, he wrote a confidential Cabinet memorandum recommending a change in industrial and social policies to help industrial areas ravaged by unemployment; he wanted job creation schemes and government money to bring in private investment. Many Cabinet members supported Heseltine; Sir Ian Gilmour, quoting Churchill, told the prime minister: 'However beautiful the strategy, you should occasionally look at the results'. Mrs Thatcher was furious and began to see Heseltine as a rival. Dismissing her critics as 'Wets', she unceremoniously removed them and replaced them with Thatcherites (1981). Two of these were self-made men – Cecil Parkinson (who became Party Chairman) was a successful industrialist and son of a railwayman from Carnforth (Lancashire); and Norman Tebbit (who became Secretary for Employment), a tough politician known in some party circles as 'the Chingford skinhead', he was a former pilot and son of a shop manager. Nigel Lawson, an economic journalist and a 'true-believer', was brought in to head the Department of Energy.

The government lost a number of by-elections, the most spectacular defeat being at Crosby, where a Conservative majority of over 19,000 was converted into a 5,000 majority for Shirley Williams, the candidate of the newly-formed Social Democratic Party (November 1981).

(c) the formation of the Social Democratic Party (SDP)

If the Conservatives had their internal squabbles, the Labour Party was in a much worse state. The right wing of the party was becoming increasingly impatient with the left because of its support for militant trade unionism, unilateral disarmament, withdrawal from the EEC and further nationalization. The election of the veteran left-winger, Michael Foot, as party leader (1980) convinced some of the right that they had no future in the Labour Party. Four of them: Roy Jenkins, Dr David Owen, Shirley Williams and William Rodgers – soon to be known as *the Gang of Four* – left the party and in a blaze of publicity launched the SDP (March 1981). Jenkins narrowly failed to win a by-election at Warrington, but after the SDP formed an alliance with the Liberals, successes followed. A Liberal, William Pitt, won Croydon; Shirley Williams won Crosby; and in March 1982 Jenkins captured Glasgow Hillhead. All three seats were taken from the Conservatives. Suddenly, soon after the Hillhead by-election, the political scene was transformed by the Falklands War.

(d) the Falklands War (April–June 1982)

1 The Argentinian claim to the British-owned Falkland Islands in the South Atlantic had been discussed on and off by the two governments for the previous twenty years. The Argentinians may well have got the impression that the British would not be averse to an eventual transfer of power; but the stumbling block was that the 1,800 Falklanders were adamant that they wished to remain under British sovereignty. Two decisions taken by the Thatcher government, on the advice of the Foreign Office, were probably interpreted by the Argentinians as signals of Britain's declining interest: the ice-breaker ship *Endurance* was removed from the Falklands, and an elderly aircraft carrier was to be scrapped, which would make it more difficult to defend the islands.

2 Argentinian forces invaded the islands (2 April) as well as their dependency, South Georgia. The UN Security Council and the EEC condemned their action and urged the Argentinians to withdraw, but to no avail. Mrs Thatcher acted decisively and astonished the world by the speed of her response. Against the advice of the Foreign Office, a British task force was swiftly assembled and sent off to recapture the Falklands. It consisted of some 79 ships including the aircraft carriers *Invincible* and *Hermes* and about 6,000 troops.

3 During the three weeks it took the task force to sail the 7,000 miles via Ascension Island to the South Atlantic, frantic attempts were made, notably by Alexander Haig, the American Secretary of State, to reach a negotiated solution. However, the British, refuting South American charges of colonialism, pointed out that the islanders wished to remain associated with Britain; and they refused to negotiate unless Argentinian troops were withdrawn. The Argentinians, safe in possession of the islands, refused to budge, and Haig's efforts came to nothing. Meanwhile, Lord Carrington, the Foreign Secretary, had resigned, accepting responsibility for 'the humiliating affront to this country'. He was replaced by Francis Pym. Mrs Thatcher showed

considerable determination and nerve, since the operation was risky in the extreme: weather conditions were highly unpredictable and there was insufficient air cover. But she viewed all attempts at negotiation as appeasement, and fortunately the opposition leaders supported her.

4 The task force arrived in Falklands waters during the final week of April and soon enjoyed complete success. South Georgia was recaptured (25 April) and the *General Belgrano,* an elderly Argentinian cruiser carrying troops and deadly Exocet missiles, was sunk by a British nuclear submarine with the loss of 368 lives (2 May). This prompted the *Sun* to come out with the triumphant front-page headline 'GOTCHA.' The sinking caused much controversy, since the vessel was outside the total exclusion zone the British had declared around the islands. HMS *Sheffield* was badly damaged by an Exocet missile (4 May), but this did not prevent successful landings at Port San Carlos (21 May) and later at Bluff Cove and Fitzroy near Port Stanley (early June); two British frigates were sunk during the landings. British troops won engagements at Darwin and Goose Green, and finally captured Port Stanley. On 14 June the Argentinian troops surrendered and the recapture of the Falklands was complete. The British lost 254 men; and the Argentinians 750. The expedition cost Britain around £1,600 million.

5 The effects of the war on the home front were little short of sensational. There was an outburst of patriotism such as had not been seen since the Second World War, and approval of the government's decisive action caused their sagging popularity to revive with a vengeance. This was reflected in the local election results in May 1982 and in two by-elections which the SDP could have been expected to win, judging from their earlier performance, but which the Conservatives won comfortably. In the euphoria of the Falklands victory, the government was able to ignore questions such as: What had it all been for? and What good did it do? To Mrs Thatcher, the answers were obvious: a military dictator had been taught a sharp lesson, and Britain's prestige in the world had been restored. Critics were given short shrift and told to 'rejoice'! On the other hand, the cost of defending the islands since then has been enormous.

(e) the election of June 1983

With over 3 million still out of work, Labour ought to have had a fighting chance of victory, but several factors worked in the Conservatives' favour:

▸ They had succeeded in bringing the annual inflation rate down to around 4 per cent, which they had claimed all along to be one of their main aims.
▸ Critics of the trade unions were pleased with the government's actions to curb trade union powers. *The 1980 Employment Act* had already restricted picketing to the pickets' own place of work. *The Employment Act of October 1982* went further, and restricted the operation of closed shops – a closed

shop could only exist when a ballot showed 85 per cent support. Trade unions were made more accountable for their actions and could be fined for unlawful strikes; and compensation was to be paid to workers who had been sacked from their jobs for non-membership of a union. The election manifesto promised more legislation to force trade unions to hold ballots before calling strikes, and ballots about whether or not to continue the political levy.

‣ The Labour Party did itself no good with a left-wing manifesto that included restoration of full trade union rights, withdrawal from the EEC and from NATO's defence policy, and unilateral nuclear disarmament. One disgruntled right-wing Labour MP called it 'the longest suicide note in history'.

‣ Above all, the continuing effect of the 'Falklands factor' was probably crucial. During the election campaign, Mrs Thatcher was able to tell the nation: 'We have ceased to be a nation in retreat ... Britain will not look back from the victory she has won.'

The Liberal/SDP Alliance conducted an impressive campaign projecting itself as the only viable alternative government to the Conservatives. Though it failed to make a breakthrough in terms of seats, it took crucial votes away from Labour. The results showed an overwhelming Conservative victory with 397 seats, against only 209 for Labour, 23 for the Alliance and 21 for others. It was a disaster for the Labour Party, which polled its lowest vote since 1935.

The Conservatives and most of the press enthused about their landslide victory. But in fact the voting figures revealed something rather different. The Conservative vote had in fact fallen from the 1979 figure (from 13.69 million to 13.01 million) suggesting not that there was a great surge of enthusiasm for Mrs Thatcher, but rather that the electors decidedly did not want a Labour government (Labour's vote fell from 11.53 million to 8.45 million). Many Labour voters and some disillusioned Tory supporters switched to the Alliance, whose 7.8 million votes were a striking feature of the election. This revealed more clearly than ever the unfairness of the British electoral system. Labour's 27.6 per cent of total votes cast entitled them to 209 seats, but the Alliance, not all that far behind with 25.4 per cent, secured only 23 seats. It was the old story of the single-vote, single-member constituency system working to the disadvantage of a party that came second in a large number of constituencies. The demand for proportional representation revived, but there was little prospect of it being introduced in the near future, since the Conservative government, not unnaturally, was happy with the existing system.

35.3 Mrs Thatcher's heyday, 1983–7

Fortified by her huge Commons majority, Mrs Thatcher reshuffled her Cabinet, bringing in more Thatcherites, and pushed ahead with her programme against a background of continuing monetarism. The government's record contained some major achievements, though all were highly controversial.

(a) privatization

This was strongly advocated on the grounds that it would increase efficiency, encourage more concern for the customer, and enable the general public and employees to become shareholders. Also attractive to the government were the proceeds – £2,500 million in 1985–6, and about £4,700 million in each of the next three years. By January 1987, no fewer than fourteen major companies (including British Aerospace, British Petroleum, British Telecom, Britoil, the Trustee Savings Bank and British Gas) had been sold off into private ownership. This was bitterly attacked by the Labour Party with its belief in nationalization, and even some Conservatives felt that things were going too far; Lord Stockton (formerly Harold Macmillan) called it 'selling off the family silver'.

(b) a tough line with the trade unions

The government continued to take a tough line with the unions, quickly introducing the new regulations about compulsory ballots. Union membership was banned at Government Communications Headquarters (GCHQ). However, the biggest confrontation came with the miners. When the National Coal Board announced the closure of twenty-one uneconomic pits, with the expected loss of 20,000 jobs, the executive of the National Union of Miners (NUM), led by Arthur Scargill, voted for a national strike. They had defeated the Heath government, so why not Thatcher too? As they saw it, this was probably their last chance to call a halt to a long series of pit closures and save whole communities which faced ruin if their local pit closed. There was an excellent response from the miners, apart from in Nottinghamshire and Derbyshire, where they were at least risk. In Mrs Thatcher's view, however, the miners were fighting parliamentary democracy and trying to bring down the government. She regarded them as 'the enemy within' as opposed to 'the enemy without' – the Argentinian aggressors: there could be no compromise.

The strike dragged on for a year (March 1984–March 1985), but it was soon clear that Scargill had miscalculated badly – the government, anticipating a strike, had made sure that large coal stocks had been built up, plenty of cheap imports were available, and demand was decreasing as summer approached. The new regulations made it more difficult for pickets to stop the movement of coal, and Scargill had made the fatal mistake of failing to hold a national ballot on whether to strike in the first place. The fact that the miners themselves were divided further weakened their stand.

There were some ugly scenes between police and strikers; and miners and their families suffered great hardship, but the government refused to compromise, and the miners were gradually forced to return to work. The strike fizzled out, ending officially in March 1985, but it had been a bitter struggle and seemed to exacerbate the divisions in society. Seumas Milne has shown the lengths to which the government, MI5 and the police Special Branch were prepared to go in order to discredit Arthur Scargill and other miners' leaders in their campaign to destroy the power of the miners' union. This included phone-tapping, constant surveillance, false reports of corruption, use of *agents provocateurs* within the NUM itself, and the seizure of NUM funds. In the words of Seumas Milne, 'with the green light from Thatcher, MI5 ran amok through the mining areas of Britain. Its freedom of manoeuvre was vastly expanded during the strike'. The government's victory was probably Mrs Thatcher's revenge against the miners for bringing Heath's government down in 1974.

A second major dispute occurred in 1986, when Rupert Murdoch, owner of Times Newspapers, sacked 5,500 workers, members of the print union, following a strike. He transferred printing to a newly built and specially fortified plant at Wapping, where he successfully resisted union attempts to prevent new work practices being introduced. The unions had to accept defeat, after being heavily fined under the new legislation. By this time, the trade union movement had lost all heart for action, though in a final show of defiance, all thirty-seven surviving unions voted to continue their payments to the Labour Party.

(c) strict maintenance of law and order, and public security

The army and police were used several times to remove peace campaigners from Greenham Common and Molesworth RAF bases, protesting against American Cruise missiles being deployed there. The BBC was continually attacked for allegedly being biased against the government; the BBC offices in Glasgow were raided and films said to threaten Britain's security were seized (February 1987). Among them was a programme about Zircon, a new spy satellite for eavesdropping on the Russians.

(d) close control of government and local authority spending

Top-spending local authorities, many of them Labour controlled, had a maximum rate placed on them (rate-capping) to force them to economize (February 1986). The Greater London Council (GLC), also Labour-controlled, and the six other English Metropolitan County Councils were abolished, on the grounds that they were a costly and unnecessary layer of government. Norman Tebbit made no secret of the fact that the real reason for the abolition of the GLC was because it was 'Labour-dominated, high-spending and at odds with the government's view of the world'. The imposing County Hall building on the Thames Embankment was sold off and now houses, among other things, two hotels and an aquarium.

(e) the Anglo-Irish Agreement (November 1985)

This was a new attempt to secure peace and stability in Northern Ireland (see Section 32.1(i)).

(f) a tough stance against international terrorism

Britain broke off diplomatic relations with Libya after a policewoman was killed by shots fired from the Libyan People's Bureau in London (April 1984). In April 1986, Mrs Thatcher supported the USA's punitive action against Libya, allowing American F-111 bombers to fly from bases in Britain to take part in air strikes on Tripoli and Benghazi that killed over a hundred people. The USA claimed that they were aiming for 'terrorist-related targets', but the raids aroused worldwide condemnation for causing the deaths of so many innocent civilians. Britain also broke off relations with Syria (October 1986), whose government was allegedly involved in an attempt to blow up a jumbo jet at Heathrow Airport.

(g) the agreement with China (1984)

Britain promised to hand Hong Kong over to China in 1997, and in return the Chinese offered safeguards, including maintaining the existing economic and social structure for at least fifty years. The handover was in accordance with the 1842 Treaty of Nanking, by which Britain leased Hong Kong until 1997.

Meanwhile, the government came under increasing fire from its critics. Unemployment stubbornly refused to come down below 3 million and it seemed that Britain was rapidly becoming 'two nations'. The government's own statistics revealed (1987) that 94 per cent of job losses since the Conservatives took office were in the North, while the South was largely thriving and prosperous. Since 1979, there had been a 28 per cent reduction in manufacturing and construction jobs, which compared badly with an 8 per cent drop in Germany, a 2 per cent drop in the USA and a 5 per cent increase in Japan. Inner cities were neglected and the public services were run down, especially the Health Service, where in 1986–7 a chronic shortage of beds caused many people to be turned away from hospital, and lengthened waiting lists for operations. When challenged before the 1983 election, the government had assured the public that the Health Service was safe, but now there seemed a real danger of creating a two-tier Health Service: for those who could afford it, a private sector which was flourishing and efficient, for those who couldn't, a public sector which was short of cash, under-staffed and generally second-rate.

In addition, the government suffered a number of embarrassments and scandals. There was a public conflict between two Cabinet ministers (Michael Heseltine and Leon Brittan) over the future of the ailing Westland Helicopter Company, the only remaining British helicopter manufacturer. No help was forthcoming from the government, though it would surely have been in Britain's defence interests to own at least one plant that could produce military helicopters, which by the mid-1980s were an essential part of a nation's armoury. Brittan, a free-marketeer and definitely 'one of us', wanted the company to be taken over by the American firm of Sikorsky, but Heseltine, a strong supporter of the EU, wanted it to become part of a European consortium. As Andrew Marr explains:

> Michael Heseltine and his business allies thought this was vital to preserve jobs and the cutting-edge science base. The United States must not be able to dictate prices and terms to Europe. So this was about where Britain stood: first with the US, or first with the EU? It was a question which would grow steadily in importance through the eighties until, in the nineties, it tore the Conservative Party apart.

Mrs Thatcher and some of her greatest business supporters, including Rupert Murdoch, backed Brittan, and the Westland company went to the USA. But she handled the affair badly and it ended with both ministers resigning (January 1986). Early in 1987 there was a scandal on the Stock Exchange when it emerged that some directors of the Guinness Company had illegally bolstered the price of their own shares during their battle to take over the Distillers' Company.

A measure of the Conservatives unpopularity was the fact that they lost four by-elections (three to the Alliance and one to Labour) between June 1984 and May 1986. However, as another election approached, the Chancellor, Nigel Lawson, suddenly announced extra spending of £7.5 billion for 1987 on education, health and social services. This seemed to be a U-turn away from monetarism, though the government did not admit it. With the inflation rate well under control at only 3 per cent and the promise of good times ahead, the opinion polls showed a revival in the Conservatives' popularity.

(h) the election of June 1987

The Labour Party, under its new leader, Neil Kinnock, was more united and better disciplined than it had been for several years. They fought a lively and professional campaign, and on the eve of the election some observers were forecasting a close result – perhaps even a hung Parliament. However, in the event the Conservatives won a third successive victory. They took 380 seats against 229 for Labour and 22 for the Alliance, giving them an overall majority of 101. *Reasons for the Conservative success were*:

‣ The relatively prosperous South and Midlands were apparently well satisfied with Tory rule and were confident that the economic recovery would continue.
‣ Some historians believe that privatization and the increase in home ownership were an important ingredient in winning working-class support, since this was part of the move towards a 'property-owning democracy'. Above all, the sale of council houses may have been a vital factor. First introduced in 1980, the sales meant that, by the time of the election in 1987, over a million council houses had passed into private ownership. As Peter Clarke puts it: 'on

council estates, a freshly painted door and a copy of the *Sun* in the letter box were a signal of Thatcher's achievement at remaking the Conservative Party'.

- Labour's defence and economic policies continued to put people off.

It was clearly a remarkable achievement by Mrs Thatcher to lead her party to three successive election victories, and in January 1988 she broke Asquith's record as the longest-serving British Prime Minister in the twentieth century. There were two other striking points about the 1987 election: the Conservatives did badly in Scotland, winning only 10 out of the 72 seats, and further entrenching the North–South divide. Over the country as a whole, *almost three people in five voted against the Conservatives.* The Conservatives took 42.2 per cent of the votes, Labour 30.8 per cent and the Alliance 22.6 per cent. Under the existing electoral system, with Labour and Alliance candidates splitting the anti-Tory vote, it was difficult to see how the Conservatives could ever lose an election.

Important developments soon took place in the Liberal/SDP Alliance camp, however. Bitterly disappointed by their poor election performance, at least in terms of seats, the two parties began talks to try to bring about a merger. The negotiations went well, and in January 1988 the new party – at first calling itself the Social and Liberal Democrats, and later the Liberal Democrats: 'Lib Dems' – was born. After twelve gruelling years as Liberal leader, David Steel decided to stand down, and Paddy Ashdown was elected leader of the new party. It remained to be seen whether the Lib Dems would be able to make any real contribution towards ending the period of Tory domination.

35.4 triumph, decline and downfall, 1987–90

(a) the triumph of Thatcherism

After her success in the 1987 election it seemed that Mrs Thatcher could be Prime Minister for life if she wished. Though she was now 62, she told interviewers that she had no thoughts of retirement and was looking forward to a fourth election victory. For about a year after the election everything seemed to go well: the economy had moved into a boom period and unemployment was falling. After reaching a peak of 3.4 million in January 1986, it fell steadily to 1.6 million in June 1990. Economic growth averaged 3.7 per cent in the years 1984–8.

Mrs Thatcher was keen to show that her government was not losing its drive; Thatcherite changes came thick and fast, though again, they were all highly controversial.

- *Privatization continued*, with the government selling off its remaining holdings in BP and going on to sell off the electricity and water utilities. By 1992, only coal and the railways out of the main industries and utilities remained in state ownership.

- *The Education Reform Act (1988)* was designed to improve what the Conservatives saw as Britain's failing education system. They blamed this on poor-quality teacher training, informal teaching methods, insufficient attention to the 'three Rs', lack of testing and streaming, and a breakdown in discipline. The Act introduced a national curriculum which all pupils had to follow, and pupils were to be tested at the ages of 7, 11, 14 and 16. Parents were given the right to choose which school they wanted their children to go to in a particular area, and control of school budgets was taken out of the hands of local authorities and given to individual head teachers. If a majority of parents wished, a school could opt out of local authority control to become 'grant-maintained'; it would then be financed directly by the government, side-stepping the local authority, and would be run by its governors.

  Critics of the Act argued that most of these changes were unnecessary and poorly thought through; the main problem with education was that it was a two-tier system. The public schools and private schools, to which most of the wealthy sent their children, were well financed and had excellent facilities, whereas the state system was underfunded, and suffered from insufficient teachers, oversized classes, and in many cases inadequate facilities and crumbling buildings.

- *The government introduced market forces into the Health Service* to make it more efficient. For example, hospitals were encouraged to opt out of the system and handle their own finances. But this had unfortunate results, as some managers went to extreme lengths in the drive for greater efficiency, running hospitals as though they were businesses instead of services. While efficiency was a laudable aim, it could hardly be called efficient that hundreds of hospital wards were closed, that thousands of nurses left the profession because of low pay, and that hospital waiting lists were getting longer; in some areas, people were having to wait over two years for operations.

- *There were further reductions in income tax.* In his budget of March 1988, seen by many as the high point of Mrs Thatcher's third government, Nigel Lawson reduced the basic rate of income tax from 27 per cent to 25 per cent, and the top rate from 60 per cent to 40 per cent. Income tax reduction had been one of the Conservatives' election promises, and Lawson could claim at this point that all his goals had been achieved: inflation, interest rates and unemployment had all been brought down, while economic growth was increasing.

(b) the government begins to lose its way

Things began to go wrong soon after Lawson's budget, however.

1 The tax cuts caused a big increase in consumer demand; this in turn fuelled inflation, which rose from 4 per cent to over 10 per cent by September 1990. To try to counteract this, interest rates were raised, from 7.5 per cent at the

time of the budget to 15 per cent in October 1989, which was highly unpopular with mortgage holders.

2 A rift gradually opened up between Mrs Thatcher and Nigel Lawson over the question of Britain joining the Exchange Rate Mechanism (ERM) (see Section 33.4(c)). Lawson had wanted Britain to enter the ERM in 1985, when the economy was in good shape. His argument was that it would steady the pound by locking it into the other major European currencies, since this would bring a more stable exchange rate and keep inflation low; 1985–6 would have been a good time to join, when the economy was booming and the exchange rate reasonably low. But Mrs Thatcher was against the idea, fearing that it would lead to a loss of government control over its own economic policy. Lawson resigned in October 1989 after Mrs Thatcher refused to sack her economic adviser, Alan Walters, who disagreed with Lawson. Mrs Thatcher was eventually persuaded to join the ERM – by John Major – in October 1990. However, by that time the exchange rate was relatively high and the economy weaker than it had been in 1985–6; this meant that the pound was over-valued and was therefore more difficult to defend.

3 The introduction of the community charge (or poll tax, as it became known), first in Scotland (1989) and then in England and Wales (1990), was the government's biggest mistake. This was a new system of financing local government, which the Conservatives had promised to reform. The old payment of rates by household was abolished and replaced by a flat-rate charge to be paid by every adult, irrespective of the size of his or her house. It was an attempt to make every taxpayer pay an equal contribution to costs under high-spending Labour councils, rather than forcing wealthy property-owners to pay well over the average.

Mrs Thatcher and Nicholas Ridley, the minister handling the introduction of the poll tax, pressed on enthusiastically with the new scheme, which was described by Mrs Thatcher as the 'flagship' of her government, though Lawson and most of the Cabinet were against it: 'Every time I hear people squeal,' said Ridley, 'I am more than ever certain that we are right.' But it didn't seem fair that 'the rich man in his castle' should pay the same as an ordinary worker living in a small terraced house. The new tax caused uproar: there were protest demonstrations and riots, and a concerted campaign to persuade people not to pay. In Liverpool in 1990, 51 per cent of adults evaded payment, and the tax became more and more difficult to collect. The government's standing in the opinion polls plummeted, and in a by-election in October 1990 the Conservatives lost the safe seat of Eastbourne to the Liberal Democrats.

(c) the downfall of Mrs Thatcher

Although things were clearly not going well for the government, Mrs Thatcher's downfall still came as a surprise to most people. The crisis began when Sir Geoffrey Howe unexpectedly resigned from the Cabinet, and on 13 November 1990 delivered a devastating speech in the Commons, criticizing Mrs Thatcher's attitude towards Europe. By 27 November, she had resigned and her successor had been chosen. Yet as Conservative leader she had won three consecutive elections with large majorities, and had never lost an election. *Why did the Conservative Party drop Mrs Thatcher?*

‣ Dissatisfaction with Mrs Thatcher's style of government had been increasing for some time in the Cabinet. Full Cabinet discussion of policies became increasingly rare, and decisions were taken by Mrs Thatcher after consultation with small groups of Cabinet members or with her personal advisers. This was one of the reasons given by Heseltine for his resignation in January 1986: 'The prime minister's methods,' he said, 'are not a proper way to carry on government and ultimately not an approach for which I can share responsibility.' An important issue, such as membership of the ERM, was never discussed in full Cabinet. Thatcher's style became increasingly dictatorial and she took to undermining ministers who criticized or displeased her by allowing press leaks from No. 10 Downing Street. She developed an irritating habit of referring to herself in the royal plural; on one famous occasion she told a group of TV reporters outside No. 10: 'We have become a grandmother.'

‣ She gradually lost touch with her original power base in the parliamentary party. This was made worse by the retirement, after the 1987 election, of William Whitelaw, an expert parliamentarian on whom she relied heavily for advice. Although he was never a Thatcherite, Whitelaw remained loyal to his leader, and according to Nicholas Ridley, 'was possessed of almost supernatural political antennae and knew when to warn Mrs Thatcher that a situation had reached breaking point.' The departure of Norman Tebbit and Lord Young, two reliable Thatcherites, left her increasingly dependent on Lawson and Howe, who, as time went on, became more impatient with her methods. Her loss of touch was never illustrated better than in her refusal to abandon her 'flagship', the poll tax.

‣ By the autumn of 1990 it was clear that Thatcherite policies had not delivered an 'economic miracle', and were seen to be a failure on all fronts (see Section 35.5).

‣ Disagreements over the government's policy towards Europe became more serious. Mrs Thatcher had never been enthusiastic about Britain's membership of the EEC, and was convinced that the sovereignty of the British government was being threatened. Her attitude to Europe had been aggressive right from the beginning. She was alarmed at the moves towards further political and economic union, especially in July 1988, when Jacques Delors, a French socialist who was President of the European Commission, made a speech in which he said that in six years there would be 'an embryo European government.' Within ten years '80 per cent of the laws affecting the economy and social policy would be passed at a European and not a national level'. Mrs Thatcher declared that Delors had 'gone over the top', and many Conservative MPs agreed with her. However, there were many pro-European Conservatives who, together with the Foreign Office, felt that Britain should play a positive role in Europe instead of the negative approach adopted by Mrs Thatcher.

The following September she responded with a speech in Bruges (Belgium) in which she attacked the whole idea of further European unity and control from Brussels: 'We have not successfully rolled back the frontiers of the state in Britain,' she said, 'only to see them reimposed at a European level.' According to Hugo Young, Mrs Thatcher's biographer, this speech 'was viewed with amazement across Europe, dismay in the Foreign Office and with especial weary horror by the Foreign Secretary, Sir Geoffrey Howe'.

However, it was not long before Howe and Lawson seemed to make some progress: they had been wanting to take Britain into the ERM, but Mrs Thatcher would not hear of it. At a summit meeting in Madrid (June 1989), they pressured her, by threatening to resign, into accepting in principle the idea of joining the ERM and a common monetary policy, when the conditions were right. Mrs Thatcher was furious at having been outmanoeuvred, and in July she sacked Howe as Foreign Secretary and replaced him with John Major. Howe became Leader of the House of Commons and Deputy Prime Minister, but he was angry at the way he had been treated. Clearly, the three senior figures in the government were on bad terms, and it was not long before Lawson resigned after further disagreement over the ERM (October 1989). At a summit meeting in Rome in October 1990, Mrs Thatcher condemned the idea of European economic and monetary union, even though at Madrid she had committed her government to it. This upset the pro-European Tories, especially when she began the usual leaks and rumours to discredit Howe, in preparation for removing him from the Cabinet.

Sir Geoffrey pre-empted these sordid goings-on by getting his resignation in first and making his sensational Commons speech. Dennis Healey once remarked that having an argument with Sir Geoffrey, a mild-mannered and quietly spoken man, was like being savaged by a dead sheep. But this speech must rank as one of the most devastating ever delivered in the House of Commons; in reality it was a signal to the party that he thought it was time for Mrs Thatcher to go.

⟩ Michael Heseltine, who had waited in the wings for a moment like this since his resignation in 1986, now challenged Mrs Thatcher for the leadership of the Conservative Party. While Mrs Thatcher won by 204 votes to 152, she was three short of the number needed to avoid a second ballot, and there were 16 abstentions. Roughly 40 per cent of Conservative MPs were not prepared to support Mrs Thatcher. In fact, even in her heyday, there was never a majority of Conservative MPs who could be described as Thatcherites. As Martin

Pugh puts it: 'This feeling spread rapidly once the Prime Minister had failed to win on the first ballot.'

Most of her Cabinet colleagues felt the same, and advised her to step down. She was clearly now seen as an electoral liability; and she therefore decided not to go forward into the second ballot. John Major and Douglas Hurd now came into the contest; in a determined effort to prevent Heseltine, who had dared to challenge her, from becoming leader, Mrs Thatcher let it be known that she supported Major. The ballot was won by John Major, who immediately became Prime Minister as well as party leader. Major had 185 votes to Heseltine's 131 and Hurd's 56.

35.5 assessment of Mrs Thatcher's governments

(a) Mrs Thatcher's achievements

There can be no doubt that it was a brilliant personal achievement by Margaret Thatcher to win three successive elections and spend eleven and a half consecutive years as Prime Minister. Only Lord Liverpool (1812–27) had spent a longer continuous period in office. She was a figure of international standing, highly respected in the USA, where she formed an excellent working relationship with her monetarist soulmate, President Reagan; in Russia, where she got on well with Mr Gorbachev; and, more grudgingly, in Europe too. *What did her policies achieve?*

Years after her retirement, when she was asked what she had changed in politics, Mrs Thatcher replied, 'Everything.' Andrew Roberts believes that she was not being egotistical, she was merely being historically accurate. He argues that between them, Thatcher and Reagan made the 1980s 'one of the most innovative and exciting decades in the history of the Free World since 1900.' True, the Left dismissed the 1980s as a time of arrogant materialism and self-indulgence, but in fact the financial excesses were

> merely the froth and spume on top of the great waves of wealth creation that were unleashed by Ronald Reagan and Margaret Thatcher during that astonishing decade. The sense of well-being that those two statesmen engendered in consumers, through cutting taxes and expressing confidence in the future, unlocked a virtuous economic circle which in turn led to further tax cuts … This in turn unlocked the energy, innovation and enterprise of the British people, just exactly as the same phenomenon was being seen in the USA.

During Mrs Thatcher's first few years in power, the 'enterprise culture' showed many successes, with a record number of small businesses being set up. Many firms, which had slimmed down during the first burst of monetarism, became extremely efficient and increased their productivity and competitiveness, so that they could rival the best in Europe. In fact, during the 1980s, productivity (the amount produced per worker) grew by over 4 per cent a year. Income tax was reduced steadily over the eleven years, and living standards improved for most people.

The most striking change in direction, which was maintained right through the Thatcher years, was privatization. The curbing of trade union powers was an important and necessary step, and resulted in fewer strikes than at any time since the 1930s. Another notable feature was the sale of council houses, which brought house ownership in Britain up from 44 per cent to about 66 per cent of the population, the highest in Western Europe. One of Mrs Thatcher's greatest achievements was to renegotiate Britain's contribution to the EEC budget (see Section 33.4(e)), and Britain became more fully integrated in Europe in spite of Eurosceptic doubts. Her policy towards Russia was a success: she formed a good relationship with Gorbachev on his first visit to Britain (December 1984): 'I like Mr Gorbachev', she told TV viewers; 'we can do business together'. During her later visit to Russia (March 1987) they had long talks, and she could claim that she had helped to pave the way for the end of the Cold War. Right at the beginning of her period in power, Mrs Thatcher presided over the granting of independence to Zimbabwe, thereby solving a long-running problem.

Thatcherism also had an effect on the Labour Party: by moving the Conservative Party firmly to the right, Mrs Thatcher forced Labour, under Neil Kinnock, John Smith and Tony Blair, to adapt to changing circumstances, modernize its image and drop most of its socialist ideals, such as nationalization and the restoration of full trade union powers. Thus Mrs Thatcher could claim, with some justification, to have set a new political agenda, changed the course of British politics and played a vital role in the disappearance of socialism from Britain.

(b) Thatcherite policy failures

On the other hand, some of Thatcher's aims had clearly not been achieved. Monetarism was quietly abandoned as unworkable and inflation had not been controlled – when she left office it had risen again to 10.6 per cent, higher than when she came to power. Pressure of public opinion prevented her from dismantling the National Health Service or from interfering too much with free education and other social services. In fact, spending in all these areas increased between 1979 and 1990, much of the extra cash being spent on unemployment benefit. In spite of her reservations about Europe, Britain had been drawn more deeply into the EEC, even joining the ERM in 1990. Nor had Mrs Thatcher 'rolled back' the state; central government ended up with more power while local government was humiliated and the universities were subjected to financial and ideological constraints from No. 10.

Mrs Thatcher's policies had some unfortunate effects:

- During the first bout of monetarism (1980–1) Britain lost between 20 per cent and 25 per cent of her manufacturing industry – sometimes referred to as a 'de-industrialization' process. Sometimes entire communities were devastated by unemployment when a vital factory closed; for example, the massive steelworks at Corby in Northamptonshire and the Consett steelworks in County Durham. There was a recovery during the years 1984–8, but this soon deteriorated into another recession, as the 'economic miracle' failed to materialize. The government, now bereft of ideas, fell back on raising interest rates, but this made the situation worse. Investment fell, borrowing was too expensive, and about 29,000 businesses went bankrupt in 1990 alone. Recent statistics show that between 1979 and 1991, the average annual rate of economic growth was only 1.75 per cent, below that of most other developed nations. This was worse than the 2.4 per cent average for the previous ten years, which had been considered poor and which the Conservatives had vowed to improve on. According to Martin Pugh, who takes a bleak view of the situation, by 1982, Britain

> had ceased to produce a wide range of sophisticated items of the sort that had once been the basis of her wealth: typewriters, computers, washing machines, television sets, sewing machines and motor cycles. Her companies had been driven out of motor cars and shipbuilding except for small remnants; and aerospace, railways and coal were fast going the same way. Also lost was the vast range of different skills associated with these industries. Whereas in the late 1950s 8 million people had worked in British manufacturing industry, by 1991 fewer than 5 million still did so.

Not surprisingly, Britain's share of total world trade continued to decline (see Table 35.1) while Japan's increased.
- The loss of so much of Britain's manufacturing industries meant that more goods had to be imported. This led to a balance of payments deficit of £13.6 billion in 1989, which rose to £16 billion by 1990. There was not enough investment in industry, so that, in the early 1990s, British capital stock – machinery, buildings and techniques – was older and smaller than that of many of its main competitors. Faced with competition from cheap imports, many British manufacturers of goods such as textiles, shoes, and consumer

table **35.1 percentage shares of world trade in manufactures, 1950–90**

	France	W. Germany	UK	Japan	USA
1950	9.9	7.3	25.5	3.4	27.3
1958	8.6	18.5	18.1	6.0	23.3
1970	8.7	19.8	10.8	11.7	18.5
1979	10.8	20.7	9.8	13.6	15.9
1989	9.0	20.4	8.2	17.6	15.8

Source: D. Childs, *Britain Since 1939: Progress and Decline* (Macmillan, 1995), p. 253.

electronics either stopped producing or set up factories in Asia, where labour was cheaper. Total output in Britain declined in 1991 and 1992.

- Unemployment had fallen from a peak of 3.4 million in 1986 to 1.6 million in June 1990; but the recession sent it up again to almost 2 million when Mrs Thatcher resigned, and it continued to rise, reaching 2.6 million by the end of 1991. However, the real unemployment figure was much higher than that, because the government's methods of counting always underestimated numbers out of work. In addition, about half a million people had been placed on official training schemes, which kept them off the official registers. The real total of unemployed at the end of 1992 was at least 3.5 million. Payment of unemployment benefit and social security was a constant drain on the budget; and so many households on low incomes meant a massive loss of purchasing power, which did nothing to help the economy recover.

- The gap between rich and poor widened. Successive income tax reductions, particularly in 1988, benefited the rich more than the poor: over the eleven and a half years of Mrs Thatcher's governments, the richest 20 per cent gained by almost a third of their income, whereas the poorest 20 per cent gained only around 1 per cent. Higher direct taxes such as VAT meant that people on low incomes had to pay the same VAT increases as those on the highest incomes; for example, on commodities such as petrol, and they were therefore relatively worse off. Although the wages of most people who were in work rose, the salaries of top people rose by much more than those of unskilled workers. By 1993, the gap between the highest and lowest wages was the widest since records began. According to the Rowntree Trust, between 1979 and 1991, the incomes of the top 10 per cent rose by more than 50 per cent, while the real incomes of the bottom sixth actually fell. Another distressing development was the deliberate casualization of the workforce: in order to maximize profits and dividends paid to shareholders, managers began to employ a higher proportion of part-time workers, who could be paid at lower rates and could be hired and fired at short notice whenever necessary. At the same time, tighter regulations made it more difficult for young people to access social security benefits, and it was no surprise when beggars began to appear on the streets again. With unemployment running permanently at around 3 million, it seemed that Thatcherite policies had created, or at least had failed to prevent, the emergence of a permanent 'underclass' for whom there was no longer any role in society. And as unemployment and poverty increased, so did the crime rate.

- Thatcherite financial policies led to freedom from regulation for the City of London and the banking system. This too had unfortunate side-effects. Many foreign banks seized the opportunity to set up in London, so that by 1991 around half the banking houses in London were foreign-owned. According to economic journalist Will Hutton, writing in 1995, in *The State We're In* (Vintage, 1996), 'the City of London has become a byword for speculation, inefficiency and cheating. Given the power to regulate their own affairs, City financial markets and institutions have conspicuously failed to meet any reasonable standard of honest dealing with the public or their own kind. There was the Guinness case, referred to earlier, and this was quickly followed by many examples of 'sleaze' and fraudulent dealings. It became commonplace for insiders with privileged information to manipulate share prices on the Stock Exchange for personal profit. Fraud and theft led to the collapse of the Barlow Clowes financial empire. In 1991, the Bank of Credit and Commerce International (BCCI) was forced to close after fraud on a huge scale was revealed; an enquiry blamed the Bank of England for not acting early enough to prevent the collapse. In the two and a half years after 1990, no fewer than 100,000 jobs were lost in the City, and it seemed likely that the Frankfurt money market might soon become more important than London. David Kynaston, in his generally sympathetic history of the City, published in 2001, describes the 1980s as 'febrile, driven by greed, pushing back the boundaries of acceptable behaviour'. Andrew Marr writes about 'the crude and swaggering "loadsamoney" years ... and the culture of excess and conspicuous display that would percolate from the City, through London, then the Home Counties, then much of southern England'. John Campbell, a recent biographer of Mrs Thatcher, points out an odd paradox of Thatcherism: it was that 'Mrs Thatcher presided over and celebrated a culture of materialism ... fundamentally at odds with her own values which were essentially conservative, old-fashioned and puritanical'.

Another failure of the City was that it tended to reward companies which concentrated on 'short-termism', including, among other practices, paying high dividends to shareholders and taking over other companies rather than spending sufficient cash on research and development (R&D). On the other hand, companies that *did* invest more of their profits in R&D were undervalued on the stock market. Shareholders were doing well, but enterprise and expansion were being discouraged, since investment was much lower than it should have been. Will Hutton provides some revealing statistics: in 1994, only thirteen British companies, four of them drug companies, appeared among the world's top 200 spenders on R&D. In British industry during the 1980s, investment rose by only 2 per cent per annum, and profits by 6 per cent per annum, while dividends jumped by 12 per cent per annum. The world's top 200 companies spent three times more on R&D than on dividends; however, in Britain, even the top research companies spent only two-thirds of the amount they paid out in dividends.

A further unhealthy trend was that the country came to rely on foreign investment to develop new industries and training. By 1995 no less than 25 per cent of British manufacturing capacity was owned by foreigners, who employed 16 per cent of all British workers. It seemed strange that a government so touchy about losing *political* control to foreigners in the European

Community should show so little concern that the country was fast losing *economic* control of its own vital industrial base.

▸ It is also possible to criticize Mrs Thatcher's foreign policies. While the public at home approved of her robust approach to the European leaders, it brought Britain's relationship with the EU to an all-time low, particularly with Germany. She refused to reduce the number of British troops stationed on the Rhine, though that would have brought a much-needed reduction in defence spending. And then in 1990 she opposed, or at least tried to delay, the reunification of Germany. Nor did Britain's European neighbours trust Mrs Thatcher's close relationship with the USA. Indeed, this reliance on the USA brought its own problems: the American attitude towards Britain was one of condescension; they had no hesitation in ignoring Britain's interests whenever it suited them. For example, in October 1983, President Reagan ordered the invasion of the Caribbean island of Grenada; the island's government, alleged by the Americans to be pro-communist, was thrown out and replaced by one approved by Washington. Reagan ignored the fact that Grenada was a member of the Commonwealth; he did not even consult Britain and did not inform them about the invasion beforehand. Yet he took for granted that the USA could use British bases to initiate the bombing of Libya in 1986, a policy that was unpopular in Britain. It led to an increase in terrorism in Britain and ultimately to the exploding of an airliner over Lockerbie in 1988. However, John Campbell argues that at least Mrs Thatcher's government was not as subservient to the USA as were Tony Blair's governments.

(c) was there a Thatcherite revolution?

No doubt the debate will go on for a long time yet about whether Margaret Thatcher really did, as she claimed, change everything. Many observers believe that her governments did not make *that* much difference. They point out that:

▸ many of the elements in her economic policies, such as attempting to limit inflation, controlling the money supply and cutting government spending, had all been introduced by the previous Labour government between 1976 and 1979;
▸ when monetarism failed to reduce the budget deficit and bring down inflation, it was quietly abandoned. It was only then that privatization – the policy Mrs Thatcher is perhaps best remembered for – became a vital policy because the government needed to find a new source of income to make up for continuing tax cuts; and
▸ the British economy during the 1980s did not perform much better than in the 1960s. Even the reduction in inflation was part of a global movement caused partly by the dramatic fall in oil prices – it would have happened without Thatcherism.

However, George L. Bernstein believes that these arguments miss the point: 'The reality of what happened was much less important than people's perceptions of what happened.' He argues that the vital change brought about by Thatcherism was that it gave people new hope: 'There was a mood of hopelessness at the end of the 1970s. Thatcher set out to reverse that mood, and she succeeded – by generating energy and new ideas ... She gets the credit, and rightly so, for this psychological change would not have occurred without her, and the psychological change was centrally important.' There was more interest in business and making money, and more attention to service and accommodating the customer.

Of course, there were other positive and lasting changes too – the reduction of the almost out of control power of the trade unions; the growth of a property-owning society; the improved efficiency of the surviving British industries; the relocation of economic activity away from manufacturing industry and into the service industries; and the de-regulation of the City. Critics claim that the latter change created a materialistic society, obsessed with quick profit and instant gratification, which is still with us today.

Arguably one of the most dramatic changes in British politics was the Labour party's move from the left into the centre. Some historians believe that Mrs Thatcher intended to destroy the Labour party as a party of socialism. Ross McKibbin claims that:

> her fundamental aim was to destroy the Labour party and 'Socialism', not to transform the British economy. Socialism was to be destroyed by a major restructuring of the electorate: in effect, the destruction of the old industrial working class. Its destruction was not at first consciously willed. The disappearance of much of British industry in the early 1980s was not intended, but it was an acceptable result of her policies of deflation and deregulation; and was then turned to advantage.

Her intention was, by encouraging home ownership and 'popular capitalism', to make people think of themselves as middle class, rather than working class, and so vote Conservative. It was this dwindling of the working class, traditionally thought of as Labour supporters, which forced the Labour party to abandon its socialist principles and move into the centre ground, in order to remain electable. In this sense, Mrs Thatcher was completely successful. Unfortunately, her theory ignored the fact that there was a large slice of the working class that had always voted Conservative, and this too was diminished by the government's policies. This aspect of the Thatcherite revolution therefore was to work to the benefit of the Labour party for at least the next ten years. Clearly, therefore, the changes of the 1980s did amount to a sort of revolution, not perhaps the one that Mrs Thatcher herself had anticipated, and certainly not a wholly positive one, but a revolution nevertheless.

35.6 John Major's governments, 1990–7

(a) Major's first term

John Major was virtually unknown to the wider public until he was unexpectedly made Foreign Secretary in 1989, and soon afterwards replacing Nigel Lawson as Chancellor. He was chosen as leader because he had received Mrs Thatcher's blessing; she thought he was 'one of us' – the best man to carry on her policies. He had the added attraction of being one of the 'new generation' of Tories – he had never been to university and had even been on the dole for a time before finding a job in a bank. He gave the impression of being a genuinely likeable man who understood the needs of ordinary people. His task now, as John Charmley puts it, 'was to move the Thatcherite agenda on to the next phase and to unite the Party in order to retain power'. According to Simon Jenkins, 'Major sought to prolong the successes of Thatcherism without the embarrassment of Thatcher herself.' He was prepared to carry privatization even further than Mrs Thatcher had done – the railways and the coal industry were next on the list (Mrs Thatcher had always regarded these as out of bounds); Major also introduced the National Lottery, much to Mrs Thatcher's disgust.

In the Gulf War (1990–1) he soon found himself carrying out a policy initiated by Mrs Thatcher. When Saddam Hussein, the ruler of Iraq, sent his forces into the neighbouring state of Kuwait (August 1990), President George H. W. Bush of the USA took the lead in pressing for action to remove the Iraqis; Saddam was ordered to withdraw his troops by 15 January 1991. Mrs Thatcher, who happened to be in the USA with Bush when the news of the invasion was announced, fully supported Bush's stand: Saddam controlled too much of the oil which the industrial West needed for him to be allowed to keep Kuwait. 'Remember, George, this is no time to go wobbly George', she told the President. By the time the 15 January deadline passed, Major was Prime Minister, and he went ahead with Britain's contribution – sending some 45,000 British military personnel to join operation *Desert Storm*, which soon chased Saddam's troops out of Kuwait.

However, Major soon showed that he had no intention of simply continuing Thatcherite policies. In the run-up to the next election (April 1992) he took a number of actions that disappointed the right wing of the party:

- he announced that he wanted a classless society;
- appointed Chris Patten, who was on the left of the party, as Party Chairman;
- dropped the disastrous poll tax and replaced it with a new council tax based on property values;
- made it clear that he believed more money would have to be spent on health and education; and

- signed *the Maastricht Treaty (December 1991)*, which committed Britain to greater integration in Europe (see Section 33.4(h)). Major negotiated a special agreement which allowed Britain to opt out of the social chapter and some aspects of the common economic policy. This was seen in many circles as a considerable achievement by the Prime Minister; however, it was not enough for the Thatcherites, who felt that he was too pro-Europe. They demanded a referendum on whether Britain should accept the treaty, but the Prime Minister refused. This disagreement over Europe was to split the Conservatives right through Major's period in office, and was to play an important part in the massive Conservative defeat in 1997.

The government faced other problems too: the economic depression grew worse, and in 1991 alone, 48,000 businesses became bankrupt. Unemployment continued to rise, and there were record numbers of house repossessions as people fell behind with their mortgage repayments.

(b) the election of April 1992

With the country in the middle of a depression, the opinion polls predicted a Labour victory, albeit a narrow one. The Labour Party had been revitalized under the leadership of Neil Kinnock: he had got rid of the militant extremists, or 'loony left' as the Conservatives called them, played down the socialist element in the manifesto, and united the party. At a big election rally in Sheffield a few days before voting, he was introduced as 'the next Prime Minister'; the evening ended in a mood of triumphal celebration, as if the election had already been won. However, against all expectations, it was the Conservatives who won a narrow victory; the figures were: Conservatives 336, Labour 271, Liberal Democrats 20, and various others 24, giving an overall Conservative majority of 21.

Reasons for John Major's victory:

- Major was a popular leader who came over as honest, caring and reliable – a sort of Stanley Baldwin figure. Despite the country suffering a severe recession, voters seemed to blame Mrs Thatcher for that, and were prepared to give the new Prime Minister a chance to prove himself. The victory was seen as a genuine personal success for Mr Major.
- Labour had not quite succeeded in throwing off its old image as a party of high spending and high taxation. John Smith, the Shadow Chancellor, had been honest enough to admit that taxes would have to go up to enable more to be spent on health, education and social services.
- Some statistics suggest that as many as one million voters, who would most probably have voted Labour or Liberal Democrat (if they had voted at all), were not registered on the electoral roll because of their refusal to pay the poll tax.
- Seven out of the eleven main daily newspapers, which accounted for two-thirds of all sales, supported the Conservatives and ran campaigns to ridicule

and discredit Neil Kinnock. His over-excited behaviour at the Sheffield rally was thought by some observers to have turned 'middle England' against Labour.

(c) a catalogue of disasters

Mr Major had very little time to enjoy his victory before things began to go wrong, however. It soon became clear that a majority of the new Conservative MPs were supporters of Thatcherite ideas; this increasingly hampered Mr Major, who was quietly trying to move the party away from Thatcherism. But the party in Parliament was probably now more Thatcherite than when Mrs Thatcher herself had been Prime Minister.

The main problems were:

1 *The recession continued,* thousands more jobs were lost and unemployment rose. The housing market remained depressed, and many house buyers found that their homes were worth less than the amount they had borrowed to buy them (this was known as 'negative equity'). The Chancellor, Norman Lamont, talked about 'the green shoots of recovery', but these were difficult to detect. In 1993, Britain's economy compared badly with those of other leading EU states: in the league table of GDP, Britain came eighth out of twelve and performed below the average (see Table 35.2).

2 *Britain was forced to take sterling out of the ERM (September 1992).* During the election campaign, Major had emphasized that Britain's membership of the ERM was his central strategy for defeating inflation and making Britain fully competitive. But it now emerged that when (as Chancellor of the Exchequer) he had taken Britain into the ERM (October 1990), the pound had been over-valued (at 2.95 German Marks). Unfortunately, because of the weak economy, the pound lost value within the ERM, and it became increasingly difficult to

table **35.2 average gross domestic product (GDP) per head, European Union states, according to purchasing power, 1993 (Average = 100)**

Greece	48
Portugal	58
Rep. Ireland	72
Spain	77
Britain	96
EU average	**100**
Germany	102
Netherlands	103
Italy	104
Belgium	106
Denmark	108
France	112
Luxembourg	130

Source: D. Childs, *Britain Since 1939: Progress and Decline* (Macmillan, 1995), p. 267.

maintain the exchange rate. The government tried to defend the pound by raising interest rates, but by September 1992 dealers were selling the currency so fast that the value continued to fall. Norman Lamont put interest rates up briefly to 15 per cent and spent £60 billion in an attempt to save the pound, but all his attempts failed: on 'Black Wednesday' (23 September 1992), sterling had to be withdrawn from the ERM and allowed to find its own level. In practice, this meant that the pound had been devalued by about 15 per cent.

This was a devastating blow for the government. Its main economic strategy had failed and the economic competence of Major and his Chancellor was now open to serious doubts. Ironically, the weaker pound made British goods cheaper abroad and exports gradually increased; but this was no thanks to the government.

3 *There was uproar when the government announced in October 1992 that in preparation for the privatization of coal, thirty-one of the remaining fifty operating pits were to be closed, throwing about 30,000 miners out of work.* This was in spite of the fact that the coal industry had become much more efficient since the miners' strike. Public opinion, on the whole, supported the miners and wanted the pits to remain open. Critics of government policy pointed out that it would be ludicrous if the country found itself at some later date having to import expensive foreign coal when it could have continued to produce British coal at lower prices. There was also the argument that all the energy industries (electricity, gas, coal, oil and nuclear power) ought to be under state control, otherwise it would be virtually impossible to have a carefully thought out, long-term, co-ordinated energy policy. Michael Heseltine, the minister responsible, agreed to reconsider the plan; but while it was postponed for a time, by June 1993 all the pits had been closed and the number of miners in the country had roughly been halved. The government had apparently committed itself to buying gas and nuclear power, though the latter was uneconomic and was having to be subsidized by the government. This was certainly not Thatcherite economics.

4 *Another unpopular step was the extension of VAT to domestic fuel (May 1993).* So great was the outcry that Lamont was forced to resign and was replaced by Kenneth Clarke. The government was losing by-elections too, both to the Liberal Democrats and Labour, and eventually its majority was reduced to one.

5 *In an attempt to rally the party, Major launched a new campaign – 'back to basics',* which seemed to be an updated version of Mrs Thatcher's Victorian values: a return to a stricter morality and a strengthening of family life. This was introduced with the best of intentions, but the party soon let Mr Major down. Within a few months the campaign backfired when eight Conservative MPs had made the headlines, amid accusations of adultery or corruption. One area where 'back to basics' might have been effective was in

cleaning up and improving standards in television. However, the government's deregulation policies made this impossible. For example, BSkyB, the satellite TV company owned by Rupert Murdoch, was freed from the regulatory standards applying to terrestrial broadcasters, partly, according to some commentators, as a political favour to Murdoch.

6 *Meanwhile the dispute in the party over Europe rumbled on as a permanent theme;* the Eurosceptics made life difficult for Mr Major every time there was a Commons vote on anything to do with Europe. As the Conservative majority dwindled, the Prime Minister had to resort to threats of resignation, and later an agreement with the Ulster Unionist MPs, to make sure that legislation got through Parliament. On one occasion, he deprived a group of nine Eurosceptic MPs of the party whip, but took them back again later, even though their attitudes had not changed; this, of course, further undermined his authority.

When rumours of a challenge to his leadership began to circulate, Mr Major boldly seized the initiative by announcing that he was offering himself for re-election in the summer of 1995 instead of waiting until the autumn. He told his critics to 'put up or shut up'. The Welsh Secretary, John Redwood, a Thatcherite and Eurosceptic, resigned from government and challenged Mr Major. However, the election resulted in a comfortable victory for Major, with 218 votes (out of 329) against 89 for Redwood. Michael Heseltine, who had earlier suffered a heart attack, decided not to stand, and his supporters voted for Major. Heseltine was rewarded with the post of Deputy Prime Minister.

7 The situation in Ireland took a turn for the better in August 1994, when the IRA called a ceasefire (see Section 32.1(j)). But while the ceasefire lasted for eighteen months, very little progress was made in the peace process. The government was in a difficult situation: the slightest sign of any concessions to the nationalists infuriated the unionists, and with such a slender majority Mr Major could not afford to alienate the Ulster Unionist MPs. The IRA called off the ceasefire in February 1996.

8 *The government mishandled the crisis over the safety of British beef.* After outbreaks of a cattle disease known as bovine spongiform encephalitis (BSE) (commonly known as 'mad cow disease'), some scientists claimed that eating beef from diseased cattle caused Creutzfeldt–Jakob disease, a fatal disease in humans. Despite government scientists denying that there could be any connection, many people in Britain stopped eating beef. It emerged that BSE was caused by contaminated cattle food, which contained animal protein made from sheep that had been suffering from a disease called 'scrapie'. There was outrage in some quarters, where it was felt that making cattle eat animal protein was something akin to cannibalism. However, it seemed that this had been going on for some time without any ill-effects, until Mrs Thatcher's government relaxed controls, so that animal feed could be

processed at lower temperatures, which was cheaper. The lower temperatures failed to destroy the BSE organisms, hence more outbreaks of the disease.

The Major government, to its credit, banned the use of cattle feed containing animal protein, and introduced new hygiene regulations in abattoirs. Unfortunately, the government then made two mistakes: it failed to ensure that the new regulations were enforced rigorously enough – some farmers continued to use up stocks of contaminated feed, and many abattoirs ignored the new rules. Second, not wanting to antagonize farmers, the government failed to introduce a sufficiently rigorous policy of slaughtering diseased animals early enough. It should have been possible, with prompt action, to eliminate all diseased herds. The result was further outbreaks of BSE. There was great public concern also when more cases of Creutzfeldt–Jakob disease were reported in humans, and there were fears of an epidemic developing.

In the end, the government got the worst of both worlds. By 1996, there was worldwide concern about the safety of British beef and the EU banned further imports. The government was therefore forced to introduce a large-scale slaughtering policy. The whole thing was a tragedy for the farmers; by the time of the next general election (May 1997) the ban on British beef exports to Europe had still not been lifted.

As the 1997 election drew nearer, the situation in the country seemed to improve and Mr Major could point to some positive achievements. Britain began to move out of the recession at last; the economy began to grow again and became the healthiest in Europe (or so the government told the public). Unemployment was falling and inflation was low and well under control. 'Britain is booming! Don't Let Labour Spoil It' urged the election posters. Another achievement was the setting up of the National Lottery, an idea rejected by Mrs Thatcher. This raised a good deal of money for charity, sports, the arts and the national heritage, though Michael White (writing in the *Guardian,* 3 May 1997) called it 'an example of degenerate Majorite radicalism.' None of this was enough to restore the Conservatives' popularity, though, and the opinion polls consistently predicted a comfortable Labour victory.

(d) the Conservative defeat, 1 May 1997

Most people seemed to expect a Labour overall majority of 40 to 50 seats and were unprepared for the huge Labour landslide victory that gave them an overall majority of 179. Labour emerged with 418 seats, their highest-ever total, beating even their famous landslide victory of 1945 (393 seats). The Conservatives had 165 seats, their lowest total since 1906, when they were reduced to 157. The Liberal Democrats won 46 seats. Seven members of the Cabinet and many former ministers lost their seats. The Conservatives were left with no seats in Scotland and Wales, suggesting that the Scots and Welsh did not like the Conservatives' opposition to devolution; and they had very few seats in the large English cities. It was a devastating rejection of a particular brand of Conservatism that had moved too far to the right. At the age of 43, Tony Blair became the youngest Prime Minister since Lord Liverpool in 1812.

There were some other remarkable points about this election. More women MPs were elected than ever before; the number just about doubled to 119, of whom 109 were Labour. The voting system as usual played some strange tricks: the Liberal Democrats doubled their number of seats, although their share of the vote fell by 1 per cent, and while the Conservatives won 31 per cent of the votes, this only brought them 25 per cent of the total seats in the UK. The Conservatives polled more votes in Scotland than the Liberal Democrats, yet won no seats, whereas the Liberal Democrats won ten. The discrepancy was even more pronounced in Wales, where the Conservatives polled twice as many votes as Plaid Cymru, who won four seats, while the Conservatives gained nothing. In the past, the system had always benefited the Conservatives; in 1997, for the first time, in Scotland and Wales, the Conservatives had to cope with the problem that usually faced the Liberal Democrats – it is difficult for minority parties, whose support is widely spread out, to win seats under the first-past-the-post system. *Why did the Conservatives lose so heavily?*

▸ Some experts feel that the Conservatives had never recovered from 'Black Wednesday', when the pound was forced out of the ERM. A financial disaster of this magnitude, resulting in a 15 per cent devaluation of the pound, had never happened before under a Conservative government. Previous financial crises – 1931, 1949, 1967 and 1976 – had all occurred under Labour. The Conservatives' reputation for economic competence had gone, and they had not succeeded in regaining it.

▸ Although the government repeatedly said that Britain was booming, many voters were clearly not feeling the benefit of it. Exit polls suggested that there was a big swing to Labour in middle-class seats among people in junior managerial and clerical jobs – the sort of people who had suffered most from negative equity when the housing market collapsed. In an age of permanent casualization and down-sizing, more and more people felt insecure in their jobs – and this included people in the South and in the London area, which were now feeling the pinch as much as the Midlands and the North.

Critics of the government claimed that the sole reason the British economy seemed to be performing better than the European economies was because Britain had an unfair advantage: its refusal to accept the social contract of the Maastricht Treaty had left the country with one of the cheapest labour markets in the Community: British workers now had very little legal protection of any kind. There was no limit on working time, no minimum wage, and no legal right to representation in the workplace. This was a return to Victorian times with a vengeance: employers were now under no legal obligation to pay their workers fairly, or to treat them as anything other than disposable commodities. Unemployment benefit (now called 'job-seekers' allowance') was limited to six months, and it was more difficult to get sickness benefit.

- Many people felt that privatization had gone far enough. While the privatized industries that had to face real competition were now competitive and sure-footed in the global marketplace (after years of hardship and job losses, both before and after privatization), it is debatable whether privatization was necessary for this to happen. The privatized utilities (such as gas, electricity and water) attracted criticism because they exploited their monopoly positions in the UK market, and their directors awarded themselves huge salary increases and share options that made them millionaires several times over. However, their increases in profit were not achieved by any particular business skill or genuine entrepreneurship, but simply by cutting staff and raising prices. Yet the government, even with its tiny majority, still pushed ahead with plans for privatizing the railways and nuclear fuels. Rail privatization aroused criticism in the South and South East; again, there were immediate staff lay-offs, and these led to poor services and left commuters struggling.

- The split in the party over Europe lost the Conservatives support. In 1906, the party had been split over tariff reform, but the result was the same; a divided party never does well in general elections. The Eurosceptics claimed that they spoke for a majority of the country, but the voting showed no obvious swing to Eurosceptic candidates. The general feeling was more that Mr Major, struggling to find an acceptable middle course for Britain's membership of the European Union, had been let down by the Eurosceptics. Sir Ian Gilmour believes that Mrs Thatcher must take much of the blame for the continuing split. He points out that, almost as soon as she had been deprived of the leadership, 'she stirred up the party's right-wingers to be fierce Europhobes, and fight the Maastricht Treaty'. Much of the Tory press aided and abetted her, in particular *The Times* and the *Daily Telegraph.* In the words of Ian Gilmour, '*The Times*, owned by Rupert Murdoch, who was an Australian and is now an American, was always chiefly concerned with its proprietor's economic interests and opinions, and the *Telegraph*, owned then by Conrad Black, a Canadian by birth, reflected Black's far right American views. Both Murdoch and Black were and are extreme Europhobes'. Chris Patten goes further, claiming that Mrs Thatcher's consistent encouragement and backing of the Eurosceptics in fact destroyed the Conservative Party for over a decade.

- Sleaze was an important issue in the election and dominated the first two weeks of the campaign. Having been in power for so long, many Conservatives, though certainly not Mr Major himself, seemed to become careless, feeling that they could get away with all sorts of corrupt practices: asking questions in the Commons to further the interests of certain companies, and accepting cash from individuals to ask questions, were two of the activities now seen to be acceptable. Two of the most notorious cases were those of junior ministers, Tim Smith and Neil Hamilton, who were accused of accepting £2,000 each and other rewards from an Egyptian financier, Mohammed Al-Fayed, to ask questions in the House. They eventually resigned from the government, as did Jonathan Aitken, who was alleged to have breached the government's own embargo on arms exports to Iraq, in his capacity as a director of a defence contracting firm. Mr Major appointed the Nolan Committee to consider how to improve standards in public life. This suggested that MPs should disclose all payments received for consultancy work; however, most Conservatives rejected this and insisted that Parliament should be left to regulate itself. However, the voters did not like sleaze. Neil Hamilton, though protesting his innocence, lost his seat to an independent 'anti-sleaze' candidate, Martin Bell, a well-known BBC TV reporter, who turned Hamilton's 20,000 majority into an 11,000 majority for himself. Jonathan Aitken also lost his seat.

› The Labour Party had been transformed almost out of recognition since 1992. The process of reform had been started by Neil Kinnock, but he resigned after Labour's defeat in 1992, and was replaced as leader by John Smith, a Scottish barrister. In 1993, Smith manoeuvred the party conference into accepting reforms that would reduce direct trade union influence on party policy. When John Smith died suddenly in May 1994 he was replaced by Tony Blair, an Oxford-educated barrister. According to Professor Anthony King (writing in the *Daily Telegraph* on 3 May 1997), 'Mr Blair was the kind of leader for the 1990s that might have been produced by computer-aided design; young, classless, squeaky-clean, with no close connections to the unions. Mr Blair knew that radical change was needed if Labour was to become electable.'

And radical change was what Mr Blair provided: the famous Clause 4 of the 1918 party constitution, which committed Labour to nationalization, was dropped, and it was made clear that a Labour government would not repeal the Conservative trade union reforms. Mr Blair promised that there would be no big tax and spending increases – *New Labour was to be a party of social democracy, not socialism*. Another new departure was the way Mr Blair wooed business leaders, explaining his plans for a partnership between New Labour and business to take Britain into the twenty-first century. He even had a meeting with Rupert Murdoch, owner of *The Times*, *The Sunday Times*, the *Sun* and BSkyB. In the end, the *Sun* and the *Evening Standard* switched support from the Conservatives to Labour, while *The Times* told people to vote for Eurosceptics of whichever party.

› Finally, tactical voting probably made an important contribution to the sheer size of Labour's majority. Blair made this possible by making a deliberate effort to improve relations with the Liberal Democrats, promising a referendum on proportional representation. In return, Paddy Ashdown said he would support a Labour government. Given the amount of common ground between the two, this made it easy for voters of either party to vote for the other in marginal constituencies, rather than splitting the anti-Conservative vote evenly. Michael Portillo, the Defence Secretary, was defeated by his Labour challenger at Enfield–Southgate, where the Liberal Democrat vote fell by 4 per cent from 1992, just enough to unseat Mr Portillo.

The defeat of Mr Portillo was a particularly serious blow for the Conservatives, since he was widely viewed as the most likely successor to Mr Major, who announced his resignation as Conservative leader the day after the election. The party was left stunned, confused, demoralized and leaderless, and the immediate need was to find a leader who could unite the various factions. In June, after a lively campaign, the Conservative MPs elected William Hague as the new party leader. At 36, the youngest Tory leader since William Pitt in 1783, Mr Hague was on the right of the party. In the *Guardian* the following day (20 June 1997), Hugo Young wrote: 'Hague's election is the delayed revenge of the Thatcherites for what happened in 1990. The party is unequivocally back in their hands, led from the right, where the noisiest heart of modern Conservatism beats'.

Sources: The statistics in this chapter are taken from the following sources:

J. Charmley, *A History of Conservative Politics 1900–1996*, Macmillan, 1996, pp. 225–51.

D. Childs, *Britain Since 1939: Progress and Decline*, Macmillan, 1995, pp. 196–267.

W. Hutton, *The State We're In*, Vintage, 1996 edn, pp. 7–8, 172, 330.

M. Pugh, *State and Society: British Social and Political History 1870–1992*, Arnold, 1994, pp. 302–34.

QUESTIONS

1 How far did Mrs Thatcher's domestic policies succeed in her aim to 'change everything' between 1979 and 1990?

2 How successful were Mrs Thatcher's foreign and defence policies?

3 'Mrs Thatcher's victories in her social and economic policies were achieved at a terrible cost.' To what extent do you think this is a fair verdict?

4 Explain why John Major and the Conservatives won the general election of 1992 against most expectations, but lost the election of 1997 so disastrously.

A document question about Thatcherism and its legacy can be found on the accompanying website www.palgrave.com/masterseries/lowe1.

the Labour party in opposition and the Blair years, 1979–2007

After their defeat in the 1979 election, the Labour party went through a difficult period. James Callaghan, who had been on the right of the party, resigned the leadership in 1980. The party faced the dilemma of what to do next: should it move to the left and become more socialist, or was the answer to go in the opposite direction, with tough policies to curb the unions? *During the first few years in opposition the left wing was in the ascendant.* The manifesto for the 1983 election was the most radical ever produced by the Labour party and the result was disastrous: Labour won only 209 seats to the Conservatives' 397. Michael Foot, the veteran left-winger who had taken over from Callaghan, resigned and *Neil Kinnock was elected leader.*

Kinnock realized that the party needed modernizing; but progress was slow, and while he was able to make a start, it was not enough for Labour to win the next election, in 1987. They could muster only 229 seats against the Conservatives' 380. Over the next five years, Kinnock succeeded in shifting control of the party back to the centre and away from the local organizations, many of which had been taken over by far-left Trotskyite groups. Labour's standing in the opinion polls steadily improved, and as the 1992 election approached, all seemed set fair for a Labour victory. Against all predictions, it was the Conservatives under John Major who won; they took 336 seats, giving them a narrow overall majority of 21. Labour did much better than in 1987, but still only managed 271 seats. Bitterly disappointed, Kinnock resigned and John Smith, the shadow Chancellor, was chosen as leader. He continued the modernization process but died suddenly in 1994.

Gordon Brown and Tony Blair were the obvious candidates for the leadership, but a deal was reached between them in which Brown did not stand for election, so enabling Blair to win. Together with a small group of supporters *they took the reform process further than many of the traditional Labour supporters had expected.* In 1995, the notorious Clause 4 (about nationalization) was dropped from the party constitution. Now firmly in the centre ground, *'New Labour' won a landslide victory in the 1997 election* with a record total of 418 seats.

During the first Blair government (1997–2001) there were important achievements: the opening of the Scottish and Welsh assemblies; the first steps in the reform of the House of Lords; the 1998 Good Friday Agreement about Northern Ireland; the introduction of the minimum wage; and overseas successes in Sierra Leone and Kosovo. There were some disappointments, but overall the government had made a good beginning and won the 2001 election with their majority only slightly reduced.

Blair's second term in office (2001–5) was overshadowed by the 'war on terror' following the 9/11 al-Qaeda attacks on the USA. Blair decided that the UK should join the USA, first in driving the Taliban government out of Afghanistan, and then in overthrowing Saddam Hussein of Iraq, who were said to be harbouring and encouraging terrorists. Both regime changes had been achieved by May 2003, but unfortunately this did not bring an end to violence. Neither country had been pacified by 2007, when Blair resigned; the decision to join in the war in Iraq was seen by most observers to be Blair's most serious mistake, and probably the thing most people will remember about his governments.

Nevertheless, New Labour was still popular enough, and the Conservatives unattractive enough, *for Blair to win a third consecutive general election in 2005*, though with a much reduced majority. Soon after the election, in July 2005, London suffered terrorist attacks when suicide bombers killed fifty-two people on the London Underground and a bus; later, other plots were thwarted by the police and security services. On a happier note, people were now enjoying the benefits of the New Labour reforms: improvements in public services and increasing prosperity for the vast majority.

But there were problems too: the government had got itself a reputation for 'spin' and sleaze, and there were financial scandals. There were controversies about immigration, ID cards and dwindling pension funds. It also became clear that Blair had made a mistake by announcing (before the 2005 election) that he would not fight a fourth election. As his third term went on, speculation about when he would resign increased, the government's authority was weakened, and Gordon Brown became more and more impatient to take over as Prime Minister. Eventually, Blair was manoeuvred into resigning in June 2007 after serving ten consecutive years in Downing Street.

36.1 the emergence of the 'New Labour' project

(a) the attempt to move the party to the left

'New Labour' as it became known, developed only gradually, following the party's defeat in the 1979 election. Callaghan resigned as leader in 1980 and a bitter struggle began about how the party should set about making itself electable again. The far left wanted it to become a genuinely radical socialist party with a programme of total nationalization of British industry, abolition of incomes policies, withdrawal from the European Community, unilateral nuclear disarmament, the closure of all American bases in Britain, and the abolition of the House of Lords. The left had even gained a majority on the National Executive Committee (NEC) of the party. A Trotskyite group known as the Militant Tendency, impatient with the Callaghan government's semi-monetarist economic policies, had been quietly infiltrating the party and gaining control of many local organizations and trade union branches. They aimed to elect Tony Benn as the new leader in preference to Denis Healey, the favourite of the party's right wing. Healey was convinced that people simply would not vote for such a radical programme. It seemed unlikely that Benn, mistakenly seen by many on the right as a dangerous revolutionary, would be able to defeat the popular Healey. Michael Foot, a veteran socialist intellectual, was persuaded to stand instead. Foot, who was probably the only left-winger acceptable to the right, won narrowly. His election turned out to be an unsatisfactory and unhappy compromise.

Despite Foot being highly respected in the party, he was unable to prevent a disastrous split. At a special party conference in 1981, new rules were accepted for the election of party leader and deputy leader. This would now be done by an electoral college in which the trade unions had 40 per cent of the votes, constituency parties 30 per cent and MPs only 30 per cent. The new rules also applied to the reselection of sitting MPs; it was clear that the left-wing activists in the constituencies and the unions were poised to take control of the party. The right wing of the party was horrified by this prospect, and four of them – Roy Jenkins, Dr David Owen, Shirley Williams and William Rodgers – decided to leave Labour; in March 1981 they formed the new Social Democratic Party (SDP), and seventeen other Labour MPs joined during the year.

For a time, the left was in the ascendant and the 1983 election manifesto was the most left-wing in the party's history. Labour was reduced to 209 seats and only 27.6 per cent of the votes, against 397 seats for the Conservatives. Even Tony Benn lost his seat in Bristol. Labour's only consolation was that the SDP–Liberal Alliance failed to replace them as the main opposition party, winning only 23 seats, from 25.4 per cent of the votes. The striking point here was that the Alliance came so close to Labour's percentage of the votes, yet won only 23 seats compared with Labour's 209. Once again the third party fell victim to Britain's 'first past the post' electoral system (see Section 35.2(e) for more about this system).

(b) the right fights back

Michael Foot resigned soon after the disastrous defeat in 1983, and Neil Kinnock was elected leader. Despite being a left-winger, he was realistic enough to accept that Labour would never win an election with a programme like the

1983 'suicide note'; the party needed radical reform. Some of the more extreme items – re-nationalization, withdrawal from the EC, ending of council house sales and the guarantee of full employment – were all dropped. However, the local left-wing activists, who ran their own newspaper, *Militant*, and were especially strong in Liverpool, where they controlled the City Council, opposed these changes. The Liverpool council, under its leader Derek Hatton, had deliberately overspent on its budget to the point of near bankruptcy, and then, claiming that it could not pay any more wages, sent out redundancy notices to all 31,000 of its staff. This, they seemed to think, would cause utter chaos which, in some mysterious way, would bring down the Thatcher government and, they hoped, would develop into the long-awaited revolution. It was clear that they would have to be brought under control. At the Labour party conference a few days later (October 1986), Kinnock launched a campaign against the militants in a dramatic speech that proved to be a turning point in Labour history. Accusing them of making implausible promises, he went on:

> I'll tell you what happens with implausible promises – they don't win victories ... You start with far-fetched resolutions. They are then pickled into a rigid dogma, and you go through the years sticking to that, outdated, misplaced, irrelevant to the real needs, and you end in the grotesque chaos of a Labour council – a *Labour* council – hiring taxis to scuttle round a city handing out redundancy notices to its own workers.

The speech ended in uproar, with the hard-left booing and heckling while the majority stood and cheered. The result was to separate the moderate or 'soft' left from the hard-liners, and soon the leaders of the militants were expelled from the party. In the words of Martin Westlake, 'the growing challenge of Militant was repulsed ... the left was permanently weakened and Kinnock's authority enhanced ... No longer could he be dismissed as a political lightweight.' There was still some way to go, but Kinnock had begun to turn the party in a new direction, and the left had lost its majority on the NEC. It came too late to defeat Mrs Thatcher in her heyday at the 1987 election, but once that was out of the way, he could begin on a thorough modernization of the party.

(c) the Kinnock–Smith reforms

Over the next five years, Kinnock introduced a number of important changes designed to centralize control of party policy. There was a new Policy Review Group made up of members of the shadow Cabinet; the power to choose by-election candidates was taken away from the local parties and given to the NEC; elections for the NEC were to be conducted on the principle of one member, one vote (OMOV) instead of block votes. This was because individual members of the party were usually more moderate than the activists. There was to be a wider franchise for selecting and re-selecting of parliamentary candidates, so there would be less chance of hard-left candidates being chosen.

The Labour MPs and the shadow Cabinet were given more control over the NEC and the Party Conference. And finally, in preparation for the next election, a radical review of party policy was carried out and published under the title *Meet the Challenge, Make the Change* (1989). The more socialist policies – high income tax, wealth tax, unilateral nuclear disarmament, price and import controls – were dropped, and the Thatcherite free market theory was accepted. There was more emphasis on education, research and development, technology, and closer co-operation between government and industry. As the 1992 election approached, everything seemed to point towards a Labour victory, so it was a bitter disappointment for Kinnock when John Major and the Conservatives won with a 21-seat majority. Some commentators blamed Labour's shadow Chancellor, John Smith, for being honest enough to admit during the campaign that taxes would have to rise if more was to be spent on education, health and social services (see Section 35.6(b) for more about this election).

Kinnock resigned in despair and John Smith was elected leader. Smith was a Scottish lawyer and a formidable Commons debater who had been President of the Board of Trade in Callaghan's government. A moderate in Labour politics, he continued the reforms, extending the OMOV principle to party conferences, constituency parties and general policy-making, in spite of strong opposition from some left-wing unions. Labour's reviving popularity was reflected in the elections for the European Parliament, when they won 62 out of 84 seats while the Conservatives could muster only 18. Smith was beginning to look increasingly like the next Prime Minister when he unexpectedly died of a heart attack in May 1994, aged only 53.

(d) the 'New Labour' project takes shape

After Smith's premature death it was widely expected that the shadow Chancellor, Gordon Brown, would become the next leader. However, the other likely candidate, Tony Blair, the shadow Home Secretary, was a charismatic young barrister who gradually moved ahead of Brown in the opinion polls. The two eventually reached an agreement, taking into account the belief that the English public-school-educated lawyer was more likely to attract middle-class voters in South and Central England. Brown would support Blair for the leadership, while he himself was to continue as shadow Chancellor, where his greatest expertise lay. Blair won the leadership election easily, and John Prescott became deputy leader. Their relationship later became strained, but in the early days Blair and Brown agreed on many things: they were both Christian socialists and they both felt that modernization of the party had not yet gone far enough; people would not trust Labour so long as it was tainted with socialism. This was enshrined above all in the famous (or notorious) Clause 4 of the 1918 Labour party constitution, which pledged the party to public ownership (nationalization) of the means of production, distribution and exchange; this was necessary to 'secure for the workers by hand or by brain the full fruit of their industry'. Hugh Gaitskell had wanted to abolish Clause 4 in 1959 but dared not press it. At a special party conference in 1995, Blair at last succeeded in getting Clause 4 dropped. It was the end of an era: the old historic socialist Labour party had been replaced by 'New Labour', as Blair called it. Social democracy had replaced socialism. There is no doubt that Blair showed considerable boldness, as well as pragmatism, in his determination to abolish Clause 4. It was a step of great significance: in a completely different political environment from that of 1918, it removed a major obstacle to Labour's electability

The next step was to re-create the party's image in time for the next election, which was due in 1997. Nothing could be taken for granted after four consecutive election defeats. Blair and his modernizing team, which included Peter Mandelson (a grandson of Herbert Morrison), Alistair Campbell and Philip Gould, began to talk about 'a third way' in politics between socialism and capitalism. This would embrace the 'enterprise of the market and the vigour of competition' while at the same time being prepared to work towards the elimination of inequality and dire poverty. The rationale behind this came partly from the fact that the size of the industrial working class – Labour's traditional supporters – had shrunk rapidly since 1980. Labour leaders believed that they had to re-position the party into the centre in order to win the middle-class vote. Blair charmed the powerful press baron, Rupert Murdoch, so that the *Sun* and the *Evening Standard* switched to support Labour. In the words of Andrew Marr, 'with his impish grin he suddenly behaved as if everything was possible, and no political allegiance was impossible to shift. He became the playful magician of political life and even took to warmly praising Margaret Thatcher ... The traditionalists looked on in silent, helpless disbelief'. The manifesto itself was a modest document. Its main promises were: to cut class sizes for five- to seven-year-olds to under 30; to speed up punishment for persistent young offenders; to cut NHS waiting times; to create more jobs for young people; not to increase income tax and to keep inflation low; and not to cancel Mrs Thatcher's trade union reforms.

The new image was apparently successful: Labour won a stunning victory with 418 seats – their highest-ever total, against the Conservatives' 165. However, some observers argued that the Labour victory was more a result of the incompetence of the Conservative government than Labour's modernization (see Section 35.6(d)for more about this election).

36.2 New Labour in power: the first Blair government, 1997–2001

(a) New Labour – Thatcherism in disguise?

When Tony Blair became Prime Minister in 1997, Mrs Thatcher was said to have remarked that her legacy would be 'safe in his hands'. The previous section showed how far New Labour had moved from old Labour; New Labour's 1997 election manifesto was the most right-wing in the party's history. But had it really moved so far to the right that it was Thatcherism under another name? There were certainly some similarities. Like Mrs Thatcher, Blair felt like an outsider in his own party trying to drag the traditionalists (in Mrs Thatcher's case, the 'Wets') further to the right than they wanted to go. Both relied on un-elected advisers and press-officers, and would by-pass their Cabinets whenever it suited them. Under Blair, Cabinet meetings often lasted only half an hour and rarely longer than an hour. Their economic policies were similar, at least for much of Blair's first government; they both believed in the dominance of market forces and the need for global free trade. Brown, as Chancellor of the Exchequer, did his best to keep big business happy, and kept Labour's election promises not to increase income tax, and to keep to the Conservatives' projected spending totals for the next two years. New Labour continued the later Thatcherite privatization policy, going ahead with privatizing the air traffic control system in spite of having promised not to do so.

However, there were more differences than similarities. Where Mrs Thatcher was abrasive and confrontational, Blair aimed for consensus. Both he and Brown, as committed Christian socialists, genuinely wanted to help the disadvantaged and to narrow the gap between rich and poor. Blair told the party conference in 1995 that he believed in the parable of the good Samaritan: 'I am my brother's keeper and I will not walk by on the other side.' Soon afterwards, his advisers told him to avoid talking in religious terms in case people dismissed him as a 'Bible-basher'; but the motivation was still there. Hence his determination to improve the NHS, education and housing, to keep unemployment to a minimum, and to eliminate child poverty. Unlike Thatcher, Blair wanted to work closely with the EU and privately favoured joining the euro system, though only when it suited Britain's economic interests. Another sharp difference from the Thatcherites, who were anti-local government, was that New Labour was in favour of de-centralization; they supported the idea of national assemblies for Northern Ireland, Scotland and Wales, as well as a reform of the House of Lords.

(b) New Labour successes

The early successes of the new government were, in their different ways, somewhat unexpected.

> Only four days after taking office, Gordon Brown, the new Chancellor of the Exchequer, transferred control of interest rates from the government to the Bank of England via a newly established Monetary Policy Committee (MPC). This proved to be a popular move: it demonstrated to the money markets that New Labour could be trusted to safeguard the capitalist system and would not necessarily favour high employment over low inflation.

- The government immediately showed a more positive attitude to Europe than the Conservatives had done. In June 1997, Blair signed up to the *Amsterdam Treaty* (see Section 33.4(i)). This put the Social Chapter, which John Major had refused to accept, back into the Maastricht Treaty after Blair had indicated Britain's willingness to accept it. On the other hand, Britain did not join the eurozone which was introduced in January 1999, though twelve of the fifteen EU member states joined. Blair was quite keen for Britain to join, and British businessmen on the whole seemed to be in favour. But much of the right-wing press was against the idea, and Gordon Brown wanted to wait until the economic situation was right; he produced five economic tests that the British economy must pass before Britain adopted the euro. This point had still not been reached when Blair resigned in 2007.

- Tragedy struck at the end of August 1997, when Princess Diana was killed in a car accident in Paris. When it became clear that the Royal Family was not going to make any public statement, Blair took the lead and paid a moving tribute on TV in which he referred to Diana as 'the people's princess'. This seemed to capture the mood of the nation, and Blair's popularity rating rose to over 90 per cent. The Queen wanted to have a quiet, private funeral for Diana, and she herself intended to keep a low profile at Balmoral, away from the scenes of public mourning in London. However, the Prime Minister persuaded her that this might be bad for her public image; eventually, it was accepted that the Queen would return to London and that there should be a public funeral in Westminster Abbey. Public resentment had been building up against the Royal Family, as there had not been a flag flown at half-mast over Buckingham Palace in acknowledgement of Diana's death. Some observers believe that Blair's advice saved the Royal Family's reputation; after the Queen returned to London and made a live broadcast, her popularity gradually revived and she regained her former standing in the country.

- The government had some success in Northern Ireland. The IRA had declared a ceasefire in 1994, but this had been broken on numerous occasions. An Irish peace settlement was high on Blair's agenda, and the IRA responded by calling for another ceasefire. But the talks were so difficult that any sort of consensus seemed unlikely. However, *the Good Friday Agreement* was signed in April 1998, setting out a step-by-step process towards devolved government for Northern Ireland and a lasting peace (see Section 32.1(k)). It was only a beginning, and it would be March 2007 before that point was reached; but the Good Friday Agreement was the vital breakthrough.

- *The Crime and Disorder Act* of July 1998 was less unexpected, since New Labour had announced its intention of being 'tough on crime and tough on the causes of crime'. The main feature of the Act was the introduction of the Anti-Social Behaviour Order (ASBO), which could be placed on troublemakers in order to ban them from certain areas; anybody breaking their ASBO conditions could be sent to gaol. These gradually began to have a positive effect: residents on many large urban estates reported that ASBOs were working and improving life. On the other hand, some social workers protested that this was the wrong way to go about it, and the civil liberties lobby also complained that sending people to gaol before they had been convicted of a crime was blurring the line between civil and criminal offences. By 2007, it was beginning to look as though ASBOs might have only a limited long-term effect, though; it was reported that in some areas they were being 'collected' as badges of honour among gang members.

- *The Human Rights Act* (November 1998) incorporated the European Convention on Human Rights into British law, allowing cases to come to court in this country. This was followed by a *Freedom of Information Act* and anti-discrimination laws.
- *The Minimum Wage* was introduced in April 1999 at £3.60 an hour (£3.00 forthe under-22s) and was to rise each year; by 2006, it had reached £5.35 an hour. The Conservatives opposed the minimum wage on the grounds that it would destroy jobs or cause inflation; neither of these predictions came about, and the Conservatives themselves made the minimum wage part of their programme for the 2005 election. There were also substantial increases in state pensions.
- *The New Deal* for young people under 25 aimed to get the young unemployed into jobs. Statistics showed that, by 2001, some 200,000 young people had moved into work, though many of the jobs had been expensive to create. The policy operated on the principle of 'carrots and sticks' – each jobseeker must take a job, train, or study; for anyone refusing all three of these, there was no fourth option.
- *Devolution for Scotland and Wales* was introduced. The Welsh assembly opened on 26 May 1999 (see Section 32.3(c)) followed by the Scottish Parliament on 9 July (see Section 32.2(e)–(f)).
- *Reform of the House of Lords.* In 2000, a start was made on the process of transforming the unelected House of Lords into a more democratic body. All the hereditary peers were removed, apart from ninety-two of them who were granted what was intended to be a temporary reprieve. Unfortunately, there were no definite plans for the next stage – a new process to choose members of the House of Lords, and the government seemed unable to decide what it wanted. Early in 2007, MPs voted in favour of a wholly elected House of Lords, but there was little prospect of any progress in the foreseeable future, since the large Conservative majority remaining in the Lords was unlikely to vote for such a proposal.
- In *foreign affairs* Blair was motivated by his Christian principles. According to Andrew Rawnsley:

> Blair saw himself as a modern version of William Gladstone. Like that Victorian liberal interventionist, his Christian faith strongly shaped his

world view ... [that] military force was a justifiable and effective instrument for pursuing the noble cause of removing dictators and spreading democracy. He was already developing this belief in using force in the name of freedom long before anyone outside Texas had ever heard of George W. Bush.

It was US President Bill Clinton who persuaded Blair to join him in disciplining Saddam Hussein, the dictator of Iraq. In December 1998, British and American planes launched Operation Desert Fox, a four-day bombing of Saddam's military establishment, after he had failed to co-operate fully with UN weapons inspectors. The operation was claimed as a success, though it was difficult to assess by exactly how much it had delayed Saddam's armaments programme.

Britain's next foreign intervention was in the *Kosovo crisis*. Kosovo was a province of Serbia, though the majority of the population were ethnic Albanian-speaking Muslims. Conflict began when the Kosovo Liberation Army launched a campaign for independence from Serbia. The Serbian forces of President Slobodan Milošević took savage reprisals, causing thousands of people to flee from their homes. Some observers began to compare this so-called ethnic cleansing with Nazi war crimes. After talks with Serb leaders failed, Blair took the lead in prompting NATO to use force against Milošević. In March 1999, the British and Americans began a controversial bombing of Serb targets in Kosovo, and then in the Serbian capital, Belgrade. However, this only succeeded in killing many innocent civilians and seemed to strengthen Milošević's determination to step up his ethnic cleansing. It is estimated that in the next few weeks as many as 12,000 ethnic Albanians were killed and around a million fled the country.

Blair realized that air attacks were not enough – only a full-scale invasion, or the threat of one, would make Milošević see sense. No support for military action was forthcoming from the EU, but eventually Blair persuaded Clinton to join Britain in threatening to invade Kosovo unless Milošević withdrew Serbian troops. Unsure whether or not this was all bluff, the Serbs backed down, withdrew their troops and accepted what was in effect an independent Kosovo under international supervision. Only a few months later, Milošević was voted out of power in Serbia and was eventually brought to the International Court of Justice at the Hague and put on trial for war crimes. With some justification, Blair could claim a victory for Britain. Sadly, when he later tried to repeat this performance in Iraq and Afghanistan, the outcomes were rather different.

Another success that received little publicity was Britain's military action in Sierra Leone, where a long and bitter civil war had officially ended in a power-sharing peace agreement in July 1999. However, some of the rebels refused to accept this and continued with the most brutal atrocities. The UN sent troops in October 2000 to implement the peace agreement, and British forces played a vital part in disarming the rebels until something approaching calm was restored.

(c) problems and failures

When New Labour took office in May 1997, the new government inherited a healthy economic situation, in which unemployment had been falling for the previous two years. Expectations of reform in many directions were high – education, the health service, housing and child poverty had all been given prominence in the election manifesto. And yet the record of Blair's first four years was disappointing; even some of his close colleagues felt that they were a wasted opportunity.

▸ One of the problems was that the Treasury was limited by the promise to keep to the Conservatives' spending estimates for the first two years. Accordingly, in December 1997, as part of the Social Security Bill, benefits to single parents were cut. Tony Benn protested to Tony Blair: 'you cannot justify taking money off the poorest to fight inflation; you can't ring-fence the rich and tax the poor. These are the poorest children of all'. In the Commons vote on the Bill's second reading, forty-seven Labour MPs voted against that particular clause, and sixty-three abstained, but it was not a big enough back-bench revolt to prevent it becoming law.

Even after the two years, Brown kept a tight control on spending and concentrated on keeping inflation low. He raised extra revenue with his controversial 'stealth taxes', as they became known. These included freezing income tax thresholds so that, as incomes rose, an extra 1.5 million people moved into the top tax band; personal allowances were frozen; stamp duty on houses and national insurance contributions were increased; and, most controversial of all, was the removal of tax credits for share dividends on investments in pensions. Until then, pension fund shareholders had been treated more favourably than normal shareholders, who had to pay 10 per cent tax on their dividends; pension fund shareholders had been exempt from paying this tax, but now they were to be treated like other shareholders – they would only receive 90 per cent of their dividends. This was felt to have a disastrous effect on the value of pension funds. However, some observers feel that its effects have been exaggerated by Brown's opponents and by the pensions industry. Nor was much of this extra cash spent on public services, since Brown chose to use £37 billion to repay the public debt.

To be fair to the Chancellor, this meant that the government's interest payments fell dramatically; it was all part of what he called an economic policy of 'prudence'. But the upshot was that, while there was some extra government funding for health, education and housing, there seemed to be little obvious improvement. The situation was retrieved to some extent in January 2000, when Blair admitted in a TV interview that the NHS needed a massive injection of money if it was to do more than just survive. This forced Brown to increase health spending in his next budget by at least 6 per cent a year above inflation for every year until 2004.

- However, John Prescott's promise to improve public transport and so reduce the number of car journeys was not fulfilled, simply because the Treasury would not allow him enough cash. Another unpopular move was the introduction of tuition fees for higher education for all but the poorest students; this came only a year after New Labour had promised not to do this. New Labour had also promised an end to sleaze, but the government soon found itself involved in a series of scandals. One of its aims was to reduce its financial dependence on the trade unions, but in doing so the leaders got themselves involved in some compromising situations with wealthy supporters. In November 1997, it was announced that Formula 1 car racing would be exempt from a general ban on tobacco advertising at sports events. A few days later it emerged that Bernie Ecclestone, who controlled Formula 1, had made a donation of £1 million to Labour before the election. While it was impossible to prove any connection between the two, it looked as though Ecclestone had bought this special favour. The first doubts were sown about New Labour's claim to be 'whiter than white'.

  A year later there was another scandal, when it was revealed that before the election Peter Mandelson, one of the leading architects of New Labour, had borrowed £373,000 from another Labour MP, Geoffrey Robinson, to buy a house. There was nothing wrong in that, but the problem arose because Robinson, an extremely wealthy businessman, had large amounts of cash in an offshore tax haven. Robinson became Paymaster General in the new government, and when Mandelson became Secretary of State for Trade and Industry it meant that he was responsible for investigations into possible suspected financial misdemeanours among MPs, including Mr Robinson. There was clearly a clash of interest there, and Mandelson would not confirm who had loaned him the cash. Though many people could see nothing wrong in the situation, it ended with both men being forced to resign. There were several similar incidents, including one in which Blair himself was accused of lying about the source of donations to the party. Finally, after being brought back into the government as Northern Ireland Secretary, Mandelson was forced to resign a second time after he was involved in a scandal over passports for two Indian businessmen who had helped to fund the Millennium Dome. Some thought these incidents were trivial, but taken together they had a damaging effect on New Labour's claim to be a party beyond reproach in its financial dealings.

- The Millennium Dome itself proved to be something of an embarrassment for the government. The project was inherited from the Conservatives, but Labour decided to continue with it, though it was going to cost around a billion pounds. In many ways it was a success: architecturally it was quite impressive, and with it came a great improvement of the surrounding area, which had been largely derelict. But the problem was that nobody could decide what to put in it. In the words of Andrew Marr:

> The range of mildly interesting exhibits was greeted as a huge disappointment. Far fewer people came and bought tickets than was hoped. It turned out to be a theme park without a theme, morphing in the public imagination into the earliest and most damaging symbol of what was wrong with New Labour: an impressively constructed big tent containing not very much at all.

▸ One of the government's most controversial policies was the increasing use of *the Private Finance Initiative (PFI)*. First introduced by Norman Lamont under the Conservatives, this took two forms:

1 Contracting-out of services such as hospital cleaning, school meals and refuse collection to private companies.
2 Privatizing major projects such as building new schools, hospitals and prisons. For example, the NHS would arrange for a private consortium to build a new hospital, and would then pay the consortium a kind of rent for the next thirty years.

It was the second type of PFI that really took off under New Labour and reached a peak during the years 2000–1. The advantage of PFI for the government is that the consortium pays for the new building, so that the cost is not included in the current Treasury accounts; it is future generations who have to foot the bill in the form of rents. Since the whole point of the exercise from the consortium's point of view is to make a profit, it follows that over the years the government will pay far more than if it had financed the building itself. Another drawback is that, once it is built, a PFI hospital cannot be altered, even if some change is vital to efficiency. Ross McKibbin feels that the government ought to have recognized that 'most people believe there are certain things in society that are the domain of the public, and from which private profit should be excluded. This might be irrational, but they believe it nonetheless'.

▸ In September 2000 there was a sudden crisis caused by rising world oil prices and high petrol taxes. Petrol prices reached record levels, and in desperation a group of lorry drivers blockaded an oil refinery in Cheshire. The idea soon caught on, and more refineries were blockaded. Within a few days most petrol stations had run dry and there were reports of food shortages and factory closures. Pressure was on Brown to promise fuel tax cuts in his forthcoming budget, but he refused. Eventually, after warnings from hospitals that people's lives were at risk, the press began to turn against the protesters, who agreed to lift their blockades. Brown made some concessions in his March budget, and things quickly returned to normal. But it had been a salutary warning for the government, which had seemed to be on the verge of panic.

(d) why did New Labour win the 2001 election?

In the election of June 2001, New Labour won another massive victory with their majority only slightly reduced from 1997. This was something of a surprise in view of the problems and disappointments of Blair's first term. Another remarkable feature of the election was the low turnout, which fell dramatically from 78 per cent in 1992 to 60 per cent in 2001. Labour's explanation was that people were too contented to bother voting. Other observers suggested that it was because people saw nothing much to choose between the two main parties, and that possibly neither of them had much to offer. According to Ross McKibbin, it was 'the adoption by the Labour Party of a neo-Thatcherite programme, modified too late for many, which persuaded so many to bid farewell to formal party politics'. *So why did Tony Blair succeed in holding on to his majority?*

‣ In spite of the disappointments, the government could point to the range of achievements outlined in Section 36.2 (b) above. Many people were in fact better off, thanks to the minimum wage, higher pensions and tax credits, though this received little acknowledgement in the media. As for the National Health Service and schools, while there may not have been any spectacular improvement, at least the decline of the Thatcherite years had been halted, and they had not deteriorated any further. Brown's commitment to put more cash into the NHS over the next three years came just in time to impress voters.

‣ Blair's policy of consensus led him to draw people from the other parties into working with the government. The Liberal Democrat, Paddy Ashdown, joined a government committee on constitutional reform; a group called 'Britain in Europe', set up to publicize the case for deeper British involvement in the EU, included the Conservatives Kenneth Clarke and Michael Heseltine, and Liberal Democrat Charles Kennedy. Even though nothing concrete was achieved, it was nevertheless a welcome and popular departure from Thatcherite confrontation.

‣ New Labour was fortunate that the Conservative party was still divided over its attitude to the EU. When John Major resigned after the 1997 defeat, the Conservatives chose William Hague as the new leader, rather than Kenneth Clarke, one of the most experienced, charismatic and popular Tories. But he was unacceptable to most of the parliamentary party because he was pro-European. Hague, chosen because he was a committed anti-European, was a talented politician and a brilliant Commons performer, and he succeeded in holding the Conservative party together. However, in the election campaign he concentrated too much on his anti-European stance and promised further tax cuts. This made the party seem narrowly British as well as unconcerned about the NHS and education. So, while voters were disappointed with the slow pace of progress under Blair, they could hope for nothing better from

Hague. There seemed no good reason to desert New Labour just when improvements were beginning to be apparent.

36.3 New Labour and the 'war on terror'

Blair's second term in power (2001–5) was dominated from very early on, at least in the media, by foreign affairs, and particularly by what George W. Bush called the 'war on terror'. On 11 September 2001, only three months after the election, terrorists attacked several targets in the USA. Blair, keen to 'stand shoulder to shoulder' with Bush, became enmeshed in the anti-terrorist campaign, which had still not been concluded successfully when Blair retired in 2007. At the same time, New Labour was responsible for a wide variety of domestic changes and reforms that made Britain safer, better-educated and generally better off (see next section). Yet most of it received relatively little publicity, as the media became more and more obsessed with the Iraq war and its aftermath.

(a) background to the 'war on terror'

Since the early 1980s there had been a series of terrorist outrages in various parts of the world, mainly directed against the USA. There was an attack on the American embassy in Beirut (Lebanon) in 1983; in 1988, an American airliner flying from Frankfurt to New York crashed on to the Scottish town of Lockerbie after a bomb exploded on board, killing all 259 passengers, the crew and eleven people on the ground. A bomb exploded in the World Trade Center in New York in 1993, killing six people and injuring several hundred; and the US embassies in Kenya and Tanzania were attacked in 1998, with a death toll of 252. Finally, in 2000, the American destroyer *Cole* was badly damaged in port at Aden in the Yemen, killing seventeen sailors. It was increasingly humiliating for the USA that, despite seeing itself as the world's most powerful state, it seemed unable to defend its property around the world.

The climax of the terrorist attacks came in the early morning of 11 September 2001, when four airliners on internal flights in the USA were hijacked. The first one was deliberately crashed into the 110-storey North Tower of the World Trade Center in New York, and a quarter of an hour later the second crashed into the South Tower. Both towers eventually collapsed, killing some 2,800 people. A third plane crashed into the Pentagon, the building near Washington that housed the US Department of Defense; the fourth one missed its target and crashed in a rural area near Pittsburgh. Over a hundred people were killed in the Pentagon and about 200 passengers on the aircraft, including the hijackers. It was the most stunning atrocity ever experienced on US soil, and it provided a stern test for the new President, George W. Bush, who had only taken office the previous January.

Once Bush had recovered from the initial shock, he took decisive action. The blame for the attack was placed on al-Qaeda (meaning 'the Base'), an Arab organization led by Osama bin Laden, which was campaigning against Western or anti-Islamic interests. Bush immediately announced 'a declaration of war on terrorism.' His aim was to overthrow the Taliban, the fundamentalist Muslim regime in Afghanistan, which was thought to be aiding and abetting al-Qaeda. This, it was hoped, would enable the Americans to capture bin Laden and destroy al-Qaeda. At the same time, Bush threatened to overthrow any regime that encouraged or harboured terrorists. First on his list after the Taliban was to be Saddam Hussein, the Iraqi dictator, and action was also threatened against Iran and Communist North Korea – three states which, according to Bush, formed an 'axis of evil.' He hoped to form a coalition of states to fight the terrorists.

Tony Blair's first reaction to 9/11 was to declare support for the USA; 'this mass terrorism,' he said, 'is the new evil in our world today.' To show Britain's solidarity with the USA, he flew to Washington and attended an emergency session of Congress. He was the only foreign leader to do so, and received a standing ovation. According to Andrew Rawnsley: 'In the build-up to the military action in Afghanistan he appointed himself an ambassador at large for the coalition, travelling more than 40,000 miles for 54 meetings with other world leaders. This helped to shape and sustain international support for the removal of the Taliban regime and the attack on the al-Qaeda bases they had harboured.' Even Clare Short, a Labour MP who was usually critical of Blair, was impressed. This was 'Tony's best moment,' she said. 'Tony bestrode the world stage, trying to hold everyone together with America.'

(b) the Taliban overthrown

A joint British and American operation against the Taliban was launched on 7 October 2001. Taliban targets and suspected al-Qaeda camps were attacked with cruise missiles fired from British submarines and heavy bombing by US planes, while troops of the Northern Alliance (Afghan opponents of the Taliban), began an offensive against Taliban strongholds in the north-west. By the end of November, the Taliban had abandoned Kabul (the capital) and had been driven out of their main power base – the province of Kandahar. Many fled into the mountains or over the border into Pakistan. The coalition's first aim had been achieved, though Osama bin Laden remained elusive and was still apparently a free man at the time of writing (2008). During the autumn and winter of 2001, Blair's popularity was at its height. He could take much of the credit for keeping the EU co-operative, and persuading Pakistan to join the American side; and he had won the admiration and gratitude of the American people for standing 'shoulder-to-shoulder' with them.

(c) Saddam Hussein becomes the next target

Blair had already made a dramatic speech at the party conference in October 2001 in which he said that he believed 9/11 was a turning point in world history. It gave the West the chance to defeat terrorism and then move on to deal with the poverty that was causing terrorism. There should be, he said, 'hope amongst all nations of a new beginning where we seek to resolve differences in a calm and ordered way; greater understanding between nations and between faiths; and above all justice and prosperity for the poor and dispossessed'. Andrew Marr believes this approach 'was the product of the Christian moralism he had developed as an Oxford student, a growing belief in his personal ability as a global leader, and a hot concentration of excited thinking utterly unlike his vaguer grasp of domestic policy ... He tied war-making and aid-giving together as Bush certainly would not have done'.

Blair was already worried about Saddam in November 1997. He seems to have genuinely believed that Saddam was on the verge of producing a nuclear weapon that might then be used by terrorists whom Iraq was supporting. He told Paddy Ashdown: 'the intelligence about Saddam really is pretty scary ... we cannot let him get away with it ... it's deadly serious'. Blair rightly saw Saddam as a man of evil who was responsible for the deaths of tens of thousands of his own people; it seemed that such a man would barely hesitate before agreeing to help terrorist groups to kill more Westerners. Bush and his close advisers, Donald Rumsfeld and Dick Cheney, had also discussed the overthrow of Saddam in 1998, long before 9/11. Their main motive was to gain control of Iraq's extensive oil supplies, though they talked a lot about bringing democracy to Iraq. Unlike Blair, they had no interest in reorganizing and improving the country after Saddam had gone. Clearly, Blair, in the words of Andrew Rawnsley, 'was not a poodle being pulled by a leash held by Bush. That caricature has been as widespread as it is wrong. He went to war alongside America because he wanted to. There were several points at which he could have chosen not to join the invasion'. The best chance was provided by Bush himself: when he realized how much opposition there was in Britain to the war, he told Blair that the US did not need British troops to take part in the actual fighting; instead, they could go in as peacekeepers once Saddam had been ejected. However, Blair insisted; he wanted Britain to play its part in overthrowing the evil dictator. There was one condition, though: he felt it was important that any military action should be approved by the United Nations.

To Blair's great disappointment there was much less enthusiasm in the rest of the world for an attack on Saddam than there had been for the campaign against the Taliban. The USA had failed to produce any evidence that Saddam was harbouring al-Qaeda terrorists, and so Bush was forced to base his justification for war on fear of Saddam's weapons of mass destruction (WMDs). Iraqi exiles who hated Saddam claimed that he already had chemical and biological weapons, and would have nuclear weapons by 2005. This suggested that there was no time to lose: Saddam must be removed; 'regime-change', as the Americans called it, was at the top of the agenda. But France, Germany and Russia believed that war should be the last resort, and that more time should be given to UN inspectors to complete their search for WMD; any military action should be sanctioned by the UN.

(d) the attack on Saddam delayed

The United Nations did not support regime-change simply on the grounds that Saddam Hussein was a wicked dictator; there had to be something specific – for example, that he was refusing to co-operate fully with the weapons inspectors, which would suggest that he had something to hide. To convince the UN, the British public and the Labour party, Blair set about producing a dossier proving that Saddam had WMD. Relying on information from Iraqi sources hostile to Saddam, British intelligence and defence experts genuinely believed that Saddam was hiding WMD somewhere in the desert. When the dossier appeared in September 2002, it seemed to prove not only that Saddam had these deadly weapons, but also that they could be ready for use in 45 minutes against targets such as the British bases in Cyprus. Consequently, the UN Security Council approved Resolution 1441, calling on Saddam to show that he had no banned weapons or 'face serious consequences'. The Iraqis accepted the resolution, and seventeen UN weapons inspectors were allowed into the country after an absence of four years. At first, Saddam did not co-operate with them fully, though at the end of February 2003 they reported that he had agreed to destroy some missiles they had discovered.

Meanwhile, Blair and Bush were getting impatient with the delay. In January 2003, Blair began to push for a second Security Council resolution to authorize an attack on Iraq, since 1441 had not given the USA full authority to launch a military attack; 'consequences' could simply mean more economic sanctions. But public opinion in Britain was moving strongly against war. On 16 February 2003, there was a massive 'stop the war' march through London, and demonstrations in cities and towns all over the country, as well as worldwide. The one in London was said to be the biggest demonstration ever seen in the capital. In the Security Council, France, Russia and China insisted that the weapons inspectors should be given more time; President Chirac of France announced that France would veto any resolution authorizing war against Iraq (10 March). The second resolution that Blair and Bush wanted so much never came.

Bush claimed that the first resolution already gave the authority to attack Iraq, and he was determined to go ahead. In spite of all opposition, Blair was equally determined to go with him, though he needed to get the support of Parliament. Robin Cook, Labour's previous Foreign Secretary, was so strongly opposed to war that he was determined to resign. In a telling resignation speech in the House of Commons (17 March) he pointed out that 'Britain is being asked to embark on a war without agreement in any of the international bodies of which we are a leading partner – not Nato, not the European Union, and, now, not the Security Council ... The British people do not doubt that Saddam is a brutal dictator, but they are not persuaded that he is a clear and present danger to Britain.' As he sat down, Cook was given a standing ovation, something unheard of in the House of Commons. Blair eventually won the support of well over half the Labour MPs, though more than a hundred rebelled. Thanks to Conservative support the Commons voted in favour of the war.

(e) the aftermath of Saddam's downfall

The USA, the UK and Spain issued a joint ultimatum to Saddam, giving him 48 hours to leave Iraq. When this was ignored, British and American forces began air attacks on Baghdad and an invasion of southern Iraq from Kuwait (20 March). Victory was not quite as swift as expected; Baghdad was captured by the Americans early in April and Basra in the south was taken by British troops. On 9 April it was announced that Saddam's 24-year dictatorship was at an end; on 1 May, President Bush declared that the war was over. Saddam disappeared temporarily, but was captured in December 2003. He was eventually put on trial in an Iraqi court, sentenced to death and executed (December 2006). The war had been a military success, but unfortunately the 'peace' that followed was disastrous. The Americans had no clear plan for reconstruction and the Iraqis grew impatient with the continued American occupation. By June 2003, armed resistance and terrorist attacks had begun; democratic elections to choose a transitional government were held in January 2005, and later there were full elections which put in place a Shia-dominated government. Yet the violence continued, reaching civil war proportions: Sunnis fought Shias, and insurgents attacked the American and British forces that were still there ostensibly to support the Iraqi army. In 2008, people were still being killed every day by suicide bombers; some observers reported that life for ordinary Iraqis was more dangerous than it had been under Saddam. Gradually, as more and more information emerged, it became clear that in the lead-up to the war, *false claims and serious mistakes had been made.*

- No weapons of mass destruction were found in Iraq, thus invalidating Blair's main justification for the war. But worse was to come: on 29 May 2003, a BBC defence correspondent, Andrew Gilligan, claimed in a Radio 4 interview that Downing Street had exaggerated the evidence of WMD and had 'sexed-up' the dossier, especially by making the claim that these weapons could be ready for use within 45 minutes. Alistair Campbell, Blair's press secretary, strongly denied the allegation and demanded an apology. This was refused and a first-class row developed between the government and the BBC.

  Neither side would admit any fault, until the government realized where Gilligan had got his information: it had come from Dr David Kelly, a Ministry of Defence scientist who did not believe that the evidence for WMD was conclusive. This was just his opinion, but the BBC had wrongly presented it as fact. Kelly had been in favour of ousting Saddam and was distressed at the turn of events, which made it appear that he had betrayed the government. Questioned aggressively by MPs, he perhaps understandably denied supplying Gilligan with inside information. It all became too much for him, and in July 2003 Dr Kelly committed suicide. Blair ordered an enquiry, led by a judge, Lord Hutton, into the whole Gilligan–Kelly affair. At the end of January 2004, Lord Hutton announced his findings which, in effect, amounted to a victory for the government. Gilligan had no grounds for claiming that the government knew that the 45-minute claim was false; the claims in the dossier were consistent with the government's intelligence at the time; Dr Kelly had probably killed himself because he felt that his reputation had been ruined; and the BBC was at fault for not exercising proper editorial control over sensation-seeking reporters. Greg Dyke, the BBC Director-General, and Gavin Davies, the BBC Chairman, both resigned immediately. Yet the seeds of doubt had been sown; Blair had always claimed that trust was one of the most important qualities in a politician. The WMD affair and the 'sexed-up' dossier did him great harm politically. The word 'Bliar' appeared on placards and many people began to wonder whether their Prime Minister could be trusted to tell the truth.

) In the meantime, other information had emerged that did nothing to improve Blair's reputation. Paul Wolfowitz, one of President Bush's inner circle, inadvertently let the truth about America's motives for the war slip out. It was nothing to do with WMD – that was just a pretext; Bush's Cabinet knew perfectly well that Saddam had none. The real reason was that, having just felt obliged to remove their troops from Saudi Arabia, a regime change in Iraq would make it possible to station them in Baghdad and Basra, and so continue to exercise control over the region's oil supplies.

) As time went on, it became obvious that the peaceful, united and democratic Iraq that Blair had promised was no more than a dream. Several mistakes were made in the weeks immediately following the overthrow of Saddam. First was the decision to disband the Iraqi army, which could have been put to good use; instead, thousands of armed young men were let loose on the community without any organization or control. No steps were taken to secure law and order in the big cities; there were no security forces and no police force; nor was there any attempt to seal the frontiers to keep out foreign troublemakers and terrorists. All this meant that Iraq was already out of control only four months after the invasion began.

Why was this allowed to happen? It seems that the US Vice-President, Dick Cheney, and Defence Secretary, Donald Rumsfeld, who had been placed in charge of post-Saddam reorganization by Bush, had simply not thought through the implications of what they were doing and had underestimated the difficulties. They had been warned of the possibility of Shia versus Sunni civil war, and the risk of anti-American terrorism, yet had blithely assumed that US troops would be able to control everything. No detailed plans had been made to secure law and order, or to move Iraq towards democracy. All they had in mind was to get control of the Iraqi nationalized oil industry, and this was the first action of Paul Bremer, the man they appointed as 'proconsul' in Iraq. There were 190 state-owned oil companies employing 650,000 people. Bremer immediately sacked half a million of them and passed a law allowing foreign takeovers and lowering corporate tax rates. He called it 'getting Iraq ready for Walmart'. No thought was given to providing 'justice and prosperity for the dispossessed' which was Blair's ultimate aim. By the end of 2004, unemployment was running at around 50 per cent. What was there to do for unemployed workers but to join the insurrections against the people they saw as responsible for their plight. The US forces could not protect the oil refineries and pipelines, and the industry was soon in ruins. Unfortunately, Blair had no control over any of this, and had no influence over Bush's 'inner circle'. All he could do was watch in dismay as these frighteningly inept people perpetrated a series of disastrous mistakes. Nor did things improve; by the spring of 2007, the International Red Cross reported that the sufferings of Iraqi civilians were 'unbearable and unacceptable'.

- One of the justifications given for going to war was that the removal of Saddam would act as a warning to other 'rogue regimes' to mend their ways and would therefore be a vital step in the war to defeat terrorism. It was true that Libya responded by abandoning its nuclear programme, but it seemed to spur Iran on to make itself into a nuclear power as quickly as possible. The result of the war was not to reduce terrorism but to increase it dramatically, and al-Qaeda was strengthened by the increase in anti-American and anti-Western feeling. A number of new networks of Islamic militants was reported, with bases in Europe as well as the Middle East. In 2004, London was named as an important centre for recruiting, fundraising and the manufacture of false documents. In March 2004, bombs exploded in Madrid, killing about 200 people on morning rush-hour trains; a Moroccan group allied to al-Qaeda was responsible. In July 2005, four suicide bombers killed 57 people on London Underground trains and a bus. The bombers were young Muslims who were British citizens; they were not members of al-Qaeda, but their motive was to make a protest against British foreign policy.

- The Americans, and by association their allies, were further discredited in the eyes of most of the world by the way in which they held terrorist suspects indefinitely without trial in dreadful conditions in a camp at Guantanamo Bay, an American base in Cuba (where American civil law did not apply), amid accusations of beatings and torture. Both American and British soldiers were found guilty of abusing, and even in some cases killing, Iraqi prisoners in the notorious Abu Ghraib gaol in Baghdad.

- The war against terrorism seemed unlikely to be successful until there was a resolution of the Palestine–Israel situation. The Arab states deplored the continued US support for Israel, which continued its illegal occupation of

Arab territories. Blair realized the importance of securing a fair deal for the Palestinians, but was unable to influence Bush in that direction.

The Americans attempted to move Iraq towards democracy: elections were held in January 2005 and the new parliament met in March. But sadly it was all overshadowed by the continuing violence. The Sunni Muslims boycotted the elections and many Iraqis considered their new government to be no more than puppets of the Americans. Even as Blair retired in May 2007, four years after Bush declared that the war was over, Iraqis were still killing each other as well as attacking American and British troops. By that time, most of the ministers who had served in Blair's Cabinet regarded the war as a complete disaster. To add to the frustration, the situation in Afghanistan had deteriorated again; the Taliban had regrouped and were carrying out a guerrilla war against the Afghan government. NATO was involved in an attempt to stabilize things, but it seemed that British troops were playing the major role in propping up the Western-backed government. At the beginning of 2009 there was little prospect of peace in Afghanistan in the near future.

36.4 domestic affairs and Blair's final years, 2001–7

Hardly had New Labour embarked on its second term when the 9/11 terrorist attacks against the USA took place, and the nation's attention became focused on the 'war on terror'. Nevertheless *the government did not neglect its domestic goals.*

(a) the NHS, education and social services

> The pre-election pledge to spend more on the NHS was not forgotten. Derek Wanless, formerly of the NatWest bank, was commissioned to produce a review of the NHS and what was needed; he concluded that only massive extra spending would bring the UK system up to the EU average. Brown accordingly imposed a 1p increase on National Insurance, and at the same time raised the ceiling so that those who were better off would have to pay proportionately more. In 2000, Britain spent 6.8 per cent of its gross domestic product (GDP) on health, while the EU average was 8 per cent. Blair pledged that Britain would catch up by 2006, and this was achieved; in fact, Scotland achieved it in 2004. The health service budget rose to over £92 billion a year from the 2001 figure of £37 billion. The results were soon apparent: by 2006, there were around 300,000 extra staff; this included about 10,000 extra senior hospital doctors (an increase of around 25 per cent), and 85,000 more nurses. Waiting lists fell, the death rate from cancer for people under 75 fell by over 15 per cent, and death rates from heart disease fell by over 35 per cent between 1996 and 2006. Since New Labour took office, 218 new hospitals and 188 new Treatment Centres have been built or are in the process of being built.

At the same time as the extra cash flooded into the NHS, so did a series of new controls, agencies, planners and targets. This sprang from Blair's view that the health service should offer patients more choice, and so allowed private companies to come in and compete with the NHS to provide quicker treatment. However, Gordon Brown and many Labour MPs had a different view. How was it possible to have competition, they asked, when for most people there was just one large local hospital? What people wanted was not more choice, but simply the best possible local hospital. The Blair argument was that you could only get the better hospitals if there was choice. Public opinion seemed to suggest that the majority agreed with Brown. In the end, a compromise was reached: just a small number of private 'foundation hospitals' would be built as a sort of trial run. Unfortunately, this had the effect of destabilizing the situation in those areas, as NHS managers were left wondering how to cope if their hospital lost to the competition; would they be forced to close? Critics claimed that there were far too many managers in any case (an extra 40,000 since 1997), and that privatization of hospital cleaning was responsible for the huge rise in hospital infections caused by bacteria such as Methicillin-resistant Staphylococcus aureus (MRSA) and Clostridium difficile (C. difficile).

› One of Blair's favourite slogans was 'education, education, education', and much was done to improve things. Between 1997 and 2007, government spending per pupil doubled (from £2,500 to £5,000), there were 36,000 extra teachers and 154,000 extra support staff; there was a 13 per cent increase (up to 58 per cent) in the number of GCSE candidates gaining five passes at C or above; and in higher education, 43 per cent of 18-to-30-year-olds were going to university – in spite of the controversial top-up tuition fees introduced in January 2004. Blair's great aim was to impose league tables and examination pressures on schools in order to give parents a choice, and encourage them to abandon the less successful ones. In order to increase choice, he pressed on with opening semi-independent schools partly financed by businesses or religious groups. These proved to be extremely popular, but critics were quick to point out that this did nothing to help the 500 or so underperforming state secondary schools in the most deprived areas, where it seemed ludicrous to talk about choice.

› During his first term, Blair announced that 'our historic aim is that ours is the first generation to end child poverty for ever … it's a 20-year mission, but I believe it can be done'. Again, a great deal was done, and long before twenty years had passed. But how is poverty measured? Probably the best way is what economists call 'median income' – this is the midway point above which half the population earns more and below which half earns less. To be officially poor was to live on less than 60 per cent of median income. In 2004, the poverty threshold was calculated as £94 a week for a single person, £172 for a couple, and £175 for a single person with two children; this was the cash they had to live on after housing costs had been paid. As Polly Toynbee and David Walker point out, 'in 1997 the UK had the highest rates of child poverty in Europe, ranking fifteenth out of the then fifteen EU member states. A third of all children in the EU classified as poor were born in the UK, a national shame.'

The government tackled the problem with a wide range of measures, including baby bonds, Child Benefit and Child Tax Credit (this replaced Working Families Tax Credit and Children's Tax Credit in 2003). This was confusing but effective: it meant that by 2005 a typical family with two children had enjoyed an 11 per cent real increase in their tax credits since 2001; in 1997 there were 4.4 million poor children – the tax credits were enough to take 1.1 million children out of poverty. Unfortunately, though, there were signs by 2006 that the number of children in relative poverty was beginning to rise again.

Sure Start nurseries were introduced to help mothers from the most deprived families with their babies and young children – 3,500 were to be completed by 2010. There were substantial extensions of the rights of workers, including flexible working hours for young mothers, and old age pensions were increased. Overall, there can be no doubt that by 2007 the poorest third of society were better off than they would have been without New Labour's policies. Interestingly, it seems likely that it was the middle classes rather than the very rich who paid for the improvements; there was very little evidence that New Labour was managing to extract more tax from the super-wealthy.

‣ In the fight against crime, 12,500 extra police officers were recruited during Labour's second term, and there was a new creation – the community support officer; 4,000 were operating in 2004, and by 2008 the number had risen to 24,000. Statistics indicated that in 2007 crime had fallen by 35 per cent since 1997, though violent crime had risen. Blair had promised that New Labour would be 'tough on crime' and certainly the UK's prisons were full; in May 2007 there were a record 80,000 inmates and numbers were rising every month. Critics questioned whether this was the best way to deal with the more petty crimes, pointing out that a third of all prisoners re-offended within a year of being released.

Much of this success received very little publicity in the media; Polly Toynbee called it 'social justice by stealth'. This was partly because Blair deliberately played down New Labour's help for the underdog, in case the middle classes disapproved. It was also because much of the media was anti-Labour; most of the newspapers had a distinct right-wing bias and only highlighted the shortcomings of Labour's policies; even the *Guardian* constantly attacked the government from a left-wing viewpoint, while, in the words of Toynbee and Walker in their book *Better or Worse? Has Labour Delivered?* (2005), the

Independent and the *Mirror* 'struck out wildly to the left in an attempt to arrest circulation decline. But a bias in favour of this Labour government was nowhere to be seen'. The BBC was equally hostile most of the time. Estelle Morris, a former teacher and a sympathetic Education Secretary, resigned in 2002, at least partly because of media harassment and bullying.

(b) more successes and problems

In their second term, Blair and New Labour responded to a number of situations and problems as they arose.

‣ Following the 9/11 outrages in the USA, the *Anti-Terrorism, Crime and Security Act* (December 2001) gave police special powers of arrest and detention without trial of foreigners suspected of being involved in supporting or stirring up terrorism. The government could not deport them because human rights laws forbade sending anyone back to a country where they might face torture or execution. Seventeen men were arrested and held at Belmarsh high security prison. This proved to be very controversial, and critics claimed it was a breach of human rights; in December 2004 the House of Lords ruled that these detentions were illegal. However, the Home Secretary, Charles Clarke, refused to release them and introduced 'control orders' to limit the movement of such detainees; control orders could also be used against British-born terror suspects. The controversy rumbled on until the situation was changed somewhat by the London bombings of July 2005.

‣ The government did a great deal for gay and lesbian rights. Early in 2002 the age of consent for gay sex was lowered to 16. A campaign called *Don't Suffer in Silence* was launched against homophobic bullying in schools. Section 28 of a Thatcher local government act forbidding teachers and councillors from 'promoting' homosexuality was repealed. It had scarcely ever been used and had been found to cause difficulties in teaching sex education. The *Civil Partnership Act* (2004) gave gay and lesbian couples the same tax and legal rights as married couples, without them actually being married; such partnerships could now be formalized in a registry office.

‣ The peace process in Northern Ireland ground to a halt; the government felt it had no choice but to suspend the assembly and return the province to direct rule from London (see Section 32.1(k)).

‣ In November 2004, a law banning the hunting of foxes with hounds was passed and became law in February 2005. This was the culmination of a long campaign by the government that was bitterly opposed by the Countryside Alliance of pro-hunting groups. But there were many loopholes in the Act, so that hounds were still used to flush out foxes, which could then be shot. In the end, after all the fuss, hunting still continued.

‣ During New Labour's second term the economy continued to perform well in spite of a global downturn. This was because Brown was able to keep the economy afloat with the help of low interest rates, low inflation and expansion in the public sector. Although the number of jobs in manufacturing declined, there was almost full employment, as businessmen invested in more up-to-date equipment. Productivity increased and the UK continued to attract increasing foreign investment, suggesting that many companies were still competitive. Most people became better off, although those in the south-east of England did better than anywhere else in the UK. A major dilemma facing the government was the question of energy: it was hoped that increasing use of renewable energy – solar, wind and wave power – would provide 10 per cent of the UK energy supply by 2010. However, this soon began to look unattainable, and the government felt obliged to take the unpopular decision to invest in a new generation of nuclear power stations rather than rely too heavily on gas, much of which would have to be obtained from unreliable foreign sources, such as Russia.

▸ As in their first term, the government suffered a series of scandals and embarrassments. David Blunkett was forced to resign as Home Secretary after the media had a field day reporting his affair with a married woman who had had a child by him; there were accusations that he had also fast-tracked visa applications for her nanny. Transport Secretary Stephen Byers resigned after allegedly lying to Parliament about details of Railtrack's bankruptcy and subsequent takeover by the government. There was criticism of the Blairs themselves for taking free holidays at the expense of rich friends, who included Cliff Richard and Geoffrey Robinson.

At the half-way mark of his second term the Prime Minister was feeling the strain. In October 2003 he had been treated in hospital for a heart problem. In the spring of 2004 he was so depressed by the situation in Iraq, the row over the notorious 'dodgy dossier', the suicide of Dr David Kelly, and rumours of plots to replace him that he came close to resigning. His wife, Cherie, and some of his closest supporters persuaded him to carry on, but in October 2004 he told Andrew Marr, the BBC's political editor, that he would lead the party into the next election but would not run for a fourth term as Prime Minister.

(c) the election of 2005

Against the predictions of many of the experts, in May 2005 Labour won an historic third term with an overall majority of 65. Though it was much reduced from 2001, it was still a substantial lead and a remarkable achievement for Tony Blair and his Chancellor, Gordon Brown. The Liberal Democrats won 62 seats, a record number for them. Yet just before the election New Labour's popularity had seemed to be at a low ebb. There was no prospect of an end to Britain's involvement in Iraq, the government was beset by scandals and resignations, and the *Telegraph, Express* and *Mail* were hostile, while the *Independent* supported the Liberal Democrats. *Why did Labour win?*

- The simple fact was that, whatever the hostile commentators might say, many people had good reason to feel pleased with the government. Blair's social reform 'by stealth' had benefited huge numbers of the poorest families. Most people had a satisfactory experience of the NHS, despite the highlighting of individual bad experiences by the media. Big business was flourishing, and New Labour did not complain about city financiers paying themselves huge salaries and bonuses; there seemed no reason for the super-rich to change their allegiance.

- The Conservatives were still in a state of crisis. William Hague had resigned after the 2001 defeat and had been replaced by Iain Duncan Smith. From the beginning, he was at a disadvantage: he had been elected because of his popularity with party members, whereas only a third of Conservative MPs wanted him as leader. He did not perform well in the Commons against Tony Blair, and in 2003 was replaced as leader by the veteran former Home Secretary, Michael Howard. In the words of Kieran O'Hara, Mr Howard was 'the terrifying Home Secretary of the Major years with "something of the night" about him (Ann Widdecombe's brilliant put-down, cleverly alluding to Mr Howard's Transylvanian ancestry and sleek vampirical appearance) ... by the 2001 landslide he had apparently left front-bench politics. But like the Prince of Darkness himself, Mr Howard rose again'. He began well and relished attacking Blair in the Commons.

However, the Conservative party was still facing the problem that had defeated them in 2001: by accepting the Thatcherite model of the economy, New Labour had forced the Tories to accept the more social democratic consensus that government must invest in public services and deliver social justice. The problem for the Conservatives was that, if they criticized Labour for not providing good enough public services, it implied that they would provide better; but since, arguably, better services can only be paid for by higher taxation, it goes against their history and instincts, which are to criticize Labour tax rises. Clearly, the Conservatives were in an awkward situation, and many voters were well aware of it.

Their other problem, as Ross McKibbin wrote at the time, was that

> at the moment there are not enough Tories. The old Tory coalition of working class deferentials and a business and professional middle class which was Conservative by birth, has been destroyed, partly by social and demographic change, partly by the (unintended) consequences of Mrs Thatcher's policies. The Tory working class has gone the way of the whole industrial working class.

(d) the final years, 2005–7

Tony Blair's last two years in office were dominated by several long-running issues. It became clear that his announcement in October 2004 that he would fight only one more election had been a serious mistake. He had also said that he would serve a full third term, but there was constant speculation in the media and among his colleagues about when exactly he would step down. Assuming that Gordon Brown was to be his successor, how long would he be given to settle in before the next election? This had the effect of making Blair into a sort of 'lame duck' Prime Minister who was fast approaching his sell-by date. Yet he refused to reveal the date, and Brown became more and more impatient.

The situation in Iraq did not improve: British troops were still losing their lives and there were accusations that the War Office had provided them with less than satisfactory equipment. The Taliban again became a serious threat in Afghanistan and more British troops were sent to prop up the hard-pressed Afghan government.

Soon after the election, dramatic events took place:

› On 6 July 2005 it was announced that London had won the vote to host the 2012 Olympic Games. Many of those involved in preparing London's bid paid tribute to Tony Blair's contribution, his support and encouragement.
› The following day, as noted earlier, four young Muslim suicide bombers killed 52 people and injured 770 more on three London Underground trains and a bus. They were not members of al-Qaeda, but two of them had been to terrorist training camps in Pakistan. It was a chilling lesson for the UK that it was just as much a target for terrorists as was the USA. Understandably, the government introduced new anti-terrorist legislation (though civil rights groups and some MPs protested), and the security services went into over-drive uncovering further plots and suspects. From that point onwards the government found itself in a difficult situation, trying to balance civil liber-ties with the need to cope with the new terrorist threats. One result was that the Commons approved the introduction of ID cards (February 2006) to combat fraud and crime, and to help prevent more terrorist attacks. However, there is considerable scepticism as to whether ID cards would be effective, and it seems unlikely that they would have prevented the London bombings, since the terrorists were all British citizens. Many critics feel that ID cards would merely increase the 'Big Brother' style surveillance society.
› During Blair's final years, the question of immigration came under close scrutiny. In 2005, it was reported that immigrants intending to stay in Britain were arriving at the rate of 1,500 a day; over 1.3 million people had arrived since 1997. There were asylum seekers from Iraq, both Shia and Sunni Muslims, as well as Kurds; there were Africans, Afghans and Chinese. There were criminal gangs of Albanians and Kosovars, and gangmasters who employed immigrants as prostitutes and in jobs such as cockle-picking. The problem hit the headlines with the dreadful tragedy of nineteen Chinese cockle-pickers who were caught by the tide and drowned in Morecambe Bay.

Many of these immigrants had entered the country illegally, and immigration officers seemed unable to prevent it happening.

- There was also an influx of workers from the new member states of the EU. In 2006 it was announced that since the EU had been enlarged in 2004, around 427,000 people, mainly from Poland, had applied to work in the UK. Many thought this was excessive; some local authorities where there were concentrations of immigrants found it hard to meet the social security bill; and in some places there was an acute shortage of accommodation. An organization called Migration Watch UK was set up to campaign for a reduction in immigration. On the other hand, opponents of this view claimed that the problem was being exaggerated. It was pointed out that most of the workers from eastern Europe would return home eventually after having earned good money for a few years. In the spring of 2008 there were complaints that if immigration were to be limited, there would be labour shortages in fruit-picking areas, and in the hotel and catering industry in all parts of the UK. In the summer of 2008 there was evidence of this beginning to happen: as British economic conditions deteriorated and the Polish economy improved, many Polish workers returned home. In addition, the problem of immigration was partly offset by the fact that around 60,000 British people emigrated every year, mainly to Australia, the USA, France and Spain, reducing the net immigration total by around a third.

- The problem of pension funds, which had been building up for several years, reached crisis proportions in 2006. The trouble stemmed from the beginning of the Blair years, when tax credits for share dividends were removed (see Section 36.2(c)). This resulted in a reduction in the value of company retirement pensions funds of £100 billion by 2006. Pensioners and workers close to retirement who had been looking forward to a comfortable pension were devastated to learn that there were great black holes in their employers' pension funds. The government, especially Gordon Brown, who had removed tax credits in the first place, was blamed, although it was not entirely his fault. In fact, many companies, in the 'good' years, had chosen to have pension 'holidays'– in other words they had not made their own contribution to their employees' pension schemes.

- On the brighter side, Blair and Brown did their best to press on with their agenda against world poverty. In 2004 they had started the Commission for Africa, which aimed to persuade the world's wealthiest states to support debt relief, in the hope that the cash would be used to pay for vital reforms. The campaign entitled 'Make Poverty History' began to take off, and Bob Geldof, who had led the successful Live Aid campaign in 1985, joined the Commission for Africa. He gathered a team of rock stars and other celebrities to lobby the representatives of the world's richest countries, who were meeting at the G8 summit at Gleneagles in Scotland. They staged a huge march of over 200,000 people through Edinburgh demanding debt cancellation for Africa's poorest countries. Soon afterwards, an agreement was signed cancelling the debts of eighteen countries and promising aid, amounting to a total of £28.8 billion.

> There was more embarrassment for the government in November 2005 when David Blunkett had to resign for the second time (this time as Work and Pensions Secretary), having failed to disclose that he had bought shares in a DNA testing company. But that was nothing compared with what was to follow. In March 2006, Scotland Yard announced that it was to investigate allegations that political parties had been accepting loans in return for seats in the House of Lords. Lord Levy, described as Blair's personal fundraiser, was arrested and questioned by police, but later released. Tony Blair himself was later questioned – the first serving Prime Minister to be interviewed by police in a criminal investigation. This was the most damaging of the various sleaze incidents that had occurred throughout his premiership; though no charges were brought against anybody, it all added to the general distrust of politicians. The year 2006 was a difficult one all round, and even members of his own party were growing tired of Blair. The May local elections were disappointing for Labour, and Blair reacted by sacking the Home Secretary, Charles Clarke, who refused to go quietly and caused further embarrassment. Then Jack Straw, the Foreign Secretary, was demoted, and the Deputy Prime Minister, John Prescott, who had also been involved in a scandal, had his role reduced so much that it became little more than a token position.

(e) Blair and Brown

By late summer 2006 the situation had reached the point where Blair was isolated from much of his party. He had fallen out with almost all his original supporters and the Brown camp felt that the time had come to launch their attack on Blair. One of the tragedies of the Blair years was the steadily deteriorating relationship between the two men. During their early years in Parliament in the 1980s they had been good friends; they were both first elected in 1983 and their approach to political and social issues was much influenced by their Christian faith. In those days, Brown was the senior partner, but after the 1992 defeat, Blair, easily the more charismatic of the two, began to overtake Brown in popularity. Then came the notorious deal (see Section 36.1(d)) in which Brown stood back, allowing Blair to be elected leader. What exactly was agreed about a handover of power from Blair to Brown is still a mystery. Some commentators believe that it would have been better for Blair if he had encouraged Brown to stand against him in the leadership election, so allowing the most popular candidate to win. It is pretty certain that Blair would have been chosen, and then Brown's hold over him would have been much less when they got into government. Together they made an extremely powerful dual leadership. In the words of Andrew Rawnsley, 'they were the rock on which New Labour was built and the rock on

Illus. **36.1 Tony Blair and Gordon Brown at the 2006 Labour Party Conference**

which it so often threatened to break apart. When they were working together their complementary talents made the government pretty much unstoppable. When they were warring with each other, it terrified the cabinet, horrified their party, astounded civil servants, obsessed the media and poisoned the government into paralysis.' The bad times became more frequent and their disagreements more fundamental. Blair always wanted to tax less and spend more than Brown thought wise. Blair wanted Britain to join the European single currency, but Brown thought it would be a great mistake; however, Brown got his way. Brown had no time for Blair's obsession with providing more consumer choice in public services.

Above all, Brown became increasingly impatient with Blair's obvious determination to stay in power as long as possible; by the summer of 2006, Brown was convinced that Blair was trying to hang on until an alternative candidate for the succession emerged. Some Labour MPs were already calling for Blair to step down, and an open letter circulated supporting this demand. Most people assumed that it was the work of the Brown camp, though this was never proved. Brown hoped to manoeuvre Blair into publicly naming the day of his retirement, since promises made in private had proved useless. Feelings were running high, and eventually, in September 2006, Blair announced that he would stand down within the next year. In the event he stayed on until 27 June 2007, thus becoming one of a special group of politicians who have been Prime Minister for ten years or more. It was fitting that he stayed long enough to see the peace process come to fruition in Northern Ireland (see Section 32.1(l)), and to receive applause in the House of Commons for the crucial role he played in the process. It was fitting too that, while there was talk of a leadership contest, nobody was willing to stand against Brown, who therefore became Prime Minister in due course.

Like Margaret Thatcher, Tony Blair had the distinction of winning three consecutive general elections, and like her, he was responsible for some important changes and for some developments that had unfortunate consequences.

▸ Blair and his New Labour colleagues moved the old Labour party from the left into the centre, and in some ways beyond that towards the right. Will Hutton argues that, in this respect, Blair was

> as important to the Labour party as Disraeli and Macmillan have been to the Tory party. They were politicians of the right who set out to appeal to the centre not as a political tactic, but because the values of the centre sat where they wanted to be, and so they invented liberal conservatism. Blair has made the same choice. He wants to associate his party with the values of the British centre … . Blair has invented a new strain of British politics – liberal Labour … and this has won three general elections.

Consequently, the Conservative leader, David Cameron, is copying Blair by trying to revive the almost extinct liberal Conservative tradition, thereby recapturing the centre ground from liberal Labour. In this way, Blair has manoeuvred Cameron into accepting that government has a responsibility to invest in public services.

On the other hand, critics point out that Blair won three elections through a systematic betrayal of the ideals on which the Labour party was founded. Ross McKibbin argues that the party's modernization had gone far enough with the Smith reforms: 'It was perfectly viable politically and electorally and there is little doubt that it would have won the 1997 election under Smith's leadership.'

▸ Perhaps the most impressive of Blair's achievements was that, by 2007, peace had been secured in Northern Ireland. For ten years he had persevered and refused to give up in his efforts to bring the most polarized parties in the province together. And in large measure because of his persistence, the hitherto inconceivable happened (see Section 32.1(l)).

▸ In many ways, the UK became a more modern, liberal and progressive country. There were more women and non-white people in Parliament than ever before. Though there were still instances of inter-racial tensions and violence, on the whole there was a greater racial tolerance than might have been expected, given the amount of immigration and terrorist threats. The police became subject to racial equality laws and more people from the ethnic minorities joined the police. Gay and lesbian people were given more equal rights, including having their partnerships acknowledged by law. On the other hand, circumstances – 9/11 and the London bombings of 2005 – forced the government to curtail some civil liberties in the struggle to control terrorism. For example, it led them, or gave them the excuse, to contemplate the introduction of ID cards.

» There were basic changes in the constitution, the most striking being the creation of the Scottish and Welsh assemblies, which by 2007 were so well-established that even the Conservatives dropped their opposition to them. It seems inconceivable that any future government would try to abolish them. There were important changes to the House of Lords. The Lord Chancellor, who had acted as a sort of chairman, the equivalent of the Speaker of the House of Commons, was replaced by an elected Speaker. As the first stage of what was meant to be a thorough-going reform of the House of Lords, all the hereditary peers (apart from the ninety-two noted earlier) were excluded, and their places were filled by suitable people nominated by the political parties. But what should be the next step? To the bitter disappointment of left-wingers who wanted a totally elected upper house, the party failed to agree on a scheme acceptable to the majority. Should all the members be elected, or should they all be nominated, or should there be a mixture? Blair seemed to be satisfied with the status quo, and in 2004 the whole idea was dropped, leaving the Lords with a huge Conservative majority.

» The government's economic policies – to the great credit of Gordon Brown – were on the whole an outstanding success. There was low inflation, low interest rates and low unemployment. Standing at around 2 million in 1997, unemployment was around 1.7 million ten years later. The country enjoyed the longest period of sustained growth in modern times, and the vast majority of people were better off. The downside was that the great consumer boom encouraged spending and borrowing; and without doubt, credit was made far too readily available. Simon Lee gives some startling statistics: by the end of November 2007, mortgage borrowing stood at £1.4 trillion; £213 billion was owed in consumer credit, including £54.9 billion on credit cards. Personal debt had rocketed to the point where the average household in the UK owed 160 per cent of its disposable income; the average household debt stood at £56,000, of which more than £47,000 were mortgage payments. Some commentators had been predicting for months that this situation could not continue indefinitely and would peak sooner or later, with dire consequences for some.

Unfortunately for Brown, this point was reached during his first year as Prime Minister, and by the end of 2008 the country was on the brink of a major recession. Many banks and building societies in the UK had taken risks in two directions. First, they had indulged in too much sub-prime lending – that is, lending to people who might well be unable to keep up their repayments. Second, they had introduced the practice of buying up parcels of debt from other lenders, including some banks in the USA; unfortunately, some of these parcels of debt were of doubtful security. When the US economy ran into problems, there was a rise in unemployment, causing many people to default on their repayments. The effects of this were felt eventually in the UK, and the crisis point came when the Northern Rock bank, arguably the bank that had taken the most risks, found itself in difficulties and had to apply to the Bank of England for a loan. This caused a rush of depositors withdrawing their cash in case the bank collapsed, which only worsened the situation. In the end, in February 2008, the government virtually nationalized Northern Rock. Other banks and building societies took fright and reduced their lending drastically, both to each other and to people seeking mortgages, so that it then became difficult to obtain a mortgage. House prices fell rapidly, loans of all types were hard to come by, and by the middle of 2008 the UK was experiencing a severe 'credit crunch'. . Unable to obtain credit, many businesses were forced to retrench, and unemployment figures began to rise.

Some of Gordon Brown's policies as Chancellor from 1997 until 2007 were now seriously being called into question. For example, he was blamed for failing to tighten up the financial regulatory system which, some critics claimed, continued to give the banks too much freedom. However, worse was to come; the government could claim that it was all part of a global financial crisis, and indeed, astonishing events were taking place in the USA. In September 2008, Lehman Brothers bank collapsed with debts of over US$600 billion, and many other leading American banks were in difficulties. In an unprecedented move, the Bush Administration provided a US$700 billion rescue package to try to restore confidence in the banking system. In Britain, HBOS (Halifax Bank of Scotland) was in severe difficulties: its shares lost almost half their value in a week, and Lloyds TSB agreed a £12 billion takeover. Brown promised that the government would 'do whatever it takes to ensure the stability of the UK financial system'. Bradford and Bingley, which seemed to be on the verge of collapse, was nationalized, and in October 2008 the government announced a £500 million rescue package for the troubled banks. Confidence in the system took a further blow when the Icelandic Landsbank failed, leaving thousands of British savers, attracted by its high interest rates, in danger of losing their investments. At the end of October 2008, official figures showed that, between July and September, the British economy had contracted for the first time in sixteen years. This caused further share price falls on the stock market and sent the pound plunging in value from around US$2 in July to US$1.53 by the end of October. Opposition politicians were soon predicting that the UK was 'on the edge of a new winter of discontent'. As job losses mounted during the early weeks of 2009, there could be little doubt that they were right.

But at the time of Blair's departure in June 2007, all this was in the future. While a few commentators and economists had been warning of dire consequences unless the banks began to show more prudence, most people, including leading bankers themselves, expected the good times to continue

- New Labour prosperity made possible what was arguably the largest increase in spending on public services in British history. The NHS and education benefited; there were pension increases; Sure Start nurseries were introduced and there was a reduction in child poverty; employee rights were increased; and, of course, the minimum wage was introduced. And in the words of Polly Toynbee, 'all this was done in the face of a mainly hostile, 75 per cent right wing British media that grew more indignant with every successive Conservative defeat'.
- In the realm of foreign affairs, Blair has to be adjudged mainly a failure. His supporters highlight the fact that Britain's overseas aid budget has more than doubled since 1997, and at the Gleneagles summit in 2005 focusing on Africa, great progress was made in debt cancellation and in securing a steady increase in global aid. But one of Blair's visions was of a united West consisting of Britain, the USA, the EU and NATO. According to Will Hutton,

> Blair believes in the West of the Christian Enlightenment. Any global initiative, whether it's action against climate change or the fight against terror, requires the West to stand collectively together, even when the US is wrong. It is why he is simultaneously pro-European and pro-American; he sees Britain's responsibility to be in the inner councils of both Washington and Brussels'.

He thought he could act as a bridge linking the USA and the leading members of the EU, particularly France and Germany. When he decided to join Bush in the attack on Iraq, he fully expected that he would be able to persuade Jacques Chirac and Gerhard Schroeder to bring France and Germany, respectively, into the coalition. When they refused to support the removal of Saddam, the bridge was on the point of collapse.

If the Iraq gamble had been completed swiftly instead of developing into a long-running disaster, all might still have been well. But the tragedy of Iraq was that it discredited Blair's whole concept of liberal interventionism by the West in support of peoples suffering at the hands of despotism. In the words of Polly Toynbee,

> he leaves a nation more alienated from Europe, more Eurosceptic than he found it. His strange alliance with Bush leaves Britain more anti-American and in that fatal bond, more disliked across the globe: the good done in Sierra Leone or Kosovo was forgotten in Baghdad. He leaves a country both more isolated and more isolationist'.

Not everybody agrees with this verdict. Andrew Roberts argues that Blair deserves praise for the way in which, 'after 9/11 he stuck to the war on terror and had the guts to support America when America most needed it'. Roberts believes that British and American policy was vindicated in December 2005, when over 10 million Iraqis voted in their general election with a 70 per cent turnout – far higher than in most Western countries – and despite all the threats to deter them.

> This showed that democracy is as popular a concept in the Middle East as it is rare. Far from being an aberration, the foreign policy pursued by the USA, Great Britain, Australia and other countries of the English-speaking peoples since 9/11 derives from the mainstream of their historical tradition … It's been a breath of fresh air to see Labour stick up for freedom around the world, as Blair has.

› One of the most striking developments of New Labour's years in power was the way in which the party that once favoured nationalization of the 'commanding heights' of the economy now accepted the belief that the private sector was superior in almost every way to the public sector. Hence the proliferation of PFI projects and other forms of privatization. These have proved extremely controversial, especially after several high-level failures, including Railtrack, the London Underground and hospital cleaning services, which in many cases led to inefficiency and the consequent spread of bacterial infections such as MRSA. Apart from PFIs being 'just an ingenious way of wasting money' (Ross McKibbin), privatized services often sacrifice efficiency in order to maximize profits.

› One of the most disappointing aspects of the Blair years was the way in which the government gained a reputation for 'spin' and sleaze. The main 'spin doctors' included Alistair Campbell (Blair's press secretary), Peter Mandelson and Lance Price. No doubt as a reaction to the earlier hostile treatment of Labour by most of the press, they developed 'spin' originally in self-defence. It involved starting rumours, often false, to divert attention away from unpleasant realities; twisting statistics; and telling downright lies. As the scandals and sleaze began to emerge, the cover-up attempts and the spin became more desperate. It all went too far and in the end many people simply stopped believing the information put out by No. 10. The government's reputation, and that of politics and politicians in general, suffered considerably.

› There seems to be general agreement among commentators that the government was weakened by the rivalry between Blair and Brown. Both camps of supporters wasted too much energy pursuing the rivalry instead of pursuing good government. Their disagreements over public services meant that their actual achievements were less than they might have been. Andrew Rawnsley, who was able to observe both men closely, believes that 'they needed each other. Neither would probably have done as much alone as they did together. The shame is that two such towering political talents might have accomplished yet more had they spent more time firing together and less time firing at each other'.

The final word on Blair? Will Hutton sums him up neatly:

> He could have done so much more and did not need to make the Iraq mistake. But what he did is still substantial. A good man; a great politician. He left his country in better shape than when he found it and established a new political system. He will be a tough act to follow.

QUESTIONS

1 Describe the changes that the Labour Party experienced in its policies and leadership between 1983 and 1997. Why did New Labour win such a dramatic victory in the 1997 general election?

2 Assess the similarities and differences between New Labour and Thatcherism during Tony Blair's first term as Prime Minister, 1997–2001.

3 Explain why and how New Labour succeeded in retaining its popularity during its first term in office.

A document question about the policies and legacy of Tony Blair can be found on the accompanying website www.palgrave.com/masterseries/lowe1.

further reading

general

Highly recommended, especially for 'AS' and 'A2' level students, are the *Modern History Review* and *20th Century History Review,* each published four times during the academic year by Philip Allan, Market Place, Deddington, Oxfordshire. Some of the most useful articles are mentioned under the appropriate chapter headings.

Statistics of general election results, population, wages and prices, and trade union membership, unless otherwise stated, are taken from Chris Cook and John Stevenson, *Handbook of Modern British History 1714–1987* (Longman, 1988).

Bernstein, G. L., *The Myth of Decline. The Rise of Britain Since 1945* (Pimlico, 2004).

Black, J., *Modern British History since 1900* (Macmillan, 2000).

Black, J. & Macraild, D.M., *Nineteenth Century Britain* (Palgrave, 2003).

Blake, R., *The Conservative Party from Peel to Thatcher* (Fontana, 1985).

Chamberlain, M.E., *Pax Britannica? British Foreign Policy 1789–1914* (Longman, 1988).

Charmley, J., *A History of Conservative Politics 1900–1996* (Macmillan, 1996).

Childs, D., *Britain Since 1939 – Progress and Decline* (Macmillan, 1995).

Clarke, P. F., *Hope and Glory – Britain 1900–1990* (Allen Lane/Penguin, 1996).

Douglas, R., *A History of the Liberal and Liberal Democratic Parties* (Hambledon Continuum, 2005).

Hennessy, P., *The Prime Minister – The Office and its Holders Since 1945* (Allen Lane, 2000).

Marquand, D., *Britain Since 1918: The Strange Career of British Democracy* (Weidenfeld, 2008).

Marr, A., *A History of Modern Britain* (Pan/Macmillan, 2007).

Marwick, A., *British Society Since 1945* (Penguin, 2nd edn, 1990).

McCord, N., *British History 1815–1906* (Oxford, 1992).

Morgan, K. O., *The People's Peace: British History 1945–1990* (Oxford, 1992).

Peden, G. C., *British Economic and Social Policy: Lloyd George to Margaret Thatcher* (Philip Allan, 1985).

Pollard, S., *The Development of the British Economy, 1914–1990* (Arnold, 4th edn, 1992).

Pugh, M., *State and Society: A Social and Political History of Britain since 1870* (Arnold, 2008).

Robbins, K., *Britain and Europe 1789–2005* (Hodder Arnold, 2005).

Roberts, A., *A History of the English-Speaking Peoples Since 1900* (Weidenfeld & Nicolson, 2006).

Royle, E., *Modern Britain: A Social History 1750–1985* (Longman, 1988).

Sked, A. and Cook, C., *Post-War Britain: A Political History* (Penguin, 1993 edn).

Stevenson, J., *British Society 1914–45* (Penguin, 1984).

Taylor, A. J. P., *English History 1914–45* (Oxford, 1965).

Thompson, F. M. L. (ed.). *The Cambridge Social History of Britain 1750–1950, vols 1–3* (Cambridge, 1993).

Wilson, A. N., *The Victorians* (Hutchinson/Arrow, 2002).

Wilson, A. N., *After the Victorians 1901–1953* (Hutchinson, 2005).

Wilson, A.N., *Our Times: The Age of Elizabeth II* (Hutchinson, 2008).

chapter 2 Britain under the Tories, 1815–30

Beales, Derek, *From Castlereagh to Gladstone, 1815–55* (Nelson, 1969).

Belchem, J., *'Orator' Hunt: Henry Hunt and English Working Class Radicalism* (Oxford University Press, 1985).

Brasher, N. H., *Arguments in History – Britain in the Nineteenth Century* (Macmillan, 1968).

Chambers, J. D. and Mingay, G. E., *The Agricultural Revolution 1750–1850* (Batsford, 1966; reprinted 1982).

Cookson, J. E., *Lord Liverpool's Administration, 1815–22* (Scottish Academic Press, 1975).

Dinwiddy, J. R., *From Luddism to the First Reform Bill* (Blackwell, 1986).

Evans, E. J., *Britain before the Reform Act: Politics and Society 1815–1832* (Longman, 1989).

Evans, E. J., 'The Premiership of Lord Liverpool', *Modern History Review*, April 1990.

Gash, N., *Aristocracy and People: Britain 1815–1865* (Arnold, 1979).

Gash, N., *Lord Liverpool* (Weidenfeld & Nicolson, 1984).

Goodlad, G., '"Liberal" and "High" Tories in the Age of Liverpool', *Modern History Review*, November 1995.

Goodlad, G. 'Liberal Toryism', *Modern History Review*, November 2002.

Hargreaves, J. A., 'Luddism', *Modern History Review*, September 1995.

Harling, P., *The Waning of 'Old Corruption': The Politics of Economical Reform in Britain 1779–1846* (Oxford University Press, 1996).

Hilton, B., *Corn, Cash and Commerce – The Economic Policies of the Tory Governments, 1815–30* (Oxford University Press, 1977).

Hilton, B., *A Mad, Bad, and Dangerous People? England 1783–1846* (Oxford University Press, 2006).

Hinde, W., *George Canning* (Collins, 1973).

Hinde, W., *Catholic Emancipation: A Shake to Men's Minds* (Blackwell, 1992).

Hurd, D., *Robert Peel* (Weidenfeld & Nicolson, 2007).

Jupp, P., *British Politics on the Eve of Reform: The Duke of Wellington's Administration, 1828–30* (Macmillan, 1998).

Longford, E., *Wellington, Pillar of State* (Weidenfeld & Nicolson, 1972).

Parry, J., *The Rise and Fall of Liberal Government in Victorian Britain* (Yale University Press, 1996).

Plowright, J., *Regency England: The Age of Lord Liverpool* (Routledge, 1996).

Reid, R., *The Peterloo Massacre* (Heinemann, 1989).

Revill, P., *The Age of Lord Liverpool* (Blackie, 1979).

Thompson, E. P., *The Making of the English Working Class* (Gollancz, 1963; Penguin, 1980).

Turner, M. J., *The Age of Unease: Government and Reform in Britain 1782–1832* (Sutton, 2000).

White, R. J., *From Waterloo to Peterloo* (Mercury, 1963).

chapter 3 foreign affairs, 1815–30

Chamberlain, M. E., *Pax Britannica? British Foreign Policy, 1789–1914* (Longman, 1988).

Chapman, T., 'A Just Equilibrium? The Congress of Vienna', *Modern History Review*, September 1996.

Derry, J. W., *Castlereagh* (Allen Lane, 1976).

Dixon, P., *Canning: Politician and Statesman* (Weidenfeld &Nicolson, 1976).

Robbins, K., *Britain and Europe 1789–2005* (Hodder Arnold, 2005).

Ward, D. R., *Foreign Affairs, 1815–1865* (Collins, 1972).

chapter 4 Parliament and the Great Reform Act of 1832

Brock, M. G., *The Great Reform Act* (Hutchinson, 1973).

Derry, J. W., *Charles, Earl Grey* (Blackwell, 1992).

Evans, E., *The Great Reform Act of 1832* (Routledge, 1983).

Goodlad, G. D., *Peel* (Collins, 2005).

Hamburger, J., *James Mill and the Art of Revolution* (Yale University Press, 1963).

Hobsbawm, E. J. and Rudé, G., *Captain Swing* (Lawrence & Wishart, 1969).

Hurd, D., *Robert Peel* (Weidenfeld & Nicolson, 2007).

Lang, S., *Parliamentary Reform 1785–1928* (Routledge, 1999).

Pearce, E., *Reform! The Fight for the 1832 Reform Act* (Jonathan Cape, 2003).

Phillips, J. A., *The Great Reform Bill in the Boroughs* (Clarendon Press, 1992).

Smith, E. A., *Lord Grey* (Oxford University Press, 1990).

Thompson, E. P., *The Making of the English Working Class* (Gollancz, 1963; Penguin, 1980).

Turner, M. J., *The Age of Unease: Government and Reform in Britain 1782–1932* (Sutton, 2000).

Wright, D. G., *Democracy and Reform* (Longman, 1970).

chapter 5 Whig reforms and failures, 1833–41

Brundage, A., *The Making of the New Poor Law, 1832–39* (Hutchinson, 1978).

Cecil, D., *Melbourne* (Constable, 1954).

Finlayson, G. B. A. M., *England in the 1830s* (Arnold, 1969).

Hague, W., *William Wilberforce* (HarperCollins, 2008).

Hilton, B., *A Mad, Bad and Dangerous People? England 1783–1846* (Oxford University Press, 2006).

Jenkins, T. A., *The Liberal Ascendancy 1830–1886* (Macmillan, 1994).

Longmate, N., *The Workhouse* (Temple Smith, 1974).

Mandler, P., 'The New Poor Law', *Modern History Review*, November 1993.

Rose, M. E., *The Relief of Poverty, 1834–1914* (Macmillan, 1972).

Watson, R., *Edwin Chadwick, Poor Law and Public Health* (Longman, 1969).

chapter 6 Chartism

Behagg, C., 'Taking Chartism Seriously', *Modern History Review*, April 1996.

Briggs, A. (ed.), *Chartist Studies* (Macmillan, 1969).

Brown, R., *Chartism* (Cambridge University Press, 1998).

Cole, G. D. H., *Chartist Portraits* (Macmillan, 1965).

Cunningham, H., 'The Nature of Chartism', *Modern History Review*, April 1990.

Jones, D., *Chartism and the Chartists* (Allen Lane, 1975).

Read, D. and Glasgow, E. L., *Feargus O'Connor* (Arnold, 1961).

Royle, E., *Chartism* (Longman, 3rd edn, 1996).

Taylor, M., *Ernest Jones, Chartism and the Romance of Politics 1819–69* (Oxford University Press, 2003).

Thompson, D., *The Chartists* (Temple Smith, 1984).

Walton, J. K., *Chartism* (Routledge, 1999).

Walton, J. K., 'What Did the Chartists Achieve?', *Modern History Review*, September 2001.

chapter 7 Sir Robert Peel, the Conservatives and the Corn Laws, 1830–46

Adelman, P., *Peel and the Conservative Party 1830–50* (Longman, 1989).

Blake, R., *The Conservative Party from Peel to Thatcher* (Fontana, 1985 edn).

Evans, E., *Sir Robert Peel* (Routledge, 1991).

Foster, R., 'Peel and his Party', *Modern History Review*, September 1993.

Gash, N., *Sir Robert Peel* (Longman, 1976).

Gash, N., 'Sir Robert Peel and the Conservative Party', *Modern History Review*, February 1990.

Goodlad, G., 'The Making of the Conservative Party', *Modern History Review*, September 2003.

Goodlad, G., *Peel* (Collins, 2005).

Grinter, R., *Disraeli and Conservatism* (Arnold, 1968).

Hilton, B., *A Mad, Bad, and Dangerous People? England 1783–1846* (Oxford University Press, 2006).

Hinde, W., *Richard Cobden: A Victorian Outsider* (Yale University Press, 1987).

Hurd, D., *Robert Peel* (Weidenfeld & Nicolson, 2007).

Jenkins, T. A., *Sir Robert Peel* (Macmillan, 1999).

Jenkins, T. A., 'Wellington, Toryism and the Nation', *History Today*, November 2002.

Kitson Clark, G., *Peel* (Duckworth, 1936).

McCord, N., *The Anti-Corn Law League* (Allen & Unwin, 1958).

Pickering, P. A. and Tyrrell, A., *The People's Bread: A History of the Anti-Corn Law League* (Continuum/Leicester University Press, 2001).

Randell, K. H., *Politics and the People 1835–1850* (Collins 1972).

Read, D., *Cobden and Bright* (Arnold, 1967).

chapter 8 domestic affairs 1846–67: Russell, Gladstone, Disraeli and the Reform Act of 1867

Blake, R., *Disraeli* (Eyre & Spottiswoode, 1966; Methuen, 1969).

Briggs, A., *Victorian People* (Penguin, 1965).

Cowling, M., *Disraeli, Gladstone and Revolution* (Cambridge, 1967).

Gash, N., 'The Peelites after Peel', *Modern History Review*, February 1994.

Hoppen, K. T., *The Mid-Victorian Generation 1846–1886* (Oxford University Press, 1998).

Jenkins, R., *Gladstone* (Macmillan, 1995).

Jenkins, T. A., *Disraeli and Victorian Conservatism* (Macmillan, 1996).

Kinealy, C., *This Great Calamity: The Irish Famine 1845–52* (Gill and Macmillan, 1994).

Kinealy, C., 'The Famine 1845–52: How England Failed Ireland', *Modern History Review*, September 1995.

Magnus, P., *Gladstone* (John Murray, 1963).

Shannon, R., *Gladstone: Peel's Inheritor 1809–1865* (Allen Lane/Penguin, 1982).

Shannon, R., *Gladstone: Heroic Minister 1865–1898* (Allen Lane/Penguin, 1999).

Smith, F. B., *The Making of the Second Reform Bill* (Cambridge, 1966).

Vincent, J., *Disraeli* (Oxford University Press, 1990).

Walton, J. K., *The Second Reform Act* (Methuen, 1987).

chapter 9 Lord Palmerston and foreign affairs, 1830–65

Chamberlain, M. E., *Lord Palmerston* (University of Wales Press, 1987).

Chamberlain, M. E., *Pax Britannica? British Foreign Policy 1789–1914* (Longman, 1988).

Chambers, J., *Palmerston – The People's Darling* (John Murray, 2004).

Goodlad, G., 'With Generous Sympathies and Hearty English Pluck', *Modern History Review*, September 1996.

Hoppen, K. T., *The Mid-Victorian Generation 1846–1886* (Oxford University Press, 1998).

Jenkins, T. A., *The Liberal Ascendancy 1830–1886* (Macmillan, 1994).

Ridley, J., *Lord Palmerston* (Constable, 1970).

Robbins, K., *Britain and Europe 1789–2005* (Hodder Arnold, 2005).

Smith, P., 'Ginger Beer or Champagne? Palmerston as Prime Minister', in Catterall, P. (ed.), *Britain 1815–1867* (Heinemann, 1994).

Southgate, D. G., *The Most English Minister: Policies and Politics of Palmerston* (Macmillan, 1966).

Steele, E. D., *Palmerston and Liberalism 1855–65* (Cambridge, 1991).

Taylor, A. J. P., *The Struggle for Mastery in Europe* (Oxford, 1954; paperback 1971).

Ward, D. R., *Foreign Affairs, 1815–1865* (Collins, 1972).

chapter 10 the Crimean War, 1854–6

Anderson, M. S., *The Eastern Question* (Macmillan, 1966).

Bostridge, M., *Florence Nightingale: The Woman and her Legend* (Viking, 2008)

Briggs, A., *The Age of Improvement 1783–1867* (Longman, 1971 edition).

Grant, S.-M., 'New Light on the Lady with the Lamp', *History Today*, September 2002.

Hibbert, C., *The Destruction of Lord Raglan* (Penguin, 1963).

Lambert, A., *The Crimean War: British Grand Strategy Against Russia, 1853–56* (Manchester University Press, 1990).

Lambert, A., 'The Crimean War: An Historical Illusion?', *Modern History Review*, November 1991.

Taylor, A. J. P., *The Struggle for Mastery in Europe* (Oxford, 1971), chs 3, 4 and 5.

Thomas, D., *Charge! Hurrah! Hurrah! A Life of Cardigan of Balaclava* (Routledge, 1974; Futura, 1976).

Woodham-Smith, C., *The Reason Why* (Constable, 1953).

chapter 11 Britain, India and the Mutiny of 1857

Chakravarty, G., *The Indian Mutiny and the British Imagination* (Cambridge University Press, 2005).

Dalrymple, W., *The Last Mughal: The Fall of a Dynasty, Delhi, 1857* (Bloomsbury, 2006).

David, S., *The Indian Mutiny 1857* (Penguin, 2002).

Edwardes, M., *British India* (Sidgwick & Jackson, 1967).

Farwell, B., *Queen Victoria's Little Wars* (Allen Lane, 1973).

Harris, J., *The Indian Mutiny* (Hart Davis MacGibbon, 1973).

Porter, B., *The Lion's Share: A Short History of British Imperialism 1850–1970* (Longman, 1975).

Spear, P., *A History of India* (Penguin, 1965).

Woodruff, P., *The Men who Ruled India* (Cape, 1953).

chapter 12 standards of living and social reform: factories, mines, public health, education, leisure, religion

Abbott, B.H., *Gladstone and Disraeli* (Collins, 1972)

Battiscombe, G., *Shaftesbury* (Constable, 1974).

Briggs, A., *Victorian Cities* (Penguin, 1963).

Chesney, K., *The Victorian Underworld* (Temple Smith, 1970).

Evans, E. J., *The Forging of the Modern State, 1783–1870* (Longman, 3rd edn, 2001).

Finer, S. E., *The Life and Times of Sir Edwin Chadwick* (Methuen, 1952).

Fraser, D., *The Evolution of the British Welfare State* (Macmillan, 1973).

Hattersley, R., *Blood and Fire – William and Catherine Booth and Their Salvation Army* (Little, Brown, 1999).

Hilton, B, *A Mad, Bad and Dangerous People? England 1783–1846* (Oxford, 2006).

Hoppen, K. T., *The Mid-Victorian Generation, 1846–1886* (Oxford, 1998).

Longmate, N., *King Cholera* (Hamish Hamilton, 1966).

McDonald, L., 'Florence Nightingale as Social Reformer', *History Today,* January 2006.

Musgrave, P. W., *Society and Education since 1800* (Methuen, 1968).

Royle, E., *Modern Britain: A Social History 1750–1985* (Arnold, 1988).

Thompson, E. P., *The Making of the English Working Class* (Gollancz, 1963; Penguin, 1980).

Thompson, F. M. L. (ed.), *The Cambridge Social History of Britain 1750–1950, Vols 1–3* (Cambridge University Press, 1993).

Waller, P. J., *Town, City and Nation. England 1850–1914* (Oxford, 1983).

Walvin, J., *English Urban Life, 1776–1851* (Hutchinson, 1984).

Wardle, D., *English Popular Education 1780–1970* (Cambridge, 1970).

Watson, R., *Edwin Chadwick, Poor Law and Public Health* (Longman, 1969).

Worrall, B. G., *The Making of the Modern Church* (SPCK, 1993 edn).

chapter 13 Gladstone's first ministry, 1868–74

Abbott, B. H., *Gladstone and Disraeli* (Collins, 1972).

Adelman, P., 'Gladstone and Liberalism', *Modern History Review,* February 1991.

Bebbington, D., *The Mind of Gladstone: Religion, Homer and Politics* (Oxford, 2004).

Biagini, E. F., *Liberty, Retrenchment and Reform: Popular Liberalism in the Age of Gladstone, 1860–1880* (Cambridge, 1992).

Chamberlain, M. E., *Pax Britannica? British Foreign Policy 1789–1914* (Longman, 1988).

Cooke, A. B. and Vincent, J., *The Governing Passion: Cabinet Government and Party Politics in Britain, 1885–86* (Harvester Press, 1974).

Feuchtwanger, E. J., *Gladstone* (Allen Lane, 2nd edn,1989).

Feuchtwanger, E.J., 'Gladstone's Irish Policy: Expediency or High Principle?', *Modern History 'Review,* November 1991.

Foot, M. R. D. (ed.), *The Gladstone Diaries* (Oxford, 1968).

Goodlad, D. G., 'Gladstone and the People: Radical or Reactionary?', *Modern History Review,* November, 1999.

Jenkins, R., *Gladstone* (Macmillan, 1996 edn).

Jenkins, T. A., *Gladstone, Whiggery and the Liberal Party, 1874–1886* (Oxford, 1988).

Jenkins, T. A., *The Liberal Ascendancy, 1830–1886* (Macmillan, 1994).

Jenkins, T. A., 'The Nonconformist Anglican', *Modern History Review,* November 1996.

Lyons, F. S. L., *Ireland Since the Famine* (Fontana, 1974).

Magnus, P., *Gladstone* (John Murray, 1963 edn).

Matthew, H. C. G., *Gladstone, 1809–1874* (Oxford, 1986).

Parry, J., *The Rise and Fall of Liberal Government in Victorian Britain* (Yale, 1993).

Shannon, R. T., *Gladstone: Heroic Minister, 1865–1898* (Allen Lane/Penguin, 1999).

Winstanley, M., *Gladstone and the Liberal Party* (Routledge, 1990).

chapter 14 Disraeli and the Conservatives in power, 1874–80

Abbott, B. H., *Gladstone and Disraeli* (Collins, 1972).

Adelman, P., *Gladstone, Disraeli and later Victorian Politics* (Longman, 1970).

Beloff, M., 'The British Empire', *History Today*, February 1996.

Blake, R., *Disraeli* (Eyre & Spottiswoode, 1966; Methuen, 1969).

Blake, R., *The Conservative Party from Peel to Thatcher* (Fontana, 1985 edn).

Blake, R., 'Disraeli – Political Outsider', *Modern History Review*, November 1989.

Farwell, B., *Queen Victoria's Little Wars* (Allen Lane, 1973).

Ferguson, N., *Empire: How Britain Made the Modern World* (Penguin, 2004).

Feuchtwanger, E., *Disraeli* (Arnold, 2000).

Grinter, R., *Disraeli and Conservatism* (Arnold, 1968).

Hobsbawm, E., *The Age of Empire 1875–1914* (Weidenfeld & Nicolson, 1987).

Jenkins, T. A., *Disraeli and Victorian Conservatism* (Macmillan, 1996).

Jenkins, T. A., 'Disraeli and the Art of Opposition', *Modern History Review*, February 1997.

Macfie, A. L., *The Eastern Question* (Longman, 1996 edn).

Porter, B., *The Lion's Share: A Short History of British Imperialism 1850–1970* (Longman, 1975).

St. John., I., 'Disraeli and Social Reform, 1874–80', *Modern History Review*, November 2004.

Shannon, R., *Gladstone and the Bulgarian Agitation, 1876* (Nelson, 1963).

Shannon, R., *The Age of Disraeli, 1868–1881* (Longman, 1992).

Smith, P., *Disraelian Conservatism* (Routledge & Kegan Paul, 1967).

Smith, P., *Disraeli: A Brief Life* (Cambridge, 1996).

Taylor, A. J. P., *The Struggle for Mastery in Europe* (Oxford, 1971 edn).

Vincent, J., *Disraeli* (Oxford, 1990).

Walton, J. K., *Disraeli* (Routledge, 1990).

chapter 15 Victorian prosperity and depression

Aldcroft, D. H., *The Development of British Industry and Foreign Competition 1875–1914* (Allen & Unwin, 1968).

Aldcroft, D. H. and Richardson, H. W., *The British Economy 1870–1939* (Macmillan, 1969).

Barker, T., 'Workshop of the World', *History Today*, June 1994.

Black, J. and Macraild, D. M., *Nineteenth Century Britain* (Palgrave/Macmillan, 2003).

Crouzet, F., *The Victorian Economy* (Columbia University Press, 1981).

Daunton, M., *The Political Economy of Britain 1850–1939* (Oxford, 1996).

Evans, E. J, *The Forging of the Modern State: Early Industrial Britain 1783–1870* (Longman, 2001 edn).

Hobsbawm, E., *Industry and Empire: The Birth of the Industrial Revolution* (Penguin, 1969).

Kennedy, W. P., *Industrial Structure, Capital Markets and the Origins of British Economic Decline* (Cambridge, 1987).

Mathias, P., *The First Industrial Nation* (Methuen, 1969).

Pugh, M., *State and Society: Political and Social History of Britain since 1870* (Arnold, 2008).

Rubinstein, W. D., *Capitalism, Culture and Decline in Britain, 1750–1990* (Routledge, 1993).

Saul, S. B., *The Myth of the Great Depression* (Macmillan, 1969).

Thompson, F. M. L., 'The Golden Age of Farming?', in *Purnell's History of the English Speaking Peoples* (BPC Publishing, 1971), pp. 3400–5.

Wiener, M. J., *English Culture and the Decline of the Industrial Spirit, 1850–1980* (Cambridge, 1981).

chapter 16 Gladstone and Salisbury, 1880–95

Adelman, P., 'Gladstone and Liberalism', *Modern History Review*, February 1991.

Chamberlain, M. E., *The Scramble for Africa* (Longman, 1974).

Coleman, B., *Conservatism and the Conservative Party in Nineteenth Century Britain* (Arnold, 1988).

Farwell, B., *Queen Victoria's Little Wars* (Allen Lane, 1973).

Flynn, K. H., 'Parnell, the Rebel Prince', *History Today*, April 2005.

Foster, R. F., *Lord Randolph Churchill: A Political Life* (Oxford, 1981).

James, R. R., *Rosebery* (Weidenfeld & Nicolson, 1963).

James, R. R., *Lord Randolph Churchill* (Weidenfeld & Nicolson, 1969).

Jenkins, R., *Gladstone* (Macmillan, 1995).

Magnus, P., *Gladstone* (John Murray, 1963 edn).

Marlowe, J., *Mission to Khartoum: General Gordon* (Gollancz, 1969).

McKinstry, L., *Rosebery: Statesman in Turmoil* (John Murray, 2006).

Moorehead, A., *The White Nile* (Hamish Hamilton, 1960).

Morton, G., *Home Rule and the Irish Question* (Longman, 1980).

Pakenham, T., *The Scramble for Africa* (Weidenfeld & Nicolson, 1991).

Parry, J., *The Rise and Fall of Liberal Government in Victorian Britain* (Yale, 1993).

Porter, B., *The Lion's Share: A Short History of British Imperialism 1850–1970* (Longman, 1975).

Roberts, A., *Salisbury: Victorian Titan* (Weidenfeld & Nicolson, 1999).

Shannon, R. T., *Gladstone: Heroic Minister 1865–1898* (Allen Lane/Penguin, 1999).

Shannon, R. T., *Gladstone: God and Politics* (Hambeldon Continuum, 2007).

Steele, D., *Lord Salisbury: A Political Biography* (Routledge, 2001).

Taylor, R., *Lord Salisbury* (Allen Lane, 1975).

Winstanley, M. J., *Ireland and the Land Question 1800–1922* (Methuen, 1984).

chapter 17 ten years of Conservative rule, 1895–1905

Chamberlain, M. E., *The Scramble for Africa* (Longman, 1974).

Chamberlain, M. E., *Pax Britannica? British Foreign Policy 1789–1914* (Longman, 1988).

Churchill, W. S., *Frontiers and Wars* (Penguin, 1972).

Charmley, J., *Splendid Isolation: Britain and the Balance of Power 1874–1914* (Hodder & Stoughton, 1999).

Coleman, B., *Conservatism and the Conservative Party in Nineteenth Century Britain* (Arnold, 1988).

Farwell, B., *Queen Victoria's Little Wars* (Allen Lane, 1973).

Fraser, P., *Joseph Chamberlain* (Cassell, 1966).

Goodlad, G. D., 'Lord Salisbury and Late Victorian Conservatism', *Modern History Review*, February 1996.

Jay, R., *Joseph Chamberlain: A Political Study* (Oxford, 1981).

Longford, E., *Jameson's Raid* (Weidenfeld & Nicolson, 1982 edn).

Magnus, P., *Kitchener: Portrait of an Imperialist* (John Murray, 1958).

Marlowe, J., *Cecil Rhodes* (Elek, 1972).

Pakenham, T., *The Boer War* (Weidenfeld & Nicolson, 1979).

Pakenham, T., *The Scramble for Africa* (Weidenfeld & Nicolson, 1991).

Roberts, A., *Salisbury: Victorian Titan* (Weidenfeld & Nicolson, 1999).

Robbins, K., *Britain and Europe 1789–2005* (Hodder Arnold, 2005).

Steele, D., *Lord Salisbury: A Political Biography* (Routledge, 2001).

Smith, P., *Lord Salisbury on Politics* (Cambridge University Press, 1972).

Taylor, R., *Lord Salisbury* (Allen Lane, 1975).

Thomas, A., *Rhodes: The Race for Africa* (BBC, 1996).

Watts, D., *Joseph Chamberlain and the Challenge of Radicalism* (Hodder & Stoughton, 1993).

Wilson, K. M., *The Policy of Entente: The Determinants of British Foreign Policy, 1904–1914* (Cambridge, 1985).

Wilson, K. M. (ed.), *Decisions for War, 1914* (Routledge, 1995).

Wilson, K. M., 'British Foreign Policy, 1900–14', *Modern History Review*, April 2001.

Young, K., *Balfour* (Bell, 1963).

chapter 18 the dominions: Canada, Australia and New Zealand before 1914

Bailyn, B., *The Peopling of British North America: An Introduction* (Vintage, 1988).

Belich, J., *Making Peoples: A History of the New Zealanders from Polynesian Settlement to the End of the Nineteenth Century* (University of Hawaii Press, 2nd edn, 2002).

Bloomfield, P., *Edward Gibbon Wakefield* (Longman, 1961).

Clark, C. M. H., *A History of Australia* (Macmillan, 1982).

Fyson, A., 'Eyewitness at Eureka', *History Today*, December 2004.

Hughes, R., *The Fatal Shore: The Epic of Australia's Founding* (Vintage, 1988).

Metge, J., *The Maoris of New Zealand* (Routledge, 1976 edn).

Morton, W. L., *The Critical Years: The Union of British North America* (Toronto, 1964).

New, C. W., *Lord Durham* (Dawson, 1969).

Welsh, F., *Australia: A New History of the Great Southern Land* (Overlook TP, 2008).

chapter 19 the growth of the trade unions and the Labour Party to 1914

Adelman, P., *The Rise of the Labour Party, 1880–1945* (Longman, 2nd edn, 1986).

Benn, C., *Keir Hardie* (Hutchinson, 1992).

Cole, G. D. H., *The Life of Robert Owen* (Cass, 1965).

Howell, D., *British Workers and the Independent Labour Party 1888–1906* (Manchester University Press, 1983).

Howson, J., 'The Dock Strike of 1889', *Modern History Review*, February 1996.

McKibbin, R., *The Evolution of the Labour Party 1910–24* (Oxford, 1974).

Morgan, K. O., *Keir Hardie: Radical and Socialist* (Weidenfeld & Nicolson, 1984).

Musson, A. E., *British Trade Unions, 1800–1875* (Macmillan, 1972).

Pelling, H., *The Origins of the Labour Party, 1880–1900* (Oxford, 1965).

Pelling, H., *A History of British Trade Unionism* (Penguin, 1968).

Pugh, M., *State and Society: British Political and Social History 1870–1992* (Arnold, 1994).

Reid, A. J., *United We Stand: A History of Britain's Trade Unions* (Allen Lane, 2004).

Tanner, D., 'The Rise of the Labour Party', *Modern History Review*, November 1989.

Tanner, D., *Political Change and the Labour Party 1900–18* (Cambridge, 1990).

Tanner, D., 'Keir Hardie and the ILP, 1900–15', *Modern History Review*, April 1994.

chapter 20 the state and the people from the 1890s to 1939

Birch, R. C., *The Shaping of the Welfare State* (Longman, 1974).

Cannadine, D., *The Decline and Fall of the British Aristocracy* (Penguin, 2005).

Chinn, C., *Poverty Amidst Prosperity: The Urban Poor in England 1834–1914* (Manchester University Press, 1995).

Constantine, S., *Unemployment in Britain between the Wars* (Longman, 1980).

Crowther, A., *British Social Policy 1914–39* (Macmillan, 1988).

Daunton, M., *Wealth and Welfare: A Social and Economic History of Britain, 1851–1951* (Oxford University Press, 2007).

Fraser, D., *The Evolution of the Welfare State* (Macmillan, 2nd edn, 1984).

Harris, J., *Private Lives, Public Spirit: A Social History of Britain 1870–1914* (Oxford, 1993).

Hattersley, R., *Borrowed Time: The Story of Britain Between the Wars* (Little, Brown, 2007).

Howkins, A., *Re-shaping Rural England: A Social History 1850–1925* (Routledge, 1991).

Lowe, R., 'The Origins of the Welfare State in Britain', *Modern History Review*, September 1989.

Peden, G. C., *British Economic and Social Policy: Lloyd George to Margaret Thatcher* (Philip Allan, 1985).

Pedersen, S., 'A Babylonian Touch', *London Review of Books*, 6 November 2008.

Pugh, M., 'We Danced All Night': A Social History of Britain Between the Wars* (Bodley Head, 2008).

Read, D., *Edwardian England* (Harrap, 1972).

Roberts, R., *The Classic Slum* (Penguin, 1973).

Searle, G. R., *A New England? Peace and War 1886–1918* (Oxford, 2004).

Stevenson, J., *British Society 1914–45* (Penguin, 1984).

Thane, P., *The Foundations of the Welfare State* (Longman, 1982).

Thane, P., 'The Impact of the Welfare State on British Society, 1906–51', *Modern History Review*, September 1989.

Thane, P., *Old Age in English History: Past Experiences, Present Issues* (Oxford, 2000).

Thompson, F. M. L. (ed.), *The Cambridge Social History of Britain 1750–1950, vols 1–3* (Cambridge, 1993).

chapter 21 the Liberals in power, 1905–14

Adelman, P., *The Decline of the Liberal Party 1910–31* (Longman, 1981).

Blewitt, N., *The Peers, the Parties and the People: The General Elections of 1910* (Macmillan, 1972).

Charmley, J., *Splendid Isolation? Britain and the Balance of Power 1874–1914* (Hodder & Stoughton, 1999).

Clarke, P. F., *Lancashire and the New Liberalism* (Cambridge, 1971).

Dangerfield, G., *The Strange Death of Liberal England 1910–14* (1936; Serif edn 1997).

Ferguson, N., *The Pity of War* (Allen Lane/Penguin, 1998).

Fisher, T., 'The Strange Death of Liberal England', *Modern History Review*, November 1999.

Green, E., 'Neutering Mr Balfour's Poodle', *Modern History Review*, April 1996.

Hamilton, R. & Herwig, H.H., *The Origins of World War 1* (Cambridge University Press, 2002)

Henig, R. (ed.), *The Origins of the First World War* (Routledge, 1993).

Jefferies, H. A., 'Germany and the First World War', *Modern History Review*, September 1995.

Jenkins, R., *Asquith* (Collins, 1964).

Joll, J., *The Origins of the First World War* (Longman, 1984).

Lemieux, S., 'The Liberal Party 1910–14. Still a Going Concern?', *Modern History Review*, September 1995.

Liddington, J., *Rebel Girls: Their Fight for the Vote* (Virago, 2006).

Liddington, J. and Norris, J., *One Hand Tied Behind Us: the Rise of the Women's Suffrage Movement* (Virago, 1979).

Lloyd, T. O., *Empire to Welfare State* (Oxford, 1970).

Murray, B. K., *The People's Budget 1909–10* (Oxford, 1980).

Pugh, M., *Lloyd George* (Longman, 1988).

Pugh, M., 'Votes for Women', *Modern History Review*, September 1990.

Pugh. M., *The Making of Modern British Politics 1867–1939* (Blackwell, 2nd edn, 1993).

Purvis, J., *Emmeline Pankhurst: A Biography* (Routledge, 2002).

Read, D., *Edwardian England* (Harrap, 1972).

Searle, G. R., *The Liberal Party: Triumph and Disintegration 1886–1939* (Macmillan, 1992).

Searle, G. R., *A New England? Peace and War 1886–1918* (Oxford, 2004).

Steiner, Z., *Britain and the Origins of the First World War* (Macmillan, 1977).

Tanner, D., 'New Liberalism 1906–14', *Modern History Review*, November 1990.

Wilson, K. M., *The Policy of Entente: The Determinants of British Foreign Policy, 1900–1914* (Cambridge, 1985).

Wilson, K. M., 'The Multiple Wars of 1914', *Modern History Review*, September 1995.

chapter 22 Britain, the First World War and its aftermath

Atkin, J., *A War of Individuals: Bloomsbury Attitudes to the Great War* (Manchester University Press, 2002).

Beckett, I. F. W. *The Great War, 1914–1918* (Longman, 2000).

Bourne, J. M., *Britain and the Great War 1914–1918* (Arnold,1989).

Constantine, S. (ed.)., *The First World War in British History* (Edward Arnold, 1995).

DeGroot, G., *Blighty* (Longman, 1996).

Ferguson, N., *The Pity of War* (Allen Lane/Penguin, 1998).

Grigg, J., *Lloyd George: War Leader* (Allen Lane, 2002).

Hart, P., *1918 – A Very British Victory* (Weidenfeld & Nicolson, 2008).

Henig, R., 'The Treaty of Versailles 80 Years On', *Modern History Review*, April 2001.

James, R. R., *Gallipoli* (Batsford, 1965).

Laffin, W. J., *British Butchers and Bunglers of World War I* (Sutton, 1988).

Liddell-Hart, B. H., *History of the First World War* (Pan, 1972).

Macdonald, L., *They Called It Passchendaele* (Michael Joseph, 1978).

Marwick, A., *The Deluge: British Society and the First World War* (Macmillan, 1973; 2nd edn, 1991).

Marwick, A., *War and Social Change in the Twentieth Century* (Macmillan, 1974)

Morgan, K. O., *Lloyd George* (Weidenfeld & Nicolson, 1974).

Pugh., M., *Lloyd George* (Longman, 1988).

Sharp, A., *The Versailles Settlement: Peacemaking in Paris, 1919* (Macmillan, 1991).

Sheffield, G., *Forgotten Victory: The First World War, Myth and Realities* (Headline, 2001).

Stevenson, D., *Cataclysm: The First World War as Political Tragedy* (Basic Books, 2004).

Strachan, H., *The First World War* (Simon & Schuster, 2003).

Taylor, A. J. P., *An Illustrated History of the First World War* (Penguin, 1963).

Terraine, J., *Douglas Haig: The Educated Soldier* (Hutchinson, 1963).

Terraine, J., *The Smoke and the Fire* (Sidgwick & Jackson, 1980).

Toye, R., *Lloyd George and Churchill: Rivals for Greatness* (Macmillan, 2007).

Winter, J. M., *The Great War and the British People* (Palgrave Macmillan, 2nd edn, 2003).

chapter 23 politics in confusion, 1918–24

Adelman, P., *The Decline of the Liberal Party 1910–1931* (Longman, 1981).

Adelman, P., *The Rise of the Labour Party 1880–1945* (Longman, 2nd edn, 1986).

Clarke, P. F., *Lancashire and the New Liberalism* (Cambridge, 1971).

Cook, C., *The Age of Alignment 1922–29* (Macmillan, 1975).

Kinnear, M., *The Fall of Lloyd George* (Macmillan, 1973).

Marquand, D., *Ramsay MacDonald* (Cape, 1977).

McKibbin, R., *The Evolution of the Labour Party 1910–24* (Oxford University Press, 1974).

Morgan, K. O., *Lloyd George* (Weidenfeld, 1974).

Morgan, K. O., 'Lloyd George and the Modern World', *Modern History Review*, November 1997.

Pelling, H., *The Origins of the Labour Party 1880–1900* (Oxford, 1965).

Phillips, G., *The Rise of the Labour Party, 1893–1931* (Routledge, 1992).

Pugh, M., *The Making of Modern British Politics, 1867–1939* (Blackwell, 1982).

Searle, G., *The Liberal Party: Triumph and Disintegration, 1886–1929* (Macmillan, 1992).

Tanner, D., *Political Change and the Labour Party, 1900–18* (Cambridge, 1990).

Taylor, A. J. P., *English History 1914–45* (Penguin, 1970).

Wilson, T., *The Downfall of the Liberal Party 1914–1935* (Collins, 1966; Fontana, 1968).

chapter 24 Baldwin, the Conservatives and the General Strike

Ball, S., 'The Conservative Dominance 1918–40', *Modern History Review*, November 1991.

Grayson, R., 'Britain in Europe. Austen Chamberlain and the Locarno System, 1924–29', *Modern History Review*, February 1999.

Hattersley, R., *Borrowed Time: The Story of Britain Between the Wars* (Little, Brown, 2007).

Howson, J., 'The General Strike: A Bluff Which Was Called?', *Modern History Review*, September 1996.

Hyde, H. M., *Baldwin – the Unexpected Prime Minister* (Hart-Davis, 1973).

Macleod, I., *Neville Chamberlain* (Muller, 1961).

Morris, M., *The General Strike* (Penguin, 1976).

Morris, M., 'The General Strike', *Modern History Review*, February 1991.

Perkins, A., *A Very British Strike: 3 May – 12 May 1926* (Macmillan, 2006).

Pugh, M., 'The General Strike', *History Today*, May 2006.

chapter 25 political and economic crises, 1929–39: the Second Labour government (1929–31), the world economic crisis and the National Governments

Adelman, P., *The Rise of the Labour Party, 1880–1945* (Longman, 1986).

Aldcroft, D. H., *The British Economy Between the Wars* (Philip Allan, 1983).

Aldcroft, D. H., 'The Locust Years? Britain's Inter-war Economy', *Modern History Review*, November 1993.

Ball, S., *Baldwin and the Conservative Party: The Crisis of 1929–31* (Yale University Press, 1988).

Bassett, R., *Nineteen Thirty One: Political Crisis* (Macmillan, 1958).

Constantine, S., *Unemployment in Britain Between the Wars* (Longman, 1980).

Cross, C., *Philip Snowden* (Barrie and Rockcliff, 1967).

Daunton, M., *Wealth and Welfare: A Social and Economic History of Britain. 1851–1951* (Oxford University Press, 2007)

Donaldson, F., *Edward VIII* (Weidenfeld & Nicolson, 1978).

Dorril, S., *Blackshirt. Sir Oswald Mosley and British Fascism* (Viking/Penguin, 2006).

Garside, W. R., *British Unemployment 1919–39* (Cambridge University Press, 1990).

Hattersley, R., *Borrowed Time: The Story of Britain Between the Wars* (Little, Brown, 2007).

Marquand, D., *Ramsay MacDonald* (Cape, 1977).

Mount, F., 'Double-Barrelled Dolts', *London Review of Books*, 6 July 2006.

Pugh, M., *Hurrah for the Blackshirts: Fascists and Fascism Between the Wars* (Pimlico, 2006).

Pugh, M., *We Danced All Night: A Social History of Britain Between the Wars* (The Bodley Head, 2008).

Skidelsky, R., *Politicians and the Slump: The Labour Government of 1929–31* (Penguin, 1970).

Skidelsky, R., *Oswald Mosley* (Papermac, 3rd edn, 1990).

Thorpe, A., *Britain in the 1930s: The Deceptive Decade* (Blackwell/Historical Association, 1992).

Thorpe, A., 'The 1931 Crisis', *Modern History Review*, November 1993.

Williamson, P., *National Crisis and National Government: British Politics, the Economy and Empire 1929–32* (Cambridge University Press, 1992).

Williamson, P., 'The King, Politicians and the 1931 Crisis', *Modern History Review*, November 1993.

chapter 26 Britain and the problems of Empire between the wars

Brown, J. M., *Gandhi: Prisoner of Hope* (Yale, 1989).

Collett, N., *The Butcher of Amritsar* (Hambledon and London, 2005).

Coogan, T. P., *Michael Collins* (Arrow, 1991).

Coogan, T. P., *De Valera, Long Fellow, Long Shadow* (Hutchinson, 1996).

De Paor, L., *Divided Ulster* (Penguin, 1971).

Foster, R. F., *Modern Ireland 1600–1972* (Penguin, 1989).

Gopal, S., *Jawaharlal Nehru: A Biography* (Oxford, 1990).

Gopal, S., 'Churchill and India', in R. Blake and W. R. Louis (eds), *Churchill* (Oxford, 1993).

Hattersley, R., *Borrowed Time: The Story of Britain Between the Wars* (Little, Brown, 2007).

Lee, J. J., *Ireland 1912–1985* (Cambridge, 1989).

Lyons, F. S. L., *Ireland Since the Famine* (Fontana, 2nd edn, 1985).

Moore, R. J., *The Crisis of Indian Unity 1917–1940* (Oxford, 1974).

Pandey, B. N., *The Break-up of British India* (Macmillan, 1969).

Porter, B., *The Lion's Share: A Short History of British Imperialism 1850–1970* (Longman, 1975).

Townshend, C., *Easter 1916: The Irish Rebellion* (Allen Lane, 2005).

Toye, G., *Lloyd George and Churchill: Rivals for Greatness* (Macmillan, 2007).

Watson, J. B., *Empire to Commonwealth, 1919–1970* (Dent, 1971).

chapter 27 appeasement and the outbreak of the Second World War: foreign affairs, 1931–9

Bullock, A., *Hitler: A Study in Tyranny* (Penguin, 1969).

Charmley, J., *Chamberlain and the Lost Peace* (Hodder & Stoughton, 1989).

Dorril, S., *Blackshirt: Sir Oswald Mosley and British Fascism* (Viking, 2006).

Gilbert, M. and Gott, R., *The Appeasers* (Weidenfeld & Nicolson, 1967).

Gregor, N., 'Hitler's Aggression: Opportunistic or Planned?', *Modern History Review*, September 2003.

Henig, R., *The Origins of the Second World War* (Routledge, 1991).

Kershaw, I., *Making Friends with Hitler: Lord Londonderry and Britain's Road to War* (Allen Lane, 2004).

Martel, G. (ed.), *'The Origins of the Second World War' Reconsidered: The A. J. P. Taylor Debate after Twenty-Five Years* (Routledge, 2nd edn, 1999.).

Neville, P., *Neville Chamberlain: A Study in Failure?* (Hodder & Stoughton, 1993).

Overy, R. J., *The Road to War* (Penguin, 1999).

Parker, R. A. C., *Chamberlain and Appeasement* (Macmillan, 1993).

Parker, R. A. C., *Churchill and Appeasement* (Papermac, 2001).

Rock, W. R., *British Appeasement in the 1930s* (Arnold, 1977).

Self, R., *Neville Chamberlain* (Ashgate, 2007).

Taylor, A. J. P., *Origins of the Second World War* (Penguin edn, 1974).

Taylor, P. M., 'Appeasement: Guilty Men or Guilty Conscience?', *Modern History Review*, November 1989.

Watt, D. C., *How War Came: The Immediate Origins of the Second World War, 1938–39* (Heinemann, 1989).

chapter 28 Britain and the Second World War, 1939–45

Addison, P., *The Road to 1945* (Pimlico, 1994 edn).

Addison, P., *Churchill: The Unexpected Hero* (Oxford University Press, 2005).

Barker, J., 'Sowing the Wind: Bomber Harris and the Wartime Bombing', *History Today*, March 2005.

Barnett, C., *The Lost Victory* (Macmillan, 1995).

Bernstein, G. L., *The Myth of Decline – The Rise of Britain Since 1945* (Pimlico, 2004).

Blake, R. and Louis, W. M. (eds), *Churchill: A Major New Assessment of His Life in Peace and War* (Oxford, 1993).

Brivati, B. and Jones, H. (eds), *What Difference Did the War Make?* (Leicester University Press, 1993).

Calder, A., *The People's War: Britain 1939–45* (Cape, 1969).

Calvocoressi, P. and Wint, G., *Total War* (Penguin, 1974).

Charmley, J., *Churchill: The End of Glory* (Hodder & Stoughton, 1993).

Friedrich, J., *The Fire: The Bombing of Germany 1940–1945*, trans. Allison Brown (Columbia University Press, 2007).

Gilbert, M., *Second World War* (Phoenix, 1996).

Jenkins, R., *Churchill* (Macmillan, 2001).

Liddell-Hart, B., *History of the Second World War* (Cassell, 1970).

Lindqvist, S., *A History of Bombing* (Granta, 2001).

Lucas, S., 'Hiroshima and History', *Modern History Review*, April 1996.

Marwick, A., 'Two World Wars: Their Impact on Britain', *Modern History Review*, September 1990.

Membery, Y., 'Stoking the Fire', *History Today*, January 2007.

Niellands, R., *The Bomber War: Arthur Harris and the Allied Bombing Offensive, 1939–45* (John Murray, 2001).

Neville, P., 'Dunkirk and the Myths of 1940', *Modern History Review*, September 1991.

Overy, R. J., *Why the Allies Won* (Penguin, 1995).

Pelling, H., *Britain and the Second World War* (Collins Fontana, 1970).

Ponting, C., *1940: Myth and Reality* (Sinclair-Stevenson, 1990).

Roberts, A., *The Holy Fox: A Biography of Lord Halifax* (Weidenfeld & Nicolson, 1991).

Roberts, A., *Eminent Churchillians* (Phoenix, 1993).

Robbins, K., *Churchill* (Longman, 1993).

Smith, H. L. (ed.), *War and Social Change* (Manchester University Press, 1986).

Taylor, A. J. P., *The Second World War* (Hamish Hamilton, 1975).

Thoms, D. W., 'Blitz, Work and Women', *Modern History Review*, November 1996.

Toye, G., *Lloyd George and Churchill: Rivals for Greatness* (Macmillan, 2007).

chapter 29 Labour in power: the Attlee governments, 1945–51

Addison, P., *The Road to 1945* (Cape, 1975).

Barnett, C., *The Lost Victory* (Macmillan, 1985).

Barnett, C., *The Audit of War* (Macmillan, 1986).

Bernstein, G. L., *The Myth of Decline – The Rise of Britain Since 1945* (Pimlico, 2004).

Cairncross, A., *Years of Recovery: British Economic Policy 1945–51* (Methuen, 1985).

Calvocoressi, P., *The British Experience, 1945–75* (Penguin,1979).

Clarke, P., *The Cripps Version: The Life of Sir Stafford Cripps* (Allen Lane, 2002).

Foot, M., *Aneurin Bevan* (Paladin paperback edn, 1975).

Fraser, D., *The Evolution of the British Welfare State* (Macmillan, 1973).

Harris, K., *Attlee* (Weidenfeld & Nicolson, 1984).

Hennessy, P., *Never Again: Britain 1945–51* (Jonathan Cape, 1992).

Jefferys, K., *The Attlee Governments 1945–51* (Longman, 1992).

Kynaston, D., *Austerity Britain, 1945–51* (Bloomsbury, 2007).

Morgan, K. O., *Labour in Power 1945–51* (Oxford, 1984).

Pearce, R., *Attlee's Labour Governments, 1945–51* (Routledge, 1993).

Pearce, R., 'Beveridge 1942: Reconstruction or Reform?', *Modern History Review*, September 1993.

Pelling, H., *The Labour Governments 1945–51* (Macmillan, 1984).

Pimlott, B., *Hugh Dalton* (Macmillan, 1986).

Saville, J., *The Labour Movement in Britain* (Faber, 1988).

Tiratsoo, N. (ed.),*The Attlee Years* (Pinter, 1991).

Tiratsoo, N., 'The Attlee Years Revisited', *Modern History Review*, February 1994.

Tiratsoo, N. and Tomlinson, J., *Industrial Efficiency and State Intervention: Labour 1939–51* (Routledge, 1993).

chapter 30 the rise and fall of consensus, 1951–79

Calvocoressi, P., *The British Experience 1945–75* (Penguin, 1979).

Campbell, J., *Edward Heath* (Weidenfeld & Nicolson, 1993).

Fisher, N., *Harold Macmillan* (Weidenfeld & Nicolson, 1982).

Goodlad, G., 'The Premiership of Harold Macmillan', *Modern History Review*, February 1997.

Healey, D., *The Time of My Life* (Michael Joseph, 1989).

Hennessy, P., *Having It So Good – Britain in the Fifties* (Allen Lane, 2006).

Hennessy, P. and Seldon, A. (eds), *Ruling Performance: British Governments from Attlee to Thatcher* (Blackwell, 1987).

Holmes, M., *The Labour Government 1974–79: Political Aims and Economic Reality* (Macmillan, 1985).

Horne, A., *Macmillan*, Vols 1 and 2 (Macmillan, 1988 and 1989).

Lamb, R., *The Failure of the Eden Government* (Sidgwick & Jackson, 1987).

Lamb, R., *The Macmillan Years 1957–63: The Emerging Truth* (John Murray, 1995).

Lapping, B., *The Labour Government 1964–70* (Penguin, 1971).

Pimlott, B., *Harold Wilson* (HarperCollins, 1993).

Ponting, C., *Breach of Promise: Labour in Power 1964–70* (Hamish Hamilton, 1987).

Ramsden, J., *The Age of Churchill and Eden, 1940–1957* (Longman, 1995).

Ramsden, J., *The Winds of Change: Macmillan to Heath* (Longman, 1996).

Sandbrook, D., *Never Had It So Good: A History of Britain from Suez to the Beatles* (Little, Brown, 2005).

Sandbrook, D., *White Heat. A History of Britain in the Swinging Sixties* (Little, Brown, 2006).

Thorpe, D. R., *Eden: The Life and Times of Anthony Eden, First Earl of Avon, 1897–1977* (Chatto & Windus, 2003).

Timmins, N., *The Five Giants: A Biography of the Welfare State* (HarperCollins, revised edn, 2001)

Turner, J., *Macmillan* (Longman, 1994).

Wilson, H., *The Labour Government 1964–70: A Personal Record* (Penguin, 1974).

chapter 31 the state of the people: social and cultural change since 1945

Black, L., 'Postwar British Immigration', *Modern History Review*, April 2004.

Halsey, A. H. and Webb, J. (eds). *Twentieth Century British Social Trends* (Macmillan, 3rd edn, 2000).

Hennessy, P., *Having It So Good: Britain in the Fifties* (Allen Lane, 2006).

Sandbrook, D., *Never Had It So Good. A History of Britain from Suez to the Beatles* (Little, Brown, 2005).

Sandbrook, D., *White Heat. A History of Britain in the Swinging Sixties* (Little, Brown, 2006).

chapter 32 Britain and its parts: England, Ireland, Scotland and Wales

Arthur, P. and Jeffery, K., *Northern Ireland Since 1968* (Blackwell, 1988).

Bartlett, C.J., *History of Postwar Britain, 1945–74* (Longman, 1977).

Buckland, P., *A History of Northern Ireland* (Holmes & Meier, 1981).

Burk, K., *The British Isles Since 1945* (Oxford University Press, 2003).

Clutterbuck, R., *Britain in Agony: The Growth of Political Violence* (Penguin, 1978).

Evans, D. G., *A History of Wales 1906–2000* (University of Wales Press, 2000).

Harvie, C., *Twentieth Century Scotland* (Edinburgh University Press, 1998 edn).

Jackson, A., *Home Rule: An Irish History 1800–2000* (Oxford University Press, 2004).

Lee, J. J., *Ireland 1912–1985* (Cambridge, 1985).

Philip, A. B., *The Welsh Question* (University of Wales Press, 1975).

Rees, M., *Northern Ireland: A Personal Perspective* (Methuen, 1985).

Wichert, S., *Northern Ireland Since 1945* (Longman, 1991).

chapter 33 Britain and its place in the world after 1945

Aldous, R. and Lee, S. (eds), *Harold Macmillan and Britain's World Role* (Macmillan, 1996).

Bernstein, G. L., *The Myth of Decline: The Rise of Britain Since 1945* (Pimlico, 2004).

Carlton, D., *Britain and the Suez Crisis* (Blackwell, 1988).

Carlton, D., 'Suez 1956: The Consequences', *Modern History Review,* February 1990.

George, S., *Britain and European Integration since 1945* (ICBH/Blackwell, 1991); and in *Modern History Review,* April 1992.

Goodlad, G. D., 'The Premiership of Harold Macmillan', *Modern History Review,* February 1997.

Horne, A., *Macmillan,* 2 vols (Macmillan, 1988–9).

Kyle, K., *Suez* (Weidenfeld & Nicolson, 1991).

Lamb, R., *The Failure of the Eden Government* (Sidgwick & Jackson, 1987).

Lamb, R., *The Macmillan Years, 1957–63: The Emerging Truth* (John Murray, 1995).

Marr, A., *A History of Modern Britain* (Macmillan, 2007).

Nutting, A., *No End of a Lesson* (Constable, 1967).

Ramsden, J., *The Winds of Change: Macmillan to Heath* (Longman, 1996).

Thorpe, D. R., *Eden: The Life and Times of Anthony Eden, First Earl of Avon, 1877–1977* (Chatto & Windus, 2003).

Turner, J., *Macmillan* (Longman, 1994).

Young, J., *Britain and European Unity 1945–1992* (Macmillan, 1993).

chapter 34 Britain and the end of Empire

Anderson, D., *Histories of the Hanged: Britain's Dirty War in Kenya and the End of Empire* (Weidenfeld, 2005).

Brasted, H., 'Decolonisation in India: Britain's Positive Role', *Modern History Review,* November 1990.

Brendon, P., *The Decline and Fall of the British Empire* (Jonathan Cape, 2007).

Brendon, P., 'A Moral Audit of the British Empire', *History Today,* October 2007.

Butler, L. J., *Britain and Empire: Adjusting to a Post-Imperial World* (I. B. Tauris, 2002).

Clarke, P., *The Last Thousand Days of the British Empire: The Demise of a Superpower, 1944–47* (Allen Lane, 2007)

Darwin, J., *Britain and Decolonisation* (Macmillan, 1988).

Elkins, C., *Britain's Gulag: The Brutal End of Empire in Kenya* (Jonathan Cape, 2005).

Ferguson, N., *Empire: How Britain Made the Modern World* (Penguin, 2003).

Hargreaves, J. D., *Decolonisation in Africa* (Longman, 1988).

Holland, R. F., *European Decolonisation 1918–81: An Introductory Survey* (Macmillan, 1985).

Holland, R. F., 'Imperial Decline: A New Historiography', *Modern History Review,* February 1992.

Porter, B., *The Absent-Minded Imperialists* (Oxford, 2004).

Porter, B., 'How Did They Get Away With It?', *London Review of Books*, 3 March 2005.

Singh, A. I., *The Origins of the Partition of India 1936–1947* (Oxford, 1990).

Thompson, A., *The Empire Strikes Back?* (Pearson, 2005).

chapter 35 Thatcherism and the New Right, 1979–97

Campbell, J., *Margaret Thatcher, Vol. 2: The Iron Lady* (Jonathan Cape, 2003).

Childs, D., *Britain Since 1939: Progress and Decline* (Macmillan, 1995).

Clark, A., *Diaries* (Weidenfeld & Nicolson, 1993).

Crick, M., *Scargill and the Miners* (Penguin, 1985).

Freedman, L., *The Official History of the Falklands Campaign*, 2 vols (Routledge, 2005).

Gilmour, I., 'Vote for the Beast!', *London Review of Books*, 20 October 2005.

Green, E. H. H., *Thatcher* (Hodder Arnold, 2006).

Howe, G., *Conflict of Loyalty* (Pan, 1994).

Hutton, W., *The State We're In* (Vintage edn, 1996).

Jenkins, S., *Thatcher and Sons: A Revolution in Three Acts* (Allen Lane, 2006).

Lawson, M., *The View From No. 11* (Bantam, 1992; Corgi, 1993).

Metz, D., 'Maggie's Lucky Strike', *History Today*, November 2004.

Milne, S., *The Enemy Within. The Secret War Against the Miners* (Verso, 3rd edn, 2004).

McKibbin, R., 'Why Did It End So Badly?', *London Review of Books*, 18 March 2004.

Riddell, P., *The Thatcher Era and its Legacy* (Blackwell, 1991).

Thatcher, M., *The Downing Street Years* (HarperCollins, 1993).

Young, H., *One of Us* (Macmillan, 1991 edn).

chapter 36 the Labour party in opposition and the Blair years, 1979–2007

Beech, M. and Lee, S., *Ten Years of New Labour* (Palgrave Macmillan, 2008).

Driver, S. and Martell, L., *New Labour* (Polity Press, 2nd edn, 2006).

Hutton, W., 'The Private Man I Knew Who Drove the Public Revolution', *Guardian*, 17 May 2007.

Lee, Simon, *Best for Britain? The Politics and Legacy of Gordon Brown* (Oneworld Publications, 2007).

Marr, A., *A History of Modern Britain* (Part 5). (Macmillan, 2007).

McKibbin, R., 'Defeatism, Defeatism, Defeatism', *London Review of Books*, 22 March 2007.

McSmith, A., *John Smith: A Life 1938–1994* (Mandarin, 1994).

O'Hara, K., *After Blair. Conservatism Beyond Thatcher* (Icon Books, 2005).

Rawnsley, A., 'Peace and War. The Reckoning', in 'The Blair Years 1997–2007', *Observer*, March 2007.

Roberts, A., 'A Great Prime Minister Who Fought for Freedom', in 'The Blair Years', *Guardian*, 17 March 2007.

Toynbee, P., 'Social Justice by Stealth', in 'The Blair Years', *Guardian*, 17 March 2007.

Toynbee, P. and Walker, D., *Better or Worse? Has Labour Delivered?* (Bloomsbury, 2005).

Westlake, M., *Kinnock: The Biography* (Little, Brown, 2001).

index